Every Decker book is accompanied by a CD-ROM.

The disc appears in the front of each copy, in its own sealed jacket. Affixed to the front of the book is a distinctive BcD sticker **"Book *cum* disc."**

The disc contains the complete text and illustrations of the book, in fully searchable PDF files. The book and disc are sold *only* as a package; neither are available independently, and no prices are available for the items individually.

BC Decker Inc is committed to providing high-quality electronic publications that complement traditional information and learning methods.

We trust you will find the book/CD package invaluable and invite your comments and suggestions.

Brian C. Decker
CEO and Publisher

Advanced Therapy of
OTITIS MEDIA

Cuneyt M. Alper, MD
Associate Professor, Department of Otolaryngology
University of Pittsburgh School of Medicine
Department of Pediatric Otolaryngology
Children's Hospital of Pittsburgh
Pittsburgh, Pennyslvania

Charles D. Bluestone, MD
Eberly Professor of Pediatric Otolaryngology
University of Pittsburgh School of Medicine
Director, Department of Pediatric Otolaryngology
Children's Hospital of Pittsburgh
Pittsburgh, Pennsylvania

Margaretha L. Casselbrant, MD, PhD
Professor, Department of Otolaryngology
University of Pittsburgh School of Medicine
Director of Research and Education
Department of Pediatric Otolaryngology
Children's Hospital of Pittsburgh
Pittsburgh, Pennsylvania

Joseph E. Dohar, MD
Associate Professor, Department of Otolaryngology
University of Pittsburgh School of Medicine
Department of Pediatric Otolaryngology
Children's Hospital of Pittsburgh
Pittsburgh, Pennsylvania

Ellen M. Mandel, MD
Research Associate Professor
Department of Otolaryngology and Pediatrics
University of Pittsburgh School of Medicine
Department of Pediatric Otolaryngology
Children's Hospital of Pittsburgh
Pittsburgh, Pennsylvania

2004
BC Decker Inc
Hamilton • London

BC Decker Inc
P.O. Box 620, LCD 1
Hamilton, Ontario L8N 3K7
Tel: 905-522-7017; 1-800-568-7281
Fax: 905-522-7839; 1-888-311-4987
E-mail: info@bcdecker.com
www.bcdecker.com

ISBN 1–55009–201-4
Printed in the United States of America

Sales and Distribution

United States
BC Decker Inc
P.O. Box 785
Lewiston, NY 14092-0785
Tel: 905-522-7017; 800-568-7281
Fax: 905-522-7839; 888-311-4987
E-mail: info@bcdecker.com
www.bcdecker.com

Canada
BC Decker Inc
20 Hughson Street South
P.O. Box 620, LCD 1
Hamilton, Ontario L8N 3K7
Tel: 905-522-7017; 800-568-7281
Fax: 905-522-7839; 888-311-4987
E-mail: info@bcdecker.com
www.bcdecker.com

Foreign Rights
John Scott & Company
International Publishers' Agency
P.O. Box 878
Kimberton, PA 19442
Tel: 610-827-1640; Fax: 610-827-1671
E-mail: jsco@voicenet.com

Japan
Igaku-Shoin Ltd.
Foreign Publications Department
3-24-17 Hongo
Bunkyo-ku, Tokyo, Japan 113-8719
Tel: 3 3817 5680; Fax: 3 3815 6776
E-mail: fd@igaku-shoin.co.jp

UK, Europe, Scandinavia, Middle East
Elsevier Science
Customer Service Department
Foots Cray High Street
Sidcup, Kent
DA14 5HP, UK
Tel: 44 (0) 208 308 5760
Fax: 44 (0) 181 308 5702
E-mail: cservice@harcourt.com

*Singapore, Malaysia, Thailand,
Philippines, Indonesia, Vietnam,
Pacific Rim, Korea*
Elsevier Science Asia
583 Orchard Road
#09/01, Forum
Singapore 238884
Tel: 65-737-3593; Fax: 65-753-2145

Australia, New Zealand
Elsevier Science Australia
Customer Service Department
STM Division
Locked Bag 16
St. Peters, New South Wales, 2044
Australia
Tel: 61 02 9517-8999
Fax: 61 02 9517-2249
E-mail: stmp@harcourt.com.au
www.harcourt.com.au

Mexico and Central America
ETM SA de CV
Calle de Tula 59
Colonia Condesa
06140 Mexico DF, Mexico
Tel: 52-5-5553-6657
Fax: 52-5-5211-8468
E-mail: editoresdetextosmex@prodigy.net.mx

Brazil
Tecmedd
Av. Maurílio Biagi, 2850
City Ribeirão Preto – SP – CEP: 14021-000
Tel: 0800 992236
Fax: (16) 3993-9000
E-mail: tecmedd@tecmedd.com.br

India, Bangladesh, Pakistan, Sri Lanka
Elsevier Health Sciences Division
Customer Service Department
17A/1, Main Ring Road
Lajpat Nagar IV
New Delhi – 110024, India
Tel: 91 11 2644 7160-64
Fax: 91 11 2644 7156
E-mail: esindia@vsnl.net

DEDICATION

We dedicate this book to our families, teachers, colleagues, house staff, and students—but especially to clinicians. They will benefit from the most up-to-date, advanced information on the management of otitis media and its complications and sequelae. In turn, we hope this knowledge will improve the health care of their patients who suffer from this common disease. The contents of this text have already helped us in the management of our patients because we have had the pleasure of editing chapters from many distinguished, world-renowned experts and have learned a great deal by contributing our own chapters.

CONTENTS

Section IV: Otitis Media with Effusion

Section VII: Complications of Otitis Media

Section VIII: Sequelae of Otitis Media

Section IX: Miscellaneous Topics on Otitis Media

PREFACE

It is common knowledge that otitis media is the most frequent diagnosis made by physicians who provide health care to infants and children. However, clinicians often confront older patients who develop this disease, which occurs in all age groups. It is estimated that over 20,000 adults have tympanostomy tubes inserted in their ears annually. Otitis media is a worldwide disease that not only has a substantial impact on patients and their families, but also is a burden on health care systems in both industrialized nations and developing countries. Thus, we now have *Advanced Therapy in Otitis Media*, which provides answers to clinical care questions from the most common problems to the relatively rare complications and sequelae of otitis media. This content is targeted at clinicians who face this disease daily, in their practice, in a variety of presentations. They include primary care physicians in the community and in tertiary care medical centers, including pediatricians, internists, family care practitioners, specialists in otolaryngology, immunology and allergy, and infectious diseases, and medical students and residents in training. Because the disease is universal, the information provided is directed toward clinicians around the world.

We are fortunate to have recruited a group of distinguished authorities in the field from many countries who are making important advances in our knowledge base related to the management of otitis media. We are unaware of any other similar text that has focused on therapy in otitis media in which there are over 100 chapters by experts on this disease entity. As editors of and contributors to this unique text, we are overwhelmed by the number of international experts in the management of otitis media who agreed to contribute chapters on relatively narrowly focused aspects of the medical and surgical treatment and prevention of otitis media and its complications and sequelae. We specifically requested that the authors provide the latest advances in one or two aspects of the management of the disease. We recognized that probably every current textbook in pediatrics, primary care, otolaryngology, and infectious diseases has one or more chapters devoted to otitis media written by one or two authors, and there are other authors who have written monographs on the other aspects of this disease (eg, epidemiology, pathogenesis, microbiology, immunology, and diagnosis), in addition to management. (Indeed, one of us is a coauthor of such a blook [Bluestone CD, Klein JO. Otitis media in infants and children. 3rd ed. Philadelphia (PA): WB Saunders; 2001]), but no other text, to our knowledge, is quite like this one. We have provided chapters on the management of not only the most common initial stages of the disease (ie, acute otitis media and otitis media with effusion) but also have included the complications and sequelae of otitis media that can be life threatening, such as meningitis and brain abscess.

We have organized the chapters in such a way that clinicians can select the specific question being asked and gain comprehensive but succinct answers from the expert. The text is directed at all health care professionals who are faced with patients with otitis media.

We are not only colleagues who provide health care on a daily basis for infants and children who have otitis media at the Children's Hospital of Pittsburgh—some of us have been together for over 20 years—we have also had a long-standing commitment to the research aspects of the management of this disease. Our Department of Pediatric Otolaryngology has had continuous funding for clinical trials and other basic and laboratory studies related to otitis media from the National Institutes of Health for the past 25 years. It is hoped that we will have more answers to important management questions in the future with our current investigations, as well as with the investigations of others who conduct research and who have contributed to this book. We hope this will prompt frequent future editions similar to other texts in this series on various common diseases published by BC Decker Inc.

Cuneyt M. Alper, MD
Charles D. Bluestone, MD
Margaretha L. Casselbrant, MD, PhD
Joseph E. Dohar, MD
Ellen M. Mandell, MD
October 2003

ACKNOWLEDGMENTS

We thank all of our invited clinicians from around the world who are authorities in the management of otitis media and who contributed chapters for this textbook. Without their commitment, hard work, and prompt submission of their manuscripts, this book could never have been published. We also want to recognize the dedicated leadership provided by Cuneyt M. Alper, MD, without whose commitment this text would not have reached the publisher. The first edition of any book that has over 100 chapters is a difficult and somewhat painstaking task, but he kept the rest of us motivated. Equally important in completing this book was Maria B. Bluestone, whom we wish to acknowledge for her outstanding editorial assistance in bringing this text into a highly readable form with her expertise in English grammar and syntax. Also, we thank Debi Hepple for her secretarial help and organization skills in contacting the contributors. Finally, we thank the editors at BC Decker Inc, our publisher, and especially Brian Decker and Rochelle Decker, who invited and inspired us to write this unique book.

CONTRIBUTORS

A. NECMETTİN AKYILDIZ, MD
Department of Otolaryngology
Gazi University Faculty of Medicine
Ankara, Turkey

GREGORY C. ALLEN, MD
Department of Otolaryngology–Head and Neck Surgery
University of Colorado Health Sciences Center
Denver, Colorado

CUNEYT M. ALPER, MD
Department of Otolaryngology
University of Pittsburgh School of Medicine
Department of Pediatric Otolaryngology
Children's Hospital of Pittsburgh
Pittsburgh, Pennsylvania

JAMES C. ANDERSON, MD
Department of Radiology
Oregon Health and Science University
Portland, Oregon

PATRICK J. ANTONELLI, MD
Department of Otolaryngology
University of Florida
Gainesville, Florida

STEPHANIE MOODY ANTONIO, MD
Department of Otolaryngology
University of Maryland
Baltimore, Maryland

ELLIS M. ARJMAND, MD, PhD
Department of Pediatric Otolaryngology
University of Pittsburgh School of Medicine
Pittsburgh, Pennsylvania

ELIZABETH D. BARNETT, MD
Department of Pediatrics
Boston University School of Medicine
Boston, Massachusetts

JAMES S. BATTI, MD
Division of Pediatric Otolaryngology
University of Connecticut School of Medicine
Hartford, Connecticut

HOWARD BAUCHNER, MD
Department of Pediatrics
Boston University School of Medicine
Boston, Massachusetts

MICHAEL J. BELMONT, MD
Department of Pediatric Otolaryngology
Children's Hospital of Pittsburgh
Pittsburgh, Pennsylvania

JOEL BERNSTEIN, MD, PhD
Departments of Otolaryngology and Pediatrics
School of Medicine and Biomedical Sciences
Department of Communicative Disorders and Sciences
State University of New York at Buffalo
Buffalo, New York

STAN L. BLOCK, MD, FAAP
Kentucky Pediatric Research, Inc.
Bardstown, Kentucky

CHARLES D. BLUESTONE, MD
Department of Otolaryngology
University of Pittsburgh School of Medicine
Department of Pediatric Otolaryngology
Children's Hospital of Pittsburgh
Pittsburgh, Pennsylvania

DERALD E. BRACKMANN, MD, FACS
House Ear Clinic
Los Angeles, California

ALEXANDER BRODSKY, MD
Department of Otolaryngology–Head and Neck Surgery
Bnai-Zion Medical Center
Haifa, Israel

CRAIG A. BUCHMAN, MD
Department of Otolaryngology–Head and Neck Surgery
University of North Carolina
Chapel Hill, North Carolina

MARGARETHA L. CASSELBRANT, MD, PhD
Department of Otolaryngology
University of Pittsburgh School of Medicine
Department of Pediatric Otolaryngology
Children's Hospital of Pittsburgh
Pittsburgh, Pennsylvania

KENNY H. CHAN, MD
Department of Otolaryngology
University of Colorado School of Medicine
Denver, Colorado

LINDA S. CHAN, PhD
Departments of Pediatrics, Emergency Medicine, and Surgery
Keck School of Medicine
University of Southern California
Los Angeles, California

DAVID H. CHI, MD
Department of Otolaryngology
University of Pittsburgh School of Medicine
Pittsburgh, Pennsylvania

TASNEE CHONMAITREE, MD
Department of Pediatrics
University of Texas Medical Branch
Galveston, Texas

PEDRO CLARÓS, MD, PhD
Department of Otolaryngology
Barcelona University
Barcelona, Spain

HARVEY COATES, MS, FRACS
Department of Otolaryngology, Head and Neck Surgery
University of Western Australia
Crawley, Western Australia

ROBERT COHEN, MD
Pediatrie
Centre Hôpital Intercommunal de Creteil
Creteil, France

MICHAEL J. CUNNINGHAM, MD
Department of Otology and Laryngology
Harvard Medical School
Boston, Massachusetts

KATHLEEN A. DALY, PhD
Department of Otolaryngology
University of Minnesota
Minneapolis, Minnesota

SUBINOY DAS, MD
Department of Otolaryngology–Head and Neck Surgery
University of North Carolina
Chapel Hill, North Carolina

NARIMAN DASH, MD
Department of Otolaryngology–Head and Neck Surgery
Eastern Virginia Medical School
Norfolk, Virginia

ANTONIO DE LA CRUZ, MD
Department of Otology
University of Southern California
Los Angeles, California

JAIMIE DE ROSA, MD
Department of Otolaryngology–Head and Neck Surgery
Boston University School of Medicine
Boston, Massachusetts

CRAIG S. DERKAY, MD
Departments of Otolaryngology and Pediatrics
Eastern Virginia Medical School
Norfolk, Virginia

JOSEPH E. DOHAR, MD, MS, FAAP, FACS
Department of Otolaryngology
University of Pittsburgh School of Medicine
Pittsburgh, Pennsylvania

ANGELA ELLISON, MD
Department of Pediatrics
Boston University School of Medicine
Boston, Massachusetts

ADELE YARRINGTON EVANS, MD
Department of Otology and Laryngology
Harvard Medical School
Boston, Massachusetts

HOWARD FADEN, MD
Department of Pediatrics
State University of New York
Buffalo, New York

JACOB FRIEDBERG, BA, MD, FRCSC
Hospital for Sick Children
Toronto, Ontario

PIERRE GEHANNO, MD
Department of Otorhinolaryngology and
    Cervico-Facial Surgery
Bichat-Claude Bernard Teaching Hospital
Paris, France

DEBORAH A. GENTILE, MD
Department of Pediatric Otolaryngology
University of Pittsburgh School of Medicine
Pittsburgh, Pennsylvania

FARYAL GHAFFAR, MD
Department of Pediatric Infectious Diseases
University of Texas Southwestern Medical Center
Dallas, Texas

NIRA A. GOLDSTEIN, MD
Department of Otolaryngology
State University of New York Downstate Medical Center
Brooklyn, New York

RICHARD L. GOODE, MD
Department of Otolaryngology
Stanford University School of Medicine
Stanford, California

MARCOS V. GOYCOOLEA, MD, PhD
Department of Otolaryngology
University of Minnesota
Minneapolis, Minnesota

KENNETH M. GRUNDFAST, MD, FACS, FAAP
Department of Otolaryngology–Head and Neck Surgery
Boston University School of Medicine
Boston, Massachusetts

ANIL GUNGOR, MD
Department of Pediatric Otolaryngology
Children's Hospital of Pittsburgh
Pittsburgh, Pennsylvania

JOSEPH HADDAD JR, MD
Department of Otolaryngology, Head and Neck Surgery
Columbia University of Physians and Surgeons
New York, New York

SEISHI HASEBE, MD
Department of Hearing and Speech Sciences
Kyoto University Graduate School of Medicine
Kyoto, Japan

TERHO HEIKKINEN, MD, PhD
Department of Pediatrics
University of Turku
Turku, Finland

EMMANUEL HELIDONIS, MD, FACS
Department of Otorhinolaryngology
University of Crete Greece
Heraklion, Greece

STEN HELLSTRÖM, MD, PhD
Department of Clinical Sciences
University Hospital of Umeå
Umeå, Sweden

BARRY E. HIRSCH, MD, FACS
Departments of Otolaryngology, Neurological Surgery,
   and Communication Science and Disorders
University of Pittsburgh Medical Center
Pittsburgh, Pennsylvania

GLENN C. ISAACSON, MD, FACS, FAAP
Department of Otolaryngology, Head and Neck Surgery
Temple University School of Medicine
Philadelphia, Pennsylvania

DAVID J. KAY, MD
Department of Pediatric Otolaryngology
Children's Hospital of Pittsburgh
Pittsburgh, Pennsylvania

YUSUF K. KEMALOĞLU, MD
Department of Otolaryngology
Gazi University Faculty of Medicine
Ankara, Turkey

HANS-GEORG KEMPF, MD, PhD
Department of Otolaryngology
Medical University of Hannover
Hannover, Germany

MARGARET A. KENNA, MD, FAAP, FACS
Department of Otolaryngology and Laryngology
Harvard Medical School
Boston, Massachusetts

JEROME O. KLEIN, MD
Maxwell Finland Laboratory for Infectious Diseases
Boston Medical Center
Boston, Massachusetts

KARI JORUNN KVAERNER, MD, PhD
Center for Health Administration
University of Oslo
Oslo, Norway

AMANDA J. LEACH, PhD
Department of Infectious Diseases
Menzies School of Health Research
Darwin, Australia

RUDOLF LEUWER, MD
ENT Department
Hamburg University Medical School
Hamburg, Germany

JAMES T.-C. LI, MD, PhD
Department of Internal Medicine
Division of Allergic Diseases
Mayo Clinic
Rochester, Minnesota

MICHAL LUNTZ, MD
Department of Otolaryngology, Head and
   Neck Surgery
Bnai Zion Medical Center
Haifa, Israel

WILLIAM M. LUXFORD, MD
House Ear Clinic
Los Angeles, California

ELLEN M. MANDEL, MD
Department of Otolaryngology and Pediatrics
University of Pittsburgh School of Medicine
Pittsburgh, Pennsylvania

DAVID L. MANDELL, MD
Department of Otolaryngology
University of Pittsburgh School of Medicine
Pittsburgh, Pennsylvania

PAOLA MARCHISIO, MD
Department of Pediatrics
University of Milan Medical School
Milan, Italy

MICHIYA MATSUMURA, MD, PhD
Department of Otolaryngology
Hokkaido University School of Medicine
Sapporo, Japan

A. RICHARD MAW, MS, FRCS
Department of Otolaryngology
University of Bristol
Bristol, England

GEORGE H. McCRACKEN JR, MD
Department of Pediatrics
University of Texas Southwestern Medical Center
Dallas, Texas

PETER MORRIS, FRACP, PhD
Department of Infectious Diseases
Menzies School of Health Research
Darwin, Australia

L. NICOLE MURRAY, MD
Department of Pediatric Otolaryngology
Louisiana State University Health Sciences Center
New Orleans, Louisiana

CHARLES M. MYER III, MD
Department of Otolaryngology–Head and Neck Surgery
University of Cincinnati
Cincinnati, Ohio

PHILIPPE OVETCHKINE, MD
Department of Pediatrics
Hopital Sainte-Justin
Montreal, Quebec

O. NURİ ÖZGİRGİN, MD
Department of Otolaryngology
Baskent University
Ankara, Turkey

TAUNO PALVA, MD
Department of Otolaryngology
University of Helsinki
Helsinki, Finland

MICHAEL M. PAPARELLA, MD
Department of Otolaryngology
University of Minnesota
Minneapolis, Minnesota

STEPHEN I. PELTON, MD
Department of Pediatrics
Boston University School of Medicine
Boston, Massachusetts

MICHAEL E. PICHICHERO, MD
Elmwood Pediatric Group
University of Rochester Medical Center
Rochester, New York

OTAVIO B. PILTCHER, MD, PhD
ENT Department
Hospital de Clinicas de Porto Alegre
Porto Alegre, Brazil

THANAI PONGDEE, MD
Department of Internal Medicine
Division of Allergic Diseases
Mayo Clinic
Rochester, Minnesota

CHRIS PRESCOTT, CAJ, FRCS
Department of Otorhinolaryngology
University of Cape Town
Cape Town, South Africa

NICOLA PRINCIPI, MD
Department of Pediatrics
University of Milan Medical School
Milan, Italy

HANS RAMSAY, MD
Department of Otolaryngology
University of Helsinki
Helsinki, Finland

YAEL RAZ, MD
Department of Otolaryngology
University of Pittsburgh School of Medicine
Pittsburgh, Pennsylvania

JAMES S. REILLY, MD
Department of Otolaryngology and Pediatrics
Thomas Jefferson Medical University
Philadelphia, Pennsylvania

JOANNE E. ROBERTS, PhD
Frank Porter Graham Child Development Center
University of North Carolina
Chapel Hill, North Carolina

RICHARD M. ROSENFELD, MD, MPH
Department of Otolaryngology
SUNY Downstate Medical Center
Brooklyn, New York

SOHAM ROY, MD
Department of Otolaryngology–Head and Neck Surgery
University of Miami
Miami, Florida

ROBERT J. RUBEN, MD, FACS, FAAP
Departments of Otolaryngology and Pediatrics
Albert Einstein College of Medicine
Bronx, New York

AINO RUOHOLA, MD
Department of Pediatrics
Turku University Hospital
University of Turky
Turku, Finland

VEDANTAM RUPA, MS, DLO
Department of ENT, Speech and Hearing
Christian Medical College and Hospital
Vellore, India

OLLI RUUSKANEN, MD
Department of Infectious Diseases
Turku University
Turku, Finland

BRITTA RYNNEL-DAGÖÖ, MD, PhD
Department of Otolaryngology
Karolinska Institute
Huddinge University Hospital
Stockholm, Sweden

BARRY SCHAITKIN, MD, FACS
Department of Otolaryngology
University of Pittsburgh School of Medicine
Pittsburgh, Pennsylvania

ANNE G. M. SCHILDER, MD, PhD
Wilhelmina Children's Hospital
University Medical Center
Utrecht, The Netherlands

RICHARD H. SCHWARTZ, MD
Department of Pediatric Allergy and Immunology
Inova Fairfax Hospital for Children
Falls Church, Virgina

UDAYAN K. SHAH, MD
Department of Otolaryngology, Head and Neck Surgery
University of Pennsylvania
Philadelphia, Pennsylvania

GORDON J. SIEGEL, MD
Department of Otolaryngology, Head and Neck Surgery
Feinberg School of Medicine
Chicago, Illinois

DAVID P. SKONER, MD
Department of Pediatrics and Otolaryngology
University of Pittsburgh School of Medicine
Pittsburgh, Pennsylvania

SVEN-ERIC STANGERUP, MD
Department of ENT
Gentofte University Hospital
Hellerup, Denmark

KARIN STENFELDT, MD, PhD
Department of Clinical Sciences
Umeå University
Umeå, Sweden

MASAHARU SUDO, MD
Department of Otolaryngology
Fukui Red Cross Hospital
Fukui, Japan

MARK J. SYMS, MD
Department of Neurosurgery
Barrow Neurological Institute
Phoenix, Arizona

HARUO TAKAHASHI, MD
Department of Translational Medical Sciences
Nagasaki University Graduate School of Biomedical Sciences
Nagasaki, Japan

TOMONORI TAKASAKA, MD, PhD
Tohoku University
Sendai, Japan

GLENN S. TAKATA, MD, MS
Department of Pediatrics
Keck School of Medicine
University of Southern California
Los Angeles, California

KAREN BORNE TEUFERT, MD
House Ear Clinic
Los Angeles, California

MIRKO TOS, MD, DMSc
Department of Otorhinolaryngology,
 Head and Neck Surgery
Gentofte University Hospital of Copenhagen
Copenhagen, Denmark

KITIRAT UNGKANONT, MD
Department of Otolaryngology
Mahidol University Siriraj Hospital
Bangkok, Thailand

ELLEN R. WALD, MD
Department of Pediatrics
University of Pittsburg School of Medicine
Pittsburgh, Pennsylvania

JANE L. WEISSMAN, MD
Department of Diagnostic Radiology
Oregon Health and Science University
Portland, Oregon

MARK E. WHITAKER, MD
Department of Otolaryngology
Geisinger Medical Center
Danville, Pennsylvania

NOBORU YAMANAKA, MD
Department of Otorhinolaryngology
Wakayama Medical College
Wakayama, Japan

ROBERT F. YELLON, MD
Department of Otolaryngology
University of Pittsburgh School of Medicine
Pittsburgh, Pennsylvania

RYO YUASA, MD
Department of Otolaryngology
Tohoku University School of Medicine
Sendai, Japan

CARLTON J. ZDANSKI, MD
Department of Otolaryngology, Head and Neck Surgery
University of North Carolina School of Medicine
Chapel Hill, North Carolina

I. Introduction

Chapter 1

Definitions of Otitis Media and Related Diseases

Charles D. Bluestone, MD

In this chapter, I provide the reader with our current state of knowledge of the terms and definitions of otitis media and related conditions. In an effort to reach consensus on the definitions and terminology of otitis media and related conditions, clinicians and scientists involved in this disease have been working for almost 25 years (Senturia et al, 1980). Prior to this period, many terms existed to describe the inflammatory conditions of the middle ear, including *secretory otitis media*, *middle ear catarrh*, and *suppurative otitis media*. This resulted in confusion and misunderstanding among clinicians who provided health care to infants and children with middle ear disease. This confusion also impeded appropriate evaluation of studies reported in the literature because interpreting the results of investigations depends on precise definitions of the disease studied. Currently, there is a consensus for using the terms *acute otitis media* and *otitis media with effusion*, but there is no consensus on many other terms and their definitions, such as chronic suppurative otitis media versus chronic otitis media, which can lead to confusion among clinicians.

The following terms, definitions, and classification of otitis media and its complications and sequelae have been used in international symposia, conferences, guidelines, and textbooks related to the disease (Bluestone, 1984; Bluestone, 1999; Bluestone and Klein, 2001; Lim et al, 1993; Lim et al, 1996; Stool et al, 1994). Also, a recently convened research meeting of international experts reached agreement on the terminology that follows (Bluestone et al, 2002), but the definitions of many other terms await future clarification and consensus.

Otitis media is an inflammation of the middle ear without reference to etiology or pathogenesis.

Acute otitis media is the rapid onset of signs and symptoms, such as otalgia and fever, of acute infection within the middle ear.

Otitis media with effusion is an inflammation of the middle ear with a collection of liquid in the middle ear space. The signs and symptoms of acute infection are absent, and there is no perforation of the tympanic membrane.

Eustachian tube dysfunction is a middle ear disorder that can have symptoms similar to otitis media, such as hearing loss, otalgia, and tinnitus, but middle ear effusion is usually absent.

Middle ear effusion designates a liquid in the middle ear but not the etiology, pathogenesis, pathology, or duration. An effusion may be (1) serous: a thin, watery liquid; (2) mucoid: a thick, viscid, mucus-like liquid; (3) purulent: a pus-like liquid; or (4) a combination of these. An effusion can be the result of either acute otitis media or otitis media with effusion. The effusion can be of recent onset, acute, or more long-lasting, subacute, or chronic.

Otorrhea is a discharge from the ear, originating at one or more of the following sites: the external auditory canal, middle ear, mastoid, inner ear, or intracranial cavity.

Classification of Otitis Media and Related Conditions

Table 1-1 is a classification derived from our present knowledge of otitis media and its complications and sequelae. The terms used in this classification are defined below.

When first encountered, otitis media can be either *acute otitis media* or *otitis media with effusion*, or its related disorder, *eustachian tube dysfunction*. Complications and sequelae of otitis media are classified into *intratemporal* (extracranial) complications and sequelae, which are those that occur within the temporal bone and those that occur within the intracranial cavity (intracranial complications). Several conditions may be complications or sequelae not of otitis media but of a related condition such as mastoiditis.

I have grouped and presented the intratemporal complications and sequelae of otitis media and related disor-

TABLE 1-1. Classification of Otitis Media and Its Complications and Sequelae

Acute otitis media

Otitis media with effusion
    Acute (short duration)
    Subacute
    Chronic

Eustachian tube dysfunction

Intratemporal (extracranial) complications and sequelae
    Hearing loss
        Conductive
        Sensorineural
    Perforation of tympanic membrane
        Acute perforation
            Without otitis media
            With otitis media (acute otitis media with perforation)
                Without otorrhea
                With otorrhea
        Chronic perforation
            Without otitis media
            With otitis media
                Acute otitis media
                    Without otorrhea
                    With otorrhea
                Chronic otitis media (and mastoiditis) (chronic suppurative otitis media)
                    Without otorrhea
                    With otorrhea
    Mastoiditis
        Acute
            Acute mastoiditis without periosteitis/osteitis
            Acute mastoiditis with periosteitis
            Acute mastoiditis with osteitis
                Without subperiosteal abscess
                With subperiosteal abscess
        Subacute
        Chronic
            Without chronic suppurative otitis media
            With chronic suppurative otitis media
    Petrositis
        Acute
        Chronic
    Labyrinthitis
        Acute
            Serous
                Localized (circumscribed)
                Generalized
            Suppurative
                Localized
                Generalized
        Chronic
            Labyrinthine sclerosis
    Facial paralysis
        Acute
        Chronic
    External otitis
        Acute external otitis
        Chronic external otitis
    Atelectasis of the middle ear
        Localized
            Without retraction pocket
            With retraction pocket
        Generalized

TABLE 1-1. continued

    Adhesive otitis media
    Cholesteatoma
        Without infection
        With infection
            Acute
                Without otorrhea
                With otorrhea
            Chronic (cholesteatoma with chronic suppurative otitis media)
                Without otorrhea
                With otorrhea
    Cholesterol granuloma
    Tympanosclerosis
    Ossicular discontinuity
    Ossicular fixation

Intracranial complications
    Meningitis
    Extradural abscess
    Subdural empyema
    Focal otitic encephalitis
    Brain abscess
    Dural sinus thrombosis
    Otitic hydrocephalus

ders, including atelectasis of the middle ear with a retraction pocket followed by adhesive otitis media and cholesteatoma, because I believe that cholesteatoma frequently progresses in this order. The suppurative complications are also grouped, including mastoiditis, petrositis, labyrinthitis, and facial paralysis.

Terminology and Definitions

Acute Otitis Media

Inflammation in the middle ear that is of rapid and short onset in association with the signs and symptoms of inflammation is characteristic of *acute otitis media*. *Acute suppurative otitis media* and *purulent otitis media* are synonyms still used by some but are not recommended terms. One or more local or systemic signs are present: otalgia (or pulling of the ear in the young infant), otorrhea, fever, recent onset of irritability, anorexia, vomiting, or diarrhea. The tympanic membrane is full or bulging, is opaque, and has limited or no mobility to pneumatic otoscopy, all of which indicate middle ear effusion. Erythema of the eardrum is an inconsistent finding. The acute onset of ear pain, fever, and a purulent discharge (otorrhea) through a perforation of the tympanic membrane (or tympanostomy tube) would also be evidence of acute otitis media. This is known as *acute otitis media with perforation*, a complication that is discussed below.

In the earliest stage of acute otitis media, only inflammation of the mucous membrane and tympanic membrane of the middle ear will be present without a middle ear effusion, that is, *acute otitis media without effusion*. Pneumatic otoscopy may reveal only myringitis in the appearance of the tympanic membrane, in which there is usually erythema and opacification of the eardrum but relatively normal mobility in response to applied positive and negative pressure. Blebs or bullae may be present when the disease is acute, and positive pressure may be present within the middle ear; positive middle ear pressure can be visualized with the pneumatic otoscope or identified by tympanometry. Children who have functioning tympanostomy tubes in place may present to their primary care physician very early at the acute onset of fever and otalgia and with an erythematous tympanic membrane but no otorrhea.

Persistent middle ear effusion is a term that is used to describe asymptomatic middle ear effusion persisting for weeks to months following the onset of acute otitis media. It should be defined, however, because this stage of acute otitis media is clinically and pathologically indistinguishable from otitis media with effusion (see below). Otitis media with effusion is not preceded by a clinically evident episode of acute otitis media, whereas persistent middle ear effusion continues following an attack of symptomatic acute otitis media. When middle ear effusion persists for 3 months or longer after an attack of acute otitis media, it is considered to be chronic.

Otitis Media with Effusion

Otitis media with effusion is the most appropriate and accepted term currently used to describe the presence of a middle ear effusion, but the signs and symptoms (eg, otalgia, fever) of acute infection are absent. Even though synonyms for relatively asymptomatic effusion developing in the middle ear have been used in the past, such as *secretory otitis media*, *nonsuppurative otitis media*, or *serous otitis media*, the most acceptable term is *otitis media with effusion*. Because the effusion may be serous (transudate), the term *secretory* may not be correct in all cases. Likewise, the term *nonsuppurative* may not be correct as asymptomatic middle ear effusion often contains bacteria (Post et al, 1995; Rayner et al, 1998) and may even be purulent (Riding et al, 1978). The term *serous otitis media* has been used if an amber or bluish effusion can be visualized through a translucent tympanic membrane but currently is not recommended. In addition, the most frequent otoscopic finding is opacification of the tympanic membrane, which prevents assessment of the type of effusion (eg, serous, mucoid, or purulent).

Pneumatic otoscopy frequently reveals either a retracted or convex tympanic membrane with impaired mobility. Fullness or even bulging may be visualized in some patients. Also, an air-fluid level, bubbles, or both may be observed through a translucent tympanic membrane. The most important distinction between otitis media with effusion and acute otitis media is that the signs and symptoms of acute infection (eg, otalgia and fever) are lacking in otitis media with effusion. Hearing loss is usually present in both conditions.

Eustachian Tube Dysfunction

Even though a patient may have symptoms similar to otitis media, such as hearing loss, otalgia, and tinnitus, middle ear effusion can be absent. This disorder is attributable to dysfunction of the eustachian tube in which the tube is either too narrow (ie, obstructed) or too wide (ie, patulous). The latter condition is most frequently associated with symptoms of autophony, that is, hearing one's own breathing and voice in the ear. This disorder can be acute and self-limited, recurrent acute, or chronic. Pneumatic otoscopy usually reveals the presence of middle ear negative pressure in which the tympanic membrane is retracted, but the otoscopic examination can be normal.

Intratemporal (Extracranial) Complications and Sequelae of Otitis Media

Intratemporal complications and sequelae of otitis media can be classified into complications and sequelae. Another disease or disorder that is concurrent with the otitis media is considered a *complication*, whereas a *sequela* of otitis media is a disease or disorder that follows, is a consequence of, or is caused by otitis media. Also, a complication or sequela may also cause another complication or sequela, for example, a cholesteatoma may cause a facial paralysis (Goldstein et al, 1998). Some conditions can be both a complication and a sequela, such as hearing loss.

Hearing Loss

The most common complication and sequela of otitis media is hearing impairment, which can be either *conductive*, *sensorineural*, or both. When conductive, the loss may be either transient or permanent. When sensorineural in origin, the impairment is usually permanent.

Conductive Hearing Loss

Fluctuating or persistent loss of hearing is present in most children who have middle ear effusion owing to acute otitis media or otitis media with effusion. The hearing loss can be either mild or moderate, with the maximum loss being no greater than 60 dB. However, the loss is usually between 15 and 40 dB. When owing to otitis media with effusion, there is an average loss of 27 dB (Fria et al, 1985). Hearing usually returns to normal thresholds when the middle ear effusion resolves. Permanent conductive hearing loss can occur, however, as a result of recurrent acute or chronic inflammation owing to adhesive otitis media or ossicular discontinuity or fixation. Negative pressure in the ear, in the absence of middle ear effusion, can also be a cause of conductive hearing loss (Finkelstein et al, 1992). Patients with eustachian tube dysfunction and intermittent or persistent high negative pressure may have an associated conductive hearing impairment.

Although controversy exists, hearing loss caused by chronic and recurrent middle ear effusions may be associated with delay or impairment of speech, language, and cognition in young children, which may or may not affect performance in school (Paradise et al, 2001; Teele et al, 1984).

Sensorineural Hearing Loss

Sensorineural hearing loss can be caused by otitis media or one of its complications or sequelae. The hearing loss can be mild, moderate, severe, or profound. Reversible sensorineural hearing impairment is generally attributed to the effect of increased tension and stiffness of the round window membrane. Permanent sensorineural hearing loss is most likely attributable to the spread of infection or products of inflammation through the round window membrane into the labyrinth (Johansson et al, 1993; Lundman et al, 1992), development of a perilymphatic fistula in the oval or round window (Weber et al, 1993), or a suppurative complication such as labyrinthitis.

Perforation of the Tympanic Membrane

When a perforation of the tympanic membrane occurs, it can be acute or chronic, otitis media may or may or not be present, and when otitis media is present, otorrhea may or may not be present.

Acute Perforation

Perforation of the tympanic membrane, when acute, is most commonly associated with otitis media (with or without otorrhea) but may also occur without otitis media. Otorrhea indicates otitis media when there is a perforation.

Most commonly, acute perforations without otitis media occur following acute perforation *with* otitis media; the middle ear inflammation resolves, but the perforation persists. Such perforations will either spontaneously heal or progress to a chronic perforation. Although relatively uncommon compared with the above pathogenesis, a perforation of the tympanic membrane can occur in the absence of otitis media. This may result from penetrating trauma, as a complication of extreme changes in middle ear pressures (eg, barotrauma), or, more rarely, from long-standing severe atelectasis.

One of the most common complications of acute otitis media is perforation of the tympanic membrane accompanied by acute drainage (otorrhea) through the defect. This is known as *acute otitis media with perforation*. Also, an acute perforation can be present in which there is otitis media but no evidence of otorrhea. Acute otitis media with perforation was more frequently encountered before the widespread use of antimicrobial therapy. It is still prevalent in developing countries, where primary health care is inadequate (Bluestone, 1998b). An acute perforation can occur, however, as a complication

of chronic otitis media with effusion, as reported in Australian Aborigines (Boswell and Nienhuys, 1996).

If an episode of acute otitis media is complicated by a perforation (usually accompanied by otorrhea), one of four outcomes is possible: (1) resolution of the acute otitis media and healing of the tympanic membrane defect; (2) resolution of the acute otitis media, but the perforation becomes chronic; (3) the perforation and otitis media persist to become chronic (ie, *chronic suppurative otitis media*); or (4) a suppurative complication of otitis media develops (Bluestone, 2000).

Chronic Perforation

Chronic perforation occurs when an acute perforation of the tympanic membrane fails to heal after 3 months or longer. It may be present with or without otitis media; the former condition may or may not be associated with otorrhea. Some clinicians have termed chronic perforation that is without otorrhea as "*inactive*" *chronic suppurative otitis media* and a chronic perforation associated with otorrhea as "*active*" *chronic suppurative otitis media* (Browning and Gatehouse, 1992). This classification is not only confusing, it is also inappropriate in some cases, such as when there is a chronic perforation and the middle ear does not become infected. Inclusion of chronic perforations under the term *chronic otitis media*, irrespective of the status of the middle ear, should be avoided. The term is confusing and potentially misleading.

When a chronic perforation is present and the middle ear becomes acutely infected, the disease is appropriately termed a *chronic perforation with acute otitis media*: otorrhea may or may not be present. The otitis media, with or without otorrhea, will have one of four possible outcomes: (1) acute otitis media occurs but resolves without progressing to the chronic stage; (2) recurrent acute otitis media occurs but does not progress to the chronic stage; (3) acute otitis media persists into the chronic stage (ie, *chronic suppurative otitis media*); or (4) recurrent acute otitis media and chronic suppurative otitis media occur periodically over time (Bluestone, 1998a).

Chronic perforation with chronic otitis media or, more commonly, *chronic suppurative otitis media* is a stage of ear disease in which chronic inflammation of the middle ear cleft is present (*middle ear cleft* is a term frequently used for the middle ear, eustachian tube, and mastoid gas cells) and there is a chronic perforation of the tympanic membrane. Mastoiditis is invariably part of the pathologic process. The condition has been called *chronic otitis media*, but this term can be confused with chronic otitis media with effusion, in which no perforation is present. It is also called *chronic suppurative otitis media and mastoiditis*, *chronic purulent otitis media*, and *chronic otomastoiditis*. The most descriptive term is *chronic otitis media with perforation, discharge, and mastoiditis* (Senturia et al, 1980), but this is not commonly used. When a cholesteatoma is also present, the term *cholesteatoma with chronic suppurative otitis media* is used; cholesteatoma can be present even if there is no acute or chronic otitis media.

Mastoiditis

Mastoiditis may or may not be a suppurative complication of otitis media because both acute otitis media and otitis media with effusion can also involve the mastoid. Mastoiditis may be acute, subacute, or chronic. The following is a classification of the stages of this suppurative complication that has recently been revised based on an understanding of the pathogenesis and pathology and on the more recent availability of computed tomographic (CT) scans (Bluestone, 1998a).

Acute Mastoiditis

Acute mastoiditis can be staged as follows:

- *acute mastoiditis without periosteitis/osteitis*
- *acute mastoiditis with periosteitis*
- *acute mastoid osteitis*

Acute mastoiditis without periosteitis/osteitis is the natural extension and part of the pathologic process of acute middle ear infection. No periosteitis or osteitis of the mastoid is present. Most likely, all patients with acute otitis media probably have extension of the middle ear disease into the mastoid gas cell system, but this stage of acute mastoiditis is not strictly a complication of otitis media. It can nevertheless be misinterpreted as a complication of otitis media, especially when CT scans are obtained for other reasons during an episode of otitis media, for example, following head trauma. Specific signs or symptoms of mastoid infection, such as protrusion of the pinna, postauricular swelling, tenderness, pain, or erythema, are not present in this most common type of mastoiditis. This stage of mastoiditis can either resolve (most common) or progress into a true complication of otitis media, that is, *acute mastoiditis with periosteitis*. This, in turn, can progress to *acute mastoid osteitis*.

Acute mastoiditis with periosteitis can develop when infection within the mastoid spreads to the periosteum covering the mastoid process. The route of infection from the mastoid cells to the periosteum is by venous channels, usually the mastoid emissary vein. This stage of acute mastoiditis should not be confused with the presence of a subperiosteal abscess. Acute mastoiditis with periosteitis is characterized by erythema, mild swelling, and tenderness in the postauricular area. The pinna may or may not be displaced inferiorly and anteriorly, with loss of the postauricular crease; sagging of the posterior external auditory canal is infrequently present (Goldstein et al, 1998).

Acute mastoid osteitis has also been termed *acute "coalescent" mastoiditis* or *acute surgical mastoiditis*, but the pathologic process is *osteitis*. When infection within the mastoid gas cell system progresses, rarefying osteitis

can cause destruction of the bony trabeculae that separate the mastoid cells. The postauricular area is usually involved, but mastoid osteitis can occur without evidence of postauricular involvement. The signs and symptoms are similar to those described above for acute mastoiditis with periosteitis; a *subperiosteal abscess* may or may not be present. The infection can spread into the neck, causing a Bezold's abscess (Marioni et al, 2001).

Subacute Mastoiditis

Although relatively uncommon, subacute mastoiditis may develop if an acute middle ear and mastoid infection fails to totally resolve within the usual 10 to 14 days. This stage has also been termed *masked mastoiditis*. The classic signs and symptoms of acute mastoiditis, such as pinna displacement, postauricular erythema, or subperiosteal abscess, are usually absent, but otalgia with postauricular pain and fever may be present. The diagnosis is made by CT scan. In this stage, the infection in the mastoid can progress into another intratemporal complication or even an intracranial complication.

Chronic Mastoiditis

When the mastoid is chronically infected, it is usually attributable to *chronic suppurative otitis media* with a *chronic perforation* of the tympanic membrane. Chronic mastoiditis may also occur in the absence of chronic suppurative otitis media. Patients with relatively asymptomatic chronic otitis media with effusion frequently have some or all of the mastoid gas cell system involved in the chronic disease process. This is commonly visualized on CT scans of the temporal bones. Chronic infection may also be present in the mastoid, even in the absence of middle ear disease owing to obstruction of the aditus ad antrum; the otitis media resolved, but the disease in the mastoid did not. Symptoms can include low-grade fever, chronic otalgia, and tenderness over the mastoid process.

Petrositis

Infection from the middle ear and mastoid gas cells can spread into the petrosal gas cells of the mastoid apex, which is called *petrositis*; it is also termed *petrous apicitis* or *apical petrositis*. This suppurative complication may be either acute or chronic and may result from acute otitis media or chronic ear disease (Somers et al, 2001). When chronic infection is the cause, it is usually attributable to chronic suppurative otitis media, cholesteatoma, or both.

Labyrinthitis

When infection spreads from the middle ear, mastoid gas cells, or both into the cochlear and vestibular apparatus, the resulting complication is termed *labyrinthitis*. The classification proposed by Schuknecht (1993) is appropriate, describing the complication as either *serous labyrinthitis* (also termed *toxic labyrinthitis*) or *suppura-*

tive labyrinthitis. Labyrinthitis may also be attributable to meningitis, which may or may not be a complication of otitis media. Serous and suppurative labyrinthitis may be acute or chronic or circumscribed or generalized, respectively. The end stage of chronic labyrinthitis is termed *labyrinthine sclerosis* or *labyrinthitis ossificans*.

Facial Paralysis

Facial paralysis caused by otitis media or one of its complications or sequelae may be either acute or chronic. It may result from acute otitis media or chronic middle ear and mastoid disease, such as cholesteatoma, chronic suppurative otitis media, or both (Shapiro et al, 1996). The grading system of the degree of injury to the face proposed by House and Brackmann (1985) is generally accepted and correlates with recovery but has been developed only for chronic facial paralysis, not acute.

External Otitis

Acute otitis media with perforation and otorrhea or chronic suppurative otitis media can cause an infection of the external auditory canal termed *external otitis*; it is also termed *infectious eczematoid external otitis*. An infection in the mastoid may also erode the bone of the ear canal or the postauricular area, resulting in dermatitis. The skin of the ear canal is erythematous, edematous, and filled with purulent drainage, and yellow-crusted plaques may be present. The organisms involved are usually the same as those found in a middle ear–mastoid infection, but the flora of the external canal usually contribute to the infectious process.

Atelectasis of the Middle Ear

Atelectasis of the middle ear is a sequela of eustachian tube dysfunction. Retraction or collapse of the tympanic membrane is characteristic of the condition; the tympanic membrane is a component of the lateral wall of the middle ear. Collapse implies passivity (absence of high negative middle ear pressure), whereas retraction implies active pulling inward of the tympanic membrane, usually from negative middle ear pressure owing to eustachian tube obstruction. Middle ear effusion is usually absent in atelectasis. The condition may be acute or chronic, localized (with or without a *retraction pocket*) or generalized, and mild, moderate, or severe.

Adhesive Otitis Media

Adhesive otitis media is a result of healing following chronic inflammation of the middle ear and mastoid. The mucous membrane is thickened by proliferation of fibrous tissue, which frequently impairs movement of the ossicles, resulting in conductive hearing loss. The pathologic process is a proliferation of fibrous tissue within the middle ear and mastoid termed *fibrous sclerosis* (Schuknecht, 1974). When cystic spaces are present, it is called *fibrocystic sclerosis*, and when there is new bone growth in the mastoid, it is termed *fibro-osseous sclerosis*.

Cholesteatoma

Cholesteatoma occurs when keratinizing stratified squamous epithelium accumulates in the middle ear or other pneumatized portions of the temporal bone. The term *aural* distinguishes this type of cholesteatoma from a similar pathologic entity that occurs outside the temporal bone. *Acquired* distinguishes it as a sequela of otitis media or related conditions (eg, retraction pocket of the tympanic membrane) distinct from aural congenital cholesteatomas. Even though this term is a misnomer—*keratoma* is more consistent with the pathology—cholesteatoma is in common use and is thus accepted (Ferlito, 1993).

Cholesteatoma can be classified as *congenital* or *acquired* (Fisch, 1994). The latter may be further subclassified as a sequela of otitis media (and certain related conditions) or as a result of implantation (iatrogenic or owing to trauma). Otitis media may also be involved in the pathogenesis of congenital cholesteatoma. *Congenital cholesteatoma* is not a sequela of otitis media, whereas *acquired cholesteatoma* is. Despite a recent and alternative acquired pathogenetic theory (Tos, 2000), classically, *congenital cholesteatoma* develops as a rest of epithelial tissue within the temporal bone in the absence of a defect in the tympanic membrane. In contrast to this strict definition, an *aural acquired cholesteatoma* develops from a retraction pocket in the pars tensa or pars flaccida, migration of epithelium through a preexisting defect of the tympanic membrane (eg, perforation), or, more rarely, metaplasia of the middle ear–mastoid mucous membrane. A cholesteatoma may involve only the middle ear, mastoid, or both and may or may not extend beyond the temporal bone.

Cholesteatoma may or may not be associated with otitis media and mastoiditis, but when otitis media is present, the infection may be acute or chronic, and otorrhea may or may not be present. A cholesteatoma that is present in association with chronic inflammation of the middle ear and mastoid is defined as *cholesteatoma with chronic suppurative otitis media*. Thus, cholesteatoma may or may not be associated with chronic suppurative otitis media. It is inappropriate to include cholesteatoma under the term *chronic otitis media* as it lacks an associated infection such as chronic suppurative otitis media.

Cholesterol Granuloma

Cholesterol granuloma is a relatively uncommon sequela of otitis media. It has often been termed *idiopathic hemotympanum*, but this term is a misnomer because there is no evidence of blood in the middle ear (Sadé et al, 1980). The blue appearance of the tympanic membrane is most likely attributable to the reflection of light from the thick liquid (granuloma) within the middle ear. The tissue is composed of chronic granulations with foreign body giant cells, foam cells, and cholesterol crystals within the middle ear, mastoid, or both (Miura et al, 2002).

Tympanosclerosis

Tympanosclerosis is characterized by whitish plaques in the tympanic membrane and nodular deposits in the submucosal layers of the middle ear. The pathologic process occurs in the lamina propria in the tympanic membrane and affects the basement membrane if within the middle ear. Hyalinization is followed in both sites by deposition of calcium and phosphate crystals. Conductive hearing loss may occur if the ossicles become embedded in the deposits. Tympanosclerosis is usually a sequela of chronic middle ear disease (chronic otitis media with effusion or chronic suppurative otitis media) but is also associated with trauma, such as following tympanostomy tube insertion. Conductive hearing loss secondary to tympanosclerosis involving only the tympanic membrane is rare, although scarring of the eardrum at the site of tympanostomy tube insertion is common (Asiri, et al, 1999).

Ossicular Discontinuity

Ossicular discontinuity, a sequela of otitis media and certain related conditions, is the result of rarefying osteitis caused by inflammation; a retraction pocket or cholesteatoma can also cause resorption of ossicles. The most commonly involved ossicle is the incus; its long process usually erodes, resulting in a disarticulation of the incudostapedial joint. The second most commonly eroded ossicle is the stapes; usually, the crural arches are initially involved. The malleus may also become eroded but not as frequently as the incus and stapes.

Ossicular Fixation

The ossicles can become fixed as a sequela of chronic middle ear inflammation, usually by fibrous tissue caused by adhesive otitis media, tympanosclerosis, or both. The ossicle itself or one of the joints (ie, incudostapedial or incudomalleolar) may be fixed.

Intracranial Complications of Otitis Media

The seven intracranial suppurative complications of otitis media may be caused by an intratemporal complication such as mastoiditis, labyrinthitis, or one or more of the other intracranial complications of otitis media (Go et al, 2000).

Meningitis

Meningitis is an inflammation of the meninges that, when a suppurative complication of otitis media or certain related conditions (eg, labyrinthitis), is usually caused by a bacterium associated with infections of the middle ear, mastoid, or both. The infection may spread directly from the middle ear–mastoid through the dura and extend to the pia-arachnoid, causing generalized meningitis. Suppurative complications in an adjacent area, such as a subdural abscess, brain abscess, or lateral sinus thrombophlebitis, may also cause an inflammation of the meninges.

Extradural Abscess

Extradural abscess, also termed *epidural abscess*, is an infection that occurs between the dura of the brain and the cranial bone. It usually results from the destruction of bone adjacent to the dura by cholesteatoma, chronic suppurative otitis media, or both. This occurs when granulation tissue and purulent material collect between the lateral aspect of the dura and the adjacent temporal bone. Dural granulation tissue within a bony defect is much more common than an actual accumulation of pus. When an abscess is present, a dural sinus thrombosis or, less commonly, a subdural or brain abscess may also be present.

Subdural Empyema

A *subdural empyema* occurs when purulent material collects within the potential space between the dura externally and the arachnoid membrane internally. Because the pus collects in a preformed space, it is correctly termed *empyema* rather than *abscess*. Subdural empyema may develop as a direct extension or, more rarely, by thrombophlebitis through venous channels.

Focal Otitic Encephalitis

Focal otitic encephalitis (also termed *cerebritis*) is a potential suppurative complication of acute otitis media, cholesteatoma, or chronic suppurative otitis media. It may also be a complication of one or more of the suppurative complications of these disorders, such as an extradural abscess or dural sinus thrombophlebitis, in which a focal area of the brain is edematous and inflamed. The signs and symptoms of this complication are similar to those associated with a brain abscess, but suppuration within the brain is not present.

Brain Abscess

Otogenic *brain abscess* is a potential intracranial suppurative complication of cholesteatoma, chronic suppurative otitis media, or both (Sennaroglu and Sozeri, 2000). It may also be caused by acute otitis media or acute mastoiditis. In addition, an intratemporal complication such as labyrinthitis or apical petrositis may be the focus, or the abscess may follow the development of an adjacent intracranial otogenic suppurative complication such as lateral sinus thrombophlebitis or meningitis.

Dural Sinus Thrombosis

Lateral and *sigmoid sinus thrombosis* or *thrombophlebitis* can occur as a result of acute otitis media, an intratemporal complication (eg, acute mastoiditis or apical petrositis), or another intracranial complication of otitis media. The superior and petrosal dural sinuses are also intimately associated with the temporal bone but are rarely affected.

Otitic Hydrocephalus

Otitic hydrocephalus describes a complication of otitis media in which there is increased intracranial pressure without abnormalities of cerebrospinal fluid. The pathogenesis of the syndrome is unknown, but because the ventricles are not dilated, the term *benign intracranial hypertension* also seems appropriate. The disease is usually associated with lateral sinus thrombosis.

References

Asiri S, Hasham A, Anazy FA, et al. Tympanosclerosis: review of literature and incidence among patients with middle-ear infection. J Laryngol Otol 1999;113:1076–80.

Bluestone CD. Definitions and classifications: state of the art. In: Lim DJ, Bluestone CD, Klein JO, Nelson JD, editors. Recent advances in otitis media with effusion. Philadelphia: BC Decker; 1984. p. 1–4.

Bluestone CD. Acute and chronic mastoiditis and chronic suppurative otitis media. Semin Pediatr Infect Dis 1998a;9:12–26.

Bluestone CD. Epidemiology and pathogenesis of chronic suppurative otitis media: implications for prevention and treatment. Int J Pediatr Otorhinolaryngol 1998b;42:207–23.

Bluestone CD. Definitions, terminology, and classification. In: Rosenfeld RM, Bluestone CD, editors. Evidence-based otitis media. Hamilton (ON): BC Decker; 1999. p. 85–103.

Bluestone CD. Clinical course, complications and sequelae of acute otitis media. Pediatr Infect Dis J 2000;19 Suppl:S37–46.

Bluestone CD. Chairman: committee report: terminology and classification of otitis media and its complications and sequelae. In: Lim DJ, Bluestone CD, Casselbrant ML, et al, editors. 7th International Symposium on Recent Advances in Otitis Media: report of the research conference. Ann Otol Rhinol Laryngol 2002;111(2 Suppl 188):102–14.

Bluestone CD, Klein JO, editors. Otitis media in infants and children. 3rd ed. Philadelphia: WB Saunders; 2001.

Boswell JB, Nienhuys TG. Patterns of persistent otitis media in the first year of life in Aboriginal and non-Aboriginal Australian infants. Ann Otol Rhinol Laryngol 1996;105:893–900.

Browning GG, Gatehouse D. The prevalence of middle ear disease in the adult British population. Clin Otolaryngol 1992;17:317–21.

Ferlito A. A review of the definition, terminology and pathology of aural cholesteatoma. J Laryngol Otol 1993;107:483–8.

Finkelstein Y, Zohar Y, Talmi YP, et al. Effects of acute negative middle ear pressure on hearing. Acta Otolaryngol (Stockh) 1992;112:88–95.

Fisch U. Tympanoplasty and mastoidectomy. New York: Thieme; 1994.

Fria TJ, Cantekin EI, Eichler JA. Hearing acuity of children with otitis media with effusion. Arch Otolaryngol Head Neck Surg 1985;111:10–6.

Go C, Bernstein JM, de Jong AL, et al. Intracranial complications of acute mastoiditis. Int J Pediatr Otorhinolaryngol 2000;52:143–8.

Goldstein NA, Casselbrant ML, Bluestone CD, Kurs-Lasky M. Intratemporal complications of acute otitis media in infants and children. Otolaryngol Head Neck Surg 1998;119:444–54.

House JW, Brackmann DE. Facial nerve grading system. Otolaryngol Head Neck Surg 1985;93:146–7.

Johansson U, Hellstrom S, Anniko M. Round window membrane in serous and purulent otitis media. Structural study in the rat. Ann Otol Rhinol Laryngol 1993;102:227–35.

Lim DL, Bluestone CD, Casselbrant ML, et al, editors. Recent advances in otitis media: proceedings of the Sixth International Symposium. Hamilton (ON): BC Decker; 1996.

Lim DJ, Bluestone CD, Klein JO, et al, editors. Recent advances in otitis media: proceedings of the Fifth International Symposium. Toronto: BC Decker; 1993.

Lundman L, Juhn SK, Bagger-Sjöbäck D, Svanborg C. Permeability of the normal round window membrane to *Haemophilus influenzae* type b endotoxin. Acta Otolaryngol (Stockh) 1992;112:524–9.

Marioni G, de Filippis C, Tregnaghi A, et al. Bezold's abscess in children: case report and review of the literature. Int J Pediatr Otorhinolaryngol 2001;61:173–7.

Miura M, Sando I, Orita Y, Hirsch BE. Histopathological study of the temporal bones and eustachian tubes of children with cholesterol granuloma. Ann Otol Rhinol Laryngol 2002;111:609–15.

Paradise JL, Feldman HM, Campbell TF, et al. Effect of early or delayed insertion of tympanostomy tubes for persistent otitis media on developmental outcomes at age of three years. N Engl J Med 2001;344:1179–87.

Post JC, Preston RA, Aul JJ, et al. Molecular analysis of bacterial pathogens in otitis media with effusion. JAMA 1995;273:1598–604.

Rayner MG, Zhang Y, Gorry MC, et al. Evidence of bacterial metabolic activity in culture-negative otitis media with effusion. JAMA 1998;279:296–9.

Riding KH, Bluestone CD, Michaels RH, et al. Microbiology of recurrent and chronic otitis media with effusion. J Pediatr 1978;93:739–43.

Sadé J, Halevy A, Klajman A, Mualem T. Cholesterol granuloma. Acta Otolaryngol (Stockh) 1980;89:233–9.

Schuknecht HF. Pathology of the ear. Cambridge (MA): Harvard University Press; 1974.

Schuknecht HF. Pathology of the ear. 2nd ed. Philadelphia: Lea & Febiger; 1993.

Sennaroglu, L, Sozeri B. Otogenic brain abscess: review of 41 cases. Otolaryngol Head Neck Surg 2000;123:751–5.

Senturia BH, Bluestone CD, Klein JO, et al. Report of the ad hoc committee on definition and classification of otitis media with effusion. Ann Otol Rhinol Laryngol 1980;89:3–4.

Shapiro NM, Schaitken BM, May M. Facial paralysis in children. In: Bluestone CD, Stool SE, Kenna MA, editors. Pediatric otolaryngology. 3rd ed. Philadelphia: WB Saunders; 1996. p. 325–6.

Somers TJ, De Foer B, Govaerts P, et al. Chronic petrous apicitis with pericarotid extension into the neck in a child. Ann Otol Rhinol Laryngol 2001;110:988–91.

Stool SE, Berg AO, Berman S, et al. Managing otitis media with effusion in young children. Quick reference guide for clinicians. Rockville (MD): Agency for Health Care Policy and Research, Public Health Service, US Department of Health and Human Services; 1994. AHCPR Publication No.: 94-0623.

Teele DW, Klein JO, Rosner B. Otitis media with effusion during the first three years of life and development of speech and language. Pediatrics 1984;74:282–7.

Tos M. A new pathogenesis of mesotympanic (congenital) cholesteatoma. Laryngoscope 2000;110:1890–7.

Weber PC, Perez BA, Bluestone CD. Congenital perilymphatic fistula and associated middle ear abnormalities. Laryngoscope 1993;103:160–4.

Chapter 2

DIAGNOSTIC METHODS

OLLI RUUSKANEN, MD, AINO RUOHOLA, MD

According to the definition of otitis media (OM), the presence of middle ear effusion (MEE) should be detected to justify the diagnosis. General symptoms of acute infection and specific signs of acute infection in the tympanic membrane (TM) are associated with acute otitis media (AOM), characterizing the acute nature of AOM. In otitis media with effusion (OME) the patient has no signs of acute illness. The presence of MEE is, however, the cornerstone of the diagnosis of AOM and OME; therefore, all efforts should be made to verify its presence or absence.

There are several options to detect MEE (Table 2-1). Tympanocentesis and aspiration of MEE are the gold standard for diagnosis of OM. At present, in everyday clinical practice, we do not use or recommend tympanocentesis because it is a painful and traumatic procedure in children. Further, the removal of MEE only once does not improve recovery from illness, and microbiologic diagnosis rarely aids treatment. Pneumatic otoscopy and tympanometry are the options of choice to indirectly detect MEE and should be carefully taught to every physician who plans to care for children. The major goal of diagnostics in research is to make a reliable diagnosis and in clinical practice to avoid overdiagnoses.

Diagnostic Signs and Symptoms

AOM almost always coincides with viral upper respiratory tract infection (URI); therefore, children with AOM and those with URI but without AOM have mainly the same symptoms, such as rhinitis (clear or purulent), cough, fever, irritability, and/or restless sleeping (Heikkinen and Ruuskanen, 1995; Kontiokari et al, 1998; Niemelä et al, 1994). The most specific symptom of AOM is earache or ear-related symptoms (eg, rubbing, pulling, or feeling of blockage), and at least one of these appears in 59 to 72% of children with AOM (Heikkinen and Ruuskanen, 1995; Kontiokari et al, 1998; Niemelä et al, 1994). It is, however, important to remember that of children with AOM, 28 to 41% do not have any ear-related symptoms, possibly owing to the inability of young children to express themselves (Heikkinen and Ruuskanen, 1995; Niemelä et al, 1994). Fever is a sign of acute infection and is thus often regarded as also related to AOM. Nonetheless, the relationship is weak as 42 to 69% of children with AOM have fever, and, comparably, fever occurs in 28 to 77% of children with uncomplicated URI (Heikkinen and Ruuskanen, 1995; Kontiokari et al, 1998; Niemelä et al, 1994). The gastrointestinal signs and symptoms seem to have no association with AOM (Kontiokari et al, 1998).

In OME, there are typically no signs or symptoms of illness. However, MEE that is present may often induce a hearing loss that cannot be reliably assessed by parents (Brody et al, 1999).

In conclusion, AOM or OME cannot be reliably predicted by the symptoms or by parental assessment, and the exploration of the TMs should therefore always be included in the clinical examination of a child.

Detection of Middle Ear Effusion

Otoscopy

Pneumatic otoscopy or otomicroscopy is used to visualize the appearance and mobility of the TM, suggestive of the presence or absence of MEE. Diagnostic differentiation of AOM and OME by otoscopy may be difficult. In one study, pediatricians overdiagnosed AOM in 27% of the cases (Pichichero and Poole, 2001). Otoscopy is highly subjective and as good as the experience of the otoscopist, and even among experts, significant interobserver variation may occur (Karma et al, 1989). However, a validated otoscopist can often reliably diagnose AOM based only on the pathologic appearance of the TM (Table 2-2).

Although time-consuming, active otoscopy training and, if possible, formal validation should have a high pri-

TABLE 2-1. Diagnostic Methods to Detect Middle Ear Effusion

Method	Level
Pneumatic otoscopy	All physicians
Tympanometry	All physicians
Acoustic reflectometry	All physicians?
Otomicroscopy	ENT–specialists
Tympanocentesis/myringotomy	ENT–specialists/pediatricians

TABLE 2-2. Appearance and Mobility of a Tympanic Membrane

Character	Normal	AOM	OME
Position	Concave	Full, bulging	Neutral, retracted
Color	Bright gray	Fire truck red Cloudy gray Green/yellow Gray blisters	Gray, pink
Translucent	Yes	No	No
Light reflex	Yes	No, dispersed	Yes, no, dispersed
Blood vessels	Not visible	Often visible	Often visible
Fluid level	No	Sometimes	Sometimes
Mobility	Free like a sail in the wind, moved by low pressure	More or less clearly decreased	Decreased

ority status in medical training (Kaleida and Stool, 1992). Sufficient lighting and careful cerumen removal are necessary for reliable otoscopy; otherwise, a considerable proportion of OM cases may be missed. Proper instruments for successful otoscopy are shown in Figure 2-1. If all essential requirements are fulfilled (most importantly that the cerumen is carefully removed), otoscopy can be a reliable diagnostic tool, which was shown in an extensive study describing the results of pneumatic otoscopy and comparing them to the presence of MEE verified by myringotomy (Karma et al, 1989). When children have acute symptoms, the best otoscopic signs predicting the presence of MEE are cloudy color, bulging position, and distinctly impaired mobility. Although slight redness is often used as a diagnostic criterion of AOM, the presence of MEE can be predicted as reliably by tossing a coin as by seeing a red ear. Further, only half of the children with a diagnosis of AOM have a red TM, and only the hemorrhagic fire truck redness is suggestive of AOM with MEE (Arola et al, 1990). Strong redness or blisters are seen in

hemorrhagic and bullous myringitis, which are early stages of AOM with the common otitis media pathogens in MEE (Palmu et al, 2001). A TM with a fully normal slightly gray color is seen in only 1 to 5% of children with MEE, and this sign, as well as the normal mobility of the TM, suggests the absence of MEE (Karma et al, 1989). A structured manner of analyzing the signs of the TM is encouraged (Kaleida, 1997). We have found a structured form to be useful in training medical students and office practitioners to pay attention not only to the color but primarily to the translucency, light reflex, and mobility of a TM. Diagnostic algorithms have their role in research but hardly in everyday practice (Le et al, 1992).

In our practice, a handheld pneumatic otoscope is often more useful than an otomicroscope. An otoscope can easily be carried and provides a good and quick visualization of the TM and its mobility. However, an otomicroscope may be superior when suctioning MEE through a tympanostomy tube, when examining granulations or other changes of a TM, and in some cases of cerumen removal.

FIGURE 2-1. Diagnostic tools. 1 = Pneumatic otoscopy with halogen bulb. 2 = 2 mm reusable speculum for otoscopy. 3 = 3 mm disposable speculum for otoscopy. 4 = 4 mm disposable speculum for otoscopy. 5 = 5 mm reusable speculum with a rubber tip for perfect seal of the ear canal. 6 = Sterile glass suction tip. 7 = Alligator forceps. 8 = Surgical head for otoscope. 9–11= Instruments for cerumen removal. 12 = Portable tympanometer.

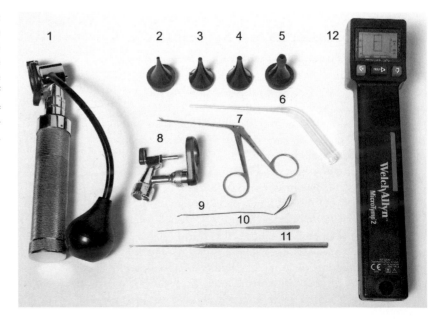

Tympanometry

Tympanometry can be used to detect MEE and/or middle ear pressure. Several different instruments, portable and table models, are available. The device screen displays a curve: a tympanogram that is a graphic presentation of the acoustic admittance of the middle ear as a function of altered air pressure (Brookhouser, 1998). Acoustic admittance means the ease with which acoustic energy transfers from one system to another. When the media on both sides of the TM have similar mechanical properties, acoustic energy transfers most effectively from the ear canal through the middle ear into the fluid of the cochlea.

The highest peak of the tympanogram is the tympanometric peak. Its position on the **y**-axis designates static admittance and indicates the maximal admittance of sound energy. Its position on the **x**-axis indicates tympanometric peak pressure. A more reliable diagnostic parameter is tympanometric width, which is the pressure interval on the **x**-axis at the 50% level of the peak static admittance. The recommended screening test criteria are static admittance and tympanometric width for which normative, age-dependent, and instrument-specific values can be given.

Tympanometry indirectly evaluates the pressure in the middle ear by the tympanometric peak pressure because that designates the equal pressure levels on both sides of the TM. Further, the tympanogram estimates the mobility of the TM because the presence of MEE decreases admittance and inhibits the pressure-provoked movement of the TM.

Tympanograms have been assorted differently by several authors (Brookhouser, 1998). Paradise and colleagues created a detailed classification into 15 types of curves from which the importance of tympanometric gradient as a predictor of MEE can easily be recognized.

Classically, tympanograms are divided according to Jerger (1970) into three types of curves as shown in Figure 2-2.

The reliability of tympanometry in the detection of MEE using myringotomy as a reference has been assessed in numerous studies but mainly in children with OME and those who are referred for tympanostomy tube placement (Brookhouser, 1998). It is widely accepted that a type A curve predicts the absence of MEE, and in the few cases in which myringotomy has revealed MEE, the amount has been subtle (Koivunen et al, 1997). The sensitivity and specificity of a type B curve vary between 60 and 90%, being higher in OME than in AOM populations. Cooperation affects the reliability of tympanometry; therefore, in children at the OM-prone age, tympanometry fails significantly more often as a result of noncooperation than in older children (Koivunen et al, 1997). Of children suspected to have OME and aged less than 2.5 years, 60% did not cooperate; therefore, half of the tympanograms did not show any curve. Furthermore, type B curves were often false-positive. Therefore, the sensitivity of tympanometry was 71% and its specificity only 38% with myringotomy as a reference. On the contrary, among cooperative children, a type B curve showed sensitivity of 79% and specificity of 93%. In another survey among infants less than 1 year of age, tympanometry was successful in 94% of cases (Palmu et al, 1999). The sensitivity of a B curve in the detection of MEE was 82% and its specificity was 98% at nonacute visits when compared with myringotomy and/or pneumatic otoscopy. Unfortunately, at acute sick visits, the sensitivity decreased to 67%. A type C curve is common during a URI, after an episode of AOM, and in children referred for tympanostomy tube placement. Its value as a predictor of MEE seems to depend on population characteristics. In a young, basically healthy pediatric population examined during health and at sick visits at an outpatient clinic, a type C curve was related to MEE in only 15 to 19% of ears

Curve	A	B	C
Static admittance	> 0.2 mmho	< 0.2 mmho	> 0.2 mmho
Tympanometric peak pressure	> −139 daPa	No peak	< −139 daPa
Hits of middle ear status	Normal	MEE	Negative middle ear pressure without/with MEE

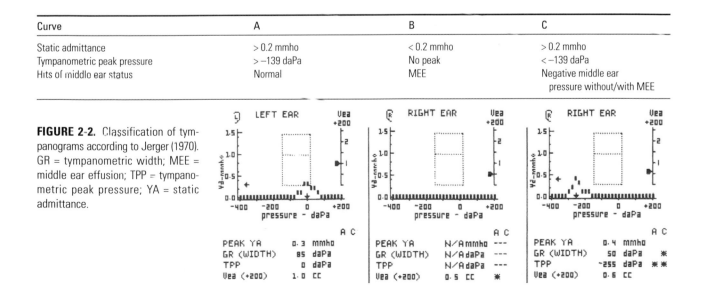

FIGURE 2-2. Classification of tympanograms according to Jerger (1970). GR = tympanometric width; MEE = middle ear effusion; TPP = tympanometric peak pressure; YA = static admittance.

(Palmu et al, 2001). The probability of MEE increased with decreasing static admittance and tympanometric peak pressure. However, interestingly, in the few cases of a type C curve connected to MEE, the bacterial culture mainly remained negative, and MEE was serous and of small volume and thus did not significantly affect hearing (Koivunen et al, 1997; Koivunen et al, 2000; Palmu et al, 2001). Thus, children with a type C curve warrant follow-up rather than active therapeutic measures.

Tympanometric findings correlate with audiometric test results, suggesting that a peaked tympanogram predicts normal hearing if sensorineural hearing impairments have been excluded (Koivunen et al, 2000; MRC Multi-Centre Otitis Media Study Group, 1999). However, tympanometry cannot replace sophisticated audiologic methods, but it could help to screen those in need (MRC Multi-Centre Otitis Media Study Group, 1999).

Our opinion is that in everyday clinical practice in a young pediatric population, curves with peaks can be considered to indicate the absence of MEE unless otoscopy reveals an air-fluid level or another clear sign of MEE, and a flat curve is highly indicative of MEE of such an amount that it possibly affects hearing.

Acoustic Reflectometry

Acoustic reflectometry is another objective measure used to predict the presence of MEE behind an intact TM. It does not require an ear seal for pressurization and thus is not as sensitive as tympanometry to artifacts caused by movement or crying. As in tympanometry, acoustic energy transfers through the TM, but part of the sound energy is reflected back depending on the status of the middle ear. The reflected sound pressure is out of phase with the incident sound, and a microphone detects the resultant sound pressure. In the redesigned model, a microprocessor analyzes the frequency spectra of reflected sound rather than the intensity of the sound, and the result can be depicted as a spectral gradient curve by a printer (Kimball, 1998). When the middle ear is healthy and the TM vibrates normally, about half of the sound energy with a broad spectrum reflects back, and the angle of the curve is wide. In contrast, when the mobility of the TM is impaired by MEE, more sound energy with a narrow spectrum is reflected, resulting in a reflectance curve with an acute angle.

The redesigned professional device (EarCheck Pro, MDI Instruments, Inc., Chester, NJ, USA), not yet available in Europe, seems to be rapid and practical in the office setting, although the ease of use varies between users, resulting in technical failure in up to 20% of recordings (Barnett et al, 1998; Block et al, 1999). If a 70° angle is used as a cut-off value, spectral gradient acoustic reflectometry may predict correctly the presence and absence of MEE in 84% of symptomatic AOM patients and in 72% of children undergoing tympanostomy tube placement (Barnett et al, 1998; Block et al, 1999). Promisingly, it seems to be as reliable as

tympanometry in detecting MEE, but more studies are needed to establish its role among the diagnostic methods.

Tympanocentesis and Myringotomy

The only reliable method to detect the presence of MEE is either tympanocentesis (needle puncture of the TM and aspiration of MEE through the TM) or myringotomy (incision in the TM providing drainage for hours to several days). Tympanocentesis as a technical procedure is a simple one. In nonanesthetized children, the TM is locally anesthetized with Bonain's solution (equal amounts of cocaine hydrochloride, menthol, and phenol) or eutectic lidocaine/prilocaine cream (EMLA) (AstraZeneca, Wilmington, DE) or 70% liquid phenol (with phenol only on the puncture point). A tympanocentesis needle (bent two times at a 70 to 90° angle to permit visualization through the magnifying lens of a surgical head) is inserted through the anteroinferior half of the TM. The other option is to make a small incision by a myringotomy knife. To obtain MEE, we have used a specific bent glass suction pipette (see Figure 2-1) connected to an electric aspirator. The other option is to attach a needle to a 1 or 3 mL syringe (Pichichero and Poole, 2001). In addition to diagnostic certainty, the advantage of these procedures is that in the era of increasing resistance of bacteria causing AOM, the microbiology of MEE can be investigated. In Finland from the 1950s to the 1990s, tympanocentesis and aspiration of MEE were recommended in the diagnosis and treatment of AOM and OME. During the 1980s, about 4,000 tympanocenteses were performed in our unit. However, as stated earlier, tympanocentesis is no longer recommended or used in Finland because in nonanesthetized children, it is a very painful and traumatizing procedure. Further, it has no therapeutic effect. In the rare cases needed, that is, in severe infections and in immunocompromised patients, tympanocentesis/myringotomy should be carried out with careful local anesthesia. The advantage of general anesthesia, when primarily indicated for other procedures, could be used to carry out a diagnostic tympanocentesis, especially in children with recurrent or prolonged OM, with exceptional cooperation difficulties, or with extremely narrow ear canals. We consider strapping a child to a papoose board unethical (Pichichero and Poole, 2001). Thus, other options instead of tympanocentesis should be used to detect MEE in clinical practice.

Conclusion

In cooperative children, tympanometry as a pleasant procedure could be the first examination followed by otoscopy with proper instruments and in unclear cases followed by pneumatic otoscopy. The future will show whether acoustic reflectometry will replace tympanometry. In noncooperative children, pneumatic otoscopy is the examination of choice.

References

Arola M, Ruuskanen O, Ziegler T, et al. Clinical role of respiratory virus infection in acute otitis media. Pediatrics 1990;86:848–55.

Barnett ED, Klein JO, Hawkins KA, et al. Comparison of spectral gradient acoustic reflectometry and other diagnostic techniques for detection of middle ear effusion in children with middle ear disease. Pediatr Infect Dis J 1998;17:556–9.

Block SL, Pichichero ME, McLinn S, et al. Spectral gradient acoustic reflectometry: detection of middle ear effusion in suppurative acute otitis media. Pediatr Infect Dis J 1999;18:741–4.

Brody R, Rosenfeld RM, Goldsmith AJ, Madell JR. Parents cannot detect mild hearing loss in children. First place—Resident Clinical Science Award 1998. Otolaryngol Head Neck Surg 1999;121:681–6.

Brookhouser PE. Use of tympanometry in office practice for diagnosis of otitis media. Pediatr Infect Dis J 1998;17:544–51.

Heikkinen T, Ruuskanen O. Signs and symptoms predicting acute otitis media. Arch Pediatr Adolesc Med 1995;149:26–9.

Jerger J. Clinical experience with impedance audiometry. Arch Otolaryngol 1970;92:311–24

Kaleida PH. The COMPLETES exam for otitis. Contemp Pediatr 1997;4:93–101.

Kaleida PH, Stool SE. Assessment of otoscopists' accuracy regarding middle-ear effusion. Otoscopic validation. Am J Dis Child 1992;146:433–5.

Karma PH, Penttilä MA, Sipilä MM, Kataja MJ. Otoscopic diagnosis of middle ear effusion in acute and non-acute otitis media. I. The value of different otoscopic findings. Int J Pediatr Otorhinolaryngol 1989;17:37–49.

Kimball S. Acoustic reflectometry: spectral gradient analysis for improved detection of middle ear effusion in children. Pediatr Infect Dis J 1998;17:552–5.

Koivunen P, Alho OP, Uhari M, et al. Minitympanometry in detecting middle ear fluid. J Pediatr 1997;131:419–22.

Koivunen P, Uhari M, Laitakari K, et al. Otoacoustic emissions and tympanometry in children with otitis media. Ear Hear 2000;21:212–7.

Kontiokari T, Koivunen P, Niemelä M, et al. Symptoms of acute otitis media. Pediatr Infect Dis J 1998;17:676–9.

Le CT, Daly KA, Margolis RH, et al. A clinical profile of otitis media. Arch Otolaryngol Head Neck Surg 1992;118:1225–8.

MRC Multi-Centre Otitis Media Study Group. Sensitivity, specificity and predictive value of tympanometry in predicting a hearing impairment in otitis media with effusion. Clin Otolaryngol 1999;24:294–300.

Niemelä M, Uhari M, Jounio-Ervasti K, et al. Lack of specific symptomatology in children with acute otitis media. Pediatr Infect Dis J 1994;13:765–8.

Palmu A, Puhakka H, Rahko T, Takala AK. Diagnostic value of tympanometry in infants in clinical practice. Int J Pediatr Otorhinolaryngol 1999;49:207–13.

Palmu A, Syrjänen R, Kilpi T, et al. Negative pressure tympanograms in children less than 2 years of age—different bacterial findings in otitis media by tympanometric results. Int J Pediatr Otorhinolaryngol 2001;61:61–9.

Palmu AA, Kotikoski MJ, Kaijalainen TH, Puhakka HJ. Bacterial etiology of acute myringitis in children less than two years of age. Pediatr Infect Dis J 2001;20:607–11.

Paradise JL, Smith CG, Bluestone CD. Tympanometric detection of middle ear effusion in infants and young children. Pediatrics 1976;58:198–210.

Pichichero ME, Poole MD. Assessing diagnostic accuracy and tympanocentesis skills in the management of otitis media. Arch Pediatr Adolesc Med 2001;155:1137–42.

Chapter 3

EXAMINATION OF THE TYMPANIC MEMBRANE FOR OTITIS MEDIA

GLENN C. ISAACSON, MD, FACS, FAAP

Otitis media (OM) is an inflammatory condition of the middle ear. Its variants—acute OM, OM with effusion, and chronic suppurative OM—are all defined clinically by a constellation of symptoms and physical signs (Bluestone, 1984; Niemela et al, 1994; Schwartz et al, 1981). Given the inconsistent reports of pain in young children and nonspecific signs, such as irritability and ear pulling, visual inspection of the tympanic membrane (TM) is of paramount importance in the diagnosis of OM (Kontiokari et al, 1998; Pelton, 1998).

Quartz-rod otoendoscopes and operating microscopes are occasionally used for visualization and documentation of the eardrum, but the workhorse instrument for OM diagnosis is the handheld halogen pneumatic otoscope (Silva and Hotaling, 1997). Accurate assessment of the eardrum and middle ear requires an ear canal clean of wax and debris, an otoscope with greater than 100 foot-candles of light output (Barriga et al, 1986), and tips capable of producing an airtight seal with the external auditory canal (Stool and Anticaglia, 1973).

There is no single physical sign that defines middle ear infection. The visual diagnosis of OM depends on the identification of physical signs of inflammation, abnormal middle ear barometric pressure, and the presence or absence of effusion.

Otoscopy of the Normal Ear

The TM provides a translucent window to the upper respiratory tract generally and to the middle ear specifically. In its healthy state, the eardrum varies in appearance from relatively opaque to completely transparent. It is variegated, with bright areas overlying the promontory and dark areas above the oval and round windows and the eustachian tube orifice (Figure 3-1). The long process of the incus is not in contact with the eardrum but is often visible in the posterosuperior quadrant.

The eardrum's blood supply is visible, radiating in a short distance from the tympanic annulus and again along the long process of the malleus, but vessels do not seem to cross the area of eardrum in between.

When both the ear canal and middle ear are at atmospheric pressure, the eardrum assumes its natural configuration. This is not conical, as described in anatomy texts, but doubly curved or "seagull" shaped (Figure 3-2). The eardrum is lowest at the annulus, curves upward toward its midspan, and curves down again toward its attachment to the malleus handle. This three-dimensional shape is best appreciated with the binocular vision of an operating microscope but can be seen with one eye as well. The seagull appearance of the eardrum is drawn down into a true cone with as little as –100 daPa of negative middle ear pressure.

Incident light from the otoscope is reflected from that surface of the eardrum that is perpendicular to it. As the eardrum forms an angle of about 140° from the long axis

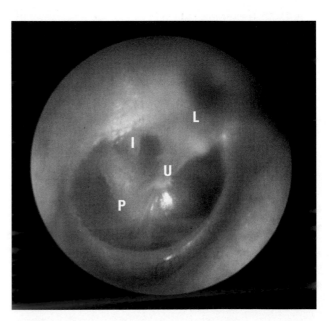

FIGURE 3-1. Normal eardrum. I = incus; L = lateral process of malleus; P = light reflex from promontory; U = umbo.

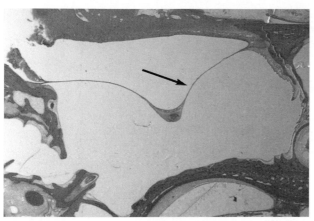

FIGURE 3-2. When both the ear canal and middle ear are at atmospheric pressure, the eardrum assumes its natural configuration, which is doubly curved or "seagull" shaped. The *arrow* indicates incident light from the otoscope and the position of light reflex.

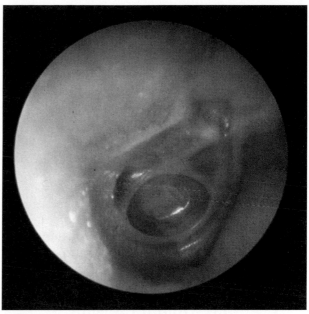

FIGURE 3-4. High negative middle ear pressure. Thinned eardrum is retracted onto the underlying promontory.

of the ear canal, the light reflex appears not at the center of the eardrum but on the outward curve of the eardrum in the anteroinferior quadrant (see Figures 3-1 and 3-2). Its position, and presence or absence, correlates poorly with any otologic disease state. As such, the observer should spend little time focused on it.

The normal eardrum is attached to the tympanic annulus and to the umbo, long process, and lateral processes of the malleus. Contact with other middle ear structures, such as the incus long process (Figure 3-3), malleus neck, or promontory (Figure 3-4), indicates retraction of the eardrum either from negative middle ear pressure or residual adherence from negative pressure in the past. The malleus long process is mobile and is drawn

inward when negative middle ear pressure is present. This is said to make the malleus seem foreshortened (Jaisinghani et al, 2000). A more easily appreciated indicator of negative middle ear pressure is the lateral process of the malleus. This is a fixed structure. When middle ear pressure is near atmospheric, the lateral process is a subtle prominence. With the development of negative pressure in the middle ear, the lateral process seems to stick out, and the eardrum is draped around it like cloth on a tent pole (Figure 3-5).

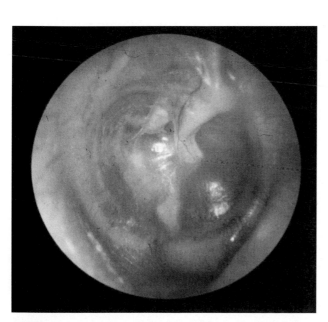

FIGURE 3-3. Negative middle ear pressure. Abnormal contact between the eardrum and the incus.

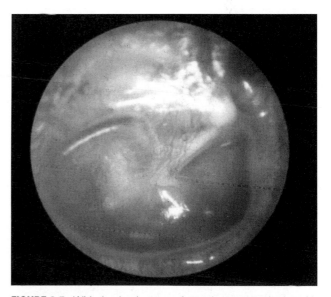

FIGURE 3-5. With the development of negative pressure in the middle ear, the malleus lateral process is prominent, and the eardrum is draped around it like cloth on a tent pole.

When the pneumatic otoscope tip is well fitted to the ear canal, only very slight pressure on the bulb is required to move the eardrum inward. On releasing the bulb, the eardrum returns to its original location. The bulb should be slightly compressed before the otoscope seals with the ear canal, which will allow changing the external ear canal pressure in both directions without breaking the seal. When negative middle ear pressure exists, the eardrum moves in slightly with bulb compression, is drawn out to normal position when pressure on the bulb is eased, and snaps down into a retracted position when the seal between the speculum and the canal is broken. If the middle ear is filled with effusion, little mobility of the eardrum can be appreciated. If air and fluid are mixed behind the eardrum, mobility is decreased, and the eardrum usually returns to a retracted position as the pneumatic otoscope is withdrawn (Bluestone and Klein, 1996).

OM without Effusion

In general, the diagnosis of acute OM is based on the presence of effusion in the middle ear. Pneumatic otoscopy, tympanometry, and tympanocentesis all depend on middle ear fluid in confirming a middle ear infection. In the first hours of acute OM, however, a child may experience severe pain, and there may be signs of inflammation before an effusion appears (Figure 3-6). In this phase, accurate observation is particularly important to avoid overdiagnosing disease.

In a screaming, thrashing, febrile child, redness of the eardrum may result from vascular engorgement rather than middle ear inflammation. If possible, the eardrum should be observed through a full respiratory cycle. When the child inhales, the redness of a Valsalva maneuver disappears, whereas true inflammatory erythema should not. It is useful to compare the two ears. If the painful one appears redder, this suggests true inflammation. A differential diagnosis of the red eardrum is considered (see Chapter 11, "The Red Eardrum").

The position of the eardrum in the early hours of OM is variable. It may fluctuate from retracted to neutral to bulging in a matter of hours. The variegated appearance of the eardrum may persist because there is no fluid to limit the transmission of light.

Sometimes it is not possible to accurately diagnose acute OM in its early phase. Re-examining the ear in a day or two can resolve this dilemma.

Acute OM with Effusion

The appearance of an acutely inflamed eardrum and a middle ear filled with pus is highly characteristic and imitated by only a few conditions. The eardrum protrudes under pressure, bulging into a doughnut shape as it is restrained only at the annulus and umbo. Middle ear

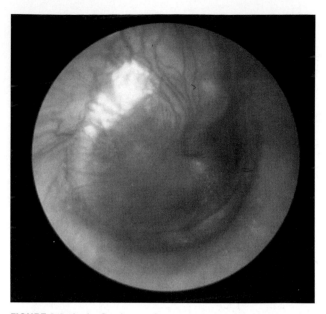

FIGURE 3-6. In the first hours of acute otitis media, however, a child may experience severe pain and there may be signs of inflammation before an effusion appears.

landmarks are obscured by opaque effusion (Figures 3-7 and 3-8). The vascularity of the eardrum is pronounced, both owing to true engorgement of the vessels and to improved visualization against the reflective background of middle ear fluid. These vessels radiate from the annulus to the umbo without interruption (Felder's sign).

Pneumatic otoscopy reveals little movement on insufflation or release of the bulb. There may be blanching of the vessels on the surface of the eardrum or in the canal when the bulb is squeezed.

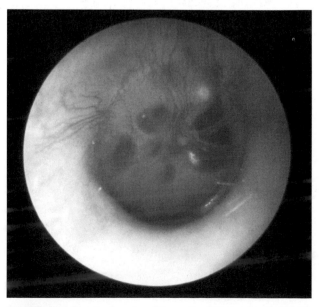

FIGURE 3-7. Day 3 of acute otitis media. Effusion is mixed with bubbles.

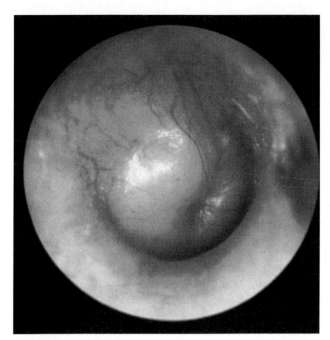

FIGURE 3-8. Bulging acute otitis media.

Within a few days, a proteinaceous exudate may appear on the surface of the eardrum, creating small whitish dots (Figure 3-9). The exudate sometimes dries and fuses into a thin membrane that peels away from the surface of the eardrum and can obscure the eardrum during the healing phase of OM (Figure 3-10).

If the eardrum perforates, pus may pool in the external auditory canal. Usually, the perforation itself is not seen, even if the pus is aspirated from the canal, because the several layers of the TM fall back into position with the release of pressure (Figure 3-11).

Two conditions that may produce the appearance of bulging acute OM with effusion are a foreign body in the distal ear canal and a congenital cholesteatoma filling the middle ear behind an intact eardrum.

OM with Effusion

Effusion may appear within the middle ear as a sequela to acute OM or may fill the ear insidiously during an upper respiratory infection. Its appearance is variable, depending on its makeup and quantity. In most cases, there are signs of negative middle ear pressure, including the loss of the seagull shape of the eardrum, foreshortening of the malleus, prominence of the lateral process, and, sometimes, cupping of the pars flaccida (Figure 3-12).

Serous effusions are relatively translucent. As such, the variegated appearance of the eardrum may persist as light is reflected from the promontory but not the recesses of the middle ear. The eardrum is pinker than normal, and small vessels course from the annulus to the umbo. If air is introduced into the middle ear from the eustachian tube, bubbles or an air-fluid level may be seen through the eardrum. The mobility of the eardrum is related to the proportion of air and liquid in the middle ear cleft but should always suggest negative pressure.

Mucoid effusions are, in general, opaque, thus hiding the normal middle ear structures. Vessels cross from the annulus to the umbo and are easily seen against the whitish background of the effusion. The malleus lateral

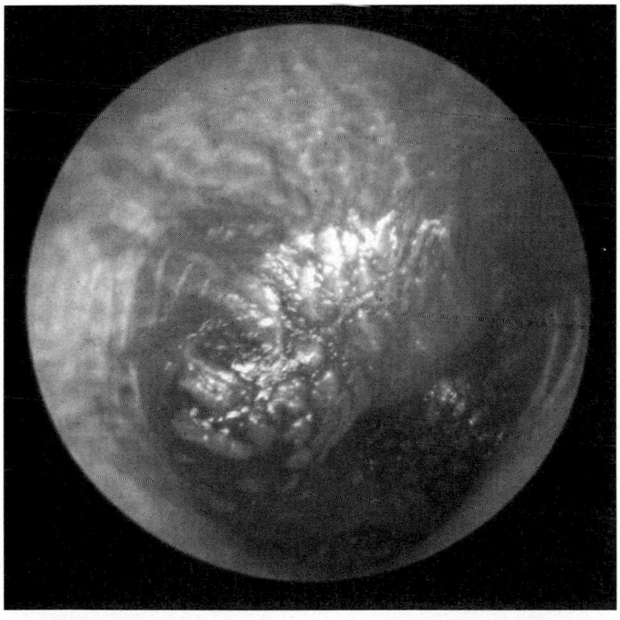

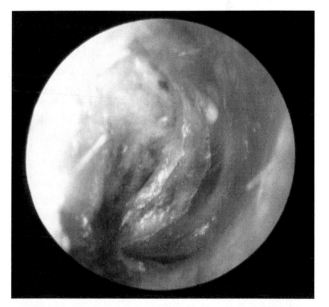

FIGURE 3-9. Within a few days, a proteinaceous exudate may appear on the surface of the eardrum, creating small whitish dots.

FIGURE 3-10. The exudate sometimes dries and fuses into a thin membrane that peels away from the surface of the eardrum and can obscure the eardrum during the healing phase of otitis media.

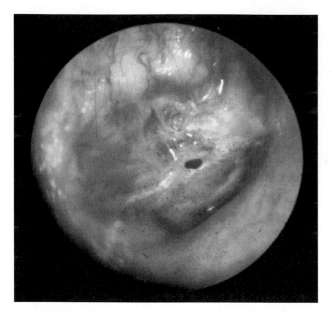

FIGURE 3-11. Usually, the perforation itself is not seen, even if the pus is aspirated from the canal, because the several layers of the tympanic membrane fall back into position with the release of pressure.

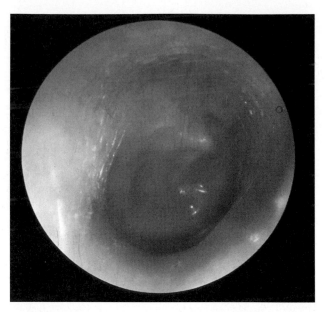

FIGURE 3-12. In most cases, there are signs of negative middle ear pressure, including the loss of the seagull shape of the eardrum, foreshortening of the malleus, prominence of the lateral process, and, sometimes, cupping of the pars flaccida.

process is prominent, and folds of the TM radiate from it. If the incus is visible in the posterosuperior quadrant, it usually represents focal retraction of the eardrum. The eardrum is typically immobile on insufflation. If bubbles appear in the middle ear, they often overlie the eustachian tube orifice anteriorly.

Chronic Suppurative OM with or without Cholesteatoma

Purulent drainage resulting from infection within the middle ear must emanate from either a perforation in the eardrum or the mouth of a retraction pocket. In differentiating chronic suppurative OM from otitis externa (Figure 3-13) or surface inflammation of the eardrum (myringitis) (Figure 3-14), it is important to visualize such a perforation or retraction. This necessitates adequate cleaning of the canal with cotton-tipped applicators, a flexible suction, or, preferably, suction under microscopic guidance. Differentiating a tympanic perforation from a retraction pocket can be difficult. Both can be centrally located, although retraction pockets have a predilection for the periphery of the eardrum (usually in the posterosuperior quadrant or the pars flaccida).

Perforations have a clean, sharp edge that can be followed around 360° (Figures 3-15 and 3-16). Moist middle ear mucosa is visible through a perforation and the structures of the middle ear, especially the ossicles, and the bony spicules of the hypotympanum are distinctly seen. The eardrum is immobile on insufflation because no pressure gradient can be created.

Retraction pockets can resemble perforations, but at some point on their periphery, squamous epithelium can be seen crawling into the middle ear. The retracted eardrum drapes over middle ear structures, producing a blunted, "Saran Wrap" appearance (see Figure 3-3). Squamous debris or granulation may be seen in the mouth of the pocket (Figure 3-17). If the middle ear is filled with fluid, the eardrum may be immobile. If the middle ear is filled with air, signs of negative pressure should be evi-

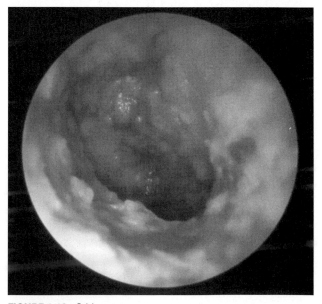

FIGURE 3-13. Otitis externa.

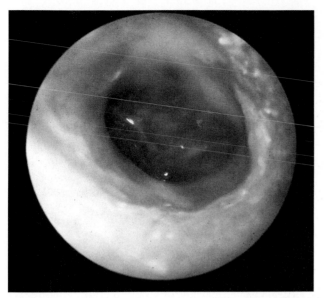

FIGURE 3-14. Surface inflammation of the eardrum (weeping myringitis).

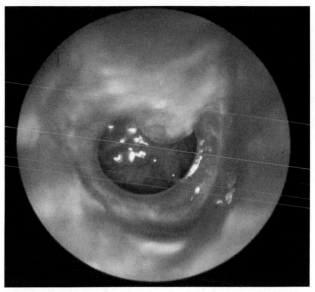

FIGURE 3-16. Moist central perforation.

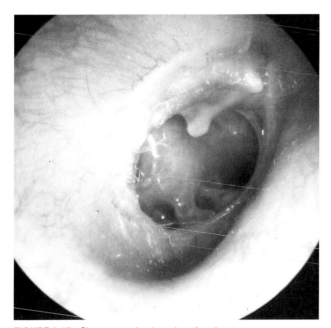

FIGURE 3-15. Clean central subtotal perforation.

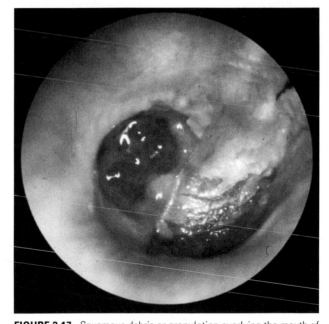

FIGURE 3-17. Squamous debris or granulation overlying the mouth of a retraction pocket cholesteatoma.

denced on insufflation and the pocket may be disproportionately mobile.

Conclusion

The clinician depends on history, physical examination, and diagnostic testing to identify the severity of middle ear pathology. Of these, careful visualization of the TM is the most accessible and, in skilled hands, the most accurate way to evaluate OM.

References

Barriga F, Schwartz RH, Hayden GF. Adequate illumination for otoscopy. Variations due to power source, bulb, and head and speculum design. Am J Dis Child 1986;140:1237–40.

Bluestone CD. State of the art: definitions and classifications. In: Lim DJ, Bluestone CD, Klein JO, Nelson JD, editors. Recent advances in otitis media with effusion: proceedings of the Third International Symposium. Philadelphia: BC Decker; 1984. p. 1–4.

Bluestone CD, Klein JO. Methods of examination: clinical examination. In: Bluestone CD, Stool SE, Kenna MA, editors. Pediatric otolaryngology. 3rd ed. Philadelphia: WB Saunders; 1996. p. 150–64.

Jaisinghani VJ, Hunter LL, Li Y, Margolis RH. Quantitative analysis of tympanic membrane disease using video-otoscopy. Laryngoscope 2000;110:1726–30.

Kontiokari T, Koivunen P, Niemela M, et al. Symptoms of acute otitis media. Pediatr Infect Dis J 1998;17:676–9.

Niemela M, Uhari M, Jounio-Ervasti K, et al. Lack of specific symptomatology in children with acute otitis media. Pediatr Infect Dis J 1994;13:765–8.

Pelton SI. Otoscopy for the diagnosis of otitis media. Pediatr Infect Dis J 1998;17:540–3.

Schwartz RH, Stool SE, Rodriguez WJ, Grundfast KM. Acute otitis media: toward a more precise definition. Clin Pediatr (Phila) 1981;20:549–54.

Silva AB, Hotaling AJ. A protocol for otolaryngology-head and neck resident training in pneumatic otoscopy. Int J Pediatr Otorhinolaryngol 1997;40:125–31.

Stool SE, Anticaglia J. Electric otoscopy—a basic skill. Notes on the essentials of otoscopic examination and on the evaluation of otoscopes. Clin Pediatr (Phila) 1973;12:420–6.

Chapter 4

EPIDEMIOLOGY

KATHLEEN A. DALY, PHD

Epidemiology is the study of disease patterns in the population and factors that influence these patterns. As disease detectives, epidemiologists focus on the who, where, when, and why of disease. Physicians concentrate on the diagnosis and treatment of individuals presenting with specific symptoms. In contrast, epidemiologists study groups that are disproportionately affected within the population to obtain clues about disease causation, susceptibility, transmission, and trends. Epidemiology plays an important role in clinical medicine by providing information about characteristics linked to disease susceptibility. Recommendations for treatment of otitis media (OM) often take these factors into account. For example, recommendations for treatment of recurrent acute OM (AOM) may differ by child's age and whether the child is cared for at home or in a child care center. This chapter reports on the incidence and prevalence of the various manifestations of OM and variation in disease rates by age, gender, and race and on time trends in OM incidence.

Background

OM continues to be one of the most common diseases of childhood. OM is a generic term for a continuum of diseases and is often used to describe the presence of middle ear effusion (MEE). The continuum includes AOM, MEE with characteristic signs and symptoms of infection; OM with effusion (OME); asymptomatic MEE (this term has also been used by researchers to describe the presence of MEE with or without symptoms); chronic OME, an effusion that persists for 2 to 3 months; chronic OM, a perforated tympanic membrane with a draining ear; and recurrent OM, more than one episode or a specified number of episodes in a given time period. Data collected by the US National Center for Health Statistics (NCHS) in the 1990s reveal that OM accounted for 18% of ambulatory care visits among 1 to 4 year olds and 14% of visits for children in the first year of life (Freid et al, 1998). Earache/ear infection was the most common reason for visiting an otolaryngologist (11.3% of visits), and OM diagnoses accounted for 17.6% of all otolaryngology office visits (Woodwell, 1992). Myringotomy with tympanostomy tubes was the most common ambulatory surgery procedure performed on children younger than 15 years in 1994 (96.9 procedures/10,000 children) (Kozak et al, 1997). Costs attributable to OM include both direct (treatment and medical care) and indirect (parental time lost from work) costs and have been estimated to be $3.5 billion per year for children with OM in the United States (Gates, 1996).

Otitis Media Rates

Data on incidence provide information about the risk of developing this disease in a given population. To determine incidence, individuals free of disease are followed and examined prospectively to ascertain disease occurrence. The cumulative incidence rate is the number developing the disease over a specified period divided by the number at risk in the population. In diseases such as OM that recur, incidence is also defined as the number of episodes of disease divided by the person-years of follow-up. For example, if 1,000 infants were followed from birth to 1 year of age and collectively experienced 2,500 episodes of OM, the incidence rate would be 250 OM episodes per 100 child-years of follow-up. In comparison, prevalence provides an indication of the disease burden (number of individuals with disease) and is the number of individuals with the disease at a particular time point divided by the population tested.

Incidence

A large number of studies around the globe have been reported on the incidence of AOM, OME, recurrent OM, and chronic OME. Besides differences in the populations being studied (age, race, risk factor profiles), differences in study design and methods, disease criteria, and method and frequency of ascertainment make direct comparison of results challenging. Community-based studies provide the best estimates of population incidence because they include all children in the community, not just those who are frequent users of the medical system or high-risk populations, for example, day-care attendees. Most studies that report OME rates are reporting the presence of MEE diagnosed with tympanometry.

Otoscopy allows assessment of changes in the tympanic membrane and middle ear, but tympanometry alone without middle ear and symptom assessment does not allow discrimination between AOM and OME.

Incidence of all types of OM decreases with age; age-specific incidence rates for AOM and OME are shown in Table 4-1. Clinical studies in the United States have shown that about half of children studied prospectively have OM onset in the first 6 months of life, and peak OM incidence occurs in the first 1.5 years of life (Daly, 1997). Cumulative incidence from studies reported in the table varies widely by disease definition, population studied, and frequency of examination, but first-year incidence exceeds second-year incidence in all studies shown. A number of factors make early infancy the period of greatest OM susceptibility. These include anatomy (infant eustachian tube angle and width provide easy access to pathogens residing in the nasopharynx), declining levels of passive antibody coupled with an immature immune system, and early entry into child care, which increases the likelihood of exposure to viral and bacterial OM pathogens, leading to early colonization and infection.

Prevalence

OME prevalence rates also decline with age. Studies of school-age children (same child in successive years or children of different ages) have shown that the likelihood of OME declines over time to 3 to 4% by age 10 or 11 years (Daly, 1997). A longitudinal study conducted in the United Kingdom followed the same group of children from 8 to 61 months and assessed their middle ear status with tympanometry every 4 to 7 months. The authors reported that the prevalence of bilateral OME during peak winter months declined from 34% at 8 months of age to 10% at 61 months of age (Midgley et al, 2000). OME is more prevalent than AOM, chiefly because MEE persists after AOM episodes. Studies of three cohorts of children followed in Denmark during the preschool years revealed that the prevalence of MEE as measured by a type B tympanogram varied by age from 1 to 19% at various points in time, but the cumulative incidence of OM by school age was 90% (Tos, 1984).

Recurrent OM, defined here as three episodes in a year, occurs in 3 to 20% of children. In younger children, and using definitions requiring fewer episodes in a speci-

TABLE 4-1. Community-Based Otitis Media Incidence Studies

Author (yr)	Country	How Ascertained	Criteria for Diagnosis	Age	Sample Size	OM Incidence*
AOM						
Biles et al (1980)	United States	Record review	MD diagnosis	0–8	1,018	35
				0–1	174	97/100 child/yr
				1–2	136	81/100 child/yr
Stewart (1989)	United States Alaskan Natives	Record review	MD diagnosis, OM not specified as chronic	0–1	344	78
Goodwin et al (1980)	United States American Indian	Medical record review	Red bulging TM with pain, fever	0–1	1,710	60
Stangerup and Tos (1986)	Denmark	Quarterly examinations for 3 mo	TM perforation, effusion at myringotomy, or red, bulging TM with pain, fever	0–1	729	22
				0–2		37
				0–3		49
Kero and Piekkala (1987)	Finland	Interview at 3, 6, 12 mo	Parent report of acute OM	0–1	4,868	35
Sipilä et al (1987)	Finland	MD examinations when OM suspected	Symptoms, signs, or effusion at myringotomy	0.5–1	1,642	28
				0.5–1.5		40
Alho et al (1991)	Finland	Medical record review	MD diagnosis of acute OM	0–1	2,512	42
				0–2		71
Ingvarsson et al (1984)	Sweden	Acute OM registry	Red, bulging TM	0–1	2,404	18
				0–5		58
Rasmussen (1994)	Sweden	Medical record review	Red TM with fever or otalgia	0–1	1,306	14
				0–3		38
				0–7		61
OME						
Lous et al (1981)	Denmark	Monthly examinations for 1 yr	Type B tympanogram	7–8	387	25/100
Birch and Elbrønd (1986)	Denmark	Biweekly examinations for 3 mo	Type B tympanogram	1–7	210	74
Owen et al (1993)	United States	Monthly examinations for 2 yr	Otorrhea, tympanometry, acoustic reflex	0–0.5	435	85
				0–1		97
				0–2		99
Zielhuis et al (1990)	Netherlands	Quarterly examinations for 2 yrs	Type B tympanogram	2–3	1,115	70
				2–4		80

*Cumulative incidence (reported as %) or number of OM episodes per 100 child/years of follow-up.
AOM = acute otitis media; OM = otitis media; OME = otitis media with effusion; TM = tympanic membrane.

fied time period, incidence can be as high as 40% (Daly, 1997). Incidence rates of chronic OME range from 4 to 27%, are inversely related to age, and are directly related to frequency of examination. Data on cumulative OME— that is, the total number of days, not necessarily contiguous, during which a child has MEE—demonstrate that in the first year of life, 33% have OME for 1 to 60 days and 25% have it for greater than 90 days (Roland et al, 1989). Mean cumulative proportion of time spent with OME in the first 2 years of life is about 20% (Paradise et al, 1997), which translates to nearly 5 months.

Natural History: Episode Duration

AOM is typically diagnosed at its onset when clinical signs and symptoms appear. Thus, duration is easily measured. Symptoms resolve rapidly, but MEE persists. Based on meta-analysis of AOM treatment studies, clinical recovery (resolution of symptoms such as fever and fussiness) occurs in 81% of untreated and 92% of treated children in 7 to 14 days, whereas only 60 to 70% resolve MEE by 30 days of follow-up (Rosenfeld et al, 1994). Studies of children followed for 12 weeks after their AOM diagnosis revealed that 15 to 25% had MEE for 8 weeks and 8 to 15% had it for 12 weeks (Daly et al, 1999). Onset of a new episode of OME, however, is difficult to pinpoint because it is likely to be asymptomatic. Because timing of onset is uncertain, so is duration. However, minimum estimates of duration can be made using the date of diagnosis and the date of resolution. MEE is labile, as evidenced by prospective studies using frequent, even daily, examinations with tympanometry in Denmark, the Netherlands, and the United States.

Age, Gender, and Race

Research has shown that the risk of developing OM decreases with age, although some studies have shown a bimodal peak, with OM rates declining from age 1 to 4 years and then rising again at school entry at age 5 years (Daly, 1997). With the advent of early entry into day-care settings over recent decades with nearly daily exposure to other young children, there may no longer be a period of secondary risk at school entry. Besides the inverse relationship between age and OM incidence and prevalence, early onset of OM also predicts later recurrent OM and chronic OME; children with OM onset in the first few months of life are two to eight times more likely to develop these conditions (Daly, 1997). The highest rate of bilateral OME occurred in 8-month-old children in the Avon study (Midgley et al, 2000). In addition, younger children are less likely to resolve MEE after treatment and more likely to have effusion that persists for > 12 weeks than older children.

Another consistent finding is that OME and AOM are more common in the winter than in the summer. Winter is the season in which respiratory infections peak. These infections increase the risk of AOM or trigger a disease process that begins as a respiratory infection and develops into a middle ear infection. Birth in the fall has also been shown to increase the risk of early-onset and recurrent OM (Biles et al, 1980; Daly, 1997). This is probably attributable to a combination of factors. Maternal antibody levels decline from the period of highest exposure in the previous winter, reaching their nadir in the fall at the infant's birth. Infants born in the fall are entering the peak respiratory disease season, when their passive antibody levels are low and they are not yet producing their own antibodies.

A few studies have ascertained OM in multiracial populations. Recent studies of more than one racial or ethnic group have reported that black and white children have similar cumulative incidence rates of AOM and OME in the first 2 years of life (Casselbrant et al, 1995; Paradise et al, 1997). Earlier studies reporting that black children were at lower risk of OM than white children did not use active surveillance for OM and thus did not control for factors that contribute to disease detection, such as access to and use of health care. Indigenous populations have been reported to have high rates of OM. In a small study comparing the history of middle ear disease in indigenous and other Australian children in early infancy, 95% of indigenous infants had MEE by 2 months of age compared with 30% of nonindigenous infants (Boswell and Nienhuys, 1995). School-age American Indian children living on reservations had much higher rates of chronic OM than a representative sample of school-age children in the general population (Daly, 1997). Among 3- to 8-year-old children in Greenland, indigenous children had a higher prevalence of chronic OM than their mixed-heritage counterparts in the same communities (Homoe et al, 1996). A stratified random sample of US school-age children tested with tympanometry as part of a US population-based survey revealed that among 6 to 10 year olds, Hispanic children had significantly higher OME prevalence rates than white children. Hispanic children also had higher hearing thresholds than the other two groups of children (Hoffman et al, 2002).

Many researchers have reported gender differences in OM rates with a male preponderance, and relative risks range from 1.2 to 2.0 for males compared with females. However, population-based studies reported relative risks at the low end of this range (Daly, 1997). These differences may be real or attributable to a possible bias in OM ascertainment for male children in clinical studies.

Trends in OM Incidence over Time

Rates of tympanostomy tube insertion increased twofold between 1976 and 1986 in England (Black, 1995). Similar trends have been observed in the United States, but changes in tube insertion rates can only be estimated.

This is attributable to gaps in the national data collection system and the fact that the vast majority of tympanostomy tube surgeries moved from hospitals to outpatient surgery centers beginning in the 1970s. Studies from Canada, the United States, and Finland have reported increasing incidence of AOM, recurrent OM, and tympanostomy tube surgeries (Croteau et al, 1990; Joki-Erkkila et al, 1998; Lanphear et al, 1997). NCHS studies have shown results consistent with these findings: a large increase in the annual visit rate for OM between 1975 and 1990 (Schappert, 1992) and a 50% increase in parent-reported AOM from 1982 to 1990 (Adams and Benson, 1991; NCHS, 1985). An increase in OM incidence seems logical given the growing increase in outside-the-home child care, especially center care. Day-care attendance and respiratory infection are the two most important risk factors for OM. However, changes in other risk factors (breast-feeding and parental smoking) are not necessarily consistent with a rise in OM incidence. Smoking rates and/or cigarette consumption declined in the United States, Canada, England, and Finland from the 1970s to the early 1990s, which would be expected to decrease rather than increase OM rates. In addition to true changes in disease incidence, other factors, such as evolving health care systems that affect access to and use of medical services, changes in physician and parent awareness of OM and OM risk factors, and changes in criteria for OM diagnosis, may influence the likelihood of a child being diagnosed with OM. This could result in an apparent increase in OM incidence. For example, if primary care physicians are currently more aware of asymptomatic MEE than they were 25 years ago, they may be more likely to perform an ear examination in the absence of symptoms, particularly in the first year of life, when asymptomatic MEE may occur in 30 to 50% of infants (Daly, 1997). Similarly, an increase in the number of physician visits for children over time could result in more ear examinations and more diagnoses of OM.

Future Projections

OM rates may decrease if pneumococcal conjugate vaccines are universally adopted during childhood, but their greatest impact is expected to be on recurrent OM and tympanostomy tube placement and on reducing nasopharyngeal carriage in both children and adults. Efficacy based on serotype-specific OM was < 60% (Eskola et al, 2001). Although the vaccine clearly prevented AOM attributable to serotypes that cross-reacted with vaccine serotypes, use of the vaccine also increased the risk of AOM attributable to nonvaccine serotypes. Therefore, the overall effect on vaccine prevention of pneumococcal OM over time remains to be seen. Trends in risk factor prevalence could also impact OM incidence. There is no evidence that use of group child care will decline in the near future. Although smaller child care settings may be preferable to reduce the risk of infectious disease, decisions about child care require parental consideration of many factors, including convenience, willingness to care for infants, regulatory oversight of the facility, and availability of structured activities for children.

References

Adams PF, Benson V. Current estimates from the National Health Interview Survey, 1990. Vital Health Stat 10 1991;(181):1–212.

Alho OP, Koivu M, Sorri M, Rantakallio P. The occurrence of acute otitis media in infants. A life-table analysis. Int J Pediatr Otorhinolaryngol 1991;21:7–14.

Biles RW, Buffler PA, O'Donell AA. Epidemiology of otitis media: a community study. Am J Public Health 1980;70:593–8.

Birch L, Elbrønd O. Prospective epidemiological study of secretory otitis media in children not attending kindergarten. A prevalence study. Int J Pediatr Otorhinolaryngol 1986;11:183–90, 191–7.

Black N. Surgery for glue ear: the English epidemic wanes. J Epidemiol Community Health 1995;49:234–7.

Boswell JB, Nienhuys TG. Onset of otitis media in the first eight weeks of life in Aboriginal and non-Aboriginal Australian infants. Ann Otol Rhinol Laryngol 1995;104:542–9.

Casselbrant ML, Mandel EM, Kurs-Lasky M, et al. Otitis media in a population of black American and white American infants, 0-2 years of age. Int J Pediatr Otorhinolaryngol 1995;33:1–16.

Croteau N, Hai V, Pless IB, Infante-Rivard C. Trends in medical visits and surgery for otitis media among children. Am J Dis Child 1990;144:535–8.

Daly K. Definition and epidemiology of otitis media with effusion. In: Roberts JE, Wallace I, Henderson F, editors. Otitis media, language, and learning in young children. Baltimore: Paul H. Brookes; 1997. p. 3–41.

Daly KA, Hunter LL, Giebink GS. Chronic otitis media with effusion. Pediatr Rev 1999;20:85–94.

Eskola J, Kilpi T, Palmu A, et al. Efficacy of a pneumococcal conjugate vaccine against otitis media. N Engl J Med 2001;344:403–9.

Freid VM, Mukuc DM, Rooks RN. Ambulatory health care visits by children: principal diagnosis and place of visit. Vital Health Stat 1998;13:1–23.

Gates GA. Cost-effectiveness considerations in otitis media treatment. Otolaryngol Head Neck Surg 1996;114:525–30.

Goodwin MH Jr, Shaw JR, Feldman CM. Distribution of otitis media among four Indian populations in Arizona. Public Health Rep 1980;95:589–94.

Hoffman HJ, MacTurk RH, Gravel JS, et al. Epidemiological risk factors for otitis media and hearing loss in school age children based on NHANES III, 1988–1994. In: Lim DJ, Bluestone CD, Casselbrant ML, et al, editors. Recent advances in otitis media—proceedings of the Seventh International Symposium. Toronto: BC Decker; 2002. p. 147–53.

Homoe P, Christensen RB, Bretlau P. Prevalence of otitis media in a survey of 591 unselected Greenlandic children. Int J Pediatr Otorhinolaryngol 1996;36:215–30.

Ingvarsson L, Lundgren K, Olofsson B. Epidemiology of acute otitis media in children—a cohort study in an urban population. In: Lim DJ, Bluestone CD, Klein JO, Nelson JD, editors. Recent advances in otitis media with effusion—proceedings of the

Third International Symposium. Philadelphia: BC Decker; 1984. p. 19–22.

Joki-Erkkila VP, Laippala P, Pukander J. Increase in pediatric acute otitis media diagnosed by primary care in two Finnish municipalities—1994–5 versus 1978–9. Epidemiol Infect 1998;121:529–34.

Kero P, Piekkala P. Factors affecting the occurrence of acute otitis media during the first year of life. Acta Paediatr Scand 1987;76:618–23.

Kozak LJ, Hall MJ, Pokras R, Lawrence L. Ambulatory surgery in the United States, 1994. National Survey of Ambulatory Surgery. Adv Data 1997;283:1–15.

Lanphear BP, Byrd RS, Auinger P, et al. Increased prevalence of recurrent otitis media among children in the United States. Pediatrics 1997;99:E1.

Lous J, Fiellau-Nikolajsen M. Epidemiology of middle-ear effusion and tubal dysfunction. A one-year prospective study comprising monthly tympanometry in 387 non-selected seven-year-old children. Int J Pediatr Otorhinolaryngol 1981;3:303–17.

Midgley EJ, Dewey C, Pryce K, et al. The frequency of otitis media with effusion in British pre-school children: a guide for treatment. Clin Otolaryngol 2000;25:485–91.

National Center for Health Statistics. Current estimates from the National Health Interview Survey, United States, 1982. Vital Health Stat 1985;10:150.

Owen MJ, Baldwin CD, Swank PR, et al. Relation of infant feeding practices, cigarette smoke exposure, and group child care to the onset and duration of otitis media with effusion in the first two years of life. J Pediatr 1993;123:702–11.

Paradise JL, Rockette HE, Colborn K, et al. Otitis media in 2253 Pittsburgh-area infants: prevalence and risk factors during the first two years of life. Pediatrics 1997;99:318–33.

Rasmussen F. Recurrence of acute otitis media at preschool age in Sweden. J Epidemiol Community Health 1994;48:33–5.

Roland PS, Finitzo T, Friel-Patti S, et al. Otitis media. Incidence, duration and hearing status. Arch Otolaryngol Head Neck Surg 1989;115:1049–53.

Rosenfeld RM, Vertrees JE, Carr J, et al. Clinical efficacy of antimicrobial drugs for acute otitis media: meta-analysis of 5400 children from thirty-three randomized trials. J Pediatr 1994;124:355–67.

Schappert SM. Office visits for otitis media: United States 1975–90. Adv Data 1992;214:1–19.

Sipilä M, Pukander J, Karma P. Incidence of acute otitis media up to the age of 1 1/2 years in urban infants. Acta Otolaryngol (Stockh) 1987;104:138–45.

Stangerup SE, Tos M. Epidemiology of acute suppurative otitis media. Am J Otolaryngol 1986;7:7–54.

Stewart JL. Otitis media in the first year of life in two Eskimo communities. Ann Otol Rhinol Laryngol 1989;98:200–2.

Tos M. Epidemiology and natural history of secretory otitis media. Am J Otol 1984;4:459–62.

Woodwell DA. Office visits to otolaryngologists 1989–90. National Ambulatory Medical Care Survey. Adv Data 1992;222:1–11.

Zielhuis FA, Straatman H, Rach GH, et al. Analysis and presentation of data on the natural time course of otitis media with effusion in children. Int J Epidemiol 1990;19:1037–44.

Chapter 5

RISK FACTORS FOR OTITIS MEDIA

MARGARETHA L. CASSELBRANT, MD, PHD, ELLEN M. MANDEL, MD

Recurrent acute otitis media (AOM) and persistent middle ear effusion (MEE) have been associated with a variety of risk factors. These risk factors can be divided into host-related factors (age, sex, race, allergy, immunocompetence, craniofacial abnormalities, genetic predisposition) and environmental factors (upper respiratory tract infection [URI], seasonality, day care, siblings, passive smoke exposure, breast-feeding, socioeconomic status, pacifier use). The results from different epidemiologic studies may vary owing to differences in definition of disease, case finding methods, observation intervals, prevalence windows, and population characteristics.

Host-Related Factors

Age

The highest incidence of AOM occurs between 6 and 11 months of age (Teele et al, 1989). Onset of the first episode of AOM before 6 months of age is a powerful predictor for recurrent AOM (Harsten et al, 1989; Teele et al, 1989).

The risk for persistent MEE after an AOM episode is also inversely correlated with age (Teele et al, 1989). Shurin and colleagues (1979) found the risk for persistent MEE after AOM to be four times higher in children under 2 years of age than in older children. Marchisio and colleagues (1988) followed 196 Italian children for 3 months after an episode of AOM and found that younger children were significantly more likely to develop chronic MEE than were older children.

Children experiencing their first episode of MEE before 2 months of age were found to be at higher risk for persistent effusion (3 months or longer) during their first year of life than were children who had their first episode later (Marchant et al, 1984).

Prematurity

Some studies have found an increased risk of MEE in premature infants, whereas others have not. Gravel and colleagues (1988), in a prospective study of 49 children who had been in the newborn intensive care unit and 19 full-term infants, did not find any association between gesta-

tional age, birth weight, or length of stay in the intensive care unit and percentage of visits with MEE during the first year. Alho and colleagues (1990), examining the records of 2,512 children from birth to 2 years of age, found no association between AOM and low birth weight (2,500 g) or prematurity (< 37 weeks). Engel and colleagues (1999a), in a prospective study of 150 full-term and 100 high-risk infants (most preterm or very low birth weight), found higher OME prevalence rates in the high-risk group. Peak prevalence was 59% in the high-risk group versus 49% in the full-term group, which was observed around the age of 10 months in both groups. When they looked at reasons for increased prevalence in the high-risk group, factors such as nasotracheal, nasopharyngeal, and nasogastric tubes; cranial growth; and neuromotor function did not appear to be significantly related in the 83 infants with available data (Engel et al, 2001).

Gender

Most investigators have reported no apparent gender-based difference in the incidence of OME (Engel et al, 1999b; Tos et al, 1978;) or in time with MEE (Paradise et al, 1997). Some studies have found males to have a significantly higher incidence of AOM and more recurrent episodes of AOM than females (Pukander et al, 1982; Teele et al, 1989), but others have not found males to have more episodes of AOM (Casselbrant et al, 1995). Males have been reported to be more prone to persistent MEE (Birch and Elbrønd, 1987). The reason for the sex difference is not known.

Race

Previous studies have suggested a lower incidence of otitis media (OM) in American black children compared with American white children (Kessner et al, 1974; Marchant et al, 1984; Schappert, 1992; Shurin et al, 1979). Kessner and colleagues (1974) reported that the prevalence of "ear pathology" (any abnormality in one or both ears, except for fibrotic scarring) in inner-city children aged 6 months to 12 years was 35.6% in 112 white children and 19.0% in 2,031 black children.

In a report from the Division of Health Care Statistics, the office visit rate for OM was much lower for black children compared with that for white children (Schappert, 1992). Marchant and colleagues (1984) reported a significantly lower incidence of OM diagnosed by otoscopy in 26 black children than in 44 white children followed from birth to 12 months of age. The rates of recurrent OM and bilateral chronic MEE in the black children who developed OM were comparable to those in white children. However, in a recent prospective study, no difference was found between black children and white children in their experience with OM when the children were from the same socioeconomic background, were examined at monthly intervals and whenever they developed signs and symptoms of ear disease, and received the same treatment for ear disease from birth to 2 years of age (Casselbrant et al, 1995). In another prospective study, 2,253 children were followed from approximately 2 months to 2 years of age, with otoscopic examinations every 6 weeks. The mean cumulative percentage of days with MEE during the first year was higher in the black infants than in the white infants, but by the second year, the rates were equal (Paradise et al, 1997). Another study of US schoolchildren, ages 6 to 10 years, evaluated with tympanometry as part of a US population-based sample survey, showed that the prevalence for otitis media with effusion (OME) was significantly higher for Hispanic children compared with white children. The prevalence of OME in this study was not significantly different in black children and in white children (Hoffman et al, 2002).

Allergy and Immunity

Allergy is a common problem in young children, occurring at a time when respiratory viral infections and OM are both very prevalent. There is still controversy regarding the role of allergy in the pathogenesis of OM. Several mechanisms have been suggested, including the middle ear functioning as a "shock organ," inflammatory swelling of the eustachian tube, and inflammatory obstruction of the nose and secondary eustachian tube dysfunction (Bluestone, 1983).

Evidence that allergic rhinitis contributes to the pathogenesis of MEE is derived from epidemiologic, mechanistic, and therapeutic lines of investigation. Kraemer and colleagues (1983) compared risk factors for persistent MEE among 76 children admitted for bilateral myringotomy and tube insertion (BM-T) and 76 controls matched by age, sex, and season of admission for a general surgical procedure. They showed a nearly fourfold increase in the risk of persistent MEE in children who had atopic symptoms for more than 15 days per month. Pukander and Karma (1988) followed 707 children with AOM and found persistence of MEE for 2 months or more to be greater in children with "atopic manifestations" (undefined) than in children without allergy. In

another study, however, allergic manifestations were not found to predispose a child to develop AOM (Pukander et al, 1985).

Tomonaga and colleagues (1988) found allergic rhinitis present in 50% of 259 Japanese patients (mean age of 6 years) in whom OME had been diagnosed. OME was present in 21% of 605 patients (mean age of 9 years) in whom allergic rhinitis had been diagnosed. The incidence of allergic rhinitis, OME, and both of these conditions was 17%, 6%, and 2%, respectively, among a control group of 108 children (aged 5 to 8 years, mean age of 6 years) in whom neither condition had been previously diagnosed. Bernstein and Reisman (1974) similarly determined the allergy status of a group of 200 children who had undergone one or more BM-T procedures. Allergy was diagnosed in 46 children (23%), but the frequency was 35% among the 88 children with multiple BM-Ts. In a follow-up study (Bernstein et al, 1983), 77 children aged 2 to 18 years who had chronic MEE and had undergone at least one BM-T procedure were examined. Middle ear immunoglobulin (Ig)E was increased in 14 of 32 children with allergic rhinitis compared with 2 of 45 children considered nonallergic.

Other investigators have proposed that defective or immature immunologic responses in children with recurrent AOM may contribute to the pathogenesis of the disease (Rynnel-Dagöö and Freijd, 1987). In general, normal serum concentrations of IgG, IgM, and IgA have been demonstrated in children with recurrent AOM (Berman et al, 1992). However, there may be more subtle immune deficiencies in otitis-prone children compared with normal children.

Human immunodeficiency virus (HIV)-infected children have a significantly higher recurrence rate of AOM than normal children (Principi et al, 1991) or children who seroconverted (Barnett et al, 1992). Infected children with a low CD4 lymphocyte count had a nearly threefold increased risk for recurrent AOM compared with HIV-infected children with normal lymphocyte counts.

Cleft Palate, Craniofacial Abnormality, and Down Syndrome

OM is present in nearly all infants under 2 years of age with unrepaired clefts of the palate (Frable et al, 1985; Paradise and Bluestone, 1974). The occurrence of OM was reduced following surgical repair of the palate (Frable et al, 1985; Paradise and Bluestone, 1974), likely owing to improvement of the eustachian tube function (Doyle et al, 1986). OM is also common in children with craniofacial abnormalities and Down syndrome (Balkany et al, 1978). The children with Down syndrome have, in addition to poor active opening function of the eustachian tube, a very low resistance of the tube. Secretions from the nasopharynx can therefore easily access the middle ear (White et al, 1984).

Genetic Predisposition

The frequency of one episode of OM occurring is so high that a genetic predisposition cannot be expected. However, a predisposition to recurrent episodes of OM and chronic MEE may have a significant genetic component. Anatomic, physiologic, and epidemiologic data suggest this. For example, the degree of pneumatization of the mastoid process, a trait believed to be linked causally to OM, was found to be more similar in monozygotic than dizygotic twins (Dahlberg and Diamant, 1945). Racial differences in eustachian tube anatomy and function have also been reported. The shorter, straighter eustachian tube found in American Indians is associated with a higher incidence of chronic suppurative OM (Doyle, 1977). Spivey and Hirschhorn (1977) found in a study of Apache Indians adopted into middle-class foster homes that the incidence of most infectious diseases decreased, but OM incidence was comparable to that reported for the reservation. The antigen HLA-A2 occurred more frequently and HLA-A3 less frequently in children with recurrent AOM than in healthy controls (Kalm et al, 1991). The frequency of HLA-A2 was significantly lower in children with chronic OME than in children with recurrent AOM (Kalm et al, 1994).

Twin and triplet studies have been used to assess heritability for OM. Two retrospective questionnaire studies have been reported. The first study of 2,750 Norwegian twin pairs estimated the heritability at 74% in females and 45% in males (Kvaerner et al, 1997). In the second study, the estimated heritability at ages 2, 3, and 4 years for acute infections was, on average, 57% (Rovers et al, 2002). In a prospective twin/triplet study from Pittsburgh, with monthly assessment of middle ear status, the heritability estimate for OM at age 2 years was 79% in females and 64% in males (Casselbrant et al, 1999).

Environmental Factors

Season and Upper Respiratory Infection

Both epidemiologic evidence and clinical experience strongly suggest that OM is frequently a complication of URI. The incidence of OME is highest during the fall and winter months and lowest in the summer months in both the northern (Casselbrant et al, 1985) and southern hemispheres (Castagno and Lavinsky, 2002), which parallels the incidence of AOM (Pukander et al, 1982) and URI (Casselbrant et al, 1985; Tos et al, 1981). This supports the hypothesis that an episode of URI plays an important role in the etiology of OM. Experimental (Buchman et al, 1994) and clinical studies (Bylander, 1984) have shown that viral URI is a risk factor for eustachian tube dysfunction and development of OM.

URIs with respiratory syncytial virus, influenza virus, and adenovirus often precede episodes of AOM (Henderson et al, 1982). Respiratory syncytial virus, rhinovirus, adenovirus, and coronavirus have been isolated in episodes of AOM (Chonmaitree et al, 1986; Pitkäranta et al, 1998).

Day Care/Home Care

The prevalence of high negative middle ear pressure and flat tympanograms (type B), indicative of MEE, has been shown to be highest in children cared for in day-care centers with many children, intermediate in children in family day care with fewer children, and lowest in children cared for at home (Fiellau-Nikolajsen, 1979; Tos et al, 1978). Another study showed that children cared for in a day-care center for at least 12 months during the first 4 years of life had 2.6 times the risk of developing persistent OME compared with children cared for at home (Rasmussen, 1993).

Alho and colleagues (1993) examined responses to questionnaires sent to parents of 2,512 Finnish children as well as the children's medical records and found an odds ratio of 2.06 for the development of AOM in children attending day-care centers compared with children cared for at home. This increased incidence of AOM in children in day-care centers was also found in a case-control study in Finland (Pukander and Karma, 1988). Children in day care have also been shown to be more likely to have a tympanostomy tube inserted than children cared for at home (Rasmussen, 1993; Wald et al, 1988).

Almost universally, studies identify day-care center attendance as a very important risk factor for developing OM, possibly explained by the increased risk for URI in young children in day care (Wald et al, 1988). Children in day-care centers are at increased risk for URI probably because of the large number of susceptible children in close contact.

Siblings

Birth order was associated with the rate of episodes of OM and percentage of time with MEE in a prospective longitudinal study by Casselbrant and colleagues (1995). The study found that firstborn children had a lower rate of AOM and less time with MEE during the first 2 years of life than did children with older siblings. Pukander and colleagues (1985) also found that children with more siblings were most likely to have recurrent episodes of AOM. Having more than one sibling was significantly related to early OM onset (Daly et al, 1999). However, Teele and colleagues (1989) reported no association between the number of siblings and risk for AOM or MEE.

The reason for the higher morbidity is probably the same as for children in day care. Paradise and colleagues (1997) combined the number of older siblings and day-care attendance into a "child exposure index" and found a significant correlation with cumulative time with MEE. The more children in the same place, the greater the opportunity for exposure to URI, which may cause eustachian tube dysfunction and increase the likelihood of developing OM.

Passive Smoking

An association between OM and passive exposure to smoking has been reported by many investigators (Etzel et al, 1992; Kraemer et al, 1983; Maw et al, 1992; Strachan et al, 1989). The risk of recurrent OM (six or more lifetime episodes) was significantly increased with combined gestational and passive smoke exposure (Lieu and Feinstein, 2002). Other investigators, however, have not been able to demonstrate such an association (Birch and Elbrønd, 1987; Zielhuis et al, 1989).

In most studies, information on smoke exposure has been obtained from the parents' report. Strachan and colleagues (1989), however, measured cotinine, a metabolite of nicotine and a marker of passive exposure to smoking, in the saliva of children 6 to 7 years of age and correlated its concentration with middle ear status as determined by tympanometry. They found that increased cotinine concentrations correlated with abnormal tympanograms and number of smokers in the household.

Etzel and colleagues (1992) measured serum cotinine concentration in children who attended a day-care center. Children exposed to tobacco smoke who had a serum cotinine concentration ≥ 2.5 ng/mL had a 38% higher rate of new episodes of MEE and OM episodes of longer duration. However, Daly and colleagues (1999) were not able to show an association between early AOM onset and cotinine-to-creatinine ratio in urine in children followed from birth to 6 months of age. More information about the pathogenesis, duration, and intensity of exposure is needed to clarify this association.

Breast-Feeding versus Bottle-Feeding

Most studies have found that breast-feeding has a protective effect against middle ear disease; however, there is controversy regarding the duration of breast-feeding necessary for protection. Some investigators have found no association between the duration of breast-feeding and the recurrence rate of AOM (Harsten et al, 1989; Tainio et al, 1988), but many have reported fewer recurrences of AOM among children who were breast-fed exclusively for a prolonged period of time (Duffy et al, 1997; Duncan et al, 1993). Duncan and colleagues (1993) followed 1,013 infants in a 1-year study and found that infants exclusively breast-fed for 4 months or longer had half the mean number of AOM episodes compared with infants who were not breast-fed at all and 40% less than infants breast-fed less than 4 months. The recurrence rate in infants exclusively breast-fed for 6 months or longer was 10% compared with 20.5% in infants who were breast-fed less than 4 months.

A cohort of 306 normal children enrolled shortly after birth was followed at well-baby visits for 2 years (Duffy et

al, 1997). The infants were examined with pneumatic otoscopy and tympanometry monthly for the first 6 months, every other month at ages 6 to 12 months, every 3 months at ages 12 to 24 months, and at interim visits after the diagnosis of OM and other recent illnesses. Between 6 and 12 months of age, the cumulative incidence of first OM episodes increased from 25 to 51% in infants exclusively breast-fed and from 54 to 76% in infants formula-fed from birth. The peak incidence of AOM and OME episodes was inversely related to rates of breast-feeding beyond 3 months of age. A twofold elevated risk of first episode of AOM or OME was observed in exclusively formula-fed infants compared with infants exclusively breast-fed for 6 months. The authors concluded that breast-feeding is a modifiable factor in the onset of AOM and OME. Saarinen (1982) found, in a prospective study of 237 children, that prolonged breast-feeding (6 months or longer) protected the child from recurrent OM not only during the period of breast-feeding but also up to 3 years of age.

The mechanism for the protective effect of breast milk is not known, but several hypotheses have been suggested. The protective mechanism may be through immunologic factors provided through the breast milk, especially secretory IgA, with antibody activity against respiratory tract viruses and bacteria (Andersson et al, 1986), or it may be through other factors preventing bacterial adhesion (Andersson et al, 1986; Hanson et al, 1985). Bluestone and Klein (1995) have suggested mechanisms in bottle-fed children that may account for these differences, including allergy to formula or cow's milk, poorer development of facial musculature needed to promote good eustachian tube function, aspiration of fluids in the middle ear with high intraoral pressures generated by bottle-feeding, and the reclining or horizontal position of the infants during feeding possibly causing reflux.

Socioeconomic Status

Socioeconomic status and access to health care are factors that may affect the incidence of OM. It has been generally thought that OM is more common among people in the lower socioeconomic strata owing to poor sanitary conditions and crowding. Paradise and colleagues (1997) followed 2,253 infants for 2 years and found an inverse relationship between the cumulative proportion of days with MEE and socioeconomic status. Castagno and Lavinsky (2002) also found a higher prevalence of OME in children in the lower socioeconomic class in southern Brazil. However, many studies revealed no correlation between socioeconomic status of the child's family and incidence of MEE (Birch and Elbrønd, 1987; Teele et al, 1989; Tos et al, 1978). Tos and colleagues (1978) found no difference in MEE rates between children living in apartments and those in houses.

Pacifier Use

Niemelä and colleagues (1994) found from parental questionnaires that among 938 5-year-old children, those who had used a pacifier had a greater risk of having had four or more episodes of AOM than those who had not, whereas thumb sucking was not associated with AOM. In a follow-up prospective study of 845 children in day-care centers, Niemelä and colleagues (1995) found that use of a pacifier increased the annual incidence of AOM and calculated that pacifier use was responsible for 25% of AOM episodes in children younger than 3 years. Warren and colleagues (2001) used questionnaires at 6 weeks and 3, 6, 9, and 12 months to determine the relationship between OM and pacifier use. Pacifier sucking was significantly associated with OM from 6 to 9 months and approached statistical significance at 9 to 12 months ($p = .056$); other time periods showed no significant relationship to OM.

References

Álho O, Kilkku O, Oja H, et al. Control of the temporal aspect when considering risk factors for acute otitis media. Arch Otolaryngol Head Neck Surg 1993;119:444–9.

Alho O, Koivu M, Hartikainen-Sorri A, et al. Is a child's history of acute otitis media and respiratory infection already determined in the antenatal and perinatal period? Int J Pediatr Otorhinolaryngol 1990;19:129–37.

Andersson B, Porras O, Hanson LA, et al. Inhibition of attachment of *Streptococcus pneumoniae* and *Haemophilus influenzae* by human milk and receptor oligosaccharides. J Infect Dis 1986; 153:232–7.

Balkany TJ, Downs MP, Jafek BW, Krajicek MJ. Otologic manifestations of Down syndrome. Surg Forum 1978;29:582–5.

Barnett ED, Klein JO, Pelton SI, Luginbuhl LM. Otitis media in children born to human immunodeficiency virus-infected mothers. Pediatr Infect Dis J 1992;11:360–4.

Berman S, Lee B, Nuss R, et al. Immunoglobulin G, total and subclass, in children with or without recurrent otitis media. J Pediatr 1992;121:249–51.

Bernstein JM, Lee J, Conboy K, et al. The role of IgE mediated hypersensitivity in recurrent otitis media with effusion. Am J Otol 1983;5:66–9.

Bernstein JM, Reisman RE. The role of acute hypersensitivity in secretory otitis media. Trans Am Acad Ophthalmol Otolaryngol 1974;78:120–7.

Birch L, Elbrønd O. A prospective epidemiological study of secretory otitis media in young children related to the indoor environment. ORL J Otorhinolaryngol Relat Spec 1987;49:253–8.

Bluestone CD. Eustachian tube function: physiology, pathophysiology, and role of allergy in pathogenesis of otitis media. J Allergy Clin Immunol 1983;72:242–51.

Bluestone CD, Klein JO. Otitis media in infants and children. Philadelphia: WB Saunders; 1995.

Buchman CA, Doyle WJ, Skoner D, et al. Otologic manifestations of experimental rhinovirus infection. Laryngoscope 1994;104: 1295–9.

Bylander A. Upper respiratory tract infection and eustachian tube function in children. Acta Otolaryngol (Stockh) 1984;97:343–9.

Casselbrant ML, Brostoff LM, Cantekin EI, et al. Otitis media with effusion in preschool children. Laryngoscope 1985;95:428–36.

Casselbrant ML, Mandel EM, Fall PA, et al. The heritability of otitis media: a twin and triplet study. JAMA 1999;282:2125–30.

Casselbrant ML, Mandel EM, Kurs-Lasky M, et al. Otitis media in a population of black American and white American infants, 0–2 years of age. Int J Pediatr Otorhinolaryngol 1995;33:1–16.

Castagno LA, Lavinsky L. Otitis media in children: seasonal changes and socioeconomic level. Int J Pediatr Otorhinolaryngol 2002;62:129–34.

Chonmaitree T, Howie VM, Truant AL. Presence of respiratory viruses in middle ear fluids and nasal wash specimens from children with acute otitis media. Pediatrics 1986;77:698–702.

Dahlberg G, Diamant M. Hereditary character in the cellular system of the mastoid process. Acta Otolaryngol (Stockh) 1945; 33:378–89.

Daly KA, Brown JE, Lindgren BR, et al. Epidemiology of otitis media onset by six months of age. Pediatrics 1999;103:1158–66.

Doyle WJ. A functional-anatomic description of eustachian tube vector relations in four ethnic populations: an osteologic study [PhD dissertation]. Pittsburgh: University of Pittsburgh; 1977.

Doyle WJ, Reilly JS, Jardini L, Rovnak S. Effect of palatoplasty on the function of the eustachian tube in children with cleft palate. Cleft Palate J 1986;23:63–8.

Duffy LC, Faden H, Wasielewski R, et al. Exclusive breastfeeding protects against bacterial colonization and day care exposure to otitis media. Pediatrics 1997;100:E7.

Duncan B, Ey J, Holberg CJ, et al. Exclusive breastfeeding for at least 4 months protects against otitis media. Pediatrics 1993; 91:867–72.

Engel J, Anteunis L, Volovics A, et al. Prevalence rates of otitis media with effusion from 0 to 2 years of age: healthy-born versus high-risk-born infants. Int J Pediatr Otorhinolaryngol 1999a;47:243–51.

Engel J, Anteunis L, Volovics A, et al. Risk factors of otitis media with effusion during infancy. Int J Pediatr Otorhinolaryngol 1999b;48:239–49.

Engel J, Mahler E, Anteunis L, et al. Why are NICU infants at risk for chronic otitis media with effusion? Int J Pediatr Otorhinolaryngol 2001;57:137–44.

Etzel RA, Pattishall EN, Haley NJ, et al. Passive smoking and middle-ear effusion among children in day care. Pediatrics 1992;90: 228–32.

Fiellau-Nikolajsen M. Tympanometry in three-year old children. Type of care as an epidemiological factor in secretory otitis media and tubal dysfunction in unselected populations of three-year old children. ORL J Otorhinolaryngol Relat Spec 1979;41:193–205.

Frable MA, Brandon GT, Theogaraj SD. Velar closure and ear tubings as a primary procedure in the repair of cleft palates. Laryngoscope 1985;95:1044–6.

Gravel JS, McCarton CM, Ruben RJ. Otitis media in neonatal intensive care unit graduates: a 1-year prospective study. Pediatrics 1988;82:44–9.

Hanson LA, Andersson B, Carlsson B, et al. Defense of mucous membranes by antibodies, receptor analogues, and nonspecific host factors. Infection 1985;13 Suppl 2:S166–70.

Harsten G, Prellner K, Heldrup J, et al. Recurrent acute otitis media. Acta Otolaryngol (Stockh) 1989;107:111–9.

Henderson FW, Collier AM, Sanyal MA, et al. A longitudinal study of respiratory viruses and bacteria in the etiology of acute otitis media with effusion. N Engl J Med 1982;306:1379–83.

Hoffman HJ, MacTurk RH, Gravel JS, et al. Epidemiological risk factors for otitis media and hearing loss in school age children based on NHANES III, 1988–1994. In: Proceedings of the Seventh International Symposium. Recent advances in otitis media [book on CD-ROM]. Hamilton (ON): BC Decker; 2002. p. 147–530.

Kalm O, Johnson U, Prellner K. HLA frequency in patients with chronic secretory otitis media. Int J Pediatr Otorhinolaryngol 1994;30:151–7.

Kalm O, Johnson U, Prellner K, Ninn K. HLA frequency in patients with recurrent acute otitis media. Arch Otolaryngol Head Neck Surg 1991;117:1296–9.

Kessner DM, Snow CK, Singer J. Assessment of medical care for children. Washington (DC): Institute of Medicine, National Academy of Sciences; 1974.

Kraemer MJ, Richardson MA, Weiss NS, et al. Risk factors for persistent middle-ear effusions—otitis media, catarrh, cigarette smoke exposure, and atopy. JAMA 1983;249:1022–5.

Kvaerner KJ, Harris JR, Tambs K, Magnus P. Distribution and heritability of recurrent ear infections. Ann Otol Rhinol Laryngol 1997;106:624–32.

Lieu JE, Feinstein AR. Effect of gestational and passive smoke exposure on ear infections in children. Arch Pediatr Adolesc Med 2002;156:147–54.

Marchant CD, Shurin PA, Turczyk VA, et al. Course and outcome of otitis media in early infancy: a prospective study. J Pediatr 1984;104:826–31.

Marchisio P, Bigalli L, Massironi E, Principi N. Risk factors for persisting otitis media with effusion in children. In: Lim DJ, Bluestone CD, Klein JO, Nelson JD, editors. Recent advances in otitis media with effusion: proceedings of the Fourth International Symposium. Philadelphia: BC Decker; 1988. p. 3–5.

Maw AR, Parker AJ, Lance GN, Dilkes MG. The effect of parental smoking on outcome after treatment for glue ear in children. Clin Otolaryngol 1992;17:411–4.

Niemelä M, Uhari M, Hannuksela A. Pacifiers and dental structure as risk factors for otitis media. Int J Pediatr Otorhinolaryngol 1994;29:121–7.

Niemelä M, Uhari M, Möttönen M. A pacifier increases the risk of recurrent acute otitis media in children in day-care centers. Pediatrics 1995;96:884–8.

Paradise JL, Bluestone CD. Early treatment of the universal otitis media of infants with cleft palate. Pediatrics 1974;53:48–54.

Paradise JL, Rockette HE, Colburn K, et al. Otitis media in 2253 Pittsburgh-area infants: prevalence and risk factors during the first two years of life. Pediatrics 1997;99:318–33.

Pitkäranta A, Virolainen A, Jero J, et al. Detection of rhinovirus, respiratory syncytial virus, and coronavirus infections in acute otitis media by reverse transcriptase polymerase chain reaction. Pediatrics 1998;102:291–5.

Principi N, Marchisio P, Tornaghi R, et al. Acute otitis media in human immunodeficiency virus-infected children. Pediatrics 1991;88:566–71.

Pukander JS, Karma PH. Persistence of middle-ear effusion and its risk factors after an acute attack of otitis media with effusion. In: Lim DJ, Bluestone CD, Klein JO, Nelson JD, editors. Recent advances in otitis media: proceedings of the Fourth International Symposium. Toronto: BC Decker; 1988. p. 8–11.

Pukander J, Karma P, Sipilä M. Occurrence and recurrence of acute otitis media among children. Acta Otolaryngol (Stockh) 1982;94:479–86.

Pukander J, Luotonen J, Timonen M, Karma P. Risk factors affecting the occurrence of acute otitis media among 2–3-year-old urban children. Acta Otolaryngol (Stockh) 1985;100:260–5.

Rasmussen F. Protracted secretory otitis media. The impact of familial factors and day-care center attendance. Int J Pediatr Otorhinolaryngol 1993;26:29–37.

Rovers M, Haggard M, Gannon M, et al. Heritability of symptom domains in otitis media: a longitudinal study of 1,373 twin pairs. Am J Epidemiol 2002;155:958–64.

Rynnel-Dagöö B, Freijd A. Immunodeficiency. In: Bernstein J, Ogra P, editors. Otitis media in immunology of the ear. New York: Raven Press; 1987. p. 363–80.

Saarinen UM. Prolonged breast-feeding as prophylaxis for recurrent otitis media. Acta Paediatr Scand 1982;71:567–71.

Schappert SM. Office visits for otitis media: United States, 1975–90. Adv Data 1992;214:1–19.

Shurin PA, Pelton SI, Donner A, Klein JO. Persistence of middle-ear effusion after acute otitis media in children. N Engl J Med 1979;300:1121–3.

Spivey GH, Hirschhorn N. A migrant study of adopted Apache children. Johns Hopkins Med J 1977;1210:43–6.

Strachan DP, Jarvis MJ, Feyerabend C. Passive smoking, salivary cotinine concentrations, and middle ear effusion in 7 year old children. BMJ 1989;298:1549–52.

Tainio VM, Savilahti E, Salmenpera L, et al. Risk factors for infantile recurrent otitis media: atopy but not type of feeding. Pediatr Res 1988;23:509–12.

Teele DW, Klein JO, Rosner B, Greater Boston Otitis Media Study Group. Epidemiology of otitis media during the first seven years of life in children in greater Boston: a prospective, cohort study. J Infect Dis 1989;160:83–94.

Tomonaga K, Kurono Y, Mogi G. The role of nasal allergy in otitis media with effusion: a clinical study. Acta Otolaryngol Suppl (Stockh) 1988;458:41–7.

Tos M, Holm-Jensen S, Sorensen CH. Changes in prevalence of secretory otitis from summer to winter in four-year-old children. Am J Otol 1981;2:324–7.

Tos M, Poulsen G, Borch J. Tympanometry in two-year-old children. ORL J Otorhinolaryngol Relat Spec 1978;40:77–85.

Wald ER, Dashefsky B, Byers C, et al. Frequency and severity of infections in day care. J Pediatr 1988;112:540–6.

Warren JJ, Levy SM, Kirchner HL, et al. Pacifier use and the occurrence of otitis media in the first year of life. Pediatr Dent 2001;23:103–7.

White BL, Doyle WJ, Bluestone CD. Eustachian tube function in infants and children with Down syndrome. In: Lim DJ, Bluestone CD, Klein JO, Nelson JD, editors. Recent advances in otitis media with effusion: proceedings of the Third International Symposium. Philadelphia: BC Decker; 1984. p. 62–6.

Zielhuis GA, Heuvelmans-Heinen EW, Rach GH, Broek PVD. Environmental risk factors for otitis media with effusion in preschool children. Scand J Prim Health Care 1989;7:33–8.

II. Acute Otitis Media

Chapter 6

FIRST-LINE TREATMENT OF ACUTE OTITIS MEDIA

Michael E. Pichichero, MD

Acute otitis media (AOM) is defined by the presence of fluid in the middle ear, a bulging tympanic membrane, plus a sign of acute local or systemic illness. The patient with AOM may have symptoms and signs specific to ear disease, including pain, otorrhea, and hearing loss, as well as systemic symptoms and signs of fever, irritability, headache, lethargy, anorexia, or vomiting. Uncommon symptoms and signs of ear infection include tinnitus, vertigo, and nystagmus. Uncomplicated AOM refers to infrequently occurring, mild to moderate infections in children who are not otitis prone, do not have persistent or recurrent infections, are beyond 6 months of age, and are not in day care. By 3 years of age, nearly 50% of all children will have experienced three or more episodes of AOM and about 40% of children experience six or more episodes of AOM by age 7 years (Teele et al, 1989).

Importance

In 1989, an estimated 31 million visits occurred and $3.5 billion was spent on treatment of AOM in the United States (Stool and Field, 1989). AOM is usually followed by a middle ear effusion (MEE) as part of the natural history of the disease. Specifically, at 2 weeks postinfection, even with appropriate therapy, 60% of patients will have a MEE; at 30 days, 50%; at 60 days, 20%; and at 90 days, 15% (Marchant et al, 1984). This persistence of effusion is generally associated with a mild hearing loss. A hearing threshold at approximately 30 dB across frequencies involving speech and language is common (Kokko, 1974). The loss of certain sounds associated with the 30 dB hearing threshold can have a significant impact on a child's ability to acquire language during the toddler years or can slow additional language acquisition in the preschool and early school-age years (Roberts et al, 1986; Teele et al, 1990).

AOM and otitis media with effusion (OME) are disease entities in the otitis media continuum. There is often a transition between OME and AOM, and the two conditions may sometimes be indistinguishable from each other diagnostically (Paradise, 1987). It is sometimes quite difficult to diagnose whether an effusion in the middle ear space is purulent (consistent with AOM) or nonpurulent (consistent with OME) and whether the effusion will be culture positive or culture negative for bacterial pathogens. As a further confounder, misdiagnosis may also occur when a patient experiencing a viral upper respiratory infection develops nasopharyngeal and eustachian tube congestion. Under this circumstance, it often occurs that the tympanic membrane (TM) becomes distorted (retracted), and the associated anatomic changes on otoscopic inspection mislead the practitioner to conclude that AOM or OME is present. Thus, a first step in treatment decisions regarding otitis media must rely on accurate diagnosis to distinguish AOM, OME, and a retracted TM without MEE from a normal TM (Pichichero, 2000a; Pichichero, 2000b). Principles of judicious use of antibiotics for otitis media have emphasized that episodes of otitis media should be classified as AOM or OME.

Etiology

The microbiologic causes of AOM have been documented on the basis of results of cultures of MEE that have been obtained by tympanocentesis (needle aspiration through the TM). Bacterial pathogens are isolated from middle ear fluids of 56 to 75% of children with AOM. Various studies from the United States, Europe, Japan, and elsewhere over the past 40 years are consistent in that they have underscored the importance of *Streptococcus pneumoniae* as the leading bacterial pathogen and nontypable *Haemophilus influenzae* as the next most important pathogen. *Moraxella catarrhalis*, group A streptococcus, and *Staphylococcus aureus* are less common causes of AOM. Respiratory viruses alone or in combination with bacterial pathogens have been identified in approximately 10 to 20% of middle ear fluids. Infection owing to *Mycoplasma pneumoniae* and *Chlamydia pneumoniae* is rare. The bacterial causes of AOM are often indistinguishable by history or physical examination.

Options for and Factors in Management

The options for management of uncomplicated AOM include watchful waiting with pain control (using acetaminophen or ibuprofen) or antibiotics.

A number of factors can be implicated in assessing the likelihood of clinical success in watchful waiting or antibiotic treatment for uncomplicated AOM. Factors associated with persistent infection include patient age less than 3 years, symptom severity, and day-care attendance. The propensity to develop AOM shows a strong genetic component.

Age

Younger children compared with older children have a greater likelihood of failing to meet the definitions of clinical success or resolution when not treated with antibiotics for AOM. The threshold appears to be sometime around 3 years of age (Kaleida et al, 1991; Laxdal et al, 1970). This may be related to anatomic factors (delayed development of optimal eustachian tube function), exposure (especially day-care attendance), or the differential incidence of resistant bacterial pathogens recovered from AOM in this age group. Children younger than 24 months tend to have a higher frequency of both penicillin-resistant *S. pneumoniae* and β-lactamase–producing gram-negative organisms than those older than 48 months of age. Pathogens recovered from children older than 48 months are more often susceptible to traditional first-line antibiotics, such as amoxicillin and trimethoprim-sulfamethoxazole.

Symptom Severity

AOM may be classified as mild, moderate, or severe based in part on the degree of otalgia and the severity of systemic symptoms, for example, fever, irritability, and anorexia. Most patients who receive placebo do well if their AOM episode is uncomplicated and mild. Kaleida and colleagues (1991) reported that 63% of children had a MEE at 2 weeks when placebo treated if the AOM was nonsevere. However, even in mild AOM, the benefit of antibiotics in the frequency of treatment failure and rate of effusion 2 weeks after disease onset significantly favors antibiotic therapy (Marcy et al, 2001).

Day-Care Attendance

The day-care environment provides a circumstance in which nasopharyngeal organisms can be easily transmitted from one child to another. As a consequence of promiscuous antimicrobial therapy in day-care children, selection and subsequent emergence of multiple antibiotic-resistant strains are common. Thus, children attending day care more often harbor resistant AOM pathogens (Henderson et al, 1988), and this should be considered in antibiotic selection.

Evidence-Based Analysis of Treatment Efficacy

Uncomplicated AOM appears to have a favorable natural history regardless of antibiotic therapy. A spontaneous resolution rate of 70 to 80% has been proposed (Marcy et al, 2001). However, overdiagnosis of AOM is common, occurring in perhaps 50% of cases (Pichichero and Poole, 2001); OME is often misdiagnosed as AOM (Pichichero and Poole, 2001). Without tympanocentesis confirmation of the diagnosis at study entry, these described high rates of spontaneous improvement may be overinflated by inclusion of many patients who did not have AOM. Of the few studies available, it is difficult to quantitate because of the lack of uniformity in the definition of outcomes, the specific outcomes monitored, and the various times of measurement. In addition, most studies do not report results, stratified by the influencing factors of age and otitis-prone state, and most report clinical criteria for administering antibiotics to placebo or observational groups during follow-up based on persistent or worsening symptoms or complications.

With the important caveats noted above, the available "evidence base" shows modest benefits from antibiotics for AOM. For uncomplicated AOM not treated with antibiotics, the clinical failure rate at 24 to 48 hours was 8% in one study (Kaleida et al, 1991) and 26% at 24 to 72 hours in another (Halsted et al, 1968). Rosenfeld and colleagues (1994) found a favorable difference of 12.9% (95% confidence interval [CI]: 8.2–19.2%) for treatment with amoxicillin compared with no antibiotics and a 13.7% (95% CI: 8.2–19.2%) favorable difference for those treated with any antibiotic compared with no antibiotic. Pooling data on failure rates at 4 to 7 days yields an estimate of 22% (three studies, 220 children; 95% CI: 10.1%–34.3%), that is, 78% of children not initially treated with antibiotics for AOM will have clinical resolution (Burke et al, 1991; Laxdal et al, 1970; Kaleida et al, 1991; Marcy et al, 2001). A pooled analysis for failure from 1 to 7 days yields an estimate of 19% (five studies, 739 children; 95% CI: 9.9%–28.0%), that is, 81% of children will have clinical resolution without treatment (Marcy et al, 2001). Resolution of pain and fever may have a significant association with age among those not treated with antibiotics for AOM; in a study of 12 children, 58% under 2 years of age had pain or fever at more than 3 days compared with 7% of children 2 years or older (Appelman et al, 1991). One study looked at the presence of MEE in relation to age in children with AOM not treated with antibiotics; the findings suggested a greater propensity to MEE with younger age (Kaleida et al, 1991).

The generalizability of findings of evidence-based analysis is difficult to assess. Only two of the nine randomized, controlled trials addressing natural history reported any outcome stratified as 2 years or less and older than 2 years (Kaleida et al, 1991; Appelman et al, 1991), and only the Kaleida and colleagues (1991) study reported early failure rate stratified in this manner. Two of the six cohort studies on natural history reported results stratified above and below 2 years of age (Froom et al, 1990; Tilyard et al, 1997). These two studies reporting outcomes by age indicate that children younger than 2 years do not resolve their clinical symptoms of AOM as quickly as older children. The studies on the clinical effectiveness of specific antibiotic regimens suffer the same problems with regard to reporting of outcomes by subject age.

In summary, evidenced-based analysis shows that antibiotics produce a short-term benefit in more rapid resolution of symptoms of uncomplicated AOM and an intermediate-term benefit in more rapid resolution of MEE. Antibiotics reduce the risk of bacteremia progressing to focal, severe infection (eg, meningitis); 2 to 4% of children younger than 2 years of age with AOM and fever have concurrent bacteremia. Antibiotics may prevent focal infections such as mastoiditis, which occur in approximately 1 in 400 untreated children. Additional advantages of antibiotic treatment include avoidance of sequential visits for patients who have not improved, as well as possibly decreasing litigation risks. There has been debate about the necessity to treat all children who have AOM with antibiotics. Yet a careful examination of the published literature would suggest that younger, febrile children are at increased risk for complications. This would apply specifically to children younger than 2 years of age. This is the age when AOM is most prevalent. If antibiotic therapy is to be withheld, perhaps it would be more appropriate for afebrile children older than 3 years of age.

Antibiotic Selection

Management of uncomplicated AOM focuses on the choice of an appropriate antibiotic. The antibiotic choice should have proven microbiologic and clinical efficacy (Dagan and McCracken, 2002; Pichichero and Casey, 2003). Microbiologic efficacy should be determined for each potential bacterial pathogen by the assessment of studies in which pretreatment tympanocentesis specimens have been obtained and assessment of efficacy occurred by predefined, appropriate clinical criteria. Cultures of middle ear aspirates obtained prior to initiation and 3 to 6 days after initiation of therapy provide definitive data about the efficacy of the drug used for sterilizing middle ear fluid. Such microbiologic efficacy of various antibiotics and placebo for treatment of AOM caused by *S. pneumoniae* and *H. influenzae* is shown in Table 6-1. Clinical efficacy should be measurable based on substantial resolution of signs and symptoms within 72 hours and prevention of relapse, recurrence, and suppurative sequelae. At least 63 trials have been published since the 1960s comparing amoxicillin, placebo, and various antibiotics (Pichichero and Casey, 2003) as treatment for AOM. Although these studies, in aggregate, evaluated over 10,000 children, none had the statistical power to detect differences among treatments (Pichichero and Casey, 2003). Trials varied in patient population size from 17 to 660 and almost always revealed successful clinical outcomes. Besides inadequate sample size problems, other study design flaws included overdiagnosis of AOM at study entry, inclusion of patients with only mild AOM, exclusion of moderate to severe and difficult to treat cases, and use of overly broad criteria (symptom resolution only) for the definition of clinical cure/improvement.

Other major considerations in antibiotic selection for AOM include comparative drug safety, compliance features, recommended duration of therapy, and cost.

There is little to distinguish one antibiotic from another in terms of safety profiles. All of the antibiotics used for AOM are generally safe. Therefore, compliance, duration of therapy, and cost become more important issues.

The main determinants of compliance are the frequency of dosing, palatability of the agent, and duration of therapy. Less frequent doses (once or twice a day) are preferable to more frequent doses, which interfere with daily routines. In many instances, the palatability of the drug ultimately determines compliance in children.

Patients (and parents) prefer a shorter course of antibiotic therapy (5 days or fewer) rather than the tradi-

TABLE 6-1. Persistence of Bacteria in Middle Ear Fluids after 3 to 5 Days of Therapy for Acute Otitis Media

Treatment	*Streptococcus pneumoniae*	*Haemophilus influenzae*
Placebo	46/57 (81)*	13/25 (52)
Amoxicillin	71/120 (59)	3/50 (6)+
		10/21 (47)++
Amoxicillin-clavulanate	2/32 (6)	10/43 (23)
Cefaclor	14/74 (18)	23/68 (33)
Cefixime	16/61 (26)	4/71 (5)
Cefuroxime axetil	0/11	1/5
Ceftriaxone	0/15	0/11
Trimethoprim-sulfamethoxazole	0/19	1/14

+ = β-lactamase negative; ++ = β-lactamase positive.
*Number still with viable bacteria (%).

tional 10-day courses often used in the United States. Many patients and parents continue antibiotic therapy only until symptoms resolve, perhaps followed by an additional 1 or 2 days; the remainder of the prescription may be saved for future use when similar symptoms arise.

Antibiotic cost is an interesting component of the treatment paradigm. Drug costs alone rarely reflect the total cost of treating an illness. For example, three office visits and three injections of intramuscular ceftriaxone would seem to greatly escalate the cost of treating AOM. However, the costs of loss of work or school attendance as a result of treatment failure and of repeat office visits for additional evaluation are also important factors, but they are often overlooked when the comparative costs of treatment include only the cost of the antibiotic.

Centers for Disease Control and Prevention Guideline Recommendations

The Centers for Disease Control and Prevention (CDC) has made recommendations with regard to the treatment of AOM with consideration to bacterial resistance (Dowell et al, 1999), as summarized in Table 6-2. Consideration should be given to antibiotic concentration achievable in middle ear fluid relative to the concentration necessary to kill the relevant pathogens. Two selection criteria were recommended: the antibiotic should be effective against most drug-resistant *S. pneumoniae* and against β-lactamase–producing *H. influenzae* and *M. catarrhalis*. On the basis of these criteria, a treatment algorithm was developed (see Table 6-2). In forming these recommendations, trials in which tympanocentesis was performed were prominently considered to avoid the problem of basing recommendations on patients who have been inaccurately diagnosed.

Important elements in the CDC treatment guideline include the recommendation to start with amoxicillin for uncomplicated AOM. The decision to continue or to switch to an alternative antibiotic should be based on clinical response on the third day of therapy, giving the selected antibiotic enough time to work or fail. Including

traditional second-line antibiotics as first-line choices may be appropriate when the patient has already been on an antibiotic within the previous month or is otitis prone.

Tympanocentesis

Tympanocentesis with a culture of middle ear fluid may be useful for patients in pain, who appear toxic, or with high fever (Pichichero, 2000a; Pichichero, 2000b). Diagnostic tympanocentesis is very helpful in guiding the choice of therapy in persistent or recurrent AOM but is not recommended in uncomplicated AOM (Pichichero, 2000a; Pichichero, 2000b). The CDC has recommended that physicians learn the skills required to perform tympanocentesis or have a referral source for patients who would benefit from the procedure (Dowell et al, 1999). Evacuation (drainage) of the MEE may be beneficial in breaking the cycle of persistent and recurrent AOM. The information provided by the culture and susceptibility report may be valuable for treating persistent and recurrent AOM (Dowell et al, 1999; Pichichero, 2000a; Pichichero 2000b). If a bacterial pathogen is reported, selecting an appropriate antibiotic will reduce the likelihood of further treatment failure; if no bacterial pathogen is isolated, the patient will not require further antibiotic treatment.

Duration of Treatment

A 10-day treatment course with an antibiotic has been standard in the United States, although shorter regimens are frequently employed in other countries. There is microbiologic and clinical evidence that shorter treatment regimens might be effective in the majority of uncomplicated AOM episodes (Pichichero and Cohen, 1997). Pediatric studies in which tympanocentesis was used to evaluate bacteria in MEE showed sterility of the middle ear space after only 3 to 6 days of antibiotic treatment (see Table 6-1). Bacterial eradication is the key determinant of treatment success; therefore, 3- to 6-day courses of antibiotic therapy might be predicted to be successful on the basis of these data. Clinical evidence supports the efficacy of shortened courses of antibiotic therapy in uncomplicated AOM. Early studies suggested that a 5-day course of therapy may be less effective than a 10-day course in children who are

TABLE 6-2. Acute Otitis Media Treatment Recommendations by the CDC Drug-Resistant *Streptococcus pneumoniae* Working Group

Antibiotics in Prior Month	Day 0	Clinically Defined Treatment Failure on Day 3	Clinically Defined Treatment Failure on Day 10–28
No	High-dose amoxicillin or usual-dose amoxicillin	High-dose amoxicillin-clavulanate or cefuroxime axetil or IM ceftriaxone	High-dose amoxicillin-clavulanate or cefuroxime axetil or IM ceftriaxone
Yes	High-dose amoxicillin or high-dose amoxicillin-clavulanate or cefuroxime axetil	IM ceftriaxone or clindamycin*; tympanocentesis	High-dose amoxicillin-clavulanate or cefuroxime axetil or IM ceftriaxone; tympanocentesis

Adapted from Dowell SF et al (1999).
*High-dose amoxicillin = 80–100 mg/kg/d. High-dose amoxicillin-clavulanate = 80–100 mg/kg/d for the amoxicillin component (requires newer formulation or combination with amoxicillin). Ceftriaxone injections recommended for 3 days. Clindamycin is not effective against *Haemophilus influenzae* or *Moraxella catarrhalis*.
CDC = Centers for Disease Control and Prevention; IM = intramuscular.

younger than 2 years of age (Pichichero and Cohen, 1997). Later, clinical efficacy of 5-, 7-, and 10-day antibiotic regimens for AOM according to patient age suggested that age was not the critical factor in predicting success in shortened antibiotic regimens (Pichichero et al, 2001). Rather, it would appear that use of antibiotic therapy within the preceding month (a known risk factor for selection of resistant pathogens) identifies a subgroup of patients who clearly benefit from longer (10 day) courses of antibiotic therapy. Regional variations to prescribing pathogen resistance patterns would therefore be relevant in considering the duration of therapy for an individual patient. In addition, patients with TM perforation are less likely to experience cure with a shortened course of therapy.

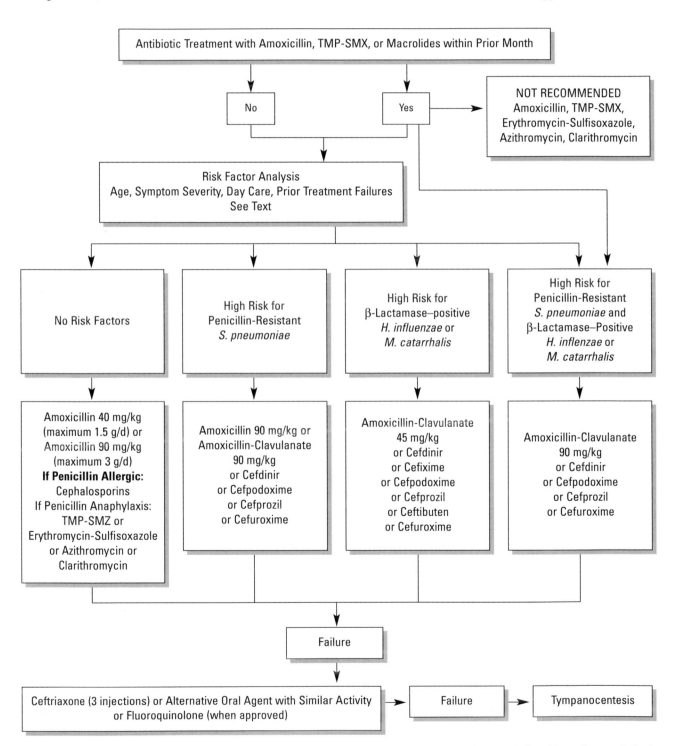

FIGURE 6-1. Algorithm for treatment of acute otitis media. *H. influenzae = Haemophilus influenzae; M. catarrhalis = Moraxella catarrhalis; S. pneumoniae = Streptococcus pneumoniae;* TMP-SMX = trimethoprim-sulfamethoxazole.

Author's Management

I treat AOM with antibiotics because they can shorten the duration of symptoms of AOM, mainly of pain and systemic illness. Antibiotics also reduce contralateral AOM by 43% and prevent suppurative complications and the risk of bacteremia with secondary bacterial seeding. Antibiotics favorably impact the impairment of hearing that occurs in association with the presence of middle ear fluid following AOM.

Amoxicillin at a dosage of 90 mg/kg/d given in two divided doses for 5 days is my first choice in most patients with uncomplicated AOM. If the patient is > 4 years old or if penicillin-resistant *S. pneumoniae* is not prevalent (< 20% of strains), then a dose of 40 mg/kg/d would be acceptable (Figure 6-1).

Resistant *S. pneumoniae*, *H. influenzae*, and *M. catarrhalis* are sometimes isolated in uncomplicated AOM. Thus, recent antimicrobial exposure (within the past month) as a risk factor for resistant pathogens would lead me to consider broader-spectrum agents. Also, children younger than 2 years of age, those in day care, and those with younger siblings in the home more often experience AOM caused by resistant pathogens; therefore, I sometimes consider use of a broader-spectrum agent in these patients.

Some patients develop a pattern of clinical failure with amoxicillin. The number of failures to be tolerated before amoxicillin is replaced with an alternative second-line therapy is subjective. I suggest that two failures with amoxicillin within a respiratory season may be sufficient to prompt the use of alternative agents in that patient. Host-specific factors may be relevant as absorption of amoxicillin (and amoxicillin-clavulanate) may be variable, leading to variable serum concentrations and secondarily reducing tissue and middle ear levels of antibiotic.

When I consider pathogen-directed antibiotic selection, I rely on the predicted efficacy of various drugs against penicillin-resistant *S. pneumoniae* and β-lactamase–producing strains of *H. influenzae* based on pharmacokinetic and pharmacodynamic principles (Tables 6-3 and 6-4). Such information is helpful in selecting second-line antibiotics when resistant organisms are suspected.

TABLE 6-3. Comparative Activity of Antibiotics against *Streptococcus pneumoniae* Based on Pharmacokinetic/ Pharmacodynamic Principles

Highest	Ceftriaxone (Rocephin)
	Double-dose amoxicillin
	Extra-strength amoxicillin-clavulanate (Augmentin)
	Cefdinir (Omnicef)
	Cefpodoxime proxetil (Vantin)
	Cefprozil (Cefzil)
	Cefuroxime (Ceftin)
	Azithromycin (Zithromax)
	Cefaclor (Ceclor)
	Clarithromycin (Biaxin)
	Loracarbef (Lorabid)
	Trimethoprim-sulfamethoxazole (Bactrim, Septa)
Lowest	Cefixime (Suprax)
	Ceftibuten (Cedax)

Drugs are listed alphabetically in each cluster.

TABLE 6-4. Comparative Activity of Antibiotics against β-Lactamase–Positive *Haemophilus influenzae* Based on Pharmacokinetic/Pharmacodynamic Principles

Highest	Cefixime (Suprax)
	Ceftibuten (Cedax)
	Ceftriaxone (Rocephin)
	Amoxicillin-clavulanate (Augmentin)
	Cefdinir (Omnicef)
	Cefpodoxime proxetil (Vantin)
	Cefprozil (Cefzil)
	Cefuroxime axetil (Ceftin)
	Azithromycin (Zithromax)
	Cefaclor (Ceclor)
	Clarithromycin (Biaxin)
	Loracarbef (Lorabid)
	Trimethoprim-sulfamethoxazole (Bactrim, Septra)
Lowest	Amoxicillin (Amoxil)
	Erythromycin

Drugs are listed alphabetically in each cluster.

References

Appelman CL, Claessen JQ, Touw-Otten FW, et al. Coamoxiclav in recurrent acute otitis media: placebo controlled study. BMJ 1991;303:1450–2.

Burke P, Bain J, Robinson D, Dunleavey J. Acute red ear in children: controlled trial of non-antibiotic treatment in general practice. BMJ 1991;303:558–62.

Dagan R, McCracken GH. Flaws in design and conduct of clinical trials in acute otitis media. Pediatr Infect Dis 2002;21:894–902.

Dowell SF, Butler JC, Giebink GS, et al. Acute otitis media: management and surveillance in an era of pneumococcal resistance—a report from the Drug-Resistant *Streptococcus pneumoniae* Therapeutic Working Group. Pediatr Infect Dis J 1999;18:1–9.

Froom J, Culpepper L, Grob P, et al. Diagnosis and antibiotic treatment of acute otitis media: report from the International Primary Care Network. BMJ 1990;300:582–6.

Halsted C, Lepow M, Balassanian N, et al. Otitis media. Clinical observations, microbiology, and evaluation of therapy. Am J Dis Child 1968;115:542–51.

Henderson FW, Gilligan PH, Wait K, et al. Nasopharyngeal carriage of antibiotic resistant pneumococci by children in group day care. J Infect Dis 1988;157:256–63.

Kaleida PH, Casselbrant ML, Rockette HE, et al. Amoxicillin or myringotomy or both for acute otitis media: results of a randomized clinical trial. Pediatrics 1991;87:466–74.

Kokko E. Chronic secretory otitis media in children. Acta Otolaryngol Suppl (Stockh) 1974;327:1–44.

Laxdal OE, Merida J, Jones RH. Treatment of acute otitis media: a controlled study of 142 children. Can Med Assoc J 1970;102:263–8.

Marchant CD, Shurin PA, Turczyk VA, et al. Course and outcome of otitis media in early infancy: a prospective study. J Pediatr 1984;104:826–31.

Marcy M, Takata G, Chan LS, et al. Management of acute otitis media. Rockville (MD): Agency for Healthcare Research and Quality, US Department of Health and Human Services; May 2001. AHRQ Publication No.: 01-E010.

Paradise JL. On classifying otitis media as suppurative or nonsuppurative, with a suggested clinical schema. J Pediatr 1987;111:948–51.

Pichichero ME. Acute otitis media: part I. Improving diagnostic accuracy. Am Fam Physician 2000a;61:2051–6.

Pichichero ME. Acute otitis media: part II. Treatment in an era of increasing antibiotic resistance. Am Fam Physician 2000b;61:2410–6.

Pichichero ME, Casey JR. Otitis, mastoiditis, and sinusitis. In: Baddour L, Gorbach S, editors. Therapy of infectious diseases. Philadelphia: WB Saunders; 2003. p. 43–85.

Pichichero ME, Cohen R. Shortened course of antibiotic therapy for acute otitis media, sinusitis and tonsillopharyngitis. Pediatr Infect Dis J 1997;16:680–5.

Pichichero ME, Marsocci SM, Murphy ML, et al. A prospective observational study of 5-, 7-, and 10-day antibiotic treatment for acute otitis media. Otolaryngol Head Neck Surg 2001;124:381–7.

Pichichero ME, Poole MD. Assessing diagnostic accuracy and tympanocentesis skills in the management of otitis media. Arch Pediatr Adolesc Med 2001;155:1137–42.

Roberts JE, Sanyal MA, Burchinal MR, et al. Otitis media in early childhood and its relationship to later verbal and academic performance. Pediatrics 1986;78:423–30.

Rosenfeld RM, Vertrees JE, Carr J, et al. Clinical efficacy of antimicrobial drugs for acute otitis media: meta-analysis of 5400 children from thirty-three randomized trials. J Pediatr 1994;124:355–67.

Stool SE, Field MJ. The impact of otitis media. Pediatr Infect Dis J 1989;8 Suppl:11–14.

Teele DW, Klein JO, Chase C, et al, the Greater Boston Otitis Media Study Group. Otitis media in infancy and intellectual ability, school achievement, speech and language at age 7 years. J Infect Dis 1990;162:685–94.

Teele DW, Klein JO, Rosner B, the Greater Boston Otitis Media Study Group. Epidemiology of otitis media during the first seven years of life in children in greater Boston: a prospective cohort study. J Infect Dis 1989;160:83–94.

Tilyard MW, Dovey SM, Walker SA. Otitis media treatment in New Zealand general practice. N Z Med J 1997;110:143–5.

Chapter 7

SHORT-COURSE ANTIBIOTICS FOR ACUTE OTITIS MEDIA

ROBERT COHEN, MD, PHILIPPE OVETCHKINE, MD, PIERRE GEHANNO, MD

The classic duration of oral antibiotic therapy was 10 days in most countries, but it is uncertain how this regimen was decided. It was probably simply extrapolated from the standard 10-day oral course treatment of penicillin for streptococcal pharyngitis (Bluestone and Klein, 1995). During the last decade, there has been an alarming worldwide increase in antibiotic resistance among the pathogens responsible for acute otitis media (AOM), particularly *Streptococcus pneumoniae*. This development is generally attributed to the extensive use of antibiotics and the selection pressure they exert on bacterial strains of nasopharyngeal flora. The increasing prevalence of multidrug-resistant *S. pneumoniae* indicates a need to reduce the use of antibiotics in respiratory tract infections, to select the most appropriate drugs, and to reduce the duration of treatment when possible.

Advantages of Shortened Treatment for AOM

There are several advantages of shorter treatment periods: the regimen is potentially less expensive, fewer side effects would be expected, compliance is better, and, finally, the impact on the commensal flora could be reduced. The advantages in terms of compliance are obvious (Cunha, 1988; Harris and Lloyd, 1994). Several studies have pointed out that compliance decreases with the daily dose frequency and the duration of treatment, and many patients tend to stop taking the medication after a few days—once symptoms have resolved. The impact of the duration of treatment on the emergence of resistant strains has recently been stressed. In a case-control study, Guillemot and colleagues (1998) showed that children treated by a treatment of long duration (> 5 days) with β-lactams was associated with an increased risk of penicillin-resistant *S. pneumoniae* carriage (odds ratio [OR]: 3.5; 95% confidence interval [CI]: 1.3–9.8; *p* = .02). Furthermore, low daily doses of an oral β-lactam induced increased risk of penicillin-resistant pneumococcal strain carriage. In a prospective randomized study in the Dominican Republic, including 791 children (ranging from 6 to 59 months) with respiratory tract illness randomly assigned to receive one of two twice-daily regimens of amoxicillin 90 mg/kg/d for 5 days or 40 mg/kg/d for 10 days, Schrag and colleagues (2001) showed that the risk of penicillin nonsusceptible pneumococcal (PNSP) carriage was significantly lower in the short-course high-dose group (24%) compared with the 10-day group (32%). The protective effect of short-course high-dose therapy was also stronger in households with three or more children (relative risk: 0.72; 95% CI: 0.52–0.98). Recently, Nasrin and colleagues (2002) suggested that the likelihood of a child carrying a PNSP is increased by 4% for each day of β-lactams used in the 6 previous months. The only potential drawback of shortened therapy is the potential loss of efficacy under certain circumstances (Paradise, 1997). The loss of chance of recovery owing to short treatment duration must be considered in light of the expectation of antibiotic treatment in AOM and with the benefits expected of shorter treatment.

Designs and Methods of Studies on Duration of Antibiotic Treatments in AOM

The first study on shorter antibiotic treatment in AOM was published by Ingvarsson and Lundgren in 1982. This comparative randomized study included 297 children aged 6 months to 7 years and compared two durations of phenoxymethylpenicillin treatment for 5 or 10 days. The dosages were not the same in the two arms: 20 or 50 mg/kg/d in two divided doses for the 5-day regimen, 25 mg/kg/d in two divided doses for the 10-day regimen. There was an insignificant difference in the outcomes of the two treatment groups. Since this first study, the efficacy of shortened treatment for AOM has been studied in many clinical trials (Pichichero and Cohen, 1997). Kozyrkij and colleagues (1998) conducted a meta-analysis of randomized, controlled trials of antibiotic treatment of

AOM in children to determine whether outcomes were comparable in children treated with antibiotics for fewer than 7 days or at least 7 days or more. The summary OR for treatment outcomes at 8 to 19 days in children treated with short-acting antibiotics (penicillin V, amoxicillin-clavulanate), cefaclor, cefixime, cefuroxime, cefpodoxime-proxetil, cefprozil) for 5 days versus 8 to 10 days was 1.52 (95% CI: 1.17–1.98), but by 20 to 30 days, outcomes between treatment groups were comparable (OR: 1.22, 95% CI: 0.98–1.54). Similar outcomes were shown with intramuscular ceftriaxone and oral azithromycin used in a short-course therapy. The authors concluded that 5 days of short-acting antibiotic use is effective treatment for uncomplicated AOM in children. However, in the conclusion of the article, the authors underlined the fact that data were not sufficient to conclude in children younger than 2 years.

In our opinion, the assessment of studies comparing two treatment durations in AOM must take into account different criteria for their interpretation and applicability to clinical practices: the study design (open, single blind, double blind, criteria of inclusion [notably tympanocentesis]), sample size (some of the trials were small and not sufficiently powered to demonstrate a difference between duration of treatment), study population, and age of patients enrolled (Paradise, 1997). The majority of the studies published have compared short courses of one antibiotic with longer courses of a second. Such a study design does not distinguish between the effect of duration of therapy versus the effect of the anti-infective drug. From our perspective, the most contributive studies are the trials using the same antibiotic with the same daily dosage in the two arms and the only variable being the duration of treatment.

Most Contributive Studies on Efficacy of Oral β-Lactams

Hendrickse and colleagues (1988) compared a 5-day regimen versus a 10-day regimen of cefaclor. Among the patients with a perforated tympanic membrane, the rate of failure was significantly higher in the 5-day regimen.

In 1996, Gooch and colleagues published the results of a large (719 children), randomized, double-blind, multicenter study comparing a short course (5 day) of cefuroxime-axetil (30 mg/kg/d) versus a longer duration of treatment (10 day) of the same drug and a 10-day regimen of amoxicillin-clavulanate (40/10 mg/kg/d). Similar results of efficacy were obtained in the three groups of children, and clinical cure occurred in 69%, 70%, and 79% of the patients, respectively. The good design of the study was compromised by the wide age range of patients included in the study: 3 months to 12 years (mean age 3.5 years).

Hoberman and colleagues (1997) studied 868 children in a comparison of amoxicillin-clavulanate (90/13 mg/kg/d) twice daily for 5 days or 10 days with amoxicillin-clavulanate (40 mg/kg/d) three times daily for 10 days. In the overall population, no significant differences in clinical outcomes were observed among the three groups; however, the twice-daily regimen for 10 days was more effective than the twice-daily regimen for 5 days in children younger than 2 years ($p = .002$).

Our group had conducted a prospective, comparative, double-blind, randomized, multicenter trial comparing amoxicillin-clavulanate in three divided doses for 10 days with an identical 5-day regimen followed by a 5-day placebo period (Cohen et al, 1998). Tympanocentesis was not performed at the enrolment. Three hundred and eighty-five children (mean age 13.3 months) were enrolled: 194 in the 5-day group and 191 in the 10-day group. In the per protocol analysis, clinical success was obtained on days 12 to 14 after the beginning of treatment in 76.7% of the children receiving the 5-day regimen and 88.1% of those receiving the 10-day regimen ($p = .006$). As the study was double-blinded and the dates of the follow-up visits were the same in the two groups, the subjects receiving the shorter treatment course had been off-therapy for longer when examined. In the short treatment groups, relapses and early recurrences were counted as failures. The curves representing patients without failure, relapse, or recurrence obtained by the Kaplan-Meier method show that most events interpreted as failures occurred not during but after treatment. Multivariate analysis showed that the 10-day course was significantly superior only among children cared for outside their homes (86.8% versus 70.8%; $p = .008$). This study showed that a 5-day regimen is not equivalent to a 10-day regimen among young children with AOM.

Our group has carried out a second study using the same type of design with cefpodoxime-proxetil: same daily dosage, 5 days versus 10 days, prospective, comparative, double-blind, randomized, multicenter. Four hundred and fifty children with a mean age of 14.3 months were included (227 in the 5-day regimen and 223 in the 10-day group). In the per protocol analysis, clinical success was obtained on days 12 to 14 after the beginning of treatment in 84.1% of the children with a shortened course of treatment and in 94.1% of those receiving the longer course of treatment ($p = .009$). The superiority of the standard treatment regimen was more marked among children cared for outside their homes, particularly those attending a day-care center (Cohen et al, 2000).

Roos and Larson (2000) carried out a single-blind, randomized, multicenter study to compare the efficacy of ceftibuten (9 mg/kg/d, once daily) in 5 versus 10 days of treatment in recurrent AOM (otitis-prone children). If 180 patients were included, only half of them were younger than 2 years of age. No statistical difference between the two treatment groups was observed on day 40: the 5-day regimen showed 35% of recurrences; the 10-day regimen showed 30%. However, the 10-day treatment was significantly better at day 14: the 5-day regimen showed 21.4% of failures or recurrences; the 10-day regimen showed 4.5% (Roos and Larson, 2000). Table 7-1 shows the relative risks of treatment failures and early recurrences for short antibiotic regimens in the previous studies.

Efficacy of Parenteral Cephalosporins

Ceftriaxone has been the most studied of a parenteral third-generation cephalosporin. A single injection of ceftriaxone has been compared with a 7- or 10-day regimen of amoxicillin, amoxicillin-clavulanate, cefaclor, and trimethoprim-sulfamethoxazole and had a similar efficacy to those of several other 10-day antibiotic regimens (Cohen et al, 1999b; Kozyrkij et al, 1998; Pichichero and Cohen, 1997). In 2000, Leibovitz and colleagues conducted an open prospective trial using the method of an "in vivo sensitivity test" comparing bacteriologic and clinical efficacy of 1-day (50 mg/kg) versus 3-day (50 mg/kg/d) intramuscular ceftriaxone. One hundred and nine patients aged from 3 to 36 months were included and 133 organisms were recovered at the onset of treatment, including 65 *S. pneumoniae*, 64 *Haemophilus influenzae*, and 4 *Moraxella catarrhalis*. Bacterial eradication of all *H. influenzae* and penicillin-susceptible *S. pneumoniae* was achieved in both treatment groups (1 and 3 days), but bacterial eradication of PNSP strains was obtained in only 52% of cases in the 1-day group compared with 97% in the 3-day group. However, a single injection of ceftriaxone is approved by the US Food and Drug Administration (FDA) and some European agencies.

Efficacy of Azithromycin

Probably because of its pharmacokinetic properties, azithromycin is one of the most studied drugs in 1-, 3-, or 5-day duration, at different dosages ranging from 10 to 30 mg/kg/d. These studies have included a large number of patients and have been well designed; however, most of those studies have included children older than 2 years of age. For any of the regimens assessed, no significant differences in clinical outcome have been observed in comparison with 10-day treatment with amoxicillin-clavulanate or 5-day treatment with clarithromycin (Dunne et al, 2001). Recently, the FDA approved azithromycin as a single-dose or 3-day treatment regimen for AOM. These regimens will deliver the same dose as the 5-day course but in less time. However, all of these studies used either no tympanocentesis or one tympanocentesis at the enrolment and clinical end point for assessment. In fact, the main problems of azithromycin in AOM are the high level of macrolide-resistant pneumococci in some countries and the poor activity against *H. influenzae* in terms of bacterial eradication of middle ear fluid (Dagan et al, 2000a; Dagan et al, 2000b).

TABLE 7-1. Relative Risk of Treatment Failures and Early Recurrences for Short Antibiotic Regimens

Study (Year)	Relative Risk	95% Confidence Interval
Hendrickse et al (1988)	1.08	0.16–7.46
Gooch et al (1996)	1.04	0.79–1.37
Hoberman et al (1997)	1.36	0.96–1.931
Cohen et al (1998)	1.93	1.12–3.05
Cohen et al (2000)	2.08	1.20–3.59

Short-Course Antibiotic Treatment

Short-course therapy may be not appropriate for young children, particularly those attending day-care centers. Some facts have to be discussed before raising the hypothesis of the lowest efficacy of short regimens in this setting:

- In the studies using the in vivo sensitivity test, bacterial eradication of middle ear fluid was achieved for most patients in less than 5 days if the strains were susceptible to the antibiotic received (Dagan and Leibovitz, 2002). However, because most patients received antibiotic treatment at the time of the second tympanocentesis, it is possible that for some patients, the bacteria will be suppressed but not totally eradicated.
- Several studies have shown that bacterial eradication of nasopharyngeal flora is more difficult to accomplish, particularly for *H. influenzae* and PNSP (Cohen et al, 1997; Varon et al, 2000).
- Most events considered as "failures" have occurred not during the antibiotic treatment but a few days after the end of the antibiotic course (Cohen et al, 1998; Cohen et al, 2000; Roos and Larson, 2000).

Among the hypotheses raised to explain the fewer efficacies in younger children, at least four have to be considered.

- Several viral pathogens of the respiratory tract (respiratory syncytial virus, parainfluenza, adenovirus, etc) are more frequent in children attending day-care centers and could explain some relapses/recurrences and clinical failures (Chonmaitree and Heikkinen, 2000).
- Pichichero (2000) suggested recently that it may be an artifact of the greater tendency of very young children than older children to experience recurrent AOM, which is associated with a high failure rate of therapy regardless of the duration of therapy.
- The role of a high level of resistant strains in young children attending day-care centers (Cohen et al, 1999a; Cohen et al, 1999b).
- The occurrence of bacterial AOM is the consequence of a cascade of events (notably viral infection, colonization of the rhinopharynx with new bacterial strains, eustachian tube dysfunction) leading to infection of the middle ear. The eradication of bacteria from middle ear fluid by antibiotic treatment is not

frequently accompanied by the eradication from the nasopharyngeal flora. The persistence of eustachian tube dysfunction for several days and the absence of eradication of potential bacterial pathogens from nasopharyngeal flora could lead to a reinfection or a superinfection. Children attending day-care centers were more likely to be colonized by *S. pneumoniae*, *H. influenzae*, and/or *M. catarrhalis* than were children cared for at home and may thus be at an increased risk of reinfection (Cohen et al, 1999a). Indeed, a strong relationship has been established between the frequency of colonization and otitis media owing to each pathogen. Recently, Dagan and colleagues (2001) demonstrated that antibiotic treatment in AOM promotes superinfection with *S. pneumoniae* carried before the onset of treatment. These mechanisms may explain that in recently treated patients, AOM becomes refractory to treatment, particularly in young children. This hypothesis is supported by an observational prospective study recently conducted by Pichichero and colleagues (2001). The authors compared 5-, 7-, and 10-day duration of antibiotic therapy for AOM in children. A total of 2,172 children were studied. No overall difference in outcome was observed comparing the three groups. However, in the subset that had an episode of AOM in the preceding month, outcome differed; the 5-day duration of treatment was followed by more frequent failure than 10-day treatment ($p < .001$). In logistic regression analysis, variables identified as contributing to a cure were age > 2 years and no AOM in the preceding month.

These aspects may explain that treating ear infections in children younger than 2 years, particularly those attending a day-care center, is more difficult than in other age groups.

Conclusion

Shorter courses of treatment are probably adequate for many patients with AOM, but some subjects may warrant longer treatment. Shorter antibiotic treatment should be used for children after 2 years of age if antibiotics are indicated. For children under 2 years, attending a day-care center, or with a ruptured tympanic membrane, the standard treatment duration is clearly more effective than short treatment. For other young patients, a short regimen was not as successful as the standard regimen. However, the difference in terms of efficacy is small and not significant for children cared for at home, and the benefits expected of shorter treatment may outweigh the risk of a higher rate of failure. Short treatment should also be used with caution in children over 2 years who have been recent antibiotic failures or with a history of several episodes of recurrent AOM.

References

Bluestone CD, Klein JO. Otitis media in infants and children. 2nd ed. Philadelphia: WB Saunders; 1995.

Chonmaitree T, Heikkinen T. Viruses and acute otitis media. Pediatr Infect Dis J 2000;19:1005–7.

Cohen R, Bingen E, Varon E, et al. Change in nasopharyngeal carriage of *Streptococcus pneumoniae* resulting from antibiotic therapy for acute otitis media in children. Pediatr Infect Dis J 1997;16:555–60.

Cohen R, Levy C, Boucherat M, et al. A multicenter, randomized, double blind trial of 5 vs 10 days of antibiotic therapy for acute otitis media in young children. J Pediatr 1998;133:634–9.

Cohen R, Levy C, Boucherat M, et al. Characteristics and outcome of children with acute otitis media attending day care. Presented at the 39th Interscience Conference on Antimicrobial Agents and Chemotherapy; 1999a Sep 26–29; San Francisco.

Cohen R, Levy C, Boucherat M, et al. Five vs ten days of antibiotic therapy for acute otitis media in young children. Pediatr Infect Dis J 2000;19:458–63.

Cohen R, Navel M, Grunberg J, et al. One dose ceftriaxone vs ten days of amoxicillin/clavulanate therapy for acute otitis media: clinical efficacy and change in nasopharyngeal flora. Pediatr Infect Dis J 1999b;18:403–9.

Cunha BA. The importance of compliance with oral antibiotic regimen. Adv Ther 1988;5:297–305.

Dagan R, Johnson C, McLinn S, et al. Bacteriologic and clinical efficacy of amoxicillin/clavulanate versus azithromycin in acute otitis media. Pediatr Infect Dis J 2000a;19:95–104.

Dagan R, Leibovitz E. Bacterial eradication in the treatment of otitis media. Lancet Infect Dis 2002;2:593–605.

Dagan R, Leibovitz E, Cheletz G, et al. Antibiotic treatment in acute otitis media promotes superinfection with resistant *Streptococcus pneumoniae* carried before initiation of treatment. J Infect Dis 2001;183:880–6.

Dagan R, Leibovitz E, Fliss D, et al. Bacteriologic efficacies of oral azithromycin and oral cefaclor in treatment of acute otitis media in infants and young children. Antimicrob Agents Chemother 2000b; 44:43–50.

Dunne MW, Latiolais T, Lewis B, et al. A randomized, double blind study of three days of azithromycin compared with amoxicillin/clavulanate for the treatment of acute otitis media. Presented at the 41st Interscience Conference on Antimicrobial Agents and Chemotherapy; 2001 Dec 16–19; Chicago.

Gooch WM, Blair E, Puopolo A, et al. Effectiveness of 5 days of therapy with cefuroxime axetil suspension for the treatment of acute otitis media. Pediatr Infect Dis J 1996;15:157–64.

Guillemot D, Carbon C, Balkau B, et al. Low dosage and long treatment duration of beta-lactam: risk factors for carriage of penicillin-resistant *Streptococcus pneumoniae*. JAMA 1998;279:394–5.

Harris CM, Lloyd DCEF. Consider short courses of antibiotics. BMJ 1994;308:919.

Hendrickse W, Kusmiesz H, Shelton S, et al. Five vs ten days of therapy for acute otitis media. Pediatr Infect Dis J 1988;7:14–23.

Hoberman A, Paradise J, Burch D, et al. Equivalent efficacy and reduced occurrence of diarrhea from a new formulation of amoxicillin/clavulanate potassium (Augmentin®) for treatment of acute otitis media in children. Pediatr Infect Dis J 1997;16: 463–70.

Ingvarsson L, Lundgren K. Penicillin treatment of acute otitis media in children. Acta Otolaryngol (Stockh) 1982;94:283–7.

Kozyrkij A, Hildes-Ripstein E, Longstaffe S, et al. Treatment of acute otitis media with shortened course of antibiotics: a meta-analysis. JAMA 1998;279:1738–42.

Leibovitz E, Piglansky L, Raiz L, et al. Bacteriological and clinical efficacy of one day vs three days intramuscular ceftriaxone for treatment of non responsive acute otitis media in children. Pediatr Infect Dis J 2000;19:1040–4.

Nasrin D, Collignon P, Roberts L, et al. Effect of beta-lactam antibiotic use in children on pneumococcal resistance to penicillin: prospective cohort study. BMJ 2002;324:28–33.

Paradise JL. Short course antimicrobial treatment for acute otitis media. Not best for infants and young children. JAMA 1997;278:1640–2.

Pichichero M. Short course antibiotic therapy for respiratory infections: a review of the evidence. Pediatr Infect Dis J 2000;19: 929–37.

Pichichero ME, Cohen R. Shortened course of antibiotic therapy for acute otitis media, sinusitis and tonsillopharyngitis. Pediatr Infect Dis J 1997;16:680–95.

Pichichero ME, Marsocci SM, Murphy ML, et al. A prospective observational study of 5-, 7-, and 10-day antibiotic treatment for acute otitis media. Otolaryngol Head Neck Surg 2001;124: 381–7.

Roos K, Larson P. Efficacy of ceftibuten in 5 versus 10 days treatment of recurrent acute otitis media in children. Int J Pediatr Otorhinolaryngol 2000;55:109–15.

Schrag SJ, Phil D, Pena C, et al. Effect of short course, high dose amoxicillin therapy on resistant pneumococcal carriage. JAMA 2001;286:49–56.

Varon E, Levy C, De La Rocque F, et al. Impact of antimicrobial therapy on nasopharyngeal carriage of *Streptococcus pneumoniae*, *Haemophilus influenzae* and *Branhamella catarrhalis* in children with respiratory tract infection. Clin Infect Dis 2000; 31:477–81.

Chapter 8

Management of Acute Otitis Media without Antibiotics

Anne G. M. Schilder, MD, PhD

The alarming rise in antimicrobial resistance has sparked worldwide interest in reducing antibiotic prescription for acute otitis media (AOM). The question is whether limiting the use of antibiotics for AOM is feasible and safe. A closer look at the Dutch policy regarding the management of AOM may answer this question.

In the Netherlands, a restrictive use of antibiotics for AOM has been practiced since the early 1990s. Based on the results of randomized trials showing that most AOM episodes resolve without antibiotics (Appelman et al, 1991; Del Mar et al, 1997; Rosenfeld et al, 1994; Van Buchem et al, 1981), guidelines on AOM developed by the Dutch College of General Practitioners (Appelman et al, 1990) advise doctors to manage AOM in children with initial observation and to limit the prescription of antibiotics to children with either a protracted course of AOM or an increased risk of complications. Consequently, only 31% of Dutch patients with AOM receive antibiotics, compared with more than 90% in most other countries (Froom et al, 1990). This chapter discusses the background of the Dutch policy regarding AOM, the general practitioner's guidelines in general, the AOM guidelines and their implementation, and the potential consequences of this policy regarding complications such as acute mastoiditis.

Background

Until the 1950s, acute mastoiditis was a common complication of AOM (Rudberg, 1954). In those preantibiotic years, the best available option to prevent complications of AOM in children was to drain the middle ear by myringotomy. This strategy for AOM was generally accepted in the Netherlands, and all children presenting with AOM to their general practitioner were referred to the local otolaryngologist for a myringotomy. Thus, in general, at the time, during a weekend on call, Dutch otolaryngologists performed between 5 and 20 myringo-

tomies on children. Few children received additional antibiotics. In the 1960s and 1970s, the work of Roddey and colleagues (1966) and Lorentzen and Haugsten (1977) suggested that myringotomy was not so effective in AOM. So in 1979, the Dutch otolaryngologist Louk van Buchem started his study on the efficacy of myringotomy and antibiotics in Dutch children with AOM (van Buchem et al, 1981). One hundred seventy-one children aged 2 to 12 years presenting with AOM in 12 general practices were randomized to receive (1) both myringotomy and antibiotics, (2) myringotomy only, (3) antibiotic only, or (4) neither therapy. All children received analgesics and decongestant nosedrops. Children were followed up by their general practitioner at days 2, 7, and 14. The study demonstrated that the clinical course did not differ significantly across the four groups. It was concluded that symptomatic therapy with analgesics and decongestant nosedrops is a good initial approach to AOM in children aged 2 years or older, and myringotomy and antibiotics can be reserved for refractory cases of AOM (symptomatic after 3 to 4 days or persistent otorrhea after 14 days). A follow-up study (van Buchem et al, 1985) evaluating the effects of this conservative approach in nearly 5,000 children with AOM showed that more than 90% had recovered within a few days. Two children developed mastoiditis: one showed signs of mastoiditis at first presentation to the general practitioner and one developed mastoiditis 7 days after myringotomy for AOM and 5 days after starting antibiotics because of an unsatisfactory clinical recovery at day 2.

These two studies have raised intense discussion, both nationally and internationally, among general practitioners, pediatricians, and otolaryngologists about the best treatment for uncomplicated AOM. In the Netherlands, this has resulted ultimately in the guidelines on AOM as published by the Dutch College of General Practitioners in 1990 (Table 8-1) (Appelman et al, 1990).

TABLE 8-1. Summary of the 1990 Guidelines on Acute Otitis Media of the Dutch College of General Practitioners

Age	Diagnosis	Management	Indication for Antibiotics	Antibiotic of First Choice
6 mo and younger	History, otoscopy	Analgesia, decongestive nosedrops, antibiotics, and re-evaluation after 24 h	Always	Amoxicillin for 7 d
6 mo–2 yr	History, otoscopy	Symptomatic (analgesia, decongestive nosedrops) and re-evaluation after 24 h	High-risk groups*; no improvement after 24 h; otorrhea for more than 14 d	Amoxicillin for 7 d
2 yr and older	History, otoscopy	Symptomatic	High-risk groups*; irregular course: earache or fever for more than 3 d; otorrhea for more than 14 d	Amoxicillin for 7 d

*High-risk groups: recurrent otitis media, Down syndrome, craniofacial malformations, immunodeficiencies.

Guidelines of the Dutch College of General Practitioners

In the Netherlands, general practitioners are considered the gatekeepers of the health care system. Every family is registered at a local general practice, which is easily accessible during office hours. During odd hours, primary care is usually offered at so-called primary care posts. Patients are seen at these posts or are visited at home. The expenses of primary care are covered by national or private insurance. In this system, conditions such as AOM are primarily managed by general practitioners, and arrangements for follow-up are made directly between the doctor and the patient or his or her caregivers.

Since 1989, the Dutch College of General Practitioners has developed 72 practice guidelines on as many subjects. It is estimated that more than 60% of the problems seen in an average practice are covered by a guideline. Guidelines are developed by general practitioners and staff based on the best available evidence. Draft guidelines are sent for comments to randomly chosen general practitioners, medical specialists in the particular field, and the Scientific Institute of Dutch Pharmacists (WINAp). After approval of the final concept by the authorization board, composed of professors of primary care, practicing general practitioners, and a representative from the National Society of General Practitioners, a guideline is published along with its scientific background in the monthly journal of the Dutch College of General Practitioners (*Huisarts en Wetenschap*). Usually, a summary of a guideline is published in the *Dutch Medical Journal* (*Nederlands Tijdschrift voor Geneeskunde*) along with a comment from a medical specialist and a reply from a gener-

al practitioner. These comments can be very critical as general practitioners and medical specialists do not always reach consensus about the guidelines. The guidelines are continually updated and revised if necessary.

The guidelines are available in Dutch on the Dutch College of General Practitioners Web site (<www.artsennet.nl/nhg>). All guidelines are presently being translated into English (Appleman, 1999b). For patients, adapted versions of guidelines on common conditions are issued by the Dutch College of General Practitioners and are made available at general practices and pharmacies.

The guidelines are not legally binding for physicians as they should have the freedom to evaluate each patient and each visit individually. Still, the guidelines are consulted in case of legal actions against a physician.

Current Guidelines on AOM of the Dutch College of General Practitioners

The Dutch guidelines on AOM were revised in 1999 (Appelman et al, 1999b). Table 8-2 summarizes these current guidelines.

The definition of AOM used in the Dutch guidelines is pragmatic: infection of the middle ear of acute onset and a characteristic appearance of the tympanic membrane. AOM is diagnosed when otoscopy demonstrates a red or bulging tympanic membrane *or* an obvious difference in redness of the left and right tympanic membrane *or* otorrhea in the presence of a tympanic membrane perforation *and* one or more signs of an acute infection: rapid onset of fever, otalgia, irritability, general illness. This definition of AOM differs from that used in the Agency of Healthcare Research and Quality evidence

TABLE 8-2. Summary of the 1999 Guidelines on Acute Otitis Media of the Dutch College of General Practitioners

Age	Diagnosis	Management	Indication for Antibiotics	Antibiotic of First Choice
6 mo and younger	History, otoscopy	Analgesia, decongestive nosedrops, antibiotics	Always	Amoxicillin for 7 d
Older than 6 mo	History, otoscopy	Symptomatic (analgesia, decongestive nosedrops)	High-risk groups*; irregular course: progressive general illness or earache, poor fluid intake, no improvement of symptoms after 3 d; otorrhea for more than 14 d	Amoxicillin for 7 d

*High-risk groups: recurrent episode of AOM within 12 months in children younger than 2 years, Down syndrome, craniofacial malformations, immunodeficiencies.

report (Marcy et al, 2000), in which the presence of middle ear fluid, as demonstrated by pneumatic otoscopy, tympanometry, or acoustic reflectometry, is a prerequisite. In the Netherlands, pneumatic otoscopy is not practiced routinely by general practitioners and tympanometry is not widely available in general practice. Using the current Dutch definition, however, agreement between general practitioners and otolaryngologists in diagnosing AOM has been shown to be good (Appelman et al, 1993; van Buchem et al, 1981).

Often the Dutch policy of managing AOM without antibiotics has been confused with withholding therapy from children with AOM. Children with AOM do receive medical care. The guidelines advise a watchful waiting policy during which adequate analgesics and symptomatic relief are given. Clear arrangements about follow-up are made with the parents. Deferring antibiotics for up to 3 days in most children has resulted in a prescription rate of antibiotics for AOM of 31% in the Netherlands as opposed to more than 90% in most other countries (Froom et al, 1990).

Against the restrictive use of antibiotics for AOM and other upper respiratory tract infections, Dutch doctors seem to be more liberal in their indications for surgical therapy for upper respiratory tract infections. The surgical rate of ventilation tubes, adenoidectomy, and tonsillectomy in children in the Netherlands is higher than in other countries of the European Union and the United States (unpublished data).

The most important change in the revised 1999 guidelines compared with the first version from 1990 has been the advice to manage AOM in children aged 6 months to 2 years in the same way as children aged 2 years or older. This advice has been based also on the study of Damoiseaux and colleagues (2000) showing that antibiotics had only a modest effect in AOM in children aged 6 months to 2 years. In this study, however, the percentage of children with persistent symptoms at day 4 was very high: 59% and 72% for the antibiotic group and placebo group, respectively. Studies of antibiotics for AOM in children aged 2 years or older have shown much lower failure rates at days 3 to 4, that is, fewer than 10% (Appelman et al, 1991; Del Mar et al, 1997; Rosenfeld et al, 1994; van Buchem et al, 1981). This confirms that these younger, immunologically immature children are at higher risk for a protracted course of and complications from AOM and therefore need closer surveillance than older children. Close monitoring of the complication rate of AOM in the Netherlands in the years to come is vital to establish whether the decision to change the guidelines in this manner has been a wise one.

Complications

The question of whether reducing antibiotic prescription for AOM is safe may be answered by comparing the inci-

dence rates of acute mastoiditis in countries with various antibiotic prescription rates for AOM.

Figure 8-1 shows incidence rates of acute mastoiditis in children aged 14 years and younger in the period 1991 to 1998 in the Netherlands, several other countries of the European Union, Canada, Australia, and the United States in relation to antibiotic prescription rates for AOM in these countries (van Zuÿlen et al, 2001). The incidence rates of acute mastoiditis in children in the United Kingdom, Canada, Australia, and the United States, where antibiotic prescription rates for AOM are all greater than 96% (Froom et al, 1990), ranged from 1.2 (95% confidence interval [CI]: 0.9–1.5) to 2.0 (95% CI: 1.8–2.2) per 100,000 person-years. The incidence rates in Norway and Denmark, where antibiotic prescription rates for AOM are 67% and 76% (van Zuÿlen et al, 2001), respectively, and in the Netherlands, where antibiotic prescription is 31% (Froom et al, 1990), were considerably higher: 3.5 (95% CI: 2.9–4.0), 4.2 (95% CI: 3.6–4.8), and 3.8 (95% CI: 3.5–4.1) per 100,000 person-years, respectively.

With the practice of myringotomy for AOM abandoned in the Netherlands in the early 1990s, it is relevant to establish whether this has had consequences for the incidence of acute mastoiditis. The incidence rates of acute mastoiditis in the Netherlands in the period 1980 to 1997 are shown in Figure 8-2.

A linear regression analysis, with incidence rate as the dependent variable and year as the independent variable, indicates that the incidence rate of acute mastoiditis in the Netherlands shows a slight but statistically significant upward trend (0.067 per 100,000 children per year; $p = .005$) over the period 1980 to 1997. The average incidence rate increased from 3 per 100,000 children in the period 1980 to 1985, to 3.7 per 100,000 children in the period 1986 to 1991, to 3.9 per 100,000 children in the period 1992 to 1997 ($p < .05$ for the period 1980–1985 versus 1986–1991 and 1992–1997). This amounts to a total of

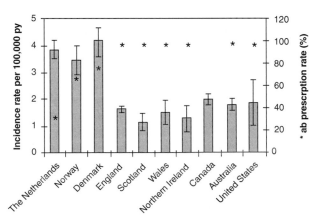

FIGURE 8-1. Comparison of the 1991–1998 incidence rates of acute mastoiditis in children age 14 years and younger (bars = 95% CI) across several countries with different antibiotic prescription rates for acute otitis media.

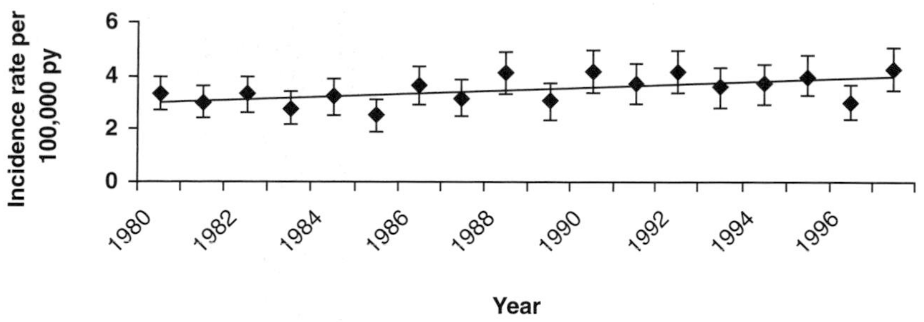

FIGURE 8-2. Dutch 1980–1997 incidence rates of acute mastoiditis in children aged 14 years and younger (bars = 95% CI).

approximately 35 patients over a period of 18 years. Unfortunately, no data on prescription rates of antibiotics for AOM in the Netherlands over the same period were available.

Both Figures 8-1 and 8-2 suggest that a watchful waiting policy for AOM is associated with one to two extra cases of acute mastoiditis per 100,000 children per year. A causal relationship between a restrictive use of antibiotics and a higher incidence of complications, however, is not fully supported by these data. For example, the incidence rate in Norway and Denmark was comparable with the rate in the Netherlands, and antibiotic prescription rates for AOM in Scandinavia are twice as high (van Zuyen et al, 2001). Also, the 1997 incidence rate in New York City and adjacent Westchester and Nassau Counties, a region with a total population of 7.6 million (twice the population of Norway) where antibiotics are prescribed to almost all children with AOM, was comparable with those of the Netherlands, Norway, and Denmark at 4 per 100,000 children (data provided by the Montefiore Medical Center Planning Department, New York City). Finally, in Norway and Germany, the incidence of acute mastoiditis has reportedly been on the rise in recent years (Fayc-Lund, 1989; Hoppe et al, 1994), even with continued high levels of antibiotic prescription. This apparent increase is based on absolute hospital figures and not on national incidence rates, making it difficult to substantiate, but it suggests that there may be other explanations for a difference in complication rates of AOM besides antibiotic prescription, such as increased virulence of pathogens.

Assuming that the higher incidence rate of acute mastoiditis in the Netherlands observed in our study is real and that it is caused by restricted use of antibiotics for AOM, the question arises as to whether two additional cases of acute mastoiditis per 100,000 children per year compared with other countries warrants abandoning of the watchful waiting strategy in AOM. The advantages of the Dutch policy of initial observation and limited use of antibiotics for AOM are obvious: fewer antibiotic prescriptions and therefore cost reduction, fewer side effects from antibiotics, and a lower antimicrobial resistance rate. The incidence rate of AOM in Dutch children younger than 15 years of age is 120 per 1,000 children per year (Bruijnzeels et al, 1993). Given the antibiotic prescription rate of 31% in the Netherlands as opposed to 96% elsewhere (Froom et al, 1990), 7,800 fewer prescriptions for AOM per 100,000 children per year are issued. As many as 20% of children receiving antibiotic therapy for OM develop diarrhea, vomiting, or skin rash, and 1 to 5% experience allergic reactions, including anaphylaxis (Ruben, 1999). This adds up to an estimated 1,600 fewer side effects from antibiotic therapy in 100,000 children with AOM annually. Furthermore, the number of antibiotic prescriptions for AOM that would be needed to prevent one episode of acute mastoiditis is extremely high: at least 2,500, in view of the low estimated incidence of acute mastoiditis in AOM of 0.4 per 1,000 AOM episodes (van Buchem et al, 1985). Moreover, not all cases of acute mastoiditis can be prevented by antibiotics. Retrospective studies (Gliklich et al, 1996; Goldstein et al, 1998; Harley et al, 1997) have shown that 36 to 87% of patients have received antibiotics for AOM prior to developing acute mastoiditis. Taking 50 as the percentage of cases of acute mastoiditis prevented by antibiotic treatment of AOM, the number needed to treat could be as high as 5,000. The 1998 percentage of penicillin-resistant *Streptococcus pneumoniae* in the Netherlands was 3.2% (Schito et al, 2000), far less than the percentage in the United States that ranged from 28 to 44% (Thornsberry et al, 1999). Although resistance to antibiotics is also affected by other factors such as day-care attendance, which is low in the Netherlands, it is universally accepted that the restriction of antibiotic prescriptions is a key element in the control of emerging antibiotic resistance and associated morbidity and mortality.

Conclusions

The alarming rise in antimicrobial resistance has prompted physicians to limit antibiotic prescription for upper respiratory tract infections and to take another look at the Dutch "observation option" for AOM. This chapter shows that prescription of antibiotics for AOM in children can be reduced safely provided that children are carefully monitored. This requires close cooperation between caregivers and their physicians. The large proportion of children younger than 2 years of age showing a protracted course of AOM indicates that these children will continue to need extra attention.

References

Appelman CLM, Bossen PC, Dunk JHM, et al. NHG-standaard otitis media acuta. Huisarts Wet 1990;33:242–5.

Appelman CLM, Claessen JQPJ, Touw-Otten FWMM, et al. Co-amoxiclav in recurrent acute otitis media: placebo controlled study. BMJ 1991;303:1450–2.

Appelman CLM, Claessen JQPJ, Touw-Otten FWMM, et al. Severity of inflammation of tympanic membrane as predictor of clinical course of recurrent acute otitis media. BMJ 1993;306:895.

Appelman CLM, van Balen FAM, van de Lisdonk EH, et al. NHG-standaard otitis media acuta (eerste herziening). Huisarts Wet 1999a;42:362–6.

Appleman CLM, van Balen FA, van de Lisdonk EA, et al. The Dutch College of General Practitioners practice guideline 'acute otitis media' E09 1999b. Available at: http://www.artsennet.nl/nhg/guidelines/E09.htm (accessed June 16, 2003).

Bruijnzeels MA, Van Suijlekom-Smit LWA, van der Velden J, van der Wouden, editors. The child in general practice [English summary]. Rotterdam: Universiteitsdrukkerij Erasmus Universiteit; 1993.

Damoiseaux RAMJ, van Balen FAM, Hoes AW, et al. Primary care based randomized, double blind trial of amoxicillin versus placebo for acute otitis media in children aged under 2 years. BMJ 2000;320:350–4.

Del Mar C, Glasziou P, Hayem M. Are antibiotics indicated as initial treatment for children with acute otitis media? A meta-analysis. BMJ 1997;314:1526–9.

Faye-Lund H. Acute and latent mastoiditis. J Laryngol Otol 1989;103:1158–60.

Froom J, Culpepper L, Grob P, et al. Diagnosis and antibiotic treatment of acute otitis media: report from International Primary Care Network. BMJ 1990;300:582–6.

Gliklich RE, Eavey RD, Iannuzzi RA, Camacho RAE. Contemporary analysis of acute mastoiditis. Arch Otolaryngol Head Neck Surg 1996;122:135–9.

Goldstein NA, Casselbrant ML, Bluestone CD, Kurs-Lasky M. Intratemporal complications of acute otitis media in infants and children. Otolaryngol Head Neck Surg 1998;119:444–54.

Harley EH, Sdralis TH, Berkowitz RG. Acute mastoiditis in children: a 12-year retrospective study. Otolaryngol Head Neck Surg 1997;116:26–30.

Hoppe JE, Köster S, Bootz F, Niethammer D. Acute mastoiditis. Relevant once again. Infection 1994;22:178–82.

Lorentzen P, Haugsten P. Treatment of acute suppurative otitis media. J Laryngol Otol 1977;91:331–40.

Marcy M, Takata G, Chan LS, et al. Management of acute otitis media. Summary, evidence report/technology assessment. Rockville (MD): Agency of Healthcare Research and Quality, US Department of Health and Human Services; 2000. AHRQ Publication No.: 01-E010.

Roddey OF, Earle R, Haggerty R. Myringotomy in acute otitis media: a controlled study. JAMA 1966;197:849–53.

Rosenfeld RM, Vertrees JE, Carr J, et al. Clinical efficacy of antimicrobial drugs for acute otitis media: meta-analysis of 5400 children from thirty-three randomized trials. J Pediatr 1994;124:355–67.

Ruben RJ. Sequelae of antibiotic therapy. In: Rosenfeld RM, Bluestone CD, editors. Evidence-based otitis media. Hamilton (ON): BC Decker; 1999. p. 303–14.

Rudberg RD. Acute otitis media: comparative therapeutic results of sulphonamide and penicillin administered in various forms. Acta Otolaryngol (Stockh) 1954;113:S1–79.

Schilder AGM, Rovers MM. International perspective on management. In: Rarenfeld RM, Bluestone CD, editors. Evidence-based otitis media. 2nd ed. Hamilton (ON): BC Decker; 2003. p. 325–32.

Schito GC, Debbia EA, Marchese A. The evolving threat of antibiotic resistance in Europe: new data from the Alexander Project. J Antimicrob Chemother 2000;46 Suppl T1:3–9.

Thornsberry C, Jones ME, Hickey ML, et al. Resistance surveillance of *Streptococcus pneumoniae*, *Haemophilus influenzae* and *Moraxella catarrhalis* isolated in the United States, 1997–1998. J Antimicrob Chemother 1999;44:749–59.

van Buchem FL, Dunk JHM, van 't Hof MA. Therapy of acute otitis media: myringotomy, antibiotics, or neither? A double-blind study in children. Lancet 1981;ii:883–7.

van Buchem FL, Peeters MF, van 't Hof MA. Acute otitis media: a new treatment strategy. BMJ 1985;290:1033–7.

van Zuÿen DA, Schilder AGM, van Balen FAM, Hoes AW. National differences in incidence of acute mastoiditis: relationship to prescribing patterns of antibiotics for acute otitis media? Pediatr Infect Dis J 2001;20:140–4.

Chapter 9

MYRINGITIS BULLOSA

L. NICOLE MURRAY, MD

Myringitis bullosa (MB), or bullous myringitis, was first described by Lowenberg during the influenza epidemic of 1889 (Lowenberg, 1891) and is characterized by the presence of vesicles on the tympanic membrane (TM), with or without other abnormalities of the eardrum and middle ear. It is an acutely painful condition that may be associated with hearing loss and generally is self-limited and not recurrent. Much has been written about the etiology of the disorder, and there has been some disagreement as to whether this is a disease entity unto itself or whether this is simply otitis media with vesicles. This chapter reviews pertinent publications and discusses the diagnosis, etiology, natural history, and management of MB.

Incidence

The actual incidence of this disorder in the general population is not known, but several studies have suggested that it occurs during the winter in children and young adults and that it is much less frequent than acute otitis media (AOM). In the largest and most recent prospective study, 82 of 2,028 children under the age of 2 years followed in the Finnish Otitis Media Vaccine Trial had MB, which suggests an incidence of around 2% in this population (Palmu et al, 2001). Other studies suggest that when compared with AOM, MB may be more common in older patients. One study, which included all children up to 17 years of age seen for ear infections, showed the mean age of MB patients to be 65 months, as opposed to 26 months for AOM patients. They showed the incidence of MB to be about 1% of that of otitis media seen in their population (Hahn et al, 1998).

Diagnosis

The disorder is diagnosed by the presence of one or more vesicles on the TM and/or canal wall skin filled with a small amount of clear to sanguineous fluid. If patients present during the vesicular stage, they will generally describe a severe stabbing or throbbing pain that seems out of proportion to their physical findings. Generally, vesicles will rupture after 4 to 12 hours and pain will subside. Scanty serosanguineous otorrhea may occur on rupture of the bullae (Karelitz, 1937). The disease is most commonly unilateral and not recurrent, although cases to the contrary have been reported. Most patients will have a middle ear effusion either at the time of diagnosis or shortly thereafter (Palmu et al, 2001). Up to 67% may have a sensorineural or mixed hearing loss, and this is further discussed later in the chapter (Hoffman and Shepsman, 1983). An audiogram is recommended to establish the presence, type, and severity of hearing loss in these patients.

MB must be distinguished from another similar disorder: granular myringitis. Granular myringitis is a variant of otitis externa and involves ulcerations of the epithelial layer of the TM with granulation tissue formation. No vesicles are present. This disorder occurs most commonly in adults and is usually unilateral. Symptoms include otorrhea, itching and stuffiness of the ear, and mild hearing loss. On examination, the eardrum and canal skin will have patchy or diffuse areas of granulation tissue, which may be crusted with otorrhea. The TM must be intact to make this diagnosis, and the middle ear is generally without fluid (Stoney et al, 1992). Granular myringitis usually responds to topical culture-directed antibiotics with steroids or oral antibiotics, but, occasionally, cauterization or tympanoplasty may be necessary (El-Seifi and Fouad, 2000).

There are no histologic data regarding the localization of bullae formation in MB as this would require full-thickness biopsy of the TM, but they are presumed to occur between the superficial epithelial layer and the middle fibrous layer. This is indirectly supported by anecdotal observations that bullae do not form in areas of tympanosclerosis but form on adjacent, nonsclerotic portions of the eardrum (Woo et al, 1992). The epithelial layer is richly supplied with pain fibers, which likely explains the severe pain that these patients report.

Etiology

There has been much controversy in the literature as to the etiology of MB, and this has been methodically and eloquently reviewed by Roberts (1980). This disorder was initially described in association with outbreaks of influenza and was thought to be attributable to the influenza virus. Several studies have reported viral cultures of middle ear fluid in these patients, and of 13 cases, only one virus has been isolated. This was an adenovirus (Roberts, 1980). Attempts have also been made to serologically document a viral cause for MB, but these studies have failed to demonstrate a rise in titers to multiple common viruses (Merifield and Miller, 1966).

The possible etiologic role of *Mycoplasma pneumoniae* was suggested when 11 of 27 healthy volunteers inoculated with the Eaton agent (the original name for the *M. pneumoniae* organism) unexpectedly developed myringitis (Rifkind et al, 1962). This study is often quoted as showing that *M. pneumoniae* is the etiologic agent of MB, but the study, in fact, did not show this. Only two of these patients had true MB with the formation of vesicles on the eardrum; the fluid from one bleb was cultured for *Mycoplasma* and was negative. Sixteen subsequent studies have reported the results of ear cultures for *M. pneumoniae* in MB, and only one ear yielded this organism. Whether other bacteria were also present in this ear was not reported. It seems most likely, as pointed out by Roberts (1980), that the *M. pneumoniae* upper respiratory infection created an inflammatory reaction that involved the ears but that this organism was not infecting the ears itself.

In contrast to the above-listed unsuccessful attempts to grow *Mycoplasma* or viruses from the ears of MB patients, a number of studies have shown great success in growing bacteria from these ears. Prior to 1980, there were reports of 66 aspirations from MB ears, of which 43 grew bacteria. The majority of organisms were *Streptococcus pneumoniae* (32%), *Haemophilus influenzae* (14%), or β-hemolytic streptococci (15%). These results are similar to those found in studies of standard AOM ears (Rifkind et al, 1962). The Finnish Otitis Media Vaccine Trial includes the largest and most recently described group of patients with MB, and 83 of 92 ears with MB were found to have a middle ear effusion. Cultures of the middle ear fluid were obtained in 74 and grew *S. pneumoniae* (32%), *H. influenzae* (29%), *Moraxella catarrhalis* (12.2%), or no bacteria (25.7%). Again, these results are similar to those from ears with AOM without MB in this study (*S. pneumoniae*, 14.5%; *H. influenza*, 28.3%; *M. catarrhalis*, 20.7%; or no bacteria, 36.6%). Only the incidence of *S. pneumoniae* was significantly different (Palmu et al, 2001).

Hearing Loss

Hearing loss can be found in 33 to 90% of patients with MB, and there have been several prospective studies of hearing in these patients. Hariri (1990) evaluated 20 ears in 18 patients and found 6 ears with sensorineural losses, 7 ears with mixed losses, and 4 ears with conductive losses. Recovery was complete in 8 of 13 ears with a sen-

sorineural component and occurred between 3 and 11 weeks. All patients received 10 days of oral antibiotics. The average degree of sensorineural loss was 28 dB, and losses were more prominent in the higher frequencies. Lashin and colleagues (1987) found 33% of 24 patients with a hearing loss. Of these, 25% had a pure sensorineural loss, 20% had a mixed loss, and 6% had a pure conductive loss. Eighty-four percent had a complete recovery of hearing with resolution of the MB, and none of these patients received treatment of any form. Hoffman and Shepsman (1983) found 14 of 21 ears with MB with a sensorineural or mixed loss and none with a pure conductive loss. The average loss was 21 dB and was also more prominent in the higher frequencies; recovery was complete in 8 of 14 ears. These patients all received erythromycin for an unknown number of days, and five patients received steroids. No conclusions were drawn with regard to any effect of steroids on hearing status. The mechanism of the sensorineural hearing loss is presumed to be attributable to the passage of toxins through the round window membrane and is supported by studies that suggest a cochlear site of lesion in these patients (Hariri, 1990).

Treatment

There have been no prospective clinical trials of treatment options for this disorder, so treatment recommendations are based on the above information in terms of etiology, natural history, and anecdotal reports. Supportive care, including warm compresses and analgesia, was successful in 90% of patients in one retrospective series, but a few of these patients needed tympanocentesis and two patients developed mastoiditis (Karelitz, 1937). Incision of blebs is not recommended as this usually does not bring about resolution of symptoms and may predispose the patient to superinfection. In the majority of cases, MB will be associated with middle ear fluid, and it seems reasonable to assume that these cases do simply represent otitis media with blisters, as suggested by Rowe in 1975. These cases should be treated as AOM with 10 days of oral antibiotics directed at the common AOM pathogens (Marais and Dale, 1997). Tympanocentesis can be considered for cases unresponsive to routine management or those with unremitting fever and discomfort, just as it would be for AOM. In MB without middle ear fluid, supportive care without antibiotics can be considered, but these patients must be compliant and followed closely. Antibiotics should be given if an effusion develops. The most conservative, and perhaps safest, approach would be to treat all cases of MB with 10 days of oral antibiotics.

There have been no studies involving hearing outcomes with regard to treatment. In the largest study of hearing in these patients, no treatment was given, and 84% had complete recovery of their hearing loss (Lashin et al, 1987). In the study with the poorest hearing recovery (57%), all patients received erythromycin, under the questionable presumption that *Mycoplasma* was the etiologic agent, and some received steroids, but no conclusions could be drawn about the efficacy of the steroids (Hoffman and Shepsman, 1983). Unfortunately, no definitive conclusions can be drawn from existing studies, and the disorder is uncommon enough that prospective randomized trials of treatment to prevent permanent hearing loss will not likely be done in the future. It seems reasonable to consider antibiotics and steroids in patients with MB and a sensorineural or mixed hearing loss and antibiotics alone for cases with a conductive loss or no hearing loss. Patients should be followed for resolution or stabilization of the hearing loss.

References

El-Seifi A, Fouad B. Granular myringitis: is it a surgical problem? Am J Otolaryngol 2000;21:462–7.

Hahn HB, Riggs MW, Hutchinson LR. Myringitis bullosa. Clin Pediatr 1998;37:265–8.

Hariri MA. Sensorineural hearing loss in bullous myringitis. A prospective study of eighteen patients. Clin Otolaryngol 1990;15:351–3.

Hoffman RA, Shepsman DA. Bullous myringitis and sensorineural hearing loss. Laryngoscope 1983;93:1544–5.

Karelitz S. Myringitis bullosa haemorrhagica. Am J Dis Child 1937;53:510–6.

Lashin N, Zaher S, Ragab A, El-Gabri TH. Hearing loss in bullous myringitis. Ear Nose Throat J 1987;67:206–10.

Lowenberg B. Influenza otitis in 1891. Trans Am Otol Soc 1891;5:70–83.

Marais J, Dale BAB. Bullous myringitis: a review. Clin Otolaryngol 1997;22:497–9.

Merifield DO, Miller GS. The etiology and clinical course of bullous myringitis. Arch Otolaryngol 1966;84:41–3.

Palmu AA, Kotikoski MJ, Kaijalainen TH, Puhakka HJ. Bacterial etiology of acute myringitis in children less than two years of age. Pediatr Infect Dis J 2001;20:607–11.

Rifkind D, Chanock R, Kravetz H, et al. Ear involvement (myringitis) and primary atypical pneumonia following inoculation of volunteers with the Eaton agent. Am Rev Respir Dis 1962;85:479–89.

Roberts D. The etiology of bullous myringitis and the role of mycoplasmas in ear disease: a review. Pediatrics 1980;65:761–6.

Rowe DS. Acute suppurative otitis media. Pediatrics 1975;56:285–94.

Stoney P, Kwok P, Hawke M. Granular myringitis: a review. J Otolaryngol 1992;21:129–35.

Woo JK, van Hasselt CA, Gluckman PGC. Myringitis bullosa haemorrhagica: clinical course influenced by tympanosclerosis. J Laryngol Otol 1992;106:162–3.

Chapter 10

ACUTE OTITIS MEDIA WITH PERFORATION

DAVID L. MANDELL, MD

Spontaneous perforation of the tympanic membrane (TM) during an episode of acute otitis media (AOM) is a relatively common occurrence. However, this clinical entity has received little attention in the otitis media (OM) literature, perhaps owing in part to the belief that perforation may be a natural sequela of the disease process of AOM rather than a complication (Bluestone and Klein, 2001). In this chapter, the incidence, pathogenesis, and management of spontaneous TM perforation in the setting of AOM are discussed.

Incidence

The reported incidence of acute perforation of the TM in the setting of AOM has ranged from 4.6 to 30% (Berger, 1989; Ingvarsson, 1982; Medical Research Council, 1957; Pukander, 1983; Schwartz et al, 1977). One reason why the incidence has varied among different studies is related to study design factors such as the inclusion criteria for AOM, level of training of the otoscopists, and setting in which the studies were performed. For example, in studies with stricter criteria for AOM, "mild" cases (red TM without middle ear effusion) have not been included, raising the calculated incidence of spontaneous perforation to 29.5 to 30% (Berger, 1989; Ingvarsson, 1982), whereas the incidence of spontaneous perforation has been lower (4.6–12%) in studies in which "mild" cases of AOM were included in the denominator (Medical Research Council, 1957; Pukander, 1983). In addition, the reported incidence of spontaneous perforation in the setting of AOM has been higher in those studies in which the TM was examined by trained otoscopists in an otolaryngology setting (29.5–30%) (Berger, 1989; Ingvarsson, 1982) versus studies in which AOM was diagnosed in large general practice settings (4.9–12%) (Medical Research Council, 1957; Pukander, 1983).

Aural discharge in the setting of an acute earache necessitates otoscopic and often otomicroscopic examination with suctioning to help distinguish between otitis externa (OE) and AOM with spontaneous TM perforation. OE alone could lead to pain and discharge that might be misinterpreted as AOM with perforation. The incidence of OE in the setting of AOM with TM perforation is not known. Sadé and Halevy (1976) postulated that OE itself may lead to ulceration of the superficial layers of the TM, contributing to perforation. In some studies, any aural discharge in the setting of an acute earache has been tallied as a sequela of AOM (with an incidence of otorrhea with AOM of 20–30%), even though no consistent otoscopic proof of a perforation was reported (Fry et al, 1969; Medical Research Council, 1957). In these studies, cases of OE without AOM could potentially have been misinterpreted as cases of otorrhea with AOM. Conversely, up to 58% of spontaneous TM perforations may not be associated with any otorrhea by the time the patient is seen by the otoscopist (Ingvarsson, 1982).

Spontaneous perforation of the TM in the setting of AOM overall has no gender predilection; it has been reported to be slightly more common in boys in one study (Pukander, 1983) and slightly more common in girls in another (Berger, 1989). Also, no significant difference between right and left sides has been noted (Berger, 1989).

The relationship between patient age and the likelihood of spontaneous TM perforation in the setting of AOM is unclear. Some investigators have found that the risk of spontaneous perforation during an attack of AOM decreases with age; among patients with documented AOM, spontaneous perforation occurred in 44% of patients under 2 years of age and only 15% of patients 8 to 15 years old (Ingvarsson, 1982). However, other studies have found that the incidence of spontaneous perforation in children with AOM does not vary significantly among age groups (Berger, 1989; Medical Research Council, 1957). In one study of patients with AOM, spontaneous TM perforation was noted in 31% of children between the ages of 0 and 3 years, 27% of patients between the ages of 3 and 6 years, and 28% of patients between the ages of 6 and 13 years (Berger, 1989).

The typical location of a spontaneous TM perforation in the setting of AOM is a matter of debate. One reference mentions that the perforation is usually in the posterior-superior quadrant of the TM (Sadé and Halevy, 1976). However, in a study of 85 spontaneous TM perforations associated with AOM, 85% of perforations were located in the anterior-inferior quadrant of the pars tensa (Berger, 1989). Perforations in this location were associated with smooth margins, good drainage of pus, and a favorable clinical course; this area was coined as the "perforation zone" (Berger, 1989). Only 15% of perforations occurred in other locations, most typically the posterior-superior quadrant. These perforations were often partially occluded with granulation tissue, had a nipple-like appearance with a tiny central opening, and did not drain pus effectively, often necessitating myringotomy (Berger, 1989).

Certain underlying factors may predispose patients to experiencing spontaneous TM rupture during an attack of AOM. One study has reported that the incidence of spontaneous TM perforation during an attack of AOM was higher (40%) in children who had a previous history of OM than in children who had no previous history of OM (24%) (Berger, 1989). In another study, it was demonstrated that the higher the annual rate of AOM, the higher the likelihood of otorrhea occurring during one of these episodes (15% otorrhea incidence in patients with one episode of AOM per year; 40% otorrhea incidence in patients with greater than three episodes of AOM per year) (Van Cauwenberge et al, 1986).

In a study from Scotland, it was noted that TM perforation and/or purulent otorrhea in association with AOM was more common in children from "less fortunate social circumstances" with single-income households, shared sleeping accommodations, and mothers who always felt "harassed" (Paterson and MacLean, 1970). Children from this type of background were felt to present to a doctor at a later stage of the illness (Paterson and MacLean, 1970). A study from Finland has reported that the frequency of spontaneous TM perforation may decrease with increased availability of emergency medical services and increased awareness of parents regarding the care of a sick child (Pukander, 1983). Implied in the results from these studies is that spontaneous TM perforation is more likely if treatment for AOM is delayed. In addition, it is believed that spontaneous perforations were more common in developed countries before the widespread use of antimicrobial therapy (Bluestone and Klein, 2001).

The propensity to develop spontaneous TM perforation in childhood may also have a genetic basis. Infants of certain ethnic groups, including the Maori children of the Ruatoki Valley and Australian Aboriginal infants, have an incidence of TM perforation as high as 54% during the first year of life (Boswell and Nienhuys, 1996; Giles and Asher, 1991). Most perforations are preceded by an attack of AOM but sometimes by otitis media with effusion (Boswell and Nienhuys, 1996).

Differences in the virulence of the infecting bacteria and decreased host resistance may also account for different incidence rates of spontaneous perforation (Bluestone and Klein, 2001).

Pathogenesis

The proposed pathogenesis of spontaneous TM perforation during an attack of AOM has been described by Bluestone (1998). As in any case of AOM, it is felt that the most common scenario is the following: an antecedent event (usually a viral upper respiratory tract infection) results in congestion of the respiratory mucosa of the nasopharynx, leading to obstruction of the eustachian tube. Subsequent development of negative middle ear pressure may lead to aspiration of potential pathogens from the nasopharynx into the middle ear. Owing to eustachian tube obstruction, adequate middle ear clearance is prevented, allowing microbial pathogens to proliferate and cause suppurative OM (Bluestone, 1998). It has been proposed that in patients with patulous eustachian tubes, a larger bolus of bacteria-laden material from the nasopharynx may be permitted to enter the middle ear, causing a more fulminant infection than would occur with a eustachian tube of normal or high resistance (Bluestone and Klein, 2001).

It has been theorized that pus accumulation in the middle ear cavity may exert pressure against blood vessels in the TM, leading to ischemic necrosis with eventual perforation and drainage of pus (Berger, 1989). Studies using fluorescein angiography have demonstrated that the anterior half of the human TM is consistently less well perfused than the posterior half of the TM (Applebaum and Deutsch, 1986), which may account for the high percentage of spontaneous perforations that occur in the anterior-inferior quadrant (Berger, 1989).

Because an acute perforation allows purulent material to drain into the external ear canal and enhances drainage of pus down the eustachian tube, a perforation may prevent further spread of infection within the temporal bone or intracranial cavity (Bluestone and Klein, 2001). Development of spontaneous perforation during an attack of AOM typically results in improvement in the clinical condition of the patient, with decreased fever and otalgia (Berger, 1989).

As outlined by Bluestone and Klein (2001), one of four possible outcomes is possible when an attack of AOM is accompanied by spontaneous perforation of the TM: (1) the acute infection resolves and the TM heals, (2) the acute infection resolves but the perforation becomes chronic, (3) both the OM and the perforation become chronic, and (4) a suppurative complication of OM develops. Most commonly, the TM will heal rapidly and spontaneously once the suppurative process in the middle ear has resolved (Sadé and Halevy, 1976), with the defect usually closed within a week (Bluestone and Klein, 2001).

In a study of 71 children with spontaneous perforation of the TM associated with AOM, 70% of the perforations had spontaneously closed by 1 week and 94% had closed by 1 month (Berger, 1989). After spontaneous closure of a perforation associated with AOM, there is nearly always evidence of a middle ear effusion, which may last from days to weeks before normal middle ear aeration is regained (Berger, 1989). Following successful antimicrobial treatment for an episode of AOM with spontaneous TM perforation, children may expect the following outcome over the subsequent 3 months: a 25% likelihood of another episode of AOM and an 85% chance of another TM perforation should another attack of AOM occur (Berger, 1989). If there has been no sign of progressive healing after 3 months despite resolution of the acute infection, the perforation should be considered chronic and managed accordingly (Bluestone and Klein, 2001). Most chronic TM perforations are the result of acute perforations that failed to heal, possibly owing to ingrowth of squamous epithelium at the edges of the perforation (Bluestone, 1998).

Treatment

The bacteria isolated from middle ear cultures in patients with AOM and spontaneous TM perforation are generally similar to those cultured from acute middle ear effusions via tympanocentesis or from acute otorrhea in patients with tympanostomy tubes (Bluestone and Klein, 2001; Mandel et al, 1994). The most commonly isolated middle ear bacteria in children with AOM and spontaneous TM rupture are *Streptococcus pneumoniae* (15–44% of ears), nontypable *Haemophilus influenzae* (15%), group A β-hemolytic streptococci (11–13%), *Moraxella catarrhalis* (8%), and *Staphylococcus aureus* (7–8%) (Brook and Gober, 2000; Hendrickse et al, 1988). It is believed that in the preantibiotic era, untreated *Streptococcus pyogenes* was distinctly associated with spontaneous TM perforation. Modern data lend support to this contention as group A β-hemolytic streptococci have been cultured from middle ear fluid during AOM in 11 to 13% of ears with spontaneous TM perforation (Brook and Gober, 2000; Hendrickse et al, 1988) versus only 3 to 4% of ears with an intact TM (Bluestone et al, 1992; Hendrickse et al, 1988). When obtaining a culture in the setting of AOM and spontaneous TM perforation, it is important to aspirate or swab the middle ear through the perforation after removal of otorrhea fluid (if present) to avoid contamination with bacteria of the external auditory canal (Brooke and Gober, 2000).

AOM with spontaneous TM perforation should be treated with the same systemic antimicrobial agents that would typically be prescribed for AOM without a perforation (Bluestone and Klein, 2001). Before initiating treatment, a culture of the otorrhea, if present, is recommended to help guide antimicrobial therapy. Otorrhea, when profuse, should be prevented from draining onto the pinna, where it may result in dermatitis (Bluestone and Klein, 2001). Aural discharge should be suctioned in the office, and a cotton ball may be placed in the external auditory canal meatus and changed as regularly as needed to keep the area dry.

In addition to systemic treatment, such as oral amoxicillin (Berger, 1989; Bluestone and Klein, 2001; Schwartz et al, 1977), an ototopical medication such as Floxin Otic (0.3%; Daiichi Pharmaceutical Corporation, Montvale, NJ) should be considered, especially if otorrhea and/or OE are present (Bluestone and Klein, 2001). Oral and ototopical medications should be started before the culture results are available. Topical ofloxacin is approved for treatment of AOM with otorrhea in children with tympanostomy tubes (Bluestone et al, 1992), although it should be equally safe and effective in the setting of an acute perforation (Bluestone and Klein, 2001). Applying ototopical drops during the acute episode may prevent secondary chronic infection with canal skin flora such as *Pseudomonas aeruginosa* (Bluestone and Klein, 2001). In cases with coincident OE and a narrow external auditory canal, an ototopical medication that contains a corticosteroid such as CiproHC Otic (0.2% ciprofloxacin hydrochloride and 1% hydrocortisone; Alcon, Fort Worth, TX) or TobraDex (0.3% tobramycin and 0.1% dexamethasone ophthalmic suspension; Alcon) should be considered. Despite the possibility of ototoxicity and the fact that these drops are not approved by the US Food and Drug Administration for use in the presence of a nonintact TM because of its lack of sterility, these preparations may hasten resolution of any external ear canal infection (Bluestone and Klein, 2001) and facilitate delivery of drops by decreasing canal skin edema. One should keep in mind that ototopical therapy alone may not be sufficient in most cases of spontaneous TM rupture because the perforation has a tendency to close early, thus preventing the drops from reaching the middle ear.

The optimal duration of antimicrobial therapy is not known, although there is some evidence to suggest that resolution of AOM with spontaneous TM perforation may require a longer duration of oral antimicrobial therapy than if the TM has remained intact (Hendrickse et al, 1988). In children with AOM, the treatment failure rate following a 5-day course of cefaclor was 53% in patients with spontaneous TM rupture versus 10% in patients with intact TMs (Hendrickse et al, 1988). The treatment failure rate in patients with AOM and spontaneous TM rupture improved to 8% following a 10-day course of cefaclor (Hendrickse et al, 1988).

If otorrhea persists despite 10 days of first-line antimicrobial therapy, a new culture should be obtained, consideration should be given to empirically changing the oral and ototopical antimicrobial agents (eg, from amoxicillin and topical ofloxacin to amoxicillin-clavulanate potassium [Augmentin, GlaxoSmithKline, Research Triangle Park, NC] and CiproHC Otic), and the external ear canal should be suctioned clean. The otomicroscope should be used to rule out another condition, such as cholesteatoma or neoplasm. If an adequate examination cannot be done with the patient awake, an examination under general anesthesia should be considered, at which time a middle ear culture can be obtained (Bluestone and Klein, 2001).

If aural discharge persists for greater than 2 to 3 weeks after onset of AOM despite treatment with adequate oral and topical antimicrobial therapy, consideration should be given to hospitalization and intravenous culture-directed antimicrobial therapy, with a thorough search for any underlying illness that would interfere with resolution of infection. A computed tomographic (CT) scan of the temporal bones with fine cuts may be obtained to rule out acute coalescent mastoiditis (osteitis). Even if the CT scan shows no evidence of coalescence, if otorrhea persists and no conditions other than a TM perforation and OM are found, exploratory tympanotomy and simple mastoidectomy may be indicated (Bluestone and Klein, 2001). During surgery, a search for other causes of persistent infection, such as cholesteatoma, should be performed. Because mastoid osteitis is the usual cause of persistent otorrhea in this setting, mastoidectomy should result in resolution of the infection (Bluestone and Klein, 2001).

In patients who are prone to recurrent AOM with spontaneous TM perforation, the most effective method to prevent another episode of TM perforation and to prevent development of chronic infection is to prevent another episode of AOM. If an episode of AOM does occur, the risk of spontaneous TM perforation is lessened by treating the patient "early, appropriately, and adequately" with antimicrobial therapy at the onset of each episode of AOM (Bluestone and Klein, 2001).

References

Applebaum EL, Deutsch EC. An endoscopic method of tympanic membrane fluorescein angiography. Ann Otol Rhinol Laryngol 1986;95:439–43.

Berger G. Nature of spontaneous tympanic membrane perforation in acute otitis media in children. J Laryngol Otol 1989;103:1150–3.

Bluestone CD. Epidemiology and pathogenesis of chronic suppurative otitis media: implications for prevention and treatment. Int J Pediatr Otorhinolaryngol 1998;42:207–23.

Bluestone CD, Klein JO. Perforation of the tympanic membrane. In: Bluestone CD, Klein JO, editors. Otitis media in infants and children. 3rd ed. Philadelphia: WB Saunders; 2001. p. 308–13.

Bluestone CD, Stephenson JS, Martin LM. Ten-year review of otitis media pathogens. Pediatr Infect Dis J 1992;11 Suppl:7–11.

Boswell JB, Nienhuys TG. Patterns of persistent otitis media in the first year of life in aboriginal and non-aboriginal infants. Ann Otol Rhinol Laryngol 1996;105:893–900.

Brook I, Gober AE. Reliability of the microbiology of spontaneously draining acute otitis media in children. Pediatr Infect Dis J 2000;19:571–3.

Dohar JE, Garner ET, Nielsen RW, et al. Topical ofloxacin treatment of otorrhea in children with tympanostomy tubes. Arch Otolaryngol Head Neck Surg 1999;125:537–45.

Fry J, Dillane JB, McNab Jones RF, et al. The outcome of acute otitis media (a report to the Medical Research Council). Br J Prev Soc Med 1969;23:205–9.

Giles M, Asher I. Prevalence and natural history of otitis media with perforation in Maori school children. J Laryngol Otol 1991;105:257–60.

Hendrickse WA, Kusmiesz H, Shelton S, Nelson JD. Five vs. ten days of therapy for acute otitis media. Pediatr Infect Dis J 1988;7:14–23.

Ingvarsson L. Acute otalgia in children—findings and diagnosis. Acta Paediatr Scand 1982;71:705–10.

Mandel EM, Casselbrant ML, Kurs-Lasky M. Acute otorrhea: bacteriology of a common complication of tympanostomy tubes. Ann Otol Rhinol Laryngol 1994;103:713–18.

Medical Research Council's Working-Party for Research in General Practice. Acute otitis media in general practice. Lancet 1957; 273:510–4.

Paterson JE, MacLean DW. Acute otitis media in children: a medical social study from general practice. Scot Med J 1970;15: 289–96.

Pukander J. Clinical features of acute otitis media among children. Acta Otolaryngol (Stockh) 1983;95:117–22.

Sadé J, Halevy A. The natural history of chronic otitis media. J Laryngol Otol 1976;90:743–51.

Schwartz R, Rodriguez WJ, Khan WN, Ross S. Acute purulent otitis media in children older than 5 years. JAMA 1977;238: 1032–3.

Van Cauwenberge PB, Declercq G, Kluyskens PM. The relationship between acute and secretory otitis media. In: Sadé J, editor. Proceedings of the International Conference on Acute and Secretory Otitis Media, Part 1. Amsterdam: Kugler Publications; 1986. p. 77–82.

Chapter 11

THE RED EARDRUM

RICHARD H. SCHWARTZ, MD

The normal eardrum is a 10 mm × 11 mm, translucent, elliptical membrane separating the middle ear cleft (mesotympanum) from the external ear canal. The margins of the eardrum are anchored by the annulus, composed of connective tissue fibers inserted into a sulcus in the proximal part of the bony ear canal. The eardrum is divided into anterior and posterior halves by a diagonal line beginning at the umbo (central depression) and continuing through the axis of the manubrium (handle) of the malleus. The eardrum directly overlying the manubrium is firmly attached to the periostium of the malleus handle. A large increase in middle ear pressure creates a biconvex shape to the distended eardrum as a result of the firm periosteal attachment. Within the layers of the eardrum is a meshwork of capillaries, which supplies oxygen and nutrients. The anterior and posterior malleolar folds demarcate the segment of the pars flaccida, located from 1 o'clock to 11 o'clock, respectively. The pars flaccida occupies about 20% of the area of the eardrum. Within the wedge-shaped pars flaccida, the eardrum is composed of two epithelial layers: modified respiratory epithelium contiguous with the lining of the middle ear cleft and squamous epithelium on its lateral surface (facing the eye of the otoscopist). The remaining 80% of the eardrum is composed of the pars tensa, a three-layered structure with a middle layer of circumferential and radial fibers for increased strength. After an episode of severely painful acute otitis media (AOM), when the bulging eardrum appears fiery red or dark purple-red, the outer, dead squamous cells of the eardrum may peel off in shaggy pieces of gray skin adherent to its lateral surface. The squamous cells may also peel off in a cast of the entire eardrum and lie in front of and obscure the actual eardrum. Only when there is an intense inflammatory myringitis superimposed on the bulging eardrum of AOM will there be the desquamation described above.

A triangular-shaped highly refractile arm known as the cone of light or, alternatively, the light reflex serves as a landmark for the eardrum. The apex of the cone of light is at the umbo. The base of the cone of light is seen from 4 o'clock to 5 o'clock on the surface of the right eardrum and from 7 o'clock to 8 o'clock on the surface of the left eardrum. Diffusion or disappearance of the cone of light had been a major criterion for AOM, but this is no longer true. Hyperemia of the capillaries of the eardrum, inequality of pressure between the middle ear and the ambient air, and the presence of middle ear effusion can dissipate or obliterate the cone of light.

Traditionally, but inaccurately, a pink or red color of the eardrum was and still is believed by some physicians, nurse practitioners, and physician's assistants to be the sine qua non of acute inflammation or infection of the middle ear cleft. Variations on this theme included redness of more than 50% of the surface of the eardrum. Even redness of only the pars flaccida was believed to be a sign of early AOM. Confirmation of this "truth" was obtained when there was a distinct incongruity between the degree of redness of one eardrum and a normal pearly luster translucency to the other eardrum. Entrenched as it is, redness of the eardrum is neither sensitive nor specific for the diagnosis of AOM; it certainly is not a sine qua non. It is well known that intense screaming or performing breath holding (Valsalva's maneuver) will cause the eardrum to redden. High fever may also produce hyperemia of the infratympanic capillaries. Physical signs for the precise diagnostic criteria for AOM are still unsettled. Many physicians and physician extenders believe that AOM is defined as whatever their viewing eye thinks it should look like, as long as the tympanic membrane (TM) is reddened. Other pediatricians insist not only on redness of the eardrum but also immobility with the pneumatic otoscope in a child with otalgia, fever, or irritability. Immobility is commonly thought to be a lack of mobility when positive pressure is applied through the pneumatic otoscope. Immobility is not absolute. Even markedly bulging eardrums in front of pus-filled middle ear clefts can indent or move a bit when excess positive pressure is applied through the pneumatic otoscope. Impairment of mobility of the eardrum must be accurately assessed only after the application of gentle negative pressure several times in succession followed by application of gentle positive pressure several times in succession.

Based on several clinical studies of bacterial AOM proven by tympanocentesis and middle ear culture, redness of the entire eardrum without bulging had poor correlation with the recovery of bacterial pathogens (Halstead et al, 1968; Karma et al, 1989). The most consistent sign that predicted recovery of bacterial pathogens in both of these studies was bulging of the TM. A growing number of experts agree that the diagnosis of AOM with an intact eardrum should rest on three mandatory major criteria: (1) bulging of the contour of the eardrum, (2) opacification regardless of the apparent color of the lateral surface of the eardrum, and (3) impaired mobility of the eardrum following application of sequential negative and positive pressure through the pneumatic otoscope. The color of the eardrum in AOM may be pink, dull red, hemorrhagic red-purple, fiery red, yellow, serum colored, off-white, or mixtures of the above colors. A survey of 82 academic pediatric infectious disease specialists and 58 academic pediatric otolaryngologists revealed that 35% of the former specialists and 31% of the latter believed that redness of the eardrum was necessary for the diagnosis of AOM (Schwartz, 2001).

We have learned that AOM caused by *Streptococcus pneumoniae* is more likely than the other major middle ear pathogens to be associated with reddened eardrums (Rodriguez and Schwartz, 1999). At least 40% of children with AOM have dull white or yellow-colored eardrums, although capillary dilatation may give a pale rosy tint to the other colors. There are two distinct presentations of AOM that may be reliably associated with intensely red eardrums. Group A streptococcal AOM or highly virulent pneumococcal AOM is sometimes associated with bulging, fiery red, or dark red-purple hemorrhagic eardrums. The eardrum will have maximum bulging, with a diagonal bisecting cleft. The cleft corresponds to the attachment of the axis of the manubrium to the eardrum.

References

Halstead C, Lepow ML, Balassanian N, et al. Otitis media. Am J Dis Child 1968;115:542–51.

Karma PH, Penttila MA, Sipilä MM, Kataja MJ. Otoscopic diagnosis of middle ear effusion in acute and non-acute otitis media. I. The value of different otoscopic findings. Int J Pediatr Otorhinolaryngol 1989;17:37–49.

Rodriguez WJ, Schwartz RH. *Streptococcus pneumoniae* causes otitis media with higher fever and more redness of tympanic membranes than *Haemophilus influenzae* or *Moraxella catarrhalis*. Pediatr Infect Dis J 1999;18:942–4.

Schwartz RH. Acute otitis media: red eardrum, bulging eardrum or neither. Infect Dis Child 2001;14:10, 11, 60.

Chapter 12

Myringotomy and Tympanocentesis

Michael J. Belmont, MD

Myringotomy is an incision in the tympanic membrane (TM) and is traditionally performed using a myringotomy knife. Tympanocentesis is a needle aspiration of the middle ear space to identify microbial pathogens. Myringotomy is often employed immediately after tympanocentesis to improve drainage of middle ear effusion (MEE). Myringotomy was first described by Sir Ashley Cooper in 1802 (Alberti, 1974). The popularity of the procedure increased until antibiotic use became commonplace in the 1940s. Since then, it has been performed for specific indications, primarily by otolaryngologists and a small number of pediatricians. As antibiotic use has increased and antibiotic resistance has bloomed, the importance of myringotomy and tympanocentesis for acute otitis media (AOM) has increased.

Procedure

Tympanocentesis and myringotomy are painful procedures. Ideally, anesthesia or analgesia should be administered. Unfortunately, constraints including nothing by mouth status, surgeon time, and operating room scheduling often dictate the setting in which they are performed. Because they are often performed on an urgent or emergent basis, most are completed without anesthesia in the office. Unfortunately, iontophoresis of topical analgesics does not provide adequate anesthesia when AOM is present. One option is to premedicate the child with acetaminophen with codeine. A second option is to topically anesthetize the TM with phenol. Unfortunately, application of phenol is not without pain.

One of the keys to a successful procedure is adequate restraint of the child. Infants can be wrapped in a sheet and immobilized by an assistant. Small children can be placed in a papoose and immobilized with the help of an assistant. Older children, who cannot hold still, require general anesthesia. Although it is possible to perform tympanocentesis and/or myringotomy with a handheld operating otoscope, better control of the needle and knife

and better depth perception are afforded by use of an operating microscope.

Cerumen is removed from the external auditory canal for better visualization that will also give an idea of how the child and/or parent will react to manipulation under restraint. The canal is then sterilized by application of 70% ethanol for 1 minute, after which the external auditory canal is suctioned dry. The tympanocentesis itself can be performed with a tuberculin syringe and an 18-gauge needle or a needle attached to an Alden-Senturia trap from Storz Instrument Co., St. Louis, MO (Figure 12-1). The needle is placed through the inferior portion (preferable anterior) of the TM and the effusion is aspirated and sent for Gram stain and culture. If a myringotomy is to be performed, a myringotomy knife can then be used to make an incision through the entire inferior half of the TM, taking care to avoid the posterior-superior quadrant. Suction is then used in the middle ear to evacuate any effusion remaining. This is followed by placement of topical antibiotic drops in the external auditory canal.

Recent works have examined the usefulness of the laser to perform myringotomy. To date, randomized clinical trials that compare the short- and long-term efficacy and complications of laser myringotomy with conventional myringotomy have not been conducted. One place where laser myringotomy may find a use is in the treatment of complications of AOM. These children may receive a tympanocentesis followed by a myringotomy and tympanostomy tube. The tube is placed to prolong drainage past the 24 to 48 hours a myringotomy stays open and to facilitate delivery of topical antibiotic drops to the middle ear. Many of these children do not have a prior indication for myringotomy and tube placement. A laser myringotomy in this setting may provide a good compromise, affording a longer period of patency without the need for a tube.

The complications of performing a myringotomy properly are few. The otorrhea that follows the procedure is the most common finding and is not considered a complication because it is the desired outcome. Dislocation of

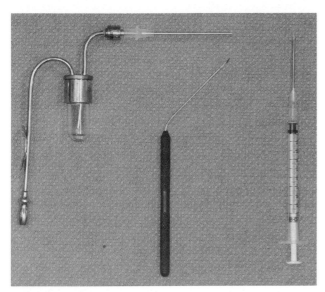

Figure 12-1. Alden-Senturia trap, myringotomy blade, and a tuberculin syringe attached to an 18-gauge needle

the incudostapedial joint, severing the facial nerve, and puncturing an exposed jugular bulb are dreaded complications but are so rare in experienced hands that they should not deter the trained practitioner from employing the procedure when indicated. The most common sequelae of the procedure are persistent perforation and an atrophic scar. Even though the incidence of these conditions has not been systematically studied in a prospective manner, the risk of either or all occurring should not outweigh the benefits of myringotomy when indicated.

Myringotomy as First-Line Treatment of Routine AOM

Prior to the widespread use of antimicrobial agents, myringotomy was routinely used to treat AOM. Nowadays, myringotomy is reserved only for selected cases of AOM and is performed primarily by otolaryngologists and a handful of primary care physicians. Eight clinical trials have evaluated the efficacy of myringotomy for routine AOM (Table 12-1). Roddey and colleagues (1966) studied 181 children, all of whom received an antimicrobial agent, and in approximately half of the subjects, myringotomy was performed as well. The only significant difference between the two groups judged by otoscopy at 2, 10, 30, and 60 days and by audiometry at 3 to 6 months was more rapid pain relief among a small group who had severe otalgia initially. Fewer children who had the myringotomy and antimicrobial therapy had MEE at the end of 6 weeks than did those who received antimicrobial agents alone, but the difference was not statistically significant.

Herberts and associates (1971) found no difference in the percentages of children with persistent effusion 10 days after either myringotomy and antimicrobial therapy or antimicrobial therapy alone. Lorentzen and Haugsten (1977) found the "myringotomy only" group to have the same recovery rate (88%) as both the group treated with penicillin V alone and the group treated with penicillin V and myringotomy. Puhakka and coworkers (1978) repeated the same study with 158 children and found that 4 weeks after the onset of AOM, 71% of the children who did not undergo myringotomy but were treated with penicillin V were cured, whereas 90% of the group that had myringotomy and penicillin V treatment had the same outcome, indicating that "myringotomy clearly accelerates the recovery rate from acute otitis media."

Qvarnberg and Palva (1980) reported the results of their study of 248 children in which they compared the efficacy of penicillin V and myringotomy, penicillin V alone, and amoxicillin and concluded that if the first attack of AOM is treated with myringotomy and antibiotics (penicillin V or amoxicillin), cure is the rule, but that if antibiotics alone (either one) are used, 10% of the patients will run a prolonged course. Schwartz and coworkers (1981) treated 776 children with a variety of antimicrobial agents, half of whom also had myringotomy (without aspiration), and found no difference in the percentage with persistent effusion 10 days after myringotomy therapy. Unfortunately, this, as well as all of the above studies, had design and methodologic flaws that make interpreting their results and answering the question of the value of myringotomy for AOM difficult.

Engelhard and coworkers (1989) avoided many of the methodologic problems in the first five studies cited above and randomly assigned 105 Israeli infants, 3 to 12 months of age, who had AOM to one of three treatment groups: (1) amoxicillin-clavulanate, (2) myringotomy plus placebo (for amoxicillin-clavulanate), and (3) amoxicillin-clavulanate and myringotomy. The two myringotomy groups were double-blinded. Using otoscopy as an outcome measure, 60% of the infants receiving the antibiotic, with or without myringotomy, recovered, whereas only 23% of subjects who received myringotomy and placebo recovered. They concluded that the addition of myringotomy to the amoxicillin-clavulanate did not appear to affect either the persistence of infection after treatment or the residual MEE.

Kaleida and colleagues (1991) randomly assigned children in Pittsburgh who had "severe" AOM to receive either 10 days of amoxicillin, myringotomy with placebo (for amoxicillin), or both amoxicillin and myringotomy; children less than 2 years of age in the trial received only amoxicillin with or without myringotomy. Outcome included an algorithm that combined otoscopy (by a validated otoscopist), tympanometry, and acoustic reflex testing. There were statistically more initial treatment failures in those children who received myringotomy alone compared with those who received amoxicillin, with or without the myringotomy. Subjects assigned to receive amoxicillin alone and those assigned to receive amoxicillin and myringotomy had similar outcomes. In addition, there was no significant difference in the number of children in each group who had persistent effusion 2 or 6 weeks later or a recurrence of AOM 2 to 6 weeks later. They concluded that amoxicillin (or an equivalent antimicrobial agent) is indicated for treatment of AOM and that the data did not support the routine use of myringotomy, either alone or in combination with amoxicillin. They did recommend myringotomy for selected infants and children, however, such as those with severe otalgia, antimicrobial treatment failures, and when a suppurative complication is present.

Thus, based on these studies, the procedure is not recommended either as the only treatment for uncomplicated AOM or in combination with an antimicrobial agent for uncomplicated AOM.

Indications for Myringotomy and/or Tympanocentesis

There are certain indications for which there is consensus at present despite the lack of evidence from clinical trials. The indications are listed in Table 12-2.

Suppurative Complications

Compared with the preantibiotic era, suppurative complications of AOM such as mastoiditis, subperiosteal abscess, and epidural abscess are relatively uncommon. Many of these complications need to be addressed with a combination of intravenous antibiotics and operative intervention

ranging from mastoidectomy to labyrinthectomy and craniotomy. However, in each case, the origin of the infection needs to be addressed. Thus, in each case, a tympanocentesis followed by a myringotomy is indicated. The aspirate is sent for Gram stain and culture. In addition, in children with suppurative complications, prolonged aeration and drainage of the middle ear are beneficial. This is accomplished by placement of a tympanostomy tube after myringotomy. This will keep the myringotomy site open longer to facilitate drainage and aeration and will serve as a conduit for topical antibiotic therapy.

Severe Otalgia

Even though some studies have failed to show that myringotomy alleviated earache, Roddey and colleagues (1966) did show that acute pain was relieved in those children who received myringotomy. Culture of the effusion is reasonable because the middle ear is being opened, but it is not absolutely necessary if there is no reason to suspect the presence of an unusual organism. This is a very uncommon indication.

Antibiotic Failure

When there is persistent otalgia or fever, or both, in spite of adequate and appropriate antimicrobial therapy, a tympanocentesis with or without myringotomy may be indicated. In an otherwise healthy child who is nontoxic and who has failed to respond to a first-line antibiotic, empiric treatment with a second-line antimicrobial agent effective against β-lactamase–producing organisms is indicated. Diagnostic tympanocentesis is indicated if the child fails to improve after another 48 to 72 hours of ther-

TABLE 12-1. Percentage of Patients with Persistent Middle Ear Effusion after Initial Myringotomy and Antimicrobial Therapy Compared with Those Receiving Antimicrobial Therapy Alone for Acute Otitis Media

| Investigator | Procedure | Number of Subjects | Percentage with Persistent Effusion after | | | Statistical Significance Achieved |
			10–14 D	4 Wk	6 Wk	
Roddey et al (1966)	AB	121	35	7	2	No
	AB + M	94	24	9	1	
Herberts et al (1971)	AB	81	10	—	—	No
	AB + M	91	18	—	—	
Lorentzen and Haugsten (1977)	AB	190	16	6		No
	AB + M	164	20	6		
Puhakka et al (1979)	AB	90	78	29	—	Yes
	AB + M	68	29	10		
Qvarnberg and Palva (1980)	AB	151	50	—	—	Yes
	AB + M	97	28	—	—	
Schwartz et al (1981)	AB	361	47	—	—	No
	AB + M	415	51			
Engelhard et al (1989)	AB	35	40	—	—	No
	AB + M	34	40		—	
Kaleida et al (1991)	AB	167*	61	—	56	No
	AB + M	104*	56	—	52	

Adapted from Bluestone CD and Klein JO (1995).
*Number of episodes.
AB = antibiotic; AB + M = antibiotic and myringotomy.

TABLE 12-2. Indications for Myringotomy and/or Tympanocentesis

Suppurative complications
Severe otalgia
Antibiotic failure
Immunocompromised patient
Neonatal patient
Intensive care unit patient

apy with the second-line antibiotic. In a child who is toxic, who has failed to respond to first-line treatment, tympanocentesis followed by myringotomy is indicated to obtain material for Gram stain and culture to direct second-line antibiotic therapy.

Immunocompromised Patient

Children with organ transplants (who are receiving medications to prevent rejection), children on chronic steroid therapy, children with hematologic malignancies, children receiving chemotherapy, and children with significant immune deficiencies do not fight infection like normal children. In this small subgroup of children, therapy for AOM requires a more aggressive approach to prevent serious suppurative complications. Children who are immunosuppressed may not manifest the typical inflammatory responses. In a nontoxic immunocompromised child with recent-onset AOM, it is reasonable to attempt a course of broad-spectrum oral antibiotics for 24 to 48 hours. Any worsening of symptoms or failure to promptly respond to treatment requires tympanocentesis to obtain material for Gram stain and culture to direct intravenous antibiotic therapy followed by myringotomy to maximize drainage and aeration. A more toxic immunocompromised child requires emergent tympanocentesis and myringotomy. Intravenous antibiotic therapy directed by Gram stain and culture can then be instituted.

Neonatal Patient

In a neonate seen as an outpatient who is otherwise healthy and who is not toxic, a trial of antibiotics and close monitoring is appropriate. On the other hand, the otolaryngologist is often asked to see a toxic neonate with otitis media who is undergoing a sepsis workup. In the neonate, gram-negative bacilli are responsible for about 20% (Arriaga et al, 1989; Berman et al, 1978; Bland, 1972; Sharon et al, 1983; Tetzlaff et al, 1977) of cases of AOM. Arriaga and colleagues (1989) demonstrated the usefulness of tympanocentesis in this group of children. Charts of 40 consecutive infants, 29 of whom were neonates, who presented with sepsis and suspected AOM and underwent tympanocentesis as part of their emergency room workup were reviewed. In 80% of these patients, clinical management was directly affected by tympa-

nocentesis data. Thus, tympanocentesis in this group of neonates should be undertaken when the presence of middle ear fluid is suspected.

Intensive Care Unit Patient

Similar to the neonatal patient, in the pediatric intensive care unit (ICU) patient, AOM cannot be assumed to be caused by *Streptococcus pneumoniae, Haemophilus influenzae,* or *Moraxella catarrhalis.* Persico and colleagues (1985) demonstrated the usefulness of myringotomy in the ICU setting. They prospectively followed 71 ICU patients with daily pneumatic otoscopy. Myringotomy was performed when the patients became febrile. They were able to demonstrate an 80% concordance between blood and middle ear cultures when both were obtained in these febrile ICU patients. Gram stain of the middle ear aspirate can provide valuable information to help direct antibiotic coverage until blood or middle ear cultures grow.

Conclusion

The importance of tympanocentesis and myringotomy has grown in recent years as the prevalence of antibiotic resistance has increased. The procedure is most often performed in the office without anesthesia. Complications associated with the procedures are rare. Indications include AOM with suppurative complications, AOM in the neonate, AOM in the immunocompromised patient, AOM in the ICU patient, AOM refractory to medical treatment, and AOM associated with severe otalgia.

References

Alberti PW. Myringotomy and ventilating tubes in the 19th century. Laryngoscope 1974;84:805–15.

Arriaga MA, Bluestone CD, Stool SE. The role of tympanocentesis in the management of infants with sepsis. Laryngoscope 1989;99:1048–51.

Berman SA, Balkany TJ, Simmons MA. Otitis media in the neonatal intensive care unit. Pediatrics 1978;62:198–201.

Bland RD. Otitis media in the first six weeks of life. Diagnosis bacteriology and management. Pediatrics 1972;49:187–97.

Bluestone CD, Klein JO. Otitis media in infants and children. 2nd ed. Philadelphia: WB Saunders; 1995.

Engelhard D, Cohen D, Strauss N, et al. Randomised study of myringotomy, amoxicillin/clavulanate, or both for acute otitis media in infants. Lancet 1989;ii:141–3.

Herberts G, Jeppsson PH, Nylen O, Branefors-Helander P. Acute otitis media: etiologic and therapeutic aspects of acute otitis media. Pract Otorhinolaryngol 1971;33:191–202.

Kaleida PH, Casselbrant ML, Rockette HE, et al. Amoxicillin or myringotomy or both for acute otitis media: results of a randomized clinical trial. Pediatrics 1991;87:466–74.

Lorentzen P, Haugsten P. Treatment of acute suppurative otitis media. J Laryngol Otol 1977;91:331–40.

Persico M, Barker GA. Mitchell DP. Purulent otitis media—a "silent" source of sepsis in the pediatric intensive care unit. Otolaryngol Head Neck Surg 1985;93:330–4.

Puhakka H, Virolainen E, Aantaa E, et al. Myringotomy in the treatment of acute otitis media in children. Duodecim 1979; 94:850–5.

Qvarnberg Y, Palva T. Active and conservative treatment in acute otitis media: prospective studies. Ann Otol Rhinol Laryngol 1980;89:269–70.

Roddey OF, Earle R, Haggerty R. Myringotomy in acute otitis media. JAMA 1966;197:849–53.

Schwartz RH, Rodriguez WJ, Schwartz DM. Office myringotomy for acute otitis media: its value in preventing middle ear effusion. Laryngoscope 1981;91:616–9.

Sharon PA, Marchant CD, Kim CH, et al. Emergence of beta lactamase producing strains of *Branhamella catarrhalis* as important agents of acute otitis media. Pediatr Infect Dis J 1983;2:34–8.

Tetzlaff TR, Ashworth C, Nelson JD. Otitis media in children less than 12 weeks of age. Pediatrics 1977;59:827–32.

Chapter 13

VIRAL OTITIS MEDIA

TASNEE CHONMAITREE, MD

Acute otitis media (AOM) has generally been considered a bacterial disease and has been treated with antibiotics. However, data generated in the past two decades have linked respiratory viruses to the pathogenesis and recovery of AOM. It is now believed that most cases of AOM occur as a bacterial complication of a viral upper respiratory tract infection (URI), and some cases of AOM have been shown to be caused by virus alone. This chapter reviews the literature on the role of viruses in AOM and provides insights into the prevention and management of the virologic elements of the disease.

Association of AOM and Viral URI

Viral URI is exceedingly common in infants and young children. On average, a young child may have two to seven episodes of URI per year. Those who attend day-care centers may have up to 14 episodes of URI per year. Respiratory viruses that commonly cause URI in infants and young children include respiratory syncytial virus (RSV), parainfluenza viruses (types 1, 2, and 3), influenza (A and B), rhinovirus, adenovirus, enterovirus, and coronavirus. Epidemiologic evidence has long suggested a close association between URI and AOM. For example, AOM generally occurs concurrently or just after viral URI, the age of peak incidence of AOM (6 to 24 months) coincides with ages when viral URIs are prevalent, and the highest incidence of AOM occurs during the winter respiratory season.

The close association between AOM and viral URI has been documented in the past two decades and is summarized in Table 13-1. In studies of children with viral URI caused by various respiratory viruses, AOM occurred in 10 to 57% of children with URI, depending on the type of viruses involved (Henderson et al, 1982; Ruuskanen et al, 1989). RSV was associated with the highest rate of AOM following URI (33 to 57%) and rhinovirus with the lowest rate (10%) (Henderson et al, 1982). In studies of more than 1,200 children with more than 1,300 episodes of URI of unknown etiology, AOM occurred in 28 to 50% of children (Heikkinen and Ruuskanen, 1994; Koivunen et al, 1999). The peak inci-

dence of AOM development was between 2 and 4 days after onset of the URI, and most children who developed AOM did so within 2 weeks following the URI episode. Studies using conventional viral diagnostic methods (viral culture and viral antigen detection) have shown respiratory viruses in the nasopharynx of approximately 40% of children with AOM (Heikkinen et al, 1999; Sarkkinen et al, 1985). More recent studies combining the more sensitive polymerase chain reaction (PCR) assay with the conventional assays detected viruses in up to 90% of respiratory secretions (Heikkinen et al, 2001). Using conventional viral diagnostic methods, the investigators at the University of Texas Medical Branch (UTMB) have shown viruses in approximately 20% of the middle ear fluid (MEF) of children with AOM (Chonmaitree, 2000). A study using the PCR technique for RSV, rhinovirus, and coronavirus has shown viruses in the MEF of 48% of children (Pitkaranta et al, 1998). Viruses associated with AOM include those that cause URI: RSV, parainfluenza virus (types 1, 2, and 3), influenza A and B, rhinovirus, adenovirus, enterovirus, and coronavirus. Less commonly, cytomegalovirus and herpes simplex virus have been reported to be associated with AOM (Chonmaitree et al, 1992b). The relative ability of different viruses to predispose individuals to AOM is difficult to determine because of different methods of diagnosis of the individual virus in various studies. However, RSV, influenza virus, parainfluenza virus, and rhinovirus seem to lead most often to the development of AOM (Heikkinen et al, 1999; Henderson et al, 1982; Pitkaranta et al, 1998).

Role of Viruses in the Pathogenesis of AOM

Although the mechanisms by which viral URI induces AOM are not fully elucidated, ample evidence derived from experimental animal studies, studies of adult volunteers infected with respiratory viruses, and clinical studies of children with URI and AOM partially elucidates the mechanisms of pathogenesis of virus-induced AOM. The bacteria known to cause AOM are those generally colonized in the child's nasopharynx without doing harm until

TABLE 13-1. Association between Upper Respiratory Tract Infection and Acute Otitis Media

Ten to 57% of children with URI caused by various respiratory viruses develop AOM.

Twenty-eight to 50% of children with URI of unknown etiology develop AOM.

Viruses are detected in respiratory secretions of 40 to 90% of children with AOM.

Viruses are detected in 20 to 48% of middle ear fluids of children with AOM.

Influenza virus vaccines and antiviral drugs may prevent AOM during influenza season.

AOM = acute otitis media; URI = upper respiratory tract infection.

there is an inflammation of the nasopharynx and eustachian tube (ET). Dysfunction of the ET leading to negative middle ear pressure is the most important factor in the pathogenesis of AOM, and respiratory viruses have been shown to cause these pathologies. Preschool children with URI and adults with experimental viral infections have been shown to have negative middle ear pressure and/or abnormal tympanograms (Buchman et al, 1994; Sanyal et al, 1980). In an experimental model of AOM in chinchillas, intranasal inoculation of influenza virus or adenovirus induces inflammation of the ET and reduces the tube's protective and transport functions (Giebink et al, 1980; Suzuki and Bakaletz, 1994). ET dysfunction results in loss of pressure equilibrium between the nasopharynx and the middle ear, impairment of the protective function of the tube, and reduced clearance by the tube, allowing bacteria and/or virus to invade the middle ear (Bakaletz et al, 1993; Chonmaitree and Heikkinen, 1997).

One important mechanism by which respiratory viruses may cause ET dysfunction is their ability to induce the production and release of cytokines and inflammatory mediators, such as histamine, bradykinin, interleukins, leukotrienes, interferon, and tumor necrosis factor, from target cells in the nasopharynx (Miyamoto and Bakaletz, 1997). Many of these substances have been shown to provoke ET dysfunction in experimental animals and in adult volunteers (Bakaletz et al, 1993; Buchman et al, 1995; Doyle et al, 1990; Ohashi et al, 1991), and ET dysfunction is believed to play a major role in aspiration of bacteria from the nasopharynx into the middle ear (Bluestone and Klein, 1994). Viruses can also promote the entrance of bacteria to the middle ear by enhancement of nasopharyngeal bacterial colonization and adherence and alteration of the host's immune defense. For example, influenza virus promoted colonization of *Streptococcus pneumoniae* in the oropharynx of adult volunteers (Wadowsky et al, 1995); RSV increased nasopharyngeal colonization of *Haemophilus influenzae* in cotton rats (Patel et al, 1992); and RSV, adenovirus, and influenza A increased adherence of *S. pneumoniae* and *H. influenzae* to epithelial cells in vitro (El Ahmer et al, 1999; Håkansson et al, 1994; Jiang et al, 1999). In addition, influenza virus has immunosuppressive effects on polymorphonuclear leukocytes, and RSV and

rhinovirus can alter cell-mediated immune function (Abramson et al, 1982; Gentile et al, 2001; Hsia et al, 1990; Ruuskanen and Ogra, 1993).

Once microbial pathogens, including bacteria and/or viruses, are in the normally sterile middle ear, local inflammation and immunologic reaction occur, leading to effusion formation and signs and symptoms of acute middle ear infection. It is still unclear how bacteria that colonize the nasopharynx without causing any harm become active pathogens once in the middle ear. However, it is likely that viruses somehow cause this event by changing the microenvironment of the nasopharynx, ET, and the middle ear, thus promoting this event. The proposed mechanisms of pathogenesis of virus-induced AOM are shown in Figure 13-1.

Does Pure Viral AOM Exist?

The information presented above suggests that viruses induce the initial process that leads to infection of the middle ear by bacteria that have colonized the nasopharynx. Evidence also suggests that viruses do enter the middle ear from the nasopharynx during the development of AOM and that viruses alone, without the presence of bacteria in the middle ear, can cause middle ear inflammation. Viral AOM has been shown to occur in both infants and children and in the animal model of AOM. Studies of infants and children with AOM for bacterial and viral etiology (using conventional viral diagnostic methods) have shown viruses in the MEF of 11 to 25% of cases. In 6 to 15% of these cases, only viruses (without bacteria) were detected in the MEF (Arola et al, 1990; Klein et al, 1982; Sarkkinen et al, 1985). Between 1992 and 1998, investigators at the UTMB studied MEF from 708 infants and children with AOM for bacteria and viruses using conventional viral diagnostic methods (Chonmaitree, 2000). Pure viral AOM was documented in 5% of these cases. In 15% of these AOM cases, viruses and bacteria were both present in the MEF. In 55%, bacteria alone were present, and in 25%, no bacteria or virus was present. The UTMB data have shown not only the presence of viruses in the MEF but also the effect of viruses on the degree of inflammation in the middle ear (see discussion below). Solid evidence suggesting that viruses alone can cause AOM has come from experimental animal data. In an earlier study in chinchillas (Giebink et al, 1980), *S. pneumoniae* and/or influenza A virus were inoculated into the animals intranasally. Bacteria alone induced AOM in 21% of animals, whereas both bacteria and virus induced AOM in 31%. Influenza A virus alone induced AOM in 4% (1 of 25) of animals; the MEF was culture positive for influenza A. In another study using adenovirus type 1, intranasal inoculation of the virus, in the absence of bacteria, caused mild to moderate tympanic membrane inflammation in 18 animals (Bakaletz et al, 1993).

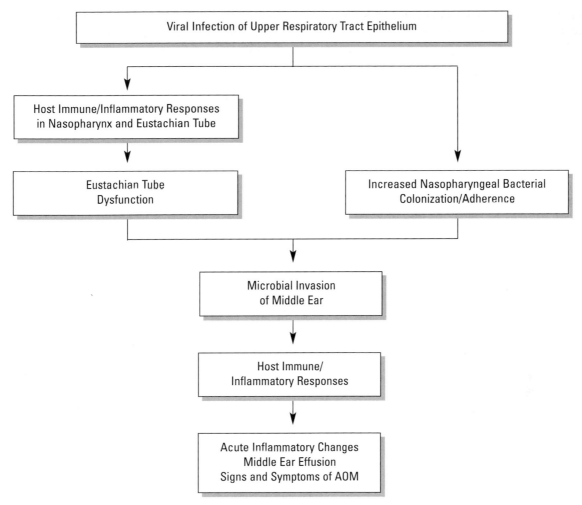

FIGURE 13-1. The proposed mechanisms of pathogenesis of virus-induced acute otitis media (AOM).

The above human and animal data elicit the ability of viruses to induce AOM in the absence of bacteria. Because it is now clear that conventional viral diagnostic assays underdetect viruses (Chonmaitree and Henrickson, 2000), the rate of viral AOM may be even higher than previously thought. Determination of the true incidence of viral AOM will require large samples and the use of more sensitive methods, such as reverse transcriptase (RT)-PCR assay for a broad spectrum of respiratory viruses.

Is AOM in Infants and Children a Pure Bacterial Disease?

Evidence to date suggests that viruses play a crucial role in both the pathogenesis and the clinical course of AOM; the disease may not be a "pure" bacterial disease (Table 13-2). Despite the availability of numerous effective antibiotics, failure of antibiotic treatment is not uncommon in AOM. Physicians generally change antibiotics when this happens, assuming that bacteria resistant to the initial antibiotic cause the treatment failure. However, resistant bacteria have been responsible for a small proportion of these cases (Pichichero and Pichichero, 1995; Teele et al, 1981). Because AOM most often occurs as a complication of viral URI, viruses also enter the middle ear during AOM development. At the time of AOM diagnosis, viruses are detected in 20% of the MEF by conventional viral diagnostic assays in 48% by RT-PCR for selected viruses (Pitkaranta et al, 1998). More importantly, the presence of viruses in the middle ear is associated with production of cytokines, chemokines, and potent inflammatory mediators in the middle ear, suggesting virus-induced inflammation. In the MEF from children with AOM, levels of interleukin-8, macrophage inflammatory protein, monocyte chemotactic protein 1, histamine, and leukotriene B_4 have been found to be higher in MEF containing both bacteria and virus than in MEF containing bacteria or virus alone (Chonmaitree et al, 1994; Chonmaitree et al, 1996; Patel et al, 1996). Finally, studies have shown that the effects of viral infection prolong AOM recovery. Bacteriologic failure at 2 to 4 days into antibiotic therapy occurred in a significantly higher

TABLE 13-2. Evidence Suggesting That Acute Otitis Media May Not Be a "Pure" Bacterial Disease

Antibiotic treatment failure in many cases is not due to resistant bacteria.
AOM occurs mostly as a complication of viral upper respiratory tract infection.
Viruses are present in the middle ear fluid of at least 20% of cases of AOM.
Viruses induce the middle ear inflammation, as evidenced by induction of potent inflammatory mediators in the middle ear.
Viruses interact with bacteria and affect the response to antibiotic treatment.

AOM = acute otitis media.

proportion of patients whose MEF contained both bacteria and virus than in the group with bacteria alone (Chonmaitree et al, 1990), and concurrent viral infection of the respiratory tract or the middle ear is associated with poor treatment outcomes (Chonmaitree et al, 1992a).

The evidence presented above suggests that in AOM, combined bacterial and viral infection of the middle ear is not uncommon, and treatment aiming at eradication of bacteria alone may not be sufficient in some cases.

Clinical Implications

Because AOM occurs as a complication of viral URI, successful prevention of URI in children will make the greatest impact on the incidence of AOM (Table 13-3). Because URI is caused by several respiratory viruses, however, successful prevention of URI in children is still a long way away. At present, prevention and treatment are available only for influenza virus. Published studies show the efficacy of influenza virus vaccines given prior to influenza season in reducing the incidence of AOM (Belshe et al, 1998; Clements et al, 1995; Heikkinen et al, 1991). Physicians may choose to recommend influenza virus vaccines for children over 6 months of age who are otitis prone, especially those attending day-care centers. The development of vaccines that effectively prevent other respiratory viruses should prove to be the most important weapons in battling AOM.

Studies on the use of antiviral drugs in the early treatment of viral URI to prevent AOM have been performed only recently. In a study of 695 children, the antiviral drug oseltamivir reduced the incidence of influenza-related AOM by 44% and reduced the overall antibiotic use for influenza complications by 31% (Whitley et al, 2001). Studies of other antiviral drugs, such as pleconaril, an investigational drug effective against rhinovirus and enterovirus, for the prevention of otitis media are ongoing.

When AOM is not a "pure" bacterial infection, the response to antibiotic can only be partial. Our knowledge about how viruses affect recovery from AOM should remind physicians that a delayed clinical response to antibiotic treatment does not always necessitate change in the type of antibiotic. Viruses, not resistant bacteria, may be responsible for the adverse clinical outcome. In this situation, persistent URI symptoms may suggest the presence of concurrent viral infection in the middle ear. The physician should consider tympanocentesis, a procedure presently underused, when resistant bacteria are suspected to be the cause of treatment failure.

Data on inflammatory mediators such as histamine and leukotriene B_4 in the MEF of children with AOM and concurrent viral infection suggest that antibiotic alone may not be adequate treatment (Chonmaitree et al, 1994; Chonmaitree et al, 1996) because the inflammatory process in the middle ear may continue even after the elimination of bacteria. Anti-inflammatory drugs may have potential benefits when used as adjuvant drugs for AOM treatment. Recent clinical trials using 5-day treatment with antihistamine and corticosteroid, however, do not show their benefits, either in reducing the levels of histamine or leukotriene B_4 in the MEF of children with AOM (McCormick et al, 2003) or in improving clinical outcome (Chonmaitree et al, 2003). Use of 5-day treatment with antihistamine unexpectedly caused an adverse effect in prolonging the duration of middle ear effusion in AOM and should be avoided (Chonmaitree et al, 2003). Further studies should be performed using a different duration of corticosteroid or other anti-inflammatory drugs, such as leukotriene antagonists. Lastly, in cases of AOM associated with combined bacterial and viral infection, an addition of an antiviral drug to antibiotic treatment may improve the clinical outcome. Studies of the efficacy of combined antibiotic and antiviral drugs are ongoing. The results may show this course of treatment to be helpful in some future cases of AOM.

Conclusion

AOM, generally considered a bacterial disease, is more likely a bacterial complication of viral URI. Viruses alone can cause the signs and symptoms of AOM. Combined bacterial and viral AOM episodes may be more common than previously thought. In these cases, viruses induce enhanced middle ear inflammation and delay bacterial clearance. Prevention or early treatment of viral URI can prevent the occurrence of AOM. Development of more vaccines and antiviral drugs targeting respiratory virus-

TABLE 13-3. Viral Acute Otitis Media: Clinical Implications

AOM may be prevented by vaccines against respiratory viruses.
AOM may be prevented by use of antiviral drugs during upper respiratory tract infection.
When AOM is not a "pure" bacterial infection, the response to an antibiotic can only be partial.
Delayed response to antibiotic treatment may be due to viral coinfection; persistent URI symptoms may be a clue. Changing the antibiotic may not help, but tympanocentesis may help with bacteriologic diagnosis.
Anti-inflammatory drugs may have some role in improving outcome of AOM.
Antiviral drugs may have a future role in the treatment of AOM.

AOM = acute otitis media; URI = upper respiratory tract infection.

es, as well as studies on the use of these tools in AOM management, will lead to new strategies for prevention and more effective treatment of this very common childhood disease.

References

Abramson JS, Giebink CS, Quie PG. Influenza A virus-induced polymorphonuclear leukocyte dysfunction in the pathogenesis of experimental pneumococcal otitis media. Infect Immun 1982;36:289–96.

Arola M, Ziegler T, Ruuskanen O, et al. Rhinovirus in acute otitis media. J Pediatr 1990;116:697–701.

Bakaletz LO, Daniels RL, Lim DJ. Modeling adenovirus type 1-induced otitis media in the chinchilla: effect on ciliary activity and fluid transport function of eustachian tube mucosal epithelium. J Infect Dis 1993;168:865–72.

Belshe RB, Mendelman PM, Treanor J, et al. The efficacy of live attenuated, cold-adapted, trivalent, intranasal influenza vaccine in children. N Engl J Med 1998;338:1405–12.

Bluestone CD, Klein JO, editors. Otitis media in infants and children. 2nd ed. Philadelphia: WB Saunders Co; 1994. p. 17–37.

Buchman CA, Doyle WJ, Skoner D, et al. Otologic manifestations of experimental rhinovirus infection. Laryngoscope 1994;104:1295–9.

Buchman CA, Swarts JD, Seroky JT, et al. Otologic and systemic manifestations of experimental influenza A virus infection in the ferret. Otolaryngol Head Neck Surg 1995;112:572–8.

Chonmaitree T. Viral and bacterial interaction in acute otitis media. Pediatr Infect Dis J 2000;19(5 Suppl):S24–30.

Chonmaitree T, Heikkinen T. Role of viruses in middle ear disease. Ann N Y Acad Sci 1997;830:143–57.

Chonmaitree T, Henrickson KJ. Detection of respiratory viruses in the middle ear fluids of children with acute otitis media by multiplex reverse transcription-polymerase chain reaction assay. Pediatr Infect Dis J 2000;19:258–60.

Chonmaitree T, Owen MJ, Howie VM. Respiratory viruses interfere with bacteriological response to antibiotic in patients with acute otitis media. J Infect Dis 1990;162:546–9.

Chonmaitree T, Owen MJ, Patel JA, et al. Effect of viral respiratory tract infection on outcome of acute otitis media. J Pediatr 1992a;120:856–62.

Chonmaitree T, Owen MJ, Patel JA, et al. Presence of cytomegalovirus and herpes simplex virus in middle ear fluids from children with acute otitis media. Clin Infect Dis 1992b;15:650–3.

Chonmaitree T, Patel JA, Garofalo R, et al. Role of leukotriene B_4 and interleukin-8 in acute bacterial and viral otitis media. Ann Otol Rhinol Laryngol 1996;105:968–74.

Chonmaitree T, Patel JA, Lett-Brown MA, et al. Virus and bacteria enhance histamine production in middle ear fluids of children with acute otitis media. J Infect Dis 1994;169:1265–70.

Chonmaitree T, Saeed K, McCormick et al. Effect of antihistamine and corticosteroid treatment in acute otitis media. Program and abstracts, 8th international symposium on recent advances on otitis media. Fort Lauderdale, FL, June 2003: p. 278, P31.

Clements DA, Langdon L, Bland C, Walter E. Influenza A vaccine decreases the incidence of otitis media in 6- to 30-month-old children in day care. Arch Pediatr Adolesc Med 1995;149:1113–7.

Doyle WJ, Boehm S, Skoner DP. Physiologic responses to intranasal dose-response challenges with histamine, methacholine, bradykinin, and prostaglandin in adult volunteers with and without nasal allergy. J Allergy Clin Immunol 1990;86:924–35.

El Ahmer OR, Raza MW, Ogilvie MM, et al. Binding of bacteria to HEp-2 cells infected with influenza A virus. FEMS Immunol Med Microbiol 1999;23:331–41.

Gentile DA, Doyle WJ, Fireman P, Skoner DP. Effect of experimental influenza A infection on systemic immune and inflammatory parameters in allergic and nonallergic adult subjects. Ann Allergy Asthma Immunol 2001;87:496–500.

Giebink GS, Berzins IK, Marker SC, et al. Experimental otitis media after nasal inoculation of *Streptococcus pneumoniae* and influenza A virus in chinchillas. Infect Immun 1980;30:445–50.

Håkansson A, Kidd A, Wadell G, et al. Adenovirus infection enhances in vitro adherence of *Streptococcus pneumoniae*. Infect Immun 1994;62:2707–14.

Heikkinen T, Ruohola A, Waris M, Ruuskanen O. Respiratory viruses in nasopharyngeal specimens from children with acute otitis media [abstract]. In: Program and abstracts of the 4th Extraordinary International Symposium on Recent Advances in Otitis Media. Sendai, Japan, 2001: p. 176, 133.

Heikkinen T, Ruuskanen O. Temporal development of acute otitis media during upper respiratory tract infection. Pediatr Infect Dis J 1994;13:659–61.

Heikkinen T, Ruuskanen O, Waris M, et al. Influenza vaccination in the prevention of acute otitis media in children. Am J Dis Child 1991;145:445–8.

Heikkinen T, Thint M, Chonmaitree T. Prevalence of various respiratory viruses in the middle ear during acute otitis media. N Engl J Med 1999;340:260–4.

Henderson FW, Collier AM, Sanyal MA, et al. A longitudinal study of respiratory viruses and bacteria in the etiology of acute otitis media with effusion. N Engl J Med 1982;306:1377–83.

Hsia J, Goldstein AL, Simon GL, et al. Peripheral blood mononuclear cell interleukin-2 and interferon-gamma production, cytotoxicity, and antigen-stimulated blastogenesis during experimental rhinovirus infection. J Infect Dis 1990;162:591–7.

Jiang Z, Nagata N, Molina E, et al. Fimbria-mediated enhanced attachment of nontypeable *Haemophilus influenzae* to respiratory syncytial virus-infected respiratory epithelial cells. Infect Immun 1999;67:187–92.

Klein BS, Dollete FR, Yolken RH. The role of respiratory syncytial virus and other viral pathogens in acute otitis media. J Pediatr 1982;101:16–20.

Koivunen P, Kontiokari T, Niemelä M, et al. Time to development of acute otitis media during an upper respiratory tract infection in children. Pediatr Infect Dis J 1999;18:303–5.

McCormick DP, Saeed K, Uchida T, et al. Middle-ear fluid histamine and leukotriene B_4 in acute otitis media: effect of antihistamine or corticosteroid treatment. Int J Pediatr Otorhinolaryngol 2003;67:221–30.

Miyamoto N, Bakaletz LO. Kinetics of the ascension of NTHi from the nasopharynx to the middle ear coincident with adenovirus-induced compromise in the chinchilla. Microb Pathog 1997;23:119–26.

Ohashi Y, Nakai Y, Esaki Y, et al. Influenza A virus-induced otitis media and mucociliary dysfunction in the guinea pig. Acta Otolaryngol Suppl (Stockh) 1991;486:135–48.

Patel J, Faden H, Sharma S, Ogra PL. Effect of respiratory syncytial virus on adherence, colonization and immunity of non-typable *Haemophilus influenzae*: implications for otitis media. Int J Pediatr Otorhinolaryngol 1992;23:15–23.

Patel JA, Sim T, Owen M, et al. Influence of viral infection on middle ear chemokine response in acute bacterial/viral otitis media. In: Lim DJ, Bluestone CD, Casselbrant ML, et al, editors. Proceedings of the Sixth International Symposium on Recent Advances in Otitis Media. Hamilton (ON): BC Decker; 1996. p. 178–9.

Pichichero ME, Pichichero CL. Persistent acute otitis media: I. Causative pathogens. Pediatr Infect Dis J 1995;14:178–83.

Pitkaranta A, Virolainen A, Jero J, et al. Detection of rhinovirus, respiratory syncytial virus, and coronavirus infections in acute otitis media by reverse transcriptase polymerase chain reaction. Pediatrics 1998;102:291–5.

Ruuskanen O, Arola M, Putto-Laurila A, et al. Acute otitis media and respiratory virus infections. Pediatr Infect Dis J 1989;8:94–9.

Ruuskanen O, Ogra PL. Respiratory syncytial virus. Curr Probl Pediatr 1993;23:50–79.

Sanyal MA, Henderson FW, Stempel EC, et al. Effect of upper respiratory tract infection on eustachian tube ventilatory function in the preschool child. J Pediatr 1980;97:11–5.

Sarkkinen HK, Ruuskanen O, Meurman O, et al. Identification of respiratory virus antigens in middle ear fluids of children with acute otitis media. J Infect Dis 1985;151:444–8.

Suzuki K, Bakaletz LO. Synergistic effect of adenovirus type 1 and nontypeable *Haemophilus influenzae* in a chinchilla model of experimental otitis media. Infect Immun 1994;62:1710–8.

Teele DW, Pelton SI, Klein JO. Bacteriology of acute otitis media unresponsive to initial antimicrobial therapy. J Pediatr 1981;98:537–9.

Wadowsky RM, Mietzner SM, Skoner DP, et al. Effect of experimental influenza A virus infection on isolation of *Streptococcus pneumoniae* and other aerobic bacteria from the oropharynges of allergic and nonallergic adult subjects. Infect Immun 1995;63:1153–7.

Whitley RJ, Hayden FG, Reisinger KS, et al. Oral oseltamivir treatment of influenza in children. Pediatr Infect Dis J 2001;20:127–33.

Chapter 14

ACUTE OTITIS MEDIA AND HIV INFECTION

Paola Marchisio, MD, Nicola Principi, MD

Since the beginning of the acquired immune deficiency syndrome (AIDS) epidemic, more than 53 million people worldwide have become infected with the human immunodeficiency virus (HIV) and about 34 million are presently living with HIV-1 (Khoury and Kovacs, 2001). Although about 90% of HIV-infected individuals live in Africa and in South Asia, HIV infection affects thousands of people living in industrialized Western countries. As of December 2001, an estimated 340,000 persons in the United States were living with AIDS, and, of these, about 3,000 were children (Figure 14-1).

Under the definition of HIV-infected children lie different subgroups of subjects, very different from one another in terms of clinical evolution and prognosis and ranging from children born to HIV-infected mothers, who carry maternal anti-HIV antibodies but who are not HIV infected, to children with full-blown AIDS, the most severe end of the clinical spectrum. Vertical transmission is by far the most important mode of acquisition of infection for children, accounting for more than 90% of cases.

Among children, the incidence of AIDS varies between 1 and 3% of the total number of cases in industrialized countries. In the United States, the total number of reported cases of AIDS in children decreased 66% in 1998 compared with 1993 (American Academy of Pediatrics, 2000; Centers for Disease Control and Prevention [CDC], 2002a). The majority of these cases are inner-city black and Hispanic children with perinatally acquired HIV infection. The decrease is greatest in children younger than 5 years of age and most likely reflects the diagnosis and treatment of women during pregnancy and chemoprophylaxis during labor and for the newborn, with a resultant decrease in perinatal transmission, which is now estimated to be only around 4 to 8%.

As in adults, HIV is associated with a gradual decrease in immunity caused by profound T-helper (CD4$^+$) cell depletion and abnormal cellular responses. Various degrees of functional defects of both T and B cells also have been found in children infected with HIV. These abnormalities, together with polyclonal hypergamma-globulinemia, predispose patients to opportunistic and recurrent infections.

One of the important features of pediatric HIV infection is the variable time of appearance of HIV-related symptomatology. Before the era of highly active antiretroviral therapy (HAART) and early treatment initiation, two patterns of disease presentation have been observed in children with perinatally acquired HIV infection. About one-fifth of children infected perinatally develop rapidly progressive disease that usually manifests within the first year of life: opportunistic infections such as *Pneumocystis carinii* pneumonia (PCP), encephalopathy, and failure to thrive are commonly seen in these infants. Early signs of HIV disease paired with precipitous loss of CD4[1] cells usually are associated with less favorable prognosis and shorter survival. Approximately 80% of vertically infected children may be clinically asymptomatic until school age and may experience only gradual progression of their clinical illness and immunosuppression. A small proportion of children do not present until the second decade of life; among them, there are subjects who received blood products in high HIV seroprevalence areas such as sub-Saharan Africa, Southeast Asia, and increasingly India, Eastern Europe, the Caribbean, Latin America, and China. If a child coming from these areas presents with symptoms possibly related to HIV (including recurrent respiratory infections, especially if unresponsive to first-line therapies), he or she should be tested for HIV.

Staging of HIV infection in children is defined according to the CDC classification. The original 1987 CDC classification divided HIV-seropositive children into three categories: P0, for children in whom the diagnosis was still indeterminate; P1, for children who are HIV infected but still clinically asymptomatic; and P2, for children who are HIV infected and have overt HIV-related symptoms. Since then, the early diagnosis of infection in children born to HIV-positive mothers has improved substantially, with the introduction of more sensitive and specific diagnostic techniques of HIV detection in blood. Confirmation that a child is definitively noninfected does not

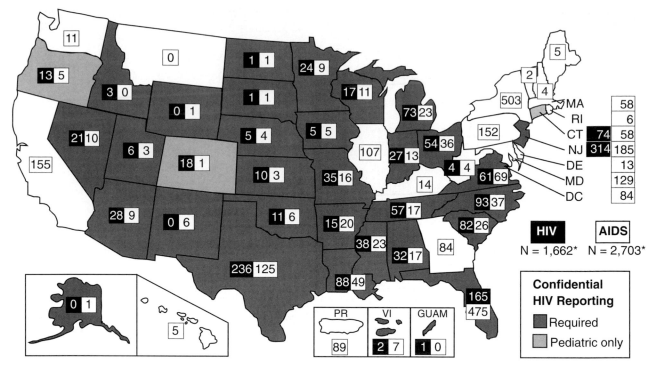

FIGURE 14-1. Children < 13 years of age living with human immunodeficiency virus (HIV) and acquired immune deficiency syndrome (AIDS), reported through 2000.

require any more loss of maternal antibodies, which may take up to 18 months of age, but two negative tests by polymerase chain reaction (PCR) or viral culture after 3 months of age suggest that a child is not infected.

In 1994, the CDC classification system was revised for children younger than 13 years in an effort to adequately detail the clinical and immunologic status of the child's HIV infection (CDC, 1994). This approach stratifies children by the two parameters of clinical status and immune impairment. There are four clinical categories (N, A, B, and C—for asymptomatic, mild, moderate, and severely symptomatic children, respectively) (Table 14-1) and three immunologic categories, which reflect age-dependent immunologic status (no suppression, moderate suppression, and severe suppression (Table 14-2). Although most asymptomatic and mildly symptomatic children range from no suppression to moderate immune suppression, those moderately and severely symptomatic are usually characterized by moderate to severe immune suppression.

As reported in the CDC classification, infectious complications have a major role in the presentation of HIV infection in children. Aside from opportunistic infections, which are common only in the late stages of the disease, when immune suppression is worst, recurrent bacterial and viral childhood infections are common and may be the first sign of HIV disease. Among the various infections that are implicated as significant contributors to the morbidity of HIV-infected children, acute otitis

media (AOM) is one of the most common. This chapter focuses on the epidemiology, pathogenesis, and etiology of AOM in children infected with HIV and provides suggestions for their evaluation and management.

Epidemiology

Several authors have reported that middle ear diseases are more common in children infected with HIV (Barnett et al, 1992; Chen et al, 1996; Gondim et al, 2000; Principi et al, 1991). In particular, a few studies have described the frequency of AOM among children infected with HIV and indicate that AOM is not only common in HIV-infected children but is also very likely to recur.

Barnett and colleagues (1992) retrospectively compared experience with AOM of 28 HIV-infected children with that of 33 children born to HIV-infected mothers but who seroreverted to HIV antibody negative by age 18 months. HIV-infected children had an experience with AOM that was similar to that of seroreverters early in the first year of life, and then they began to show an increased incidence of AOM starting at the end of the first year of life that persisted through the second and third years of life. In detail, the mean number of episodes of AOM during the first year of life was 1.89 in HIV-infected children and 1.33 in seroreverters. The annual rate decreased to 0.13 by the third year of life among seroreverters, whereas the mean number of episodes/year increased to 2.4 in

TABLE 14-1. Clinical Categories of the Pediatric HIV Classification

Category N: asymptomatic

Category A: mildly symptomatic
 At least two of lymphadenopathy, hepatomegaly, splenomegaly, parotitis, dermatitis, recurrent or persistent upper respiratory tract infection, sinusitis, and otitis media

Category B: moderately symptomatic
 Single episode of a severe bacterial infection (meningitis, pneumonia, or sepsis)
 Lymphocytic interstitial pneumonitis
 Anemia, neutropenia, thrombocytopenia
 Cardiomyopathy, nephropathy, hepatitis, diarrhea
 Candidiasis, severe varicella-zoster, or herpes simplex virus

Category C: severely symptomatic (AIDS)
 Two severe bacterial infections
 Encephalopathy (acquired microcephaly, cognitive delay, abnormal neurology)
 Wasting syndrome (severe failure to thrive)
 Opportunistic infections (*Pneumocystis carinii* pneumonia, cytomegalovirus, toxoplasmosis, disseminated mycosis)
 Disseminated mycobacterial disease
 Cancer (Kaposi's sarcoma, lymphoma)

AIDS = acquired immune deficiency syndrome; HIV = human immunodeficiency virus.

the HIV-infected cohort. By age 3 years, all HIV-infected children had experienced at least one episode of AOM and 80% had experienced six or more, whereas 75% of children who seroreverted had experienced one or more episodes and none had had six or more.

In our comparative cohort study (Principi et al, 1991) (Table 14-3), we observed prospectively 27 pairs of children (each pair comprising a HIV-infected child and a closely matched control not infected with HIV) for 543 cumulative months (mean period of observation 19.4 ± 11 months). Data were evaluated considering HIV-infected children both as a whole and by HIV classification status, identified as either asymptomatic (P1) or symptomatic (P2). During the observation period, the number of children who experienced AOM was similar in HIV-infected subjects compared with control subjects, both considering total population and P1 and P2 groups

separately. However, 46 episodes of AOM were diagnosed in 15 HIV patients and 22 episodes in 16 control children; thus, the mean number of episodes per child was significantly higher in HIV-infected children than in normal controls. When P1 and P2 groups were considered separately, HIV-infected children showed a higher average number of episodes of AOM even if the difference versus normal control children did not reach statistical significance. Among the 24 children followed up for at least 6 months, recurrent AOM (three or more episodes) was diagnosed in seven HIV-infected children compared with two control children. The difference is not statistically significant. When the total population was subdivided according to symptomatology, the proportion of children with recurrences was not significantly different in P1 case patients compared with control patients (3/23 versus 2/23) but was significantly higher in P2 children than in paired controls (4/10 versus 0/10).

The tendency to recur was confirmed by Chen and colleagues (1996), who prospectively followed 145 children with HIV infection acquired vertically and 153 seroreverted children: 64 (44%) HIV-infected children had recurrent AOM compared with 13 (8.5%) seroreverters ($p < .001$).

Pathogenesis

Local and systemic immunodeficiency, which is the typical feature of advanced HIV infection, could be considered to account, at least in part, for the predisposition to recurrent and persistent otitis media among children with symptomatic HIV infection.

However, the exact role of immunodeficiency as regards AOM in HIV-infected children has not yet been fully clarified. In fact, the results of the studies regarding otitis media are conflicting. Barnett and colleagues (1992) reported that abnormally low CD4+ lymphocyte counts (< 1,500/mmc) were associated with a significantly greater mean number of episodes of AOM during the first year of life (2.35 versus 1.18). The children with lower CD4+ counts also had a nearly threefold risk of recurrent (three or more episodes) AOM (47% versus 18%) compared with

TABLE 14-2. Centers for Disease Control and Prevention Immunologic Categories Based on Age-Specific CD4+ T-Lymphocyte Counts and Percentage of Total Lymphocytes

Immunologic Category	Age of Child		
	< 12 Mo µL (%)	1–5 Yr µL (%)	6–12 Yr µL (%)
1 No evidence of suppression	≥ 1,500 (≥ 25)	≥1,000 (≥ 25)	≥ 500 (≥ 25)
2 Evidence of moderate suppression	750–1,499 (15–24)	500–999 (15–24)	200–499 (15–24)
3 Severe suppression	< 750 (< 15)	< 500 (< 15)	< 200 (< 15)

Adapted from Centers for Disease Control and Prevention (1994).

TABLE 14-3. Occurrence of Acute Otitis Media in HIV-Infected Children and Paired Normal Controls

Variable	Total HIV-Infected Children	P1	P2
Number of subjects	27 (27)*	24 (24)	12(12)
Number of episodes of AOM	46 (22)	27 (17)	19 (5)
Number of subjects with AOM	15 (16)	11 (13)	6 (4)
Number of subjects with recurrent AOM	7/24 (2/24)	3/23 (2/23)	4/10 (0/10)

Adapted from Principi N et al (1991).
*Data for paired control children are in parentheses.
AOM = acute otitis media; HIV = human immunodeficiency virus.

HIV-infected children with adequate CD4$^+$ cell counts. Chen and colleagues (1996) reported that the frequency of recurrent otitis media increased as the immunologic status of HIV-infected subjects declined. In contrast, we were not able to find any significant association between neutrophil count, CD4$^+$ count, or CD4$^+$-to-CD8$^+$ ratio and the risk of either recurrent AOM, treatment failure, or persistence of middle ear effusion (Principi et al, 1991).

As regards immunoglobulins, most HIV-infected children show hypergammaglobulinemia, but they behave paradoxically as if they were functionally hypogammaglobulinemic. In addition, abnormalities of IgG subclasses, including high concentrations of IgG1 and IgG3 and low concentrations of IgG2 and IgG4, have been described. It is probable that other abnormalities in the protection against infectious agents play a role in modifying the response to antibiotic therapy and in increasing the risk of recurrence. Local production of inflammatory cytokines (interleukin [IL]-1β, IL-6, tumor necrosis factor-α) in nasopharyngeal secretions has been demonstrated to be poor in children with recurrent AOM compared with children not affected by recurrent middle ear diseases (Lindberg et al, 1994).

Clinical Presentation

The clinical presentation of AOM in HIV-infected children does not differ from that encountered in normal children. Spontaneous perforation of the tympanic membrane with purulent drainage is more likely in HIV-infected children than in children not infected with HIV. Shapiro and Novelli (1998), in a cohort of 32 HIV-infected children, noted otorrhea in 14 patients from either tympanic membrane perforation or middle ear granulation tissue.

Middle ear fluid may contain HIV: the virus was identified in four HIV-infected adults with AOM with PCR. In the same ears, bacterial genomic sequences were also present, so the role of HIV as a pathogenic organism for AOM is still not clarified (Liederman et al, 1998). HIV has been isolated from several body fluids, but only blood, semen, cervical secretions, and human milk have been implicated epidemiologically in the transmission of infection (American Academy of Pediatrics, 2000). Therefore, no special precautions in cases of purulent otorrhea should be taken (as for nasal secretions, they can be discarded in routine waste containers). In cases of bloody otorrhea, instruments and specula should be cleaned according to the recommended standard precautions.

Microbiology

In the first years of the AIDS epidemic, little information was available regarding causative organisms for AOM in HIV-infected children. Krasinski and colleagues (1988) recovered *Staphylococcus epidermidis*, pneumococcus,

enterococcus, *Escherichia coli*, and *Pseudomonas aeruginosa* from middle ear aspirates from four episodes of otitis media in three patients. Our group performed two studies on this subject. In the first one (Principi et al, 1991), we observed that the bacterial etiology of AOM in a small group of HIV-infected children was similar to that encountered in children not exposed to HIV: by tympanocentesis performed in 17 of 19 episodes of AOM diagnosed in children with signs and/or symptoms of HIV infection, middle ear fluid yielded *Streptococcus pneumoniae* (six cases, 33.5%), *Haemophilus influenzae* nontypable (two cases, 11.7%), *Streptococcus pyogenes* (two cases, 11.7%), *Proteus mirabilis* (two cases, 11.7%), and *E. coli* (one case, 5.9%); in four cases, no growth was demonstrated. In the second study (Marchisio et al, 1996), which involved a larger group of HIV-infected children analyzed according to the severity of their immunosuppression, similar results were achieved. The microbiology of 60 episodes of AOM diagnosed in 21 symptomatic HIV-infected children (ages 9 months to 12 years) was compared with that of 121 episodes of AOM occurring in 113 immunocompetent HIV-negative children (ages 6 months to 12 years) in the period from 1990 to 1995. The prevalence of the three most common pathogens (*S. pneumoniae*, *H. influenzae*, and group A β-hemolytic streptococcus) was similar in HIV-infected and normal children (Table 14-4). *Staphylococcus aureus* was significantly more frequent in AOM diagnosed in severely immunosuppressed stages (Table 14-5). A significantly lower proportion of middle ear effusions obtained in HIV-infected children yielded no bacteria compared with normal children: this finding could be the result of the local immune dysfunction probably present in HIV-infected children and of the consequent higher nasopharyngeal colonization rate of both *S. pneumoniae* and *S. aureus* (Cruciani et al, 1993).

Resistant bacteria were as common in HIV-infected children as in normal children. In our study, β-lactamase production among isolates of *H. influenzae* was a rare phenomenon both in HIV-infected and normal children, and no penicillin-resistant *S. pneumoniae* was found. These observations agreed with the results derived from microbiologic surveys conducted in Italy in the early 1990s, which showed a lower prevalence of resistant bacteria than in other European countries.

No specific data are available on the actual prevalence of resistant strains in HIV-infected children with AOM. However, it is conceivable that as resistance has rapidly become a major problem among pathogens causing AOM in normal, immunocompetent children, the same phenomenon would be found among pathogenic organisms of HIV-infected children.

Reports of middle and external ear canal infections associated with unusual or opportunistic pathogens in adults with HIV infection include cases of otomastoiditis caused by *Aspergillus fumigatus* (Strauss and Fine, 1991)

TABLE 14-4. Pathogens Isolated in Acute Otitis Media in HIV-Infected Children and Healthy Controls

Bacteria	HIV-Infected Children (AOM n = 60) (%)	Normal Children (AOM n = 121) (%)
Streptococcus pneumoniae	14 (23.3)	16 (13.3)
Haemophilus influenzae	14 (23.3)	34 (28.3)
Group A streptococcus	11 (18.3)	16 (13.3)
Staphylococcus aureus	6 (10.0)	3 (2.5)
Enteric bacilli	8 (13.3)	9 (7.5)
Pseudomonas aeruginosa	3 (5.0)	2 (1.7)
Moraxella catarrhalis	1 (1.7)	1 (0.8)
No growth	9 (15.0)	40 (33.3)*

Adapted from Marchisio P et al (1996).
*Difference between no growth in HIV-infected children versus normal children, *p* = .016.
AOM = acute otitis media; HIV = human immunodeficiency virus.

and otitis media caused by *Nocardia asteroides* (Forrett-Kamisky et al, 1991) or *Pneumocystis carinii* (Smith et al, 1988). *P. carinii* has not been reported to cause ear infections in children infected with HIV.

Outcome

The outcome of AOM after a 10-day amoxicillin treatment was studied in a group of HIV-infected children in comparison with paired healthy controls (Barnett et al, 1992). The cure rate of AOM was similar in HIV-infected but asymptomatic children (24/27, 88.9%) compared with control healthy children (15/17, 88.2%) but was substantially and significantly reduced in HIV-infected symptomatic children (10/19, 52.6%). The reason for the high rate of failure of amoxicillin treatment of AOM was not clear; no resistant bacteria were isolated by tympanocentesis. Eight of the 10 children were then successfully treated with amoxicillin-clavulanic acid, whereas 2 patients developed chronic purulent middle ear drainage resistant to any form of treatment. It is possible that the impairment in local immunity may play a role in determining failures in immunosuppressed HIV-infected children. It is well known that when immune response is abnormal, the in vivo efficacy of in vitro active antibiotics is reduced and the sterilization of the site of infection is enormously slowed or even impossible to reach.

Persistence of OME after an episode of AOM is much higher in children with symptomatic HIV infection compared with normal controls and children who are HIV infected but still asymptomatic. Persistence of middle ear effusion for weeks to months after the onset of AOM is frequent among normal children, but after 3 months, only about 10% of children still have effusion. On the contrary, chronic OME (lasting ≥ 12 weeks) was observed in about 30% of asymptomatic HIV-infected children and in about 100% of symptomatic HIV-infected children (Principi et al, 1991).

In the cohort of Shapiro and Novelli (1998), a total of 6 (moderately to severely immunocompromised) of 32 HIV-infected children with a history of otitis media developed systemic complications, secondary to middle ear pathology despite treatment with oral antibiotic therapy (Table 14-6); bacteremia and recalcitrant otorrhea requiring intravenous antibiotic therapy were the most common. In total, 14 of the 32 patients were noted to have otorrhea from either tympanic membrane perforation, the presence of a tympanostomy tube, or middle ear granulation tissue.

Treatment

Given the observations that children with AOM who have HIV infection are at significantly increased risk of recurrences of AOM, treatment failures, and prolonged middle ear effusion, antibiotic therapy should be regarded as the first step in the management of AOM in every child known to be HIV infected.

As the microbiology of AOM on HIV-infected children is similar to that associated with AOM in normal children, related to both the prevalence and the susceptibility pattern, the selection of empiric therapy should follow the same recommendations given for immunocompetent children of the same geographic area (Marchisio et al, 1996). In general, amoxicillin should still be regarded as first-line therapy.

Only in severely immunosuppressed children does the role of *S. aureus* suggest the use of an antibiotic with a spectrum extended to this pathogen whenever first-choice drugs fail. Tympanocentesis should not be regarded as a universal first-line procedure for HIV-infected children but should be indicated only in patients who fail to respond to first-choice antibiotics.

Even if specific studies are lacking, the duration of antibiotic therapy of AOM should follow the same recommendations for immunocompetent children when

TABLE 14-5. Pathogens Isolated in Acute Otitis Media in HIV-Infected Children According to Immunologic Categories

Bacteria	Category 1 (AOM n = 19) (%)	Category 2 (AOM n = 19) (%)	Category 3 (AOM n = 22) (%)
Streptococcus pneumoniae	4 (21.0)	3 (15.8)	7 (31.8)
Haemophilus influenzae	4 (21.0)	4 (21.0)	6 (27.3)
Group A streptococcus	3 (15.8)	2 (10.5)	6 (27.3)
Staphylococcus aureus	1 (5.2)	2 (10.5)	3 (13.6)
Enteric bacilli	4 (21.0)	4 (21.0)	0
Pseudomonas aeruginosa	1 (5.2)	0	2 (9.1)
Moraxella catarrhalis	0	0	1 (4.5)
No growth	4 (21.0)	5 (26.3)	0

Adapted from Marchisio P et al (1996).
AOM = acute otitis media; HIV = human immunodeficiency virus.

TABLE 14-6. Complications of Otitis Media in HIV-Infected Children

Age (yr)	Gender	HIV Category	Complication/Treatment
2	Male	B2	Bacteremia (*Streptococcus viridans*)/intravenous antibiotics
3	Male	B3	Fever/acute otitis media/intravenous antibiotics
3	Male	B3	Fever/otorrhea/intravenous antibiotics
3	Female	A2	Bacteremia (*Streptococcus pneumoniae*)/intravenous antibiotics
2	Male	C1	Recalcitrant otorrhea (*Pseudomonas aeruginosa*, *Enterobacter cloacae*, *Acinetobacter*)/intravenous antibiotics
11	Female	B3	Fever/acute otitis media/intravenous antibiotics

Adapted from Shapiro NL and Novelli V (1998).
HIV = human immunodeficiency virus.

HIV-infected children who are still asymptomatic or mildly symptomatic are concerned. On the contrary, it seems reasonable to extend the duration of therapy for approximately 2 to 3 weeks (or for at least 1 week beyond the complete resolution of symptoms) in children who have symptomatic HIV infection.

The indications for and effect of myringotomy and ventilation tubes are probably the same as for immunologically competent children, although there have been no trials to confirm this (Hadfield et al, 1996).

Prevention

Immunoprophylaxis

Because *S. pneumoniae* and *H. influenzae* are common in the community, no effective way exists to reduce exposure to these bacteria. This is also true for HIV-infected children, who are actually allowed to attend day care and schools without any particular restriction. In August 2000, the American Academy of Pediatrics (2000) issued new recommendations for use of the heptavalent pneumococcal vaccine in high-risk populations, which include children with HIV infection. The vaccination schedule is age specific and requires a four-dose regimen for children younger than 24 months, whereas for older children (between ages 24 and 59 months), only two doses are suggested. In addition, all HIV-infected children aged < 5 years should be administered the Hib vaccine and a yearly influenza vaccine.

Regarding passive immunoprophylaxis, intravenous immunoglobulins at a dose of 400 mg/kg given once a month appear to be safe and associated with a measurable reduction in serious and minor bacterial infections in HIV-infected children with mild immunodeficiency and in those not receiving trimethoprim-sulfamethoxazole (TMP-SMX) for prophylaxis of PCP. In the first years of the epidemic, the National Institutes of Health demonstrated that in children with entry CD4+ counts of at least 200/mmc, intravenous immunoglobulin was associated with a 36% decrease in the rate of ear infections per 100 patients/years (Mofenson et al, 1992). Actually, the CDC (2002) suggests the use of intravenous immunoglobulins to prevent serious bacterial infections only in HIV-infected children who have hypogammaglobulinemia (IgG < 400 mg/dL).

Antibiotic Prophylaxis

According to the CDC (2002), clinicians can administer antibiotic chemoprophylaxis to HIV-infected subjects who have "frequent recurrences of serious bacterial respiratory infections." Zuccotti and colleagues (2001) have studied the efficacy of a 6-month course of low-dose cefaclor (20 mg/kg once daily) in the prevention of recurrent AOM in 17 HIV-infected children. Cefaclor administration was associated with a reduction of the number of episodes of AOM: 12 of 17 children experienced no episodes, and 5 children had only one episode. The benefit of prophylaxis was long-lasting as during the 6 months after prophylaxis, nine children had no episodes, seven had only one episode, and one child had two. TMP-SMZ (administered for PCP prophylaxis) and clarithromycin or azithromycin (administered for *Mycobacterium avium* complex [MAC] prophylaxis) are also appropriate as chemoprophylaxis for recurrent AOM if drug-sensitive organisms are likely to be involved. Actually, given the emergence and spread of macrolide resistance among isolates of *S. pneumoniae*, chemoprophylaxis with macrolide should be considered with great caution.

Conclusion

With the improvement of the immune function of many HIV-positive children receiving HAART, the quality of life of children infected with HIV has changed dramatically. Rapid diagnosis of HIV infection is largely available, and this gives the opportunity for early initiation of potent therapy. Efficient suppression of viral replication and maintenance of normal immune function are now achievable for many children infected with HIV. Even before the introduction of HAART, mortality rates from HIV were decreasing, probably because of increased use of prophylaxis to reduce opportunistic infections. HAART has led to further reductions in disease progression and mortality in Europe and North America. It is conceivable that otitis media and its complications will also have a less important role in HIV-infected children if adequately treated. It is likely that in the near future, pediatric HIV disease will no longer be considered a rapidly fatal illness but a chronic one with a long period of relative well-being. But HIV infection has not disappeared. It is estimated that 2.7 million children are living with HIV, of whom only 1% live in Europe and the United States. In many sub-Saharan countries, for one-third to half of all children under 5 years, mortality is now a result of AIDS. Even in developed countries, including the United States, HIV affects disproportionately those subgroups who have limited access to medical and preventive services because of poverty and social disadvantage: more recently, the majority of new HIV infections were diagnosed in non-Hispanic blacks and a substantial number were reported in Hispanics, whereas persons with AIDS at the time of initial HIV diagnosis were more likely to be Asians/Pacific Islanders (CDC, 2002). Especially in these subgroups, HIV infection should still be considered in the differential diagnosis of a wide range of otolaryngologic pediatric conditions, including recurrent, unresponsive, and/or persistent rhinosinusitis and otitis media. Should HIV infection be diagnosed, it should be managed by pediatric multidisciplinary teams.

References

American Academy of Pediatrics. Policy statement: recommendations for the prevention of pneumococcal infections, including the use of pneumococcal conjugate vaccine (Prevnar), pneumococcal polysaccharide vaccine, and antibiotic prophylaxis. Pediatrics 2000;106:362–6.

American Academy of Pediatrics. Human immunodeficiency virus infection. In: Pickring LK, editor. 2000 Red Book: report of the Committee on Infectious Diseases. 25th ed. Elk Grove Village (IL): American Academy of Pediatrics; 2000. p. 325–50.

Barnett ED, Klein JO, Pelton SI, Luginbuhl LM. Otitis media in children born to human immunodeficiency virus-infected mothers. Pediatr Infect Dis J 1992;11:360–4.

Centers for Disease Control and Prevention. 1994 Revised classification system for human immunodeficiency virus infection in children less than 13 years of age. MMWR Morb Mortal Wkly Rep 1994;43:1–19.

Centers for Disease Control and Prevention. Diagnosis and reporting of HIV and AIDS in States with HIV/AIDS surveillance—United States, 1994–2000. MMWR Morb Mortal Wkly Rep 2002a;51:595–8.

Centers for Disease Control and Prevention. Update: AIDS—United States, 2000. MMWR Morb Mortal Wkly Rep 2002b;51:592–5.

Centers for Disease Control and Prevention. 2002 USPHS/IDSA guidelines for the prevention of opportunistic infections among HIV-infected persons. MMWR Morb Mortal Wkly Rep 2002c;51:1–52.

Chen AY, Ohlms LA, Stewart MG, Kline MW. Otolaryngologic disease progression in children with human immunodeficiency virus infection. Arch Otolaryngol Head Neck Surg 1996;122:1360–3.

Cruciani M, Luzzati R, Fioredda F, et al. Mucosal colonization by pyogenic bacteria among children with HIV infection. AIDS 1993;7:1533–4.

Forrett-Kamisky MC, Sherer C, Berner M, et al. Otite moyenne à Nocardia asteroides au cours du SIDA. Presse Med 1991;20:1512–3.

Gondim LA, Zonta RF, Fortkamp E, Schmeling RO. Otorhinolaryngological manifestations in children with human immunodeficiency virus infection. Int J Pediatr Otorhinolaryngol 2000;54:97–102.

Hadfield PJ, Birchall MA, Novelli V, Bailey CM. The ENT manifestations of HIV infection in children. Clin Otolaryngol 1996;21:30–6.

Khoury M, Kovacs A. Pediatric HIV infection. Clin Obstet Gynecol 2001;44:243–75.

Krasinski K, Borkowsky W, Bonk S, et al. Bacterial infections in human immunodeficiency virus-infected children. Pediatr Infect Dis J 1988;7:323–8.

Liederman EM, Post JC, Aul JJ, et al. Analysis of adult otitis media: polymerase chain reaction versus culture for bacteria and viruses. Ann Otol Rhinol Laryngol 1998;107:10–6.

Lindberg K, Rynnel-Dagöö B, Sundquist KG. Cytokines in nasopharyngeal secretions: evidence for defective IL-1 beta production in children with recurrent episodes of acute otitis media. Clin Exp Immunol 1994;97:396–402.

Marchisio P, Principi N, Sorella S, et al. Etiology of acute otitis media in human immunodeficiency virus-infected children. Pediatr Infect Dis J 1996;15:58–61.

Mofenson LM, Moye J, Bethel J, et al. Prophylactic intravenous immunoglobulin in HIV-infected children with CD4+ counts of 0.20×10^9/L or more. JAMA 1992;268:483–8.

Principi N, Marchisio P, Tornaghi R, et al. Acute otitis media in human immunodeficiency virus infected children. Pediatrics 1991;88:566–71.

Shapiro NL, Novelli V. Otitis media in children with vertically-acquired HIV infection: the Great Ormond Street Hospital Experience. Int J Pediatr Otorhinolaryngol 1998;45:69–75.

Smith M, Hirrschfield L, Zahtz G, Siegal F. Pneumocystis carinii otitis media. Am J Med 1988;85:745–6.

Strauss M, Fine E. Aspergillus otomastoiditis in acquired immunodeficiency syndrome. Am J Otol 1991;12:49–53.

Zuccotti GV, D'Auria E, Torcoletti M, et al. Clinical and pro-host effects of cefaclor in prophylaxis of recurrent otitis media in HIV-infected children. J Intern Med Res 2001;29:349–54.

Chapter 15

Acute Otitis Media in Children with Penicillin/Antibiotic Allergy

Thanai Pongdee, MD, James T.-C. Li, MD, PhD

Acute otitis media (AOM) is the leading cause of pediatric office visits in the United States, accounting for almost 30 million physician visits yearly among children younger than 12 months of age. Almost two-thirds of all children have at least one episode and approximately one-third have three or more episodes of AOM per year. Complications of AOM, occurring in fewer than 1% of patients, include mastoiditis, bacterial meningitis, cerebral abscess, and bacteremia (Blumer, 1999).

The Centers for Disease Control and Prevention (CDC) and the American Academy of Pediatrics released a consensus statement supporting the use of antimicrobial therapy for the treatment of AOM (Dowell et al, 1998). A second consensus statement from the Drug-resistant *Streptococcus pneumoniae* Therapeutic Working Group of the CDC concluded that amoxicillin should be the first-line antibiotic for treating AOM. Second-line therapies consisted mainly of other β-lactam antibiotics (Dowell et al, 1999). Neither consensus statement addressed the management of the child with AOM who is allergic to penicillins or other β-lactam antibiotics. Simply withholding indicated penicillin therapy in these children may result in several adverse clinical consequences such as treatment failures, increased toxicity of alternative agents, and increased costs (Salkind et al, 2001). A proper understanding of the evaluation and management of these children with penicillin allergy is essential to select the optimal course of therapy.

Definitions

Adverse drug reactions refer to any undesirable response caused by therapeutic doses of a drug (Anderson, 1992). An allergic or hypersensitivity reaction to a drug is defined as an adverse reaction mediated by immunologic mechanisms. Although allergic reactions account for only 5 to 10% of all adverse drug reactions, they represent the most serious, with 1 in 10,000 resulting in death (Boguniewicz and Leung, 1995). Antibiotics as a group constitute the most frequent cause of allergic drug reactions (Boguniewicz and Leung, 1995). Overall, penicillin represents the most common cause of allergic drug reactions and anaphylaxis (deShazo and Kemp, 1997).

Prevalence

The prevalence of penicillin allergy in the general population has been estimated to be 2%. The reported incidence varies widely from 1 to 10%, depending on factors such as the history of exposure, route of administration, duration of treatment, elapsed time between the reaction and diagnostic testing or re-exposure, and nature of the initial reaction (deShazo and Kemp, 1997). Anaphylactic reactions to penicillin occur in 0.01 to 0.05% of treatment courses. The incidence of death from penicillin anaphylaxis has been estimated to be 1 death per 50,000 to 100,000 treatment courses, which translates to 400 to 800 deaths annually in the United States. Anaphylactic reactions from penicillin are fatal approximately 10% of the time (Boguniewicz and Leung, 1995).

Risk Factors for Allergic Reactions

Age

Acute allergic reactions to penicillin occur more frequently in those individuals between the ages of 20 and 49 years. Although penicillin reactions occur less frequently in elderly individuals, the risk of fatality from penicillin-induced anaphylaxis is higher, probably owing to age and/or disease-associated compromised cardiopulmonary function. Children have been shown to have faster declines in antipenicillin IgE antibody titers, which may explain their lower risk of allergic drug reactions when compared with adults (Boguniewicz and Leung, 1995).

History of Previous Penicillin-Allergic Reaction

Patients with a history of anaphylaxis and urticaria have higher reaction rates than those with a vague or unknown history of penicillin reactions. Individuals with a prior penicillin reaction have a four- to sixfold increased risk of subsequent reactions to penicillin compared with those without a previous history of reactions (Weiss and Adkinson, 1988). However, the more remote the occurrence of a penicillin-allergic reaction, the lower the risk for anaphylaxis with readministration (deShazo and Kemp, 1997).

History of Atopy or Other Allergy

An atopic background does not predispose individuals to penicillin allergy. However, sensitized atopic individuals may have increased risk for severe anaphylactic reactions if IgE antibodies are produced (Weizz and Adkinson, 1988).

Route and Dose of Administration

Orally administered penicillin produces fewer allergic reactions than parenteral administration of penicillin (Weiss and Adkinson, 1988). The parenteral route is less immunogenic than subcutaneous or intramuscular routes (Kishiyama and Adelman, 1994). Frequent inter-mittent courses of therapy are more likely to result in drug sensitization than prolonged treatment without drug-free intervals (Anderson, 1992).

Concomitant β-Blocker Therapy

An increased risk and severity of allergic penicillin reactions have been linked to the concomitant use of β-blocker drugs (Anderson, 1992).

Drug Metabolism

Allergic reactions result from the interaction between penicillin metabolites and components of the immune system. Owing to its small molecular size, penicillin must first form covalent conjugates with macromolecular host proteins to elicit an immune response. These conjugates form multivalent immunogenic complexes, which act as antigens (Figure 15-1). The penicilloyl antigenic group is the most abundant metabolite and is therefore called the "major determinant." Other metabolites such as penicilloate and penilloate constitute a small portion of antigenic moieties and are thus called "minor determinants." Both major and minor determinants can elicit drug-specific immune responses that ultimately give rise to the clinical manifestations of allergic reactions to penicillin (Boguniewicz and Leung, 1995).

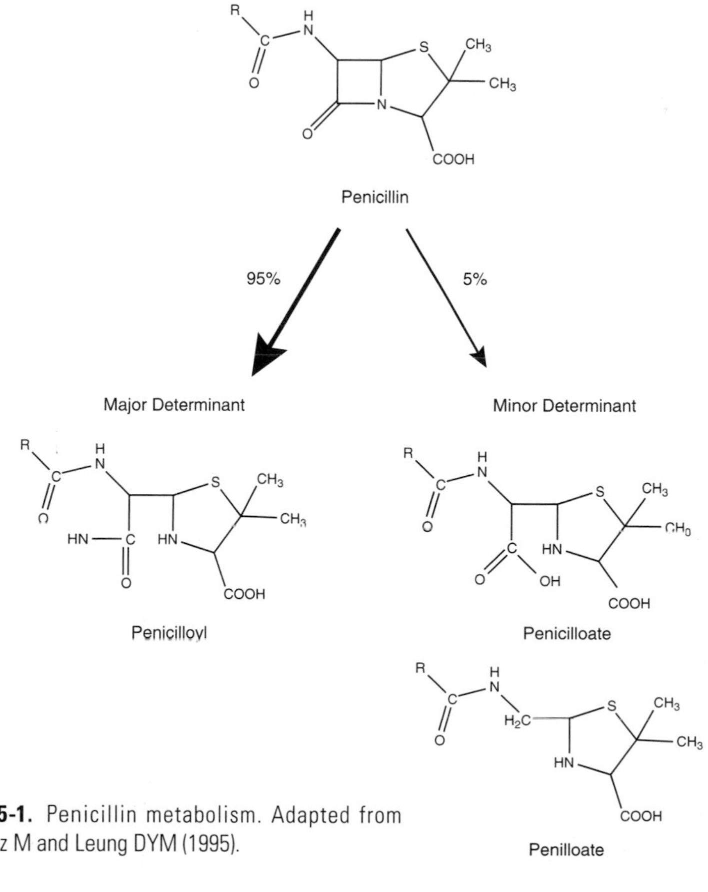

FIGURE 15-1. Penicillin metabolism. Adapted from Boguniewicz M and Leung DYM (1995).

Types of Reactions

Allergic reactions to penicillin have been categorized by two different classification systems (Table 15-1). The Gell and Coombs classification system for immunologic reactions organizes allergic reactions into four categories by their immune mechanism and clinical syndrome (Coombs and Gell, 1975). These four categories include immediate hypersensitivity reactions (type I), cytotoxic antibody reactions (type II), immune complex reactions (type III), and delayed-type hypersensitivity reactions (type IV). Levine (1966) classified adverse reactions to penicillin by their time of onset. Immediate reactions begin within the first hour after penicillin administration. Accelerated penicillin reactions occur from 1 to 72 hours after drug use. Late reactions do not appear until after 72 hours from penicillin administration. Immediate and accelerated reactions typify type I reactions. Late reactions encompass type II, III, and IV reactions (Weiss and Adkinson, 1988). Understanding the different classifications of penicillin-allergic reactions immensely aids the evaluation of individuals with potential penicillin allergy.

Type I, or immediate hypersensitivity, reactions occur when penicillin-antigenic metabolites cross-link the penicillin-specific IgE antibodies bound to tissue mast cells and/or circulating basophils, leading to cell activation, degranulation, and mediator release. These released mediators include histamine, prostaglandins, leukotrienes, platelet-activating factor, proteases, and eosinophil and neutrophil chemotactic factors (Gruchalla, 1998). The most serious clinical manifestation is anaphylaxis with a significant risk of death. Other signs and symptoms of IgE-mediated allergic reactions include urticaria, pruritus, angioedema, bronchospasm, cutaneous flushing, nausea, vomiting, diarrhea, sneezing, and nasal congestion (Boguniewicz and Leung, 1995).

Cytotoxic antibody (type II) reactions occur when penicillin determinants become chemically bound to circulating blood cells, leading to their accelerated destruction via IgG or IgM antibodies and complement. This reaction clinically results in hemolytic anemia or thrombocytopenia (Weiss and Adkinson, 1988).

Immune complex (type III) reactions occur when penicillin-specific IgG or IgM antibodies form circulating immune complexes with penicillin antigens. These circulating immune complexes deposit in basement membranes, resulting in complement activation and subsequent tissue injury. The classic clinical manifestation is serum sickness characterized by fever, rash, lymphadenopathy, arthralgias, nephritis, hepatitis, and vasculitis (Gruchalla, 1998).

Delayed-type hypersensitivity (type IV) reactions are caused by activated T lymphocytes that recognize penicillin antigens. These reactions are usually manifested in the skin, with allergic contact dermatitis being the most common (Gruchalla, 1998).

A number of allergic drug reactions are difficult to classify according to the Gell and Coombs system because the exact immunologic mechanisms for these reactions are unknown. These reactions include maculopapular eruptions, Stevens-Johnson syndrome, and exfoliative dermatitis (Weiss and Adkinson, 1988).

Diagnostic Evaluation

Penicillin Skin Testing

Penicillin skin testing is a well-established, generally accepted method to evaluate for IgE-mediated sensitivity to penicillin. The penicillin testing reagents should include both major and minor determinants (Lin, 1992). The preparation of test reagents and technique of penicillin skin testing have been well described previously (Van Dellen et al, 1971); thus, a detailed description will not be discussed here. Skin testing with penicillin polylysine (major determinant) alone has a sensitivity rate of 76%. Sensitivity rates climb to 97 to 99% when both penicillin polylysine and either freshly prepared penicillin G potassium or freshly prepared minor determinant mixtures are used for penicillin skin testing. Thus, patients at risk for anaphylaxis can be missed if minor determinant mixtures are not used (Boguniewicz and Leung, 1995). The risk of conversion from a negative to a positive skin test following the testing procedure is negligible (Anderson, 1992).

Skin testing is safe when performed by sequential scratch or puncture followed by intradermal testing if the scratch or puncture tests are negative. Systemic reaction rates to penicillin skin testing range from 0.12 to 0.5%. In those who are skin test positive, systemic reaction rates

TABLE 15-1. Classification of Penicillin Reactions*

Classification	Time of Onset (h)	Mediator(s)	Clinical Manifestations
Immediate reaction	< 1 after exposure		
Type I		Penicillin-specific IgE antibodies	Anaphylaxis and/or urticaria, bronchospasm, angioedema, pruritus
Late reactions	> 72 after exposure		
Type II		IgG, IgM, complement	Hemolytic anemia, thrombocytopenia
Type III		IgG, IgM immune complexes	Serum sickness, tissue injury
Type IV		Sensitized T lymphocytes	Contact dermatitis
Other (idiopathic)	Usually > 72 after exposure		Stevens-Johnson syndrome, toxic epidermal necrolysis

*Adapted from Salkind A et al (2001).

are 2.3% or less. When systemic IgE-mediated reactions do occur, they are typically mild and promptly respond to treatment. Fatalities from penicillin skin testing are extremely rare (Valyasevi and Van Dellen, 2000).

Skin testing proves valuable for establishing penicillin sensitivity status in individuals with positive or unknown histories of penicillin allergy (Boguniewicz and Leung, 1995). In patients with no history of penicillin allergy, skin tests are positive in 2 to 7% (mean 6%) of patients. In patients with no history of allergy but with positive skin test results, 1 to 10% will experience an acute allergic reaction when given penicillin (deShazo and Kemp, 1997). Previous studies have shown that the administration of penicillin in patients with positive histories but negative skin tests to both major and minor determinants resulted in an overall reaction rate of 4.5%, which is similar to rates in the general population. The most common reactions observed were urticaria or other mild allergic reactions (Lin, 1992). Penicillin anaphylaxis has not been reported in individuals who have negative skin tests to both major and minor determinants (Weiss and Adkinson, 1988). On the other hand, penicillin is contraindicated in patients who have both a positive history and a positive skin test for penicillin because the chance for an immediate reaction if penicillin is given again is 50 to 70% (deShazo and Kemp, 1997). Thus, skin testing is an effective method to identify patients in whom penicillin can or cannot be administered safely.

In Vitro Testing

Radioallergosorbent tests (RASTs) are available for detection of specific IgE antibodies to penicillin determinants. However, these assays are much less sensitive, more time-consuming, and more expensive than penicillin skin testing. RAST should be reserved for patients who cannot undergo skin testing (Boguniewicz and Leung, 1995). When used in these circumstances, penicillin RAST results should be interpreted cautiously as their significance is still under investigation. Positive in vitro tests may suggest a diagnosis of penicillin allergy, but negative tests are not reliable for excluding penicillin hypersensitivity (Disease Management of Drug Hypersensitivity, 1999).

Cross-Reactivities with Penicillin

All β lactam antibiotics (penicillins, cephalosporins, monobactams, carbapenems, and carbacephems) share a common chemical structure, consisting of a four-member β-lactam ring that, except for monobactams, is fused to a second five- or six-member ring (Figure 15-2). Various side chains are attached to the β-lactam ring. Some cephalosporins, carbapenems, and carbacephems possess a side chain attached to the second ring (deShazo and Kemp, 1997). Cross-reactivity between penicillin and other β-lactam antibiotics exists because of their related bicyclic core structure (Boguniewicz and Leung, 1995).

Semisynthetic Penicillins

Most individuals allergic to penicillin will also be allergic to semisynthetic penicillins (such as ampicillin, amoxicillin, nafcillin, or oxacillin) because of the shared β-lactam ring (deShazo and Kemp, 1997). Nevertheless, patients who have reacted to semisynthetic penicillins and not to penicillin have been reported (Vega et al, 1994). This unique sensitivity is presumably attributable to specific IgE antibodies for the particular side chains that differentiate these antibiotics from penicillin. Therefore, these individuals may not be identified by penicillin skin testing (deShazo and Kemp, 1997). The incidence of side chain–specific hypersensitivity has yet to be determined (Lin, 1992). Two specific types of rashes do not represent IgE-mediated reactions and do not place an individual at increased risk for a life-threatening reaction to penicillin. First, ampicillin and amoxicillin are associated with the development of a maculopapular rash in 5 to 10% of patients. Second, if patients with Epstein-Barr infections are given ampicillin or amoxicillin, almost 100% will develop a nonpruritic rash (Disease Management of Drug Hypersensitivity, 1999).

Cephalosporins

Allergic reactions to cephalosporins occur at a low incidence, an overall rate of about 1%. The cross-reactivity between penicillins and cephalosporins remains unclear largely owing to the fact that the specific haptens involved in cephalosporin hypersensitivity have not been identified. Retrospective studies report a four- to eightfold increased risk of allergic reactions to cephalosporins in patients with a history of penicillin allergy compared with those without such a history (Kelkar and Li, 2001). Immunologic cross-reactivity between penicillin and cephalosporins is greatest for first-generation cephalosporins and least for third-generation cephalosporins (deShazo and Kemp, 1997). In patients with a history of penicillin allergy who are not skin tested but are given a second- or third-generation cephalosporin directly, the chance for an allergic reaction is likely less than 1% (Anne and Reisman, 1995). Reactions to cephalosporins overall occur in approximately 3 to 7% of patients with a positive history of penicillin allergy (Saxon et al, 1987). Fewer than 2% of patients with a history of penicillin allergy but negative skin tests have reactions to cephalosporins (Shepherd, 1991). Thus, penicillin skin testing may be useful in those with a history of penicillin allergy who require cephalosporin therapy. Patients with a history of penicillin allergy but negative skin tests are not at increased risk for allergy to cephalosporins (Kelkar and Li, 2001).

The package inserts for cephalosporin antibiotics all state the following:

> Before therapy with [the cephalosporin] is instituted, careful inquiry should be made to determine whether the

patient has had previous hypersensitivity reactions to the [cephalosporin], other cephalosporins, penicillins, or other drugs. If this product is to be given to penicillin-sensitive patients, caution should be exercised because cross-sensitivity among beta-lactam antibiotics has been clearly documented and may occur in up to 10 percent of patients with a history of penicillin allergy.

Monobactams

Aztreonam is the prototypical monobactam antibiotic, which has a monocyclic ring structure rather than the bicyclic structure of other β-lactam antibiotics. Antibodies specific for aztreonam are mainly side chain specific (Boguniewicz and Leung, 1995). Minimal cross-reactivity occurs between aztreonam and other β-lactam antibiotics (deShazo and Kemp, 1997).

Carbapenems

Cross-reactivity is high between penicillin and carbapenems, of which imipenem is prototypical. Imipenem metabolism results in determinants analogous to penicillin major and minor determinants. These similar determinants, which are highly cross-reactive, suggest that imipenem should be contraindicated in patients with positive penicillin skin tests (Boguniewicz and Leung, 1995).

Carbacephems

Loracarbef represents the carbacephem class of β-lactam antibiotics. The degree of cross-reactivity between loracarbef and the penicillins or cephalosporins is unknown (Kishiyama and Adelman, 1994).

Approach to Penicillin Allergy in Children with Acute Otitis Media

Previous studies report that 80 to 90% of patients who report a penicillin allergy are not truly allergic to the drug when properly evaluated and tested (Salkind et al, 2001). The most salient factor in the diagnosis of an allergic drug reaction is the patient's history. The following important historical information should be obtained (Gruchalla, 1998):

- Determine the patient's age at the time of the reaction.
- Determine when penicillin therapy was initiated and establish a temporal relationship between the initiation of therapy and the onset of symptoms.
- Determine the characteristics of the reaction.
- Distinguish between maculopapular skin eruptions and urticaria as only the latter is likely to be IgE mediated.
- Determine if any mucous membranes were involved as the presence of this finding suggests the possibility of

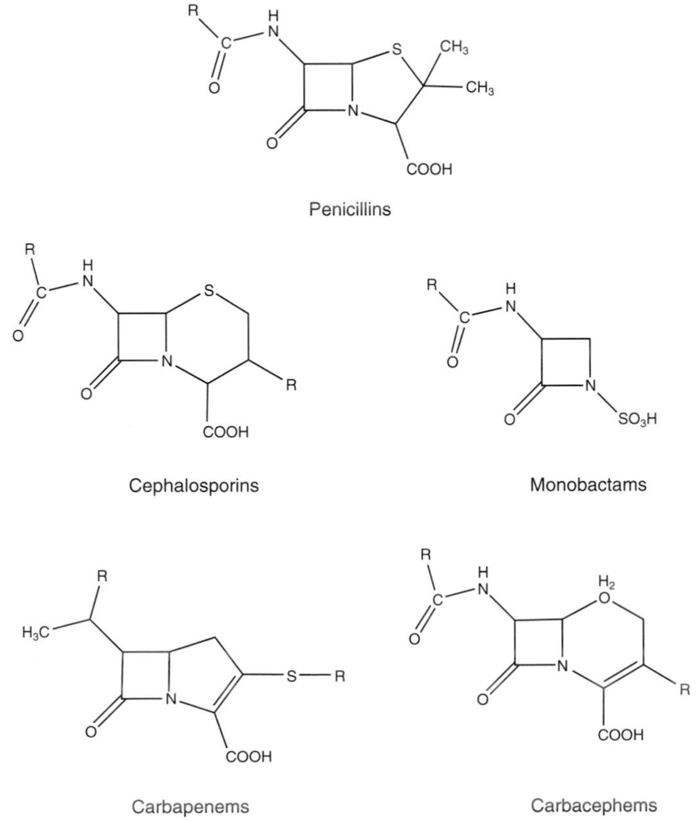

FIGURE 15-2. General structures of β-lactam antibiotics.

potentially life-threatening reactions such as Stevens-Johnson syndrome and toxic epidermal necrolysis.

- Determine the route of administration.
- Determine the reasons for which penicillin was being taken.
- Determine other medications the patient was taking and their temporal relationship to penicillin use.
- Determine what happened when the penicillin was discontinued.
- Determine if the patient has taken antibiotics similar to penicillin before or after the reaction. If so, determine the results of these other antibiotics.

A thorough history including these important components can help determine the likelihood that an individual has penicillin allergy. A retrospective analysis (Salkind et al, 2001) calculated that a clinical history suggesting penicillin allergy increases the likelihood that the patient will be penicillin allergic as assessed by skin testing (summary positive likelihood ratio: 1.9; 95% confidence interval [CI]: 1.5–2.5). The absence of a suggestive history for penicillin history decreases the likelihood of a positive skin test result by more than half (summary negative likelihood ratio: 0.5; 95% CI: 0.4–0.6).

Diagnostic and Therapeutic Options

For children who have received amoxicillin in the past and whose history is suggestive of an allergic reaction, the most straightforward management choice for subsequent episodes of AOM is to avoid amoxicillin and consider alternative antibiotics. According to the national consensus statement issued by the CDC, alternatives to amoxicillin that would provide adequate antimicrobial coverage include amoxicillin-clavulanate, cefuroxime axetil, and ceftriaxone. Cefprozil and cefpodoxime were also considered as alternatives to amoxicillin for treatment failures. However, limited evidence for efficacy against drug-resistant *S. pneumoniae* prevented their official endorsement as alternative agents. Other agents less active against pneumococci, and thus not recommended, include cefaclor, cefixime, loracarbef, and ceftibuten (Dowell et al, 1999).

With the recommended alternative antibiotics all being β-lactams, specifically cephalosporins, two options exist. First, the cephalosporin may be given directly without further testing. Because all of the alternative antibiotics are either a second- or third-generation cephalosporin, the chance for an allergic reaction is probably less than 1% (Anne and Reisman, 1995). However, fatal anaphylactic reactions to cephalosporins have been reported (Kelkar and Li, 2001). A second option would be to perform penicillin skin testing. If skin testing is negative, either amoxicillin or a cephalosporin may be used with the same risk of allergic reactions as that of the general population. If penicillin skin testing is positive, the risk for an allergic reaction

to cephalosporins increases significantly to about 7% (Saxon et al, 1987); therefore, both amoxicillin and cephalosporins should be avoided.

Another possible solution for allergic reactions to amoxicillin would be to avoid amoxicillin and use non–β-lactam antibiotics. Trimethoprim-sulfamethoxazole and macrolide regimens have traditionally been useful as first- and second-line antibiotics for AOM. However, pneumococcal surveillance studies indicate that resistance to trimethoprim-sulfamethoxazole and to macrolides is substantial, thereby resulting in increased treatment failures (Dowell et al, 1999). An additional factor to consider is that trimethoprim-sulfamethoxazole may cause a number of hypersensitivity reactions, including delayed-type skin reactions, urticaria, drug fever, Stevens-Johnson syndrome, and, rarely, anaphylaxis (Boguniewicz and Leung, 1995). Macrolides may be advantageous because they have low immunogenic potential (Boguniewicz and Leung, 1995), but children often refuse these antibiotics because of taste or gastrointestinal upset (Klein, 1999).

Clindamycin is another non–β-lactam antibiotic that may be useful in individuals allergic to amoxicillin. Clindamycin is effective against drug-resistant pneumococci but is not active against *Haemophilus influenzae* or *Moraxella catarrhalis*. Therefore, clindamycin should be used only in culture-confirmed pneumococcal disease or after completing at least 3 days of effective treatment for these pathogens (Dowell et al, 1999).

To eliminate potential allergic reactions, observation may be considered for those with AOM who are allergic to amoxicillin. The observation option involves deferring antibiotics and providing only symptomatic care for selected children for the first 3 days. This practice is based on a number of studies that suggest that antibiotics may be unnecessary or provide only a marginal benefit for AOM (Culpepper and Froom, 1997). The Agency for Healthcare Research and Quality (AHRQ) recently completed an evidence report that concluded that the majority of children with AOM will have clinical resolution within the first week after presentation without the need for antibiotics. However, the AHRQ acknowledged that further research is needed to definitively address this issue (Marcy et al, 2001).

In cases of AOM when penicillins are absolutely indicated and no appropriate substitution is available, desensitization may be considered for patients who are allergic to penicillin (Anderson, 1992). In patients with positive penicillin skin tests, desensitization substantially reduces the risk of anaphylaxis. However, desensitization does not affect the risk for non–IgE-mediated reactions. Patients allergic to β-lactam antibiotics have been successfully desensitized using either oral or parenteral protocols. Oral desensitization is preferred because of the lower risk of provoking an acute allergic reaction (Boguniewicz and Leung, 1995).

Desensitization involves the administration of twofold dose increments every 15 minutes, beginning with one ten-thousandth of a conventional dose (Table 15-2) (Anderson, 1992). Complications of oral β-lactam desensitization include mild pruritus and pruritic rashes in approximately 5% during the procedure and in 25% during subsequent full-dose therapy. Adjustments in dosage and dose intervals may be required if acute reactions occur during desensitization. Approximately 5% of patients experience drug-induced serum sickness, hemolytic anemia, or nephritis during the course of full-dose therapy (deShazo and Kemp, 1997).

Desensitization should be performed only by an experienced physician with emergency treatment readily available, preferably in an intensive care setting (Boguniewicz and Leung, 1995). The effects of desensitization are transient. For penicillin to be tolerated following desensitization, ongoing drug exposure is required. If the drug administration is interrupted, clinical hypersensitivity may return within 48 hours (deShazo and Kemp, 1997).

Summary

The standard of care for treating AOM involves either amoxicillin or other β-lactam antibiotics. Treating children with AOM who are allergic to penicillin represents an important clinical challenge. The evaluation and management of penicillin-allergic children require knowledge concerning the details of previous allergic reactions, the available testing procedures, and potential cross-reactive antibiotics. By having a proper understanding of the therapeutic options available to these children, clinicians will have the necessary foundation to choose the optimal course of therapy.

TABLE 15-2. β-Lactam Oral Desensitization Protocol*

Stock Drug Concentration, mg/mL[†]	Dose No.	Amount, mL	Drug Dose, mg	Cumulative Drug, mg
0.5	1[‡]	0.05	0.025	0.025
	2	0.10	0.05	0.075
	3	0.20	0.10	0.175
	4	0.40	0.20	0.375
	5	0.80	0.40	0.775
5.0	6	0.15	0.75	1.525
	7	0.30	1.50	3.025
	8	0.60	3.00	6.025
	9	1.20	6.00	12.025
	10	2.40	12.00	24.025
50	11	0.50	25.00	49.025
	12	1.20	60.00	109.025
	13	2.50	125.00	234.025
	14	5.00	250.00	484.025

*Reproduced from Anderson J (1992).

[†]Dilutions using 250 mg/5 mL of pediatric syrup.

[‡]Dose approximately doubled every 15 to 30 minutes.

References

Anderson J. Allergic reactions to drugs and biologic agents. JAMA 1992;268:2845–57.

Anne S, Reisman RE. Risk of administering cephalosporin antibiotics to patients with histories of penicillin allergy. Ann Allergy Asthma Immunol 1995;74:167–70.

Blumer J. Fundamental basis for rational therapeutics in acute otitis media. Pediatr Infect Dis J 1999;18:1130–40.

Boguniewicz M, Leung DYM. Hypersensitivity reactions to antibiotics commonly used in children. Pediatr Infect Dis J 1995; 14:221–31.

Coombs R, Gell PGH. Classification of allergic reactions responsible for clinical hypersensitivity and disease. In: Gell PCR, Lachman PJ, editors. Clinical aspects of immunology. Oxford (UK): Blackwell Scientific Publications; 1975. p. 761–81.

Culpepper L, Froom J. Routine antimicrobial treatment of acute otitis media: is it necessary? JAMA 1997;278:1643–45.

deShazo R, Kemp SF. Allergic reactions to drugs and biologic agents. JAMA 1997;278:1895–906.

Disease management of drug hypersensitivity: a practice parameter. Ann Allergy Asthma Immunol 1999;83:665–700.

Dowell S, Butler JC, Giebink GS, et al. Acute otitis media: management and surveillance in an era of pneumococcal resistance—a report from the Drug-resistant Streptococcus pneumoniae Therapeutic Working Group. Pediatr Infect Dis J 1999;18:1–9.

Dowell S, Marcy SM, Phillips WR, et al. Otitis media: principles of judicious use of antimicrobial agents. Pediatrics 1998;101 (Suppl Pt 2):165–71.

Gruchalla R. Drug allergies. Primary Care Clin North Am 1998;25: 791–807.

Kelkar PS, Li JTC. Cephalosporin allergy. N Engl J Med 2001;345: 804–9.

Kishiyama J, Adelman DC. The cross-reactivity and immunology of beta-lactam antibiotics. Drug Saf 1994;10:318–27.

Klein J. Review of consensus reports on management of acute otitis media. Pediatr Infect Dis J 1999;18:1152–5.

Levine B. Immunologic mechanisms of penicillin allergy: a haptenic model system for the study of allergic diseases in man. N Engl J Med 1966;275:1115–25.

Lin R. A perspective on penicillin allergy. Arch Intern Med 1992; 152:930–7.

Marcy M, Takata G, Shekelle P, et al. Management of acute otitis media. Evidence Report/Technology Assessment No. 15. Rockville (MD): Agency for Healthcare Research and Quality; May 2001. AHRQ Publication No.: 01-E010.

Salkind A, Cuddy PG, Foxworth JW. Is this patient allergic to penicillin? JAMA 2001;285:2498–505.

Saxon A, Beall GN, Rohr AS, Adelman DC. Immediate hypersensitivity reactions to beta-lactam antibiotics. Ann Intern Med 1987;107:204–15.

Shepherd G. Allergy to beta-lactam antibiotics. Immunol Allergy Clin North Am 1991;11:611–33.

Valyasevi M, Van Dellen RG. Frequency of systematic reactions to penicillin skin tests. Ann Allergy Asthma Immunol 2000;85: 363–5.

Van Dellen RG, Walsh WE, Peters GA, Gleich GJ. Differing patterns of wheal and flare skin reactivity in patients allergic to the penicillins. J Allergy 1971;47:230–6.

Vega J, Blanca M, Garcia JJ, et al. Immediate allergic reactions to amoxicillin. Allergy 1994;49:317–22.

Weiss M, Adkinson NF. Immediate hypersensitivity reactions to penicillin and related antibiotics. Clin Allergy 1988;18:515–40.

Chapter 16

Antibiotic Management of Refractory Acute Otitis Media

Stan L. Block, MD, FAAP

"Lives of great men all remind us
We can make our lives sublime,
And departing, leave behind us
Footprints on the sands of time."

Henry W. Longfellow, *A Psalm of Life* (1838)

The prevalence of penicillin-nonsusceptible *Streptococcus pneumoniae* (PNSP) and β-lactamase–producing *Haemophilus influenzae* in acute otitis media (AOM) has increased dramatically throughout the United States since Block and colleagues first reported the onslaught of PNSP in AOM as beginning in 1992 (Block et al, 1995). Consequently, clinicians should no longer expect Pollyanna-like efficacy rates, such as those published in the 1980s, for antibiotic treatment of AOM (Marchant et al, 1992). Recent data suggest that the efficacy rate even for better oral broad spectrum antibiotics used in first-line therapy of AOM now approaches 75% in younger children (Black et al, 2000; Hoberman et al, 1996). Also, the rate of naturally occurring spontaneous resolution of AOM probably becomes insignificant in refractory AOM. Moreover, in contrast to therapy for new-onset AOM, the rate of antibiotic efficacy even for more active oral broad spectrum agents will more likely approach 65% and 50%, respectively, for second- and third-line therapy.

This chapter examines the bacteriology and antibiotic management of children who have persistent or refractory AOM. Persistent AOM is defined as the child with AOM who has persistent signs and symptoms of AOM during antibiotic therapy. Refractory AOM is defined as the child who develops signs and symptoms of AOM within 1 to 7 days after completing a course of antibiotics. For simplicity's sake, persistent AOM has been included as a subset of refractory AOM because the etiology is likely to be the same. Researchers from Israel have reported that causative pathogens of antibiotic failures within 7 days following therapy appear to be predominantly persistent pathogens (Leibovitz et al, 2000).

Harsh Reality of Efficacy of Second-Line Antibiotics

The practitioner must realize that comparative clinical efficacy trials for AOM have been conducted almost universally in children with new-onset AOM and have included paltry sample sizes of children < 24 months. The highest rates of refractory AOM occur in children younger than 24 months (Block et al, 2000; Carlin et al, 1991; Hoberman et al, 1996). We have limited comparative US data regarding how efficacious each second-line antibiotic could be in the treatment of refractory AOM or primarily in younger children. Therefore, to make our best-educated estimate as to antibiotic efficacy for second-, third-, and even fourth-line therapy for refractory AOM with their more resistant pathogens, we must synthesize data from the following sources:

- older in vivo clinical trials conducted in "virgin ears" (new-onset AOM)
- sparse newer in vivo data from noncomparative and comparative antibiotic trials in children with refractory AOM
- evolving annual in vitro antibiotic susceptibility patterns of otopathogens

Although none of these data by themselves are ideal, together they can provide a framework for predicting antibiotic efficacy for children with refractory AOM in the changing milieu of antibiotic resistance and implementation of new antibacterial vaccines.

TABLE 16-1. Causes of Treatment Failure in Acute Otitis Media

Microbiologic/pharmacodynamic factors
  Highly resistant pathogen (MIC exceeds MEE concentration)
  Inadequate MEE concentration of an antibiotic for a usually susceptible
    pathogen
  Protection by a copathogen:
    Virus
    β-Lactamase–producing organism
    Chlamydia pneumoniae
  Inadequate spectrum of empiric antimicrobial coverage (eg,
    trimethoprim-sulfamethoxazole for *Streptococcus pyogenes*, cefixime,
    or ceftibuten for *Streptococcus pneumoniae*)
Host factors
  Nonadherence: parental vs child
  Reduced absorption: gastroenteritis or antibiotic-induced increased
    motility
  "Bad plumbing": poor eustachian tube function: anatomic or functional (cleft
    palate, infancy, otitis prone)
Environmental factors
  Day-care environment with secondary reinfection by viral URI or AOM
    bacterial pathogen
  Smoking household

Adapted from Block SL and Harrison CJ (2001).
AOM = acute otitis media; MEE = middle ear effusion; MIC = minimum inhibitory concentration; URI = upper respiratory infection.

Table 16-1 shows many of the common reasons for antibiotic failures, several of which are unrelated to bacterial resistance. In fact, when we examined our epidemiologic data on AOM (Figure 16-1), we found that the rate of refractory AOM had not changed between an earlier cohort of children (1989–1990) who had no exposure to PNSP and another later cohort (1993–1994) whose rate of PNSP in AOM was documented as ~ 33% (Block et al, 2001a). The same experienced validated otoscopists evaluated all children in this general population.

Microbiology of Refractory AOM

Unlike an episode of new-onset AOM, the bacteriology of refractory AOM may differ markedly depending on the antibiotic recently used (Block et al, 2001b). For instance, the pathogens recovered in new-onset AOM are usually reported in most series as *S. pneumoniae* (35–45%), with about one-third as PNSP strains (Block et al, 1995; Block et al, 2002; Pichichero et al, 1997); nontypable *H. influenzae* (25–35%), with about half as β-lactamase–producing strains; and *Moraxella catarrhalis* (5–15%), with nearly all as β-lactamase–producing strains. Similar to other sites looking carefully at middle ear data, we have not seen *H. influenzae* type B in over 15 years in our practice as a consequence of routine use of the Hib vaccine in infants.

Pichichero and Pichichero (1995) reported that from 1989 to 1992, causative pathogens of refractory AOM (within 4 days following therapy) were almost twice as likely to be penicillin-susceptible *S. pneumoniae* (PSSP)

than β-lactamase–producing strains of *H. influenzae* and *M. catarrhalis*. However, as we previously reported, from 1992 to 1994 in the era of PNSP, recent antibiotic therapy seemed to select particularly for PNSP strains in children with AOM (Block et al, 1995). Evaluating an even larger cohort of children from rural Kentucky (1992–1998) who were recently treated within the 3 days prior to culture compared with those not recently treated, PNSP was nearly three-fold more likely to be recovered (36% versus 13%) (unpublished data) (Figure 16-2). Among children who have *S. pneumoniae* recovered in AOM after receiving numerous courses of antibiotics, the rate of PNSP appears to burgeon to a range between 77 and 90% (Del Castillo et al, 1998; Gehanno et al, 1998; Leibovitz et al, 1998).

But when certain antibiotics fail because of their unique in vitro spectrum of coverage, they will also likely select for particular pathogens (discussed below.) The in vitro spectrum of coverage of some of the more commonly used second-line antibiotics is examined below.

In Vitro Antibiotic Spectrum of Activity

Generally, for an antibiotic to be considered a suitable choice for treatment of refractory AOM, it must provide reasonable activity against the two critical otopathogens commonly encountered in refractory AOM: PNSP and β-lactamase–producing *H. influenzae*. Tables 16-2 and 16-3 show the minimum inhibitory concentration (MIC) 50/90 values for some of the more commonly used antibiotics for AOM compared with the usual otopathogens. The MIC values of this compilation of isolates obtained from patients of all ages in three multicenter surveillance studies (Credito et al, 2001; Spangler et al, 1996; Thornsberry et al, 1999) correspond almost identically to the included rural Kentucky data obtained exclusively from children with AOM. For comparison, the table also includes the peak middle ear effusion (MEE) concentrations reported for each respective antibiotic (Block and Harrison, 2001).

According to the mouse model for antibiotic efficacy proposed by Craig and Andes (1996), the amount of drug available in the serum must exceed the MIC of the invading bacteria > 40% of the time to eradicate the organism. Others surmise that the peak MEE concentration must exceed the bacterial MIC during the dosing interval (Harrison, 1997). The mouse model using serum concentrations is an adequate surrogate model for efficacy of many oral β-lactam antibiotics. However, it may not account for at least the modest efficacy of certain antibiotics, such as azithromycin, which are heavily concentrated intracellularly and also achieve minimal serum concentrations. Furthermore, despite the serum concentrations for cephalexin and erythromycin being fairly reasonable, neither drug penetrates the MEE very well. They also lack

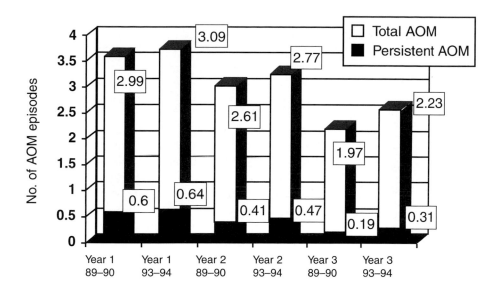

FIGURE 16-1. Epidemiology of acute otitis media (AOM) in rural Kentucky children 1989–1990 versus 1993–1994. Total episodes of AOM versus episodes of persistent AOM annually. Adapted from Block SL et al (2001a).

efficacy for AOM. Furthermore, some additional new antibiotics will not gain approval for AOM in the United States because of a lack of MEE penetration or poor in vitro activity and lack of clinical efficacy against one of the two primary otopathogens. In addition, as will be shown, occasionally the in vivo pathogens recovered from antibiotic failures may not necessarily match the expected in vitro predictions.

In Vitro Activity against PNSP

The spontaneous cure rate at 5 to 7 days for *S. pneumoniae* in AOM approaches only 20% (Howie, 1993). Unlike gram-negative otopathogens, *S. pneumoniae* also tends to cause invasive disease. Moreover, PNSP has become an increasingly predominant pathogen of AOM in the 1990s, accounting for one-third to half of all pneumo-

coccal strains. As seen in Table 16-2, no oral antibiotic for AOM has high activity against fully resistant PNSP strains (r-PNSP) (penicillin MIC > 1.0 µg/mL). Ceftriaxone (parenteral) is the most active antibiotic, followed by aminopenicillins (amoxicillin ± clavulanate), two third-generation cephalosporins (cefdinir and cefpodoxime), and two second-generation cephalosporins (cefprozil and cefuroxime). But peak MEE antibiotic concentrations frequently will not exceed bacterial MIC values, except for parenteral ceftriaxone.

About half of strains of r-PNSP continue to be quite susceptible to azithromycin and clarithromycin, whereas the other half is markedly resistant. Clindamycin is the most active oral antibiotic for r-PNSP but is not approved for AOM, provides no activity against gram-negative otopathogens, and is very unpalatable. Although a dose of parenteral ceftriaxone achieves high and sustained pene-

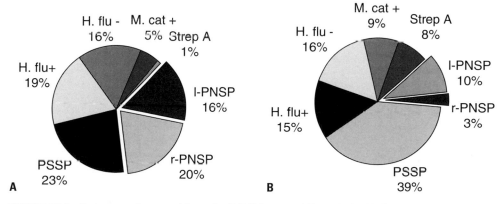

FIGURE 16-2. Pathogens of acute otitis media (AOM) from rural Kentucky (1992–1998). Treatment within 3 days (A) versus no treatment for 4 days (B). H. flu = *Haemophilus influenzae*; M. cat = *Moraxella catarrhalis*; i-PNSP = intermediate-level penicillin-nonsusceptible *Streptococcus pneumoniae*; PSSP = penicillin-susceptible *Streptococcus pneumoniae*; r-PNSP = resistant penicillin-nonsusceptible *Streptococcus pneumoniae*; Strep A = group A streptococcus. (A) *n* = 150; (B) *n* = 631.

TABLE 16-2. In Vitro Susceptibility of *Streptococcus pneumoniae* Isolates*

Antibiotic	Peak MEE Concentration µg/mL (dose)	Resistant PNSP[†] MIC$_{50}$	Resistant PNSP[†] MIC$_{90}$	Intermediate PNSP[†] MIC$_{50}$	Intermediate PNSP[†] MIC$_{90}$	PSSP MIC$_{50}$	PSSP MIC$_{90}$
Penicillin[††]		4.0	4.0	0.5	1.0.	0.06	0.06
Amoxicillin-clavulanate[§]	4.0–6.3 (30–45 g/kg bid)	2–4	4–8	0.25–0.5	1	0.06	0.06
Cefprozil	2.0 (15 mg/kg bid)	8–16	16–32	1–2	4	0.12	0.25–0.5
Cefuroxime	0.2–1.2 (15 mg/kg bid)	4	16	1–2	4	0.12	0.25
Loracarbef	3.9 (15 mg/kg bid)	16–> 32	> 32.0	4–16	> 32.0	0.5–1	1–2
Cefdinir	0.72 (14 mg/kg qd)	4	8–16	0.5–1	4	0.12	0.25
Cefpodoxime	0.5–0.87 (5 mg/kg bid)	4	4–8	0.5	1–2	0.03	0.06
Cefixime	1.2 (8 mg/kg qd)	4–32	64	2–4	16	0.25	0.5
Ceftriaxone	35 @ 24 h, 19 @ 48 h (50 mg/kg, one dose)	1–2	2–4	0.25	0.5–1	0.03	0.03
Azithromycin	8.6 (10 mg/kg) day 1, then 5 mg/kg 4 d	2–8	8–> 64	0.25–2	4–> 64	0.06–0.12	0.06–0.25
Clarithromycin	7.4 (7.5 mg/kg bid)	2–4	4–> 64	0.06–1	2–> 64	0.03–0.25	0.06–0.25
Trimethoprim-sulfamethoxazole[ǁ]	1.4–2.0 (4 mg/kg bid)	2–8	16	0.5–2	8	0.12–0.25	1–2
Clindamycin	3.6 (10 mg/kg bid)	0.06	0.06–> 8	0.06	0.06–> 8	0.06	0.06

*Numbers are expressed in µg/mL.

[†]Resistant PNSP, penicillin MIC ≥ 2.0 µg/mL; intermediate PNSP, penicillin MIC > 0.06 to 1.0 µg/mL.

[††]No MEE concentrations available.

[§]Amoxicillin-clavulanate at 2:1.

[ǁ]Concentrations and doses are for trimethoprim-sulfamethoxazole at 19:1.

MEE = middle ear effusion; MIC = minimum inhibitory concentration; PNSP = penicillin-nonsusceptible *Streptococcus pneumoniae*; PSSP = penicillin-susceptible *Streptococcus pneumoniae*.

tration into the MEE at 24 and 48 hours, MEE concentrations probably wane markedly by 4 or 5 days. In fact, we observed recrudescence of symptoms at 48 hours among children with PNSP AOM treated with alternate-day ceftriaxone (Block et al, 1995). Others have also observed high failure rates in children with PNSP treated with a single dose of ceftriaxone (Leibovitz et al, 2000).

Many second-line antibiotics continue to be relatively active against intermediate-level PNSP strains (i-PNSP) (penicillin MIC = 0.1 to 1.0 µg/mL). Aminopenicillins, cefdinir, cefpodoxime, cefprozil, cefuroxime, and macrolides each possess modest activity against i-PNSP. However, the higher peak MEE concentrations of amoxicillin achieved with high-dose (80–90 mg/kg/d) aminopenicillins offer

TABLE 16-3. In Vitro Susceptibility of Gram-Negative Isolates of Acute Otitis Media*

Antibiotic	Peak MEE Concentration	β-Lactamase (+) *H. influenzae* MIC$_{50}$	β-Lactamase (+) *H. influenzae* MIC$_{90}$	β-Lactamase (−) *H. influenzae* MIC$_{50}$	β-Lactamase (−) *H. influenzae* MIC$_{90}$	β-Lactamase (+) *M. catarrhalis* MIC$_{50}$	β-Lactamase (+) *M. catarrhalis* MIC$_{90}$
Amoxicillin-clavulanate[†]	4.0–6.3 (30–45 g/kg bid)	0.5–1	2.0	0.25–0.5	0.5–1	0.25–1	0.25–1
Cefprozil	2.0 (15 mg/kg bid)	4	16–32	2	4–8	2	8
Cefuroxime	0.2–1.2 (15 mg/kg bid)	0.5	1–2	0.5	1	1–2	2–4
Loracarbef	3.9 (15 mg/kg bid)	2–4	16	1–2	2–4	2	4
Cefdinir	0.72 (14 mg/kg qd)	0.25	0.5	0.25	0.25	0.25	0.25
Cefpodoxime	0.5–0.87 (5 mg/kg bid)	0.06	0.12–0.25	0.06	0.025	1	1
Cefixime	1.2 (8 mg/kg qd)	0.06	0.12	0.06	0.06	0.25	0.5
Ceftriaxone	35 @ 24 h, 19 @ 48 h (50 mg/kg, 1 dose)	< 0.06	< 0.06	< 0.06	< 0.06	< 0.06	< 0.06
Azithromycin	8.6 (10 mg/kg) day 1, then 5 mg/kg qd for 4 d	1–4	2–8	1–2	2–8	0.06–0.12	0.12–0.25
Clarithromycin	7.4 (7.5 mg/kg bid)	8–16	16	4–16	8–16	0.03–0.25	0.06–0.25
Trimethoprim-sulfamethoxazole[‡]	1.4–2.0 (4 mg/kg bid)	0.12	2–4	0.12–0.25	0.5–1.0	0.12	≤ 0.5–2

*Numbers are expressed in µg/mL (dose).

[†]Amoxicillin-clavulanate at 2:1.

[‡]Trimethoprim-sulfamethoxazole at 19:1.

MEE = middle ear effusion; MIC = minimum inhibitory concentration.

pharmacodynamic advantages over other β-lactam antibiotics for the treatment of PNSP. Note that third-generation cephalosporins diverge markedly with regard to *S. pneumoniae* coverage. Cefdinir and cefpodoxime possess moderately good activity against both PSSP and i-PNSP. In contrast, cefixime and ceftibuten possess poor activity against any PNSP strains (ceftibuten $MIC_{50/90}$ values, $> 32/> 32$ μg/mL), and ceftibuten is minimally active against PSSP ($MIC_{50/90}$ values, 4/8 μg/mL) compared with cefixime ($MIC_{50/90}$ values, 0.25/0.5 μg/mL) (Neu, 1995).

In Vitro Activity against *H. influenzae*

Although the spontaneous cure rate for *H. influenzae* in AOM is purportedly as high as ~ 50%, this has been documented only in children with new-onset AOM (Howie, 1993). Clinicians must be aware that more than half of strains of *H. influenzae* found in AOM produce β-lactamase enzymes, rendering it particularly less vulnerable to certain β-lactam antibiotics. In addition, all strains of *H. influenzae* have become increasingly resistant to non–β-lactam antibiotics such as the sulfonamides ± trimethoprim and macrolides (see Table 16-3).

The second-generation cephalosporins, with the exception of cefuroxime, generally have an Achilles heel for coverage of β-lactamase–producing *H. influenzae*. Cefprozil has particularly high $MIC_{50/90}$ values (4/16 μg/mL) and should not be prescribed when *H. influenzae* is likely, such as in otitis-conjunctivitis syndrome. Similarly, erythromycin ± sulfisoxazole and the second-generation macrolide clarithromycin possess poor activity against most strains of *H. influenzae*. At least in vitro, the spectrum of coverage for azithromycin against *H. influenzae* appears to be adequate ($MIC_{50/90}$ values, 2/4 μg/mL) when compared with the measurable concentrations in the MEE. However, many argue that azithromycin is so heavily concentrated in the intracellular compartment that available concentrations in the MEE will unlikely exceed the MICs of most *H. influenzae*—a predominantly extracellular organism.

Third-generation cephalosporins generally possess excellent coverage of gram-negative pathogens of AOM, with $MIC_{50/90}$ values ranging from 0.03 to 0.125 μg/mL. Ceftibuten is the exception because it has marginal activity against *M. catarrhalis* ($MIC_{50/90}$ values, 0.5/4 μg/mL) (Neu, 1995). Amoxicillin-clavulanate (AMC) has reasonably good activity against β-lactamase–producing *H. influenzae*, but data from AOM isolates and other recent series show recent modest increases in $MIC_{50/90}$ values (0.5/2 μg/mL) (Block et al, 2001; Credito et al, 2001; Spangler et al, 1996). This could become clinically relevant in the 15 to 20% of patients who do not absorb amoxicillin very well (Block et al, 2001b). About 25% of *H. influenzae* is resistant to trimethoprim-sulfamethoxazole.

In Vivo Antibiotic Data in Clinical Trials: "Shifty Sands"

The clinician should also evaluate in vivo data regarding how effectively the antibiotic eradicates the infection in the child with AOM. Three different clinical methodologies, each with different end points for efficacy, have been used in the past to assay antibiotic efficacy: (1) clinical efficacy without tympanocentesis—clinical outcome data at the end of therapy; (2) single-tympanocentesis data—clinical outcome at the end of therapy; and (3) double-tympanocentesis (initially and midtherapy) data—microbiologic outcome at midtherapy (or "in vivo sensitivity test") (Howie, 1993). The "test of cure" visit (28 days following therapy) advocated by some authorities provides minimal information about drug efficacy because of high rates of reinfection in AOM.

Only tympanocentesis trials reveal microbiologic efficacy, a critical issue because nearly every comparative clinical trial has been conducted in new-onset AOM and is powered to show equivalency. But the practitioner must rely on other data to uncover how effective an antibiotic should perform when used in children with refractory AOM—the purported target population for each second-line antibiotic. Remember also that most published clinical trials in the United States were conducted before 1993 and thus had virtually no cases of AOM caused by PNSP and only 10 to 20% of cases caused by β-lactamase–producing *H. influenzae*.

Nontympanocentesis Trials: "Washed Out Sands"

In essence, nontympanocentesis comparative antibiotic trials have rarely shown any difference between two antibiotics for full-course treatment at the end of therapy time point, thus explaining Marchant and colleagues' proposed "Pollyanna effect" in AOM clinical trials (Marchant et al, 1992). Reasons include overdiagnosis of AOM by less experienced practitioners, a high spontaneous cure rate of AOM, and the inclusion of high rates of children who were older, with new-onset AOM, and with mild to moderate AOM. With the exception of short-course versus standard 10-day antibiotic trials as follows, nontympanocentesis data should generally be disregarded for efficacy.

Single-dose ceftriaxone was significantly less efficacious than AMC in "difficult-to-find" first-line therapy patients (no antibiotics for 28 days). But these data can be gleaned only by examining the *Physician's Desk Reference* (PDR) (1997). Five days of therapy with AMC (45 mg/kg/d) were as effective as 10 days of therapy with the same dose of AMC (Hoberman et al, 1996). But in the subset of children younger than 2 years, again in whom most refractory AOM is found, 5-day therapy was significantly less effective. More recently, single-dose azithromycin (30 mg/kg) was shown to be as effective and as well tolerated as AMC (45 mg/kg/d bid) for 10 days (Block et al, 2000). This clinical trial is similarly limited by the following: a small sample size ($n = 184$ in each group) was evaluated, only cases of new-onset AOM and a mostly older population (over 60% were older than 2 years) were studied, and tympanocentesis was not performed.

Single-Tympanocentesis Trials: "Common as Desert Sands"

Most experts concur that single tympanocentesis is justified in a child with bulging AOM who is significantly symptomatic, ill appearing, or refractory to several courses of antibiotics (see below). Children in tympanocentesis trials must have bona fide more severe and symptomatic AOM along with documented pus behind the tympanic membrane (TM). Single-tympanocentesis trials using end of therapy end points are the most widely available and reliable data for assessing antibiotic efficacy relative to actual clinical practice. Investigators performing tympanocentesis must be highly experienced otoscopists. These trials also often reveal potential significant differences between antibiotics in efficacy rates by pathogen. Likewise, they are not numerically powered to show overall differences in efficacy between two antibiotics and are usually limited by exclusive enrolment of first-line therapy patients with AOM.

Furthermore, clinical trials evaluating new antibiotics for AOM in the United States during the 1990s have uniformly selected AMC as the gold standard with which to compare in tympanocentesis trials. Unfortunately, some of these clinical trials have not been published or have selected certain subpopulations for publication. For instance, bacteriologic efficacy data for ceftriaxone in AOM were obtained overseas. To obtain an unbiased viewpoint of the entire AOM data sample used in a drug trial, the reader may have to resort to examining overall and by-pathogen cure rate as published in the *PDR*—an unbiased, objective, published source. The absence of a disclaimer in the *PDR* for comparative efficacy data in AOM reveals that only three drugs—cefdinir, cefpodoxime, and cefuroxime— have demonstrated efficacy statistically equivalent to AMC in first-line therapy patients at the end of therapy. But all of these data are older than a decade, and most were obtained before the emergence of PNSP in AOM. Even before PNSP was widespread in AOM, the following commonly used antibiotics for AOM have demonstrated a particular bacterial "Achilles heel" in by-pathogen analysis in the *PDR* (1997) (see the following section):

- cefprozil: β-lactamase–producing *H. influenzae*
- cefixime: PSSP
- ceftibuten: PSSP
- clarithromycin: all strains of *H. influenzae*

These data suggest that antibiotic selection after clinical failure with any of these drugs should target their respective in vivo and in vitro (see Tables 16-2 and 16-3) Achilles heel pathogen.

As for antibiotic efficacy for PNSP in US single-tympanocentesis trials, the data are sparse. Four antibiotics—cefprozil, AMC, clindamycin, and cefdinir— have been evaluated in primarily noncomparative US trials in about 10 to 40 patients each. Each antibiotic demonstrated similar satisfactory response rates of 60 to 70% for PNSP. The trial design and small sample size provide a limited basis for recommendations to treat refractory AOM caused by PNSP.

Double-Tympanocentesis Data: "About as Fun as Sand in Both Eyes"

In the 1970s and 1980s, before PNSP and β-lactamase–producing *H. influenzae* emerged as problems in AOM, Howie (1993) was the first to espouse the use of double tympanocentesis as a marker for antibiotic efficacy for respective pathogens. Using this methodology, a second tympanocentesis is performed between 2 and 7 days into therapy in children who have already undergone an initial tympanocentesis. Double-tympanocentesis data are particularly valuable for revealing by-pathogen comparative and noncomparative differences in efficacy rates between antibiotics (or even placebo) using a small sample size. For example, before PNSP was documented in AOM, double-tympanocentesis data corroborate much of the above single-tympanocentesis data showing that *H. influenzae* was the particular Achilles heel for cefprozil, clarithromycin, cefaclor, and trimethoprim-sulfamethoxazole (Table 16-4) (Howie, 1993).

Double-tympanocentesis data are somewhat helpful in determining final outcome at the end of therapy. Even when an antibiotic has *not* eradicated an organism midtherapy, nearly two-thirds of patients will still achieve a successful outcome at the end of therapy (Dagan et al, 2000; Howie, 1993; Leibovitz et al, 2000). On the other

TABLE 16-4. Antibiotic Efficacy Midtherapy Using Double Tympanocentesis: Bacteriologic Pitfalls

Drug	Bacterial Achilles Heel
Placebo	Penicillin-susceptible *Streptococcus pneumoniae* 19% ($n = 57$)
Cefixime	Penicillin-susceptible *Streptococcus pneumoniae* 74% ($n = 61$)
Cefpodoxime	*Moraxella catarrhalis* 60% ($n = 15$)
Cefprozil	*Haemophilus influenzae* 43% ($n = 14$)
Cefaclor	*Haemophilus influenzae* 67% ($n = 82$)
Clarithromycin	*Haemophilus influenzae* 20% ($n = 15$)
Trimethoprim-sulfamethoxazole	*Haemophilus influenzae* 75% ($n = 61$)

Adapted from Howie VM (1993).

hand, 90% of children whose MEE is sterile midtherapy will show resolution of AOM at the end of therapy.

Dagan and colleagues (2000) showed that AMC was clearly superior to azithromycin midtherapy, particularly for AOM caused by *H. influenzae*. This midtherapy inferior response rate suggested that azithromycin behaved more like a bacteriostatic drug, especially for an extracellular organism such as *H. influenzae*. On the other hand, at the end of therapy, azithromycin, surprisingly, was equally as efficacious as AMC for *S. pneumoniae*, despite many PNSP strains. Furthermore, the 16% advantage in overall efficacy at the end of therapy in favor of AMC over azithromycin was quite similar to the earlier difference (12%) reported in the *PDR* (1997) using single tympanocentesis in a small sample size.

Double-tympanocentesis data may be limited by the following issues:

- publication of few randomized comparative clinical trial using patients residing in the United States
- extreme difficulty in obtaining permission from parents to enrol their children in such an onerous trial—thus the need to obtain most of the data outside the United States
- extreme difficulty in obtaining approval from ethical review boards because of a lack of any patient benefit along with the invasiveness of the second tympanocentesis
- significant difference in early outcome midtherapy may likely be a consequence of comparing bacteriostatic with bacteriocidal drugs
- high early withdrawal rate in the trials
- methodologic difficulties in assessing an already distorted TM to perform a second tympanocentesis and in obtaining a "true" culture from an already draining TM
- additional invasive risk, anesthetic risk, and pain for the patient when most patients are clinically improved by midtherapy
- enrolment of children mostly with new-onset AOM

Palatability Issues: "Some Taste Like Sand"

Although many antibiotics may possess a unique spectrum of bacterial coverage or may even be considered quite broad spectrum, palatability issues of liquid formulations can present an insurmountable barrier. Four oral antibiotic suspensions are particularly troublesome to use. Two cephalosporins, cefpodoxime proxetil and cefuroxime axetil, although they possess quite good in vitro activity, can be so unpleasant tasting as to frequently jeopardize their routine use in children (Steele et al, 2001). Clarithromycin and clindamycin are also poorly palatable. Taste problems may be circumvented in some cases by mixing with FlavorRX or administering "chasers" of chocolate milk or fruit punch before and after dosing. But the rate of patient refusal appears to be unacceptable for most practitioners to routinely prescribe these medications.

Management of Refractory AOM: "Shifting Sands"

The Centers for Disease Control and Prevention (CDC) convened an expert panel to determine the optimal approach to manage AOM in the era of PNSP. Selecting among the currently available antibiotics, the Drug-resistant *Streptococcus pneumoniae* (DRSP) Therapeutic Working Group formalized a treatment algorithm for both recurrent AOM and AOM refractory to a single course of amoxicillin, as shown in Table 16-5 (Dowell et al, 1999). The approach showed much promise, particularly by further advocating tympanocentesis in refractory AOM, use of high-dose amoxicillin as a first-line agent, and acknowledging the use of a different approach for the child with new-onset versus recurrent AOM (Dowell et al, 1999). Although this algorithm presented an excellent springboard for discussion, many thought leaders expressed the following concerns:

TABLE 16-5. CDC Drug Resistant Working Group Pneumocococcus Guidelines for Antibiotic Treatment of Refractory and Recurrent AOM

Appearance of Clinical Signs	Switch Therapy to
If treatment failure after day 3 or at end of therapy (refractory AOM)	High-dose amoxicillin-clavulanate,* or cefuroxime axetil, or intramuscular ceftriaxone × 3 d
If treated with an antibiotic within 30 d (recurrent AOM)	High-dose amoxicillin, or high-dose amoxicillin-clavulanate or cefuroxime axetil
If treatment failure	Consider clindamycin if penicillin-nonsusceptible *Streptococcus pneumoniae* identified; consider tympanocentesis + susceptibility testing to select drug

Adapted from Dowell S et al (1999).
*High-dose amoxicillin or amoxicillin-clavulanate refers to a 90 mg/kg/d dose of the amoxicillin component. Augmentin ES is currently available.
AOM = acute otitis media.

- no option for patients allergic to penicillin
- no algorithm for management of third- or fourth-line patients
- poor palatability of cefuroxime suspension
- expense and burden of three consecutive daily injections of ceftriaxone as recommended for those simply failing one course of amoxicillin
- virtually no clinicians were aware of how to or were being taught how to perform tympanocentesis
- absence of an efficacious cephalosporin (cefpodoxime) with good in vitro activity in the algorithm (cefdinir was not approved until 1 month after publication)

New Antibiotic Algorithm for Refractory OM: "Solid as Sand in Concrete"

Second-Line Therapy

β-Lactamase–producing strains of *H. influenzae* and *M. catarrhalis* rather than *S. pneumoniae* are customarily thought to be predominant pathogens recovered in children who fail amoxicillin. Counterintuitively, our recent data (Table 16-6) (Block et al, 2001b), similar to those of Pichichero and Pichichero (1995), showed that *S. pneumoniae* of all levels of penicillin susceptibility was the most common pathogen in amoxicillin failures before availability of the heptavalent pneumococcal conjugate vaccine (PCV-7). The algorithm for AOM shown in Figure 16-3 has been a practical and reliable approach for children with refractory AOM in our practice. Second-line therapy in this algorithm is also quite consistent with recent guidelines regarding the treatment of sinusitis from the American Academy of Pediatrics (AAP) (2001). Thus, when practitioners confront a child who has recently failed amoxicillin therapy, second-line therapy would include either high-dose AMC (45 mg/kg/dose bid) or third-generation cephalosporins such as cefdinir

TABLE 16-6. Pathogens Recovered in Acute Otitis Media Recently Treated within 7 Days with Amoxicillin vs Amoxicillin-Clavulanate (*Not* Overall Efficacy Data)

Bacteria	Amoxicillin, % (*n* = 38)	AMC, % (*n* = 59)
Haemophilus influenzae (–)	16	29
Haemophilus influenzae (+)	11	22
Moraxella catarrhalis (+)	13	7
i-PNSP	20	10
r-PNSP	13	17
PSSP	26	12

Adapted from Block SL et al (2001b).
AMC = amoxicillin-clavulanate; i-PNSP = intermediate-level penicillin-nonsusceptible *Streptococcus pneumoniae*; PSSP = penicillin susceptible *Streptococcus pneumoniae*; r-PNSP = resistant penicillin-nonsusceptible *Streptococcus pneumoniae*.

(14 mg/kg/dose qd) or cefpodoxime (5 mg/kg/dose bid). Although approved for twice-daily therapy, cefdinir should be used as a once-daily dose for 10 days to treat refractory AOM (Block et al, 2000). The overall satisfactory response rate was significantly better for once-daily than twice-daily dosing for children younger than 24 months—the hotbed for refractory AOM. Cefpodoxime has significant palatability issues, whereas cefdinir can also be prescribed once daily and is among the best-tasting antibiotics (Steele et al, 2001). For children with refractory AOM, clinicians should uniformly prescribe a full course of antibiotics and avoid short-course therapy.

Third-Line Therapy

Because refractory AOM is so widespread (20–25%) in young children, particularly for those enrolled in day care, this part of the algorithm differs notably from the AAP sinusitis guidelines. They recommend intravenous ceftriaxone or cefotaxime at this point, which would be quite expensive and onerous for young children. Moreover, the practitioner's office would grind to a standstill during the winter months. In my experience using this new proposed algorithm in Figure 16-3, the majority of children will still respond to one of the more effective oral antibiotics or especially so to a few doses of parenteral ceftriaxone. Adjunctive tympanocentesis might also improve outcome.

When a child has failed a third-generation cephalosporin, the purported most likely pathogen would be PNSP or β-lactamase (+) *H. influenzae*. Thus, high-dose AMC provides reasonable coverage, second only to parenteral ceftriaxone. On the other hand, if the child fails second-line therapy with AMC, conventional wisdom and in vitro data (see Tables 16-2 and 16-3) suggest that the most likely pathogen would be PNSP. Thus, clindamycin and parenteral ceftriaxone have been obvious judicious choices that we often selected in the past. However, when Block and colleagues (2001b) recently examined the causative pathogens of AOM recently treated with AMC (before PCV-7) (see Table 16-6), they deduced the same conclusion (pre-PNSP) as Patel and colleagues (1995): *H. influenzae* was the primary culprit. Patel and colleagues found *H. influenzae* in 11 of 12 failures with AMC, whereas we observed *H. influenzae* more than twice as often than PNSP (51 versus 27%). *H. influenzae* was also recovered in 8 of 12 patients treated with high-dose AMC. Thus, a third-generation oral cephalosporin seems well suited to treat AMC failures at this juncture (see below). Clinicians could also justify the use of parenteral ceftriaxone for two or three daily doses as a third-line option as well.

Fourth-Line Therapy

For fourth-line therapy in the child who is not highly otitis prone, two or three doses of ceftriaxone (50 mg/kg/d) administered on consecutive or alternate days would be preferred. Alternatively, clindamycin, with its fairly good PNSP coverage, coupled with either cefixime or trimethoprim-sulfamethoxazole, could be selected. But one should be quite cautious regarding the problems of poor palatability or severe diarrhea when using potent oral antibiotics simultaneously. At this juncture, many clinicians may forego anticipation of an antibiotic cure and instead refer the child for pressure equalization (PE) tubes as fourth-line therapy, particularly if the child is highly otitis prone or quite symptomatic with AOM.

Tympanocentesis: "Sand in One Eye"

Although tympanocentesis is suggested as possible adjunctive therapy for second-line failures by the DRSP Working Group (Dowell et al, 1999), very few practitioners perform tympanocentesis. I prefer to advocate this invasive procedure as an adjunct to third- or fourth-line therapy in children with more severe illness or for families who will allow it. One could speculate that tympanocentesis at this point might occasionally help to avoid PE tubes because the spe-

cific causative pathogen can be identified and targeted, and the chronic MEE abscess is drained. The procedural details regarding in-office tympanocentesis have been thoroughly explained in an article by Block in the March 1999 issue of *Contemporary Pediatrics*.

Refractory AOM in the Penicillin-Allergic Child: "Sand in Your Britches"

If the child has suffered an anaphylactic-type reaction to an aminopenicillin in the past, then all β-lactam antibiotics should be avoided. Clinicians will be relegated to using macrolides or trimethoprim-sulfamethoxazole. However, I would recommend the use of high-dose azithromycin (20 mg/kg/d for 3 days) based on preliminary efficacy data from a small single-tympanocentesis study (Arrieata et al, 2002). For the child who had a less severe hypersensitivity reaction, customary effective oral cephalosporins in the algorithm should be acceptable

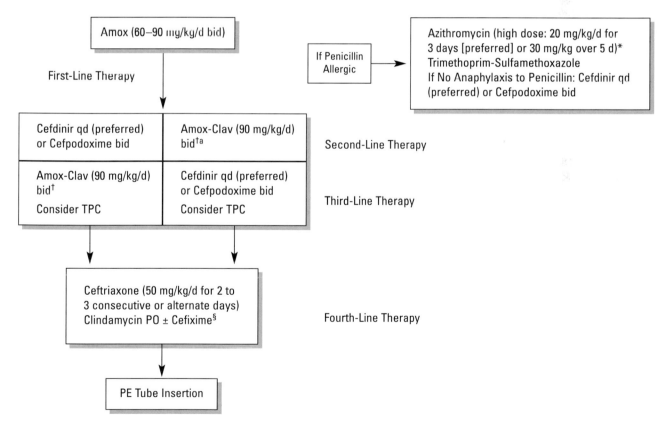

FIGURE 16-3. Antibiotic algorithm for refractory acute otitis media when penicillin-nonsusceptible *Streptococcus pneumoniae* is a moving target in light of the PCV-7 vaccine. All antibiotics prescribed at standard doses for 10 days unless otherwise specified. *Azithromycin standard approved dosing is 10 mg/kg/day 1 and then 5 mg/kg/d for 4 days. †Available as Augmentin ES. ‡As a third-line therapy, practitioners may consider using a higher dose (25 mg/kg) of cefdinir administered on an empty stomach. §Use caution regarding pseudomembranous colitis when two broad-spectrum oral antibiotics are prescribed; notable palatability issues with clindamycin. Amox = amoxicillin; Amox-clav = amoxicillin-clavulanate; PE = pressure equalization; TPC = tympanocentesis.

therapy. If these young children become otitis prone, they should be referred for insertion of PE tubes much more quickly than their nonallergic counterparts owing to a lack of a full antibiotic armamentarium.

Impact of Heptavalent Pneumococcal Conjugate Vaccine: "Quicksand for PNSP"

The remarkable heptavalent pneumococcal conjugate vaccine PCV-7 was only recently (March 2000) implemented in the routine vaccination schedule for infants in the United States. PCV-7's effects on invasive disease have been quite robust, with a nearly 10-fold reduction in *S. pneumoniae*–invasive disease in 2 years of routine use (Black et al, 2001). What about the impact of PCV-7 on AOM? Will it make the historically predominant pathogens (PNSP) of refractory AOM a shifting or waning target? In light of currently available data, much of the following is the author's speculation regarding AOM.

First, the important influence that age has on serotypes recovered in pneumococcal AOM prior to use of PCV-7 should be examined. Figure 16-4 shows that almost 80% of the serotypes recovered in children 7 to 24 months of age are either vaccine or vaccine-related serotypes. Most importantly, nearly all r-PNSP and most i-PNSP serotypes are included in the vaccine. Also, data from Eskola and colleagues (2001) showed that the PCV-7 reduced vaccine and vaccine-related serotypes by 57% and 51%, respectively. Although nonvaccine serotypes increased by about one-third, these serotypes so far rarely show a propensity to develop into PNSP. Thus, full immunization with PCV-7 could make many cases of refractory AOM somewhat easier to treat.

As for the effectiveness of PCV-7 in reducing the overall rates of AOM, both the Northern California (Black et al, 2000) and Finnish (Eskola et al, 2001) data showed a very modest reduction of about 6 to 7%. Interestingly, Black and colleagues also showed a greater than 20% reduction in PE tube insertion, along with a greater than 40% reduction in children with severe recurrent AOM after the booster dose at 12 months. Neither study could account for the possibility of "herd immunity" as an entire community becomes adequately vaccinated. This phenomenon, which has occurred with other vaccines such as Hib or influenza virus, has been documented somewhat with PCV-7 (Dagan et al, 2001). This could even further reduce rates of pneumococcal and PNSP AOM in young children. On the other hand, the overall effect of PCV-7 on older children will be quite minimal, as suggested by our data (Block et al, 2002). Nearly 60% of the serotypes recovered in children older than 24 months are non–vaccine-related serotypes, which are much less likely to be PNSP as well (see Figure 16-4).

Our observations from 2001 to 2003 in the 98% + vaccinated population in our practice suggest that PCV-7 may be having an impact on pathogens recovered in children < 24 months who have been vaccinated with PCV-7. Since 2001, we have noted a 50% reduction in the rates of overall pneumococcal AOM. Consequent rates of *H. influenzae* have increased to the point where they account for nearly half of AOM pathogens. Likewise, gram-negative β–lactamase-positive organisms account for 45% of all AOM organisms (Block et al, 2003). But with the insufficient availability of PCV-7 in 2002 and much of 2003 and the subsequent vaccination with a maximum of only two or three doses of PCV-7 as infants, the effects of herd immunity may not be as pronounced until a few years in the future. Now that the PCV-7 vaccine is in full supply, the off-label use of pneumococcal 23-valent polysaccharide vaccine might be considered as a booster dose for children older than 24 months who are otitis prone and who have been primed with at least two or three doses of PCV-7. Data from Finland (Kayhty et al, 1996) and our site (Block et al, 1997) have shown this regimen to be quite immunogenic and well tolerated in children who had received two or three priming doses of either CRM PCV-5 or the outer membrane protein version of PCV-7 from another manufacturer, respectively.

Following a fourth dose of PCV-7 it is necessary to confer moderate protection against PNSP and vaccine serotypes of AOM, then the algorithm in Figure 16-3 for refractory AOM continues to be applicable. Prior to availability of PCV-7, for those children who failed amoxicillin as first-line therapy for AOM, *S. pneumoniae* was the most likely pathogen to be recovered (see Table 16-6). Thus, when high-dose amoxicillin was prescribed initially, high-dose AMC as second-line therapy provided only additional coverage of the clavulanic acid component, that is, for β-lactamase–producing organisms. However, if *H. influenzae* becomes a more predominant pathogen of refractory AOM, then cefdinir/cefpodoxime and AMC become the best options to cover both nonvaccine PSSP and *H. influenzae*. Cefprozil and possibly the macrolides become even less attractive options when *H. influenzae* predominates.

Arguably, one could use cefixime, which is quite active against gram-negative organisms, as a second-line agent in fully PCV-7–vaccinated children. However, coverage of PSSP, which will continue to be one of the major pathogens of refractory AOM, is suspect. Ceftibuten, although quite active against *H. influenzae*, possesses minimal activity against either PSSP, PNSP, or *M. catarrhalis* (Neu, 1995).

Other Antibiotic Options: "Diamond in the Rough or Cubic Zirconia?"

Preliminary data from a recent single-tympanocentesis clinical trial showed that high-dose azithromycin (20 mg/kg/d for 3 days) was as efficacious both overall and for *H.*

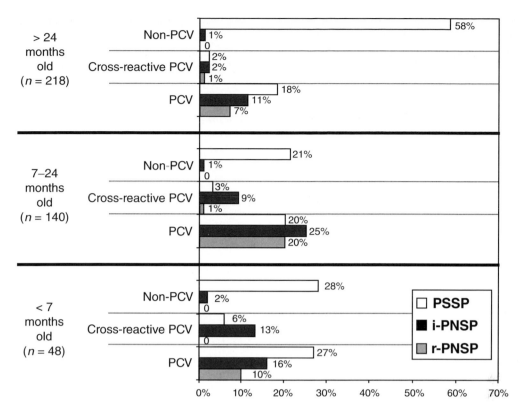

FIGURE 16-4. Level of penicillin resistance versus age distribution of pneumococcal serotypes in children with acute otitis media (1992–1998). Adapted from Block SL et al (2002). i-PNSP = intermediate-level penicillin-nonsusceptible *Streptococcus pneumoniae*; PCV = pneumococcal conjugate vaccine; PSSP = penicillin-susceptible *Streptococcus pneumoniae*; r-PNSP = resistant penicillin-nonsusceptible *Streptococcus pneumoniae*.

influenzae as high-dose AMC (90 mg/kg/d for 10 days) (Block et al, 2002). In addition, clinicians may want to evaluate high-dose cefdinir (25 mg/kg/d given twice daily), which is currently undergoing clinical investigation. But higher-dose cefdinir should be administered on an empty stomach. Finally, PNSP continues to become increasingly resistant to clindamycin and even somewhat to ceftriaxone. Thus, newer antibiotic options, such as the available linezolid suspension (0% resistance to PNSP) and gatifloxacin and telithromycin (< 5% resistance to PNSP), which are undergoing clinical trials for refractory AOM, may become empiric treatment of choice for refractory AOM when PNSP is known or suspected in refractory AOM. Gatifloxacin also has excellent activity against *H. influenzae*, whereas linezolid does not. The two former drugs may also have a role in children who have refractory PE tube otorrhea when methicillin-resistant *Staphylococcus aureus* is known or suspected.

Conclusion

Of course, practitioners should opt for an otolaryngologic referral for PE tubes for the child with refractory AOM who fails fourth-line therapy and even earlier after third-line therapy, especially in the child who is markedly symptomatic or highly otitis prone.

References

American Academy of Pediatrics, Subcommittee on Management of Sinusitis and Committee on Quality Improvement. Clinical practice guideline: management of sinusitis. Pediatrics 2001; 108:798–808.

Arrieata A, Block SL, Arguedas A, et al. High-dose azithromycin versus high-dose amoxicillin clavulanate in recurrent or persistent acute otitis media. Third World Congress of Pediatric Infectious Disease; 2002 Nov 19; Santiago, Chile.

Black S, Shinefield H, Fireman B, et al. Efficacy, safety, and immunogenicity of heptavalent pneumococcal conjugate vaccine in children. Pediatr Infect Dis J 2000;19:187–95.

Black SB, Shinefield HR, Hansen J, et al. Postlicensure evaluation of the effectiveness of seven valent pneumococcal conjugate vaccine. Pediatr Infect Dis J 2001;12:1105–17.

Block SL. Tympanocentesis: why, when, how. Contemp Pediatr 1999;16:103–27.

Block SL, Arrieta A, Seibel M, et al. Single dose azithromycin (30 mg/kg) in acute otitis media. Presented at Infectious Disease Society of America; 2000 Sept 8; Philadelphia.

Block SL, Harrison CJ. Diagnosis and management of acute otitis media. New York: Professional Communications; 2001.

Block SL, Harrison CJ, Hedrick JA, et al. Penicillin-resistant *Streptococcus pneumoniae* in acute otitis media: risk factors, susceptibility patterns, and antimicrobial management. Pediatr Infect Dis J 1995;14:751–9.

Block SL, Harrison CJ, Hedrick JA, et al. Restricted use of antibiotic prophylaxis for recurrent acute otitis media in the era of penicillin non-susceptible *Streptococcus pneumoniae*. Int J Pediatr Otorhinolaryngol 2001;61:47–60.

Block SL, Hedrick JA, Harrison CJ, et al. Pneumococcal serotypes from acute otitis media in rural Kentucky. Pediatr Infect Dis J 2002;21:859–65.

Block SL, Hedrick JA, Harrison CJ. Routine use of Prevnar in a pediatric practice profoundly alters the microbiology of acute otitis media. Society for Pediatric Research; 2003 May 3–6; Seattle, WA.

Block SL, Hedrick JA, Smith RA, et al. Pneumococcal conjugate vaccine vs. pneumococcal polysaccharide 23 in 6-month old infants after 2 prior doses of conjugate vaccine. Presented at 37th Interscience Conference on Antimicrobial Agents and Chemotherapy; 1997 Sept 18–Oct 1; Toronto.

Block SL, Hedrick JA, Tyler RD, et al. Microbiology of acute otitis media recently treated with aminopenicillins. Pediatr Infect Dis J 2001;20:1017–21.

Block SL, McCarty JM, Hedrick JA, et al, and the Cefdinir Otitis Media Study Group. Comparative safety and efficacy of cefdinir vs. amoxicillin/clavulanate for treatment of suppurative acute otitis media in children. Pediatr Infect Dis J 2000;19: S159–65.

Carlin SA, Marchant CD, Shurin PA, et al. Host factors and early therapeutic response in acute otitis media. J Pediatr 1991;118: 178–83.

Craig WA, Andes D. Pharmacokinetics and pharmacodynamics of antibiotics in otitis media. Pediatr Infect Dis J 1996;15:255–9.

Credito KL, Gengrong L, Pankuch GA, et al. Susceptibilities of *Haemophilus influenzae* and *Moraxella catarrhalis* to ABT-773 compared to their susceptibilities to 11 other agents. Antimicrob Agents Chemother 2001;45:67–72.

Dagan R, Johnson CE, McLinn S, et al. Bacteriologic and clinical efficacy of amoxicillin/clavulanate vs. azithromycin in acute otitis media. Pediatr Infect Dis J 2000;19:95–104.

Dagan R, Sikuler-Cohen M, Zamir O, et al. Effect of a conjugate pneumococcal vaccine on the occurrence of respiratory infections and antibiotic use in day-care center attendees. Pediatr Infect Dis J 2001;20:951–8.

Del Castillo F, Baquero-Artigao F, Garcia-Perrea A. Influence of recent antibiotic therapy on antimicrobial resistance of *Streptococcus pneumoniae* in children with acute otitis media in Spain. Pediatr Infect Dis J 1998;17:94–7.

Dowell S, Butler J, Giebink G, et al. Acute otitis media: management and surveillance in an era of pneumococcal resistance— a report from the Drug-Resistant *Streptococcus pneumoniae* Therapeutic Working Group. Pediatr Infect Dis J 1999;18:1–9.

Eskola J, Kilpi T, Palmu A, et al. Efficacy of a pneumococcal conjugate vaccine against acute otitis media. N Engl J Med 2001;344: 403–9.

Gehanno P, N'Guyen L, Derriennic M, et al. Pathogens isolated during treatment failures in otitis. Pediatr Infect Dis J 1998;17: 885–90.

Harrison CJ. Using antibiotic concentrations in middle ear fluid to predict potential clinical efficacy. Pediatr Infect Dis J 1997;16: S12–6.

Hoberman A, Paradise JL, Block S, et al. Efficacy of amoxicillin/ clavulanate for acute otitis media: relation to *Streptococcus pneumoniae* susceptibility. Pediatr Infect Dis J 1996;15 Suppl:955–62.

Howie VM. Otitis media. Pediatr Rev 1993;14:320–3.

Kayhty H, Ahman H, Vuorela A, et al. Response at 24 months to a booster dose of pneumococcal polysaccharide vaccine in children immunized with pentavalent Pnc conjugate vaccine in infancy. Presented at the 36th Interscience Conference on Antimicrobial Agents and Chemotherapy; 1996 Sept 15–18; New Orleans.

Leibovitz E, Greenberg D, Porat N, et al. Clinical relapse of acute otitis media within 1 month after completion of treatment: bacteriologic correlates. Presented at the 40th Interscience Conference on Antimicrobial Agents and Chemotherapy; 2000a; Sept 19; Toronto.

Leibovitz E, Piglansky L, Raiz S, et al. Bacteriologic and clinical efficacy of one day vs. three day intramuscular ceftriaxone for treatment of nonresponsive acute otitis media in children. Pediatr Infect Dis J 2000b;11:1040–5.

Leibovitz E, Raiz S, Piglansky L, et al. Resistance pattern of middle ear fluid isolates in acute otitis media recently treated with antibiotics. Pediatr Infect Dis J 1998;17:463–69.

Marchant CD, Carlin SA, Johnson CE, et al. Measuring the comparative efficacy of antibacterial agents for acute otitis media: the "Pollyanna phenomenon." J Pediatr 1992;120:72–7.

Neu HC. Ceftibuten: minimal inhibitory concentrations, postantibiotic effect and beta-lactamase stability—a rationale for dosing programs. Pediatr Infect Dis J 1995;16:S88–92.

Patel JA, Reisner B, Vizirinia N, et al. Bacteriologic failure of amoxicillin-clavulanate in treatment of acute otitis media caused by nontypeable *Haemophilus influenzae*. J Pediatr 1995; 126:799–806.

Physician's desk reference. 50th ed. Montvale (NJ): Medical Economics Data Production Company; 1997.

Pichichero ME, McLinn S, Aronovitz G, et al. Cefprozil treatment of persistent and recurrent acute otitis media. Pediatr Infect Dis J 1997;16:471–8.

Pichichero ME, Pichichero CL. Persistent acute otitis media, I: causative pathogens. Pediatr Infect Dis J 1995;14:178–83.

Spangler SK, Jacobs MR, Appelbaum PC. Activities of RPR 106972, cefditoren, two new oxazolidinones, and other oral and parenteral agents against 203 penicillin-susceptible and resistant pneumococci. Antimicrob Agents Chemother 1996;40:481–4.

Steele RW, Thomas MP, Begue RE. Compliance issues related to the selection of antibiotic suspensions for children. Pediatr Infect Dis J 2001;20:1–5.

Thornsberry C, Ogilvie PT, Holley HP, Sahm DF. Survey of susceptibilities of *Streptococcus pneumoniae*, *Haemophilus influenzae*, and *Moraxella catarrhalis* isolates to 26 antimicrobial agents: a prospective U.S. study. Antimicrob Agents Chemother 1999; 43:2612–23.

Chapter 17

Management of Acute Otitis Media in an Antibiotic-Resistant Era Worldwide

Faryal Ghaffar, MD, George H. McCracken Jr, MD

Acute otitis media (AOM) in children continues to be a major challenge for health care providers. With the emergence of resistant organisms, particularly *Streptococcus pneumoniae*, management of this disease has become increasingly complex.

Pneumococci had been among the most highly susceptible bacteria throughout the first quarter-century of the chemotherapeutic use of penicillin. The first clinical isolate of penicillin-resistant *S. pneumoniae* was described in 1967; the isolate was recovered from a patient in Papua, New Guinea. Between 1967 and 1977, sporadic reports of penicillin-resistant clinical isolates were published from various parts of the world. The next dramatic event in the epidemiology of antibiotic-resistant pneumococci was the outbreak of pneumococcal disease caused by multidrug-resistant strains in South African hospitals in 1977. In contrast to the first isolate, which was susceptible to chloramphenicol, tetracycline, erythromycin, and sulfa drugs, the multidrug-resistant South African strains recovered in 1977 were shown to have greatly increased minimum inhibitory concentrations (MICs), not only for penicillin (a 1,000-fold increase) but also for tetracycline, erythromycin, chloramphenicol, clindamycin, streptomycin, and, for some strains, rifampin (Appelbaum, 1992).

In the United States, more than 30% of pneumococcal strains are penicillin nonsusceptible (PNSP). Some areas, such as Atlanta and Dallas, report higher levels of resistance, up to 50% of strains (Spika et al, 1991). These strains are frequently multidrug resistant. In the United States between 1991 and 1992, a total of 6.6% of hospital strains of *S. pneumoniae* were PNSP; between 1993 and 1994, the total was 15.7%; and between 1994 and 1995,

the total had risen to 23.6%. This is an approximate 350% increase in less than 5 years. From 1979 to 1995, an even bigger increase in PNSP occurred: from 1.8 to 23.6%, although over a longer period of time (Appelbaum, 1996). The rate of PNSP varies widely in other parts of the world, ranging from 40 to 70% in France (Gehanno et al, 1995), Spain (Fenoll et al, 1991), Israel (Dagan et al, 1994), South Africa (Friedland and Istre, 1992), and some Asian countries (Mastro et al, 1993).

One of the highest levels of resistance was seen in Cadiz, Spain, where 89% of the pneumococcal strains were found to be resistant to penicillin in 1995 (Appelbaum, 1996). This is a dramatic increase since 1991, when the percentage of resistant strains was 29% (Garcia-Martos et al, 1997). Lower rates are seen in Finland, the Slovak Republic, the Netherlands, and Australia, where isolates are rarely resistant (Hermans et al, 1997; Manninen et al, 1997; McLaughlin et al, 1997; Trupl et al, 1997). In countries with high rates of pneumococcal resistance, such as Spain and France, widespread use of oral antibiotics and poor treatment compliance have been implicated as predisposing factors. In contrast, Italy has a low rate of pneumococcal resistance, where we see a lower use of oral antibiotics, widespread use of injectable antibiotics, and therapy with a wider range of antibiotics (Klein, 1998).

The worldwide spread of resistant pneumococci is thought to be related to human-to-human spread of relatively few clonal groups such as serotypes 6B, 19F, and 23F that harbor resistant determinants to multiple classes of antibiotics. This phenomenon has been particularly highlighted by the worldwide spread of the serotype 23F pneumococcal clone (the "Spanish" clone), first identified in Spain in the early 1980s and resistant to penicillin, chloramphenicol, and tetracycline. This clone has now been found in the United States, South Africa, the United Kingdom, South America, several other countries in Europe, and the Far East. Serotype 19F, 14, 19A, 9N, and 3 and serogroup 6 variants of this clone have also been reported in various regions of the world. A recent study in the United States showed that close to 40% of all highly penicillin-resistant pneumococci belong to this Spanish 23F clone (Richter et al, 2002; Tomasz, 1997).

The rapid spread of resistant clones and the emergence of new variants of resistance mechanisms mandate the establishment of effectively functioning surveillance systems, through which the powerful methods of molecular epidemiology could help to identify reservoirs and modes of transmission of the resistant bacteria (Appelbaum, 2002).

The increasing rate of β-lactamase–producing *Haemophilus influenzae* and *Moraxella catarrhalis*, coupled with pneumococcal resistance, further complicates the choice of appropriate antibiotic therapy for AOM, particularly for those patients who have failed an initial course of amoxicillin therapy. Up to 40% of nontypable *H. influenzae* isolates and more than 90% of *M. catarrhalis* isolates from middle ear fluid (MEF) are β-lactamase producers (Block et al, 1994; Bluestone, 1992).

Management Options

To prevent treatment failure caused by resistant pathogens, physicians should be aware of the likely bacteria causing AOM and the relative effectiveness of available antimicrobial agents. Selection of therapy for AOM should be based on susceptibility patterns of the etiologic agents in that particular geographic location, on consideration of risk factors in a child for carriage of resistant *S. pneumoniae,* and on pharmacokinetics (ie, drug concentration in body fluids) and pharmacodynamics (ie, interaction of drug concentrations in relation to MIC values) of antibi-

otics in MEF (Table 17-1) (Craig and Andes, 1996; Doern et al, 1996; Dowell et al, 1999). The tolerability, frequency of administration of an antibiotic, and cost of therapy should be taken into consideration for parents and patients to comply with therapy. Cost includes the office visits and the acquisition cost of the drug itself, which vary based on reimbursement, formulary restrictions, and whether patients' medical care is covered by public assistance or is paid out of pocket. In addition, cost includes ancillary expenses in parents' lost time at work and additional therapy if the initial treatment fails.

Controlling the spread of resistant pneumococci through appropriate and judicious prescribing to reduce selective pressure is necessary. Promoting the judicious use of antimicrobial agents is one step in managing drug resistance. This includes the principles discussed as well as a restriction of their use in illnesses such as colds, bronchitis, and otitis media with effusion. Other important actions include increasing the accuracy of diagnosis and educating parents to ensure a complete course of therapy. Appropriate empiric drug choices can be made if local surveillance data are understood and applied in conjunction with the results of susceptibility testing and pharmacokinetic and pharmacodynamic data. The recommendations of the Drug-resistant *Streptococcus pneumoniae* Therapeutic Working Group, which were published in 1999, follow the principles of judicious antimicrobial use and should be implemented (Dowell et al, 1999).

How does the practitioner know about the prevalence of PNSP if tympanocentesis is not commonly performed? One way is to perform susceptibility testing on nasopharyngeal isolates of *S. pneumoniae* collected from children with or without an underlying AOM (Zenni et al, 1995). An active surveillance system could be established by the local hospital to provide information to the community practitioner. Another strategy is to provide training to practitioners who care for children to perform tympanocentesis to obtain an isolate for susceptibility testing (Pichichero, 2002).

Table 17-1. Activity of β-Lactams against Isolates of *Streptococcus pneumoniae*

Agent (dosage)	Peak Serum Concentration (µg/mL)	Peak MEF Concentration (µg/mL)	Penicillin Intermediate			Penicillin Resistant		
			MIC50	MIC90	T > MIC	MIC50	MIC90	T > MIC
Amoxicillin 13.3 mg/kg tid	3.5–7	1–6	0.25	1	83–59	2	4	59–46
Cefuroxime 250 mg bid	2–7	1–2	0.5	4	53–33	8	16	23–0
Ceftriaxone 50 mg IM qd	171*	35*	0.25	1	100	2	4	100
Cefpodoxime 5 mg/kg bid	1–4	0.2–1	0.5	2	54–0	4	16	0
Cefprozil 15 mg/kg bid	6–10	2.0	1	8	66–28	16	32	28–0
Cefaclor 13.3 mg/kg tid	7–13	0.5–4	4	64	0	128	> 128	0
Loracarbef 15 mg/kg bid	13–19	2–4	8	64	26–0	128	> 128	0
Cefixime 8 mg/kg qd	3–4	1–2	4	16	0	32	64	0

Adapted from Dowell SF et al (1999); Craig WA and Andes D (1996); and Doern GV et al (1996).
*Peak concentration after a single dose

MEF = middle ear fluid; MIC = minimum inhibitory concentration; MIC50 and MIC90 = MICs at which 50 and 90% of the isolates are inhibited, respectively; T > MIC = time above MIC50 and MIC90 = time concentration of drug in serum is above the MIC50 and MIC90 expressed as a percentage of the dosing interval.

Initial Empiric Therapy

Amoxicillin remains the antibiotic of choice for initial empiric treatment of AOM, even in areas where there is a high prevalence of antibiotic-resistant strains of *S. pneumoniae*. This is because it is safe, well tolerated, and inexpensive and has been effective for the management of AOM for many years. Amoxicillin has the lowest MICs against penicillin-intermediate and -resistant *S. pneumoniae* strains when compared with other oral β-lactam antibiotics.

Conventional dosages of amoxicillin (40–45 mg/kg/d) in two or three divided doses are effective when there is a low prevalence of PNSP (up to 10%) in the community or when the patient is at low risk for infection with resistant strains. Factors to be considered in assessing the risk for infection with PNSP include antimicrobial exposure, age, and day-care attendance. Younger patients are more likely to harbor resistant pneumococcal strains. Block (1997) found that more than half of infants and children younger than 2 years of age were infected with a resistant pathogen, primarily intermediate and resistant *S. pneumoniae*. By 3 years of age, the incidence of resistant infection decreased to 18%. A number of factors are responsible for emergence of resistance secondary to antibiotics. The likelihood of resistance is influenced by the MIC in relation to the pharmacokinetic profile of the drug (Craig and Andes, 1996). Subinhibitory concentrations promote the emergence of resistant mutants in vitro; similarly, subinhibitory concentrations seen during trough levels in clinical dosing allow resistant organisms to emerge (Craig and Andes, 1996). Based on this information, short-term exposure to a potent agent is less likely to select for resistant strains than is long-term exposure to low antibiotic concentrations, as can occur with long-acting antibiotics (long half-life values) given infrequently. This phenomenon is exacerbated by the poor compliance often seen in clinical settings. New studies show the remarkable ability of antibiotics to rapidly promote nasopharyngeal carriage and the spread of antibiotic-resistant AOM pathogens. Increase in carriage of antibiotic-resistant *S. pneumoniae* can occur as early as 3 to 4 days after initiation of antibiotic treatment and can last for weeks to months. Children colonized with antibiotic-resistant organisms transmit those organisms to their family members and to those in day care, creating a vicious cycle in which increased antibiotic resistance is associated with decreased therapeutic response when causing AOM, which can lead to increased antibiotic use and, in turn, a further increase in resistance. Also, day-care centers, especially large-group day-care centers, contribute to the likelihood of resistance in several ways: extensive antimicrobial use, large numbers of children, and frequent, person-to-person contact (Friedland et al, 1994). Thus, patients who were not exposed to antibiotics in the preceding 3 months, are

older than 2 years of age, and did not attend day care are appropriate candidates for conventional amoxicillin therapy. In the standard dosage of 40 to 45 mg/kg/d, amoxicillin achieves peak MEF concentrations in the range of 1 to 6 µg/mL, which would fail to eradicate some intermediate and most highly resistant *S. pneumoniae* (Friedland and McCracken, 1994).

If there is a high prevalence of PNSP in the community (> 10%) or the patient is at risk for infection with PNSP, a higher dosage of amoxicillin should be considered.

Higher dosages of amoxicillin (80–90 mg/kg/d) divided into two or three doses produce MEF concentrations > 1 µg/mL for at least 50% of the dosing interval (Canafax et al, 1998). More importantly, the MEF concentrations are at least threefold greater than the MIC_{90} value (2 µg/mL) for penicillin-intermediate strains of pneumococci in at least 30% of the subjects (Canafax et al, 1998). To achieve a satisfactory response against highly resistant strains of *S. pneumoniae* with penicillin MIC of 2 to 4 µg/mL, it is necessary to use dosages of amoxicillin of at least 80 to 90 mg/kg/d in two divided doses (Canafax et al, 1998). In France, dosages as large as 150 mg/kg/d have been used in some children with persistent otitis media. Amoxicillin should be given for a total of 10 days. Shorter courses of antibiotic therapy are often inadequate for treatment of AOM in infants and young children (≤ 2 years of age). Compared with a 5-day regimen, outcome is significantly better when children less than 2 years of age receive 10 days of therapy (Klein, 1998).

Children who receive frequent antibiotic treatments, high-dose amoxicillin treatment, or amoxicillin prophylaxis are at greatest risk for having disease caused by β-lactamase–positive *H. influenzae*. In such children, high-dose amoxicillin-clavulanate (90/6.4 mg/kg/d, Augmentin ES-600) or cefdinir (Guay, 2000) may be considered as an initial therapy. The new 14 to 1 formulation of amoxicillin-clavulanate (90/6.4 mg/kg/d, Augmentin ES) has twice the concentration of amoxicillin compared with the 7 to 1 formulation of amoxicillin-clavulanate (45/6.4 mg/kg/d) but maintains the clavulanate dosage at 6.4 mg/kg/d to provide coverage for PNSP and β-lactamase positive *H. influenzae* and to minimize potential adverse effects, especially diarrhea (Dagan et al, 2001).

Alternative Choices for Treatment

If a patient fails to show clinical improvement after 3 to 4 days of the initial regimen, an alternative agent should be used. In some patients who do not respond to antibiotic therapy, myringotomy or tympanocentesis may be required to recover the causative agent for identification and susceptibility testing. The selection of an antibiotic can be made on the basis of results of susceptibility studies and the known pharmacodynamics of the agent. If a middle ear aspirate is not obtained, the agent chosen should be effective against highly resistant *S. pneumoniae* and β-lactamase–producing *H. influenzae*. Antibiotics that meet these two criteria include high-dose amoxicillin-clavulanate (90/6.4 mg/kg/d, Augmentin ES-600) and intramuscular ceftriaxone in one or more dosages, depending on the clinical response. Cefdinir is also appropriate in children who fail initial empiric therapy, although it would not be effective against highly resistant pneumococci. Clindamycin is effective for highly resistant *S. pneumoniae* but lacks coverage for *H. influenzae*. The appropriate use of clindamycin is for culture-proven resistant *S. pneumoniae* or second-line treatment for suspected highly resistant *S. pneumoniae* after adequate treatment for β-lactamase–producing organisms.

Treatment failure is characterized by both clinical symptoms and otoscopic findings of tympanic membrane inflammation that persist after 72 hours of antibiotic therapy. Symptoms and signs of AOM persist more frequently when antibiotic therapy fails to eradicate the pathogen from MEF than when it succeeds (Dagan et al, 1998). If assessments are done at 10 days or later, it is critical to distinguish between patients who failed to respond to initial treatment and those who have persistence of middle ear effusion without signs of local inflammation. Cefdinir is not more effective than high-dose amoxicillin-clavulanate. If a child fails therapy with high-dose amoxicillin-clavulanate, it is unlikely that cefuroxime axetil/cefdinir would be beneficial. Penetration of cefdinir (14 mg/kg dose) into the middle ear is modest (median concentration approximately 0.72 μg/mL), which is borderline for some intermediate-resistant pneumococci (Guay, 2000). Block and colleagues (2000) showed that therapy with cefdinir resulted in a bacteriologic eradication rate of 72.7% and 50% for patients with penicillin-intermediate and -resistant *S. pneumoniae* isolates, respectively.

Ceftriaxone is a potent agent against the principal pathogens of AOM, including PNSP. Ceftriaxone is bactericidal, and fewer than 2% of pneumococcal isolates have MIC values of > 2 μg/mL. The pharmacodynamics of ceftriaxone in MEF are unique and provide an explanation of its effectiveness. After a 50 mg/kg dose in infants and children, peak ceftriaxone concentrations in plasma are 170 μg/mL, and in MEF, they are approximately 35 μg/mL. The peak MEF concentrations are greater than the MICs of *S. pneumoniae* and *H. influenzae* for 100 to 150 hours (Gudnason et al, 1998). For ceftriaxone-resistant pneumococci (MIC_{90}, 1–2 μg/mL), the maximum MEF concentration exceeds the MIC by 35-fold and remains above the MIC for approximately 100 hours (Gudnason et al, 1998).

The advantages of ceftriaxone therapy over oral agents are better compliance and effective bactericidal activity. A series of three daily injections may improve the effectiveness of ceftriaxone, particularly among children who have failed a recent course of another antibiotic. In one study, single-dose ceftriaxone therapy failed to eradicate PNSP

from MEF cultures in 7 of 13 patients 3 to 5 days after the dose, whereas three daily doses resulted in bacteriologic cure in 16 of 17 patients. Eradication of *H. influenzae* and *M. catarrhalis* occurs in all patients after a single 50 mg/kg ceftriaxone dose (Leibovitz et al, 2000). Similarly, Gehanno and colleagues (1997) recently reported an 89% eradication rate using a 3-day regimen of ceftriaxone for resistant *S. pneumoniae* (MIC > 1 μg/mL) from the MEF of children who had nonresponsive AOM. A series of three daily injections, rather than the single injection, may be more effective for highly resistant *S. pneumoniae*.

It is likely, but remains to be demonstrated, that a regimen consisting of a second intramuscular ceftriaxone dose in only those patients with continued clinical signs of acute infection 48 to 72 hours after the first 50 mg/kg dose would also be effective. This proposed regimen is consistent with the pharmacokinetic and pharmacodynamic properties of ceftriaxone in MEF. An alternative approach could be a single dose of ceftriaxone followed by 10 days of amoxicillin in a dosage of 80 to 90 mg/kg/d in two doses.

Clindamycin has excellent in vitro activity against many strains of PNSP and has been used successfully in children with PNSP that did not respond to β-lactam antibiotics (Nelson et al, 1994). The empiric use of clindamycin for refractory AOM requires an additional antibiotic to cover *H. influenzae* if a β-lactamase–stable drug has not been used previously. The appropriate use of clindamycin is for culture-proven highly resistant *S. pneumoniae* or second-line treatment for suspected highly resistant *S. pneumoniae* after adequate treatment for β-lactamase–producing pathogens.

Cefdinir, a new oral third-generation cephalosporin, has good activity against β-lactamase–producing *H. influenzae* and moderate activity against intermediate penicillin-resistant pneumococci. The in vitro activity of cefdinir is comparable with those of cefpodoxime and cefuroxime (Guay, 2000). Cefdinir became available 1 month after AOM recommendations by the Centers for Disease Control and Prevention (CDC) Working Group were published. A wide spectrum of in vitro activity against middle ear pathogens, a low incidence of gastrointestinal adverse reactions, excellent palatability, and a convenient dosing schedule of cefdinir QD should make it the most appropriate oral cephalosporin alternative for second-line therapy of AOM relative to the CDC Working Group guidelines. High dosages (eg, 25 mg/kg daily) are currently being evaluated.

Rifampin remains extremely active against PNSP, but its use as a single agent is not recommended because it readily induces bacterial resistance.

Newer fluoroquinolones (levofloxacin, gatifloxacin, moxifloxacin) are more effective than the older fluoroquinolones (ofloxacin, ciprofloxacin) against *S. pneumoniae*, but none of these fluoroquinolones is approved in children because of an association between their use and the development of arthrotoxicity in juvenile animal models. Fluoroquinolones should not be used for routine treatment of AOM because other antibiotics have adequate efficacy but should be considered for recurrent and nonresponsive AOM. Gatifloxacin, given as 10 mg/kg for 10 days to children between 6 months and 7 years of age (> 90% were < 2 years of age) with recurrent or nonresponsive AOM, had an overall clinical cure rate of 87% (150/173); among evaluable patients with *S. pneumoniae*, the clinical cure rate was 91% (30/33). The bacteriologic cure rate for all patients was 96%. The most frequent drug-related adverse events were vomiting (15%) and diarrhea (5%). There have been no reports of arthropathy (Arguedas et al, 2001).

In summary, standard dosage amoxicillin remains the antibiotic of first choice for treatment of AOM. If the child has risk factors for carriage of PNSP or there is a high prevalence of PNSP in the community (> 10%), a larger initial dosage (80–90 mg/kg/d) should be considered. If clinical failure occurs after 48 to 72 hours and compliance is ensured, then amoxicillin-clavulanate (90/6.4 mg/kg/d, Augmentin ES-600), cefdinir, and intramuscular ceftriaxone for 1 to 3 days are reasonable alternatives for treatment of penicillin-resistant *S. pneumoniae* and β-lactamase–producing organisms. Clindamycin should be used for suspected highly resistant *S. pneumoniae* after adequate coverage for β-lactamase–producing organisms. Myringotomy for MEF culture and susceptibility testing should be considered in all cases of treatment failures.

The emergence of disease caused by penicillin-resistant and multidrug-resistant pneumococci has become a global concern, necessitating the identification of the epidemiologic spread of such strains. The rapid spread of resistant clones and the emergence of new variants of resistance mechanisms call for effective surveillance systems and collaboration among clinicians, scientists, the pharmaceutical industry, and regulatory and public health agencies.

Universal use of the pneumococcal conjugate vaccine is expected to result in few cases of AOM caused by antibiotic-resistant pneumococcal serotypes contained in the vaccine and possibly in an increased percentage of *Haemophilus* cases.

References

Appelbaum PC. Antimicrobial resistance in *Streptococcus pneumoniae*: an overview. Clin Infect Dis 1992;15:77–83.

Appelbaum PC. Epidemiology and in vitro susceptibility of drug-resistant *Streptococcus pneumoniae*. Pediatr Infect Dis J 1996;15:932–9.

Appelbaum PC. Resistance among *Streptococcus pneumoniae*: implications for drug resistance. Clin Infect Dis 2002;34:1613–9.

Arguedas A, Sher L, Lopez E, et al. Gatifloxacin treatment of recurrent/non-responsive acute otitis media [abstract]. In: Programs and abstracts of the 41st Interscience Conference on Antimicrobial Agents and Chemotherapy, Chicago. American Society for Microbiology; 2001. p. 372.

Block SL. Causative pathogens, antibiotic resistance and therapeutic considerations in acute otitis media. Pediatr Infect Dis J 1997;16:449–56.

Block SL, Hedrick JA, Kratzer J, et al. Five-day twice daily cefdinir therapy for acute otitis media: microbiologic and clinical efficacy. Pediatr Infect Dis J 2000;19(12 Suppl):S153–8.

Block SL, Hedrick J, Wright P, et al. Drug-resistant *Streptococcus pneumoniae*: Kentucky and Tennessee, 1993. MMWR Morb Mortal Wkly Rep 1994;43:23–5.

Bluestone CD. Current therapy for otitis media and criteria for evaluation of new antimicrobial agents. Clin Infect Dis 1992;14 Suppl 2:S197–203.

Canafax DM, Yan Z, Chonmaitree T, et al. Amoxicillin middle-ear fluid penetration and pharmacokinetics in children with acute otitis media. Pediatr Infect Dis J 1998;17:149–56.

Craig WA, Andes D. Pharmacokinetics and pharmacodynamics of antibiotics in otitis media. Pediatr Infect Dis J 1996;15:255–9.

Dagan R, Hoberman A, Johnson C, et al. Bacteriologic and clinical efficacy of high dose amoxicillin/clavulanate in children with acute otitis media. Pediatr Infect Dis J 2001;20:829–37.

Dagan R, Leibovitz E, Greenberg D, et al. Dynamics of pneumococcal nasopharyngeal colonization during the first days of antibiotic treatment in pediatric patients. Pediatr Infect Dis J 1998;17:880–5.

Dagan R, Leibovitz E, Greenberg D, et al. Early eradication of pathogens from middle-ear fluid during antibiotic treatment of acute otitis media is associated with improved clinical outcome. Pediatr Infect Dis J 1998;17:776–82.

Dagan R, Yagupsky P, Goldbart A, et al. Increasing prevalence of penicillin-resistant pneumococcal infections in children in southern Israel: implications for future immunization policies. Pediatr Infect Dis J 1994;13:782–6.

Doern GV, Brueggemann A, Holley HP, Rauch AM. Antimicrobial resistance of *Streptococcus pneumoniae* recovered from outpatients in the United States during the winter months of 1994 to 1995: results of a 30-center national surveillance study. Antimicrob Agents Chemother 1996;40:1208–13.

Dowell SF, Butler JC, Giebink GS, et al. and the Drug-resistant *Streptococcus pneumoniae* Therapeutic Working Group. Acute otitis media: management and surveillance in an era of pneumococcal resistance—a report from the Drug-resistant *Streptococcus pneumoniae* Therapeutic Working Group. Pediatr Infect Dis J 1999;18:1–9.

Fenoll A, Bourgon CM, Muñóz R, et al. Serotype distribution and antimicrobial resistance of *Streptococcus pneumoniae* isolates causing systemic infections in Spain, 1979–89. Rev Infect Dis 1991;13:56–60.

Friedland IR, Istre GR. Management of penicillin-resistant pneumococcal infections. Pediatr Infect Dis J 1992;11:433–5.

Friedland IR, McCracken GH Jr. Management of infections caused by antibiotic-resistant *Streptococcus pneumoniae*. N Engl J Med 1994;331:377–82.

Garcia-Martos P, Galan F, Marin P, et al. Increase in high resistance to penicillin of clinical isolates of *S. pneumoniae* in Cadiz, Spain. Chemotherapy 1997;43:179–81.

Gehanno P, Berche P, N'Gyen L, et al. Resolution of clinical failure in acute otitis media confirmed by in vivo bacterial eradication—efficacy and safety of ceftriaxone injected once daily, for 3 days [abstract]. In: Programs and abstracts of the 37th Interscience Conference on Antimicrobial Agents and Chemotherapy, Toronto, 1997. Washington (DC): American Society for Microbiology, 1997. p. 372.

Gehanno P, Lenoir G, Berche P. In vivo correlates for *Streptococcus pneumoniae* penicillin resistance in acute otitis media. Antimicrob Agents Chemother 1995;39:271–2.

Guay DR. Pharmacodynamics and pharmacokinetics of cefdinir, an oral extended spectrum cephalosporin. Pediatr Infect Dis J 2000;19(12 Suppl):S141–6.

Gudnason T, Gudbrandsson F, Barsanti F, et al. Penetration of ceftriaxone into the middle ear fluid of children. Pediatr Infect Dis J 1998;17:258–60.

Hermans P, Sluijter M, Elzenaar K, et al. Penicillin-resistant *Streptococcus pneumoniae* in the Netherlands: results of a 1-year molecular epidemiologic study. J Infect Dis 1997;175:1413–22.

Klein JO. Protecting the therapeutic advantage of antimicrobial agents used for otitis media. Pediatr Infect Dis J 1998;17:571–5.

Leibovitz E, Piglansky L, Raiz S, et al. Bacteriologic and clinical efficacy of one day vs. three day intramuscular ceftriaxone for treatment of nonresponsive acute otitis media in children. Pediatr Infect Dis J 2000;19:1040–5.

Manninen R, Hudvinen P, Nissinen A, et al. Increasing antimicrobial resistance in *Streptococcus pneumoniae*, *Haemophilus influenzae*, and *Moraxella catarrhalis* in Finland. J Antimicrob Chemother 1997;40:387–92.

Mastro TD, Nomani NK, Ishaq Z, et al. Use of nasopharyngeal isolates of *Streptococcus pneumoniae* and *Haemophilus influenzae* from children in Pakistan for surveillance for antimicrobial resistance. Pediatr Infect Dis J 1993;12:824–30.

McLaughlin V, Riley T, Roberts C. Invasive *Streptococcus pneumoniae* in Perth teaching. Commun Dis Int 1997;21:73–6.

Nelson CT, Mason EO, Kaplan SL. Activity of oral antibiotic in middle ear and sinus infections caused by penicillin resistant *Streptococcus pneumoniae*: implications for treatment. Pediatr Infect Dis J 1994;13:585–9.

Pichichero ME. Diagnostic accuracy, tympanocentesis training performance, and antibiotic selection by pediatric residents in management of otitis media. Pediatrics 2002;110:1064–70.

Richter SS, Heilmann KP, Coffman SL, et al. The molecular epidemiology of penicillin-resistant *Streptococcus pneumoniae* in the United States, 1994–2000. Clin Infect Dis 2002;34:330–9.

Spika JS, Facklam RR, Plikaytis BD, et al, and the Pneumococcal Surveillance Working Group. Antimicrobial resistance of *Streptococcus pneumoniae* in the United States, 1979–1987. J Infect Dis 1991;163:1273–8.

Tomasz A. Antibiotic resistance in *Streptococcus pneumoniae*. Clin Infect Dis 1997;24 Suppl 1:S85–8.

Trupl J, Hupkova H, Appelbaum PC, et al. The incidence of penicillin-resistant pneumococci in the Slovak Republic. Chemotherapy 1997;43:316–22.

Zenni MK, Cheatham SH, Thompson JM, et al. *Streptococcus pneumoniae* colonization in the young child: association with otitis media and resistance to penicillin. J Pediatr 1995;127:533–7.

Chapter 18

Intramuscular Antimicrobial Therapy for Acute Otitis Media

Angela Ellison, MD, Howard Bauchner, MD

The cost and complexity involving the management and treatment of otitis media are increasing, especially in the era of drug-resistant bacterial pathogens. Even with a wide array of available antibiotics and the introduction of the pneumococcal conjugate vaccine, it is unlikely that there will be a significant reduction in the incidence of otitis media in the immediate future. Therefore, the development of antimicrobial agents with increased clinical and bacteriologic efficacy against drug-resistant pathogens is crucial in decreasing the morbidity and health care burden associated with treating this infection.

Problems with Resistance

The emergence of multidrug-resistant pathogens has created an environment in which health care providers are faced with high rates of treatment failure and recurrent infections. The ability of penicillin-resistant pneumococci to alter penicillin-binding proteins within their cell wall, as well as the production of β-lactamase by *Haemophilus influenzae* and *Moraxella catarrhalis*, has allowed pathogens to become resistant to many of our first-line antimicrobial agents. *Streptococcus pneumoniae* is the most common bacterial cause of acute otitis media (AOM), pneumonia, meningitis, and sinusitis in developed countries. As such, penicillin-resistant *S. pneumoniae* pose a significant threat to child health. In addition, AOM owing to *S. pneumoniae* is also less likely to resolve spontaneously than is disease owing to *H. influenzae* and *M. catarrhalis* (Klein, 1994). Health care providers must therefore continue to update their knowledge about changing the susceptibility patterns of pneumococci and appropriate antimicrobial treatment.

Therapeutic Options

Numerous therapeutics options exist for the treatment of AOM. However, oral amoxicillin continues to remain the drug of choice for the treatment of uncomplicated infection (Klein, 1991). Amoxicillin has established efficacy against *S. pneumoniae* with documented clinical success for at least the past two decades. The second-line choice of treatment if amoxicillin fails has remained controversial. The most popular oral alternatives include amoxicillin-clavulanate, azithromycin, cefdinir, cefpodoxime, and cefuroxime (Klein, 2002).

Trimethoprim-sulfamethoxazole (TMP-SMX) and macrolide regimens have been used as first- and second-line treatment in the past, but concern over increasing resistance to these agents has limited their use. Pneumococcal surveillance studies have shown that resistance to these agents is more common than resistance to penicillin (Thornsberry et al, 1997). There is also an increased likelihood of resistance to macrolides and TMP-SMX in cases in which initial therapy with amoxicillin has failed (Dowell et al, 1999).

The decreased bacteriologic success of many orally administered antimicrobial agents has emphasized the need for newer alternatives. Multiple studies performed over the past two decades have demonstrated that pathogens recovered from the middle ear fluid (MEF) of patients with nonresponsive AOM are likely to be resistant to various antibiotic drugs than the pathogens recovered in cases of simple, uncomplicated AOM (Del Castillo et al, 1998; Harrison et al, 1985; Leibovitz et al, 1998a; Teele et al, 1981). Numerous intramuscular (IM) options exist for the treatment of uncomplicated bacterial infections, such as IM penicillin for streptococcal pharyngitis.

However, investigations in the use of IM therapy for the treatment of complicated and uncomplicated AOM have focused on ceftriaxone.

Pharmacokinetics and Pharmacodynamics of Ceftriaxone

The clinical and bacteriologic efficacy of ceftriaxone for the treatment of AOM is determined by its ability to reach a concentration in MEF that exceeds the minimum inhibitory concentrations (MICs) of the common bacterial pathogens. The time period for which antimicrobial concentrations remain above the MIC and the MEF-to-MIC ratio have been shown to be predictors of bacteriologic efficacy in otitis media (Craig and Andes, 1996).

Ceftriaxone has demonstrated very favorable pharmacokinetics and pharmocodynamics in the treatment of bacterial infections. A single 50 mg/kg dose is rapidly and completely absorbed following IM administration, with an estimated plasma half-life of 6 hours (Gudnason et al, 1998). In 1998, Gudnason and colleagues conducted a randomized pharmacokinetic study in an effort to determine the pharmacokinetics and pharmacodynamics of ceftriaxone in the MEF in children. The total concentration (bound and unbound) of ceftriaxone in the MEF was obtained during the insertion of tympanostomy tubes in 42 pediatric patients with otitis media. Patients enrolled in the study had documented chronic middle ear effusion for at least 3 months, requiring insertion of tympanostomy tubes. Patients were randomized to one of six groups based on the time interval between ceftriaxone administration and sampling of both the MEF and plasma. MEF sampling times were from 1 to 50 hours after a single IM injection of 50 mg/kg of ceftriaxone. Mean ceftriaxone levels in the middle ear reached a peak of 35 µg/mL at 24 hours and remained at 19 µg/mL at 48 hours, with a calculated MEF half-life of 25 hours. The concentration maximum of ceftriaxone in the MEF was shown to be 35 to 580 times higher than the MIC_{90} for the three major causative pathogens in otitis media. The time in which the concentration of ceftriaxone exceeded the MIC_{90} was between 100 and > 200 hours (4–8 days). Good bacteriologic efficacy could therefore be predicted for a single 50 mg/kg IM dose of ceftriaxone for the treatment of AOM, including that caused by penicillin-resistant pneumococci (Craig and Andes, 1996).

Clinical Trials of Ceftriaxone

Numerous clinical trials have been conducted to determine the efficacy of IM ceftriaxone for the treatment of AOM (Table 18-1). Green and Rothrock (1993) conducted a double-blind, randomized study comparing a single dose of intramuscularly administered ceftriaxone with oral amoxicillin. A total of 233 patients in a pediatric emergency room, aged 5 months to 5 years, with uncomplicated AOM were randomized to either single IM therapy (50 mg/kg) plus oral placebo for 10 days or to placebo injection plus oral amoxicillin for 10 days. Uncomplicated AOM was defined as symptoms of fever, otalgia, or irritability and compatible otoscopic findings of either discoloration, bulging, impaired mobility, or opacity other than scarring. Successful treatment was defined as resolution of AOM symptoms and the absence of these symptoms within 10 days of the visit to the emergency department; treatment of those subjects not meeting these criteria was judged as unsuccessful. Successful treatment was clinically and statistically similar in the two groups: 107 of the 117 patients given amoxicillin (91%) and 105 of the 116 patients given ceftriaxone (91%) ($p = .803$). The investigators concluded that a single IM injection of ceftriaxone (50 mg/kg) is as effective as 10 days of oral amoxicillin for the treatment of uncomplicated AOM in children.

Barnett and colleagues (1997) conducted a larger randomized, single-blind trial comparing the clinical efficacy of single-dose IM ceftriaxone with 10 days of oral TMP-SMX. A total of 484 patients, aged 3 months to 3 years, with the diagnosis of acute AOM were randomized to either a single IM dose of ceftriaxone (50 mg/kg) or to 10 days of oral TMP-SMX. Acute AOM was defined as signs of acute illness (fever, ear pain or pulling, ear discharge, vomiting, lethargy, or irritability) plus an abnormal tympanic membrane with objective evidence of middle ear effusion. Patients were evaluated at scheduled visits at 3, 14, and 28 days. On day 3, 223 of 241 (92.5%) children in the ceftriaxone group and 231 of 243 (95.1%) children in the TMP-SMX group were cured (defined as no clinical signs of AOM) or improved (defined as fewer signs of illness, afebrile, and nearly back to baseline status). On day 14, 158 of 197 (80.2%) children in the ceftriaxone group and 174 of 212 (82.1%) children in the TMP-SMX group were cured (defined as remaining well since the previous visit). On day 28, 108 of 136 (79.4%)

TABLE 18-1. Clinical Trials of Intramuscular Ceftriaxone for the Treatment of Acute Otitis Media

Name	Publication Date	Type of Trial	No. of Subjects	Subjects' Age	Findings
Green et al	January 1993	Randomized, double blind	233	5 mo–5 yr	CFTX and AMOX; equal efficacy in uncomplicated AOM
Barnett et al	January 1997	Randomized, single blind	484	3 mo–3 yr	CFTX and TMP-SMX comparable; efficacy in uncomplicated AOM
Leibovitz et al	December 1998	Prospective	92	3–36 mo	3-d IM CFTX efficacious in nonresponsive AOM
Leibovitz et al	November 2000	Randomized	109	3–36 mo	3-d IM CFTX superior to 1-d IM CFTX in nonresponsive AOM

AMOX = amoxicillin; CFTX = ceftriaxone; IM = intramuscular; TMP-SMX = trimethroprim-sulfamethoxazole.

children in the ceftriaxone group and 124 of 155 (80%) children in the TMP-SMX group were cured. The investigators concluded that a single dose of ceftriaxone is comparable in clinical efficacy to 10 days of oral TMP-SMZ for the treatment of AOM.

Leibovitz and colleagues conducted two important studies involving the bacteriologic efficacy and the appropriate duration of treatment of IM therapy in nonresponsive AOM. The first (Leibovitz et al, 1998b) was a prospective trial in which 92 patients (aged 3–36 months) with culture-proven nonresponsive AOM underwent treatment with IM ceftriaxone for 3 days. Nonresponsive AOM was defined as persistent or relapsing AOM for which an antibiotic was administered for any period of time > 48 hours during the 14 days preceding tympanocentesis. MEF was aspirated for culture by tympanocentesis on the day of enrolment, and a second tap was performed on days 4 to 10. Bacteriologic failure was defined by positive culture on days 4 to 10. Bacteriologic eradication was achieved in 100 of 105 (95%) cases. Bacteriologic success occurred in 13 of 13 (100%) penicillin-susceptible *S. pneumoniae* versus 28 of 34 (82%) *S. pneumoniae* intermediately resistant to penicillin. The investigators concluded that a 3-day IM ceftriaxone regimen is efficacious for the treatment of nonresponsive AOM.

Leibovitz and colleagues (2000) next conducted a randomized trial to determine the bacteriologic and clinical efficacy of 1 day versus 3 days of an IM ceftriaxone regimen in the treatment of nonresponsive AOM in children. Nonresponsive AOM was defined in the same manner as above. One hundred and nine patients ages 3 to 36 months with culture-proven, nonresponsive AOM were randomized to receive 1 (50 mg/kg) or 3 days (50 mg/kg/d) of IM ceftriaxone. MEF was once again aspirated for culture by tympanocentesis on the day of enrolment and again on days 4 to 5. *S. pneumoniae* isolates with penicillin MIC values of 0.1 to 1.0 μg/mL were considered intermediately susceptible to penicillin, whereas those with MIC > 1.0 μg/mL were defined as fully resistant. These two groups constitute penicillin-nonsusceptible strains. Bacteriologic failure was defined by a positive culture on days 4 to 5. Bacteriologic eradication of 14 of 27 (52%) and 33 of 34 (97%) penicillin-nonsusceptible *S. pneumoniae* isolates was achieved in the 1-day and 3-day groups, respectively. The investigators concluded that a 3-day IM ceftriaxone regimen was superior to a 1-day IM regimen in the treatment of nonresponsive AOM caused by penicillin-resistant *S. pneumoniae*.

Potential Benefits of Intramuscular Therapy

In addition to bacteriologic cure, a major potential benefit of IM therapy is improved adherence. Missed doses, spillage, and vomiting are just a few of the reasons why patient adherence with oral medications is poor. Incomplete administration and interrupted antibiotic courses may result in recurrent infection and increased selection of drug-resistant pathogens. Therefore, ceftriaxone may be warranted in cases in which adherence or tolerance of oral medication is problematic.

Parental satisfaction is another potential advantage. In 1996, Bauchner and colleagues published the results of a randomized, controlled trial comparing parental preference for single-dose IM therapy versus standard 10-day oral therapy (amoxicillin-clavulanate given three times a day) for the treatment of AOM. Six hundred and forty-eight children, aged 3 months to 6 years, were randomly assigned to receive IM ceftriaxone or oral therapy. The results showed that 85% of parents expressed a preference for a single dose of IM therapy at enrolment. At days 14 to 16, more parents in the IM group reported being "very satisfied" with the antibiotic (95%) compared with parents whose children were assigned to the oral therapy group (38% $p < .001$). In comparing current therapy with past oral therapy for AOM, 71% of parents with children in the IM therapy group reported more satisfaction with current therapy, in contrast to 21% of parents with children in the oral therapy group ($p < .001$). Overall, the majority (83%) of parents indicated that they would prefer single-dose IM therapy for AOM in the future.

Potential Disadvantages of Intramuscular Therapy

There are a number of potential disadvantages of IM therapy, including the emergence of bacterial resistance, pain, and cost.

There are few data about the emergence of penicillin-resistant bacteria after treatment with ceftriaxone. Heikkinen and colleagues (2000) determined the effect of a single 50 mg/kg dose of ceftriaxone on the nasopharyngeal bacterial flora in 167 children with diagnosed AOM. Nasopharyngeal swabs were obtained at enrolment and at the first follow-up visit 5 days after initiation of treatment. Before treatment, 60% of pneumococcal isolates were sensitive to penicillin, 26% were of intermediate susceptibility, and 14% were penicillin resistant as opposed to 24%, 59%, and 16% after treatment, respectively. The relative proportion of pneumococcal strains with decreased susceptibility to penicillin was significantly increased after treatment with ceftriaxone (Heikkinen et al, 2000).

Cohen and colleagues (1999) reported similar findings. This group conducted a randomized trial (in an area with a high rate of resistant pneumococcal strains) comparing the efficacy and safety of one 50 mg/kg dose of ceftriaxone with 10 days of amoxicillin-clavulanate therapy for AOM. Five hundred and thirteen children with diagnosed AOM were randomized to either treatment group and 463 children were evaluated for efficacy. A nasopharyngeal swab for bacterial culture was performed before treatment and at days 12 to 14. Among children carrying *S. pneumoniae*, the percentage of strains resistant to penicillin increased from 53% before treatment to 63% after treatment in the ceftriaxone group. Of note, there was a greater percentage increase of resistant strains in the amoxicillin-clavulanate group after treatment (an increase from 51 to 83%).

These studies are important because they illustrate the concern for the risk of developing resistant pneumococcal strains after use of IM ceftriaxone. However, the study conducted by Cohen and colleagues (1999) showed no evidence that a single dose of ceftriaxone contributed more to the emergence of resistance than 10 days of treatment with an oral antibiotic.

IM administration of ceftriaxone is associated with pain and induration and warmth at the injection site. Given advances in therapy for pain, numerous approaches are possible that will reduce the pain. For example, topical anesthetics, such as EMLA cream, and ethyl chloride spray (vapocoolant) may be used. Interestingly, despite the pain, as mentioned above, under certain circumstances, parents still prefer single-dose therapy to giving a drug two to three times a day for 5 to 10 days.

A single dose of IM ceftriaxone is more expensive than 10 days of amoxicillin and most other oral alternatives. However, the cost is highly dependent on where the drug is being dispensed. In addition, the additional cost is often not paid directly by the patient because many insurance plans cover injectibles.

Centers for Disease Control and Prevention Recommendations

In January 1999, the Drug-resistant *Streptococcus pneumoniae* Therapeutic Working Group of the Centers for Disease Control and Prevention (CDC) published new recommendations for the management of AOM in the era of pneumococcal resistance (Dowell et al, 1999). The group concluded that oral amoxicillin should remain the first-line antimicrobial agent for the treatment of uncomplicated AOM. It was recommended that the initial dosage of amoxicillin be increased from 40 to 45 mg/kg/d up to 80 to 90 mg/kg/d. These recommendations were based on the increasing prevalence of drug-resistant pneumococci, safety of high-dose amoxicillin, and evidence that higher dosages of amoxicillin can achieve effective MEF concentrations (Dowell et al, 1999).

If clinical treatment failure occurs after 3 days of the therapy, it is suggested that an alternative agent be used. Such alternative agents should be selected after considering the risk of infection with resistant strains. The three recommended antimicrobial alternatives include oral amoxicillin-clavulanate, cefuroxime axetil, and IM ceftriaxone. It was suggested that IM ceftriaxone be given as three daily doses. The group also notes that in some difficult cases, diagnostic tympanocentesis with culture and susceptibility testing of isolates may be necessary to guide treatment.

Current Uses of Ceftriaxone

IM ceftriaxone has a wide variety of uses in both acute and nonacute settings. One of the most popular uses is in the management of febrile, nontoxic-appearing children at risk for bacteremia. It is our experience that in the emergency room setting, IM ceftriaxone is often used to treat infants with fever who also have AOM. This approach helps protect children against possible bacteremia. The use of ceftriaxone in these cases may soon decline following the introduction and widespread use of the pneumococcal conjugate vaccine.

There are few data about the use of ceftriaxone for the treatment of AOM in the office setting. In our discussions with practitioners and in our own clinical practice, its use in this setting has been limited. In general, practitioners are comfortable with the array of oral therapies that are available and are concerned about the overuse of ceftriaxone. Whether this will change in the coming years because of the continuing rise of resistant *S. pneumoniae* is unclear. How the increase in rates of resistant *S. pneumoniae* will interact with the introduction of the conjugate pneumococcal vaccine and impact on practice is also uncertain.

Conclusion

We believe that ceftriaxone, as IM therapy for AOM, does have an important but limited role. The clinical data are impressive. Overall, ceftriaxone is as effective as any oral antibiotic. The levels achieved in the middle ear are sufficient to treat even most resistant bacterial organisms. Although the CDC recommends that patients receive three daily doses and the data from Leibovitz and colleagues (1998b) suggest that this is necessary if the child has resistant *S. pneumoniae*, for the clinician who does not perform tympanocentesis, no microbiologic data are available. Understanding that young infants who are in day care and have received antibiotic therapy in the past 30 to 60 days are at high risk of having resistant organisms may help to guide follow-up. For these children, very close follow-up is warranted. If they continue to be ill after 24 hours, they likely require additional doses of ceftriaxone.

Ceftriaxone will continue to play a limited but important role in the treatment of AOM. Given all that we have learned about bacterial resistance and the importance of using effective but targeted treatment, it should be an alternative therapy. Whether its importance in the initial treatment of AOM increases will depend on the impact of conjugate pneumococcal vaccine and the rates of resistant *S. pneumoniae*.

References

Barnett ED, Teele DW, Klein J, et al. Comparison of ceftriaxone and trimethoprim-sulfamethoxazole for acute otitis media. Pediatrics 1997;99:23–8.

Bauchner H, Adams W, Barnett E, Klein JO. Therapy for acute otitis media: preferences of parents for oral or parenteral antibiotic. Arch Pediatr Adolesc Med 1996;150:396–9.

Cohen R, Navel M, Grunberg J, et al. One dose ceftriaxone vs. ten days of amoxicillin/clavulanate therapy for acute otitis media: clinical efficacy and change in nasopharyngeal flora. Pediatr Infect Dis J 1999;18:403–9.

Craig WA, Andes D. Pharmacokinetics and pharmacodynamics of antibiotics in otitis media. Pediatr Infect Dis J 1996;15:255–9.

Del Castillo F, Baquero-Artigao F, Garcia-Perea A. Influence of recent antibiotic therapy on antimicrobial resistance of *Streptococcus pneumoniae* in children with acute otitis media in Spain. Pediatr Infect Dis J 1998;17:94–7.

Dowell SF, Butler JC, Giebink GS, et al. Acute otitis media: management and surveillance in an era of pneumococcal resistance—a report from the Drug-resistant *Streptococcus pneumoniae* Therapeutic Working Group. Pediatr Infect Dis J 1999;18:1–9.

Green SM, Rothrock SG. Single dose intramuscular ceftriaxone for acute otitis media in children. Pediatrics 1993;91:23–30.

Gudnason T, Gudbrandsson F, Barsanti F, Kristinsson KG. Penetration of ceftriaxone into the middle ear fluid of children. Pediatr Infect Dis J 1998;17:258–60.

Harrison CJ, Marks MI, Welch DF. Microbiology of recently treated acute otitis media compared with previously treated otitis media. Pediatr Infect Dis J 1985;4:641–6.

Heikkinen T, Saeed KA, McCormick DP, et al. A single intramuscular dose of ceftriaxone changes nasopharyngeal bacterial flora in children with acute otitis media. Acta Paediatr 2000;89:1316–21.

Klein JO. Review of consensus reports on management of acute otitis media. Pediatr Infect Dis J 1991;18:1152–5.

Klein JO. Otitis media. Clin Infect Dis 1994;19:823–33.

Klein JO. Accurate acute otitis media diagnosis equals good antibiotic use. Infect Dis Child 2002;15:41–2.

Leibovitz E, Piglansky L, Raiz S, et al. Bacteriologic efficacy of a three day IM ceftriaxone regimen in nonresponsive acute otitis media. Pediatr Infect Dis J 1998a;17:1126–31.

Leibovitz E, Piglansky L, Raiz S, et al. Bacteriologic and clinical efficacy of one day vs. three-day intramuscular ceftriaxone for treatment of nonresponsive acute otitis media in children. Pediatr Infect Dis J 2000;19:1040–5.

Leibovitz E, Raiz S, Piglansky L, et al. Resistance pattern of middle ear fluid isolates in acute otitis media recently treated with antibiotics. Pediatr Infect Dis J 1998b;17:463–9.

Teele DW, Pelton SI, Klein JO. Bacteriologic efficacy of acute otitis media: I. Causative pathogens. Pediatr Infect Dis J 1981;98:537–9.

Thornsberry C, Ogilvie P, Kehn J, Mauriz Y. Surveillance of antimicrobial resistance in *Streptococcus pneumoniae*, *Haemophilus influenzae* and *Moraxella catarrhalis* in the United States 1996–97 reporting season. Diagn Microbiol Infect Dis 1997;29:249–57.

III. Recurrent Acute Otitis Media

Chapter 19

WHEN IS ACUTE OTITIS MEDIA TOO OFTEN?

KARI JORUNN KVAERNER, MD, PhD

Acute otitis media (AOM) is a common and self-limiting inflammation of the middle ear (Klein et al, 1989), and its peak incidence is at age 6 to 15 months (Prellner et al, 1984). Studies of histopathologic changes in the middle ear have shown that the clinical manifestations of AOM, secretory otitis media (OM), and chronic OM are different stages of the same disease—a disease continuum (Paparella et al, 1990). Single AOM episodes are relatively easy to manage, but children with recurrent AOM represent a clinical challenge (Giebink, 1994). Because frequent AOM episodes may lead to delayed speech acquisition, hearing loss, and otologic sequelae, early identification and follow-up of these children are important.

Forty percent of all children have experienced one or more episodes of OM by age 2 years (Kvaerner et al, 1997; Prellner et al, 1994). Although most children normally recover without sequela, 5 to 10% of children experience recurrent episodes of OM (Kvaerner et al, 1997; Prellner et al, 1984). Figure 19-1 shows how the first AOM episode is distributed in children who develop recurrent AOM compared with nonrecurrent AOM children.

Although acute suppurative OM refers to a clinically identifiable infection in the middle ear with sudden onset and short duration (Klein et al, 1989), there is no general classification agreement on the definitions of recurrent OM. For research purposes, the term "recurrent acute otitis media" is normally defined as four or more AOM episodes during a 12-month period or three or more episodes during a 6-month period, with an intermediate period of at least 1 month between two consecutive episodes (Alho et al, 1990; Kvaerner et al, 1997).

Persistent OM is associated with mild to moderate hearing loss and subsequent longer-term effects on behavior and quality of life (Vernon-Feagans, 1999). Evidence from auditory deprivation research indicates that the earlier the identification and habilitation occur, the greater the level of

speech production and linguistic competence achieved by the children during their early years of life (Mauk and Behrens, 1993). Further, more intractable pathology, such as granulation tissue and cholesteatoma, can develop in the middle ear as a complication of OM (Tos, 1984).

When Should We Consider Managing AOM Differently?

Although there is a lack of uniform definitions of recurrent AOM, clinically, these children are easy to identify. For the treating physician, children present at an early age with recurrent ear infections (Alho et al, 1990; Kvaerner et al, 1997; Prellner et al, 1984). It is often difficult to determine whether children present with a new ear infection or whether the second consultation involves unsuccessful treatment of the primary AOM episode. By the time the recurrence of infections leads to a more or less chronic illness, AOM is "too often," and the child is in an otitis-prone condition. In neonates, neither the mastoid system nor the immune apparatus is fully developed, and the nasopharyngeal dimensions will subsequently be changed with increasing age (Maw et al, 1991). As part of the maturation of the immune system, children experience four to eight subclinical upper respiratory infections yearly, with a varying number presenting as clinically identifiable infections (Prellner et al, 1984). In otitis-prone children, infections may be more likely to develop into AOM episodes (Prellner et al, 1984).

Treatment and Followup of Otitis-Prone Children: Case History

Matthew is 6 months old and the youngest of three children. At 7 weeks of age, he had acute onset of fever at night. The general physician diagnosed AOM with perforated eardrum at consultation the following day. Matthew recovered clinically

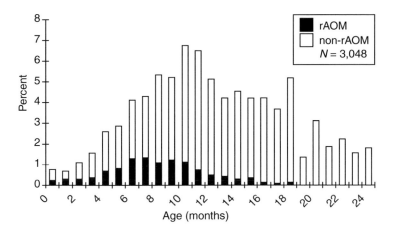

FIGURE 19-1. Frequency distribution of the first acute otitis media episode among children with recurrent acute otitis media (rAOM) and nonrecurrent acute otitis media (non-rAOM) within 1 year after the first episode. Data from a prospective cohort of Oslo-born children followed from birth to age 2 years (*N* = 3,048).

overnight but received antibiotic treatment because of his young age. Nevertheless, the ear discharge continued, and growth of bacteria revealed nonencapsulated β-hemolytic streptococci resistant to the first-choice antibiotics he was given (penicillin). On the second antibiotic treatment, the discharge cleared up. Unfortunately, Matthew was subject to another AOM episode within a few weeks, with fever and systemic illness symptoms. The third visit to his physician in a short period of time resulted in another antibiotic treatment. By the age of 4 months, Matthew had experienced three AOM episodes, and his parents were worried about the recurrence of the disease and the intermittent episodes of discharge associated with the infectious episodes. Additionally, he was still a demanding baby who, because of the frequency of illness, had not adopted a regular sleeping pattern. Subsequently, his parents were becoming "worn out" by the chronic pattern of his illness.

How Do the Criteria "Too Often" Vary in Different Clinical Presentations?

Some children are more susceptible to AOM than others (Kvaerner et al, 1997; Prellner et al, 1984). Therefore, the criterion "too often" will vary according to different age groups, risk groups, and clinical presentations. There is a genetic susceptibility for recurrent AOM (Casselbrant et al, 1999; Kvaerner et al, 1995) that is probably precipitated by exposure to respiratory pathogens at early age. Physicians should therefore make an effort to identify and follow high-risk infants and, in cases of recurrent ear infections, refer them to otolaryngology specialists to optimize treatment.

Case History (continued)

Because Matthew's father had recurrent OM in childhood, his parents were aware of the probability for OM in their son. Additionally, the oldest sibling in the family, now 6 years old, also had recurrent episodes of ear infections in the first years of life. Both older siblings attended day care, and there was an allergy predisposition in the family. The family was regularly exposed to upper respiratory pathogens and common colds, and chronic rhinitis and intermittent secretory OM almost became a regular condition among the children in the family.

Children with a family history of AOM and with the first episode prior to 9 months are at increased risk for AOM (Kvaerner et al, 1997). In addition to genetic involvement (Casselbrant et al, 1999; Kvaerner et al, 1995), early exposure to respiratory pathogens with subsequent AOM increases the probability for recurrence (Kvaerner et al, 1996; Kvaerner et al, 1997). As many as 5 to 10% of all children with ear infections experience recurrent episodes (Kvaerner et al, 1997; Prellner et al, 1984). In Table 19-1, an overview of factors associated with AOM is shown.

Both clinical and population-based investigations published since 1995 have the findings of many previous studies: young age, age at onset, and male gender are significant risk factors for recurrent OM (Alho et al, 1990; Kvaerner et al, 1995). Most recent studies evaluating child care and OM report that exposure to other children at home or in a day-care setting increases the risk of AOM, recurrent AOM, and OM with effusion (Kvaerner et al, 1996; Paradise et al, 1997). Recent studies confirm that risk increases as the number of children increases, particularly children under age 2 years (Kvaerner et al, 1996; Paradise et al, 1997). Kvaerner and colleagues (1996) found that the most important risk factors in early AOM among Norwegian infants were attendance at day care with many children and having siblings in day care and that recurrent AOM was associated with having siblings and attending day care. Daly and colleagues (1999) reported that day care and siblings, but not siblings in day care, increased the risk of early OM onset. These disparate findings probably reflect the fact that many children in the

TABLE 19-1. Factors Associated with Increased Risk for Recurrent Acute Otitis Media

Genetic predisposition
Early age at onset of first ear infection
Day care
Siblings in day care
Gender (male)
Allergic predisposition
Passive smoking?

United States enter day care in the first few months of life, whereas children in Norway typically enter day care at about 1 year of age. Only one retrospective study reported that day care alone was not a risk factor, but the combination of day care, allergy, and passive smoking increased the risk of recurrent AOM (Stenstrom and Ingvarsson, 1997).

Reported racial differences (Paradise et al, 1997) and familial aggregation (Daly et al, 1999; Kvaerner et al, 1997; Stenstrom and Ingvarsson, 1997) suggest genetic involvement in OM. Twin studies from Norway (Kvaerner et al, 1995) and Pittsburgh (Casselbrant et al, 1999) have reported that OM has a large heredity component. The Norwegian study, applying multivariate modeling, found that genetic factors are major contributors for OM. Heredity was estimated at 74% for females and 45% for males. A similar study by Casselbrant and colleagues (1999) confirmed the substantial genetic variability of OM. A segregation analysis of first-degree relatives from 176 families suggests that OM susceptibility is likely to be attributable to more than one gene (Rich et al, 2002).

The effect of age at the first AOM episode (Prellner et al, 1984) and male gender on subsequent otitis proneness (Kvaerner et al, 1997) may be related to genetically determined anatomic or physiologic variability. The finding that infants with cord blood antibody levels to *Streptococcus pneumoniae* types 14 and 19F in the lowest quartile had significantly earlier onset of OM than infants with higher antibody levels adds evidence that delayed maturation of certain immunoglobulin subgroups is one of the mechanisms for such susceptibility (Salazar et al, 1997). This finding also suggests a new prevention strategy: vaccination of pregnant women to increase infant antibody levels during the first few months of life to prevent early OM onset. Evidence that some children are particularly susceptible to many types of upper respiratory infections confirms reports of the association between viral and bacterial upper respiratory tract infections (Prellner et al, 1984).

General Management Aspects for Recurrent AOM

Case History (continued)

At 4 months, Matthew was referred to an otolaryngologist. Because the ear symptoms and discharge returned every time the antibiotic treatment was stopped, Matthew received surgical treatment with myringotomy of his nondischarging ear and intravenous antibiotics. By the time the ear discharge ceased and the clinical situation improved, oral antibiotics were prescribed for another couple of weeks and ventilation tubes were inserted. An otolaryngologist followed Matthew every 6 weeks. Despite long-term treatment, Matthew's ear did not clear up. At the age of 6 months, he received in-patient treatment with bilateral cortical mastoidectomy. Outpatient follow-up with antibiotic treatment at each sign of AOM was given. Subsequently, at age 12 months, ventilation tubes were

inserted again. The following year, the infection rate declined somewhat, but the parents did not feel that Matthew's situation was under control until age 3 years. As a high-risk infant, Matthew received regular outpatient follow-up with otomicroscopy and audiologic investigations throughout childhood.

Management of the otitis-prone child has three different treatment considerations: (1) medical treatment of current AOM episodes, (2) medical prophylaxis between infections, and (3) nonmedical environmental precautions prior to onset of the first infection. Further, the choice of treatment and follow-up should take into consideration that chronic and prolonged disease in young children has an impact on the total family structure. Accordingly, treatment and follow-up should have familial considerations in mind when individual factors such as frequency of infections, age, and the general health state of the child determine the choice of treatment. Table 19-2 provides an overview of the various treatment aspects in otitis-prone children. Antibiotic prophylaxis is the most effective method to reduce the frequency of new episodes of OM in children with recurrent AOM, but it should be used with caution (Prellner et al, 1994). Tympanostomy tube placement and/or adenoidectomy are supplemental treatment alternatives.

Antibiotics

As opposed to children with single, uncomplicated AOM episodes, in which antibiotics have only a limited effect on the clinical course and outcome (Williams et al, 1993), antibiotics are indicated in children with recurrent ear infections at an early age (Prellner et al, 1984). Antibiotics appear to have a beneficial but limited effect on recurrent OM; improvement was found in one of nine children after 2 months of treatment in a large meta-analysis of 958 children (Williams et al, 1993). Nevertheless, long-term, low-dose antibiotic treatment is an alternative to surgical treatment in otitis-prone children in whom preexisting, low, specific IgG antibody levels against AOM-associated pneumococcal types have been shown, with

TABLE 19-2. Management Overview in Otitis-Prone Children

	Prior to First Infection	Current Infections	Preventing Recurrences
Risk factor reduction			
Day care	Avoid for 1 yr		
Parental smoking	Avoid		
Vaccination	X		
Antibiotics			
Intermittent		X	X
Long term		X	X
Surgery			
Myringotomy		X	
Ventilation tube insertion			X
Adenoidectomy			X
Cortical mastoidectomy		X	

subsequent increased vulnerability for development of recurrent AOM (Prellner et al, 1994). Benefits from intermittent penicillin prophylaxis of upper respiratory infections have been reported. Low-dose penicillin V given to otitis-prone children at onset of upper respiratory infections has been reported to reduce the number of AOM episodes by 50% compared with children who did not receive antibiotics (Prellner et al, 1994).

Surgery

Early surgical intervention with ventilation tubes has been effective in 50% of children with recurrent AOM (Genhart, 1981). In some children in whom infection symptoms and ear discharge continue in spite of ventilation tube insertion, cortical mastoidectomy is necessary to clear up the infection.

Prevention and Prophylaxis

Breast-feeding, using family or small-group day care for infants and toddlers, and avoiding exposure to household tobacco smoke are the main preventive measures against AOM. It is also useful to immunize children who have recurrent OM with influenza and pneumococcal vaccines. Thirty to 40% of episodes of AOM are caused by *S. pneumoniae* (Williams et al, 1993). Clinical studies have shown that the heptavalent pneumococcal vaccine that is recommended for infants to protect against invasive disease also has a moderate amount of protection against ear infections while reducing frequent OM (Fireman et al, 2003). Although *Haemophilus influenzae* type b is principally responsible for invasive infections, it is traditionally said to play only a minor role in otitis, which is usually caused by noncapsulated *Haemophilus* strains beyond the vaccine's reach. In most studies, it has been observed that 2 to 5% of cases of *Haemophilus* otitis are attributable to *Haemophilus* type b (Reinert, 1997).

Early Identification

Infectious exposure caused by siblings or other children is the main risk factor for early AOM (Kvaerner et al, 1996; Stenstrom and Ingvarsson, 1997; Vernon-Feagans, 1999). Children with the first AOM episode prior to 9 months of age are at increased risk for subsequent otitis proneness (Kvaerner et al, 1997). Because frequent AOM episodes may lead to delayed speech and hearing loss (Mauk and Behrens, 1993; Vernon-Feagans, 1999), surgical treatment, and otologic sequelae, physicians should follow high-risk infants.

References

Alho OP, Koivu M, Sorri M, Rantakallio P. Risk factors for recurrent acute otitis media and respiratory infection in infancy. Int J Pediatr Otorhinolaryngol 1990;19:151–61.

Casselbrant ML, Mandel EM, Fall PA, et al. The heritability of otitis media: a twin and triplet study. JAMA 1999;282:2125–30.

Daly KA, Brown JE, Lindgren BR, et al. Epidemiology of otitis media onset by six months of age. Pediatrics 1999;103:1158–66.

Fireman B, Black SB, Shinefield HR, et al. Impact of the pneumococcal vaccines on otitis media. Infect Dis J 2003;22:10–6.

Genhart D. Tympanostomy tubes in the otitis prone child. Laryngoscope 1981;91:849–66.

Giebink GS. Preventing otitis media. Ann Otol Rhinol Laryngol Suppl 1994;163:20–3.

Klein JO, Tos M, Hussl B, et al. Recent advances in otitis media. Definition and classification. Ann Otol Rhinol Laryngol Suppl 1989;139:10–5.

Kværner KJ, Nafstad P, Hagen JK, et al. Early acute otitis media and siblings' attendance at nursery. Arch Dis Child 1996;55:338–41.

Kvaerner KJ, Nafstad P, Hagen JA, et al. Recurrent acute otitis media: the significance of age at onset. Acta Otolaryngol (Stockh) 1997;117:578–84.

Kværner KJ, Tambs K, Harris JR, Magnus P. Distribution and heritability of recurrent ear infections. Ann Otol Rhinol Laryngol 1997;106:624–32.

Mauk GW, Behrens TB. Historical, political and technological context associated with early identification of hearing loss. Semin Hear 1993;14:1–17.

Maw AR, Smith IM, Lance GN. Lateral cephalometric analysis of children with otitis media with effusion: a comparison with age and sex matched controls. J Laryngol Otol 1991;105:71–7.

Paparella MM, Schachern PA, Yoon TH, et al. Otopathologic correlates of the continuum of otitis media. Ann Otol Rhinol Laryngol Suppl 1990;148:17–22.

Paradise JL, Rockette HE, Colborn DK, et al. Otitis media in 2253 Pittsburgh-area infants: prevalence and risk factors during the first two years of life. Pediatrics 1997;99:318–33.

Prellner K, Fogle-Hansson M, Jørgensen F, et al. Prevention of recurrent acute otitis media in otitis-prone children by intermittent prophylaxis with penicillin. Acta Otolaryngol (Stockh) 1994;114:182–7.

Prellner K, Kalm O, Pedersen FK. Pneumococcal antibodies and complement during and after periods of recurrent otitis. Int J Pediatr Otorhinolaryngol 1984;7:39–49.

Reinert P. The role of pneumococcal and *Haemophilus* type B vaccination in the prevention of acute otitis media. Clin Microbiol Infect 1997;3:59–61.

Rich SS, Spray B, Daly K, et al. Evidence for single gene effects in the familial risk of chronic/recurrent otitis media. In: Lim DJ, Bluestone CD, Casselbrant, ML, et al, editors. Proceedings of the Seventh International Symposium on Recent Advances in Otitis Media. Hamilton (ON): BC Decker; 2002.

Salazar JC, Daly KA, Giebink GS, et al. Low cord blood pneumococcal immunoglobulin G (IgG) antibodies predict early onset acute otitis media in infancy. Am J Epidemiol 1997;145:1048–56.

Stenstrom C, Ingvarsson L. Otitis-prone children and controls: a study of possible predisposing factors. 1. Heredity, family background and perinatal period. Acta Otolaryngol (Stockh) 1997;117:87–93.

Tos M. Incidence, etiology and pathogenesis of cholesteatoma in children. Am J Otol 1984;5:459–62.

Vernon-Feagans L. Impact of otitis media on speech, language, cognition and behavior. In: Rosenfeld RM, Bluestone CD, editors. Evidence-based otitis media. Hamilton (ON): BC Decker; 1999. p. 353–73.

Williams RL, Chalmers TC, Stange KC, et al. Use of antibiotics in preventing recurrent acute otitis media and in treating otitis media with effusion. A meta-analytic attempt to resolve the brouhaha. JAMA 1993;270:1344–51.

Chapter 20

THE OTITIS-PRONE CHILD

DAVID J. KAY, MD

The otitis-prone child traditionally refers to a child with recurrent acute otitis media (AOM). Although many different parameters exist in the literature for defining recurrent AOM, one of the more established ones is the occurrence of three episodes in a 6-month period or four episodes in a 12-month period (Bluestone and Klein, 2001). The exceptions to these criteria are very young children, in whom even a single episode in the first 6 months of life or two episodes in the first 12 months of life may qualify them for consideration as "otitis prone" if these episodes are accompanied by a strong family history of middle ear disease (Bluestone and Klein, 2001).

Using these definitions, it is estimated that by 3 years of age, children will be distributed among three roughly equal-sized groups: one-third will be otitis prone, one-third will be otitis free, and the remaining third will have only occasional episodes of otitis media (OM) (Bluestone and Klein, 2001). This has been confirmed by epidemiologic studies showing that by 24 months of age, one in seven children will have experienced over six episodes of OM (Howie et al, 1975). A similar study showed that 16% of children will have had six or more episodes of OM by the age of 3 years (Teele et al, 1989).

Etiology and Pathogenesis

It is likely that the single most important factor in those children who are otitis prone is some degree of eustachian tube dysfunction (Bluestone and Klein, 2001). This was confirmed in one study showing that children with more than 11 episodes of OM had poorer active eustachian tube function, measured via pressure chamber testing, than did control children (Stenstrom et al, 1991). Nevertheless, eustachian tube dysfunction is but one of many potential contributing factors in the otitis-prone child.

Environmental factors have been shown to play a large role in recurrent AOM. Day-care attendance has been demonstrated in a half-dozen independent studies to increase the risk of OM when compared to children who stay at home (Bluestone and Klein, 2001). This likely represents a significant increase among these children of exposures to respiratory pathogens. The use of pacifiers has been shown to increase the risk of recurrent AOM (Niemelä et al, 1995; Uhari et al, 1996); moreover, the mechanism had been shown to be something other than bacteria on the pacifiers (Brook and Gober, 1997). The effects of tobacco smoke exposure can now be studied more scientifically by measuring cotinine in body fluids rather than relying on history alone. Using cotinine as a measure, tobacco smoke exposure was shown to increase the incidence of recurrent AOM (Etzel et al, 1992), with a higher increase in incidence for both prenatal and postnatal exposure together compared with just postnatal exposure alone (Ey et al, 1995). There are also many studies associating breast-feeding with a decrease in recurrent AOM incidence (Bluestone and Klein, 2001). The protective mechanism may be either the mechanics of the feeding itself, the properties of the breast milk compared with other liquids, or a combination of the two. A breast-feeding infant uses a different assortment of muscles and generates less negative pressure than a bottle-fed infant. Breast milk itself may be more immunologic and anti-inflammatory and may offer other protective factors and be less allergenic compared with formula or cow's milk. These properties of the breast milk itself are likely the most significant as breast milk fed via an artificial feeder to children with cleft palates still showed a protective effect against recurrent AOM (Paradise and Elster, 1994).

Although there is no conclusive evidence demonstrating that allergies definitely play a causative role in recurrent AOM, there are several proposed mechanisms (Bluestone and Klein, 2001). The middle ear mucosa may itself be a target organ. Alternatively, the end-effects of an allergic reaction may yield swelling of the eustachian tube mucosa, nasal obstruction, and entry of nasopharyngeal secretions (including bacteria) into the middle ear. At the very least, allergies increase inflammatory mediators, which may play a nonspecific role in middle ear and eustachian tube inflammation.

The presence of a dampened immune system may predispose a child to recurrent AOM. Such immunodeficiencies may be overt, such as agammaglobulinemia or chronic granulomatous diseases, or rather subtle, such as immunoglobulin subclass deficiencies. The workup for such deficiencies will be discussed below.

Nasopharyngeal obstruction may present as recurrent AOM if blockage of the eustachian tube orifice occurs. This obstruction may be the result of simple hypertrophic adenoid tissue, a marked posterior nasal septal deviation, or even a more serious nasopharyngeal tumor.

Gastroesophageal reflux disease (GERD) is emerging as another causative entity of OM, particularly otitis media with effusion (Tasker et al, 2002). Its role in the pathogenesis of recurrent AOM has yet to be elucidated.

Diagnostic Workup

The first step in management is the diagnostic workup. A careful history, including not only past medical history but also a detailed family and social history, should be elicited. Parents should be asked if any of the child's first- or second-degree relatives have a history of ear disease, raising the suspicion of an underlying genetic predisposition. Inquiries must be made concerning environmental factors such as day-care attendance, tobacco smoke exposure, pacifier use, and breast-feeding, as described above.

Children should be carefully examined to determine the extent of adenotonsillar hypertrophy and may be questioned concerning the signs and symptoms of GERD as well. In older children with unilateral effusion, one should keep in mind the possibility of a nasopharyngeal tumor, such as Wegener's granulomatosis or a carcinoma; this may be evaluated by visual examination of the nasopharynx via flexible fiberoptic nasopharyngoscopy. Any questionable mass or fullness should undergo a nasopharyngeal biopsy.

Children who experience recurrent AOM in spite of repeated tympanostomy tube placements should undergo a formal allergy and immunology workup. Care must be taken to ensure that all of the child's vaccinations are up to date, particularly the pneumococcal vaccine and an annual influenza vaccine. Recurrent AOM is common in many primary immunodeficiencies and may be the presenting symptom (Church, 1997). A comprehensive investigation should be considered in children with recurrent AOM in conjunction with other symptoms, including infections with opportunistic organisms; recurrent or chronic wheezing, dermatitis, or diarrhea; failure to thrive or developmental delay; a family history of any immunologic deficiency; or remarkable signs on the physical examination such as enlarged lymph nodes or the absence of lymphatic tissue, hepatosplenomegaly, clubbing, petechiae, or ecchymosis (Church, 1997). The initial immunological workup is performed with limited laboratory testing, including a complete blood count with differential; serum concentrations of IgG, IgA, and IgM and their subclasses; and antibody levels to tetanus, *Haemophilus influenzae* type b (Hib) (Church, 1997), and pneumococ-

ci. If it is prevalent in the population or suspected through the history and physical examination, human immunodeficiency virus (HIV) testing should also be performed.

Treatment Options

Treatment should begin with the least invasive maneuvers first, namely environmental changes. For infants, breast-feeding should be encouraged and pacifier use discouraged. Exposure to tobacco smoke should be eliminated; if caregiver cessation is unrealistic, then smoking should be limited to outside the home. Day-care attendance should be discouraged. If the social situation mandates attendance, then an appropriate facility should be chosen that provides the most hygienic environment, as well as the smallest number of children per classroom, thus minimizing the risk of upper respiratory tract infections.

The initial major intervention is generally a surgical one, namely the performance of bilateral myringotomies and tympanostomy tube placement. Tymanostomy tubes have been shown to reduce the total time with OM to a greater extent than prophylactic antibiotics, although the measured difference missed statistical significance (Casselbrant et al, 1992). Moreover, tympanostomy tubes are preferred to antibiotic prophylaxis because of the growing concern regarding the development of resistant bacteria (Dowell et al, 1999). Children who are truly otitis prone may require multiple sets of grommets; alternatively, longer-lasting T tubes may be placed to avoid repeated procedures. Although tube placement is performed with the intention of reducing the risk of OM, it may, in fact, increase the incidence of otorrhea after intubation in children with patulous eustachian tubes.

Tympanostomy tube placement, because of its relative ease and low morbidity, is generally considered a better first-line surgical therapy than adenoidectomy. Nevertheless, there are many trials demonstrating that adenoidectomy reduces the frequency of middle ear disease (Bluestone and Klein, 2001). There are two proposed mechanisms for this effect. The adenoid pad may alter eustachian tube function, or the adenoid pad may harbor pathogenic bacteria in its crypts. Most likely, the result is from a combination of the two. There are only limited data on adenoidectomy as a first-line therapy in young children. Compared with initial tympanostomy tube placement, adenoidectomy offers an increase in the risks and costs without any longer-term benefit. Studies have shown only minimal benefit of initial adenoidectomy in recurrent AOM and only for a short duration (Paradise et al, 1990). Therefore, adenoidectomy should be used as a second-line treatment after initial tympanostomy tube failure. For children who have failed prior tympanostomy tube placement, adenoidectomy reduces the incidence of further recurrent AOM (Paradise et al, 1990), although it may not be an appropriate procedure for young infants. Moreover, performing a concurrent tonsillectomy offers no additional benefit in preventing recurrent AOM (Paradise et al, 1999).

Many studies have documented that antibiotic prophylaxis is effective in preventing recurrent AOM (Bluestone and Klein, 2001). Amoxicillin or trimethoprim-sulfamethoxazole has been shown to work better than sulfisoxazole (Thompson et al, 1999). The medication should be administered at half the therapeutic dose once daily during winter and spring for up to 6 months. If the child fails antibiotic prophylaxis, one may proceed to bilateral myringotomies and tympanostomy tube placement. It is important to recall, however, that tympanostomy tubes are preferred to antibiotic prophylaxis because of the growing concern regarding the development of resistant bacteria (Dowell et al, 1999). Prophylaxis should therefore be reserved for children whose parents refuse initial tympanostomy tube placement.

Other prophylactic medications aside from antibiotics have been used in attempts to treat recurrent AOM, with limited success. Xylitol, a five-carbon sugar alcohol, has been demonstrated to have a small effect in reducing recurrent AOM incidence (Uhari et al, 1998). However, the tremendous dosage required to prevent a single infection drastically reduces the usefulness of this and similar medications.

Vaccination has been shown to play an important role in the prevention of recurrent AOM. The heptavalent pneumococcal conjugate vaccine has been successful in reducing the incidence of OM, including the absolute number of OM episodes, the rate of recurrent AOM, and the need for tympanostomy tubes (Black et al, 2000; Fireman et al, 2003). The 23-type pneumococcal polysaccharide vaccine covers only a few of the responsible subtypes and may not be immunogenic enough to protect against recurrent AOM (Bluestone and Klein, 2001). Nonetheless, it may be considered in older children who have already received the heptavalent pneumococcal conjugate vaccine. Similarly, administration of the influenza vaccine has shown a 36% reduction in OM episodes in children attending day care (Clements et al, 1995). Unlike the pneumococcal vaccines, the influenza vaccine must be readministered each winter until the child outgrows his or her otitis-prone state.

Conclusion

Recurrent AOM is a common problem, affecting up to a third of young children. Most children can be successfully treated with tympanostomy tubes, although prophylactic antibiotics are also effective. Children failing tympanostomy tubes will benefit from an adenoidectomy as well as pneumococcal and influenza vaccines. Children who fail secondary therapy or who have other suspicious symptoms should be considered for comprehensive immunologic testing.

References

Black S, Shinefield H, Fireman B, et al. Efficacy, safety and immunogenicity of heptavalent pneumococcal conjugate vaccine in children. Pediatr Infect Dis J 2000;19:187–95.

Bluestone CD, Klein JO. Otitis media in infants and children. 3rd ed. Philadelphia: WB Saunders; 2001.

Brook I, Gober AE. Bacterial colonization of pacifiers of infants with acute otitis media. J Laryngol Otol 1997;111:614–5.

Casselbrant ML, Kaleida PH, Rockette HE, et al. Efficacy of antimicrobial prophylaxis and of tympanostomy tube insertion for prevention of recurrent acute otitis media: results of a randomized controlled trial. Pediatr Infect Dis J 1992;11:278–86.

Church JA. Immunologic evaluation of the child with recurrent otitis media. Ear Nose Throat J 1997;76:31–42.

Clements DA, Langdon L, Bland C, Walter E. Influenza A vaccine decreases the incidence of otitis media in 6- to 30-month-old children in day care. Arch Pediatr Adolesc Med 1995;149:1113–7.

Dowell SF, Butler JC, Giebink GS, et al. Acute otitis media: management and surveillance in an era of pneumococcal resistance—a report from the Drug-Resistant *Streptococcus pneumoniae* Therapeutic Working Group. Pediatr Infect Dis J 1999;18:1–9.

Etzel RA, Pattishall EN, Haley NJ, et al. Passive smoking and middle ear effusion among children in day care. Pediatrics 1992;90:228–32.

Ey JL, Holberg CJ, Aldous MB, et al. Passive smoke exposure and otitis media in the first year of life. Pediatrics 1995;95:670–7.

Fireman B, Black SB, Shinefield HR, et al. Impact of the pneumococcal conjugate vaccine on otitis media. Pediatr Infect Dis J 2003;222:10–6.

Howie VM, Ploussard JH, Sloyer J. The "otitis-prone" condition. Am J Dis Child 1975;129:676–8.

Niemelä M, Uhari M, Mottonen M. A pacifier increases the risk of recurrent acute otitis media in children in day care centers. Pediatrics 1995;96:884–8.

Paradise JL, Bluestone CD, Colborn DK, et al. Adenoidectomy and adenotonsillectomy for recurrent acute otitis media: parallel randomized controlled trials in children not previously treated with tympanostomy tubes. JAMA 1999;282:945–53.

Paradise JL, Bluestone CD, Rogers KD, et al. Efficacy of adenoidectomy for recurrent acute otitis media in children previously treated with tympanostomy-tube placement: results of parallel randomized and non-randomized trials. JAMA 1990;263:2066–73.

Paradise JL, Elster BA. Breast milk products against otitis media with effusion. Pediatrics 1994;94:853–60.

Stenstrom C, Bylander-Groth A, Ingvarsson L. Eustachian tube function in otitis-prone and healthy children. Int J Pediatr Otolaryngol 1991;21:127–38.

Tasker A, Dettmar PW, Panelli M, et al. Is gastric reflux a cause of otitis media with effusion in children? Laryngoscope 2002;112:1930–4.

Teele DW, Klein JO, Rosner B. Epidemiology of otitis media during the first seven years of life in children in greater Boston: a prospective, cohort study. J Infect Dis 1989;160:83–94.

Thompson D, Oster G, McGarry LJ, Klein JO. Management of otitis media among children in a large health insurance plan. Pediatr Infect Dis J 1999;18:239–44.

Uhari M, Kontiokari T, Niemelä M. A novel use of xylitol sugar in preventing acute otitis media. Pediatrics 1998;102:897–84.

Uhari M, Mantysaari K, Niemelä M. A meta-analytic review of the risk factors for acute otitis media. Clin Infect Dis 1996;22:1079–83.

Chapter 21

Ventilation Tubes for Recurrent Acute Otitis Media

Margaretha L. Casselbrant, MD, PhD

Recurrent acute otitis media (AOM) is common in infants and children and requires different management strategies than isolated episodes of AOM. Howie and colleagues (1975) popularized the term "otitis prone." They reported that 6% of children had six or more episodes of AOM before age 6 years, whereas Teele and coworkers (1989) found that 39% of children had six or more episodes of AOM by the age of 7 years.

For clinical and research purposes, recurrent AOM is most often defined as three or more well-documented and separate AOM episodes in the preceding 6 months or four or more episodes in the preceding 12 months, with at least one episode in the previous 6 months. The episodes of AOM should be separated by effusion-free intervals, but in many children, the short duration between episodes of AOM may prevent the resolution of the effusion.

The two most common treatment options for recurrent AOM besides watchful waiting are antimicrobial prophylaxis and tympanostomy tube insertion. With the increase in resistant organisms causing otitis media, tympanostomy tube insertion has, for most children, become the initial treatment of choice.

Tympanostomy tube insertion is the most common pediatric surgical procedure, with more than 1 million operations performed in the United States and Canada per year (Gates, 1996; To et al, 1996). This number may increase owing to the increase in resistant organisms.

Results of Clinical Trials

Three clinical trials have shown tympanostomy tube insertion to be efficacious in preventing recurrent AOM. The three trials have varying entry and follow-up criteria, but in all three studies, the children were evaluated at monthly intervals and whenever an ear, nose, or throat illness occurred. The first clinical trial was conducted by Gebhart (1981), who randomized 108 otitis-prone infants and children below the age of 3 years with a history of three or more episodes of AOM in the previous 6 months to tympanostomy tube insertion or antibiotic therapy for each episode of AOM (controls). The presence of middle ear effusion (MEE) at entry did not preclude inclusion. During the 6-month follow-up, 45% of the children in the tube group had one episode of AOM (otorrhea through the tube) and 9% had two or more episodes, whereas 39% of the children in the control group had one episode of AOM and 56% had two or more episodes ($p < .001$).

The second trial was a multicenter study conducted by Gonzalez and coworkers (1986). They enrolled 65 otitis-prone children 4 years or younger who had three or more episodes of AOM in the previous 6 months or four or more episodes in the previous 18 months and randomly assigned them to three treatment groups: daily sulfisoxazole prophylaxis (500 mg bid, < 5 years of age; 1 g bid, ≥ 5 years of age), placebo, and tympanostomy tube insertion. In this study, the children were also entered with and without MEE and were also followed for only 6 months. The number of episodes of AOM per child (attack rate) in the 6 months of follow-up was 2.0 in the placebo group, 1.38 in the sulfisoxazole group, and 0.86 in the tympanostomy tube group ($p = .005$). Treatment failure was defined as two or more episodes of AOM or otorrhea in 3 months. Five of 22 children in the tympanostomy tube group failed compared with 12 of 20 children in the placebo group ($p = .02$). There were eight treatment failures in 21 children in the sulfisoxazole group. Children in the tympanostomy tube group who had MEE at entry had significantly less middle ear disease when treated with tympanostomy tube insertion. However, the attack rates of AOM were not significantly reduced in those subjects who were effusion free at the time of random assignment.

The third clinical trial, conducted in Pittsburgh, randomly assigned 264 children 7 to 35 months of age to one of three treatment groups: amoxicillin prophylaxis (20 mg/kg/d in one dose at bedtime), placebo, or myringotomy and tube insertion (Casselbrant et al, 1992). All children had experienced three or more episodes of AOM in the previous 6 months or four or more episodes in 1 year with at least one episode in the previous 6 months; only patients who were effusion free were entered. Subjects were followed for 2 years. The average rate of new episodes of AOM, including otorrhea, was significantly reduced in those subjects in the amoxicillin prophylaxis group compared with the tube or placebo group (Table 21-1). There was no significant difference between the tube and placebo groups for this outcome measure. However, for episodes with OM, which includes AOM, otitis media with effusion (OME), and otorrhea, there were statistically significantly fewer episodes in the tube group than in the placebo group. Also, time with otitis media of any type (ie, AOM, otorrhea, or OME) was 6% in the tube group compared with 10% in the amoxicillin group and 15% in the placebo group in the 2-year follow-up period. The difference between the tympanostomy tube group and the amoxicillin and placebo groups translates to 26 and 61 fewer days with otitis media, respectively, over 2 years. The authors concluded that prophylactic antimicrobial therapy and tympanostomy tube insertion were efficacious in treating children with AOM. However, in those days before widespread development of resistant organisms, the authors recommended prophylactic antimicrobial therapy as the initial treatment option, and if this failed, the next step was tympanostomy tubes.

Rationale for Tympanostomy Tubes

Tympanostomy tubes are effective in preventing recurrent episodes of AOM because the tympanostomy tube bypasses the child's immature and poorly developed eustachian tube and replaces two of the three eustachian tube functions, providing ventilation and drainage of the middle ear and mastoid (Bluestone and Klein, 2001). Ambient pressure is maintained in the middle ear and mastoid with ventilation tubes. However, the insertion of a tympanostomy tube may predispose the child to reflux of nasopharyngeal secretions into the middle ear through the eustachian tube as the tympanostomy tube eliminates the middle ear air cushion present in an intact middle ear system. This should be considered in some older children who have previously done well but later develop recurrent episodes with otorrhea. This can be an indication that the child's eustachian tube has matured and become more patulous and nasopharyngeal secretion is refluxing up into the middle ear as there is no middle ear cushion. In such a child, removal of the tympanostomy tubes and patching of the tympanic membrane may resolve the problem. Episodes of otorrhea can also occur after water has been introduced through the external ear canal during showering, bathing, swimming, or diving.

Complications and Duration of Tubes

The most common adverse effect associated with a functioning tympanostomy tube is otorrhea. Acute otorrhea was observed at least once in 50% of 246 infants and children, mean age 3.6 years at entry, who were followed prospectively with monthly evaluations in three randomized clinical trials (Mandel et al, 1994). The children received tympanostomy tubes for recurrent AOM or chronic OME. Recurrent episodes of otorrhea were documented in 22% of the children. The highest prevalence of otorrhea was documented in the study enrolling children 35 months or younger who received tubes for recurrent episodes of AOM (Casselbrant et al, 1992). In a recent meta-analysis that included 134 articles, 70 case series, and 64 randomized clinical trials, transient otorrhea occurred early in 16% of patients and late in 26% of patients. Recurrent otorrhea was reported in 7.4% of patients and chronic otorrhea in 3.5% (Kay et al, 2001). The indication for tympanostomy tube insertion and the ages of the subjects were not reported, which could have accounted for the lower prevalence of otorrhea in this study.

Armstrong tympanostomy tubes were inserted for the episodes of recurrent AOM in the study by Casselbrant and colleagues (1992). Fifty percent of the tympanostomy tubes were extruded or became nonfunctional within

TABLE 21-1. Amoxicillin Prophylaxis and Placebo versus Tympanostomy Tube Insertion for Recurrent AOM

| Outcomes | Treatment Groups | | | | | |
| | 1 | 2 | 3 | p Value Groups | | |
	Amoxicillin	Placebo	Tympanostomy Tube	1 vs 2	3 vs 2	1 vs 3
Rates of AOM/otorrhea (child yr)	0.60	1.08	1.02	< .001	NS	.001
Rates of OM (AOM, OME, otorrhea)	1.31	1.70	1.39	.008	.020	.700
Mean percent of time with OM (AOM, OME, or otorrhea)	10.00	15.00	6.60	.030	< .001	NS
Median time to first episode of AOM/otorrhea (in mo)	22.10	8.20	11.20	.003	NS	.008

Adapted from Casselbrant ML et al (1992).
AOM = acute otitis media; NS = not significant; OM = otitis media; OME = otitis media with effusion.

13.8 months after insertion. During the 2-year observation period, tympanostomy tube insertion was performed only once in 72% of the 76 children, whereas 26% of the children received two procedures and 1% of the children received three procedures.

The meta-analysis by Kay and colleagues (2001) reported that the most common sequelae after tympanostomy tube extrusion included tympanosclerosis and focal atrophy, in 32% and 25% of ears, respectively. A perforation persisted in 2.2% of ears after extrusion of a short-term tube and 16.6% of ears after extrusion of a long-term tube.

In addition, insertion of tympanostomy tubes in infants and young children requires general anesthesia, which is very safe in normal children but can be associated with an increased risk of complications, such as reaction to medications or airway problems.

Clinical Implications

Tympanostomy tube insertion is indicated for treatment of infants and children with recurrent episodes of AOM. Previously, a trial of long-term antimicrobial prophylaxis was usually recommended and mandated by some insurance company utilization review boards as the initial treatment of choice for recurrent AOM, and insertion of tympanostomy tubes was not considered until antimicrobial prophylaxis had failed or the family could not comply with the treatment regimen. However, during the past 10 years, long-term antimicrobial prophylaxis has been associated with the emergence of drug-resistant *Streptococcus pneumoniae* strains. The incidence of resistant *S. pneumoniae* varies with geographic location and is highest in children 2 years or younger. It is higher if the child received antimicrobial treatment within 30 days and is more commonly isolated from middle ear secretions than blood and cerebrospinal fluid (Wald et al, 2000). Tympanostomy tube insertion is now considered the initial treatment of choice to prevent recurrent AOM. Antimicrobial prophylaxis is still a treatment option for recurrent AOM but is reserved for selected children.

After an episode of AOM, middle ear fluid may persist for weeks to months. In a child with recurrent AOM, the cumulative time with MEE may be significant. In some children with only a short interval between the episodes of AOM, the MEE might not resolve. The fluid in the middle ear causes a mild to moderate hearing loss (Fria et al, 1985), which could affect the child's speech and language development or school performance. Thus, certain groups of children such as children with a permanent hearing loss (sensorineural or conductive), speech delay, or developmental delay are more affected by the fluctuating or persistent fluid in the middle ear, which would resolve by insertion of tympanostomy tubes. Most episodes of otorrhea are quite asymptomatic and of short duration, and the effect on hearing is usually negligible.

Another advantage of tubes is that an episode of otorrhea in an otherwise asymptomatic child can be treated with ototopical therapy alone, whereas a child with an episode of AOM behind an intact tympanic membrane usually requires systemic antimicrobial therapy.

Children with tympanostomy tubes should be closely followed and episodes of otorrhea should be treated to avoid chronic disease. Use of earplugs is recommended for water exposure. After tympanostomy tube extrusion or blockage of the tube, the children should be followed and assessed for recurrence of disease.

Author's Experience

In any child who has recurrent AOM, which I define as a minimum of three episodes of AOM in 6 months or four episodes of AOM in 12 months, with one episode within the last 6 months, I consider tympanostomy tube insertion. However, prior to this, I consider the child's age, family history, daily environment, season, prior tympanostomy tubes, and anesthesia risk. I educate parents about the possible effect of risk factors such as day-care attendance and second-hand smoke. I recommend changing the child's daily environment if possible. It is important to be very sensitive during such a discussion as for many families, this might not be possible, and you do not want to make the parents feel upset or guilty.

I recommend early tympanostomy tube insertion for the following groups of children: those who develop recurrent AOM at a very early age and have a strong family history of otitis media; have episodes of AOM year round; have persistent MEE between episodes of AOM; develop recurrent disease immediately after a tympanostomy tube has extruded; are at high risk for recurrent AOM, such as children with craniofacial abnormalities, sensorineural hearing loss, speech delay, or developmental delay; have a systemic disease such as asthma that worsens during an episode of AOM; or have febrile seizures.

Parents should be informed that episodes of otorrhea can occur after tympanostomy tube insertion but that such episodes are usually asymptomatic and require, in most cases, only ototopical drops.

In older children with recurrent AOM, especially if the episodes occur in the spring, children with nonsevere disease, or children who are at risk for anesthesia, watchful waiting or prophylactic antimicrobial therapy should be considered.

References

Bluestone CD, Klein JO. Physiology, pathophysiology and pathogenesis. In: Bluestone CB, Klein JO, editors. Otitis media in infants and children. 3rd ed. Philadelphia: WB Saunders; 2001. p. 34–57.

Casselbrant ML, Kaleida PH, Rockette HE, et al. Efficacy of antimicrobial prophylaxis and of tympanostomy-tube insertion for prevention of recurrent acute otitis media: results of a randomized clinical trial. Pediatr Infect Dis J 1992;11:278–86.

Fria TJ, Cantekin EI, Eichler JA. Hearing acuity of children with otitis media with effusion. Arch Otolaryngol Head Neck Surg 1985;111:10–6.

Gates GA. Cost-effectiveness considerations in otitis media treatment. Otolaryngol Head Neck Surg 1996;114:525–30.

Gebhart DE. Tympanostomy tubes in otitis media prone children. Laryngoscope 1981;91:849–66.

Gonzales C, Arnold JE, Woody EA, et al. Prevention of recurrent acute otitis media: chemoprophylaxis versus tympanostomy tubes. Laryngoscope 1986;96:1330–4.

Howie VM, Ploussard JH, Sloyer J. The "otitis media-prone" condition. Am J Dis Child 1975;129:676-8.

Kay DJ, Nelson M, Rosenfeld RM. Meta-analysis of tympanostomy tube sequelae. Otolaryngol Head Neck Surg 2001;124:374–80.

Mandel EM, Casselbrant ML, Kurs-Lasky M. Acute otorrhea: bacteriology of a common complication of tympanostomy tubes. Ann Otol Rhinol Laryngol 1994;103:713–8.

Teele DW, Klein JO, Rosner BA, and the Greater Boston Otitis Media Study Group. Epidemiology of otitis media during the first seven years of life in children in Greater Boston: a prospective, cohort study. J Infect Dis 1989;160:83–94.

To T, Coyte PC, Feldman W, et al. Myringotomy with insertion of ventilation tubes. In: Goel V, Williams JI, Anderson GM, editors. Patterns of health care in Ontario. The ICES practice atlas. 2nd ed. Ottawa (ON): Canadian Medical Association; 1996. p. 297–300.

Wald ER, Mason EO, Bradley JS, et al, and the US Pediatric Multicenter Pneumococcal Surveillance Group. Acute otitis media caused by *Streptococcus pneumoniae* in children's hospitals between 1994 and 1997. Pediatr Infect Dis J 2001;20: 34–9.

Chapter 22

Antibiotic Prophylaxis for Recurrent Acute Otitis Media

Richard M. Rosenfeld, MD, MPH

Howie and colleagues (1975) coined the term "otitis prone" after noting that certain children have a remarkable tendency for recurrent infection. Recurrent acute otitis media (AOM) is best defined as three or more well-documented and separate AOM episodes in the preceding 6 months or four or more episodes in the preceding 12 months (Dowell et al, 1998). "Well documented" is emphasized because issues of diagnostic certainty become paramount when dealing with recurrent infection. "Separate" is also emphasized because true recurrent AOM has an effusion-free interval between episodes.

The efficacy of antimicrobial prophylaxis for recurrent AOM is well established by meta-analysis of randomized controlled trials (RCTs) (Rosenfeld, 1999; Williams et al, 1993). Effective use of this evidence in making decisions about individual patients requires knowing both the natural history of recurrent AOM and the incremental benefit of prophylaxis on outcomes. This chapter summarizes existing knowledge and the author's approach to judicious use of antimicrobial prophylaxis. Ongoing concerns about the impact of antibiotics on accelerated bacterial resistance, however, suggest a diminishing role for prophylaxis in managing children with recurrent AOM.

Natural History of Recurrent AOM

The prognosis of recurrent AOM is summarized in Table 22-1 for 13 RCTs comparing antimicrobial prophylaxis with placebo (Casselbrant et al, 1992; Gaskins et al, 1982; Gonzalez et al; 1986, Liston et al, 1983; Mandel et al, 1996; Maynard et al, 1972; Perrin et al, 1974; Prellner et al, 1994; Principi et al, 1989; Roark and Berman, 1997; Schuller, 1983; Sih et al, 1993; Varsano et al, 1985). Although children in the placebo groups received antimicrobial agents for individual AOM episodes when they occurred (typically for 10 days), they remain the best source of prog-nostic information against which to judge the impact of prophylaxis. To qualify for study inclusion, most children experienced three or more episodes of AOM over the preceding 6 to 12 months. The mean baseline rate of AOM recurrence was at least 0.42 episodes/patient-month (≥ 5 AOM per child per year) for the studies in which the rate was directly stated (Perrin et al, 1974; Principi et al, 1989; Schuller, 1983; Sih et al, 1993) or a minimum rate was calculable from the entry criteria (Casselbrant et al, 1992; Gonzalez et al, 1986; Liston et al, 1983; Prellner et al, 1994; Roark and Berman, 1997; Varsano et al, 1985).

The cumulative recurrence rate was 0.13, reflecting 770 AOM episodes in 6,072 patient-months of observation (95% confidence interval [CI]: 0.12–0.14). Therefore, about 1.6 annual episodes of AOM occurred per child. In the four studies that specified a baseline rate of AOM (Perrin et al, 1974; Principi et al, 1989; Schuller, 1983; Sih et al, 1993), the incidence decreased from 0.44 episodes per patient-month at baseline to 0.27 episodes per patient-month during the study. From the standpoint of prognosis, this equates to 0.17 fewer AOM episodes per patient-month (95% CI: 0.14–0.20) or an annual decrease of 2.0 AOM episodes per patient (95% CI: 1.7–2.4 episodes). For the studies in which a minimum baseline rate of AOM could be calculated from entry criteria (Casselbrant et al, 1992; Gonzalez et al, 1986; Liston et al, 1983; Prellner et al, 1994; Roark and Berman, 1997; Varsano et al, 1985), the incidence decreased by at least 0.11 episodes/patient-month (≥ 1.4 annual AOM episodes per patient).

Review of the data in Table 22-1 suggests a favorable prognosis for recurrent AOM. During a median observation period of 6 months, 51% of children had no further acute infections (95% CI: 46–55) and 87% had fewer than three AOM episodes (95% CI: 83–90). Alternatively, only 13% of children had three or more total AOM while enrolled in the study (95% CI: 7–10). Although the study

TABLE 22-1. Spontaneous Improvement of Recurrent Acute Otitis Media in Children Randomized to Placebo in Clinical Trials

| Author (Year) | Country | Entry Rate* | Study Duration | AOM Episodes, n (%)[†] | | | AOM/Patient-Month (Rate)[‡] | |
				None	2 or Fewer	Baseline	During Study	
Casselbrant et al (1992)	USA	3/6; 4/12	2 yr	32/80 (40)	61/80 (76)	(≥ 0.33)	173/1,920	(0.09)
Gaskins et al (1982)	USA	3/18; 5	6 mo	3/11 (27)	11/11 (100)	NS	8/66	(0.12)
Gonzalez et al (1986)	USA	3/6; 5/18	6 mo	3/20 (15)	—	(≥ 0.28)	40/120	(0.33)
Liston et al (1983)	USA	3/6	3 mo	14/34 (41)	27/34 (79)	(≥ 0.50)	43/102	(0.42)
Mandel et al (1996)	USA	3/12[§]	1 yr	24/51 (47)	46/51 (90)	(≥ 0.25)	46/531	(0.09)
Maynard et al (1972)	Alaska	NS	1 yr	115/191 (60)	171/191 (90)	NS	141/2,292	(0.06)
Perrin et al (1974)	USA	3/18; 5	3 mo	33/54 (61)	—	(0.31)	28/162	(0.17)
Prellner et al (1994)	Sweden	3/6	5 mo	—	—	(≥ 0.50)	78/187	(0.42)
Principi et al (1989)	Italy	3/6	6 mo	11/30 (37)	—	(0.52)	25/180	(0.14)
Roark and Berman (1997)	USA	3/6	NS	37/59 (63)	—	(≥ 0.50)	20/92	(0.22)
Schuller (1983)	USA	4/12	2 yr	—	—	(0.45)	118/288	(0.41)
Sih et al (1993)	Brazil	3/12	3 mo	10/20 (50)	19/20 (95)	(0.50)	14/60	(0.23)
Varsano et al, 1985	Israel	3/6	10 wk	12/32 (38)	—	(≥ 0.50)	36/74	(0.49)
Total				294/582 (51)	335/387 (87)		770/6074	(0.13)

Adapted from Rosenfeld RM (1999).

*Baseline rate of AOM recurrence to enter study in episodes/month or total episodes.

[†]Number of children with specified number of AOM episodes divided by the total number of children in the placebo group.

[‡]Rate of occurrence of AOM episodes per patient-month of observation (incidence density); baseline rate is listed (if stated by authors) or calculated from entry criteria when possible.

[§]Eligibility based on recurrent middle ear effusion, not just recurrent AOM.

AOM = acute otitis media; NS = not specified.

durations were not equal, only about one in eight enrolled children continued to have recurrent AOM (roughly defined as three or more AOM episodes during the study).

Many studies excluded children with baseline otitis media with effusion (OME), so the results should be extrapolated to this population with caution. Children were also generally excluded if they had immune deficiency, cleft palate, craniofacial anomalies, or Down syndrome. Unfortunately, these are also the children most likely to develop recurrent AOM. Spontaneous rates of improvement are likely to be lower in populations with baseline OME or with underlying predisposing factors for AOM or OME.

Efficacy of Antimicrobial Prophylaxis

Thirteen RCTs have compared antimicrobial prophylaxis with placebo therapy for the prevention of recurrent AOM (Table 22-2) (Casselbrant et al, 1992; Gaskins et al, 1982; Gonzalez et al, 1986; Liston et al, 1983; Mandel et al, 1996; Maynard et al, 1972; Perrin et al, 1974; Prellner et al, 1994; Principi et al, 1989; Roark and Berman, 1997; Schuller, 1983; Sih et al, 1993; Varsano et al, 1985). Study duration ranged from several months to 2 years (median of 6 months), during which time children in the study group received daily antimicrobial therapy at half the usual dosage for AOM. Amoxicillin (or ampicillin) was used most often, followed by sulfisoxazole, trimethoprim-sulfamethoxazole (TMP-SMX), and penicillin. AOM episodes, if they occurred, were treated with a therapeutic dosage of an alternative antibiotic. Eleven of the

13 trials in Table 22-2 had statistically better outcomes for the study group.

The overall absolute decrease in AOM recurrence attributable to therapy was 0.12 (95% CI: 0.08–0.16) episodes per patient-month (about 1.5 annual episodes). Therefore, preventing a single AOM episode requires treating one child for 8 months or eight children for 1 month (95% CI: 6–12). For comparison, the mean reduction in AOM recurrence from baseline in the placebo group (eg, spontaneous resolution) was 0.21 episodes/patient-month (2.5 annual episodes) for studies that specified a baseline rate (Perrin et al, 1974; Principi et al, 1989; Schuller, 1983; Sih et al, 1993) and at least 0.11 episodes/patient-month (≥ 1.4 annual episodes) for studies in which a minimum baseline rate was calculable from the entry criteria (Casselbrant et al, 1992; Gonzalez et al, 1986; Liston et al, 1983; Prellner et al, 1994; Roark and Berman, 1997; Varsano et al, 1985).

The greatest benefits of antimicrobial prophylaxis were observed in studies using sulfisoxazole and those with high AOM recurrence in the placebo group. The absolute rate difference (RD) for five trials using sulfisoxazole (Gonzalez et al, 1986; Liston et al, 1983; Perrin et al, 1974; Schuller, 1983; Varsano et al, 1985) was 0.22 (95% CI: 0.12–0.32) compared with a significantly lower RD of 0.04 (95% CI: 0.03–0.05) for the remaining eight trials. Consequently, the clinical effort needed to prevent an AOM episode with sulfisoxazole prophylaxis (treating one child for 4.5 months) is substantially less than for other antimicrobial agents (treating one child for 25 months). When the placebo group had an AOM recur-

TABLE 22-2. Efficacy of Antimicrobial Prophylaxis for Recurrent Acute Otitis Media: Incidence Density of Acute Otitis Media

Author (Year)	Country	Entry Rate*	Drug and Duration	AOM/Patient-Month (Rate)[†]		Absolute RD[‡] (95% CI)
				Study Group	Placebo Group	
Casselbrant et al (1992)	USA	3/6; 4/12	AMX 2 yr	103/2064 (0.05)	173/1,920 (0.09)	0.04 (0.02–0.06)[§]
Gaskins et al (1982)	USA	3/18; 5	TMP-SMX 6 mo	0/60 (0)	8/66 (0.12)	0.12 (0.04–0.20)[§]
Gonzalez et al (1986)	USA	3/6; 5/18	SSX 6 mo	29/126 (0.23)	40/120 (0.33)	0.10 (−0.01–0.22)
Liston et al (1983)	USA	3/6	SSX 3 mo	25/102 (0.25)	43/102 (0.42)	0.18 (0.05–0.30)[§]
Mandel et al (1996)	USA	3/12[‖]	AMX 1 yr	14/610 (0.02)	46/531 (0.09)	0.06 (0.04–0.09)[§]
Maynard et al (1972)	Alaska	NS	AMP 1 yr	73/2076 (0.04)	141/2292 (0.06)	0.03 (0.01–0.04)[§]
Perrin et al (1974)	USA	3/18; 5	SSX 3 mo	4/162 (0.02)	28/162 (0.17)	0.15 (0.09–0.21)[§]
Prellner et al (1994)	Sweden	3/6	PCN 5 mo	45/167 (0.27)	78/187 (0.42)	0.15 (0.06–0.25)[§]
Principi et al (1989)	Italy	3/6	AMX or TMP-SMX 6 mo	20/396 (0.05)	25/180 (0.14)	0.09 (0.03–0.14)[§]
Roark and Berman (1997)	USA	3/6	AMX 45 d	36/146 (0.25)	20/92 (0.22)	−0.03 (−0.14–0.08)
Schuller (1983)	USA	4/12	SSX 2 yr	28/288 (0.10)	118/288 (0.41)	0.31 (0.25–0.38)[§]
Sih et al (1993)	Brazil	3/12	AMX or TMP-SMX 3 mo	8/120 (0.07)	14/60 (0.23)	0.17 (0.05–0.28)[§]
Varsano et al (1985)	Israel	3/6	SSX 10 wk	9/74 (0.12)	36/74 (0.49)	0.36 (0.23–0.50)[§]
Overall						0.12 (0.08–0.16)[§]

Adapted from Rosenfeld RM (1999).

*Baseline rate of AOM recurrence to enter study in episodes/month or total episodes.

[†]Rate of occurrence of AOM episodes per patient-month of observation (incidence density).

[‡]RD is the absolute decrease in AOM episodes per patient-month attributable to prophylaxis; positive values favor the study group and negative values favor the control group.

[§]$p < .05$ when the 95% CI does not contain 0.

[‖]Eligibility based on recurrent middle ear effusion, not just recurrent AOM.

AMP = ampicillin; AMX = amoxicillin; AOM = acute otitis media; CI = confidence interval; PCN = penicillin; RD = rate difference; SSX = sulfisoxazole; TMP-SMX = trimethoprim-sulfamethoxazole.

rence rate of at least 0.2 episodes per patient-month (Gonzalez et al, 1986; Liston et al, 1983; Prellner et al, 1994; Roark and Berman, 1997; Schuller, 1983; Sih et al, 1993; Varsano et al, 1985), the RD was 0.18 (95% CI: 0.08–0.28). In contrast, studies with a rate less than 0.2 had an RD of 0.06 (95% CI: 0.04–0.09).

Children treated with antimicrobial prophylaxis were significantly more likely to have no further AOM during the study period (median 6 months) than children treated with placebo (Table 22-3). The overall RD was 25% (95% CI: 15–35), with a number needed to treat of four. Similarly, the likelihood of having fewer than three fur-

TABLE 22-3. Efficacy of Antimicrobial Prophylaxis for Recurrent Acute Otitis Media: Chance of Having No Further Acute Otitis Media Episodes

Author (Year)	Country	Entry Rate*	Drug and Duration	AOM Episodes, n (%)[†]		Absolute RD[‡] (95% CI)
				Study Group	Placebo Group	
Casselbrant et al (1992)	USA	3/6; 4/12	AMX 2 yr	50/86 (58)	32/80 (40)	18 (3–33)[§]
Gaskins et al (1982)	USA	3/18; 5	TMP-SMX 6 mo	10/10 (100)	3/11 (27)	73 (46–99)[§]
Gonzalez et al (1986)	USA	3/6; 5/18	SSX 6 mo	5/21 (24)	3/20 (15)	9 (−15–33)
Liston et al (1983)	USA	3/6	SSX 3 mo	18/35 (51)	14/34 (41)	10 (−13–34)
Mandel et al (1996)	USA	3/12[‖]	AMX 1 yr	42/55 (76)	24/51 (47)	29 (12–47)[§]
Maynard et al (1972)	Alaska	NS	AMP 1 yr	131/173 (76)	115/191 (60)	16 (6–25)[§]
Perrin et al (1974)	USA	3/18; 5	SSX 3 mo	50/54 (93)	33/54 (61)	31 (17–46)[§]
Principi et al (1989)	Italy	3/6	AMX or TMP-SMX 6 mo	48/66 (73)	11/30 (37)	36 (16–56)[§]
Roark and Berman (1997)	USA	3/6	AMX 45 d	62/99 (63)	37/59 (63)	0 (−16–16)
Sih et al (1993)	Brazil	3/12	AMX or TMP-SMX 3 mo	33/40 (82)	10/20 (50)	33 (8–57)[§]
Varsano et al (1985)	Israel	3/6	SSX 10 wk	25/32 (78)	12/32 (38)	41 (19–63)[§]
Overall						25 (15–35)[§]

Adapted from Rosenfeld RM (1999).

*Baseline rate of AOM recurrence to enter study in episodes/month or total episodes.

[†]Number of children with no AOM during study (median duration 6 mo) divided by total number of evaluable children.

[‡]Eligibility based on recurrent middle ear effusion, not just recurrent AOM.

[§]$p < .05$ when the 95% CI does not contain zero.

[‖]RD is the absolute percentage increase in positive outcomes attributable to prophylaxis; positive values favor the study group and negative values favor the control group.

AMP = ampicillin; AMX = amoxicillin; AOM = acute otitis media; CI = confidence interval; PCN = penicillin; RD = rate difference; SSX = sulfisoxazole; TMP-SMX = trimethoprim-sulfamethoxazole.

ther AOM episodes during the study period was significantly reduced by therapy (Table 22-4). The RD, however, was only 8% (95% CI: 4–11), making it necessary to treat 12 children to benefit 1 child.

Clinical Implications

The favorable prognosis of recurrent AOM suggests that most children who resolve between episodes (eg, no chronic middle ear effusion) should be observed for 3 to 6 months before considering antimicrobial prophylaxis. Although children enter comparative trials with a history of at least 3 to 6 AOM episodes during the previous year, they average only 1.6 annual episodes while on placebo (0.13 AOM per patient-month). Further, about half experience no additional episodes of AOM while on placebo for a median duration of 6 months, and nearly 90% have only two or fewer episodes over a similar time period.

Antimicrobial prophylaxis may be considered for selected children with recurrent AOM, but for most, the risk of accelerated bacterial resistance exceeds the modest benefit of daily antibiotic consumption (especially for children who attend group day care). Candidates for prophylaxis should have well-documented recurrent AOM ($\geq$ 3 episodes in the past 6 months or $\geq$ 4 in the past 12 months) with clearing of effusion between infections. In contrast, children with baseline or intercurrent OME do not benefit from antimicrobial prophylaxis (Schwartz and Rodriquez, 1982; Varsano et al, 1985). Parent expectations for prophylaxis should be appropriately modest (see Table 22-2), reflecting only a 0.12 episode per month decrease in AOM frequency attributable to therapy (about 1.0 to 2.0 AOM per year for 95% of children).

Sulfisoxazole and amoxicillin are the agents of choice for antibiotic prophylaxis; TMP-SMX is contraindicated (*Physician's Desk Reference*, 2000), and cephalosporins have not been demonstrated to be effective. Choosing between sulfisoxazole and amoxicillin is largely a matter of personal preference. Sulfisoxazole may be more efficacious (a 0.22 AOM episodes per month decrease) (Gonzalez et al, 1986; Liston et al, 1983; Perrin et al, 1974; Schuller, 1983; Varsano et al, 1985) and less likely to promote pharyngeal colonization with resistant pneumococci or β-lactamase–producing bacteria (Brook and Gober, 1996). Amoxicillin, however, is a safe, well-tolerated, established standard for treating AOM. Adverse reaction rates for sulfonamides are also favorable, estimated at only 11 events per 100 person-years at risk among children younger than 2 years of age (Uhari et al, 1996). Hematologic reactions are related more to TMP-SMX than sulfisoxazole, but concerned clinicians can obtain a baseline complete blood count with platelets (Cunningham, 1990).

To minimize the risk of resistant bacteria, prophylactic therapy should be limited to 6 months (Dowell et al, 1998). The ideal time for prophylaxis is during the season for upper respiratory tract viruses, which in the northeastern United States runs from October through May. Breakthrough episodes of AOM should be anticipated because prophylaxis is unlikely to eliminate all AOM. When episodes occur, they are treated with a full therapeutic course of an alternate antimicrobial agent. Two or more breakthrough infections are a criterion for prophylaxis failure.

Antimicrobial prophylaxis for recurrent AOM should be offered only to families who are likely to comply with therapy and are comfortable with their child receiving a daily dose of antibiotic. The modest benefits of prophylaxis demonstrated under ideal circumstances in RCTs are likely to be smaller in real-life situations in which compliance may be less than optimal. For example, when 80

TABLE 22-4. Efficacy of Antimicrobial Prophylaxis for Recurrent Acute Otitis Media: Chance of Having Fewer than 3 Further Acute Otitis Media Episodes

Author (Year)	Country	Entry Rate*	Drug and Duration	< 3 AOM Episodes, n (%)[†]		Absolute RD[‡] (95% CI)
				Study Group	Placebo Group	
Gaskins et al (1982)	USA	3/18; 5	TMP-SMX 6 mo	10/10 (100)	3/11 (27)	73 (46–99)[§]
Casselbrant et al (1992)	USA	3/6; 4/12	AMX 2 yr	75/86 (87)	61/80 (76)	11 (–1–23)
Gaskins et al (1982)	USA	3/18; 5	TMP-SMX 6mo	10/10 (100)	11/11 (100)	0 (–24–22)
Liston et al (1983)	USA	3/6	SSX 3 mo	34/35 (97)	27/34 (79)	18 (3–32)[§]
Mandel et al (1996)	USA	3/12[‖]	AMX 1 yr	55/55 (100)	46/51 (90)	10 (2–18)[§]
Maynard et al (1972)	Alaska	NS	AMP 1 yr	165/173 (95)	171/191 (37)	6 (1–11)[§]
Sih et al (1993)	Brazil	3/12	AMX or TMP-SMX 3 mo	40/40 (100)	19/20 (95)	5 (–5–15)
Overall						8 (4–11)[§]

Adapted from Rosenfeld RM (1999).

*Baseline rate of AOM recurrence to enter study in episodes/month or total episodes.

[†]Eligibility based on recurrent middle ear effusion, not just recurrent AOM.

[‡]Number of children with no AOM during study (median duration 6 mo) divided by total number of evaluable children.

[§]$p < .05$ when the 95% CI does not contain 0.

[‖]RD is the absolute percentage increase in positive outcomes attributable to prophylaxis; positive values favor the study group and negative values favor the control group.

AMP = ampicillin; AMX = amoxicillin; AOM = acute otitis media; CI = confidence interval; PCN = penicillin; RD = rate difference; SSX = sulfisoxazole; TMP-SMX = trimethoprim-sulfamethoxazole.

inner-city children with recurrent AOM were given prophylactic antibiotics, fewer than half complied with maintenance medication (Goldstein and Sculerati, 1994). Greater compliance is achieved with intermittent prophylaxis at the onset of an upper respiratory infection, but RCTs have shown inconsistent benefits (Heikkinen et al, 1995; Prellner et al, 1994). Intermittent prophylaxis is not recommended because of decreased efficacy compared with continuous drug administration (Berman et al, 1992; Foglé-Hannson et al, 2001).

References

Berman S, Nuss R, Roark R, et al. Effectiveness of continuous vs. intermittent amoxicillin to prevent episodes of otitis media. Pediatr Infect Dis J 1992;11:63–7.

Brook I, Gober AE. Prophylaxis with amoxicillin and sulfisoxazole for otitis media: effect on recovery of penicillin-resistant bacteria from children. Clin Infect Dis 1996;22:143–5.

Casselbrant ML, Kaleida PH, Rockette HE, et al. Efficacy of antimicrobial prophylaxis and of tympanostomy tube insertion for prevention of recurrent acute otitis media: results of a randomized clinical trial. Pediatr Infect Dis J 1992;11:278–86.

Cunningham MJ. Chemoprophylaxis with oral trimethoprim-sulfamethoxazole in otitis media: relevance of hematologic abnormalities. Clin Pediatr 1990;29:273–7.

Dowell SF, Marcy MS, Phillips WR, et al. Otitis media—principles of judicious use of antimicrobial agents. Pediatrics 1998;101 Suppl:165–71.

Foglé-Hannson M, White P, Hermansson A, Prellner K. Short-term penicillin-V prophylaxis did not prevent acute otitis media in infants. Int J Pediatr Otorhinolaryngol 2001;59:119–23.

Gaskins JD, Holt RJ, Kyong CU, et al. Chemoprophylaxis of recurrent otitis media using trimethoprim/sulfamethoxazole. Drug Intell Clin Pharm 1982;16:387–9.

Goldstein NA, Sculerati N. Compliance with prophylactic antibiotics for otitis media in a New York City clinic. Int J Pediatr Otorhinolaryngol 1994;28:129–40.

Gonzalez C, Arnold JE, Woody EA, et al. Prevention of recurrent acute otitis media: chemoprophylaxis versus tympanostomy tubes. Laryngoscope 1986;96:1330–4.

Heikkinen T, Ruuskanen O, Ziegler T, et al. Short term use of amoxicillin-clavulanate during upper respiratory tract infection for prevention of acute otitis media. J Pediatr 1995;126:313–6.

Howie VM, Ploussard JH, Sloyer J. The "otitis-prone" condition. Am J Dis Child 1975;129:676–8.

Liston TE, Foshee WS, Pierson WD. Sulfisoxazole chemoprophylaxis for frequent otitis media. Pediatrics 1983;71:524–30.

Mandel EM, Casselbrant ML, Rockette HE, et al. Efficacy of antimicrobial prophylaxis for recurrent middle-ear effusion. Pediatr Infect Dis J 1996;15:1074–82.

Maynard JE, Fleshman JK, Tschopp CF. Otitis media in Alaskan Eskimo children: prospective evaluation of chemoprophylaxis. JAMA 1972;219:597–9.

Perrin JM, Charney E, MacWhinney JB Jr, et al. Sulfisoxazole as chemoprophylaxis for recurrent otitis media: a double-blind crossover study in pediatric practice. N Engl J Med 1974;291:664–7.

Physician's desk reference. 54th ed. Montvale (NJ): Medical Economics Company; 2000.

Prellner K, Foglé-Hansson M, Jørgensen F, et al. Prevention of recurrent acute otitis media in otitis-prone children by intermittent prophylaxis with penicillin. Acta Otolaryngol (Stockh) 1994;114:182–7.

Principi N, Marchisio P, Massironi E, et al. Prophylaxis of recurrent acute otitis media and middle-ear effusion: comparison of amoxicillin with sulfamethoxazole and trimethoprim. Am J Dis Child 1989;143:1414–8.

Roark R, Berman S. Continuous twice daily or once daily amoxicillin prophylaxis compared with placebo for children with recurrent acute otitis media. Pediatr Infect Dis J 1997;16:376–81.

Rosenfeld RM. What to expect from medical therapy. In: Rosenfeld RM, Bluestone CD, editors. Evidence-based otitis media. Hamilton (ON): BC Decker; 1999. p. 179–206.

Schuller DE. Prophylaxis of otitis media in asthmatic children. Pediatr Infect Dis 1983;2:280–3.

Schwartz RH, Rodriguez WJ. Trimethoprim-sulfamethoxazole treatment of persistent otitis media with effusion. Pediatr Infect Dis 1982;1:333–5.

Sih T, Moura R, Caldas S, Schwartz B. Prophylaxis for recurrent acute otitis media: a Brazilian study. Int J Pediatr Otorhinolaryngol 1993;25:19–24.

Uhari M, Nuutinen M, Turtinen J. Adverse reactions in children during long term antimicrobial therapy. Pediatr Infect Dis J 1996;15:404–8.

Varsano I, Volvitz B, Mimouni F. Sulfisoxazole prophylaxis of middle-ear effusion and recurrent acute otitis media. Am J Dis Child 1985;139:632–5.

Williams RL, Chalmers TC, Stange KC, et al. Use of antibiotics in preventing recurrent acute otitis media and in treating otitis media with effusion: a meta-analytic attempt to resolve the brouhaha. JAMA 1993;270:1344–51.

Adenoidectomy with and without Tonsillectomy for Recurrent Acute Otitis Media

Jacob Friedberg, BA, MD, FRCSC

The common wisdom is that adenoids and, to a lesser degree, tonsils can impair eustachian tube function either on the basis of obstruction owing to size or secondary to inflammatory swelling, predisposing children to recurrent acute otitis media (AOM) or resulting in otitis media with effusion (OME). The role of adenoidectomy with and without tonsillectomy in the management of recurrent AOM (and similarly for OME) has been a source of argument among clinicians for decades and continues to be a controversial treatment modality. With the increasing prevalence of antibiotic-resistant pathogens, we have become obliged to look critically at any treatment option for the effective management of AOM and OME that can minimize the use of precious antibiotics, preserving them for conditions for which there may be no other satisfactory treatment.

The incidence of major complications from AOM has significantly decreased in both developed and developing countries (Rutka and Lekagul, 1998; Sorensen, 1977). Although the availability of effective antibiotics has had a major impact on the natural history of AOM and its life-threatening sequelae, socioeconomic factors such as improved nutrition, housing, and vaccination have also played a significant role in greatly reducing the incidence of what were once common complications.

The incidence of uncomplicated AOM has not similarly decreased. Indeed, there is evidence of an increased incidence, at least in the United States (Lanphear et al, 1997). AOM is responsible for a significant degree of morbidity in the pediatric population, and there is increasing concern over the educational and psychosocial sequelae of recurrent, mild, and/or fluctuating hearing loss during the early years of language development.

It is the rare child who does not have at least one episode of AOM before entering school, and the "otitis-prone" child may suffer dozens of such infections by age 4 or 5 years. Even if no apparent long-term anatomic damage or language impairment results from these infections, they can leave behind a history of repeated distress for both patient and parents. Any safe interventional modality that can significantly reduce this burden of disease is welcome.

A generation ago, any one of a number of first-generation antibiotics was effective in the "cure" of most episodes of AOM. Major suppurative complications had not disappeared but were a far cry from the preantibiotic era incidence. Antibiotics were widely prescribed for most cases of definitively diagnosed AOM and likely even more often in cases that would surely fail to be so diagnosed today. Prophylactic antibiotics, whose efficacy in limiting the frequency of recurrent ear infections was well established and not in question, were regularly prescribed for a month, a season, or even a year. The success of antibiotic treatment resulted in a general reluctance to recommend a surgical option such as myringotomy and tympanostomy tube insertion let alone a significantly more invasive (and costly) intervention such as adenotonsillectomy or adenoidectomy alone. The resulting excessively liberal use of antibiotics has now been recognized as a major contributor to the worldwide epidemic of antibiotic-resistant microorganisms.

Surgical Options for Otitis Media

In the past, surgical options have often been considered only as a last resort for cases of failed medical management, as if to suggest that there was little to lose and possibly something to gain (Berman, 1995). The further implication was, and often still is, that medical management is by definition "conservative," whereas any form of surgical intervention is "radical." There ought to be no reason not to consider an earlier surgical intervention if the effectiveness of such a policy can be supported by sound evidence.

The more judicious use of antibiotics and the selective insertion of middle ear tympanostomy tubes are effective treatments in the management of most patients with recurrent AOM. Nevertheless, there is still a cohort of otherwise normal, healthy children who continue to suffer recurrent acute ear infections in spite of these measures. The acceptability of other surgical options such as adenoidectomy, adenotonsillectomy, and even cortical mastoidectomy is inversely proportional to the relative morbidity of these procedures.

Bilateral myringotomy with insertion of tympanostomy tubes is an accepted treatment option for recurrent AOM and has little associated morbidity. Although tympanosclerosis, or, more correctly, myringosclerosis, is common, it is largely of cosmetic concern. Residual tympanic membrane perforations are rare with the more commonly used tympanostomy tubes and, should they occur, can be readily repaired. Local or general anesthetic complications are extremely rare.

In contrast, adenoidectomy and particularly adenotonsillectomy have a significant associated morbidity and even mortality for the surgery and the required anesthetic (Coyte et al, 2001; Crysdale and Russel, 1986; Vayda et al, 1977). The clinician must decide on an individualized basis whether any benefit to be obtained from surgical intervention in the management of recurrent AOM is worth this risk of increased morbidity.

In 1973, Shambaugh and Quic stated that prophylaxis for recurrent otitis media (OM) in children should first be the removal of the adenoids (Shambaugh and Quie, 1973). Such a categorical recommendation would be difficult to support today.

Paradise and colleagues (1990) found that adenoidectomy was of value for those children who developed recurrent AOM following extrusion of tympanostomy tubes. In the first and second years following surgery, the randomized group spent 47% and 37% less time with OM and had 28% and 35% fewer episodes of AOM compared with their controls.

In a later randomized clinical trial, Paradise and colleagues (1999) found that both adenoidectomy and adenotonsillectomy, with some advantage to the latter, had a significant but limited effect compared with no treatment on reducing the number of episodes of AOM and the duration of time with OM. The study did not include children under 3 years of age and found that the benefits of the surgery were largely limited to the first year following

the surgery. The authors concluded that given the associated cost and morbidity of these surgical procedures and the modest improvement in disease control, adenoidectomy or adenotonsillectomy should not be considered as a first option in the management of recurrent AOM.

Van Damme and colleagues (1999) found that OM-prone children were significantly more likely to harbor typical middle ear pathogens such as *Streptococcus pneumoniae, Moraxella catarrhalis*, and *Haemophilus influenzae* in their adenoids than were those children who were not prone to OM. In addition, this nasopharyngeal colonization was reduced after adenoidectomy. This supports the concept that factors other than adenoid size are involved in the pathogenesis of AOM.

Maw and colleagues, in several studies in children with OME, demonstrated that adjuvant adenoidectomy in combination with tympanostomy tube insertion decreased the need for subsequent tube insertion and that adenoidectomy alone was as effective as tympanostomy tube insertion. The inclusion of tonsillectomy did not appear to enhance the outcome (Maw and Bawden, 1993; Maw and Bawden, 1994; Maw and Herod, 1986). Gates and colleagues (1987) demonstrated that in children with OME, adenoidectomy with and without tympanostomy tube insertion was effective in reducing the need for subsequent tympanostomy tube insertion compared with children undergoing myringotomy or myringotomy and tube insertion without adenoidectomy. Also, contrary to popular belief, this effect was independent of adenoid size at the time of surgery, suggesting that the effect of the adenoids on the eustachian tube and middle ear space was not simply mechanical (Gates et al, 1987). This study was limited to a review of children 4 to 8 years of age, and the authors could not make recommendations for younger children. One cannot necessarily extrapolate the findings regarding OME to younger children or to recurrent AOM.

On the basis of these and other studies, the authors of the 1994 Agency for Health Care Policy and Research guidelines supported the role of adenoidectomy in the management of OME in children over 4 years of age but not in younger children (Stool et al, 1994).

In a study reviewing the records of over 37,000 children undergoing myringotomy and tube insertion as the first surgical treatment for OM, Coyte and colleagues (2001) found that adjuvant adenoidectomy significantly reduced the chance of a subsequent tympanostomy tube reinsertion. Adenotonsillectomy still further reduced the need for such surgery or readmission for OM-related conditions (Coyte et al, 2001). In contrast to other studies, the benefit of adjuvant surgery was seen in children of all age groups but was greatest for those 3 years of age and older. In this study, the prior history of the children, that is, frequency of ear infection, duration of effusion, and adenoid size, was not available, and, undoubtedly, the many surgeons used diverse criteria for treatment selection. Although this study demonstrated the reduction of subsequent hospital admissions for further surgical interventions, it could infer only that there were fewer or less distressing ear infections experienced by those children who did not undergo further surgery. One can conclude from these data that there is a group of children who would benefit from primary adjuvant surgery for AOM. However, the criteria for selecting the appropriate candidates are not known at this point.

Recommendations

The issue of adjuvant surgery beyond myringotomy and tympanostomy tube insertion for recurrent AOM hinges around risk/cost versus benefit.

There is now a sizable body of evidence demonstrating the efficacy of adenoidectomy, when performed as an isolated procedure or as an adjuvant to insertion of tympanostomy tubes, in decreasing the number of subsequent episodes of AOM. Significant complications are recognized but exceedingly rare.

It is therefore recommended that adjuvant adenoidectomy be considered in any child who is a candidate for a second or third set of tympanostomy tubes. It should also be considered for the child who has functioning tympanostomy tubes in place and continues to have repeated infections or protracted bouts of otorrhea and has failed medical management or is allergic to one or more antibiotics commonly used to treat AOM.

The benefit of adenoidectomy at least for the treatment of AOM does not appear to be related to adenoid size.

There is convincing evidence that adenoidectomy is effective in children over 3 or 4 years of age both by itself and as an adjunct to tympanostomy tube insertion. There is less evidence to support its role in the younger child, but adenoidectomy should be considered in selected patients with refractory disease and with full appreciation of the small but very real associated morbidity.

Tonsillectomy, on the other hand, is subject to more significant complications, which include wound infection, serious hemorrhage, and even death, albeit rarely. In view of the uncertain or marginal advantage over that afforded by adenoidectomy alone, I would not recommend tonsillectomy solely for the purpose of limiting further ear infections. Tonsillectomy for the management of primary tonsil disease, for example, recurrent tonsillitis, and airway obstruction, should be considered a separate issue.

Ideally, if it were possible to select a priori those children who would benefit from adenoidectomy for the management of their recurrent AOM, adenoidectomy could be recommended as a primary surgical intervention (shades of Shambaugh!), but this is not currently the situation.

References

Berman S. Otitis media in children. N Engl J Med 1995;332:1560–5.

Coyte PC, Croxford R, McIsaac W, et al. The role of adjuvant adenoidectomy and tonsillectomy in the outcome of the insertion of tympanostomy tubes. N Engl J Med 2002;344:1188–95.

Crysdale WS, Russel D. Complications of tonsillectomy and adenoidectomy in 9409 children observed overnight. Can Med Assoc J 1986;135:1139–42.

Gates GA, Avery CS, Prihoda TJ, Cooper JC. Effectiveness of adenoidectomy and tympanostomy tubes in the treatment of chronic otitis media with effusion. N Engl J Med 1987;317:1444–51.

Lanphear BP, Byrd RS, Auinger P, Hall CB. Increasing prevalence of recurrent otitis media among children in the United States. Pediatrics 1997;99:E1.

Maw AR, Bawden R. Spontaneous resolution of severe chronic glue ear in children and the effect of adenoidectomy, tonsillectomy and insertion of ventilating tubes (grommets). BMJ 1993;306:756–60.

Maw AR, Bawden R. The long-term outcome of secretory otitis media in children and the effects of surgical treatment: a ten-year study. Acta Otorhinolaryngol (Belg) 1994;48:317–24.

Maw AR, Herod F. Otoscopic, impedance and audiometric findings in glue ear treated by adenoidectomy and tonsillectomy. A prospective randomized study. Lancet 1986;i:1399–402.

Paradise JL, Bluestone CD, Colborn DK, et al. Adenoidectomy and adenotonsillectomy for recurrent acute otitis media: parallel randomized clinical trials in children not previously treated with tympanostomy tubes. JAMA 1999;282:945–53.

Paradise JL, Bluestone CD, Rogers KD, et al. Efficacy of adenoidectomy for recurrent otitis media in children previously treated with tympanostomy tube placement. JAMA 1990;263:2066–73.

Rutka J, Lekagul S. No therapy: use, abuse, efficacy and morbidity—the European versus the third-world experience. J Otolaryngol 1998;27 Suppl 2:43–8.

Shambaugh GE, Quie PG. Acute otitis media and mastoiditis. In: Paparella MM, Shumrick DA, editors. Otolaryngology. Vol. 2. Philadelphia: WB Saunders; 1973. p. 113–20.

Sorensen H. Antibiotics in suppurative otitis media. Otolaryngol Clin North Am 1977;10:45–50.

Stool SE, Berg AO, Berman S, et al. Otitis media with effusion in young children. Clinical practice guideline number 12. Rockville (MD): Agency for Health Care Policy and Research, US Department of Health and Human Services; July 1994. AHCPR Publication No.: 94-0622.

Van Damme D, Vaneechoutte M, Claeys G, et al. Role of nasopharyngeal bacterial flora in the evaluation of recurrent middle ear infections in children. Clin Microbiol Infect 1999;5:530–4.

Vayda E, Lyons D, Anderson GD. Surgery and anesthesia in Ontario. Can Med Assoc J 1977;116:1263–6.

Chapter 24

ROLE OF NASOPHARYNGEAL COLONIZATION IN RECURRENT OTITIS MEDIA

HOWARD FADEN, MD

The importance of nasopharyngeal colonization in the development of acute otitis media (AOM) has recently generated wide interest, even though the nasopharynx has long been acknowledged as the reservoir for potential middle ear pathogens. At the same time, the nasopharynx is also the normal habitat for nonpathogens. The balance between the nonpathogens and pathogens ultimately decides the evolution of disease. This chapter describes the differences in colonization patterns that exist in normal children and children predisposed to recurrent AOM. The latter children are often referred to as "otitis prone."

Normal Colonization

The nasopharynx rapidly becomes colonized after birth, and the pattern of colonization is surprisingly similar among the multitude of newborn babies. The flora is predominantly composed of α-hemolytic streptococci, nonhemolytic streptococci, diphtheroids, and *Neisseria* species. Little is known about anaerobes in the newborn; however, anaerobes are presumed to be uncommon in edentulous individuals. Opportunity for colonization actually begins at birth when the infant passes through the birth canal, but, few data are available on the potential of vaginal flora to colonize the upper airway of newborns. Unlike the rapid appearance of nonpathogens in the nasopharynx, pathogens such as *Streptococcus pneumoniae*, *Haemophilus influenzae*, and *Moraxella catarrhalis* colonize gradually throughout the first year of life; colonization with a fourth important pathogen, group A streptococcus, occurs uncommonly early in life (Faden, 1998; Faden et al, 1997). *M. catarrhalis* is the first of the pathogens to colonize, followed shortly by *S. pneumoniae* and *H. influenzae*. By 6 months of age, cumulative acquisition rates are 55% for *M. catarrhalis*, 38% for *S. pneumoniae*, and 19% for *H. influenzae*. Prevalence rates at 6 months are 26% for

M. catarrhalis, 24% for *S. pneumoniae*, and 9% for *H. influenzae* (Faden et al, 1997). Children typically acquire a number of different strains of each pathogen over time. At any one time, there is usually one dominant strain; several others may exist concurrently. Individual strains tend to colonize for several months, although the duration of colonization varies from less than 1 month to more than 6 months. The timing of the initial colonization, the duration of colonization, and the frequency of colonization with different strains of a particular pathogen, as well as colonization with different types of pathogens, are important in the subsequent evolution of middle ear disease.

Factors Affecting Colonization

Exposure to pathogens in the environment is the single most important factor leading to acquisition. Thus, the home is the initial reservoir for pathogens. Although parents may contribute to the colonization of newborns, siblings are more likely to disseminate pathogens because they are more often colonized. As the number of siblings in a household increases, so does the risk of spread. Day care is a more important environmental hazard than the home in the acquisition of pathogens. Day care allows contact with a larger number of infants who are colonized with many different strains of pathogens. The pathogens found in day-care centers often represent bacterial populations with a high degree of antibiotic resistance. Lest we forget, day care also enhances the spread of respiratory viruses that enable these nasopharyngeal bacterial pathogens to cause AOM. Public schools contribute to colonization in a like manner but to a lesser degree because the contact is less intimate and personal hygiene is improved in the older child.

Diet has long been known to affect colonization. In our own experience, breast-fed infants experience less nasopharyngeal colonization and delayed colonization with pathogens than formula-fed infants do (Duffy et al, 1997). This pattern results in a lower incidence of AOM among breast-fed infants (Duffy et al, 1997). The mechanism by which breast milk reduces colonization with pathogens is unclear. Breast milk is known to contain numerous defense mechanisms, including cellular elements such as neutrophils, macrophages, and lymphocytes, as well as pathogen-specific antibody, lysozyme, and lactoferrin. Pathogen-specific antibody may prove to be the most important protective element in human milk. The level of antibody in human milk is inversely related to the frequency of colonization with the pathogens (Harabuchi et al, 1994a).

Seasons of the year affect colonization. Colonization with pathogens tends to be more common in the winter months. This may not reflect the climate as much as seasonal outbreaks of respiratory viruses. Viruses such as respiratory syncytial virus and influenza characteristically appear in the winter. During viral infections, cilia motility decreases, mucus production increases, and mucus stagnation ensues. These changes may enhance bacterial replication and adherence.

It would seem reasonable to assume that the immune system plays some role in eliminating pathogens from the airway. At birth, infants possess placentally acquired maternal antibody to a number of pathogens. These antibodies have the potential to protect infants from disease, such as AOM, but are not able to affect colonization (Bernstein et al, 1991). In contrast, local antibody is ideally situated to prevent colonization. Prior to exposure to a specific pathogen, infants lack local antibody; after colonization, almost every infant generates pathogen-specific local antibody in the nasopharynx (Harabuchi et al, 1994b). The robustness of the local antibody response is inversely related to the duration of colonization (Harabuchi et al, 1994b). Children with a poor immune response experience prolonged colonization with the same strain or recurrent colonization with different strains.

Antibiotics affect colonization. The effects of antibiotics are broad and indiscriminate. That is to say, they alter the normal flora even as they eradicate pathogens. The effect of the antibiotics depends on the susceptibility of the flora and on the ability of the drug to enter the nasopharynx. Antibiotics reduce colonization with the most susceptible strains of organisms. The effect on colonization begins early in the treatment and dissipates after the antibiotics are discontinued; colonization with pathogens quickly returns to pretreatment levels. Often the pathogens that recolonize the nasopharynx appear to be resistant to the antibiotic. The increased resistance most often represents an overgrowth of resistant strains that were present at the start of treatment rather than the induction of mutations in previously susceptible strains (Varon et al, 2000). The proliferation of these resistant

strains during AOM treatment may contribute to the spread of resistant strains and enhance the probability that a recurrent episode may be caused by resistant organisms.

Differences in Colonization Patterns between Normal Children and Otitis-Prone Children

Researchers often describe *S. pneumoniae*, *H. influenzae*, and *M. catarrhalis* as normal flora because these organisms may be cultured from healthy children. However, our experiences demonstrate that normal, healthy children are only occasionally colonized with these pathogens, and after they become colonized, they rapidly eliminate the pathogens. In contrast, otitis-prone children are colonized earlier, more frequently, and for longer periods (Faden et al, 1991). This pattern is associated with persistent, recurrent, and chronic otitis media and very much resembles the situation among the indigenous populations of New Guinea and Australia. For example, 100% of infants in Papua, New Guinea, are colonized with pathogens by 3 months of age (Gratten et al, 1986). Similarly, the aboriginal population in Australia becomes colonized with the same pathogens very early in life (Leach et al, 1994). Both populations experience early, recurrent, and chronic otitis media as a result of their precocious colonization patterns. Our own study demonstrated colonization with pathogens in the first year of life greatly increases the risk of becoming otitis prone when compared with children who escape colonization (Faden et al, 1997). When the frequency of colonization is compared between normal and otitis-prone children, colonization with pathogens is increased throughout the year in the otitis-prone group, that is, during periods of health and during respiratory illness (Table 24-1).

At this point, it is reasonable to ask why otitis-prone children experience increased colonization with pathogens. Is it simply increased exposure? In all likelihood, otitis-prone children are different than normal children. For example, the immune response to each of the

TABLE 24-1. Comparison of Nasopharyngeal Colonization Rates (%) in Normal and Otitis-Prone Children during Well Visits and Respiratory Illness Visits

	Normal	Otitis Prone	p
Healthy			
SP	14	25	NS
NTHI	5	33	< .01
MC	12	31	NS
III			
SP	24	41	< .05
NTHI	22	58	< .001
MC	25	40	< .05

Adapted from Faden HS et al, 1991.
MC = *Moraxella catarrhalis*; NTHI = nontypable *Haemophilus influenzae*; SP = *Streptococcus pneumoniae*.

middle ear pathogens is reduced in the otitis-prone group (Harabuchi et al, 1998; Hotomi et al, 1999; Yamanaka and Faden, 1993). In addition, otitis-prone children fail to mount an anamnestic antibody response on second exposure to pathogens such as *H. influenzae* (Yamanaka and Faden, 1993). Studies from our laboratory further suggest that T lymphocyte responses to *H. influenzae* are impaired in subjects experiencing recurrent infections (Abe et al, 2000; Kodama et al, 1999). These studies suggest that recurrent infection and, perhaps, colonization occur because immunologic memory is impaired. It is unclear whether this abnormality is congenital or acquired or represents a delay in maturation of the immune system.

Colonization Risk Factors for Persistent and Recurrent AOM

Colonization with multiple pathogens during AOM is associated with persistent symptoms and relapses (Faden et al, 2002). This association is intriguing because it suggests that the persistence or relapse may have been due to a second pathogen residing in the nasopharynx at the time of the initial episode. This is supported by the work of Carlin and colleagues (1987), who discovered that the etiology of recurrences was due to different pathogens in 75% of the episodes. In the case of *H. influenzae* AOM, recurrences are more often due to the same organism, suggesting that *H. influenzae* has a penchant for persistence at the site of infection and possibly on the mucosal surface as well (Barenkamp et al, 1984). More than 50 years ago, Bjuggren and Tunevall (1952) noted that *H. influenzae* was prominent in recurrent and persistent episodes of AOM, and their explanation for this was that *H. influenzae* had the ability to persist in the respiratory tract. Thus, persistent or recurrent episodes of AOM may represent nasopharyngeal isolates that enter the middle ear during or soon after completing the initial course of antibiotics.

Our studies on nasopharyngeal colonization also suggest that persistent disease or recurrent disease occurs when antibiotic-resistant strains of *S. pneumoniae* are present (Faden et al, 2002). Dagan and colleagues (2001) recently demonstrated that recurrent episodes of AOM appearing soon after the successful treatment of AOM owing to antibiotic-susceptible *S. pneumoniae* may result from antibiotic-resistant isolates that were present in the nasopharynx during the treatment of the first episode. The second organism may invade the middle ear so quickly that the first infection appears to be unresolved by the time the second one begins.

Preventing Colonization

This chapter described the importance of nasopharyngeal colonization in the development of otitis media and demonstrated that normal children are colonized with pathogens much less frequently than otitis-prone children. Thus, it is imperative to avoid colonization early in life if one is to avoid AOM, especially recurrent episodes. Immunization may be the best tool to prevent colonization. At present, there are two commercially available vaccines, *H. influenzae* type b and *S. pneumoniae*, proven to reduce colonization (Adegbola et al, 1998; Dagan et al, 1996). Of the two vaccines, the pneumococcal vaccine is most important in AOM because *S. pneumoniae* is more likely to cause AOM. Unfortunately, the current pneumococcal vaccine for use in children less than 2 years old contains only 7 of 90 types of *S. pneumoniae*.

Future Directions

Although there are no commercial vaccines for nontypable *H. influenzae* or *M. catarrhalis*, several are under investigation. Because neither of these organisms has a high potential for invasive disease, there has been a focus on developing intranasal vaccines that will have a greater capacity to produce local immunity than systemic immunity.

Even before these vaccines become available, it may be possible to reconsider the possibility of eliminating the heavy nasopharyngeal bacterial burden in otitis-prone children. We have already noted that breast-feeding, home care, and immunization with the pneumococcal vaccine may prevent nasopharyngeal colonization with pathogens. These should all be recommended for families with otitis-prone children.

Based on data presented in this chapter, it also seems reasonable to explore the possibility of reducing the bacterial burden with the judicious use of antibiotics known to affect nasopharyngeal carrier states. For example, rifampin, ciprofloxacin, and ceftriaxone are all approved for the eradication of the meningococcal carrier state. Rifampin has also been proven to be effective in eliminating carriage of *H. influenzae* type B. Although systemic ciprofloxacin is not approved for use in children younger than 18 years of age, there is a topical preparation that is used in children with chronic suppurative otitis media. Each of the antibiotics deserves study in the elimination of *S. pneumoniae*, *H. influenzae*, and *M. catarrhalis* from the nasopharynx. This approach may be associated with several problems. As is the case with all antibiotics, treatment adversely affects the nonpathogens that comprise normal flora. Second, frequent or prolonged use of these drugs will result in an increase of resistance. Third, the inhibitory effects on the pathogens may be short-lived, and recolonization may quickly occur.

A more physiologic approach to the problem would be to restore the normal flora. Roos and colleagues (1993) demonstrated an inhibition of recurrent streptococcal pharyngitis following the application of known inhibitory strains of α-hemolytic streptococci to the throats of patients 2 to 34 years of age. More recently, the same group of investigators applied a similar preparation to the nasopharynxes of children 6 months to 6 years of age who had experienced recurrent otitis media (Roos et al, 2001). They demonstrated a 50% reduction in disease. Their preparations included three strains of *Streptococcus sanguis* and one strain of *Streptococcus mitis* in the first study and two strains of *S. sanguis*, two strains of *S. mitis*, and one strain of *Streptococcus oralis* in the second study. The mechanisms of protection by these probiotics are not known but may include the production of an acid environment, release of hydrogen peroxide, depletion of nutrients in the microenvironment, or the production of antibiotic-like substances. Bernstein and our group have also been investigating the possible use of a probiotic-like viridans streptococcus to recolonize the airways of otitis-prone children. After screening hundreds of strains, they identified a number of isolates that inhibited the growth of *S. pneumoniae*, *H. influenzae*, and *M. catarrhalis* on agar plates (Bernstein et al, 1994). One particular strain, designated Parker, inhibited all pathogens tested. Parker proved to be a strain of *S. oralis*.

Conclusion

AOM is common in childhood. A subpopulation of children, representing 5 to 10% of the pediatric population, experiences more than four episodes in a single year and is classified as otitis prone. These children differ from normal children in several respects. One important difference relates to the pattern of nasopharyngeal colonization. Otitis-prone children become colonized with pathogens earlier, for more prolonged periods, and more often. The reason for this difference is complex. However, prevention of colonization with pathogens or elimination of colonization with pathogens may be crucial in protection against recurrent otitis media.

References

Abe T, Murphy TF, Sethi S, et al. Lymphocyte proliferative response to P6 of *Haemophilus influenzae* is associated with relative protection from exacerbations of chronic obstructive pulmonary disease. Am J Respir Crit Care Med 2000;165:967–71.

Adegbola RA, Mulholland EK, Secka O, et al. Vaccination with a *Haemophilus influenzae* type b conjugate vaccine reduces oropharyngeal carriage of *H. influenzae* type b among Gambian children. J Infect Dis 1998;177:1758–61.

Barenkamp SJ, Shurin PA, Marchant CD, et al. Do children with recurrent *Haemophilus influenzae* otitis media become infected with a new organism or reacquire the original strain? J Pediatr 1984;145:533–7.

Bernstein JM, Faden HS, Ogra PL. Nasopharyngeal colonization by nontypeable *Haemophilus influenzae* in children: the effect of serum bactericidal antibody. Otolaryngol Head Neck Surg 1991;105:406–10.

Bernstein JM, Sagahtaheri-Altaie S, Dryja DM, Wactawski-Wende J. Bacterial interference in nasopharyngeal bacterial flora of otitis-prone and non-otitis-prone children. Acta Otorhinolaryngol Belg 1994;48:1–9.

Bjuggren G, Tunevall G. Otitis in childhood. Acta Otolaryngol (Stockh) 1952;42:311–28.

Carlin SA, Marchant CD, Shurin PA, et al. Early recurrences of otitis media: reinfection or relapse? J Pediatr 1987;110:20–5.

Dagan R, Leibovitz E, Cheletz G, et al. Antibiotic treatment in acute otitis media promotes superinfection with resistant *Streptococcus pneumoniae* carried before initiation of treatment. J Infect Dis 2001;183:880–6.

Dagan R, Melamed R, Muallem M, et al. Reduction of nasopharyngeal carriage of pneumococci during the second year of life by a heptavalent conjugate pneumococcal vaccine. J Infect Dis 1996;174:1271–8.

Duffy LC, Faden H, Wasielewski R, et al. Exclusive breastfeeding protects against bacterial colonization and day care exposure to otitis media. Pediatrics 1997;100:1–8.

Faden HS. Monthly prevalence of group A, B and G *Streptococcus*, *Haemophilus influenzae* types E and F and *Pseudomonas aeruginosa* nasopharyngeal colonization in the first two years of life. Pediatr Infect Dis J 1998;17:255–6.

Faden HS, Duffy L, Wasielewski R, et al. Relationship between nasopharyngeal colonization and the development of otitis media in children. J Infect Dis 1997;175:1440–45.

Faden HS, Hotomi M, Yamanaka N. The importance of *Streptococcus pneumoniae* colonization on the course of acute otitis media [abstract]. Pediatr Res 2002;49:244.

Faden HS, Waz MJ, Bernstein JM, et al. Nasopharyngeal flora in the first three years of life in normal and otitis-prone children. Ann Otol Rhinol Laryngol 1991;100:612–5.

Gratten M, Gratten H, Poli A, et al. Colonisation of *Haemophilus influenzae* and *Streptococcus pneumoniae* in the upper respiratory tract of neonates in Papua, New Guinea: primary acquisition, duration of carriage, and relationship to carriage in mothers. Biol Neonate 1986;50:114–20.

Harabuchi Y, Faden H, Yamanaka N, et al. Human milk secretory IgA antibody to nontypeable *Haemophilus influenzae*: possible protective effects against nasopharyngeal colonization. J Pediatr 1994a;124:193–8.

Harabuchi Y, Faden H, Yamanaka N, et al. Nasopharyngeal colonization with nontypeable *Haemophilus influenzae* and recurrent otitis media. J Infect Dis 1994b;170:862–966.

Harabuchi Y, Murakata H, Goh M, et al. Serum antibodies specific to CD outer membrane protein of *Moraxella catarrhalis*, P6 outer membrane protein of nontypeable *Haemophilus influenzae* and capsular polysaccharides of *Streptococcus pneumoniae* in children with otitis media with effusion. Acta Otolaryngol (Stockh) 1998;118:826–32.

Hotomi M, Yamanaka N, Saito T, et al. Antibody responses to the outer membrane protein P6 of non-typeable *Haemophilus influenzae* and pneumococcal capsular polysaccharides in otitis-prone children. Acta Otolaryngol (Stockh) 1999;119:703–7.

Kodama H, Faden H, Harabuchi Y, et al. Cellular immune response of adenoidal and tonsillar lymphocytes to the P6 outer membrane protein of non-typeable *Haemophilus influenzae* and its relation to otitis media. Acta Otolaryngol (Stockh) 1999;119:377–83.

Leach AJ, Boswell JB, Asche V, et al. Bacterial colonization of the nasopharynx predicts very early onset and persistence of otitis media in Australian aboriginal infants. Pediatr Infect Dis J 1994;13:983–9.

Roos K, Grahn E, Holm SE, et al. Interfering α-streptococci as a protection against recurrent streptococcal tonsillitis in children. Int J Pediatr Otorhinolaryngol 1993;15:141–8.

Roos K, Hakansson EG, Holm S. Effect of recolonisation with "interfering" α streptococci on recurrences of acute and secretory otitis media in children: randomized placebo controlled trial. BMJ 2001;322:210–2.

Varon E, Levy C, De La Rocque F, et al. Impact of antimicrobial therapy on nasopharyngeal carriage of *Streptococcus pneumoniae*, *Haemophilus influenzae*, *Branhamella catarrhalis* in children with respiratory tract infections. Clin Infect Dis 2000;31:477–81.

Yamanaka N, Faden H. Antibody response to outer membrane protein of nontypeable *Haemophilus influenzae* in otitis-prone children. J Pediatr 1993;122:212–8.

Chapter 25

VIRAL VACCINES FOR RECURRENT ACUTE OTITIS MEDIA

TERHO HEIKKINEN, MD, PhD

The high incidence of acute otitis media (AOM) in children and the substantial impact of this disease on families and the health care system have made the development of an effective vaccine against AOM a high-priority area of research. Although the multifactorial etiology of AOM constitutes a serious problem in the development of an otitis vaccine, the vaccine approach is considered to hold the greatest promise for the ultimate prevention of AOM (Giebink, 1994).

Rationale for Viral Vaccines in the Prevention of AOM

Although AOM is usually regarded as a bacterial infection, research into the etiology and pathogenesis of AOM carried out during the past two decades has produced strong evidence for the crucial role of viruses in the development of AOM (Heikkinen and Chonmaitree, 2003). Extensive clinical studies have documented the tight association between AOM and viral respiratory infections (Arola et al, 1990; Henderson et al, 1982; Ruuskanen et al, 1989), and studies of the temporal development of AOM have demonstrated that the peak incidence of AOM occurs on day 3 or 4 after the onset of symptoms of viral upper respiratory infection (Heikkinen and Ruuskanen,

1994; Koivunen et al, 1999). In the majority of cases in children, viral infection of the upper respiratory mucosa initiates the whole cascade of events that finally leads to the development of AOM, and AOM can be clearly regarded as a complication of a preceding or concomitant viral infection (Heikkinen and Chonmaitree, 2003).

The well-established role of viruses in the etiology and pathogenesis of AOM justifies the consideration of viral vaccines in the prevention of AOM. In terms of prevention of AOM by vaccination, there is a fundamental difference between viral and bacterial vaccines (Figure 25-1). Bacterial vaccines are able only to prevent the bacterial complication of a viral infection. Because most young children harbor in the nasopharyngeal mucosa at least two of the three major bacterial pathogens causing AOM (Heikkinen et al, 2000), even a 100% effective vaccine against a single bacterial pathogen would not result in a striking decrease in the total incidence of AOM because the complication could be caused by any of the other bacterial pathogens (Eskola et al, 2001). Viral vaccines, on the other hand, act at an earlier stage in the pathogenesis of AOM. Effective vaccines against viruses predisposing to AOM have the potential to prevent the whole preceding viral infection, thereby also preventing the development of AOM as a complication by any bacterial strains in the nasopharynx.

FIGURE 25-1. Sites of action of viral and bacterial vaccines in the prevention of acute otitis media. *Bold arrow* denotes a decrease in otitis media owing to the vaccine. *H. influenzae = Haemophilus influenzae; M. catarrhalis = Moraxella catarrhalis;* RSV= respiratory syncytial virus; *S. pneumoniae = Streptococcus pneumoniae.*

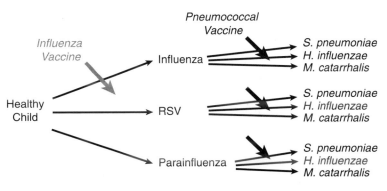

Clinical Studies of AOM Prevention by Viral Vaccines

At present, influenza vaccine is the only commercially available vaccine for the control of viral respiratory infections. Several clinical studies have assessed the efficacy of influenza vaccine in the prevention of AOM in different subgroups of children. The first of these trials included 374 day-care children aged 1 to 3 years in Finland (Heikkinen et al, 1991). The mean number of previous attacks of AOM in the children was 4.4, and 66% of the participants had a history of at least two episodes of AOM. Half of the children received two doses of a trivalent inactivated influenza vaccine before the expected influenza epidemic, whereas the other half served as unvaccinated controls. The parents of all participating children were asked to bring their children to the study office for clinical examination whenever fever or signs of a respiratory tract infection appeared. A nasopharyngeal aspirate was obtained during each episode of infection for viral antigen detection. During the 6-week study period, 3 children in the vaccine group and 18 children in the control group had AOM during influenza infection, indicating a statistically significant decrease by 83% in the incidence of influenza-associated AOM (Figure 25-2). More importantly, although influenza vaccination does not have an impact on the development of AOM during other viral infections, the substantial decrease in influenza-associated AOM resulted in a 36% reduction in the overall morbidity owing to AOM in the vaccine group regardless of the viral etiology.

Another study carried out in North Carolina involved 186 day-care children aged 6 to 30 months (Clements et al, 1995). Ninety-four children were randomized to receive trivalent subvirion influenza vaccine, whereas the other children received hepatitis B vaccine or ear examinations only. During a 4-month winter period, including the time of the influenza A epidemic, the children were examined biweekly using otoscopy and tympanometry. During the 6-week period of peak influenza activity in the community, AOM was diagnosed in 21.5% of children in the influenza vaccine group and in 36.4% of children in the control group. There was a statistically significant 32% reduction in the episodes of AOM during the influenza season. No significant differences were observed between the groups either before or after the influenza epidemic.

The efficacy of the newly developed live attenuated, cold-adapted, trivalent intranasal influenza vaccine was studied in a multicenter, double-blind, placebo-controlled trial among 1,602 children aged 15 to 71 months (Belshe et al, 1998). A total of 1,070 children were assigned to receive either one or two doses of the vaccine (> 80% of them received two doses) and 532 children were assigned placebo. After the beginning of the influenza outbreak in

the community, the participating families were contacted weekly by telephone, and children with fever or respiratory or other symptoms were cultured for influenza viruses and advised to be examined by their primary care provider. The overall efficacy of the vaccine against culture-confirmed influenza was 93%, and children receiving the influenza vaccine had 30% fewer episodes of febrile otitis media than those in the placebo group.

Investigators in Italy evaluated the efficacy of an intranasal, inactivated, virosomal subunit influenza vaccine in the prevention of AOM in children with a history of recurrent AOM, defined as three or more episodes in the preceding 6 months or four or more episodes in the preceding 12 months (Marchisio et al, 2002). A total of 133 children aged 1 to 5 years were assigned randomly to the vaccine group (*n* = 67) or to the unvaccinated control group (*n* = 66). The children were followed for 6 months, during which period they were routinely examined every 4 to 6 weeks. In addition, the families were contacted by telephone twice per week to inquire about the status of the children and to remind the parents to bring the children to the study clinic whenever they developed any symptoms of respiratory illness. The investigator responsible for the clinical examinations was blinded to group assignment until the end of the follow-up period. The diagnosis of AOM was based on clinical symptoms, pneumatic otoscopy, and tympanometry. During the 6-month follow-up period, 36% of the vaccine recipients and 64% of the control children had at least one episode of AOM, constituting a statistically significant 44% reduction (Figure 25-3). The efficacy of the vaccine was even greater (63%) when the number of children with two or more episodes of AOM was considered as the end point.

A recent study carried out in Pittsburgh, PA, evaluated the efficacy of inactivated trivalent influenza vaccine in reducing the incidence of AOM in children 6 to 24 months of age (Hoberman et al, 2002). In this randomized, double-blind, placebo-controlled trial, 417 and 376

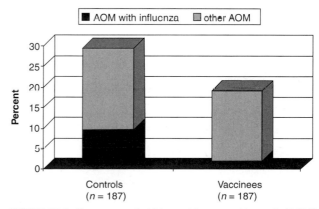

FIGURE 25-2. Percentage of children with acute otitis media (AOM) in the influenza vaccine group and the control group during the influenza epidemic. Adapted from Heikkinen T et al, 1991.

children received two doses of influenza vaccine or placebo during the respiratory seasons of 1999 to 2000 and 2000 to 2001, respectively. The children were seen biweekly during the respiratory season, and the parents were additionally instructed to contact the investigators at any time if the child developed signs or symptoms of respiratory tract infection. Twenty percent of the children had had recurrent AOM (at least three episodes in the preceding 6 months or four episodes in the preceding year) and 27% of them attended day care. In addition, 70% of children enrolled during the second season had received at least one dose of pneumococcal vaccine. No significant differences were observed between the vaccine and placebo groups in the proportions of children with at least one episode of AOM either during the influenza season or the entire respiratory season. However, no data are available on the efficacy of vaccination in the prevention of influenza-associated AOM. Moreover, the general activity of influenza was low during the study period; the attack rate in the placebo group was 16% in the first winter and only 3% in the second winter. Because of the very low incidence of influenza in the study population during the second winter, influenza vaccine could not even be proven to be effective against influenza infection.

Effectiveness of Viral Vaccines against AOM

The overall effectiveness of viral vaccines in the prevention of AOM depends on several factors. Although virtually all respiratory viruses are capable of predisposing a child to AOM and have also been found in the middle ear fluid (Heikkinen and Chonmaitree, 2003), recent data indicate that some viruses, for example, respiratory syncytial virus (RSV), influenza viruses, parainfluenza viruses, and rhinoviruses, may have a more active role in the pathogenesis of AOM than some other viruses (Heikkinen et al, 1999; Pitkäranta et al, 1998). In children with AOM during laboratory-confirmed RSV infection, the same virus was found in the middle ear fluid in 74% of the

cases, which was significantly higher than the corresponding rates for parainfluenza viruses (52%) or influenza viruses (42%) (Heikkinen et al, 1999). On the other hand, the relative prevalences of these viruses were significantly higher than those for enteroviruses (11%) or adenoviruses (4%). Several other studies have also indicated that RSV may be the principal virus leading to the development of AOM as a complication (Henderson et al, 1982; Ruuskanen et al, 1989; Uhari et al, 1995). It is logical to assume that vaccines against those viruses that most frequently predispose the child to AOM would show the greatest effect in the prevention of AOM.

Other crucial factors affecting the overall effectiveness of viral vaccines for AOM include the duration of the follow-up period and the relative incidence of different viral infections in the population during that period. Theoretically, a 100% effective vaccine against any respiratory virus could be expected to prevent all episodes of AOM occurring as a complication of viral infection during a period when only that particular virus circulated in the community. However, it is usual that several different viruses cocirculate among children during any respiratory season. The protective efficacy of any viral vaccine against AOM depends on the relative incidence of that virus in the population during any defined period of time. For example, it could be expected that the use of an effective influenza vaccine would result in high rates of AOM prevention during the peak epidemic activity of influenza, but the overall effectiveness of influenza vaccine against AOM would be substantially decreased during periods of low influenza activity that occurs during the early and late stages of the epidemic. Similarly, no efficacy could be anticipated outside the influenza season. Because of great variation in the duration of the follow-up and other aspects of study design, the results of AOM prevention in different clinical trials are not directly comparable.

The effectiveness of a viral vaccine in the prevention of AOM is also dependent on the features of the population under study. Some demographic factors that affect the estimates of effectiveness include age, recent history of AOM episodes, day-care attendance, and the number of siblings. It is conceivable that the greatest benefit from viral vaccination could be expected to be observed in those children who suffer most from viral infections and AOM.

Use of Viral Vaccines in Children

The discussion on the potential use of viral vaccines in children is limited to influenza because no vaccines for other respiratory viruses are currently available. Influenza vaccination is officially recommended for children older than 6 months with any high-risk condition. During recent years, however, increasing evidence for the great disease burden of influenza in children has initiated a discussion as to whether previously healthy children

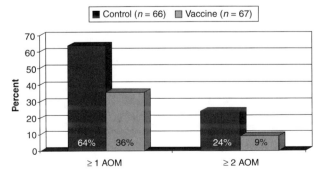

FIGURE 25-3. Percentage of children with one or more or two or more episodes of acute otitis media (AOM) during the 6-month follow-up period. Adapted from Marchisio P et al (2002).

would also benefit from influenza vaccination (Izurieta et al, 2000; Neuzil et al, 2000). Based on recent studies, in 2002, the Advisory Committee on Immunization Practices decided to encourage influenza vaccination of all children 6 to 23 months of age to the extent feasible. Although this is still short of a full recommendation, such a recommendation could be expected in a few years. Meanwhile, considering the well-established safety of influenza vaccine and its efficacy in preventing both influenza and AOM as a complication of influenza, it seems prudent to offer the vaccine to any child older than 6 months who is at risk of developing recurrent episodes of AOM. However, it should always be emphasized to the parents that influenza vaccine cannot prevent illnesses caused by other viruses; therefore, the child may continue to develop AOM during other viral infections.

Future Considerations

Because rhinoviruses are estimated to cause approximately 30 to 50% of all viral respiratory infections and these viruses are also closely associated with AOM, an effective vaccine against rhinoviruses could have the greatest impact on the overall incidence of AOM. However, because of more than 100 different serotypes of rhinoviruses and the absence of a suitable common antigen across all rhinovirus serotypes, the prospects for development of a vaccine against rhinoviruses seem poor. Several different types of vaccines against RSV and parainfluenza viruses are currently being developed, and some of them are already in early clinical trials (Ison et al, 2002). Based on our knowledge of the central role of viruses in the pathogenesis of AOM and the results of influenza vaccine trials, it is also likely that vaccines against RSV and parainfluenza viruses would be effective in preventing the development of AOM as a complication of these viral infections.

Finally, it is important to emphasize that viral and bacterial vaccines are not competing or mutually exclusive approaches in the prevention of AOM; rather, they would well complement each other. However, from the larger viewpoint of respiratory illnesses in children, viral vaccines have the additional advantage of preventing the whole underlying viral illness and thereby also preventing other virus-induced complications than AOM. Considering the direct and indirect costs of viral respiratory illnesses and their complications in society, the larger potential of vaccines against major respiratory viruses could also be anticipated to make them more cost-effective than bacterial vaccines in the context of AOM.

References

Arola M, Ruuskanen O, Ziegler T, et al. Clinical role of respiratory virus infection in acute otitis media. Pediatrics 1990;86:848–55.

Belshe RB, Mendelman PM, Treanor J, et al. The efficacy of live attenuated, cold-adapted, trivalent, intranasal influenzavirus vaccine in children. N Engl J Med 1998;338:1405–12.

Clements DA, Langdon L, Bland C, Walter E. Influenza A vaccine decreases the incidence of otitis media in 6- to 30-month-old children in day care. Arch Pediatr Adolesc Med 1995;149:1113–7.

Eskola J, Kilpi T, Palmu A, et al. Efficacy of a pneumococcal conjugate vaccine against acute otitis media. N Engl J Med 2001;344:403–9.

Giebink GS. Preventing otitis media. Ann Otol Rhinol Laryngol 1994;103:20–3.

Heikkinen T, Chonmaitree T. Importance of respiratory viruses in acute otitis media. Clin Microbiol Rev 2003;16:230–41.

Heikkinen T, Ruuskanen O, Waris M, et al. Influenza vaccination in the prevention of acute otitis media in children. Am J Dis Child 1991;145:445–8.

Heikkinen T, Ruuskanen O. Temporal development of acute otitis media during upper respiratory tract infection. Pediatr Infect Dis J 1994;13:659–61.

Heikkinen T, Saeed KA, McCormick DP, et al. A single intramuscular dose of ceftriaxone changes nasopharyngeal bacterial flora in children with acute otitis media. Acta Paediatr 2000;89:1316–21.

Heikkinen T, Thint M, Chonmaitree T. Prevalence of various respiratory viruses in the middle ear during acute otitis media. N Engl J Med 1999;340:260–4.

Henderson FW, Collier AM, Sanyal MA, et al. A longitudinal study of respiratory viruses and bacteria in the etiology of acute otitis media with effusion. N Engl J Med 1982;306:1377–83.

Hoberman A, Greenberg DP, Paradise JL, et al. Efficacy of inactivated influenza vaccine in preventing acute otitis media (AOM) in young children [abstract]. Pediatric Academic Societies' Annual Meeting; 2002 May 4–7; Baltimore, MD.

Ison MG, Mills J, Openshaw P, et al. Current research on respiratory viral infections: Fourth International Symposium. Antiviral Res 2002;55:227–78.

Izurieta HS, Thompson WW, Kramarz P, et al. Influenza and the rates of hospitalization for respiratory disease among infants and young children. N Engl J Med 2000;342:232–9.

Koivunen P, Kontiokari T, Niemelä M, et al. Time to development of acute otitis media during an upper respiratory tract infection in children. Pediatr Infect Dis J 1999;18:303–5.

Marchisio P, Cavagna R, Maspes B, et al. Efficacy of intranasal virosomal influenza vaccine in the prevention of recurrent acute otitis media in children. Clin Infect Dis 2002;35:168–74.

Neuzil KM, Mellen BG, Wright PF, et al. The effect of influenza on hospitalizations, outpatient visits, and courses of antibiotics in children. N Engl J Med 2000;342:225–31.

Pitkäranta A, Virolainen A, Jero J, et al. Detection of rhinovirus, respiratory syncytial virus, and coronavirus infections in acute otitis media by reverse transcriptase polymerase chain reaction. Pediatrics 1998;102:291–5.

Ruuskanen O, Arola M, Putto-Laurila A, et al. Acute otitis media and respiratory virus infections. Pediatr Infect Dis J 1989;8:94–9.

Uhari M, Hietala J, Tuokko H. Risk of acute otitis media in relation to the viral etiology of infections in children. Clin Infect Dis 1995;20:521–4.

Chapter 26

Bacterial Vaccines for Prevention of Acute Otitis Media

Jerome O. Klein, MD

The approval by the US Food and Drug Administration (FDA) in February 2000 of a heptavalent conjugate pneumococcal vaccine (PCV-7) was based on large-scale clinical trials that identified the efficacy of the vaccine for prevention of invasive disease, pneumonia, and acute otitis media (AOM). The efficacy was robust for prevention of invasive disease and pneumonia but less so for prevention of AOM. Subsequent microbiologic data raised questions about the possibility of increased incidence of disease owing to nonvaccine serotypes. Nevertheless, the vaccine was effective in reducing the incidence of AOM and was most useful in decreasing the number of children who had recurrent disease and who had myringotomy and placement of ventilating tubes. The subjects of this review include the availability of bacterial vaccines for prevention of AOM, the results of clinical and microbiologic trials of pneumococcal vaccines for prevention of AOM, current recommendations for use of PCV-7, and the implications for the efficacy of bacterial vaccines for prevention of AOM in the future. The interested reader should review the proceedings of a symposium, *Otitis Media: A Preventable Disease?* held in February 2000 and published in *Vaccine* (2000) and should visit the Web site <http://www.pneumo.com> for the latest information about pneumococcal diseases and the conjugate pneumococcal vaccine.

Bacterial Vaccines for Prevention of AOM

Eleven bacterial vaccines are available in the United States as of April 2002 (Table 26-1). Most have no effect on the incidence of AOM; four have potential or limited effect on infections known to cause otitis media (OM) in selected patients (*Mycobacterium tuberculosis, Corynebacterium diphtheriae, Haemophilus influenzae* type b, and *Clostridium tetani*). Because only 10% of *Haemophilus* species responsi-

ble for OM were type b, the *H. influenzae* type b conjugate vaccine (Hib) had minimal effect on the incidence of AOM. *H. influenzae* is responsible for approximately 25 to 50% of episodes of AOM. Thus, the Hib vaccine would prevent 5% or fewer cases of AOM. Only the pneumococcal polysaccharide and conjugate polysaccharide vaccines have had a substantial influence on the incidence of OM. Vaccines for nontypable *H. influenzae* and *Moraxella catarrhalis* are in the early stages of development.

Pneumococcal Polysaccharide Vaccines

A 23-type vaccine composed of capsular polysaccharide antigens was licensed in the United States in 1983, replacing a 14-type vaccine licensed in 1977. Each polysaccharide antigen is prepared separately and stimulates a type-specific immune response. Currently, there are two licensed pneumococcal polysaccharide vaccines available in the United States. The serotypes present in the 23-type vaccine are listed in Table 26-2. Protective levels of antibody are available for 5 to 10 years in adults. However, the polysaccharide vaccine is not immunogenic for infants 2 years of age and younger. In children older than 2 years of age who received the polysaccharide vaccine, concentrations of antibody will fall to unprotective levels in 3 to 5 years. Based on these serologic data, it is recommended that the children who are at high risk for invasive pneumococcal disease or are still suffering recurrent episodes of AOM be reimmunized after 3 to 5 years.

Investigations of 8- and 14-type pneumococcal vaccines to prevent recurrent episodes of AOM were initiated in 1975. The clinical experience of AOM in children younger than 2 years of age in the vaccine groups was similar to that of children in the control groups, and the duration of middle ear effusion was similar in the immunized and control groups (Teele et al, 1981). Finnish children ages 2 to 7 years who received the polysaccharide vaccines

TABLE 26-1. Currently Available Bacterial Vaccines in the United States, 2002

Vaccine	Type	Efficacy for Prevention of AOM
Anthrax	Inactivated bacteria	0
Bacille Calmette-Guérin	Live bacteria	±
Diphtheria	Toxoid	±
Haemophilus influenzae type b	Conjugate polysaccharide	±
Lyme disease	Recombinant outer-surface protein	0
Meningococcal	Polysaccharides A/C/Y/W-135	0
Pertussis	Antigens	0
Plague	Inactivated bacteria	0
Pneumococcal	Polysaccharide (23 types)	+
	Conjugate polysaccharide (7 types)	+
Tetanus	Toxoid	±
Typhoid	Live or inactivated bacteria or polysaccharide	0

AOM = acute otitis media.

0 = no known effect; ± = limited or uncertain effect; + = substantial effect.

had 50% fewer episodes of OM caused by types present in the vaccine (Makela et al, 1980). AOM was also reduced in a Swedish study of children between 2 and 5 years of age who received the 14-type vaccine (Rosen et al, 1983).

The pneumococcal polysaccharide vaccine was ineffective in preventing AOM in children under 2 years of age but was effective in reducing the number of episodes of AOM in children 2 years of age and older. The implication of the results of the polysaccharide vaccine trials is that the vaccine should be considered a supplement to the conjugate pneumococcal vaccine (PCV-7) in children who are 2 years of age or older and still suffering from recurrent AOM.

Pneumococcal Conjugate Vaccines

The first pneumococcal vaccine capable of eliciting protective antibodies in infants, a heptavalent pneumococcal conjugate polysaccharide vaccine (PCV-7), was approved by the FDA in February 2000. The vaccine contains the polysaccharides of *Streptococcus pneumoniae* conjugated to a nontoxic diphtheria protein CRM 197. The serotypes in PCV-7 are responsible for approximately two-thirds of cases of pneumococcal AOM in the United States (Table 26 2). The vaccine elicits an antibody response to all serotypes after primary immunization and produces an amnestic response following a booster dose. Protective titers were achieved after doses administered at ages 2, 4, and 6 months, but concentrations of antibody waned during the following 6 months, requiring a booster dose between ages 12 and 15 months. The vaccine was effective in preventing vaccine-type invasive disease (97.4% in fully immunized infants) and pneumonia (35% decrease for radiographically identifiable disease) (Black et al, 2000).

Clinical Trials for Prevention of AOM

Beginning in October 1995, PCV-7 was administered to almost 38,000 children in northern California in a double-blind trial (Black et al, 2000). For OM, data were available from clinical records of office visits, emergency department visits, and hospitalizations. Efficacy against visits, episodes, recurrent disease (five episodes in 6 months or six episodes in 12 months), and placement of ventilating tubes was 8.9%, 7.0%, 22.8%, and 25%, respectively. In a study using a similar protocol with PCV-7, the efficacy of the vaccine in prevention of episodes of AOM was 6% (Eskola et al, 2001). Thus, the vaccine was modestly effective for prevention of single episodes of AOM but was more effective for children who were destined to have recurrent AOM; fewer immunized children had recurrent episodes of AOM and fewer immunized children had surgery for placement of ventilating tubes.

TABLE 26-2. Serotypes of Pneumococcal Polysaccharide and Conjugate Vaccines (PCV-7)

Serotype	Polysaccharide Vaccine	Conjugate Vaccine
1	+	
2	+	
3	+	
4	+	+
5	+	
6B	+	+
7F	+	
8	+	
9N	+	
9V	+	+
10A	+	
11A	+	
12F	+	
14	+	+
15B	+	
17A (Wyeth)	+	
17Γ (Merck)	+	
18C	+	+
19A	+	
19F	+	+
20	+	
22F	+	
23F	+	+
33F	+	

Microbiologic Efficacy of PCV-7 for Prevention of AOM

The bacteriologic efficacy of PCV-7 was evaluated in the Finnish children (Eskola et al, 2001). The bacteriologic diagnosis was based on aspiration of middle ear fluids in patients with AOM. The reduction in the number of episodes in the per-protocol analysis was 57% against culture-confirmed, serotype-specific AOM, 34% against culture-confirmed pneumococcal AOM (irrespective of the serotype), and 6% against AOM irrespective of the etiology. The number of episodes attributed to serotypes that are cross-reactive with those in the vaccine was reduced by 51%, whereas the number of episodes owing to all other serotypes increased by 33%. Children who received PCV-7 had more episodes of AOM owing to *H. influenzae* (11%) but no difference in episodes owing to *M. catarrhalis* (Table 26-3).

Was PCV-7 Effective for Prevention of AOM?

The conjugate pneumococcal vaccine was extraordinarily effective for prevention of invasive disease (including bacteremia, meningitis, and bacteremic pneumonia) and for radiologically defined pneumonia (including any infiltrative disease and more so for single- or multilobe consolidations) but only modestly effective for prevention of AOM. PCV-7 was most effective in decreasing the number of children with recurrent disease and in decreasing the number of children who needed placement of ventilating tubes. The possibility of increased AOM owing to serotypes not in the vaccine (serotype switching) is raised by the microbiologic data presented by Eskola and colleagues (2001). Although there was a decrease in AOM owing to serotypes in the vaccine and in AOM owing to serologically related serotypes, there were more episodes of nonvaccine types in immunized children. Is it possible that immunized children had decreased nasopharyngeal carriage owing to serotypes in PCV-7 but had replacement by

serotypes not in the vaccine and that these strains were capable of causing AOM? Preliminary data suggest that carriage of pneumococci owing to types present in the vaccine is reduced, but there may be an increase in nonvaccine-type pneumococci (Mbelle et al, 1999).

Recommendations for Use of PCV-7

The Committee on Infectious Diseases of the American Academy of Pediatrics (2000) recommended universal immunization of infants 2 years of age and younger with PCV-7. By April 2003, more than 42 million doses had been distributed (personal communication, Wyeth Laboratories). For children 2 to 5 years of age, use of PCV-7 is recommended for children at high risk (eg, those with immunodeficiencies, sickle cell disease, human immunodeficiency virus [HIV] infection) and is considered optional for children at moderate risk, such as those in day care or in families with low socioeconomic status. Use of the vaccine for prevention of recurrent AOM is included in the category of moderate risk for optional use of the vaccine. The strategy for prevention of recurrent AOM in children 2 to 5 years should include protection by immunization, including influenza virus vaccine each fall and pneumococcal vaccines. The child should complete the appropriate schedule of PCV-7 followed by administration of the 23-type pneumococcal polysaccharide vaccine (no sooner than 8 weeks after the last dose of PCV-7). The strategy of two pneumococcal vaccines provides high concentrations of serum antibody for the seven common types associated with AOM in PCV-7 and broadens the coverage of serotypes by adding the antigens provided by the 23-type vaccine.

The Future

Although prevention of episodes of AOM by the conjugate pneumococcal vaccine has not been as robust as for invasive pneumococcal disease and pneumonia, PCV-7 is an important part of the strategy of reducing the incidence of AOM. Over the next few years, a number of questions need to be answered about the conjugate vaccine:

- Why are the results different for AOM and invasive pneumococcal disease?
- Does the vaccine need to provide more antibody or a different type of antibody to prevent AOM?
- Will nonvaccine types replace vaccine serotypes in the nasopharynx and reduce the efficacy of the vaccine for prevention of AOM?
- Will there be an increase in AOM owing to other pathogens that will replace the pneumococcus?
- Will use of the vaccine alter prescribing patterns of physicians for AOM?
- Will the serotypes represented in PCV-7 need to be changed owing to altered serotype disease patterns?

TABLE 26-3. Microbiology of Acute Otitis Media and Estimates of the Protective Efficacy of PCV-7

Etiology of Acute Otitis Media	Number of Episodes		Vaccine Efficacy (Point Estimate)
	PCV-7	Control Vaccine	
Any	1,251	1,345	6
Culture-confirmed pneumococcus	271	414	34
Pneumococcal serotypes in PCV-7*	107	250	57
Cross-reactive pneumococcal serotypes†	41	84	51
Other pneumococcal serotypes‡	125	96	−33
Haemophilus influenzae	315	287	−11
Moraxella catarrhalis	379	381	

Adapted from Eskola et al (2001).
*Serotypes 4, 6B, 9V, 14, 18C, 19F, 23F.
†Serotypes 6A, 9N, 18B, 19A, 23A.
‡Serotypes 3, 11, 15, 16, 22, 33, 35, 38.

These and other questions about AOM and the efficacy of the vaccine will be answered only over time as investigators follow the clinical and microbiologic patterns of the disease.

We need a common antigen for a pneumococcal vaccine so that we do not have to rely on vaccines based on specific serotypes, but this concept remains an elusive goal. We need vaccines for nontypable *H. influenzae* and *M. catarrhalis*. Prevention of viral disease by vaccines such as the current parenteral influenza virus vaccines and the future cold-adapted intranasal influenza vaccines have been demonstrated to reduce the incidence of AOM in immunized infants and children and should be considered part of the strategic plan for children with recurrent AOM. Other respiratory viral vaccines are in various stages of development and are likely to prevent a certain proportion of episodes of AOM. Other products, such as the oligosaccharides that block receptor sites on the mucosa of the upper respiratory tract, are attractive in providing an immune basis for protection that is not species specific.

References

Black S, Shinefield H, Fireman B, et al. Efficacy, safety and immunogenicity of heptavalent pneumococcal conjugate vaccine in children. Northern California Kaiser Permanente Vaccine Study Center Group. Pediatr Infect Dis J 2000;19:187–95.

Committee on Infectious Diseases, American Academy of Pediatrics. Policy statement: recommendations for the prevention of pneumococcal infections, including the use of pneumococcal conjugate vaccine (Prevnar), pneumococcal polysaccharide vaccine, and antibiotic prophylaxis. Pediatrics 2000;106:362–6.

Eskola J, Kilpi T, Palmu A, et al. Efficacy of a pneumococcal conjugate vaccine against acute otitis media. N Engl J Med 2001;344: 403–9.

Makela PH, Sibakov M, Herva E, Henricksen J. Pneumococcal vaccine and otitis media. Lancet 1980;ii:547–51.

Mbelle N, Wasas A, Huebner R, et al. Immunogenicity and impact on carriage of a 9-valent pneumococcal conjugate vaccine given to infants in Soweto, South Africa. J Infect Dis 1999;180: 1171–5.

Otitis media: a preventable disease? Proceedings of an international symposium. 2000 Feb 13–16; Annecy, France. Vaccine 2000;19 Suppl 1:1–152. Guest editors: Dagan R, Klein V, Charmaitree T, et al.

Rosen C, Christensen P, Hovelius B, et al. Effect of pneumococcal vaccination on upper respiratory tract infections in children. Design of a follow-up study. Scand J Infect Dis 1983;39 Suppl:39–44.

Teele DW, Klein JO, Bratton L, et al. Use of pneumococcal vaccine for prevention of recurrent acute otitis media in infants in Boston. The Greater Boston Collaborative Otitis Media Study. Rev Infect Dis 1981;3 Suppl:S113–8.

Chapter 27

Mucosal Immunity and Nasal Immunization in the Treatment of Infectious Diseases of the Upper Respiratory Tract

Joel Bernstein, MD, PhD, Noboru Yamanaka, MD

Naturally acquired mucosal infections or specific immunization with a variety of vaccine antigens administered in the respiratory or intestinal tract has been shown to result in the development of specific antibody and T cell–mediated immunologic responses (Ogra et al, 2001). Such responses are often associated with the development of significant protection against reinfection and/or clinical disease in the mucosal epithelium (Russell et al, 2000). The nasal route for vaccination offers some important opportunities, especially for the prophylaxis of respiratory diseases, including those of the middle ear and paranasal sinuses. Vaccination via the respiratory tract is reviewed in this chapter and the deposition and clearance of antigens in the nose and nasopharynx are described.

In humans, the structure known as Waldeyer's ring (the tonsils and adenoids) is important as an induction site (Bernstein, 1999). The immune response following intranasal administration can provide protection both at the administration site and at various effector sites as part of the common mucosal immune system. The common mucosal immune system consists of inductive sites in the nasopharynx (adenoid), palatine tonsils, Peyer's patches of the small bowel, and appendix. These inductive sites consist of well-developed lymphoid follicles, surrounded by a mantle zone and intrafollicular areas that consist mainly of T cells and follicular areas that consist mainly of B cells. A full description of the mucosal-associated lymphoid tissue is described in this chapter because it is particularly related to the upper respiratory tract and its

potential for control and prevention of bacterial and viral infections in the upper respiratory tract, particularly in the middle ear and paranasal sinuses. Despite the enormous research and publications that have addressed the potential role of immunization via the nasal and oral cavity, there is not yet any commercially available nasal vaccine for upper respiratory tract infections. However, the availability of an influenza viral vaccine is very close to the marketplace.

Vaccination via the Respiratory Tract

Almost all viral, bacterial, and parasitic agents causing common infectious diseases of the respiratory, intestinal, and genital tract enter or infect through the large surface area made available by mucosal membranes (Chen, 2000). The nasal mucosa is an important arm of the mucosal immune system because it is often the first point of contact for inhaled antigens. As a consequence, intranasal immunization has emerged as possibly the most effective route for vaccination for both peripheral and mucosal immunity (McGhee et al, 1999; Ogra, 2002). There are several reasons why the nose is an attractive route for immunization. It is highly accessible and vascularized. After intranasal immunization, both mucosal and systemic responses can be induced (van Ginkel et al, 2000). Immune responses can be induced at a distant mucosal site, such as the genital tract, following intranasal vaccination owing to the dissemination of effector immune cells in the common mucosal immune system. The nose can be used for easy immunization of large population groups, and nasal immunization does not require needles and syringes, which are potential sources of infection and pain for children. However, it should also be noted that oral or intranasal immunization can lead to systemic tolerance. Although secretory immunoglobulin (sIg)A, the most important sIg in the mucosa-associated lymphoid tissue, functions primarily to prevent colonization and absorption of specific infectious disease antigens, there may also be a decreased immunoglobulin (Ig)G systemic response. In some cases, this may be beneficial—as in autoimmune diseases and in some allergic diseases—but the concept of tolerance following oral immunization or nasal immunization could be potentially harmful when the antigen breaches the mucosal protection and enters the systemic system. In this case, down-regulation of IgG caused by immune tolerance may allow the infection to become chronic.

An overview of the mucosal immune system is therefore required to understand the great potential of the nasal mucosa as a source of protection against incoming bacterial or viral antigens as well as allergens from both inhaled particles and possibly food antigens. A schematic summary of the mucosal immune system is seen in Figure 27-1. M cells are present in the mucosal inductive sites in both the upper respiratory tract and the small bowel, specifically in the tonsils, adenoids, and Peyer's patches in the gastrointestinal tract (Neutra et al, 1996). M cells are thought to play an important role in antigen processing and possibly the induction of antigen-specific immunity in mucosal effector sites. Following uptake by M cells, antigen is then presented to either antigen-presenting cells in the lamina propria of the tonsils and adenoids or directly to T or B cells in the reticular epithelium. These cells, whether T or B cells, may then become activated and may be transferred to follicular dendritic cells, where they may mature into B cells. These mature B

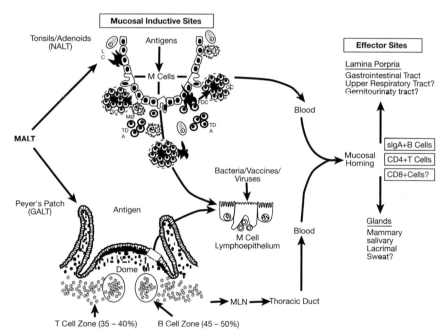

FIGURE 27-1. The role of inductive sites for mucosal immunoglobulin (Ig)A responses. Antigen uptake by M cells occurs in both the tonsils and adenoids, as well as in the Peyer's patches. This results in the initial induction of the immune response. Antigen-sensitized, precursor surface IgA+ B cells, CD4+ T helper cells, and CD8+ T suppressor cells in these inductive sites leave via efferent lymphatics and migrate to regional lymph nodes and then either via the blood or thoracic duct to reach the bloodstream. These migrating cells enter the IgA effector sites, where terminal differentiation, synthesis, and transport of secretory IgA occur. In the upper respiratory tract, this may occur in the salivary glands, the nasal mucosa, the middle ear during acute otitis media, and the paranasal sinuses in acute rhinosinusitis. The induction in mucus-associated lymphoid tissue and exodus of cells to effector sites is termed the common mucosal immune system. It should be emphasized that in addition to the transfer of the IgA B cells to these effector sites, there is increasing evidence that T cells are also involved in this migration pattern. However, the integrins and the counter-receptors on the endothelium of small blood vessels have not yet been completely worked out for the upper respiratory tract. Adapted from McGhee JR et al (1999). FDC = follicular dendritic cell; GALT = gastrointestinal-associated lymphoid tissue; GO = ; MALT = mucosa-associated lymphoid tissue; MLN = mesentric lymph node; MØ = macrophage; TD = tonsillar dendritic cells.

cells and possibly T cells are then exported from the mucosal inductive site in the tonsils and adenoids or the Peyer's patch to the blood or lymphatics and may home to other areas of the common mucosal immune system. In general, however, there is compartmentalization of the mucosal immune system. This phenomenon results in seeding of mature B cells and probably T cells to areas that are close to the inductive site. For example, in the tonsil and adenoids, the B and T cells may migrate to the nasal mucosa, lacrimal gland, parotid gland, and paranasal sinuses and middle ear during acute infectious disease because the paranasal sinuses and the middle ear are essentially sterile in the normal healthy state. In contrast to the tonsils and adenoids, the Peyer's patch mature B cells primarily seed the gut and the lower gastrointestinal tract via the mesenteric lymph nodes. Another significant difference between the upper respiratory tract and the lower respiratory tract is that the subclass IgA1 is more common in the upper respiratory tract, whereas IgA2 is more common as the sIg in the gastrointestinal tract (Brandtzaeg and Haneberg, 1997). Thus, it is more likely that intranasal immunization would result in seeding of B cells that are destined to secrete sIgA1 and T helper (Th) or T suppressor cells to areas of the upper respiratory tract, middle ear, and paranasal sinuses during acute bacterial or viral infectious diseases. However, it has also been demonstrated that intranasal immunization may also seed distant areas of a common mucosal immune system, especially the genitourinary tract (Mestecky and Fultz, 1999).

The best defense against pathogens that invade the eustachian tube, paranasal sinuses, oral pharynx, and nasopharynx would be vaccines. Preferably, they would be mucosal vaccines capable of inducing both mucosal immunity to prevent adherence or colonization of the nasopharynx and systemic immunity, mainly of the IgG classes, to prevent invasion of the body, and with complement and neutrophils, these vaccines would destroy the bacteria once they have invaded the middle ear or paranasal sinuses.

Mucosal defenses against pathogens consist of innate barriers such as mucus and epithelial barriers and innate immune mechanisms such as lactoferrin, defensins, and adaptive host immunity, which, at mucosal surfaces, consist predominantly of sIgA and cytotoxic lymphocytes.

This chapter now focuses on antigen-specific mucosal immune responses. Figure 27-2 summarizes the differentiation and regulation of Th subsets in the immune response in the mucosal compartments, which include the tonsils, adenoids, and Peyer's patches (Xu-Amano et al, 1993). An encounter of pathogen-derived antigen or vaccine antigen will stimulate Th cells to secrete cytokines. Depending on the stimulus, a Th1 (interleukin [IL]-2 and interferon [IFN]-γ as the major cytokines) or Th2 cell response (IL-4, IL-5, IL-10, and IL-13 as major cytokines) is induced. For example, intracellular pathogens will

induce production of IL-12/IL-18 by macrophages, activated by IFN-γ production by natural killer cells, and induce differentiation to a Th1-mediated immune response, which supports cell-mediated immunity (CMI) and production of complement-fixing antibodies, presumably by production of cytokines such as IFN-γ, IL-2, and tumor necrosis factor (TNF)-β. A Th2 response can be observed on infection of parasites or on vaccine administration; this response is characterized by the production of cytokines such as IL-4, IL-5, IL-6, IL-10, and IL-13, which support humoral immunity. However, for induction of a sIgA response, transforming growth factor (TGF)-β1 is required to enable B cells to switch to IgA. TGF-β1 production is associated with inhibition of IL-4 production by Th2 cells inhibiting IgE production.

Mucosal sIgA Antibody Responses

The hallmark of the humoral mucosal immune response is the synthesis of sIgA (Figure 27-3). Figure 27-3 demon-

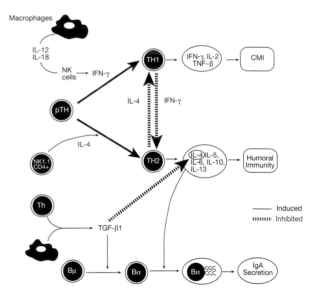

FIGURE 27-2. A schematic overview of a local immune response following intranasal or oral immunization with a vaccine. This diagram illustrates the development of cell-mediated immunity (CMI), as well as humoral immunity and the role of transforming growth factor-(TGF)β1 on the development of immunoglobulin (Ig)A plasma cells and IgA secretion at the level of the nasopharynx. Professional antigen-presenting cells such as macrophages release interleukin (IL)-12 and IL-18, which stimulate natural killer (NK) cells to produce interferon (IFN)-γ. IFN-γ, in turn, up-regulates T helper (Th)1 cells with the production of IFN-γ, IL-2, and tumor necrosis factor (TNF)-β, which results in CMI at the level of the nasopharynx. In addition, NK cells releasing IL-4 stimulate pre-Th cells to develop into Th2 cells. Th2 cells release a number of cytokines, which result in humoral immunity, including IgE hypersensitivity. Th cells may also produce TGF-β1, which inhibits IL-4 and turns off the production of IgE development but specifically enhances the production of B cells, which produce IgA. Adapted from van Ginkel FW et al (2000).

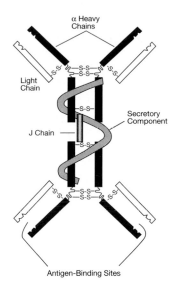

FIGURE 27-3. A highly schematized diagram of a dimeric immunoglobulin (Ig)A found in secretions. In addition to the two IgA monomers, there is a single J chain and an additional polypeptide chain called the secretory component, which is thought to protect the IgA molecules from being digested by proteolytic enzymes in the secretions. The secretory component molecule is found on the basolateral surface of the epithelial cells and appears to be the receptor for the J chain.

strates a highly schematized diagram of dimeric IgA molecule found in secretions. In addition to the two IgA monomers, there is a single J chain and an additional polypeptide chain called the secretory component, which is thought to protect IgA molecules from being digested by proteolytic enzymes in the secretions. The secretory component molecules found in the basolateral surface of the epithelial cells appear to be the receptor for the J chain.

sIgA results from transcytosis of polymeric IgA across the epithelium through binding of the polymeric Ig receptor (Figure 27-4). Figure 27-4 demonstrates the mechanism of transport of a dimeric IgA molecule across an epithelial cell. The IgA molecule, as a J chain–containing dimer, binds to a specialized transmembrane Fc receptor protein on the nonluminal surface of the secretory epithelial cell. The surface of the receptor-IgA complexes is ingested by receptor-mediated endocytosis, transferred across the epithelial cell cytoplasm in vesicles, and then secreted into the lumina of the opposite side of the cell by exocytosis. When exposed to the lumen, the part of the Fc receptor protein that is bound to the IgA dimer (the secretory component) is cleaved from its transmembrane tail, therefore releasing the antibody in the form shown in Figure 27-3. The major immunologic role for sIgA is its ability to prevent adsorption and absorption of antigens from bacteria and viruses and other foreign substances through the mucosal epithelium of the nose and nasopharynx, as well as the gastrointestinal tract and perhaps the genitourinary tract (McGhee et al, 1999). In addition, if viral antigen does cross the epithelial barrier, IgA has the ability to neutralize the viral antigen intracellularly in the nasal and gastrointestinal mucosa. Thus, the major function of sIgA is the prevention of the bacterial or viral particle from entering the mucosa of the upper respiratory tract from the external environment. Unlike IgG and IgM, it does not fix complement. Thus, it is not important in phagocytosis or in killing of bacteria of the upper respiratory tract. As is mentioned later, the role of sIgA, which is synthesized in the middle ear mucosa, is still controversial (Ogra et al, 1974).

In conclusion, virus-specific intraepithelial IgA can inhibit viral entry and replication at the level of the nasopharynx and the nasal mucosa. Elimination of the virus in the upper respiratory tract is critical to the prevention of both acute bacterial rhinosinusitis and acute suppurative otitis media (OM). Thus, intranasal vaccines would be extremely important in eliminating the absorption of these viruses and bacteria and inhibiting their transport to upper respiratory tract cavities.

CMI at Mucosal Surfaces

Figure 27-5 summarizes CMI at mucosal surfaces. Pathways of intracellular pathogen clearance from infected cells by cytotoxic cells are schematically represented.

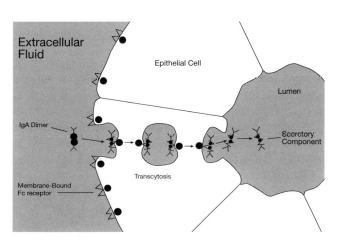

FIGURE 27-4. The mechanism of transport of a dimeric immunoglobulin (Ig)A molecule across an epithelial cell. The IgA molecule, as a J chain–containing dimer, binds to a specialized transmembrane Fc receptor protein on the nonluminal surface of the secretory epithelial cell. The surface of the receptor-IgA complexes is ingested by receptor-mediated endocytosis, transferred across the epithelial cell cytoplasm in vesicles, and then secreted into the lumina of the opposite side of the cell by exocytosis. When exposed to the lumen, the part of the Fc receptor protein that is bound to the IgA dimer (the secretory component) is cleaved from its transmembrane tail, thereby releasing the antibody in the form shown in Figure 27-3.

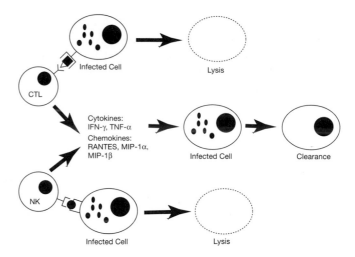

FIGURE 27-5. Cell-mediated immunity at mucosal surfaces. This diagrammatic figure demonstrates the pathways of intracellular pathogen clearance from infected cells by cytotoxic cells. Intracellular pathogen-derived antigens complexed to major histocompatibility antigen (MHC) class I molecules are recognized by cytotoxic lymphocytes, whereas natural killer (NK) cells recognize the absence of suppressed levels of MHC class I molecules on infected cells. Both of these cells are able to lyse the infected cells and allow for clearance of the infected cell. The natural killer cell releases regulated and activated normal T-cell expressed and secreted (RANTES), macrophage inflammatory (MIP)-1α, and MIP-1β, whereas the cytotoxic lymphocytes (CTLs) release interferon (IFN)-γ and tumor necrosis factor (TNF)-α.

Intracellular pathogen-derived antigens complexed to major histocompatibility antigen (MHC) class I molecules are recognized by cytotoxic lymphocytes, whereas natural killer cells recognize the absence of suppressed levels of MHC class I molecules on infected cells. The activated cytotoxic cells deliver apoptotic signals through Fas ligand and perforin to infected cells. They also secrete the cytokines IFN-γ and TNF-α and the chemokines RANTES, MIP-1α, and MIP-1β to inhibit or suppress intracellular pathogen replication (Gallichan and Rosenthal, 1996; Yang et al, 1997).

Thus, in addition to sIgA, which is the major humoral antibody responsible for inhibition of adherence and replication of virus and bacteria at the surface of the nasopharynx and the nasal mucosa, CMI at mucosal surfaces is primarily the result of T cells that can recognize peptides derived from core proteins of the pathogens such as influenza virus. Core proteins are usually expressed and presented earlier during infection than proteins targeted for neutralizing antibodies. Subsequently, CMI occurs before the induction of antibodies and forms an early line of defense, as summarized in Figure 27-5 (Offit et al, 1991).

Summary of the Common Mucosal Immune System

Thus far, this chapter has emphasized the immunobiology of the common mucosal immune system. Antigenic exposure at mucosal sites such as the tonsils and adenoids in the upper respiratory tract and Peyer's patches in the small bowel activates mucosal B and T lymphocytes to emigrate from these inductive sites to various mucosal effector sites, such as in the upper respiratory tract, lacrimal gland, parotid gland, nasal mucosa, and middle ear during acute OM (Bernstein et al, 1999). The common mucosal immune system involves homing of antigen-specific lymphocytes to mucosal effector sites other than the site where the initial antigen exposure occurred, such as the adenoid or nasopharynx. This pathway has almost exclusively been documented for sIgA antibody responses at mucosal surfaces mediated by B cells, but similar events are assumed to take place with T cells. Thus, both Th and T suppressor cells, as mentioned above, are involved in the local immune response. The fact that nasal immunization can induce antibodies in a broader range of tissues, such as secretions, and tissues such as the nasal mucosa, the paranasal sinuses, the middle ear, and the genitourinary tract, reflects the wide range of possibilities for protection against viruses and bacteria following nasal immunization (Ogra et al, 2001).

Summary of Mucosal and Nasal Vaccines

Although mucosal application of vaccines is attractive for many reasons, only a few mucosal vaccines, mostly oral, have been approved for human use. These vaccines include poliovirus, *Salmonella typhi*, and the recently approved tetravalent rotavirus vaccine (*Morbidity and Mortality Weekly Report*, 1999). The latter vaccine, however, has been removed from the market because of the relatively high incidence of intussusception. Mucosal vaccines approved for humans so far involve live attenuated pathogens, and for this reason, oral polio vaccine is recommended after receiving the injected inactivated virus because a limited number of polio cases occur after immunization with a live attenuated virus. Because the live virus induces better, longer-lasting protection, it is given after some level of systemic immunity has been achieved to limit possible problems. The cold-adaptive influenza virus, which is in advanced clinical trials, will be the first mucosal vaccine given intranasally to humans and has been shown to generate protective immune responses (Belshe et al, 1998).

An alternate approach is the use of deoxyribonucleic acid (DNA) vaccines. Plasmid DNA has been used in clinical trials to induce protection against several pathogens, including hepatitis B virus, herpes simplex virus, human immunodeficiency virus (HIV), malaria, and influenza (Braciale, 1993; Fynan et al, 1993).

Another promising avenue for mucosal vaccines is the use of bacterial adhesins. Mucosal antibodies to these proteins block the pathogen's ability to penetrate mucosal barriers. Our laboratory has isolated various bacterial adhesins from pathogenic bacteria (Bernstein and Reddy, 2000), and antibodies directed against these adhesins might play a role in protecting the host against the attachment of these bacteria to the nasopharyngeal mucosa or to the mucus overlying the nasopharyngeal mucosa. The importance of blocking the initial attachment and entry into the host cell has been recognized for some time for viruses such as influenza, but the use of this approach for bacteria is still in its infancy and has enormous potential for intranasal vaccination.

There is increasing interest in the development of a vaccine directed against the bacteria that are responsible for OM. The interest is driven by the high incidence of this disease, the ineffectiveness of empiric antimicrobial treatment, and the rapid emergence of microorganisms resistant to antibiotics. Nontypable *Haemophilus influenzae* (NTHi) is a leading causative pathogen for OM. Many studies for developing an effective vaccine against NTHi have focused on outer membrane proteins (OMPs), conserved in the cell envelope. One specific OMP, P6, is highly conserved among strains and is antigenically stable. Our previous studies using purified P6 from NTHi showed that intranasal immunization with P6 evoked mucosal immunity against P6 and enhanced nasopharyngeal clearance of inoculated live NTHi (Hotomi et al, 2002). The findings suggested that P6 is an attractive candidate for a preventive bacterial vaccine. However, there has been considerable difficulty in getting P6 from NTHi. Recombinant versions of the protein may be a promising alternative, and for this reason, a study was designed to determine the immunogenicity of the recombinant version of P6 (rP6) as an intranasal vaccine candidate to induce specific mucosal immunity against NTHi. Intranasal immunization with rP6 and cholera toxin elevated anti-rP6–specific IgG in sera 1 week after the final immunization. The immune responses were highly maintained for 3 weeks after the final immunization. In controls, lower levels of anti-rP6–specific IgG in sera were identified (Figure 27-6).

The rP6 index for IgA was elevated in the nasopharyngeal secretions 1 week after the final immunization. The immune response was also highly maintained for 3 weeks after the final immunization. In controls, anti-rP6–specific IgA in nasopharyngeal washings was low (Figure 27-7).

Nasopharyngeal colonization with potential middle ear pathogens is the first step in the development of OM

(Harabuchi et al, 1994). Children who are colonized with NTHi in the first year of life are at increased risk of developing OM compared with children who remain free of NTHi. Effectively preventing NTHi adhesion by immunization with common antigens of NTHi could result in selective reduction of NTHi alone in the nasopharynx. The induction of specific mucosal immunity by intranasal application of rP6 mixed with cholera toxin has been demonstrated as an effective method of enhancing both mucosal immunity with sIgA and systemic immunity with specific IgG against NTHi. However, as with most studies, this was performed in a Balb/c mouse. There have been no human studies, although P6 is an excellent candidate for a human intranasal vaccine.

It is obvious that if the success in many animal studies can be duplicated in humans, intranasal immunization with recombinant OMPs of other bacteria may be extremely important in preventing bacterial upper respiratory infections, especially in the otitis-prone child, and hopefully will be a routine procedure in the future of medical therapy in this era of serious emergence of resistant bacteria. An extensive review of nasal vaccines has recently been published by Davis (2001). In this review, a large number of nasal vaccines were used in both mice and humans. Also, the various adjuvants that can be used for nasal vaccines are also reviewed in that study. Specifically, those vaccines that have been used via the intranasal route in humans are reviewed in Table 27-1. They include group B meningococcus, influenza hemagglutinin, and neuraminidase from the influenza virus; cold-adaptive live virus of influenzae; *Streptococcus mutans* using liposomes as the adjuvant; diphtheria and tetanus using polysorbate-capric glycerides as an adjuvant; respiratory syncytial virus as a live cold-adapted virus; and pertussis using whole-cell bacteria.

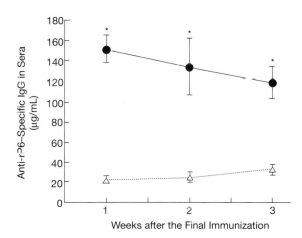

FIGURE 27-6. Anti-recombinant P6 (rP6)–specific immunoglobulin (Ig)G in the serum of animals receiving intranasal immunization with rP6 antigen of nontypable *Haemophilus influenzae*. The *closed circles* represent the immunized group; the *open triangles* represent the non-immunized control.

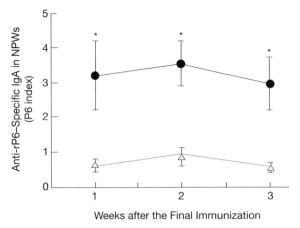

FIGURE 27-7. Anti–recombinant P6 (rP6)–specific immunoglobulin (Ig)A in nasopharyngeal washings (NPWs) following intranasal immunization with rP6 from nontypable *Haemophilus influenzae*. The *closed circles* represent the immunized group; the *open triangles* represent the nonimmunized control.

It is clear that the performance of the nasal vaccine can be influenced by the physical nature of the antigen and the chosen delivery system. Theoretically, the best intranasal vaccine would produce sIgA at the level of the nasopharyngeal mucus membrane and IgG as a systemically induced immune response.

Again, it is emphasized that mucosal immunization can lead to tolerance. In some cases, this can be detrimental because the antigen may enter the systemic circulation and antibody of the IgG subclasses would not be available to prevent disseminated infection. However, in certain autoimmune diseases, this oral tolerance or nasal immunization leading to tolerance might be beneficial.

Conclusion and Future Directions

It appears that lymphoid tissue in the nasopharynx, tonsils, and adenoids is able to process antigens, mount a specific immune response locally, and spread to regional epithelia via distinct homing mechanisms. Such immunologic reactivity may also home to other mucosal sites, such as gut-associated lymphoid tissue (GALT) or bronchus-associated lymphoid tissue (BALT) and possibly the genital tract and mammary glands. Other observations have suggested that it is also possible to induce an effective immune response in the middle ear cavity by the introduction of antigens in the GALT or BALT. The available evidence, based on vaccine antigens appropriate for prevention of OM, has suggested that intranasal immunization can be used to produce sIgA, which will prevent the colonization of bacteria at the level of the nasopharynx. The models employing immunization with P6, as mentioned in this chapter, are a classic model for what can be considered for human intranasal vaccination. Intranasal immunization against *Streptococcus pneumoniae*, *Pseudomonas* species, and respiratory syncytial virus may eventually be available for humans as well. As a result of these observations, the interest in vaccine delivery systems has shifted to immunization via the nasal route. It appears to be as effective as the oral route, may require smaller antigen doses, can be effective even with nonreplicating agents, and can frequently induce mucosal and systemic responses that may be equal or even superior to all immunization. Finally, it is again emphasized that these vaccines, particularly those that possess replicating agents, interact specifically with mucosal epithelium and induce the synthesis of a variety of immunoregulatory and proinflammatory cytokines and chemokines. Currently, however, most vaccines available for human use cannot be delivered or are not effective via mucosal routes and, as a result, are administered systemically. Such immunizations consistently induce specific antibody responses in the circulation and other systemic sites. Thus, the ability to induce a balanced mucosal response and systemic immune response following mucosal immunization is the future goal of most immunization programs. The success of intranasal immunization will be determined by multiple factors, including the nature of the vaccine antigens, intestinal or respiratory mucosal microenvironment, concurrent use of adjuvants and delivery systems employed for vaccine administration, and potential for induction of systemic tolerance.

TABLE 27-1. Recent Studies on Nasal Vaccination in Man

System	Antigen	Species	Comment
OMP	Group B meningococcus	Humans	—
Liposome	*Streptococcus mutans*	Humans	—
OMV	Norwegian group B meningococcus	Humans	Good T cell responses
Liposome (plus HLT)	Influenza hemagglutinin and neuraminidase	Humans	HLT needed to provide good response
Live cold-adapted and inactivated influenza vaccines	Trivalent influenza	Humans	Cold-adapted system more protective than inactivated vaccine
Whole cell	Pertussis	Humans	—
rCTB	CTB	Humans	Responses in upper respiratory tract and vagina

Adapted from Davis SS (2001).
CTB = cholera toxin subunit B; HLT = heat-labile toxin; OMP = outer membrane protein; OMV = outer membrane vesicle.

References

Belshe RB, Mendelman PM, Treanor J, et al. The efficacy of live attenuated, cold-adapted, trivalent, intranasal influenza virus vaccine in children. N Engl J Med 1998;338:1405–12.

Bernstein JM. Waldeyer's ring and otitis media: the nasopharyngeal tonsil and otitis media. Int J Pediatr Otorhinolaryngol 1999;49 Suppl 1:S127–32.

Bernstein JM, Gorfien J, Brandtzaeg P. The immunobiology of the tonsils and adenoids. In: Ogra PL, Mestecky J, Lamm ME, et al, editors. Mucosal immunology. San Diego: Academic Press; 1999. p. 1339–62.

Bernstein JM, Reddy M. Bacteria-mucin interaction in the upper aerodigestive tract shows striking heterogeneity: implications in otitis media, rhinosinusitis and pneumonia. Otolaryngol Head Neck Surg 2000;122:514–20.

Braciale TJ. Naked DNA and vaccine design. Trends Microbiol 1993;1:1323–5.

Brandtzaeg P, Haneberg B. Role of nasal-associated lymphoid tissue in the human mucosal immune system. Mucosal Immunol Update 1997;5:4–7.

Chen H. Recent advances in mucosal vaccine development. J Control Release 2000;67:117–28.

Davis SS. Nasal vaccines. Adv Drug Deliv Rev 2001;51:21–42.

Fynan EF, Webster RG, Fuller DH, et al. DNA vaccines: protective immunization by parental, mucosal, and gene-gun inoculations. Proc Natl Acad Sci U S A 1993;90:11478–82.

Gallichan WS, Rosenthal KL. Long-lived cytotoxic T lymphocyte memory in mucosal tissues after mucosal but not systemic immunization. J Exp Med 1996;184:1879–90.

Harabuchi Y, Faden H, Yamanaka N, et al. Nasopharyngeal colonization with non-typable *Haemophilus influenzae* and recurrent otitis media. J Infect Dis 1994;170:862–6.

Hotomi M, Yamanaka N, Shimada J, et al. Intranasal immunization with recombinant outer membrane protein 6 induces specific immune responses against non-typable *Haemophilus influenzae*. Int J Pediatr Otorhinolaryngol 2002;65:109–16.

Intussusception among recipients of rotavirus vaccine—United States, 1998–1999. Morb Mortal Wkly Rep 1999;48:577–81.

McGhee JR, Lamm ME, Strober W. Mucosal immune responses: an overview. In: Ogra PL, Mestecky J, Lamm ME, et al, editors. Mucosal immunology. San Diego: Academic Press; 1999. p. 485–506.

Mestecky J, Fultz PN. Mucosal immune system of the human genital tract. J Infect Dis 1999;179 Suppl 3:S470–4.

Neutra MR, Frey A, Kraehenbuhl JP. Epithelial M cells: gateways for mucosal infection in immunization. Cell 1996;86:345–8.

Offit PA, Cunningham SL, Dudzik KI. Memory and distribution of virus-specific cytotoxic T lymphocytes (CTLs) and CTL precursors after rotavirus infection. J Virol 1991;65:1318–24.

Ogra PL. Mucosal vaccines and nasal immunization. In: Lim D, Bluestone CD, Casselbrant ML, et al, editors. Recent advances in otitis media: proceedings of the 7th International Symposium. Hamilton (ON): BC Decker; 1999. p. 36–8.

Ogra PL, Bernstein JM, Yurchak AM, et al. Characteristics of secretory immune system in human middle ear: implications in otitis media. J Immunol 1974;112:488–95.

Ogra PL, Faden H, Welliver R. Vaccination strategies for mucosal immune responses. Clin Microbiol Rev 2001;14:430–45.

Russell MW, Martin MH, Hong-Yin W, et al. Strategies of immunization against mucosal infections. Vaccine 2000;19:122–7.

van Ginkel FW, Nguyen HH, McGhee JR. Vaccines for mucosal immunity to combat emerging infectious diseases. Emerg Infect Dis 2000;6:123–32.

Xu-Amano J, Kiyono H, Jackson RJ, et al. Helper T cell subsets for immunoglobulin-A responses: oral immunization with tetanus, toxoid and cholera toxin as adjuvant selectively induces TH_2 cells in mucosal associated tissues. J Exp Med 1993;178:1309–20.

Yang OO, Kalims SA, Trocha A, et al. Suppression of human immunodeficiency virus type 1 replication by CD8[+] positive cells: Evidence for HLA class 1-restricted triggering of cytolytic and non-cytolytic mechanisms. J Virol 1997;71:3120–8.

Chapter 28

ALLERGY TESTING/TREATMENT FOR OTITIS MEDIA

DEBORAH A. GENTILE, MD, DAVID P. SKONER, MD

Retrospective and prospective epidemiologic surveys have shown that allergic rhinitis is closely associated with or may be a causative factor in asthma, sinusitis, and otitis media (OM). The high prevalence of OM among patients with allergic rhinitis strongly suggests that IgE-mediated allergies are involved in the pathogenesis of middle ear disease. Of children with allergy, 21% have OM, whereas 50% of children with chronic OM have nasal allergy (Skoner, 2000; Skoner and Casselbrant, 1998).

In and of itself, allergic rhinitis can have a significant impact on quality of life, psychological well-being, and capacity to function in activities of daily living. Individuals with allergic rhinitis are more likely to exhibit shyness, depression, anxiety, fearfulness, and fatigue than are those without the condition. Furthermore, children with allergic rhinitis miss 2 million school days each year, and, even when they are in school, their ability to learn and to process cognitive input has been found to be significantly impaired relative to the abilities of their nonallergic peers. Additionally, allergic rhinitis accounts for nearly 2 billion dollars in annual health care spending, along with costly but undetermined indirect expenses (Corren, 2000; Druce, 1998; Fireman, 2000). In addition to these psychosocial, performance, and economic problems, allergic rhinitis, when left untreated, may exacerbate and contribute to the symptoms of several comorbid conditions in both the upper and lower airways.

Allergic rhinitis and atopy, in general, are caused by the interaction of a genetically predisposed patient and the environment. Genetics clearly plays an important role. Approximately 20 to 30% of the general population and 10 to 15% of children are atopic. When both parents are atopic, this risk more than quadruples, reaching 50%. The risk increases further, to nearly 72%, when both parents have the same atopic manifestation (whether allergic rhinitis, asthma, or atopic dermatitis) (Druce, 1998; Skoner et al, 1997).

The role of the environment is essential because allergens, which are ubiquitous in virtually all environments, initiate and then, on subsequent exposure, trigger the genetically predetermined immune response. When an allergen comes into contact with a nasal mucosa that has been previously sensitized by that allergen, it binds to specific IgE antibodies on the cell surface of the nasal mucosal mast cells, which then degranulate. In the early, or immediate, phase of the allergic reaction, re-exposure to the allergen will cause mast cells to release and generate inflammatory mediators such as histamine, leukotrienes, and prostaglandins, which increases vascular permeability, tissue edema, and cellular recruitment and produces the localized symptoms of rhinorrhea, pruritus, sneezing, and congestion. The late-phase response usually occurs 4 to 8 hours after the initial exposure, during which time symptoms recur (Barnes, 1998). The predominant symptom in the late phase is congestion, and this phase is primarily driven by cellular infiltration.

A model has been developed to explain the pathogenesis of OM. This model hypothesizes that nasal inflammation caused by allergens or viral upper respiratory tract infections (URTIs) leads to inflammatory swelling and obstruction of the eustachian tube, which, in turn, leads to increased negative pressure in the middle ear and improper ventilation. Middle ear underpressure allows fluids to accumulate in the middle ear. Transient eustachian tube opening can occur in the middle ear with an underpressure and effusion, which results in insufflation or aspiration into the middle ear cavity of nasopharyngeal secretions that contain bacteria, virus, and/or allergens. Bacteria in the middle ear fluid can cause acute bacterial OM. Sustained obstruction and dysfunction of the eustachian tube (eg, because of inflammation caused by perennial allergic rhinitis), persistent effusion, and unresolved bacterial infections can lead to chronic OM. This model has been extensively tested because of the accessibility of the middle ear to assessment of function. A number of studies on the pathogenesis of OM have described interactions among nasal allergic reactions, viral URTIs, eustachian tube dysfunction, and middle ear disease (Doyle, 2002; Gentile and Skoner, 2002; Skoner and Casselbrant, 1998).

Signs and Symptoms of Allergic Rhinitis in Children

Allergic rhinitis may present with a wide range of signs and symptoms (Table 28-1). Unfortunately, many of the symptoms of allergic rhinitis may go unrecognized in children because of their inability to verbalize and describe their symptoms. Therefore, the signs of the condition are particularly important in recognizing this condition in the pediatric population. Some characteristic signs of allergic rhinitis in children include the "allergic shiner," a darkening of the lower eyelid because of chronic nasal obstruction and suborbital edema; the "allergic crease," visible as a transverse skin line above the tip and below the bridge of the nose caused by constant rubbing; and the "allergic salute," characterized by upward rubbing of the nose with the palm of the hand as a means of trying to reduce itching and temporarily open the nasal passages (Druce, 1998; Skoner, 2001; Skoner et al, 1997).

In addition to these more localized signs and symptoms, many children with allergic rhinitis experience systemic symptoms, including weakness, malaise, fatigue, irritability, and poor appetite. Children are often unable to express these symptoms or may attribute them to other causes. Therefore, the presence of these symptoms may not be recognized unless they are specifically elicited. In addition, children with allergic rhinitis often do not sleep soundly and do not feel well, a combination that may have deleterious effects on both school performance and self-esteem. Also, children presenting with a history of recurrent or chronic URTIs may have allergic rhinitis (Fireman, 2000).

Evaluating and Diagnosing Allergic Rhinitis

The diagnosis of allergic rhinitis is highly dependent on a comprehensive history. Children, particularly older ones, may be able to provide accurate information in this regard if skillfully questioned. When evaluating younger children, however, the clinician will need to depend primarily on information provided by parents or other care-givers. In addition to questioning about the signs and symptoms discussed above, the clinician may find it useful to ask about the presence of allergens in the home and school environment, including pets, cockroaches, moisture, humidity, and irritants such as smoke, cleaning agents, and air sprays (Druce, 1998; Skoner, 2001).

Once a decision to evaluate for allergy has been made, the patient should be tested for allergy to a panel of geographically appropriate inhalant substances. There is no well-documented role for food allergy in triggering OM. To test for the presence of allergen-specific IgE antibodies to inhalant substances, several methods are available, including in vivo skin testing and in vitro serum testing. Generally, skin tests are preferable because they are more sensitive, are less costly, and provide a vivid teaching example to allergic patients about their tissue inflammatory process. However, expertise in interpretation, such as that provided by a board-certified allergist/clinical immunologist, is desirable. Exceptions to the general recommendation for skin testing include patients who have extensive skin disease that precludes use of the skin for testing, are unable to discontinue invalidating antihistamine or other therapies, or are using β-blocker therapy, which increases the risk of skin testing. In vitro testing should be used in these patients (Demoly et al, 1998).

The allergy evaluation should include the following allergens, which may vary geographically: pollens (grasses, trees, weeds), molds, dust mites, cats, dogs, and cockroaches. Because two or more seasons of pollen exposure are required for sensitization, allergy testing for seasonal allergens such as trees, grasses, and weeds is typically performed after 2 or 3 years of age. However, allergy to perennial inhalant allergens such as house dust mite, dog, cat, and cockroach can manifest after several months of daily exposure. In these instances, allergy testing to perennial allergens may be performed in children younger than 2 years of age if clinically indicated. However, these children may exhibit a smaller wheal and flare in the event of a positive allergy skin test than will older children and adults. Skin tests must be interpreted in the context of reactions to both a positive (histamine) and a negative (saline) control skin test. Both puncture and intradermal testing may be warranted in the evaluation (Demoly et al, 1998).

Treating Allergic Rhinitis

Specific treatment options include environmental control for allergen avoidance, pharmacotherapy, and immunotherapy. In all cases, the primary goal of treatment is to control the symptoms and improve the quality of life without altering the patient's ability to function. A second but equally important goal is to prevent the development of sequelae of allergic rhinitis, including OM (Dykewicz et al, 1998; Skoner, 2000).

TABLE 28-1. Signs and Symptoms of Allergic Rhinitis

Itching of the nose, ears, palate, or throat
Sneezing episodes
Thin, clear rhinorrhea
Nasal congestion
Sinus headache
Eustachian tube dysfunction
Mouth breathing or snoring
Chronic postnasal drip
Chronic, nonproductive cough
Frequent throat clearing
Sleep disturbance
Daytime fatigue

Environmental Control for Allergen Avoidance

Educating families about avoiding exposure to allergens is an essential part of the treatment of allergic rhinitis (Table 28-2). Unfortunately, it is also often highly impractical. Moreover, it may have negative psychosocial ramifications for children that should not be ignored. Avoiding outdoor sports in the springtime and banishing furred pets from the home, for example, may have adverse effects on children that range beyond allergen control. Nevertheless, families should be taught about the importance of environmental control measures and advised to adhere to them to the extent possible (Dykewicz et al, 1998; Fireman, 2000).

Oral Antihistamines

The Joint Task Force on Practice Parameters in Allergy, Asthma and Immunology recently published guidelines on the diagnosis and management of allergic rhinitis. These guidelines review the considerations in selecting an antihistamine for the treatment of allergic rhinitis. As with any medication, the choice of an antihistamine should be considered in the context of an individual patient's needs and response to a given agent regarding the benefit obtained versus the risk of adverse effects (Dykewicz et al, 1998). Adherence issues are also important because treatment is usually administered chronically.

Three generations of antihistamines are currently available: the first-generation (sedating) antihistamines, which are available without prescription; the second-generation (hyposedating or nonsedating) agents, most of which require a prescription; and the third-generation (nonsedating metabolites of second-generation agents), all of which require a prescription (Table 28-3). Antihistamines act primarily by blocking the histamine$_1$ receptor, but several of the newer agents have also been shown to have mild anti-inflammatory properties. The problems that limited treatment with the first-generation antihistamines including sedation and frequent dosing have been largely eliminated by the second- and third-generation agents. The second- and third-generation agents have several advantages over the first-generation agents, including preferential binding to peripheral histamine$_1$ receptors, which results in minimal penetration of the central nervous system; minimal antiserotoninergic, anticholinergic, and α-adrenergic blocking activity; and minimal sedative and performance-impairing effects (Barnes, 1998; Fireman, 2000; Gentile et al, 2000).

As a general rule, antihistamines reduce the symptoms of sneezing, pruritus, and rhinorrhea but have little or no effect on nasal congestion. Consequently, a topical or oral decongestant may need to be added. Many antihistamine-decongestant formulations are available. The major advantage of these combinations is their convenience. The disadvantages are intolerance of the fixed dosage of decongestant in certain patients and an inability to titrate each agent independently (Barnes, 1998; Fireman, 2000; Gentile et al, 2000).

Patients should be educated about the appropriate use of antihistamines. For optimal results, antihistamines should be administered prophylactically (2 to 5 hours before allergen exposure) or on a regular basis if needed chronically. Although antihistamines are effective on an as-needed basis, these agents work best when they are administered in a maintenance fashion (Gentile et al, 2000).

Decongestants

Decongestants produce vasoconstriction within the nasal mucosa through α-adrenergic receptor activation and are therefore effective in relieving the symptoms of nasal

TABLE 28-2. Environmental Control of Allergen Exposure

Allergens	Control Measures
Dust mites	Encase bedding in airtight covers
	Wash bedding in water > 130°F
	Remove wall-to-wall carpeting
	Remove upholstered furniture
	Do not use fans
Animal dander	Avoid furred pets
	Keep animals out of patient's bedroom
Cockroaches	Control available food supply
	Keep kitchen/bathroom surfaces dry and free of standing water
	Professionally exterminate
Mold	Destroy moisture-prone areas
	Avoid high humidity in patient's bedroom
	Repair water leaks
	Check basements, attics, and crawl spaces for standing water and mold
Pollen	Keep car and house windows closed
	Control timing of outdoor exposure
	Restrict camping, hiking, and raking leaves
	Drive in air-conditioned car
	Air-condition the home
	Install portable high-efficiency particulate air filters

TABLE 28-3. Second- and Third-Generation Antihistamines

Medication	Onset of Action (h)	Formulations	Recommended Dosage
Azelastine	3	Nasal spray	> 12 yr: 2 sprays per nostril bid
Cetirizine	1–2	Tablets, 10 mg	> 12 yr: 10 mg, qd; 6–11 yr: 5–10 mg qd
		Syrup, 5 mg/5mL	2–5 yr: 5 mg qd
Fexofenadine	1–2	Capsules, 60 mg	> 12 yr: 60 mg bid or 180 mg qd
		Tablets, 30 mg	6–11 yr: 30 mg bid
		Tablets, 60 mg	
		Tablets, 180 mg	
Loratidine	1–2	Tablets, 10 mg	>12 yr: 10 mg, qd
		Syrup, 5 mg/5 mL	6–11 yr: 5–10 mg qd; 2–5 yr: 5 mg qd
Desloratidine	1–2	Tablets, 5 mg	> 12 yr: 5mg qd

obstruction. However, these agents have no effect on other symptoms such as rhinorrhea, pruritus, or sneezing. Therefore, they may be most effective when used in combination with other agents, such as antihistamines (Corren, 2000; Fireman, 2000; Gentile et al, 2000).

A number of decongestants are available for oral use, but the most commonly used is pseudoephedrine. The most common side effects of oral decongestants include central nervous system (nervousness, insomnia, irritability, headache) and cardiovascular (palpitations, tachycardia) effects. In addition, these drugs may elevate blood pressure, raise intraocular pressure, and aggravate urinary obstruction (Gentile et al, 2000).

Topical intranasal decongestants are sometimes used by patients with allergic rhinitis. However, when these agents are used for longer than 3 to 5 days, many patients will experience rebound congestion after withdrawal of the drug. If patients continue to use these medications over several months, a form of rhinitis, rhinitis medicamentosa, will develop, which can be difficult to treat effectively (Gentile et al, 2000).

Intranasal Corticosteroids

Topical intranasal corticosteroids represent the most efficacious agents for the treatment of allergic rhinitis and are useful in relieving symptoms of nasal pruritus, rhinorrhea, sneezing, and congestion (Table 28-4). These drugs exert their effects through multiple mechanisms, including vasoconstriction and reduction of edema, suppression of cytokine production, and inhibition of inflammatory cell influx. Physiologically, prophylactic treatment before nasal allergen challenge reduces both early- and late-phase allergic responses (Barnes, 1998; Dykewicz et al, 1998; Fireman, 2000).

These agents work best when taken regularly on a daily basis or prophylactically in anticipation of an imminent pollen season. However, because of their rapid onset of action (within 12 to 24 hours for many agents), there is increasing evidence that they may also be effective when used intermittently. A number of glucocorticoid

compounds are now available for intranasal use in both aerosol and aqueous (intravenous) formulations. Although the topical potency of these agents varies widely, clinical trials have been unable to demonstrate significant differences in efficacy (Dykewicz et al, 1998).

The most important pharmacologic characteristic differentiating these agents is systemic bioavailability. After intranasal administration, the majority of the dose is swallowed. Most of the available compounds, including beclomethasone dipropionate, budesonide, flunisolide, and triamcinolone acetonide, are absorbed readily from the gastrointestinal tract into the systemic circulation and subsequently undergo significant first-pass hepatic metabolism. The resulting bioavailabilities can be as high as 50%. However, neither fluticasone propionate nor mometasone furoate is well absorbed through the gastrointestinal tract, and the small amount of drug that reaches the portal circulation is rapidly and thoroughly metabolized. The low systemic availabilities of these two newer agents may be most important in growing children and in patients who are already using inhaled corticosteroids for asthma (Dykewicz et al, 1998; Schenkel et al, 2000; Skoner et al, 2000).

Patients using intranasal corticosteroids experience dryness and irritation of the nasal mucous membranes in 5 to 10% of mild cases and mild epistaxis in approximately 5%. For mild symptoms, the dose of intranasal corticosteroid may be reduced if tolerated, and/or saline nasal spray should be instilled before spraying the drug (Druce, 1998).

Mast Cell Stabilizers

Mast cell stabilizers, such as cromolyn sodium, can be useful in relieving nasal pruritus, rhinorrhea, and sneezing; however, they have minimal effect on congestion. Cromolyn sodium is generally well tolerated and is most efficacious when taken prophylactically, well in advance of allergen exposure. In addition, because of its short duration of action, it should be taken four times a day; as a result, compliance is difficult for many patients (Barnes, 1998; Dykewicz et al, 1998; Fireman, 2000).

Ipratropium Bromide

Topical intranasal ipratropium bromide, 0.03% solution, reduces the volume of watery secretions but has little or no effect on other symptoms. Therefore, this agent is most helpful in allergic rhinitis when rhinorrhea is refractory to topical intranasal corticosteroids and/or antihistamines. The most common side effects include nasal irritation, crusting, and mild epistaxis (Barnes, 1998; Dykewicz et al, 1998).

Allergen Immunotherapy

Specific-allergen immunotherapy continues to be a useful and important treatment for many patients with severe

TABLE 28-4. Intranasal Corticosteroid Sprays

Corticosteroid	Dose per Actuation (μg)	Recommended Dosage
Beclomethasone or dipropionate	42 84	> 6 yr: 168–336 μg/d qd or bid
Budesonide	32	> 12 yr: 64–256 μg/d qd; 6–11 yr: 64–128 μg/day qd
Flunisolide	25	> 14 yr: 200–400 μg/d bid; 6–14 yr: 15–200 μg/d bid
Fluticasone propionate	50	> 4 yr: 100–200 μg/d qd or bid
Mometasone furoate	50	> 12 yr: 200 μg/d qd; 3–11 yr: 100 μg/d qd
Triamcinolone acetonide	55	> 12 yr: 220–440 μg/d qd or bid; 6–11 yr: 220 μg/d qd

allergic rhinitis. Research performed during the last decade has demonstrated that allergen immunotherapy induces a state of allergen-specific T-lymphocyte tolerance with a subsequent reduction in mediator release and tissue inflammation. When administered to appropriately selected patients, immunotherapy is effective in most cases. In addition to short-term benefits, recently published data suggest that the improvement in rhinitis symptoms persists for several years after the treatment is discontinued. Immunotherapy should be considered in patients who (1) do not respond to a combination of environmental control measures and medications, (2) experience substantial side effects with medications, (3) have symptoms for a significant portion of the year that require daily therapy, or (4) prefer long-term modulation of their allergic symptoms. In making the decision to prescribe this therapy, the clinician should consider the positive and potentially negative effects of regular office visits for the administration of injections. If the decision is made to prescribe immunotherapy, it must be administered by a physician who is experienced in its use and whose office is set up for dealing with the management of adverse allergic reactions, including anaphylaxis should this rare event occur (Barnes, 1998; Dykewicz et al, 1998; Fireman, 2000).

Efficacy of Allergy Treatment in OM

Despite the epidemiologic evidence implicating a role for allergy in OM and the common approach of evaluating and treating allergy in otitis-prone children, there is a striking lack of well-designed efficacy trials to test the various allergy therapies (Skoner, 2000). Most of the previously conducted trials have been confined to the evaluation of relatively "nonspecific" medical therapies, such as antihistamine/decongestant preparations, and have not extended to more specific allergy therapies, including environmental controls and immunotherapy. Studies of the former type have largely produced negative results, but design limitations have restricted the interpretation and generalization of these results. Despite these negative results, there is some evidence to support the efficacy of both antihistamines and decongestants in OM (Flynn et al, 2001; Suzuki et al, 1999). A recent meta-analysis in children with OM demonstrated that subjects treated with a combination of an antihistamine and decongestant demonstrated significantly lower rates of persistent OM 2 weeks after diagnosis (Flynn et al, 2001). However, there were no differences in any of the other outcome parameters, including quality of life or assessments of language restrictions. The results from studies using corticosteroids have been mixed. In one recent study, intranasally administered fluticasone did not prevent the development of OM during URTIs in children (Ruohola et al, 2000). Indeed, that study demonstrated an increased

incidence of OM in the group treated with intranasal fluticasone. The limitations of this study included failure to examine the effect of this medication in subjects with allergic rhinitis and failure to use this medication in prophylaxis prior to the development of URTI symptoms. In another meta-analysis, systemic corticosteroids alone or combined with an antibiotic led to a quicker resolution of OM in the short term (Butler and van Der Voort, 2001). However, there was no evidence for a long-term benefit from treating hearing loss associated with OM. To date, no well-designed studies have examined the effect of allergy environmental control measures on the development of OM.

Conclusion

A number of publications have documented the need to focus on the role of allergy in OM. One set of guidelines on OM concluded that, if validated, the proposed linkage between allergy and OM might open up important new avenues for intervention (Chan et al, 2001). This highlights the need for randomized, controlled studies of therapy, focusing on clinically important outcomes.

References

Barnes PJ. Pathophysiology of allergic inflammation. In: Middleton E, Reed CE, Ellis EF, et al, editors. Allergy principles and practice. 5th ed. St. Louis: Mosby; 1998. p. 356–66.

Butler CC, van Der Voort JH. Steroids for otitis media with effusion: a systematic review. Arch Pediatr Adolesc Med 2001;155:641–7.

Chan LS, Takata GS, Shekelle P, et al. Evidence assessment of management of acute otitis media: II. Research gaps and priorities for future research. Pediatrics 2001;108:248–54.

Corren J. Allergic rhinitis: treating the adult. J Allergy Clin Immunol 2000;105(6 Pt 2):S610–5.

Demoly P, Michel F-B, Bousquet J. In vivo methods for study of allergy skin tests, techniques and interpretations. In: Middleton E, Reed CE, Ellis EF, et al, editors. Allergy principles and practice. 5th ed. St. Louis: Mosby; 1998. p. 430–9.

Doyle WJ. The link between allergic rhinitis and otitis media. Curr Opin Allergy Clin Immunol 2002;2:21–5.

Druce HM. Allergic and nonallergic rhinitis. In: Middleton E, Reed CE, Ellis EF, et al, editors. Allergy principles and practice. 5th ed. St. Louis: Mosby; 1998. p. 1005–16.

Dykewicz MS, Fineman S, Skoner DP, et al. Diagnosis and management of rhinitis: complete guidelines of the Joint Task Force on Practice Parameters in Allergy, Asthma and Immunology. American Academy of Allergy, Asthma and Immunology. Ann Allergy Asthma Immunol 1998;81:478–518.

Fireman P. Therapeutic approaches to allergic rhinitis: treating the child. J Allergy Clin Immunol 2000;105:S616–21.

Flynn CA, Griffin G, Tudiver R. Decongestants and antihistamines for acute otitis media in children. Cochrane Database Syst Rev 2001;2:CD001727.

Gentile DA, Friday GA, Skoner DP. Management of allergic rhinitis: antihistamines and decongestants. Immunol Allergy Clin North Am 2000;20:355–68.

Gentile DA, Skoner DP. Otitis media. In: Lieberman PL, Blaiss MS, editors. Atlas of allergic diseases. Philadelphia: Current Medicine Inc.; 2002. p. 225–33.

Ruohola A, Heikkinen T, Waris M, et al. Intranasal fluticasone propionate does not prevent acute otitis media during viral upper respiratory infection in children. J Allergy Clin Immunol 2000;106:467–71.

Schenkel EJ, Skoner DP, Bronsky EA, et al. Absence of growth retardation in children with perennial allergic rhinitis following 1 year of treatment with mometasone furoate aqueous nasal spray. Pediatrics 2000;105:E22.

Skoner D, Urbach AH, Fireman P. Pediatric allergy and immunology. In: Davis H, Zitelli B, editors. Atlas of pediatric physical diagnosis. 3rd ed. St. Louis: Mosby; l997. p. 75–110.

Skoner DP. Complications of allergic rhinitis. J Allergy Clin Immunol 2000;105(6 Pt 2):S605–9.

Skoner DP. Allergic rhinitis: definition, epidemiology, pathophysiology, detection and diagnosis. J Allergy Clin Immunol 2001; 108:S2–8.

Skoner DP, Casselbrant ML. Otitis media. In: Middleton E, Reed CE, Ellis EF, et al, editors. Allergy principles and practice. 5th ed. St. Louis: Mosby; 1998. p. 1036–49.

Skoner DP, Rachelefsky GS, Meltzer EO, et al. Detection of growth suppression in children during treatment with intranasal beclomethasone dipropionate. Pediatrics 2000;105:E23.

Suzuki M, Kawauchi H, Mogi G. Clinical efficacy of an antiallergic drug on otitis media with effusion in association with allergic rhinitis. Auris Nasus Larynx 1999;26:123–9.

Chapter 29

Prevention of Acute Otitis Media during the Common Cold

Craig A. Buchman, MD, Subinoy Das, MD

Upper respiratory tract infection (URI), otherwise known as the "common cold," is the most frequent illness suffered by Americans (Adams et al, 1999). According to the National Center for Health Statistics, an estimated 62 million cases of the common cold in the United States required medical attention or resulted in restricted activity in 1996. This disease is caused by a viral infection of the epithelium lining the respiratory tract. Although this illness is typically self-limiting, it may lead to complications such as sinusitis, acute otitis media (AOM), and pneumonia. Substantial evidence supports a causal role for viral URIs in the pathogenesis of AOM. In this regard, a significant impact on the incidence and prevalence of AOM could be realized by rational interventions in viral URI pathogenesis. The prevention of AOM resulting from a URI would significantly reduce patient morbidity and health care expenditures.

Role of URIs in AOM

AOM has been historically considered to be a simple bacterial infection of the middle ear space. However, substantial evidence now indicates that viral URIs play a critical role in the pathogenesis of AOM. This evidence has come from four classes of studies. First, epidemiologic studies have shown a temporal relation between URIs and AOM. Culture studies have found respiratory viruses in the middle ear fluids (MEFs) and nasopharyngeal aspirates of patients with AOM. Experimental studies in humans and animals have demonstrated that nasal inoculation with various respiratory viruses can induce the formation of AOM. Finally, clinical studies have shown that virus-specific therapies for URIs reduce the incidence of AOM. Together, these studies provide compelling evidence for the causal role of respiratory viruses in AOM.

The epidemiology of AOM is fully discussed in Chapter 4, "Epidemiology." Epidemiologic studies have revealed a relationship between AOM and viral respiratory infection. In the 1980s, a large, 14-year longitudinal study demonstrated that viral respiratory infections increased the relative risk for AOM by 220% (Henderson et al, 1982). A study of 4,524 patients in Finland in the 1980s showed a significant correlation between AOM and respiratory viral infections, particularly during viral epidemics (Ruuskanen et al, 1989). A 1-year prospective trial of 363 patients with AOM demonstrated that 94% of these patients had symptoms of a URI preceding the development of their AOM (Arola et al, 1990). Another prospective study of 596 patients showed that a URI was the greatest risk factor for developing AOM (Daly et al, 1999). Finally, the peak onset of AOM has been found to be 3 to 4 days following the onset of a URI. Thus, these studies and others support an initiating role for viral URIs in the pathogenesis of AOM.

Various microbiologic assays performed on both nasopharyngeal aspirates and MEF samples have also revealed the significant interrelationship between respiratory viruses and AOM (Table 29-1). In one meta-analysis that summarized the results of 15 studies using either standard culture techniques or virus-specific antigen detection methods, 10% ($n = 1,221$; range 0–55%) of middle ear effusions (MEEs) were positive for at least one of the respiratory viruses during episodes of AOM (Ruuskanen et al, 1989). Modern studies using reverse transcriptase polymerase chain reaction (RT-PCR) have revealed a much greater incidence of respiratory virus detection in MEF. For instance, in a study examining 92 patients with AOM, viral-specific ribonucleic acid from rhinovirus, respiratory syncytial virus (RSV), or coronavirus was detected in the MEF or nasopharyngeal aspirates of 75% of patients (Pitkäranta et al, 1998). These studies and others have confirmed the frequent presence of respiratory viruses in nasal fluids and MEFs from

TABLE 29-1. Prevalence of Viruses in Upper Respiratory Infections and Acute Otitis Media

Etiologic Agent	Nasopharyngeal Aspirates in Children with URI (%)		MEF Aspirates in Children with URI + AOM (%)			
			Standard Detection Methods (n = 456)		Advanced Detection Methods* (n = 92)	
	Standard Detection Methods (n = 10,000)	Advanced Detection Methods* (n = 200)	URI Type†	Virus Found in MEF	URI Type†	Virus Found in MEF
Rhinoviruses	34	53			30	24
Coronaviruses	14	9			15	8
Influenza viruses	9	6	5	2		
Respiratory syncytial virus	4	2	14	11	23	18
Parainfluenza virus	4	2	6	3		
Adenoviruses	2	1	5	0		
Other viruses	2	1				

Adapted from Heikkinen T et al (1999); Makela MJ et al (1998); Monto AS (2002); and Pitkäranta A et al (1998).
*Includes the use of polymerase chain reaction, fluoroimmunoassays for antigens, and serologies.
†Viral diagnosis confirmed via nasopharyngeal aspirates, cultures, and/or serologies.
AOM = acute otitis media; MEF = middle ear fluid; URI = upper respiratory infection.

patients with AOM, thus supporting the conclusion that respiratory viruses are critical for the development of AOM.

The results from human experimental investigations suggest that the temporal association between viral URIs and episodes of AOM represents a causal relationship (see Table 29-1). In a series of studies performed in Pittsburgh, as many as 20% of individuals infected with one of the common respiratory viruses (influenza A, rhinovirus, or RSV) developed AOM following nasal inoculation (Buchman et al, 1994; Buchman et al, 1995; Buchman et al, 2002). In contrast to the previously mentioned epidemiologic findings, comparative analysis between the various virus-infected groups showed that influenza A infection was significantly more likely to result in AOM than either RSV or rhinovirus. Nevertheless, these studies and others confirm a clear, causal role for viral URIs in the pathogenesis of AOM.

Furthermore, a respiratory viral etiology for AOM has been supported by clinical trials for antiviral therapies. Significant reductions in the incidence of AOM (in selected pediatric populations) were achieved using inactivated, live, attenuated influenza vaccines, RSV-enriched immunoglobulin, or anti-influenza drugs. In one study examining 374 children in day care during an influenza epidemic, influenza A vaccine was shown to decrease the overall rate of AOM by 36% and decrease the rate of AOM associated with influenza A by 83% (Heikkinen et al, 1991). Another study showed that high-dose RSV immunoglobulin significantly decreased the incidence of AOM in 109 children (Simoes et al, 1996). Finally, intranasal zanamivir, a neuraminidase inhibitor effective against influenza, was shown to decrease middle ear pressure abnormalities (a known precursor to AOM) by 41% in a randomized, controlled group of subjects inoculated

with influenza A (Hayden et al, 2001). These studies again provide strong evidence for a respiratory viral etiology for the development of AOM.

Pathogenesis of Acute Otitis Media

The mechanism(s) whereby viral URIs result in middle ear inflammation (ie, otitis) and effusion formation have not been well characterized. Respiratory viruses can directly invade the middle ear cleft, resulting in inflammation. Viruses can also disrupt normal eustachian tube–middle ear physiology and immune function, thereby predisposing the middle ear to secondary bacterial or viral infection or sterile effusion formation by unknown mechanisms (ie, hydrops ex vacuo theory). Viruses may also have unique mechanisms that contribute to the pathogenesis of AOM.

Substantial evidence supports the notion that direct invasion of the middle ear space by respiratory viruses plays a role in the pathogenesis of AOM. Viruses can invade the middle ear as either the sole pathogen or as a coinfectious agent with bacteria and rarely with other viruses. As previously mentioned, viruses have been identified in the effusions of patients with AOM (see Table 29-1). In one recent study, in 168 children who had AOM and a virus-positive nasopharyngeal aspirate, 77 of them (46%) were positive for the same virus in their MEF specimen (Heikkinen et al, 1999). In addition, this study found RSV in MEFs at higher rates than other respiratory viruses, suggesting that RSV may be more virulent with regard to AOM formation. These results support the fact that some respiratory viruses can directly invade the middle ear space and possibly contribute to the pathogenesis of AOM.

Viruses may also cause inflammatory and/or mucosal changes that create an environment that promotes an ascending bacterial superinfection. For example, certain viruses seem to lead to an increased rate of coinfection with other specific types of bacteria (Table 29-2). In one study, 8 of 24 MEF cultures that contained influenza also grew one or more types of bacteria. Interestingly, all eight of these cultures grew *Streptococcus pneumoniae* (Heikkinen et al, 1999). In addition, MEF obtained from a patient with AOM following intranasal influenza inoculation revealed the same strain of influenza and *S. pneumoniae* (Buchman et al, 1995). These findings suggest that although respiratory viruses may share some common aspects of their pathogenesis of AOM, each species of respiratory virus likely has unique methods of causing AOM.

Respiratory viruses are also known to cause eustachian tube dysfunction. This outcome may also be an important event in the initiation of AOM. During naturally occurring URIs, abnormal middle ear pressures and eustachian tube dysfunction have been documented using standard testing protocols. In human experimental studies, intranasal inoculation of healthy adult volunteers with a variety of respiratory viruses reliably resulted in eustachian tube opening failure, abnormal middle ear pressures, and AOM. The temporal pattern of the observed otologic consequences (ie, eustachian tube obstruction, followed by middle ear underpressure, followed by AOM) suggests a causal mechanism. That is, viral URIs disrupt normal eustachian tube opening function, which results in middle ear underpressures and subsequent MEE formation. Because the middle ear is essentially a noncollapsible gas pocket, middle ear underpressures are believed to predispose to effusion formation by either aspiration of infectious nasopharyngeal secretions through the eustachian tube, with consequent exudation (ie, inflammation), or underpressure-induced transudation (ie, hydrops ex vacuo theory).

Finally, individual viruses also have unique molecular and cellular mechanisms that may promote the formation of AOM. Rhinovirus, a member of the picornavirus family and the most common cause of URIs, has been shown to inhibit nuclear import in infected cells. This may prevent the infected epithelium from using its innate immunity pathways, such as those transduced by the nuclear factor κB (NF-κB) and signal transducer and activator of transcription (STAT) pathways, thus preventing an effective immune response to other pathogens.

RSV is also known to lead to prolonged activation of NF-κB. This effect on epithelial immunity remains unclear. The fact that RSV has been found in substantially higher frequencies in the MEFs of patients with AOM than with other respiratory viruses implies that this virus may be more "otogenic" than other viruses. By contrast, influenza A virus typically produces a more severe constellation of symptoms during a URI and seems to preferentially predispose patients to *S. pneumoniae* infections. It is theorized that the neuraminidase of influenza virus may promote streptococcal adherence to the respiratory tract epithelium. The advent of advanced viral assays and culture techniques will undoubtedly reveal greater insight into the intracellular pathology that occurs with these viral infections.

Clinical Scenario

An otherwise healthy 18-month-old boy presents with a 2-day history of fussiness, tugging at his right ear, and crying repeatedly throughout the night. This child has had two prior ear infections in the last 4 months; both resolved with antibiotic therapy. In the week prior to this episode, the child had a cold for 3 days accompanied by cough, low-grade fever, and clear rhinorrhea. Physical examination is unremarkable except for otologic findings of a bulging right tympanic membrane with purulent fluid in the middle ear. The child is successfully treated with high-dose amoxicillin with resolution of symptoms in 3 days. Two months later, the child's parent calls the clinic to inform the treating physician that the child now has another "cold," and the parent is worried that this will progress to another episode of AOM.

This clinical scenario is a common one that faces primary care physicians and otolaryngologists daily. The diagnosis and management of these patients with regard to prevention of AOM following URI are discussed below.

Diagnosis

Currently, the diagnosis of a viral URI is made almost exclusively by history and physical examination. Unfortunately, as there is great overlap in the various clinical presentations for the various URI syndromes, specific viral identification is not possible based on clinical examination alone. Moreover, rapid detection methods for the var-

TABLE 29-2. Percentage of Specific Microorganisms in Middle Ear Fluid Samples Containing Both Viruses and Bacteria*

Bacterial Species	RSV (*n* = 22)	Parainfluenza (*n* = 10)	Influenza (*n* = 8)	Enterovirus (*n* = 3)
Streptococcus pneumoniae	36	10	100	33
Haemophilus influenzae	45	50	25	0
Moraxella catarrhalis	27	50	38	33
Pseudomonas aeruginosa	0	0	0	66

Adapted from Heikkinen T et al (1999).
*Some middle ear fluid samples grew more than one type of bacteria.

ious viruses causing URIs are currently not widely available for routine clinical use. Thus, intervention into URIs as they relate to recurrent AOM prevention is empiric. In the future, as molecular-based viral detection kits become more rapid, more accurate, and more economical, the use of viral assays may become more common. In addition, as better therapies are learned to prevent the complications of URIs, more accurate diagnoses of particular viral infections will become increasingly important.

Management

Management schemes for children with recurrent AOM related to URIs include (1) observation with antibiotic therapy for each episode of AOM; (2) risk factor assessment and alteration (ie, day care, second-hand smoke, bottle feeding, etc); (3) URI prophylaxis; (4) antibacterial prophylaxis; (5) allergy and immune system assessment and vaccination; and (6) surgical prophylaxis with tympanostomy tubes with or without adenoidectomy. Generally, the choice of therapy should be based on a risk-benefit analysis for each individual patient. Children with nonsevere episodes of AOM or those at low risk for complications can be managed expectantly with modification of risk factors and appropriate antimicrobial therapy for each episode. Specifically, second-hand smoke exposure should be eliminated, day-care requirements assessed, and consideration given to breast-feeding when practical. High-risk individuals are those who have a greater frequency and/or severity of AOM episodes or carry a significant risk for complications related to AOM episodes. For the purposes of this discussion, high-risk individuals include children with a history of recurrent AOM (greater than three episodes in 6 months or greater than four episodes in 1 year), craniofacial malformations, premature infancy, immunodeficiency (ie, human immunodeficiency virus [HIV], sickle cell disease, or immunosuppression), asthma, febrile seizures, particular ethnic backgrounds (Native American), central nervous system developmental abnormalities (spina bifida, encephaloceles, inner ear malformations, or previous meningitis), and cochlear implants. Some adults may also be high-risk individuals, including those with sensorineural hearing loss, immunosuppression, and cochlear implants; hospitalized patients; and the elderly. For these special patient populations, more aggressive intervention may be warranted. This chapter focuses on URI prevention and AOM prevention as it relates to URIs in both low- and high-risk patients.

Recurrent AOM Prevention
Related to URIs in Low-Risk Patients

The prevention of URIs has been extensively studied. Because most URIs are transmitted by either hand-to-hand contact or exposure to aerosolized infectious materials, contact avoidance is the primary mode of prevention.

This includes barrier precautions and frequent handwashing, particularly in high-risk areas such as health care facilities and day-care centers. Teaching children to cover their mouth with their forearms instead of their hands has decreased the transmission of viruses in schools. Sharing of various eating utensils, drinking glasses, foods, napkins, and tissues should be discouraged. Moreover, children with acute febrile illnesses or those with significant nasal discharge and cough should be asked to stay home from school or day care to avoid transmission.

Specific antiviral therapies in the form of drugs and vaccines for patients with uncomplicated URIs are currently not justified for most viral etiologies. This is primarily because there are currently no rapid and accurate diagnostic tests available for viral identification, and reliable antiviral therapies are lacking. Vaccination is discussed in detail elsewhere in this book. One exception to this is the influenza vaccine, which is recommended annually for elderly patients and those at high risk for developing influenza or an influenza-related complication, including health care workers. In addition, "because young, otherwise healthy children are at increased risk for influenza-related hospitalization," the Centers for Disease Control and Prevention (CDC) encourages influenza vaccination of healthy children aged 6 to 23 months when feasible. Influenza vaccination of children older than 6 months who have certain medical conditions continues to be strongly recommended by the CDC. Other drugs such as ribavirin, monoclonal antibodies to RSV, and neuraminidase inhibitors such as zanamivir are used to prevent viral respiratory infections for high-risk patients. Studies of these clinical outcomes are limited.

Recurrent AOM Prevention
Related to URIs in High-Risk Patients

Many therapies have been studied for their ability to prevent the development of AOM following a URI. In addition to those preventive measures discussed above, both virus-nonspecific and virus-specific therapies should be considered for the prevention of AOM during viral URIs. Virus-nonspecific therapies include antibacterial therapy, nonantimicrobial medical therapies, and surgical prophylaxis with tympanostomy tubes with or without adenoidectomy. Virus-specific therapies may include either antiviral drugs or virus-specific vaccinations.

Antibacterial therapies include antibiotics and antibacterial vaccines. Generally, antibiotic therapy can be instituted either immediately after the onset of a URI or as seasonal, long-term prophylaxis. Few studies have specifically examined whether antibiotics were useful in decreasing the incidence of AOM when given promptly after the onset of URI symptoms. These studies have failed to show prophylactic efficacy (Giebink, 2001; Fogle-Hansson et al, 2001). Other studies have demonstrated that antibiotic therapy is futile and possibly harmful in the treatment of isolated URIs. Seasonal or long-term antimicrobial prophylaxis for recurrent AOM has been studied extensively and is discussed in detail elsewhere in this book. Briefly, a meta-analysis from 33 randomized clinical trials examined the use of seasonal antibiotic prophylaxis for otitis-prone children and showed that prophylaxis decreased one episode of AOM every 9 months. However, many of these trials did not adequately control for confounding variables. An Italian study provided evidence for the use of antibiotic prophylaxis for patients with recurrent AOM without chronic otitis media with effusion, but studies have also shown that long-term use of antibiotics promotes antibiotic resistance, particularly with resistant *S. pneumoniae* (Giebink, 2001). Currently, prophylactic antibiotic use appears justified only for those patients with recurrent AOM and significant risk factors for complications, as previously described. Moreover, children with tympanostomy tubes in place with recurrent AOM (otorrhea) may also benefit from antibiotic prophylaxis. Antibacterial prophylaxis is not appropriate in children with chronic MEE.

Antibacterial vaccines currently available for the potential prevention of AOM include the *S. pneumoniae* vaccine and the *Haemophilus influenzae* type B vaccine. *S. pneumoniae* (ie, pneumococcus) has the greatest propensity for causing bacterial episodes of AOM. Pneumococcal conjugate vaccines have shown success in two large preliminary trials. In February 2000, Prevnar, produced by Wyeth-Lederle of Madison, NJ, was approved by the US Food and Drug Administration (FDA). In a large American study, this vaccine led to a 7.8% reduction ($p < .0001$) in visits for AOM, decreased antibiotic prescriptions by 5.7%, reduced the number of visits for those with recurrent AOM by up to 26%, and led to a 24% reduction in the future need for tympanostomy tubes (Fireman et al, 2003). In a Finnish study, this vaccine reduced serotype-specific episodes of AOM by 57% and increased episodes from other nonreactive serotypes by 33%. These findings are concerning in that the vaccine, over time, may simply alter the microbiology of AOM in a phenomenon known as serotype replacement. This also lends credence to the theory that viruses may be able to independently promote AOM regardless of a particular bacterial serotype. Nevertheless, the CDC currently recommends the pneumococcal conjugate vaccine for all children between 2 and 23 months (primarily for its prophylaxis against meningitis). This should produce modest reductions in the AOM attack rate during viral URIs. Confirmation of vaccination should be assessed in all children with recurrent AOM and those children at high risk for AOM and its complications.

Many nonantimicrobial medical therapies have been studied as preventive therapies for recurrent AOM, although very few have found positive results. One exception is xylitol, a sugar alcohol referred to as birch sugar. Xylitol inhibits *S. pneumoniae* and was found to be effec-

tive in preventing AOM in three clinical trials when given in high doses (Uhari et al, 2001).

Other studies have found negative or conflicting results for nonantimicrobial remedies. Decongestants alone and decongestant-antihistamine mixtures have been shown to be noneffective in preventing the development of AOM following a URI. Similarly, intranasal corticosteroids have been shown to be ineffective in preventing the development of AOM following a URI and, in fact, may significantly increase the development of AOM following rhinovirus URIs. Many other adjunctive therapies have been studied, including garlic, red wine, intranasal ice, and herbal remedies—all with conflicting results.

For high-risk patients or those severely affected by AOM, surgical intervention as a means of prophylaxis may be warranted. This topic is extensively addressed in this book in numerous chapters. Surgical benefits have been examined for the prevention of AOM, although no studies have specifically addressed surgical procedures for the prevention of AOM related to URIs. Generally speaking, tympanostomy tube insertion is appropriate for those children severely affected with recurrent AOM or those children with significant risk factors for developing intratemporal, intracranial, and systemic complications. In selected children, tympanostomy tube insertion has had a significant positive impact on disease incidence, particularly within the first 12 months of follow-up. Tympanostomy tubes reduced the incidence of AOM by a mean of 56% and decreased the prevalence of MEE by 115 child-days per year. Within several weeks of tympanostomy tube placement, 79% of children had an improved quality of life and had significant changes in activity limitations and speech development (Rosenfeld, 2001). Adenoidectomy has also shown significant benefit for the prevention of recurrent AOM. Although not directly studied for children with URIs, adenoidectomy performed in children with prior tube extrusion reduced the risk of future tube placement by 50% and decreased the incidence of AOM by 26% (Rosenfeld, 2001). Myringotomy and tonsillectomy alone have been shown to be ineffective for the prevention of AOM.

Virus-specific therapies have also been extensively studied, although limited data exist regarding efficacy in AOM prevention. RSV immunoglobulin in high doses was shown to reduce the incidence of AOM. However, this finding may have been attributable to other antibodies in these immunoglobulin preparations (Simoes et al, 1996). Drugs that bind the capsid of picornaviruses, rhinovirus protease inhibitors, and recombinant interferon have been used experimentally against human rhinovirus, all with limited success (Hayden, 2001). Rimantadine, an anti-influenza drug, showed no benefit for ear symptoms in one study when given near the onset of an episode of influenza. However, newer drugs for influenza, such as zanamivir and oseltamivir, have shown beneficial effects in experimental infections in preventing the development of middle ear underpressures, a known prerequisite for the development of AOM following a URI (Hayden, 2001). Because specific virus identification remains problematic, the use of these medications should probably be limited to high-risk individuals during known viral epidemics.

Viral vaccines will clearly play a significant role in the future for preventing AOM. Currently, only the influenza vaccine is available for routine clinical use. Preliminary experience with a liquid, trivalent, cold-adapted, intranasal influenza vaccine is very encouraging. In preliminary trials, febrile AOM was decreased by 36% and antibiotic use for febrile AOM decreased by 35% (Glezen, 2001). In June 2003, the FDA approved licensure for this drug, FluMist™ (Influenza Virus Vaccine Live, Intranasal, Medimmune, Gaithersburg, MD). The drug is approved for healthy children and healthy adults between 5 and 49 years of age and will be released in the fall of 2003. A vaccine against RSV also holds great promise in the fight against AOM. Unfortunately, experimental vaccines against RSV produced in the 1960s led to increased morbidity and mortality in patients who subsequently contracted RSV. The true mechanism of illness was never identified, and work on a live vaccine for RSV was halted. The development of vaccines against the common respiratory viruses continues to be an active area of investigation and will ultimately result in great reductions in AOM attack rates in the future.

Conclusion

In conclusion, AOM continues to have significant effects on patient morbidity and health care costs. Substantial evidence supports a causal role for common respiratory viruses in the pathogenesis of AOM. Thus, a major thrust of current research has been devoted to elucidating the inflammatory mechanisms of viral infections in the hopes of developing virus-specific therapies to prevent the development of AOM. Because the accurate diagnosis of specific viruses remains difficult and often impractical, virus-specific therapies are still somewhat limited. Nevertheless, there currently remain numerous rational nonspecific therapies as well as a few vaccines and antiviral drugs that are useful in the prevention of URI-related AOM. Future advances in our understanding of the inflammatory mechanisms of viral URI will undoubtedly lead to improved antiviral therapies and vaccines. This will decrease the incidence and severity of AOM and bring us closer to the goal of making AOM a truly preventable disease.

Acknowledgment

This work was supported, in part, by a grant from the National Institutes of Health (DC00187).

References

Adams PF, Hendershot GE, Marano MA. Current estimates from the National Health Interview Survey 1996. National Center for Health Statistics. Vital Health Stat 1999;10(200).

Arola M, Ruuskanen O, Ziegler T, et al. Clinical role of respiratory virus infection in acute otitis media. Pediatrics 1990;86:848–55.

Buchman CA, Doyle WJ, Pilcher O, et al. Nasal and otologic effects of experimental respiratory syncytial virus infection in adults. Am J Otolaryngol 2002;23:70–5.

Buchman CA, Doyle WJ, Skoner D, et al. Otologic manifestations of experimental rhinovirus infection. Laryngoscope 1994;104: 1295–9.

Buchman CA, Doyle WJ, Skoner DP, et al. Influenza A virus–induced acute otitis media. J Infect Dis 1995;172:1348–51.

Daly KA, Brown JE, Lindgren BR, et al. Epidemiology of otitis media onset by six months of age. Pediatrics 1999;103:1158–66.

Fireman B, Black SB, Shinefield HR, et al. Impact of the pneumococcal conjugate vaccine on otitis media. Pediatr Infect Dis J 2003;22:10–6.

Fogle-Hansson M, White P, Hermansson A, Prellner K. Short-term penicillin-V prophylaxis did not prevent acute otitis media in infants. Int J Pediatr Otorhinolaryngol 2001;59:119–23.

Giebink GS. Otitis media prevention: non-vaccine prophylaxis. Vaccine 2001;19 Suppl 1:S129–33.

Glezen WP. Prevention of acute otitis media by prophylaxis and treatment of influenza virus infections. Vaccine 2001;19 Suppl 1:S56–8.

Hayden FG. Influenza virus and rhinovirus-related otitis media: potential for antiviral intervention. Vaccine 2001;19 Suppl 1:S66–70.

Heikkinen T, Ruuskanen O, Waris M, et al. Influenza vaccination in the prevention of acute otitis media in children. Am J Dis Child 1991;145:445–8.

Heikkinen T, Thint M, Chonmaitree T. Prevalence of various respiratory viruses in the middle ear during acute otitis media. N Engl J Med 1999;340:260–4.

Henderson FW, Collier AM, Sanyal MA, et al. A longitudinal study of respiratory viruses and bacteria in the etiology of acute otitis media with effusion. N Engl J Med 1982;306:1377–83.

Makela MJ, Puhakka T, Ruuskanen O, et al. Viruses and bacteria in the etiology of the common cold. J Clin Microbiol 1998; 36:539–42.

Monto AS. Epidemiology of viral respiratory infections. Am J Med 2002;112:4–12.

Pitkäranta A, Virolainen A, Jero J, Hayden FG. Detection of rhinovirus, respiratory syncytial virus, and coronavirus infections in acute otitis media by reverse transcriptase polymerase chain reaction. Pediatrics 1998;102:1–5.

Rosenfeld RM. Surgical prevention of otitis media. Vaccine 2001;19 Suppl 1:S134–9.

Ruuskanen O, Arola M, Putto-Laurila A, et al. Acute otitis media and respiratory virus infections. Pediatr Infect Dis J 1989; 8:94–9.

Simoes EA, Groothuis JR, Tristram DA, et al. Respiratory syncytial virus-enriched globulin for the prevention of acute otitis media in high risk children. J Pediatr 1996;129:214–9.

Uhari M, Tapeline T, Kontiokari T. Xylitol in preventing acute otitis media. Vaccine 2001;19 Suppl 1:S144–7.

Chapter 30

Rhinosinusitis in Recurrent Acute Otitis Media

Anil Gungor, MD

Physicians treating otitis media (OM) are enjoying an evidence-based, analytic classification system with detailed management algorithms. Classification and management of rhinosinusitis (RS), compared with advances in OM, are still in their infancy. There are still no objective clinical criteria, objective classification system, or objective tests for the diagnosis of RS. Access to the sinuses is limited by the unacceptable invasiveness of most procedures. Computed tomographic scans do not provide 100% accuracy and cannot be used as screening tests because of the associated exposure to radiation and expense. Cultures obtained from the nose do not have the desired correlation with the pathogen in the sinus. We do have a conceptual understanding about the function and purpose of the middle ear–mastoid system that has stood the test of time reasonably well. In the first few years of the twenty-first century, we still do not know why we have sinuses. We have an imperfect understanding of the physiology and, to a very limited extent, the pathology of the sinuses. We do not know how to make the sinuses function better because we do not know their function. We do not know how to define a normal sinus because we do not have a test to assess normalcy in the sinus. In health, we do not notice the workings of the sinuses. When there is a disease affecting the sinus, the signs and symptoms are nonspecific, and we still do not become aware of the lack of a specific function. In short, clinicians and researchers alike are in the dark, looking for evidence, and most of what we do in the management of RS is approximated from imperfect data. However, using analogies between the middle ear–mastoid system and the sinuses, we can still be good clinicians by using data available from OM studies and adapting them for use in the diagnosis and treatment of RS.

An interesting relationship between OM and RS can be observed in diseases presenting with both. When OM and sinonasal disease occur, persist, and recur in concert, a detailed evaluation and assessment of possible underlying disease processes are justified. However, it must be realized that more often than not, OM and RS of childhood are temporary and limited diseases that eventually resolve spontaneously.

Appropriate medical intervention provides cure for most, and surgical intervention, at least for sinusitis, is rarely necessary. This chapter provides a perspective on evaluating and treating OM with persistent or recurrent sinonasal disease in the pediatric group and their proposed mechanism(s). This perspective is maintained by the following similarities between OM and RS:

- Both the middle ear–mastoid system and the sinuses are essentially air-filled cavities in bone covered by respiratory epithelium and have a narrow outflow tract that opens into the nasopharynx.
- Both systems increase in size (pneumatization) with age, and their health is maintained by an active mucociliary clearance system.
- The most common and best-defined factors in the etiology of disease states of both systems include adenoid hypertrophy, outflow obstruction, viral upper respiratory tract infection (URI), mucociliary clearance, anatomic deformities, immune immaturity/deficiency, allergy, and day-care/environmental factors.
- Both disease states are common to a particular age group.

It is difficult to establish the true incidence of RS in the pediatric population as signs and symptoms often are not different from those of a URI or "seasonal allergy." Reportedly, RS affects 31 million individuals in the United States, making it the most common of all health care complaints (Moss and Parsons, 1986). As is true for OM, there is evidence that more frequent exposure to ill contacts, such as in day-care settings, increases the incidence and protracts the length of RS (Bjuggren et al, 1949; Wald, 1985). Like OM, the most common predisposing factor for RS is believed to be a viral URI. The incidence of acute OM (AOM) is greater during viral respiratory epidemics, especially those caused by respiratory syncytial virus. Viral

URIs alone or in combination with bacteria are present in up to 50% of children with AOM. Rhinovirus genomic material is detectable in 50% of sinus aspirates and in the nasal secretions of up to 70% of children with colds (Pitkäranta et al, 1997; Rakes et al, 1995). Rhinovirus infection is associated with minimal damage to the nasal mucosa (Winther et al, 1990) and exerts its clinical effects through triggering the release of inflammatory mediators (Proud et al, 1988; Rees and Eccles, 1994; Winther, 1994). The inflammatory response to the viral infection could obstruct the ostiae of the sinuses. The leukocyte enzymes elastase and collagenase can destroy cells and inhibit ciliary movement. Temporarily acquired ciliary defects have been observed in the nasal mucosa of children with acute viral URIs (Mygind et al, 1983).

The adenoids have been shown to be a key factor in OM, but their role in RS is less clear (van Cauwenberge et al, 1995). Large adenoid tissue can obstruct nasal air and mucus flow; however, an adenoid pad may interfere with nasal mucociliary clearance even without reaching obstructive dimensions. Adenoids act as a reservoir for bacteria and may thus cause recurrent sinus infections by retrograde spread of bacteria into the nose and sinuses (Lee and Rosenfeld, 1997; Sorbin et al, 1992). There is a high incidence of mucosal thickening on sinus films in children undergoing adenotonsillectomy and bilateral tympanostomy tube insertion (Rosenfeld, 1995). Adenoidectomy causes a reduction in the number of bacterial pathogens and an increase in commensal microorganisms (Tallat et al, 1989). Adenoidectomy may provide complete or near-complete resolution of RS symptoms (Vandenberg and Heatley, 1997).

The incidence of sinus disease is high in patients with cleft palate, in whom OM is almost universal (Gungor and Corey, 1997). In repaired clefts of the palate, several factors, including an incompetent velopharynx and a deviated nasal septum, are potential explanations for the association. In unrepaired clefts of the palate, continuous oropharyngeal contamination of the sinuses predisposes to RS. OM risk factors in repaired and unrepaired clefts include anatomic deficiencies of the eustachian tube and the paratubal muscles and functional deficiencies of the velopharyngeal closure.

Allergic inflammation is an important contributor to the development, recurrence, and persistence of OM (Gungor and Corey, 1997; Hurst and Fredens, 1997). However, only circumstantial evidence supports allergic rhinitis as a risk factor for RS. RS can persist in allergic subjects despite medical and surgical treatment.

Laryngopharyngeal reflux (LPR) is emerging as a possibly important factor in the development and persistence of both RS and OM. Pepsin is identified in the middle ear fluid (Tasker et al, 2002), and otalgia is associated with LPR (Gibson and Cochran, 1994). Nasopharyngeal pH is lower (Contencin and Narcy, 1991), and esophageal biopsies are frequently positive for reflux in children with RS (Yellon et al, 2000). LPR is more prevalent in children with chronic RS, and sinus disease improves with antireflux treatment (Bothwell et al, 1999; Phipps et al, 2000).

Local factors that decrease the mucociliary transport from the sinuses are likely to contribute to the development of sinus disease. Various physical conditions, chemicals, and pharmacologic agents affect the effectiveness of the cilia in clearance (Proctor, 1982). Defects in ciliary transport, such as those associated with viral infections or primary ciliary dyskinesia (PCD), lead to ineffective mucociliary clearance.

Kartagener's syndrome is an autosomal, recessively transmitted disease involving the triad of situs inversus, bronchiectasis, and OM. RS usually accompanies this triad. The cilia of these patients lack the adenosine triphosphatase–containing dynein arms. Other defects in the cilia include reduced numbers of dynein arms, absent radial spokes, translocation of microtubule doublets, abnormal length, an abnormal basal apparatus, and even aplasia (de Iongh and Rutland, 1995). A number of patients with the clinical features of PCD have been identified in whom no ciliary ultrastructural defect has been found (Herzon and Murphy, 1980; Pederson, 1983).

Otitis-Sinusitis–Prone Child

A child is designated as "sinusitis prone" if he/she suffers three or more episodes of RS within a year or if he/she requires antibiotic therapy for control of sinusitis for 3 or more months during a year. This description is similar to the description of the "otitis-prone" child. In my clinical practice, the majority of children who are designated "otitis-sinusitis prone" have previously undiagnosed or untreated allergies and/or LPR. A much smaller fraction is immunodeficient. Respiratory allergy occurs in 8 to 20% of children, whereas estimates of the incidence of all immunodeficiency diseases of childhood combined are less than 0.5% (Stiehm, 1989). OM occurs in high frequency in both allergic and immunodeficient children (Lusk et al, 1991; Shapiro, 1988). Recurrent OM precedes RS in both groups. The importance of LPR in both is just beginning to emerge, and we are experiencing a paradigm shift in the management of children with OM and/or RS.

The undiagnosed immunodeficient child is virtually always taking antibiotics and experiences a recurrence of symptoms shortly after antibiotic treatment is completed. In the most common immunodeficiencies, recurrent RS with OM is the only indication that a patient may be immunodeficient. Immunoglobulin (Ig)A and IgG are the primary Igs in nasal secretions (Kaliner, 1991). Selective IgA deficiency is the most prevalent human immunodeficiency. IgG is derived mainly from the plasma, and its distribution in the nasal mucosa is a function of vascular permeability. The remainder arises from IgG production by plasma cells present within the mucosa. Common variable immune deficiency (CVID) is a rare heterogeneous group of familial immunologic disorders characterized by panhypogammaglobulinemia and recurrent infections. Chronic and recurrent OM and RS are common. IgG, IgA, and IgM are usually significantly reduced in serum. IgG levels are generally less than 200 mg/dL. The response to primary immunization is poor, and retention of antibody from previous immunizations is variable (Karlsson et al, 1985).

IgG Subclass Deficiencies

Four IgG subclasses have been identified on the basis of antigenic differences in the heavy-chain (Fc) portion of the IgG molecule. Antibody responses to bacterial protein antigens are primarily in the IgG1 subclass. Infections caused by bacteria with polysaccharide capsules, such as *Haemophilus influenzae* and *Streptococcus pneumoniae*, are associated with IgG2 subclass deficiencies (Karlsson et al, 1985; Normansell, 1987). Immunoglobulin G3 is the main subclass involved in the primary response to various viral agents (Soderstrom et al, 1987). IgG4 is capable of mast cell activation and is believed to be the blocking antibody responsible for the effect of immunotherapy (Heiner et al, 1986; Herrmann et al, 1995); IgG2 or IgG2-IgG4 deficiency frequently occurs in association with IgA deficiency, as well as in ataxia telangiectasia (Oxelius et al, 1981; Oxelius et al, 1982). In children, about half of all IgG subclass deficiencies are of the IgG2 type, and most are transient (Soderstrom et al, 1988). The true incidence and natural history of clinically significant IgG subclass deficiencies are not known. Some individuals with documented IgG subclass deficiencies are healthy.

Vaccine hyporesponsiveness in the form of defective antibody response to pneumococcal polysaccharide and unconjugated *H. influenzae* type b polysaccharide may exist alone or in combination with selective IgG subclass deficiency (usually IgG2 or IgG2-IgG4 deficiency) (Shapiro et al, 1991).

Patients with X-linked agammaglobulinemia (XLA) are severely deficient in all immunoglobulin classes and are unable to synthesize antibodies to almost any antigen. B cells are absent from blood, whereas plasma cells are absent from bone marrow, mucous membranes, and lymph nodes. Peripheral lymph nodes are decreased in size (Smith et al, 1994).

Hyperimmunoglobulinemia E with impaired neutrophil chemotaxis (Job's syndrome) is characterized by eczema, recurrent staphylococcal skin abscesses, RS, and OM (Schopfer et al, 1979).

Immunologic Laboratory Evaluation

A relatively small number of tests are required to establish a diagnosis in the majority of sinusitis-otitis–prone children with immunodeficiency disease. Serum Ig levels (G, A, M, E) and IgG subclass levels, diphtheria and tetanus antitoxin titers, pre- and postimmunization pneumococcal antibody levels, complement C4, and total hemolytic complement (CH50) are ordered. If the history and the examination suggest allergies, an in vitro or an in vivo allergy screen limited to the most common allergens in the area needs to be performed.

Treatment of the Child with Rhinosinusitis and AOM

AOM and RS are usually self-limiting diseases, and patients may experience clinical improvement despite ineffective or no treatment. Sinus punctures and ear taps show exudate and high bacterial concentrations in the sinus and middle ear. The percentage of β-lactamase–producing *H. influenzae* strains is 25% in the United States. Most strains of *Moraxella catarrhalis* produce β-lactamase. The rate of isolation of multidrug-resistant *S. pneumoniae* strains is increasing in the United States (Dowell et al, 1998). Fifty-four percent of strains of *H. influenzae* and 74% of strains of *M. catarrhalis* recovered from sinus aspirates have been ampicillin resistant (Gwaltney et al, 1992). In addition, the development of resistance of *S. pneumoniae* to multiple antibiotics is of great concern. Some strains are only sensitive to vancomycin, cefuroxime axetil, or cefotaxime. In spite of penicillin-resistant pneumococci, amoxicillin-clavulanate, cefuroxime axetil, and cefpodoxime still provide satisfactory antimicrobial coverage for the initial treatment of acute community-acquired RS. Patients with severe infection or with orbital or intracranial extension of disease require initial treatment directed against highly resistant *S. pneumoniae* delivered intravenously. A combination of vancomycin and a third-generation cephalosporin (ceftriaxone or cefotaxime) is indicated in such patients until the sensitivity pattern of the causative bacteria is available to guide therapy (Gwaltney et al, 1992). The clinician should be alert for treatment failure following institution of empiric therapy, especially in areas where the prevalence of resistant *S. pneumoniae* is high.

The treatment of a child with RS and OM, when other risk factors are absent, is not different from the treatment of a child with RS only. In acute RS with AOM, treatment consists of antibiotics with nasal saline irrigations when possible. The difference between the treatments of chronic versus acute RS is in the duration of the antibiotic treatment. The duration of antibiotic treatment in chronic RS is 4 to 6 weeks. In chronic RS, nasal steroids are used as an adjunct. If a patient has an opacified sinus that is not draining, it may be necessary to perform a sinus tap, especially for the immunocompromised patient, the patient with an intraorbital or intracranial extension, or the patient in whom the chance of an infection from a resistant organism is high. In acute RS, antibiotic treatment should last for a minimum of 2 weeks and may be reasonably continued for 1 month if the symptoms are not completely resolved. If the patient is maintained on antibiotic therapy for longer than 2 weeks, a diet that includes *Lactobacillus acidophilus* (in yogurt or pill form) should be encouraged to prevent diarrhea resulting from a depletion of normal intestinal flora. Topical decongestants are an important adjunct to antibiotic therapy in managing acute and chronic RS.

Initiation of topical nasal steroids may hasten the resolution of symptoms through anti-inflammatory action over a longer term. They also may provide prophylaxis over prolonged periods in patients who have recurrent episodes of acute RS by lessening edema in the osteomeatal complex. They are not typically recommended during the early phase of some viral illnesses such as varicella or measles because, in some circumstances, there is a possibility of exacerbating these infections. Oral steroids are rarely required to treat acute RS but may be necessary to quiet inflammation in a particularly recalcitrant case or when intraorbital/intracranial complications are present. In patients with reactive airway disease, in whom RS leads to serious pulmonary complications, oral steroids are often necessary. Saline irrigation may also assist in the clearing of thickened secretions in the nasal cavity and can provide significant symptomatic relief.

Initial therapy for children with mild disease who have not received antibiotics in the previous 4 to 6 weeks includes amoxicillin-clavulanate (45–90 mg/kg/d), cefdinir, cefpodoxime proxetil, and cefuroxime axetil. Azithromycin, erythromycin, or trimethoprim-sulfamethoxazole (TMP-SMX) is recommended only if the patient has a history of immediate type I hypersensitivity reaction to β-lactams. These antibiotics have limited effectiveness against the major pathogens of RS, and bacterial failure of 20 to 25% is possible. The use of TMP-SMX is associated with a large increase in the risk of life-threatening toxic epidermal necrolysis (Roujeau et al, 1995). Children with immediate hypersensitivity reactions to β-lactams may need desensitization and culture-directed antibiotics.

LPR has to be assessed by the physician and addressed with antireflux measures such as lifestyle changes, dietary adjustments, antacids, histamine₂ blockers, or proton pump inhibitors as appropriate.

Presently, I use the treatment protocol for chronic RS as outlined below:

1. Amoxicillin + clavulanate: A total of 90 mg/kg orally daily of amoxicillin in two divided doses up to a maximum of 3,000 mg/d. In patients allergic to amoxicillin and penicillin, cefdinir (7 mg/kg orally every 12 hours to a maximum of 600 mg/d) is used instead of amoxicillin + clavulanate. Treatment is used for 14 days.
2. Nasal steroid spray (in RS): One puff into each nostril once a day in the morning for children less than 12 years old and two puffs into each nostril for children 12 years

and older. I prefer to use preparations that have no benzalkonium chloride as a preservative, which can cause irritation and inflammation in the nose.
3. Hypertonic saline nasal wash: Parents/patients are given written instructions and a recipe detailing the preparation of a buffered hypertonic saline solution at home and the irrigation of the nasal passages with the help of a bulb syringe or nasal irrigation bottle. This nasal wash is done twice a day: once in the morning before the nasal steroid spray and once in the evening. The solution can be prepared at home by adding two to three heaping teaspoons of "pickling/canning" salt and one rounded teaspoon of baking soda (sodium bicarbonate) to one quart of bottled water.
4. Topical decongestant oxymetazoline is prescribed to facilitate the use of nasal steroid sprays and hypertonic saline nasal wash. Oxymetazoline spray is used before the nasal steroid spray (in RS) up to twice a day, one to two sprays into each nostril. Oxymetazoline will not be used longer than 5 days.
5. Dietary and lifestyle changes to address LPR (verbal information supported by a take-home document) combined with a trial of histamine₂ blocker or proton pump inhibitor in select cases.

Judicious use of antibiotics and regular administration of antibodies are the only effective treatments for B-cell disorders. For patients with global Ig deficiencies, such as CVID and XLA, Ig replacement therapy is indicated (Sorensen and Polmar, 1987). For patients with selective Ig or IgG subclass deficiencies, Ig replacement therapy may also be efficacious, as indicated by some uncontrolled studies in small numbers. The most common form of replacement therapy is with intravenous immunoglobulin (IVIG). Broad antibody deficiency should be documented before such therapy is initiated. In hyperimmunoglobulinemia E syndrome and neutrophil function defects, antibiotic prophylaxis with antistaphylococcal antibiotics is appropriate. IVIG may be useful (Buckley et al, 1972) but should not be used in IgG subclass–deficient patients unless they are shown to have a deficiency of antibodies to a broad array of antigens.

Role of Surgery in the Treatment of OM with RS

In my experience, adenoid hypertrophy and/or adenoid infection are the most common causative factors for a child to have RS and OM. If treatment with an appropriate protocol as described in the preceding text fails, adenoidectomy should be considered. Adenoid size as determined by endoscopy or lateral neck radiography is not a regulating element in surgical decision making. In the older child without other risk factors for eustachian tube dysfunction or OM, the insertion of ventilation tubes may be postponed, and simple myringotomy to remove middle ear effusion present at the time of the adenoidectomy may suffice. Nasal and endoscopic surgery should be considered only if there is evidence of anatomic abnormalities, ciliary dyskinesias, or cystic fibrosis. Adenoidectomy with ventilation tubes or simple myringotomies as the first surgical step addressing RS with OM is safe and effective in the great majority of children. If LPR or gastroesophageal reflux disease is documented to be attributable to hiatal hernia or relaxation at the lower esophageal sphincter, surgery is considered.

References

Bjuggren G, Kraepelien S, Lind J. Sinusitis in children at home and in day nurseries. Ann Paediatr 1949;173:205–21.

Bothwell MR, Parsons DS, Talbot A, et al. Outcome of reflux therapy on pediatric chronic sinusitis. Otolaryngol Head Neck Surg 1999;121:255–62.

Buckley RH, Wray BB, Belmaker EZ. Extreme hyperimmunoglobulinemia E and undue susceptibility to infection. Pediatrics 1972;49:59–70.

Contencin P, Narcy P. Nasopharyngeal pH monitoring in infants and children with chronic rhinopharyngitis. Int J Pediatr Otorhinolaryngol 1991;22:249–56.

de Iongh RU, Rutland J. Ciliary defects in healthy subjects, bronchiectasis, and primary ciliary dyskinesia. Am J Respir Crit Care Med 1995;151:1559–67.

Dowell SF, Marcy SM, Philips WR, et al. Otitis media—principles of judicious use of antimicrobial agents. Pediatrics 1998;101: 165–71.

Gibson WS Jr, Cochran W. Otalgia in infants and children: a manifestation of gastroesophageal reflux. Int J Pediatr Otorhinolaryngol 1994;28:213–8.

Gungor A, Corey JP. Relationship between otitis media with effusion and allergy. Curr Opin Otolaryngol 1997;5:46–8.

Gwaltney JM Jr, Scheld WM, Sande MA, Sydnor A. The microbial etiology and antimicrobial therapy of adults with acute community acquired sinusitis: a fifteen-year experience at the University of Virginia and review of other selected studies. J Allergy Clin Immunol 1992;90:457–62.

Heiner DC, Lee SI, Short JA. IgG4 subclass deficiency syndromes. Monogr Allergy 1986;20:149–56.

Herrmann D, Herzgen M, Frank E, et al. Effect of hyposensitization for tree pollinosis on associated apple allergy. J Invest Allergol Clin Immunol 1995;5:259–67.

Herzon F, Murphy S. Normal ciliary ultrastructure in children with Kartagener's syndrome. Ann Otol Rhinol Laryngol 1980;89: 81–3.

Hurst DS, Fredens K. Eosinophil cationic protein in mucosal biopsies from patients with allergy and otitis media with effusion. Otolaryngol Head Neck Surg 1997;117:42–8.

Kaliner MA. Human nasal respiratory secretions and host defense. Am Rev Respir Dis 1991;144(3 Pt 2):52–6.

Karlsson G, Hansson HA, Petruson B, et al. The nasal mucosa in immunodeficiency. Surface morphology, mucociliary function and bacteriological findings in adult patients with common variable immunodeficiency or selective IgA deficiency. Acta Otolaryngol (Stockh) 1985;100:456–69.

Lee D, Rosenfeld RM. Adenoid bacteriology and sinonasal symptoms in children. Otolaryngol Head Neck Surg 1997;116:301–7.

Lusk RP, Polmar SH, Muntz HR. Endoscopic ethmoidectomy and maxillary antrostomy in immunodeficient patients. Arch Otolaryngol Head Neck Surg 1991;117:60–3.

Moss AJ, Parsons VL. Current estimates from the National Health Interview Survey, US—1985. Vital Health Stat 10 1986;160: 1–182.

Mygind N, Pederen M, Nielsen MH. Primary and secondary ciliary dyskinesia. Acta Otolaryngol (Stockh) 1983;95:688–94.

Normansell DE. Human immunoglobulin subclasses. Diagn Clin Immunol 1987;5:115–28.

Oxelius VA, Berkel IA, Hanson LA. IgG2 deficiency in ataxia telangiectasia. N Engl J Med 1982;306:515–7.

Oxelius VA, Laurrell AB, Lindquist B, et al. IgG subclasses in selective IgA deficiency. Importance of IgG2IgG4 deficiency. N Engl J Med 1981;304:1476–7.

Pedersen M. Specific types of abnormal ciliary motility in Kartagener's syndrome and analogous respiratory disorder. Eur J Respir Dis 1983;64 Suppl 127:78–90.

Phipps CD, Wood WE, Gibson WS. Gastroesophageal reflux contributing to chronic sinus disease in children. Arch Otolaryngol Head Neck Surg 2000;126:831–6.

Pitkäranta A, Arruda E, Malmberg H, Hayden FG. Detection of rhinovirus in sinus brushings of patients with acute community-acquired sinusitis by reverse transcription PCR. J Clin Microbiol 1997;35:1791–3.

Proctor DF. The mucociliary system. In: Proctor DF, Andersen I, editors. The nose: upper airway physiology and the atmospheric environment. Amsterdam: Elsevier Biomedical Press; 1982. p. 245–78.

Proud D, Reynolds CJ, Lacapra S, et al. Nasal provocation with bradykinin induced symptoms of rhinitis and a sore throat. Am Rev Respir Dis 1988;137:613–6.

Rakes GP, Arruda E, Ingram JM, et al. Human rhinovirus in wheezing children: relationship to serum IgE and nasal eosinophil cationic protein. J Respir Crit Care Med 1995;151:362A.

Rees GL, Eccles R. Sore throat following nasal and oropharyngeal bradykinin challenge. Acta Otolaryngol (Stockh) 1994;114: 311–4.

Rosenfeld RM. Pilot study of outcomes in pediatric sinusitis. Arch Otolaryngol Head Neck Surg 1995;121:729–36.

Roujeau JC, Kelly JP, Naldi L, et al. Medication use and the risk of Stevens-Johnson syndrome or toxic epidermal necrolysis. N Engl J Med 1995;333:1600–7.

Schopfer K, Baerlocher K, Price P, et al. Staphylococcal IgE antibodies, hyperimmunoglobulinemia E and Staphylococcus aureus infections. N Engl J Med 1979;300:835–8.

Shapiro G, Virant F, Furukama C, et al. Immunologic defects in patients with refractory sinusitis. Pediatrics 1991;87:311–6.

Shapiro GG. Sinusitis in children. J Allergy Clin Immunol 1988;81: 1025–7.

Smith CI, Islam KB, Vorechovsky I, et al. X-linked agammaglobulinemia and other immunoglobulin deficiencies. Immunol Rev 1994;138:159–83.

Soderstrom T, Soderstrom R, Andersson R, et al. Factors influencing IgG subclass levels in serum and secretions. Monogr Allergy 1988;23:236–43.

Soderstrom T, Soderstrom R, Avanzini A, et al. Immunoglobulin G subclass deficiency. Int Arch Allergy Appl Immunol 1987; 82:476–80.

Sorbin J, Engquist S, Nord CE. Bacteriology of the maxillary sinus in healthy volunteers. Scand J Infect Dis 1992;24:633–5.

Sorensen RY, Polmar SH. Immunoglobulin replacement therapy. Ann Clin Res 1987;19:293–304.

Stiehm ER. Immunologic disorders in infants and children. Philadelphia: WB Saunders; 1989.

Tallat AM, Baghdat YS, El-Ghazawy E, et al. Nasopharyngeal bacterial flora before and after adenoidectomy. J Laryngol Otol 1989;103:372–4.

Tasker A, Dettmar PW, Panetti M, et al. Reflux of gastric juice and glue ear in children. Lancet 2002;359:493.

van Cauwenberge PB, Bellussi L, Maw AR, et al. The adenoid as a key factor in upper airway infections. Int J Pediatr Otorhinolaryngol 1995;32 Suppl:S71–80.

Vandenberg SJ, Heatley DG. Efficacy of adenoidectomy in relieving symptoms of chronic sinusitis in children. Arch Otolaryngol Head Neck Surg 1997;123:675–8.

Wald ER. Epidemiology, pathology, and etiology of sinusitis. Pediatr Infect Dis 1985;4:551–4.

Winther B. The effect on the nasal mucosa of respiratory viruses (common cold). Danish Med Bull 1994;41:193–204.

Winther B, Gwaltney JM Jr, Hendley JO. Respiratory virus infection of monolayer cultures of human epithelial cells. Am Rev Respir Dis 1990;141:839–45.

Yellon RF, Coticchia J, Dixit S, et al. Esophageal biopsy for the analysis of gastroesophageal reflux-associated otolaryngologic problems in children. Am J Med 2000;108 Suppl 4: S131–8.

Chapter 31

Immune Workup/Management for Recurrent Otitis Media

Stephen I. Pelton, MD

Management of the otitis-prone child represents a challenge for the clinician with regard to selection of specific antimicrobial therapy for each acute episode, implementation of strategies for prevention, and counseling of parents regarding the potential for morbidity, as well as underlying risk features that enhance susceptibility. The pathogenesis of disease is multifactorial, with bacterial otopathogens ascending from the nasopharynx to the middle ear most often in the setting of concomitant viral infection. For each event in the pathogenesis, risk features have been established. Nasopharyngeal colonization with bacterial otopathogens is more frequent in infants who are formula-fed, as well as in infants with siblings in the household and for toddlers in day-care settings, reflecting reduced resistance to colonization with bacterial otopathogens and greater exposure to bacterial and viral respiratory pathogens, respectively. Additional environmental features, such as smoking in the household or exposure to wood-burning stoves, are also likely risk features. Anatomic abnormalities, most commonly cleft palate, demonstrate one end of the spectrum of eustachian tube (ET) dysfunction, resulting in near-universal occurrence of recurrent otitis media (ROM), and establish poor ET function as a critical risk feature. Similarly, children with other anatomic or physiologic causes for ET dysfunction are at increased risk for ROM. Third, the immune system plays a critical role in children by influencing susceptibility to bacterial otitis media (OM) through its effect on nasopharyngeal colonization and/or middle ear invasion by bacterial otopathogens.

Evidence in Support of a Critical Role for the Immune System

The evidence that the immune system has a critical role in protection from acute bacterial OM is derived from three types of studies. Descriptive studies identify ROM as a common clinical problem in children with a spectrum of immune deficiencies (Berdal et al, 1976; Bernstein, 2002; Moss et al, 1992; Williams, 1987). Both Barnett and colleagues (1992) and Principi and colleagues (1991) observed a greater number of episodes of acute otitis media (AOM) in human immunodeficiency virus (HIV)-infected children compared with uninfected controls. Principi and colleagues (1991) further observed that more frequent episodes occurred in children with a greater degree of immune dysfunction (classified as P2 immune status) compared with HIV-infected children with a lesser degree (classified as P1 immune status). They also reported a greater rate of persistent disease following standard therapy with amoxicillin. ROM has also been reported as a common feature in children with primary immunodeficiencies, most often in children with B-cell dysfunction and the associated hypogammaglobulinemia (Hausser et al, 1983; Stocks et al, 1999; Umetsu et al, 1995). These observations are consistent with a recent report of decreased B-cell proliferation and diminished interleukin-2 receptors (on B cells) in HIV-infected patients with active HIV replication in plasma, resulting in a functional hypogammaglobulinemia even though measured concentrations are elevated. Additional evidence for the importance of humoral antibody in determining susceptibility to OM is suggested by the observed reduction in AOM in premature infants passively immunized with high-dose respiratory syncytial virus (RSV) immunoglobulin (Ig) (RSVIG) but not RSV monoclonal antibody (Englund and Glezen, 2001). Both preparations (RSVIG and RSV monoclonal antibody) prevent lower respiratory tract RSV disease. Only RSVIG, which alone has very high concentrations of antibody against bacterial otopathogens, significantly reduces the frequency of AOM, further demonstrating the sufficiency of humoral antibody for prevention and supporting the hypothesis that the failure to make antibody would be a critical risk feature for recurrent disease. Similar support for the importance of humoral antibody in susceptibility to and prevention of ROM is provided by the observed 57% reduction in type-specific pneumococcal OM following immunization with 7-valent pneumococcal conjugate vaccine.

Immune Disorders Frequently Associated with ROM

A number of immunologic disorders are associated with frequent OM (Table 31-1). Increasing evidence has emerged that many otitis-prone children demonstrate subtle deficits in response to pneumococcal polysaccharide antigens or the outer membrane protein P6 from *Haemophilus influenzae*; however, the clinical relevance of such defects remains uncertain as these children are not susceptible to infections other than AOM (Epstein and Gruskay, 1995; Freijd et al, 1984; Yamanaka et al, 1997; Zora et al, 1993). In clinical practice, most children in whom the only concern is ROM do not have a quantifiable immunologic abnormality (Berman et al, 1992; Church, 1997). When an immune defect is detected, the abnormality is usually limited to partial IgG subclass or IgA deficiency (Berman et al, 1992; Gross et al, 1992). These abnormalities have been identified in 10% and 30% of children with ROM, respectively (Berman et al, 1992). Gross and colleagues (1992) reported partial IgA deficiency in one-third of 267 children with ROM and partial IgG1 deficiency in 3 (1%), IgG3 in 5 (2%), IgG2 or IgG4 deficiency in 6 (2%) each, and more than one partial deficiency in 6 additional patients. Umetsu and colleagues (1995) detailed 20 children with recurrent sinopulmonary infection, including ROM, sinusitis and/or pneumonia, and IgG subclass deficiency.

The identification of IgG subclass deficiency is challenging in children younger than 2 or 3 years of age. Total IgG and all four subclasses decay over the first months of life and reach a nadir at 4 to 8 months of age. Total IgG, IgG1, and IgG3 begin to increase during the latter half of

the first year of life and usually achieve adult concentrations by age 5 years, whereas IgG2 and IgG4 often demonstrate a delay before increasing and may not achieve adult concentrations until 10 years of age. Karma and colleagues (1976) reported that 14 (24%) of 59 children with ROM had reduced concentrations of serum Igs or Ig subclasses, yet only one case persisted when tested after a few years. These observations confirm the difficulty of making a diagnosis of IgG subclass deficiency in early infancy.

In children with signs and symptoms beyond ROM, more significant immunologic defects must be considered. Severe combined immunodeficiency syndrome (SCIDS) is characterized by defective humoral and cell media antibody. A diverse spectrum of genetic mutations has been associated with the same resultant immunologic defects. These children present before 6 months of age with ROM in conjunction with severe diarrhea, failure to thrive, oral candidiasis, and interstitial pneumonia often due to *Pneumocystis carinii* (Stocks et al, 1999). Stocks and colleagues (1999) reported that 70% of cases of SCIDS presented with otolaryngologic signs and/or symptoms.

Children with DiGeorge syndrome may have immune defects as severe as those seen in SCIDS in addition to thymic hypoplasia, hypoparathyroidism, and cardiac defects. Common variable Ig deficiency (also referred to as common variable hypogammaglobulinemia) is also characterized by recurrent upper and lower respiratory tract infection, chronic diarrhea, and bronchiectasis (Hausser et al, 1983). The immune defect is characterized by panhypogammaglobulinemia and can be differentiated from X-linked agammaglobulinemia by the presence of circulating B cells. In addition, autoimmune manifestations such as arthralgia and hemolytic anemia may be present.

Defects in phagocytic function also predispose to recurrent respiratory tract infection and recurrent OM (Church, 1997; Hill et al, 1997; Voss and Rhodes, 1992). In addition, these children frequently manifest cutaneous abscesses (pyoderma), gingivitis, candidal diaper dermatitis, or perianal abscesses. Voss and Rhodes (1992) described an infant with leukocyte adhesion deficiency

TABLE 31-1. Immune Disorders Associated with Recurrent Otitis Media

Immune Disorder	Immune Deficit
SCIDS; DiGeorge syndrome	↓ IgG; ↓ cell-mediated immunity
X-linked agammaglobulinemia	↓ IgG; absence of B cells (humoral immunity)
Combined variable immunoglobulin deficiency	↓ IgG; abnormal B cells (humoral immunity)
Hypogammaglobulinemia of infancy	↓ IgG (transiently low)
IgG subclass deficiency	↓ IgG1; ↓ IgG2; ↓ IgG3; or ↓ IgG4 alone or in combination
IgA deficiency	↓ IgA
Leukocyte adhesion deficiency	↓ Phagocytic function
Chronic granulomatous disease	↓ Phagocytic function
HIV	↓ Cell-mediated and B-cell function (humoral immunity)
Decreased responsiveness to polysaccharide antigen	↓ Specific antibody

HIV = human immunodeficiency virus; Ig = immunoglobulin; SCIDS = severe combined immunodeficiency syndrome.

who presented with ROM and soft tissue abscess, a persistently elevated leukocyte count, and delayed separation of the umbilical cord. The defect is characterized by impaired leukocyte migration, chemotaxis, and phagocytosis. A clue to the diagnosis may be the absence of pus at the site of infection. A syndrome of ROM, chronic diarrhea, and defective neutrophil granulocyte chemotaxis has also been reported and provides additional support for a link between defective leukocyte function and enhanced susceptibility to ROM (Hill et al, 1997). Similarly, Church (1997) identified chronic granulomatous disease in one child with ROM referred for immunologic evaluation. Children with Job's syndrome, hyperimmunoglobulinemia E and neutrophil dysfunction, may also suffer recurrent episodes of AOM. An absolute linkage between phagocyte disorders and AOM remains to be confirmed. Because AOM is common, it may be happenstance rather than causation that the two are observed in the same child.

ROM is also very common in children infected with HIV (Barnett et al, 1992; Chen et al, 1996; Principi et al, 1991; Williams, 1987). In general, additional signs of immunodeficiency such as recurrent thrush, lymphadenopathy, hepatomegaly or splenomegaly, failure to thrive, or chronic diarrhea are present, although ROM may be the presenting feature and/or dominant feature early in the course of disease. Both Barnett and colleagues (1992) and Principi and colleagues (1991) have reported increased episodes in this population. Barnett and colleagues (1992) observed that children with HIV continued to have frequent episodes of AOM beyond their first year of life. Principi and colleagues (1991) reported that those HIV-infected children with more severe immunologic dysfunction had a greater burden of disease compared with those with less evidence of immunologic decay. They also observed an inadequate response to amoxicillin therapy in 30% of HIV-infected children compared with only 10% in uninfected controls. Marchisio and colleagues (1996) defined the bacterial etiology of AOM in 60 episodes in 21 HIV-infected children. *Streptococcus pneumoniae*, nontypable *H. influenzae*, and group A streptococcus were recovered from the middle ear in 56.5% of cases, a proportion similar to that seen in immunocompetent children. *Staphylococcus aureus* was also identified in several HIV-infected children with severe immunosuppression.

Evaluation of the Child with ROM

Criteria to initiate an immune evaluation in a child with ROM have not been established. The goal of the clinician when determining if an immune evaluation is warranted is to identify immunologic defects that are potentially curable or warrant intervention to prevent more serious infectious disease morbidity or to provide reassurance (to the family) that no major immune defect is present. In general, the benefit of an immune evaluation for the child

whose manifestations are limited to ROM in the absence of additional concerns for enhanced susceptibility to infection or signs or symptoms such as failure to thrive, chronic diarrhea, lymphadenopathy, or organomegaly is controversial. Even when the diagnosis of an IgA or IgG subclass deficiency is suggested from the measurement of Igs and Ig subclasses, it is often maturational and transient. For the two most commonly considered management strategies, prophylactic antibiotics and intravenous immunoglobulin (IVIG) treatment, it is not necessary to demonstrate a specific immune defect as the otitis-prone child is likely to benefit from either even in the absence of a specific deficit.

In children with a family history of immunodeficiency, an at-risk profile for HIV, or additional concerns, as detailed in Table 31-2, an extensive immune workup is indicated. Table 31-3 identifies the spectrum of evaluation that should be considered and the abnormality that would likely be observed in children with immunodeficiency and ROM. Some of these tests, complete blood count, Igs and Ig subclasses, HIV antibody detection, nitroblue tetrazolium testing of neutrophil function, and flow cytometry, are likely to be readily available; however, more specialized testing of leukocyte function will usually require consultation with an immunologist. If a specific defect is identified, genetic evaluation and subsequent counseling are indicated to identify specific syndromes, implications for family members, and potential specific therapies such as bone marrow transplantation or gene transfer.

Management

The management of the child with ROM in whom a specific immune defect has been identified must address two questions: the treatment of acute episodes and the prevention of subsequent episodes. Few studies have been performed to specifically identify the bacterial pathogens in children with immune defects. The largest reported the results of tympanocentesis in 60 acute episodes in 21 HIV-infected children 9 months to 12 years of age (Marchisio et al, 1996). The study identified *S. aureus* as a pathogen in several children with the most severe immunodeficiency.

TABLE 31-2. Indications for Immune Evaluation in Children with Recurrent Otitis Media

Recurrent pneumonia or bronchiectasis
Invasive bacterial disease
Absence of tonsils, lymph nodes, or thymus (on chest radiographs)
Infection with opportunistic pathogens
Persistent dermatitis
Recurrent or chronic diarrhea
Failure to thrive
Family history of immune deficiency, risk features for human immunodeficiency virus
Recurrent thrush and/or gingivitis
Hepatosplenomegaly

TABLE 31-3. Laboratory Evaluation of Children with Recurrent Otitis Media

Laboratory Test	Observation	Potential Diagnosis
Complete blood count	Lymphopenia	SCIDS; HIV; DiGeorge syndrome
	Leukocytosis (persistent)	LAD
Total Ig	↓ IgG	X-linked agammaglobulinemia; combined variable immunoglobulin deficiency; transient hypogammaglobulinemia of infancy
	↓ IgA	IgA deficiency; ataxia-telangiectasia
	↑ IgE	Job's syndrome
IgG subclasses	↓ IgG1, ↓ IgG2, ↓ IgG3, ↓ IgG4	IgG subclass deficiency
Rebuck skin window	↓ Neutrophil migration	LAD
Boyden chamber	↓ Chemotaxis	LAD
Chemiluminescence or nitroblue tetrazolium	↓ Oxidative burst	Chronic granulomatous disease
	±	LAD
Flow cytometry analysis of neutrophils	↓ CD11, ↓ CD18	LAD
HIV antibody	ELISA and Western blot	HIV*

ELISA = enzyme-linked immunosorbent assay; HIV = human immunodeficiency virus; Ig = immunoglobulin; LAD = leukocyte adhesion deficiency; SCIDS = severe combined immunodeficiency syndrome.
*For children younger than 18 months old, demonstration of HIV by polymerase chain reaction or culture is necessary for diagnosis.

Additional studies, not in immunocompromised children, provide evidence that isolates of *S. pneumoniae* and nontypable *H. influenzae* in children on prophylactic antibiotics are more likely to demonstrate reduced susceptibility to β-lactam and macrolide antibiotics.

Both prophylactic antibiotics and IVIG have been reported to reduce episodes of AOM in children with and without identifiable immune defects, specifically IgG3 deficiency (Barlan et al, 1993). Prophylactic administration of amoxicillin (20–40 mg/kg as a single daily dose) is likely to be beneficial in this population. The use of IVIG is more controversial as reports of both successful reduction in the number of episodes and a lack of success are plentiful (Barlan et al, 1993; Ishizaka et al, 1994; Jorgensen et al, 1990; Kalm et al, 1986). Most of the studies reporting a lack of success are in either healthy children or those with limited immune defects (failure to respond to polysaccharide antigens). However, this is a time-consuming and difficult intervention strategy and should be considered cautiously for children whose manifestations of immune deficiency are limited to ROM. We have advocated IVIG only for children with IgG subclass deficiency when broader immunologic dysfunction was present with risk for or evidence of invasive disease, recurrent pneumonia, or bronchiectasis. An alternative approach might be the early insertion of pressure equalization tubes in the child with ROM and immune deficits. Pressure equalization tubes have been demonstrated to reduce the duration of middle ear effusion associated with AOM and possibly the frequency of episodes.

References

Barlan IB, Geha RS, Schneider LC. Therapy for patients with recurrent infections and low serum IgG3 levels. J Allergy Clin Immunol 1993;92:353–5.

Barnett ED, Klein JO, Pelton SI, Luginbuhl LM. Otitis media in children born to human immunodeficiency virus-infected mothers. Pediatr Infect Dis J 1992;11:360–4.

Berdal P, Brandtzaeg P, Proland SS, et al. Immunodeficiency syndromes with otorhinolaryngological manifestations. Acta Otolaryngol (Stockh) 1976;82:185–92.

Berman S, Lee B, Nuss R, et al. Immunoglobulin G, total and subclass, in children with or without recurrent otitis media. J Pediatr 1992;121:249–51.

Bernstein JM. Immunologic aspects of otitis media. Curr Allergy Asthma Rep 2002;2:309–15.

Chen AV, Ohlms LA, Stewart MG, Kline MW. Otolaryngologic disease progression in children with human immunodeficiency virus infection. Arch Otolaryngol Head Neck Surg 1996;122:1360–3.

Church JA. Immunologic evaluation of the child with recurrent otitis media. Ear Nose Throat J 1997;76:31–42.

Englund JA, Glezen WP. Passive immunization for the prevention of otitis media. Vaccine 2001;19 Suppl 1:S116–21.

Epstein MM, Gruskay F. Selective deficiency in pneumococcal antibody response in children with recurrent infections. Ann Allergy Asthma Immunol 1995;75:125–31.

Freijd A, Hammarstrom L, Persson MA, Smith CI. Plasma antipneumococcal antibody activity of the IgG class and subclasses in otitis prone children. Clin Exp Immunol 1984;56:233–8.

Gross S, Blaiss MS, Herrod HG. Role of immunoglobulin subclasses and specific antibody determinations in the evaluation of recurrent infection in children. J Pediatr 1992;121:516–22.

Hausser C, Virelizier JL, Buriot D, Griscelli C. Common variable hypogammaglobulinemia in children. Clinical and immunologic observations in 30 patients. Am J Dis Child 1983;137:833–7.

Hill HR, Book LS, Hemming VG, Herbst JJ. Defective neutrophil chemotactic responses in patients with recurrent episodes of otitis media and chronic diarrhea. Am J Dis Child 1977;131:433–6.

Ishizaka A, Sakiyama Y, Otsu M, et al. Successful intravenous immunoglobulin therapy for recurrent pneumococcal otitis media in young children. Eur J Pediatr 1994;153:174–8.

Jorgensen F, Andersson B, Hanson LA, et al. Gamma-globulin treatment of recurrent acute otitis media in children. Pediatr Infect Dis J 1990;9:389–94.

Kalm O, Prellner K, Christensen P. The effect of intravenous immunoglobulin treatment in recurrent acute otitis media. Int J Pediatr Otolaryngol 1986;11:237–46.

Karma P, Palva A, Kokko E. Immunological defects in children with chronic otitis media. Acta Otolaryngol (Stockh) 1976;82:193–5.

Marchisio P, Principi N, Sorella S, et al. Etiology of acute otitis media in human immunodeficiency virus-infected children. Pediatr Infect Dis J 1996;15:58–61.

Moss RB, Carmack MA, Esrig S. Deficiency of IgG4 in children: association of isolated IgG4 deficiency with recurrent respiratory tract infection. J Pediatr 1992;120:16–21.

Principi M, Marchisio P, Tornaghi R, et al. Acute otitis media in immunodeficiency virus-infected children. Pediatrics 1991;88: 566–71.

Stocks RMS, Thompson JW, Church JA, et al. Severe combined immunodeficiency: otolaryngological presentation and management. Ann Otol Rhinol Laryngol 1999;108:403–7.

Umetsu DT, Ambrosino DM, Quinti I, et al. Recurrent sinopulmonary infection and impaired antibody response to bacterial capsular polysaccharide antigen in children with selective IgG-subclass deficiency. N Engl J Med 1995;313:1247–51.

Voss LM, Rhodes KH. Leukocyte adhesion deficiency presenting with recurrent otitis media and persistent leukocytosis. Clin Pediatr 1992;31:442–5.

Williams MA. Head and neck findings in pediatric acquired immune deficiency syndrome. Laryngoscope 1987;97:713–6.

Yamanaka N, Hotomi M, Shimada J, Togawa A. Immunologic deficiency in "otitis-prone" children. Ann N Y Acad Sci 1997;830: 70–81.

Zora JA, Silk HJ, Tinkelman DG. Evaluation of postimmunization pneumococcal titers in children with recurrent infections and normal levels of immunoglobulin. Ann Allergy 1993;70: 283–8.

Chapter 32

Immunoglobulins for Recurrent Acute Otitis Media

Michiya Matsumura, MD, PhD

The number of cases of intractable recurrent otitis media (OM) has increased. Intractable recurrent OM has become resistant to the regular clinical treatments for outpatients, and in some cases, hospitalization is required. An increase of multidrug-resistant bacteria, the decline of immunocompetence of carriers (Ishizaka et al, 1994), and environmental factors such as group nursing are thought to be the cause of spread. I have measured immunoglobulin (Ig)G subclass and specific IgG2 antibody to *Streptococcus pneumoniae* in infants with intractable recurrent OM and administered Ig substitution therapy for those particularly intractable cases (Matsumura et al, 2001).

Table 32-1 shows the values of IgG subclass and specific IgG2 antibody to *S. pneumoniae* in six cases of infants with serious recurrent OM. IgG subclass deficiency is observed only in IgG1 in case 1 and in IgG2 in case 6. IgG2 is the major neutralizing antibody against *Haemophilus influenzae*, *S. pneumoniae*, or *Neisseria meningitidis*; it was normal in all cases except case 6. On the other hand, specific IgG2 antibody to *S. pneumoniae* was low in all cases, suggesting that the total IgG2 value does not necessarily reflect the disease state. Furthermore, it is thought that

IgG2 deficiency may occur not only by the decline of total IgG2 but also by impaired production of specific antibodies that belong to IgG2 (Suetake et al, 1995). Patients in cases 1 and 2 developed OM in both ears with complaints of fever. They were resistant to our outpatient treatments, such as oral administration of antibiotics or tympanotomy, for several months. The condition was alleviated only when antibiotics were administered intravenously under hospitalization, but it deteriorated as soon as the treatment was altered to oral administration. It was continuation of the disease rather than recurrence.

Sulfonated human Ig was administered to patients under the following circumstances: (1) when antibiotics had been administered intravenously under hospitalization with poor response or the disease recurred within a month, although the treatment was temporarily effective, and (2) either IgG subclass or specific IgG2 antibody to *S. pneumoniae* was at a markedly low level. Understanding and consent were obtained from the parents for administration of the Ig and its attendant risks, namely, that it is synthesized from human blood product, various vaccinations have to be avoided for 3 months after the treatment, and serious side effects, such as shock, may occur, albeit

TABLE 32-1. Serum Level of Immunoglobulin G Subclass (mg/dL)

Case	Age/Sex	IgG1	IgG2	IgG3	IgG4	Total	Serum Level of Specific IgG2 Antibody to *Streptococcus pneumoniae* (µ/mL)
1	9 mo/F	310	56	142	12	519	2.8
2	1 yr, 4 mo/F	769	87	62	29	947	2.2
3	9 mo/M	904	220	46	5	1,175	1.5
4	1 yr, 10 mo/M	1,220	113	53	4	1390	1.4
5	1 yr, 1 mo/M	789	113	44	2	948	2.6
6	11 mo/M	838	44	57	4	943	0.9
Abnormal level			< 350	< 50	< 10	< 0.05	< 3.0

rarely. The initial dose is 300 mg/kg, which is generally followed by three sessions of 200 mg/kg every 4 weeks. The therapy is stopped if no clinical effect is observed after the three sessions. After the three sessions of therapy, chronologic examination of IgG subclass and specific IgG2 antibody to *S. pneumoniae* is continued, and we discuss whether the therapy is to be further continued in consideration of the patient's clinical condition and antibody levels. We evaluated the therapeutic effect of Ig by whether the tympanic membrane was intact, a tympanogram was type A, the serum level of IgG subclass was above 50 mg/dL, and the serum level of specific IgG2 antibody to *S. pneumoniae* was above 3.0 μg/mL.

After discussion with the parents, Ig therapy was performed on an outpatient basis in cases 1 and 2. In both cases, antibiotics were combined and administered orally. The changes over time in IgG2 (Figure 32-1) and in specific IgG2 antibody to *S. pneumoniae* (Figure 32-2) showed an expected increase of antibody values after the therapy. The IgG2 value remained above the cutoff value for 4 weeks after completion of therapy, and the specific IgG2 antibody to *S. pneumoniae* value was also above the cutoff value. However, both of them declined below the cutoff value 8 weeks after therapy. Clinically, temperatures returned to normal the following day after therapy, and examination of the tympanic membranes improved. Tympanograms showed type A graphs in both cases from 3 days onward. However, in case 2, the level of specific IgG2 antibody to *S. pneumoniae* declined to nearly the pretreatment level 8 weeks after completion of the therapy, and the IgG2 level also declined below the cutoff value. Simultaneously, OM recurred by 8 weeks after completion of the substitute therapy, and *H. influenzae* was recovered.

Although our protocol of Ig therapy specifies the initial dose of 300 mg/kg and 200 mg/kg for the second session onward on an outpatient basis every 4 weeks, there is a report advocating one treatment for every

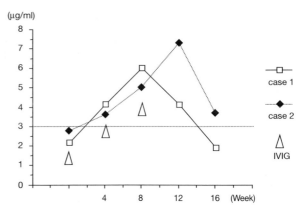

FIGURE 32-2. Changes in *Streptococcus pneumoniae*–specific immunoglobulin G2 antibody with immunoglobulin therapy. IVIG = intravenous immunoglobulin.

2 months for similar OM (Suetake et al, 1995). We believe that the 4-week interval is appropriate for maintaining the antibody levels because they declined 8 weeks after completion of the therapy, and, in case 2 in particular, OM recurred.

Compared with that of other studies (Suetake M et al, 1995; Ishizaka et al, 1994), our formula consisted of fewer sessions of three. Although antibody levels will rise well between the ages of 1.5 and 2 years in healthy infants, the increase is slow in those with recurrent OM, starting around the age of 4 years. On the one hand, it may be desirable to continue the therapy. On the other hand, because we do not know when antibody production starts if the therapy is continued and because we hope to limit the therapy session to as few treatments as possible, we maintain our policy of discussing the treatment with parents at the time of recurrence.

In infants, particularly those who cannot have vaccinations, OM is suspected to become even more intractable. For recurrent OM, none of the available antibiotics is effective. However, Ig therapy is effective and worth applying. At the same time, we must note that the Ig is prepared from human blood and that it has to be applied cautiously because of cost and its possible side effects (Englund and Glezen, 2000), and its abuse must be prohibited.

References

Englund JA, Glezen WP. Passive immunization for the prevention of otitis media. Vaccine 2000;19 Suppl 1: S116–21.

Ishizaka A, Sakiyama Y, Otsu M, et al. Successful intravenous immunoglobulin therapy for recurrent pneumococcal otitis media in young children. Eur J Pediatr 1994;153:174–8.

Matsumura M, Fukuda S, Chida E, et al. Therapy for otitis-prone children in Tenshi hospital. Auris Nasus Larynx 2001;28 Suppl:S29–32.

Suetake M, Endo H, Shimoda H, et al. [Immunoglobulin therapy for otitis-prone children.] Otol Jpn 1995;5:132–7.

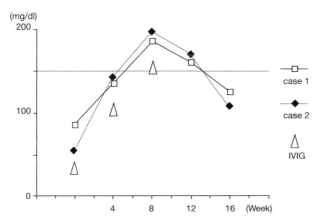

FIGURE 32-1. Changes in immunoglobulin G2 antibody with immunoglobulin therapy. IVIG = intravenous immunoglobulin.

Chapter 33

WATCHFUL WAITING FOR OTITIS MEDIA WITH EFFUSION

MICHAEL J. BELMONT, MD

Otitis media with effusion (OME) is an inflammation of the middle ear with fluid collected in the middle ear space. The signs and symptoms of an acute infectious process are not present. Much has been written about bilateral myringotomy and tympanostomy tube placement and adenoidectomy for OME. At times, however, it is appropriate to employ watchful waiting in the management of OME.

Natural History of Untreated OME

Five studies have reported the persistence of OME after an episode of acute otitis media (AOM) for children randomized to initially receive placebo (Burke et al, 1991; Claessen et al, 1994; Kaleida et al, 1991; Mygind et al, 1981; Thalin et al, 1985). Pooled data from these studies demonstrated that 1 month after an episode of AOM, 40% of children still have OME. This decreases to 26% after 3 months. Teele and colleagues (1980) reported the prevalence rates of OME after antibiotic-treated AOM; 40% of children had fluid at 1 month, but only 10% had OME at 3 months. Similarly, OME detected in surveillance studies also had high rates of spontaneous resolution. Fifty-one percent of children clear the fluid by 1 month, 74% by 6 months, and 95% by 1 year (Buckley and Hinton, 1991; Lous and Fiellau-Nikolajsen, 1981; Reves et al, 1985; van Balen et al, 1996; Williamson et al, 1994; Zeisel et al, 1995). These data demonstrated that OME is a common sequela of AOM and that the majority of children with fluid after an episode of AOM, or fluid found on routine examination, clear the fluid without intervention by 3 months.

Conversely, four studies have documented that spontaneous resolution of bilateral OME present for 3 months or longer is very low. Only 27% of ears have cleared by 6 months, 32% by 1 year, 49% by 3 years, and 59% by 4 years (Casselbrant et al, 1985; Dempster et al, 1993; Lieberman and Bartal, 1986; Maw and Bawden, 1994).

Sequela of Untreated OME

Treatment of OME is based in part on the assumption that it is associated with hearing loss and vestibular dysfunction and that this hearing loss is significant enough to result in speech and language developmental delay.

Hearing Loss and Speech and Language Developmental Delay

OME is most certainly associated with hearing loss. The mean three-frequency pure-tone average hearing level associated with OME is 27 dB in infants and 25 dB in older children (Fria et al, 1985); however, the range is 0 to 60 dB. Although, on average, this is only a "mild" loss, hearing function is tested in a soundproof booth and may not truly reflect real-life listening situations. Indeed, Rosenfeld and colleagues (1996) demonstrated that children with OME and "normal hearing" had substantial difficulties with word recognition at soft listening levels and in the presence of background noise.

Thus, OME is associated with hearing loss and difficulty hearing in normal listening environments. Whether it is associated with long-term speech and language developmental delay is yet unclear. In 1994, the Agency for Health Care Policy and Research (AHCPR) reviewed the results of many studies of the association of OME and speech and language development (Stool et al, 1994). Several studies reviewed reported lower scores for children with histories of OME versus children without such histories on tests of vocabulary, auditory comprehension, semantics and syntax, and narrative skills. Other studies reviewed, however, failed to find significant differences in these measures between the two groups

Children treated for chronic otitis media with effusion (COME) do indeed spend less time with OME and less time with hearing loss. Gates and colleagues (1987) randomly assigned 578 children with COME into one of four treatment groups: myringotomy, myringotomy and adenoidectomy, myringotomy and tympanostomy tube placement, or myringotomy and tympanostomy tube placement and adenoidectomy. Although a control group composed of children not receiving surgery was lacking, the three latter treatment groups spent less time with OME and less time with hearing loss greater than 20 dB than the myringotomy-only group. Mandel and colleagues (1989; 1992), in two separate studies, randomly assigned children with COME to one of three treatment groups: myringotomy, myringotomy and tympanostomy tube placement, or no surgery. They demonstrated that myringotomy and tympanostomy tube placement provided more effusion-free time and better hearing than no surgery or myringotomy without tube placement.

Thus, children with COME who receive treatment do spend less time with effusion and less time with hearing loss. However, does this hearing improvement result in improved speech, language, cognition, and psychosocial development? Rach and colleagues (1991) compared verbal expression and comprehension in a group of children with COME randomized to tympanostomy tube placement or watchful waiting. At the 6-month follow-up, they reported an improvement in language scores that favored the treatment group but did not reach statistical significance. Maw and colleagues (1999) and Wilks and colleagues (2000) compared early surgery with bilateral myringotomy and tympanostomy tube placement and watchful waiting for persistent bilateral COME. All children had bilateral OME for at least 3 months and a hearing loss greater than 25 dB. The main outcome measures were behavioral problems measured by the Richmond Behavior Checklist and hearing loss. By 9 months, early surgical intervention had significantly reduced behavioral problems by 17%. At 9 months, verbal comprehension and expressive language scores were significantly better in the early surgery group than in the watchful waiting group, whose scores were below expected scores for the age of the children in the study.

In a more recent study, Paradise and colleagues (2001) were unable to document any difference in speech, language, and cognition among children who received early treatment (tympanostomy tube placement) compared with those whose operation was delayed up to 9 months later if effusion persisted (delayed treatment). Unfortunately, only 73 children in the study had bilateral, continuous effusion. Three hundred and twenty-nine children (82%) of the study group had unilateral or discontinuous effusion, which would be less likely to be associated with hearing loss and developmental delay. Moreover, detection of a significant difference in treatment groups was made more difficult as only 82% of children assigned to the early treatment group actually received tympanostomy tubes, whereas 34% of the children assigned to the late treatment group did receive tympanostomy tubes. Lastly, hearing was described as abnormal in 75% of children with bilateral and 50% of children with unilateral middle ear effusion. Thus, only 60% of the group as a whole had "abnormal" hearing, which could potentially be causally associated with developmental delay. This further limits the ability of this study to detect a difference in groups.

Vestibular Dysfunction

Parents of children with OME often report clumsiness and balance problems. Casselbrant and colleagues (1995) demonstrated that children with OME have a significantly higher velocity of sway than normal children on dynamic platform posturography testing. Casselbrant and colleagues (1998) also demonstrated that children with OME may be more visually dependent for balance than healthy age-matched controls. Hart and colleagues (1998) demonstrated that children with OME had significantly lower performance in two separate standardized tests of balance. More recently, Casselbrant and colleagues (1998) were able to demonstrate continued vestibular abnormalities in a group of children with a past history of recurrent or persistent middle ear effusion but no OME at the time of testing. This may indicate some lasting effect of OME on the vestibular labyrinth.

A number of studies have demonstrated improvement of vestibular function after tube placement. Casselbrant and colleagues (1995) demonstrated a statistically significant improvement in velocity of sway after tube placement in a group of children with OME. Golz and colleagues (1998) demonstrated a significantly poorer Bruininks-Oseretsky balance score in children with OME than controls. Moreover, after tympanostomy tube placement, the score significantly improved and was not different from the control group. Golz and colleagues (1991) evaluated the effect of long-standing OME on vestibular function in a group of 97 children with no recent evidence of AOM. Abnormal electronystagmography (ENG) findings were documented in 69 (71%) patients. Moreover, after tube insertion, all but one patient had normal postoperative ENG results.

Structural and Functional Ear Changes

OME is an inflammatory process associated with a cellular infiltrate composed of macrophages, fibroblast plasma cells, and neutrophils (Ruah et al, 1992). Chronic inflammation has been shown to result in a thinning fibrous layer of the tympanic membrane (Ruah et al, 1992) and may also result in tympanosclerosis, a process characterized by the formation of whitish plaques in the submucosal layer of the middle ear. These plaques can result in limitation of ossicular movement and conductive hearing loss. Moreover, the eustachian tube dysfunction associated with COME combined with an atelectatic tympanic membrane can result in more significant problems such as retraction pocket formation, adhesive otitis, ossicular erosion, and cholesteatoma. Indeed, this can be seen in children with cleft palates, who serve as an in vivo model of eustachian tube dysfunction. The reported incidence of cholesteatoma in children with cleft palates varies from 2.6 to 9.2%, significantly higher than the 0.0047 to 0.0092% in the general population (Bluestone and Klein, 2003; Kemppainen et al, 1999). Tube placement improves middle ear ventilation and allows nonadhesive pars tensa and often pars flaccida retraction pockets to improve or resolve, thus preventing progression to adhesive otitis, ossicular erosion, or cholesteatoma formation.

Management Options

Healthy Children with Bilateral OME of Less than 3 Months or Unilateral OME of Less than 6 Months

It is evident that most effusions that develop after an episode of AOM and effusions found on routine examination in an otherwise healthy child will resolve spontaneously. Watchful waiting for these children is indicated. At this time, discussion of environmental risk factors with the family is appropriate. Breast-feeding, along with avoidance of second-hand smoke, large-group day care, and pacifier use, may be useful.

In addition, a single course of oral antibiotics may be given in an attempt to clear the effusion. Nine randomized, controlled, blinded trials have been conducted to assess the efficacy of antimicrobial therapy in OME. Six demonstrated a statistically significant rate of OME resolution compared with placebo. Meta-analysis of these nine studies demonstrated a modest (15%) but statistically significant effect.

Healthy Children with Bilateral OME of 3 Months or More or Unilateral OME of 6 Months or More

It is clear that COME is associated with hearing loss and vestibular abnormalities. In addition, there is some evidence, although far from conclusive, to suggest an association with speech and language developmental delays. Moreover, there is evidence to show that early treatment results in less time with effusion, less time with hearing loss, and resolution of vestibular abnormalities. In addition, there is some limited evidence to suggest an improvement in speech and language development after early surgical treatment. Coupled with the fact that docu-

mented bilateral OME for 3 months or greater takes a very long time to resolve spontaneously and can be associated with pathologic changes in the middle ear and tympanic membrane, placement of tubes is more appropriate than watchful waiting regardless of associated hearing loss. In an otherwise healthy child with unilateral OME for 6 months without hearing loss, developmental delays, or middle ear/tympanic membrane abnormalities, it would be appropriate to continue watchful waiting. However, if there is any significant hearing loss, aural fullness, school performance problems, or tympanic membrane/middle ear abnormalities, tube placement is more appropriate.

Children with Comorbidities

The studies cited above, by design, included only healthy children. They exclude children with comorbidities. Similarly, the clinical practice guideline for OME in young children released by the AHCPR limits its discussion and management of OME to otherwise healthy children 1 to 3 years of age with no craniofacial or neurologic abnormalities or sensory deficits (Stool et al, 1994). The following year, Bluestone and Klein (1995) published their opinions of the guidelines. Children with craniofacial or neurologic abnormalities or sensory deficits require more aggressive treatment. The 20 dB hearing level criterion proposed by the AHCPR should not be used to manage these patients.

Children with a concurrent conductive or sensorineural hearing loss may have a very significant hearing loss as the result of OME. The additional 20 to 30 dB of hearing loss may place these children's hearing loss into the moderate to severe range. Children with speech and language delay or mental retardation may be more significantly affected by the hearing loss associated with OME than normal children. These children may best be served by earlier tube placement if the effusion is associated with any hearing loss.

Children with cleft palates almost universally have OME. Palate repair seems to improve middle ear and eustachian tube function, but OME is not infrequent after repair. If fluid is present, it is appropriate to place tubes when the cleft lip is repaired. Children with trisomy 21 also have a high incidence of OME and conductive hearing loss, and more aggressive tube placement is reasonable.

Lastly, when there is significant pathology of the middle ear or tympanic membrane, earlier placement of a tube is appropriate to restore normal intratympanic pressure and possibly prevent long-term sequelae such as cholesteatoma and ossicular erosion.

References

Bluestone CD, Klein JO. Clinical practice guideline on otitis media with effusion in young children: strengths and weaknesses. Otolaryngol Head Neck Surg 1995;112:507–11.

Bluestone CD, Klein JO. Intratemporal complications and sequelae of otitis media. In: Bluestone CD, Stool SE, Alper CM, et al, editors. Pediatric otolaryngology. 4th ed. Philadelphia: WB Saunders; 2003. p. 687–764.

Buckley G, Hinton A. Otitis media with effusion in children shows a progressive resolution with time. Clin Otolaryngol 1991;16:354–7.

Burke P, Bain J, Robinson D, Dunleavey J. Acute red ear in children: controlled trial of nonantibiotic treatment in general practice. BMJ 1991;303:558–62.

Casselbrant M, Redfern MS, Furman JM, et al. Visual-induced postural sway in children with and without otitis media. Ann Otol Rhinol Laryngol 1998;107:401–5.

Casselbrant ML, Brostoff LM, Cantekin EI, et al. Otitis media with effusion in preschool children. Laryngoscope 1985;95:428–36.

Casselbrant ML, Furman JM, Rubenstein E, Mandel EM. Effect of otitis media on the vestibular system in children. Ann Otol Rhinol Laryngol 1995;104:620–4.

Claessen JQPJ, Appelman CLM, Touw-Otten FWMM, et al. Persistence of middle-ear dysfunction after recurrent acute otitis media. Clin Otolaryngol 1994;19:35–40.

Dempster JH, Browning GG, Gatehouse SG. A randomized study of the surgical management of children with persistent otitis media with effusion associated with a hearing impairment. J Laryngol Otol 1993;107:284–9.

Fria TJ, Cantekin EI, Eichler JA. Hearing acuity of children with otitis media with effusion. Arch Otolaryngol 1985;111:10–6.

Gates GA, Avery CA, Prihoda TJ, Cooper JC Jr. Effectiveness of adenoidectomy and tympanostomy tubes in the treatment of chronic otitis media with effusion. N Engl J Med 1987;317:1444–51.

Golz A, Angel-Yeger B, Parush S. Evaluation of balance disturbances in children with middle ear effusion. Int J Pediatr Otorhinolaryngol 1998;43:21–6.

Golz A, Westerman ST, Gilbert LM, et al. Effect of middle ear effusion on the vestibular labyrinth. J Laryngol Otol 1991;105:987–9.

Hart MC, Nichols DS, Butler EM, Barin K. Childhood imbalance and chronic otitis media with effusion: effect of tympanostomy tube insertion on standardized tests of balance and locomotion. Laryngoscope 1998;108:665–70.

Kaleida PH, Casselbrant ML, Rockette HE, et al. Amoxicillin or myringotomy or both for acute otitis media: results of a randomized clinical trial. Pediatrics 1991;87:466–74.

Kemppainen HO, Puhakka HJ, Laippala PJ, et al. Epidemiology and aetiology of middle ear cholesteatoma.. Acta Otolaryngol (Stockh) 1999;119:568–72.

Lieberman A, Bartal N. Untreated persistent middle-ear effusion. J Laryngol Otol 1986;100:875–8.

Lous J, Fiellau-Nikolajsen M. Epidemiology of middle-ear effusion and tubal dysfunction. A one-year prospective study comprising monthly tympanometry in 387 non-selected 7-year-old children. Int J Pediatr Otorhinolaryngol 1981;3:303–17.

Mandel EM, Rockette HE, Bluestone CD, et al. Myringotomy with and without tympanostomy tubes for chronic otitis media with effusion. Arch Otolaryngol Head Neck Surg 1989;115:1217–24.

Mandel EM, Rockette HE, Bluestone CD, et al. Efficacy of myringotomy with and without tympanostomy tubes for chronic otitis media with effusion. Pediatr Infect Dis J 1992;11:270–7.

Maw RA, Bawden R. The long-term outcome of secretory otitis media in children and the effects of surgical treatment: a ten-year study. Acta Otorhinolaryngol Belg 1994;48:317–24.

Maw R, Wilks J, Harvey I, et al. Early surgery compared with watchful waiting for glue ear and effect on language development in preschool children: a randomized trial. Lancet 1999;353:960–3.

Mygind N, Meistrup-Larsen KI, Thomsen J, et al. Penicillin in acute otitis media: a double-blind, placebo-controlled trial. Clin Otolaryngol 1981;6:5–13.

Paradise JL, Feldman HM, Campbell TF, et al. Effect of early or delayed insertion of tympanostomy tubes for persistent otitis media on developmental outcomes at the age of three years. N Engl J Med 2001;344:1179–87.

Rach GH, Zielhuis GA, Van Baarle PW, Van Den Brok P. The effect of treatment with ventilating tubes on language development in preschool children with otitis media with effusion. Clin Otolaryngol 1991;16:128–32.

Reves R, Budgett R, Miller D, et al. Study of middle-ear disease using tympanometry in general practice. BMJ 1985;290:1953–6.

Rosenfeld RM, Madell JR, McMahon A. Auditory function in normal-hearing children with middle ear effusion. In: Lim DJ, Bluestone CD, Casselbrant M, et al, editors. Recent advances in otitis media. Proceedings of the Sixth International Symposium. Hamilton (ON): BC Decker; 1996. p. 354–6.

Ruah CB, Schachern PA, Paparella MM, Zelterman D. Mechanism of retraction pocket formation in the pediatric tympanic membrane. Arch Otolaryngol Head Neck Surg 1992;118:1298–305.

Stool SE, Berg AO, Berman S, et al. Otitis media with effusion in young children. Clinical practice guideline number 12. Rockville (MD): US Department of Health and Human Services, Agency for Health Care Policy and Research, Public Health Service; July 1994. AHCPR Publication No.: 94-0622.

Teele DW, Klein JO, Rosner BA. Epidemiology of otitis media in children. Ann Otol Rhinol Laryngol Suppl 1980;68:5–6.

Thalin A, Densert O, Larsson A, et al. Is penicillin necessary in the treatment of acute otitis media? In: Sade J, editor. Proceedings of the International Conference on Acute And Secretory Otitis Media. Amsterdam: Kugler Publications; 1985. p. 441–6.

van Balen FAM, de Melker RA, Touw-Otten FWMM. Double-blind randomised trial of co-amoxiclav versus placebo for persistent otitis media with effusion in general practice. Lancet 1996;348:713–6.

Wilks J, Maw R, Peters TJ, et al. Randomised controlled trial of early surgery versus watchful waiting for glue ear: the effect on behavioural problems in preschool children. Clin Otolaryngol 2000;25:209–14.

Williamson IG, Dunleavey J, Bain J, Robinson D. The natural history of otitis media with effusion—a three-year study of the incidence and prevalence of abnormal tympanograms in four South West Hampshire infant and first schools. J Laryngol Otol 1994;108:930–4.

Zeisel SA, Roberts JE, Gunn EB, et al. Prospective surveillance for otitis media with effusion among black infants in group child care. J Pediatr 1995;127:875–80.

Chapter 34

ANTIBIOTICS FOR OTITIS MEDIA WITH EFFUSION

RICHARD M. ROSENFELD, MD, MPH

Management of patients with otitis media with effusion (OME) remains controversial. At the center of this controversy lies the most commonly used treatment option: antimicrobial agents. Although there are different theories for the pathogenesis of OME, there is an agreement that acute otitis media (AOM) precedes most of the OME episodes. Consensus on the bacterial etiology of most cases of AOM has historically led to the concept that OME is inadequately treated AOM, and the use of repeated and more potent antimicrobial agents should be the reasonable approach to the management of OME. This bias was further fed by the Pollyanna effect, that is, a high resolution rate attributed to the effect of antibiotics. Moreover, failure of clinicians to accurately distinguish the ears with AOM from those with OME resulted in repeated treatment of patients, leading to enormous cost of management of otitis media. Although evidence started to build up, leading to frustration related to the use of antimicrobial agents in the scientific community, general pediatric practice continued to use the only tool available as a result of pressure arising from tradition and lack of alternatives.

It was not until recently that the accurate value of antimicrobial agents in the management of OME has been demonstrated. Despite the presence of a now large volume of evidence against the use of antibiotics in OME, it continues to be managed in the community with multiple courses of antibiotics.

The rationale for antimicrobial therapy of OME is based on a 30% prevalence of viable bacteria in aspirated effusions and an 80% prevalence of bacterial genomic material (Hendolin et al, 1997; Post et al, 1995). Unfortunately, the impact of antimicrobial therapy on OME resolution is less than what might be expected from bacteriologic studies. Impact is best assessed by double-blind randomized controlled trials (RCTs) that compare antimicrobial therapy with placebo. Study results are compared using the absolute rate difference (RD), defined as the absolute difference in successful outcomes between the antimicrobial and placebo groups. A positive RD favors antimicrobial therapy and is statistically significant when the corresponding 95% confidence interval (CI) does not contain zero.

This chapter summarizes RCTs of antimicrobial therapy for OME individually and in aggregate using random effects meta-analysis. The results are assessed for validity and compared with those of published systematic reviews. All analyses demonstrate consistent short-term and modest benefits, suggesting a limited role for judicious antimicrobial therapy in selected children with OME.

Evidence for Antimicrobial Efficacy

Nine placebo-controlled RCTs (Table 34-1) have assessed the efficacy of antimicrobial therapy for OME (Daly et al, 1991; Mandel et al, 1987; Mandel et al, 1991; Marks et al, 1981; Møller and Dingsør, 1990; Podoshin et al, 1990; Schloss et al, 1988; Thomsen et al, 1989; van Balen et al, 1996). To avoid bias in outcome assessment, four unblinded studies (Corwin et al, 1986; Ernstson and Anari, 1985; Giebink et al, 1990; Healy, 1984) are excluded in which the control group received no drug instead of placebo. Prior analysis has shown that including unblinded studies inflates combined efficacy estimates by nearly 50% (Rosenfeld, 1999). Also excluded were a nonrandomized study of antimicrobial therapy (Sundberg, 1984), three randomized trials that used a prophylactic dose of antibiotic (half of the recommended daily therapeutic dosage) (deCastro et al, 1982; Schwartz and Rodriguez, 1982; Varsano et al, 1985), and a controversial reanalysis (Cantekin et al, 1991) of data originally published by Mandel and coworkers (1987).

Review of Table 34-1 shows that seven of the nine RCTs had results favoring antimicrobial therapy (RD greater than zero), of which six were statistically significant. The overall RD, obtained by pooling data with random effects meta-analysis (Borenstein and Rothstein, 2000), was .15, with a 95% CI of .06 to .24. An RD of .15 means that, on average, about seven children need treat-

TABLE 34-1. Efficacy of Antibiotic Therapy for Complete Resolution of OME at 10 Days to 8 Weeks (Median 4 Weeks)

Author (Year)	Country	Duration (Diagnosis)[†]	Drug and Duration[‡]	Complete Resolution, N (%)[§]		Absolute RD[‖] (95% CI)
				Antibiotic	Placebo	
Marks et al (1981)	England	NS (t)	TMP/SMX 28 d	16/25 (64)	7/26 (27)	.37 (.12–.63)*
Mandel et al (1987)	USA	Most ≥ 4 wk (a)	AMX 14 d	96/318 (30)	22/156 (14)	.16 (.09–.24)*
Schloss et al (1988)	Canada	NS (o, t)	ERY/SSX 14 d	6/25 (24)	8/27 (30)	−.06 (−.30–.18)
Thomsen et al (1989)	Denmark	12 wk (t)	AMX/CLV 30 d	69/111 (62)	34/110 (31)	.31 (.19–.44)*
Møller and Dingsør (1990)	Norway	12 wk (o, t)	ERY 14 d	12/69 (17)	19/72 (26)	−.09 (−.23–.05)
Podoshin et al (1990)	Israel	8 wk (t)	AMX 14 d	20/49 (41)	5/37 (14)	.27 (.10–.45)*
Daly et al (1991)	USA	NS (o, t)	TMP/SMX 14 d	5/21 (24)	2/21 (10)	.14 (−.08–.36)
Mandel et al (1991)	USA	Most ≥ 4 wk (a)	VAR 14 d	59/236 (25)	11/78 (14)	.11 (.01–.20)*
van Balen et al (1996)	Netherlands	12 wk (t)	AMX/CLV 14 d	18/79 (23)	5/74 (7)	.16 (.05–.27)*
Combined**				301/933 (32)	113/60 (19)	.15 (.06–.24)*

AMP = ampicillin; AMX = amoxicillin; AOM = acute otitis media; CEF = cefaclor; CLV = clavulanate; ERY = erythromycin; OME = otitis media with effusion; PCN = penicillin; RD = rate difference; SSX = sulfisoxazole; SMX = sulfamethoxazole; TMP = trimethoprim; VAR = various antibiotics (AMX, CEF, or ERY/SSX).

[†]Minimum duration of OME to enter study and method of diagnosis: algorithm (a), otoscopy (o), or tympanometry (t).

[‡]Outcomes are reported at completion of therapy for all studies except Podoshin et al (1990), who reported 6 weeks later, and for Mandel et al (1987) and Møller and Dingsør (1990), who reported 2 weeks later.

[§]Number of children with clearance of OME from all initially affected ears divided by the total number of evaluable children.

[‖]Absolute change in OME complete resolution attributable to therapy; positive values favor the antibiotic group.

*$p < .05$ when the 95% CI does not contain zero.

**Combined $p = .001$; test for heterogeneity $Q = 27.00$, df = 8, $p < .001$.

ment to achieve one additional cure beyond natural history. The number needed to treat (NNT) is easily calculated as the reciprocal of the RD ($1.00 \div 0.15 = 6.7$). The NNT is a useful measure of clinical importance because it reflects the amount of clinical effort that must be expended to achieve one additional treatment success (Laupacis et al, 1988). There was significant heterogeneity among studies ($p < .001$) in Table 34-1, with results ranging from an RD of .37 to −.09 (negative results favor placebo). The study (Møller and Dingsør, 1990) with the poorest result used erythromycin as single-agent therapy.

Whereas other meta-analyses (Stool et al, 1994; Williams et al, 1993) of OME have included RCTs with a prophylactic dosage of an antimicrobial agent (deCastro et al, 1982; Schwartz and Rodriguez, 1982; Varsano et al, 1985), these studies were excluded from Table 34-1 because a subtherapeutic level of drug could unfavorably bias results. Prophylaxis studies generally administer half of the recommended therapeutic drug dosage, which might reduce clinical efficacy. As shown in Table 34-2, the overall impact of antimicrobial prophylaxis on OME resolution is not statistically significant (RD = .12, 95% CI = −.11, .35). Only one study (Varsano et al, 1985) showed a significant benefit, but the sample size was too low to define the magnitude of benefit with an acceptable degree of clinical certainty (95% CI = .06–.56).

Antimicrobial prophylaxis is an option for selected effusion-free children with histories of chronic or recurrent OME. Mandel and colleagues (1996) compared the efficacy of amoxicillin prophylaxis with that of placebo for managing recurrent middle ear effusion (MEE) (either AOM or OME) in 111 children in Pittsburgh. Inclusion criteria were at least three episodes of MEE or 3

cumulative months of MEE during the past year. Amoxicillin prophylaxis reduced AOM incidence by 0.76 episodes/year and OME incidence by 0.62 episodes/year; the overall time with MEE was also reduced by 13%. Although statistically significant, clinical benefits of this magnitude may be relevant only for high-risk children with recurrent OME and effusion-free periods.

As noted above, prophylaxis is ineffective as therapy for persistent OME without effusion-free intervals. One later study found that azithromycin prophylaxis of OME for 12 weeks improved middle ear pressures versus decongestant alone, but the clinical relevance is unclear, and the duration of benefit (if any) beyond the prophylactic period was not studied (Safak et al, 2001).

Validity of Existing Evidence

Three published meta-analyses (Rosenfeld and Post, 1992; Stool et al, 1994; Williams et al, 1993) have shown that antibiotic therapy confers a modest, but statistically significant, short-term benefit for resolution of OME. Rosenfeld and Post (1992) obtained a higher RD than that shown in Table 34-1 (.23 versus .15) because they included several unblinded studies that inflated the treatment effect. Conversely, Stool and colleagues (1994) emphasized blinded studies, but their effect size was slightly lower (RD = .14, 95% CI = .04–24) because one RCT (van Balen et al, 1996) was not yet published and three included studies (deCastro et al, 1982; Schwartz and Rodriguez, 1982; Varsano et al, 1985) using a prophylactic dosage of antibiotic. The same observations apply to Williams and coworkers (1993), who obtained an RD of .16 (95% CI = .03–.29), with some unblinded studies included.

The earlier RCT by Mandel and colleagues (1987) in Table 34-1 was the subject of considerable controversy because a dissenting analysis (Cantekin et al, 1991) using tympanometry as an outcome measure reduced the RD from .16 to .08 (based on 51/309 tympanometric successes in the study group and 13/150 successes with placebo). Because of this controversy, Williams and colleagues (1993) used the dissenting analysis and Stool and colleagues (1994) used neither. When viewed in perspective as only one link in a chain of RCT evidence, however, the impact of this controversy on meta-analysis results is extremely small. When recalculated using data from the dissenting analysis, the RD in Table 34-1 decreases by one percentage point to .14 (95% CI = .05–.23).

Most of the children in RCTs of medical therapy for OME have established preexisting effusion(s) lasting weeks to months (see Table 34-1). Consequently, the results may not apply to OME of very recent onset or of lesser duration. The cause of OME is generally unknown but more often of spontaneous onset rather than persistent effusion after a discrete episode of AOM. As in most otitis media RCTs, children were often excluded who had immune deficiency, cleft palate, craniofacial anomalies, prior tympanostomy tubes, or Down or other syndromes. Meta-analysis results may not apply to these populations.

The modest 15% increase in OME resolution attributable to antimicrobial therapy must be viewed in the context of a short-term benefit; the impact on long-term resolution is smaller, if not negligible, based on the limited evidence available. Mandel and colleagues (1987) reported an RD of .16 at 2 weeks but only .06 at 4 weeks. Giebink and colleagues (1990) reported RDs of .55 and .18, respectively, at similar time points. Similarly, Williams and coworkers (1993) reported no significant intermediate or long-term benefits to antimicrobial therapy for OME in their meta-analysis. The same trend is observed with corticosteroid therapy, alone or in combination with an antibiotic (Stool et al, 1994).

The relatively modest benefit of antimicrobial therapy for OME explains the "brouhaha" that has permeated the medical literature over the past decade (Williams et al, 1993). When the focus of attention is only statistical significance, the results of individual trials appear conflicting, and even a single study (Cantekin et al, 1991; Mandel et al, 1987) can yield discrepant conclusions based on the method of outcome assessment (algorithm versus tympanometry). When the focus of attention is clinical importance, however, the individual and pooled 95% confidence limits show remarkably consistent findings: a small benefit of antimicrobial therapy that on aggregate is statistically significant. Three independent meta-analyses (Rosenfeld and Post, 1992; Stool et al, 1994; Williams et al, 1993) support this conclusion, making the "brouhaha" more of a historical curiosity than a clinically meaningful issue.

Clinical Implications and Recommendations

Recommendations with respect to the management of OME should start with emphasizing the accurate diagnosis of OME. Although assessment of the actual rate of misdiagnosis of OME in the community is not straightforward, the known challenges in evaluation of the signs of the tympanic membrane should have an impact on the accuracy of the diagnosis.

Besides the misconception that antibiotics are indicated each time OME is diagnosed, probably the most common reason for overtreating an ear with OME is the thought that it is AOM. Education and training, as well as use of pneumatic otoscopy, serve to limit this common mistake. In the absence of signs and symptoms of an acute infection, primary care physicians should be encouraged to avoid treating children with antibiotics because of parental concerns and expectations exacerbated with minor symptoms of ear tugging, irritability, and hearing loss, sometimes coupled with impression of hyperemia and fullness owing to engorged blood vessels and possibly insufflated air during the otoscopic examination (especially when pneumatic otoscopy is not used to assess the mobility of the eardrum).

TABLE 34-2. Efficacy of Antibiotic Prophylaxis versus Placebo for Complete Resolution of OME

Author (Year)	Country	Duration (Diagnosis)[†]	Drug and Duration	Blind Study	Complete Resolution, N (%)[‡]		Absolute RD[§] (95% CI)
					Prophylaxis	No Prophylaxis	
DeCastro et al (1982)	USA	NS (t)	SSX	Y	5/15 (33)	0/15 (0)	.31 (.06–.56)*
Schwartz and Rodriguez (1982)	USA	≤ 15 d (t)	TMP/SMX	N	19/33 (58)	21/36 (58)	−.01 (−.24–.23)
Varsano et al (1985)	Israel	NS (o)	SSX	Y	10/19 (53)	8/16 (50)	.03 (−.31 .36)
Combined**					34/67 (51)	29/67 (43)	.12 (−.11–.35)

OME = otitis media with effusion; RD = rate difference; SMX = sulfamethoxazole; SSX = sulfisoxazole; TMP = trimethoprim.
[†]Minimum duration of OME to enter study and method of diagnosis: algorithm (a), otoscopy (o), or tympanometry (t).
[‡]Number of children with clearance of OME from all initially affected ears divided by the total number of evaluable children.
[§]Absolute change in OME complete resolution attributable to therapy; positive values favor the prophylaxis group.
*$p < .05$ when the 95% CI does not contain zero.
**Combined $p = .323$; test for heterogeneity Q = 3.77, df = 2, $p = .152$.

The evidence for the actual role of antibiotics should be repeatedly presented to the physicians as well as the community. Approximately one in seven children derive a short-term therapeutic benefit from antimicrobial therapy for OME. Randomized trials with blinded outcome assessment (Daly et al, 1991; Mandel et al, 1987; Mandel et al, 1991; Marks et al, 1981; Møller and Dingsør, 1990; Podoshin et al, 1990; Schloss et al, 1988; Thomsen et al, 1989; van Balen et al, 1996) show only a 15% absolute increase in OME resolution attributable to antimicrobial therapy, which increases to 22% when nonblinded trials (Laupacis et al, 1988; Mandel et al, 1996; Stool et al, 1994; Williams et al, 1993) are also included. The latter estimate, however, is artificially high because of bias related to less rigorous study design (no placebo controls). In contrast, antimicrobial prophylaxis offers no benefits beyond spontaneous resolution (deCastro et al, 1982; Schwartz and Rodriguez, 1982; Varsano et al, 1985) and should not be used when managing persistent OME.

A 1994 clinical practice guideline suggested that antimicrobial therapy is optional for most OME (Stool et al, 1994) but failed to provide advice on who might benefit from therapy. Reasonable candidates for a single course of antimicrobial therapy include the following (Rosenfeld and Bluestone, 2003):

- High-risk children, with OME lasting 4 weeks or longer who are at risk for adverse learning-language sequelae from persistent MEE
- Surgical candidates who have not had recent prior antibiotics
- Selected children with recurrent OME, particularly if high risk

Whereas no prospective trials demonstrate improved outcomes with this approach, even a modest short-term reduction in OME persistence may benefit high-risk children and help avoid a small percentage of surgery. There is no definitive evidence, however, to mandate a trial of antimicrobial therapy before tympanostomy tube placement.

When antimicrobial therapy is considered for a child with OME, clinicians are advised to consider the following (Rosenfeld and Bluestone, 2003):

- Expectations should reflect that only approximately one in seven children derive a short-term benefit from antimicrobial therapy; hopes for a dramatic and lasting response are likely to yield disappointment.
- A single 5- to 10-day course of therapy is appropriate; no benefits have been documented for prolonged, repetitive, or aggressive therapeutic regimens.
- Prophylactic antimicrobial agents have no role in managing chronic OME; randomized studies show comparable outcomes with placebo therapy.
- Placebo-controlled studies show no difference in antimicrobial efficacy related to the bacterial spectrum of the prescribed drug (Rosenfeld and Post, 1992; Williams et al, 1993).
- Comparative antimicrobial studies generally show equivalent efficacy between established standards (amoxicillin) and newer, broader-spectrum agents; however, one RCT showed slightly better outcomes with amoxicillin-clavulanate than penicillin V (Thomsen et al, 1997).
- A single intramuscular dose of ceftriaxone is not recommended for OME; this agent is approved only for treating AOM, and the efficacy for OME is unknown.

Although not included in this chapter either owing to absence of evidence or relative insignificance, some other factors play a role in our day-to-day management of children with OME. When the indication of antibiotics for the treatment of OME is this controversial and is advised to be considered in selected children with OME, a few words may be necessary on how to select those children.

The factors that influence our decision on treating OME with antibiotics may be individual or environmental. A definition of "high-risk" subjects with OME is usually brought for the selection of a surgical treatment. Consideration of ventilation tube placement under anesthesia suggests that application of the one in seven chance of eliminating this surgical risk by using antibiotics may be justified in children with no history of prior antibiotic use. Whereas speech delay, development of tympanic membrane sequelae such as retraction pocket or atelectasis, a history of ventilation tube placement (especially with recurrence of OME immediately after the extrusion of tubes), the presence of other physical or mental impairments, or having OME in an only hearing ear may be considered important factors for placement of ventilation tubes, a trial of antibiotics before surgery may be appropriate for children with non-advanced problems. Similarly, a strong family history for recurrent and persistent ear problems, day-care attendance, and immune deficiency may be clues for selecting subjects with ongoing middle ear inflammation owing to an infectious process. If tubes are not considered, whereas fall and winter months decrease our hope of spontaneous resolution, perhaps because of a new infection, spring and early summer may reduce the desire to give antibiotics. Probably the strongest contraindication for use of antibiotics would be the presence of air bubbles or the presence of an air-fluid level. Although it is not unusual for such children to be a little more symptomatic and to have complaints of popping, pain, and discomfort, these should not be indications for any medical management.

If antibiotics are considered, it is due to the concept of targeting ongoing infection, despite the absence of signs and symptoms of AOM. Therefore, it makes sense to apply the concepts of treatment of AOM to the treatment of OME and to consider the high prevalence of resistant bacteria, with increased incidence in children recently treated with antibiotics, in day care, or who are diagnosed during winter or late spring. High-dose amoxicillin with or without clavulanic acid would therefore be the choice. The presence of penicillin allergy or, more importantly, multidrug allergy would, on the other hand, reduce the enthusiasm of selection of other antibiotics.

Conclusion

Restrictive antimicrobial use is essential to limit the spread of multidrug resistant bacteria, particularly *Streptococcus pneumoniae*. Antimicrobial agents are not indicated for initial treatment of sporadic OME, as noted appropriately by the American Academy of Pediatrics and Centers for Disease Control and Prevention (Dowell et al, 1998). There is, however, a role for judicious antimicrobial therapy in managing selected children with OME. The guidelines presented above should help target children most likely to benefit from therapy, while preventing excessive antimicrobial use in the general community.

References

Borenstein M, Rothstein H. Comprehensive meta-analysis: a computer program for research synthesis (version 1.0.25). Englewood (NJ): Biostat Inc; 2000.

Cantekin EI, McGuire TW, Griffith TL. Antimicrobial therapy for otitis media with effusion ('secretory' otitis media). JAMA 1991;266:3309–17.

Corwin MJ, Weiner LB, Daniels D. Efficacy of oral antibiotics for the treatment of persistent otitis media with effusion. Int J Pediatr Otorhinolaryngol 1986;11:109–12.

Daly K, Giebink GS, Batalden PB, et al. Resolution of otitis media with effusion with the use of a stepped treatment regimen of trimethoprim-sulfamethoxazole and prednisone. Pediatr Infect Dis J 1991;10:500–6.

deCastro FJ, Jaeger RW, Martin L, et al. Serous otitis media: a double-blind trial with sulfisoxazole. Mo Med 1982;79:629–30.

Dowell SF, Marcy M, Phillips WR, et al. Otitis media—principles of judicious use of antimicrobial agents. Pediatrics 1998;101 Suppl:165–71.

Ernstson S, Anari M. Cefaclor in the treatment of otitis media with effusion. Acta Otolaryngol Suppl (Stockh) 1985;424:17–21.

Giebink GS, Batalden PB, Le CT, et al. A controlled trial comparing three treatments for chronic otitis media with effusion. Pediatr Infect Dis J 1990;9:33–40.

Healy GB. Antimicrobial therapy of chronic otitis media with effusion. Int J Pediatr Otorhinolaryngol 1984;8:13–7.

Hendolin PH, Markkanen A, Ylikoski J, Wahlfors JJ. Use of multiplex PCR for simultaneous detection of four bacterial species in middle ear effusions. J Clin Microbiol 1997;35:2854–8.

Laupacis A, Sackett DL, Roberts RS. An assessment of clinically useful measures of the consequences of treatment. N Engl J Med 1988;318:1728–33.

Mandel EM, Casselbrant ML, Rockette HE, et al. Efficacy of antimicrobial prophylaxis for recurrent middle-ear effusion. Pediatr Infect Dis J 1996;15:1074–82.

Mandel EM, Rockette HE, Bluestone CD, et al. Efficacy of amoxicillin with and without decongestant-antihistamine for otitis media with effusion in children: results of a double-blind randomized trial. N Engl J Med 1987;316:432–7.

Mandel EM, Rockette HE, Paradise JL, et al. Comparative efficacy of erythromycin-sulfisoxazole, cefaclor, amoxicillin or placebo for otitis media with effusion in children. Pediatr Infect Dis J 1991;10:899–906.

Marks NJ, Mills RP, Shaheen OH. A controlled trial of cotrimoxazole therapy in serous otitis media. J Laryngol Otol 1981;95:1003–9.

Møller P, Dingsør G. Otitis media with effusion: can erythromycin reduce the need for ventilating tubes? J Laryngol Otol 1990;140:200–2.

Podoshin L, Fradis M, Ben-David Y, Faraggi D. The efficacy of oral steroids in the treatment of persistent otitis media with effusion. Arch Otolaryngol Head Neck Surg 1990;116:1404–6.

Post JC, Preston RA, Aul JJ, et al. Molecular analysis of bacterial pathogens in otitis media with effusion [comment]. JAMA 1995;273:1598–604.

Rosenfeld RM. What to expect from medical therapy. In: Rosenfeld RM, Bluestone CD, editors. Evidence-based otitis media. Hamilton (ON): BC Decker; 1999. p. 179–206.

Rosenfeld RM, Bluestone CD. Clinical pathway for otitis media with effusion. In: Rosenfeld RM, Bluestone CD, editors. Evidence-based otitis media. 2nd ed. Hamilton (ON): BC Decker; 2003. p. 303–24.

Rosenfeld RM, Post JC. Meta-analysis of antibiotics for the treatment of otitis media with effusion. Otolaryngol Head Neck Surg 1992;106:378–86.

Safak MA, Kilic R, Haberal I, et al. A comparative study of azithromycin and pseudoephedrine hydrochloride for otitis media with effusion in children. Acta Otolaryngol (Stockh) 2001;121:925–9.

Schloss MD, Dempsey EE, Rishikof E, et al. Double blind study comparing erythromycin-sulfisoxazole (Pediazole) t.i.d. to placebo in chronic otitis media with effusion. In: Lim DJ, Bluestone CD, Klein JO, Nelson JD, editors. Proceedings of the Fourth International Symposium on Recent Advances in Otitis Media. Toronto: BC Decker; 1988. p. 261–3.

Schwartz RH, Rodriguez WJ. Trimethoprim-sulfamethoxazole treatment of persistent otitis media with effusion. Pediatr Infect Dis J 1982;1:333–5.

Stool SE, Berg AO, Berman S, et al. Otitis media with effusion in young children. Clinical practice guideline number 12. Rockville (MD): Agency for Health Care Policy and Research, Public Health Service, US Department of Health and Human Services; July 1994. AHCPR Publication No.: 94-0622.

Sundberg L. Antibiotic treatment of secretory otitis media. Acta Otolaryngol Suppl (Stockh) 1984;407:26–9.

Thomsen J, Sederberg-Olsen J, Balle V, Hartzen S. Antibiotic treatment of children with secretory otitis media. Arch Otolaryngol Head Neck Surg 1997;123:695–9.

Thomsen J, Sederberg-Olsen J, Balle V, et al. Antibiotic treatment of children with secretory otitis media: a randomized, double-blind, placebo-controlled study. Arch Otolaryngol Head Neck Surg 1989;115:447–51.

van Balen FAM, de Melker RA, Touw-Otten FWMM. Double-blind randomised trial of co-amoxiclav versus placebo for persistent otitis media with effusion in general practice. Lancet 1996;348:713–6.

Varsano I, Volvitz B, Mimouni F. Sulfisoxazole prophylaxis of middle ear effusion and recurrent acute otitis media. Am J Dis Child 1985;139:632–5.

Williams RL, Chalmers TC, Stange KC, et al. Use of antibiotics in preventing recurrent acute otitis media and in treating otitis media with effusion: a meta-analytic attempt to resolve the brouhaha. JAMA 1993;270:1344–51.

Chapter 35

STEROIDS FOR CHRONIC OTITIS MEDIA WITH EFFUSION IN CHILDREN

ELLEN M. MANDEL, MD

The role of steroids in the management of otitis media with effusion (OME) is controversial. Glucocorticosteroids in various forms (systemic, inhaled, intranasal, intratympanic) have been tried with varying degrees of success, but the question of steroid efficacy has not been settled.

Mechanisms of Action

Glucocorticosteroids have many effects that, at least theoretically, should make them efficacious for the treatment of middle ear disease. The anti-inflammatory activity of steroids comes from inhibition of phospholipase A_2 with the subsequent prevention of the formation of arachidonic acid and its metabolites (Schweibert et al, 1996); this then prevents the synthesis of inflammatory mediators (Fergie and Purcell, 1998; Jung et al, 1988). Steroids have recently been shown to up-regulate transepithelial sodium transport in the middle ear epithelium, promoting the removal of fluid from the middle ear space (Tan et al, 1997). Also, steroids have been shown to decrease mucin production in vitro by suppressing MUC5AC (Fergie et al, 2000). Although the relation of otitis media and allergy is unsettled, these actions of steroids in lessening inflammation may ameliorate the allergic diatheses that are thought to be responsible for middle ear effusion (MEE) (Hurst, 1996). Other proposed mechanisms of steroid action are an increase in surfactant in the eustachian tube (Persico et al, 1978) and shrinkage of peritubal lymphoid tissue (Crysdale, 1984; Schwartz et al, 1980a), allowing for better tubal function.

Oral Steroids

Many studies of oral steroids for OME have been reported, but, owing to a small sample size, differences in definitions of middle ear status, or other limitations in study design, their role has been difficult to determine. Of six studies with more than 100 subjects, three were nonrandomized and nonblinded (Oppenheimer, 1968; Persico et al, 1978; Rosenfeld, 1995), and a fourth reported the outcome of 14 days of treatment at only 2 months after the start of treatment (Podoshin et al, 1990). The steroid used, as well as the dose and the length of time of treatment, varied widely. Outcome measures varied; some studies defined the presence/absence of disease by tympanometry and/or audiometry only, others used otoscopy (some used validated observers [Stool and Flaherty, 1983], whereas others did not) or otomicroscopy, and others used combinations of these. Study populations were often not characterized for possible confounders such as laterality of effusion, previous history of middle ear disease, duration of effusion, or allergy status. The use of a concurrent antimicrobial agent was also not consistent. In animal studies, concurrent use of an antimicrobial agent and a steroid was more effective than each alone in clearing MEE and in lowering the levels of anti-inflammatory mediators in MEE (Jung et al, 1988). Some of these studies tested steroid plus antibiotic against placebos, not clarifying whether the positive outcome in the treated group was attributable to the steroid, the antibiotic, or the combination. In spite of the many variations in design and population, most studies have found at least a short-term positive effect of oral steroid, including three large studies reported in the past 10 years. Rosenfeld (1995) reported the results of his experience of treatment of chronic OME with prednisolone (1 mg/kg for 10 days) given with various antimicrobial agents (all β-lactamase resistant) versus no treatment in a nonrandomized, nonblinded, study design in 122 children. At the first follow-up visit, 3 to 4 weeks after the start of treatment, 32% of subjects whose parents chose treatment with steroid and antibiotic were effusion free compared with 2% in the group who remained untreated. Children in the treated group whose effusion had resolved were given sulfisoxazole prophylaxis for a minimum of 6 weeks or "until the end of the viral season (October through to May)." At a second visit 6 months after entry, resolution of OME was noted in 25% of children who received steroid treatment; relapse between the first and second follow-up visits occurred in 12 of 28 (43%) of subjects. No comparative data were available for the children in the control group because most had undergone myringotomy and tube insertion. Hemlin and colleagues (1997) published their randomized, double-blind trial of cefixime for 10 days with and without one dose of betamethasone versus placebo for both in children with OME for at least 3 months. Of 140 evaluable subjects at the first follow-up visit 2 to 11 days after completing treatment, 26 (44.1%) of 59 subjects receiving both active medications were considered "cured," as were 12 (19.7%) of 61 receiving only cefixime and 1 (5%) of 20 in the placebo group. However, subjects were considered "cured" at follow-up if they had at least one "normal" ear if they had bilateral MEE at entry, or, if they had unilateral MEE at entry, both ears were clear. Children considered "cured" at the first follow-up visit were seen at 6 weeks and 6 months. Recurrence was common in all groups, and no statistically significant difference in middle ear status was noted at either follow-up visit.

In the most recent study (Mandel et al, 2002), 144 children 1 to 9 years of age with MEE of at least 2 months duration were entered in a double-blind, randomized trial and were assigned to one of four treatment arms: (1) steroid + amoxicillin for 14 days and then amoxicillin for 14 more days; (2) steroid + amoxicillin for 14 days and then placebo for amoxicillin for 14 more days; (3) placebo (for steroid) + amoxicillin for 14 days and then amoxicillin for 14 more days; (4) placebo (for steroid) + amoxicillin for 14 days and then placebo for amoxicillin for 14 more days. Subjects were examined by otoscopy, tympanometry, and audiometry at entry and 2 and 4 weeks after entry; those without MEE at the 4-week visit returned monthly for up to three more visits or until recurrence of effusion. Allergy skin testing was performed at the 4-week visit. One hundred thirty-five subjects (94%) returned for the 2-week visit, and 132 subjects (92%) were seen for the 4-week visit. At the 2-week visit, 33.3% of subjects in the steroid + amoxicillin group had no MEE compared with 16.7% in the placebo + amoxicillin group ($p = .03$, adjusting for stratification variables; 95% confidence interval [CI] on the difference in proportions: 2.4%, 31.0%). At the 4-week visit, the percentage of subjects with no MEE in the steroid-treated group was 32.8%, whereas that in the placebo group was 20% ($p = .12$, adjusting for stratification variables and treatment received during weeks 3 and 4; 95% CI for the difference in proportions in the two groups: −2.0%, 27.7%). Comparing change in middle ear status from the 2- to 4-week visit, there were no significant differences in recurrence of MEE or further clearance of MEE between those treated with amoxicillin for 2 weeks and those treated for 4 weeks. Interestingly, for the subgroup of subjects who still had MEE at the 2-week visit, hearing measures were statistically significantly better in the steroid-treated groups than in the nonsteroid-treated groups, but these differences were no longer present by the 4-week visit. By the 4-month visit, 68.4% of subjects in the steroid group who had no MEE at the 4-week visit had recurrence of MEE, as did 69.2% of such subjects in the placebo group. We therefore concluded that treatment with the dose and type of steroid used in this study should not be universally recommended for treatment of chronic OME.

Nonsystemic Steroids

To avoid the systemic side effects of oral steroids, other ways to deliver the drug have been tried. Direct delivery of steroid into the middle ear space has been proposed. Torrey (1971) reported the case of an adult with chronic OME managed by repeated injections of hydrocortisone acetate directly into the middle ear space through the tympanic membrane. Sato and colleagues (1988) reported the results of iontophoresis of dexamethasone and fosfomycin in 48 children (68 ears) aged 3 to 6 years with OME of unspecified duration. Half of the children received treatment, whereas the other half remained untreated. Treatment was performed three times per week for 10 treatments. All entered ears had type B tympanograms at entry; at the 1-month follow-up, 42.4% of ears in the treated group had type B tympanograms, as did 88.5% of untreated ears. Hearing was also shown to improve with treatment. No further follow-up was reported.

Intranasal steroids have been widely used in the treatment of allergic rhinitis and have also been proposed for the treatment of middle ear disease. In 1982, Shapiro and colleagues and Rees and colleagues reported the results of their studies using nasal dexamethasone phosphate and nasal flunisolide, respectively, in children with "eustachian tube dysfunction," defined by tympanometric parameters. These reports showed early modest improvement in the groups treated with steroid. Schwartz and colleagues (1980b) reported the results of the use of 10 days of intranasal beclomethasone in an uncontrolled trial in 25 children aged 9 months to 12 years with OME from 2 to 12 weeks duration; 8 children also received sulfisoxazole nightly as prophylaxis for AOM. Ten of the 25 children were noted to have resolved their effusion at the 2-week and 5-week visits, and two additional children had "partial clearance," that is, resolution in one ear. Of note, 6 of 8 children also treated with sulfisoxazole were effusion free or had partial clearance, compared with 6 of 17 who did not receive antibiotic. The authors then contrasted the results of intranasal steroid to a previous study by their group using oral steroid (Schwartz et al, 1980a) and found the oral steroid to be more efficacious than the inhaled steroid (62.5% clearance versus 48%, respectively). Intranasal beclomethasone was tested in a randomized, double-blind trial by Lildholt and Kortholm (1982), in which 70 children above the age of 4 years with OME of unspecified duration received either active drug or placebo (vehicle only), two sprays twice a day for 1 month. At the end of the treatment period, there was no difference between the two groups in middle ear status, nor was any difference found on follow-up 1 month after treatment was discontinued. The subject of the efficacy of intranasal steroid was re-examined by Tracy and colleagues (1998), who randomly assigned 61 children, aged 3 to 11 years, with MEE for at least 3 months, to receive either antibiotic (amoxicillin in a prophylactic dose of 20 mg/kg/d), antibiotic and intranasal beclomethasone, or antibiotic and intranasal placebo for 12 weeks. The final otoscopic "scores" (a composite of scores for mobility, effusion, and retraction) were improved in all three treatment groups, with the most improvement seen in the beclomethasone + antibiotic group. Resolution of MEE by otoscopic examination was noted more often in the antibiotic + beclomethasone group, but statistical significance between treatment groups (antibiotic alone and antibiotic + placebo were combined) was achieved only for analyses based on ears and not for subjects.

Results of Steroid Treatment for Chronic OME in Allergic Children

Allergy has been proposed as a risk factor for OME because of the suggestion that OM occurs more frequently in allergic children (Corey et al, 1994). Because steroids are often used to treat allergic diseases, one might expect that steroid would be particularly effective in treating MEE in allergic children. In our recent study of oral steroid for chronic OME (Mandel et al, 2002), 41.8% of the study patients had one or more positive allergy skin tests. The percentage of children with positive skin tests increased with increasing age: 22.7% in the 1- to 2-year-old group, 39.3% in the 2- to 5-year-old group, and 54.% in the 6- to 9-year-old group. This observed frequency of positive allergy skin tests in children with otitis media is greater than that reported in a general pediatric population in the United Kingdom at 4 years of age of 20% (Arshad et al, 2001) but similar to the 39% reported in a population of healthy children followed to age 6 years in Tucson, AZ (Wright et al, 1994). However, there was no significant difference in the resolution of MEE according to allergic status in those children treated with steroids compared with placebo at either 2 or 4 weeks of study within the parameters of this study design. The possibility exists that a higher dose of steroid is needed to promote

greater resolution of MEE in those children who were skin test positive. Tracy and colleagues (1998), in their study of 61 children with otitis media, 25% of whom had positive allergy skin tests, also did not show any difference in outcome of intranasal beclomethasone therapy for otitis media when analyzed by allergy skin test status.

Safety Issues with the Use of Steroids

Physicians and patients alike are concerned with the safety issues surrounding the use of steroids. Concern about increased severity of disease during viral infections such as measles and especially varicella in patients using steroids has received much attention and is still controversial. Case reports linking use of steroids to severe and often fatal varicella have appeared (Kasper and Howe, 1990; Lantner et al, 1990; Silk et al, 1988), and in 1991, the US Food and Drug Administration (FDA) required manufacturers of all oral, parenteral, and aerosolized glucocorticoid products to add a warning to the package inserts regarding potential fatal outcomes in patients receiving these preparations and who were exposed to varicella (Spahn and Kamada, 1995). In 1993, Dowell and Bresee published a case-control study showing an odds ratio of 178 of developing severe varicella in children who received systemic steroids within 30 days of onset of their rash. However, the study design was criticized for choosing children who did not have varicella as the control group, which cast doubt on the link between steroids and severe varicella. Patel and colleagues (1996) also used a case-control design but used children with uncomplicated varicella as the control group and found no increased risk of complicated varicella-zoster infection. Live attenuated varicella vaccine was licensed by the FDA in March 1995 for use in individuals 12 months and older who have not had varicella. Unpublished information from the vaccine manufacturer relates that the protection against any disease in vaccinees after household exposure was approximately 70%, but protection against severe disease was greater than 95%. When varicella does occur in vaccinated children, it is mild and the rash may be atypical, resembling insect bites. Rarely, such children may be potentially infectious to susceptible persons (American Academy of Pediatrics, 2000b). Varicella vaccine is now recommended by the American Academy of Pediatrics to be given to all healthy children routinely at 12 months of age. For unimmunized children up to 13 years of age who have no reliable history of varicella, one dose is recommended; after the age of 13 years, two doses of vaccine, 4 to 8 weeks apart, are recommended. If a nonimmunized child without a history of previous varicella infection who has recently received steroids is exposed to varicella, varicella-zoster immune globulin (VZIG) can be used to prevent severe infection, but it is only effective within 96 hours after exposure (American Academy of Pediatrics, 2000b). If more than 96 hours have elapsed since exposure, acyclovir can be given. Oral acyclovir can be given to patients on nonimmunosuppressive doses of steroid (< 1 mg/kg/d of oral steroid or inhaled steroid), but intravenous acyclovir is recommended for patients who received high-dose therapy (≥ 1 mg/kg/d) of steroid (Spahn and Kamada, 1995).

Another potential problem with the use of corticosteroids is interference with and safety of immunizations in children receiving or who have just finished a course of steroid. Detailed recommendations are available in the Red Book 2000 (Report of the Committee on Infectious Diseases) from the American Academy of Pediatrics (2000a).

Other problems with steroids are of concern, such as effect on growth, changes in mental status and mood, cataracts, osteoporosis, and aseptic necrosis of the femoral head. However, these should not be major problems when a short course of steroids is used. Temporary increases in appetite and change in mood, both resolving after cessation of the steroid, have been reported with short-term treatment of OME (Mandel et al, 2002).

Reviews and Recommendations Concerning Steroid Use for OME

In 1992, the Working Group on Steroid Use, Antimicrobial Agents Committee of the Infectious Diseases Society of America, published *Guidelines for the Use of Systemic Glucocorticoids in the Management of Selected Infections*, in which a recommendation for or against steroid use was made for many types of infections (McGowan et al, 1992). The recommendation for "chronic effusion after otitis media" was "moderate evidence for use," even though the extent of benefit had not been determined. Rosenfeld and colleagues (1991) published a meta-analysis of six randomized clinical trials involving the use of oral steroids for OME and concluded from the available trials that children receiving steroids for 7 to 14 days were 3.6 times more likely than placebo-treated subjects to be effusion free at the end of therapy. The authors also concluded that "the presence of significant heterogeneity among these studies suggests that additional trials will be needed to identify the specific subset(s) of children most likely to benefit from steroid therapy." Rosenfeld (1992), in another publication aimed at clinicians, reviewed the evidence for the efficacy of steroid for chronic OME and recommended its use prior to surgery. The clinical practice guideline on otitis media with effusion in young children published by the Agency for Health Care Policy and Research (Stool et al, 1994) concluded that steroid medications were not recommended for the treatment of OME in a child of any age. This recommendation was based on their expert panel's meta-analyses of studies of steroid with and without antibiotic compared with placebo or antibiotic alone. Papp (1996) published a summary and critique of these guidelines, in which he felt that the expert panel "minimized a cost-benefit analysis done

when coming to their conclusions" (referring to a study published by Berman et al in 1994). Papp did not dismiss the possible efficacy of steroids but felt that the issue of steroid efficacy had not been settled. More recently, Butler and van der Voort (2001) published their meta-analysis of randomized, controlled trials of oral and topical nasal steroids and concluded that although steroid treatment led to resolution of OME in the short term, there is no evidence of long-term benefit; therefore, treatment with oral or topical nasal steroids is not recommended.

Role for Steroid Treatment in Chronic OME

Although there seems to be short-term benefit from the use of steroids, the long-term benefit is in doubt and remains controversial. Berman and colleagues (1994) showed a cost saving to the use of systemic steroid, and Rosenfeld's non-randomized study (1995) showed that fewer children went on to have tympanostomy tube insertion when treated with steroid. In our recent study (Mandel et al, 2002), we found only a short-term benefit to steroid use in terms of MEE status. We therefore did not recommend steroid in the dose used in our study for universal use in chronic OME. However, in addition to short-term benefit in the clearance of MEE, we found that even children with effusion who had been treated with steroid had improved hearing compared with those with effusion who did not receive steroid treatment. This speaks to some beneficial effect of steroid on the middle ear, and the mechanisms of such effects should be further explored in an effort to develop even better, more targeted treatments for this common problem.

References

American Academy of Pediatrics. Immunization in special clinical circumstances. In: Pickering LK, editor. 2000 Red Book: report of the Committee on Infectious Diseases. 25th ed. Elk Grove Village (IL): American Academy of Pediatrics; 2000a. p. 61–2.

American Academy of Pediatrics. Varicella-zoster infections. In: Pickering LK, editor. 2000 Red Book: report of the Committee on Infectious Diseases. 25th ed. Elk Grove Village (IL): American Academy of Pediatrics; 2000b. p. 624–38.

American Academy of Pediatrics. Policy statement. Recommendations for the use of live attenuated varicella vaccine (RE9524). Pediatrics 1995;95:791–6.

Arshad SH, Tariq SM, Matthews S, Hakim E. Sensitization to common allergens and its association with allergic disorders at age 4 years: a whole population birth cohort study. Pediatrics 2001;108:E33.

Berman S, Roark R, Luckey D. Theoretical cost effectiveness of management options for children with persisting middle ear effusion. Pediatrics 1994;93:353–63.

Butler CC, van der Voort JH. Steroid for otitis media with effusion: a systematic review. Arch Pediatr Adolesc Med 2001;155:641–7.

Corey JP, Adham RE, Abbass AH, Seligman I. The role of IgE-mediated hypersensitivity in otitis media with effusion. Am J Otolaryngol 1994;15:138–44.

Crysdale WS. Medical management of serous otitis media. Otolaryngol Clin North Am 1984;17:653–7.

Dowell SF, Bresee JS. Severe varicella associated with steroid use. Pediatrics 1993;92:223–8.

Fergie JE, Purcell K. The role of inflammatory mediators and anti-inflammatory drugs in otitis media. Pediatr Ann 1998;27:76–81.

Fergie N, Guo L, Pearson JP, Birchall JP. The influence of prednisolone on the secretion of MUC5AC from TH29-MTX cell culture. Clin Otolaryngol 2000;25:570–6.

Hemlin C, Carenfelt C, Papatziamos G. Single dose of betamethasone in combined medical treatment of secretory otitis media. Ann Otol Rhinol Laryngol 1997;106:359–63.

Hurst DS. Association of otitis media with effusion and allergy as demonstrated by intradermal skin testing and eosinophil cationic protein levels in both middle-ear effusions and mucosal biopsies. Laryngoscope 1996;106:1128–37.

Jung TTK, Hwang S-J, Olson D, et al. Effects of penicillin, ibuprofen, corticosteroid, and tympanostomy tube insertion on experimental otitis media. In: Lim DJ, Bluestone CD, Klein JO, Nelson JD, editors. Recent advances in otitis media—proceedings of the Fourth International Symposium. Toronto: BC Decker; 1988. p. 231–5.

Lantner R, Rockoff JB, DeMasi J, et al. Fatal varicella in a corticosteroid-dependent asthmatic receiving troleandomycin. Allergy Proc 1990;11:83–7.

Lildholt T, Kortholm B. Beclomethasone nasal spray in the treatment of middle-ear effusion: a double-blind study. Int J Pediatr Otorhinolaryngol 1982;4:133–7.

Kasper WL, Howe PM. Fatal varicella after a single course of corticosteroids. Pediatr Infect Dis J 1990;10:729–32.

Mandel EM, Casselbrant ML, Rockette HE, et al. Systemic steroid for chronic otitis media with effusion in children. Pediatrics 2002;110:1071–80.

McGowan JE, Chesney PJ, Crossley KB, LaForce FM. Guidelines for the use of systemic glucocorticoids in the management of selected infections. J Infect Dis 1992;165:1–13.

Oppenheimer P. Short-term steroid therapy: treatment of serous otitis media in children. Arch Otolaryngol 1968;88:138–40.

Papp C. Management of otitis media with effusion in young children. Ann Pharmacother 1996;30:1291–7.

Patel H, Macarthur C, Johnson D. Recent corticosteroid use and the risk of complicated varicella in otherwise immunocompetent children. Arch Pediatr Adolesc Med 1996;150:409–14.

Persico M, Podoshin L, Fradis M. Otitis media with effusion: a steroid and antibiotic therapeutic trial before surgery. Ann Otol 1978;87:191–6.

Podoshin L, Fradis M, Ben-David Y, Faraggi D. The efficacy of oral steroids in the treatment of persistent otitis media with effusion. Arch Otolaryngol Head Neck Surg 1990;116:1404–6.

Rees T, Bierman CW, Shapiro GG, et al. Double-blind evaluation of nasal flunisolide for modifying eustachian tube dysfunction in allergic children. J Allergy Clin Immunol 1982;69 Suppl 1:149.

Rosenfeld RM. New concepts for steroid use in otitis media with effusion. Clin Pediatr 1992;31:615–21.

Rosenfeld RM. Nonsurgical management of surgical otitis media with effusion. J Laryngol Otol 1995;109:811–6.

Rosenfeld RM, Mandel EM, Bluestone CD. Systemic steroids for otitis media with effusion in children. Arch Otolaryngol Head Neck Surg 1991;117:984–9.

Sato H, Takahashi H, Honjo I. Transtympanic iontophoresis of dexamethasone and fosfomycin. Arch Otolaryngol Head Neck Surg 1988;114:531–3.

Schwartz RH, Puglese J, Schwartz DM. Use of a short course of prednisone for treating middle-ear effusion: a double-blind crossover study. Ann Otol Rhinol Laryngol 1980a;89 Suppl 68:296–300.

Schwartz RH, Schwartz DM, Grundfast KM. Intranasal beclomethasone in the treatment of middle ear effusion: a pilot study. Ann Allergy 1980b;45:284–7.

Schweibert LM, Beck LA, Stellato C, et al. Glucocorticoid inhibition of cytokine production: relevance to antiallergic actions. J Allergy Clin Immunol 1996;97:143–52.

Shapiro GG, Bierman CW, Furukawa CT, et al. Treatment of persistent eustachian tube dysfunction in children with aerosolized nasal dexamethasone phosphate versus placebo. Ann Allergy 1982;49:81–5.

Silk HJ, Guay-Woodford L, Perez-Atayde AR, et al. Fatal varicella in steroid-dependent asthma. J Allergy Clin Immunol 1988;81:47–51.

Spahn JD, Kamada AK. Special considerations in the use of glucocorticoids in children. Pediatr Rev 1995;16:266–72.

Stool SE, Berg AO, Berman S, et al. Otitis media with effusion in young children. Clinical practice guideline number 12. Rockville (MD): Agency for Health Care Policy and Research, Public Health Service, US Department of Health and Human Services; July 1994. AHCPR Publication No.: 94-0622.

Stool SE, Flaherty MR. Validation of diagnosis of otitis media with effusion. Ann Otol Rhinol Laryngol 1983; 92 Suppl 107:5–6.

Tan C-T, Escoubet B, van den Abbeele T, et al. Modulation of middle ear epithelial function by steroids: clinical relevance. Acta Otolaryngol (Stockh) 1997;117:284–8.

Torrey EH. Treatment for chronic otitis media. Arch Otolaryngol 1971;93:435.

Tracy JM, Demain JG, Hoffman KM, Goetz DW. Intranasal beclomethasone as an adjunct to treatment of chronic middle-ear effusion. Ann Allergy Asthma Immunol 1998;80:198–206.

Wright AL, Holberg CJ, Martinez FD, et al. Epidemiology of physician-diagnosed allergic rhinitis in childhood. Pediatrics 1994;94:895–901.

Chapter 36

Adjuvant Therapy for Otitis Media with Effusion

David L. Mandell, MD

The multifactorial pathogenesis of otitis media with effusion (OME) and the tendency of OME to recur after treatment may account for the complexity encountered in attempting to optimally manage the disorder. Traditional treatment options for OME are covered elsewhere in this text and include watchful waiting, antimicrobial therapy, corticosteroid therapy, otoventilation, ventilation tube placement, and adenoidectomy with or without tonsillectomy. The purpose of this chapter is to review some of the adjuvant and alternative therapies that have been investigated for treatment of OME. These therapies can be grouped into the following categories: mucolytic agents, surfactant therapy, and anti-inflammatory medications.

Mucolytic Agents

A universal characteristic of OME is nonspecific inflammation of the middle ear mucosa and secretory transformation of the epithelial layer, with accumulation of fluid in the middle ear (Ovesen et al, 2000; Pignataro et al, 1996). Thick mucoid middle ear effusions contain mucopolysaccharides, which are large, complex molecules that make the mucus so sticky that it cannot be transported through the eustachian tube by the epithelial mucociliary apparatus (Bauer, 1968). Attempts have been made to decrease the viscosity of mucoid middle ear effusions by chemical means, breaking down the molecules contributing to high viscosity to facilitate emptying of the mucus through the eustachian tube into the nasopharynx, thus restoring middle ear aeration, improving hearing, and decreasing the need for surgery (Bauer, 1968; Gessert et al, 1960; Kumazawa and Ushiro, 1988). Three general classes of mucolytic agents have been investigated in subjects with OME: proteolytic enzymes, amides, and cysteine derivatives (Bauer, 1968).

Proteolytic Enzymes

The earliest attempts at decreasing the viscosity of thick mucoid middle ear effusions in patients with OME used proteolytic enzymes such as trypsin and chymotrypsin (Auslander, 1958; Gessert et al, 1960; Mawson, 1967). These agents act by hydrolyzing peptide bonds and have been shown to decrease the viscosity of aspirated human middle ear effusions in vitro (Gessert et al, 1960). The first clinical series was reported by Auslander (1958), in which 106 patients with secretory otitis media (SOM) were treated with myringotomy, politzerization, and aspiration of serous fluid, followed by intramuscular injection of trypsin into the buttock twice a day for 5 days, with repeated politzerization until the middle ear became clear. The cure rate was 84% with just one myringotomy and trypsin treatment. In 1967, Mawson performed myringotomy, middle ear aspiration, and injection of α-chymotrypsin directly into the middle ear followed by Politzer bag compression of the meatus in 63 ears with OME, with a cure rate of 76%. Although control subjects were not used in either of these two studies, it was claimed that during the period before proteolytic enzyme therapy, most similar cases had required two or more myringotomies (up to 10) to clear the middle ear (Auslander, 1958).

Attempts to develop noninjectable routes of administration for proteolytic agents in patients with chronic OME were unsuccessful (Gessert et al, 1960). Buccal absorption of chymotrypsin was abandoned owing to episodes of severe buccal mucosal ulceration (Gessert et al, 1960). Experimentation with a 5- to 7-day course of enteric-coated oral chymotrypsin in subjects with OME demonstrated no chemical or clinical evidence of resolution of middle ear effusion (Gessert et al, 1960). Thus, since the 1960s, no further human experimentation with proteolytic agents has been pursued.

Amides

Amides are felt to decrease the viscosity of mucus by unfolding its three-dimensional structure via breakage of hydrogen bonds (Bauer, 1968). In a 1968 publication, Bauer reported on the direct injection of carbamide (urea) into the middle ear space in cases of "glue ear." After several minutes, the mucoid effusion had softened enough that it could be aspirated, leading to immediate improvement in hearing, no cases of inner ear damage, and only one recurrence of middle ear effusion in 18 children. Despite these promising results, the technique did not catch on, likely owing to the fact that tympanocentesis was required for drug administration.

Cysteine Derivatives

Of all of the experimental mucolytic agents that have been used to treat OME, the most studied is S-carboxymethylcysteine (SCMC). This agent is a blocked thiol derivative of the amino acid cysteine that has mucolytic properties (Majima et al, 1990; Ramsden et al, 1977), is administered orally as a syrup, and has not been associated with any major adverse reactions. Its use in patients with SOM or glue ear was first reported in 1975 (Taylor and Dareshani, 1975). In a double-blind, placebo-controlled trial of 46 patients with SOM, oral administration of SCMC syrup for 1 month resulted in resolution of the effusion in approximately one-third of subjects, whereas only 2% of patients treated with placebo experienced resolution (Taylor and Dareshani, 1975).

Other double-blind prospective studies have demonstrated mixed results with respect to treatment of OME. In a study by Khan and colleagues (1981), average pure-tone audiometry results improved significantly in children with OME treated with myringotomy and 3 months of oral SCMC compared with myringotomy and placebo. In 1988, a Japanese study found that children with OME who were randomized to a 4-week course of SCMC attained a significant decrease in the amount of effusion as determined by otoscopy and a significant improvement in pure-tone audiometric results when compared with placebo-treated controls (Kumazawa and Ushiro, 1988). However, in a double-blind prospective study by Ramsden and colleagues (1977), the rate of resolution of glue ear was not significantly different in children with OME randomized to 3 months of either oral SCMC or placebo, contradicting the encouraging results of other reports.

In 1996, Pignataro and colleagues published a meta-analysis of 10 placebo-controlled trials evaluating the therapeutic relevance of SCMC therapy in children with OME. Using a new outcome measure ("overall clinical improvement") and a combined total of 430 subjects, it was calculated that children with OME receiving oral SCMC benefit approximately 2.3 times more often than similar patients receiving placebo. The rate of overall clinical improvement was 52% for subjects who received SCMC and 39% for subjects who received placebo.

Since the meta-analysis was published, two other clinical trials using cysteine derivatives in the treatment of children with OME have emerged. In a randomized, placebo-controlled study from Denmark, N-acetylcysteine was instilled into the middle ears of children at the time of tympanostomy tube placement and again on postoperative days 3 and 7 (Ovesen et al, 2000). N-Acetylcysteine is believed to possess anti-inflammatory and antioxidative properties in addition to its mucolytic properties. Although there was no difference in the rate of tube otorrhea, the rate of recurrent OME necessitating tympanostomy reinsertion was significantly less (14%) in patients who had been treated with topical N-acetylcysteine versus placebo (37%). In another double-blind, randomized, placebo-controlled trial from the United Kingdom, children with chronic OME who received 6 weeks of oral SCMC were 1.68 times more likely to experience resolution of the effusion at an 8-week follow-up when compared with patients treated with placebo (Commins et al, 2000).

The therapeutic potential of cysteine derivatives in children with OME has inspired multiple clinical trials spanning the past four decades. However, this form of adjuvant therapy has failed to achieve widespread popularity, most likely owing to the fact that its modest success may not be dramatic enough to significantly impact disease outcome on a large scale. Commins and colleagues (2000) stated that anything less than an additional 20% improvement on the background resolution of chronic OME is not clinically important; thus, there is not sufficient evidence to support widespread use of SCMC in the clinical setting.

Surfactant Therapy

In recent years, a multitude of reports have established the presence of surfactant, a complex mixture of lipids, phospholipids, and proteins, in the eustachian tube and middle ear of animals and humans (McGuire, 2002). Traditionally, surfactant has been thought to function in the eustachian tube as a surface tension-lowering agent (Flisberg et al, 1963), leading to a reduction in eustachian tube opening pressure, better middle ear aeration, and reduction of middle ear effusion (McGuire, 2002). Surfactant may also function as an antiadherent agent and is known to have promacrophage, prophagocytic, and anti-inflammatory properties (McGuire, 2002). Multiple animal studies have established a clear relationship between recovery time from experimental acute otitis media and surfactant administration (McGuire, 2002).

Only two studies have investigated the potential therapeutic role of surfactant-stimulating oral medications in otitis media in human subjects, and the results have not been uniform. In a prospective, double-blind, placebo-controlled study from Italy, children with SOM who were treated with 15 days of oral ambroxol (a product stimulating synthesis of phospholipids in vivo) were found to have significantly greater improvement in audiometric and tympanometric results and in resolution of the subjective sensation of ear "occlusion" when compared with the placebo group (Passàli and Zavattini, 1987). The degree of improvement of opacification of the tympanic membrane, however, was similar between the two groups. In another randomized, double-blind, placebo-controlled study from Sweden, children with OME who were treated with 2 weeks of oral terbutaline (a β2-selective agonist known to cause secretion of surfactant from alveolar type II cells and possibly from the eustachian tube) were found to have no significant difference in clinical outcome when compared with the placebo group (Malm and White, 1992). Although no clinical studies describing topical application of surfactant have been published, it has at least been theorized that surfactant ear drops could be used after tympanostomy tube placement to help counteract oxygen-mediated changes in the middle ear (McGuire, 2002). Also, surfactant nasal spray is a potential avenue of exploration, although clinical studies are lacking.

Anti-inflammatory Medications

The nonspecific inflammatory changes in the middle ear mucosa of subjects with OME may be initiated and perpetuated by multiple agents, including bacteria, lipopolysaccharides, arachidonic acid metabolites, primary cytokines (interleukin-1β, tumor necrosis factor-α), and oxygen-derived free radicals produced by inflammatory cells (Giebink et al, 1990; Ovesen et al, 2000; Testa et al, 2001). These findings have led to experimental investigations into the potential therapeutic benefits of anti-inflammatory agents in OME, such as ibuprofen (a nonsteroidal anti-inflammatory agent), glutathione (an extracellular antioxidant), kampo medicine (an anti-inflammatory Japanese traditional herbal medicine), and ozone.

Ibuprofen

Ibuprofen is a nonsteroidal anti-inflammatory agent that inhibits cyclooxygenase, the enzyme that converts arachidonic acid to the direct precursors of prostaglandins (Giebink et al, 1990). The middle ear mucosa is capable of producing prostaglandins, and increased concentrations of prostaglandins and leukotrienes have been found in experimental serous and purulent middle ear effusions (Giebink et al, 1990). There is only one prospective, randomized study investigating the potential role of ibuprofen in the treatment of chronic OME in the literature, and that study failed to demonstrate any improvement in the rate of resolution or relapse of middle ear effusion when ibuprofen was compared with trimethoprim-sulfamethoxazole,

prednisone, and no treatment (Giebink et al, 1990). One reason for ibuprofen's lack of clinical effectiveness in resolving chronic middle ear effusions may be attributable to its inability to inhibit the production of the lipoxygenase metabolites of arachidonic acid (leukotrienes), which may themselves contribute to chronic middle ear inflammation (Giebink et al, 1990). The only beneficial effect that ibuprofen has been shown to possess in otitis media is a significant reduction in otalgia (but not an improvement in otoscopic findings) in children with AOM when compared with placebo (Bertin et al, 1996).

Glutathione

In a prospective, randomized study from Italy, children with chronic OME who received 2 weeks of nasal aerosolized glutathione (GSH), an extracellular antioxidant, demonstrated significant improvement in otoscopic, audiometric, and tympanometric findings at 1 and 3 months of follow-up (Testa et al, 2001). At 3 months of follow-up, 67% of GSH patients and 8% of placebo patients showed clinical improvement. It was concluded that after its introduction into the nasal cavity, GSH allows for clearance of middle ear effusion owing to its antioxidant effects.

Kampo Medicine

In Japan, kampo is known for its anti-inflammatory properties. It has been reported to inhibit the activity of inflammatory mediators such as prostaglandins, immune complexes, complement, and cellular mediated responses (Ikeda and Takasaka, 1998). The effectiveness of kampo medicine in the treatment of OME, however, has yet to be convincingly demonstrated. In an open trial from Japan, children with SOM were treated with oral kampo medicine for 4 weeks, following which 15% recovered normal hearing and 40% recovered normal tympanometry (Ikeda and Takasaka, 1988). No controls were included. In another Japanese trial, the rate of resolution of middle ear effusion in children with OME following initial myringotomy was similar between groups that had been randomized to 4 weeks of either oral kampo medicine or SCMC (Majima et al, 1990).

Conclusion

All of the adjuvant therapies for OME discussed herein represent creative treatment attempts targeting specific abnormalities associated with this disease of multifactorial pathogenesis. Although none of these novel approaches has yet to demonstrate any major therapeutic impact on OME, and although none has achieved widespread acceptance, further understanding of the pathologic changes of the middle ear in OME will certainly stimulate further experimental trials, one or more of which may someday yield new breakthroughs in therapy.

References

Auslander MM. Serous otitis media: treatment with injectable trypsin. Arch Otolaryngol 1958;67:24–7.

Bauer F. Treatment of "glue ear" by intratympanic injection of urea. J Laryngol Otol 1968;82:717–22.

Bertin L, Pons G, d'Athis P, et al. A randomized, double-blind, multicentre controlled trial of ibuprofen versus aceta-minophen and placebo for symptoms of acute otitis media in children. Fundam Clin Pharmacol 1996;10:387–92.

Commins DJ, Koay BC, Bates GJ, et al. The role of Mucodyne® in reducing the need for surgery in patients with persistent otitis media with effusion. Clin Otolaryngol 2000;25:274–9.

Flisberg K, Ingested PS, Ortegren U. The valve and 'locking' mechanism of the eustachian tube. Acta Otolaryngol (Stockh) 1963;182:57–68.

Gessert CF, Baumann ES, Senturia BH. The action of enzymes on human middle-ear effusions. Ann Otol Rhinol Laryngol 1960;69:936–55.

Giebink GS, Batalden PB, Le CT, et al. A controlled trial comparing three treatments for chronic otitis media with effusion. Pediatr Infect Dis J 1990;9:33–40.

Ikeda K, Takasaka T. Treatment of secretory otitis media with kampo medicine. Arch Otorhinolaryngol 1988;245:234–6.

Khan JA, Marcus P, Cummings SW. S-Carboxymethylcysteine in otitis media with effusion (a double-blind study). J Laryngol Otol 1981;95:995–1001.

Kumazawa T, Ushiro K. Clinical evaluation of S-CMC syrup applied in the treatment of otitis media with effusion. Acta Otolaryngol Suppl (Stockh) 1988;458:56–62.

Majima Y, Takeuchi K, Sakakura Y. Effects of myringotomy and orally administered drugs on viscosity and elasticity of middle-ear effusions from children with otitis media with effusion. Acta Otolaryngol Suppl (Stockh) 1990;471:66–72.

Malm L, White P. Beta-agonists and surfactant in eustachian tube function. Acta Otolaryngol Suppl (Stockh) 1992;493:133–6.

Mawson SR. Myringotomy, α-chymotrypsin and reverse politzerization for "glue" ears. J Laryngol Otol 1967;81:147–50.

McGuire JF. Surfactant in the middle ear and eustachian tube: a review. Int J Pediatr Otorhinolaryngol 2002;66:1–15.

Ovesen T, Felding JU, Tommerup B, et al. Effect of N-acetylcysteine on the incidence of recurrence of otitis media with effusion and reinsertion of ventilation tubes. Acta Otolaryngol Suppl (Stockh) 2000;543:79–81.

Passàli D, Zavattini G. Multicenter study on the treatment of secretory otitis media with ambroxol: importance of a surface-tension-lowering substance. Respiration 1987;1 Suppl:52–9.

Pignataro O, Pignataro LD, Gallus G, et al. Otitis media with effusion and S-carboxymethylcysteine and/or its lysine salt: a critical overview. Int J Pediatr Otorhinolaryngol 1996;35:231–41.

Ramsden RT, Moffat DA, Gibson WPR, Jay MM. S-Carboxymethylcysteine in the treatment of glue ear: a double blind trial. J Laryngol Otol 1977;91:847–51.

Taylor PH, Dareshani N. S-Carboxy-methyl-cysteine syrup in secretory otitis media. Br J Clin Pract 1975;29:177–80.

Testa B, Testa D, Mesolella M, et al. Management of chronic otitis media with effusion: the role of glutathione. Laryngoscope 2001;111:1486–9.

Chapter 37

Autoinflation for the Treatment of Otitis Media with Effusion

Cuneyt M. Alper, MD

Otitis media with effusion (OME) has been a treatment challenge in the pediatric population. There has been a marginal response to medical management with antibiotics. Knowledge of the crucial role of eustachian tube (ET) dysfunction in the development and persistence of OME has led to exploration of alternative methods of ventilation of the middle ear (ME). Myringotomy results in reaccumulation of the effusion after healing of the tympanic membrane (TM), but placement of ventilation tubes has been the method to maintain aeration of the ME, which is particularly important in chronic OME. Significant morbidity associated with the disease, its complications and sequelae, and placement of ventilation tubes has stimulated efforts to seek alternative noninvasive approaches to ventilate the ME.

Previous Studies

The idea of forcing air through the ET by autoinsufflation to ventilate the ME is three centuries old. Politzer developed an insufflation bulb with a nasal olive applicator 100 years ago. In 1962, Gottschalk (1962) suggested treatment of "serous otitis" using a continuous source of compressed air, claiming that a Politzer bulb would not provide sufficient pressure and volume. He directly visualized the TM during inflation to monitor the success of insufflation. He also used pneumotoscopy to drain effusion down the ET by repeated inward displacement of the TM with positive pressure, which he termed "pneumomassage." He applied this method to serous otitis media cases and achieved an 81.5% success in clearing the fluid for a period of 1 month or longer. Whereas children 12 years of age and older and adults had a 92.6% success rate, in children younger than 12 years, removal of fluid with this method was only 59.2% successful. Not being a popular method among the pediatric population in

whom OME is prevalent, alternative functional and appealing devices have been designed. A carnival blower was introduced for maintaining ME ventilation in children by Hunt-Williams in 1968. He monitored the achieved pressure with a blowmanometer and the opening of the ET by an otophone. Although intermittent "catarrhal" cases responded quickly to his treatment, he found that "secretory otitis" cases needed prolonged treatment or application of a balloon to the nosepiece to achieve higher pressures. Shea (1971) used concurrent swallowing of water to close the soft palate while squeezing a rubber nasal bulb to facilitate the opening of the ET. Misurya (1975) presented a physiologic method of ET inflation by the patient squeezing the inflated cheeks that coincided with the late phase of swallowing. In 1977, Fraser compared autoinflation using the carnival blower introduced by Hunt-Williams with topical decongestant and oral antihistamine-decongestant agents in a clinical trial. No difference in middle ear effusion (MEE) between groups was seen in that study with the application of any combination of these treatments for 6 weeks.

Schwartz and colleagues (1978) monitored the middle ear pressure (MEP) with a tympanometer for 30 minutes after the insufflation of ears with the Shea method and demonstrated that ears with high negative pressures failed to maintain postinflation pressures. Bylander and colleagues (1983) tested the efficacy of mouth-to-nose inflation and found that 29% of the children could not inflate their MEs. Chan and colleagues (1987) introduced an autoinflation unit that consisted of an anesthesia mask connected to an airflow meter. A clinical trial with this instrument demonstrated a lack of efficacy (Chan and Bluestone, 1989). Stangerup and colleagues (Stangerup and colleagues, 1992; Stangerup and Tos, 1994) reported 64% improvement for up to 2 weeks in a clinical trial in children who used a balloon mounted to a nasal tube, the

Otovent (Invotec International Inc., Jacksonville, FL) device (Figures 37-1 and 37-2). Brooker and McNiece (1992), on the other hand, reported a worse outcome in the autoinflation group that used a carnival blower attached to a balloon. The Otovent device was used in another trial by Blanshard and colleagues (1993) and demonstrated both otoscopic and tympanometric improvement at 1 month and only otoscopic improvement at 2 months but no improvement at 3 months.

Factors Influencing Outcome

The results of autoinsufflation for treatment or prevention of OME have been highly variable. This variability in outcome may be attributable to the instrument, technique, small sample sizes, or different study populations with differing characteristics or severity of the disease.

The common concept in these methods was to achieve high enough nasopharyngeal pressure to open the ET with a safe, effective, feasible, and appealing method for the subjects. By introducing different methods and instruments, authors implied that the key to success lay behind the technique of insufflation. On the surface, different instruments to open the ET could make a difference. However, these devices have more common features than differences. First of all, they all rely on the individual's ability to comply with the method. All have the aim of increasing the nasopharyngeal pressure above the threshold for ET opening. Although regular blow-out devices raise the nasopharyngeal pressure up to 30 mm Hg, the addition of a balloon to this blow-out increases the ability of the device up to 60 mm Hg (Hunt-Williams, 1968). Investigators claimed to provide an appealing form (blow-

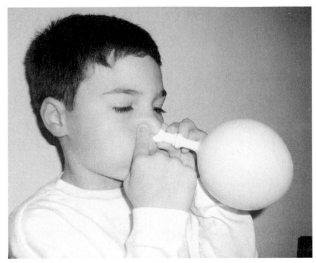

FIGURE 37-2. A 6-year-old child blowing the balloon with his nose while pinching his other nostril.

outs or balloons) or function (anesthesia mask with a flowmeter) to the target population. Some preferred to reduce the opening pressure of the ET by adding an act of synchronous swallowing (Shea, 1971). However, the basic principle and mechanism of action of these devices did not differ from each other. Therefore, the device types may not be the likely cause of the differences in clinical outcomes in those studies.

The difference in the ability to autoinsufflate has clearly been related to age. Bylander and colleagues (1983) have shown that only 71% of normal children could voluntarily increase the MEP compared with 100% of adults. Young children have difficulty in ventilating their ME with autoinflation. A wide range of variability in the ability to perform autoinflation is another potential bias in the group assignment of the study subjects. Assessment of the successful opening of the ET has therefore been part of the methodology in some studies. For this purpose, methods such as auscultation, otoscopy (Gottschalk, 1962), otophone (Hunt-Williams, 1968), tympanometry (Fraser et al, 1977), and tubosonometry (Chan et al, 1987; Chan and Bluestone, 1989) have been used. Inability to open the ET is a well-known etiologic factor in the development of OME in the first place and would a priori restrict the outcome of autoinflation treatment. When Chan and colleagues (1987) prescreened subjects for their ability to achieve tubal opening and stratified them equally in the study and control groups, there were no differences in the outcome between the study groups.

It was noticed long ago that all clinical types of MEE were not the same, and a different response to the treatment could be observed with insufflation related to the type and severity of the disease (Hunt-Williams, 1968). In fact, a course of treatment that could be sufficient for "intermittent catarrhal" or "mild secretory otitis" was not

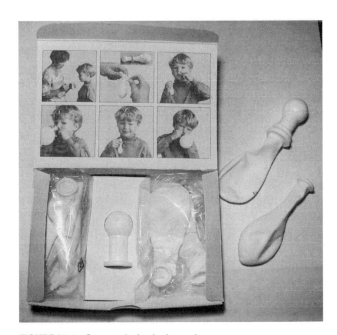

FIGURE 37-1. Otovent device in the package.

enough for "severe secretory otitis" or "cleft palate deafness," as noted by Hunt-Williams (1968). This potential difference within the target population may be the selection bias in various studies. Also, multifactorial etiopathogenesis and the variable course of the disease may limit the ability to assess the efficacy of this treatment.

Blanshard and colleagues (1993) pointed out better results in the group compliant with treatment compared with the low-compliance group. However, the high-compliance group also had a lower number of type B tympanograms and more type C2 tympanograms at entry. This supports the point that different outcomes may be related to the severity of the disease. It is also interesting that subjects who entered the study in the winter months had lower compliance with treatment. Worse course of the disease and higher rates for recurrence in the winter may have led to negative reinforcement for compliance. On the other hand, subjects who feel the difference, which is more likely in summer, may be more compliant and therefore may be more eager to continue their treatment until the completion of the study.

In most studies that claim success, autoinsufflation lacks long-term success. In the Stangerup and colleagues' study, the duration of improvement was as short as 2 weeks (Stangerup et al, 1992; Stangerup and Tos, 1994). Although all of the children, including the nonresponders at 2 weeks, continued the treatment for another 2 weeks, there was no longer a statistical difference at the 4-week visit. Also, the study by Blanshard and colleagues (1993) revealed early improvement but failure later.

Safety of the insufflation is important in its applicability to the treatment of patients. No known serious complications have been associated with nasal insufflation of the ME. However, the possibility of causing acute OM by forcing nasopharyngeal secretions with virus and bacteria into the ME has been a concern. Nasal decongestants and suctioning of the nasopharynx as well as antibiotic prophylaxis for the first 3 days of autoinsufflation treatment were recommended because of the potential adverse outcome (Gottschalk, 1962). Although not stated by the authors, a worse outcome in the autoinsufflation group compared with the control group in a study brings this possibility to mind (Brooker and McNiece, 1992).

Possible Mechanisms of Failure

The impression of improvement as long as the treatment is continued and recurrence soon after stopping the treatment may be consistent with the observation of Gottschalk (1962), that is, keeping the ME clear by repeatedly blowing the fluid away into the mastoid.

Insufflation may displace the effusion in the ME to the more distal and peripheral air cells within the temporal bone. Gottschalk (1962) described this observation and modified his method to otoscopically monitor and displace the fluid with pneumomassage. He described insufflation only as the starting point of the treatment. Displacement of the TM with pneumatic otoscopy was then supposed to redistribute the fluid, which may have been blown into the aditus and mastoid antrum. He observed that the tympanum would frequently empty completely on the first insufflation and would then fill again from the mastoid following several minutes of pneumomassage. It is possible that the newly created gas cushion in the ME may continue to keep the effusion in the distant regions. Some authors suggested that the positive pressure created with insufflation would naturally result in displacement of any residual fluid down the ET with the next swallow (Shea, 1971). The mechanism by which the insufflated gas remains in the ME and the fluid drains has not been addressed.

Interesting observations were also made by Schwartz and coworkers (1978) when they followed the change in MEP after insufflation. Even though this observation was limited to only 30 minutes, the changes that occurred over that period in the insufflated ears are extremely important in terms of understanding the possible mechanism of failure. The ears that had relatively low negative pressures maintained the postinsufflation levels over the 30-minute period. On the other hand, the more negative the baseline MEP was in an ear, the sooner the pressure returned to preinsufflation levels.

There are some possible explanations for this rapid drop in MEP, which occurred in the study conducted by Schwartz and colleagues (1978). Insufflated gas may have leaked back into the nasopharynx through the ET. This explanation is not likely because postinsufflation pressure levels were not high enough to passively open the ET. A second possibility is reduction of MEP because of the gradual redistribution of the insufflated gas bolus from a limited initial volume around the anterior mesotympanum to a relatively larger volume in the entire ME and mastoid gas cells. This may be possible because of the physical properties of fluids and gas, surface tension, and limitations of the anatomy formed by narrow recesses, tendons, and membranes. Limited volume of gas bolus within the temporal bone may initially appear as high MEP and also will give an impression that the ME was sufficiently insufflated. However, the same amount of gas bolus may gradually bubble out to the distal portions of the temporal bone, resulting in a rapid decrease in the measured MEP.

This phenomenon was observed during serial magnetic resonance imaging (MRI) in a controlled trial of insufflation to prevent development of MEE in monkeys with unilaterally paralyzed tensor veli palatini muscles (Alper and Doyle, 1999b). In that study, an animal with tympanometric improvement demonstrated little amount of effusion in the ME, whereas the mastoid was filled, giving a false impression of resolution. This animal subsequently progressed to flat tympanograms. In a similar trial in the monkey model, a set of pre- and postin-sufflation MRIs clearly demonstrated displacement of effusion from ME to mastoid cells (Alper et al, 2000).

Summary of the Literature

In summary, previous experience with autoinflation in the literature demonstrates that autoinflation methods and techniques (1) may not make a clinically important difference; (2) cannot be successfully performed in all ages; (3) may not be effective in all types or durations of effusion; (4) may have an increased risk for viral or bacterial inoculation; and (5) may lead to improvement of short duration.

With knowledge of the controversial results on autoinflation in the literature and the possible role of differences in the study population, methodology, techniques of insufflation, and modes of monitoring the outcome, and having done several studies on monkeys and human subjects on the mechanism of efficacy and failure (Alper and Doyle, 1999a; Alper and Doyle, 1999b; Alper et al, 1996; Alper et al, 1999; Alper et al, 2000), a clinical trial of the efficacy of autoinflation with and without steroids in children with chronic OME is currently being conducted at Children's Hospital of Pittsburgh. Because the study is not complete and the results are not available, discussion of the study is not the subject of this chapter.

Potential Indications

1. In chronic OME, with the duration of bilateral MEE longer than 3 months, there is little evidence that effusion will resolve with autoinflation or, if it resolves, that the improvement will last. The outcome of the study that is currently under way may change my practice, but, currently, if they are not eligible for the study, I recommend ventilation tubes for patients with chronic OME.
2. When the duration of OME is less than 3 months (if bilateral or less than 6 months if unilateral), I may consider autoinflation as an alternative to waiting if the patient has had at least one course of antibiotics in the past for this episode of OME.
3. If the season is late spring or summer, there is a higher chance of spontaneous resolution and a higher chance of possible resolution with autoinflation. With the thought of a better chance for autoinflation in a favorable season, I may consider autoinflation as an alternative to ventilation tubes.
4. If a child has recurrent episodes of OME with durations not long enough to warrant ventilation tubes with each episode, and if there is no significant hearing loss or other risk factors such as speech delay, I may consider autoinflation.
5. When there is a contraindication for ventilation tube

placement or anesthesia, I may consider the possibility of autoinflation as an alternative.
6. If the child wants to participate in water sports and there is concern regarding the high risk for otorrhea after ventilation placement, or if the child has developed this complication in the past, I consider autoinflation.
7. Some parents may inquire about the alternatives, mostly in children with a history of multiple sets of tubes. Although I present the alternatives, including watchful waiting, I offer tubes as the standard of care for chronic OME.
8. Another population that may benefit from autoinflation is patients with ET dysfunction without MEE. Although this condition does not directly apply to patients discussed in this chapter, some individuals may suffer discomfort owing to either chronic negative MEP or intermittent underpressures after episodes of upper respiratory infection, which may proceed to MEE. This population may benefit by using a device for autoinflation or after learning how to perform the Valsalva maneuver to equalize their MEP with the atmospheric pressure. Similarly, in the risk of barotrauma, either related to aviation, scuba diving, or hyperbaric oxygen treatment, autoinflation may be a measure to prevent the development of OME.

Patient Selection

Naturally, these considerations of autoinflation are for selected patients who would use and may benefit from this treatment. Appropriate identification of the patients capable of performing the method and who may be compliant enough to anticipate a response is crucial to avoid the frustration of patients, parents, and clinicians.

One of the critical factors in the outcome seems to be the ability and willingness to perform the autoinflation with the recommended method. Providing a test or practice autoinflation device in the physician's office may allow parents and the child to see and understand the concept and the method much better than long conversations or written material. Explanation of the concept with a device would allow screening the parents and patients, who may find this treatment interesting and promising. Actual practice with the device would then eliminate the patients who would not use the device effectively to open the ET.

I use Otovent as the device for autoinflation because it is simple, user friendly, available (through most pharmacies), and safe (limiting the highest possible pressure achieved); is studied the most; and has a potential benefit according to some studies (Blanshard et al, 1993; Brooker and McNiece, 1992; Stangerup and Tos, 1994).

I instruct parents to keep the nasal probe tip clean, personalize the use to eliminate any cross-contamination between children, avoid use when sick and with increased nasal secretions, and immediately stop the treatment with autoinflation and seek medical advice if use of the device is associated with ear pain. I suggest inflating the balloon three times a day, when possible, each time once on each nostril. I suggest continuing treatment for at least 1 month to avoid a false improvement and an early recurrence.

I treat my patients with autoinflation relatively rarely. Perhaps the limited eligibility and lack of parental enthusiasm impact the number of patients who receive this treatment as well as the enrolment rate for the study that I am conducting. The study will hopefully clarify the controversy regarding this treatment and lead to better and more appropriate treatment of patients.

Disclaimer

The author does not have any relationship with the producers or distributors of the Otovent.

References

Alper CM, Doyle WJ. MRI validation of the accuracy of tympanometric gradient for the diagnosis of OME. Br J Audiol 1999a; 33:223–9.

Alper CM, Doyle WJ. Repeated middle ear inflation does not prevent otitis media with effusion in a monkey model. Laryngoscope 1999b;109:1074–80.

Alper CM, Swarts JD, Doyle WJ. Middle ear inflation for the diagnosis of otitis media with effusion. Auris Nasus Larynx 1999; 26:479–86.

Alper CM, Swarts JD, Doyle WJ. Prevention of otitis media with effusion by repeated air inflation in a monkey model. Arch Otolaryngol Head Neck Surg 2000;126:609–14.

Alper CM, Tabari R, Seroky JT, Doyle WJ. Magnetic resonance imaging of otitis media with effusion caused by functional obstruction of the eustachian tube. Ann Otol Rhinol Laryngol 1996;106:422–31.

Blanshard JD, Maw AR, Bawden R. Conservative treatment of otitis media with effusion by autoinflation of the middle ear. Clin Otolaryngol 1993;18:188–92.

Brooker DS, McNiece A. Autoinflation in the treatment of the glue ear in children. Clin Otolaryngol 1992;17:289–90.

Bylander A, Tjernstom O, Ivarsson A. Pressure opening and closing functions of the eustachian tube by inflation and deflation in children and adults with normal ears. Acta Otolaryngol (Stockh) 1983;96:255–68.

Chan KH, Bluestone CD. Lack of efficacy of middle-ear inflation: treatment of otitis media with effusion in children. Otolaryngol Head Neck Surg 1989;100:317–23.

Chan KH, Cantekin EI, Karnavas WJ, Bluestone CD. Autoinflation of eustachian tube in young children. Laryngoscope 1987;97: 668–74.

Fraser JG, Mehta M, Fraser PM. The medical treatment of secretory otitis media. A clinical trial of three commonly used regimes. J Laryngol Otol 1977;91:757–65.

Gottschalk GH. Serous otitis: treatment by controlled middle ear inflation. Laryngoscope 1962;72:1379–90.

Hunt-Williams R. A method for maintaining middle-ear ventilation in children. J Laryngol Otol 1968;82:921–6.

Misurya V. Physiologic eustachian tube inflation. Arch Otolaryngol 1975;101:730–2.

Schwartz DM, Schwartz RH, Redfield NP. Treatment of negative middle ear pressure and serous otitis media with Politzer's technique. An old procedure revisited. Arch Otolaryngol 1978;104:487–90.

Shea JJ. Autoinflation treatment of serous otitis media in children. J Laryngol Otol 1971;85:1254–8.

Stangerup SE, Sederberg-Olsen J, Balle V. Autoinflation as a treatment of secretory otitis media. A randomized controlled study. Arch Otolaryngol Head Neck Surg 1992;118:149–52.

Stangerup SE, Tos M. Autoinflation in the treatment of eustachian tube dysfunction, secretory otitis media and its sequelae. In: Mogi G, editor. Proceedings of the Second Extraordinary International Symposium on Recent Advances in Otitis Media. Amsterdam: Kugler; 1994. p. 759–63.

Chapter 38

Myringotomy and Tympanostomy Tubes for Otitis Media with Effusion

Charles D. Bluestone, MD

Myringotomy with tympanostomy tube insertion is the most common minor surgical procedure performed in children and is frequently performed in the adult population. It is estimated that about 550,000 patients younger than 15 years of age receive tympanostomy tubes per year, but approximately 14,000 individuals 15 to 44 years of age also have this surgery every year. The indications for placement of tympanostomy tubes are the following: (1) chronic/recurrent otitis media with effusion (OME), (2) recurrent acute otitis media (AOM), (3) suppurative complications of otitis media (OM), (3) eustachian tube dysfunction, and (4) prevention of barotrauma (Bluestone and Lee, 1999). The most common of these indications are for chronic OME, prevention of recurrent AOM, or both. In this chapter, I discuss only the indications for tympanostomy tube placement for OME that is chronic or is frequently recurrent in both children and adults. Related to my discussion is the question of the effect of OME on the ear and the child when the disease becomes chronic.

Does chronic middle ear effusion (MEE) cause any long-term sequelae in children because of impairment of hearing? Much has been written about the handicap imposed on the severely hearing-impaired child, but less is known about the effects on the young child of the mild and fluctuating hearing loss associated with OM. The results of many studies of the association of OM and development of speech, language, and cognitive abilities have been reviewed by Stool and associates (1994). Some of these studies identified associations of recurrent OME and lower scores on tests of vocabulary, auditory comprehension, and language skills. Other studies failed to find significant differences among children with and without histories of prolonged time spent with MEE. A more recent study by Paradise and colleagues (2000) failed to find any difference in speech, language, and cognition in those children who had had early tympanostomy tube insertion compared with those whose operation was delayed for 3 to 6 months.

Even though there is still doubt as to the possible effect of hearing loss owing to OME on child development, there is an effect on vestibular, balance, and motor functions even in the absence of MEE at the time of testing (Casselbrant et al, 2000). Also, structural sequelae within the middle ear owing to long-lasting MEE are possible. These include ossicular discontinuity and fixation, although the degree of risk in the individual child is unknown.

Results of Clinical Trials

Three important randomized clinical trials have addressed the question of the efficacy of myringotomy and the insertion of tympanostomy tubes for the treatment of chronic OME:

1. Gates and colleagues (1987) evaluated 578 Texas children in a trial that randomly assigned children 4 to 8 years of age who had chronic OME unresponsive to antimicrobial therapy into one of four surgical treatment groups: (1) myringotomy, (2) myringotomy and tympanostomy tube insertion, (3) adenoidectomy and myringotomy, and (4) adenoidectomy, myringotomy, and tympanostomy tube insertion. The study did not include a control group of no surgery, but all three of the other treatments did statistically better than myringotomy, without tympanostomy tube placement (Table 38-1).

2. We conducted a study in 109 children who had chronic OME that had been unresponsive to antimicrobial therapy and randomly assigned subjects to receive either myringotomy, myringotomy and tympanostomy tube insertion, or no surgery (control) (Mandel et al, 1989). During this 3-year trial, in which subjects

TABLE 38-1. Effectiveness of Various Treatments in 578 Children with Chronic Otitis Media with Effusion

Outcome*	Myringotomy	Myringotomy and Tube Insertion	Adenoidectomy and Myringotomy	Adenoidectomy, Myringotomy, and Tube Insertion
Time with effusion (%)	49.1	34.9	30.2	25.8
Time with hearing loss† (%)	37.5	30.4	22.0	2.4
Median time to first recurrence (d)	54	222	92	240
Number of surgical retreatments	66	36	17	17

Adapted from Gates GA et al (1987).
*During 2-year follow-up.
†Hearing loss ≥ 20 dB.

were evaluated monthly and whenever an ear, nose, and throat illness occurred, patients who had tympanostomy tubes inserted had less middle ear disease and better hearing than either children who had only myringotomy or those subjects in whom no surgery had been performed. In addition, half of the subjects in the myringotomy group had to have tympanostomy tubes inserted during the first year of the trial owing to an excessive number of myringotomies to control their disease. Likewise, half of the subjects in the control group required tympanostomy tube insertion during the course of the year because of development of "significant" hearing loss associated with their chronic MEE, even though none of the children had this degree of hearing loss when they entered the trial.

Approximately 50% of the children, however, had at least one bout of otorrhea when the tubes were in place, but these episodes were usually easily treated and short lasting, although two children did develop chronic otorrhea that required intravenous antimicrobial therapy to eliminate the drainage. In addition, one subject who had tubes inserted eventually had to have bilateral tympanoplasties to repair chronic tympanic membrane perforations that persisted after the tubes spontaneously extruded. Myringotomy (without tympanostomy tube insertion) provided no major advantage over no surgery (ie, control) regarding the percentage of time with MEE, number of bouts of AOM, and the number of subsequent surgical procedures. We concluded that myringotomy and

tympanostomy tube placement provided more effusion-free time and better hearing than either myringotomy without tympanostomy tube insertion or no surgery, but some patients who received tubes did develop otorrhea, and perforation was a problem in one of the children. Because the researchers considered the interpretation of this trial to be difficult owing to the complexities of the design, the protocol was revised and a second clinical trial was conducted.

3. We conducted a second trial with 111 children who were randomized into the same three groups as in the first study: myringotomy, myringotomy and tympanostomy tube insertion, and no surgery (control) (Mandel et al, 1992). As in the first trial, subjects were re-examined at least every month for 3 years. Similar outcomes were observed in this trial as were reported in the first study. Again, subjects in the myringotomy and tube group had less time with MEE and better hearing than either those children who had only a myringotomy performed or in the group that had had no surgery (Table 38-2). Similar to the initial trial, otorrhea occurred in 41% of those who were randomized to the tympanostomy tube group, and three subjects developed chronic perforations after the tubes extruded; two of these children eventually required a tympanoplasty when the perforation failed to spontaneously heal after 2 years.

We concluded, based on these two randomized clinical trials that evaluated a total of 220 subjects, that for

TABLE 38-2. Morbidity for First Year of Randomized Trial of Myringotomy, Myringotomy and Tympanostomy Tube, and No Surgery (Control) in 109 Pittsburgh Infants and Children with Chronic Otitis Media with Effusion

Outcome Measure	Treatment Groups			Statistically Significant Difference
	1: No Surgery (n = 35)	2: Myringotomy (n = 38)	3: Myringotomy and Tympanostomy Tube (n = 36)	
Treatment failure (proportion of subjects)	0.56	0.70	0.06	Yes*
Acute otitis media (episodes/person-year)	0.95	0.81	0.23	< .001†
Middle ear effusion (proportion of time)	0.64	0.61	0.17	< .001†

Adapted from Mandel EM et al (1992).
*Actuarial rate: 90% confidence intervals for group 3 vs groups 1 and 2.
†For group 1 vs group 3.

children who have OME that is unresponsive to nonsurgical treatment and became chronic, myringotomy and tympanostomy tube insertion would be the first surgical procedure to perform as opposed to myringotomy alone. Even though Gates and colleagues (1987) recommended an adenoidectomy and myringotomy (without tympanostomy tube insertion) as "the initial surgical procedure," we recommended reserving adenoidectomy for those children who required another surgical procedure if OM recurred following extrusion of the initial tube. This recommendation was made because the study by Gates and colleagues in 1987 showed that adenoidectomy in their population was only somewhat better than myringotomy and tube and because in the two studies by Mandel and coworkers (1989, 1992), about 50% of the subjects required only one myringotomy and tube insertion during the 3-year trial, that is, adenoidectomy would not have been necessary. But if the child has significant nasal obstruction owing to obstructive adenoids, then adenoidectomy and myringotomy (with or without tube insertion) as an initial procedure are a reasonable option.

Advantages versus Disadvantages of Tympanostomy Tubes

These three clinical trials have shown that tympanostomy tube insertion can be beneficial in selected infants and children because middle ear disease is reduced and hearing is restored, although there are known complications and sequelae associated with the surgery. Kay and colleagues (2001) concluded from their meta-analysis that sequelae are common following tympanostomy tube placement but are usually only transient (16% of patients develop transient otorrhea in the immediate postoperative period and 26% later on) or cosmetic (tympanosclerosis or focal atrophy).

The advantages versus the disadvantages of the procedure can be related to certain physiologic and pathophysiologic aspects of the nasopharynx, eustachian tube, and middle ear and mastoid gas system that are related to the pathogenesis of OM. The eustachian tube has three important physiologic functions in relation to the middle ear–mastoid: (1) middle ear pressure regulation, (2) drainage of secretions down the eustachian tube, and (3) protection of the middle ear from the entrance of unwanted nasopharyngeal secretions (Bluestone and Klein, 2001). A patent tympanostomy tube would maintain ambient pressure within the middle ear and mastoid and provide adequate drainage both down the eustachian tube and through the tympanostomy tube into the external auditory canal. Therefore, two physiologic functions of the eustachian tube are fulfilled by the tympanostomy tube. However, the protective function of the eustachian tube is impaired by tympanostomy tube insertion because the middle ear is exposed to the ear canal, and

water contamination of the middle ear is a distinct possibility. Also, a tympanostomy tube violates the integrity of the middle ear cleft's physiologic middle ear gas cushion, which promotes reflux of nasopharyngeal secretions into the middle ear that can result in "reflux otitis media" and otorrhea (Bluestone, 1998).

The proven success of the tympanostomy tube placement in prevention of most, but not all, episodes of OM is most likely related to the tube's pressure regulation function of the middle ear. During an episode of an upper respiratory tract infection, there is inflammation of the nasopharynx and the nasopharyngeal end of the eustachian tube followed by negative pressure in the middle ear. This middle ear negative pressure can then lead to either aspiration of nasopharyngeal secretions (with virus and bacteria) into the middle ear or an accumulation of sterile fluid in the middle ear secondary to the negative pressure. Because a functioning tympanostomy tube maintains ambient pressure in the middle ear, the sequence of events that leads to MEE is prevented. Also, patients who have chronic eustachian tube obstruction (usually functional, ie, failure of pressure regulation), such as children with an unrepaired cleft palate, will have middle ear negative pressure and MEE. Thus, the tympanostomy tube prevents chronic negative pressure, which, in turn, prevents the transudation of effusion into the middle ear. But because the tympanostomy tube is not a substitute for a normal eustachian tube because the protective function is lost, reflux of nasopharyngeal secretions or contamination of the middle ear can result in OM.

Recommendations for Tympanostomy Tube Placement

Factors to be taken into account in the decision-making process to insert tympanostomy tubes for chronic MEE include duration of MEE, degree of hearing loss, type of MEE, presence of atelectasis/retraction pocket, and concurrent permanent hearing loss.

Duration of MEE

When bilateral OME is unresponsive to nonsurgical treatment, which should include a course of an antimicrobial agent, and persists for at least 3 months, insertion of tympanostomy tubes is a reasonable management option. This recommendation is made because natural history studies have indicated that approximately 90% of children who have OME will be effusion free in about 90 to 120 days. For children who have unilateral effusion, the duration can probably be extended to 6 months prior to consideration for tube placement because hearing is assumed to be good in the unaffected ear (Bluestone and Klein, 1995). For some children, the time of onset will not be known, but the parents may relate that hearing loss was present from a known date. Thus, the clinician can determine the duration by a "best guess." But when the duration is totally unknown at the time of diagnosis, the time of onset is when the diagnosis is made, and the child should be re-examined in 3 months.

Even though randomized clinical trials have not been reported that assessed the efficacy of tympanostomy tube placement in children who have had recurrent OME, in which each episode did not progress to the chronic stage, it seems reasonable to recommend tube insertion if the cumulative duration of effusion appears excessive, such as 6 or more cumulative months during the preceding year. Also, the presence of recurrent AOM, even when the criteria for placement of tympanostomy tubes are not met (eg, three or more episodes in 6 months or four or more in the preceding year, with at least one episode being recent), may signal the need for tympanostomy tube insertion at an earlier duration than 3 months of OME. In addition, the natural history of OME has not been systematically studied in children who have had one or more tympanostomy tube insertions in the past, but these patients are more severely affected with middle ear disease than those who are potential candidates for a first tube insertion. Thus, the duration of effusion probably should be shorter in these patients than those who never had a previous tympanostomy tube placement. Likewise, in children who have a known chronic eustachian tube obstruction, such as those who have a cleft palate and have had multiple tympanostomy tube procedures, the duration of recurrent OME will be less than the customary 3 months.

Degree of Hearing Loss

Elimination of chronic MEE that is asymptomatic, especially when significant hearing loss is absent, is still a subject of debate (Stool et al, 1994). All such children have some degree of conductive hearing loss if followed closely. Indeed, in the first clinical trial conducted by Mandel and coworkers (1989), patients with "significant" hearing loss were not randomized into the no surgery (control) group. However, half of these subjects developed "significant" hearing loss at the end of the first year, became "treatment failures," and had tympanostomy tubes inserted. At present, it seems to be reasonable to insert tympanostomy tubes in selected children to remove chronic effusion, restore hearing, and prevent possible complications and sequelae of chronic OME.

The clinical practice guideline *Managing Otitis Media with Effusion in Young Children*, by Stool and colleagues (1994), concluded that myringotomy and tympanostomy tube placement are an option to antimicrobial treatment when the duration of OME persists for longer than 3 months, is bilateral, and is associated with a hearing deficit (defined as 20 dB hearing threshold level or worse in the better hearing ear). Tympanostomy tube placement is recommended when the effusion meets the above criteria and persists for longer than 4 months. In contradis-

tinction to the recommendations of the guideline that limits tube insertion to those children who have bilateral chronic effusion and a bilateral hearing loss (greater than 20 dB), we recommend the procedure irrespective of the child's hearing assessed at one point in time (Bluestone and Klein, 1995).

Type of MEE

The type and amount of effusion thought to be within the middle ear cleft are factors in the decision to place a tympanostomy tube. When only a small amount of serous effusion is observed behind a translucent tympanic membrane, especially when an air-fluid level or bubbles are visualized, the clinician should observe and follow the patient rather than insert a tympanostomy tube. In contrast, a completely opaque, immobile tympanic membrane might indicate that a mucoid effusion is present that would benefit from a tube insertion. However, the degree of hearing loss is related to the amount of MEE rather than the viscosity of the effusion, that is, mucoid versus serous.

Presence of Atelectasis/Retraction Pocket

The presence of chronic atelectasis of the middle ear–tympanic membrane, especially when a retraction pocket is present, would signal the need to insert a tympanostomy tube to eliminate the effusion and restore the tympanic membrane to a more normal position. Earlier insertion than waiting the recommended 3 months may be indicated if the atelectasis is generalized and severe or the retraction pocket is deep. If the extent of the retraction pocket cannot be adequately determined by otomicroscopy with the aid of a pneumatic otoscope (Siegle or Bruening) in the outpatient setting, then the tympanostomy tube placement should be performed in a timely fashion and the extent of the retraction pocket can be more adequately assessed under general anesthesia. Taking advantage of nitrous oxide anesthesia, in an attempt to inflate the atelectatic tympanic membrane/retraction pocket, is an invaluable aid when these tympanic membrane abnormalities are present. Also, when the atelectatic tympanic membrane is attached to the incudostapedial joint, placement of a tympanostomy tube is more compelling than continued observation because erosion of the joint is a known sequela of this abnormality.

Concurrent Permanent Hearing Loss

When the patient has a concurrent permanent conductive hearing loss (eg, ossicular pathology, adhesions, or tympanosclerosis) or a sensorineural hearing loss, or when both types of hearing loss are present, insertion of tympanostomy tubes may be indicated earlier than the recommended duration of 3 months. Earlier placement should be considered when the patient relies on a hearing aid, which is not effective when hearing loss is worse owing to the MEE.

Mattsson C, Marklund SL, Hellström S. Application of oxygen free radical scavengers to diminish the occurrence of myringosclerosis. Ann Otol Rhinol Laryngol 1997b;106:513–8.

Olsson M, Dalsgaard CJ, Haegerstrand A, et al. Accumulation of T-lymphocytes and expression of interleukin-2 receptors in non-rheumatic stenotic aortic valves. J Am Coll Cardiol 1994;23:1162–70.

Rae D, Gatland DJ, Youngs R, Cook J. Aspiration of middle ear effusions prior to grommet insertion an etiological factor in tympanosclerosis. J Otolaryngol 1989;18:229–31.

Schiff M, Yoo TJ. Immunological aspects of otologic disease: an overview. Laryngoscope 1985;95:259–69.

Schilder AG. Assessment of complications of the condition and of the treatment of otitis media with effusion. Int J Pediatr Otorhinolaryngol 1999;49:247–51.

Spratley JE, Hellström SO, Mattsson CK, Pais-Clemente M. Topical ascorbic acid reduces myringosclerosis in perforated tympanic membranes. A study in the rat. Ann Otol Rhinol Laryngol 2001;110:585–91.

Tos M, Bonding P, Paulsen G. Tympanosclerosis of the drum in secretory otitis media after insertion of grommets: a prospective, comparative study. J Laryngol Otol 1983;97:489–96.

Chapter 40

Management of Otitis Media and Otitis Media with Effusion in the Speech-Delayed Child

Robert J. Ruben, MD, FACS, FAAP

Language delay or deviance is associated with and appears to be exacerbated by the hearing loss caused by otitis media (OM) and otitis media with effusion (OME). The recognition of language abnormality in a child with OM or OME is a critical factor in the decision as to what type of intervention and when an intervention should be taken. The specific association of OM and diminished language function was articulated and documented by Holm and Kunze (1969) in their landmark article, "The Effect of Chronic Otitis Media on Language and Speech Development."

Since then, numerous studies have examined various aspects of the effect of OM and the associated hearing loss on speech and language. There are two types of associated hearing loss. The least common is the effect of a permanent conductive loss as a result of destruction of a portion of the transformer mechanism of the middle ear. The most common is the temporary and intermittent conductive hearing loss associated with middle ear fluid: OME and/or severe retraction of the tympanic membrane. Studies of the temporary and intermittent form of hearing loss occurring in the first few years of life have reported an effect or lack of an effect on subsequent language depending on the populations examined, the severity of the hearing loss (duration and intensity), and the form of outcome measure used. When these reports are looked at as a whole, speech and language morbidity results from the intermittent and temporary hearing loss of OME (Ruben, 2002). The severity of the resultant language disorder depends on the amount and length of time of hearing loss—the disease vector—and, what appears to be most critical, the child's intrinsic qualities and extrinsic linguistic environment—the condition(s) of the host (Ruben, 2003). A child with either a cognitive and/or a sensory deficit is at greater risk for deviant lin-guistic development than an otherwise healthy child. Likewise, the child who is linguistically deprived will have substantial linguistic deviance associated with OME during the beginning of life when compared with the child reared in a similar environment who did not have OME and the associated hearing loss (Wallace et al, 1996). The effect of a poor linguistic environment is also found when different populations are studied using identical metrics for ascertainment and outcome (Shriberg et al, 2000).

Incidence

The incidence of childhood ear infection with resultant OME is essentially 100%. However, only about 10% of children will have a residual of OME for more than 4 to 6 weeks. About 5 to 6% of children will have multiple recurrent episodes of acute otitis media (AOM) and then associated OME. Approximately 5 to 10% of all children are at risk of having prolonged periods of OME and hearing loss. This alone may not be sufficient to result in substantial linguistic deviance. The effect of the vector—OME and hearing loss—must be evaluated in regard to the susceptibility of the host. The incidence of the more common intrinsic conditions that make a child more susceptible to the effect of OME, such as specific language impairment, ranges from 5 to 8% of the population. Additionally, there are all of the other sensory and cognitive disorders, such as sensorineural hearing loss, visual impairment, or mental retardation, that exacerbate the effect of OME on language development. The incidence of these disorders is in the range of 10% of the population. There is no estimate of the incidence of inadequate linguistic environments, but this situation is mostly likely, but not exclusively, associated with social dysfunction, as seen in poverty and foster care. The child at risk for deviant speech and language development from OME is the child who has both long-standing hearing loss (vector) and intrinsic and/or extrinsic risk factors (a susceptible host).

Diagnosis

The clinician has the opportunity to prevent probable adverse speech and language outcomes from OME by recognition of that patient who is both susceptible (host) and has considerable OME (vector). The importance of this form of preventive medicine is that the child will then be able to more fully develop his/her communication skills, which are essential for social and economic success in the contemporary communication society. The cognitively impaired child, as exemplified in a study of children with Down syndrome, will be able to reach a higher level of function with hearing restored (Ruben, 2003). Those with the greatest handicaps—the most vulnerable hosts—need the closest observation and the prompt institution of appropriate care.

The identification of the child who is at risk and/or who is being adversely affected is the critical aspect of the care of the child with OME and the associated hearing loss in regard to speech and language function. Table 40-1 lists the main areas and some examples of intrinsic host factors and Table 40-2 lists the extrinsic host factors.

The health care provider should evaluate the expressive and receptive language of each child to determine whether the child has language deviance as manifest by delay. Consistent data show that OME in the first year of life affects expressive language during the second year of life (Wallace et al, 1988). An accurate screening evaluation of the child's language is accomplished by using any number of speech/language inventories. I have used the Early Language Milestone (ELM©) successfully for many years (Ruben, 1991). Each new patient 36 months of age or younger is screened with the ELM. This test notes the level of expressive and receptive language. Additionally, there is information concerning the visual function of the child up to 18 months and the speech intelligibility from 18 to 36 months of age (Figure 40-1). If a child has a history and/or physical finding of OME, such as a type B flat tympanogram, a conductive hearing loss, or otoscopic presence of OME, and the ELM shows delay of language or that receptive language is more advanced than expressive language, even though the expressive language is within the level expected for the child's age, then the child is considered as being at risk for deviant speech and language. As language is partly socially dependent, a child from a high-functioning linguistic environment, such as where one or both parents are lawyers, would be expected to have more advanced language function than a child with a parent or parents who are manual laborers. The linguistic environment of the child is considered when

TABLE 40-1. Intrinsic Host Factors Resulting in Increased Susceptibility to Deleterious Speech and Language Effects from Otitis Media

Susceptible Condition	Examples
Anatomic abnormality	Craniofacial malformations
	Submucosal cleft palate (American Indian, Turner's syndrome)
Cognitive deficiency	Down syndrome
	Velocardiofacial syndrome
	22Q11.2 microdeletion syndrome
	Fetal alcohol syndrome
	Kabuki make-up syndrome
	Learning disabled
	Williams syndrome
Enzymatic	Beckwith-Wiedemann syndrome
	Mucopolysaccharidoses
Immune deficiency	Human immunodeficiency virus (HIV)
	Immotile cilia syndrome
	Specific immune deficiencies
	Specific immune deficiencies (transitory, developmental)
Linguistic deficiency	Specific language impairment (SLI) —expressive
	SLI—receptive
	SLI—mixed
	Pervasive developmental delay (autism, Asperger's syndrome)
Physiologic abnormality	Muscular dystrophy
	Neurologic impairments (cerebral palsy)
Psychiatric	Fragile X syndrome
Sensory deficiency	Auditory-mixed loss (Stickler's syndrome)
	Auditory-mixed loss (CHARGE association)
	Auditory—central
	Auditory—neural
	Auditory—sensory mild to moderate loss
	Auditory—sensory moderate to severe loss
	Auditory—sensory profound loss
	Auditory—sensory unilateral loss
	Visual
Speech	Speech dysfunction

CHARGE = coloboma of the eye, heart anomaly, choanal atresia, retardation, and genital and ear anomalies.

making a judgment as to whether the child is showing signs of language delay or deviance.

There are two additional inputs into the decision as to whether there should be intervention for the child in regard to a potential or an actual language delay. These are the physical examination and a measure of the child's hearing threshold and a tympanogram. The physical examination looks for the condition of the middle ear cleft, whether there is a malformation such as a submucosal cleft of the palate that would be associated with eustachian tube malfunction with an increased incidence of OME and whether there is speech pathology such as hypernasality or articulation abnormality. The hearing evaluation allows for determination of both the threshold at the time of the testing and the detection of a conductive loss, and the tympanogram will serve as confirmation or as an independent measure of the condition of the middle ear cleft.

TABLE 40-2. Extrinsic Host Factors Resulting in Increased Susceptibility to Deleterious Speech and Language Effects from Otitis Media

Susceptible Conditions	Examples
Low socioeconomic class, poverty	Low income, poverty
	American Indian, Australian Aborigine
Inadequate parental language input	Inner city
	American Indian
Sensory deprivation	Orphanage
	Prolonged hospitalization

The decision to intervene in the care of OM /OME for language abnormality and/or risk is a product of three factors:

- The nature of the host: intrinsic and extrinsic physical examination, audiogram, and tympanogram (see Tables 40-1 and 40-2).
- The magnitude of the vector: duration, age, and extent of the hearing loss
- The language status of the child (see Figure 40-1)

Management

There are several management options for the care of OM/OME and the associated hearing loss. The first is watchful waiting. This option is used when there appears to be little risk or evidence of language deviance and there is minimal effect from the OME in hearing or changes in the middle ear cleft. Additionally, if there is a reasonable suspicion of a potential linguistic effect, follow-up should be ensured. If a child is in a social situation in which follow-up is problematic because of economic and/or social disintegration, the health care provider may consider a lower threshold for intervention because this may be a child who is potentially at greater risk because of the extrinsically poorer linguistic environment and the probability that the child may not receive optimal care for recurrent episodes of OM.

The care of OME for the child with potential or actual linguistic deviance is twofold. All of the children who show a substantial linguistic deviation at the time of initial examination need to have definitive evaluations and implementation of appropriate habilitation therapy, usually carried out in the United States by speech/language pathologists and in many other countries by logopedists.

The second option is to try to restore hearing and prevent or diminish the incidence of OM/OME. Children younger than 2 years of age with recurrent OM and/or persistent OME are cared for with the insertion of a long-lasting tympanostomy tube such as a T tube. The parents are informed that this tube will be in place for 1 or more years, that there is a need for water precautions, that there is a higher incidence of perforation after the tube is removed, and that there probably will be episodes of otorrhea, among other risks. The benefits are that there will probably be a hearing improvement and a reduction in the number of episodes of OM and/or OME. The child over age 2 years who has no contraindication for adenoidectomy such as a submucosal cleft or a severe speech disorder will undergo an adenoidectomy with the insertion of a small grommet-type tympanostomy tube, which has an approximate half-life of 6 months. The adenoidectomy is performed to decrease the need for a second operative procedure (Gates et al, 1987). If the tubes are extruded and the OME recurs, then the T tube is put in place in a second surgical procedure. There will be a number of children, typically with immune defects such as immotile cilia syndrome, in whom the use of the tympanostomy tube incurs almost continuous otorrhea. In these cases, the tympanostomy tubes are removed, the ears are observed for any changes that would lead to cholesteatoma and/or chronic OM, and the hearing is restored with a hearing aid(s) (Maheshwar et al, 2002).

Studies have shown the efficacy of tympanostomy tubes for language improvement (Wilks et al, 2000). There are also studies that show no effect. Typical of the latter is the one by Paradise and colleagues (2001). This study excluded almost all of the intrinsic and extrinsic host factors that cause a child to be more susceptible to the deleterious effects of OM. Ninety-one percent of their population had only minimal hearing loss, as evidenced by OME as intermittent and unilateral, and a hearing threshold greater than 20 dB and up to 25 dB to age 23 months and 15 dB after age 23 months. It is not surprising that the study showed no effect of the intervention as their subjects had minimal otitis—a small vector occurring in very resistant/resilient hosts. It is essential to take into account the intrinsic and extrinsic host factors to determine the effect of OM and of the efficacy of any intervention. Not doing so may mislead many and inadvertently deny care to those

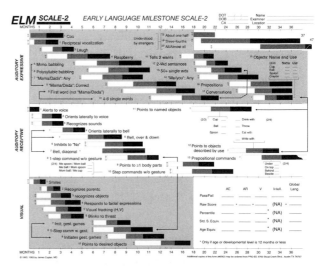

FIGURE 40-1. Early Language Milestone (ELM) form.

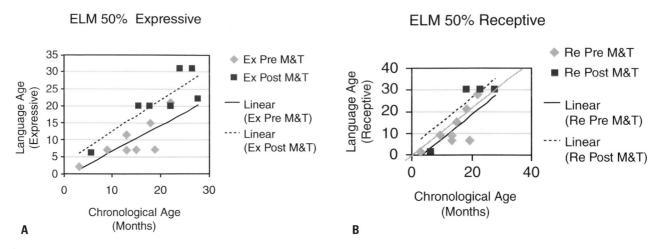

FIGURE 40-2. *A,* Expressive language level before and after insertion of tympanostomy tubes and restoration of hearing as evaluated with the Early Language Milestone (ELM) in a consecutive series of nine patients. The *dark lines* are linear regression lines. *B,* Receptive language level before and after insertion of tympanostomy tubes and restoration of hearing as evaluated with the ELM in a consecutive series of nine patients. The *dark lines* are linear regression lines. Ex = expressive language; M&T = myringotomy and tube; Re = receptive language.

for whom it would be beneficial. The decision for an intervention in a child with a form of OM depends primarily on the intrinsic and extrinsic host characteristics.

The care of the child with potential or actual language deviance associated with OM is continued until the OM/OME is cured. The child is periodically monitored otoscopically, audiometrically, and linguistically, the latter with repeated ELM evaluations. Tympanostomy tubes can be removed when the child has been free of OM for one or two winters and, preferably, when there is an indication of eustachian tube function. Each ear needs to be considered separately. An ear with an extruded tympanostomy tube that has no further difficulty does not mean that the tube in the intubated ear will do the same. If a child with an open tympanostomy tube is able to decrease the pressure in his/her middle ear cleft, this is an indication of improved eustachian tube function. This is observed when the child can release the pressure difference established with a tympanogram by swallowing. Equally important is the monitoring of language development with the ELM, which allows the health care provider to determine if cure of the OM-associated morbidity did or did not result in language improvement. Positive outcomes (Figures 40-2A [expressive] and 40-2B [receptive]) show the language development of nine consecutive children who had an ELM before the placement of a tympanostomy tube and restoration of hearing. All had expressive language that was more delayed than receptive language, and several had receptive delay. Six months or longer postoperatively with restoration of hearing, there was improvement of expressive and receptive language to age level or better. If the language does not reach age level within a few months, then the patient is referred to the appropriate health service.

References

Gates GA, Avery CA, Prihoda TJ, Cooper JC Jr. Effectiveness of adenoidectomy and tympanostomy tubes in the treatment of chronic otitis media with effusion. N Engl J Med 1987;317:1444–51.

Holm VA, Kunze LH. Effect of chronic otitis media on language and speech development. Pediatrics 1969;43:833–9.

Maheshwar AA, Milling MA, Kumar M, et al. Use of hearing aids in the management of children with cleft palate. Int J Pediatr Otorhinolaryngol 2002;66:55–62.

Paradise JL, Feldman HM, Campbell TF, et al. Effect of early or delayed insertion of tympanostomy tubes for persistent otitis media on developmental outcomes at the age of three years. N Engl J Med 2001;344:1179–87.

Ruben RJ. Language screening as a factor in the management of the pediatric otolaryngic patient. Effectiveness and efficiency. Arch Otolaryngol Head Neck Surg 1991;117:1021–5.

Ruben RJ. Otitis media: is there a relationship to language development? In: Accardo P, Rogers B, Capute A, editors. Disorders of language development. Timonium (MD): York Press; 2002. p. 81–91.

Ruben RJ. Host susceptibility to otitis media sequelae. In: Rosenfeld R, Bluestone C, editors. Evidence-based otitis media. Hamilton (ON): BC Decker; 2003. p. 505–14.

Shriberg LD, Flipsen P Jr, Thielke H, et al. Risk for speech disorder associated with early recurrent otitis media with effusion: two retrospective studies. J Speech Lang Hear Res 2000;43:79–99.

Wallace IF, Gravel JS, McCarton CM, Ruben RJ. Otitis media and language development at 1 year of age. J Speech Hear Disord 1988;53:245–51.

Wallace IF, Gravel JS, Schwartz RG, Ruben RJ. Otitis media, communication style of primary caregivers, and language skills of 2 year olds: a preliminary report. J Dev Behav Pediatr 1996;17: 27–35.

Wilks J, Maw R, Peters TJ, et al. Randomised controlled trial of early surgery versus watchful waiting for glue ear: the effect on behavioral problems in pre-school children. Clin Otolaryngol 2000;25:209–14.

Chapter 41

LASER-ASSISTED MYRINGOTOMY IN OTITIS MEDIA

JAMES S. REILLY, MD, GORDON J. SIEGEL, MD

Lasers are high-energy tools that can be employed for vaporization of tissue, often with an absence of bleeding through the destruction of small blood vessels. The beam of electrons from the laser has enabled delicate, "hands-off" precision to laryngeal and ear surgery for the last three decades (Goode, 1982). Laser myringotomy (LM) is a recent and different approach to myringotomy (MT) and affords the immediate benefit of temporary middle ear ventilation. The circular tympanic membrane (TM) opening is created without bleeding from vaporization of the eardrum by the laser beam.

Newer LM systems combine carbon-dioxide laser technology with video otoendoscopy to provide a closed and safer system for using the laser within the ear canal plus a magnified TM image. When the laser beam is activated, a small disk-shaped portion of the TM (1–3 mm) is vaporized. The procedure can be performed in the office or in the operating room.

The laser creates an MT opening that is achieved without any handheld instrument touching the TM or possibly injuring the middle ear ossicles. The precision of the opening is extremely remarkable, and the absence of bleeding permits excellent visualization of the TM during the healing period. The LM permits middle ear fluid to drain, topical medications to be applied directly to the middle ear mucosa, and air to equalize pressures by entering the middle ear for a 2- to 3-week period (Cohen et al, 1998; DeRowe et al, 1994; Silverstein et al, 1996).

The attraction of LM is the potential to provide longer-term ventilation of the middle ear space without the placement of plastic or metal ear ventilating tubes. The physician who treats patients with otitis media (OM) on a daily basis can select ears that are producing symptoms, such as pain or temporarily decreased hearing from middle ear fluid, and create a reliable opening to release the fluid. The benefits of LM are now beginning to be explored.

Carbon-Dioxide Laser Physics and Flash Scanners

Twenty years ago, Goode (1982) first introduced carbon-dioxide lasers to create LM in the TM. Two fundamental improvements over MT with a blade were immediately noted. The most important finding was that the laser openings lasted longer than incisions created by an MT knife (7 versus 2 days). Also, the risk of holding a knife in the ear canal that could damage the middle ear ossicles was avoided.

LM never gained widespread popularity because there were technical, safety, and financial challenges. The carbon-dioxide laser needed to be attached to a microscope, which remained cumbersome if the patient moved. Second, the laser beam was fired in an open system, and the beam-to-target distance was 40 cm. An errant energy beam could cause tissue damage or fire if it was reflected off-course and injure the patient or the staff. In addition, the energy of the laser beam delivered a wide distribution curve of thermal energy to the center of the focal point. When excessive thermal damage is delivered to the central portion of the MT opening (eg, gaussian), the depth of tissue penetration is uneven. The greatest vaporization will occur in the very central portion. If an effusion is not present, this uneven distribution of thermal energy could potentially cause injury to the middle ear mucosa or even to the cochlea (DeRowe et al, 1994).

Modification over the past decade in laser technology design has produced improvements in carbon-dioxide delivery systems by computer chip–driven "flash scanners."

Flash scanners spiral the laser beam concentrically over the surface of the skin or other tissue to vaporize the most superficial layers of tissue and pinpoint the depth of injury. The vaporization avoids deeper penetrations that could not be achieved by handheld knives or scalpels (Cohen et al, 1998).

About 4 years ago, the advantages of flash scanner technology were combined with video otoendoscopy to permit a magnified video image for examination of the TM (OtoLam, Sharplan, Tel Aviv, Israel). The inventors created an attractive marriage of image and function because they combined the visual focal plane and the flash scanner focal plane to make an identical overlapping image. This technical advance gave the physician, for the very first time, a handheld instrument that permitted accurate imaging of the TM and the ability to create precise, circular TM perforations either in the office or in the operating room.

Clinical Reports

LM is a distinct and promising advance in the treatment of OM. Numerous clinical reports have emerged. However, although encouraging, prospective randomized clinical trials of LM have not yet been initiated. Reports must be compared with larger studies of OM (antimicrobial agents or other surgical interventions, such as tube placement or adenoidectomy). The outcomes of these reports are hampered from analysis and must be analyzed from published historical clinical controls.

The first LM clinical report for OM used the former microslad technique to control the LM on 70 ears. Silverstein and colleagues (1996) noted that with an average TM opening size of 1.6 mm, the LM remained patent for an average of 3.14 weeks. The duration of patency of LM achieved was eight times longer than an MT created with a knife and three times longer than that achieved in Goode's (1982) study. Follow-up showed that 80% of these adults and children were free of effusion at 90 days, rekindling interest in the benefits of LM.

A pilot investigation of LM for children with OM ($N = 306$) took place at four different pediatric care facilities (Brodsky et al, 1999; Brodsky et al, 2001; Cook et al, 2001a; Reilly et al, 2000; Siegel et al, 2000). Children were entered during office visits and subdivided into clinical categories of either acute otitis media (AOM) or chronic otitis media (COM). Both arms of this study combined LM with antibiotic therapy (both systemic and topical).

The children (male = 63%; median age 18 months) in the AOM arm had immediate relief of symptoms in 97% of 136 children's ears treated with LM during the first 24 hours after combined office treatment. Overall, 92% (90/98) remained free of symptoms over the 90-day period of observation when treated with a 7-day course of amoxicillin plus topical ofloxacin drops to the middle ear.

The children with COM who were candidates for MT were also offered LM. This part of the study had 55 children (100 ears) with persistent effusions averaging 4 months. There was a larger percentage of boys (68%). These children were older (45 versus 18 months) in this study. About two-thirds of these children remained effusion free for 90 days (Brodsky et al, 1999).

Cook and colleagues (2001a) selected 61 ears from 127 children in the above study for tympanostomy tube placement in the office setting. LM plus MT was successfully performed in all 61 ears. Selected children had 43 ears with recurrent AOM, 8 ears with acute OM, and 10 ears with COM. Fifteen ears had purulent effusions, 5 had serous effusions, and 23 had mucoid effusions. Eighteen ears had no middle ear fluid. Two ear tubes blocked early despite administering otic drops. Tube blockage was associated with thicker TMs or mucoid effusions. At 2-week follow-up, 4 of 5 ears (79%) were disease free, although 13 ears (21%) had not resolved their infections completely. MT in the nonsedated child is technically much more difficult (Friedman et al, 2001). Other studies have supported these findings (Hoffman and Li, 2001; Siegel and Chandra, 2002).

Siegel and Chandra (2002) compared parent satisfaction and the costs of LM performed in the office with those of MT performed in the operating room. The office setting had 35 children with a comparable group of 29 children whose families preferred that the procedure (MT) be performed in the traditional setting of an operating room or outpatient surgical center. The overwhelming factor toward office was parental desire for avoidance of general anesthesia (30/35).

Siegel and Chandra found that 37% (8/35) of parents felt that the temporary discomfort was worse than they had anticipated. However, they point out that health care costs are greatly reduced. Typical costs of outpatient surgical centers were $2,375 compared with hospital costs of $3,040. The office charges were only $240 (90% less).

LM has been reported to be useful for treating other patients with eustachian tube dysfunction and granular myringitis of the TM. Eustachian tube blockage in patients with osteomyelitis requiring pressurized hyperbaric oxygen often leads to serous middle ear effusions. LM is superior to tympanostomy tube placement for short-term ventilation. When granulation myringitis is a complication of OM, superficial removal of granulation tissue using the carbon-dioxide laser treatments with LM have proven to be beneficial. (Bent et al, 2000; Bent et al, 2001; Cook et al, 2001b)

Sufficient topical anesthesia for pain control to the TM using 8% tetracaine is successful in over 90% of patients (Hoffman and Li, 2001). Children sometimes do not get the proper level of anesthesia to the TM, which remains a significant and erratic problem. We have increased the concentration to 32% tetracaine, but the pledget with the tetracaine may not come into direct contact with the eardrum. The pledget remains for 60 minutes. Younger children (< 6 years) seem more tearful than older children, and this fear may be both ear pain and the noise associated with the TM movement. Physicians who have busy practices may be distracted with other activities within the office setting and will find LM unreliable. Also, parents or children who are anxious and do not cooperate may be poor candidates for proper topical anesthesia.

The complications of the LM reported to date are few. One TM perforation in an ear did not heal within the 90 days of the study (Brodsky et al, 1999). Damage to the ossicular chain can occur if the beam is not properly aligned or aimed. One case report has been published to date, and more will come if persons are not properly trained and judicious.

Conclusion

LM appears to be a very effective way to perform an MT in the office setting and the operating room. Bleeding is minimal, and the circular opening in the eardrum facilitates the drainage of middle ear effusions. Also, the beam touches the TM so gently that the middle ear can be entered almost by layers. The opening from the created LM permits the safe introduction of topical antibiotic eardrops. OM often resolves more quickly and may require a shorter duration of oral antimicrobial agents. Antibiotics are used less frequently and at less cost, based on these very preliminary studies when compared with protracted courses of antibiotics alone.

Refractory cases of OM can also benefit with placement of ear tubes. However, MT placement with LM, although at a fraction of the cost, is still technically more difficult than with general anesthesia. Surgical procedures in the office setting may also be associated with increased anxiety for the parents and the child, particularly if adequate pain control is not achieved with topical anesthetics. Therefore, otolaryngologists must develop expertise to perform this regularly and permit adequate time to avoid hasty procedures that might alarm the child or parent.

The initial investment and costs of laser technology are high. Costs for carbon-dioxide lasers remain very high (over $40,000 US) because the number of units produced remains small. To balance costs, hospitals have required an offset of high-volume use. Such financial concerns dictate that the lasers be located where multiple physicians are available to use them either in hospitals or outpatient surgical centers.

Initial concerns remain about making a costly investment when the reimbursement for office-based procedures remains lower than that for hospital-based procedures. The instruments are portable, yet this process is cumbersome to use. A single site designed for LM and/or tube placement is much more efficient and less likely to be damaging to the instruments.

The potential for savings in health care costs for the treatment of OM should not be ignored. LM has the potential to provide safe, less costly, and quicker resolution of effusions and associated symptoms if widely adopted.

References

Bent JP, April MM, Ward RF. Atypical indications for OtoScan laser-assisted myringotomy. Laryngoscope 2001;111:87–9.

Bent JP, April MM, Ward RF, Packard AM. Role of otoscan-assisted laser myringotomy in hyperbaric oxygen therapy. Undersea Hyperb Med 2000;27:159–61.

Brodsky L, Brookhouser P, Chait D, et al. Office based insertion of pressure equalization tubes: the role of laser assisted tympanic membrane fenestration. Laryngoscope 1999;109:2009–14.

Brodsky L, Cook SP, Deutsch E, et al. Optimizing effectiveness of laser tympanic membrane fenestration in chronic otitis media with effusion. Int J Pediatr Otorhinolaryngol 2001;58:59–64.

Cohen D, Siegel G, Krespi J, et al. Middle ear laser office ventilation (LOV) with a CO_2 laser flashscanner. J Clin Laser Med Surg 1998;16:107–9.

Cook SP, Brodsky L, Reilly JS, et al. Effectiveness of adenoidectomy and laser tympanic membrane fenestration. Laryngoscope 2001a; 111:251–4.

Cook SP, Deutsch ES, Reilly JS. Alternative indications for laser-assisted tympanic membrane fenestration. Lasers Surg Med 2001b;28:320–3.

DeRowe A, Ophir D, Katzir A. Experimental study of CO_2 laser myringotomy with a hand-held otoscope and fiberoptic delivery system. Lasers Surg Med 1994;15:249–53.

Friedman O, Deutsch ES, Reilly JS, Cook SP. The feasibility of office-based laser assisted tympanic membrane with tympanostomy tube insertion. Int J Pediatr Otorhinolaryngol 2001;58:59–64.

Goode R. CO_2 laser myringotomy. Laryngoscope 1982;92:420–3.

Hoffman RA, Li CL. Tetracaine topical anesthesia for myringotomy Laryngoscope 2001;111:1636–8.

Reilly JS, Deutsch ES, Cook SP. Laser assisted myringotomy: a feasibility study with short-term follow-up. Ear Nose Throat J 2000;79:654–7.

Siegel GJ, Brodsky L, Waner M, et al. Office based laser assisted tympanic membrane fenestration in adults and children: pilot data to support an alternative to traditional approaches to otitis media. Int J Pediatr Otorhinolaryngol 2000;53:111–20.

Siegel GJ, Chandra RK. Laser office ventilation of ears with the insertion of tubes. Otolaryngol Head Neck Surg 2002;127:67–72.

Silverstein H, Jackson LE, Rosenberg SI, Conlon WS. Pediatric laser-assisted tympanostomy. Laryngoscope 2001;111:905–6.

Silverstein H, Kuhn J, Choo D, et al. Laser-assisted tympanostomy. Laryngoscope 1996;106:1067–74.

ADENOIDECTOMY WITH AND WITHOUT TONSILLECTOMY FOR OTITIS MEDIA WITH EFFUSION

A. RICHARD MAW, MS, FRCS

During the last 20 years, there has been continuing worldwide controversy regarding the role of surgery for otitis media with effusion (OME). This has been in large part related to the variable rates of operation reported in different centers and in different cultures. Surgery has been directed toward either the ears or the upper airway. The transient benefit of myringotomy alone led to the use of ventilation tube insertion. Alternatively, adenoidectomy was performed in an effort to alter the pathogenesis and natural history of OME, and, in the past, tonsillectomy was performed for similar reasons. Early meta-analyses showed the flawed study design of surgical trials (Bodner et al, 1991). There were often small numbers of cases with variable entry criteria, such as failure to exclude previously treated cases, inclusion of unilateral and bilateral cases, differing age groups, and differing duration of disease prior to trial entry. Outcome measures were also variable, including subjective hearing impairment, otoscopic examination, audiometric or appropriate age-related hearing threshold estimation, tympanometric change, time with effusion, and parental observations. A few trials have attempted more sophisticated and relevant end-point assessments (eg, speech, language, learning, and behavior) but often using a variety of different test methodologies. Finally, adequate control of a nonsurgical nature has frequently been lacking, and there has been use of both within- and between-patient controls. Invariably, exclusion of the most severely affected cases has skewed results.

Incidence

Since 1992, various trials have been reported in the United States and Europe. However, there has been a failure to precisely define the condition itself and its natural history.

Consequently, this has resulted in wide variation in descriptions of the process of spontaneous resolution of the untreated disease. The variation is most obvious between data for placebo-controlled, randomized trials of medical treatment and data obtained from the unoperated ears in cases of bilateral disease in randomized, controlled trials of surgical treatment. Furthermore, there is only a single study of very long-term spontaneous resolution of more than 3 years, and in this, significant cases are lost to follow-up, affecting recall rates (Maw and Bawden, 1993).

Table 42-1 summarizes the available results of trial data and meta-analyses of randomized, controlled trials for medical and surgical treatment, showing mean rates of spontaneous resolution of OME with 95% confidence intervals where available (Maw and Bawden, 1993; Rosenfeld, 1999). It is obvious from the data of spontaneous resolution at 6 months, 1 year, and 2 years that medical trials have included cases with much less severe disease than surgical trials, such that 97% of effusions resolve at 2 years

TABLE 42-1. Spontaneous Resolution of Otitis Media with Effusion (%)

Spontaneous Resolution	Medical Trials (95% CI)	Surgical Trials (95% CI)
1 mo	52 (47–58)	
3 mo	63 (60–66)	
6 mo	76 (73–79)	27 (20–35)
1 yr	88 (84–90)	32 (24–40)
2 yr	97 (95–99)	31 (25–37)
3 yr		49
4 yr		59
5 yr		69
7 yr		85
10 yr		95

Adapted from Rosenfeld (1999) and Maw and Bawden (1993).

in medical trials compared with 31% in surgical trials. Only after 10 years is the spontaneous resolution rate in surgical trials similar to the 2-year rate for medical trials. The results of treatment must be judged against these data, taking into account the very significant differences.

Importance

There is no doubt that surgery has a role in the management of OME. In properly selected cases, all otolaryngologists are familiar with the parental opinion postoperatively that their offspring has been rendered a "different child." We now have evidence that part of the observed improvement relates to parental expectation of benefit (G. G. Browning, personal communication, 2002). But beneficial measurable differences can be demonstrated in audiometric hearing gain in addition to changes in reported hearing difficulty by parents. Other studies in our own department have shown changes in expressive language, verbal comprehension, and behavior following ventilation tube insertion for OME (Maw et al, 1999; Wilks et al, 2000). It is probable that we lack appropriate tests with sufficient sensitivity to demonstrate all of the beneficial changes that accrue following ventilation tube insertion and particularly following adenoidectomy for OME. However, the consensus of results of such studies does show benefit in terms of hearing improvement and reduced time with OME following adenoidectomy, with less need for retreatment with ventilation tubes if initial tube surgery is combined with adenoidectomy. This is not surprising if adenoidectomy does indeed reduce the overall time with OME. The need for retreatment with further ventilation tube insertion is 37% at 1 year, 66% at 3 years, and 67% at 5 years following tube insertion alone. However, if the initial operation is combined with adenoidectomy, tube reinsertion rate is 9% at 1 year, 32% at 3 years, and 34% at 5 years. Overall, we have demonstrated a 54% rate for further tube insertion where the operation is carried out alone compared with 36% if initially combined with adenoidectomy (Maw, 1995). What needs to be shown is whether there will be a reduction in longer-term middle ear sequelae following adenoidectomy.

Pathogenesis

We have reasonable data demonstrating nasopharyngeal and adenoid growth in normal, nonaffected children (Maw, 1995), and we have shown significant changes in these parameters in those children with persistent OME. Both bony and soft tissue changes occur, and the latter almost entirely relate to adenoid tissue. Children with OME have a smaller nasopharynx, and in some areas, there is a delay in the normal rate of growth compared with controls. This may be attributable in part to changes in the skull base growth together with altered sinus pneumatization. Such changes may result in eustachian tube dysfunction and provide a mechanism for nasopharyngeal infection to spread more easily via the eustachian tube to the middle ear cleft (Maw, 1995). It was presumably on the basis of acting as a site of potential infection that tonsillectomy was formally recommended for treatment of OME, but our early studies have failed to show a relationship between tonsillectomy and resolution of persistent OME (Maw, 1983).

Management Options

Reviewing the pertinent trials relating to adenoidectomy or adenotonsillectomy, with or without ventilation tube insertion during the last 20 years, demonstrates the options for treatment that have been considered. The data included in Table 42-2 show most of the important features of each trial, including the number of children studied, their age range, the various treatment options included in the trial, the outcome measures, and the duration of each trial. Bearing in mind that annually in the United Kingdom there are approximately 60,000 operations for OME, it is surprising that the studies include so few cases, even when multicenter trials are included. What is clear is that surgical trials have almost invariably included only somewhat older children of more than 3 years of age who have more severe disease than those children included in medical trials.

Surprisingly, national guidelines have somewhat erroneously advised generic treatment recommendations for OME based on these children, with few guidelines for younger children in whom earlier surgical treatment might have disproportionately greater benefit by altering the natural history of the condition at an early stage in the disease process rather than treating its effects. Such trials are certainly required provided that they are properly conducted.

My Experience

Having personally conducted many of these investigations, I feel empowered to discuss with parents the natural history of the condition and the options for treatment from a position of strength. Otolaryngologists must know the data and then be in a position of empowerment. Having taken a proper history and conducted a detailed examination of the upper respiratory tract and ears, including pneumatic otoscopy and microscopy, I examine the audiometric and tympanometric data together with the parents. I describe the etiology and natural history of OME together with risk factors for the disease, especially in relation to age and the effect of season and contact with other children. Where adenoidectomy might be involved, I then describe the natural history of the nasopharynx and adenoids. Simple line diagrams are an essential aid. I draw a logarithmic regression curve of age

TABLE 42-2. Recent Randomized Trials of Treatment of Otitis Media with Effusion

Trial Reference (Year)	n	Range (mean)	Surgery	Outcome Measures	Duration
Maw (1983)	103	3–9 (5.25)	AD, AT, unilateral VT, nil	Otoscopic clearance	1 yr
Black et al (1986)	100	(6.3)	AD + VT, VT	Audiometry, tympanometry, parental opinions	1 yr
Gates et al (1987)	576	4–8	Bilateral MYR, bilateral VT, AD + bilateral MYR, AD + bilateral VT (dry tap 32%)	Mean time OME, mean time hearing > 20 dB, postoperative otorrhea, retreatment (19%)	2 yr
Black et al (1990)	149	4–9	AD, bilateral MYR, unilateral VT; AD, unilateral MYR, bilateral VT; bilateral MYR, unilateral VT; unilateral MYR, unilateral VT	Audiometry, mean worst 250–4000 Hz, tympanometry, parental opinion	2 yr
Mandel et al (1992)	111	7 1/2–12 yr	Bilateral VT, bilateral MYR, nil	Audiometry, tympanometry, otoscopy	3 yr
Maw, 1993	228	2–9	AD, unilateral VT; AD; unilateral VT; nil (AD + AD or AT)	Otoscopy, tympanometry, audiometry, duration OME	12 yr
Dempster et al (1993)	78	5–8	AD, unilateral VT; AD; unilateral VT; nil (dry tap–0)	Audiometry (0.5, 1,000, and 2,000 Hz), otoscopy, tympanometry	2 yr
Browning and Haggard (2002)	253	3 1/2–7 yr	AD, bilateral VT; bilateral VT; nil	Audiometry, tympanometry, reported hearing disability, behavior	2 yr

AD = adenoidectomy; AT = adenotonsillectomy; MYR = myringotomy; nil = following no intervention; OME = otitis media with effusion; VT = ventilation tube insertion.

against the incidence of OME, and then I draw the seasonal incidence from January to December, indicating the prevalence of bilateral type B tympanograms in the winter (at about 20% compared with 4% in the summer, taken from data from our longitudinal study of normal children [Dewey et al, 2000]). In selected cases, in addition to referring to the anatomy of the nasopharynx and adenoids, further demonstration may be shown on a lateral postnasal space radiograph, which can usually be taken at the time of the appointment.

Advice on management largely depends on the season in which the consultation is taking place and the age of the child, together with the severity of the condition as judged by the history and audiometric investigations. Generally, at the first consultation, I adopt a watchful waiting policy. However, many children have already been seen several months previously in community clinics by audiologists or clinicians with special experience in pediatric audiology. Frequently, these children have failed screening tests for hearing ability carried out by health visitors or general practitioners. Thus, in these children, there is a documented history with contemporaneous audiometric and impedance tests, and often there are letters from schoolteachers or nurses substantiating the history. In these children, the watchful waiting policy may need to be revised and shortened. My own period of watchful waiting is variable. For children seen in the winter months, from October to January, I would review them in April or May and possibly again in midsummer. If effusions are still present with hearing loss and other associated problems at the subsequent examination, I would then recommend surgery. Children seen in the spring or early summer months would be reviewed in September or October, and if they still had effusions and hearing loss, they would be treated surgically before the winter.

Provided that there is no evidence of significant recurrent infection or pain, in most cases, I give no medical treatment. In all children, I recommend amplification of parental speech, and for older children, there should be liaison with nursery or schoolteachers who should be aware of the problem. Sometimes I recommend use of an Otovent balloon with regular autoinflation in children old enough to comply. For very young children and particularly those with a history of superadded recurrent acute otitis media, where there is a personal history of allergy or a strong family history of allergy, I recommend change of diet from cow's milk to goat or soy milk. Otherwise, with persistent OME accompanied by symptoms of demonstrable hearing loss, I proceed with surgery.

Generally, for children younger than 3 years of age, I advise insertion of bilateral ventilation tubes alone. For those older than 3 years, ventilation tube insertion may be combined with adenoidectomy. If there is a history of nasal obstruction, mouth breathing, or snoring, or if there is speech hyponasality on examination, I proceed with adenoidectomy. Adenoid enlargement in these cases is often supported by a lateral radiograph of the postnasal space, confirming reduction of the airway. Without any such symptoms, particularly in younger children aged less than 3 years, I defer adenoidectomy, thus reserving it in these children who progress to persistent, recurrent disease following initial treatment with ventilation tubes alone. However, there is a need for studies to show the effects of adenoidectomy in children younger than 3 years old and with persistent OME. We may be able to reduce the overall time with effusion and so prevent sequelae. Such a suggestion is supported by our studies in older children, which have demonstrated the best reduction of duration of OME assessed otoscopically from 6.1 years without treatment to 3.5 years with ventilation tubes alone, to 3.4 years with adenoidectomy alone, and to 2.3 years with a combination of adenoidectomy and ventilation tubes. Objective assessment with tympanometry shows a longer duration because of its greater sensitivity compared with otoscopy, and durations of 7.8 years, 4.9 years, 4.0 years, and 2.8 years, respectively, have been shown by tympanometric change. The otoscopic and tympanometric improvements are associated with improvements in mean hearing threshold. These children were aged 2 to 9 years with a mean of 5.25 years, and we have no data for the effects of adenoidectomy in a younger, mean group of 3 years or younger (Maw and Bawden, 1993).

A similar age range was included in the multicenter Trial of Alternative Regimens for Glue Ear Treatment (TARGET) in the United Kingdom. The trial compared the effect of ventilation tube alone against tube insertion and adenoidectomy and against medical treatment. There was a hearing gain of 3.7 dB in the first year and a 3.3 dB gain in the second year in favor of adenoidectomy. In standard deviation terms, the effect of ventilation tubes alone is large and the adenoidectomy effect is very large. The associated improvement in reported hearing difficulty, which is a measure of disability, also shows a very large effect, which is greater than that predicted from the hearing level. The increase may be accounted for by parental expectation of benefit (Browning and Haggard, 2002). Thus, these early results from 13 centers in the United Kingdom support those of my previous work, indicating an additional benefit from adenoidectomy compared with that owing to ventilation tube insertion alone. We must now assess the effect of adenoid removal in younger children with severe persistent OME.

References

Black NA, Crowther J, Freeland A. The effectiveness of adenoidectomy in the treatment of glue ear: a randomised controlled trial. Clin Otolaryngol 1986;11:149–55.

Black NA, Sanderson CFB, Freeland AP, Vessey MR. A randomised controlled trial of surgery for glue ear. BMJ 1990;300:1551–6.

Bodner EE, Browning GG, Chalmers FT, Chalmers TL. Can meta-analysis help uncertainty in surgery for otitis media in children? J Laryngol Otol 1991;105:812–9.

Browning GG, Haggard MP. Trial of Alternative Regimens for Glue Ear Treatment (TARGET). Presented at the Eighth International Congress in Paediatric Otorhinolaryngology; 2002 Sept 11–4; Oxford, England.

Dempster JH, Browning GG, Gatehouse SG. A randomized study of surgical management of children with persistent otitis media with effusion associated with learning impairment. J Laryngol Otol 1993;107:284–9.

Dewey C, Midgley E, Maw AR. The relationship between otitis media with effusion and contact with other children in a British cohort studied from 8 months to $3\frac{1}{2}$ years. Int J Pediatr Otorhinolaryngol 2000;55:33–45.

Gates GA, Avery CS, PriLoda TJ, Cooper JC. Effectiveness of adenoidectomy and tympanostomy tubes in the treatment of chronic otitis media with effusion. N Engl J Med 1987;317:1444–51.

Mandel EM, Rockette HE, Bluestone CD, et al. Efficacy of myringotomy with and without tympanostomy tubes for chronic otitis media with effusion. Pediatr Infect Dis J 1992;11:270–7.

Maw AR. Chronic otitis media with effusion (glue ear) and adeno-tonsillectomy: prospective randomised controlled study. BMJ 1983;287:1586–8.

Maw AR. Glue ear in childhood. Clinics in developmental medicine no. 135. London: MacKeith Press; 1995.

Maw AR, Bawden R. Spontaneous resolution of severe glue ear in children and the effect of adenoidectomy, tonsillectomy and insertion of ventilation tubes (grommets). BMJ 1993;306:756–60.

Maw AR, Wilks J, Harvey I, Golding J. Early surgery compared with watchful waiting for glue ear and effect on language development in pre-school children: a randomised trial. Lancet 1999;353:960–3.

Rosenfeld RM. Natural history of untreated otitis media. In: Rosenfeld RM, Bluestone CD, editors. Evidence-based otitis media. Hamilton (ON): BC Decker; 1999. p. 165–70.

Wilks J, Maw AR, Peters TJ, et al. Randomised controlled trial of early surgery versus watchful waiting for glue ear: the effect on behavioral problems in pre-school children. Clin Otolaryngol 2000;25:209–14.

Chapter 43

Long-Lasting Tubes for Otitis Media with Effusion

Richard L. Goode, MD

Insertion of a ventilation tube in the tympanic membrane (TM) for the treatment of recurrent or chronic otitis media with effusion (OME), unresponsive to an adequate trial of medical therapy, is well known. The indications for the use of standard short-term tubes have been described in detail in other chapters and are not reviewed here. It is less clear when to select a long-lasting ventilation tube, arbitrarily defined as a tube that stays in place longer than 12 months, with an average duration of 24 to 36 months and occasionally much longer. Standard or short-lasting tubes usually remain less than 12 months, on average 6 to 8 months and, again, occasionally much longer. This chapter discusses the role of long-lasting tubes in the treatment of OME. Long-term tubes can also be used in the treatment of recurrent acute otitis media, but that is not the focus of this chapter.

The goal of tube insertion in OME is to provide ventilation of the middle ear for an adequate period of time to avoid recurrence of OME after tube extrusion or removal. This duration of ventilation is not known in every case, but the literature supports the contention that durations of 4 months provide resolution of OME in around 80% of ears (Armstrong, 1968). This cure rate has not changed over 28 years (Todd, 1999). Failure is defined as a recurrence of OME after tube extrusion requiring reinsertion of a ventilation tube. In adults and older children, errors in proper tube selection are less significant because repeat tube insertion can usually be performed in the office under local or topical anesthesia. Some otolaryngologists insert tubes in this manner in younger children, but this is not the norm. The expense, inconvenience, and risk are primarily attributable to the need for general anesthesia in an operating room.

If the exact time in which a tube must remain in a given case to produce a cure were known, we would want to select a tube that remained in place that length of time but no longer, all else being equal. A reasonable alternative would be a tube that could be painlessly removed in the office at any time if it was known that adequate

eustachian tube function had been restored. This is because the longer a tube is in place, the higher the complication rate. The most serious complication is a chronic perforation of the TM requiring surgical closure after tube removal or extrusion. This appears to be a problem with transcutaneous tubes elsewhere, such as catheters and drains; the longer a foreign body is in place through the skin, the greater the complication rate. A recent meta-analysis of 134 articles quantitated the relative risk of complications when long-term tubes were used compared with short-term tubes (Kay et al, 2001). The long-term tubes were the Butterfly (a modified shorter inner flange T tube), Paparella II, Per-Lee, and Goode T tube. The incidence of otorrhea was 2.2 times greater, chronic perforation was 3.5 times greater, and cholesteatoma, an uncommon late complication, was 2.6 times greater. The important relationship of the length of time the tubes were in place versus the cure rate and the incidence of complications was not evaluated in the meta-analysis but was addressed in several of the individual articles. In a previous review of 12 studies reporting the incidence of permanent TM perforation after long-term (years) middle ear ventilation with a T tube, the mean incidence was 11.5%, with a range from 3 to 47.5% (Goode, 1996). If the lowest and highest incidences were eliminated, the mean was 8.8%. As previously noted, complications increased the longer the tube was in place in a relatively linear fashion. There were other contributing factors, which are discussed below.

Advantages of a Long-Term Tube

The reason to select a long-lasting tube over a short-lasting tube is to produce a higher cure rate and avoid the need to reinsert a second or third ventilation tube, usually requiring general anesthesia with increased expense, discomfort, inconvenience, and risk.

A commonly used clinical approach in children is to routinely insert a standard short-term tube in the usual case of OME. If the OME returns after tube extrusion or removal, a long-term tube is inserted. Some surgeons will wait until a second or even third short-term tube placement fails before considering insertion of a long-term tube. This approach is based on accepting an 80% cure rate as reasonable after 6 to 8 months of ventilation. Whereas some short-term tubes remain in place for 12 months and longer, most do not. What is not known is whether a second short-term tube insertion will produce an 80% cure after initial tube failure to cure OME. If true, this would suggest that two tube insertions would produce an overall cure of 96% (80% cure the first time and 80% cure of the 20% failures the second time). It would also imply that a longer ventilation time of 12 to 16 months (equal to the time in which two short-term tubes would be in place) should produce the same higher percentage cure. Furthermore, because the child is getting older and larger, eustachian tube function would be expected to improve, all else being equal, predisposing the patient to a higher cure rate.

Unfortunately, it does not appear that a second short-term tube will have the same percentage cure as a primary tube because failure of a primary tube to control OME selects out the more difficult cases. Some ears need prolonged or even permanent ventilation to effect a cure. If we could diagnose these cases prior to initial tube insertion, primary insertion of a longer duration tube would be indicated rather than insertion of a short-term tube with a high failure percentage. Again, a long-term tube that could be easily and painlessly removed in the office at any desired time would also meet this requirement. Certainly, two or more short-term tube insertions are not as desirable as one longer-term tube insertion, assuming the same cure rate and an acceptable incidence of complications.

We do know that some patients are much more likely to require longer ventilation times and are candidates for primary insertion of a longer-duration tube. These include children with the following conditions:

- nasal allergies
- small stature
- immune and nutritional deficiencies
- anatomic deformities such as cleft palate
- radiotherapy to the nasopharynx

Large obstructing adenoids are another factor but can be treated with an adenoidectomy at the time of tube insertion.

Why Do Long-Term Tubes Stay in Longer?

Retention of a ventilating tube appears to be based on the diameter and rigidity of the internal flange. The larger the diameter and the more rigid the flange material, the longer the retention, all else being equal (Moore, 1990). The status of the TM is an important variable; atrophic, flaccid TMs do less to prevent tube extrusion than normal TMs, so retention times are shorter. Inserting tubes so that part of the internal flange is under the malleus handle appears to lengthen retention time, particularly in tubes with rigid flanges. The TM status prior to tube insertion also appears to have an effect on the incidence of chronic perforations. Matt and colleagues (1991) found a 0% permanent perforation incidence with marked TM retraction. Various sites on the TM do not appear to be important for chronic perforations, assuming that the TM is normal in each site (Hampton and Adams, 1996).

Not All Long-Term Tubes Are Alike

My experience is with the T tube used as both a short- and a long-term tube (Goode, 1983; Goode, 1996). The T tube has several features that differ from the long-term tubes with a large lumen and large circumferential inner flange, such as the Paparella II and the Per-Lee; retention times are similar. The T-tube inner flanges comprise only a small percentage of the circumference of the tube, about 30% compared with 100% in the larger tubes, and can be easily cut to any desired length. The shaft inner diameter (ID) is similar to that of short-term tubes (1.1 mm), and the inner flanges collapse on insertion and removal so that the myringotomy diameter is the same as with short-term tubes. The result is a smaller hole after removal or extrusion compared with larger-lumen tubes with circumferential flanges. For example, the ID of the Paparella II tube is 1.27 mm and the inner flange diameter is 4.3 mm; the Per-Lee ID is 1.5 mm with an inner flange diameter of 7.8 mm. For comparison, the inner flange diameters of the commonly used short-duration Sheehy, Donaldson, and Shepard tubes are 3.0, 2.3, and 2.4 mm, respectively. Variations in size exist, depending on the manufacturer.

The standard T tube is of silicone rubber and has a shaft length of 12 mm, an ID of 1.1 mm, and an inner flange length of 4 mm on each side; the total inner flange width is 9.5 mm. This tube was designed to be long in all dimensions to allow the otosurgeon to customize the tube to the desired size. We usually shorten the shaft length to 5 to 6 mm because longer lengths increase the likelihood of later obstruction (Figure 1A). The inner flange length is shortened depending on the desired tube retention time. This is discussed in more detail later.

A variety of modified T tubes are now commercially available. Some are of slightly larger diameter and shorter shaft length; some have outer flanges similar to grommet tubes (Figure 1B). Others have shorter flange lengths (3 versus 4 mm) and are made of softer durometer silicone rubber (called soft silicone or supersoft silicone). There is evidence that tubes with flanges of softer silicone rubber and shorter length (3 mm or less) are less likely to

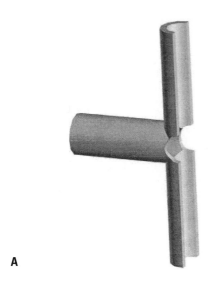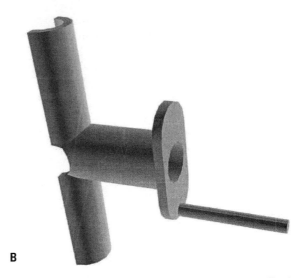

A

B

FIGURE 43-1. Examples of T tubes for mid- and long-term ventilation. *A,* Standard T tube. The shaft has been shortened to 5 mm. The inner flanges can be shortened, if desired, to any length. *B,* T-grommet tube with an external flange and pullout tab.

produce permanent perforations on extrusion (Inglis et al, 1990; Talmon et al, 2001).

An advantage of T tubes over other short- and long-term tubes is that they can be removed in the office without pain at any time. The length of time in which the tube remains in place is under the control of the surgeon, so removal under general anesthesia is rarely required, whereas this is the norm for removal of other ventilation tubes. This feature is underused, particularly in the treatment of recurrent OME after primary ventilation tube failure. Removal of T tubes appears to produce fewer perforations than extrusion. Matt and colleagues (1991) reported a 0% incidence of perforation when T tubes were removed rather than allowed to extrude (Matt et al, 1991). When T tubes were removed, the duration in place is usually less than if they are allowed to extrude. In the case of T tubes, it is duration rather than tube design that is the major variable producing permanent perforations after extrusion. This may not be true for the other long-term tubes.

What Is the Ideal Duration in which a Long-Term Tube Should Be in Place?

In individual OME cases, the minimum ventilation time needed to achieve a cure is not known. This is particularly true when a previous tube has failed, presumably because it came out too soon. This suggests that a longer ventilation time is required but does not define how long. Because the incidence of complications increases the longer a tube is in place, one way to decrease complications is to remove the tube sooner than the average 36-month retention time. The most serious complication is a TM perforation that requires later closure with a myringoplasty after recovery of eustachian tube function.

Although iatrogenic cholesteatoma is also a serious complication, it is rare. Recurrent otorrhea is greater with long-term tubes but responds well to topical antibiotic drops such as ciprofloxacin or ofloxacin. Tube obstruction can be a problem and may require replacement of the tube if it cannot be opened in situ.

Reasonable Treatment Time That Is Likely to Be Successful with an Acceptable Perforation Incidence

In the usual case, I would suggest 16 to 18 months as the time to consider removal. This period is about two to three times longer than the average duration of a short-term tube and would be expected to produce a perforation incidence about two to three times that of a short-term tube, around 4 to 6%. In my opinion, this is an acceptably low perforation rate. After this time period, the incidence gradually increases to 8.8% (average of 10 studies previously described) at 24 to 36 months and then levels off. Inglis and colleagues (1990) found that the average time for T-tube retention with no perforations was 17.5 months, whereas the average time in the perforation group was 21.5 months. They also recommended consideration of removal at 18 months. Talmon and colleagues (2001) described their experience with a polyethylene T tube in 306 children. The tubes were electively removed after 15 to 24 months ventilation time with a mean duration of 20 months. The persistent perforation incidence was 1.49%, and 4.9% of ears required reinsertion of tubes. Siddiqui and colleagues (1997) used a T tube with short inner flanges of soft silicone rubber, similar to that used by Inglis and colleagues (1990), to treat 191 patients with OME. The inner flange diameter was 4.75 mm, with an individual flange length of 1.7 mm. The mean duration to spontaneous extrusion was 29.3 months, with a permanent perforation incidence of 9.6%. They found that ventilation times beyond 36 months were "an important factor" in the incidence of complications and recommended removal at 3 years. Lentsch and colleagues (2000), in an analysis of 273 tube removals, found a 3% persistent TM perforation incidence when tubes were removed before 3 years and a 15% incidence after 3 years. Nichols and colleagues (1998) also found that ventilation tube retention beyond 36 months produced a significantly increased perforation rate after removal. Paper patching did not improve healing.

Because the T tube has a unique property that allows it to be removed painlessly in the office without anesthesia, its duration is under the control of the physician. Unfortunately, it may not be obvious whether 18 months or so is an adequate duration so that a tube removal is not followed by recurrence of OME. In many cases, it may be wiser to warn the parents of the increasing complication rate but to leave the tubes in place. Other factors are important in this decision, including age, size, other tube complications (drainage, plugging), time of year, and so forth. Eustachian tube testing during the ventilation period using a tympanometer may be useful in determining whether adequate function has returned (Goode, 1983). Although such testing can be helpful in the removal decision, repeated eustachian tube testing is not routinely used because it is not thought to be sensitive enough.

Early summer is a good time to consider removal because OME and upper respiratory infections are less common and water sports are more popular. In bilateral cases, one tube can be removed at a time; the second tube can be removed 4 to 6 weeks later if the first ear is doing well. If the OME recurs, the tubes are reinserted at a different site in the TM.

Midterm Tube

Another solution is to modify a T tube so that it extrudes at around 18 months (Goode, 1996). It is my impression that the average retention time correlates roughly with the flange length; shortening the flange length by half, from 4 to 2 mm, decreases the retention time by half, all else being equal. This would decrease the mean retention time of a standard T tube from 36 to 18 months, producing a medium duration or midterm tube that appears to be a reasonable compromise between adequate ventilation in primary tube failure cases and an acceptable incidence of post-tube chronic perforations. Talmon and colleagues (2001) have made the same suggestion. Soft silicone rubber tubes are preferred. The tube could still be removed in the office at any time, if desired. Insertion would also be easier than with longer-flanged tubes.

Conclusion

In summary, I suggest that the best treatment solution after failure of a short-term tube for OME in children is to insert a soft silicone rubber T tube, ideally though a normal area of the TM, and to reassess it at 6-month intervals regarding need. Shortening the flanges to 2 to 3 mm may be advantageous in some cases. A T tube may be considered as a primary tube in cases in which longer ventilation times are anticipated. At around 18 months, assuming no evidence of continuing eustachian tube dysfunction, tube removal in the office can be considered and discussed with the parents. If perforation rates greater than 4 to 6% are considered too high, the tubes can be removed; otherwise they should stay until the physician believes that a cure has been obtained. It is hoped that with improved eustachian tube testing, identification of when a tube can be removed will become a science rather than an art, as it is now.

References

Armstrong BW. What your colleagues think of tympanostomy tubes. Laryngoscope 1968;78:1303–13.

Goode RL. Advantages of the T-tube for short- and long-term middle ear ventilation. Laryngoscope 1983;93:376–8.

Goode RL. Long-term middle-ear ventilation with T-tubes: the perforation problem. Otolaryngol Head Neck Surg 1996;115:500–1.

Hampton SM, Adams DA. Perforation rates after ventilation tube insertion: does the positioning of the tube matter? Clin Otolaryngol 1996;21:548–9.

Inglis AF, Richardson MA, Higgins TS. Lowering the incidence of perforation following Goode T-tubes removal. Presented at the 1990 meeting of the American Society of Pediatric Otolaryngology; 1990 May 19; Toronto.

Kay DJ, Nelson M, Rosenfeld RM. Meta-analysis of tympanostomy tube sequalae. Otolaryngol Head Neck Surg 2001;124:374–80.

Lentsch EJ, Goudy S, Ganzel TM, et al. Rate of persistent perforation after elective tympanostomy tube removal in pediatric patients. Int J Pediatr Otorhinolaryngol 2000;54:134–8.

Matt BH, Miller RP, Meyers RM, et al. Incidence of perforation with Goode T-tubes. Int J Pediatr Otorhinolaryngol 1991;21:1–16.

Moore PJ. Ventilation tube duration versus design. Ann Otol Rhinol Laryngol 1990;99:722–3.

Nichols PT, Ramadan HH, Wax MK, Santrock RD. Relationship between tympanic membrane perforations and retained ventilation tubes. Arch Otolaryngol Head Neck Surg 1998;124:417–9.

Siddiqui N, Toynton S, Mangat KS. Results of middle ear ventilation with "Mangat" T-tubes. Int J Pediatr Otorhinolaryngol 1997;20:90–6.

Talmon Y, Gadban H, Samet A, et al. Medium-term middle-ear ventilation with self-manufactured polyethylene T-tubes for the treatment of children with middle-ear effusion. J Laryngol Otol 2001;115:699–703.

Todd NV. What your colleagues think of tympanostomy tubes—28 years later. Laryngoscope 1999;109:1028–32.

Chapter 44

MASTOIDECTOMY IN CHRONIC OTITIS MEDIA WITH EFFUSION

O. NURİ ÖZGİRGİN, MD

Chronic otitis media with effusion (COME) is defined as persistent inflammation of the middle ear mucosa and the presence of free fluid in the middle ear space and the mastoid. Eustachian tube dysfunction is the causative factor that initiates the inflammatory changes in the middle ear mucosa. The main mechanisms involved in COME are hypoventilation and changes in partial gas pressures in the middle ear compartments. These conditions induce mucosal metaplasia, which leads to increased numbers of secretory cells in the mucosal lining of the middle ear (Bluestone and Doyle, 1988). The other factors that play a role in the pathophysiology of COME are the presence of viral and bacterial infections, allergy, immotile cilia syndrome, and congenital disorders such as cleft palate and Down syndrome.

The eustachian tube functions are to ventilate, protect, and drain the middle ear. Its dysfunction is the most frequent cause of middle ear and mastoid air cell hypoventilation and can be a major contributor to COME. The common treatment options, such as ventilation tube (VT) insertion, for secretory conditions of the middle ear and mastoid are usually effective. However, when these measures fail, mastoidectomy may be necessary to remove irreversible pathology and create a larger air reservoir.

Mastoid Mucosa in COME

In COME, the middle ear mucosa consists of pseudo-stratified columnar epithelium, increased numbers of goblet cells, and nonciliated cells that contain secretory granules (Özgirgin et al, 1989). The middle ear and mastoid are derived from the first branchial pouch, and both structures are lined by respiratory mucosa. Therefore, the response to bacterial and inflammatory stimuli in these two structures is similar. Also, the mucosal lining of the mastoid air cells shows similar changes to that of the middle ear in COME. The mastoid lining is composed of stratified epithelium, and the main ultrastructural findings in the inflammatory state are enlarged nuclei with a high nucleocytoplasmic ratio, prominent nucleoli, abundant Golgi bodies, and increased numbers of free polysomes (Newberg et al, 1985).

During human fetal life, mesenchyme is the dominant tissue in the temporal bone and mastoid antrum. In the second half of gestation, the embryonic mesenchyme gradually regresses to form the antral space and open air cells. Eventually, a thin mucoperiosteal layer replaces the thick submucosa in the antrum and mastoid cells. Pneumatization of the mastoid occurs via osteoclastic activity of the periosteum in the form of bone resorption. Simultaneously, osteoblastic new bone development continues to meet the requirements of the growing skull. Normally, genetic coding produces a pneumatized mastoid of a size specific to the individual, and this process can be greatly influenced by environmental factors. Consequently, different stages of arrested pneumatization are possible.

When normal regression of the mesenchyme is arrested, intercellular septa remain thick and the air cell compartments may be filled with fluid, granulation tissue, or small or large cholesterol granulomas. If arrest of mesenchyme regression occurs in early childhood, the original hematopoietic tissue in the mastoid tip may still be present or may have turned to fat by the time pneumatization stops (Palva and Ramsay, 2002).

In normal development, mesenchyme is expected to disappear by age 5 years. Interestingly, Jaisinghani and colleagues (1999) identified mesenchyme in 38 (2.7%) of 1,404 adult human temporal bones. In all 38 cases, the mesenchyme tissue showed histopathologic features of otitis media. Disruption of mesenchyme regression causes abnormal tissue changes that are usually not affected by VT insertions. These irreversible tissue changes are known contributing factors in chronic mastoid disease and can be treated only by mastoidectomy.

Granulation tissue filling the periantral cells and the mastoid antrum is the common surgical finding in COME for which mastoidectomy is performed. This irreversible tissue also blocks the aditus, which is the only air passage between the middle ear and the antrum (Figures 44-1 and 44-2).

Körner's Septum

Körner's septum is also a predisposing factor that makes the mastoid reluctant to conventional treatment methods in COME. It is a compact, bony, petrosquamosal lamina that is situated lateral to the facial canal. This structure appears as a result of a defect during the resolving process of the petrosquamous lamina, which should disappear following the twenty-second gestational week. It extends inferiorly from the posterior aspect of the glenoid fossa to the mastoid apex just above the middle ear cavity. Whether or not Körner's septum predisposes to hypocellularity of the mastoid is still a matter of debate; however, this structure definitely complicates infection and inflammation of the mastoid (Akyildiz et al, 1991).

In my experience, Körner's septum is a frequent finding in patients with COME who require mastoidectomy. This suggests that the structure is somehow associated with development of irreversible pathology in the mastoid. It is possible that Körner's septum facilitates isthmus blockage during inflammation of the middle ear. In COME cases that do not respond to recurrent VT insertion or cases with chronic ear discharge through the VT, the presence of Körner's septum may influence the decision of whether to perform a mastoidectomy.

Mastoid Pneumatization

Two hypotheses have been proposed to explain the pathogenesis of the hypocellular mastoid. Supporters of the "environmental theory" claim that previous middle ear

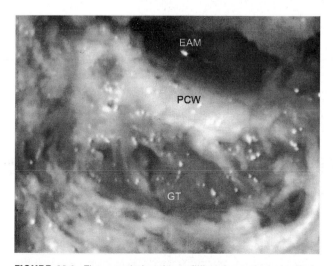

FIGURE 44-1. The granulation tissue filling the periantral cells in chronic otitis media with effusion. EAM = external auditory meatus; GT = granulation tissue; PCW = posterior canal wall.

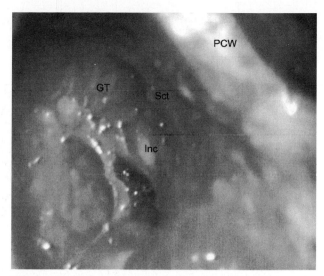

FIGURE 44-2. The blockage of the aditus ad antrum by the granulation tissue in chronic otitis media with effusion. GT = granulation tissue; Inc = incus; PCW = posterior canal wall; Sct = scutum.

infections ultimately cause hypocellularity. Those who believe in the "hereditary theory" maintain that genetic factors determine small mastoid size, which, in turn, predisposes to acute or chronic otitis media. Investigation has shown the environmental hypothesis to be more logical, and many studies support this concept.

In a study conducted on guinea pigs, Aoki and colleagues (1990) experimentally induced COME in one ear of each newborn and left the other ear as a control. They then examined the mastoid cells in adult life. In the COME ears, the cortical mastoid bone was considerably thicker than the normal mastoid. In addition, each cell contained a thick layer of mesenchymal tissue infiltrated with round inflammatory cells.

In contrast, Sadé and Fuchs (1996), proponents of the hereditary theory, identified poor mastoid pneumatization (less than 6 cm^2) as a predictor of COME in adult humans. The etiopathogenesis of COME involves poor mastoid pneumatization and fluctuations of gas diffusion into and out of circulation, as well as eustachian tube obstruction. The authors found that negative pressure did not induce COME when there was good pneumatization of the mastoid. They concluded that disease results only when there is a combination of negative pressure and poor pneumatization (Sadé and Fuchs, 1997).

Between these two theories, the environmental theory is backed by many studies (Aoki et al, 1990; Homoe et al, 1992; Ikarashi et al, 1994; Palva et al, 2002; Roizen et al, 1994; Stangerup and Tos, 1986; Tos and Stangerup, 1984, 1985; Tos et al, 1984, 1985).

By itself, reduced mastoid cell volume, which the environmental theory indicates is a result of COME, is not an indication for mastoidectomy. Mastoid surgery is performed only when such disease-induced small mastoid cavities are lined by granulation tissue or cholesterol granulomas.

Gas-Exchange Function of the Mastoid

Honjo and colleagues (1998) used nitrous oxide methodology to study the gas exchange in the mastoid cell system. Their work demonstrated that gas exchange takes place only when there is an air space in the middle ear. The same investigation revealed that a larger mastoid is advantageous in patients with COME because it helps maintain the air space in the middle ear. The authors speculated that ears with larger mastoids are less susceptible to COME and have a higher curability rate. They concluded that impaired gas-exchange function of the mastoid is related to lack of aeration of the middle ear and that medical treatment will fail without adequate ventilation of middle ear compartments.

Takahashi and colleagues (1994) compared gas exchange in the middle ear and mastoid of patients with COME with that in normal subjects. This study analyzed tympanogram data and data from micropressure sensors that were inserted into the mastoid cavity during general anesthesia with nitrous oxide. The results showed that gas-exchange function was impaired in 50% of the ears with COME. The researchers also assessed previously operated mastoidectomy cavities and showed zero or minimal pressure increase, indicating no gas exchange in the mastoid cavity. They concluded that obliteration of the mastoidectomy cavity was necessary in these cases.

As the above authors indicated, zero or minimal gas exchange in mastoidectomy cavities does not abandon the air reservoir function of the mastoid. The mastoidectomy cavity forms an "air reservoir," which, in the setting of eustachian tube dysfunction, helps prevent detrimental negative pressure buildup in the middle ear. The tympanic membrane essentially acts as an air-pressure regulator. When small mastoid cell volume is coupled with eustachian tube dysfunction, tympanic membrane displacement will be more pronounced. This eventually causes deep retraction pockets to form. In such cases, mastoidectomy basically "repneumatizes" the mastoid, creating a larger air reservoir. Expanding this reservoir size reduces volume changes that occur with eustachian dysfunction and also facilitates eradication of any infection that might develop in the mastoid (Jackler and Schindler, 1984).

Role of VTs on Mastoid Mucosa

Research has shown that the time of onset of middle ear inflammation is important with respect to inhibition of mastoid air cell development. If inflammation occurs early in life, development of the mastoid air cell system is significantly inhibited. In contrast, when eustachian tube dysfunction develops later in life, they merely aggravate inflammatory effects in the mastoid (Ikarashi et al, 1994).

In patients with COME, VT placement helps equalize middle ear pressure and drain the middle ear and mastoid. Both of these functions may increase mastoid air cell volume. One study of 21 patients with COME revealed significant volumetric expansion in the first 3 months after VT insertion. The authors attributed this improvement to drainage of accumulated effusion and relief of mucosal edema. The mastoid air cell volume remained unchanged over the long term in these chronic cases. The effect of VT placement on mucosal edema in the mastoid remains a matter of controversy. Some researchers contend that relief of mucosal edema is confined to the middle ear space and antrum, whereas others indicate that there is also a marked effect in the mucosa of the mastoid air cells (Tashima et al, 1986).

Hasebe and colleagues (2000) analyzed 107 ears of 85 patients who underwent VT insertion for COME that was resistant to medical treatment. They used high-resolution computed tomography (CT) to investigate residual soft tissue densities and found that the mastoid cells were filled with soft tissue in 29.9% of the ears. The problem was even more frequent (80%) in the ears with severe attic retraction. They attributed the higher rate in the patients with retraction pockets to reduced gas exchange and the presence of tissue changes (eg, granulation tissue). The latter are irreversible forms of mastoid pathology that contribute to the development of deep retraction pockets and thus lead to cholesteatoma formation in the long term. The same researchers noted that COME-related soft tissue changes were much more frequent in adult patients than pediatric patients.

Tos and Stangerup (1984) found that VT insertion did not increase the extent of pneumatization. They attributed this to previous middle ear infections that the child had.

Radiologic Evaluation of the Mastoid in COME

Opacification of the mastoid air cell system is a common radiographic finding in COME and indicates latent mastoiditis or previous infection (Figure 44-3). According to reports in the literature, patients who have a higher number of otitis media episodes prior to tympanostomy show more marked opacification. In COME, either with a draining ear or an ear resistant to multiple VT insertions, CT of the temporal bone is always done to examine the mastoid air cells. There is a strong correlation between radiographic mastoid opacification and abnormal findings in the mastoid air cell system during mastoidectomy.

Mastoidectomy Indications

A number of treatment strategies have been proposed for COME. Medical treatment consists of antibiotics and corticosteroids. VT placement is currently the gold stan-

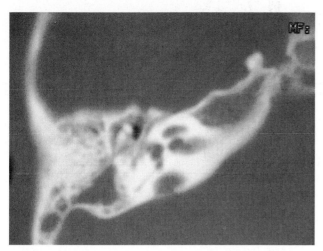

FIGURE 44-3. Axial computed tomographic scan of the temporal bone. The soft tissue fills all the cells and surrounds the ossicular chain.

dard therapy. VTs help eliminate secretions and ventilate the middle ear and mastoid. The guidelines of the US Agency for Health Care and Research Quality recommend VT insertion for children who have a 3-month or longer history of COME and exhibit 20 dB or worse bilateral hearing loss.

Children may require multiple sets of tubes before they grow out of middle ear disease. However, in those children, an underlying persistent mucosal disease of the mastoid as well as the small volume of the mastoid air cells may be a contributing factor. Besides considering a long-lasting type of tube such as a T tube, especially in children who repeatedly develop otitis media with effusion immediately after the extrusion of the VTs, mastoidectomy may be considered. Although VT placement is the gold standard, this procedure does not lead to healthy mastoid mucosa in every case. In most cases of COME, VT insertion effectively reduces inflammation, edema, and excessive secretion from the middle ear mucosa; however, this method cannot address the problems posed by cholesterol granuloma and granulation tissue lesions. Granulation tissue and cholesterol granuloma within the mastoid air cells and antrum are both irreversible. These pathologies are the main reasons for failure to achieve full recovery with VT, and mastoidectomy is the only effective solution for such cases.

Cholesterol granuloma (blue eardrum) develops in COME accompanied by bloody effusion. Characteristic findings are a hypocellular mastoid and hyperplastic and metaplastic mucoperiosteal lining, including the presence of glands, cysts, and cholesterol granuloma. In spite of medical therapy and VT insertion, the condition may progress, and mastoid surgery is indicated for these patients (Paparella, 1976).

Sometimes the granulation tissue filling the antrum also blocks the aditus, resulting in the accumulation of the secretions in the mastoid despite the presence of a patent VT, and may exhibit itself with "deep dull pain." Mastoidectomy would be indicated in this situation.

Persistent otorrhea is the most common complication of VT insertion. Otitis externa, formation of granulation tissue around the tube, and foreign body reactions are some of the factors that cause otorrhea that are beyond the scope of this chapter. These patients present to the otolaryngologist having already used several courses of ear drops and/or systemic antibiotics. In these cases, intravenous antibiotics and local treatment with frequent suctioning may help. However, the otorrhea that starts immediately after tube insertion and that does not resolve despite maximal medical treatment may be attributable to the mucosal disease of the mastoid as a result of COME. In this situation, the chronic discharge after the VT placement may be attributable to the persistence of inflammation in the mastoid. The fact that secretion through the VT stops after mastoidectomy confirms that the secretory process is closely related to the pathologic mucosa in the mastoid. The swollen mucosal lining of the mastoid air cells and the granulation tissue filling these spaces are the typical radiologic findings of the mastoid in these cases. Surgical exploration of the mastoid may reveal osteitis, thick mucoid fluid, cholesterol granuloma, or granulomatous polypoid mucosa. Creation of an aerated cavity to be lined with healthy mucosa by removing all of the diseased cells will be the only choice to cure the condition in this case. VTs should be left in place even after mastoidectomy is performed. It is reasonable to remove the tubes 1 or 2 years postsurgery if they do not extrude spontaneously. Allergy and/or immunology workup also have to be performed before attempting any treatment (Heaton and Mills, 1993; Jung and Rhee, 1991). In the 1980s, Holmquist and colleagues (1980) reported that the mucosal changes within the mastoid that occurred owing to COME are relieved by mastoidectomy only.

Development of atelectasis of the middle ear and/or tympanic membrane retraction pockets is a sequela of eustachian tube dysfunction and COME, and small mastoid volume and an underlying diseased mastoid may be the cause of this process. Mastoidectomy may be the only solution to stop the progression of this sequela. The possibility of cholesteatoma formation should also be kept in mind in cases in which retraction pockets have not responded to multiple VT insertions. Stangerup and Tos (1986), proponents of the environmental theory, believe that middle ear ventilation increases the size of the cell system to some degree. These authors advocate creating a large air reservoir by mastoidectomy to obtain better functional results. Takahashi and colleagues (1998) have indicated that preservation of the mastoid mucosa, mainly the epitympanic mucosa, is important to promote reaeration of the mastoid after ear surgery and prevent re-retractions and cholesteatoma formation.

Mastoidectomy may also be considered during closure of the eardrum perforations to increase the chance of an aerated middle ear following the tympanoplasty in patients with a long history of COME or in patients who still demonstrate ongoing eustachian tube problems on the contralateral ear.

My common indications for mastoidectomy related to COME are persistent otorrhea after VT placement that cannot be controlled otherwise and recurrences of COME despite VT reinsertions. The development of cholesterol granuloma is relatively rare, but mastoidectomy becomes the only choice when present. The retraction pockets may evolve to cholesteatoma when they are deep and when there is persistent negative middle ear pressure. In cases with grade III or deeper retraction pockets, I perform a mastoidectomy during the excision of the retraction pocket and reconstruction of the tympanic membrane with fascia and cartilage graft.

Surgical Technique

The incision for mastoidectomy is the classic retroauricular type. Initially, an anteriorly pedicled periosteal flap is raised. This flap is important as it is replaced in its original position at the end of the operation to prevent skin retraction toward the mastoidectomy cavity in the long term. The antrum and all diseased air cells must be opened to remove any irreversible tissue and create a uniform cavity. Simple mastoidectomy is not the surgery of choice in these cases. Drilling out the mastoid air cells without establishing a wide opening to the epitympanic recess and the middle ear will not achieve cure. The aditus ad antrum and facial recess have to be explored, and the granulation tissue has to be removed. It is important to maintain the connection with the middle ear space by performing either posterior atticotomy or posterior tympanotomy to allow better drainage and aeration of the mastoidectomy cavity. An effective mastoidectomy should stabilize the inflammatory process and restore normal middle ear function in these patients. In each case, VT insertion and adenoidectomy, if not done before, are also performed in the same session.

Özbilen and colleagues (1991) studied a series of 26 patients with COME who were operated on and also compared with a control group that only had VTs placed. Seventeen individuals underwent complete mastoidectomy with extended posterior tympanotomy and VT insertion, and nine underwent simple mastoidectomy and VT insertion. At surgery, the noted findings were hypertrophy of the mucosal lining of the mastoid antrum and cellules, similar mucosal changes in the ossicular chain, granulation tissue, and effusion. The aditus ad antrum was blocked by mucosal pathology in 17 cases, and cholesterol granulomas were detected in 8 cases. During follow-up, four patients required revision mastoidectomies owing to

obstruction of the aditus ad antrum by mucosal folds. The success rate in the COME ears was 65%, whereas the rate in control ears was only 45%.

Holmquist and colleagues (1980) suggest that the surgical technique for COME cases that require mastoidectomy should include opening of the epitympanic recess and the space anterior to the malleus head, opening of the facial recess, Silastic sheeting, and VT insertion.

In the large majority of cases, the middle ear heals once the mastoid pathology is removed. Experience to date indicates that only a small number of COME ears exhibit extensive mastoid bone inflammation. This suggests that performing mastoid surgery as soon as the pathology is detected offers a better chance for full recovery.

Conclusion

In summary, VT insertion is still the gold standard for managing COME. However, some cases cannot be cured despite multiple VT insertions. Otorrhea developing immediately after the tympanostomy tube insertion is not always resolved by routine measures such as systemic or topical antibiotic treatment or VT removal. In such cases, radiologic findings in the mastoid show reduced cellularity and opacification of cellules, suggesting persistent inflammation in the mastoid. In patients with these problems, mastoidectomy may be the only effective way to achieve a dry, normal-functioning middle ear.

References

Akyildiz N, Göksu N, Özbilen S, et al. Körner's septum: Does it contribute to retraction and adhesion process? Presented at The Politzer Society International Conference on Reality in Ear Surgery and Otoneurosurgery; 1991 Jun 16–19; Maastricht, The Netherlands.

Aoki K, Esaki S, Honda Y, Tos M. Effect of middle ear infection on pneumatization and growth of the mastoid process. An experimental study in pigs. Acta Otolaryngol (Stockh) 1990;110: 399–409.

Bluestone CD, Doyle WJ. Anatomy and physiology of eustachian tube and middle ear related to otitis media. J Allergy Clin Immunol 1988;81:997–1003.

Hasebe S, Takahashi H, Honjo I, Sudo M. Organic change of effusion in the mastoid in otitis media with effusion and its relation to attic retraction. Int J Pediatr Otorhinolaryngol 2000;53:17–24.

Heaton JM, Mills RP. Otorrhoea via ventilation tubes in adults and children. Clin Otolaryngol 1993;18:496–9.

Holmquist J, Jarlstedt J, Tjellstrom A. Surgery of the mastoid in ears with middle ear effusion. Ann Otol Rhinol Laryngol 1980; 89:322–3.

Homoe P, Lynnerup N, Videbaek H. CT-scanning of ancient Greenlandic Inuit temporal bones. Acta Otolaryngol (Stockh) 1992;11:674–9.

Honjo I, Takahashi H, Sudo M, et al. Pathophysiological and therapeutic considerations of otitis media with effusion from viewpoint of middle ear ventilation. Int J Pediatr Otorhinolaryngol 1998;43:105–13.

Ikarashi H, Nakano Y, Okura T. The relationship between the degree of chronic middle ear inflammation and tympanic bulla pneumatization in the pig as animal model. Eur Arch Otorhinolaryngol 1994;251:100–4.

Jackler RK, Schindler RA. Role of the mastoid in tympanic membrane reconstruction. Laryngoscope 1984;94:495–500.

Jaisinghani VJ, Paparella MM, Schachern PA, et al. Residual mesenchyme persisting into adulthood. Am J Otolaryngol 1999; 20:363–70.

Jung TK, Rhee CK. Otolaryngologic approach to the diagnosis and management of otitis media. Otolaryngol Clin North Am 1991;24:931–45.

Newberg LB, Ling V, Shamsuddin AM. Microscopic analysis of the mastoid bone in chronic serous otitis media. Laryngoscope 1985;95:921–3.

Özbilen S, Akyildiz N, Göksu N, et al. Mastoid surgery in chronic secretory otitis media. Presented at The Politzer Society International Conference on Reality in Ear Surgery and Otoneurosurgery; 1991 Jun 16–19; Maastricht, The Netherlands.

Özgirgin N, Akbay C, Saran Y, et al. Otitis media with effusion: an ethiopathogenetic (ultrastructural) approach. An Otorrinolaringol Ibero Am 1989;4:9–16.

Palva T, Ramsay H. Fate of the mesenchyme in the process of pneumatization. Otol Neurotol 2002;23:192–9.

Paparella MM. Blue ear drum and its management. Ann Otol Rhinol Laryngol 1976;85:293–5.

Roizen NJ, Martich V, Ben-Ami T, et al. Sclerosis of the mastoid air cells as an indicator of undiagnosed otitis media in children with Down's syndrome. Clin Pediatr (Phila) 1994;33:439–43.

Sadé J, Fuchs C. Secretory otitis media in adults: I. The role of mastoid pneumatization as a risk factor. Ann Otol Rhinol Laryngol 1996;105:643–7.

Sadé J, Fuchs C. Secretory otitis media in adults: II. The role of mastoid pneumatization as a prognostic factor. Ann Otol Rhinol Laryngol 1997;106:37–40.

Stangerup SE, Tos M. Treatment of secretory otitis and pneumatization. Laryngoscope 1986;96:680–4.

Takahashi H, Honjo I, Naito Y, et al. Cause of posterior canal wall retraction after surgery from the viewpoint of mastoid conditions. Am J Otol 1998;19:131–5.

Takahashi H, Sugimaru T, Honjo I, et al. Assessment of the gas exchange function of the middle ear using nitrous oxide. A preliminary study. Acta Otolaryngol (Stockh) 1994;114: 643–6.

Tashima K, Tanaka S, Saito H. Volumetric changes of the aerated middle ear and mastoid after insertion of tympanostomy tubes. Am J Otolaryngol 1986;7:302–5.

Tos M, Stangerup SE. Mastoid pneumatization in secretory otitis. Further support for the environmental theory. Acta Otolaryngol (Stockh) 1984;98:110–8.

Tos M, Stangerup SE. Secretory otitis and pneumatization of the mastoid process: sexual differences in the size of mastoid cell system. Am J Otolaryngol 1985;6:199–205.

Tos M, Stangerup SE, Andreassen UK. Size of the mastoid air cells and otitis media. Ann Otol Rhinol Laryngol 1985;94(4 Pt 1): 386–92.

Tos M, Stangerup SE, Hvid G. Mastoid pneumatization. Evidence of the environmental theory. Arch Otolaryngol 1984;110:502–7.

Chapter 45

INCIDENTAL MIDDLE EAR/ MASTOID FLUID IN COMPUTED TOMOGRAPHY/MAGNETIC RESONANCE IMAGING

CUNEYT M. ALPER, MD

The diagnosis and management of otitis media (OM) have not changed significantly over the past several decades. The main advance in the diagnosis has been the widespread use of sensitive imaging modalities such as computed tomographic (CT) scans and magnetic resonance imaging (MRI). However, the routine use of these diagnostic tools for OM remains limited to the diagnosis of complications and some sequelae. When used for the temporal bones, the oversensitivity and somewhat lack of specificity of these techniques related to inflammation or effusion and in the middle ear (ME) and mastoid gas cell system may create diagnostic and therapeutic dilemmas. On the other hand, much broader use of these imaging modalities for other systems and pathologies may introduce incidental temporal bone findings or, more commonly, incidental finding of a middle ear effusion (MEE). Moreover, while targeting other pathologies, because of not using the specific imaging protocols for the temporal bone with the necessary detail and format, these powerful techniques often end up highlighting an abnormality in the ear without the ability to adequately differentiate or rule out pathologies. This brings the need for differential diagnosis and a question of repeat imaging with temporal bone imaging protocols.

How Common Is MEE?

It is important to know the prevalence of ME fluid in the population that could be identified as an incidental finding on a CT scan or MRI.

It is possible that there may be an acute otitis media (AOM) at the time of the imaging study. Although AOM is usually symptomatic, the severity of the symptoms may

vary and may be unnoticed owing to any coexisting symptoms or signs or a biased approach that might be attributable to the problem that required the imaging study in the first place.

A study of the epidemiology of OM by Teele and colleagues (1989) demonstrated that by the age of 3 years, 38% of children develop one or two episodes of AOM and 33% develop three or more, with the remaining 29% of children having no history of OM. Although the chance of a concurrent AOM during an imaging study is small, it is more likely in young children between the ages of 6 and 18 months, when there is an age-specific peak attack rate.

It is also well known that after an episode of AOM, there is a period of persistent MEE without significant signs or symptoms. A well-known study from Boston (Teele et al, 1980) found that 70% of the children still had effusion 2 weeks after an AOM. There was still effusion present in 40% of children at 1 month, 20% at 2 months, and 10% at 3 months. The mean periods of time spent with MEE after the first, second, and third episodes of AOM were almost identical, ranging from 39 to 44 days. Various studies demonstrated similar incidences of MEE after initiation of antibiotic therapy for AOM, with a 41 to 85% incidence in 10 to 14 days, a 23 to 73% incidence at 1 month, a 12 to 29% incidence at 2 months, and a 5 to 25% incidence at 3 months (Bluestone and Klein, 2001). The prospective study by Paradise and colleagues (1997) indicated that children had a mean of 20.4 and 16.6 days with MEE in the first and second years of life, respectively.

Surveys of otherwise healthy children for the presence of MEE have identified a high prevalence of asymptomatic fluid. In a survey of 2- to 5-year-old black children in day care, the mean proportion of examinations demonstrating bilateral effusion ranged from 12% between the ages of 24 and 30 months and 4% between the ages 54 and 60 months (Zeisel et al, 1999). In Pittsburgh children, aged 2 to 6 years and observed monthly for a 2-year period, approximately two-thirds of the episodes of otitis media with effusion (OME) cleared within 1 month (Casselbrant et al, 1985).

In a surveillance study with daily tympanometry and symptom diary and weekly otoscopy, 40 children (20 families) were followed in Pittsburgh during the fall through winter and spring months (Antonio et al, 2002; Moody et al, 1998). Of the 40 children, 14 were between the ages of 18 months and 3 years, and the others were ages 4 to 6 years. Sixty-seven episodes (17 bilateral) of OM (either AOM or OME) were identified in 16 children. Only 11 children were treated with antibiotics for five episodes of AOM and six episodes of OME. The average duration of OM was 20.5 days, with a range of 3 to 129 days. Of 67 ear episodes, 16 (24%), 6 (9%), and 1 (1.5%) lasted more than 30, 60, and 90 days, respectively. Sixty-three percent of these mostly asymptomatic OME episodes were temporally related to a cold.

It is relatively rare to obtain an imaging study in the newborn period. However, there is probably a higher incidence of asymptomatic effusion in this age group. OME was identified at 2 months in 34% of the otherwise normal infants in one study (Marchant et al, 1984). Half of the infants with OME were asymptomatic.

These numbers suggest that a significant proportion of an otherwise healthy pediatric population may have an incidental finding of MEE on an imaging study obtained for another reason. This chance is higher in younger children, children in day care, or those with a recent history of a cold.

The incidence of asymptomatic effusion in an adult should be very small. In the absence of a surveillance study in adults, it may not be possible to declare an incidence or prevalence of MEE in otherwise healthy adults. CT scans performed in 31 healthy adults with a common cold demonstrated 87% abnormalities in the paranasal sinuses (Gwaltney et al, 1994). Although the presence of MEE after a cold is not documented with an imaging study, development of significant negative ME pressures after experimental viral upper respiratory infections suggests that CT or MRI could demonstrate changes consistent with effusion (Alper et al, 1996b; Alper et al, 1998; Doyle et al, 1999). After 2 weeks without any treatment, 11 (79%) of the 14 subjects who had a repeat CT scan demonstrated clearance or marked improvement of the abnormalities. The relatively rare incidence of MEE, coupled with the potential of underlying serious pathologies, such as nasopharyngeal tumor, makes an incidental finding of MEE in an adult a distinct clinical entity with specific diagnostic challenges.

What Is the Chance of Diagnosing Incidental ME Fluid with Imaging?

All of the studies and discussion above were related to asymptomatic MEE in an otherwise healthy normal patient. It is not unusual for MEE to be diagnosed during a well-child visit. However, our subject is MEE that is incidentally identified on a CT scan and MRI as an occult finding. However, imaging studies are not obtained in completely healthy children and adults unless it is due to the extremely small possibility of being part of a study that requires them. The imaging study that may incidentally reveal MEE is usually a study of the head and neck. This suggests the possibility of an underlying pathology directly causing MEE, making the patient's ear more prone to the development of effusion or an overall systemic pathologic condition making the patient prone to MEE. The chance of the presence of MEE incidentally diagnosed on an imaging study is therefore relatively higher in patients who need this study compared with the prevalence of effusion in an otherwise healthy population.

An obstacle in diagnosing the changes on the imaging study consistent with MEE is the potential bias of the radiologist to focus on the region and the potential pathology of interest and either not notice those changes or not report them. It is naturally very difficult to find any information on the rate of missing incidental findings. My experience with reviewing all imaging studies personally is that overlooking an incidental radiologic finding that could have some significance happens often. Similar to the clinicians, a radiologist may also overlook a sign or finding or may fail to report it if the study was requested for another reason. However, the undiagnosed portion of incidental findings on imaging studies is naturally not the subject of this chapter.

Another obstacle in the differential diagnosis of the abnormalities on imaging studies of the ME and mastoid is the limitations of the imaging protocol. Temporal bone imaging with CT scan or MRI has a specific protocol, and there are different temporal bone imaging protocols for diagnosing and ruling out specific pathologies of concern. The routine mechanism for processing and evaluating imaging studies is to conduct the entire preplanned protocol and either not have it reviewed by the radiologist before the patient leaves the imaging suite or have a brief review of the imaging for the purpose of a planned study. Therefore, it is rare that a modification to the imaging protocol would be possible and conducted on intraimaging notice of an incidental finding of MEE. Many clinicians would suggest that in the absence of clinical information, including a history and physical examination, such a modification would not be indicated at all. Limiting the scope of findings in the imaging consistent with MEE, very few would argue against that statement, knowing the relatively high prevalence of asymptomatic MEE in the population.

One other potential obstacle in the diagnosis of MEE with an imaging study in the presence of a radiology report mentioning such abnormalities is the level of concern and interest in further investigation by the physician who requested the imaging. Some clinicians may ignore this finding owing to the importance of the primary indication for the study, and some may rely on the unimportance of the effusion or expectation that spontaneous resolution is likely and not investigate further. Other clinicians may refer the patient to an otolaryngologist for further diagnosis and workup.

How often a patient is referred to an otolaryngologist owing to an imaging study consistent with OM is not known. There are no statistics or specific studies on this matter. My personal opinion is that it is very rare. I may get a referral once or twice a year of a patient with an incidental finding of fluid in the ME (Figure 45-1). I probably notice more cases with fluid in the ME or mastoid while personally reviewing the imaging studies for other reasons. This is consistent with underdiagnosing or underreporting of ME fluid.

What Does a CT Scan See?

For proper use of CT for the imaging of temporal bone, high-definition CT is used to offer high-contrast images, which allows excellent recognition of bony and soft tissue structures and pathology (Valvassori et al, 1995). The speed of image acquisition may be as fast as 1 second per slice. Recent developments allow continuous acquisition of data using spiral rather than axial slice-by-slice scanning. This allows high-speed examinations over a wide area of coverage. High-definition CT images are obtained with the use of special software reconstruction techniques that reduce pixel size to 0.25 mm. Slice thickness is reduced to 1.5 mm, and serial sections at 1.00 mm are achieved by overlapping sections by 0.5 mm. Two or more sections are necessary for proper examination of the temporal bone. In the routine CT examination of the temporal bone, contrast enhancement is not necessary. If the patient can cooperate, direct coronal and sagittal imaging can be performed. Otherwise, electronic reconstruction techniques allow a multiplanar display of anatomy acquired with axial slices only. Three-dimensional surface reconstruction of bone or soft tissue is possible from axial slices.

Cortical bone bony septations and ossicles are seen as white in the CT scan. Air (gas) in the ME and mastoid is black. Any soft tissue or fluid is viewed as gray. The radiologist can measure tissue absorption with the cursor of variable size on a CT and obtain densitometric readings of selected areas of the temporal bone. This technique, however, is not reliable in differentiating fluids and soft tissues filling the mastoid air cells and ME because of partial volume averaging effects.

What Does an MRI See?

MRI is an imaging technique that produces cross-sectional images without exposing the patient to radiation (Valvassori et al, 1995). The intensity of the MRI signal depends on the concentration of the hydrogen nuclei in the examined tissue and on two tissue-specific relaxation times in the magnetic field, T_1 and T_2. Variation of relaxation times is obtained by changing the interval between the radio frequencies, the repetition time (TR), and the time the signal or echo is measured after the signal, or echo time (TE).

The signal intensity of different tissues is directly proportional to the amount of free protons present in the tis-

FIGURE 45-1. Magnetic resonance imaging requested for a history of delayed growth of a 12-year-old female demonstrating bilateral effusion in mastoids. She had ear infections before 2 years of age and had symptoms consistent with nasal allergies. She denied hearing loss. An otolaryngology visit 3 weeks later revealed effusion in the left ear. She was treated with 10 mg daily cetirizine (Zyrtec) and a 10-day course of amoxicillin because she had not received any recent antibiotics. Ears were clear in the visit 6 weeks after. When she developed bilateral effusions a few weeks later that lasted more than 3 months, ventilation tubes were placed, and an adenoidectomy was performed. Postoperatively, she had left-sided otorrhea that responded to ofloxacin ear drops. A repeat imaging study was not requested.

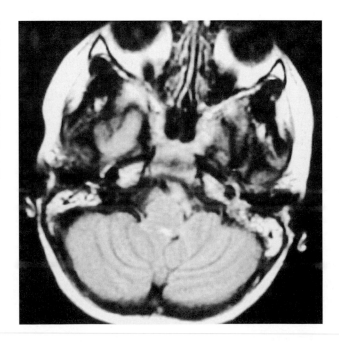

sue. Fat and body fluids contain large amounts of free protons and therefore emit strong MRI signals displayed as bright areas. Air, cortical bone, and calcified tissue appear as dark areas because they contain few free protons. Pathologic processes can be recognized when the proton density and relaxation times of the abnormal tissue are different from those of the normal tissue. Different projections are obtained by changing the orientation of the magnetic field without changing the position of the patient. T_1 images obtained by a short TR and TE offer the best anatomic delineation. T_2 images obtained with long TR and TE differentiate normal from pathologic tissues. The intravenous injection of ferromagnetic contrast agents (gadolinium) has improved the differentiation of pathologic processes.

Because cortical bone and air (gas) emit no signal, a normal mastoid, external auditory canal, and ME cavity appear on MRIs as black areas, and contours of these structures are not visualized. The petrous apex is also dark, except for inner ear and internal auditory canal structures that appear bright.

Fluid and soft tissue changes caused by trauma, infection, or tumor of the temporal bone are seen in MRI as high signal intensity. MRI is more sensitive than CT in detecting small soft tissue lesions or effusion in the temporal bone. However, the anatomic site of the lesion and presence and extent of bony destruction cannot be determined by MRI because anatomic landmarks are absent, except the fluid in the labyrinth. MRI has recently been shown to be an excellent noninvasive tool for the diagnosis and quantification of MEE in animal models and humans (Alper and Doyle, 1999a; Alper and Doyle, 1999b; Alper et al, 1996b; Alper et al, 1999a; Alper et al, 1999b; Alper et al, 1999c; Alper et al, 2000).

Are All Abnormal Findings Effusion?

Incidental findings on a CT scan or MRI may not necessarily be effusion, and, as stated above, it may be difficult to differentiate effusion from other pathologies. It would be of great importance to differentiate and not overlook any other potential pathologies. Table 45-1 outlines the imaging characteristics of some of the normal structures and tissues and some pathologies in the temporal bone. MEE may have similar characteristics on a CT scan with granulation tissue, bone marrow, cholesteatoma, or cholesterol granuloma that did not cause bony erosion. Effusion on an MRI may have similar signal intensity features with cholesteatoma, mucocele, petrous apicitis, and arachnoid cyst.

An effusion may be silent (such as in OME) or may be attributable to an AOM or mastoiditis without bony erosion. Any acute inflammatory process would change the imaging characteristics, specifically with an increase in contrast enhancement. Although an AOM or mastoiditis is typically not asymptomatic and does not fall under the category of incidental finding, "silent" OM or "masked mastoiditis" under the use of antibiotics may end up being incidentally picked up.

Another presentation of MEE as an abnormal finding is on a temporal bone imaging for evaluation of trauma. Opacification on a CT scan or increased signal intensity in MRI would either suggest a hemorrhage or cerebrospinal fluid leak into the ME or mastoid. The increased chance in any patient with significant maxillofacial trauma of developing MEE, with or without any procedure, packing, or intubation or nasogastric tube placement, would only make any differentiation more difficult.

There are very few reports on the incidental diagnosis of ME or mastoid disease. A report of 644 MRIs for cerebellopontine angle (CPA) tumors ordered by an otolaryngology department demonstrated abnormalities in 45% of the studies in patients between the ages of 43 and 76 years (Mirza et al, 2000). Whereas CPA tumors were diagnosed in 4%, sinus findings were present in 8.7%, and ME and mastoid disease were present in 5.3%. The authors stated that the high signal intensity in the ME or mastoid region was in patients with known ME disease, indicating that these cases were not, in fact, incidental.

It is worthwhile to state once more that studies with incidental temporal bone findings will most likely not be in temporal bone protocols. Images may not have adequate slices, high definition, the best orientation, or contrast enhancement that may be necessary to differentiate effusion from other pathologies. Printouts may not have the optimal window settings for temporal bone pathologies or a complete and adequate set of printouts of the temporal bone imaging. Therefore, the imaging characteristics outlined in Table 45-1 may not be too helpful in the differential diagnosis.

What to Do When CT/MRI Identifies "Fluid" in the ME or Mastoid

The initial approach to a diagnosis of an incidental finding of fluid in the ME or mastoid should include a thorough history and physical examination. The primary goal of this approach is to find out if the history and otoscopic examination are consistent with the imaging. The second goal is to rule out any acute inflammatory process that could need immediate attention. The third goal is to rule out any other underlying pathologies consistent with the abnormalities in the imaging or that may have caused the MEE.

Complete History and Physical Examination

Often the history would provide information on the likelihood of a current or recent inflammatory process in the ME or age-appropriate symptoms consistent with OME. The most common symptom in the history for an AOM

TABLE 45-1. Imaging Characteristics of the Temporal Bone

Tissue or Diagnosis	CT		MRI		
	Bone Erosion	Contrast Enhancement	T_1 Signal Intensity	T_2 Signal Intensity	Contrast Enhancement
Air/gas	NA	None	None	None	None
Cortical bone	NA	None	None	None	None
Inner ear fluid	NA	None	Low	High	None
Effusion	None	None	Low	High	Rim or none
Granulation tissue	None	Rim or yes	Low	Intermediate	Yes
Bone marrow	None	None	High	Low	None
Cholesteatoma	Smooth	None	Low	High	None
Cholesterol granuloma	Smooth	None	High	High	None
Mucocele	Smooth	Rim or none	Low	High	Rim or none
Petrous apicitis	Irregular	Rim	Low	High	Rim
Arachnoid cyst	Smooth	None	Low	High	None
Neoplasm	Variable	Yes	Isointense or variable	High or variable	Yes
Carotid aneurysm	Smooth	Yes	Low	Inhomogeneous	Rim
Encephalocele	Smooth	Yes	Isointense or variable	High or variable	Isointense with brain

NA = not applicable.

would be otalgia in older children or irritability and tugging of ears in infants. Although "incidental" implies unknown or unexpected finding (ie, occult), the symptoms or signs are often known either to the primary physician or to the patient. Reviewing all of the ear-related history may therefore explain the imaging findings, relieve the excitement, and prevent unnecessary workup.

The otoscopic examination may also be consistent with MEE, depending on the interval between the imaging study and re-examination of the patient by the primary physician or the referred specialist. Diagnosis of MEE is usually not a challenge for an experienced pneumatic otoscopist. Moreover, this examination may often give clues related to a previous history of OM, the duration of MEE, and the possibility of spontaneous resolution.

Treatment

Combined with the otoscopic examination, evaluation of the history should focus on the potential need for treatment. The condition of the ear with the supporting history should dictate the treatment modality irrespective of the presence of an imaging study as long as the imaging findings are consistent with the clinical diagnosis. Of course, while determining the most appropriate mode of management, the underlying or coexisting illnesses or pathology that prompted the imaging study in the first place should be kept in mind in terms of selection of the method and timing of the ear disease. Again, in that condition, existence of fluid in the ME cleft visualized on a CT scan or an MRI should not bias the physician on one mode of treatment or another, but it should be viewed just as a "confirmation" of the clinical diagnosis of the ME disease. For the conditions of ME imaging findings consistent with the clinical assessment, treatment choices of watchful waiting, antibiotics, tympanocentesis or myringotomy, ventilation tube placement,

or any other treatment should be considered. Treatment of "masked mastoiditis" may be less aggressive than for acute mastoiditis with periosteitis, and tympanocentesis and culture-directed antimicrobial therapy may be adequate (Bluestone, 1998).

The timing of any of these treatments may be moderated by the "main" concern in the diagnosis and treatment of the patient and the potential association of MEE with that concern. An infectious process in the central nervous system in the presence of any "incidental" ME fluid would require an urgent approach to the ear not only for treatment but also for diagnostic purposes, that is, to obtain a microbiologic specimen.

If the patient with incidental ME fluid goes to the operating room for another reason, this opportunity should not be missed to examine the ears under general anesthesia. This may provide valuable information that may otherwise be difficult to obtain owing to the patient's age or degree of cooperation. Again, if indicated, the necessary treatment for the ear should be coordinated employing the same anesthesia.

Although not indicated as per the known history, the other diagnoses and anticipated prognosis and condition of the patient may also indicate planning a treatment such as placement of ventilation tubes under the same anesthesia. Even if neither the past history nor the anticipated prognosis indicates a need for ventilation tubes, there may be questions on the diagnosis, as well as the possibility of increasing the chance of resolution; thus, a myringotomy may be performed in the presence of an imaging consistent with MEE if the patient is already going to the operating room.

Need for Repeat Imaging?

When clinical assessment of MEE is consistent with the imaging, even though not done with an optimal protocol, there is no need for repeat imaging before the appropriate treatment. But the clinician should proceed with the indicated treatment. However, there will still be a question remaining on whether to perform follow-up imaging after treatment. The answer to this question is squeezed between the concerns on residual abnormality or the potential for missing important pathology and the concern of requesting an imaging study with extremely small potential yield that is also well supported by the pressure from a managed care environment. Therefore, there is no magic answer. If the history is consistent with recurrent AOM, or OME, or if there is a recent episode of AOM or a recent cold, and if the otoscopic examination before any treatment is consistent with the imaging, and MEE resolves with the treatment option that the patient receives (from watchful waiting to ventilation tubes), I do not obtain another imaging study of any kind. If I plan a treatment and a follow-up, I may wait to obtain a hearing test and wait for the completion of the treatment unless imaging, history, or otoscopy reveals any unusual feature.

This same approach applies to the conditions that have spontaneously resolved even before the first history and physical examination after the imaging study. If it is likely—based on history and risk factors—that MEE had been present at the time of imaging, even though my physical examination does not confirm the effusion, accepting the high probability of spontaneous resolution, I do not obtain a repeat imaging study. However, I prefer to obtain an audiogram and a tympanogram at that visit to confirm the normal ME status.

For these two conditions for which I do not plan a repeat imaging study, I have an extensive discussion with the patient or the family, informing them about the risks and the benefits of each option. There we compare the extremely low chance of abnormal repeat imaging with the further exposure to x-ray (if it is a CT scan that is necessary), the possible need for contrast, and, in small children, the need for sedation. Through this discussion, it is no longer my decision but becomes the family's informed decision not to obtain repeat imaging.

If there are some unusual features in the imaging, history, or physical examination or the audiologic evaluation is not necessarily consistent with MEE, although the otoscopic examination confirms the presence of effusion, I prefer to obtain repeat imaging study. The timing of the study can be determined as per the specific conditions of the patient. However, if there is a time for a course of treatment or a need for ventilation tubes, it is preferable to wait 4 to 6 weeks for the complete resolution of the ME inflammation before a repeat imaging to avoid a similar dilemma.

If the imaging characteristics of the abnormal CT or MRI have the likelihood of another pathology, or an underlying potentially serious pathology is causing the effusion, there is a relatively urgent need for repeat imaging with the appropriate temporal bone imaging protocols.

In adults, especially those with unilateral MEE, attention should be directed at the neck for any lymph node enlargement and to the nasopharynx for a mass. This applies to any effusion at an age in which this condition is not prevalent, especially when there is no past history or risk factors.

Choice of Repeat CT versus MRI

If the initial imaging study of concern was an MRI, if/whenever I order a repeat study, I prefer a high-resolution CT scan with both axial and coronal sections. CT has the advantages of cost, easier scheduling (at least in most institutions) than MRI, shorter data collection time, less chance of needing sedation, less sensitivity to patient motion, and excellent bony detail. This last feature, which MRI lacks, is critical for an organ of essentially bone and because the most critical differentiating factor is bony erosion. This repeat imaging study to confirm the resolution of effusion and to rule out rare pathologies does not need to be with contrast.

A repeat CT scan will still be my first choice, even if the initial imaging study of concern was a CT scan, because, as stated before, the first study will most likely lack the definition, frequency, and orientation for the temporal bone. In cases of persistent imaging features consistent with ME or mastoid effusion, if the prior treatment modality did not include ventilation tubes, I would then place tubes and discuss the risks and benefits of one more imaging study. Any effusion-like imaging abnormalities limited to the mastoid or any section of the temporal bone will then require either surgical exploration and possible biopsy, and if it was not obtained before, I may obtain an MRI. At any phase when clinical or imaging information leads to a specific diagnosis, treatment is planned accordingly.

References

Alper CM, Doyle WJ. MRI validation of the accuracy of tympanometric gradient for the diagnosis of OME. Br J Audiol 1999a; 33:223–9.

Alper CM, Doyle WJ. Repeated middle ear inflation does not prevent otitis media with effusion in a monkey model. Laryngoscope 1999b;109:1074–80.

Alper CM, Doyle WJ, Seroky JT, et al. Pre-challenge antibodies moderate infection rate, and signs and symptoms in adults experimentally challenged with rhinovirus type 39. Laryngoscope 1996a;106:1298–305.

Alper CM, Doyle WJ, Seroky JT. Higher rates of pressure decrease in inflamed compared to non-inflamed middle ears. Otolaryngol Head Neck Surg 1999a;121:98–102.

Alper CM, Doyle WJ, Skoner DP, et al. Pre-challenge antibodies moderate disease expression in adults experimentally exposed to rhinovirus strain Hanks. Clin Infect Dis 1998;27:119–28.

Alper CM, Sabo DL, Doyle WJ. Validation by magnetic resonance imaging of tympanometry for diagnosing middle ear effusion. Otolaryngol Head Neck Surg 1999c;121:523–7.

Alper CM, Swarts JD, Doyle WJ. Middle ear inflation for the diagnosis of otitis media with effusion. Auris Nasus Larynx 1999b; 26:479–86.

Alper CM, Swarts JD, Doyle WJ. Prevention of otitis media with effusion by repeated air inflation in a monkey model. Arch Otolaryngol Head Neck Surg 2000;126:609–14.

Alper CM, Tabari R, Seroky JT, Doyle WJ. Magnetic resonance imaging of otitis media with effusion caused by functional obstruction of the eustachian tube. Ann Otol Rhinol Laryngol 1996b;106:422–31.

Antonio SM, Don D, Doyle WJ, Alper CM. Daily home tympanometry to study the pathogenesis of otitis media. Pediatr Infect Dis J 2002;21:882–5.

Bluestone CD. Acute and chronic mastoiditis and chronic suppurative otitis media. Semin Pediatr Infect Dis 1998;9:12–26.

Bluestone CD, Klein JO. Epidemiology. In: Bluestone CD, Klein JO, editors. Otitis media in infants and children. 3rd ed. Philadelphia: WB Saunders; 2001. p. 58–78.

Casselbrant ML, Brostoff LM, Cantekin EI, et al. Otitis media with effusion in preschool children. Laryngoscope 1985;95:428–36.

Doyle WJ, Alper CM, Buchman CA, et al. Illness and otological changes during upper respiratory virus infection. Laryngoscope 1999;109:324–8.

Gwaltney JM, Phillips CD, Miller DR, Riker DK. Computed tomographic study of the common cold. N Engl J Med 1994;330: 25–30.

Marchant CD, Shurin IM, Turcyzk VA, et al. Course and outcome of otitis media in infancy: a prospective study. J Pediatr 1984; 105:633–8.

Mirza S, Malik TH, Ahmed A, et al. Incidental findings on magnetic resonance imaging screening for cerebellopontine angle tumours. J Laryngol Otol 2000;114:750–4.

Moody SA, Alper CM, Doyle WJ. Daily tympanometry in children during the cold season: association of otitis media with upper respiratory tract infections. Int J Pediatr Otolaryngol 1998;45: 143–50.

Paradise JL, Rockette JE, Colborn K, et al. Otitis media in 2253 Pittsburgh-area infants: prevalence and risk factors during the first two years of life. Pediatrics 1997;99:318–33.

Teele DW, Klein JO, Rosner BA. Epidemiology of otitis media in children. Ann Otol Rhinol Laryngol 1980;89:5–6.

Teele DW, Klein JO, Rosner BA. Epidemiology of otitis media during the first seven years of life in children in greater Boston: a prospective, cohort study. J Infect Dis 1989;160:83–94.

Valvassori GE, Mafee MF, Carter BL, editors. Imaging of the head and neck. Stuttgart: Thieme; 1995.

Zeisel SA, Roberts JE, Neebe EC, et al. A longitudinal study of otitis media with effusion among 2- to 5-year-old African-American children in day care. Pediatrics 1999;103:15–9.

Chapter 46

TYPE OF TUBE TO INSERT

DAVID J. KAY, MD

The placement of tympanostomy tubes for ventilation of the middle ear is a frequent practice: it is the main reason a child receives general anesthesia in the United States (Owings and Kozak, 1998) and is second only to neonatal circumcision in being the most common surgical procedure in childhood (Derkay, 1993). Armstrong first described tympanostomy tubes in 1954, with an initial series of five patients receiving a straight vinyl tube with a 45° bevel. Over the following half-century, tubes have evolved to encompass a myriad of design styles and construction materials.

Tubes are currently placed for a variety of reasons, including chronic otitis media with effusion, recurrent acute otitis media, tympanic membrane (TM) retraction pockets or severe atelectasis (Potsic et al, 1997), idiopathic hemotympanum (Gates, 1994), and hyperbaric oxygen therapy to eliminate the high incidences of middle ear complications (Presswood et al, 1994). In deciding what particular type of tube to place, there are two primary variables to consider: the material from which the tube is constructed and the design or shape into which the material is constructed.

Tube Materials

Tympanostomy tubes may be manufactured from a variety of materials, most commonly from plastics or metals (Table 46-1). Based on the current literature, fluoroplastic (see below) appears to be the gold standard of tympanostomy tube materials, given its inert nature and nonadhesive qualities. Most comparative studies of other tube materials use fluoroplastic as a benchmark. Originally developed under the brand name Teflon, polytetrafluoroethylene (PTFE) consists of fluorine atoms covalently bound to carbon atoms (Karlan et al, 1980). This offers not only high heat resistance but also a very low coefficient of friction.

Tube Designs

Although there are scores of different tube designs available (Table 46-2), they can fundamentally be divided into two major categories: short-term tubes and long-term tubes. The two categories differ on the intended retention times of the tubes: 8 to 18 months with short-term tubes and 15 months to years with long-term ones (Kay et al, 2001; Rosenfeld and Isaacson, 1999). In general, each category has a representative design style (although many variations exist, as will be discussed below): grommets as short-term tubes and T tubes as long-term ones. The fundamental difference between the two is the presence of an outer flange.

The differing duration of ventilation between the two categories is related to the underlying mechanism of tube extrusion. The squamous layer of the TM keratinizes, and as the keratin migrates, it forms currents that push the tube posteroinferiorly (van Baarle and Wentges, 1975). The keratin then accumulates between the TM and the tube (either the outer flange or the tube itself) and thereby pushes out the tube. Because it is more difficult to push the tube out if there is no outer flange or if the inner flange is very large, the T tube design results in a significantly longer intubation period compared with grommets.

Table 46-2 outlines the major categories of tube designs. Grommets feature both an inner and an outer flange; the stiffer and larger the flange, the longer the tube stays in (Inglis, 1998). T tubes are so named because they are shaped like the letter " T," as a long straight tube with an inner flange. The T tube shaft is too long to fit in the middle ear (Rosenfeld and Isaacson, 1999), preventing the entire tube from entering the tympanic cavity. T grommets combine the large inner flange of T tubes with

TABLE 46-1. Common Tympanostomy Tube Materials

Metal
Stainless steel
Titanium
Gold
Plastic
Fluoroplastic (Teflon)
Silicone (Silastic)
Polyethylene (vinyl)
Ceramic
Calcium phosphate (hydroxyapatite)

TABLE 46-2. Common Tympanostomy Tube Design Styles

Style	Characteristics
Grommets	
Armstrong beveled grommets	Beveled inner flange, consistent with TM angle; lumen parallels EAC
Modified Armstrong beveled grommets	Less acute inner flange angle vs regular Armstrong; offset inner flange diameter
Armstrong V grommets	Forward projecting tab on anterior inner flange
Baldwin butterfly ventilation tube	Curvilinear trim to lateral outer flanges
Baxter beveled buttons	Large beveled lumen
Berger "V" bobbin ventilation tube	Conical flanges
Boston ventilation tube	Conical beveled outer flange
Beveled bobbins	Bell-shaped lateral flange
Canale ventilation tube	Angled tab on outer flange; notch on inner flange
Collar button ventilation tube	Equal inner and outer flanges; beveled shaft; flap tab on inner flange
Donaldson tube	Similar inner and outer flanges; outer may have tab for removal
Lindman-Silverstein Arrow	Arrow-shaped inner flange; rotate tube 90° after insertion to lock into place
Minireversible ventilation tube	Notched flanges of different diameters; either can be inner or outer
Moretz tab vent tube	Tab on inner flange
Paparella I vent tube	Notched inner flange; twist insertion into small incision
Paparella type II	Similar to Paparella I, with notched inner flange but with very large inner diameter (1.52 mm) and inner flange diameter (4.45 mm)
Pope beveled grommet	Beveled inner and outer flange; lumen in line of sight while tube in TM
Reuter Bobbin	With or without holes in flanges; flat profile (only 1 mm inner flange distance)
Rock ventilation tube	Tapered outer flange
Shah ventilation tubes	"Shoehorn" inner flange tab for insertion in small incision; hourglass shape; mini version has small (0.76 mm) inner diameter
Shea ventilation tube	Tab on thick outer flange; flat tab on thin inner flange
Shea parasol ventilation tube	Sides of inner flange beveled inward rather than outward
Sheehy collar button	
Shepard grommet	Thin inner flange, thick outer flange; hourglass shape
Spoon bobbin	Extended tab on inner flange
Sultan ventilation tube	Hourglass shape; straight tab on inner flange
Umbrella ventilation tube	Only of soft (eg, silicone) material; inner flange collapses for insertion, inverts on removal; tab on outer flange
Venturi ventilation tube	Sloped lumen at inner and outer flanges
T tubes	
T-type vent tube	Flat inner flanges
Butterfly ventilation tubes	Shaft has tapered end
Goode T tubes	Long length, small (1.14 mm) diameter; inner flanges curved
Modified Goode T tube	Larger lumen (1.27 mm), shorter length
Mangat	
Richards T tube	Long shaft
Modified Richards T tube	Shorter, wider shaft
Per-Lee tube	60° angled flange; inner flange is a circular disk rather than a true T
Siegel T grommets	
Baxter beveled T grommets	Beveled outer flange, T inner flange
Cohen T grommets	Standard grommet outer flange
Duravent tubes	Outer flange is beveled cone; inner flanges are two tabs
Goode T grommets	
Paparella 2000 ventilation tubes	Inner flange has notch for ossicle; outer flange has curvilinear profile
Rube T grommet	Short flanges, no need to trim
Touma beveled T grommet	Beveled outer flange for improved visibility; flat inner flange
Touma T-type grommets	Flat inner flange; tab on outer flange
V-T ventilation tube	Beveled outer flange; flat inner flanges
Shank tubes	
Plain straight shank	Long shaft; small inner flange
Armstrong beveled straight shank	Beveled inner flange, consistent with TM angle; lumen parallels EAC
Armstrong V tube	Forward projecting tab on inner flange; notch in outer end of shank
Feuerstein split tube	Shank is split: larger straight segment, smaller angled segment
Hubbard airplane tubes	No inner flange; has outer flange

EAC = external auditory canal; TM = tympanic membrane.

the outer flange of grommets. Straight tubes feature no inner flange, although they may have a small outer flange and are used for very short-term intubation periods. Ultimately, the lumen diameter and shaft length will determine the ventilation ability of any given tube.

Factors in Choosing Ventilation Tubes

In choosing what type of tympanostomy tube to insert, there are a multitude of factors to consider. Issues for tube selection include but are not limited to biocompatibility, tube surface qualities and biofilm formation, otorrhea incidence, extrusion rates, retention times, occlusion rates, ease of insertion and removal, and rates of possible sequelae. Unfortunately, there are relatively few randomized trials comparing different tube designs and materials.

Biocompatibility

To be effective as a tympanostomy tube, the substance must be biocompatible with the middle ear (Rosenfeld and Isaacson, 1999). Because of their relative inertness, many metals, particularly stainless steel, have been used to manufacture tympanostomy tubes. Gold tubes, among others, have been advocated because, in theory, they offer little tissue rejection (Tami et al, 1987).

Fluoroplastic (Teflon, PTFE) has very high heat resistance in addition to being chemically inert (Karlan et al, 1980). Silicone consists of alternating silicone and oxygen atoms, with methyl side groups covalently bound to the silicone atoms (Karlan et al, 1980). The resulting polymer is flexible and stable over a wide temperature range.

The body will mount less of a foreign body reaction to the tube, and thus less granulation tissue will be formed as biocompatibility increases. In a randomized trial of 31 children receiving titanium tubes placed in one ear and a Shepard fluoroplastic tube in the other, there was more granulation tissue observed around titanium tubes (Shone and Griffith, 1990).

Biocompatibility can also be determined by the structural changes induced in the TM. In a study of 10 rats undergoing myringotomy and tube placement with different tube materials, the TMs were evaluated histologically (Soderberg and Hellström, 1988). There were slightly more structural changes seen with stainless steel than with fluoroplastic, and both showed fewer changes than with plain polyethylene tubes.

In clinical studies, in which histologic sectioning cannot be performed, structural changes to the TM can be determined by the otoscopic evidence of tympanosclerosis. A systematic literature review of tube sequelae (Kay et al, 2001) showed that among 7,197 ears in 41 studies, there were no differences in rates of tympanosclerosis in comparing short-term (eg, grommets) and long-term (eg, T tubes, Paparella II, Per-Lee, etc) tubes.

Tube Surface Qualities

The manufacturing processes of tympanostomy tubes, together with the innate properties of the materials themselves, will affect the qualities of the surface of the tubes, particularly the lumen. Gold tubes have a diamond-drilled mirror-like surface to resist bacterial adhesion, which may result in the tube being relatively more bacteria repellant (Tami et al, 1987). Titanium, like gold, offers a highly polished surface with the possibility of decreased bacterial and mucus adherence, which may also slow the extrusion rates (Handler et al, 1988; Shone and Griffith, 1990).

Fluoroplastic (Teflon, PTFE) has a very low coefficient of friction, making the tubes relatively nonadhesive (Karlan et al, 1980). Silicone, with its alternating silicone and oxygen atoms, is one of the more flexible polymers (Karlan et al, 1980). Electron microscopy performed on each showed that fluoroplastic has a smoother and the silicone a rougher surface quality, although there were considerable variations among members of both groups (Karlan et al, 1980).

In addition to their underlying component material, the tubes may be coated with a variety of substances designed to reduce their bioadherence. Both fluoroplastic and silicone tubes may be impregnated with silver oxide (Chole and Hubbell, 1995). Teflon tubes may be coated with phosphorylcholine, a zwitterionic compound that attracts water molecules, thereby repelling other molecules (Berry et al, 2000). Silicone tubes may be coated with high-energy ionized argon atoms (Biedlingmaier et al, 1998). These atoms smooth the surface of the silicone, increasing the critical surface tension and thereby decreasing the tube's adhesiveness.

Closely related to the quality of the tube surface is the propensity of that surface to develop a persistent biofilm. Although no clinical comparisons have been done to date, an in vitro scanning electron microscopic study was performed comparing phosphorylcholine versus silver oxide coating of fluoroplastic tubes (Berry et al, 2000). Silver oxide–coated tubes had a biofilm formation after soaking in a solution for 5 days with either *Pseudomonas aeruginosa* or *Staphylococcus aureus*. Noncoated control tubes had biofilms after inoculation with *P. aeruginosa* but not *S. aureus*. The phosphorylcholine-coated tubes had biofilms for neither bacteria.

A similar in vitro scanning electron microscopic study was performed comparing high-energy ionized argon atoms versus silver oxide–coated silicone tubes (Biedlingmaier et al, 1998). Both the silver oxide–coated and control (uncoated) tubes had biofilms after soaking for 5 days in *P. aeruginosa*, *S. aureus*, or *Staphylococcus epidermidis*. The ionized argon tubes, in contrast, had no biofilm formation. Similar to the fluoroplastic tubes, clinical studies have yet to be conducted.

Incidence of Otorrhea

Biocompatibility, tube surface qualities, and tube design type all work together in influencing the incidence of tympanostomy tube otorrhea. Much effort has been made in designing tympanostomy tubes that will decrease the occurrences of tube drainage. Both fluoroplastic and silicone tubes have been impregnated with silver oxide, as described above, in an effort to lower the rate of otorrhea (Chole and Hubbell, 1995). Additionally, semipermeable membranes have been placed within the lumen of tympanostomy tubes to try to decrease otorrhea while maintaining adequate ventilation (Levinson et al, 1982; Plotkin, 1981).

In one clinical study, 86 children had fluoroplastic tubes inserted in one ear and silicone in the other ear (Karlan et al, 1980). The fluoroplastic tubes showed significantly less otorrhea, although the data, when broken down by time, were significant only for early otorrhea (fewer than 3 weeks postoperatively). In a similar study, 28 children had a fluoroplastic Sheehy collar button tube placed in one ear and a Microtek gold tube placed in the other, both with an equivalent inner diameter (1.25 mm) (Tami et al, 1987). After the 12-month follow-up, there was no significant difference in otorrhea. Another study featured 31 children receiving titanium tubes in one ear and a Shepard fluoroplastic tube in the other (Shone and Griffith, 1990). There was a nonsignificant trend (likely owing to the low power of the study) toward an increased number of episodes of purulent otorrhea with the titanium tubes in place.

One of the only prospective randomized studies of multiple (ie, more than two) tubes compared Shepard fluoroplastic, Armstrong beveled fluoroplastic, Reuter-Bobbin stainless steel, and Goode T tubes (Weigel et al, 1989). For 75 children, a T tube was placed in the right ear, the left ear was randomized to one of the other three tubes, and the children were followed for a mean of 17 months. The T tubes showed the highest otorrhea incidence. The incidence of otorrhea among the short-term tubes was significantly lower with the fluoroplastic Shepard; the Reuter-Bobbins and Armstrong beveled tubes had statistically equivalent otorrhea rates.

In a systematic literature review of tube sequelae, otorrhea was 2.2 times more likely ($p < .001$) and otorrhea significant enough to require tube removal was 14.4 times more likely ($p < .001$) with long-term tubes compared with short-term tympanostomy tubes (Table 46-3) (Kay et al, 2001). That same study included a meta-analysis of sequelae, which required articles that directly compared short-term versus long-term tubes (Table 46-4) (Kay et al, 2001). In six studies comparing 1,539 ears, the incidence of otorrhea increased with long-term tubes by 13.7% (or 2.1 times), yet this was of only borderline statistical significance.

Extrusion Rates/Retention Times

Tympanostomy tubes are functional only while they remain in the TM. The retention time—and its correlate, the extrusion rate—is related not only to the tube material but also to the tube design.

As discussed above in the biocompatibility section, the presence of a tympanostomy tube will initiate a foreign body reaction by the host patient. Minimizing this reaction will therefore maximize the tube's retention time.

The highly polished metals, as well as the fluoroplastics, have smooth surfaces with decreased mucus adherence. Among the metals, titanium is relatively lightweight, which may additionally slow the extrusion rates (Handler et al, 1988; Shone and Griffith, 1990). In one study, 31 children had titanium tubes placed in one ear and a Shepard fluoroplastic tube in the other (Shone and Griffith, 1990). There were no differences in the extrusion rates after 1 year. After the 12-month follow-up, there was a significantly earlier extrusion rate seen with the gold tubes, of which 43% (versus 7% of the fluoroplastic tubes) extruded before 1 year.

Regarding tube design, different tubes may offer differing diameters of the lumen itself, with larger lumens leading to longer retention times. Similarly, the longer the length of the lumen, the longer the tube will be retained. There is much variability in regard to flange design. Straight tubes feature no inner flange, although they may have a small outer flange and are used for very

TABLE 46-3. Impact of Tube Type (Short Term vs Long Term) on Incidence of Sequelae

Sequelae	Long-Term Tube, n/N (%)*	Short-Term Tube, n/N (%)*	Relative Risk[†] (95% CI)	p Value
Otorrhea, unspecified type	690/2122 (32.5)	678/4593 (14.8)	2.2 (2.0–2.4)	< .001
Otorrhea needing tube removal	198/1464 (13.5)	30/3196 (0.9)	14.4 (9.9–21.0)	< .001
Chronic perforation	556/3356 (16.6)	175/8107 (2.2)	7.7 (6.5–9.1)	< .001
Cholesteatoma	24/1899 (1.4)	62/8231 (0.8)	1.7 (1.1–2.7)	.041
Atrophy or retraction at tube site	107/460 (23.3)	374/1467 (25.5)	0.9 (0.8–1.1)	.366
Tympanosclerosis	62/295 (21.0)	923/3671 (25.1)	0.8 (0.7–1.1)	.132
Blockage of tube lumen	96/1060 (9.1)	169/2271 (7.4)	1.2 (0.9–1.5)	.125

Adapted from Kay DJ et al (2001).

*Number of ears with sequelae (n) divided by total number of evaluable ears (N).

[†]Ratio of sequelae incidence for long-term tubes versus short-term tubes; values > 1.0 indicate greater risk with long-term tubes.

TABLE 46-4. Meta-Analysis of Tympanostomy Tube Sequelae: Increase in Sequelae from Long-Term vs Short-Term Tubes

Outcome Assessed	No. of Studies	No. of Ears	Rate Difference, % (95% CI)*	Relative Risk (95% CI)†
Otorrhea	6	1,539	13.7 (−0.7–28.0)	2.1 (1.0–4.1)
Chronic perforation	8	3,965	7.3 (1.3–13.3)	3.5 (1.5–7.1)
Cholesteatoma	6	6,998	1.3 (0.4–2.2)	2.6 (1.5–4.4)

Adapted from Kay DJ et al (2001).
*Absolute difference in outcomes between groups; $p < .05$ when the 95% CI does not include 0.
†Ratio of sequelae incidence between groups; $p < .05$ when the 95% CI does not include 1.

short term intubation periods. Grommets feature both an inner and an outer flange; the stiffer and larger the flange, the longer the tube stays in (Inglis, 1998). Whereas a larger inner flange will increase retention times, a larger outer flange will decrease retention times as more keratin may accumulate underneath it. For example, because it is more difficult to push the tube out if there is no outer flange or if the inner flange is very large, the T tube design results in a significantly longer intubation period compared with grommets.

In a prospective, randomized study of four tubes comparing Shepard fluoroplastic, Armstrong beveled, Reuter-Bobbin, and Goode T tubes, there was no difference in extrusion rates among the three short-term tubes (Weigel et al, 1989). The T tubes, however, had significantly longer retention times than the other three.

Myringotomy Location and Tube Retention Times

A discussion of tympanostomy tube extrusion rates would not be complete without addressing the location of the myringotomy itself. An anteroinferior radial myringotomy incision may last as long as an anterosuperior placement and is easier to perform. In one study, 35 patients treated with bilateral Paparella I tubes received radial incisions, with the tubes placed in the anterosuperior quadrant of the left and the anteroinferior quadrant on the right: the tubes showed equivalent extrusion rates (April et al, 1992). Moreover, anteroinferior perforations, should they arise, are easier to repair than anterosuperior perforations (Inglis, 1998). However, the anterior position is favorable to the posterior one, where tubes extrude sooner. One study placed an anterior tube in one ear and a posterior tube in the other; significant differences were seen in two-thirds of the 52 patients (van Baarle and Wentges, 1975).

Although radial incisions may be more common, their sequelae are not that different when compared with circumferential incisions. In one study, 125 patients received an anterosuperior incision followed by placement of Paparella I tubes (Guttenplan et al, 1991). The incisions were circumferential in one ear and radial in the other, with the ears chosen randomized by birth month. Although no significant differences were seen, there was a slightly longer retention time with the radial approaches that did not meet statistical significance.

Occlusion Rates

The lumen diameter and length of the tube will determine not only the ventilation ability but also the propensity for the tube lumen to clog. In a study of 75 children receiving a T tube in the right ear with the left ear randomized to one of three short-term tubes (Shepard, Armstrong beveled, Reuter-Bobbin), there was an increased rate of tube obstruction for the Reuter-Bobbin tube only (Weigel et al, 1989). However, this was also the narrowest of the tubes used, with an inner diameter of 1.0 mm compared with 1.14 mm for the Armstrong and Shepard tubes and 1.1 mm for the T tubes. The increased occlusion rates may therefore more likely be secondary to the narrowed lumen diameter rather than the specific tube design.

This theory is supported by a systematic literature review of tube sequelae that noted that different tube types (long term versus short term) had no effect on rates of tube blockage (Kay et al, 2001). Similarly, occlusion rates may be comparable among different tube materials. A study of 28 children receiving a fluoroplastic Sheehy collar button tube placed in one ear and a Microtek gold tube placed in the other, both with an equivalent inner diameter (1.25 mm), showed no significant difference in tube occlusion rates after 12-month follow-up (Tami et al, 1987).

Ease of Insertion, Removal, and Office Examination

Ease of insertion may be related to both tube design and tube material. Both the shapes and the angles of either the inner or the outer flanges may be constructed to provide a unique tube design. For example, tubes with angled inner flanges may facilitate ease of insertion. For short-term tubes, a stiffer tube (eg, fluoroplastic or metal) is generally easier to insert, whereas for T tubes, the large inner flanges require a softer, more pliable material (eg, silicone). Although silicone tubes may be coated with high-energy ionized argon atoms (Biedlingmaier et al, 1998), the resulting tube may become more flaccid than a standard silicone one, increasing the difficulty of tube placement.

Tympanostomy tubes made from silicone, because of their softness, facilitate their removal in the office rather than in the operating room. For all tubes, outer flanges may be provided with tabs or fine wires to facilitate removal. If wires are used, they should be trimmed to the appropriate length before insertion. However, office removal of retained grommets is performed so infrequently that the true utilities of tabs and wires are limited. Once the tubes have extruded into the ear canal, they can generally be easily removed with cerumen curettes or alligator forceps.

Tubes of similar materials are often available in different colors in an effort to make the tube itself more visible to primary care physicians. Angled flanges may impact the visibility through the lumen of the tube as the TM itself is angled rather than perpendicular relative to the external auditory canal.

Rates of Residual Perforations and Cholesteatoma

Residual TM perforations occur infrequently after tympanostomy tube placement but have been noted to occur more commonly with long-term tubes. In a prospective, randomized study of four tube types, residual perforations were seen in the T tube group only (Weigel et al, 1989). A systematic literature review of tube sequelae showed that chronic perforations were uncommon with short-term tubes (2.2%) but 7.7 times more common with long-term tubes (16.6%) (see Table 46-3) (Kay et al, 2001). A more rigorous meta-analysis showed that in comparison with short-term tubes, perforations increased by 7.3% (3.5 times more likely) when long-term tubes were used (see Table 46-4) (Kay et al, 2001). That same review showed that tube type had no effect on the rates of focal atrophy or retraction.

Cholesteatoma is a far more rare complication and again is noted to be more common with long-term tubes. The above-mentioned systematic review found that cholesteatoma had 70% higher rates with long-term tubes compared with short-term tubes ($p = .041$) yet had a low absolute rate difference given the rarity of this sequela (1.4% with a long-term tube, 0.8% with a short-term tube) (see Table 46-3) (Kay et al, 2001). Similarly, the meta-analysis showed that the incidence of cholesteatoma increased by 1.3% (2.6 times more likely) with long-term rather than short-term tube use (see Table 46-4) (Kay et al, 2001).

Special Situations

In certain situations, the nature of the patient's ear will dictate which types of tubes will be able to be inserted. One common example is the patient with narrow external auditory canals, particularly in very young children.

The tube may not fit through the speculum itself, requiring the surgeon to first place the tube through the canal toward the TM and only then apply the speculum. If the canal is very narrow, then a rigid tube (eg, fluoroplastic or metal) may not fit at all, and a softer compressible tube (eg, silicone) will be needed to fit through the external auditory canal; often either a silicone grommet or T tube will serve this purpose.

In cases of a severely atelectatic middle ear or adherent TM, there may not be sufficient middle ear space to fit rigid inner flanges (eg, fluoroplastic or metal) or even enough middle ear space to accommodate circular flanges (eg, grommets). Efforts should be made to create a small middle ear space with right-angled instruments, but even so, one may only be able to fit a T tube with the flanges trimmed rather short. In situations such as this one, it is often easier to insert a T tube than a grommet as the flanges can be inserted one at a time with a blunt pick.

Additionally, there are those selected children with anticipated long-term eustachian tube dysfunction. These include children with cleft palates, craniofacial syndromes, or chronic ear disease who have already undergone multiple sets of tubes. With these children, the surgeon and parents must carefully weigh the risks and benefits of long-term tube placement versus future multiple short-term tube insertions (see below).

Conclusions

Tube Material

Although there are multiple materials for the manufacture of tympanostomy tubes, from the standpoint of clinical outcomes, fluoroplastic tubes are the benchmark. In addition to their low adhesiveness and chemical inertness, they offer a long track record of use, yielding predictable clinical results.

For the longer-lasting tubes such as T tubes, silicone is the more appropriate choice to facilitate both tube insertion and tube removal (if spontaneous extrusion does not occur). Although the use of silicone for grommets may facilitate office removal of tympanostomy tubes, the retention rate is low enough that removal is an uncommon procedure. Moreover, tube removal is often accompanied by paper-patch myringoplasty, a challenging procedure to perform in children outside an operating room.

Finally, the newly developed coatings show future promise, particularly with their demonstrated in vitro ability to resist the formation of biofilms. However, we still need to produce in vivo data demonstrating clinically significant improvements in reducing otorrhea, maintaining tube lumen patency, or increasing tube retention time. Until then, their increased costs per tube must be weighed against what is only a hypothetical clinical benefit.

Tube Design

In comparing different types of tube designs, it is essential to distinguish between severe and nonsevere (eg, tympanosclerosis, atrophy) sequelae. Although serious sequelae requiring intervention (eg, perforation, cholesteatoma, severe otorrhea) are at least twice as common with long-term tubes, they still remain relatively rare (Kay et al, 2001). The increased sequelae risks are most likely secondary to the greater masses of the tubes, coupled with the larger inner flanges that must pass through the TM on extrusion.

Long-term tubes offer longer periods of ventilation (several years) than short-term tubes (8–14 months), thereby decreasing the need for as frequent procedures and general anesthesia in children who require prolonged ventilation (Kay et al, 2001). One must therefore weigh the increased complication rate associated with long-term tubes versus the increased reoperation rate associated with short-term tubes and discuss all of the options with the child's parents (Gates, 1998). Ultimately, each case must be judged on its own to determine if the additional risks of long-term tubes outweigh the benefits of the prolonged ventilation they provide.

Overall

Having chosen which subtype of tube (short term or long term) to place, the ultimate choice among the myriad of design styles rests with the surgeon's preference as there are few objective data to support one style over another. Based on ease of insertion and ease of office care, each surgeon's personal experience will dictate the tube design with which they are most comfortable.

Although tympanostomy tubes are safe and efficacious for most children with refractory otitis media, they are associated with significant sequelae. Fortunately, most sequelae result in more of a short-term inconvenience rather than a long-term morbidity, and serious complications requiring surgical intervention are uncommon. Although some objective data exist comparing different types of tube materials and designs, the ultimate decision lies with the experience and preferences of the operating surgeon.

References

April MM, Portella RR, Orobello PW Jr, Naclerio RM. Tympanostomy tube insertion: anterosuperior vs. anteroinferior quadrant. Otolaryngol Head Neck Surg 1992;106:241–2.

Armstrong BW. A new treatment for chronic secretory otitis media. Arch Otolaryngol 1954;69:653–4.

Berry JA, Biedlingmaier JF, Whelan PJ. In vitro resistance to bacterial biofilm formation on coated flouroplastic tympanostomy tubes. Otolaryngol Head Neck Surg 2000;123:246–51.

Biedlingmaier JF, Samaranayake R, Whelan P. Resistance to biofilm formation on otologic implant materials. Otolaryngol Head Neck Surg 1998;118:444–51.

Chole RA, Hubbell RN. Antimicrobial activity of Silastic tympanostomy tubes impregnated with silver oxide: a double blind randomized multicenter trial. Arch Otolaryngol Head Neck Surg 1995;121:562–5.

Derkay CS. Pediatric otolaryngology procedures in the US: 1978–1987. Int J Pediatr Otorhinolaryngol 1993;25:1–12.

Gates GA. Surgery of ventilation and mucosal disease. In: Brackmann DE, Shelton C, Arriaga MA, editors. Otologic surgery. Philadelphia: WB Saunders; 1994. p. 85–102.

Gates GA. Adenoidectomy in the management of otitis media in children. In: Lalwani AK, Grundfast KM, editors. Pediatric otology and neurotology. Philadelphia: Lippincott Raven; 1998. p. 214–50.

Guttenplan MD, Tom LW, DeVito MA, et al. Radial vs. circumferential incision in myringotomy and tube placement. Int J Pediatr Otorhinolaryngol 1991;21:211–5.

Handler SD, Miller L, Potsic WP, et al. A prospective study of titanium ventilation tubes. Int J Pediatr Otorhinolaryngol 1988; 16:55–60.

Inglis AF. Tympanostomy tubes. In: Cummings CW, Frederickson JM, Harker LA, et al, editors. Otolaryngology head and neck surgery. St. Louis: Mosby; 1998. p. P478–87.

Karlan MS, Skobel B, Grizzard M, et al. Myringotomy tube materials: bacterial adhesion and infection. Otolaryngol Head Neck Surg 1980;88:783–95.

Kay DJ, Nelson M, Rosenfeld RM. Meta-analysis of tympanostomy tube sequelae. Otolaryngol Head Neck Surg 2001;124:374–80.

Levinson SR, Gill AJ, Teich L. Semipermeable membrane tubes: a prospective study. Otolaryngol Head Neck Surg 1982;90:622–8.

Owings MF, Kozak LJ. Ambulatory and inpatient procedures in the United States, 1996. Vital Health Statistics 13 (139). Hyattsville (MD): National Center for Health Statistics; 1998.

Plotkin RP. Middle ear ventilation with the Castelli membrane tube. Laryngoscope 1981;7:1173–5.

Potsic WP, Cotton RT, Handler SD. Surgical pediatric otolaryngology. New York: Thieme; 1997.

Presswood G, Zamboni WA, Stephenson LL, Santos PM. Effect of artificial airway on ear complications from hyperbaric oxygen. Laryngoscope 1994;104:1383–4.

Rosenfeld RM, Isaacson GC. Tympanostomy tube care and consequences. In: Rosenfeld RM, Bluestone CD, editors. Evidence-based otitis media. Hamilton (ON): BC Decker; 1999. p. 315–36.

Shone GR, Griffith IP. Titanium grommets: a trial to assess function and extrusion rates. J Laryngol Otol 1990;104:197–9.

Soderberg O, Hellström SOM. Effects of different tympanostomy tubes (Teflon and stainless steel) on the tympanic membrane structures. In: Lim DJ, Bluestone CD, Klein JO, Nelson JD, editors. Recent advances in otitis media—proceedings of the Fourth International Symposium. Toronto: BC Decker; 1988. p. 280–2.

Tami TA, Kennedy KS, Harley E. A clinical evaluation of gold-plated tubes for middle ear ventilation. Arch Otolaryngol Head Neck Surg 1987;113:979–80.

van Baarle PWL, Wentges RT. Extrusion of transtympanic ventilating tubes, relative to the site of insertion. ORL J Otorhinolaryngol Relat Spec 1975;37:35–40.

Weigel MT, Parker MY, Manning M, et al. A prospective randomized study of four commonly used tympanostomy tubes. Laryngoscope 1989;99:252–6.

V. Complications of Ventilation Tubes

Chapter 47

POST-TYMPANOSTOMY TUBE OTORRHEA

TERHO HEIKKINEN, MD, PhD

Otorrhea through the lumen of a tympanostomy tube is a frequent problem for pediatricians, otolaryngologists, and primary care physicians. In fact, otorrhea is the most common complication of tympanostomy tube placement. A meta-analysis of the incidence of otorrhea reported in studies between 1966 and 1999 indicated that transient otorrhea occurred in 16% of patients in the early postoperative period and in 26% of patients later during the follow-up (Kay et al, 2001). Substantially higher figures were reported in a recent long-term prospective study of children who underwent tympanostomy tube placement between 6 and 36 months of age and were followed carefully thereafter (Ah-Tye et al, 2001). The proportion of children with indwelling tubes who developed at least one episode of otorrhea was 75% by 12 months of follow-up, and it increased to 83% by 18 months of follow-up. The mean number of episodes of otorrhea was approximately 1.5 per child-year, and the episodes were distributed evenly throughout the seasons of the year.

In most cases of otorrhea, the parents have already noticed the aural discharge at home, and it is the primary reason for the appointment. The parents may be anxious or disappointed because they may have expected that subjecting their child to surgical treatment would finally bring the problem of recurring or persistent ear infections to an end. The parents should be educated about the frequency and usually benign nature of this complication in normal, healthy children to relieve their potential anxiety about any major immunologic disorder or other severe underlying disease of the child.

Although the majority of episodes of otorrhea resolve rapidly with treatment, the high incidence rate of this complication makes it a non-negligible disease entity. Apart from the costs of medications, repeated visits to doctors' offices, and parental time lost from work, otor-

rhea also has a clearly negative impact on the general quality of life in families (Rosenfeld et al, 2000).

Early Postoperative Otorrhea

Otorrhea occurring in the early postoperative period (within 2 to 4 weeks) after tympanostomy tube insertion has been reported in approximately 10 to 20% of children (Golz et al, 1998; Kay et al, 2001). The presence of purulent or mucoid effusions in the middle ear cavity at the time of tube insertion has been especially associated with a higher incidence of otorrhea (Baldwin and Aland, 1990). The association of postoperative otorrhea with the presence and quality of the middle ear effusion suggests that this type of otorrhea is generally the consequence of the middle ear condition before surgery rather than contamination from the ear canal. Although sterile precautions are part of standard surgical procedures, disinfection of the ear canal with alcohol or povidone-iodine before tube insertion has not been shown to decrease the incidence of otorrhea in the immediate postoperative period (Baldwin and Aland, 1990; Giebink et al, 1992). Some studies have suggested that saline irrigation of the middle ear cavity at the time of myringotomy might help reduce otorrhea after the placement of tympanostomy tubes (Balkany et al, 1986; Gross et al, 2000).

Antimicrobial agents (eg, neomycin, polymyxin B, gentamicin, and ciprofloxacin) administered as OTIC drops either at the time of surgery or several days afterward have been used frequently to prevent postoperative otorrhea. The combined results of several randomized, controlled trials suggest that topical use of these drugs may slightly decrease the incidence of otorrhea (reviewed in Rosenfeld and Isaacson, 1999). However, the modest decrease in the rate of otorrhea achieved with such prophylaxis should be balanced with the potential ototoxicity of many of these drugs (Russell et al, 2001). Prevention of otorrhea with topical antimicrobial drugs could be considered reasonable in selected children, especially in those with purulent middle ear effusion at the time of tube insertion. The use of antimicrobial agents in such cases might be more accurately called early treatment instead of prophylaxis. Although no data are currently available on the efficacy of ofloxacin ear drops in the prevention of postoperative otorrhea, this recently approved drug might be the most suitable one in the child with tympanostomy tubes because of no demonstrable ototoxicity (Gates, 2001). Alternatively, a short course of systemic antibiotics could be used to prevent otorrhea in children with clearly inflamed middle ear mucosa at the time of surgery (Baldwin and Aland, 1990).

If otorrhea occurs soon after the placement of tympanostomy tubes, it is advisable to obtain a routine bacterial culture of the discharge to rule out any infrequent bacterial species as etiologic agents. If treatment with antimicrobial drugs is deemed necessary, the choice of the drug can be based on knowledge of the bacterial etiology and the susceptibility of that particular bacterial strain to various antimicrobial agents. In the majority of bacteria-positive cases, the cultures yield either *Streptococcus pneumoniae*, *Haemophilus influenzae*, or *Moraxella catarrhalis*, which generally respond rapidly to short courses of oral antibiotics. Mild cases of postoperative otorrhea often resolve spontaneously without any treatment. When the cause is *Pseudomonas aeruginosa*, staphylococci, or other infrequent causes of otorrhea, topical treatment with ofloxacin ear drops could be expected to be effective.

Acute Otorrhea after the Postoperative Period

The majority of episodes of otorrhea in children with tympanostomy tubes occur several months after tube placement (Mandel et al, 1994). Most of these episodes are clearly associated with viral upper respiratory tract infections, and otorrhea can generally be considered as a bacterial complication of the preceding or concomitant viral illness (Ruohola et al, 1999). Such acute onset of purulent discharge through a tympanostomy tube is also clear evidence of acute otitis media (AOM) (Bluestone and Klein, 2001). It is understandable that great amounts of pus coming out of the ear may look dramatic and sometimes cause substantial anxiety in persons unfamiliar with the origin of the discharge. Parents should be informed that the difference in AOM between children with intact tympanic membranes and those with tympanostomy tubes is that the effusion that usually accumulates in the middle ear behind an intact tympanic membrane is drained from the middle ear to the external

auditory canal in children with tubes; otherwise, the situation resembles normal AOM.

If acute otorrhea occurs in a child with clear signs and symptoms of a preceding or concomitant viral respiratory infection, the bacterial etiology of the discharge is most likely similar to that in children with AOM with intact tympanic membranes, that is, *S. pneumoniae*, *H. influenzae*, or *M. catarrhalis* (Ruohola et al, 1999). Therefore, the choice of the antibiotic can be based on the same criteria as in any child with AOM, considering the susceptibility patterns of these bacteria to various antimicrobial drugs in the local area. Treatment with oral antibiotics for 7 days is usually sufficient, and in most cases, the aural discharge discontinues within 3 to 5 days of the start of the antibiotic therapy (Ruohola et al, 1999).

Oral antibiotics are usually preferable to OTIC drops because parents and children are used to oral administration of drugs, and systemic antibiotics are effective in treating the disease. Although OTIC drops could also be used, their role in treating acute otorrhea in everyday clinical practice is small. First, the viscosity of many eardrops raises concerns about whether the administered drops can enter the middle ear cavity through the narrow lumen of the tympanostomy tube by gravity alone (Arnold and Bressler, 1999). Second, although ofloxacin drops have been reported to be less viscous than many others (Goldblatt, 2001), the outbound direction of the purulent drainage from the middle ear cavity to the ear canal could be thought to effectively decrease the amount of drug entering the middle ear. Effective use of OTIC drops in children with purulent drainage from the middle ear would require daily cleansing of the ear canal. This is not feasible in outpatients in most clinical situations.

Although empiric antibiotic treatment of acute otorrhea can be started without knowledge of the bacterial etiology, it is prudent to obtain a routine bacterial culture of the discharge before beginning the treatment. Acute otorrhea provides an excellent opportunity to collect a specimen of the middle ear fluid without tympanocentesis. The bacterial findings in the cultures can also be used to determine any changes or trends in the general susceptibility patterns of the major otitis pathogens in the local area. More importantly, the availability of the results of the bacterial culture is crucial in cases in which the drainage does not cease within several days of antibiotic treatment. In these cases, antibiotic therapy can be judiciously changed and targeted according to the known bacterial etiology and the detailed susceptibility of the bacterial strain to different drugs. In addition to production of β-lactamase by many strains of *H. influenzae* and most strains of *M. catarrhalis*, the increasing prevalence of penicillin-resistant strains of *S. pneumoniae* poses a great challenge to the treatment of acute otorrhea. Many penicillin-resistant strains of pneumococci are also resistant to one or more other antibiotics generally used to treat AOM. Furthermore, although the great majority of cases of acute otorrhea are caused by these three bacterial species, in some cases, the etiology of the purulent drainage may be *P. aeruginosa*, *Staphylococcus aureus*, or some other infrequent pathogen. Early detection of these rare causes of otorrhea is obviously beneficial for successful management of the disease.

In collecting the middle ear specimen for bacterial culture, it would be best to try to avoid contamination of the sample by the normal bacterial flora of the external auditory canal. To achieve this, the ear canal should first be cleaned by suction or with cotton applicators to the extent that the tympanostomy tube is clearly visible. The specimen for bacterial culture is then obtained by careful suction of the middle ear fluid from as close to the tubal orifice as possible. In clinical practice, the interpretation of the bacterial culture results is not problematic when the culture yields either *S. pneumoniae*, *H. influenzae*, or *M. catarrhalis*. In contrast, the interpretation of the results may be difficult if the specimen has been obtained from the outer ear canal and the pathogens found in the culture are *P. aeruginosa* or *S. aureus*, which can also belong to the commensal flora of the external auditory canal. Coagulase-negative staphylococci are frequently cultured in specimens obtained from the ear canal. However, these strains are part of the normal flora of the external auditory canal and are most likely not the true cause of the middle ear discharge.

The bacterial etiology of otorrhea is related to the age of the child and the season of the year. In children younger than 3 years of age and during the winter season, *S. pneumoniae*, *H. influenzae*, and *M. catarrhalis* are clearly the most frequent causes of the middle ear discharge (Mandel et al, 1994; Ruohola et al, 1999; Schneider, 1989). However, the relative frequencies of *P. aeruginosa* and staphylococci are increased in older children and during the summer months, potentially reflecting increased swimming or other aquatic activities (Mandel et al, 1994; Schneider, 1989). These findings suggest that in older children and in the summertime, the cause of otorrhea may sometimes be contamination of the middle ear with pathogen-containing water via the tympanostomy tube. These findings also underscore the importance of obtaining a bacterial specimen from the discharge, especially in children without signs and symptoms of a preceding or concomitant respiratory infection.

Recently, we demonstrated that a combination of a 3-day course of oral prednisolone with antibiotic treatment significantly shortened the duration of acute otorrhea in children (Ruohola et al, 1999). The median duration of otorrhea in children receiving both prednisolone and antibiotic was 1 day, compared with 3 days in children receiving antibiotic only. In the majority of children who received the steroid, the middle ear discharge stopped during the first day of the treatment. Despite these promising results of a short course of steroid as an adjuvant therapy of otorrhea, steroids should not be used in children with recent exposure to an individual with chickenpox because of the potential risk of disseminated varicella in the child (Dowell and Bresee, 1993). In selected cases, however, particularly in children with a history of varicella or who have been vaccinated against it, the use of a short course of steroids together with antibiotics could be considered.

In most cases of acute otorrhea, the management of the situation is rather simple and straightforward. After initial cleansing of the ear canal and visual verification of middle ear discharge through the tympanostomy tube, a specimen of the discharge is obtained for bacterial culture. Empiric antibiotic treatment can be started immediately without waiting for the results of the culture. As in any case of AOM, amoxicillin and amoxicillin-clavulanate are still the first-line drugs, but, obviously, the choice of the antibiotic must be individualized on the basis of potential allergies or other factors. Once the results of the bacterial culture are available, the treatment may have to be modified, especially in the case of drug-resistant strains of bacteria or production of β-lactamase. If the initial culture yields *P. aeruginosa*, the major management options include antipseudomonal OTIC drops, oral ciprofloxacin, or intravenous antipseudomonal drugs. Depending on the situation, especially in older, cooperative children, ambulatory treatment with ototopical drugs and/or oral ciprofloxacin is often a reasonable choice. However, in young children and also in older ones in whom otorrhea seems refractory, admission to hospital for intensive systemic and/or topical treatment may be necessary.

Usually, otorrhea discontinues within several days of the start of the antibiotic treatment. It is, however, strongly recommended that the ears be re-examined soon after the cessation of otorrhea to confirm that the middle ear discharge has been stopped and that the absence of visible discharge to the ear canal has not been caused by obstruction of the tubal lumen.

Persistent Otorrhea

If the middle ear discharge continues for longer than a week despite appropriate antibiotic therapy that is based on bacterial culture and known susceptibility of the bacterial strain to the drug used, re-examination of the child is necessary. If the persistence of otorrhea is not attributable to poor compliance to the antibiotic treatment, it is most often advisable to refer the child to the hospital or to an otolaryngologist for closer examination and more intensive therapy, including daily cleansing of the ear canal and combination of effective ototopical treatment with oral antibiotics. Sometimes the reason for the persistent discharge is granulation tissue around the tube or a cholesteatoma. In selected cases, even removal of the tube may be necessary to stop the discharge.

In cases of persistent otorrhea, the bacterial etiology often changes during the continuing discharge, and repeated sampling of the middle ear fluid for bacterial culture is often necessary (Brook and Frazier, 1996). The role of anaerobic bacteria in the etiology of persistent otorrhea is still controversial. This is because their presence can be considered a reflection of the long duration of the inflammatory process in the middle ear, which creates good conditions for the proliferation of anaerobic bacteria. However, the clinical importance of anaerobes may be greater than has been realized because antibiotic treatment targeted against anaerobic bacteria has been shown to advance the resolution of chronic otorrhea (Brook, 1994). One potential explanation for this is that many anaerobic bacteria produce β-lactamase, and in mixed infections, this β-lactamase may inhibit the efficacy of the antibiotic in killing the aerobic bacteria that otherwise would be susceptible to the drug. Because culturing of anaerobic organisms is often difficult, empiric addition of an antibiotic effective against anaerobic bacteria (eg, clindamycin) is often reasonable in cases of persistent otorrhea.

References

Ah-Tye C, Paradise JL, Colborn DK. Otorrhea in young children after tympanostomy-tube placement for persistent middle-ear effusion: prevalence, incidence, and duration. Pediatrics 2001; 107:1251–8.

Arnold DJ, Bressler KL. Permeability of tympanostomy tubes to ototopical preparations. Otolaryngol Head Neck Surg 1999; 121:35–7.

Baldwin RL, Aland J. The effects of povidone-iodine preparation on the incidence of post-tympanostomy otorrhea. Otolaryngol Head Neck Surg 1990;102:631–4.

Balkany TJ, Arenberg IK, Steenerson RL. Ventilation tube surgery and middle ear irrigation. Laryngoscope 1986;96:529–32.

Bluestone CD, Klein JO. Definitions, terminology, and classification. In: Bluestone CD, Klein JO, editors. Otitis media in infants and children. 3rd ed. Philadelphia: WB Saunders; 2001. p. 1–15.

Brook I. Management of chronic suppurative otitis media: superiority of therapy effective against anaerobic bacteria. Pediatr Infect Dis J 1994;13:188–93.

Brook I, Frazier EH. Microbial dynamics of persistent otitis media in children. J Pediatr 1996;128:237–40.

Dowell SF, Bresee JS. Severe varicella associated with steroid use. Pediatrics 1993;92:223–8.

Gates GA. Safety of ofloxacin otic and other ototopical treatments in animal models and in humans. Pediatr Infect Dis J 2001;20: 104–7.

Giebink GS, Daly K, Buran DJ, Satz M, Ayre T. Predictors for postoperative otorrhea following tympanostomy tube insertion. Arch Otolaryngol Head Neck Surg 1992;118:491–4.

Goldblatt EL. Efficacy of ofloxacin and other otic preparations for acute otitis media in patients with tympanostomy tubes. Pediatr Infect Dis J 2001;20:116–9.

Golz A, Ghersin T, Joachims HZ, et al. Prophylactic treatment after ventilation tube insertion: comparison of various methods. Otolaryngol Head Neck Surg 1998;119:117–20.

Gross RD, Burgess LP, Holtel MR, et al. Saline irrigation in the prevention of otorrhea after tympanostomy tube placement. Laryngoscope 2000;110:246–9.

Kay DJ, Nelson M, Rosenfeld RM. Meta-analysis of tympanostomy tube sequelae. Otolaryngol Head Neck Surg 2001;124:374–80.

Mandel EM, Casselbrant ML, Kurs-Lasky M. Acute otorrhea: bacteriology of a common complication of tympanostomy tubes. Ann Otol Rhinol Laryngol 1994;103:713–8.

Rosenfeld RM, Bhaya MH, Bower CM, et al. Impact of tympanostomy tubes on child quality of life. Arch Otolaryngol Head Neck Surg 2000;126:585–92.

Rosenfeld RM, Isaacson GC. Tympanostomy tube care and consequences. In: Rosenfeld RM, Bluestone CD, editors. Evidence-based otitis media. Hamilton (ON): BC Decker; 1999. p. 315–36.

Ruohola A, Heikkinen T, Jero J, et al. Oral prednisolone is an effective adjuvant therapy for acute otitis media with discharge through tympanostomy tubes. J Pediatr 1999;134:459–63.

Russell PT, Church CA, Jinn TH, et al. Effects of common topical otic preparations on the morphology of isolated cochlear outer hair cells. Acta Otolaryngol (Stockh) 2001;121:135–9.

Schneider ML. Bacteriology of otorrhea from tympanostomy tubes. Arch Otolaryngol Head Neck Surg 1989;115:1225–6.

Chapter 48

Water Precautions with Tympanostomy Tubes

Nira A. Goldstein, MD

Tympanostomy tube insertion is one of the most commonly performed surgical procedures in children, with approximately 700,000 cases performed annually in the United States (Kleinman et al, 1994). Otorrhea through a functioning tympanostomy tube is a common complication of tube insertion, occurring at some time in 30 to 83% of children with tubes (Ah-Tye et al, 2001; Mandel et al, 1994; Rosenfeld and Isaacson, 1999). Otorrhea results from either infection of the middle ear space with pathogens from the nasopharynx as in acute otitis media seen with intact tympanic membranes or from infection of the middle ear space with organisms from external sources, such as bath or swimming water. Otolaryngologists have traditionally forbidden water exposure of ears with tympanostomy tubes to prevent water from penetrating the external auditory canal. However, recent prospective studies have challenged the need for strict water precautions.

Scientific Models

Theoretic and practical models have been developed to determine if water enters the middle ear via a patent tympanostomy tube with different types of water exposure. Marks and Mills (1983) calculated a theoretic pressure of 12.8 to 22.8 cm H_2O to push water through a tympanostomy tube, assuming normal eustachian tube function. In vivo measurements of 17 patients (1 adult, 16 children) demonstrated that a mean of 13.3 cm H_2O was required for a droplet of sterile water placed on the grommet to traverse the tube and enter the middle ear, a pressure much higher than that found with normal surface swimming, bathing, and hair washing. Pashley and Scholl (1984) calculated that a similar pressure of 12 to 22 cm H_2O was required to push water through a patent tympanostomy tube in a model of an ear with normal eustachian tube function. Changes in the diameter of the tympanostomy tube resulted in insignificant changes to the

required pressure. Bath water lowered the surface tension in the tube lumen but still required a pressure of 11 to 21 cm H_2O to penetrate the tube. They theorized that even higher pressures would be required in patients with poor eustachian tube function.

Using an in vitro model of the human head with an auricle, external auditory canal, tympanic membrane with a Sheehy-style collar button tympanostomy tube, middle ear, eustachian tube, and mastoid cavity, Herbert and colleagues (1998) tested for water entry under different conditions. No water entry occurred for showering, hair rinsing, head submersion, and filling of the external auditory canal with clean tap water. Soapy water increased the incidence of middle ear contamination to 14.6%. Head dunking in chlorinated water at depths greater than 60 cm (2 feet) significantly increased the incidence of water entry. In contrast to the above studies, Morgan (1987), using a fluorescein dye powder, demonstrated that water contacted the tympanic membrane in 13.5% of adult ears during hair washing and 52% of adult ears after head submersion.

Although tap water and chlorinated pool water are unlikely to contain significant numbers of bacteria, bath water has been found to contain *Staphylococcus aureus*, *Pseudomonas aeruginosa*, *Klebsiella* sp, *Proteus* sp, and *Escherichia coli*, with concentrations as high as 10^6 organism/mL (Ayliffe et al, 1969; Ayliffe et al, 1975). In a guinea pig model of ears with Per-Lee grommets, Smelt and Monkhouse (1985) found more pronounced histologic inflammatory changes after irrigation with dirty bath water compared with controls but not with swimming pool or sea water. Water from lakes, rivers, and ponds also has a high bacterial count.

Methods of Ear Protection

Depriving children of swimming enjoyment is distressing to the children and their families and prevents the acquisition of swimming and life-saving skills. The most common method of ear protection is the use of a barrier such as an earplug, ear putty, bathing cap, headband, or cotton wool with or without treatment with petroleum jelly. Although cotton wool is not an effective barrier to water absorption, the moldable soft plastic and silicone plugs are an effective barrier during showering, bathing, and surface swimming (Laitakari et al, 1986; Sheehy and Robinson, 1983). Some authors have questioned whether the use of earplugs may increase the rate of otorrhea because the use of ear canal–occlusive equipment has been shown to increase the number of organisms in the ear canal (Brook and Coolbaugh, 1984). An alternative method of water precautions is the use of ototopical antimicrobial drops after swimming. Although animal studies have demonstrated ototoxic effects of drops containing polymyxin, aminoglycosides, and propylene glycol, this ototoxicity has not been confirmed in humans as reports are limited to a few anecdotal case reports (Welling et al, 1995). The new ofloxacin drop has no demonstrable ototoxicity (Barlow et al, 1994). However, concerns about potential ecologic effects in noninfected ears have rendered ototopical prophylaxis a less popular method of water precautions.

Prospective Studies of Water Precautions

In addition to scientific model studies addressing the conditions required for water to pass through the tympanostomy tube, there have been several recent prospective studies of swimming with tympanostomy tubes (Becker et al, 1987; Parker et al, 1994; Salata and Derkay, 1996; Sharma, 1986; Smelt and Yeoh, 1984). These studies have not shown higher rates of otorrhea in children who swim versus children who do not swim. A meta-analysis by Lee and colleagues (1999) of five previously published articles involving 619 children also showed statistically equivalent rates of otorrhea between children who swam without ear protection and nonswimmers (Table 48-1). The mean age of the children ranged from 2.67 to 5.98 years, and restric-

tions were placed on the depth of swimming allowed in two of the studies (diving and swimming more than 180 cm [6 feet] beneath the surface [Salata and Derkay, 1996] and jumping from a high board [Sharma, 1986]). No significant differences in otorrhea rates were noted in any of the studies, and four of the five studies demonstrated a trend toward less otorrhea in the swimmers. The results have been attributed to the association of otorrhea with young age and concurrent viral upper respiratory infection and not with water penetration through the tube (Arcand et al, 1984; Giannoni, 2000; Rosenfeld and Isaacson, 1999; Salata and Derkay, 1996). Of the five studies, however, none were blinded and only one was randomized.

Five studies have addressed the issue of the use of water precautions when swimming and bathing (Table 48-2). Arcand and colleagues (1984), in an uncontrolled study, randomly assigned 816 children to either swimming and bathing while occluding the ear canal and wearing a bathing cap ("closed canal") or to swimming and bathing without protection but using a polymyxin B/gramicidin eardrop at bedtime on the day of swimming ("open canal"). Diving was not permitted. They found that 22.3% of patients in the "open canal" group presented with at least one episode of otorrhea compared with 27.6% of patients in the "closed canal" group—rates that were not significantly different. In both groups, episodes were more common in the younger children, with 45% of the children younger than 2 years having at least one episode. There was no seasonal variation in otorrhea rates, and otorrhea was associated with a concurrent upper respiratory infection in over 50% of the patients in both groups.

In a prospective, nonrandomized study by Becker and colleagues (1987), parents of 85 children with tympanostomy tubes chose to have their children swim and bathe without earplugs, swim and bathe with earplugs, or not to swim. There were no restrictions on the frequency, duration, location, or type of swimming. The incidence of otorrhea was not significantly different between each group: 16% in the swimming without earplugs group, 30% in the swimming with earplugs group, and 30% in the no swim-

TABLE 48-1. Prospective Studies of Otorrhea Rates in Nonswimmers versus Swimmers*

Author (Year)	Otorrhea Rate, n (%)[†]		Absolute RD (95% CI)[‡]	Statistically Significant?
	Nonswimmers	Swimmers		
Smelt and Yeoh (1984)	6/40 (15)	3/43 (7)	8 (−5–21)	No
Sharma (1986)	12/58 (21)	11/72 (15)	5 (−8–19)	No
Becker et al (1987)	9/30 (30)	5/32 (16)	14 (−6–35)	No
Parker et al (1994)	18/30 (60)	42/62 (68)	−8 (−29–13)	No
Salata and Derkay (1996)	41/116 (35)	44/138 (32)	3 (−8–15)	No
Overall	86/274 (31)	105/347 (30)	5 (−2–12)	No

Adapted from Rosenfeld RM and Isaacson GC (1999).
*Data from Lee and colleagues (1999) and pooled using random effects meta-analysis.
[†]Number of children with otorrhea divided by the total number of evaluable children.
[‡]RD is the absolute percentage change in otorrhea rates attributable to not swimming: a negative RD indicates better outcomes (less otorrhea) for nonswimmers.
RD = rate difference.

TABLE 48-2. Prospective Studies of the Incidence of Otorrhea in Children Swimming and Bathing with and without the Use of Water Precautions

Author (Year)	Otorrhea Rate, n (%)*			Statistically Significant?
	Earplugs or Barrier	Ototopical Prophylaxis	No Ear Protection	
Arcand et al (1984)	116/413 (28)	89/403 (22)	—	Not reported
Becker et al (1987)	7/23 (30)	—	5/32 (16)	No
Parker et al (1994)	13/15 (87)	—	42/62 (68)	No
Salata and Derkay (1996)†	27/44 (61)	74/101 (73)	76/138 (55)	No
Goldstein, unpublished data	42/90 (47)	—	46/82 (56)	No

*Number of children with otorrhea divided by the total number of evaluable children.
†Sum of swimming-related, upper respiratory tract infection–related, and bathing-related otorrhea.

ming group. Parker and colleagues (1994) randomized 212 children into swimming or nonswimming groups, but 15 children who had been randomized to no swimming self-selected to a swimming group and used some form of water precautions. Of the 107 children with 1-year follow-up, the incidence of otorrhea was not significantly different between groups: 67.7% in the swimming without precautions group, 86.7% in the swimming with precautions group, and 60% in the no swimming group.

The parents of 533 children with tympanostomy tubes self-selected for their children to swim without precautions; swim without ear protection but to have polymyxin B sulfate, neomycin sulfate, and hydrocortisone instilled into their ears at bedtime after swimming; and swim with earplugs in a prospective study by Salata and Derkay (1996). A control group was composed of the children who never went swimming during the study period. Diving and swimming more than 180 cm (6 feet) beneath the surface were not permitted, and parents were advised not to allow water to enter the ears during bathing. Of the 261 children with comprehensive follow-up information, 65% had at least one episode of otorrhea. There was no significant difference in the overall rate of otorrhea between swimmers (68%) and nonswimmers (59%). The mean age of the children who swam with earplugs was 5 years, whereas the mean age of the children in the other groups was 2 years. There was no significant difference between groups in otorrhea specifically related to swimming—11% in the no precautions group, 14% in the ototopical prophylaxis group, and 20% in the earplugs group—although there was a trend toward increased otorrhea in the children who wore earplugs. Otorrhea associated with upper respiratory infections occurred in 40% of the children, but there was no significant difference between groups. The location of swimming did not influence the otorrhea rates.

Goldstein and colleagues (2001) performed a prospective, randomized, investigator-blinded, controlled study of 172 children aged 6 months to 6 years with tympanostomy tubes who were randomized to swimming and bathing with or without earplugs. Diving and underwater swimming were not permitted. The mean age of the children in both groups was 2 years. There was no significant differ-

ence in the incidence of otorrhea between the children who wore earplugs (47%) and the children who did not wear earplugs (56%). There was also no significant difference between groups in otorrhea related to swimming (9% in the earplugs group versus 11% in the no earplugs group) and otorrhea related to upper respiratory infections (38% in the earplugs group and 42% in the no earplugs group). Although the children who did not wear earplugs had a higher rate per month of otorrhea (0.10 episodes) than the children who wore earplugs (0.07 episodes), the difference just approached statistical significance ($p = .05$). A logistic regression model demonstrated that follow-up of at least 12 months, age under 4 years at entry, age of onset of otitis media of less than 1 year, and no prior history of adenoidectomy were prognostic for predicting the occurrence of otorrhea. Although there were too few episodes of swimming-related otorrhea to correlate the occurrence of otorrhea with the location of water exposure or type of swimming, there was a relatively higher incidence of otorrhea after swimming in the ocean in the children who did not wear earplugs.

Conclusion

Given the results of the above studies, which demonstrate either no benefit or very minimal benefit to the use of water precautions in children with tympanostomy tubes, children should be allowed to surface swim and bathe without the routine use of ear protection. Because most of the studies did not permit children to dive or swim underwater, children should be cautioned against these activities. There are also not enough data regarding swimming in nonchlorinated water; therefore, ear protection is advised when swimming in lakes, rivers, ponds, and oceans. For the few children who develop repeated episodes of otorrhea, ear protection with an earplug or other barrier can be recommended.

References

Ah-Tye C, Paradise JL, Colborn DK. Otorrhea in young children after tympanostomy-tube placement for persistent middle-ear effusion: prevalence, incidence, and duration. Pediatrics 2001; 107:1251–8.

Arcand P, Gauthier P, Bilodeau G, et al. Post-myringotomy care: a prospective study. J Otolaryngol 1984;13:305–8.

Ayliffe GAJ, Babb JR, Collins BJ, et al. Disinfection of baths and bathwater. Nurs Times 1975;71:22–3.

Ayliffe GAJ, Brightwell KM, Collins BJ, Lowbury EJL. Varieties of aseptic practice in hospital wards. Lancet 1969;ii:1117–20.

Barlow DW, Duckert LG, Kreig CS, Gates GA. Ototoxicity of topical otomicrobial agents. Acta Otolaryngol (Stockh) 1994;115: 231–5.

Becker GD, Eckberg TJ, Goldware RR. Swimming and tympanostomy tubes: a prospective study. Laryngoscope 1987;97:740–1.

Brook I, Coolbaugh JC. Changes in the bacterial flora of the external ear canal from the wearing of occlusive equipment. Laryngoscope 1984;94:963–5.

Giannoni C. Swimming with tympanostomy tubes. Arch Otolaryngol Head Neck Surg 2000;126:1507–8.

Goldstein NA, Mandel EM, Janosky JE, Casselbrant ML. Water precautions and tympanostomy tubes: a randomized, controlled trial. Presented at the American Society of Pediatric Otolaryngology 16th Annual Meeting; 2001 May 10; Scottsdale, AZ.

Herbert RL, King GE, Bent JP. Tympanostomy tubes and water exposure: a practical model. Arch Otolaryngol Head Neck Surg 1998;124:1118–21.

Kleinman LC, Kosecoff J, Dubois RW, Brook RH. The medical appropriateness of tympanostomy tubes proposed for children younger than 16 years in the United States. JAMA 1994;271: 1250–5.

Laitakari K, Sorri M, Pirilä T, et al. Ear protection against waterborne infection: an objective evaluation. J Laryngol Otol 1986; 100:1337–40.

Lee D, Youk A, Goldstein NA. A meta-analysis of swimming and water precautions. Laryngoscope 1999;109:536–40.

Mandel EM, Casselbrant ML, Kurs-Lasky M. Acute otorrhea: bacteriology of a common complication of tympanostomy tubes. Ann Otol Rhinol Laryngol 1994;103:713–18.

Marks NJ, Mills RP. Swimming and grommets. J R Soc Med 1983; 76:23–6.

Morgan NJ. Penetration of water down the external auditory meatus to the tympanic membrane. J Laryngol Otol 1987;101:536–7.

Parker GS, Tami TA, Maddox MR, Wilson JF. The effect of water exposure after tympanostomy tube insertion. Am J Otolaryngol 1994;15:193–6.

Pashley NRT, Scholl PD. Tympanostomy tubes and liquids—an in vitro study. J Otolaryngol 1984;13:296–8.

Rosenfeld RM, Isaacson GC. Tympanostomy tube care and consequences. In: Rosenfeld RM, Bluestone CD, editors. Evidence-based otitis media. Hamilton (ON): BC Decker; 1999. p. 315–36.

Salata JA, Derkay CS. Water precautions in children with tympanostomy tubes. Arch Otolaryngol Head Neck Surg 1996;122: 276–80.

Sharma PD. Swimming with grommets. Scand Audiol Suppl 1986; 26:89–91.

Sheehy JL, Robinson JV. Doc's proplugs. Otolaryngol Head Neck Surg 1983;91:94–5.

Smelt GJC, Monkhouse WS. The effect of bath water, sea water and swimming pool water on the guinea pig middle ear. J Laryngol Otol 1985;99:1209–16.

Smelt GJC, Yeoh LH. Swimming and grommets. J Laryngol Otol 1984;98:243–5.

Welling DB, Forrest LA, Goll F. Safety of ototopical antibiotics. Laryngoscope 1995;105:472–4.

Chapter 49

EARDROPS FOR OTORRHEA

JOSEPH E. DOHAR, MD, MS, FACS, FAAP

A decade ago, there would have been little reason to include a chapter such as this in a text on advanced therapy in otitis media (OM) as few data existed that supported the formulation, safety, and efficacy of ototopical antimicrobial agents. Until recently, there had been little research and development of new ototopical preparations. Lore and anecdote supported most practices. Although the *Physician's Desk Reference* (*PDR*) listed several otic preparations (Table 49-1), they, by and large, only had US Food and Drug Administration (FDA)-approved indications for use in the external auditory canal (Mandel et al, 1989). The product labels of these preparations carried contraindications or cautions for use in the middle ear. This changed in the 1990s owing to several new developments and some that are currently evolving. Otic formulations of one of the newest classes of antibiotics, the quinolones, led to the first FDA-approved ototopical antimicrobial agent in the middle ear.

The other significant advance that accompanied new ototopical drug development was a paradigm shift from the treatment of otorrhea primarily with systemic antibiotics to treatment of uncomplicated cases with topical agents alone. Treating acute otorrhea through a tympanostomy tube (AOT) is a common problem for clinicians, and current data suggest that the incidence of this disease is increasing (Ah-Tye et al, 2001; Baker and Chole, 1988; Mandel et al, 1989; Mandel et al, 1994). Today, the most common initial treatment of AOT is systemic antimicrobial therapy, ototopical medication, or both (Nelson, 1988). In the United States alone, it is estimated that 1 million tympanostomy tube insertions are performed

TABLE 49-1. Otic Preparations

Americaine Otic Topical Anesthetic Ear Drops (Medeva)
Auralgan Otic Solution (Wyeth-Ayerst)
Cerumenex Drops (Purdue Frederick)
Cipro HC Otic Suspension (Alcon)
Cortisporin-TC Otic Suspension (Monarch)
Decadron Phosphate Sterile Ophthalmic Solution (Merck & Co., Inc.)
Floxin Otic Solution (Daiichi)
Otic Domeboro Solution (Bayer)
Pediotic Suspension Sterile (Monarch)
Vosol HC Otic Solution (Wallace)
Vosol Otic Solution (Wallace)

annually (Theone and Johnson, 1991). Although it has traditionally been stated that the rate of post–tympanostomy tube otorrhea is 5 to 15%, the incidence has varied by study, and an average figure of 20% had been estimated (Lusk, 1986). Herzon (1980) reported that of 140 patients with tympanostomy tubes who were followed for at least 1 year, 21% developed otorrhea one or more times, whereas McLelland (1980) reported that drainage developed in 19.9% of 697 ears with tympanostomy tubes. Other reports have suggested even higher incidences, up to 50% (Ah-Tye et al, 2001; Baker and Chole, 1988; Mandel et al, 1989; Mandel et al, 1994). Mandel and colleagues (1989) have reported that of 34 subjects with chronic middle ear effusion who were treated with tympanostomy tubes and observed for 3 years, 68% developed at least one episode of otorrhea through a tube. More recent data have suggested post–tympanostomy tube otorrhea rates as high as 84% within an 18-month follow-up (Ah-Tye et al, 2001). This trend is attributable to several factors, although day-care attendance has been highlighted as most significant. Clinicians should anticipate much more of this disease in the future and must devise the most appropriate, cost-effective, safe, and efficacious treatments to manage it. Eardrops are the cornerstone of therapy and the focus of this chapter.

Topical versus Systemic Therapy

There are many advantages of using topical rather than systemic therapy. First, topical medications are delivered directly to the target organ. By bypassing the systemic circulation, pharmacokinetic factors such as solubility, intestinal absorption, and hepatic first-pass effects do not affect ultimate tissue concentrations. Perhaps more important is the advantage that topical antibiotics lead to the development of resistance less often. The FDA has stated that it "is unaware of any evidence that…topical antibiotics…have led to an increase in infection in the general population by resistant organisms… The agency believes that if resistance were a problem…it would have been known by now" (Langford and Benrimoj, 1996). This tenet on resistance and topical therapy holds for short-term use in the community provided that drug delivery is effective. This point was corroborated by a study done in Pittsburgh. Two-hundred and thirty-one consecutive children presenting to the outpatient otolaryngology clinic with draining ears from which *Pseudomonas aeruginosa* was isolated were studied (Dohar et al, 1996). Of these, 99.6% showed a sensitivity to polymyxin B, one of the active ingredients in Cortisporin Otic Suspension, used in the community since the 1970s. Only one strain of *P. aeruginosa* proved resistant to polymyxin B. The authors concluded that despite widespread use of ototopical Cortisporin Otic Suspension for nearly three decades, *P. aeruginosa* remained sensitive to it. This failure to invoke resistance has been observed for topical skin antibiotics and topical eyedrops. The likely reason for this is that the concentrations of topical antibiotics exceed the minimal inhibitory concentration at the site of infection to such a degree that eradication is more rapid and complete. Also, topical therapy is generally used in relatively short treatment courses. When reports of resistance to a topical agent are made, a critical reviewer must carefully search for an explanation. For example, a recent report by Berenholz and colleagues (2002) concluded that an increased resistance to ciprofloxacin (available as an ototopical formulation Cipro-HC) by *P. aeruginosa* was observed in a select population of otitis externa patients. The key here is that ciprofloxacin is in common use systemically and its systemic, not its ototopical, use is likely responsible for the emergence of increased resistance. Another factor that may lead to the emergence of bacterial resistance to topical antibiotics is inadequate drug delivery. This has been the case in lower respiratory and sinus infections. Generally speaking, this should not occur with middle ear infections. Five major pathogens isolated from draining ears, *P. aeruginosa*, *Streptococcus pneumoniae*, *Staphylococcus aureus*, *Haemophilus influenzae*, and *Moraxella catarrhalis*, are of concern for their propensity to develop resistance. This, coupled with the high prevalence of OM and the substantial public health concern of bacterial resistance, strongly supports the development of topical strategies to minimize resistance in the future.

The next major advantage of a topical over a systemic strategy is the lower incidence of adverse events with the former. The typical product labels of systemic antibiotics include such common side effects as diarrhea, nausea, rash, vomiting, abdominal pain, and headache, along with more severe side effects such as Stevens-Johnsons syndrome, aplastic anemia, seizure, and anaphylaxis. With the newer topical agents, only minor local irritative and allergic effects are seen—a marked advantage. A recent trial comparing the efficacy and safety of topical ofloxacin with amoxicillin-clavulanate found an incidence of 6% for treatment-related side effects associated with the ototopical agent compared with 31% for the systemic agent (Goldblatt et al, 1998). The improved safety profile of topical over systemic antimicrobial agents is unequivocal.

More notable is that this study is unprecedented in demonstrating that in uncomplicated cases of otorrhea without severe constitutional signs or additional sites of bacterial infection, topical therapy alone is sufficient. Oral antibiotics should be reserved for treatment failure or suspected poor delivery of the topical agent (Figure 49-1).

A higher incidence of adverse events has been reported for older ototopical agents. Most of these were local sensitivity reactions and, by and large, were seen with neomycin-containing products. The major disadvantage of neomycin is its propensity to lead to sensitization. This manifests as allergic inflammation, most often of the skin of the external auditory canal (EAC) and pinna. Van Ginkel and colleagues (1995) stated that "Because of the high risk of sensitization, topical preparations containing neomycin...should not be used routinely." In patients with otitis who have been treated topically, neomycin is invariably the most important sensitizer (Fraki et al, 1985; Holmes et al, 1982; Pigatto et al, 1991; Rasmussen, 1974; Smith et al, 1990; Van Ginkel et al, 1995). Neomycin sensitization is vastly underestimated. When used in the EAC, the package insert of the *PDR* (1995) states that the manifestation of sensitization to neomycin is usually a low-grade reddening with swelling, dry scaling, and itching. It may manifest as failure to heal. By extrapolation of nasal allergy, we know that mucosa responds to allergic triggers with edema and drainage. In both skin and mucosa, the inflammatory manifestations of allergy and infection are clinically similar, if not indistinguishable.

Formulation Issues

When evaluating systemic drugs, most of the emphasis is on the active ingredients of the formulation. Although this way of thinking spills over to the evaluation of topical agents, one must resist the temptation to ignore other components of the formulation as they are important in several ways. First, vehicular components may possess antimicrobial activity either primarily or synergistically. Second, vehicular components may contribute more significantly to the side-effect profile of the active ingredients. Third, the biocompatibility of the drug may be heavily influenced by these components.

Role of pH

One of the most fundamental considerations in formulating an ototopical agent is deciding on its pH. Most traditional preparations are formulated as acidic solutions or suspensions with an average pH of 3.0 to the low 4.0s. According to the *PDR* (1995), the pH of Cortisporin Otic Suspension is 3.0. It is unclear from the literature as to why older ototopical agents were formulated at such a low pH. One explanation is that they were steroid-containing combinations for which acidic pH was necessary to solubilize the steroid. From an anti-infective standpoint, two benefits were realized. First, acid is bactericidal to *P. aeruginosa*, the major pathogen isolated from otorrhea (Thorp et al, 1998). This is why Vosol, a 2% solution of acetic acid with 3% propylene glycol, is effective in treating some discharging ears. Adding aluminum to acetic acid to form aluminum acetate (Burow's solution) results in even greater inhibition of growth of *P. aeruginosa* and also of *S. aureus*, *Proteus mirabilis*, and *Streptococcus pyogenes* owing to a synergistic effect (Thorp et al, 1998). Second, some fungi are suppressed by acid as well (Glassman et al, 1978). The role of

fungi in ear disease is debated, and there is a question as to whether they warrant specific treatment. Fungi are known pathogens in other regions of the body. In a draining ear, the environment is humid, dark, and warm—conditions known to ideally support the growth of fungi. Their presence in aural drainage may only be as saprophytes and not as opportunistic primary pathogens. If this is the case, simply drying up the ear should eliminate the fungi that are present. Curiously, fungi are rarely isolated from acute otorrhea. One study found that fungi were isolated from

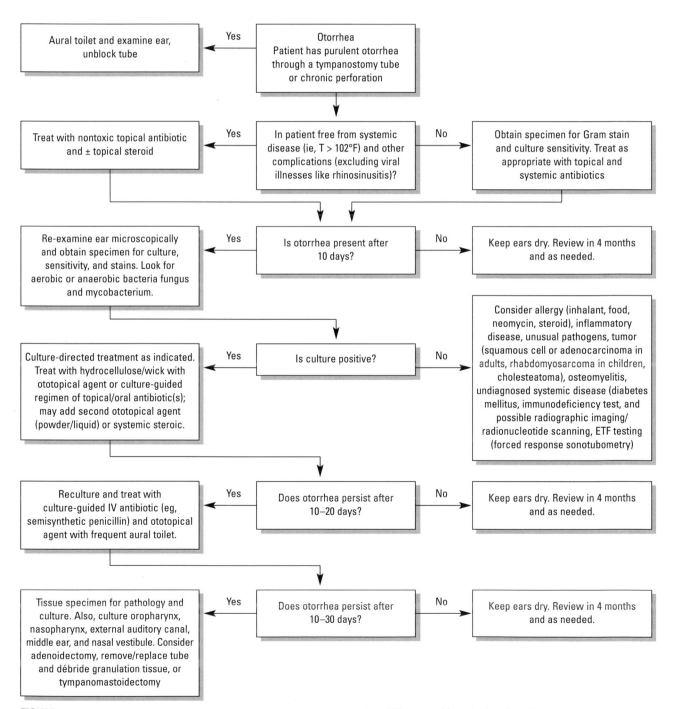

FIGURE 49-1. An algorithm for the treatment of post–tympanostomy tube otorrhea. ETF = eustachian tube function; IV = intravenous.

otorrhea originating from the middle ear in only 2% of cases (Glassman et al, 1978). The physiologic pH of the EAC is acidic. It has been hypothesized that restoring the pH of the external auditory canal, which is often altered by otorrhea, may prevent the opportunistic proliferation of yeast, which, in turn, results in a secondary superinfection. This hypothesis has been supported by the finding of increased isolation of yeast in ears treated with topical ofloxacin (pH 6.8) (Jackman et al, 2002). Further study is necessary before a definitive conclusion may be drawn. The chief disadvantage of an acidic formulation is the discomfort it causes that may compromise compliance. Until definitive studies are done, the decision of whether to use a nonacidic formulation that is less likely to burn or an acidic one with theoretic antimicrobial advantages is left to the individual clinician.

Viscosity

The key to using topical agents is delivering them. Theoretically, the more viscous the preparation, the less readily it will traverse a tympanostomy tube, overcome its high surface tension, and gain access to the middle ear. In general, suspensions are more viscous than solutions.

Because of pH issues (and thus comfort), otic suspensions are far more common than their solution counterparts. No pharmacokinetic studies have been performed in which delivery to the middle ear through a tympanostomy tube has been compared. It is likely that this issue is less relevant in treating otitis externa. Unless comparative delivery studies are done, less viscous agents are preferable when delivery to the middle ear is the goal. A second disadvantage of more viscous suspensions relates to otowicks. Although less often used with middle ear infections, there are instances in which a cannulated otowick may be useful in treating OM. Because the principle of otowicks relies on drug delivery via capillary action, solutions with all components solubilized would be absorbed and delivered most efficiently. Again, no comparative trials of solutions and suspensions with otowicks are available.

Other Components

The components of the vehicle may increase inflammation. For example, many older ototopical formulations contained propylene glycol. This is one of the compounds sold as antifreeze. Although seemingly irrelevant, there is a considerable irritative effect on mucosa by such a compound. Barlow and colleagues (1994) found that Cortisporin Otic Suspension produced moderate to severe middle ear mucosal thickening, moderate periosteal thickening, inflammatory cell infiltration, and resultant thickening of the tympanic membrane.

Recent attention has also focused on the excipient preservatives of topical agents. Most of this research has been done with topical intranasal steroids, although there

is little reason to believe that a significant difference would exist between middle ear mucosa and nasal mucosa. Benzalkonium chloride is the most widely used preservative in topical nasal corticosteroids and newer ototopical preparations, such as Floxin Otic. It may also be found in dermatologic topical products as well. It is a quaternary ammonium compound first introduced in 1935 as an antiseptic agent. Mucosal changes such as squamous metaplasia, loss of cilia, loss of goblet cells, and a lack of mucus-covering epithelium have been observed (Berg et al, 1997). Ciliostasis was promoted, and a reduction in mucociliary transport was measured. Reflex mucosal congestion was also noted with long-term use. Additionally, systemic reactions to topical exposures such as hypersensitivity lung syndrome with circulating immune complexes were seen. As an aside, benzalkonium, which is found in most Dutch ototopical preparations, as well as the newer preparations being developed in the United States, hardly elicited any allergic reaction at all, with only 1 of 34 patients demonstrating a positive skin test to it (Van Ginkel et al, 1995).

Polyvinyl alcohol is yet another preservative found in more recently released ototopical preparations (Cipro HC). Anecdotes of polymerization of this substance leading to obstructed tympanostomy tubes and cast formation within the EAC were reported. Although thought to be a function of higher than recommended dosages or longer than recommended treatment courses, neither seemed to have occurred in some cases. The critical point for all of these examples is that no ototopical agent is FDA approved for prolonged use. Although it is possible that many preservative effects are reversible when a short-treatment course (ie, fewer than 14 days) is prescribed, longer off-label use may present a variety of problems, with these attributable to the preservative being among them. Future research efforts are focusing on compounds with intrinsic properties that obviate the need for a preservative. Until such products are available, such agents must be used judiciously.

Contribution of Elements

Until recently, the standard of care in the United States was to use combination agents with either more than one antibiotic, a steroid with the antibiotic, or both. The FDA has become less likely to approve combination preparations unless a separate significant contribution of each component is shown. Although this regulatory attitude has been recently adopted in the United States, it has long been a standard in other countries throughout the world. This is a prudent approach because as the number of agents increases, so does the potential for toxicity—and cost. Further, it makes little sense to risk sensitization to a compound that may benefit the patient later in life if its inclusion in a combination product does not make a significant contribution.

Steroids

The need for a steroid has become the most debated issue of ototopical preparation. The rationale for including a steroid is theoretically sound. The problem, however, is that there are no conclusive published clinical trials demonstrating the added benefit.

Studies that lend support, albeit weak, for the inclusion of a steroid with an antibiotic are discussed initially. The first study compared the treatment of otorrhea with gentamicin alone with a colistin-neomycin-hydrocortisone combination (Gyde et al, 1982). The authors concluded that the steroid-antibiotic combination was more effective in relieving inflammation in a shorter period of time, whereas gentamicin alone was more effective in eradicating the infecting organisms. There were several problems with this study. The sample size was small, and the comparators were unmatched. The study would have been more convincing had the same antibiotic been used in both groups. In another study of 163 patients with chronic OM, combined gentamicin-steroid therapy was compared with placebo. More clinical cures (52% versus 30%) resulted with the combination (Browning et al, 1988). Again, the study would have been more compelling had the combined gentamicin-steroid group been compared with a gentamicin-only group. The best clinical trial available to date was recently presented. The investigators demonstrated in a multi-institutional, prospective, randomized, blinded clinical trial, enrolling 201 pediatric patients with AOT, a net difference of 1.09 days shortening of mean time to cessation of drainage when treated with ciprofloxacin plus dexamethasone compared with treatment with ciprofloxacin alone (Roland, 2001).

On the other side of the debate are clinical trials that lead one to question the need for a combination of steroid and antibiotic in all cases. A multicenter, prospective, open-label trial examined the safety and efficacy of topical ofloxacin 0.3% to treat chronic suppurative otitis media (CSOM) (Agro et al, 1998). Adolescents and adults $\geq$ 12 years of age with purulent otorrhea through a chronic perforation in the tympanic membrane were studied. Note that the defining clinical feature of CSOM in this trial was not by the duration of drainage but by the fact that the drainage occurred through a chronic perforation of the tympanic membrane, present $\geq$ 21 days. In spite of this definition, the mean duration of drainage in the United States was 50.5 ± 142.0 days, with a median of 10.0 days. In patients from Latin America, the mean duration of drainage was 214.3 ± 265.7 days, with a median of 100 days. Overall, the mean duration of drainage for all sites combined was 97.8 ± 199.7 days, with a median of 28.5 days. This trial is important because chronic inflammation is one of the clinical circumstances for which most feel the contribution of a steroid to be significant. This is especially true when an obvious manifesta-

tion of inflammation, such as granulation tissue, is present. Most infections were unilateral. The overall clinical response in topical ofloxacin-treated subjects was cure (meaning "dry ear") for 91% of the subjects. Pathogens eradicated included *S. aureus*, *P. mirabilis*, and *P. aeruginosa*. Although there was no steroid-containing comparator in this trial, it would be hard to improve this cure rate with the addition of a steroid.

The addition of a steroid might shorten the time to cessation of the otorrhea. In this trial, this was difficult to assess as the second visit was not until days 4 to 6, likely too late to have measured an effect. The study did reveal that at visit 2 (days 4 to 6), 94% of clinically evaluable subjects from Latin American sites and 85% of those from US centers showed improvement. Another interesting finding in this study was that only 59% of the US subjects had valid pathogens at baseline. One would suspect that the drainage in these subjects was a result of continued inflammation and not persistent infection.

Finally, many believe that the addition of a steroid "may help but cannot hurt." This is not true. The *PDR* states, in a warning for Cortisporin Otic Suspension regarding the steroid component, that "Since corticoids may inhibit the body's defense mechanism against infection, a concomitant antimicrobial drug may be used when this inhibition is considered to be clinically significant in a particular case" (*PDR*, 1995). More concerning, we think of steroids as anti-inflammatory agents, yet the opposite can be observed. In spite of their intrinsic anti-inflammatory activity, topical steroids can also enhance the inflammation owing to sensitization (Van Ginkel et al, 1995). One study showed that 6 of 34 patients (18%) with chronic otorrhea (ie, > 3 months) treated with a steroid-containing ototopical agent had positive patch tests to steroids. This is particularly concerning for two reasons. First, it causes one to question if those patients with refractory CSOM who have been treated with a steroid-containing topical agent may, in fact, be experiencing allergic inflammation perpetuated by continued exposure to the steroid. Further, otolaryngologists use steroids for protracted lengths of time to treat other diseases, such as allergic rhinitis. The question again is whether sensitization to the steroids causes the symptoms to persist. Clearly, much more study is necessary. Until better data are available, the evidence supports treating with single-antibiotic monotherapy in most routine cases of acute otorrhea without a steroid unless an associated vigorous inflammatory host response is present (eg, obstructing aural granuloma). The clinical setting in which steroids may play a prominent role might be chronic otorrhea. The data suggest that several of these cases have either no pathogen present or a sole fungal isolate. Both scenarios would likely benefit from treatment with an anti-inflammatory agent. Presently, most of the available steroid-containing combination ototopical agents contain hydrocortisone as the anti-inflammatory agent. It is known that hydrocortisone is a relatively weak steroid. If it is a clinician's judgment that anti-inflammatory action is necessary, use of a more potent steroid seems prudent. More potent topical steroids are available, and still others are currently under investigation.

Multiple Antimicrobial Agents

The last issue relating to combination products is the need for more than one antimicrobial agent in any single formulation. Cortisporin, Pediotic Suspension, and Colymycin are all examples of preparations that contain one or more antibiotics. The rationale for the combination of antibiotics in these preparations is unclear. Polymyxin B sulfate (10,000 U/mL), represented in most topical ear preparations, is effective against *P. aeruginosa* and other gram-negative bacteria, including strains of *Escherichia* (*PDR*, 1988). Similarly, colistin sulfate (3 mg/mL) is effective against most gram-negative organisms, notably *P. aeruginosa*, *Escherichia coli*, and *Klebsiella* species (Jackman et al, 2002). Neomycin sulfate (3.3 mg/mL) is an aminoglycoside, again with primary effectiveness against many gram-negative organisms and some activity against *S. aureus* as well. Surprisingly, from an anti-infective perspective, it is the activity against the gram-positive staphylococci that probably led to the inclusion of neomycin, activity not generally emphasized for antibiotics belonging to the aminoglycoside class. The other possible rationale for the inclusion of neomycin was to provide a second antibiotic to act synergistically with polymyxin B against *Pseudomonas*. It has been traditionally taught that "dual" antibiotic therapy is necessary when treating *Pseudomonas* infections causing pneumonia or infection in immunocompromised patients (Menzies and Gregory, 1996). This premise has been based on the rationale that the synergy of two drugs with different modes of activity reduces the likelihood of treatment-induced resistance and more effectively eradicates the organism. The data on the treatment of aural *Pseudomonas* infections have not supported the need for dual therapy. A study from Pittsburgh revealed excellent in vitro susceptibility of aural isolates of *P. aeruginosa* to the semisynthetic penicillins. Single-agent intravenous therapy from this class of antibiotics has been the standard treatment for CSOM owing to *P. aeruginosa* in children, refractory to outpatient management, with excellent results (Dohar et al, 1995). The fluoroquinolones, as mentioned previously, achieve the appropriate coverage of both the gram-positive and gram-negative bacterial pathogens commonly recovered in OM with a nonintact tympanic membrane. Studies have shown that 0.3% ofloxacin used topically eradicated 94% or more of *P. aeruginosa*, *H. influenzae*, *S. pneumoniae*, *S. aureus*, and *M. catarrhalis*, the five major pathogens isolated from otorrhea through a tympanostomy tube in children aged 1 to 12 years with acute OM with tympanostomy tubes (Jackman et al, 2002). Interestingly, none of the antibiotic components of Cortisporin Otic Suspension or Pediotic Suspension cover *S. pneumoniae* (*PDR*, 1997). Yet *S. pneumoniae* is one of the three most common pathogens isolated from otorrhea through tympanostomy tubes in children (Dohar et al, 1999). Physicians usually treat children with draining ears empirically. Choosing an antibiotic that does not cover a primary pathogen is unwise. In such a setting, Cortisporin Otic Suspension would have to be combined with a systemic antibiotic to cover the *Pneumococcus*, defeating the advantage of topical therapy alone.

My Experience

Although there are other chapters that address post–tympanostomy tube otorrhea, CSOM, and oral antibiotics for otorrhea, the concepts put forward are best brought together in a treatment algorithm presented in Figure 49-1. The algorithm presented addresses the diagnosis and treatment of otorrhea.

I have found in my clinical practice that "troubleshooting" in patients with otorrhea is not as simple as some may believe. With regard to lower airway disease, just as it is said that all that wheezes is not asthma, it should also be said that all that drains is not necessarily infectious otorrhea. As a product of several clinical trials, as well as basic science animal studies and clinical practice experience, I have generated the algorithm outlined in Figure 49-1 to guide the practitioner.

In general, if a patient has purulent otorrhea through a tympanostomy tube or chronic perforation, it is reasonable to begin by treating the ear conservatively if there is no evidence of bacterial disease in other sites beyond the ear or of substantial systemic manifestations of infection such as an elevated temperature above 102°F by using only ototopical therapy with aural toilet. Alternatively, if the patient manifests signs and symptoms of systemic illness or complications, then a specimen for Gram stain, as well as culture and sensitivity, should be obtained and both ototopical and systemic antimicrobial therapy initiated on an empiric basis. Later, culture-guided changes may be made as appropriate. If the otorrhea persists beyond 10 days, it is reasonable to obtain a culture that, in otherwise uncomplicated patients, is not routine at initial presentation. The key, however, in obtaining this culture is to identify any potential pathogens that would not likely be treatable with standard ototopical drops. Most commonly encountered in this group are fungal pathogens. Culture-directed treatment is instituted, and the addition of a systemic antibiotic adjunctively to the ototopical therapy may be warranted as well. The latter is especially beneficial if there is a suspicion that the patient is not compliant with ototopical therapy or that the ototopical therapy is not being adequately delivered. It is rare in the case of bacterial otorrhea that treatment failure is a result of in vitro "drug-bug" issues if topical antibiotics are adequately delivered. What is far more likely is that the ototopical antimicrobial agent is not adequately delivered. At times, this can be corrected with attention to aural toilet to remove cerumen, squamous debris, or otorrhea from the ear canal or lumen of the tympanostomy tube. In other instances, the patient or guardian may require instruction on optimal delivery techniques for ototopical eardrops to the middle ear. Attention on retraction of the auricle posteriorly and superiorly to straighten the course of the EAC and instruction on sufficient tragal pumping to deliver the medication are beneficial. Finally, the addition of a fenestrated otowick are prudent in some patients. The fenestration allows continued drainage of the middle ear fluid, while at the same time, the wick, via capillary action, facilitates medial delivery of the ototopical agent. In the absence of an identifiable infectious cause for the otorrhea, alternative diagnosis must be entertained. It is important to consider allergy not only to the topical agents used but also to things such as the material from which the tympanostomy tube is constructed. Bearing in mind that the primary manifestations of allergic inflammation in the nose are mucosal edema and suppuration, these same findings associated with the middle ear mucosa may lead the unsuspecting clinician to presume treatment failure as a result of an incompletely eradicated infection as opposed to an alternative noninfectious etiology underlying the otorrhea. Unusual pathogens such as mycobacterium and fungi should be considered, and sometimes alternative transport media must be used to isolate other, more fastidious pathogens. Also, consultation with a microbiologist may be helpful to ensure that the appropriate culture techniques and isolation techniques are used for some of the less common pathogens. One must also bear in mind tumors, undiagnosed systemic diseases such as diabetes mellitus, and immunodeficiencies that might result in protracted clinical courses. Finally, imaging studies and radionucleotide scans may be necessary to explore the mastoid as a contributing factor to the recidivism of the disease process as well as to rule out complications and spread beyond the pneumatized spaces of the middle ear cleft. If eustachian tube function testing is available within a clinical practice, this evaluation is sometimes helpful in distinguishing between patients who have continued otorrhea because of an unresolved process in the middle ear cleft proper as opposed to those whose otorrhea is a manifestation of eustachian tube abnormalities, such as a patulous eustachian tube. Certain syndromes, such as velocardiofacial syndrome and syndromes that include in part or in total either complete clefts of the secondary palate or submucous clefts of the palate, are associated with nasopharyngeal reflux, and this may underlie the clinician's inability to resolve the otorrhea. Along these same lines, some studies have suggested that reflux of gastric contents via the eustachian tube into the middle ear cleft, such as acid, pepsin, and bile salts, may lead to a secondary noninfectious inflammation of the middle ear and mastoid mucosa, causing secondary CSOM. Occult cholesteatoma must always be considered in the differential of CSOM, and this should be diagnosed with microscopic evaluation of the ear and possibly computed tomography scanning. Based on this evaluation, if it is still believed that an infectious etiology is responsible for the refractory process, a trial of culture-guided intravenous antibiotic therapy with more frequent aural toilet is reasonable. If in spite of this final attempt to medically clear the process the patient continues to manifest drainage from the ears, a tissue specimen for pathology and a culture should be obtained under anesthesia. Consideration of culture of alternative sources of potential pathogens such as the nasopharynx, EAC, middle ear, and nasal vestibule should be undertaken. We have encountered patients who have field colonization with refractory organisms such as methacillin-resistant S. aureus and at times directed topical therapy to such pathogens using agents such as mupiracin. Alternatively, should the nasopharynx be harboring pathogens that are unable to be eradicated with systemic antibiotic therapy, adenoidectomy in those cases in which the eustachian tube is not patulous might be of benefit. If one feels that the tympanostomy tube itself, either by virtue of an allergic hypersensitivity response or by virtue of chronic colonization with either planktonic bacteria or possibly biofilm, might lead one to consider replacing the tympanostomy tubes with a different tube pending the circumstances and at the same time débriding any granulation tissue present. There is a suggestion that topical steroids, systemic steroids, or both may be useful adjunctively in these difficult to treat patients, and if the empiric ototopical agent chosen did not contain a steroid at the onset, consideration of treatment with a steroid or possibly a short 2- to 3-day course of systemic steroids may be of value. Finally, in refractory cases in which mastoiditis occurs in association with OM, tympanomastoid surgery may be necessary. In general, canal wall up procedures with care taken to open the aditus ad antrum to ensure free communication between the middle ear and the mastoid and adequate ventilation of the mastoid space are necessary. It may be necessary to review with the patient the importance of avoiding external contamination of the middle ear in cases in which it is suspected that infection is a result of infectious pathogens gaining access to the middle ear via entry through the perforation or tympanostomy tube. Avoiding high-risk activities such as swimming at considerable depths or in known contaminated water sources such as lakes and ponds may also be beneficial. Finally, in the case of suspected nasopharyngeal reflux or suspected external contamination, in spite of reasonable precautions that fail, an attempt to reconstruct the tympanic membrane should be made. The patient should be clinically observed with a nonventilated middle ear. The danger of the latter approach is that in the event of continued eustachian tube dysfunction, recurrent OM or chronic OM with effusion may result, in which case, further intervention may be necessary.

Conclusion

After reviewing the evidence presented in this chapter, it is my hope that the reader appreciates that the use of the often taken for granted category of ototopical medications should be given more thought than it has been given in the past. We have entered into a new era. More questions have been raised than are answered. As of this writing, research continues to be active in ototopical therapy, with the hope that even more progress may be realized.

References

Agro AS, Garner ET, Wright JW III, et al. Clinical trial of ototopical ofloxacin for treatment of chronic suppurative otitis media. Clin Ther 1998;20:744–59.

Ah-Tye C, Paradise JL, Colborn DK. Otorrhea in young children after tympanostomy tube placement for persistent otitis media with effusion: prevalence, incidence, and duration. Pediatrics 2001;108:E1.

Baker RS, Chole RA. A randomized clinical trial of topical gentamicin after tympanostomy tube placement. Arch Otolaryngol Head Neck Surg 1988;114:755–7.

Barlow DW, Duckert LG, Kreig SC, Gates GA. Ototoxicity of topical otomicrobial agents. Acta Otolaryngol (Stockh) 1994;115:231–5.

Berenholz L, Katzenell U, Harell M. Evolving resistant Pseudomonas to ciprofloxacin in malignant otitis externa. Laryngoscope 2002;112:1619–22.

Berg OH, Lie K, Steinsvag SK. The effects of topical nasal steroids on rat respiratory mucosa in vito, with special reference to benzalkonium chloride. Allergy 1997;52:627–32.

Browning GG, Gatehouse S, Calder IT. Medical management of active chronic otitis media: a controlled study. J Laryngol Otol 1988;102:491–5.

Dohar JE, Garner ET, Nielsen RW, et al. Topical ofloxacin treatment of otorrhea in children with tympanostomy tubes. Arch Otolaryngol Head Neck Surg 1999;125:537–45.

Dohar JE, Kenna MA, Wadowsky RM. Therapeutic implications in the treatment of aural Pseudomonas infections based on in vitro susceptibility patterns. Arch Otolaryngol Head Neck Surg 1995;121:1022–5.

Dohar JE, Kenna MA, Wadowsky RM. In vitro susceptibility of aural isolates of P. aeruginosa to commonly used ototopical antibiotics. Am J Otol 1996;17:207–9.

Fraki JE, Kalimo K, Tuohimaa P, Aantaa E. Contact allergy to various components of topical preparations for treatment of external otitis. Acta Otolaryngol (Stockh) 1985;100:414–8.

Glassman JM, Pillar J, Soyka JP. Otitis externa: comparative in vitro sensitivities of clinical isolates of bacteria and fungi to nonantibiotic and antibiotic otic preparations. Curr Ther Res Clin Exp 1978;23:S29–38.

Goldblatt EL, Dohar JE, Nozza RJ, et al. Topical ofloxacin versus sys-temic amoxicillin/clavulanate in purulent otorrhea in children with tympanostomy tubes. Int J Pediatr Otorhinolaryngol 1998;46:91–101.

Gyde MC, Norris D, Kavalec EC. The weeping ear: clinical re-evaluation of treatment. J Intern Med Res 1982;10:333–40.

Herzon FS. Tympanostomy tubes. Arch Otolaryngol 1980;106:645–7.

Holmes RC, Johns AN, Wilkinson JD, et al. Medicament contact dermatitis in patients with chronic inflammatory disease. J R Soc Med 1982;75:27–30.

Jackman A, Bent J, April M, Ward R. Topical antibiotics induced otomycosis. Presented at the 17th annual meeting of the American Society of Pediatric Otolaryngology; 2002 May 11–14; Boca Raton (FL).

Langford JH, Benrimoj SI. Clinical rationale for topical antimicrobial preparations. J Antimicrob Chemother 1996;37:399–402.

Lusk RP. Tympanostomy membrane-ventilating tubes. In: Cummings CW, editor. Otolaryngology—head and neck surgery. 1st ed. St. Louis: Mosby-Year Book; 1986. p. 3064.

Mandel EM, Casselbrant ML, Kurs-Lasky M. Acute otorrhea: bacteriology of a common complication of tympanostomy tubes. Ann Otol Rhinol Laryngol 1994;103:713–8.

Mandel EM, Rockette HE, Bluestone CD, et al. Myringotomy with and without tympanostomy tubes for chronic otitis media with effusion. Arch Otolaryngol Head Neck Surg 1989;115:1217–24.

McLelland CA. Incidence of complications from use of tympanostomy tubes. Arch Otolaryngol 1980;106:97–9.

Menzies B, Gregory DW. Pseudomonas. In: Schlossberg D, editor. Current therapy of infectious disease. St. Louis: Mosby-Year Book; 1996. p. 446–50.

Nelson JD. Management of chronic suppurative otitis media: a survey of practicing pediatricians. In: Bluestone CD, Kenna MA, Scheetz MD, editors. Workshop on chronic suppurative otitis media: etiology and management. Ann Otol Rhinol Laryngol 1988;97 Suppl 131:26–8.

Physician's desk reference. 42nd ed. Montvale (NJ): Medical Economics Data Production Company; 1988.

Physician's desk reference. 49th ed. Montvale (NJ): Medical Economics Data Production Company; 1995.

Physician's desk reference. 51st ed. Montvale (NJ): Medical Economics Data Production Company; 1997.

Pigatto PD, Bigardi A, Legori A, et al. Allergic contact dermatitis prevalence in patients with otitis externa. Acta Derm Venereol 1991;71:162–5.

Rasmussen PA. Otitis externa and allergic contact dermatitis. Acta Otolaryngol (Stockh) 1974;77:344–7.

Roland PS. Topical dexamethasone enhances resolution of acute otitis media with a tympanostomy tube. Presented at the Combined otolaryngological spring meetings of the Triological Society and the American Society of Pediatric Otolaryngology annual meeting; 2001 May 14; Boca Raton (FL).

Smith IM, Keay DG, Buxton PK. Contact hypersensitivity in patients with chronic otitis externa. Clin Otolaryngol 1990;15:155–8.

Theone DE, Johnson CE. Pharmacotherapy of otitis media. Pharmacotherapy 1991;11:212–21.

Thorp MA, Kruger J, Oliver S, et al. The antibacterial acidity of acetic acid and Burow's solution as topical otological preparations. J Laryngol Otol 1998;112:925–8.

Van Ginkel CJ, Bruintjes TD, Huizing EH. Allergy due to topical medications in chronic otitis externa and chronic otitis media. Clin Otolaryngol 1995;20:326–8.

Chapter 50

OTOTOXICITY OWING TO EARDROPS

Marcos V. Goycoolea, MD, PhD

Ototoxicity owing to eardrops involves the concept that under specific circumstances, when placed in the middle ear, some of the components of these preparations can reach the inner ear and cause sensory damage. This concept and the common use of eardrops in patients raise a number of questions regarding the risks and benefits of this practice.

There are at least nine reports totaling 165 documented patients who developed sensorineural hearing loss owing to the use of otic drops for otitis media (Linder et al, 1995). In a survey composed of 2,235 otolaryngologists, 3.4% reported having seen irreversible cochlear damage owing to otic drops (Lundy and Graham, 1993). If each of these otolaryngologists would have seen at least one case, this would represent 76 additional cases. Moreover, if 3.4% of otolaryngologists worldwide (eardrops are used universally) would see, at the very least, one case (a very conservative estimate), ototoxicity to eardrops would constitute a significant problem. Therefore, to avoid this complication while benefiting from the use of these preparations, it is important to review the experimental and clinical evidence available and the pathogenesis of these events. With this information in hand, safer means of using otic drops can be developed.

It is well established that substances placed experimentally in the middle ear can be recovered in the perilymph (directly or indirectly), observed to cause morphologic inner ear changes, noted to cause detectable neurophysiologic changes, or localized in the perilymph, cochlea, vestibular labyrinth, and endolymphatic sac (Goycoolea and Jung, 1991; Morizono, 1991). In fact, pharmacologic labyrinthectomy in humans (placement of vestibulotoxic drugs through a ventilation tube) is one of the established treatment modalities for severe Meniere's disease and is based on the passage of these substances from the middle to the inner ear.

Pathophysiology

Possible routes from the middle to the inner ear include round and oval windows, bony fistulae, microfissures, blood, and/or lymph vessels. Bony fistulae, microfissures, and the oval window do not seem to play a role, and lymphatics, which are abundant in the round window membrane, seem to participate in a peripheral rather than in a central direction. This is because the inner ear is of neuroectodermal origin; therefore, it should not have prominent lymphatic conduits (Goycoolea and Jung, 1991). Blood vessels are an important route to consider (which requires further investigation) because of the abundant vascular connections between the middle and the inner ear in the round window (Axelsson, 1968; Goycoolea and Jung, 1991; Nakashima and Ito, 1981).

The predominant pathway—and the most evaluated—seems to be the round window membrane. This membrane is the only soft tissue barrier between the middle and the inner ear. It is located inferiorly in the medial wall of the middle ear and lies in a niche, being therefore susceptible to exposure to fluids in the middle ear cavity.

Ultrastructural studies of the round window membrane of humans, monkeys, felines, and rodents have disclosed three basic layers: an outer epithelium, a middle core of connective tissue, and an inner epithelium. Despite being formed by three layers, experimental evidence has suggested that it behaves like a semipermeable membrane. Such evidence suggests that the layers of the round window participate in resorption and secretion of substances to and from the inner ear. Different substances, including antibiotics and tracers, when placed in the middle ear, traverse the membrane. Permeability is selective. Factors affecting permeability include size, concentration, electrical charge, thickness of the membrane, and facilitating agents (Goycoolea, 2001; Goycoolea et al, 1988).

Ototoxicity of the components of commonly used eardrops, when placed experimentally in the round window niche, has been detected directly or indirectly in the inner ear and is listed in Table 50-1 (Goycoolea and Jung, 1991; Goycoolea et al, 1988; Palomar and Palomar, 2001). Ototoxicity of the components of commonly used eardrops, when placed in the middle ear of humans, has been reported to cause an effect in the inner ear (Table 50-2) (Goycoolea et al, 1988; Parnes et al, 1999).

Available Evidence of Inner Ear Effects of Otic Drop Components

Experimental Animal Studies (Normal Middle Ears)

Chloramphenicol, neomycin, and polymyxin B have been shown to cause hair cell damage (Goycoolea and Jung, 1991; Palomar and Palomar, 2001; Smith and Myers, 1979). Instillation of gentamicin (Smith and Myers, 1979; Wersall et al, 1969) has also resulted in labyrinthine changes. On the other hand, ciprofloxacin traverses the membrane from middle to inner ear and seems to be nontoxic (Bagger-Sjöbäck et al, 1992). Local anesthetics diffuse across the round window membrane and can act as facilitating agents for an increase in permeability (Goycoolea and Jung, 1991; Hoft, 1969).

Propylene glycol has been shown not only to be ototoxic but also to cause significant inflammatory reactions in the middle ear mucosa (Wright and Meyerhoff, 1984). Antiseptics that are used in ear surgery, such as chlorhexidine, povidone-iodine scrub, and ethanol, can also cause labyrinthine changes (Goycoolea et al, 1988; Palomar and Palomar, 2001).

Human Studies (Normal Middle Ears)

Dexamethasone, hydrocortisone, and methylprednisolone have been documented to traverse the round window membrane (Parnes et al, 1999). When used intratympanically in humans (for the treatment of inner ear disorders), methylprednisolone and dexamethasone (Itoh and Sakata, 1991; Parnes et al, 1999) appear to be safe.

Gentamicin has well-known toxic effects in the inner ear. When this drug is placed transtympanically (in normal middle ears), its effects are manifested in the inner ear. This has been extensively documented and is so well established that it is currently used as a standard form of therapy for severe Meniere's disease. Moreover, gentamicin placed in the round window niche of patients before undergoing labyrinthectomy or translabyrinthine surgery can be recovered in the labyrinthine fluids in significant levels (Becvarovski et al, 2002).

The question that comes up is what happens to the permeability of otic drop components in middle ears with otitis media. The round window membrane in otitis media

TABLE 50-1. Ototoxicity of the Components of Commonly Used Eardrops That Can Be Detected Directly or Indirectly in the Inner Ear after Placing Them Experimentally in the Round Window Niche

Antibiotics
  Chloramphenicol
  Gentamicin
  Neomycin
  Polymyxin B
Antiseptics
  Acetic acid
  Ethanol
Local anesthetics
  Lidocaine
Solvents
  Propylene glycol

Corticosteroids (hydrocortisone and betamethasone) have also been detected in the inner ear after placing them experimentally in the round window niche; however, their effects are beneficial.

undergoes the same histopathologic changes that the mucoperiostium of the middle ear mucosa does (it is part of it). These changes suggest that in early stages (the first 3 to 5 days of active inflammation), there may be an increase in permeability but that, as the inflammatory process develops (1 week of inflammation and thereafter), the membrane becomes thicker and develops protective mechanisms in terms of decreased permeability. As the active inflammatory process decreases (and the membrane regains its normality), so do the thickness and the protective mechanisms developed by the membrane decrease. Experimental evidence in cats, chinchillas, and guinea pigs using tracers and neomycin has confirmed this suggestion (Goycoolea, 2001; Palomar and Palomar, 2001).

There is an apparent discrepancy between experimental studies and clinical impressions in terms of ototoxicity of eardrops. As mentioned, animal studies have shown that during an established active inflammatory process (draining ears), round window membrane permeability drastically decreases owing to an increase in the thickness of the membrane to defensive mechanisms in the mem-

TABLE 50-2. Ototoxicity of the Components of Commonly Used Eardrops That Have Been Reported to Cause an Effect in the Inner Ear When Placed in the Middle Ear of Humans

Antibiotics
  Chloramphenicol
  Framycetin
  Gentamicin
  Gramicidin
  Neomycin
  Polymyxin B
Local anesthetics
  Lidocaine

Dexamethasone has also been reported to cause effects in the inner ear; however, its effects are beneficial.

brane (Goycoolea and Lundman, 1997) and dilution effects by the middle ear effusion. In my opinion, this is what happens in clinical cases because the physician uses otic drops once the active inflammatory process is already established. Therefore, in light of the available experimental evidence, it comes as no surprise that in these cases, ototoxic drugs traverse the membrane less readily and are less likely to cause inner ear damage, leading to an "apparent discrepancy." However, once the active inflammatory process decreases or subsides, the defensive mechanisms decrease, and the membrane becomes more permeable. Moreover, if one reviews the documented cases of patients who have developed sensorineural hearing loss owing to the use of otic drops for otitis media (Linder et al, 1995), these tend to coincide with this explanation. Most of the reported cases are related to prolonged use of drops and/or in patients who continued their use once the drainage had subsided. That is to say, ototoxicity occurred once the active inflammatory process had subsided, the defensive mechanisms had decreased, and the membrane had become more permeable.

Which Drops Are Safe to Use?

Based on the available evidence, our indications and rationale for the use of otic drops are as follows:

- In chronic otitis media (chronic draining ears), topical treatment is our main modality. In our department at Clinica Las Condes, we consider it safe to use quinolones as a first-line treatment, based on their safety profile. It is also possible that shorter courses of other drops may be safe and reasonable should quinolones be either unavailable or contraindicated (eg, allergy) or that the bacteria are resistant to them, assuming that the round window membrane has an established inflammatory process and its permeability is drastically reduced.
- In recently draining ears, we consider it safe to use quinolones and, if needed, other types of otic drops while drainage persists, assuming that the round window membrane has an inflammatory process and that there are dilution effects from the effusion. The patients are closely monitored, and as soon as the drainage decreases, if needed, we switch to quinolone drops (eg, ciprofloxacin), assuming that the inflammatory process is decreasing and the membrane is becoming more permeable.
- In ears without drainage (eg, placement of ventilation tubes in patients with "cloudy" effusion), we use only quinolone drops. No other type of otic drops is used.

Future Trends

In terms of future trends or alternatives, some of our experimental approaches include the following:

- Developing slow-release biodegradable membranes that could release substances over time in the middle ear (Goycoolea et al, 1991) because otic drops achieve adequate local levels for very short periods of time.
- Developing spheres of a size that would not traverse the round window membrane or be absorbed by the middle ear mucosa, to which ototoxic drugs could be attached (provided that they would stay attached and remain effective) (Goycoolea and Jung, 1991).
- Developing means of defining the stage of reactivity of the middle ear mucosa and of permeability of the round window membrane to use ototoxics safely. The stage of reactivity should eventually be determined by evaluating middle ear effusions because they are a reflection of that of the middle ear mucosa (Goycoolea et al, 1979).
- Better defining the "defense mechanisms" of the round window membrane (round window membrane defense system) (Goycoolea and Jung, 1991).
- Developing research protocols that would evaluate not only passage but also mechanisms, routes, and distribution in the inner ear. This would also allow the eventual development of therapeutic approaches.

References

Axelsson A. The vascular anatomy of the cochlea in the guinea pig and man. Acta Otolaryngol (Stockh) 1968;243:1–30.

Bagger-Sjöbäck D, Lundman L, Nilsson-Ehle I. Ciprofloxacin and the inner ear: a morphological and round window permeability study. ORL J Otorhinolaryngol Relat Spec 1992;54:5–9.

Becvarovski Z, Bojrab DI, Michaelides EM, et al. Round window gentamicin absorption: an in vivo human model. Laryngoscope 2002;112:1610–3.

Goycoolea MV. Clinical aspects of round window permeability under normal and pathological conditions. Acta Otolaryngol (Stockh) 2001;121:437–47.

Goycoolea MV, Jung TK. Complications of suppurative otitis media. In: Paparella MM, Shumrick DA, Gluckman JL, Meyerhoff WL, editors. Otolaryngology. Vol. 2. Philadelphia: WB Saunders; 1991. p. 1381–403.

Goycoolea MV, Lundman L. Round window membrane. A review. Microsc Res Tech 1997;36:201–11.

Goycoolea MV, Muchow D, Schachern PA. Experimental studies on round window membrane structure function and permeability. Laryngoscope 1988;98 Suppl 44:1–20.

Goycoolea MV, Muchow D, Sirvio L, Winandy RM. In search of missing links in otology. Part II. Development of an implantable middle ear drug delivery system: initial studies of sustained ampicillin release for the treatment of otitis media. Laryngoscope 1991;101:727–32.

Goycoolea MV, Paparella MM, Juhn SK, Carpenter AM. A longitudinal study of cellular changes in otitis media. Otolaryngol Head Neck Surg 1979;87:685–700.

Hoft J. The permeability of the round window membrane and its changes by pontocaine (tetracaine). Arch Klin Exp Ohr Nas Kehlkopfheilk 1969;193:128–37.

Itoh A, Sakata E. Treatment of vestibular disorders. Acta Otolaryngol Suppl (Stockh) 1991;481:617–23.

Linder TE, Zwuky S, Brandle P. Ototoxicity of ear drops: a clinical perspective. Am J Otol 1995;16:653–7.

Lundy LB, Graham MD. Ototoxicity and ototopical medications: a survey of otolaryngologists. Am J Otol 1993;14:141–6.

Morizono T. Middle ear inflammatory mediators and cochlear function. Otolaryngol Clin North Am 1991;24:835–43.

Nakashima T, Ito A. Blood flow of the round window. Arch Otorhinolaryngol 1981;230:57–9.

Palomar GV, Palomar AV. Are some ear drops ototoxic or potentially ototoxic? Acta Otolaryngol (Stockh) 2001;121:565–8.

Parnes LS, Sun AH, Freeman DJ. Corticosteroid pharmacokinetics in the inner ear fluids: an animal study followed by clinical application. Laryngoscope 1999;109 Suppl 91:1–17.

Smith BM, Myers MG. The penetration of gentamicin and neomycin into perilymph across the round window membrane. Otolaryngol Head Neck Surg 1979;87:888–91.

Wersall J, Lundquist PG, Bjokroth B. Ototoxicity of gentamicin. Infect Dis J 1969;119:410–5.

Wright CG, Meyerhoff WL. Ototoxicity of otic drops applied to the middle ear in the chinchilla. Am J Otolaryngol 1984;5:166–76.

Chapter 51

ORAL ANTIBIOTIC TREATMENT FOR PURULENT EAR DISCHARGE

PIERRE GEHANNO, MD, ROBERT COHEN, MD

Acute purulent ear discharge in a child is a common reason for physician visits. Two situations should be distinguished: when the ear discharge is obviously related to spontaneous perforation of the tympanic membrane (TM), revealing acute otitis media (AOM), and when the ear discharge occurs in a child who has a tympanostomy tube (Table 51-1).

In the first situation, the ear discharge is related to spontaneous perforation of the TM. The patient has a history of upper respiratory tract infection over the previous few days, sometimes with low-grade fever but without symptoms suggesting otitis media (OM). The ear discharge, often first noted in the morning, abruptly reveals AOM. Alternatively, a fever and reports by the parents of behaviors or complaints indicating ear pain make AOM likely, and the ear discharge simply confirms this diagnosis.

In this situation, the physician must select the best agent for antibiotic treatment of simple AOM. Fever > 38°C and intense pain suggest *Streptococcus pneumoniae* and indicate amoxicillin therapy. If the patient lives in a country with a majority of penicillin-resistant *S. pneumoniae*, amoxicillin at a standard dose of 80 mg/kg/d should be used. If this is not the case, amoxicillin at a dose of 40 mg/kg/d is enough.

Concomitant conjunctivitis suggests infection by *Haemophilus influenzae* because this organism can produce β-lactamase. Appropriate choices in these cases include amoxicillin-clavulanic acid or second- or third-generation cephalosporins. After 3 years of age, *Streptococcus pyogenes* seems to be one of the leading causes of AOM with otorrhea (Coffey, 1968). This species remains susceptible to many antibiotics, including the penicillins and macrolides. When there is no clinical orientation

TABLE 51-1. Possible Diagnoses and Strategies Regarding Acute Otitis Media

Presentation	Possible Diagnosis	Strategy
Bilateral otorrhea, ongoing rhinopharyngitis	AOM or spontaneous perforation	Common antibiotic therapy according to clinical correlation and local resistance levels
Children with a tympanostomy tube		
Bilateral otorrhea, ongoing rhinopharyngitis	Almost certain AOM	Common oral antibiotic therapy according to clinical correlation and local resistance levels
No rhinopharyngitis; clinical signs of unilateral otorrhea	Possible external otitis (*Pseudomonas aeruginosa* is possible pathogen)	Eardrops (ofloxacin, ciprofloxacin)
If otorrhea is not cured after 1 week		
With persistant granuloma around tympanostomy tube	External otitis remains probable diagnosis	Ventilation tube removal or general antibiotic therapy if small granuloma
No granuloma; tympanic membrane almost normal	AOM	Otorrhea may isolate *Haemophilus influenzae*, *Streptococcus pneumoniae*, or *P. aeruginosa*

AOM = acute otitis media.

regarding the causative organism, both possibilities should be taken into account, according to the local rates of resistance of *S. pneumoniae* to penicillin and macrolides and of *H. influenzae* to β-lactams.

In cases of failure of antibiotic treatment, a culture of otorrhea should be performed to identify the pathogen (usually *S. pneumoniae*) (Cohen et al, 1994; Gehanno et al, 1998; Jacobs et al, 1998; Pichichero and Pichichero, 1995) and assess which antibiotics should be used, using the maximum inhibitory concentration (MIC). If the MIC of *S. pneumoniae* is between 1 and 2 mg/L, amoxicillin at a dose of 150 mg/kg/d should be used (Gehanno et al, 2001). If the MIC of *S. pneumoniae* is higher than 2 mg/L, a parenteral treatment is indicated, such as ceftriaxone at a dose of 50 mg/kg/d (Gehanno et al, 1999; Leibovitz et al, 1998).

In the second situation in which the ear discharge occurs in a child who has a tympanostomy tube, the situation is far more complex. If the ear discharge is concomitant with an episode of upper respiratory infection, the diagnosis is probably AOM in a child with tympanostomy tubes (perhaps because of recurrent OM). Acute occurrence of a discharge from both ears increases the likelihood of this diagnosis, even though this clue does not have a positive predictive value of 100%. In this setting, conventional antibiotic therapy for AOM, as discussed above, is appropriate.

In patients with no constitutional or local manifestations of upper respiratory infection, insidious onset of a unilateral ear discharge may indicate otitis externa, often caused by *Pseudomonas aeruginosa* triggered by the "foreign body" effect of the tympanostomy tube or OM secondary to middle ear contamination from external water sources. This diagnostic hypothesis cannot be confirmed by the general practitioner because the discharge obscures the TM. Nevertheless, it should lead to prescription of eardrops that do not contain aminoglycosides. At present, preference should be given to ototopical fluoroquinolones (ciprofloxacin or ofloxacin). The addition of topical or systemic steroids could be considered. In general, the situation should be re-evaluated after 5 or 6 days.

A pediatrician or ear, nose, and throat specialist who can aspirate the external auditory canal and examine the TM under the microscope can confirm the hypothesis that the patient has otitis externa generated by the tympanostomy tube acting as an intratympanic foreign body. This examination shows tympanoscopic abnormalities with a granuloma circling the implantation site of the tube into the TM.

At the follow-up visit, if there is no response to the first-line ototopical fluoroquinolone treatment, two options are possible. In patients who have persistent TM alterations with a granuloma circling the site of implantation of the tympanostomy tube, the diagnosis is foreign body–related otitis externa refractory to ototopical antibiotics, although *P. aeruginosa* is usually susceptible to fluoroquinolones, particularly ciprofloxacin. Either the tube can be removed or it can be left in place and the patient given the trimethoprim-sulfamethoxazole combination. When the tympanostomy tube is removed, we usually prefer not to replace a new one and just follow the patient. In cases of recurrent or serous OM, a new tympanostomy tube will be replaced.

In patients with few or no TM abnormalities and, in particular, no granuloma, collection of an ear specimen for microbiologic studies can be useful for determining the cause of the discharge and, if needed, guiding the selection of antimicrobial agents.

Because none of these following bacterial species are a part of commensal flora of the external auditory canal, the recovery of *H. influenzae*, *S. pneumoniae*, *S. pyogenes*, or *M. catarrhalis* indicates that the discharge comes from the middle ear fluid and suggests strongly the diagnosis of AOM. In this situation, if this has not been done already, conventional antibiotic therapy for AOM based on susceptibility test results should be given.

Growing a *P. aeruginosa* strain or, more rarely, a staphylococcus should be interpreted according to the appearance of the TM: one possibility is otitis media due to *P. aeruginosa*. The susceptibility of the *P. aeruginosa* to fluoroquinolones supports this diagnosis. The need for systemic antibiotic therapy should be considered in this situation. The trimethoprim-sulfamethoxazole combination can be used if indicated by susceptibility tests. Another possibility is parenteral antibiotic therapy, usually ceftazidime for about 8 days. For most practitioners, the risk of cartilage damage related to fluoroquinolone use in young children is not worth taking in this condition, the outcome of which is favorable in the overwhelming majority of cases. Nevertheless, the large amount of knowledge regarding the low incidence of adverse events with the use of these antibiotics could lead one to reconsider the risk-benefit ratio.

Conclusion

Likely the best strategy in a child with a purulent ear discharge may not be immediately obvious and may require adjustments, particularly in patients with tympanostomy tubes. These adjustments are made according to the local course, which should be evaluated either by a pediatrician experienced in the evaluation of the TM or by an ear, nose, and throat specialist.

References

Coffey JD. Otitis media in the practice of pediatrics. Pediatrics 1968;38:25–9.

Cohen R, de la Roque F, Boucherat M, et al. Treatment failure in otitis media: an analysis. J Chemother 1994;6 Suppl:17–22.

Gehanno P, Nguyen L, Barry B, et al. Eradication by ceftriaxone of *Streptococcus pneumoniae* isolates with increased resistance to penicillin in cases of acute otitis media. Antimicrob Agents Chemother 1999;43:16–20.

Gehanno P, Nguyen L, Derriennic M, et al. Pathogens isolated during treatment failures in otitis. Pediatr Infect Dis J 1998;17:885–90.

Gehanno P, Vu Thien H, Olivier C, et al. Efficacité bactériologique de l'amoxicilline orale à la posologie de 150 mg/kg/j en 3 prises sur le pneumocoque de sensibilité diminuée à la pénicilline G (PSDP) chez des enfants de 6 à 30 mois en échec de traitement antibiotique d'une otite moyenne aiguë (OMA) [abstract]. In: 21ème Reunion Interdisciplinaire de Chimiotherapie Anti-Infectieuse. Paris: 2001: abstract 77/C13. p. 112.

Jacobs MR, Dagan R, Appelbaum C, Burch DJ. Prevalence of antimicrobial resistant pathogens in middle ear fluid: multinational study of 917 children with acute otitis media. Antimicrob Agents Chemother 1998;42:589–95.

Leibovitz E, Piglansky L, Raiz S, et al. Bacteriologic efficacy of a three-day intramuscular ceftriaxone regimen in nonresponsive acute otitis media. Pediatr Infect Dis 1998;17:1126–31.

Pichichero ME, Pichichero CL. Persistent acute otitis media: causative pathogens. Pediatr Infect Dis J 1995;14:178–83.

Chapter 52

INTRAVENOUS ANTIBIOTICS FOR OTORRHEA

MARGARET A. KENNA, MD, FAAP, FACS

Chronic suppurative otitis media (CSOM) is a stage of ear disease in which there is chronic inflammation of the middle ear and mastoid and in which a nonintact tympanic membrane (TM) (perforation or tympanostomy tube [TT]) and discharge (otorrhea) are present (Bluestone and Klein, 2003b; Dohar, 2003). Although it most commonly follows an episode of acute otitis media (AOM), pathogens may also enter the middle ear from the ear canal through the nonintact TM. Other names used for CSOM include CSOM and mastoiditis, chronic purulent otitis, and chronic otomastoiditis. Mastoiditis (inflammatory involvement of the mastoid) is always part of the pathologic process (Bluestone and Klein, 2003b). CSOM may or may not be associated with cholesteatoma. In patients with cholesteatoma, surgery continues to be the mainstay of therapy, with medical management being used in an adjunctive fashion (Bluestone and Klein, 2003a).

Until the 1980s, patients with CSOM that did not resolve with conventional medical management underwent tympanomastoid surgery. However, in some patients, otorrhea would continue (Shambaugh and Glasscock, 1980). In 1986, two articles were published that addressed the bacteriology of CSOM without cholesteatoma in children and the nonsurgical management of these patients. In 36 children with CSOM, *Pseudomonas aeruginosa* was the most commonly isolated bacteria, followed by *Staphylococcus aureus* and diphtheroids (Kenna and Bluestone, 1986). In all 36 children, intravenous (IV) antimicrobials against the major identified bacterial pathogen(s) and daily aural toilet were used to initially manage the CSOM, with an 89% (32/36) success rate for medical therapy alone (Kenna et al, 1986). Many others, including Dagan and colleagues (1992) in Israel and Arguedas and colleagues (1993) in Costa Rica, have subsequently reported similar results. The success of IV antimicrobials in the management of CSOM sparked an interest in other nonsurgical medical options, especially topical antimicrobial therapy. Many published studies have since demonstrated the efficacy of topical antimicrobial therapy either alone or in combination with systemic therapy for the medical management of CSOM (Klein, 2001; Myer, 2001). This raises the question of whether IV antimicrobial therapy is still a useful and effective option in the nonsurgical management of CSOM without cholesteatoma.

Incidence and Epidemiology

CSOM is not rare, although an exact incidence is difficult to ascertain because many studies include patients both with and without cholesteatoma, with or without TTs, and with varying durations of otorrhea. In a 1991 study from Israel, Fliss and colleagues estimated the yearly incidence to be 39 in 100,000 children ages birth to 15 years, whereas a 2002 study from Nigeria (Ologe and Nwawolo, 2002) found a prevalence of 73 per 1,000 pupils studied. In the Nigerian study, the highest incidence was seen in the 2- to 5-year age group, with unilateral disease being most prevalent (79.5%). Other racial and ethnic groups are also known to have a high incidence of CSOM with draining TM perforations, including American Indians, Canadian and Alaskan (Eskimo) natives, and Australian aboriginal children (Bluestone and Klein, 2003a; Coates et al, 2002). Other factors that may contribute to an increased incidence of CSOM include lack of breast-feeding, overcrowding, poor hygiene, poor nutrition, passive cigarette smoking, high rates of colonization of the nasopharynx with pathogenic organisms, and inadequate access to health care (Bluestone and Klein, 2003b). More commonly, otorrhea is seen in children with TTs in place. Herzon, in 1980, reported that 21% of his patients had otorrhea one or more times while the TTs were in place, whereas, in the same year, McLelland reported an incidence of chronic TT otorrhea of 3.6%. In a published discussion in *The Pediatric Infectious Disease Journal* in 2001, Bluestone noted an incidence of otorrhea of about 50%

in children with TTs who were followed closely for 2 to 3 years in clinical studies of children with otitis media in Pittsburgh, whereas Paradise reported that 80% of children under the age of 3 years who had tubes placed for persistent otitis media with effusion eventually had at least one episode of otorrhea through a TT (Bluestone, 2001). However, the vast majority of children with TT-related otorrhea have resolution of the otorrhea with either oral or topical antimicrobials, with only a small number having chronic otorrhea refractory to conventional medical therapy.

Etiology and Pathogenesis of CSOM

It is likely that CSOM often occurs secondary to an episode of AOM. This can happen in the presence of an intact TM owing to reflux of organisms from the nasopharynx, with subsequent perforation and drainage. Most AOM is due to *Streptococcus pneumoniae*, *Haemophilus influenzae*, or *Moraxella catarrhalis*, although organisms more frequently associated with CSOM, such as *P. aeruginosa* and *S. aureus*, have been detected in middle ear effusions from behind intact TMs (Bluestone and Klein, 2003b; Li et al, 2001). Additionally, Kim and colleagues (2002) detected fungal deoxyribonucleic acid (DNA) in 34% of middle ear effusions of patients undergoing myringotomy and tube placement, suggesting that these organisms may have entered the middle ear from the nasopharynx. CSOM may result when acute middle ear infection occurs, either with otorrhea through a resultant acute perforation or through an existing TT, with the occurrence of a subsequent secondary bacterial infection resulting from an organism(s) that most likely enters from either the external auditory canal or the nasopharynx. In the presence of an already nonintact TM, bacteria can also enter from either the nasopharynx or the external auditory canal. Populations with a high prevalence of CSOM may also have eustachian tube function that predisposes the patient to reflux of pathogens from the nasopharynx, making chronic infection more likely (Velepi et al, 2000). As noted, the most common bacteria isolated in CSOM reported by Kenna and Bluestone from Pittsburgh from both an initial (1986) and a follow-up study (Kenna et al, 1993) were *P. aeruginosa* and *S. aureus*, with few anaerobes detected. *P. aeruginosa* has also been reported as a very commonly detected bacterial organism in CSOM in patients in many other countries, including Japan (Nakagawa et al, 1994), Africa (van Hasselt and van Kregten, 2002), and Spain (Miro, 2000). Although the authors of these reports did not document significant numbers of anaerobes, Brook (1985) found *Bacteroides melaninogenicus* in 40% and *Peptococcus* species in 35% of middle ear exudates. Other uncommonly identified organisms in cultures from patients with CSOM include *Mycobacterium tuberculosis*, atypical mycobacteria, *Aspergillus* species, *Actinomyces* species, and *Candida* species (Bluestone and Klein, 2003a; Khanna et al, 2000; Kim et al, 2002).

The role of anaerobes, fungi, and yeast in the pathogenesis of CSOM, either as initial causative organisms, copathogens, or colonizers, has not been clearly defined. Otorrhea from which these organisms are isolated may resolve when only topical antimicrobials are used, suggesting that eradication of the underlying aerobic bacterial organism may often be sufficient and therefore should be the primary goal. In other cases, CSOM resistant to initial treatment with conventional therapy in which fungal isolates are subsequently cultured will often resolve with the use of antifungal agents. However, there are currently no ototopical antifungal agents approved by the US Food and Drug Administration (FDA), making management of fungal otitis potentially problematic. Clearly, further work in this area is needed.

Pathology

Schuknecht (1993), in discussing CSOM, states that "the mucous membrane may be thickened by edema, submucosal fibrosis and infiltration with chronic inflammatory cell. Mucosal edema may proceed to formation of aural polyps. …Persistent suppuration may cause mucosal ulceration, the formation of granulation tissue and bone resorption." In more advanced cases, osteitis of the ossicles, mastoid bone, and labyrinth may occur. In the stage at which significant permanent bony changes have not occurred (inflammation is confined to the mucosa), appropriate medical therapy may be able to reverse these pathologic changes without surgical intervention. When considering the diagnosis of CSOM, other entities in the differential diagnosis need to be excluded, including external otitis, foreign body, cholesteatoma, Langherhans' cell histiocytosis or another neoplasm, Munchausen syndrome, and branchial cleft anomalies. Other medical conditions that may predispose the patient to or act as possible contributors to ongoing middle ear and mastoid infection include chronic sinusitis, adenoiditis, anatomic abnormalities of the craniofacial structures (especially the palate and midface), immune deficiency, ciliary dyskinesia, poorly controlled diabetes, allergy, and nasopharyngeal or gastroesophageal reflux. Not infrequently, identification and effective management of the associated medical conditions will result in significant improvement of CSOM or will at least make the management more effective.

Management Options

Options in the management of CSOM are medical and/or surgical. If cholesteatoma is present, surgery is the primary mode of therapy, and cholesteatoma must always be considered if medical management fails or there is early recurrence of otorrhea. If otorrhea is accompanied by any signs or symptoms of an intracranial complication of otitis media, then medical management, as outlined below, may not be appropriate. If a patient with CSOM fails appropriate oral, IV, and topical medical therapies, then tympanomastoid surgery should be considered.

The medical options for uncomplicated CSOM owing to bacterial pathogens include oral, topical, and IV antimicrobial agents. Initial management can be directed empirically by the known probable pathogens. If otorrhea continues despite initial appropriate antimicrobial therapy, cultures and sensitivities should be obtained for aerobic, anaerobic, and fungal organisms, with special attention to uncommon or difficult-to-grow organisms, such as *M. tuberculosis*. Although cultures can often be obtained in the outpatient office setting, examination of the ear under general anesthesia may be needed for children who are unable to cooperate, if the anatomy is difficult to examine in the awake child (narrow external auditory canal, previous mastoid surgery, congenital anomalies of the ear), or there is a suspicion of foreign body, cholesteatoma, or other middle ear pathology. These cultures should be obtained, if possible, directly from the middle ear through the TM perforation or TT. Care should be taken to avoid culturing any material from the external auditory canal because these culture results may well represent contaminants rather than the actual middle ear pathogen. Polyps or other tissue obtained should be submitted both for culture and sensitivities and histopathologic examination.

In the 1980s, IV antimicrobial therapy was considered for further medical management of CSOM because there were no readily available oral agents that were effective against the most commonly isolated pathogens in CSOM, *P. aeruginosa* and *S. aureus* (Kenna et al, 1986). With the introduction of the quinolone and antistaphylococcal oral antimicrobials, non-IV systemic therapy may now be a more available option in the treatment of CSOM secondary to *P. aeruginosa* and other pathogens prior to considering IV antimicrobials. In addition, *P. aeruginosa* is occasionally sensitive to trimethoprim-sulfisoxazole, a readily available and well-tolerated oral antimicrobial combination (Dohar et al, 1996). A potential limiting factor for oral quinolones is the fact that they are not approved by the FDA for routine use in children under the age of 18 years, although they have been used with great success and a minimum of side effects in teenagers with cystic fibrosis (Church et al, 1997). In addition, there was concern about possible ototoxicity from the topical medications in use in the 1980s, especially the constituents of Cortisporin (polymyxin B, neomycin, hydrocortisone, propylene glycol, and thimerosal) (Myer, 2001). However, since the initial reports of successful IV antimicrobial therapy for CSOM were published, there have been many studies about the effective use of topical antimicrobial therapy for CSOM, either alone or in combination with IV therapy. The introduction of the quinolone antimicrobials has made topical therapy much more feasible. This is due to their efficacy against *P. aeruginosa* and other pathogens, as well as the apparent absence of ototoxicity when used either topically or systemically (Klein, 2001). Currently, there are no FDA approved topical agents effective against *Candida* species, *Aspergillus* species, or similar organisms. What seems clear from these studies is that aural toilet is a key part of any medical regimen, and, in many cases, topical therapy and diligent aural débridement may be all that are needed to promote resolution of CSOM. In addition, in rural areas where access to medical care is limited, aural toilet with topical medications may be the only option for many patients.

In many children, CSOM is associated with the presence of a TT, and there have been many anecdotal reports of tube removal alone resulting in cessation of otorrhea. Certainly, if the tube is associated with granulation tissue or possible squamous debris, tube removal (and possible replacement, depending on the clinical situation), along with the granulation tissue and squamous debris, would be an obvious first step in managing otorrhea as part of aural toilet.

If the patient fails management with appropriate culture-guided oral and/or topical antimicrobials (or antifungals if that is the isolated pathogen), then IV antimicrobials should be considered. Most patients can be treated on an outpatient basis once IV access has been established and the choice of antimicrobial has been made. Frequent examination of the ear with débridement of drainage is necessary to allow instillation of topical medications and to evaluate when otorrhea has resolved. If otorrhea persists after 7 days of therapy, the ear should be recultured and the choice of antimicrobial adjusted accordingly. At this point, if there continues to be significant granulation tissue and/or polyps, an examination of the ear under anesthesia should be performed, if not already accomplished, to rule out cholesteatoma or another pathology and to obtain possible biopsies. If the otorrhea has not significantly improved after at least 1 to 2 weeks of appropriate systemic therapy, aural toilet, and repeat culture of the ear with adjustment for any new pathogens or sensitivities, a computed tomographic scan of the temporal bones should also be considered to rule out other pathology not evident by otomicroscopic examination. If the patient fails IV medical management, diligent aural toilet, and treatment of any other medical problems that may be contributing to the CSOM, then surgical intervention should be entertained.

Although antimicrobial therapy for CSOM is very effective, it is not without concern. The child must have a long-term IV line placed, usually by the department of anesthesia or general surgery. A decision about whether a central or peripherally inserted central catheter (PICC) line is appropriate hinges on how long the IV antimicrobials will be needed, with a central line more appropriate for more than 2 weeks of therapy. Based on published studies, 2 weeks of antimicrobial therapy is usually enough to result in cessation of otorrhea and a dry middle ear. Each patient, however, needs to be considered individually, with unusual craniofacial anatomy or an immunodeficiency being possible factors in prolonging the duration of CSOM before resolution. Additional issues that need to be considered for IV therapy include the possible need for sedation or general anesthesia for the placement of PICC or central lines, access to an appropriate home care company for IV site care and provision of medications, the training of parents in IV line care, and the probable need for an on-site nurse in any school setting. In addition, there will almost inevitably be insurance-related issues for either inpatient or outpatient care. Finally, there are potential complications of long-term IV placement that include local wound infection, systemic infection from organisms that gain access through the line, discomfort at the line site, line nonfunction owing to clotting or kinking, and need for line replacement if the line stops working but the CSOM still has not resolved.

The question arises, therefore, about when to use IV antimicrobial therapy in the management of CSOM. A recent article in the Cochrane Database of Systematic Reviews assessed 24 clinical trials involving 1,660 people with CSOM (Acuin, 2002). The authors noted that the definition and severity of CSOM were variable, the methodologic quality of the trials was generally poor, and follow-up was short. With these caveats, they found that aural toilet combined with topical therapy with antibiotics or antiseptics was more effective in resolving otorrhea and eradicating bacteria from the middle ear than systemic antibiotics and that combining the two therapeutic modalities did not improve the outcome. Topical quinolones were more effective than nonquinolones. Long-term outcomes such as preventing recurrences, closure of TM perforations, and hearing improvement were not assessed. and further evaluation was felt to be indicated. Therefore, based on this review, as well as the information now available about topical therapy, it would be reasonable to consider IV antimicrobials for CSOM as part of a stepwise approach to the management of CSOM. A proposed algorithm is in Figure 52-1.

Conclusion

CSOM without cholesteatoma continues to be a not uncommon complication of otitis media. Systemic and topical antimicrobials effective against the most common bacteria associated with CSOM are widely available. The decision to use IV antimicrobials in the medical management of CSOM depends on the patient's response to prior therapy as well as his/her current clinical situation. If the patient does not have prompt resolution of otor-

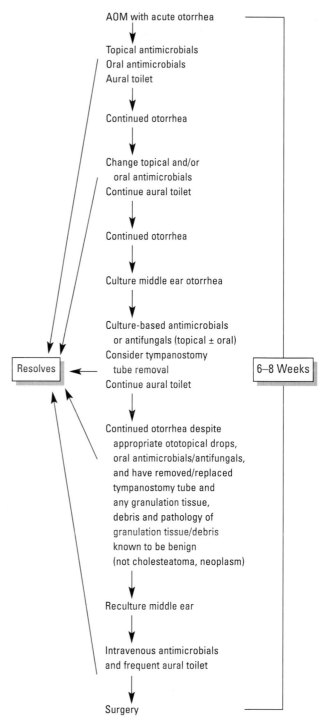

FIGURE 52-1. Treatment of chronic suppurative otitis media. AOM = acute otitis media.

rhea with appropriate medical therapy, cholesteatoma or other pathology should be suspected and investigated.

References

Acuin J, Smith A, Mackenzie I. Interventions for chronic suppurative otitis media. Cochrane Database of Systemic Reviews 2002;4.

Arguedas AG, Herrera JF, Faingezicht I, Mohs E. Ceftazidime for therapy of children with chronic suppurative otitis media without cholesteatoma. Pediatr Infect Dis J 1993;12:246–8.

Bluestone CD. Efficacy of ofloxacin and other ototopical preparations for chronic suppurative otitis media in children. Pediatr Infect Dis J 2001;20:120–2.

Bluestone CD, Klein JO. Intratemporal complications and sequelae of otitis media. In: Bluestone CD, Stool SE, Alper CM, et al, editors. Pediatric otolaryngology. 4th ed. Philadelphia: WB Saunders; 2003a. p. 687–764.

Bluestone CD, Klein JO. Otitis media and eustachian tube dysfunction. In: Bluestone CD, Stool SE, Alper CM, et al, editors. Pediatric otolaryngology. 4th ed. Philadelphia: WB Saunders; 2003b. p. 475–686.

Brook I. Prevalence of beta-lactamase producing bacteria in chronic suppurative otitis media. Am J Dis Child 1985;139:280–3.

Church DA, Kanga JF, Kuhn RJ, et al. Sequential ciprofloxacin therapy in pediatric cystic fibrosis: comparative study vs. ceftazidime/tobramycin in the treatment of acute pulmonary exacerbations. The Cystic Fibrosis Study Group. Pediatr Infect Dis J 1997;16:97–105.

Coates HL, Morris PS, Leach AJ, Couzos S. Otitis media in Aboriginal children: tackling a major health problem. Med J Aust 2002;177:176–7.

Dagan R, Fliss DM, Einhorn M, et al. Outpatient management of chronic suppurative otitis media without cholesteatoma in children. Pediatr Infect Dis J 1992;11:542–6.

Dohar JE. Otorrhea. In: Bluestone CD, Stool SE, Alper CM, editors. Pediatric otolaryngology. 4th ed. Philadelphia: WB Saunders; 2003. p. 297–305.

Dohar JE, Kenna MA, Wadowsky RM. In vitro susceptibility of aural isolates of P. aeruginosa to commonly used ototopical antibiotics. Am J Otol 1996;17:207–9.

Fliss DM, Shoham I, Leiberman A, et al. Chronic suppurative otitis media without cholesteatoma in children in Southern Israel: incidence and risk factors. Pediatr Infect Dis J 1991;10:895–9.

Herzon FS. Tympanostomy tubes: infectious complications. Arch Otolaryngol 1980;106:645–7.

Kenna MA, Bluestone CD. Microbiology of chronic suppurative otitis media in children. Pediatr Infect Dis J 1986;5:223–5.

Kenna MA, Bluestone CD, Reilly JS, Lusk RP. Medical management of chronic suppurative otitis media without cholesteatoma in children. Laryngoscope 1986;96:146–51.

Kenna MA, Rosane B, Bluestone CD. Update on medical management of chronic suppurative otitis media. Am J Otol 1993;14:469–73.

Khanna V, Chander J, Nagarkar NM, Dass A. Clinicomicrobiologic evaluation of active tubotympanic type chronic suppurative otitis media. J Otolaryngol 2000;29:148–53.

Kim EJ, Catten MD, Lalwani AK. Detection of fungal DNA in effusion associated with acute and serous otitis media. Laryngoscope 2002;112:2037–41.

Klein JO. In vitro and in vivo antimicrobial activity of topical ofloxacin and other ototopical agents. Pediatr Infect Dis J 2001;20:120–3.

Li WC, Chiu NC, Hsu CH, et al. Pathogens in the middle-ear effusion of children with persistent otitis media: implications of drug resistance and complications. J Microbiol Immunol Infect 2001;34:190–4.

McClelland CA. Incidence of complications from use of tympanostomy tubes. Arch Otolaryngol 1980;106:97–9.

Miro N. Controlled multicenter study on chronic suppurative otitis media treated with topical applications of ciprofloxacin 0.2% solution in single-dose containers of combination of polymyxin B, neomycin, and hydrocortisone suspension. Otolaryngol Head Neck Surg 2000;123:617–23.

Myer CM. Historical perspective on the use of otic antimicrobial agents. Pediatr Infect Dis J 2001;20:98–101.

Nakagawa T, Yadohisa O, Komune S, Uemura T. A 16-year survey of changes in bacterial isolates associated with chronic suppurative otitis media. Eur Arch Otorhinolaryngol 1994;119 Suppl 1:S27–32.

Ologe FE, Nwawolo CC. Prevalence of chronic suppurative otitis media (CSOM) among school children in a rural community in Nigeria. Niger Postgrad Med J 2002;9:63–6.

Schuknecht HF. Infections. In: Schuknecht HF, editor. Pathology of the ear. 2nd ed. Philadelphia: Lea and Febiger; 1993. p. 191–254.

Shambaugh GE, Glasscock ME. Pathology and clinical course of inflammatory disease of the middle ear. In: Surgery of the ear. 3rd ed. Philadelphia: WB Saunders; 1980. p. 186–220.

van Hasselt P, van Kregten E. Treatment of chronic suppurative otitis media with ofloxacin in hydroxypropyl methylcellulose ear drops: a clinical/bacteriological study in a rural area of Malawi. Int J Pediatr Otorhinolaryngol 2002;63:49–56.

Velepi M, Rozmani V, Velepi M, Bonifacic M. Gastroesophageal reflux, allergy and chronic tubotympanal disorders. Int J Pediatr Otorhinolaryngol 2000;55:187–90.

Chapter 53

Evaluation and Treatment of Recurrent Post-Tympanostomy Otorrhea

Patrick J. Antonelli, MD

Tympanostomy tubes (TTs) are commonly used because of their ability to reduce the frequency of symptomatic acute otitis media (AOM) and the time spent with persistent otitis media with effusion (OME), thereby increasing the amount of time that children have normal hearing. It is not widely appreciated that TTs do not dramatically reduce the incidence of middle ear inflammation (Casselbrant et al, 1992). Otitis media after TT placement—with a patent TT—is manifest as otorrhea. Fortunately, many episodes of post-tympanostomy otorrhea (PTO) will be transient and mild and possibly not even noticed by the patient or parent. PTO has been demonstrated in at least half of the children who have received TTs (Ah-Tye et al, 2001).

PTO may recur, generally in association with viral upper respiratory tract infections (URIs) or external contamination of the middle ear (Gates et al, 1988; Gates et al, 1989). Isolated recurrences of PTO are usually attributable to these common causes, and no special concern is necessary. PTO should not, however, be anticipated with every URI or episode of ear canal contamination. Clinically apparent, recurrent PTO that occurs with regularity or immediately following a treated episode occurs in fewer than 5% of patients with TTs. Recurrent PTO mandates special consideration regarding possible underlying causes and treatment alternatives.

Recurrent PTO can be more than a nuisance. Recurrent PTO may impart conductive hearing loss, interfere with a child's ability to attend school, and, less commonly, lead to social alienation. Although failure to accurately diagnose and treat recurrent PTO is unlikely to result in dire consequences, a wide range of potentially serious complications may develop from the suppurative process or its underlying condition. Recurrent PTO may also be a tremendous drain on a family's financial resources. In addition to the costs of repeated physician visits and multiple courses of medical therapy, parents of children with recurrent PTO must deal with income lost from staying home with a child not allowed to return to school or day care because of the purulent otorrhea. This financial burden is far greater when the cost of additional treatments, such as additional surgery, is included. Thus, for the child and the family, recurrent PTO demands intensive evaluation and treatment.

Pathogenesis

As indicated above, viral URIs and external contamination of the middle ear, such as with swimming, are far and away the most common causes of recurrent PTO. Children may experience up to one viral URI per month. Day-care attendance, particularly with larger play-group sizes, increases the risk of URI and AOM (Kvaerner et al, 1997). Changing day-care settings may seem reasonable, but this may prove difficult for all but the most affluent families. Fortunately, most viral URIs do not lead to PTO. Contamination of the ears by swimming may be more readily controlled, but this is less commonly a significant factor in the pathogenesis of recurrent PTO than viral URI and usually does not lead to PTO (ie, restriction on swimming is usually not necessary) (Lee et al, 1999).

Bacterial URIs may also predispose children to recurrent PTO (Kvaerner et al, 2000). In younger children, these commonly present with purulent or mucopurulent rhinorrhea. Clinical signs of chronic rhinosinusitis or adenoiditis can be relatively subtle (eg, recurrent cough) or altogether lacking.

Many other causes must be considered when evaluating children with recurrent PTO. These causes, listed in Table 53-1, may be classified as infectious-immunologic and noninfectious. In addition to recurrent viral URIs, difficult pathogens must be considered. Some may be routine middle ear pathogens, such as *Streptococcus pneumoniae*, but with resistance to multiple antibiotics (Brook and Gober, 1999). Although this can occur, it is more common to encounter more difficult strains with recurrent or persistent PTO. These would include *Pseudomonas aeruginosa* and *Staphylococcus aureus* (Mandel et al, 1994). PTO that appears to be recurrent may, in fact, be persis-

TABLE 53-1. Causes of Recurrent Post-Tympanostomy Otorrhea

Infectious and immunologic
  Recurrent upper respiratory tract infection
    Viral upper respiratory infection
    Day care
    Bacterial upper respiratory infection
      Rhinosinusitis
      Adenoiditis
  Difficult pathogen
    Antibiotic resistant
    Atypical
      Mycobacteria
      Fungus
  Bacterial biofilm formation
    Epithelial or tympanostomy tube surface
    Increased resistance to antibiotics
    Absolute resistance to immunoglobulins
    Collateral damage by defense systems
    Persistent disease
  Immunologic deficiency
    Cell mediated
    Humoral
    Combined
  Occult nidus
    Cholesteatoma
    Branchial cleft anomaly
Noninfectious
  Reflux
    Gastropharyngeal
    Nasopharyngeal (ie, lack of back-pressure)
  Foreign body reaction
    Tympanostomy tube related
      Hypersensitivity/allergy
      Glove powder
      Cotton fibers
    Other
      Ossicular prosthesis
      Surgical plastic sheeting
      Welding slag
      Hearing aid mold material
  Respiratory tract pathology
    Noninfectious inflammation
      Allergy
      Irritants
        Tobacco smoke
        Air pollution
    Ciliary dyskinesia
  Neoplasia
  Cerebrospinal fluid leak

tent or chronic PTO that has waned with insufficient treatment. After frequent administration of systemic and topical antibacterial therapy, fungal colonization or superinfection (eg, *Candida albicans*) may develop (Kim et al, 2002). In rare circumstances, mycobacteria, both typical and atypical species, may cause recurrent or persistent PTO (Franklin et al, 1994).

Immunodeficiencies, particularly immunoglobulin subclass deficiencies (eg, IgG2) have long been associated with children prone to recurrent AOM (Breukels et al, 1999). Such deficiencies would be expected to increase the risk of recurrent PTO as well, but reports of immune deficiencies in children with recurrent PTO are lacking. Children with more serious immune deficiencies may be even more vulnerable to recurrent PTO.

In recent years, bacterial biofilms—complex bacterial colonies that form on tissue and TT surfaces—have been implicated in the pathogenesis of chronic otitis media (Post, 2001). TT surfaces are vulnerable to biofilm formation. The biofilms may impart resistance to antibiotics and host immune responses, rendering the TT into a nidus for persistent or recurrent PTO. The importance of biofilms in recurrent PTO has yet to be elucidated.

On occasion, an occult nidus will be responsible for recurrence of PTO. Small attic cholesteatomas may go unnoticed on diagnostic pneumatic otoscopy and otomicroscopy, even by experienced otoscopists. First branchial cleft anomalies may present similarly but are extremely rare.

Noninfectious causes of recurrent PTO are less intuitive but potentially more common. For example, TTs equilibrate middle ear pressure with environmental pressure. If the eustachian tube and TT are both patent, swallowing may lead to reflux of nasopharyngeal mucus into the tubotympanum (Bluestone and Klein, 1996). This may be manifest as recurrent PTO. Reflux of gastric secretions (ie, pepsin) has been demonstrated in over 80% of children with chronic OME (Tasker et al, 2002). If reflux persists after TT placement, recurrent PTO may result.

TTs are essentially foreign bodies, and it is expected that the host will ultimately treat them as such, contributing to extrusion. TT composition (especially certain plastics) may lead to a hypersensitivity reaction, but this is very unusual. If meticulous care is not taken during the process of TT insertion, powder from surgical gloves or fibers from drapes and sponges may be inadvertently inserted along with the TT. Such materials are notoriously proinflammatory. In rare circumstances, TT placement may expose a reaction to materials residing in the middle ear for desired (eg, Silastic sheeting) or undesired (eg, welding slag) reasons.

Noninfectious respiratory tract pathology commonly contributes to the development of PTO (Kvaerner et al, 2000). Upper respiratory tract allergy and exposure to environmental tobacco smoke and air pollution are widespread. Symptoms of rhinosinusitis typically accompany any middle ear involvement.

Ciliary dyskinesia is not a common cause of recurrent PTO, but recurrent PTO is not uncommon in children with ciliary dyskinesia. Most children with this disorder will have the diagnosis established prior to TT placement. On occasion, the recurrent PTO will be the primary presenting complaint.

Cerebrospinal fluid leaks and middle ear neoplasms may present with middle ear effusions or PTO. Otorrhea in these conditions is more often chronic than recurrent.

Evaluation and Focused Management

The key to management of recurrent PTO is determining the underlying cause (Table 53-2). Effecting treatment is usually relatively easy if the cause can be determined (Table 53-3). Thus, it is critical that all possible etiologies be considered (see Table 53-1).

Families are questioned about contributing factors, such as day-care play-group size, smoking in the home, exposure to allergens, and feeding habits that may contribute to reflux. With the exception of avoiding external contamination, these factors can be difficult for many families to control satisfactorily.

In addition to a complete history, a thorough ear examination is necessary. This usually requires suction débridement with either an operating otoscope or a microscope. In the process, foreign bodies may be identified and removed. Débridement allows sampling of middle ear effusion with minimal contamination from the external canal flora. It also facilitates delivery of topical agents through the TT and into the middle ear. Finally, complete débridement is absolutely necessary to identify occult pathology, such as attic cholesteatoma. Repeated

examination and débridement may be necessary. It is not uncommon for cholesteatomas to be diagnosed after years of recurrent otorrhea. Examination at the end of therapy may be necessary to distinguish recurrent PTO (ie, the ear clears with treatment) from inadequately treated chronic PTO (ie, the ear merely becomes less inflamed with treatment).

A full head and neck examination may yield helpful information. Diffuse adenopathy may lead to the diagnosis of an immune deficiency (eg, human immunodeficiency virus [HIV] or hematogenous malignancy). Nasopharyngoscopy may demonstrate insidious rhinosinusitis or adenoiditis.

Middle ear aspirates may be submitted for a wide range of analysis, including salivary and gastric enzymes. However, most clinicians send middle ear exudates only for bacterial culture and antibiotic sensitivities. Bacteriologic information is critical, particularly after standard empiric regimens have failed, because resistant and atypical pathogens are more common in such circumstances. Pathogens resistant to oral antibiotics frequently respond to parenteral antibiotic therapy. Culture of middle ear fluids alone may not be sufficient to isolate fastidious organisms, such as mycobacteria. Tissue cultures may be necessary if no pathogens can be identified.

Nasal and nasopharyngeal cultures may identify a reservoir for resistant middle ear pathogens. Culture-directed ototopical, systemic, and nasotopical therapy will generally lead to eradication of these pathogens. Remote sites (especially skinfolds) should be evaluated for sources of fungal infection, which may lead to an id reaction in the middle ear.

Systemic laboratory evaluation commonly includes screening for immunoglobulin deficiency, HIV, and upper respiratory allergies. If IgG2 deficiency, the most common immunologic defect in recurrent otitis media, is found, pneumococcal vaccination may be beneficial (Breukels et al, 1999). Consultation with an allergist or immunologist should be considered even if initial screening batteries do not reveal common anomalies.

The utility and timing of radiographic imaging are less certain. Small cholesteatomas and other subtle middle ear pathology may be indistinguishable from middle ear exudates on radiographic studies. Ideally, imaging would be obtained when the ear is dry, particularly if sedation is required, but this may be difficult to achieve.

TABLE 53-2. Evaluation of Recurrent Post-Tympanostomy Otorrhea

Evaluation
  History
  Examination
    Ear
      Débridement
      Microscopy
    Nasopharynx
    Neck
  Laboratory
    Otorrhea sample
      Microbiology (culture)
      Pepsin
    Systemic
      Immunoglobulin
        Subclass deficiency
        Allergy
      Human immunodeficiency virus (HIV)
  Radiographic
    Computed tomography
      Temporal bones
      Paranasal sinuses
  Ancillary: gastroesophageal probe

TABLE 53-3. Postevaluation Management of Recurrent Post-Tympanostomy Otorrhea

Social
  Day-care modification (reduced play-group size)
  Smoke avoidance
  Allergy precautions
  Reflux precautions
  Contamination avoidance and earplugs

Maximal medical therapy, including parenteral antibiotic therapy, should be administered to optimize the middle ear status prior to imaging. Imaging should include both the temporal bones and the paranasal sinuses. Computed tomography is the modality of choice, and contrast is generally not needed. Imaging should definitely be obtained if atypical findings, such as neurologic deficits or anatomic irregularities, are encountered.

Evaluation for gastric reflux is typically performed by a dual pH probe. Some clinicians will forego this study in favor of an empiric trial of antireflux medications, but the role of these agents in the treatment of PTO remains uncertain.

Empiric Management: My Approach

If a predisposing factor can be identified, treatment can generally be focused (Table 53-3). If the underlying cause of recurrent PTO is not apparent or PTO recurs despite addressing any identified patient-centric factors, empiric therapy may be necessary. As with any therapy, this begins with the least invasive intervention and progresses to surgical management. Empiric treatment of recurrent PTO should begin similarly to isolated PTO, with topical and systemic antimicrobial agents, as has been addressed elsewhere in this text. The issues addressed below will therefore focus on treatment of PTO that has failed such conservative management.

Prophylactic antibiotic therapy may be administered systemically or topically and chronically or episodically. There are no data to support the use of antibiotic prophylaxis in the presence of TTs. The use of topical antimicrobial therapy has been studied most closely relative to external contamination with swimming and found to be of no significant value (Kim et al, 2002). Systemic prophylaxis was widely used to avoid TT placement. Its use has been discouraged because of the emergence of resistant pathogens with their use (Brook and Gober, 1996).

Medical therapy directed at contributing factors may be of more value than antimicrobial prophylaxis. Maintaining strict nasal toilet with saline irrigations is a very safe means of reducing the proinflammatory burden on the eustachian tube, but no research has supported its use. Nasal toilet may be of more value for children with nasopharyngeal reflux secondary to cleft palate with velopharyngeal insufficiency. Administration of influenza vaccine reduces the rate of recurrent otitis media (Clements et al, 1995). Similar benefits may be expected with recurrent PTO. Pneumococcal vaccination has also been shown to yield a modest reduction in AOM and, presumably, recurrent PTO (Fireman et al, 2003). As the risk associated with these vaccines is acceptably low, consideration should be given to administering these vaccines to children with recurrent PTO. Chronic oral administration of the natural sweetener xylitol, either in gum (pellet) or syrup formulation, has been shown to significantly reduce the incidence of AOM (Uhari et al, 1996). Although data on xylitol in recurrent PTO are lacking, its benefits demonstrated in AOM and its safety profile warrant consideration for use in recurrent PTO. Empiric treatment of reflux has been advocated by some clinicians, but the safety profile of acid blockers is not as favorable as xylitol. Formal pH measurements would be recommended prior to empiric treatment of reflux. Intravenous immunoglobulin therapy may be beneficial, particularly in children with refractory PTO and subtle immunoglobulin deficiencies.

If medical management fails, a variety of surgical interventions may be efficacious. Tube removal or replacement will often correct the problem, suggesting that the underlying problem may have been a foreign body reaction or development of a biofilm on the TT. When the TT is replaced, a TT model that can be easily removed in the clinic should be used. Recurrent or chronic PTO after TT replacement should force the clinician to consider the value of the TT, particularly if the indication for TT placement was painless OME. Amplification (ie, hearing aids) can be effectively used to rehabilitate children with conductive hearing loss owing to chronic OME—much more so than chronically or recurrently draining ears (Flanagan et al, 1996). If a child is to undergo general anesthesia to remove or replace a TT, one should consider simultaneous adenoidectomy, which has been shown to be effective in the treatment of recurrent OME (Gates et al, 1987). Although sinus disease may be present in a significant proportion of children with recurrent or chronic otitis media, surgical intervention is rarely necessary. If PTO continues or recurs, consideration must be given to leaving the TTs out entirely. Tympanoplasty with mastoidectomy is rarely indicated for recurrent PTO. Middle ear surgery should be reserved for cases in which otorrhea recurs following tube removal and maximal medical therapy or in cases suspicious for cholesteatoma on physical (eg, polyp formation) or radiographic (eg, ossicular or scutal erosion) examination. If gastric reflux is demonstrated and medical therapy fails, Nissen fundoplication may be necessary.

References

Ah-Tye C, Paradise JL, Colborn DK. Otorrhea in young children after tympanostomy-tube placement for persistent middle-ear effusion: prevalence, incidence, and duration. Pediatrics 2001;107:1251–8.

Bluestone CD, Klein JO. Otitis media, atelectasis, and eustachian tube dysfunction. In: Bluestone CD, Stool SE, Kenna MA, editors. Pediatric otolaryngology. Vol. 1. Philadelphia: WB Saunders; 1996. p. 388–582.

Breukels MA, Rijkers GT, Voorhorst-Ogink MM, et al. Pneumococcal conjugate vaccine primes for polysaccharide-inducible IgG2 antibody response in children with recurrent otitis media acuta. J Infect Dis 1999;179:1152–6.

Brook I, Gober AE. Prophylaxis with amoxicillin or sulfisoxazole for otitis media: effect on the recovery of penicillin-resistant bacteria from children. Clin Infect Dis 1996;22:143–5.

Brook I, Gober AE. Resistance to antimicrobials used for therapy of otitis media and sinusitis: effect of previous antimicrobial therapy and smoking. Ann Otol Rhinol Laryngol 1999;108:645–7.

Casselbrant ML, Kaleida PH, Rockette HE, et al. Efficacy of antimicrobial prophylaxis and of tympanostomy tube insertion for prevention of recurrent acute otitis media: results of a randomized clinical trial. Pediatr Infect Dis J 1992;11:278–86.

Clements DA, Langdon L, Bland C, Walter E. Influenza A vaccine decreases the incidence of otitis media in 6- to 30-month-old children in day care. Arch Pediatr Adolesc Med 1995;149:1113–7.

Fireman B, Black SB, Shinefield HR, et al. Impact of the pneumococcal conjugate vaccine on otitis media. Pediatr Infect Dis J 2003;22:10–6.

Flanagan PM, Knight LC, Thomas A, et al. Hearing aids and glue ear. Clin Otolaryngol 1996;21:297–300.

Franklin DJ, Starke JR, Brady MT, et al. Chronic otitis media after tympanostomy tube placement caused by *Mycobacterium abscessus*: a new clinical entity? Am J Otol 1994;15:313–20.

Gates GA, Avery CA, Cooper JC Jr, Prihoda TJ. Chronic secretory otitis media: effects of surgical management. Ann Otol Rhinol Laryngol Suppl 1989;138:2–32.

Gates GA, Avery CA, Prihoda TJ, Cooper JC Jr. Effectiveness of adenoidectomy and tympanostomy tubes in the treatment of chronic otitis media with effusion. N Engl J Med 1987;317:1444–51.

Gates GA, Avery CA, Prihoda TJ, Holt GR. Delayed onset posttympanotomy otorrhea. Otolaryngol Head Neck Surg 1988;98:111–5.

Kim EJ, Catten MD, Lalwani AK. Detection of fungal DNA in effusion associated with acute and serous otitis media. Laryngoscope 2002;112:2037–41.

Kvaerner KJ, Nafstad P, Hagen J, et al. Early acute otitis media: determined by exposure to respiratory pathogens. Acta Otolaryngol Suppl (Stockh) 1997;529:14–8.

Kvaerner KJ, Nafstad P, Jaakkola JJ. Upper respiratory morbidity in preschool children: a cross-sectional study. Arch Otolaryngol Head Neck Surg 2000;126:1201–6.

Lee D, Youk A, Goldstein NA. A meta-analysis of swimming and water precautions. Laryngoscope 1999;109:536–40.

Mandel EM, Casselbrant ML, Kurs-Lasky M. Acute otorrhea: bacteriology of a common complication of tympanostomy tubes. Ann Otol Rhinol Laryngol 1994;103:713–8.

Post JC. Direct evidence of bacterial biofilms in otitis media. Laryngoscope 2001;111:2083–94.

Tasker A, Dettmar PW, Panetti M, et al. Reflux of gastric juice and glue ear in children. Lancet 2002;359:493.

Uhari M, Kontiokari T, Koskela M, Niemela M. Xylitol chewing gum in prevention of acute otitis media: double blind randomized trial. BMJ 1996;313:1180–4.

Chapter 54

WORKUP AND MANAGEMENT OF CHRONIC OTORRHEA

CHARLES D. BLUESTONE, MD

Chronic otorrhea can be the result of chronic infection in the external or middle ear, or both, or from the inner ear and brain (perilymphatic or cerebrospinal fluid) (Schloss and Pearl, 1996). In this chapter, I limit my discussion to the evaluation and management of chronic suppurative otitis media.

Chronic suppurative otitis media is the stage of ear disease in which there is chronic inflammation of the middle ear and mastoid and in which a nonintact tympanic membrane (chronic perforation or tympanostomy tube) is present. This complication of otitis media has also been commonly called chronic otitis media, but this term can be confused with chronic otitis media with effusion, which is not a complication of otitis media, and no perforation of the tympanic membrane is present (Bluestone, 1999). Also, the term chronic otitis media has been inappropriately used when a chronic perforation of the tympanic membrane is present, but the middle ear and mastoid are free of infection (see Chapter 1, "Definitions of Otitis Media and Related Diseases"). Otorrhea may or may not be evident; a discharge may be present in the middle ear or mastoid, or both, but otorrhea is not evident through the perforation—or tympanostomy tube—or in the external auditory canal. There is no consensus regarding the duration of otitis media to be designated chronic suppurative otitis media. Even though 3 or more months appears to be appropriate, some clinicians consider a shorter duration of otitis media, such as 3 weeks, as being chronic, especially when the causative organism is *Pseudomonas*. When acute otorrhea fails to improve after initial, appropriate, and adequate ototopical therapy (and systemic antibiotic treatment), the disease can progress to the chronic stage if not effectively managed. Thus, the distinction between acute and chronic otorrhea is based not only on duration but also on response to management, the causative bacterial pathogens, and the underlying pathology. When a cholesteatoma is also present, the term cholesteatoma with chronic suppurative otitis media is appropriately used (Bluestone et al, 2002).

However, because an acquired aural cholesteatoma does not have to be associated with chronic suppurative otitis media, cholesteatoma is not part of the pathologic features of the type of ear disease described in this chapter (see Chapter 83, "Cholesteatoma").

Chronic suppurative otitis media, without cholesteatoma, is preceded by acute otitis media, in which a perforation of the tympanic membrane or tympanostomy tube is present (Bluestone, 2000).

Workup

The character of the discharge can be helpful in the differential diagnosis between the presence of chronic suppurative otitis media versus another cause (Dohar, 2003). Otorrhea that is clear or "watery" fluid can be from the inner ear (perilymphatic fluid) or the intracranial cavity (cerebrospinal fluid), especially if there is copious clear otorrhea following trauma to the ear or head. Although relatively rarely encountered, congenital malformations or tumors of the inner ear or middle ear cleft can also be the cause. Computed tomography (CT) of the temporal bones/intracranial cavity, radionucleotide scanning, or testing the fluid for glucose or β_2-transferrin would provide confirmation. Mucoid, purulent, or mucopurulent drainage usually indicates an infectious etiology. Likewise, bloody or sanguineous drainage usually points to an infectious etiology, but there may be another underlying etiology, such as tumor. Table 54-1 lists the anatomic sites that can be the origin of chronic otorrhea. A chronic, purulent, mucoid, or serous discharge through a perforation of the tympanic membrane or tympanostomy tube is evidence of chronic suppurative otitis media. Frequently, a polyp will be seen emerging through the perforation or tympanostomy tube. The size of the perforation has no relation to the duration or severity of the disease, but, frequently, the defect involves most of the pars tensa. There is no otalgia, mastoid or pinna tenderness, vertigo, or fever. When any of these signs or symptoms are present, the

TABLE 54-1. Differential Diagnosis of Chronic Otorrhea Related to Anatomic Site

External ear
  Otitis externa
  Perichondritis
  Myringitis
  Foreign body
  Herpes zoster oticus
  Congenital canal cyst
  Furuncle
  Trauma
  Cerebrospinal/perilymphatic fluid
  Tumor
  Parotid salivary fluid
Middle ear cleft* (tympanic membrane is nonintact)
  Acute otitis media
  Otitis media with effusion
  Barotrauma
  Chronic suppurative otitis media
  Cholesteatoma/retraction pocket
  Cerebrospinal/perilymphatic fluid
  Tumor
Inner ear (tympanic membrane is nonintact)
  Cerebrospinal/perilymphatic fluid

*Middle ear, eustachian tube, mastoid.

examiner should look for a possible suppurative intratemporal complication, such as mastoiditis or labyrinthitis, or an intracranial complication. The disease must be distinguished from cholesteatoma or a neoplasm; both may cause chronic otorrhea. When either of these entities is suspected, CT scans should be obtained (see below).

A complete history and physical examination of the head and neck are indicated because there may be an underlying cause of the infection, such as the presence of paranasal sinusitis. This condition must be actively treated because the ear infection may not respond to medical treatment until the sinusitis resolves. An upper respiratory tract allergy, an immunologic deficiency, or a nasopharyngeal tumor may also contribute to the pathogenesis of chronic suppurative otitis media and will need to be managed appropriately. More recently, smoking and gastroesophageal reflux have been implicated as possible etiologic factors in chronic middle ear disease.

The otomicroscope should be used to completely evaluate the external ear canal and tympanic membrane. This will help assess the defect in the tympanic membrane or tympanostomy tube and rule out the possible presence of a cholesteatoma or tumor. If a satisfactory examination cannot be performed with the child awake, then an examination under general anesthesia will be necessary. At this time, the discharge can be aspirated and a culture from the middle ear can be obtained.

Culture, Susceptibility Testing, and Microbiology

When a chronic aural discharge is present, it is desirable to culture the drainage. The antimicrobial regimen can

then be adjusted according to the results of the Gram stain, culture, and susceptibility testing. The most effective method to obtain a sample of the discharge is to remove as much of the purulent material as possible from the external canal by suction or cotton-tipped applicator and then aspirate the pus directly at or through the perforation or tympanostomy tube using a blunt-nosed needle attached to a tuberculin syringe or an Alden-Senturia trap (Storz Instrument Co., St. Louis, MO) and suction. This procedure is most effectively accomplished employing the otomicroscope.

The bacteria that cause the initial episode of acute otitis media and perforation or acute otorrhea through a tympanostomy tube are usually not those that are isolated from chronic suppurative otitis media (Mandel et al, 1994). The most common organism isolated from around the world is *Pseudomonas aeruginosa*; *Staphylococcus aureus* is also found, but less commonly. Table 54-2 shows the frequency of bacteria isolated from children with chronic suppurative otitis media at the Children's Hospital of Pittsburgh (Kenna et al, 1993). Anaerobic bacteria were isolated infrequently in this study. Anaerobic bacteria have been isolated from ears with chronic suppurative otitis media, but whether they are true pathogens remains to be demonstrated. Brook (1985) isolated *Bacteroides melaninogenicus* in 40% and *Peptococcus* species in 35% of middle ear exudates; the collection of exudate was performed through the perforation in

TABLE 54-2. Microbiology of Chronic Suppurative Otitis Media in 51 Children (80 Ears)

Bacteria Isolated	Number of Isolates* ($n = 118$)
Pseudomonas aeruginosa	56
Staphylococcus aureus	18
Diphtheroids	8
Streptococcus pneumoniae	7
Haemophilus influenzae (nontypable)	6
Bacteroides sp	3
Candida albicans	2
Candida parapsilosis	2
Enterococcus	2
Acinetobacter	2
Staphylococcus epidermidis	1
Morganella morganii	1
Providencia stuartii	1
Klebsiella sp	1
Proteus sp	1
Serratia marcescens	1
Moraxella	1
Pseudomonas cepacia	1
Providencia rettgeri	1
Pseudomonas maltophilia	1
Achromobacter xylosoxidans	1
Eikenella	1

Adapted from Kenna MA, Rosane BA, Bluestone CD. Medical management of chronic suppurative otitis media without cholesteatoma in children—update 1992. Am J Otolaryngol 1993;14:469–73.

*Number exceeds 80 owing to more than one organism isolated in 38 ears.

the tympanic membrane using an 18-gauge needle covered by a plastic cannula.

There have also been reports of isolating unusual organisms, such as *Mycobacterium tuberculosis, Mycobacterium chelonae, Mycobacterium avium-intracellulare, Blastomyces dermatitidis, Actinomyces, Alcaligenes piechaudii,* and *Candida* species.

Assessment of Hearing

Evaluation of the hearing is an important part of the workup because the degree of hearing loss is important in the decision-making process, for example, a moderate to severe hearing loss may indicate a middle ear defect, such as a cholesteatoma. But a conductive hearing loss usually accompanies chronic suppurative otitis media. If a hearing loss greater than 20 to 30 dB is found, the ossicles may be involved. However, the patient may also have a sensorineural component, which is most likely attributable to a serous labyrinthitis. Impedance testing may be helpful if purulent material in the ear canal prevents visualization of the eardrum adequately enough to identify a possible perforation. If perforation is present, the measured volume of the external canal will be larger than expected. However, the tympanometric pattern may be flat, despite the presence of a perforation, if the volume of air in the middle ear and mastoid is small. When this is suspected, the pressure on the pump manometer of the impedance bridge can be increased in an attempt to force open the eustachian tube. If the tube can be opened with positive air pressure from the pump manometer, a perforation must be present.

Imaging

CT scans of the middle ear and mastoid should be obtained when intensive medical treatment (including intravenous antimicrobial therapy) fails, the child has an early recurrence, or, initially, a cholesteatoma is suspected. In the typical case, the sclerotic or undeveloped mastoid will appear "cloudy." If a defect in the bone owing to osteitis is present, however, the area will appear on the CT scans. Discontinuity of the ossicular chain, if present, may be visualized on the CT scans. Unusual causes of a chronic draining ear, including neoplasms and eosinophilic granuloma, must be considered in the differential diagnosis of chronic suppurative otitis media, and in such cases, CT scans should be obtained initially. Erosion of portions of the temporal bone, especially the labyrinth, on the CT scan is suggestive of tumor.

Management

Chronic suppurative otitis media, which is uncomplicated, is initially treated medically. Because the bacteria most frequently cultured are gram negative, antimicrobial agents should be selected to be effective against these organisms, but the antibiotic treatment should be culture directed. As I describe below, medical treatment consists of aural toilet, ototopical medication, and possible administration of systemic antimicrobial agents, first orally and, if this fails, intravenously. Tympanomastoid surgery is reserved for those patients in whom intensive medical treatment has failed or when a cholesteatoma or neoplasm is diagnosed or suspected; evidence of these disease entities may not be apparent from the CT scans.

Aural Toilet

An important part of the management of chronic suppurative otitis media is frequent use of aural toilet. The most effective manner in which to clean the external canal is by carefully and completely aspirating the discharge from the external auditory canal with the aid of the otomicroscope. Thoroughly cleaning the ear canal will enhance the use of ototopical agents. Aural toilet as the sole method of treatment of chronic suppurative otitis media had been advocated for management of this disease in developing nations, but a study failed to show that it was as effective as combining this treatment with ototopical agents (Smith et al, 1996) (see below).

Ototopical Medications

A suspension containing polymyxin B, neomycin sulfates, and hydrocortisone (Pediotic) and one that has neomycin, polymyxin E, and hydrocortisone (Coly-Mycin) have been used in the past but are no longer used in the United States. Caution is advised owing to the concern over the potential ototoxicity of these agents (Perry and Smith, 1996). Some clinicians use topical tobramycin (with dexamethasone) (Tobradex) or gentamicin (Garamycin) ophthalmic drops instilled into the ear when *Pseudomonas* is isolated, but, again, these agents are aminoglycosides and may therefore be ototoxic (Ikeda and Morizono, 1991). More importantly, none of these popular medications are approved for use when there is a nonintact tympanic membrane. Nevertheless, these ototopical agents are used widely and appear to be effective for treating chronic suppurative otitis media (Smith et al, 1996). Clinicians who have employed them with apparent success think that if the infection is not eliminated, it, too, may cause damage to the inner ear.

Ofloxacin (Floxin Otic) is the only ototopical agent approved by the US Food and Drug Administration (FDA) when the tympanic membrane is not intact. It is used in children when acute otitis media with otorrhea occurs when a tympanostomy tube is in place. At present, it is the only topical antimicrobial agent that has been demonstrated to be safe and effective (Dohar et al, 1999; Gates, 2001; Goldblatt, 2001; Goldblatt et al, 1998) and approved for this indication in children. It is also approved for adults who have chronic suppurative otitis media, but it is currently not approved for this indication in children (Agro et al, 1998), even though it has been reported to be effective in this age group (Kaga and Ichimura, 1998). The common bacterial pathogens isolated from these infections are susceptible to this topical agent (Klein, 2001). Also, topical ofloxacin has been shown to be more effective than the combination of neomycin-polymyxin B-hydrocortisone otic drops in adults with chronic suppurative otitis media (Tong et al, 1996). Thus, the lack of reported clinical trials in children notwithstanding, it seems reasonable today to use ofloxacin initially in children who have uncomplicated chronic suppurative otitis media.

Ciprofloxacin with hydrocortisone (Cipro HC) is approved by the FDA to treat external otitis in both children and adults. Even though ciprofloxacin is not approved for chronic suppurative otitis media, it appears to be effective (Aslan et al, 1998; Dohar et al, 1996; Esposito et al, 1990, Esposito et al, 1992). One study showed that topical ciprofloxacin was more effective than topical gentamicin for chronic suppurative otitis media in adults (Tutkun et al, 1995), and another showed that this antibiotic was equally as effective as tobramycin in adults with this infection (Fradis et al, 1997). No apparent ototoxicity has occurred after using this ototopical agent in patients with chronic suppurative otitis media (Ozagar et al, 1997). In addition, topical ciprofloxacin did not cause ototoxicity in the monkey model of chronic suppurative otitis media (Alper et al, 1999). There is still no consensus about the potential efficacy of adding a corticosteroid component to the antimicrobial agent, but steroids may hasten resolution of the inflammation (Crowther and Simpson, 1991). Recently, Alper and associates (2000) reported that the combination of tobramycin and dexamethasone was more effective than tobramycin alone in the monkey model of chronic suppurative otitis media. Tobramycin with and without dexamethasone was not only effective but also safe, that is, there was no cochlear damage.

Some clinicians, especially in developing countries that have limited health care financial resources, recommend antiseptic drops as an alternative to antibiotic topical agents. An antiseptic ototopical agent (aluminum acetate) was found to be as effective as topical gentamicin sulfate for otorrhea in a randomized clinical trial reported from the United Kingdom (Clayton et al, 1990). Thorp and colleagues (1998) evaluated the in vitro activity of acetic acid and aluminum subacetate (Burow's solution) and found both to be effective against the major pathogens causing chronic suppurative otitis media. Burow's solution was somewhat more effective than acetic acid. Antiseptic drops (eg, acetic acid) are commonly used in underdeveloped countries and are reputed to be effective. Owing to cost and availability, antibiotic ototopical agents are used when antiseptic drops are ineffective.

Ototopical agents currently approved by the FDA (2002) for ear infections are listed in Table 54-3. As stated above, only ofloxacin otic solution is approved for children when the tympanic membrane is nonintact, and then only when a tympanostomy tube is present. Nevertheless, other agents, such as ciprofloxacin with hydrocortisone, may be beneficial for use in children with this middle ear and mastoid infection. The advantage of quinolone topical agents is that there is no evidence of ototoxicity in animal models, which had been reported using the aminoglycosides. Also, with the growing concern regarding the emergence of multidrug-resistant bacterial otic pathogens, the use of an ototopical agent is desirable because using a high concentration of the drug directed at the site of infection will hopefully prevent emergence of resistant organisms.

When ototopical antibiotic medications are elected, the patient should ideally return to the outpatient facility daily to have the discharge thoroughly aspirated or swabbed (ie, aural toilet, ear mopping) and to have the ototopical medication directly instilled into the middle ear through the perforation or tympanostomy tube using an otoscope or otomicroscope. Frequently, the discharge will rapidly improve within a week with this type of treatment, after which the eardrops may be administered at home until there is complete resolution of the middle ear–mastoid inflammation. When daily administration by the physician is not feasible, a family member/caregiver can administer the drops.

Oral Antimicrobial Agents

Oral antibiotics that are approved to treat acute otitis media may be effective if the bacterium is susceptible, but

TABLE 54-3. Ototopical Agents Used in the Treatment of Chronic Suppurative Otitis Media*

Generic Name	Trade Name (Company)
Acetic acid (2%) otic solution	Vosol (Wallace Laboratories, Cranbury, NJ)
Acetic acid (2%) and hydrocortisone (1%) otic solution	Vosol HC (Wallace Laboratories, Cranbury, NJ)
Acetic acid 2% in aqueous aluminum acetate otic solution	Otic Domeboro (Bayer Corporation, West Haven, CT)
Ciprofloxacin hydrochloride and hydrocortisone otic suspension	Ciprofloxin HC Suspension (Alcon, Humacao, PR)
Colistin sulfate-neomycin sulfate-thonzonium bromide-hydrocortisone acetate otic suspension	Cortisone-TC Otic Suspension (Monarch Pharmaceuticals, Bristol, TN)
Neomycin, polymycin B sulfate, and hydrocortisone otic suspension	Pediotic Suspension (Monarch Pharmaceuticals, Bristol, TN)
Ofloxacin otic solution 0.3%	Floxin Otic (Daiichi Pharmaceutical Corp., Montvale, NJ)

*Agents listed are commonly used in children and adults; only Floxin Otic has US Food and Drug Administration approval for this indication, but only for adults.

because the organism is usually *P. aeruginosa*, agents that are currently approved for children will usually not be effective; currently, systemic quinolone antibiotics are not FDA approved in the United States. However, orally administered ciprofloxacin has been shown to be effective in adults and children who had chronic suppurative otitis media (Lang et al, 1992; Piccirillo and Parnes, 1989). Despite the potential drawbacks of prescribing oral antibiotics that are not effective when *Pseudomonas* is the causative organism, many clinicians still administer a broad-spectrum oral antibiotic, hoping that the underlying infection is caused by the usual bacteria that are isolated from ears with acute otitis media. In a report of a randomized clinical trial conducted in Kenya, Smith and colleagues (1996) compared (1) oral amoxicillin-clavulanate, dry mopping of the ear, and ototopical antibiotic-cortisone drops; (2) dry mopping alone; and (3) no treatment. They found that the combination of oral antibiotic and topical agents was statistically more effective than dry mopping alone or no treatment. But one randomized clinical trial found that topical ofloxacin was more effective than systemic amoxicillin-clavulanate (without eardrops) in adults with chronic suppurative otitis media (Yuen et al, 1994).

The patient should be re-examined in about 7 to 10 days when ototopical agents or oral antimicrobial agents, or both, are used. At that time, any adjustments can be made in the medications following the results of the microbiologic studies. After approximately 1 week, there should be cessation of the discharge or marked improvement. If the otorrhea is improving, the child should be re-examined periodically thereafter until resolution occurs. If after 1 to 2 weeks there is no improvement, other treatment options such as parenteral antimicrobial therapy should be considered.

Parenteral Antimicrobial Agents

If the child is a treatment failure following the administration of ototopical agents, with or without an oral antimicrobial agent, parenteral antimicrobial therapy should be considered. Of 173 children followed prospectively following tympanostomy tube placement, Ah-Tye and colleagues (2001) reported that 5 (3%) required parenteral antibiotic therapy to eliminate chronic infection that was unresponsive to ototopical and oral antimicrobial therapy. When intravenous therapy is indicated, the patient should receive a parenteral β-lactam antipseudomonal drug, such as ticarcillin, piperacillin, or ceftazidime; empirically, ticarcillin-tazobactam is usually selected because *Pseudomonas*, with and without *S. aureus*, is frequently isolated. The results of the culture and susceptibility studies dictate the antimicrobial agent ultimately chosen (Kenna et al, 1986; Kenna et al, 1993). Dagan and colleagues (1992) in Israel and Arguedas and associates (1993) in Costa Rica reported excellent results using ceftazidime. In Finland, Vartiainen

and Kansanen (1992) also recommended a trial of intravenous antimicrobial therapy before considering mastoid surgery. The regimen can be altered when the results of culture and susceptibility tests are available. Also, the external canal purulent material and debris (and middle ear, if possible) are aspirated and the ototopical medication instilled daily. This method of treatment is usually performed on an ambulatory basis (Dagan et al, 1992; Esposito, 2000), but hospitalization may be required on an individualized basis, such as when daily aural toilet is inconvenient or compliance in giving the medication is uncertain as an outpatient.

In approximately 90% of children, the middle ear will be free of discharge and the signs of chronic suppurative otitis media will be greatly improved or absent within 5 to 7 days. My colleagues and I conducted a study in 36 pediatric patients with chronic suppurative otitis media in which all received parenteral antimicrobial therapy and daily aural toilet (Kenna et al, 1986). Medical therapy alone resolved the infection in 32 patients (89%); 4 children required tympanomastoidectomy. We later increased the study group to 66 children and reported similar short-term results; 89% had dry ears following intravenous antibiotic therapy (Kenna and Bluestone, 1988). In a follow-up of that study, 51 of the original 66 children were evaluated for their long-term outcomes (Kenna et al, 1993). Of these 51 children, 40 (78%) had resolution of their initial or recurrent infection following medical treatment and 11 (22%) had to eventually have mastoid surgery. Failure was associated with older children and as early recurrence. If the patient had recurrence of the otorrhea with the same type, medical therapy usually failed and the patient required mastoid surgery.

If resolution does occur with intravenous antimicrobial therapy and hospitalization is required, the child can be discharged and receive the parenteral antibiotic and eardrops (by the parent/caregiver) for a period of 10 to 14 days at home. The patient should be followed at periodic intervals to watch for signs of spontaneous closure of the perforation, which frequently happens after the middle ear and mastoid are no longer infected. Appropriate intensive medical treatment should be attempted before recommending major ear surgery because the outcome of surgery is not as favorable when medical treatment is withheld (Vartiainen and Vartiainen, 1996).

Surgery

Placement of a tympanostomy tube may be helpful if the chronic suppurative otitis media is associated with a perforation that is too small to permit adequate drainage or the perforation frequently closes, only to reopen with episodic drainage. On the other hand, if the chronic infection is related to a tympanostomy tube (ie, the middle ear air cushion is absent), some clinicians advocate removal of the tube, hoping that the infection will subsequently subside. However, the recurrent/chronic ear infections for which the tube was inserted originally frequently recur. There may be some merit in attempting this approach in a patient who has had a long-standing retained tube.

When chronic suppurative otitis media fails to respond to intensive medical therapy (ie, intravenous antibiotics, aural toilet, and ototopical medications) within several days, surgery on the middle ear and mastoid, that is, tympanomastoidectomy, may be required to eradicate the infection. A CT scan should be obtained (see above). Failures usually occur when there is (1) an underlying blockage of the communication between the middle ear and mastoid (ie, aditus ad antrum), (2) irreversible chronic osteitis, (3) cholesteatoma (or tumor), or (4) an early recurrence with the same causative organism (Kenna et al, 1993).

The tympanomastoidectomy procedure that is preferred combines a complete (simple, cortical) mastoidectomy with middle ear surgery to remove the infection (eg, purulent material, granulation tissue, and the involved mastoid bone), which frequently includes a tympanoplasty, that is, tympanomastoidectomy with tympanoplasty. Cultures of all infected tissue (including infected bone) are assessed for Gram stain, aerobic and anaerobic bacteria, fungi, and susceptibility testing. The goals of this surgery, in addition to eradication of the disease process, are to maintain the intact posterior and superior canal walls and maintain, or reconstruct, the tympanic membrane and ossicular chain. This procedure is preferred over performing a modified radical, or radical, mastoidectomy, especially in children. Peri- and postoperative culture-directed intravenous antimicrobial therapy is advised to aid in eliminating the chronic infection and to prevent postoperative wound breakdown. Placement of a tympanostomy tube is optional but is preferred, at least in the immediate postoperative course, to provide adequate middle ear and mastoid drainage, particularly if the infection has been long-lasting.

Prevention of Recurrence

The most effective way to prevent recurrence of otorrhea when the tympanic membrane is intact and an attack of acute otitis media occurs is to promptly, appropriately, and adequately treat the infection with the usual oral antimicrobial agents recommended for acute otitis media. If the tympanic membrane is not intact (ie, perforation or a tympanostomy tube is present without evidence of infection), early treatment of acute otorrhea (ie, acute otitis media) should likewise be effective. Treatment with an oral antimicrobial agent may be enhanced by adding an ototopical agent(s) to prevent a secondary infection with external ear canal organisms such as *Pseudomonas*.

A recent meta-analysis of post-tympanostomy tube otorrhea revealed that approximately 16% will have it in the immediate postoperative period, 26% will have it later, 7% will have recurrent episodes, and about 4% will

develop chronic otorrhea (Kay et al, 2001). It is important to remember that chronic infection is always preceded by acute infection: if the acute infection is eliminated, chronic infection does not occur (Bluestone, 2001).

If a perforation (or tympanostomy tube) is present, in the absence of middle ear–mastoid infection, and it is desirable to maintain middle ear ventilation through a nonintact eardrum, recurrent episodes of otorrhea can usually be prevented with antimicrobial prophylaxis, for example, amoxicillin. If a tympanostomy tube is present and the middle ear is now disease free, its removal may restore middle ear–eustachian tube physiology (ie, prevent reflux or insufflation of nasopharyngeal secretions). Yet removal of tympanostomy tubes may not be desirable, especially in infants and young children, and in these cases, antimicrobial prophylaxis, despite the current concern about emergence of antibiotic-resistant bacteria, should also be considered until the tubes spontaneously extrude.

If the patient has a chronic perforation and otitis media (and mastoiditis) has been eliminated, tympanoplastic surgery should be considered. The same factors should be considered when deciding to repair an eardrum perforation in children as described above related to removing a tympanostomy tube (Bluestone, 2002).

References

Agro AS, Garner ET, Wright JW 3rd, et al. Clinical trial of ototopical ofloxacin for treatment of chronic suppurative otitis media. Clin Ther 1998;20:744–59.

Ah-Tye C, Paradise JL, Colburn DK. Otorrhea in young children after tympanostomy-tube placement for persistent middle-ear effusion: prevalence, incidence, and duration. Pediatrics 2001; 107:1251–8.

Alper CM, Dohar JE, Gulhan M, et al. Treatment of chronic suppurative otitis media with topical tobramycin and dexamethasone. Arch Otolaryngol Head Neck Surg 2000;126:165–73.

Alper CM, Swarts JD, Doyle WJ. Middle ear inflation for diagnosis and treatment of otitis media with effusion. Auris Nasus Larynx 1999;26:479–86.

Arguedas AG, Herrera JF, Faingezicht I, et al. Ceftazidime for therapy of children with chronic suppurative otitis media without cholesteatoma. Pediatr Infect Dis J 1993;12:246–8.

Aslan A, Altuntas A, Titiz A, et al. A new dosage regimen for topical application of ciprofloxacin in the management of chronic suppurative otitis media. Otolaryngol Head Neck Surg 1998; 118:883–5.

Bluestone CD. Eustachian tube function and dysfunction. In: Rosenfeld RM, Bluestone CD, editors. Evidence-based otitis media. Hamilton (ON): BC Decker; 1999. p. 137–56.

Bluestone CD. Clinical course, complications and sequelae of acute otitis media. Pediatr Infect Dis J 2000;19:S37–46.

Bluestone CD. Efficacy of ofloxacin and other ototopical preparations for chronic suppurative otitis media in children. Pediatr Infect Dis J 2001;20:111–8.

Bluestone CD. Mastoidectomy and cholesteatoma. In: Bluestone CD, Rosenfeld RM, editors. Surgical atlas of pediatric otolaryngology. Hamilton (ON): BC Decker; 2002. p. 91–122.

Bluestone CD, Gates GA, Klein JO, et al. Chairman: committee report: terminology and classification of otitis media and its complications and sequelae. Ann Otol Rhinol Laryngol 2002;111(3 Suppl 188 Pt 2):8–18.

Brook I. Prevalence of beta-lactamase-producing bacteria in chronic suppurative otitis media. Am J Dis Child 1985;139:280–3.

Clayton MI, Osborne JE, Rutherford D, Rivron RP. A double-blind, randomized, prospective trial of a topical antiseptic versus a topical antibiotic in the treatment of otorrhea. J Otolaryngol 1990;15:7–10.

Crowther JA, Simpson D. Medical treatment of chronic otitis media: steroid or antibiotic with steroid ear-drops? Clin Otolaryngol 1991;16:142–4.

Dagan R, Fliss DM, Einhorn M, et al. Outpatient management of chronic suppurative otitis media without cholesteatoma in children. Pediatr Infect Dis J 1992;11:542–6.

Dohar JE. Otorrhea. In: Bluestone CD, Stool SE, Alper CM, et al, editors. Pediatric otolaryngology. 4th ed. Philadelphia: WB Saunders; 2003. p. 297–305.

Dohar JE, Garner ET, Nielsen RW, et al. Topic ofloxacin treatment of otorrhea in children with tympanostomy tubes. Arch Otolaryngol Head Neck Surg 1999;125:537–45.

Dohar JE, Kenna MA, Wadowsky RM. In vitro susceptibility of aural isolates of *P. aeruginosa* to commonly used ototopical antibiotics. Am J Otol 1996;17:207–9.

Esposito S. Outpatient parenteral treatment of bacterial infections: the Italian model as an international trend? J Antimicrob Chemother 2000;45:724–7.

Esposito S, D'Errico G, Montanaro C. Topical and oral treatment of chronic otitis media with ciprofloxacin. Arch Otolaryngol Head Neck Surg 1990;116:557–9.

Esposito S, Noviello S, D'Errico G, Montanaro C. Topical ciprofloxacin vs. intramuscular gentamicin for chronic otitis media. Arch Otolaryngol Head Neck Surg 1992;118:842–4.

Fradis M, Brodsky A, Ben-David J, et al. Chronic otitis media treated topically with ciprofloxacin or tobramycin. Arch Otolaryngol Head Neck Surg 1997;123:1057–60.

Gates GA. Safety of ofloxacin otic and other ototopical treatments in animal models and in humans. Pediatr Infect Dis J 2001;20:104–7.

Goldblatt EL. Efficacy of ofloxacin and other otic preparations for acute otitis media in patients with tympanostomy tubes. Pediatr Infect Dis J 2001;20:116–9.

Goldblatt EL, Dohar J, Nozza RJ, et al. Topic ofloxacin versus systemic amoxicillin/clavulanate in purulent otorrhea in children with tympanostomy tubes. Int J Pediatr Otorhinolaryngol 1998;46:91–101.

Ikeda K, Morizono T. Effect of ototopic application of a corticosteroid preparation on cochlear function. Am J Otolaryngol 1991;12:150–3.

Kaga K, Ichimura K. A preliminary report: clinical effects of otic solution of ofloxacin in infantile myringitis and chronic otitis media. Int J Pediatr Otorhinolaryngol 1998;42:199–205.

Kay DJ, Nelson M, Rosenfeld RM. Meta-analysis of tympanostomy tube sequelae. Otolaryngol Head Neck Surg 2001;124:374–80.

Kenna MA, Bluestone CD. Medical management of chronic suppurative otitis media without cholesteatoma. In: Lim DJ, Bluestone CD, Klein JO, Nelson JD, editors. Proceedings of the Fourth International Symposium on Otitis Media. Burlington (ON): BC Decker; 1988. p. 222–6.

Kenna MA, Bluestone CD, Reilly J. Medical management of chronic suppurative otitis media without cholesteatoma in children. Laryngoscope 1986;96:146–51.

Kenna MA, Rosane BA, Bluestone CD. Medical management of chronic suppurative otitis media without cholesteatoma in children—update 1992. Am J Otolaryngol 1993;14:469–73.

Klein JO. In vitro and in vivo antimicrobial activity of topical ofloxacin and other ototopical agents. Pediatr Infect Dis J 2001;20:102–3.

Lang R, Goshen S, Raas-Rothschild A, et al. Oral ciprofloxacin in the management of chronic suppurative otitis media without cholesteatoma in children: preliminary experience in 21 children. Pediatr Infect Dis J 1992;11:925–9.

Mandel EM, Casselbrant ML, Kurs-Lasky M. Acute otorrhea: bacteriology of a common complication of tympanostomy tubes. Ann Otol Rhinol Laryngol 1994;103:713–8.

Ozagar A, Koc A, Ciprut A, et al. Effects of topical otic preparation on hearing in chronic otitis media. Otolaryngol Head Neck Surg 1997;117:405–8.

Perry BP, Smith DW. Effect of Cortisporin Otic Suspension on cochlear function and efferent activity in the guinea pig. Laryngoscope 1996;106:1557–61.

Piccirillo JF, Parnes SM. Ciprofloxacin for the treatment of chronic ear disease. Laryngoscope 1989;99:510–3.

Schloss MD, Pearl AJ. Otorrhea. In: Bluestone, CD, Stool SE, Kenna MA, editors. Pediatric otolaryngology. 3rd ed. Philadelphia: WB Saunders; 1996. p. 243–8.

Smith AW, Hatcher J, Mackenzie IJ, et al. Randomised controlled trial of treatment of chronic suppurative otitis media in Kenyan schoolchildren. Lancet 1996;348:1128–33.

Thorp MA, Kruger J, Oliver S, et al. The antibacterial acidity of acetic acid and Burow's solution as topical otological preparations. J Laryngol Otol 1998;112:925–8.

Tong MCF, Woo JKS, van Hasslet CA. A double-blind comparative study of ofloxacin otic drops versus neomycin-polymyxin B-hydrocortisone otic drops in the medical treatment of chronic suppurative otitis media. J Laryngol Otol 1996;110:309–14.

Tutkun A, Ozagar A, Koc A, et al. Treatment of chronic ear disease: topical ciprofloxacin vs. topical gentamicin. Arch Otolaryngol Head Neck Surg 1995;121:1414–6.

Vartiainen E, Kansanen M. Tympanomastoidectomy for chronic otitis media without cholesteatoma. Otolaryngol Head Neck Surg 1992;106:230–4.

Vartiainen E, Vartiainen J. Effect of aerobic bacteriology on the clinical presentation and treatment results of chronic suppurative otitis media. J Laryngol Otol 1996;110:315–8.

Yuen PW, Lau SK, Chau PY, et al. Ofloxacin eardrop treatment for active chronic suppurative otitis media: prospective randomized study. Am J Otol 1994;15:670–3.

Chapter 55

METHICILLIN-RESISTANT *STAPHYLOCOCCUS AUREUS* OTORRHEA

CHARLES M. MYER III, MD

An almost universal problem following tympanostomy tube placement is otorrhea. With approximately 1 million tympanostomy tubes inserted on an annual basis in the United States, and with otorrhea occurring in at least one-third of these individuals, it is clear that the development of a treatment protocol for this problem is essential. In general, children under 3 years of age more often have those organisms associated with acute otitis media, including *Streptococcus pneumoniae*, *Haemophilus influenzae*, and *Moraxella catarrhalis*. In contrast, children over 3 years of age more often have infections marked by *Staphylococcus aureus* and *Pseudomonas aeruginosa*. Similarly, these last two organisms can be found as opportunistic pathogens in those individuals who have received prolonged antimicrobial therapy. In most situations, otorrhea is not cultured and ototopical antimicrobial therapy is instituted, often with an ototopical fluoroquinolone as a single agent. When there is an associated respiratory infection that has been present for several weeks, or if the drainage does not improve over a few days, oral antimicrobial therapy may be instituted. Should the drainage not clear over 1 to 2 weeks, the patient is brought in for suctioning, and, in refractory situations, a culture is obtained (Myer, 2001). Regardless, all patients should be examined at the conclusion of treatment to ensure tube patency and absence of middle ear effusion. When methicillin-resistant *S. aureus* (MRSA) is identified, a cascade of events ensues, which requires the cooperation of otolaryngologists, primary care physicians, and infectious disease specialists (Hartnick et al, 2000).

Although staphylococcal infections are relatively common in medical practice, these organisms have shown an ability to develop resistance to the antibiotics to which they are exposed (Jevons, 1961). The initial strains of MRSA were noted in 1961, and it has been reported that up to 61% of hospital-acquired staphylococcal infections are methicillin resistant (*Lancet*, 1988). Because vancomycin, the agent that has been used most often to treat MRSA, requires parenteral administration and has potential side effects, alternative treatment strategies have been described with variable success in the treatment of this condition (Hartnick et al, 2000). Additionally, one must consider that vancomycin-resistant strains of *S. aureus* have been seen in Europe and the United States (Hartnick et al, 2000).

Reports of MRSA otorrhea following tympanostomy tube placement have been few. However, Suh and colleagues (1998) reported a 23% incidence of otorrhea with an 8% incidence of MRSA otorrhea after middle ear surgery. Once MRSA is identified, it is imperative that the clinician develops a treatment protocol for the disease process itself in addition to addressing the public health concerns raised by the discovery of MRSA. Specifically, the clinician must be aware that the major mode of transmission of MRSA in the hospital setting is by direct contact between patients and health care workers. Colonization sites include the anterior nares, axilla, and perirectal area. In point of fact, in our institution, patients are labeled as "MRSA positive" until three sets of surveillance cultures are obtained from these areas at least 7 days or more apart and are reported as negative. Patients are off antimicrobial therapy for at least 48 hours before these cultures are obtained. Until such time, institutions that use isolation precautions for patients with MRSA must do so according to local guidelines developed in conjunction with infectious disease experts.

Although treatment of infectious conditions such as MRSA otorrhea usually focuses on antimicrobial therapy, prevention of the development of this condition may be equally valuable in the overall public health scheme. Possible measures may include the screening of health care workers as potential carriers and the use of aseptic techniques. Routine hand washing and the use of gloves when performing tympanostomy tube placement and when suctioning draining ears are inexpensive, time-honored, and effective practices (Hartnick et al, 2000).

Strict adherence to isolation protocols also serves to minimize or prevent the spread of MRSA. In Children's Hospital Medical Center, Cincinnati, Ohio (CHMCC), children with positive MRSA cultures are managed by a standard protocol. In addition to the primary site, cultures are obtained from the surveillance areas as described previously. For children who are inpatients, these individuals are placed in isolation units in which gowns, gloves, and masks are worn by health care workers. Noncritical medical equipment, including stethoscopes, blood pressure cuffs, and thermometers, is left in the patient's room. Children are not permitted to leave the isolation unit. Although family and friends may enter and leave as they wish, they are instructed about strict hand washing, and gowns, gloves, and masks are made available, although they are not required. Once the child leaves the hospital, the room is thoroughly sanitized.

As stated previously, patients remain MRSA positive until negative cultures are obtained from the primary site and the surveillance regions on three separate occasions at least 7 days apart. Until that time, should the child return to the hospital, he or she again goes to the isolation unit. However, once the child leaves the hospital, he or she returns to school or day care and resumes normal activities without any isolation precautions. This philosophy is based on the rationale that an otherwise healthy child who is exposed to MRSA will shed the organism quickly, in contradistinction to the ill child in a hospital setting who is continuously exposed to MRSA and will not shed the organism and, thus, is more likely to become infected.

The general issue of isolation of patients with MRSA is more complex when patients are seen in an outpatient setting. These are usually otherwise healthy patients who are being seen in a clinic or office setting. Although our initial protocol had these patients coming at the end of the day so that the room could be thoroughly cleaned following the visit without hindering patient flow, the current policy at CHMCC requires strict hand-washing procedures and makes certain that all sites with which the child might come into contact are cleaned and wiped down after the visit. Thus, the patients no longer need to come at the end of the day, and it is no longer necessary to shut the room for a specific period of time. However, such policies are specific to each institution and each office and must be developed in conjunction with local infectious disease consultants. Our current procedure is felt to be both safe and cost effective.

Although vancomycin is regarded almost universally as the standard therapy for MRSA infections, it is neither practical nor effective to use this aggressive parenteral antimicrobial agent for most cases of MRSA otorrhea. Although the traditional treatment of otorrhea has included such agents as chloramphenicol, gentamicin, tobramycin, and 1% hydrocortisone-polymyxin-neomycin drops, one must always consider the possibility of ototoxicity owing to either the drug or the carrier. However, the ototopical fluoroquinolones have not demonstrated ototoxicity and are effective against almost all of the bacterial organisms encountered with tympanostomy tube otorrhea (Myer, 2001). Thus, when treating a child with MRSA otorrhea, the otolaryngologist should request a full sensitivity panel to multiple antimicrobial agents to derive the most efficacious and safe treatment regimen. Although use of ototopical fluoroquinolones may be ideal in the treatment of otorrhea, their lack of efficacy in certain cases of MRSA otorrhea may force the clinician to add systemic therapy. Choices may include trimethoprim-sulfamethoxazole, vancomycin, or, potentially, an aminoglycoside. These agents are typically added after several weeks of topical therapy and aural toilet if the otorrhea persists. As previously described, surveillance cultures are obtained once the drainage stops. If the external auditory canal cultures remain positive, topical therapy alone is generally continued for several weeks, but ventilating tube removal must be considered if positive cultures continue as this may be the source of infection. In general, however, topical therapy is stopped after the first negative culture.

Conclusion

An emerging problem in the treatment of otorrhea is MRSA. In addition to developing an office protocol for the management of this condition, the clinician must be aware of the infectious disease implications of this diagnosis and request a full antibiotic sensitivity panel when culturing the patient. If a potentially ototoxic mediation is necessary, families should be informed and the information documented in the chart. If conservative treatment using aural toilet, an ototopical antimicrobial agent, and oral antimicrobial therapy is not effective, parenteral administration of vancomycin must be considered. Given the low rate of postoperative otorrhea, antiseptic irrigation of the ear canal prior to myringotomy and tube placement does not appear warranted. On the other hand, hand washing and the use of gloves at the time of the procedure are recommended. In managing patients with MRSA otorrhea, the otolaryngologist must establish a dialogue with infectious disease consultants to minimize spread of the disease while developing an effective treatment plan for the affected individual (Hartnick et al, 2000).

References

Ciprofloxacin resistance in epidemic methicillin-resistant *Staphylococcus aureus* [letter]. Lancet 1988;ii:843.

Hartnick CJ, Shott S, Willging JP, Myer CM III. Methicillin resistant *Staphylococcus aureus* otorrhea after tympanostomy tube placement: an emerging concern. Arch Otolaryngol Head Neck Surg 2000;126:1440–3.

Jevons MP. "Celbenin"-resistant staphylococci. BMJ 1961;1:124–5.

Myer CM III. Post-tympanostomy tube otorrhea. Ear Nose Throat J 2001;80 Suppl 6:4–7.

Suh HK, Jeon YH, Song JS, Cheong HJ. A molecular epidemiologic study of methicillin-resistant *Staphylococcus aureus* infection in patients undergoing middle-ear surgery. Eur Arch Otorhinolaryngol 1998;255:347–51.

Chapter 56

Other Complications of Tympanostomy Tubes

Adele Yarrington Evans, MD, Michael J. Cunningham, MD

Multiple complications other than otorrhea and tympanic membrane perforation are associated with the placement or presence of tympanostomy tubes (Table 56-1). These can occur in the operating room at the time of tube placement, during the time in which the tube is in place, or after the tube has extruded or been removed. Many of these additional complications are unusual or very uncommon, existing only as case reports.

When Placing the Tube

Anesthesia-Related Complications

Complications directly related to the administration of general anesthesia for tube placement do occur. The most common anesthesia-related complications are agitation and prolonged recovery from anesthetics. Upper airway obstruction during or following mask anesthesia technique can complicate myringotomy with tympanostomy tube placement procedures, both intra- and postoperatively (Hoffman et al, 2002; Markowitz-Spence et al, 1990). The majority of obstructive airway events are minor, managed with simple head repositioning, jaw thrust, oral airway placement, or positive pressure ventilation. Severe events necessitating emergent endotracheal intubation are rare.

Vomiting is a risk intraoperatively but more commonly occurs postoperatively (Hoffman et al, 2002; Markowitz-Spence et al, 1990). Intraoperative vomiting poses the additional risk of aspiration. Transient cardiac arrhythmias, hyperthermia, or hypothermia may also occur.

Factors suspected to influence the likelihood of occurrence of anesthesia-associated complications are the patient's age, the level of experience of the anesthesiologist, and the presence of a preexisting medical condition or acute illness. A personal or family history of prior problems with anesthesia, particularly a family history of malignant hyperthermia, is of particular importance. Under such circumstances, anesthesia consultation is necessary to arrange for the use of a "clean" anesthesia machine and operating room in which inhalational agents have not yet been used. The additional preoperative use of sedation and the intraoperative manipulation of anesthetic agents to avoid depolarizing muscle relaxants and inhalation agents such as halothane can ensure safe anesthesia administration (Dudley et al, 1990).

Many surgical procedures require administration of antibiotic prophylaxis for subacute bacterial endocarditis when performed in patients with structural heart disease. The American Heart Association does not recommend the use of prophylactic antibiotics for myringotomy with

TABLE 56-1. Other Complications of Tympanostomy Tubes

When placing the tube
    Anesthesia-related complications
    Upper airway obstruction
    Nausea/vomiting
    Arrhythmias
    Hyper-/hypothermia
    Agitation with or without self-harm
    Vascular anomalies and injury
    Anomalous internal carotid artery
    High-riding/dehiscent jugular venous bulb
    Persistent stapedial artery
    Middle ear trauma
    Ossicular disruption/dislocation
    Facial nerve injury
    Promontory (round or oval window) injury
While the tube is in place
    Otorrhea
    Immediate otorrhea
    Delayed otorrhea
    Chronic/persistent otorrhea
    Tube obstruction
    Granulation tissue and aural polyp formation
    Premature tube extrusion
    Medial tube displacement
    Hearing loss
After tube extrusion or removal
    Persistent perforation
    Tympanosclerosis (myringosclerosis)
    Focal/segmental atrophy
    Cholesteatoma
    Failure of tube extrusion
    Ear canal stenosis

tube placement, and this recommendation has been substantiated (Brown et al, 1995).

Bleeding disorders such as factor VIII deficiency (classic hemophilia), factor IX deficiency (Christmas disease), and von Willebrand's disease typically pose minimal risk during tympanostomy tube placement because there is usually very limited bleeding from the tympanic membrane during myringotomy. Bleeding is more likely to occur with an inflamed eardrum, and any bleeding can potentially result in obstruction of the tympanostomy tube. Postoperative drainage that is bloodstained can be a harrowing experience for both the patient and the family. The benefit of administration of perioperative factor replacement, desmopressin (DDAVP, Stimate) or ε-aminocaproic acid (Amicar) must be weighed against the risk, cost, and time factors. Such measures may be more appropriate in the setting of an emergent otopathologic situation and marked coagulopathy.

Vascular Anomalies and Injury

Aberrant Internal Carotid Artery

Vascular injuries may result from the myringotomy incision when anomalous vessels are present within the middle ear. The internal carotid artery (ICA) normally courses anteromedial to the middle ear space. Congenital anomalies of the ICA exist, and middle ear exposure of the ICA can result from osseous erosion secondary to trauma, neoplasm, infection, or cholesteatoma. An aberrant carotid artery is usually asymptomatic. Its presence can be suggested by complaints of pulsatile tinnitus, aural fullness, and hearing loss or by visualization of a red, pulsatile mass on otoscopy. Otoscopic documentation can be difficult in patients with otitis media owing to the presence of a middle ear effusion or postinflammatory changes of the tympanic membrane. Most aberrant carotid arteries are typically identified incidentally. When this anomaly is suspected, diagnostic imaging is necessary. Options include contrast-enhanced computed tomography (CT) or magnetic resonance angiography. CT is often the diagnostic study of choice as it elucidates the vascular anomaly relative to the osseous anatomy of the middle and inner ear. The established presence of an aberrant carotid artery is a relative contraindication to incisional myringotomy or laser tympanotomy for tympanostomy tube placement (Brodish and Woolley, 1999). The exceptional case is that situation wherein the drainage of the middle ear space is an absolute necessity. Under such circumstances, tube positioning must be dictated by precise preoperative localization of the anomalous ICA.

Anomalous Internal Jugular Vein

The internal jugular vein normally lies beneath the floor of the middle ear cavity. Like the ICA, the internal jugular vein is normally protected by bone. When anomalously positioned, the so-called "high-riding" jugular venous bulb may have only a thin osseous covering or may be entirely unprotected. The presence of a high-riding jugular venous bulb can be suggested by the complaint of pulsatile rhythmic tinnitus exacerbated by physical activity or stress, especially if such tinnitus is relieved by gentle pressure over the internal jugular vein in the neck. The characteristic otoscopic finding is that of a blue mass arising from the floor of the middle ear cavity. This visual characteristic can be obscured by a middle ear effusion or by tympanic membrane scarring. When it is suspected, contrast-enhanced CT is again the study of choice for identification. In addition to hemorrhage, laceration of the jugular bulb can result in an air embolus or transverse sinus thrombosis secondary to infection. Fortunately, these are rare complications (Brodish and Woolley, 1999). Documentation of a high-riding jugular venous bulb is not an absolute contraindication to myringotomy but warrants detailed otomicroscopic examination and precise anterosuperior myringotomy placement.

Persistent Stapedial Artery

A persistent stapedial artery may exist in the middle ear space when the second branchial artery fails to calcify during embryologic development. This congenital anomaly is extremely rare, occurring in 1 in 5,000 to 1 in 10,000 ears. The persisting vessel courses through the middle ear space, is 1.5 mm in diameter, and traverses the obturator foramen of the stapes (Schuknecht, 1993). It is potentially at risk of laceration secondary to incisional myringotomy or laser tympanotomy.

Management

Injury to a middle ear vascular anomaly during incisional myringotomy or laser tympanotomy results in immediate brisk bleeding. Initial management consists of immediate tamponade, either with absorbable cellulose, antibiotic-infused gauze, or a combination thereof. Once the bleeding is successfully controlled, immediate arrangements for the performance of a radiologic evaluation to identify the anomalous vessel are necessary. The packing is usually left in place for several days to allow for healing of the traumatized vessel wall and is subsequently removed under general anesthesia anticipating possible operative middle ear exploration. An ICA injury refractory to conservative management such as packing may require angiographic embolization. Only in extreme circumstances is surgical vessel ligation considered (Brodish and Woolley, 1999).

Middle Ear Trauma

Dislocation or disruption of the ossicles can potentially occur during tympanostomy tube placement. The most common site of injury is the incudostapedial joint (Wang et al, 1999). Ossicular dislocation or disruption should be suspected when postoperative audiologic evaluation reveals persistent conductive hearing compromise in the presence of a healthy-appearing tympanic membrane and patent tympanostomy tube, especially if this conductive hearing loss is near maximum severity. CT can suggest the diagnosis. For example, lateral dislocation of the incus results in a "Y-shaped" appearance of the malleoincudal complex as opposed to the typical "ice-cream cone" (Meriot et al, 1997). Surgical exploration of the middle ear often proves necessary for definitive diagnostic and therapeutic purposes. Avoidance of the posterosuperior quadrant during myringotomy should prevent this complication.

Injury to the facial nerve, chorda tympani, promontory, or oval or round windows is also theoretically possible. The facial nerve may be exposed in the middle ear owing to an anomalous course or to bony dehiscence of the horizontal canal. Such anomalies of the facial nerve are more common in patients with other congenital malformations of the middle ear and should be anticipated (Jahrsdoerfer, 1981). Oval or round window fistula formation is a risk with any penetrating trauma to the middle ear (Guyot, 1992).

While the Tube Is in Place

The most common complication associated with the presence of a tympanostomy tube is otorrhea. Additional potential sequelae include obstruction of the os of the tube, foreign body reaction to the tube with granulation tissue and occasional aural polyp formation, premature extrusion of the tube, medial displacement of the tube into the middle ear cleft, and failure of tube extrusion (Kay et al, 2001).

Tube Obstruction

The os of the tube may become obstructed with blood, cerumen, or inspissated secretions (Figure 56-1). Obstructed tubes are typically nonfunctional. Tympanostomy tube obstruction may lead to premature tube extrusion as well as to recurrence of inherent eustachian tube dysfunction and its related sequelae. Tube obstruction may be prevented by the immediate postoperative application of various otic drops. These may contain antibiotics, steroids, or topical vasoconstrictors such as phenylephrine or oxymetazoline (Altman et al, 1998; Jamal, 1995). Once obstructed, management options include the application of topical drops to soften debris followed by otomicroscopic suctioning or instrumental clearing of crusts from the os of the tube. If such efforts are unsuccessful, surgical tympanostomy tube removal and replacement may be indicated (Cunningham et al, 1993).

Granulation Tissue and Aural Polyp Formation

Controversy exists as to whether granulation tissue formation is a reaction to the tube itself or to the entrapment of squamous epithelium around the tube. Medical management consists of the application of topical antibiotic

drops to eradicate any associated infection. Such drop preparations should ideally also contain a topical steroid to help reduce local inflammation. If persistent and unresponsive, operative tympanostomy tube and granulation tissue removal may be warranted. Tube replacement at the same operative setting is dictated by the indications for which the original tube was placed, the current middle ear disease status, and the size of any residual tympanic membrane perforations at the prior tube site.

Aural polyps represent an organized mass of granulation tissue in response to a multitude of potential etiologies. When a tympanostomy tube serves as the nidus, it is possible that the tube itself may be completely obscured. If the origin of the aural polyp is uncertain, CT prior to polyp removal is recommended to identify a possible inciting foreign body (such as a tympanostomy tube) and to rule out associated tympanomastoid disease, particularly that resulting in osseous destruction (Gliklich et al, 1993). In the absence of the latter, transcanal aural polypectomy is recommended with removal of the associated tympanostomy tube. Tube replacement in the same operative setting depends on the same factors as outlined above (Figures 56-2 and 56-3).

Premature Tube Extrusion

Premature tube extrusion may be attributable to technical error in placement, tube obstruction and subsequent middle ear disease, or local inflammatory rejection of the composite materials of the tube itself. In the latter situation, the use of a replacement tube of a different composition may reduce inflammation, allowing "engraftment" of the tube until the usual mechanisms of extrusion ensue.

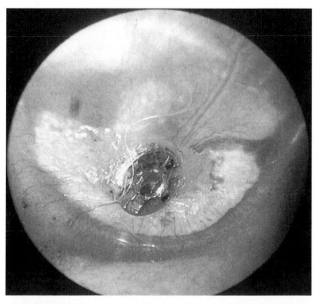

FIGURE 56-1. Obstructed stainless steel Reuter bobbin tube. Note surrounding tympanic membrane tympanosclerosis (myringosclerosis).

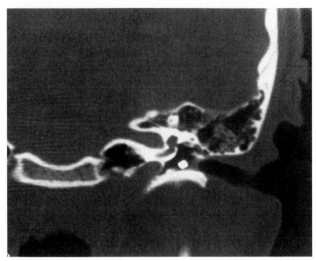

FIGURE 56-2. Coronal computed tomographic scan of left temporal bone demonstrating a radiopaque foreign body consistent with a tympanostomy tube within the middle ear space, medial to a thickened tympanic membrane. Otomicroscopic examination had revealed an aural polyp filling the medial left external ear canal.

Medial Tube Displacement

A tympanostomy tube may become medially displaced. Early medial displacement may result from the creation of too large a myringotomy. The reasons for late medial displacement are not entirely clear but may be related to the effects of tympanostomy tube shape or composition on tube migration. A medially displaced tube behind an intact tympanic membrane may cause a foreign body response within the middle ear cleft, promoting the development of otitis media with or without mastoiditis. A medialized tube can also potentially obstruct the eustachian tube orifice with resultant eustachian tube dysfunction (Cunningham et al, 1993; Green et al, 1997; Weber and Rosner, 1997;

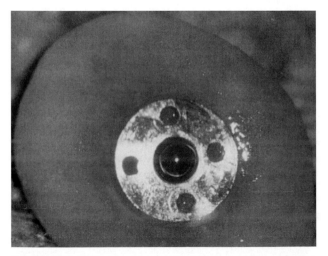

FIGURE 56-3. Surgically excised aural polyp surrounding a stainless steel Reuter bobbin tympanostomy tube.

Yanta et al, 1996). Given these potential sequelae, the operative removal of a medially displaced tympanostomy tube is recommended as long as the middle ear exploration does not put the ossicular chain at risk.

Hearing Loss

The issue of hearing loss associated with tympanostomy tube placement is complex. Sensorineural hearing loss has been documented in approximately 1% of the pediatric population undergoing myringotomy and tympanostomy tube placement (Derkay et al, 2000; Emery and Weber, 1998; Manning et al, 1994). This is not necessarily a cause and effect relationship but rather highlights the importance of age-appropriate hearing evaluations in all children undergoing the placement of tympanostomy tubes (Derkay et al, 2000; Manning et al, 1994).

Conductive hearing loss is a common indication for tympanostomy tube placement. On occasion, conductive hearing loss may persist while a tube is in place. This could be caused by tube obstruction and recurrent middle ear disease. It is controversial as to whether the tube itself can cause a conductive hearing loss. The position of the tube within the tympanic membrane, the size of the tympanostomy tube os, and the shape of the tube have been suspected to be factors that influence conductive hearing loss after tube placement (Voss et al, 2001). Theoretically, any perforation as represented by the os of a tube can cause hearing loss by impedance mismatch. Perforations in specific locations within the tympanic membrane may allow the sound waves to be presented directly to the round window and cancel waves presented by the ossicular chain. This effect is greatest at very low and, to a lesser degree, very high frequencies. It is rare for true symptomatic conductive hearing loss to persist when the tube is well positioned and patent (Estrem and Batra, 2000).

After Tube Extrusion or Removal

Adverse sequelae can occur following the extrusion or removal of a tympanostomy tube from the tympanic membrane. Such complications include tympanosclerosis (myringosclerosis), dimeric membrane formation with focal atrophy or retraction pocket development, residual tympanic membrane perforation, possible cholesteatoma formation, and ear canal stenosis (Yanta et al, 1996). These complications may relate to the middle ear disease process that dictated tube placement as well as to the surgical procedure itself. This statement is supported by the observation that tympanosclerosis (myringosclerosis), focal atrophy, and retraction pocket formation also occur frequently in ears that have never been intubated (Kay et al, 2001).

Tympanosclerosis (Myringosclerosis)

Tympanosclerosis is a subepithelial hyalinization of the mucosa of the middle ear attributed to inflammation

(Friedman et al, 2001). When it occurs specifically in the tympanic membrane, the term myringosclerosis is commonly used. There is no unifying explanation for tympanosclerosis (myringosclerosis) development; associated factors include inflammatory middle ear disease and tympanostomy tube insertion (Russell and Giles, 2002). Tympanosclerotic (myringosclerotic) changes occur in both intubated and nonintubated chronically diseased ears, although the rate is higher in ears in which tympanostomy tubes have been placed: 59% of treated ears compared with 13% of nonintubated control ears in one study (Tos and Stangerup, 1989). Despite its prevalence, the hearing loss attributable to tympanosclerosis is actually quite minimal, approximating only 0.5 dB. Tympanosclerosis may be more significant for its ability to obscure the contents of the middle ear than in terms of its effect on hearing.

Cholesteatoma

The chance of developing a cholesteatoma in association with a tympanostomy tube site has been estimated to approximate 0.5%. The incidence increases in ears that have undergone multiple surgeries, that have had intubations of prolonged duration, and that have experienced frequent infections (Golz et al, 1999). The significance of the latter as a risk factor as opposed to merely a symptom is debatable. The overall incidence of cholesteatoma has decreased by half since the commonplace use of tympanostomy tubes began (Rakover et al, 2000). This observation suggests that the risk of developing cholesteatoma is comparatively much greater in nonintubated ears with significant eustachian tube dysfunction.

Tympanic Membrane Atrophy

Focal/segmental tympanic membrane atrophy—so-called dimeric membrane formation—can result from tympanostomy tube placement (Figure 56-4). More generalized tympanic membrane retraction is a well-documented sequela of eustachian tube dysfunction. Dimeric tympanic membranes appear to be at increased risk for retraction pocket formation as well as spontaneous perforation (Maw and Bawden, 1994).

Necessity for Operative Tube Removal

The need for operative removal of tympanostomy tubes can be considered a complication of tympanostomy tube placement. Failure of extrusion of a tympanostomy tube may require that it be manually extracted (Cunningham et al, 1993). The timing of tube removal remains controversial. A review of the indications for operative tube removal at our institution demonstrated refractory otorrhea and granulation tissue formation to be the most common reasons. Tube obstruction, failure of tube extrusion, and tube displacement into the middle ear followed in order of frequency (Cunningham et al, 1993).

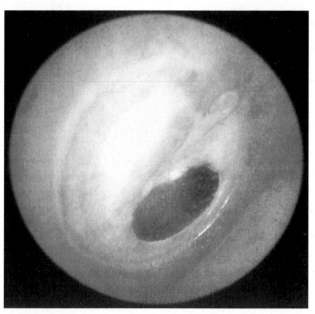

FIGURE 56-4. Focal atrophy of the anterior portion of the tympanic membrane. This dimeric membrane contrasts significantly with the surrounding tympanosclerotic (myringosclerotic) tympanic membrane.

Summary

In a recently published multicenter study conducted by the American Society of Pediatric Otolaryngology, nearly 80% of children who underwent tympanostomy tube placement experienced an improvement in their quality of life. This was based on composite evaluation of their physical symptoms, caregiver concerns, emotional distress, hearing loss, activity limitations, and speech impairment (Rosenfeld et al, 2000). Although associated with an array of potential complications, the use of tympanostomy tubes has clearly afforded benefits that significantly outweigh their associated risks.

References

Altman JS, Haupert MS, Hamaker RA, Belenky WM. Phenylephrine and the prevention of postoperative tympanostomy tube obstruction. Arch Otolaryngol Head Neck Surg 1998;124: 1233–6.

Brodish BN, Woolley AL. Major vascular injuries in children undergoing myringotomy for tube placement. Am J Otolaryngol 1999;20:46–50.

Brown OE, Manning SC, Phillips DL. Lack of bacteremia in children undergoing myringotomy and tympanostomy tube placement. Pediatr Infect Dis J 1995;14:1101–2.

Cunningham MJ, Eavey RD, Krouse JH, Kiskaddon RM. Tympanostomy tubes: experience with removal. Laryngoscope 1993;103:659–62.

Derkay CS, Carron JD, Wiatrak BJ, et al. Post-surgical follow-up of children with tympanostomy tubes: results of the American Academy of Head and Neck Surgery Pediatric Otolaryngology Committee National Survey. Otolaryngol Head Neck Surg 2000;122:313–8.

Dudley JP, Reynolds R, Dubrow T. Malignant hyperthermia in the otolaryngology patient: prospective anesthetic and surgical management of eight children. Ann Otol Rhinol Laryngol 1990;99:297–9.

Emery M, Weber PC. Hearing loss due to myringotomy and tube placement and the role of preoperative audiograms. Arch Otolaryngol Head Neck Surg 1998;124:421–4.

Estrem SA, Batra PS. Conductive hearing loss associated with pressure equalization tubes. Otolaryngol Head Neck Surg 2000; 122:349–51.

Friedman EM, Sprecher RC, Simon S, Dunn JK. Quantitation and prevalence of tympanosclerosis in a pediatric otolaryngology clinic. Int J Pediatr Otorhinolaryngol 2001;60:205–11.

Gliklich R, Cunningham M, Eavey R. The cause of aural polyps in children. Arch Otolaryngol Head Neck Surg 1993;119:669–71.

Golz A, Goldenberg D, Netzer A, et al. Cholesteatoma association with ventilation tube insertion. Arch Otolaryngol Head Neck Surg 1999;125:754–7.

Green KM, de Carpentier JP, Curley JW. An unusual complication of T-tubes. J Laryngol Otol 1997;111:282–3.

Guyot JP. Penetrating wounds of the ear with oval window fistulas. Reports of 2 cases. ORL J Otorhinolaryngol Relat Spec 1992; 54:282–4.

Hoffman KK, Thompson GK, Burke BL, Derkay CS. Anesthetic complications of tympanostomy tube placement in children. Arch Otolaryngol Head Neck Surg 2002;128:1040–3.

Jahrsdoerfer RA. The facial nerve in congenital middle ear malformations. Laryngoscope 1981;91:1217–25.

Jamal TS. Avoidance of postoperative blockage of ventilation tubes. Laryngoscope 1995;105:833–4.

Kay DJ, Nelson M, Rosenfeld RM. Meta-analysis of tympanostomy tube sequelae. Otolaryngol Head Neck Surg 2001;124:374–80.

Manning SC, Brown OR, Roland PS, Phillips DL. Incidence of sensorineural hearing loss in patients evaluated for tympanostomy tubes. Arch Otolaryngol Head Neck Surg 1994;120:881–4.

Markowitz-Spence L, Brodsky L, Syed N, et al. Anesthesia complications of tympanostomy tube placement in children. Arch Otolaryngol Head Neck Surg 1990;116:809–12.

Maw AR, Bawden R. Tympanic membrane atrophy, scarring, atelectasis and attic retraction in persistent, untreated otitis media with effusion and following ventilation tube insertion. Int J Pediatr Otorhinolaryngol 1994;30:189–204.

Meriot P, Veillon F, Garcia JF, et al. CT appearances of ossicular injuries. Radiographics 1997;17:1445–54.

Rakover Y, Keywan K, Rosen G. Comparison of the incidence of cholesteatoma surgery before and after using ventilation tubes for secretory otitis media. Int J Pediatr Otorhinolaryngol 2000;56: 41–4.

Rosenfeld RM, Bhaya MH, Bower CM, et al. Impact of tympanostomy tubes on child quality of life. Arch Otolaryngol Head Neck Surg 2000;126:585–92.

Russell JD, Giles JJ. Tympanosclerosis in the rat tympanic membrane: an experimental study. Laryngoscope 2002;112: 1663–6.

Schuknecht HF. Persistent stapedial artery. In: Nadol JB, Schuknecht HF, editors. Surgery of the ear and the temporal bone. New York: Raven Press; 1993. p. 235.

Tos M, Stangerup SE. Hearing loss in tympanosclerosis caused by grommets. Arch Otolaryngol Head Neck Surg 1989;115:931–5.

Voss SE, Rosowski JJ, Merchant SN, Peake WT. How do tympanic membrane perforations affect human middle ear sound transmission? Acta Otolaryngol (Stockh) 2001;121:169–73.

Wang LF, Ho KY, Tai CF, Kuo WR. Traumatic ossicular chain discontinuity—report of two cases. Kaohsiung J Med Sci 1999;15: 504–9.

Weber DC, Rosner D. An unusual cause of eustachian tube dysfunction. Otolaryngol Head Neck Surg 1997;117:S142–4.

Yanta MJ, Brown OE, Fancher JR. Bilateral ear canal stenosis from retained Goode T-tubes. Int J Pediatr Otorhinolaryngol 1996; 37:173–8.

Chapter 57

Persistent Tympanic Membrane Perforation Following Surgical Insertion of Ventilation Tubes

Emmanuel Helidonis, MD, FACS

Myringotomy with tube insertion is the most common pediatric procedure for recurrent otitis media and for persistent otitis media with effusion (OME) (Armstrong, 1954). Tympanostomy tube placement in the United States is estimated to be 4 million cases per year, at an annual cost of about 3 to 4 billion dollars. Among the few complications following tube insertion, the most serious is persistent perforation of the tympanic membrane that is greater in patients requiring repeated myringotomies. A perforation is considered persistent if the eardrum has not adequately healed within 3 months after tube extrusion or removal (Lentsch et al, 2000; Nickols et al, 1998).

Healing of the perforation may not occur owing to the presence of squamous epithelium at the edges of the perforation, which prevents spontaneous repair (Bluestone and Klein, 2001). Persistent perforation of the tympanic membrane following tube insertion varies from 0.5 to 2% for short-term tubes and from 3 to 47.5% for long-term tubes (Hughes et al, 1974; Levine et al, 1994). If we accept a rate of perforation of 1%, then 10,000 permanent perforations per year occur requiring some form of tympanoplasty.

Conventional tubes are associated with the lowest rate of permanent perforations, whereas permanent tubes are associated with the highest rate of permanent perforations (Table 57-1). Kay and colleagues (2001) showed that after tube extrusion, a perforation rate of 2.2% with short-term tubes and a perforation rate of 16.6% with long-term tubes were observed. For this reason, they concluded that long-term tubes should be used only on a selective and individualized basis (Kay et al, 2001).

In another study in which 273 tubes were removed from 201 patients, 11% of the ears, 29 of 273, had a per-sistent perforation. This was true especially for those cases in which the tubes were in place for more than 3 years (Levine et al, 1994). Casselbrant and colleagues (1992) also showed that of 215 children prospectively observed for at least 2 to 3 years in three clinical trials of efficacy and safety of tympanostomy tube insertion conducted in Pittsburgh, 2.4% had to eventually have a tympanoplasty for chronic perforation.

Etiology and Pathogenesis

For a persistent tympanic membrane perforation to occur, several factors play a role, the main one being the duration of intubation (Levine et al, 1994). We agree with the findings of Lentsch and Nickols concerning a higher rate of perforation when the duration of intubation is more than 36 months, although we believe that a ventilation tube staying even less time, for example, 18 to 36 months, will likely have the same possibility of leaving a permanent perforation. The logical question that has to be answered is the following: under what circumstances does the squamous epithelium grow to the margin of the

TABLE 57-1. Incidence of Perforation Rate after Extrusion of Tubes

Authors (Year)	Perforation Rate (%)		
	Short-Term Tubes	Long-Term Tubes	Overall
Hughes et al (1974)	0.5–2	3–47.5	
Levine et al (1994)			11
Kay et al (2001)	2.2	16.6	
Casselbrant et al (2001)			2.4

287

perforation, impeding its healing, and how long does it take to do that? The answer is a difficult one owing to the presence of other parameters that may also be responsible for the appearance and persistence of a perforation.

Our experience showed that other crucial factors for the appearance of a permanent tympanic membrane perforation following tube extrusion or removal are the persistent dysfunction of the eustachian tube, the presence of sinusitis and allergy, false myringotomy techniques, the condition and structure of the tympanic membrane (as in atelectatic ear cases), repeated attacks of acute otitis media (AOM) not adequately treated with antibiotics, and the use of long-term tubes.

A permanent perforation of the tympanic membrane usually appears after tube extrusion or removal. Criteria for tube removal usually include persistent otorrhea, the presence of granulation tissue around the tube, a blocked tube with reappearance of persistent middle ear effusion (MEE), and a prolonged period of tube presence (Cunningham et al, 1993).

At the Department of Otolaryngology of the Medical School of the University of Crete, it was observed that the most common reasons for tube removal are the presence of granulation tissue at the site of tympanostomy, persistent otorrhea, and the prolonged presence of tubes past the expected period of extrusion of 3 to 12 months for short-term tubes and over a year for long-term tubes.

Long-term tubes that are larger in diameter and have longer flanges are designed to remain in place for extended periods of time and are responsible for the higher rate of perforation. The blocking of tubes with mucus or cerumen is seldom a reason for them to be removed because they can usually be unblocked with the use of cortisone or hydrogen peroxide eardrops or with a fine straight needle. However, sometimes the MEE is so thick that it necessitates the placement of a wider tube and frequent visits for suctioning.

One of the major causes for the appearance of an eardrum perforation is persistent eustachian tube dysfunction, which may be responsible for several ear problems such as repeated attacks of AOM, serous otitis media, and atelectatic ears.

In patients who have undergone radiotherapy for head and neck carcinoma, in particular of the nasopharynx, the chances of developing chronic OME, which necessitates tube placement, are rather high. Owing to the irradiation, side effects develop, causing chronic dysfunction of the eustachian tube and impairment of hematosis or even necrosis of the tympanic membrane, thus increasing the possibility of having a permanent perforation after the tube is extruded or removed.

The type of local anesthesia used for myringotomy may also play a role in the appearance of perforation, especially in cases in which the tympanic membrane is very thin, as in the atelectatic ear. In these cases, it is better

to avoid using phenol; instead, we use other types of anesthesia, such as local injections of an anesthetic or iontophoresis. One should also avoid using strong suction on the edges of the tympanostomy, and, instead, when the drum is thin, pass the suction tip beyond the tympanostomy. Otherwise, the strong suction may enlarge the tympanostomy or even avulse a piece of the eardrum. One should also be careful to use suction tips that are not too large or have beveled tip edges. In cases in which hard cerumen develops around the tube, preventing its normal extrusion, it is better to soften the cerumen with cortisone or hydrogen peroxide drops and then remove it to avoid the danger of having a permanent perforation.

Another factor causing a tube to stay longer is a narrow external auditory canal or the presence of exostoses, which do not allow the tube to be extruded because it impinges on the canal walls. In these cases, before inserting the tube, the surgeon has to carefully inspect the drum surface and then try to put it in the area where the tube has the best chance to extrude.

Recurrent middle ear infection may also contribute to the weakening of the tympanic membrane favoring a permanent perforation after the extrusion of a tube.

Inexperience may also play an important role in creating complications. Too large a myringotomy incision or extended trauma to the eardrum may lead to the appearance of a permanent perforation.

A perforation may also occur in patients who have had a tympanoplasty and subsequently developed chronic OME necessitating tube insertion. Their tympanic membrane may have less healing ability, a factor that increases the chances of having a perforation.

Treatment

One of the best measures to avoid a permanent tympanic membrane perforation following tube insertion is prevention. Guidelines for tube insertion recommend surgical intervention after 4 months following initial diagnosis of bilateral OME and a 20 dB hearing loss. Adherence to strict criteria for surgery will reduce the number of tube insertions and thus the rate of complications and the subsequent high financial and emotional costs for the patient and his or her family.

A sensitive question frequently asked by the patient or his or her parents is what the possible complications are following tube insertion. The physician must clearly inform the patient about the advantages of inserting the tube, the possible complications, the need to avoid water entering the ear, the need for frequent follow-ups, and the need to follow instructions.

After a myringotomy procedure, patients must be advised to visit their physician at frequent intervals to have the positioning of the tube and the appearance of the drums evaluated with the surgical microscope.

When a permanent perforation occurs, several factors have to be taken into consideration before deciding on its repair. One of them is the patient's age. When a permanent perforation takes place in a child following myringotomy tube insertion, it is better to wait for some time before deciding to repair the perforation. Like a tympanostomy tube, a perforation may be beneficial for a child with recurrent AOM or chronic OME. If the child is free of ear infections for over a year and is 8 years old, then a tympanoplasty can be performed provided that a persistent eustachian tube dysfunction is not present. If it is present, then it is better to wait until the child becomes 12 years or older, when the development of the eustachian tube is over and the incidence of upper respiratory tract infections decreases.

An indicator for the possible presence of a eustachian tube dysfunction is the appearance of the other ear. If the other ear is atelectatic, then it is better to wait. It is also very important to exclude other causes of eustachian tube dysfunction, such as chronic sinusitis, large adenoids, and allergy. If such problems are found, then they should be treated accordingly before the tympanoplasty to increase the chances of a successful operation.

The size of the perforation also plays a role. Large perforations need more extensive procedures and have a higher rate of postoperative complications, and the patient needs more care. This is why when we deal with a child, it is better to wait until he or she is 12 years old because at that age, children may more consistently follow instructions regarding their postoperative care.

Small perforations can easily be repaired following methods such as a paper patch and/or a graft of fat, connective tissue, or fascia according to the perforation's size. In large perforations with persistent eustachian tube dysfunction, a tragal cartilage graft is the method of choice because it resists retraction.

The condition of the tympanic membrane is another factor that has to be observed. There are cases of postintubation perforations in the presence of an atrophic or tympanosclerotic eardrum. When the drum is very atrophic, it is better to use a large graft to replace the atrophic drum, whereas when the drum has tympanosclerosis, it may be necessary to remove some tympanosclerotic plaques to adjust the graft in a better way.

In cases in which the mucosa of the middle ear is edematous or thickened and a tympanoplasty is decided on, a piece of Silastic has to be inserted in the middle ear to avoid adhesions.

A meta-analysis of tympanoplasty in children showed that the success rate increased with advancing age and that none of the parameters, such as recurrence of MEE, high negative pressure, or atelectasis, played any role as significant predictors of success (Kay et al, 2001). However, a question that has to be answered is whether to leave the perforation open in a patient who has been irradiated and presents severe problems of healing owing to the irradiation side effect on the eustachian tube, external auditory canal skin, and tympanic membrane.

Conclusion

As far as the treatment plan is concerned regarding the repair of a perforation, the physician has to study each case separately, taking into consideration the family environment, age of the patient, existence of other diseases, previous history, and size of the perforation. Sometimes watchful waiting is an acceptable alternative. Some perforations, even large ones, especially in children, have the tendency to heal spontaneously, whereas all of the rest need some type of tympanoplasty, at the time when the physician judges best.

References

Armstrong BW. A new treatment for chronic secretory otitis media. Arch Otolaryngol 1954;59:653–4.

Bluestone CD, Klein OJ. Otitis media in infants and children. Philadelphia: WB Saunders; 2001.

Casselbrant ML, Kaleida PH, Rockette HE, et al. Efficacy of antimicrobial prophylaxis and of tympanostomy tube insertion for prevention of recurrent acute otitis media; results of a randomized clinical trial. Pediatr Infect Dis J 1992;11:278–86.

Cunningham MJ, Eavey RD, Krause JH, Kiskaddon RM. Tympanostomy tubes: experience with removal. Laryngoscope 1993;103:659–62.

Hughes LA, Warder FR, Hudson WR. Complications of tympanostomy tubes. Arch Otolaryngol 1974;100:151–4.

Kay DJ, Nelson M, Rosenfeld RM. Meta-analysis of tympanostomy tube sequelae. Otolaryngol Head Neck Surg 2001;124:374–80.

Lentsch EJ, Goudy S, Ganzel TM, et al. Rate of persistent perforation after elective tympanostomy tube removal in pediatric patients. Int J Pediatr Otorhinolaryngol 2000;54:143–8.

Levine S, Daly K, Gilbink GS. Tympanic membrane perforation and tympanostomy tubes. Ann Otol Rhinol Laryngol Suppl 1994;163:27–30.

Nickols RT, Ramadan HH, Wax MK, Santrak RD. Relationship between tympanic membrane perforation and retained ventilation tubes. Arch Otolaryngol Head Neck Surg 1998;124:417–9.

Chapter 58

RETAINED TUBES

KARIN STENFELDT, MD, PhD

Placement of a ventilating tube in the tympanic membrane is a common surgical procedure in children. Ventilation of the middle ear brings positive effects on the child's hearing by resolving otitis media with effusion (OME), and the treatment is also known to reduce the incidence of recurrent otitis media. The procedure is quick and safe for the child. However, there are a few side effects, including otorrhea, persistent perforation, and development of myringosclerosis. In most cases, the tube is extruded within 1 or 2 years, but in a few cases, the tube is not extruded but stays in place in the tympanic membrane for prolonged periods. Although most textbooks cover the indications for tube placement, indications for removal of a ventilation tube have not been dealt with. The management of retained tubes has thus been left to local traditions and the judgment and experience of the individual physician. This chapter discusses the management of retained tubes.

Incidence

The incidence of retained tubes is not found in the literature, and there is not even a generally accepted definition of the meaning of "retained tubes." There is thus a need for prospective studies on the incidence and management of retained tubes. The time of retention differs between different types of tubes, but most tubes extrude spontaneously within 2 years. T tubes are designed for long-term treatment, and about 70% are in place at 30 months (Rothera and Grant, 1985). Different authors consider tubes as retained when they are in place more than 1.5 years, 2 to 3 years, or even 4 years (Caetano et al, 1999; Chevretton et al, 1987; Courteney-Harris et al, 1992; Iwaki et al, 1998; Lentsch et al, 2000). For reasons to be discussed in this chapter, I suggest that a tube is defined as being "retained" when not extruded within 3 years after placement.

Importance

Even though most tubes extrude from the tympanic membrane spontaneously, the small number that are retained adds up to a large number of children because treatment with ventilation tubes is such a common procedure. Strangely, there is no general recommendation for how to handle these cases. The lack of guidelines leaves the decision to the individual physician, and the patient may receive conflicting recommendations at consultations. When the decision is made to remove the tube, surgery is usually performed under general anesthesia, which introduces a dilemma: general anesthesia involves a risk for the patient and should be avoided if removal of the tube is not necessary. On the other hand, leaving a tube may cause problems. Many otolaryngologists have discovered that tubes, when left in the ear for a long time, will cause a persistent perforation of the tympanic membrane. Lentsch and colleagues (2000) found that 15% of tympanic membranes showed persistent perforation after removal when the tube had been in place over 3 years compared with 3% when the tube had been in place less than 3 years. In a recent study, a higher perforation risk was observed after tube removal when tubes were retained more than 4 years (El-Bitar et al, 2002): 6.1% persistent perforation was reported when tubes were retained 3 to 4 years compared with 40% when tubes were retained 4 to 5 years. Children older than 7 years had a markedly higher risk of persistent perforation after tube removal compared with younger children, in whom the risk of persistent perforation was negligible in cases of tube retention up to 4 years. Nichols and colleagues (1998) found that the perforation rate was significantly higher in children with tubes retained beyond 3 years. In the group of children in whom the tympanic membranes eventually healed, the duration of ventilating tubes was an average of 2.5 years. In the group of children who ended up with perforation of the tympanic membrane, the mean time for ventilation tube retention was 3.9 years. The perforation rate was also higher in children with a history of receiving more than three sets of tubes, in whom the perforation rate was 42% compared with 24% in those receiving fewer than three sets of tubes (Nichols et al, 1998). After removal of ventilation tubes, Pribitkin and colleagues (1992) found a healing rate of

92% in those receiving less than three sets of tubes versus 61% in those receiving more than three sets of tubes. In a study including T tubes and Paparella type II tubes, which are designed for long-time intubation, Saito and colleagues (1996) found that the longer the tube stayed in place, the higher the risk of persistent perforation after removal of the tube. The perforation rate increased when the intubation period exceeded 12 and 24 months.

A persistent perforation might lead to conductive hearing loss, problems with swimming and concurrent infections, and a need for surgical correction by means of a myringoplasty. Adding up the positive effects of tube placement with the negative factors, including the cost for continuous follow-up visits with checks of ears and ventilation tube function, removal of tubes under general anesthesia, and permanent perforations in need of myringoplasty, certainly makes up a highly complex cost-benefit picture that is difficult to evaluate.

Etiology/Pathogenesis

Persistent perforations as a complication of treatment with T tubes are well known. Tubes designed to stay longer in the tympanic membrane have a larger diameter and larger flanges. On the other hand, because short-term tubes with a narrow diameter are easily extruded, the use of such tubes may lead to multiple tube insertions, which are also a risk factor for developing a persistent perforation (Nichols et al, 1998). The location of the tube does not seem to make any difference for the development of a persistent perforation (Hampton and Adams, 1996; Pribitkin et al, 1992; Walker, 1997). Healing of the perforation is better after spontaneous extrusion than after removal of the tube. The perforation rate was 4% in ears in which tubes spontaneously extruded and 14.3% when intentionally extruded (Saito et al, 1996). Lentsch and colleagues (2000) found an 11% perforation rate after tube removal. One may assume that there is some reason why a certain individual does not extrude the tubes spontaneously. Retention of the ventilation tube might be associated with reduced "healing activity" of the tympanic membrane with less epithelial migration and, when the tube is pulled out, a reduced healing capacity. Thus, the healing capacity of the tympanic membrane, as a characteristic of the individual person, is probably of importance.

Granulation tissue around the myringotomy opening and drainage from the middle ear are factors that do not reduce the healing rate (Pribitkin et al, 1992). It is probable that the inflammatory process may even facilitate healing, which has been observed in studies on pneumococcal otitis media and myringotomy, in which infected ears healed more quickly than noninfected ones (Magnuson et al, 1996). On the other hand, myringosclerosis in the tympanic membrane is an inhibitory factor with regard to healing because the sclerotic area around the perforation margins interferes with blood supply and collagen production. Myringosclerosis of the tympanic membrane is related to the elevated oxygen concentration in the middle ear in the presence of a ventilating tube (Mattsson et al, 1999). This process starts early after the tube insertion, and removing a retained tube to avoid myringosclerosis is probably of no benefit as the injury has already been caused.

Children with Down syndrome tend to have persistent perforations more frequently than other patients (Pribitkin et al, 1992). Possibly, this patient category has a reduced healing capacity of the tympanic membrane, or the healing capacity may be disturbed by an impaired tubal function with induction of negative middle ear pressure. Previous adenoidectomy predicts a poorer outcome concerning tympanic membrane healing after tube removal (Nichols et al, 1998). After controlling for other factors, adenoidectomy was found to be a single predictor for poorer outcome in this study. However, a child who has undergone adenoidectomy is usually a child with recurrent OME and multiple tube insertions, which is a predictor for persistent perforation. El-Bitar and colleagues (2002) found a higher incidence of persistent perforations after tube removal in children older than 7 years, whereas in other studies, the age and sex of the patient were not prognostic factors (Nichols et al, 1998; Pribitkin et al, 1992).

Management Options

Some colleagues remove the tubes after only 1 year to prevent persistent perforations, whereas others do not extract a tube on the indication that it has been in place for a prolonged period (Cunningham et al, 1993; El-Bitar et al, 2002; Solomon et al, 1993). Considering the fact that the risk of persistent perforation is greater when a tube has remained in place for more than 3 years (Lentsch et al, 2000; Nichols et al, 1998), this time limit is used in the present chapter as a definition of a retained tube. However, the decision to remove the tube is based not only on the intubation time but also on several other facts. The clinical outcome after removing the tube is only a calculation of probability, and the physician must judge what is best for the individual patient and give the appropriate advice. The information below is meant to provide guidelines to the treating physician in his or her decision as to when to remove the tube.

Indications for leaving a retained tube in place are as follows:

- The patient has ongoing OME or recurrent otitis media in the contralateral ear.
- The patient has not passed the age of OME or recurrent otitis media, and the disease is assumed to return after tube removal.
- The patient is an adult and has no discomfort from the tube.

Indications for removing a retained tube are as follows:

- There is no longer any indication for ventilation tube treatment. The patient is assumed to have passed the age of OME, which is indicated by the absence of fluid in the contralateral ear and/or the fact that the patient has passed preschool age.
- The patient wishes to have a diving ear.
- The tube is dislocated into the middle ear.

A healthy ear on the contralateral side strengthens a decision to remove the tube. Similarly, a child who is able to actively blow air into the middle ear space, which can be observed in the ear microscope after the child has performed a Valsalva's maneuver, indicates that the child will be able to equalize negative pressure in the middle ear and that there is less risk for OME after tube removal. When the patient has bilateral retained tubes or a perforation in the contralateral ear, the state of the contralateral ear cannot serve as a guide. When a patient has a perforation in the contralateral ear, on the basis of chronic otitis media, or after tube extrusion or removal, one should bear in mind that this patient might have a higher risk for also developing a persistent perforation in the ear under consideration. This statement is not based on previous publications but rather on the author's own experience.

If your choice is to extract the tube, you can do this with or without general anesthesia. In children, general anesthesia is preferred. The edge of the perforation can be freshened up by gentle scraping it with a surgical pick. There is also the option to cover the perforation with a paper or tape patch, which in some studies has been shown to promote healing of the tympanic membrane after extraction of long-term tubes (Courteney-Harris et al, 1992; Saito et al, 1996) and in ears with more than three previous tube placements (Pribitkin et al, 1992) (Table 58-1). In other studies, scraping the edge or patching the perforation did not seem to promote healing (El-Bitar et al, 2002; Lentsch et al, 2000; Nichols et al, 1998). These studies were retrospective, however, and might include more severe cases with poor prognosis. Different

patching materials have been tried, such as contact lens patching (Caetano et al, 1999). Gelfoam and hyaluronan application could promote healing after tube removal. These materials have been successfully used in the repair of chronic perforations (Baldwin and Loftin, 1992; Stenfors, 1989). There are a few publications on the use of Gelfoam application after tube removal (El-Bitar et al, 2002; Hekkenberg and Smitheringale, 1995; Nichols et al, 1998), and Gelfoam was found beneficial in one study (Hekkenberg and Smitheringale, 1995). The extremely high cost of hyaluronan would be a disadvantage for the use of this material. A few cases of fat myringoplasty in combination with tube removal have been reported (El-Bitar et al, 2002; Nichols et al, 1998).

If the perforation does not heal after tube removal, traditional myringoplasty with fascia or the more simple procedure with blocking of the perforation with lobulus fat is possible (Mitchell et al, 1997). Most perforations that ultimately heal will do so within 6 months, but because a few more will heal up to 1 year after removal of the tube, a myringoplasty should be postponed until 1 year has elapsed after tube removal (Bingham et al, 1989).

My Experience

I make an assumption as to whether a patient will need the tube in the future. If the individual patient is likely to need more tube placements, this will most certainly be as bad as leaving a tube in place for a long time because multiple tube insertions are one risk factor for developing a persistent perforation (Nichols et al, 1998; Pribitkin et al, 1992).

If it is assumed that the patient will not need the tube any longer, and there is indication for removing the ventilation tube, I perform a freshening of the perforation margins after tube removal. If the patient has an increased risk of developing a persistent perforation, I place a paper or tape patch over the perforation. This is indicated when the tube has stayed for a long time, when a tube of the long-term type is present (large flange, T tube), or when the patient has had many tube insertions or if the patient has Down syndrome.

TABLE 58-1. Rate of Persistent Perforation after Retained Tube Removal

Study (Year)	Removal of Tube (%)	Removal of Tube and Freshening of Perforation Margin (%)	Removal of Tube and Patching (%)
Solomon et al (1993)	10.3		
Chevretton et al (1987)	20	3	
Bingham et al (1989)	20	3	
Nichols et al (1998)	26	26	30 (paper)
Lentsch et al (2000)		11	40 (paper)
Saito et al (1996)		13	3.3 (tape patch)
Courteney-Harris et al (1992)		16.5	6.8 (Silastic sheeting)
Pribitkin et al (1992)	15		13 (paper)
Hekkenberg and Smitheringale (1995)	10.3		4.5 (Gelfilm)

Case Studies

Case 1

A 4.5-year-old girl on a control visit has bilateral ventilation tubes that were inserted 20 months earlier. She was first diagnosed with OME at the age of 1 year, and this is her second set of tubes. Ventilation tubes were first inserted at the age of 14 months and were extruded within the first year of placement, whereafter she developed AOM and long-lasting OME. In this example, OME is likely to return if the tubes would be extracted, and there is no indication for removal.

Case 2

An adult male was referred by a general practitioner because of a retained T tube that was placed 12 years previously. The tube caused no discomfort, and removal of the tube would carry a substantial risk for a permanent perforation. In this particular case, removing the tube would cause the patient more discomfort than leaving it in place. In a case of a permanent perforation, there is an increased risk for infection when water and bacteria enter the middle ear. Water is unlikely to enter the middle ear through the narrow tube opening as long as the patient does not dive underwater. I thus let the tube stay in place and ask the patient to return if otorrhea or discomfort develops.

Case 3

A 6-year-old boy had tubes placed bilaterally 2 years previously because of recurrent otitis media and long-lasting OME with hearing impairment. The left tube was still in place, whereas the right one had extruded spontaneously, with subsequent healing of the tympanic membrane. The boy had no problems with recurrent otitis media or OME since the time of tube placement, and his hearing had normalized. As there was no ongoing OME in the ear with the healed tympanic membrane, and as the boy wished to be able to dive, the remaining tube was removed under general anesthesia, which allowed refreshening of the perforation margins.

Medialized Ventilation Tubes

I have also met patients with a trapped tube in the middle ear behind an intact tympanic membrane. The rate for displacement of a ventilating tube into the middle ear was estimated at 0.5% in a meta-analysis and is thus a rather unusual complication (Kay et al, 2001). Some colleagues claim that such a displaced tube can be left in place, provided that it does not cause any hearing impairment. Others, including myself, would prefer to remove the tube. I saw a boy with a tube in the middle ear that was clearly visible in the upper rear quadrant behind an intact tympanic membrane when he was examined in the sitting position in the clinic, but, in the horizontal position, when the patient was under general anesthesia in the operating room, the tube could no longer be seen. The same situation has also been described by Cunningham and colleagues (1993), who stated that the location of a medialized tube can be highly variable and can change with the position of the patient, and they suggested removal of a tube that is displaced into the middle ear cleft. Roy and colleagues (2002) presented four cases with tubes trapped in the middle ear with the complication of granulation tissue formation and conductive hearing loss. Performing a small myringotomy and removing the tube would be less risky than the potential complication of leaving the tube. As it is a foreign body, the tube might contribute to chronic infection. In the presence of purulent otitis media, the tube may be difficult to find because of severe mucosal swelling. Furthermore, a trapped tube may later slip forward into the protympanon and no longer be visible through the external meatus.

Conclusion

Ventilation tubes should be left in place until the child is expected to have resolved the problems with OME and recurrent purulent otitis media. In adults, there is no time range when the problems are expected to resolve; therefore, the tube can be left in place until spontaneously extruded. A tube that has become trapped in the middle ear cavity should be removed.

References

Baldwin RL, Loftin L. Gelfilm myringoplasty: a technique for residual perforations. Laryngoscope 1992;102:340–2.

Bingham BJG, Gurr PA, Owen G. Tympanic membrane perforation following the removal of ventilation tubes in the presence of persistent aural discharge. Clin Otolaryngol 1989;14:525–8.

Caetano HM, Maw J, Bernard P, Bonn G. Tympanic membrane patching with bandage contact lens after removal of ventilation T tubes. J Otolaryngol 1999;28:65–7.

Chevretton E, Bingham BJG, Firman E. The prevention of tympanic membrane perforation following the removal of long-term Paparella type II ventilation tubes. Clin Otolaryngol 1987;12:377–81.

Courteney-Harris RG, Ford GR, Ganiwalla TMJ, Mangat KS. Closure of tympanic membrane perforation after the removal of Goode-type tympanostomy tubes: the use of Silastic sheeting. J Laryngol Otol 1992;106:960–2.

Cunningham MJ, Eavey RD, Krouse JH, Kiskaddon RM. Tympanostomy tubes: experience with removal. Laryngoscope 1993;103:659–62.

El-Bitar MA, Pena MT, Choi SS, Zalzal GH. Retained ventilation tubes. Should they be removed at 2 years? Arch Otolaryngol Head Neck Surg 2002;128:1357–60.

Hampton SM, Adams DA. Perforation rates after ventilation tube insertion: does the positioning of the tube matter? Clin Otolaryngol 1996;21:548–9.

Hekkenberg RJ, Smitheringale AJ. Gelfoam/Gelfilm patching following the removal of ventilation tubes. J Otolaryngol 1995;24:362–3.

Iwaki E, Saito T, Tsuda G, et al. Timing for removal of tympanic ventilation tube in children. Auris Nasus Larynx 1998;25: 361–8.

Kay DJ, Nelson M, Rosenfeld RM. Meta-analysis of tympanostomy tube sequelae. Otolaryngol Head Neck Surg 2001;124:374–80.

Lentsch EJ, Goudy S, Ganzel TM, et al. Rate of persistent perforation after elective tympanostomy tube removal in pediatric patients. Int J Pediatr Otorhinolaryngol 2000;54:143–8.

Magnuson K, Hermansson A, Hellström S. Healing of tympanic membrane after myringotomy during *Streptococcus pneumoniae* otitis media. An otomicroscopic and histologic study in the rat. Ann Otol Rhinol Laryngol 1996;105:397–404.

Mattsson C, Johansson C, Hellström S. Myringosclerosis develops within 9 hours of myringotomy. ORL J Otorhinolaryngol Relat Spec 1999;61:31–6.

Mitchell RB, Pereira KD, Lazar RH. Fat graft myringoplasty in children—a safe and successful day-stay procedure. J Laryngol Otol 1997;111:106–8.

Nichols PT, Ramadan HH, Wax MK, Santrock RD. Relationship between tympanic membrane perforations and retained ventilation tubes. Arch Otolaryngol Head Neck Surg 1998;124:417–9.

Pribitkin EA, Handler SD, Tom LWC, et al. Ventilation tube removal. Indications for paper patch myringoplasty. Arch Otolaryngol Head Neck Surg 1992;118:495–7.

Rothera MP, Grant HR. Long-term ventilation of the middle ear using the Goode T-tube. J Laryngol Otol 1985;99:335–7.

Roy S, Josephson GD, Lambert P. Retained tympanostomy tubes in the middle ear cleft: an uncommon complication of tube placement. In: Lim DJ, Bluestone CD, Casselbrant MI, et al, editors. Recent advances in otitis media: proceedings of the Seventh International Symposium on Recent Advances In Otitis Media. Hamilton (ON): BC Decker Inc; 2002. p. 661–3.

Saito T, Iwaki E, Kohno Y, et al. Prevention of persistent ear drum perforation after long-term ventilation tube treatment for otitis media with effusion in children. Int J Pediatr Otorhinolaryngol 1996;38:31–9.

Solomon PR, Lax MJ, Smitheringale AJ. Tympanic membrane perforation following ventilation tube removal in a pediatric setting: a historical study. J Otolaryngol 1993;22:48–9.

Stenfors LE. Repair of tympanic membrane perforations using hyaluronic acid. An alternative to myringoplasty. J Laryngol Otol 1989;103:39–40.

Walker P. Ventilation tube duration versus site of placement. Aust N Z J Surg 1997;67:571–2.

VI. *Chronic Suppurative Otitis Media*

Chapter 59

CHRONIC SUPPURATIVE OTITIS MEDIA WITH CHOLESTEATOMA

WILLIAM M. LUXFORD, MD, MARK J. SYMS, MD

The term *cholesteatoma* was first used by Johannes Muller in 1838 to describe a neoplasm (Ferlto, 1993). The term is a misnomer because cholesteatoma is not a true neoplasm and does not contain cholesterol. Despite attempts to develop more appropriate terminology, cholesteatoma remains the terms used by otolaryngologists.

Cholesteatoma has been defined by Abramson and colleagues (1977) as "...a three dimensional epidermal and connective tissue structure, usually in the form of a sac and frequently conforming to the architecture of the various spaces of the middle ear, attic and mastoid. This structure has the capacity for progressive and independent growth at the expense of underlying bone and has a tendency to recur after removal."

Cholesteatoma is classified as congenital and acquired. Acquired cholesteatoma occurs in the presence of chronic suppurative otitis media (CSOM).

The incidence of cholesteatoma in the United States is 6 per 100,000 in the general population (Harker and Koontz, 1977). Cholesteatoma was most prevalent in the 10- to 19-year-old age group, with an incidence of 9.2 per 100,000. Cholesteatoma is more common in children with cleft palate, with a reported incidence of 8% (Kemppainen et al, 1999).

The pathogenesis of cholesteatoma has been debated for more than a century. There are three theories of the pathogenesis of cholesteatoma: metaplasia of the middle ear epithelium, basal cell hyperplasia, and invagination of epithelium through a preexisting retraction pocket or perforation. Sadé and colleagues (1983) observed in histopathologic studies the occurrence of squamous metaplasia in the middle ear in patients with cholesteatoma. The metaplasia was particularly prominent in ears with

granulation tissue. It is doubtful whether metaplastic changes can lead to the clinical features of cholesteatoma. The consistent location of cholesteatoma in the pars flaccida also makes the validity of this theory questionable. In the basal cell hyperplasia theory, the cholesteatoma is formed by ingrowth of epithelium through its own basement membrane. Ruedi (1959) demonstrated that in experimental animals, cholesteatoma could be induced by application of foreign material to the medial aspect of the pars flaccida. From this demonstration, Ruedi theorized that cholesteatoma could be generated by an inflammatory reaction in the pars flaccida. The most widely supported theory for the generation of acquired cholesteatoma is an invagination of epithelium through a preexisting retraction pocket or perforation. The process is initiated by eustachian tube obstruction, leading to impaired middle ear and mastoid ventilation. The impaired ventilation results in negative pressure in the middle ear, which leads to the tympanic membrane becoming flaccid or retracted. The retraction pocket deepens secondary to negative middle ear pressure and repeated inflammation. As the pocket deepens, desquamated debris cannot be cleared, and a cholesteatoma results.

Cholesteatoma and CSOM are related. The two conditions share the common factor of eustachian tube dysfunction. However, CSOM is very common and cholesteatoma is relatively uncommon. Persistent CSOM has been shown to be associated with greater inflammation in the posterior quadrant of the pars tensa and pars flaccida (Ruah et al, 1992).

Not only has the pathogenesis of cholesteatoma been controversial, but the surgical management of cholesteatoma has been surrounded by controversy as well. Prior to the introduction of reliable tympanoplasty techniques in the 1950s, either a modified radical mastoidectomy or a radical mastoidectomy was performed to manage aural cholesteatoma. The introduction of tympanoplasty techniques made maintenance of normal anatomic contours of the canal wall possible (Sheehy and Patterson, 1967; Wullstein, 1956; Zollner, 1955). When performing surgery, the primary goal is to eradicate the disease. When performing canal wall intact (CWI) mastoidectomies, the philosophy is to avoid an open mastoid cavity where possible, perform the operation in two stages if necessary, and re-explore the mastoid and middle ear for residual cholesteatoma when indicated (Sheehy et al, 1977). A canal wall down (CWD) mastoidectomy has the disadvantages of lifelong mastoid care and the possible recurrence of discharge. Despite the disadvantages associated with CWD mastoidectomy, the extent of the disease or other factors often necessitates this approach.

To better understand factors associated with performing CWI and CWD mastoidectomies, a retrospective review of cholesteatoma surgeries performed at the House Ear Clinic was recently performed (Syms and Luxford, 2003). Charts of all patients undergoing mastoid surgery at the clinic during the period between January 1995 and December 2000 were reviewed ($n = 972$). Only ears that had no history of prior mastoidectomy or ears in which all previous surgeries were performed at the clinic and that had the presence of cholesteatoma were used in the final analysis. These criteria yielded 486 ears in 464 patients for inclusion.

The presence of recurrent and residual cholesteatoma at surgeries subsequent to the first surgery was assessed. Recurrent cholesteatoma is defined as cholesteatoma developing from a posterosuperior retraction pocket. Residual cholesteatoma is defined as disease left behind during the previous surgery that has continued to develop. Figure 59-1 details the number of CWI and CWD surgeries. Overall, there were 333 (68.5%) CWI ears, whereas the canal wall was taken down in 153 (31.5%) ears. Of the 153 ears with a CWD mastoidectomy, 130 ears had the canal wall taken down during the first operation, 15 during a second operation, and 8 during the third operation.

At the conclusion of each procedure, the need for another operation (staging the procedure) is recorded in the medical record. The possible reasons for staging the operation are residual cholesteatoma, mucosal problems, or "other." Residual cholesteatoma is selected when the surgeon suspects incomplete removal of the cholesteatoma. If residual cholesteatoma is suspected, an additional procedure is performed 6 to 18 months later to inspect the mastoid and middle ear for residual cholesteatoma. Mucosal problems are selected when the middle ear mucosa is either diseased or absent. Silastic is placed in the middle ear space, and middle ear mucosa is allowed to regenerate or the inflammation of the mucosa resolves during the healing

time prior to the next surgery. The Silastic prevents adhesions between the middle ear mucosa and the tympanic membrane. Once the mucosal disease is resolved, ossicular reconstruction can be performed without the concern for adhesions within the middle ear space.

If a reason for staging was selected at the prior operation, the additional surgery is considered to be "planned." When no reason for staging was selected, the disease was considered to be resolved. If another procedure was performed after the disease was considered to be resolved, the additional surgery is considered to be "unplanned." Figure 59-2 details the number of planned and unplanned procedures. A second stage was planned in 341 of the 486 (70.2%) ears, a third stage was planned in 21 (14.3%) ears, and a fourth stage was planned in 4 (0.8%) ears. Some patients had an additional stage planned yet did not undergo the procedure.

In some ears, another operation was not planned, yet another operation was performed. In our series, 6 ears had

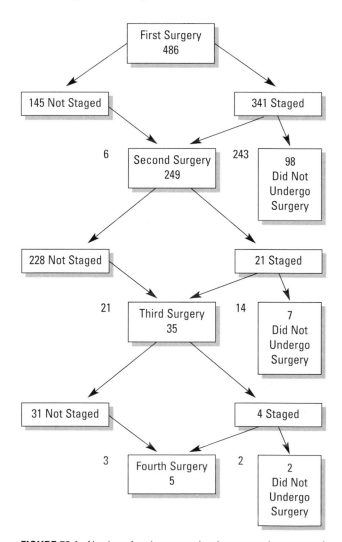

FIGURE 59-1. Number of patients experiencing a staged or unstaged surgery by number of surgeries. Adapted from Syms MJ and Luxford WM (2003).

an unplanned second procedure, 21 ears had an unplanned third procedure, and 3 ears had an unplanned fourth procedure. Twenty-eight patients had a total of 30 unplanned operations. Of the unplanned procedures, almost half (46.7%) were revision tympanoplasties. This suggests that approximately half of the revisions occurred to correct hearing problems or a perforation. Cholesteatoma was found in 12 (40%) of the 30 unplanned procedures. That is, of the total 486 ears treated, 2.5% had recurrent cholesteatoma that needed an additional procedure that was not planned. The incidence of residual cholesteatoma once an ear is declared disease free, usually after a second stage, is very small.

Of those patients who underwent a planned second surgery, 203 of the 243 were staged owing to residual cholesteatoma and 66 (32.5%) showed cholesteatoma at the second surgery. For patients undergoing a planned third operation, three of the eight patients who were staged because of residual cholesteatoma had cholesteatoma at the third operation. For patients undergoing a planned fourth operation, the one patient with residual cholesteatoma as a reason for staging had no cholesteatoma at the fourth operation. Overall, a total of 69 (32.5%) of the 212 ears that were staged for residual cholesteatoma had cholesteatoma at the later operation. In ears staged for reasons other than residual cholesteatoma, 13 of 40 had cholesteatoma found at the second surgery and 3 of 6 at the third surgery. The one patient staged for reasons other than cholesteatoma had cholesteatoma at the fourth surgery. Overall, 17 (36%) of 47 ears staged for reasons other than residual cholesteatoma did have cholesteatoma at the subsequent surgery.

Our findings in this series corroborate earlier reports from our institution that the canal wall will be taken down in approximately 30% of cases (Sheehy and Robinson, 1982). In this series, the majority of the CWD mastoidectomies were performed during the first procedure. Only 23 of the 153 CWD mastoidectomies were performed during a second or third surgery. Mastoid obliteration, offering the best possibility of a low-maintenance bowl, was performed in 50 patients who underwent a CWD mastoidectomy for the first procedure. After correctly performing the procedure and with proper healing, the end result is a bowl the size of an enlarged external auditory canal. There was no association found between the severity of the disease and the status of the canal wall. Factors such as mastoid size, ability to follow-up, and age determined the status of the canal wall.

Some authors have recommended that a CWD mastoidectomy be performed as the surgical management of cholesteatoma (Chang and Chen, 2000; Karmarkar et al, 1995; Roden et al, 1996). Some authors have argued that CWI mastoidectomies lead to patients undergoing additional procedures. Our findings demonstrate that 70% of patients will have an indication for a second stage proce-

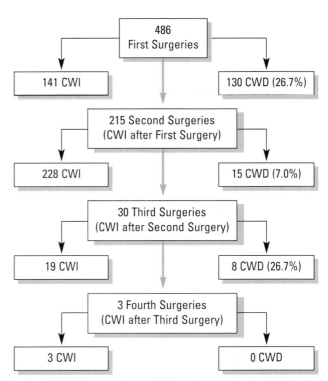

FIGURE 59-2. Number of patients undergoing canal wall intact (CWI) and canal wall down (CWD) procedures. Adapted from Syms MJ and Luxford WM (2003).

dure. Of the 486 ears in this series, only 35 required a third stage and 5 required a fourth stage procedure. Cholesteatoma was found in 13 (2.7% of all ears) ears undergoing a third procedure and 2 (0.4% of all ears) patients undergoing a fourth procedure. A range of 6 to 13% has been reported as the incidence of residual cholesteatoma in patients with a CWD mastoidectomy (Cody and Taylor, 1977; Karmarkar et al, 1995; Sadé, 1987). We found an incidence of 14.6%. A proposed advantage of CWD mastoidectomy is that patients will undergo only one procedure. With CWI mastoidectomy with a planned second stage, the patients are expected to undergo two procedures. CWI patients undergo fewer unplanned procedures because residual cholesteatoma is found in 3.2% of patients after a planned second stage and the incidence of residual for CWD mastoidectomy patients had been reported to be between 6 and 13%. Additionally, CWI mastoidectomy avoids cavity infections. Some authors reported an incidence of infections in CWD cavities in the range of 9.6 to 30% (Brown, 1982; Chang and Chen, 2000).

Chronic otitis media with cholesteatoma can be effectively managed using a CWI or a CWD procedure when necessary. The canal wall remained intact in approximately 69% of ears and will usually be taken down, if needed, during the first surgery. Any patient with a planned second stage should be strongly encouraged to undergo the procedure because 27% of patients will have a residual cholesteatoma. Management of cholesteatoma with a CWI mastoidectomy results in 10% of patients undergoing procedures in addition to the planned second stage.

References

Abramson M, Gantz BJ, Asarch RG, Litton WB. Cholesteatoma pathogenesis: evidence for the migration theory. In: McCabe BF, Sadé J, Abramson M, editors. Cholesteatoma. First international conference. Birmingham (AL): Aesculapius; 1977. p. 176–86.

Brown JS. A ten year statistical follow-up of 1142 consecutive cases of cholesteatoma: the closed vs. the open technique. Laryngoscope 1982;92:390–6.

Chang C, Chen M. Canal-wall-down tympanoplasty with mastoidectomy for advanced cholesteatoma. J Otolaryngol 2000;29:270–3.

Cody DTR, Taylor WF. Mastoidectomy for acquired cholesteatoma. In: McCabe BF, Sadé J, Abramson M, editors. Cholesteatoma. First international conference. Birmingham (AL): Aesculapius; 1977. p. 337.

Ferlto A. A review of the definition, terminology and pathology of aural cholesteatoma. J Laryngol Otol 1993;107:483–8.

Harker LA, Koontz FP. The bacteriology of cholesteatoma. In: McCabe BF, Sadé J, Abramson M, editors. Cholesteatoma. First international conference. Birmingham (AL): Aesculapius; 1977. p. 264–7.

Karmarkar S, Bhatia S, Saleh E, et al. Cholesteatoma surgery: the individualized technique. Ann Otol Rhinol Laryngol 1995;104:591–5.

Kemppainen HO, Puhakka HJ, Laippala PJ, et al. Epidemiology and aetiology of middle ear cholesteatoma. Acta Otolaryngol (Stockh) 1999;119:568–72.

Roden D, Honrubia V, Wiet R. Outcome of residual cholesteatoma and hearing in mastoid surgery. J Otolaryngol 1996;25:178–81.

Ruah CB, Schachern PA, Paparella MM, Zelterman D. Mechanism of retraction pocket formation in the pediatric tympanic membrane. Arch Otolaryngol Head Neck Surg 1992;118:1298–305.

Ruedi L. Cholesteatoma formation in the middle ear in animal experiments. Acta Otolaryngol (Stockh) 1959;50:233.

Sadé J. Treatment of cholesteatoma. Am J Otol 1987;8:524–33.

Sadé J, Babiacki A, Pinkus G. The metaplastic and congenital origin of cholesteatoma. Acta Otolaryngol (Stockh) 1983;93:119–29.

Sheehy JL, Brackmann DE, Graham MD. Cholesteatoma surgery: residual and recurrent disease: a review of 1,024 cases. Ann Otol Rhinol Laryngol 1977;86:451–62.

Sheehy JL, Patterson ME. Intact canal wall tympanoplasty with mastoidectomy. A review of eight years experience. Laryngoscope 1967;77.1532–42.

Sheehy JL, Robinson JV. Cholesteatoma surgery at the otologic medical group: residual and recurrent disease. Am J Otol 1982;3:209–15.

Syms MJ, Luxford WM. Management of cholesteatoma: status of the canal wall. Laryngoscope 2003;113:443–8.

Wullstein H. Theory and practice of tympanoplasty. Laryngoscope 1956;66:1076–93.

Zollner F. Principle of plastic surgery of the sound conducting apparatus. J Laryngol Otol 1955;69:637–52.

Chapter 60

Chronic Suppurative Otitis Media without Cholesteatoma

Harvey Coates, MS, FRACS

The World Health Organization's (WHO) definition of chronic suppurative otitis media (CSOM) is a stage in ear disease in which there is a chronic infection of the middle ear cleft (eustachian tube, middle ear, and mastoid) in the presence of a persistent tympanic membrane (TM) perforation (World Health Organization, 1998). There may be intermittent or constant purulent otorrhea. Mastoiditis is a consistent part of the pathologic process. This definition of chronic otorrhea varies between various groups from 2 weeks to 3 months or longer. I believe that 2 months minimum is necessary to distinguish this process from acute otitis media (AOM) with perforation.

Synonyms, many of which are inaccurate and inappropriate, include chronic otitis media (OM) (active and inactive), suppurative OM, and chronic perforation. For the purposes of this chapter, CSOM is characterized by recurrent or persistent bacterial infection of the ear with conductive hearing loss, mucopurulent otorrhea, and a chronic perforation of the TM.

Incidence

CSOM is a disease affecting especially indigenous people with poor health, hygiene, and nutrition throughout the world. In developing countries, in cases in which CSOM accounted for 60 to 80% of middle ear disease, suppurative intracranial complications occurred in about 10% (Davidson et al, 1989). The WHO reported that a prevalence of CSOM greater than 4% in a defined child population indicated a massive public health problem needing urgent attention in targeted populations (World Health Organization, 1998). In many underdeveloped countries throughout the world, the incidence of CSOM is significantly higher than this.

In Inuit Indians, the prevalence of CSOM varies up to 66%, whereas in Australia, the prevalence of CSOM in the

Aboriginal population is similarly high. The majority of children with CSOM have associated conductive hearing loss as a result of a perforated TM, otorrhea, granulation, polyps, cholesteatoma, and ossicular chain problems. In Australia, screenings of conductive hearing loss in Aboriginal children in one series showed 41% to have a hearing loss of 25 dB or greater in at least one ear (Watson et al, 1992). In nonindigenous Australian children, hearing loss in a large series was in the range of 4 to 5% of children, with an average hearing loss of 20 dB (McPherson, 1990).

Importance

Mortality and Morbidity

In 1993, the WHO reported that OM (principally CSOM) was responsible for the deaths of 51,000 children under the age of 5 years each year in developing countries (WHO, 1994). Combining this loss of life from early death with loss from disability—a term known as disability-adjusted life-years—OM resulted in an impact similar to meningitis and trachoma. This burden of suffering was assessed cumulatively in Australia, and Aboriginal children would be expected to have 32 months with OM between the ages of 2 and 20 years (McGilchrist and Hills, 1986) and non-Aboriginal children only 3 months with OM for the same time period.

CSOM in children will often continue into adulthood if improperly treated in childhood. Nunez and Browning (1990) reported that the annual risk of developing an abscess was approximately 1 in 10,000 in an adult with active chronic OM, with males three times more likely to develop this. They commented that although this risk appeared to be low, the lifetime expectancy of an adult aged 30 years with active chronic OM developing an abscess was 1 in 200 (Nunez and Browning, 1990).

Hearing Loss

Up to one-third of the population in developing countries has their quality of life affected by CSOM and its precursors, OM and otitis media with effusion (OME). CSOM is the most common cause of hearing impairment in children in developing countries. Between 30 and 80% of Aboriginal children suffer from hearing loss. The impact of OM on development of language in Aboriginal children with the early onset of OM shortly after birth, persistent otorrhea, and hearing loss is much greater than in non-Aboriginal children. Difficulties in acquisition of language, particularly when English may be a second language, together with auditory processing problems, create a milieu in which educational success is difficult to accomplish.

Difficulty hearing in class leads to poor scholastic performance, behavior problems, poor self-esteem and social isolation, truancy, and, subsequently, unemployment and interaction with the judicial system.

Pathogenesis

CSOM is a sequela of acute or unresolved OM, particularly in children with poor socioeconomic conditions, and usually presents within the first 5 years of life. In the presence of a preexisting perforation or ventilation tube, infection may develop secondary to contamination from ear canal organisms or with an upper respiratory tract infection. Reflux of nasopharyngeal secretions and possibly reflux of gastric secretions may occur secondary to loss of the protective middle ear air cushion with a perforation. This is in addition to the fact that children have shorter eustachian tubes, making them more prone to reflux. Recent studies by Tasker and colleagues (2002) showed that in OME, up to 83% of children had high levels of pepsin/pepsinogen in their effusions, suggesting that the reflux of gastric juice into the middle ear could be more common than previously thought.

Active middle ear infection leads to increased vascularity of the middle ear mucosa and submucosa with infiltration by acute and chronic inflammatory cells, subsequent mucosal edema, and osteitis. This infection leads to mucosa/ulceration and chronic infection and metaplasia of the columnar epithelium, which changes to a cuboidal-type epithelium with capillary proliferation, development of granulation, polyps, osteitis, and new bone formation. Pathologic changes in the temporal bone occur with almost 100% ossicular involvement, osteitis of the temporal bone, and development of granulation tissue and polyps. In about 25% of cases, cholesterol granuloma or tympanosclerosis is present. Progression of CSOM may lead to complications both within the temporal bone and intracranially. Temporal bone complications include mastoiditis, ossicular chain destruction, facial nerve involvement, secondary cholesteatoma development, labyrinthitis, and sensorineural hearing loss. Intracranial complications may include meningitis, extradural and intracranial abscesses, and sigmoid sinus thrombosis.

Bacteriology

The usual organisms cultured in CSOM are aerobic organisms, although anaerobic organisms and fungi have been implicated in the disease process. The most common organism is *Pseudomonas aeruginosa*, followed by *Staphylococcus aureus*, and these bacteria may derive from external ear canal contamination of the middle ear (Brook and Finegold, 1979). Brook (1989) believes that the role of anaerobes has been underplayed and that it is important to culture for these organisms from the middle ear aspirates. The importance of culturing from the middle ear rather than the ear canal is stressed. He found that 56% of ear aspirates in patients with CSOM isolated anaerobic organisms, and other studies have shown isolation of anaerobic organisms of between 8 and 59%. The most common anaerobic bacteria isolated are *Bacteroides fragilis* and *Bacteroides melaninogenicus* group 9. Fungal isolates are principally *Aspergillus* species and *Candida albicans* (Attallah, 2000). Tuberculosis has also been implicated as a cause of CSOM in developing countries.

No discussion of CSOM would be complete without consideration of the effects of biofilm formation by bacteria in middle ear disease.

Biofilm formation occurs when microorganisms present in middle ear fluid lead to a quorum with deposition of sessile bacteria with protective biofilm production on mucosal surfaces and foreign bodies. This biofilm acts to provide an almost impervious layer to many systemic and topical antibiotics and may increase the resistance to antibiotics (eg, to tobramycin by *P. aeruginosa* and *S. aureus*) from 20 to 100 times. Within the glycocalyx formed by the heaping of bacteria and supporting substances, some bacterial changes to an almost inert form may occur. The presence of a viral stimulation such as an upper respiratory tract infection may encourage these spore-like bacteria to become activated and undergo planktonic changes, reactivating otorrhea. Biofilm has been noted to attach to osteitic bone, epithelial pits, and foreign bodies in CSOM (Post, 2001). I have isolated bacterial biofilm from the middle ear mucosa of a child with CSOM (Figure 60-1).

Future management strategies for CSOM may need to take into account treatment for biofilm. These strategies could include using appropriate messages to signal the biofilm to "go planktonic," where it could be available to systemic and topical antibiotics, disrupting the biofilm mechanically, using other chemicals or detergents that may break down the biofilm layer or using

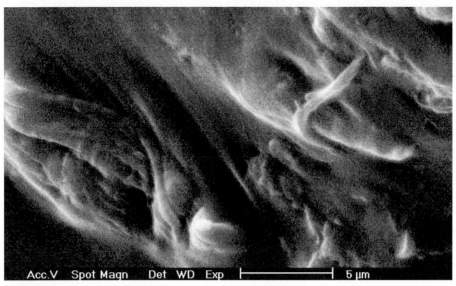

FIGURE 60-1. Scanning electron micrograph of middle ear mucosa from a child with chronic suppurative otitis media showing bacterial biofilm formation.

penetrance enhancers or antipolymerases to block the synthesis of biofilm.

Management: Treatment Options

Management of uncomplicated CSOM initially consists of conservative management with local treatment and topical medications and, occasionally, systemic antibiotic therapy. In complicated and persistent CSOM in which medical treatment has failed, consideration of surgical options using the principles of removal of disease and reconstruction and repair of the anatomy becomes an option. Treatment of CSOM is difficult because of structural and anatomic problems that prevent direct access to the diseased middle ear and mastoid for cleaning. Also, problems with diffusion of systemic antibiotics into the temporal bone tissues to give sufficiently high mean inhibitory concentrations to eradicate the bacteria and problems of bacterial resistance and the new concept of the nonplanktonic growth modes of biofilm and other factors mitigate against easy control of the CSOM infection.

Conservative Management

After a full history and clinical examination, consideration must be made to rule out underlying associated factors such as chronic rhinosinusitis, allergy, immunoglobulin deficiency, and unusual infections. This demands examination under the operating microscope with a culture of the middle ear discharge looking for aerobic, anaerobic, fungal, and acid-fast bacilli. Thorough cleansing of the ear canal and middle ear using suction or ear toilet syringing with either a dilute povidone-iodine solution or a 3% hydrogen peroxide solution is recommend-

ed. Dry mopping has been shown to be ineffective for cleaning ears (Smith et al, 1996).

In addition, it may be possible in older children to control some granulation tissue and polyps by office débridement, although this is best done under a general anesthetic in most children. The other mainstay of treatment in the first instance for CSOM is topical antibiotic eardrops, which are often combined with steroids for their anti-inflammatory effect. In the past, aminoglycoside antibiotics and other potentially ototoxic eardrops have been used, but there have been reports of ototoxicity leading to sensorineural hearing loss with prolonged use of these drops. Fluoroquinolone eardrops, which are nonototoxic, have become the treatment of choice for management of otorrhea in CSOM (Acuin et al, 2001). Prolonged treatment using these drops (eg, ciprofloxacin hydrochloride) for 14 to 28 days may be necessary for control of the discharge. Aslan and colleagues (1998) noted an 83.3% clinical cure rate with ciprofloxacin solution at a concentration of 125 μg/mL and a 100% clinical cure rate and complete bacteriologic eradication after 21 days (Aslan et al, 1998). Caution must be exercised with those solutions and eardrops that are not approved for use with perforated TMs.

Failure of topical ear toilets and antibiotic and steroid eardrop treatment requires consideration for admission for intravenous (IV) antibiotics or outpatient IV management. Although there have been reports of oral ciprofloxacin causing joint complications, oral ciprofloxacin is perhaps a viable alternative to hospital or outpatient therapy. Systemic therapy is given with IV-extended penicillins, ciprofloxacin, the aminoglycosides, or cephalosporins for up to 10 to 14 days, usually in addition to local therapy.

Surgical Treatment

Myringoplasty

Generally, if a TM perforation has persisted for longer than 3 to 6 months and shows no sign of healing, then TM repair should be considered. The principal reasons for repairing a TM are

- to restore the TM and improve hearing,
- to prevent ingrowth of the TM edge and cholesteatoma formation, and
- to allow the child to swim without ear protection.

Myringoplasty (or type 1 tympanoplasty) is performed to heal TM perforations where there is no ossicular chain involvement and no persistent chronic otorrhea, which may require mastoid surgery. Myringoplasty may be via a transcanal, endaural, or postauricular approach. Tympanoplasty with ossicular chain reconstruction is indicated in most cases in which there is evidence of ossicular chain discontinuity or loss of the ossicles from chronic disease. Where there is chronic otorrhea unresponsive to conservative management, or if there are significant signs and symptoms such as profuse otorrhea, facial nerve involvement, vertigo, otalgia, and headaches, then a computed tomographic (CT) scan may indicate significant mastoid disease or cholesteatoma.

Mastoidectomy

Mastoidectomy may be performed with the canal wall up (cortical mastoidectomy) or may be combined with a facial recess approach. Often, particularly in children, canal wall up procedures will need to have a second stage to ensure eradication of disease, and reconstruction of the ossicular chain will have to be considered if it has been involved in the disease process.

Management of Complications

Management of complications of CSOM, including otogenic abscesses, generally follows the surgical principles of decompression of the abscess with drainage and meticulous attention to the mastoid cavity with closure of fistulae or defects between the temporal bone and intracranial cavity. A detailed description of surgical management of each complication of CSOM is beyond the scope of this chapter.

My Preferences

After obtaining a history and performing an examination, particularly under the operating microscope, I recommend obtaining an audiogram with air and bone testing and speech discrimination scores. Under the operating microscope, the ear is cleaned and an initial culture is taken from the middle ear. If there is profuse otorrhea, ear toilets using a 5% povidone-iodine solution two to three times daily should be carried out. Fluoroquinolone eardrops (eg,

ciprofloxacin hydrochloride) are instilled (three drops twice daily for 10 to 14 days) using an injection technique by compressing the tragus against the ear canal. The child is reviewed after a month, and if the otorrhea persists, then a CT scan of the mastoid and the temporal bone is considered to rule out underlying cholesteatoma and/or mastoiditis and to define the mastoid cavity size. On occasion, prior to considering surgical management for these patients, they will be admitted for broad-spectrum and culture-sensitive antibiotics, together with intensive ear toilets.

If the chronic discharge does not settle with conservative management or there is failure of straightforward myringoplasty, then one should consider a mastoidectomy procedure.

Dry Perforation

If the perforation remains dry after appropriate ear toilets, a myringoplasty with or without ossicular chain reconstruction can be considered. For a very small perforation occupying less than one-quarter or one-third of the TM, I use a technique of inlay myringoplasty using thinned tragal cartilage, as described by Eavey (1998).

In cases in which the perforation is larger and occupies greater than one-third of the TM, then I use a classic transcanal underlay myringoplasty with inspection of the ossicular chain. I use either tragal perichondrium or temporalis fascia in this technique. If the perforation is anterior and difficult to expose, then a postauricular approach may be necessary or a canalplasty may be performed. On occasion, particularly where there is a question of mastoid surgery or an attic exploration being necessary, then an endaural approach is performed.

Postoperative antibiotics are given to reduce the incidence of postoperative infection, particularly in indigenous children.

Ossicular Chain Reconstruction

Essentially, ossicular chain reconstruction replaces the malleus and incus assembly or replaces all of the ossicles with an oval window to TM prosthesis. The partial ossicular replacement between the stapes head and the foreshortened long handle of the incus is performed by interposing tragal cartilage or transpositioning the incus head. Occasionally, in the absence of the malleus handle and long process of the incus, a layered tragal cartilage graft directly apposing the TM to form a type 3 tympanoplasty is performed. My preferred partial ossicular chain replacement prostheses are oval top columellars and spanner malleus-stapes assemblies, as described by Black (1995). Tragal cartilage is used as a table on the undersurface of the TM to reduce extrusion of the prosthesis.

Total ossicular replacement is performed by using a spanner assembly, which connects the malleus to the footplate. Oval top columellar prostheses with autograft cartilage are also used.

Elimination Surgery

In cases of canal wall down procedures, in which there has been no recurrence of otorrhea or chronic mastoiditis, consideration of reconstruction of the posterior canal wall and obliteration of the mastoid cavity can be made after a year of a dry mastoid cavity. The indications for this are to avoid the open cavity and reduce the chance of chronic otorrhea. In addition, vertigo secondary to air or water caloric effects, particularly when swimming, may be eliminated, and hearing aid fitting is easier than with a large cavity. Staged reconstruction may be preferred to allow optimal hearing and canal restoration. I prefer the method described by Black (1995), in which large low facial ridge cavities are managed with hydroxyapatite and high facial ridge small cavity sites are managed with an attic defect plate technique using tragal cartilage. Obliteration of the mastoid cavity and revascularization of the wall using a middle temporal artery flap lead to improved success rates.

My Preferences in Specific Cases

Under 5-Year-Old Child

Early myringoplasty is important for optimal language, hearing, and educational development, particularly in indigenous children. In those cases in which there is CSOM with bilateral perforations and greater than 30 dB hearing loss and recurrent otorrhea, I perform early myringoplasty using an inlay technique for small perforations and an underlay transcanal or postauricular approach for large perforations.

Postoperative antibiotics are given for 7 days to reduce the possibility of secondary infection and loss of the graft. Where there are bilateral perforations, I perform the transcanal or postauricular myringoplasty on the larger perforation on the ear with the worst hearing and may perform a circumcision of the TM edge and patching with Silastic sheeting on the contralateral side.

My experience parallels that of Denoyelle and colleagues (1999). In their series, the age of the patient and the size and location of the perforation did not affect the outcome, but poor prognostic factors were inflammatory changes in the middle ear mucosa, contralateral TM perforation, and contralateral cholesteatoma. They felt that the presence of one of these latter factors preoperatively should lead to a consideration of a more durable graft material, such as autologous cartilage.

CSOM with Severe Granulation Tissue Formation

Merchant and colleagues (1997) noted that CSOM with granulation was more difficult to treat than CSOM with cholesteatoma. This is also my experience, and in these cases, canal wall down mastoidectomy, together with careful removal of granulation tissue from the middle ear and mastoid, is performed. Care must be taken with the

obscuring of normal anatomic markers by the destructive disease, with the facial nerve, semicircular canals, and stapes superstructure being particularly at risk. A preoperative CT scan may help in preoperative planning and to avoid complications.

In those cases in which the surgeon is reluctant to proceed further owing to concerns regarding perilymph fistula formation or facial nerve injury, a planned staged procedure with intensive antibiotic eardrop therapy prior to the second procedure may be the best option. Often, after removal of the bulk of the infected granulation tissue and creation of an open mastoid bowl, the remaining granulation tissue may respond to topical therapy more easily.

Children with Down Syndrome

In my experience, children with Down syndrome have long-standing eustachian tube dysfunction and anatomic differences requiring an aggressive approach with a canal wall down procedure with a meatoplasty to allow adequate exposure of the cavity, in view of the usual narrow external auditory canal.

Justification for My Preferences

Conservative Management

The majority of children with CSOM will respond to conservative management with intensive ear toilets using suction or irrigation followed by the use of antibiotic steroid eardrops, preferably one that is nonototoxic (fluoroquinolone). Topical therapy must be continued for an adequate period of time to allow eradication of bacterial disease. Rarely, persistent otorrhea, despite appropriate topical therapy, may require admission to the hospital or outpatient IV therapy with broad-spectrum culture-sensitive antibiotics.

My current first-line management for topical therapy in the presence of a wet perforation is fluoroquinolone antibiotic/steroid eardrops, such as ciprofloxacin hydrochloride, which are nonototoxic and have an excellent antibacterial spectrum.

Failure of this medical treatment despite patient compliance necessitates hospital or outpatient IV antibiotic therapy. If this is unsuccessful after 5 to 6 days with appropriate antibiotic therapy, a CT scan is performed to rule out significant mastoiditis or cholesteatoma. On occasion, an examination of the ear under anesthesia may be warranted for biopsy purposes and to rule out cholesteatoma and unusual conditions (eg, tuberculosis). This may be followed by a cortical mastoidectomy with or without myringoplasty.

Myringoplasty

For simple myringoplasty with small perforations, the inlay tragal myringoplasty has a number of advantages:

1. In the absence of a significant hearing loss, this technique allows relatively straightforward and rapid closure of the TM perforation without tympanomeatal flap elevation.

2. The results appear similar to those of underlay myringoplasty but have the advantage of less discomfort. Also, the technique is a more straightforward procedure, particularly with anterosuperior perforations that might otherwise require a postauricular approach.

3. Even in the presence of postoperative infection, the graft may survive with the low oxygen and nutrition requirements of the cartilage and perichondrium

4. The procedure may be done as a same-day care procedure, and the child would be able to fly in the immediate postoperative period, which is not necessarily the case with other forms of myringoplasty.

Although there are concerns that this technique may mask an underlying cholesteatoma at the margins of the perforation, the advantages in most cases outweigh the disadvantages.

Underlay myringoplasty using temporalis fascia or tragal perichondrium for medium-size dry perforations remains my treatment of choice for medium- or large-size perforations, using either an endaural or a postauricular approach. These autograft tissues have graft-take rates of over 90% in many cases.

In the absence of cholesteatoma and in the presence of a large mastoid air cell system, a canal wall up technique is preferable to avoid a large mastoid cavity. Generally, however, if there is a small relatively sclerotic mastoid bone, then a canal wall down procedure will leave, in the presence of a wide meatoplasty, a small smooth cavity with a well-vascularized lining and an intact drum with objectives similar to those of elimination surgery (Black, 1995). However, canal wall down procedures in the presence of significant mastoid disease may be the only effective means of the eradication of the disease in children. Reconstruction of the canal wall can be considered in the future if the cavities remain dry and free of disease.

Ossicular Chain Reconstruction

My preferred technique of ossicular chain reconstruction is to use spanner assemblies or oval top columellars because of the ease of use and reported reduction in extrusion through the TM.

Alternative Approaches

My principles of otologic surgery dictate that if I perform two procedures on a patient and the procedure, whether it is myringoplasty, ossicular chain reconstruction, or mastoidectomy, is unsuccessful, then I will consider obtaining a second opinion from a colleague who specializes solely in otology. Generally, the success rate of myringoplasty on the first occasion is between 85 and 90%, but in special populations, such as indigenous children, the graft-take rate may be as low as 50%, particularly when factors such as early postoperative swimming in potentially contaminated water (eg, waterholes) and failure to comply with postoperative care are included.

With the inlay tragal cartilage myringoplasty, failure may be attributable to a small defect at the edge of the rim, and this can often be closed with a simple fat/subcutaneous tissue graft with good success. If the inlay technique fails, then an underlay temporalis fascia graft myringoplasty is performed, and at this procedure, careful examination of the status of the middle ear mucosa and the patency of the eustachian tube and consideration of a biopsy to exclude unusual disease are undertaken. If the middle ear mucosa is very thickened and polypoid, then clearance of this tissue in the middle ear cavity may result in successful revision myringoplasty.

The wet and open cavity remains a difficult problem for the otologist and may be related to exposed respiratory epithelium, failure of healing, or failure of the normal epithelial migration that is self-cleaning (Black, 1995). In the presence of a wet cavity, a number of surgical factors may have led to the presence of persistent otorrhea. These are stated in Table 60-1.

The factors in Table 60-1, together with postoperative infection, avascular changes, or problems with epithelial migration in the mastoid cavity, must be considered. These surgical factors and postoperative conditions may interact to create a poor prognosis for a dry mastoid cavity (Sadé et al, 1982). Prevention of a wet mastoid cavity requires appropriate surgical procedure selection and attention to those factors. Black (1995) noted a number of clinical features that will indicate a poor ossiculoplasty prognosis (Black, 1995) (Table 60-2).

A number of these conditions, including otorrhea, severe mucosal damage, myringitis, TM collapse, or a radical cavity, can be ameliorated by staging the surgery. Middle ear fluid or an absent malleus or stapes, together with severe audiologic losses, is more difficult to manage. Failure of canal wall reconstruction or complications of this surgery may be related to infection preoperatively, an excessively large mastoid cavity, the presence of a low facial ridge with its shorter healing distance, avascular atrophic cavity skin lining, or a lack of the pars tensa in radical mastoidectomy cavities (Black, 1995). Canal wall repair complications can be prevented by avoiding the

TABLE 60-1. Surgical Factors Leading to Persistent Cavity Otorrhea

Small meatus with inadequate cavity cleaning
Large cavity with exposed respiratory epithelium
Retained high facial ridge
Failure to close off the middle ear
Failure to adequately remove chronic infection and granulation
Failure to revascularize the mastoid cavity lining

TABLE 60-2. Poor Prognostic Factors for Ossiculoplasty

Absent malleus or absent stapes
Large, low-frequency air–bone gap
Unremitting otorrhea or chronic myringitis
Poor middle ear mucosa
Middle ear effusion or severe eardrum collapse at surgery
First-stage radical mastoidectomy reconstruction

factors mentioned above, in particular ensuring that there is no infection present and that a good vascular canal skin flap is used.

References

Acuin J, Smith A, Mackenzie I. Interventions for chronic suppurative otitis media. Cochrane Database Syst Rev 2001(3).

Aslan A, Altuntas A, Titiz A, et al. A new dosage regimen for topical application of ciprofloxacin in the management of chronic suppurative otitis media. Otolaryngol Head Neck Surg 1998; 118:883–5.

Attallah MS. Microbiology of chronic suppurative otitis media with cholesteatoma. Saudi Med J 2000;21:924–7.

Black B. Mastoidectomy elimination. Laryngoscope 1995;105 Suppl:1–30.

Brook I. Pediatric anaerobic infection: diagnosis and management. St. Louis: Mosby; 1989.

Brook I, Finegold SM. Bacteriology of chronic otitis media. JAMA 1979;241:487–8.

Davidson J, Hyde ML, Alberti PW. Epidemiologic patterns in childhood hearing loss: a review. Int J Pediatr Otorhinolaryngol 1989;17:239–66.

Denoyelle F, Roger G, Chauvin P, Garabedian EN. Myringoplasty in children: predictive factors of outcome. Laryngoscope 1999; 109:47–51.

Eavey RD. Inlay tympanoplasty: cartilage butterfly technique. Laryngoscope 1998;108:657–61.

McGilchrist CA, Hills LJ. Estimation of cumulative illness using cross sectional data. J Chron Dis 1986;39:929–31.

McPherson B. Hearing loss in Australian Aborigines: a critical evaluation. Austral J Audiol 1990;12:67–78.

Merchant SN, Wang P, Jang CH, et al. Efficacy of tympanomastoid surgery for control of infection in active chronic otitis media. Laryngoscope 1997;107:872–7.

Nunez DA, Browning GG. Risks of developing an otogenic intracranial abscess. J Laryngol Otol 1990;104:468–72.

Post CJ. Direct evidence of bacterial biofilms in otitis media. Laryngoscope 2001;111:2083–94.

Sadé J, Weinberg J, Berco E, et al. The marsupialized (radical) mastoid. J Laryngol Otol 1982;96:869–75.

Smith AW, Hatcher J, Mackenzie IJ, et al. Randomized controlled trial of treatment of chronic suppurative otitis media in Kenyan schoolchildren. Lancet 1996;348:1128–33.

Tasker A, Dettmar PW, Panetti M, et al. Reflux of gastric juice and glue ear in children. Lancet 2002;359:493.

Watson DS, Clapin M. Ear health of Aboriginal primary school children in the Eastern Goldfields region of WA. Aust J Public Health 1992;16:26–30.

World Health Organization. World development report 1993: investing in health. Oxford (UK): Oxford University Press; 1994.

World Health Organization. Prevention of hearing impairment from chronic otitis media. Report of WHO/CIBA Foundation Workshop. London, 19–21 November 1996. Geneva: World Health Organization; 1998.

Chapter 61

EXTERNAL EAR CANAL POLYP VERSUS MASS IN THE EXTERNAL EAR CANAL

TAUNO PALVA, MD, HANS RAMSAY, MD

The skin in the ear canal is thick on the lateral cartilaginous portion and contains ceruminous, sebaceous, and sweat glands. In the medial bony portion, it is much thinner and consists only of the keratinizing epithelium joined tightly with the periosteum. Ceruminous masses rarely block the ear canal and are easy to diagnose. Fault in the horizontal transport of keratin out of the ear canal may result in the rare keratosis obturans, but this condition is not difficult to diagnose. Adenomas or adenocarcinomas deriving from the glandular structures occur almost exclusively in adults, similarly to spinocellular and basal cell carcinomas, and are not discussed here.

For the differential diagnosis of polyps versus masses in the external ear canal, we deal with three diseases in which the mass may mimic genuine inflammatory polyps or granulation tissue: rhabdomyosarcoma (RMS); the multisystemic disease of Langerhans' cell histiocytosis (LCH), of which—in terms of the ear—the eosinophilic granuloma (EG) is of special interest; and myxoma. All of these are difficult to diagnose if primarily not considered as alternatives to inflammatory diseases of the external ear canal or middle ear.

Incidence, Clinical Characteristics, and Histology

Aural polyps are distinctly more common than the three above-mentioned diseases, but even they are seldom seen in children. The current antibiotic treatment of middle ear infections has minimized the necrotic changes both in the pars tensa and in Shrapnell's membrane, and the perforations through which the edematous mucosa or polypoid granulation tissue gains entrance to the ear canal have become rare. There are no global figures for the incidence; a recent 20-year retrospective study identified 35 pediatric patients with aural polyps, 95% of which were

associated with chronic otitis media, cholesteatoma, or retained tympanostomy tubes (Gliklich et al, 1993). In one of these children, the polyps proved to be attributable to LCH.

Polyps are soft formations of a tissue that bulges outward from its normal surface level with either a narrow stalk or with a relatively broad base. In the presently discussed context, they originate from the respiratory epithelium of the middle ear. An edematous promontory mucosa may protrude through a pars tensa perforation. It appears as a soft, reddish mass on the tympanic membrane and may create an impression of a granular myringitis. In the former, there is generally a history of preexisting otitis media and impaired hearing. In the latter, hearing is normal.

Polyps in the area of Shrapnell's membrane are more frequent. They originate from Prussak's space and the lower lateral attic (Palva et al, 2001). Owing to the declining frequency of cholesteatomatous disease, these polyps have also become rare. If such small formations are primarily seen in the area of Shrapnell's membrane, the diagnosis of a chronic inflammatory ear disease is likely. There may or may not be discharge, and hearing is still normal. In neglected cases, the polyps may become large, partly occluding the view to the tympanic membrane, or they may fill the entire ear canal.

Aural polyps vary greatly in their microscopic appearance. They are covered by cuboidal epithelium of the middle ear but may also show squamous epithelium, which derives from the perforation edges or from the ingrowth of papillary projections into Prussak's space (Palva et al, 2001). The stroma may be highly edematous, containing a sparse collagen matrix, fibrocytes, and a few round cells. Fresh polyps have a high cellular content. Stretches of columnar epithelium may become trapped inside the granulation tissue but disappear with the maturation and shrinking of the tissues. The newly formed delicate blood vessels disrupt easily, and areas with hemosiderin pigment appear. Polyps of long duration become dense owing to fibrosis.

RMS is the most common malignant mesenchymal tumor in children. The overall estimate in the white population has been given as 0.44 in 100,000 and distinctly less (0.13/100,000) for the African population (Young and Miller, 1975). Of 688 such patients in the final report (Maurer et al, 1988) of the Intergroup Rhabdomyosarcoma Study Group (IRS), 14% appeared at the parameningeal sites and 7% involved the temporal bone. In another study of 60 children with head and neck RMS (Anderson et al, 1990), the ear was involved in 10%, the predominant sites being the orbit and nasopharynx (both in 25%).

RMS appears in different locations, grows fast, and metastasizes early. In the region of the ear, the great majority of RMSs appear initially in the temporal bone, the mass in the ear canal being a late presentation. An initial site of RMS is rarely in the ear canal. There is an easily bleeding friable reddish mass that may fill the meatus completely. There is frequently pain, which is lacking in benign polyps, and the discharge may be purulent or reddish in color. With the temporal bone location, the patient may sometimes be brought for examination when a posterior extension has already caused facial paralysis. In advanced cases, the granulomatous masses fill all compartments of the middle ear.

RMS derives from the primitive striated muscle cells, either of those in the muscles of the ear canal or apparently those in the middle ear. Of the subtypes (Feldman, 1982), the embryonal form, most frequent in children under the age of 10 years, consists of evenly distributed cells, which may be long, thin, and spindle-shaped or small and round. Mitoses are frequent. The botryoid subtype is lobulated and resembles a cluster of grapes (hence the name from Greek). It is characterized by multilayered bands of short spindle cells parallel to the mucous membrane, and the deeper layers consist of myxoid cells. In older children, the alveolar type is more common and the tumor cells are grouped around spaces resembling pulmonary alveoli. Cross-striation in the large spindle cells is diagnostic for RMS but is not commonly found. Feldman (1982) estimated that half of the cases are initially wrongly diagnosed.

Immunohistochemistry has shown RMS to be a heterogeneous group of tumors with respect to their molecular basis and degree of differentiation. In the modern diagnostic workup and in the differential diagnosis inside the RMS, the main emphasis is on the immunostaining for muscle-related antigens, for example, staining for desmin (Figure 61-1), muscle-actin, myosin, and myoglobin. In differentiation between the subtypes of RMS, staining for the myogenic regulatory genes expressed in the RMS cells is the most recent addition employed in the academic pathology centers. Fresh tissue specimens are needed for differentiation of RMS from other small cell tumors such as lymphoblastomas or lymphomas.

EG forms part of the disease complex of LCH, which has been estimated to have an incidence of 1 in 200,000 in children under 15 years of age (Thomas et al, 1996). LCH in young children is a highly malignant, multisystemic disease. Its less malignant intermediate forms involve several tissues, and EG is the localized form with an initial, relatively benign, single-bone involvement. An early study (McCaffrey and McDonald, 1979) from a period between 1926 and 1978 contained 22 patients with histiocytosis of the temporal bone—15% of all LCH patients seen during that period. In a recent study (Quraishi et al, 1993) over a 33-year period (1959–1992), there were 54 LCH patients, of whom 15 had only the temporal bone lesion at presentation.

EG starts as an osteolytic lesion of the temporal bone and is initially silent; hence, radiography is the only helpful noninvasive method for an early diagnosis. Erosion of the cortical bone may cause a postauricular swelling, sug-

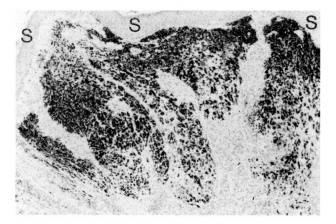

FIGURE 61-1. Biopsy of ear canal mass, immunostaining for desmin (×100 original magnification). The black-staining rhabdomyosarcoma (RMS) cell infiltration is massive under the ear canal skin (S). This 4-year-old boy presented in December 1987 with a mass in the right ear canal. Diagnosis of botryoid embryonal RMS was made after a delay of 3 months. Immunostaining was positive for desmin, muscle-related actin, and myf4 transcript factor. Computed tomographic scanning placed the process to group 3 in the Intergroup Rhabdomyosarcoma Study Group (IRS) clinical classification. Multidrug chemotherapy and irradiation were started according to protocol IRS 3. The ear became deaf after 6 months. As biopsies from canal skin and promontory mucosa remained positive, late surgery was performed in March 1989. The medial half of the canal skin was removed with remnants of the tympanic membrane, the canal closure being aided by the musculoperiosteal flap. Necrotic tumor was removed from the mastoid, around the labyrinth and facial nerve. The bare dural and sigmoid sinus surfaces were débrided with a large diamond drill. Viable tumor from the carotid region, petrous apex, and peritubal cells was removed by drilling to healthy surfaces. The large cavity was obliterated with abdominal fat. Chemotherapy ended in May 1990. The tumor-free period is now 13 years.

gesting mastoid involvement in otitis media. Spread to the ear canal makes the skin edematous and granulating. Combined with a painless discharge, the condition simulates chronic otitis media associated with external otitis. Large tissue masses and polyps appear less often, but tumor masses occluding the ear canal combined with extensive involvement of the entire temporal bone have been seen in very young children suffering from multisystem LCH (Yu et al, 1994).

LCH is a disease with an idiopathic proliferation of Langerhans' cells or their marrow precursors, a large resident population being present, for example, in skin and bone marrow. The cells have a more or less kidney-shaped nucleus and a rich cytoplasm with an eosinophilic staining. Earlier EG was often misinterpreted as a foreign body granuloma or simple granulation tissue. In electron microscopy, Birbeck granules in the histiocytes are diagnostic but not demonstrable in all cases. The diagnosis became reliable with the use of monoclonal antibodies, first the OKT 6 surface marker reacting with the CD1-positive Langerhans' cells. Presently, the immunohistochemical detection of S-100 antigens in the tissue samples is used for this purpose (Figure 61-2).

Myxomas in the external ear canal are rare benign mesenchymal tumors, and there appear to be no general estimates of their incidence. However, they seem to be relatively frequent among the patients in a recently described Carney's symptom complex, a familial disorder transmitted as an autosomal dominant trait. The signs of the complex include myxomas, spotty pigmentation, endocrine overactivity, and melanotic schwannomas (Carney, 1995; Ferreiro and Carney, 1994). In a series of 152 such patients, there were 22 with a myxoma in the external ear and/or the ear canal, and in 2, it was the presenting sign of the complex. The individual case reports (Palva et al, 1991) reflect the rarity of solitary myxomas in the ear canal without relation to Carney's complex. We suspect, however, that there are cases with a misinterpreted diagnosis as it may be possible to remove a pedunculated narrow stalk myxoma without recurrence under a label of an ear canal polyp or cyst.

Myxomas may appear as single or multiple tumors in the external ear, ear canal, or both. In the ear canal, they often form multiple round, circumscribed, and translucent mucoid "pearls," varying in diameter from 1 to 20 mm, surfaced by the canal skin. At times they may extend onto the tympanic membrane (Palva et al, 1991). They also appear as pedunculated polypoid formations or more seldom as a soft tissue mass filling the entire external ear canal (Ferreiro and Carney, 1994). There is seldom pain, and discharge is absent, except in cases with large tumor masses. When considering the diagnosis, the otolaryngologist should examine the patient's face and oral cavity for spotty pigmentation, which is the most frequent associated sign. Simultaneously, signs for the less

often appearing endocrine disorders, Cushing's syndrome and acromegaly, are observed. When the diagnosis becomes confirmed, a transthoracal echocardiography is ordered to exclude myxomas of the heart.

Myxoid lesions derive from connective tissue and are histologically subdivided into a large variety of tumors, which, in the ear canal, represent the cutaneous subtype of the mainstream myxomas. They consist chiefly of polyhedral and stellate fibroblastoid cells, loosely embedded in the soft mucoid matrix. Scattered multinucleated cells appear regularly. The gelatinous material in the ground substance stains positively with alcian blue and periodic acid–Schiff. Lacking specific elements, the diagnosis is often misinterpreted. The correct one was initially made in only 3 of 15 patients with ear canal myxoma (Ferreiro

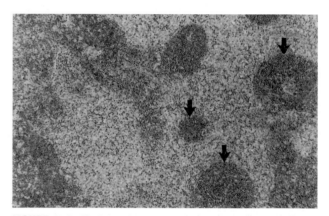

FIGURE 61-2. Neck lymph node, normal architecture destroyed by eosinophilic granuloma cells with kidney-shaped nuclei, and large eosinophilic cytoplasm. *Arrows* point to normal remaining follicles (hematoxylin-eosin stain; ×100 original magnification). This boy was 13 years old when presenting in 1977 with a cauliflower-type tumor in the left ear canal; biopsy gave a diagnosis of eosinophilic granuloma (EG). A few months earlier, a solitary lesion had been found in the femur, and during successive years, he had several similar lesions in the long bones, treated with irradiation. Both temporal bones became involved, and he received surgery in 1978 followed by full doses of irradiation. The right ear became deaf owing to tumor-caused osteolysis of the promontory in 1987; extensive surgery resulted in facial nerve injury. In 1990, a massive recurrence became apparent in the left ear. The granulomatous canal skin was excised and the ear canal was closed. Tumor masses were meticulously removed from the mastoid, perilabyrinthine spaces, and peritubal cells, and the bare dural surfaces were débrided with the diamond. Injury to the facial nerve occurred. The extensive cavity was treated with a solution of 5-fluorouracil and filled with abdominal fat. In 1993, a positive neck node was removed; its normal structure was largely replaced by tumor cells (figure), which reacted positively with S-100 antibody. A similar node appeared in 2000; both areas received 7 Gy irradiation. In 2002, the left ear had a hearing level of 55 dB with good bone conduction. Eye closure is satisfactory, and there is good tonus around the mouth with limited movements. Owing to involvement of several tissues, the initial diagnosis of EG has been changed to an intermediate form of LCH. At present, after 25 years of disease, the patient appears healed but is followed annually.

and Carney, 1994). In the presence of an extensive amount of blood vessels, the cutaneous form is also referred to as angiomyxoma. Myxomas arising from the peripheral nerve sheath (neurothekeomas) are extremely rare; only one such case has been reported (Youngs et al, 1989).

The problem with these three groups of tumors, together with some other extremely rare malignancies involving the ear canal, is that an average practitioner hardly even remembers their existence. Rather, he or she proceeds with a treatment of chronic otitis media, assuming the mass in the ear canal to belong automatically to the group of innocent polyps or simple granulation tissue. This may delay arrival to a proper diagnosis by several months, and in RMS and LCH, this may be fatal to the patient.

Differential Diagnosis, Biopsy, and Other Immediate Measures

At present, if we see a patient with small polyps or granulation tissue in the region of Shrapnell's membrane with a history of chronic otitis media, we do not perform a biopsy but order computed tomographic (CT) scans of the temporal bones. If there is a cholesteatoma that is limited to Prussak's space and to the attic compartments, radiologic osteolytic changes appear at the same site, whereas the mastoid air cells remain cloudy without osteolysis. In such a case, we consider the small polyps to indicate a cholesteatomatous process in Prussak's space and schedule the patient for tympanoplastic/mastoid surgery.

The finding of a solitary, roundish osteolytic lesion with well-defined edges involving the mastoid, with a uniform soft tissue density, suggests the presence of an EG. In such a situation, as much polypoid tissue that can conveniently be biopsied will be sent to the pathologist with a note of a suspicion for EG. Similarly, if a cholesteatoma also involves the mastoid, a radiologic differential diagnosis may not succeed, and it would be wise to make the biopsy first, in preparation for more extensive surgery necessary in EG.

When large polyps or granulation tissue fill the ear canal, it is important to remember that malignant lesions mimic inflammatory diseases and that they may coexist. A gentle evaluation of the lesion and of its attachments to the ear canal skin is made. Some RMS cases are limited to the ear canal, similarly to cutaneous myxomas, and the CT scans return negative. These two diseases should then be considered as the likely diagnoses. At present, soft tissue masses in different middle ear compartments suggest—in developed countries—RMS or, more seldom, a multisystem LCH rather than chronic otitis media. In developing countries, such extensive changes are frequently seen in chronic otitis media.

Unplanned biopsies in RMS should be avoided as they may activate the tumor to progression. We concur

with the thinking (Anderson et al, 1990) that the child should be admitted to an academic pediatric hospital for a full general evaluation regarding RMS and LCH, the workup being followed by a planned biopsy under general anesthesia. The entire mass from the ear canal is removed together with the involved portion of the canal skin. Under the same anesthesia, the nasopharynx is examined, and the pediatrician can perform bone marrow aspiration or a lumbar puncture.

In the past, the procedures did not always follow this protocol (see Figure 61-1), or biopsies reported negative may have been made elsewhere. Both the otologist and the pathologist may initially miss the diagnosis, the former by inexperience and the latter by making use of only routine histologic staining methods. If we see a reply of "polyps and/or granulation tissue" in such cases, the protocol starts from the beginning. Both formalin-fixed and fresh tissue from the mass is sent with a note of the likely clinical diagnoses.

We saw an example of improper management of ear canal tumors in a case in which an attempt had been made nine times to remove a recurrence. The otologist had interpreted them as polyps and repeatedly obtained reports confirming "cystic or polypoid changes." When the circumscribed tumors involving both the anterior canal skin and a portion of the tympanic membrane were removed with a clear margin, the pathologist was asked to look for a myxoma. This diagnosis was also consistent with the earlier specimens (Palva et al, 1991).

General Outlines for Further Special Treatment

The treatment of children in whom simple polyps and granulation tissue in the ear canal are attributable to chronic otitis media is the responsibility of otolaryngology departments. We outlined earlier the necessary steps for aural microsurgery (Palva et al, 2001) and will not repeat them in detail. In changes limited to Prussak's space, the surgical steps include laser evaporation of its anterior membrane and removal of the granulation tissue from the posterior pouch. Prussak's space then becomes open via the anterior pouch to the anterior mesotympanum and via the lower lateral attic to the posterior mesotympanum. A small piece of cartilage placed into the lateral malleal space medial to the skin at the site of Shrapnell's membrane eliminates retractions. An inflammatory process in the major compartments superior to the epitympanic diaphragm suggests that the aeration pathway via the tympanic isthmus is reduced or blocked. In such cases, we emphasize the necessity of simultaneous removal of the tensor fold, creating a large new aeration route from the supratubal recess directly to the anterior epitympanum.

The treatment of RMS of the ear has changed radically during the latter half of the twentieth century. During the early decades from the 1950s, the initial treatment was surgery combined with radiation therapy, and the patients generally died of intracranial extension of the disease. With the development of new and more potent chemotherapeutic agents, the chances for a cure have become much better for RMS patients in general, and, presently, multiagent chemotherapy is of decisive importance in treatment.

If the extent of the lesion is favorable for a complete resection, in our organization, the ear surgeon removes the tumor as early as possible without sacrificing vital structures, and pediatric oncologists continue with multidrug chemotherapy and irradiation in accordance with the latest IRS treatment protocols. Applied in the early stage, chemotherapy has the best effect against microscale metastatic spread of RMS. In patients not operated on initially, it results in rapid diminution in the size of the tumor. If magnetic resonance imaging still suggests rests of tumor tissue, late-stage surgery is considered. It is always performed by a highly experienced ear surgeon who is used to working around the labyrinth, facial nerve, and carotid canal (see Figure 61-1).

Children with LCH and EG also need a team of otologists and pediatricians for effective treatment. After assessment of the findings, surgery is the first line of treatment in solitary lesions in EG. The entire tumor in the temporal bone is removed as totally as possible without harming the facial nerve or the labyrinth. If the removal is considered incomplete for any reason, treatment is continued in the first place with full-dose irradiation. However, chemotherapy is another possibility and must be weighed individually. In multisystem LCH, and especially in young children with a fulminant disease, only the ear canal tumor is removed for biopsy, and multiagent chemotherapy is started as first-line treatment.

The treatment of ear canal myxomas is surgery. The skin carrying the lesion(s) is excised with a clear margin. This may also necessitate partial removal of the pars tensa adjacent to the annular rim. The defect is patched with a thin fascia, which, in the ear canal, should also surface the bare bone and extend under the cut edge of the intact skin.

Prognosis

In inflammatory polyps, the prognosis is excellent up to healing of the chronic ear inflammation and restitution of hearing. The results are better if the surgeon is experienced and used to handling different forms of chronic ear disease. Ear surgery in children should never be left to learning members of the staff without strict supervision.

In RMS of the temporal bone, the prognosis used to be poor. Of 12 patients from 1966 to 1988 (Wiatrak and Pensal, 1989), there were two survivals when treated using varying combinations of treatment modalities. In another series (Anderson et al, 1990) of 60 children with a head and neck RMS, the overall mortality of 50% in 1970 to 1979 decreased to 23% between 1980 and 1987, but none of the 6 patients with RMS of the ear survived. In the final IRS study (Maurer et al, 1988), the overall survival in RMS rose to 70 to 80%. The latest study (Hawkins et al, 2001) of the total IRS material of 179 children with middle ear RMS, between 1972 and 1997, gave a 67% 5-year failure-free survival. When successive IRS studies were compared, there was great improvement in the 3-year failure-free survival rates, from the initial 42% to the last 88%. The development of new drugs and methods for multiagent chemotherapy and the earlier diagnosis were the reasons for this outcome. Prognosis is good in the rare cases limited to the ear canal (Markkanen et al, 1996) and in localized tumors in which the surgical removal appears complete (Hawkins et al, 2001).

For multisystem disseminated LCH, the mortality rate has been estimated as 40% (Anderson et al, 1990). In very young children with disseminated fulminant disease, the prognosis has been poor, but encouraging reports exist when, for example, a disease involving the ear canal as well as the entire temporal bone up to the petrous apex healed with chemotherapy using etoposide (Yu et al, 1994). The intermediate forms with lesions of bone, skin, and mucous membranes and with organ dysfunctions may have a semimalignant, varyingly long, indolent course, whereas solitary lesions of bone are considered curable.

Clinical experience has shown that EG in the temporal bone differs unfavorably from solitary lesions in the long bones, which heal after surgical curettage or irradiation or without any treatment. The difference may be attributable to the clonality of the lesion with a highly varying biologic behavior (Beverley and Abbas, 1994). In EG of the temporal bone, when diagnosed early, surgery may be decisive. Recurring tumors may show involvement of the canal skin and of all middle ear crevices and be extremely resistant to all modes of treatment (see Figure 62-2). Recent studies indeed suggest that in this disease, the changes might not just be attributable to polyclonal reactive proliferations of Langerhans' cells but would represent clonal neoplastic processes with varying degrees of malignancy (Beverley and Abbas, 1994; Willman et al, 1994).

Cutaneous myxomas of the ear are not life-threatening but demand excision with a good margin. Otherwise, recurrences are certain. It is important to make a correct diagnosis and thus identify patients at risk for Carney's complex. The most serious component of this syndrome, cardiac myxoma, is lethal if undiagnosed and, when diagnosed late, may be associated with serious complications of surgery. It should also be remembered that they appear generally in the age range of 35 to 60 years and may be preceded for long periods by cutaneous myxomas (Carney, 1995; Ferreiro and Carney, 1994).

Conclusion

There is often delay in the treatment of malignant tumors of the ear because they are so rare and the inflammatory diseases are so much more frequent. Early diagnosis of malignomas, of both RMS and LCH, is of great importance for successful treatment. Every time the examining physician of whatever schooling notices a soft tissue mass in the ear canal of a child, he or she should, as the first choice, consider it malignant and send the patient to an academic center for further evaluation. Obtaining the right biopsy diagnosis without delay contributes to better survival of these patients. Improved percentages for permanent cure rest basically in the continuous development of new chemotherapeutic agents for both RMS and LCH. Multicenter trials should be encouraged, and each center should have a team of specialists who evaluate the patients jointly and who are, in turn, responsible for the specific phases of treatment.

References

Anderson GL, Tom LWC, Womer, RB, et al. Rhabdomyosarcoma of the head and neck in children. Arch Otolaryngol Head Neck Surg 1990;116:428–31.

Beverley PCL, Abbas AK. The scientific challenge of Langerhans' cell histiocytosis. Br J Cancer 1994;70 Suppl 70:61–4.

Carney JA. Carney complex: the complex of myxomas, spotty pigmentation, endocrine overactivity, and schwannomas. Semin Dermatol 1995;14:90–8.

Feldman BA. Rhabdomyosarcoma of the head and neck. Laryngoscope 1982;92:424–40.

Ferreiro JA, Carney JA. Myxomas of the external ear and their significance. Am J Surg Pathol 1994;18:274–80.

Gliklich RE, Cunningham MJ, Eavey RD. The cause for aural polyps in children. Arch Otolaryngol Head Neck Surg 1993; 119:669–71.

Hawkins DS, Anderson JR, Paidas CN, et al. Improved outcome for patients with middle ear rhabdomyosarcoma: a children's oncology study group. J Clin Oncol 2001;19:3073–9.

Markkanen A, Vornanen M, Riikonen P. Rhabdomyosarcoma in the external ear canal in a 3-year old boy [in Finnish]. Duodecim 1996;112:1005–9.

Maurer HM, Beltangady M, Gehan EA, et al. The Intergroup Rhabdomyosarcoma Study-1. A final report. Cancer 1988;61: 209–20.

McCaffrey TV, McDonald TJ. Histiocytosis X of the ear and temporal bone: review of 22 cases. Laryngoscope 1979;89:1735–42.

Palva T, Ramsay H, Northrop C. Color atlas of the anatomy and pathology of the epitympanum. Basel: Karger; 2001.

Palva T, Saksela E, Ramsay H. Myxoma of the external auditory meatus. J Laryngol Otol 1991;105:364–6.

Quraishi MS, Blaynay AW, Breatnach F. Aural symptoms as primary presentation of Langerhans' cell histiocytosis. Clin Otolaryngol 1993;18:317–23.

Thomas C, Donnadieu J, Emile JF, Brousse N. Langerhans' cell histiocytosis [in French]. Arch Pediatr 1996;3:63–9.

Wiatrak BJ, Pensak ML. Rhabdomyosarcoma of the ear and temporal bone. Laryngoscope 1989;99:1188–92.

Willman CL, Busque L, Griffith BB, et al. Langerhans' cell histiocytosis (histiocytosis X) a clonal proliferative disease. N Engl J Med 1994;331:154–60.

Young JL Jr, Miller RW. Incidence of malignant tumors in U.S. children. J Pediatr 1975;86:254–8.

Youngs R, Kwok P, Hyams M, Hyams VJ. Neurothekeoma (peripheral nerve sheath myxoma) of the external auditory canal. J Otolaryngol 1989;18:90–3.

Yu LC, Schenoy S, Ward K, Warrier RP. Successful treatment of multisystem Langerhans' cell histiocytosis (histiocytosis X) with etoposide. Am J Pediatr Hemat Oncol 1994;16:275–7.

VII. Complications of Otitis Media

Chapter 62

WHEN TO SUSPECT COMPLICATED SUPPURATIVE OTITIS MEDIA

VEDANTAM RUPA, MS, DLO

Complications of suppurative otitis media (SOM) were a major cause of mortality and morbidity in the preantibiotic era but have shown a considerable decline in recent times. In 1935, Kafka reported a prevalence of 6.4% for intracranial complications. Sixty years later, in the antibiotic era, the prevalence of such cases was reported as < 0.36% (Kangsanarak et al, 1995). At our hospital, we have found the annual incidence of complicated SOM to have decreased from 12 to 15 cases per year in the 1980s to approximately 6 per year in the 1990s (Rupa and Jacob, unpublished data, 2002). The advent of broader-spectrum antimicrobial agents, greater availability of medical care, widespread immunization, and an aggressive surgical intervention to remove mastoid foci of infection are some of the factors that seem to have contributed significantly to the decline.

Complications occur when the underlying disease process spreads beyond the confines of the middle ear cleft through direct bone erosion, osteothrombophlebitis, or preformed pathways. Intracranial complications that occur owing to extension of infection to the cranial compartment include meningitis, brain abscess (temporal lobe abscess or cerebellar abscess), extradural abscess, subdural empyema, lateral sinus thrombosis, and otitic hydrocephalus. Extracranial complications, which are produced by spread of infection within the temporal bone, include mastoid abscess, labyrinthitis, facial paralysis, and petrositis. Complications may occur secondary to either acute suppurative otitis media (ASOM) or chronic suppurative otitis media (CSOM). Definitions of ASOM and CSOM vary from one publication to another, and the need to clearly define the entity being described has been stressed

(Bluestone et al, 2002). ASOM is defined here as an acute infection of the middle ear cleft characterized by recent (< 2 days) onset of earache and fever with or without otorrhea and the presence of a dull or congested tympanic membrane (TM) with or without a perforation. CSOM is defined here as an entity characterized by the presence of purulent ear discharge in a patient with a perforation or retraction of either the pars tensa or pars flaccida of the TM along with granulations and/or cholesteatoma.

What clinical factors predispose a patient to develop complications? In an analysis of 360 patients with CSOM operated on at our hospital (Rupa and Raman, 1991), we found that the 122 patients who had complications were younger ($p < .001$) and had a shorter duration of ear discharge ($p < .001$) (Tables 62-1 and 62-2). The presence of cholesteatoma was not predictive of a complication as patients with granulations alone were equally prone (Table 62-3). Knowledge of such predictors assists us in determining which type of patient is more likely to develop a complication.

TABLE 62-1. Age Distribution of Patients with and without Complications of Chronic Suppurative Otitis Media

Age (yr)	Number of Patients (%)		p Value
	Uncomplicated	Complicated	
< 10	23 (9.7)	42 (34.4)	< .001
11–20	120 (50.4)	52 (42.6)	
21–30	63 (26.5)	16 (13.1)	
> 40	32 (13.4)	12 (9.8)	
	238	122	

TABLE 62-2. Duration of Ear Discharge in Patients with and without Complications

| Duration (yr) | Number of Patients (%) | | p Value |
	Uncomplicated	Complicated	
< 1	16 (6.7)	23 (18.9)	< .002
1–5	94 (39.5)	47 (38.5)	
> 5	128 (53.8)	52 (42.6)	
	238	122	

Intracranial Complications

Concomitant with the decline in the number of cases of complicated SOM, the clinical presentation of patients, particularly those with intracranial complications, has changed considerably. This is largely owing to the masking effect on clinical features by the widespread use of antibiotics. A high index of suspicion and familiarity with the clinical features of impending complications are essential to avoid missing a complication.

In up to one-third of cases, more than one complication may be present simultaneously (Ludman, 1997). When two or more complications occur simultaneously, the clinical features of one complication may be prominent and the others may be diagnosed only on further testing. Table 62-4 lists the common symptoms and signs in patients with SOM that should alert the clinician to an impending complication. The symptoms have been subdivided into nonspecific and specific categories (see Table 62-4) in those in whom an intracranial complication is suspected. In a patient with CSOM, the recent onset of two or more nonspecific symptoms or one specific symptom or sign is sufficient to initiate investigations to exclude a complication. In a patient with ASOM, complications should be suspected if after 1 week of appropriate antibiotic therapy, symptoms such as fever and earache do not resolve or if otorrhea persists. The development of additional symptoms and signs, as detailed in Table 62-4, should also be carefully ascertained.

Classic descriptions of symptoms and signs in conditions such as brain abscess and lateral sinus thrombosis (Shambaugh, 1990) are seldom seen in this era. In our experience, the clinical distinction between early and late symptoms and signs as noted by some authors (Schwaber et al, 1989) cannot be made in patients who have had prior antibiotic therapy. Analysis of a series of 40 patients who presented to our hospital within the last 5 years with suspected complications of SOM revealed that there was no statistically significant difference between the 29 patients with radiologically evident intracranial complications and the 11 patients without (Table 62-5) when symptoms such as headache, earache, fever, and increased otorrhea are considered (Rupa and Jacob, unpublished data, 2002). Further, clinical differentiation between the various intracranial complications so lucidly described in descriptions of cases from the preantibiotic era is currently impossible. We have found that high-grade fever (> 100°F), headache, papilledema, and neck stiffness, although suggestive of a complication, might occur with equal frequency in a patient with either subdural abscess, cerebellar abscess, or meningitis.

Diagnosis in these patients is best made by radiologic imaging. We have found that a contrast-enhanced computed tomographic (CECT) scan of the brain is perhaps the most valuable investigation in patients with suspected complications. Although magnetic resonance imaging (MRI) provides better soft tissue definition, it is considerably more expensive. CT provides considerable bony detail, which is essential to demonstrate bone erosion and is preferred for this reason.

Besides providing conclusive evidence of a space-occupying complication of SOM, a CECT scan of the brain is also important in differentiating such a patient from one with meningitis. Too often has a CECT scan of the brain been omitted in favor of lumbar puncture because of a suspicion of meningitis (most often in a sick, febrile child with papilledema). The resultant herniation

TABLE 62-3. Otoscopic Findings in Patients with and without Complications

| Otoscopic Finding | Number of Patients (%) | | p Value |
	Uncomplicated	Complicated	
Cholesteatoma	182 (75.3)	93 (76.3)	0.8
Granulations	60 (24.8)	29 (23.7)	
	238	122	

TABLE 62-4. Clinical Features in Suspected Complicated Otitis Media

Intracranial Complications

Symptoms	Signs
Nonspecific	Neck stiffness
Headache	Contralateral upper motor neuron
Fever	facial paresis
Increased otorrhea	Aphasia (left temporal lobe lesion)
Earache	Cerebellar signs (ataxia, past-pointing,
Specific	nystagmus)
Drowsiness	Papilledema
Altered sensorium	Sixth nerve palsy
Seizures	Tenderness along internal jugular vein
Ataxia	Positive Kernig's sign
Diplopia	
Blurred vision	

Extracranial Complications

Increased otorrhea	Mastoid tenderness
Earache	Postaural swelling/fistula
Headache	Sensorineural hearing loss on audiometry
Increasing hearing loss	Sixth cranial nerve palsy
Vertigo	Lower motor neuron seventh cranial
Vomiting	nerve palsy
Deviation of angle of	Swelling around mastoid/zygoma
mouth	Spontaneous nystagmus
Diplopia	Positive fistula sign

TABLE 62-5. Distribution of Clinical Features at Presentation in Patients with Suspected and Documented Intracranial Complications of Chronic and Acute Suppurative Otitis Media

| Clinical Feature | Number of Patients (%) | | |
	Uncomplicated (n = 29)	Complicated (n = 11)	p Value
Headache	28 (96.6)	11 (100)	1.000
Increased otorrhea	10 (34.5)	3 (27.3)	1.000
Earache	10 (34.5)	7 (63.6)	.153
Fever	19 (65.5)	5 (45.5)	.295
Features of meningeal irritation*	14 (48.3)	1 (9.1)	.030[†]
Features of raised intracranial tension[‡]	15 (51.7)	2[§] (18.2)	.079
Focal neurologic deficit[‖]	9 (31.0)	0 (0)	.043[†]

*Neck stiffness, positive Kernig's sign.
[†]Statistically significant.
[‡]Papilledema, sixth cranial nerve palsy.
[§]Two patients without radiologic evidence of intracranial complication were diagnosed to have papilledema by the attending physician.
[‖]Homonymous hemianopia, upper motoneuron lesion seventh cranial nerve palsy, aphasia, cerebellar signs.

of the cerebellar tonsils owing to a sudden fall in pressure (coning) in the presence of an underlying, undetected brain abscess is the unfortunate cause of death in these patients. It has been our practice to emphasize to pediatricians and internists who may be unfamiliar with the changing presentation of complicated SOM that it is important to exclude an intracranial suppurative space-occupying lesion by CECT scanning of the brain prior to performing lumbar puncture, however "typical" the case may be. Figure 62-1 outlines our recommended protocol for the management of patients with suspected intracranial complications.

Individual intracranial complications owing to ASOM/CSOM are described below to highlight certain diagnostic features.

Meningitis

In patients with suspected meningitis, headache, fever, and neck stiffness are usually present but are not diagnostic. After excluding an intracranial space-occupying complication such as an abscess with CECT scanning of the brain, a lumbar puncture may be performed to confirm the diagnosis. In meningitis, cerebrospinal fluid (CSF) is turbid, usually with raised pressure, pleocytosis, raised protein, low sugar, and low chloride levels. Bacteriologic examination may be positive in untreated cases. Although a brain abscess leaking into the subarachnoid space or subdural empyema may produce a similar CSF picture, the CSF sugar levels are generally not so low.

A case of partially treated pyogenic meningitis may occasionally be confused with tuberculous meningitis based on the CSF picture of pleocytosis with lympho-

cytes predominant. This is a dilemma occasionally faced by us and probably by physicians in other developing countries where tuberculosis is highly prevalent and can manifest as meningitis. The suspicion is heightened if the otoscopic picture is one of CSOM with granulations and no cholesteatoma suggesting tuberculous OM with mastoiditis. Diagnosis here depends on response to appropriate antibiotic therapy and surgical treatment of the mastoid focus. A negative acid-fast bacillus (AFB) smear and culture of both CSF and ear granulations, as well as absence of granulomata on the histopathology of ear granulations, are confirmatory. However, a patient presenting with meningitis and otoscopic evidence of SOM is more likely to have pyogenic rather than tuberculous meningitis.

In patients with meningitis following ASOM, particularly if the history of meningitis has been recurrent, it is also important to exclude a congenital inner ear defect such as Mondini's deformity. High-resolution CT scans with 1.5 mm sections of the temporal bone or thin-slice T_2-weighted MRIs are invaluable in arriving at this diagnosis.

Brain Abscess

The early stages of temporal lobe or cerebellar abscess formation produce symptoms of an infective focus with fever, headache, and earache. If antibiotics have been administered, fever is not present. The later stages produce symptoms of raised intracranial pressure and focal neurologic deficit. For a temporal lobe abscess, this includes altered sensorium, homonymous hemianopia, aphasia (if the abscess is left-sided), and facial hemiparesis. For cerebellar abscess, gait ataxia, coarse intention tremor, nystagmus, and past-pointing are typical.

The early symptoms of brain abscess may be masked by antibiotics prescribed by a general practitioner. The patient is often not brought to a specialist until the later symptoms and signs appear. Features of concomitant meningitis or lateral sinus thrombosis may predominate while the abscess enlarges; hence, clinical features at this stage are unreliable. CECT scanning of the brain is diagnostic. In brain abscess, the classic ring lesion produced by a hypodense central area (owing to pus) and an enhancing rim (produced by the abscess wall) is characteristically seen. When the abscess capsule has not formed, only hypodense areas with patchy enhancement suggestive of cerebritis or cerebellitis are visible. At our hospital, we have found that cerebellar abscesses are slightly more common than temporal lobe abscesses.

Extradural Abscess

Extradural abscesses are a common intracranial complication that may present with earache and increased otorrhea or be asymptomatic and a chance finding at surgery. In CECT scanning of the brain, an extradural abscess is visualized as a hypodense area between the dura and

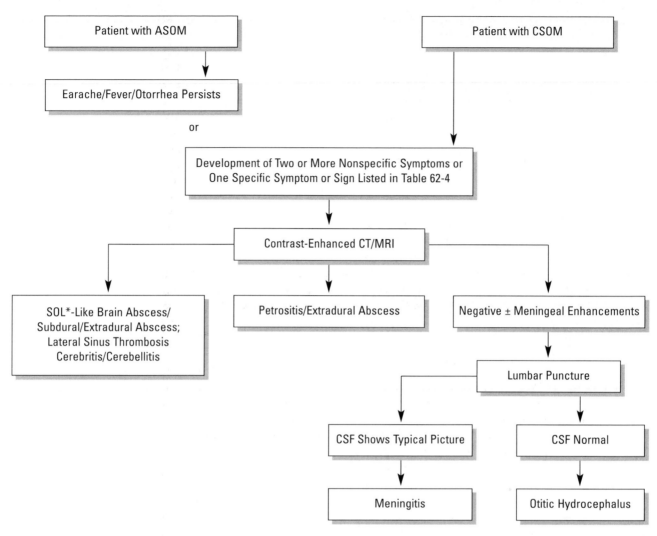

FIGURE 62-1. Diagnostic protocol for suspected complications of suppurative otitis media. ASOM = acute suppurative otitis media; CSF = cerebrospinal fluid; CSOM = chronic suppurative otitis media; CT = computed tomography; MRI = magnetic resonance imaging; SOL = space-occupying lesion.

tegmen or between the sinus plate and sigmoid sinus (perisinus abscess). We have found perisinus abscesses to be more common than extradural abscess related to the tegmen (Rupa and Jacob, 2002).

Subdural Empyema

Patients with subdural empyema present initially with fever and headache similar to patients with brain abscess. However, unlike those with brain abscess, there is rapid progression of symptoms. The onset of seizures, hemiparesis, aphasia, and hemianopia often occurs within a few hours. The patient also appears very toxic. In our series of 29 patients with intracranial complications, only patients with subdural empyema presented with seizures (Rupa and Jacob, unpublished data, 2002). CECT scanning of the brain shows hypodense areas owing to pus collection in the subdural space and is diagnostic.

Lateral Sinus Thrombosis

Persistent fever, otalgia, and neck pain along the upper end of the sternocleidomastoid muscle are the usual features of lateral sinus thrombosis. We rarely encounter patients with isolated lateral sinus thrombosis. Cerebellar abscess and meningitis are the two other complications often occurring concomitantly, and their presence may mask the clinical features of sinus thrombosis. CECT scanning of the brain, if positive, is diagnostic. In lateral sinus thrombosis, the classic "delta" sign, a triangular area with central hypodensity (owing to the thrombus) and peripheral dural enhancement, may occasionally be seen. The more definitive investigation is MRI. The radiologic findings on MRI are highly variable and depend on the degree of residual flow and the age of the thrombus (Marks, 2002). In the early or acute phase (first 3 to 5 days) of venous thrombosis, an isointense signal on T_1-weighted images and a hypointense signal on T_2-weighted images have been described. In the subacute phase (5 to 30 days later), the thrombus becomes hyperintense on T_1- and T_2-weighted images. In our experience, diagnosis is easily established in the majority of cases by intraoperative findings of discolored dura over the sinus and absence of blood on aspiration of the sinus with a wide-bore needle. Associated perisinus abscess with granulations is commonly seen.

Otitic Hydrocephalus

This complication is rarely seen by itself and is usually associated with lateral sinus thrombosis. It may be suspected in a patient with papilledema, drowsiness, headache, and blurred vision in whom CT scanning is normal and lumbar puncture shows CSF that is normal except for high pressure. In our recent series of 29 cases with intracranial complications of SOM, we did not encounter a single patient with this condition (Rupa and Jacob, unpublished data, 2002).

Extracranial Complications

The diagnosis of extracranial complications is more clearcut. They occur secondary to the spread of infections intratemporally beyond the confines of the middle ear cleft and include mastoid abscess, facial paralysis, labyrinthitis, and petrositis. Table 62-4 lists common symptoms and signs in extracranial complications.

Mastoid Abscess

Mastoid abscesses may follow ASOM or CSOM. In our experience, they are commonly seen following CSOM and are generally located subperiosteally in the postaural region. In a series of 122 patients with complicated CSOM we operated on, more than 50% of those with extracranial complications were found to have mastoid abscess (Rupa and Raman, 1991). Occasionally, cases of Bezold's abscess with pus deep to the sternocleidomastoid muscle and Citelli's abscess with pus deep to the posterior belly of the digastric muscle are seen. Luc's abscess, a collection in the zygomatic area, is infrequently seen. The abscess location depends on the degree of pneumatization of the mastoid air cell system. Occasionally, the abscess may have burst, and a postaural fistula results.

Patients with ASOM present with high-grade fever and postaural swelling pushing the pinna outward. In children, irritability, failure to feed, and vomiting are common. Patients with CSOM present less dramatically and fever may not be present, although earache is a common feature. We have found that in patients with CSOM and a postaural fistula, differentiation from tuberculous mastoiditis is important, particularly in patients who have noncholesteatomatous ear disease. Thorough exenteration of air cells and submission of excised granula-

tions for histopathology, as well as culture and sensitivity (both routine and for AFB), are essential in these cases.

Labyrinthitis

Labyrinthitis following ASOM or CSOM may be either diffuse or circumscribed. The diffuse type may be further subclassified as serous or suppurative. Serous labyrinthitis is characterized by the presence of vertigo, vomiting, and sensorineural hearing loss. A positive fistula sign is present. The patient may complain of diplacusis or sound distortion. Pure-tone audiometry reveals a high-frequency hearing loss initially that progressively spreads to the other frequencies. If treated promptly, vestibular symptoms resolve completely, and hearing gain may occur. The diagnosis of serous labyrinthitis is, therefore, usually made in retrospect, after hearing assessment.

In suppurative labyrinthitis, which is less common, there is progression of hearing loss, which may become severe to profound. Fistula sign is negative because of the absence of a functioning labyrinth. Spontaneous nystagmus with the fast component beating toward the affected ear is present. The patient has gross imbalance, and differentiation from ataxia of cerebellar origin is important. Clinical differentiation from a patient with intracranial complications is difficult, and CECT scanning of the brain will be required for exclusion.

Circumscribed labyrinthitis, which is most often seen in CSOM and produced by localized cholesteatomatous bone erosion, for example, over the lateral semicircular canal, is the most common type of labyrinthitis we see. Such patients present with symptoms of imbalance and vertigo, which is often positional. Occasionally, nausea and vomiting are present, particularly when microscopic suction clearance of the ear is performed. Fistula sign is usually positive. Sensorineural hearing loss may or may not be present. Diagnosis is usually evident at surgery.

Facial Paralysis

Facial paralysis secondary to ASOM has a dramatic onset accompanied by fever, earache, and, occasionally, pus discharge. It may be partial or complete. In patients with CSOM, paralysis is most often secondary to erosion of the bony facial canal by cholesteatoma or granulations; hence, the onset of facial weakness, as evidenced by the inability of the patient to close his eyes and deviation of the angle of mouth, occurs gradually. CT scanning is not essential in facial paralysis secondary to ASOM unless a concomitant intracranial complication is suspected.

Petrositis

Petrositis is a comparatively less frequently encountered complication of SOM. The condition more often follows ASOM than CSOM because it occurs in well-pneumatized bones. In CSOM, there is often considerable mastoid sclerosis, which limits the spread of infection to the petrous apex. Rarely, erosion of bone right up to the petrous apex by cholesteatoma or granulations may occur.

Petrositis should be suspected in any patient with ASOM or CSOM who develops deep-seated earache and retro-orbital pain, increased or persistent otorrhea, and sixth cranial nerve palsy. All of the components of this classic triad (which constitutes Gradenigo's syndrome) are not always seen because of modification by antimicrobial therapy. Associated seventh cranial nerve palsy and vertigo may be present. In 2 of 29 patients with complicated SOM that we have recently seen, petrositis occurred secondary to ASOM. These patients had the complete triad of Gradenigo's syndrome.

CECT scanning of the temporal bone with axial and coronal cuts of the petrous apex is useful in delineating the presence of petrositis and differentiating it from an extradural abscess in relation to the petrous apex, which may present in a similar fashion. Per orbital view of the petrous pyramids or Stenvers view may be useful in those situations in which CT scanning facilities are not available.

Conclusion

Complications of SOM are rarer today than ever before and have a markedly different presentation from the pre-antibiotic era. Complications should be suspected in any patient with ASOM who has persistent earache, fever, or otorrhea or who develops characteristic clinical features, as described above. In CSOM, the development of new clinical features in addition to otorrhea may herald a complication. Familiarity with the common clinical presentation of complications, as seen currently in an era in which antibi-

otic therapy masks early symptoms and signs in many, is essential. However, awareness that clinical features alone are, at best, unreliable is important. The need for CECT scanning of the brain in cases of suspected intracranial complications, primarily to establish a diagnosis and secondarily to provide a green light to proceed with lumbar puncture if CT is negative for a space-occupying lesion, should be recognized by the attending clinician.

References

Bluestone CD, Gates GA, Klein JO, et al. Panel reports. Definitions, terminology and classification of otitis media. Ann Otol Rhinol Laryngol 2002;111 Suppl 188:8–18.

Kafka MM. Mortality of mastoiditis and cerebral complications with review of 3225 cases of mastoiditis with complications. Laryngoscope 1935;45:790–822.

Kangsanarak J, Navacharoen N, Fooanant S, Ruckphapunt K. Intracranial complications of suppurative otitis media: 13 years' experience. Am J Otol 1995;16:104–9.

Ludman H. Complications of chronic suppurative otitis media. In: Booth JB, Kerr AG, editors. Scott-Brown's otolaryngology. Oxford (UK): Butterworth-Heinemann; 1997. p. 12–29.

Marks MP. Cerebral ischemia and infarction. In: Atlas SW, editor. Magnetic resonance imaging of the brain and spine. Philadelphia: Lippincott, Williams & Wilkins; 2002. p. 249.

Rupa V, Raman R. Chronic suppurative otitis media: complicated versus uncomplicated disease. Acta Otolaryngol (Stockh) 1991;111:530–5.

Schwaber MK, Pensak ML, Bartels LJ. The early symptoms and signs of neurotologic complications of chronic suppurative otitis media. Laryngoscope 1989;99:373–5.

Shambaugh GE. Intracranial complications of otitis media. In: Glasscock ME, Shambaugh GE, Johnson CD, editors. Surgery of the ear. Philadelphia: WB Saunders; 1990. p. 249–75.

Chapter 63

PERIAURICULAR/ POSTAURICULAR/EXTERNAL EAR CANAL SWELLING

NIRA A. GOLDSTEIN, MD

The differential diagnosis of periauricular/postauricular/ external ear canal swelling includes infections, tumors, and trauma (Table 63-1). Proper diagnosis requires a thorough history, a physical examination, directed radiologic and laboratory studies, and an evaluation of the patient's response to therapy. A lack of improvement with treatment may indicate the need for tissue biopsy.

Otitis Externa

Acute otitis externa is a diffuse cellulitis of the external auditory canal (EAC) that may involve surrounding structures. Accumulation of moisture, removal of protective cerumen, and localized trauma allow invasion of bacteria or fungus into the underlying skin of the EAC. Symptoms include mild to severe otalgia, itching, tenderness with manipulation of the auricle, hearing loss, and otorrhea. Physical examination demonstrates erythema and edema of the EAC skin with exudate. EAC occlusion results in conductive hearing loss. Pinna manipulation or tragal palpation elicits pain. Pre- and postauricular tender adenopathy may be present. Extension of the infection to the auricle and periauricular skin may occur, producing a surrounding cellulitis. Because the skin of the EAC is continuous with the outer epithelial layer of the tympanic membrane, the tympanic membrane may appear inflamed. The middle ear and mastoid are usually normal (Hirsch, 1996).

Cleaning and débridement of the desquamated epithelium and debris are important for diagnosis and treatment. The most common causative bacteria are *Pseudomonas aeruginosa* and *Staphylococcus aureus*, but a variety of other gram-positive cocci and gram-negative rods may be found (Clark et al, 1997; Roland and Stroman, 2002). Both bacterial and fungal cultures are obtained for patients with recurrent or persistent infec-

tion or immunocompromised patients. If possible, the tympanic membrane is visualized to determine whether the otitis externa is secondary to acute otitis media with otorrhea through a tympanic membrane perforation or chronic otitis media with or without cholesteatoma. The presence of either of these conditions or the extension of the infection beyond the confines of the EAC warrants systemic therapy (Thompson, 2001). Ototopical medication is prescribed after the ear is cleaned. If the ear canal

TABLE 63-1. Differential Diagnosis of Periauricular/ Postauricular/External Ear Canal Swelling

Infections
   Otitis externa
      Acute bacterial
      Otomycosis
      Chronic
      Eczematous/allergic
      Bullous myringitis
      Herpes zoster oticus
      Furunculosis
   Acute mastoiditis
   Malignant (necrotizing) otitis externa
   Perichondritis
      Relapsing perichondritis
   Exostoses/osteomas
Common pediatric tumors*
   Fibrous dysplasia
   Langerhans' cell histiocytosis
   Rhabdomyosarcoma
Auricular trauma
   Auricular hematoma
   Bites
   Frostbite
   Burns
Postauricular epidermoid inclusion cyst
External auditory canal cholesteatoma

*A complete listing of pediatric ear and temporal bone tumors is presented in Table 63-4.

swelling prohibits instillation of the eardrops, a wick is placed to facilitate treatment. A variety of ototopical medications may be prescribed to lower the EAC pH, reduce the inflammation, and eliminate the bacteria (Table 63-2). The fluoroquinolone drops have demonstrated efficacy with no risk of ototoxicity, which may be a concern in cases of perforated tympanic membranes. Adjunctive analgesics are indicated when the pain is severe. Water precautions are also instituted.

Chronic otitis externa may result from partially treated acute otitis externa and is usually characterized by symptoms of ear fullness, itchiness, and otorrhea. Predisposing factors must be eliminated, and treatment with ototopical antibiotics and steroid preparations is instituted. Eczematous otitis externa or atopic dermatitis represents the cutaneous expression of systemic aberrant immune reactivity. In the initial stages, there is an erythematous swelling of the pinna and conchal bowl with moist vesicles and pustules. Self-inflicted trauma results from intense itching. The chronic stage is characterized by irritated, dry, scaly skin. Contact dermatitis presents similarly and results from exposure to purulent drainage, nickel and chromium found in earrings, plastic or Silastic found in earmolds, hairsprays, insecticides, poison ivy, and topical neomycin. Treatment is topical and sometimes systemic steroids with topical astringents for acute oozing or weeping and removal of the offending agent if present (Hirsch, 1996).

Acute fungal otitis externa or otomycosis is usually caused by *Aspergillus* species and *Candida albicans*. Aural pruritus and ear fullness are more common complaints than otalgia. Examination reveals mild inflammation and debris with visible hyphae and mycelia. Thorough débridement of the EAC and treatment with acidifying agents, clotrimazole, or antifungal creams (see Table 63-2) are required. In rare cases of local cellulitis, oral fluconazole may be necessary.

Bullous myringitis is characterized by vesicles or bullae seen on the bony portion of the EAC and on the tympanic membrane. It is one of the forms of acute myringitis. The other, hemorrhagic myringitis, consists of hemorrhagic redness of the tympanic membrane. The typical presentation is that of very severe, throbbing otalgia during the course of an upper respiratory infection usually in children, adolescents, and young adults. If the blisters rupture, there is short-lived, blood-stained, watery otorrhea. Sensorineural hearing loss, which is usually self-limited, has been reported, but the mechanism is unknown (Hoffman and Shepsman, 1983; Wetmore and Abramson, 1979). Although early reports associated bullous myringitis with the influenza virus, other viruses, and *Mycoplasma pneumoniae*, more recent investigators have found the same otologic pathogens as in acute otitis media, with *Streptococcus pneumoniae* being the most common (Marais and Dale, 1997; Palmu et al, 2001). In addition, middle ear fluid

has been found in the vast majority of cases in children younger than 2 years of age. Children in this age group should be treated as for acute otitis media. There is no consensus for the treatment of older children and adults, but, generally, analgesics and ototopical agents are recommended, with the addition of oral antibiotics if there is middle ear disease or purulent drainage. Rupture of the vesicles has not been shown to be efficacious. Herpes zoster oticus (Ramsay Hunt syndrome) is characterized by herpetic vesicles on the auricle or in the EAC. Topical acyclovir ointment and systemic acyclovir, valacyclovir, or famciclovir are used for treatment.

Furunculosis arises from an infection of a hair follicle occurring at the junction of the conchal and canal skin. Otalgia, fever, localized subcutaneous swelling and tenderness of the region, and tender lymphadenopathy are found. The tympanic membrane may not be visualized if the abscess is large or there is a diffuse otitis externa. The causative organism is usually *S. aureus*. Early-stage lesions

TABLE 63-2. Medications for Acute Otitis Externa

Acidifying agents
  Acetic acid 2%
  Benzoic acid
  Boric acid
  Salicylic acid
Phenols and alcohols
  Alcohol 95%
  Phenol
  Thymol 1%
General antiseptics
  m-Cresyl acetate 25%
  Gentian violet 2%
  Thimerosal 1:1000
  Povidone-iodine 1%
Antibiotics
  Amphotericin B
  Chloramphenicol
  Ciprofloxacin
  Colistin
  Gentamicin
  Neomycin
  Ofloxacin
  Oxytetracycline
  Polymyxin B
  Sulfanilamide
  Tobramycin
Antifungals
  Clotrimazole
  Fluorocytosine (5-FC)
  Iodochlorhydroxyquin
  Miconazole
  Nystatin
Anti-inflammatories
  Betamethasone
  Desonide
  Dexamethasone
  Hydrocortisone
  Prednisolone

Adapted from Hirsch BE (1996).

with mild swelling may be treated with an oral antistaphy-lococcal agent and possibly a topical antistaphylococcal agent, such as mupirocin ointment. If an abscess develops, incision and drainage are necessary. A wick or a rubber band Penrose drain may be placed for drainage, and warm compresses and analgesia provide temporary relief.

The severe pain, postauricular lymph node swelling, and erythema, edema, and tenderness of the pinna and periauricular soft tissues may mimic acute mastoiditis (Schapowal, 2002). Computed tomographic (CT) scanning of the temporal bone is useful to evaluate for middle ear and mastoid soft tissue density, bony destruction of mastoid air cells, and subperiosteal abscess (Goldstein et al, 1998). The management of acute mastoiditis is discussed elsewhere in this book. Even in the absence of acute mastoiditis, systemic therapy with antibiotics directed against *P. aeruginosa* and *S. aureus* is necessary for treatment of periauricular cellulitis or perichondritis. Intravenous therapy may be required if there are signs of toxicity (fever, chills, malaise) or while the patient is undergoing workup of acute mastoiditis.

Malignant Otitis Externa

Malignant (necrotizing) otitis externa occurs in immuno-compromised or diabetic patients and represents the spread of infection, resulting in osteomyelitis of the EAC bone and the skull base. *P. aeruginosa* is almost always the responsible pathogen. Although 90% of adult patients have some form of glucose intolerance, affected children are either healthy adolescents with diabetes or children with immune dysfunction from leukemia, malnutrition, or solid tumors. Symptoms are aural discomfort, otorrhea, and hearing loss, which progresses to unrelenting otalgia. Examination classically reveals granulation tissue on the floor of the EAC at the bony-cartilaginous junction. There may be edema and erythema of the preauricular area and pinna. The tympanic membrane is often necrotic in children, whereas the tympanic membrane and the middle ear are normal in adults. Facial paralysis, which may be permanent, is more common in children. Multiple cranial neuropathies, most commonly cranial nerves IX, X, and XI, may occur in adults but have not been reported in children. A deforming chondritis may also be found in children but is uncommon in adults (Table 63-3) (Rubin et al, 1988).

The diagnosis of malignant otitis externa should be suspected in diabetic or immunocompromised patients with *Pseudomonas* external otitis refractory to topical therapy. Cultures and débridement and biopsy of the EAC tissue are required to establish that the process is one of inflammation and to rule out an occult malignancy. An elevated erythrocyte sedimentation rate is a helpful sign. In adults, CT determines the extent of involvement by identifying bony erosion and changes in soft tissue around the EAC and the skull. Because young children have limited development of the tympanic ring and mastoid bone, bony destruction may not be appreciated on CT. The technetium 99m radionuclide scan identifies the areas of osteomyelitis, although the signal may remain indefinitely. Gallium binds to actively dividing cells such as white blood cells, and resolution of the inflammatory process eliminates the activity. Therefore, the gallium radionuclide scan demonstrates the resolution of osteomyelitis and may be used to determine the end point of therapy.

Treatment is hospitalization, frequent ear cleaning with débridement of devitalized tissue, intravenous antipseudomonal antibiotics, and topical antibiotic drops. Combination intravenous therapy consisting of an aminoglycoside and an antipseudomonal semisynthetic penicillin is usually given for 4 to 6 weeks in adults. In children, a 2- to 3-week course is usually adequate (Rubin et al, 1988). Oral ciprofloxacin has been used as an alternative therapy in adults. Although not yet approved by the US Food and Drug Administration for use in children, ciprofloxacin has been used extensively in the cystic fibrosis population and other children with pseudomonal infections without demonstration of arthropathy (Jick, 1997). Recurrence and mortality rates of 20% have been reported in adults. Children have a lower recurrence rate, and there have been no reported fatalities.

Perichondritis

Perichondritis may occur after surgical procedures of the ear, including acupuncture to the pinna and high ear piercing, traumatic injuries to the pinna, frostbite, or burns. Clinical features include pain, erythema, edema, and induration of the affected areas, which classically spares the lobule because it is devoid of cartilage. Causative organisms are usually *P. aeruginosa* and

TABLE 63-3. Comparison of Adults and Children with Malignant Otitis Externa

	Adults (*n* = 162)	Children (*n* = 15)
Diabetes mellitus	94%*	20%*
Male:female ratio	2:1	1:1
Pseudomonas aeruginosa	99%	93%
Facial paralysis	34%	53%
Recovery	15%*	13%
Permanent	87%*	88%
Other cranial nerve pareses	23%*	0
Necrotic tympanic membrane	NA	56%*
Anti-*Pseudomonas* agents	89%*	100%
Surgery	44%*	48%
Mortality	19%	0
Recurrence	22%*	7%

Adapted from Rubin J et al (1988).
NA = not available.
*Data available on fewer than the total number of patients.

S. aureus. Treatment is intravenous antibiotics. A fluid collection may develop between the perichondrium and cartilage. This can be managed by serial aspirations but may require incision and drainage. Relapsing perichondritis is a systemic autoimmune disorder affecting multiple cartilaginous structures, including the pinnae, ribs, joints, and nasal, laryngeal, tracheal, and eustachian tube cartilages. The disease is uncommon in children and usually occurs in the fourth decade, affecting women more often than men. In addition to the pinna findings, patients may have hoarseness or dyspnea. The diagnosis is usually made clinically but may require biopsy. Treatment is corticosteroids, but chemotherapeutic and other anti-inflammatory agents are also used.

Exostoses/Osteomas

Exostoses are multiple, diffuse, broad-based growths of bone arising from the tympanic bone of the EAC, lying just lateral to the tympanic annulus. They are usually bilateral and occur in people engaged in cold-water swimming. Osteomas are usually unilateral, discrete, pedunculated bony masses with a narrow base arising along the tympanomastoid or tympanosquamous suture lines. Generally, exostoses and osteomas are incidental findings, and no treatment is necessary. If cerumen accumulates in the EAC medial to the exostoses, conductive hearing loss and otitis externa may develop. Cleaning of the cerumen and treatment of the otitis externa with top-ical drops may be necessary. Surgery may be necessary for lesions that obstruct the EAC. Osteomas can often be removed from the EAC with a curette. Removal of exostoses requires a postauricular approach, elevation of skin flaps, removal of the exostoses with the aid of a cutting or diamond bur or mallet and chisel, replacement of flaps, and, occasionally, split-thickness skin grafting (Whitaker et al, 1998).

Tumors of the Ear and Temporal Bone

Pediatric tumors of the ear and temporal bone are rare. Of the 25,000 reports of pediatric neoplasms on file at the Armed Forces Institute of Pathology, only 100 are primary neoplasms of the ear (Cunningham and Myers, 1988). Children often present insidiously with a clinical presentation of acute otitis media, chronic otitis media, or external otitis. Aural polyps are often present but may be assumed to be inflammatory in nature. Pain out of proportion to physical findings, a failure to improve after medical therapy, or the presence of sensorineural hearing loss, facial paralysis, or vertigo suggests the presence of a neoplastic process. A tissue biopsy is critical for proper diagnosis. A wide spectrum of benign and malignant neoplasms may arise in the ear and temporal bone (Table 63-4) (Cass, 1996). The more common lesions causing periauricular and ear canal swelling are presented. Specifically excluded are the vascular, neural, skin, leukemic, and metastatic lesions.

TABLE 63-4. Neoplastic and Paraneoplastic Lesions Reported Involving the Temporal Bone in Children

Benign Tumors	Malignant Tumors	Congenital and Paraneoplastic Conditions
Adenoma	Adenocarcinoma	Bone cyst, aneurysmal and unicameral
Carcinoid tumor	Adenoid cystic carcinoma	Carotid artery, aberrant and aneurysmal
Chondroblastoma	Squamous cell carcinoma	Choristoma, neural and salivary
Chondromyxoid fibroma	Rhabdomyosarcoma	Congenital and acquired cholesteatoma
Endodermal sinus tumor	Chondrosarcoma	Dermoid reparative granuloma
Ossifying fibroma	Ewing's sarcoma	Fibrous dysplasia
Giant cell tumor	Fibrosarcoma	Langerhans' cell histiocytosis
Glomus tumor	Desmoid tumor	Wegener's granulomatosis
Granular cell tumor	Juvenile fibromatosis	
Hamartoma	Fibrous histiocytoma	
Hemangioma	Ganglioneuroblastoma	
Hemangiopericytoma	Granulocytic sarcoma	
Lipoma	Hemangiosarcoma	
Lymphangiomatosis	Liposarcoma	
Melanotic neuroectodermal tumor of infancy	Burkitt's lymphoma	
Meningioma	Lymphosarcoma	
Neurofibroma	Metastatic neuroblastoma of adrenal	
Osteoblastoma	gland origin	
Osteoma		
Acoustic schwannoma		
Chorda tympani schwannoma		
Facial nerve schwannoma		
Jugular foramen schwannoma		
Trigeminal schwannoma		
Teratoma		

Adapted from Cass SP (1996).

Fibrous Dysplasia

Fibrous dysplasia is a disorder of proliferating fibro-osseous tissue that replaces normal medullary bone. Most believe that it is a congenital bone anomaly, but others attribute it to an aberrant reparative process that occurs in response to trauma or an arrest in bony maturation. It is classified into three types: monostotic (single bone), polyostotic (multiple bones), and McCune-Albright syndrome. McCune-Albright syndrome consists of polyostotic fibrous dysplasia, skin pigmentation, and endocrinopathies. Fibrous dysplasia tends to develop in late childhood and adolescence. The skin and endocrine changes are rare in the monostotic form, which becomes quiescent after puberty. The polyostotic form may progress beyond the third decade.

The head and neck bones are involved in 20 to 25% of cases of monostotic fibrous dysplasia and 40 to 50% of polyostotic fibrous dysplasia. The maxilla and mandible are most frequently involved (Tran et al, 1996). The temporal bone is involved in 18% of cases with head and neck involvement. Presenting symptoms are temporal bone enlargement, which may be peri-, pre-, or supra-auricular; conductive hearing loss; progressive external canal occlusion; and facial paralysis. Stenosis of the EAC may give rise to canal cholesteatoma. Temporomandibular joint distortion results in trismus. The otic capsule is usually spared, but involvement may cause vertigo and sensorineural hearing loss.

Plain films demonstrate bony enlargement and sclerosis or a uniform ground-glass appearance. CT demonstrates the expansile growth of the lesions, thinning of the surrounding cortical bone, and displacement of adjacent structures. The otic capsule appears to float within the lesion. Magnetic resonance imaging (MRI) delineates the margins better than CT. Conservative management is indicated for this benign disease, and CT is useful for monitoring disease progression. Surgical indications are for diagnostic biopsy, cholesteatoma, hearing loss, cranial nerve dysfunction, and correction of significant cosmetic deformity. Simple curettage, as well as complex resection and reconstruction of the EAC, may be performed. Decompression of the internal auditory canal or fallopian canal may be required in selected cases. Malignant degeneration has been reported in 1 of 200 cases of fibrous dysplasia, of whom half have received radiation therapy. Therefore, radiation therapy is contraindicated. Clinical signs of developing malignancy are pain, rapid swelling, and elevation in alkaline phosphatase levels.

Langerhans' Cell Histiocytosis

Langerhans' cell histiocytosis (histiocytosis X) is a group of disorders characterized by the idiopathic proliferation of histiocytes called the Langerhans' cells. Diagnosis requires pathologic identification of Langerhans' cells under electron microscopy by identifying Birbeck granules, which are rod-shaped organelles present within the nuclear cytoplasm. The disorder is not considered malignant and may have an immunologic basis. The disorder is divided into three categories according to severity and prognosis. Eosinophilic granuloma is the localized and mildest form of the illness. One bony site is typically affected, although multifocal lesions can occur. The skull is the most frequently affected site, but lesions can occur in the long bones of the extremities, pelvis, ribs, mandible, maxilla, and vertebrae. Approximately 50% of patients are diagnosed before the age of 5 years and 75% before the age of 20 years.

Hand-Schüller-Christian disease is a more severe systemic form of Langerhans' cell histiocytosis. The classic triad of diabetes insipidus secondary to posterior pituitary and/or hypothalamic disease, proptosis from orbital bone involvement, and osteolytic skull lesions is present in less than 25% of the cases. Multifocal osseous lesions associated with limited extraskeletal involvement of skin, lymph nodes, and viscera are characteristic. The disease typically affects children between 1 and 5 years of age, but it can present in young adulthood. The clinical course is chronic, with significant morbidity. Letterer-Siwe disease is a disseminated form of Langerhans' cell histiocytosis characterized by multiorgan involvement. The disease presents with fever, rash, lymphadenopathy, hepatosplenomegaly, dyspnea, and blood dyscrasias in children under 3 years of age. The disease is rapidly progressive with a high mortality rate.

Temporal bone involvement occurs in 15 to 61% of cases of Langerhans' cell histiocytosis. Signs and symptoms include otorrhea unresponsive to medical therapy, postauricular swelling, conductive hearing loss, and the presence of aural polyps or granulation tissue. Facial paralysis, sensorineural hearing loss, and vertigo are rare. CT demonstrates the sharply marginated lytic lesions, erosion of the ossicles and otic capsule, and the soft tissue margins of the histiocytic mass. Diagnosis is established by biopsy of the bony lesion. Localized osseous lesions can be managed by surgical curettage, low-dose radiation therapy, or cortical mastoidectomy. Multiorgan or systemic disease requires chemotherapy.

Rhabdomyosarcoma

Rhabdomyosarcoma, the most prevalent soft tissue sarcoma in children, accounts for 5 to 15% of all childhood neoplasms (Wiatrak and Pensak, 1989). The peak age of incidence is between ages 2 and 5 years, with a second peak incidence between ages 15 and 19 years. The tissue of origin is striated skeletal muscle. The four subtypes are pleomorphic, embryonal, alveolar, and botryoid, with the embryonal subtype being the most common in the head and neck. The tumor is highly aggressive and locally destructive, with a high rate of regional and distant metastases. The most common sites of distant metastases are the lungs, skeletal system, brain, breast, and intestines. Middle ear rhabdomyosarcoma may spread to the fallopian canal, internal auditory canal, and posterior fossa. Petrous apex tumors will also follow this pathway. Other pathways of intracranial extension are from the mastoid to the middle cranial fossa, from the labyrinth through the cochlear and vestibular aqueducts, inferiorly through the jugular bulb, styloid process, and carotid artery, and direct extension from the infratemporal fossa or the nasopharynx. Death results most commonly from direct meningeal extension or metastatic disease.

Clinical presentation resembles chronic otitis media with otalgia, purulent or bloody otorrhea, aural polyps, and granulation tissue unresponsive to treatment. Headaches, cranial nerve palsies, especially of the seventh nerve, and sensorineural hearing loss also occur. A tissue biopsy is critical for diagnosis. CT defines the extent of the lesion and the extent of bone destruction in the temporal bone. MRI demonstrates intracranial extension. A complete metastatic workup, including complete blood cell count, chest radiography, chest and abdominal CT, urinalysis, blood chemistries, liver enzymes, bone scan, liver spleen scan, bone marrow aspirate, and lumbar puncture, is obtained. The lesion is staged according to the International Rhabdomyosarcoma Study Group classification (Table 63-5). Surgery is performed for localized tumors that can be excised completely or with only microscopic residual without causing significant disability (group I or II). Recent advances in cranial base surgery have allowed more lesions to be approached surgically. Chemotherapy should be administered to control distant metastases. Chemotherapy is administered to patients whose tumors are unresectable (group III) or metastatic (group IV). Surgical excision may be possible after completion of chemotherapy. Radiation therapy is also administered. Survival remains poor, ranging from an 82% 5-year survival for group I patients to 24% for group IV patients.

Auricular Trauma

Trauma to the auricle may present as auricular swelling. Perichondritis may result (see "Perichondritis," above). An auricular hematoma separates the perichondrium from its underlying cartilage on the anterior surface. If not treated, the cartilage will die, leading to a cauliflower ear deformity. The hematoma must be evacuated, with placement of a drain and an external pressure dressing. Systemic antibiotics are usually prescribed. Bites to the auricle should be repaired if they have occurred within 12 hours of presentation; otherwise, they should be allowed to heal by secondary intention (Lassen, 2001). Human bites must be aggressively treated with antibiotic prophylaxis. The most common organisms are *Staphylococcus*, α-hemolytic streptococcus, and *Bacteroides*. Because of the high incidence of β-lactamase–producing bacteria, treatment with amoxi-

TABLE 63-5. Intergroup Rhabdomyosarcoma Study: Classification of Head and Neck Rhabdomyosarcoma Patients

Group I	Localized disease, completely resected (regional nodes not involved)
	Confined to muscle or organ of origin
	Contiguous involvement: infiltration outside the muscle or organ of origin, as through fascial planes
Group II	Grossly resected tumor with microscopic residual disease (nodes negative)
	Regional disease, completely resected (nodes positive or negative)
	Regional disease with involved nodes, grossly resected, but with evidence of microscopic residual disease
Group III	Incomplete resection or biopsy with gross residual disease
Group IV	Metastatic disease present at onset

Adapted from Wiatrak BJ and Pensak ML (1989).

cillin-clavulanate potassium provides good coverage. If there is evidence of chondritis, parenteral ticarcillin disodium and clavulanate potassium have been recommended (Goodman, 1992). Insect bites are usually self-limited but may cause significant pinna swelling and protrusion. They can be differentiated from acute mastoiditis because the patient is not toxic or ill and the tympanic membrane and middle ear are normal. Frostbite should be treated with rapid rewarming with wet saline soaks, sedatives, analgesia, and antibiotics for deep infections (Sessions et al, 1971). Burned ears should be treated by gentle washing with soap, administration of topical and oral antibiotics, hair trimming, and avoidance of pressure to the ear. If chondritis develops, it must be aggressively managed with systemic antibiotics, débridement with cultures, and direct antibiotic irrigation via catheters (Skedros et al, 1992).

Miscellaneous Conditions

Postauricular epidermoid inclusion cysts usually present as an asymptomatic mass, although they may become acutely infected. Treatment of the acute infection requires systemic antibiotic therapy directed against *S. aureus* with incision and drainage if an abscess is present. Definitive treatment is surgical excision. Cholesteatoma can rarely originate from the EAC (Martin et al, 1999). There are five groups according to cause: postsurgical, post-traumatic, congenital ear canal stenosis, ear canal obstruction, and spontaneous. Examination reveals EAC cholesteatoma in the presence of a normal tympanic membrane. A fistulous communication with the mastoid is often present. Many can be treated locally, but mastoidectomy is required if there is erosion into the mastoid cavity.

Summary

The differential diagnosis of periauricular swelling has been presented. Whereas the more common conditions usually do not present a diagnostic challenge, the uncommon lesions often require a high index of suspicion for proper diagnosis and treatment.

References

Cass SP. Tumors of the ear and temporal bone. In: Bluestone CD, Stool SE, Kenna MA, editors. Pediatric otolaryngology. 3rd ed. Philadelphia: WB Saunders; 1996. p. 707–17.

Clark WB, Brook I, Bianki D, Thompson DH. Microbiology of otitis externa. Otolaryngol Head Neck Surg 1997;116:23–5.

Cunningham MJ, Myers EN. Tumors and tumorlike lesions of the ear and temporal bone in children. Ear Nose Throat J 1988;67:726–49.

Goldstein NA, Casselbrant ML, Bluestone CD, Kurs-Lasky M. Intratemporal complications of acute otitis media in infants and children. Otolaryngol Head Neck Surg 1998;119:444–54.

Goodman A. Soft tissue injuries to the face. In: Papel ID, Nachlas NE, editors. Facial plastic and reconstructive surgery. St. Louis: Mosby-Year Book; 1992. p. 449–59.

Hirsch BE. Diseases of the external ear. In: Bluestone CD, Stool SE, Kenna MA, editors. Pediatric otolaryngology. 3rd ed. Philadelphia: WB Saunders; 1996. p. 378–87.

Hoffman RA, Shepsman DA. Bullous myringitis and sensorineural hearing loss. Laryngoscope 1983;93:1544–5.

Jick S. Ciprofloxacin safety in a pediatric population. Pediatr Infect Dis J 1997;16:130–4.

Lassen LF. Auricular trauma. In: Alper C, Myers EN, Eibling DE, editors. Decision-making in ear, nose and throat disorders. Philadelphia: WB Saunders; 2001. p. 56–7.

Marais J, Dale BAB. Bullous myringitis: a review. Clin Otolaryngol 1997;22:497–9.

Martin DW, Selesnick SH, Parisier SC. External auditory canal cholesteatoma with erosion into the mastoid. Otolaryngol Head Neck Surg 1999;121:298–300.

Palmu AAI, Kotikoski MJ, Kaijalainen TH, Puhakka HJ. Bacterial etiology of acute myringitis in children less than two years of age. Pediatr Infect Dis J 2001;20:607–11.

Roland PS, Stroman DW. Microbiology of acute otitis externa. Laryngoscope 2002;112:1166–77.

Rubin J, Yu VL, Stool SE. Malignant external otitis in children. J Pediatr 1988;113:965–70.

Schapowal A. Otitis externa: a clinical overview. Ear Nose Throat J 2002;81 Suppl 1:21–2.

Sessions DG, Stallings JO, Mills WJ, Beal DD. Frostbite of the ear. Laryngoscope 1971;81:1223–32.

Skedros DG, Goldfarb IW, Slater H, Rocco J. Chondritis of the burned ear: a review. Ear Nose Throat J 1992;71:359–62.

Thompson SW. Otitis externa. In: Alper C, Myers EN, Eibling DE, editors. Decision-making in ear, nose and throat disorders. Philadelphia: WB Saunders; 2001. p. 28–9.

Tran LP, Grundfast KM, Selesnick SH. Benign lesions of the external auditory canal. Otolaryngol Clin North Am 1996;29:807–25.

Wetmore SJ, Abramson M. Bullous myringitis with sensorineural hearing loss. Otolaryngol Head Neck Surg 1979;87:66–70.

Whitaker SR, Cordier A, Kosjakov S, Charbonneau R. Treatment of external auditory canal exostoses. Laryngoscope 1998;108:195–9.

Wiatrak BJ, Pensak ML. Rhabdomyosarcoma of the ear and temporal bone. Laryngoscope 1989;99:1188–92.

Chapter 64

ACUTE MASTOIDITIS

MICHAL LUNTZ, MD, ALEXANDER BRODSKY, MD

Acute mastoiditis is an acute inflammatory disease of the mastoid process (Bluestone and Klein, 1983; Shambaugh, 1967) in a patient with no history of simple chronic otitis media (chronic perforation of the tympanic membrane) or cholesteatoma. The clinical criteria for diagnosis of acute mastoiditis are signs of acute otitis media (AOM) on otoscopy and local inflammatory findings over the mastoid area (pain, redness, local sensitivity, protrusion of the auricle, or sagging of the posterosuperior wall of the external auditory canal) or local inflammatory findings over the mastoid process and roentgenographic or surgical findings of mastoiditis (with no signs of AOM).

A history of chronic otitis media excludes the diagnosis of "simple" acute mastoiditis (the entity discussed in this chapter), although the clinical presentation of the two entities may be similar. The non-"simple" type of mastoiditis can be termed "acute mastoid inflammatory presentation of chronic middle ear disease" and is not discussed here.

Incidence

The incidence of acute mastoiditis has declined since the introduction of antibiotics (House, 1946; Mygind, 1910). In 1959, it was reported that 0.4% of acute episodes of otitis media developed into acute mastoiditis (Palva and Pukkinen, 1959), whereas the reported incidence during the 1980s was 0.004% (Palva et al, 1985). In recent years, however, the number of children admitted to hospital with acute mastoiditis seems to have risen (Hoppe et al, 1994; Luntz et al, 1994; Ogle and Lauer, 1986). Suggested reasons include the fact that most cases of AOM are treated by pediatricians without performing myringotomy and the emergence of antibiotic-resistant organisms associated with incorrect and abusive use of antibiotics (Spratley et al, 2000).

Clinical Presentation and Course

The following description of clinical characteristics is based on our retrospective multicenter study of a series of 223 consecutive cases of acute mastoiditis treated at nine secondary or tertiary referral centers in Israel between 1984 and 1998 (Luntz et al, 2001) and on an updated review of the literature. The ages of patients with acute mastoiditis ranged from 3 months to almost 80 years (mean 5.3 years). Approximately 30% of the patients were 1 year or younger (Antonelli et al, 1999; Harley et al, 1997; Luntz et al, 2001) and over 80% were under 8 years of age (Hoppe et al, 1994; Luntz et al, 2001; Ogle and Lauer, 1986; Spratley et al, 2000).

One-third of patients with acute mastoiditis had a history of recurrent AOM (Harley et al, 1997; Luntz et al, 2001). A second episode of acute mastoiditis had occurred in a significant number of patients, all of whom had been characterized as otitis prone prior to the first episode (Luntz et al, 2001). A history of recurrent AOM therefore increases the risk of recurrence of acute mastoiditis.

The duration of middle ear symptoms prior to the diagnosis of acute mastoiditis ranged between 1 and 60 days in our multicenter study, with a mean of around 6 days (Luntz et al, 2001). However, shorter periods have been reported (Holt and Young, 1981; Luntz et al, 1994; Luntz et al, 2001; Rosen et al, 1986). We found that 30% of patients had experienced middle ear symptoms for not more than 48 hours prior to the diagnosis (Luntz et al, 2001), suggesting that at least some of the disease processes in the middle ear cleft that express themselves clinically as acute mastoiditis involve the mastoid bone from the outset and are not a complication of a neglected otitis media, as previously thought (Shambaugh, 1967). Thus, even when routine oral antibiotics are given for AOM, there is a good chance that these processes will not readily subside because most antibiotics do not penetrate the bony tissue as well as they penetrate soft tissue.

In line with this information, it is worth noting that in a significant number of cases (21–58% in different studies), acute mastoiditis develops despite prior antibiotic treatment given for a clinically diagnosed AOM (Antonelli et al, 1999; Harley et al, 1997; Holt and Young, 1981; Luntz et al, 1994; Luntz et al, 2001; Rosen et al, 1986; Petersen et al, 1998; Prellner and Rydel, 1986; Spratley et al, 2000). Thus, the routine use of antibiotics for AOM cannot be considered an absolute safeguard against the development of acute mastoiditis and its complications.

At presentation, most patients, but not all, showed signs of AOM and a bulging tympanic membrane on otoscopy. Postauricular erythema, postauricular edema, and fluctuation were present in 86%, 87%, and 17% of patients, respectively (Luntz et al, 2001; Spratley et al, 2000). Fever was usually present, but its absence did not exclude acute mastoiditis (Harley et al, 1997; Luntz et al, 2001; Vera-Cruz et al, 1999). The white blood cell count was usually high (Harley et al, 1997; Luntz et al, 2001). A discharging ear was seen at presentation in about 30% of patients, some of whom had undergone myringotomy prior to admission, but in most cases, it was attributable to a spontaneous perforation of the eardrum (Luntz et al, 2001).

In some patients with periauricular edema and swelling of the external ear canal, clinical differentiation between severe external otitis and mastoiditis may be difficult. Local sensitivity on tragal manipulation characterizes external otitis. In some of these cases, computed tomography (CT) may be helpful in differentiating between the two entities (in cases of external otitis, the middle ear and the mastoid cavity are expected to be well aerated).

In some patients, the tympanic membrane may have a normal appearance, but there may be other clinical signs of acute mastoiditis, such as postauricular erythema and edema, protrusion of the auricle, and fever. Such patients were typically found to have middle ear symptoms of longer duration and to have received antibiotic treatment prior to the diagnosis of acute mastoiditis (Luntz et al, 2001). Thus, the resolution of tympanic membrane signs in these patients may be attributable to the antimicrobial therapy. An entity that includes signs of acute mastoiditis with a tympanic membrane of normal or almost normal appearance is commonly termed "masked mastoiditis" (Faye-Lund, 1989; Holt and Gates, 1983).

Causative Organisms

The following information about causative organisms in acute mastoiditis was obtained from studies carried out over the last two decades and is presented in Table 64-1 (Antonelli et al, 1999; Ginsburg et al, 1980; Gliklich et al, 1996; Luntz et al, 2001; Petersen et al, 1998; Ronis et al, 1968; Spratley et al, 2000; Vera-Cruz et al, 1999). The results of bacterial cultures were available for a significant proportion of the patients studied. Cultures were taken from the middle ear during myringotomy, from purulent discharge in the external auditory canal, from the mastoid cavity during mastoidectomy, or from the subperiosteal abscess cavity. The incidence of negative cultures ranged from 16 to 43% in the different studies (Antonelli et al, 1999; Harley et al, 1997; Holt and Young, 1981; Luntz et al, 2001; Petersen et al, 1998; Prellner and Rydel, 1986; Rosen et al, 1986; Vera-Cruz et al, 1999). Of patients with negative cultures, 47% had received antibiotics prior to the bacterial sampling (Luntz et al, 2001). A similar percentage (50%) of patients with positive cultures had been treated with antibiotics prior to bacterial sampling.

In the positive cultures, the most commonly isolated pathogens were *Streptococcus pneumoniae*, *Streptococcus pyogenes*, *Staphylococcus aureus*, and *Staphylococcus* coagulase negative. In most studies, the frequency of isolation of *Haemophilus influenzae* and of *Branhamella catarrhalis* was surprisingly low (0–8% and 0%, respectively) (Antonelli et al, 1999; Ginsburg et al, 1980; Gliklich et al, 1996; Luntz et al, 2001; Petersen et al, 1998; Ronis et al, 1968; Spratley et al, 2000; Vera-Cruz et al, 1999) compared with their incidence in AOM (Bluestone et al, 1992) (23% and 14%, respectively). Also, the incidence of *S. pneumoniae* colonization was lower in acute mastoiditis (9.9%) than in AOM (35%) (Bluestone et al, 1992; Spratley et al, 2000). Because the rate of preadmission antibiotic therapy seems to be similar in patients with positive cultures and with negative cultures (50% and 46.7%, respectively [Luntz et al, 2001]), the extremely low incidence of *H. influenzae* and *B. catarrhalis* colonization might be explained by the greater sensitivity of these microorganisms to the conventional antibiotics prescribed for the AOM symptoms presented by patients prior to the appearance of a full-blown picture of acute mastoiditis. It is therefore possible that the group of patients with negative cultures includes those in whom these two bacteria were the causative organisms for the acute mastoiditis. The practical implication of this information is that in spite of the low isolation rates of *H. influenzae* and *B. catarrhalis* in patients with acute mastoiditis, the activity range of antibiotics chosen for the treatment of acute mastoiditis should include these two bacteria.

The high incidence of *S. aureus*–positive cultures found in acute mastoiditis (5–19%) relative to AOM (1%)

TABLE 64-1. Incidence (%) of Causative Organisms in Acute Mastoiditis

Microorganisms	Luntz et al (2001) (223 ears) (1984–1998)	Prellner and Rydel (1986) (22 ears) (1970–1984)	Petersen et al (1998) (79 ears) (1977–1996)	Ginsburg et al (1980) (57 ears) (1955–1979)	Gliklich et al (1996) (124 ears) (1964–1987)	Vera-Cruz et al (1999) (35 ears) (1993–1997)	Antonelli et al (1999) (31 ears) (1987–1997)	Spratley et al (2000) (23 ears) (1993–1998)
Streptococcus pneumoniae	9.9	31	31	28	21	22	35	13
Streptococcus pyogenes	9.2	19	13	16	12	—	13	13
Staphylococcus aureus	8.6	9	5	16	10	11	19	—
Haemophilus influenzae	2.6	9	8	2	5	—	—	4

(Antonelli et al, 1999; Ginsburg et al, 1980; Gliklich et al, 1996; Luntz et al, 2001; Petersen et al, 1998; Ronis et al, 1968; Spratley et al, 2000; Vera-Cruz et al, 1999) might be attributable to a greater tendency of this organism than of other organisms to invade bone. This possibility is supported by the high incidence of *S. aureus* as a causative organism in osteomyelitis. Marked colonization by *S. aureus* in acute mastoiditis has also been reported by other authors (Ginsburg et al, 1980; Gliklich et al, 1996; Prellner and Rydel, 1986). Whatever the reason, this finding should prompt clinicians to include a potent antistaphylococcal agent in the treatment of acute mastoiditis even before culture results are available.

Complications

The incidence of complications in acute mastoiditis is still relatively high (Table 64-2) (Gliklich et al, 1996; Go et al, 2000; Luntz et al, 2001). Possible complications of acute mastoiditis are classified as extracranial or intracranial. Extracranial complications include subperiosteal abscess, facial nerve paralysis, labyrinthitis, petrositis (which might later develop into a severe intracranial complication), and Bezold's abscess. Intracranial complications include meningitis, encephalitis, epidural abscess, subdural and subarachnoid empyema or abscess, sinus thrombosis, brain abscess, and otitic hydrocephalus. Complications may be present at the time of the diagnosis of mastoiditis or may appear later in the course of disease in spite of what seems to be adequate treatment (Ginsburg et al, 1980; Gliklich et al, 1996; Go et al, 2000; Ronis et al, 1968; Rosen et al, 1986; Zoller, 1972).

Two groups at risk of developing complications have been identified: those who have already experienced a spontaneous perforation of the tympanic membrane and purulent discharge by the time that acute mastoiditis is diagnosed and those in whom the causative agents are *S. pyogenes* and *S. aureus* (Luntz et al, 2001). Patients who undergo myringotomy prior to a clinical diagnosis of acute mastoiditis have a lower tendency to develop severe complications (Luntz et al, 2001).

Outcome

The outcome of acute mastoiditis is usually favorable owing to a better understanding of the disease and better availability of focused antibiotic treatment, CT, and operating room facilities. However, severe intracranial complications still carry their known risks (Go et al, 2000; Luntz et al, 2001).

Management

Although the incidence of acute mastoiditis has declined significantly since the advent of antibiotics, the prevalence

TABLE 64-2. Complications in 223 Patients with Acute Mastoiditis

Complication	Number of Patients		
	Complication on Admission*	Complications developed during Hospitalization	Total*
Extracranial			
Subperiosteal abscess	37	13	50
Labyrinthitis	1		1
Facial nerve palsy	1	2	3
Intracranial			
Meningoencephalitis	6	1	7
Perisinus empyema	2	1	3
Sigmoid or lateral sinus thrombosis	3		3
Perisinus empyema and lateral sinus thrombosis	1		1
Lateral sinus thrombosis and pulmonary emboli	1	1	2
Subdural abscess	1		1
Cerebellar abscess	1		1
Petrous apex suppuration and cavernous sinus thrombosis	1		1
Other			
Myocardial infarction		1	1
Total	49	19	68

*Some patients present with more than one complication; hence, the column totals exceed the sum of each column.

of severe complications in acute mastoiditis is still high. This fact calls for prompt and focused treatment once the diagnosis is made. The key to successful treatment and favorable outcome is early identification of the exact causative organism and a possible intracranial complication. The latter requires, on the part of the physician, a high level of clinical suspicion and prompt performance of a temporal bone and brain CT. A CT scan of the brain (with and without intravenous contrast) and temporal bones is therefore a mandatory part of the very early workup of these patients (Go et al, 2000; Spratley et al, 2000).

The chances of isolating the causative organism are best when an uncontaminated sample for bacterial culture is taken prior to the initiation of antibiotic treatment.

Most authors agree that surgical drainage via myringotomy (with or without placement of a ventilation tube [VT]) in combination with intravenous antibiotic therapy is the standard treatment regimen in uncomplicated cases (Niv et al, 1998; Spratley et al, 2000). Treatment on an outpatient basis may be feasible provided that close daily monitoring can be guaranteed (Niv et al, 1998). Most authors, however, prefer hospitalization. Development of an extracranial or intracranial complication requires more aggressive surgical treatment (drainage of subperiosteal abscess, cortical mastoidectomy, and surgical treatment of intracranial complications as indicated) (Go et al, 2000).

The scheme in Figure 64-1 presents a recommended treatment protocol. Once acute mastoiditis has been clinically diagnosed, the patient can be allocated to one of two groups. Group A comprises patients in whom a subperiosteal abscess is already apparent on presentation. Group B comprises patients in whom there is no subperiosteal abscess. Both groups should undergo CT of the brain and temporal bone, surgical drainage with sampling for bacterial culture, and prompt initiation of systemic antibiotic treatment. Initial antibiotic treatment should cover the above-mentioned possible causative organisms in acute mastoiditis, which are somewhat different from those in AOM. Considering the high incidence of *S. pneumoniae*, *S. pyogenes*, *S. aureus*, and *Staphylococcus* coagulase negative, we recommend intravenous amoxicillin-clavulanate (75 mg/kg/d) or cefuroxime (150 mg/kg/d) as the first choice of antibiotic therapy. If necessary, the antibiotic treatment can later be changed to a culture-based therapy, based on the results of the sample taken before starting antibiotic treatment.

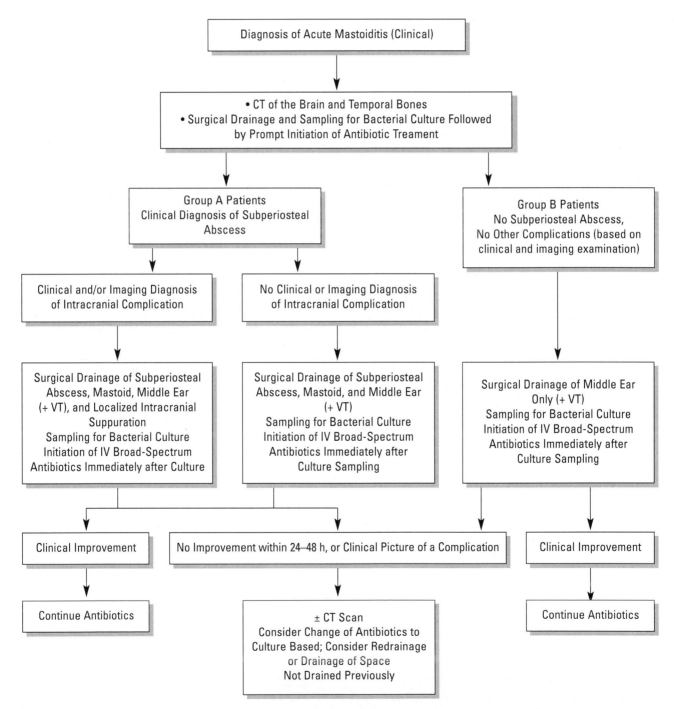

FIGURE 64-1. Recommended treatment protocol in acute mastoiditis. CT = computed tomography; IV = intravenous; VT = ventilation tube.

The procedure of surgical drainage differs in the two groups. In group A patients, who presented with a subperiosteal abscess, it should include drainage of the mastoid via a retroauricular incision together with cortical mastoidectomy and drainage of the tympanic cavity via myringotomy and VT insertion. In group B patients, who did not have a subperiosteal abscess on presentation, drainage can be accomplished by VT insertion alone. As long as these VTs are draining, local treatment by frequent suctioning and wick (soaked with ototopic drops) replacement is recommended.

It should be re-emphasized that three factors are crucial for a favorable outcome of acute mastoiditis: early initiation of antibiotic treatment, obtaining a culture sample for isolation of causative microorganisms *before* starting antibiotics, and prompt performance of a brain CT scan to check for possible complications. Because the last-mentioned factor, when performed in babies and young children, often requires deep sedation or general anesthesia, proper planning of the sequence of handling these three factors is essential. The physician should also consider the possibility of the presence of an intracranial complication, which might call for extension of the surgical drainage to include further surgical treatment (drainage) of this intracranial complication. Thus, with optimal planning, after clinical diagnosis of an acute mastoiditis, the patient will be referred for immediate CT—under sedation or general anesthesia if necessary—and the same anesthesia will be used for the drainage procedure. Immediately after the culture sample is taken, broad-spectrum systemic antibiotics should be initiated (while the patient is still in the operating room).

If the patient shows improvement, no change in treatment is required. If there is no improvement within 24 to 48 hours or development of a complication is suspected, appropriate surgical measures and a change in the antibiotic, preferably based on culture findings, are considered.

References

Antonelli PJ, Dhanani N, Giannoni CM, Kubilis PS. Impact of resistant pneumococcus on rates of acute mastoiditis. Otolaryngol Head Neck Surg 1999;121:190–4.

Bluestone CD, Klein JO. Intratemporal complications and sequelae of otitis media. In: Bluestone CD, Stool SE, editors. Pediatric otolaryngology. Philadelphia: WB Saunders; 1983. p. 549–52.

Bluestone CD, Stephenson JS, Martin LM. Ten year review of otitis media pathogens. Pediatr Infect Dis J 1992;11:7–11.

Faye-Lund H. Acute and latent mastoiditis. J Laryngol Otol 1989;103:1158–60.

Ginsburg CM, Rudoy R, Nelson JD. Acute mastoiditis in infants and children. Clin Pediatr 1980;101:87–91.

Gliklich RE, Eavey RD, Iannuzzi RA, Camacho AE. A contemporary analysis of acute mastoiditis. Arch Otolaryngol Head Neck Surg 1996;122:135–9.

Go C, Bernstein JM, de Jong AL, et al. Intracranial complications of acute mastoiditis. Int J Pediatr Otorhinolaryngol 2000;52:143–8.

Harley EH, Sdralis T, Berkowitz RG. Acute mastoiditis in children: a 12-year retrospective study. Otolaryngol Head Neck Surg 1997;116:26-30.

Holt GR, Gates GA. Masked mastoiditis. Laryngoscope 1983;93:1034–7.

Holt GR, Young WC. Acute coalescent mastoiditis. Otolaryngol Head Neck Surg 1981;89:317–21.

Hoppe JE, Kostern S, Bootz F, Niethammer D. Acute mastoiditis—relevant once again. Infection 1994;22:178–82.

House HP. Acute otitis media. A comparative study of the results obtained in therapy before and after the introduction of the sulfonamide compounds. Arch Otolaryngol Head Neck Surg 1946;43:371–8.

Luntz M, Brodsky A, Nusem S, et al. Acute mastoiditis—the antibiotic era: a multicenter study. Int J Pediatr Otorhinolaryngol 2001;57:1–9.

Luntz M, Keren G, Nusem S, Kronenberg J. Acute mastoiditis—revisited. Ear Nose Throat J 1994;73:648–54.

Mygind H. Subperiosteal abscess of the mastoid region. Ann Otol Rhinol Laryngol 1910;19:254–65.

Niv A, Nash M, Peiser J, et al. Outpatient management of acute mastoiditis with periosteitis in children. Int J Pediatr Otorhinolaryngol 1998;46:9–13.

Ogle JW, Lauer BA. Acute mastoiditis. Am J Dis Child 1986;140:1178–82.

Palva T, Pukkinen K. Mastoiditis. J Laryngol Otol 1959;73:573–88.

Palva T, Virtanen H, Makinen J. Acute and latent mastoiditis in children. J Laryngol Otol 1985;99:127–36.

Petersen CG, Ovesen T, Pedersen CB. Acute mastoiditis in a Danish county from 1977 to 1996 with focus on the bacteriology. Int J Pediatr Otorhinolaryngol 1998;45:21–9.

Prellner D, Rydel R. Acute mastoiditis. Acta Otolaryngol (Stockh) 1986;1002:52–6.

Ronis B, Ronis M, Liebman E. Acute mastoiditis as seen today. Eye Ear Nose Throat Mon 1968;47:502–7.

Rosen A, Ophir D, Marshak G. Acute mastoiditis: a review of 69 cases. Ann Otol Rhinol Laryngol 1986;95:222–4.

Shambaugh GF Jr. Surgery of the ear. 2nd ed. Philadelphia: WB Saunders; 1967. p. 187–203.

Spratley J, Silvera H, Alvarez I, Pais-Clemente M. Acute mastoiditis in children: review of the current status. Int J Pediatr Otorhinolaryngol 2000;56:33–40.

Vera-Cruz P, Farinha RR, Calado V. Acute mastoiditis in children—our experience. Int J Pediatr Otorhinolaryngol 1999;50:113–7.

Zoller H. Acute mastoiditis and its complications. South Med J 1972;65:477–80.

Chapter 65

CHRONIC MASTOIDITIS

STEPHANIE MOODY ANTONIO, MD, DERALD E. BRACKMANN, MD, FACS

Chronic mastoiditis is a protracted disease characterized by the presence of granulation tissue, cholesteatoma, or low-grade pathogens. The disease may present with otorrhea, otalgia, or fever, but often the symptoms are subtle. Chronic mastoiditis may progress without otologic symptoms or signs until serious complications occur.

As an infectious or inflammatory process, it may be manifested in several different ways. First, it can be associated with chronic suppurative otitis media (OM) with or without cholesteatoma and declare itself with persistent or recurrent otorrhea that is refractory to medical treatment. In this case, it is often associated with chronic OM with perforation or with a chronically draining mastoid cavity. Conversely, incompletely treated acute OM or acute mastoiditis may persist as latent disease. If an attic blockage isolates the mastoid from the middle ear, the extent of disease may be unsuspected after adequate resolution of middle ear physical findings and symptoms. This condition is often called "masked," "silent," or "latent" mastoiditis. Finally, chronic mastoiditis may present as benign-appearing serous OM that is unexpectedly unresponsive to ventilation tubes. This presentation has been labeled chronic serous mastoiditis, idiopathic hemotympanum, and cholesterol granuloma; is noninfectious in nature; and is probably related to eustachian tube blockage. The focus of this chapter is on latent mastoiditis because other chapters extensively discuss the differentiated entities, including cholesteatoma and cholesterol granuloma.

Description

Classically, chronic mastoiditis can be diagnosed by eliciting a history of intermittent otorrhea, acute OM, or acute mastoiditis. Often there is recent or repeated use of antibiotics, both oral and ototopical. Patients may report failure of antibiotics to resolve symptoms, requiring prolonged courses of increasingly broader-spectrum drugs or recurrence of symptoms a few weeks after completing a full course of treatment for acute OM or acute mastoiditis. Symptoms such as aural fullness, pressure, pulsatile tinnitus, and dull otalgia may be subtle. The duration of complaints may range from months to years.

As mentioned, chronic mastoiditis is most commonly intimately associated with chronic OM and is suspected after examination reveals purulent malodorous discharge through a perforated tympanic membrane (TM) or ventilation tube. In this case, the TM is vasculitic and thickened or may be covered with epithelialitis or granulation tissue. The TM can also be retracted and adhered to middle ear mucosa. The diseased middle ear mucosa seen through a perforation is erythematous and polypoid. Cholesteatoma may be evident.

On the other hand, active disease may be silent within the mastoid at the same time the middle ear appears inactive. In this case, suspicion must be high to make a timely diagnosis. Obstruction of the antrum by adhesions, fibrosis, or granulation tissue isolates the mastoid from the middle ear. Unlike acute mastoiditis, which often coexists with acute OM and can be quickly recognized by concurrent fever, tenderness over the mastoid process, or sagging of the posterosuperior wall of the external auditory canal, latent chronic mastoiditis is unsuspected in the absence of these classic signs. Symptoms associated with intratemporal or intracranial complications such as fever, headache, meningeal signs, lethargy, vomiting, deep boring head pain, or focal neurologic symptoms may be the first indication of active disease. When serious complications arise, the onset is abrupt, the diagnosis can be evasive, and treatment may be delayed.

Incidence and Importance

Chronic mastoiditis is probably much more common than currently appreciated. With the development of antibiotic agents successful in treating OM and mastoiditis, acute complications have greatly declined. However, insidious inflammation may persist despite the control of acute suppurative infections. Of 90 patients (123 adult temporal bones) with histologic evidence of chronic OM, Paparella and colleagues (1980) found that only 24 patients had symptoms of otologic disease and fewer had an associated TM perforation. In the same study, 24 ears of 111 infant temporal bones were found to have significant histologic evidence of OM without middle ear symptoms or findings. Several case studies have highlighted the presentation of masked chronic mastoiditis (Holt and Gates, 1983; Palva et al, 1985). In one case series, nine patients (in 4 years reviewed) were diagnosed with masked mastoiditis after presenting with vague ear symptoms and intracranial complications of meningitis, facial paralysis, cerebritis, epidural abscess, and brain abscess. Four of nine patients had intact tympanic membranes (Holt and Gates, 1983).

Interestingly, one group of authors presented an association between infants with intractable diarrhea and latent mastoiditis (De Sousa et al, 1980). In their report of 20 infants with diarrhea found to have persistent mastoiditis, 10 underwent surgical intervention. Of those 10 infants, 9 had resolution of the diarrhea postoperatively. The association is not understood.

Despite its inconspicuous features, chronic mastoiditis may result in all of the serious sequelae of acute mastoiditis, including hearing loss, facial palsy, labyrinthitis, extradural abscess, thrombophlebitis of the sigmoid or lateral sinus, petrositis, meningitis, and temporal lobe abscess. Newborns and diabetic, elderly, and immunosuppressed patients may be at higher risk for complications.

Etiology and Pathogenesis

The pathophysiology of mastoiditis usually parallels disease of the middle ear because the two spaces are confluent. However, if the aditus ad antrum becomes blocked by either cholesteatoma or granulation tissue, the two spaces may begin to act independently. Under the influence of antibiotics, acute infectious processes may be controlled. On examination, the middle ear may be normal. However, within the mastoid, aeration via the eustachian tube has ceased, exposing the cavity to decreasing oxygenation and decreasing pressure. The resulting environment with low oxygen tension and acidic pH fosters the growth of anaerobic bacteria. Production of pus is minimal with these low-grade pathogens. Mucosal edema and effusion occur as a result of the initial infectious process and are aggravated by negative pressure, hypoxia, and hypercapnia. Other factors blamed for roles in the pathogenesis of OM, such as inflammatory mediators and by-products, ciliary dyskinesia, and altered bacterial properties, including adherence and biofilms, likely contribute to disease in the mastoid.

Predominant pathologic features include granulation tissue, osteitis, and bone destruction. Histologic changes of the mucous membrane include metaplasia, inflammatory cell infiltrate, edema, fibrosis of the submucosa, ulceration, and granulation tissue. Demineralization and osteoclastic activity result in resorption of the mastoid trabeculae. This is associated with the radiographic diagnosis of "coalescent mastoiditis." Osteitic bone is replaced by vascular tissue and inflammatory infiltrate. The inflammatory and resorptive process may cause erosion of the ossicles, mastoid cortex, sigmoid sinus plate, or tegmen (Schuknecht, 1993) (Figures 65-1 to 65-4).

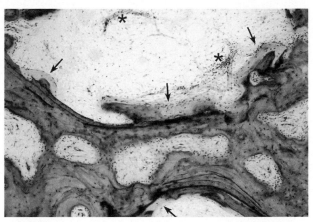

FIGURE 65-1. Osteitis in mastoid. Air cells are filled with fibrous tissue. New bone forming in osteoid tissue (*arrows*). Inflammatory round cell accumulation (*asterisk*). Hematoxylin and eosin stain; ×100 original magnification.

A high index of suspicion is critical when evaluating patients with a history of acute OM or mastoiditis and subtle persisting complaints or with acute meningitis or other intracranial infection without an obvious primary source. High-resolution computed tomography will demonstrate evidence of mastoid disease, osteitis, and bone destruction (Figure 65-5). Magnetic resonance imaging is useful to further delineate mucosal disease but, more importantly, to survey for sigmoid sinus thrombosis, epidural abscess, and cerebral edema or abscess. Radionucleotide studies can suggest increased metabolic activity consistent with osteitis. In the absence of ear symptoms or radiographic findings, the diagnosis may be made only with surgical exploration (Neely and Wallace, 2001).

Management Options

Mastoiditis is a spectrum of progressive inflammation and with it is a sequence of management protocols. Mastoid disease without osteitis associated with middle ear disease will often respond to antibiotic therapy. When chronic OM presents with suppuration and TM perforation, associated mastoid disease will often reverse if the infection is managed with antibiotics and the middle ear and mastoid are sealed by tympanoplasty. In this case, we perform lateral graft tympanoplasty with canalplasty. The canalplasty is important to gain adequate exposure for removal of cholesteatoma and to prepare for placement of the graft flat over the tympanic ring. To prevent adhesions and maintain a middle ear space, diseased mucosa is covered with Gelfilm and antibiotic-soaked Gelfoam before the graft is placed. If a second stage is planned, we use reinforced Silastic to cover denuded mucosa of the promontory, facial recess, and epitympanum.

We perform mastoidectomy when irreversible mastoid disease is suspected based on history, radiographic

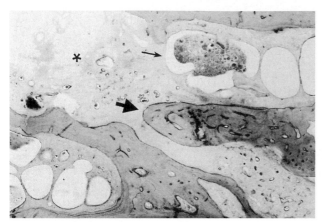

FIGURE 65-2. Mastoid antrum blocked by fibrous tissue (*asterisk*) at the level of the short process of incus (*large arrow*). Air space filled with fluid that has contracted owing to fixation dehydration (*small arrow*). Hematoxylin and eosin stain; ×25 original magnification.

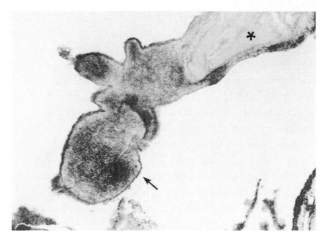

FIGURE 65-4. Granuloma (*arrow*) filled with inflammatory round cells emanating from a mastoid trabeculum (*asterisk*). Hematoxylin and eosin stain; ×60 original magnification.

evidence of osteitis, or intraoperative findings. The surgical goals are to exonerate infection and provide adequate drainage and aeration. In the past, a radical mastoidectomy was thought obligatory; however, an intact canal wall mastoidectomy can effectively eliminate both the mucosal disease and the antral obstructing lesion. A radical or modified radical mastoidectomy may be performed only when it is impossible to remove extensive cholesteatoma or if avoidance of a second surgery is paramount because of the patient's medical condition or the diseased side is the only hearing ear (Sheehy, 1994). A wide facial recess will improve access to disease and aeration to the middle ear and eustachian tube. Dissection of the epitympanum and zygomatic root cells should be performed for the same purpose. With wide exposure, all disease should be eliminated, including in the osteitic

bone and granulation tissue. A curet is useful to remove granulation tissue from hard bone and small air cells.

When a patient presents with chronic drainage from a mastoid bowl, we often perform revision mastoidectomy and mastoid obliteration. After creation of a clean cavity, bone pate collected from the outer cortex of the temporal squamosa and rinsed in antibiotic saline is lightly packed into the mastoid bowl to restructure a posterior canal wall. Elimination of the cavity liberates the patient from irritating cavity-related infections and cleaning routines.

If the ossicular chain is intact but covered with diseased mucosa or adhesions but not cholesteatoma, it can be left intact. A cup forceps or laser can be used to remove bulky disease. With control of infection and improved aeration, the remaining diseased mucosa will normalize. If the incudostapedial joint is not intact, the incus should be removed and a second-stage hearing reconstruction planned. A prosthesis should not be placed in the face of mastoiditis with complications.

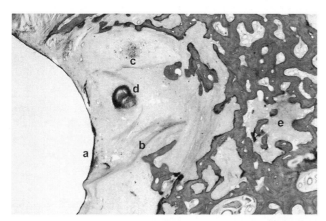

FIGURE 65-3. Antrum blocked by fibrosis and new bone. Keratinizing squamous epithelium (*a*). Tympanosclerosis in fibrous tissue (*b*). Inflammatory round cell accumulation (*c*). Tip of a squamous epithelium–lined pocket projecting into fibrous tissue (*d*). Fibrous tissue in new bone of the antrum (*e*). Hematoxylin and eosin stain; ×25 original magnification.

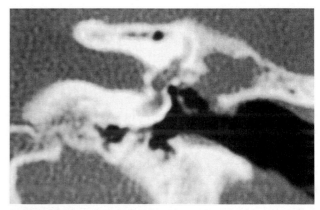

FIGURE 65-5. Coronal computed tomographic scan of left temporal bone demonstrates an aerated normal-appearing middle ear space and diseased obstruction of the antrum.

The facial nerve should be examined for pathologic exposure. If inflammation or edema of the nerve is identified, the nerve should be decompressed to expose healthy epineurium at both ends. The sheath should not be opened in the presence of infection (McCabe et al, 1977).

The bone over the dura should be thinned so that the dura can be examined. Diseased dura and epidural abscess should be treated with wide exposure of diseased bone. Granulation tissue on the dura can be controlled with curettage but does not have to be entirely removed. Caution should be used when excising inflamed tissue because prolapsed dura can be mistaken for granulation tissue (Graham and Lundy, 2001). Too much manipulation of the friable, bloody dura can cause injury and cerebrospinal fluid (CSF) leak. Monopolar cautery should not be used on dura because it is also likely to cause injury. Most of the time, the dura is intact, and communication with CSF can be avoided. If a lesion communicates intradurally, intracranial disease can be managed simultaneously. In this case, the dura should be primarily repaired. Small defects may be managed with a muscle plug or fascia graft.

As discussed, mastoiditis in the face of an intact TM may not be realized until a serious complication has occurred. Management of these complications includes hospital admission, immediate institution of intravenous broad-spectrum antibiotics, and mastoidectomy. A complete neurologic examination should be performed to identify papilledema, facial nerve palsy, meningismus, or other signs of intracranial involvement. Lumbar puncture for CSF pressure and studies should be included in the initial evaluation to rule out otic hydrocephalus and meningitis. Neurosurgical consultation should be sought for definitive management of intracranial complications. Often mastoidectomy is delayed during acute treatment for meningitis, brain abscess, cerebritis, or cerebral edema. Surgical intervention should typically take place as soon as the patient is stabilized for anesthesia.

Conclusion

Chronic mastoiditis is a protracted diseased condition of the mastoid that is refractory to medical therapy and is characterized by the presence of granulation tissue, cholesteatoma, or low-grade pathogens. Careful follow-up should be maintained when treating acute OM and mastoiditis. Recurrent or persistent otologic symptoms should be viewed with a high index of suspicion for chronic latent mastoiditis and associated intratemporal or intracranial complications. Treatment consists of appropriate radiographic study and surgical management of mastoid disease and related complications.

References

DeSousa JS, DaSilva A, DaCosta R. Intractable diarrhea of infancy and latent otomastoiditis. Arch Dis Child 1980;55:937–40.

Graham MD, Lundy LB. Dural herniation and cerebrospinal fluid leaks. In: Brackmann DE, Shelton C, Arriaga MA, editors. Otologic surgery. 2nd ed. Philadelphia: WB Saunders; 2001. p. 216–23.

Holt RG, Gates GA. Masked mastoiditis. Laryngoscope 1983;93:1034–7.

McCabe BF, Katz AE, Sadé J, Ziv M. Acute and chronic mastoiditis. Ann Otol Rhinol Laryngol 1977;86:402–9.

Neely JG, Wallace MS. Surgery of acute infections and their complications. In: Brackmann DE, Shelton C, Arriaga MA, editors. Otologic surgery. 2nd ed. Philadelphia: WB Saunders; 2001. p. 155–65.

Palva T, Virtanen H, Makinen J. Acute and latent mastoiditis in children. J Laryngol Otol 1985;99:127–36.

Paparella MM, Meyerhoff WL, Goycoolea MV. Silent otitis media. Laryngoscope 1980;90:1089–98.

Schuknecht HF. Pathology of the ear. 2nd ed. Philadelphia: Lea & Febiger, 1993.

Sheehy JL. Surgery of chronic otitis media. In: English GM, editor. Otolaryngology: diseases of the ear and hearing. Philadelphia: Lippincott; 1994. p. 1–87.

Chapter 66

FACIAL PARALYSIS IN OTITIS MEDIA

BARRY SCHAITKIN, MD, FACS

Facial paralysis is a worrisome and fortunately infrequent complication of otitis media (OM). However, it can be one of the earliest symptoms of acute otitis media (AOM). All patients presenting with facial paralysis should have a complete head and neck examination, and in children, a particular focus should be the performance of otoscopy, preferably with the operating microscope. Immediate referral to an otolaryngologist should be carried out in all cases for both diagnosis and treatment.

Involvement of the facial nerve from infection differs completely with the type of OM, whether acute or chronic, so each type is dealt with separately in this chapter.

Acute Otitis Media

Incidence

It is difficult to obtain meaningful data on the incidence of facial paralysis from AOM. Older studies suffer from the changes over the years in both the microbiology and the availability of antibiotics. Because AOM is managed extensively by the pediatrician and general otolaryngologists, those series that look at facial paralysis probably do not capture the vast majority of cases. Ellefsen and Bonding (1996) reviewed the preantibiotic incidence of facial paralysis owing to AOM. In 1899, Vogt estimated the incidence at 0.5% in patients with AOM. In 1937, Pollmann reported an incidence of 0.7%, and Kettle found an incidence of 0.5% in 10,000 patients he studied in 1943 (Ellefsen and Bonding, 1996). Telischi and coworkers (2000) reviewed the causes of facial paralysis in 3,650 consecutive patients. Bell's palsy, which makes up the most common etiology of inflammatory facial paralysis, made up 50% of this series, which was skewed toward cases referred to a tertiary care center. Overall, infection made up less than 4% of the total. Table 66-1 reviews the causes of facial paralysis in this group.

Ellefsen and Bonding (1996) reviewed 17 years of admissions of patients with facial paralysis from AOM to the hospitals of Copenhagen and found only 23 patients, for an incidence of 2.3 cases per million inhabitants.

Their data would suggest a contemporary incidence of 0.005%. Sixty-one percent of their 23 patients were children, and all were younger than 3 years of age. This is most likely in keeping with the high frequency rates of OM in this age group. However, they did have 26% of the patients in the 50 years of age and older group. In the Telischi and coworkers series, 48% of the patients were over the age of 18 years (Telischi et al, 2000).

Pathophysiology

Involvement of the facial nerve from AOM is felt to be secondary to the organism gaining entry to the nerve through dehiscences in the fallopian canal. Such dehiscences have been described by multiple authors (Baxter, 1971). It is, of course, true that no one knows for sure that this is the mechanism of action. Joseph and Sperling (1998) pointed out that this proposed mechanism is based on extremely limited information and is primarily circumstantial based on the intimacy between the facial nerve and the middle ear and the fact that dehiscences in

TABLE 66-1. Inflammatory Causes of Facial Paralysis

Disease	Cases (*n*)
Acute bacterial otitis media	61
Chronic otitis media	28
With cholesteatoma	24
Without cholesteatoma	4
Malignant (necrotizing) external otitis	4
Acute otitis externa	1
Other inflammatory disorders	36
Chickenpox	8
Poliomyelitis	7
Infectious mononucleosis	5
Lyme disease	3
Myringitis bullosa hemorrhagica	2
HIV+/AIDS	2
Other	9
Total	130

Adapted from Telischi FF et al (2000).
AIDS = acquired immune deficiency syndrome; HIV = human immunodeficiency virus.

this segment have been described in as high as 83% of patients. Other possible causes include the fact that the nerve is affected by a toxic by-product of the organisms, ischemia, or some type of pressure phenomenon. It is also possible that the inflammatory process does not affect the nerve through these areas of dehiscences but gets there through preformed vascular spaces. White and McCans (2000) discussed the possible mechanisms of facial paralysis, listing direct bacterial invasion, mechanical compression, acute toxic neuritis, and bacterial toxin leading to demyelinization as possible etiologies.

Microbiology

The organisms that cause facial paralysis are those that are seen for OM in general. Here there is also not a great deal of data, but in Ellefsen and Bonding's study (1996), two-thirds of the patients had either no growth or saprophytes on culture. The remaining patients had primarily *Haemophilus influenzae*, although group A streptococcus, pneumococcus, and *Staphylococcus aureus* were all seen.

Treatment

Medical

The treatment of facial paralysis associated with AOM is primarily medical and involves therapeutic doses of appropriate antibiotics.

Myringotomy

In addition to antibiotic therapy, a wide myringotomy and drainage both for culture and treatment are recommended for all cases of AOM associated with facial paralysis. Some authors recommend myringotomy and tympanostomy tube insertion.

Mastoid Surgery

Surgery other than myringotomy has an extremely limited role in this setting. Surgery should be restricted to those who develop a subperiosteal abscess or coalescent mastoiditis or have persistent purulent drainage through the myringotomy. In the immunocompromised setting, mastoid surgery may be indicated both for diagnosis and for culturing unusual organisms.

In the rare event when surgery is performed, mastoid surgery should clear infected bone and soft tissue. There is no evidence that opening the sheath is indicated in this setting, and my preference would be to let the disease dictate the extent of mastoidectomy required.

Telischi and coworkers (2000) reported on 37 patients with facial paralysis owing to AOM who were seen in the first 14 days. Table 66-2 reviews the patients' final House-Brackmann score (Table 66-3 describes the House-Brackmann grading system). Goldstein and coworkers (1998) reported on 22 cases and recommended surgery based on nerve conduction studies. They found that evoked electromyography (EEMG) correlated with outcome in

TABLE 66-2. Recovery of Facial Function in 37 Patients with Facial Paralysis owing to Acute Otitis Media

Type of Recovery	Number of Patients	%
Satisfactory		92
Grade I	31	
Grade II	3	
Unsatisfactory		8
Grade III	3	
Grade IV		
Total	37	100

Grade refers to the House-Brackmann grading system.

patients with a complete paralysis but not in those with an incomplete paralysis. However, EEMG is designed for predicting outcome in the complete paralysis setting, and it is here that it has value. It is to be expected that patients with an incomplete paralysis will have a good outcome.

In general, the advantage of EEMG is that it is capable of determining if the nerve has been severely affected. Because most pathologies affect the nerve in the temporal bone, EEMG, measuring down field potentials, will require time to show a loss of potentials. Even nerve transection requires 3 days to show a decreased response.

TABLE 66-3. House-Brackmann Grading System

Grade	Description	Characteristics
I	Normal	Normal facial function in all areas
II	Mild dysfunction	Gross: slight weakness noticeable on close inspection; may have very slight synkinesis
		At rest: normal symmetry and tone
		Motion
		Forehead: moderate to good function
		Eye: complete closure with minimum effort
		Mouth: slight asymmetry
III	Moderate dysfunction	Gross: obvious but not disfiguring difference between two sides; noticeable but not severe synkinesis, contracture, and/or hemifacial spasm
		At rest: normal symmetry and tone
		Motion
		Forehead: slight to moderate movement
		Eye: complete closure with effort
		Mouth: slightly weak with maximum effort
IV	Moderate severe dysfunction	Gross: obvious weakness and/or disfiguring asymmetry
		At rest: normal symmetry and tone
		Motion
		Forehead: none
		Eye: incomplete closure
		Mouth: asymmetric with maximum effort
V	Severe dysfunction	Gross: only barely perceptible motion
		At rest: asymmetry
		Motion
		Forehead: none
		Eye: incomplete closure
		Mouth: slight movement
VI	Total paralysis	No movement

Adapted from Telischi FF et al (2000).

Surgical decompression is recommended in traumatic lesions when the amplitude of the summation potential is 10% or less than that of the contralateral normal side within 6 days of the onset of the paralysis because this most likely represents a divided nerve requiring reconstitution. In Bell's palsy, some authors recommend decompression if there is a 90% loss of summation potentials within 10 days and the EEMG shows no voluntary action potentials. This therapeutic approach would be reasonable for patients with AOM causing a complete facial paralysis who lose 90% of their summation potential during the first 10 days of treatment.

Chronic Suppurative Otitis Media

Incidence

Again, one must look historically to see the change in the incidence of this complication. In the preantibiotic era, mortality from chronic OM was 4%. In the Telischi and coworkers study (2000) within the infectious etiologies, AOM occurred more than 2 to 1 over chronic OM. The majority of cases of chronic OM were associated with cholesteatoma. Because of this, most cases of facial paralysis occur at the anatomic point, where cholesteatoma is commonly near the facial nerve, particularly in the region of the cochleariform or pyramidal process. It is in these two locations that cholesteatoma tissue may become trapped between a fixed bony prominence and the compressible facial nerve. Patients then present either acutely with infection in a chronic ear or in a slowly progressive manner owing to the compression and toxic products at the edge of the cholesteatoma. In the 28 patients with chronic OM whom Telischi and coworkers studied (2000), 24 of them had cholesteatoma, and their ages ranged from 2 to 83 years. Only 1 of these 24 patients with cholesteatoma was younger than 18. In contrast, 2 of the 4 patients with chronic OM without cholesteatoma were under 8 years of age.

Pathophysiology

It is unclear whether facial paralysis in chronic OM is from toxic products, inflammation, ischemia, or pressure.

Patients who present with chronic OM and facial paralysis should have preoperative imaging studies, primarily high-resolution computed tomographic scans both in an axial and a coronal plane. In patients who remain unclear, magnetic resonance imaging may add additional information.

Treatment

Patients with facial paralysis in this setting require exploratory mastoidectomy. The nerve must be explored and decompressed throughout the area of disease. I allow the extent of pneumatization to dictate the type of mastoidectomy, reserving canal wall down procedures for poorly pneumatized temporal bones. It goes without saying that all landmarks and disease should be cleared away from the facial nerve prior to embarking on decompression of that structure.

Recovery of facial function in this group depends on intervening within 10 days of onset of the paralysis with good preoperative electrical testing. In six patients whom Telischi and coworkers (2000) treated beyond 3 weeks from the onset of their paralysis and in whom EEMG was now absent, none had a complete recovery, two had a grade VI, three had a grade V, and two had a grade IV. All of the patients with normal electrophysiology had a full recovery. EEMG is the electrical test of choice for decision making in the setting of inflammatory disease and facial paralysis.

Harker and Pignatar (1992) operated on six patients without cholesteatoma and achieved grade I in five and grade II in one.

Conclusion

Fortunately, the vast majority of patients with facial paralysis from OM can be successfully treated. Treatment should be offered on an urgent to emergent basis from the time of onset of the paralysis. For those with AOM, once the diagnosis is certain, wide myringotomy is effective in 92% of patients, and in this setting, we can usually achieve a House-Brackmann grade I or II. Patients who are immunocompromised or are slow to recover with this initial treatment should be treated aggressively. There is a need for surgical intervention in some cases.

All of the patients with chronic OM require surgical therapy. The vast majority of these patients have cholesteatoma that will need to be treated with some form of mastoidectomy. If the patients are seen within 10 days of the onset of their facial paralysis and have good preservation of electrical testing, the likelihood of a good recovery is still excellent.

References

Baxter A. Dehiscence of the fallopian canal. An anatomical study. J Laryngol Otol 1971;85:587–94.

Ellefsen B, Bonding P. Facial palsy in acute otitis media. Clin Otolaryngol 1996;21:393–5.

Goldstein NA, Casselbrant ML, Bluestone CD, Kurs-Lasky M. Intratemporal complications of acute otitis media in infants and children. Otol Head Neck Surg 1998;119:444–54.

Harker LA, Pignatar. Facial nerve paralysis secondary to chronic otitis media without cholesteatoma. Am J Otol 1992;13:372–4.

Joseph EM, Sperling NM. Facial nerve paralysis in acute otitis media: cause and management revisited. Otol Head Neck Surg 1998;118:694–6.

Telischi FF, Chandler JR, May M, Schaitkin B. Infection: otitis media, cholesteatoma, necrotizing external otitis, and other inflammatory disorders. In: May M, Schaitkin B, editors. The facial nerve: May's 2nd ed. New York: Thieme; 2000. p. 383–91.

White N, McCans KM. Facial paralysis secondary to acute otitis media. Pediatr Emerg Care 2000;16:343–5.

Chapter 67

BALANCE AND OTITIS MEDIA

MARGARETHA L. CASSELBRANT, MD, PHD

Eustachian tube dysfunction with and without middle ear effusion (MEE) has long been considered one of the most common causes of balance disturbances in young children (Blayney and Colman, 1984; Busis, 1976; Fried, 1980; Mercia, 1942). Although balance has not traditionally been included as one of the considerations guiding therapy of otitis media with effusion (OME) and eustachian tube dysfunction, recent data suggest that it should be. Persistent and recurrent episodes of MEE could potentially cause impairment of balance with possible long-term consequences such as a delay in the development of motor functions and achievement of motor milestones. Because otitis media (OM) is one of the most common diseases in children, this could have important clinical implications.

This chapter reviews the existing literature on the effect of OM and eustachian tube dysfunction and balance in children. Clinical implications are outlined and implications for therapy are discussed.

Previous Studies

Only recently have studies been performed in children that have concerned the anecdotal evidence that vestibular, balance, and motor function may deteriorate during an episode of MEE. Many different methodologies have been used to assess balance, such as electronystagmography (ENG), forced and moving posture platforms, gross motor function testing, and other methods. In most studies, the children have been compared with a control group of children or have been used as their own control when studied pre- and post-tympanostomy tube insertion.

Electronystagmography

ENG includes oculomotor, caloric, and positional testing and involves recording of eye movements (nystagmus). It provides a record of spontaneous nystagmus or induced nystagmus (caloric and positional testing) with objective measurements of the response. In the studies reported in this chapter, only spontaneous nystagmus and nystagmus induced by positional changes have been reported.

Golz and colleagues (1991) evaluated 97 children with MEE aged 4 to 7 years, using ENG, which included spontaneous and positional nystagmus recordings. Abnormal ENG was found in 71% of the children with MEE compared with only 4% in a control group of 50 age-matched children with no MEE. The abnormal ENG findings resolved in 99% of the children after tympanostomy tubes were inserted. A correlation was found between abnormal ENG findings and subjective balance disturbances as reported by the parents.

In 1998, Golz and colleagues tested 136 children, aged 4 to 9 years, using ENG before and after tympanostomy tube insertion and compared the results with those obtained in 74 healthy age- and sex-matched children with no history of middle ear disease (Golz et al, 1998b). In this study, pathologic ENG findings were found in 58% of the children with MEE compared with only 4% of the control group ($p < .001$). Balance disturbance was found to occur as frequently in children with unilateral as with bilateral effusion. The symptoms and signs of balance disturbances resolved in 96% of the 77 children who were tested at least 1 month after tube insertion.

ENG, Romberg's test, and past pointing testing were performed in 30 children with MEE aged 8 to 13 years and in 15 age- and sex-matched controls (Koyuncu et al, 1999). Spontaneous nystagmus was documented in 3% and positional nystagmus in 33%. The Romberg's test showed abnormalities in 33% of the children and the past pointing test in 10% of the children with MEE compared with none in the controls ($p < .05$). After tympanostomy tube insertion, vestibular test results returned to normal and symptoms related to vestibular disturbances improved.

Platform Posturography

Postural control is maintained by vestibular, visual, and proprioceptive sensory integration and can be evaluated using platform posturography testing. Postural stability is assessed by measuring body sway. The influence of vision can be evaluated by measuring the body sway when the eyes are open or closed. Using a moving posture platform, the influence of proprioception on postural stability can also be assessed by measuring the body sway while the subject is standing on a platform when it is stable and when it is moving. This can be performed with eyes open and eyes closed. When the subject is tested on a moving platform while moving and with eyes closed, the subject is relying on the vestibular system alone for postural stability.

In a pilot study, nine children, 4 to 9 years of age, with a history of recurrent or persistent MEE were examined pre- and post-tympanostomy tube insertion using a moving posture platform (Casselbrant et al, 1983). No difference in postural stability was found between children with bilateral and unilateral MEE as long as they could use vision or proprioception. However, when these sensory inputs were eliminated, the two children with unilateral MEE lost their balance. After tympanostomy tube placement, these two children with unilateral effusion could perform all parts of the test.

Body sway measurements (speed of sway) were assessed using a fixed-force body sway platform in 34 chil-

FIGURE 67-1. EquiTest system shows the child standing on the platform surrounded by a visual scene. A safety harness is attached to the child should loss of balance occur. The platform surface and visual surround are capable of moving independently or simultaneously. Pressure-sensing strain gauges beneath the platform's surface detect the patient's sway by measuring vertical or horizontal forces applied to the surface. Reproduced with permission from NeuroCom International, Inc.

dren aged 3 to 5 years with chronic MEE and in 34 age- and sex-matched controls (Jones et al, 1990). Prior to tympanostomy tube insertion, body sway parameters were significantly greater in children with MEE than in controls ($p < .05$). Four months after tympanostomy tube insertion, there was no longer any significant difference between the two groups. There was no correlation between a parental history of imbalance and poor test results.

A moving posturography platform (NeuroCom, International, Inc., Clackamas, OR) (Figure 67-1) was used to evaluate 41 children 3 to 12 years of age with OME before and after tympanostomy tube insertion and 50 children with normal middle ear status (Casselbrant et al, 1995). The children were tested on the moving posture platform under six standard sensory conditions (Figure 67-2). Children with MEE had a significantly higher mean velocity of sway than children with normal middle ear status ($p < .05$). For both groups, younger children (< 7 years) had a significantly higher velocity than older children (> 7 years) ($p < .001$). The velocity of sway for condition VI (most difficult) decreased significantly ($p < .05$) in 22 children tested within a month after tube insertion. Only 8% of the children with normal middle ear status fell during posturography testing compared with 63% of the children with MEE. There was also a significant difference in the proportion of children falling pretube versus post-tube ($p < .05$). Most of the children fell on conditions V and VI.

In a later study, Casselbrant and colleagues (1998) investigated the effects of moving visual environments (optic flow) on body sway in 11 children aged 3 to 9 years with MEE and 11 age-matched children with normal middle ears. The subjects were placed on a posture platform with a visual surround (NeuroCom, International, Inc.), which moved back and forth sinusoidally at two frequencies, 0.10 and 0.25 Hz. The results indicate that children with MEE have increased body sway in response to moving visual scenes. This was particularly evident for the higher frequencies (0.25 Hz) ($p = .04$). Children with MEE are more reliant on vision for maintaining balance.

Gross Motor Function Testing

The two most common tests to assess gross motor function are the Peabody Developmental Motor Scale (PDMS-GM) and the Bruininks Oseretsky Tests for Motor Proficiency (BOTMP). These two tests are standardized, and normative age-appropriate data are available. The PDMS-GM test includes five domains over 17 age levels and includes reflexes, balance, nonlocomotion mobility, and ability to catch and throw. The BOTMP test evaluates bilateral coordination, strength, and running speed and agility.

Golz and colleagues (1998a) evaluated 64 children, age 4 to 7 years, using the BOTMP test before and after tube insertion and compared the results with those obtained in 57 age- and sex-matched healthy children with no history of middle ear disease. Of the 64 children with MEE, 61% performed significantly below the expected scores for their age compared with 7% of the controls ($p < .001$). Forty-eight children were tested after tympanostomy tube insertion, and only 4% ($p < .001$) continued to perform below expected scores for age. Following tympanostomy tube insertion, there was no difference in the BOTMP test scores between the two groups of children. A correlation was found between low test scores and parents reporting balance disturbance in their child.

Cohen and colleagues (1997) tested 25 children with MEE (19 bilateral and 6 unilateral disease) aged 13 to 47 months using the gross motor subtests of the PDMS test and compared the results with those of age-matched controls. Bilaterally, but not unilaterally, affected children performed significantly worse compared with controls on balance ($p < .02$), locomotion ($p < .01$), and total scores ($p < .01$). The parents' perception of the children's balance correlated poorly with the test results (total PDMS score; $p < .34$).

Orlin and colleagues (1997) investigated preschool children aged 24 to 60 months using the gross motor portion of the PDMS-GM test. Thirteen children with MEE were compared before and after tympanostomy tube placement with 12 children without MEE and no history

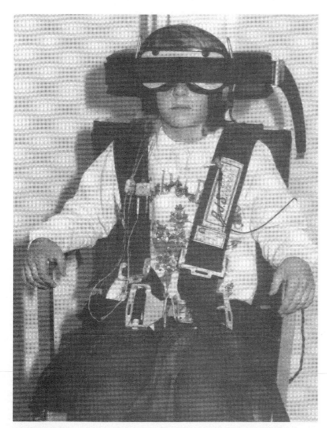

FIGURE 67-2. The six sensory testing conditions of the EquiTest posturography platform. Reproduced with permission from NeuroCom International, Inc.

of middle ear disease. The children with MEE had significantly reduced scores preoperatively compared with those without MEE on the PDMS-GM ($p < .05$). After surgery, the children with MEE had higher scores than those without MEE.

Using both the PDMS and the BOTMP, Hart and colleagues (1998) showed that MEE significantly affected balance and motor skills in 19 children with MEE aged 4 to 6 years when compared with 14 age- and sex-matched controls with a minimal history of middle ear disease. Children with MEE showed a significantly lower performance in the balance subscales than children with no MEE ($p < .01$). Both groups of children improved when retested. The improvement after tube insertion in children with MEE was much greater than the improvement seen in the controls on retest ($p = .05$). The improvement in children with normal middle ears could be attributed to a learning effect.

Motor performance was evaluated in two groups of children aged 5 to 6 years (Von et al, 1988). One group consisted of 16 children with a history of OM who had had tympanostomy tubes inserted within the 20 months preceding testing, whereas none of the 16 children in the other group had a history of OM. The Motor Accuracy Test-Revised, the Stott Test of Motor Impairment, and a measure of standing balance were used to assess fine motor coordination, overall motor skills, and balance, respectively. On each of these measures, the children with a history of OM scored lower than the children without a history of OM, but the differences were not statistically significant.

Other Methods

Denning and Mayberry (1987) examined balance function in 18 4- to 5-year-old children with and 17 children without a history of OM (six or more episodes) using the Southern California Postrotatory Nystagmus Test (SCPNT) and five tests from the Miller Assessment for Preschoolers. Children with a history of OM had significantly decreased percentile rank scores on the Stepping test (72% versus 18%; $p < .001$) and on Vertical Writing (67% versus 24%; $p < .01$) compared with children without a history of OM. There was no significant difference for duration of nystagmus as measured by the SCPNT ($p = .93$).

Fifty children, age 4 to 9 years, with MEE and 20 age-matched children with normal middle ear status were evaluated using a rotating chair oscillation test and craniocorpography (CCG) (Ben-David et al, 1993). The CCG is a stepping test in which the movements of the head and shoulder are recorded. There were no significant differences in the CCG deviation between children with MEE and children with normal middle ears, nor were there any significant differences between the CCG results recorded before tympanostomy tube insertion and those obtained 2 months after surgery in the children with MEE. However, they recorded a significant difference between the two groups in regard to right postrotatory nystagmus ($p = .04$).

Factors Influencing the Assessment of Balance

Method of Testing

Several different methods, including ENG, posture platform testing, and gross motor function testing, have been used to evaluate the effect of OM on balance function. Children with MEE have usually been compared with an age- and often sex-matched control group of children with no or a minimal history of middle ear disease. In addition, in many of the studies, the children have been used as their own control because they have also been tested pre– and post–tympanostomy tube insertion. In the majority of the studies, balance function was affected when there was fluid in the middle ear compared with balance function in the control subjects or after tympanostomy tubes had been inserted.

Only two of the studies (Ben-David et al, 1993; Von et al, 1988) did not demonstrate an effect of MEE on balance function. In the study by Von and colleagues (1988), the children had undergone tympanostomy tube insertion 20 months prior to testing, but there was no information regarding middle ear status at the time of testing. It is possible that all children had patent tympanostomy tubes or the middle ear status was normal at the time of testing, which would explain why there was no difference between the two groups pre– and post–tympanostomy tube insertion. In the second study (Ben-David et al, 1993), balance function in children with MEE was compared with that of normal controls as well as of themselves after tympanostomy tube insertion using the CCG testing. The CCG method is not a commonly used test method, and it is possible that it is not sensitive enough to demonstrate any differences in balance function.

Asymmetry of MEE

In the first pilot study by Casselbrant and colleagues (1983), the two children with unilateral disease performed worse than the children with bilateral middle ear disease. This finding could have been caused by the small number of the children tested because this difference between children with unilateral and bilateral disease was not found when a large cohort of children was tested (Casselbrant et al, 1995). Golz and colleagues (1998b) reported that balance disturbance was as frequent in children with unilateral disease as it was in children with bilateral disease. However, Cohen and colleagues (1997) reported that children with bilateral disease performed worse than children with unilateral disease. In none of the studies is the exact duration of the MEE or the amount of fluid in the middle ears known at the time of

testing. A high negative pressure in the middle ear could cause the same effect on balance as fluid in the ear.

Correlation between Test Results and Parents' Perception

In some studies, information regarding the parents' perception of the child's motor performance was obtained. Golz and colleagues (1991, 1998a, 1998b) reported a positive correlation between abnormal ENG and BOTMP test results and balance disturbance such as frequent falling, clumsiness, or unsteadiness reported by the parents. The parents also reported improvement in the child's balance after tympanostomy tube insertion. Contrary to these results, Cohen and colleagues (1997) and Jones and colleagues (1990) reported that the parents' perception of the child's balance performance correlated poorly with the test results. The poor correlation between the parents' perception of the child's performance in some studies could have been caused by poor knowledge about the child's motor development. Thus, because OM is most common in younger children, it is important to educate parents about a child's motor development and achievement of milestones.

Clinical Implications

The pathophysiology behind the effect of OM on balance function is not known, but it may reflect an impairment of the peripheral vestibular system through passage of toxic substances or transmission of pressure through the middle ear via the round or oval window affecting the labyrinth.

The integrity of the vestibular apparatus is considered critical for motor development. Infants with a hypoactive labyrinth are delayed in standing and walking (Rapin, 1974; Tsuzuku and Kaga, 1992), and abnormalities of the semicircular canals found in children with CHARGE association (coloboma of the eye, heart anomaly, choanal atresia, retardation, and genital and ear anomalies) are associated with delayed motor development (Murofushi et al, 1997; Wright et al, 1986). Also, children with both congenital and acquired vestibular deficits have more difficulties with balance in sensory conflict situations (Pykko et al, 1986; Selz et al, 1996).

Children with MEE are more reliant on visual cues than on vestibular and proprioceptive impulses for maintaining balance (Casselbrant et al, 1998). They behaved similarly to adult patients with vestibular deficits and patients with anxiety and space and motion discomfort, who also have demonstrated reliance on visual cues for postural stability (Jacobs et al, 1995; Redfern and Furman, 1994). This increased reliance on vision for balance may indicate that vestibular function is reduced or vestibular input is disregarded. In a child with MEE who depends on visual cues for balance, play may simulate moving visual surrounds. Adaptive strategies may fail, and the child may become clumsy and more prone to accidents or falls, leading to injury. In support of this notion, a retrospective study from Sweden (Stenstrom and Ingvarsson, 1994) that compared otitis-prone children with control children with no or a minimal history of OM in regard to ambulatory visits to the orthopedic clinic found a statistically significant difference between the two groups in the number of total visits per child (0.32 versus 0.21; $p < .01$) and the number of children involved (26.9% versus 17.8%; $p < .05$), indicating that otitis-prone children seem to be more accident prone.

OM is one of the most common diseases in young children and causes a mild to moderate hearing loss (Fria et al, 1985), which may cause developmental delays or learning disabilities. The presence of a hearing loss has been an important factor in the consideration regarding treatment intervention. On the contrary, very little attention has been focused on the effect of OM on balance and the necessity for treatment intervention. The Agency for Health Care Policy and Research (AHCPR) guidelines (Stool et al, 1994) included only hearing loss and duration of fluid as indications for tympanostomy tube insertion, but in a response by Bluestone and Klein (1995) to the AHCPR guidelines, it was emphasized that balance disturbance should also be considered as an indication for tympanostomy tube insertion. Middle ear disease is usually a disease of young children, who often cannot express their symptoms, but if there is concern about the child being "clumsy" or having delayed developmental milestones, this should be considered in the decision regarding treatment of the child's ear disease.

It should be pointed out that for the normal child with MEE whom the parents perceive as being "clumsy" and who improves after tympanostomy tube insertion, no additional testing needs to be done. However, any child who expresses complaints about dizziness, experiences balance problems, or does not improve after tympanostomy tube insertion should undergo additional testing. This is usually an older child because he/she can verbalize the symptoms. Such a child should be worked up for dizziness of unknown etiology, which includes a thorough history, a complete physical and otoneurologic examination, hearing testing, imaging (computed tomography or magnetic resonance imaging), and vestibular testing including ENG, rotational testing, and posturography testing. In addition, a child who complains of dizziness during an episode of AOM should be evaluated for complication of the disease, such as labyrinthitis or meningitis.

Author's Experience

With the knowledge of the results from the studies presented above on the effect of OM on balance in children and my own clinical experience, I consider it very important to obtain a history regarding each child's motor development and balance from every parent whose child is being evaluated for OM. Some parents may report that their child is clumsy during an episode of OM or that their child's balance has improved after tympanostomy tube insertion. However, many parents may not spontaneously report these observations until they are specifically asked, but then they may confirm that they have noticed an improvement in the child's balance after the tympanostomy tube insertion. If there are any concerns regarding balance in a child with fluid in the middle ear, I strongly recommend tympanostomy tube insertion.

Conclusion

In an otherwise normal child whose balance seems to be affected by fluid in the middle ear, tympanostomy tube insertion should be considered because a child who is clumsy may be prone to accidents. In addition, we do not yet know the long-term effect of MEE on balance. This is being addressed in an ongoing, prospective study of children with a documented history of middle ear disease since early infancy who have undergone yearly vestibular, balance, and motor development testing from 2 to 9 years of age. Preliminary results indicate that for the older children, the long-term effect of OM on balance seems to be minimal (Casselbrant et al, 2000).

References

Ben-David J, Podoshin L, Fradis M, Faraggi D. Is the vestibular system affected by middle ear effusion? Otolaryngol Head Neck Surg 1993;109:421–6.

Blayney AW, Colman BH. Dizziness in childhood. Clin Otolaryngol 1984;9:77–85.

Bluestone CD, Klein JO. Clinical practice guideline on otitis media with effusion in young children: strengths and weaknesses. Otolaryngol Head Neck Surg 1995;112:507–11.

Busis SN. Vertigo in children. Pediatr Ann 1976;2:478–81.

Casselbrant ML, Black FO, Nashner L, Panion R. Vestibular function assessment in children with otitis media. Ann Otol Rhinol Laryngol 1983;107:46–7.

Casselbrant ML, Furman JM, Mandel EM, et al. Past history of otitis media and balance in four-year-old children. Laryngoscope 2000;110:773–8.

Casselbrant ML, Furman JM, Rubenstein E, Mandel EM. Effect of otitis media on the vestibular system in children. Ann Otol Rhinol Laryngol 1995;104:620–4.

Casselbrant ML, Redfern MS, Furman JM, et al. Visual-induced postural sway in children with and without otitis media. Ann Otol Rhinol Laryngol 1998;107:401–5.

Cohen H, Friedman EM, Lai D, et al. Balance in children with otitis media with effusion. Int J Pediatr Otorhinolaryngol 1997;42:107–15.

Denning J, Mayberry W. Vestibular dysfunction in preschool children with a history of otitis media. Occup Ther J Res 1987;7:335–48.

Fria TJ, Cantekin EI, Eichler JA. Hearing acuity of children with otitis media with effusion. Arch Otolaryngol 1985;11:10–6.

Fried MP. The evaluation of dizziness in children. Laryngoscope 1980;90:1548–60.

Golz A, Angel-Yeger B, Parush S. Evaluation of balance disturbances in children with middle ear effusion. Int J Pediatr Otorhinolaryngol 1998a;43:21–6.

Golz A, Netzer A, Angel-Yeger B, et al. Effects of middle ear effusion on the vestibular system in children. Otolaryngol Head Neck Surg 1998b;119:695–9.

Golz A, Westerman ST, Gilbert LM, et al. Effect of middle ear effusion on the vestibular labyrinth. J Laryngol Otol 1991;105:987–9.

Hart MC, Nichols DS, Butler EM, Barin K. Childhood imbalance and chronic otitis media with effusion: effect of tympanostomy tube insertion on standardized tests of balance and locomotion. Laryngoscope 1998;108:665–70.

Jacob RG, Redfern MS, Furman JM. Optic flow-induced sway in anxiety disorders associated with space and motion discomfort. J Anxiety Disord 1995;9:411–25.

Jones NS, Radomskij P, Prichard AJN, Snashall SE. Imbalance and chronic secretory otitis media in children: effect of myringotomy and insertion of ventilation tubes on body sway. Ann Otol Rhinol Laryngol 1990;99:477–81.

Koyuncu M, Muhittin S, Tanyeri Y, et al. Effects of otitis media with effusion on the vestibular system in children. Otolaryngol Head Neck Surg 1999;120:117–21.

Mercia FW. Vertigo due to obstruction of the eustachian tube. JAMA 1942;118:1282–4.

Murofushi T, Ouvrier RA, Parker GD, et al. Vestibular abnormalities in CHARGE association. Ann Otol Rhinol Laryngol 1997;106:129–34.

Orlin MN, Effgen SK, Handler SD. Effect of otitis media with effusion on gross motor ability in preschool-aged children: preliminary findings. Pediatrics 1997;99:334–7.

Pykko I, Starck J, Scholtz HG, et al. Evaluation of vestibular deficiency using posturography. In: Claussen CF, Krane MV, editors. Vertigo, nausea, tinnitus and hearing loss in cardiovascular diseases. New York: Elsevier Science Publishers; 1986. p. 363–70.

Rapin I. Hypoactive labyrinths and motor development. Clin Pediatr (Phila) 1974;13:922–3.

Redfern M, Furman J. Postural sway in response to optic flow stimuli in vestibular patients. J Vestib Res 1994;4:221–30.

Selz PA, Girardi M, Konrad HR, Hughes LF. Vestibular deficits in deaf children. Otolaryngol Head Neck Surg 1996;115:70–7.

Stenstrom C, Ingvarsson L. General illness and need of medical care in otitis prone children. Int J Pediatr Otorhinolaryngol 1994;29:23–32.

Stool SE, Berg AO, Berman S, et al. Otitis media with effusion in young children. Clinical practice guideline number 12. Rockville (MD): US Department of Health and Human Services, Agency for Health Care Policy and Research; July 1994. AHCPR Publication No.: 94-0622.

Tsuzuku T, Kaga K. Delayed motor function and results of vestibular function tests in children with inner ear anomalies. Int J Pediatr Otorhinolaryngol 1992;23:261–8.

Von T, Deitz JC, McLaughlin J, et al. The effects of chronic otitis media on motor performance in five and six-year-old children. Am J Occup Ther 1988;42:421–6.

Wright CG, Brown OE, Meyerhoff WL, Rutledge JC. Auditory and temporal bone abnormalities in CHARGE association. Ann Otol Rhinol Laryngol 1986;95:480–6.

Chapter 68

Sensorineural Hearing Impairment

Ellis M. Arjmand, MD, PhD

Although it is generally accepted that acute otitis media (AOM) can lead to sensorineural hearing impairment (SNHI), the mechanism by which this occurs, the frequency with which it occurs, and the severity of the resulting hearing impairment are not well known. Consequently, the implications for therapy of AOM are not defined. Even less is known about the likelihood of SNHI developing from other forms of otitis media (OM) (eg, chronic suppurative OM, chronic serous OM, adhesive OM).

Relevant reports in the literature include animal studies (in which middle ear [ME] bacterial inoculation or direct application of toxin to the round window [RW] membrane is performed), case review studies (in which the contralateral ear is often the control), and case reports of SNHI in patients with a history of OM. Unfortunately, the literature on this subject is difficult to manage. The definition of OM varies, cholesteatoma may or may not be present, and the use of potentially ototoxic topical antibiotics is confounding.

It seems clear that SNHI does not frequently develop as a consequence of OM because, if it did, the incidence of SNHI in children would likely be much higher than it is. However, it may be that OM accounts for a much higher percentage of pediatric SNHI than is currently recognized. Evidence in support of this comes from experimental findings that ME pathogens and inflammatory agents can enter the inner ear and from human case series, which, although less than completely convincing, indicate that many patients with chronic OM develop permanent SNHI, typically of a mild degree.

Some authors attribute a high percentage of pediatric SNHI to chronic OM (Billings and Kenna, 1999). Although this is not widely accepted and is difficult to establish with certainty, in many cases, it is also difficult to exclude OM as a cause. Logic suggests, however, that OM would most likely cause unilateral or asymmetric SNHI, given its relatively rare occurrence relative to the incidence of OM (ie, it is unlikely that both ears would be affected equally and simultaneously). In addition, several studies demonstrate that the effects of ME or RW mem-

brane toxin application are dose dependent, and the endotoxin and exotoxin used in many studies are derived from organisms not commonly causing OM. It is difficult to know how findings from these studies relate to actual cases of OM.

This chapter reviews the recent literature on SNHI related to OM. The reader should note that the terminology for various forms of OM is not used consistently in the literature, and in some cases, the definitions in the primary references are not entirely clear. Here the references are cited with attention to acute or chronic OM, with or without cholesteatoma, with or without otorrhea, and adhesive OM is included as a separate category. A brief review of experimental data precedes a discussion of the relevant clinical studies.

Background

Complications of OM that may lead to SNHI are well known and well described. Traditionally, serous and suppurative labyrinthitis are described. More recently, labyrinthitis has been categorized as acute, subacute, chronic, and labyrinthitis ossificans (Bluestone and Klein, 1995). Labyrinthitis as a disease entity is discussed elsewhere in this text. There are several mechanisms by which labyrinthitis may develop but, when occurring as a consequence of OM, all involve continuity between the ME and the inner ear. The usual places of entry are the RW, oval window (OW), and lateral semicircular canal (especially in the case of erosion by cholesteatoma).

The degree to which normal RW and OW membranes are permeable to pathogens is controversial. In some patients with inner ear anomalies, these sites allow a greater likelihood of transmission of pathogens from the ME to the inner ear. This subject has recently received increased attention owing to the finding of an unexpectedly high incidence of meningitis in cochlear implant recipients (O'Donoghue et al, 2002). It is thought that the subset of these cochlear implant recipients with inner ear anomalies is predisposed to otitic meningitis owing to

RW or OW abnormalities; others develop meningitis from the spread of OM through the cochleostomy. Although this is a special case of inner ear infection developing from OM, and it may not bear directly on the pathogenesis of SNHI from OM in otherwise healthy individuals, the potential effects of ME disease on the inner ear are demonstrated.

Experimental Data

The literature relating to inner ear effects of OM is extensive, and a thorough review is beyond the scope of this chapter. A brief summary of some relevant findings is provided.

Goycoolea and colleagues, in a series of articles published in the 1980s (Goycoolea et al, 1980a; 1980b; Paparella et al, 1984), determined that the RW membrane is the likely route of spread for ME contents into the inner ear. Anatomic changes of the RW membrane were reported in a cat model of eustachian tube obstruction; the oval window was essentially unchanged (Goycoolea et al, 1980b). A subsequent study demonstrated that human serum albumin applied to the RW niche passed through the RW membranes of cats with eustachian tube obstruction but not in control animals (Goycoolea et al, 1980a). Furthermore, time-dependent changes in RW membrane permeability were demonstrated, with a reduction in permeability following 1 to 2 weeks of eustachian tube obstruction (Schachern et al, 1987).

More recent studies have demonstrated inner ear damage from *Pseudomonas* exotoxin applied to the chinchilla RW membrane; the effects were dose dependent (Lundman et al, 1992). Bacterial endotoxin (*Salmonella* derived) applied to the chinchilla ME crossed the RW membrane, resulting in a marked inflammatory response in the inner ear (Kawauchi et al, 1988). The passage of macromolecules, such as proteases, from the ME to the inner ear may be facilitated by the effects of toxins in the ME. This was shown experimentally using ME application of radioiodinated streptolysin O and albumin in the guinea pig (Engel et al, 1998).

In a rat model, a single ME application of *Escherichia coli* lipopolysaccharide caused a change in auditory brainstem response (ABR) thresholds; the effect was greatest at higher frequencies (ie, the cochlear regions closest to the RW). Interestingly, morphologic changes in the inner ear were not detected by light microscopy in this study (Spandow et al, 1989). A dose-dependent effect of ME endotoxin (*E. coli* lipopolysaccharide) on the ABR has been demonstrated (Kim and Kim, 1995).

Clinical Data

Clinical reports of SNHI in patients with OM involve patients with chronic otitis media with effusion (COME), chronic OM with otorrhea, chronic OM with cholesteatoma, adhesive OM, and AOM. Patient ages vary widely, as does the duration of the disease. It is difficult to draw strong conclusions because the patient populations are quite heterogeneous, but some patterns and trends emerge. A number of recent and significant reports are reviewed here.

COME

In a study of 71 children with COME, audiometric data from 119 affected ears were reported (Mutlu et al, 1998). Eight children had evidence of SNHI, defined as a bone-conduction loss of at least 25 dB for one or more frequencies between 250 and 4,000 Hz. The determination that SNHI was due to OM was based solely on the clinical history. Six children had SNHI at a single frequency, with rapid clinical improvement. The other two children had SNHI at two or more frequencies, with complete resolution in one patient but permanent SNHI in the other. The permanent SNHI was of mild degree, and it appears that the cases of transient SNHI were also mild.

A 19% incidence of SNHI was reported in a large clinical series of 1,372 children and adults with COME (Harada et al, 1992). The incidence of SNHI attributed to COME was 1%. Half of the patients in this series were children younger than 10 years of age. The incidence of SNHI increased with increasing patient age. Of 14 patients with SNHI, acute onset and gradual improvement were seen in 5, all of whom were adults. Nine patients had gradually progressive, permanent SNHI; five of these nine patients were children. The severity of permanent SNHI ranged from mild to profound. Interestingly, all nine patients who developed permanent SNHI had preexisting SNHI, ranging in severity from minimal to moderate.

A small case series identified permanent SNHI attributable to COME in two adults and one child (Aviel and Ostfeld, 1982). The severity of SNHI was variable: one patient had unilateral severe SNHI, one had bilateral high-frequency SNHI, and one had bilateral predominantly low-frequency SNHI. Both adult patients had experienced symptoms of dysequilibrium.

These reports illustrate a shortcoming typical of case series on this topic, namely that it is difficult to know with certainty if the SNHI can be attributed to the COME, despite the authors' contention that there were no other known etiologic factors.

In general, it appears that permanent SNHI develops only rarely as a consequence of COME. The severity is variable but typically mild. Some patients with permanent SNHI had preexisting SNHI of a milder degree, and some adults who developed SNHI had symptoms of vestibular dysfunction. There are also reports of mild, reversible SNHI associated with COME. Whether any patients in these studies who developed SNHI had inner ear anomalies is not described.

Chronic OM with Otorrhea and/or Cholesteatoma

Chronic suppurative OM,* without cholesteatoma, has been shown in some studies to have no effect on cochlear function (ie, bone-conduction hearing thresholds) in children (Kaplan et al, 1996). Eighty-seven children between 2 and 16 years of age, some with bilateral disease, were studied. All had a history of otorrhea, via a tympanic membrane perforation, of at least 2 months duration. Hearing was assessed following medical therapy, 3 days after achieving a dry ear. The contralateral ears of patients with unilateral otorrhea served as controls.

In contrast, others have reported permanent SNHI in patients with chronic otorrhea. As many as 18% of chronically infected ears were found to have permanent high-frequency SNHI; hearing impairment was seen more frequently in patients with cholesteatoma and in older patients. Patients younger than 10 years and older than 60 years were excluded, but those who had been treated with ototoxic topical agents were not (Vartiainen and Karjalainen, 1987).

Similarly, Paparella and colleagues (1980) attributed SNHI occurring at 1,000, 2,000, and 4,000 Hz to chronic OM. Data from 47 patients were reviewed; patients with other known causes of SNHI were excluded. Longer duration of ear drainage was thought to be associated with more severe hearing impairment, although this is not clearly demonstrated. The average effect on hearing is mild, even for patients with 20 to 30 years of otorrhea. Localized tympanogenic labyrinthitis, via invasion through the RW membrane, was proposed as the cause of SNHI based on temporal bone studies and preliminary laboratory data.

Others have reported that chronic otorrhea is associated with SNHI, but cholesteatoma is not (Blakeley and Kim, 1998). Records were reviewed from 123 patients at least 15 years of age, some with cholesteatoma, who had chronic unilateral otorrhea. Hearing was assessed at 500, 1,000, and 2,000 Hz, with the contralateral, noninfected ears serving as controls. An average difference in a bone-conduction threshold of 5 dB was seen between the infected and control ears, with great variability among patients. The presence of cholesteatoma was not a significant determinant of hearing threshold; the percentage of patients with cholesteatoma is not given.

A significant degree of SNHI was also reported in a group of 161 patients (ages 5 to 87 years) with chronic unilateral otorrhea (Levine et al, 1989). The difference in pure-tone average averaged 9.1 dB, and there was a significant difference at each frequency from 250 to 4,000 Hz, ranging from 5.6 to 12.8 dB. Most patients had a small difference in bone-conduction thresholds between diseased and control ears, but a few had a pronounced difference. The range is not given, but 20% had differences greater than 20 dB between ears. Ossicular erosion, the presence of cholesteatoma, and the extent of mucosal disease were associated with slightly more severe SNHI. Patients who had received potentially ototoxic topical antibiotics were not excluded.

Summarizing and drawing conclusions from these reports are difficult. Otorrhea, cholesteatoma, and longer duration of disease have been shown to be associated with SNHI in some series, but the literature is far from conclusive. The positive findings of SNHI in patients with chronic otorrhea suggest a small effect overall, but there appears to be significant variability among individuals. Unfortunately, the intersubject variability is not well described in many of these studies. The negative findings seem to indicate that SNHI in patients with otorrhea is uncommon, not that it does not occur. The practice of looking for differences in average bone-conduction thresholds may fail to reveal a clinically significant difference in a small number of patients; in this instance, case reports may be more revealing than case series.

Chronic OM

Several other studies of chronic OM, involving both pediatric and adult patients, have demonstrated a small yet significant average difference in bone-conduction thresholds. The effect is greater at higher frequencies, which some authors have taken as evidence for RW invasion at the route for cochlear damage. Average differences in bone-conduction thresholds between the diseased and control (contralateral) ears are less than 10 dB (MacAndie and O'Reilly, 1999; Noordzij et al, 1995). All patients in both of these studies underwent ear surgery, but the definition of chronic OM was not precisely given (eg, presence or absence of otorrhea, duration of symptoms), and patients who had used ototoxic topical antibiotics were not excluded.

The potential for severe SNHI in some patients with chronic OM is demonstrated in a study of 897 patients (80% older than 16 years of age), 3% of whom had profound SNHI in the affected ear (Vartiainen and Vartiainen, 1995). Profound SNHI was more common in elderly patients. Some degree of SNHI was seen in 12% of the 115 pediatric patients, but only 1.7% had profound SNHI.

Adhesive OM

Adhesive OM has been shown to have similar effects on hearing to chronic OM with otorrhea in a study with a similar design (Dommerby and Tos, 1986). Sixty-seven patients with unilateral adhesive OM, some of whom had cholesteatoma, were treated and followed for a minimum of 2 years (96% were followed for more than 2 years). In 76% of the ears, bone-conduction thresholds in the treated ear were at least 10 dB poorer at one or more frequencies. Overall, the finding of SNHI in affected ears was common, but the average differences were small, there was wide variability between subjects, and all patients had undergone surgery. The hearing loss was not progressive over the time of observation in the study.

AOM

The effect of AOM on hearing is perhaps of greatest interest clinically with regard to pediatric OM. Rahko and colleagues (1989) did not see any significant differences in air- or bone-conduction thresholds as a function of the number of episodes of AOM in a group of 359 children (5 years of age). The children were studied when the otologic examination and tympanograms were normal. The number of episodes of AOM ranged from zero to more than eight, but the number of children in each group is not provided. Given the apparently low incidence of SNHI as a consequence of OM, it may be that the sample size in this study is too small to demonstrate an effect.

Anecdotal evidence indicates that both transient and permanent SNHI can result from AOM. SNHI that was more pronounced at higher frequencies (eg, 4,000 to 8,000 Hz) developed in two adults with documented purulent ME effusions (Paparella et al, 1984). One patient had a permanent, severe, high-frequency SNHI.

Treatment Recommendations

SNHI should be suspected in children with AOM who develop symptoms of dysequilibrium or a marked subjective change in hearing. Similarly, SNHI should be suspected in patients with chronic OM (adhesive, chronic suppurative, chronic otorrhea, chronic OME) who develop vestibular symptoms or a marked subjective change in hearing. These patients should have an immediate hearing assessment, including high-frequency audiometric testing if available. If SNHI is confirmed or cannot be excluded owing to patient age and lack of cooperation, aggressive treatment of OM should be instituted. In cases of AOM, immediate myringotomy should be performed, with or without tympanostomy tube placement. Broad-spectrum antibiotics should be used; intravenous antibiotics should be considered in patients with chronic forms of OM. For patients with chronic OM, imaging studies (preferably computed tomography [CT]) are recommended to rule out cholesteatoma or other bone-erosive disease processes. In cases of AOM with secondary SNHI, imaging by CT or magnetic resonance imaging should be performed to evaluate for inner ear anomalies that may be associated with preformed ME to inner ear pathways.

In patients with known inner ear anomalies, for whom the likelihood of preformed pathways from the ME to the inner ear is thought to be increased, routine treatment of AOM should include broad-spectrum antibiotics (ie, more aggressive initial treatment of AOM than is customary). The same principle applies to cases of AOM in children with preexisting SNHI of any etiology because the consequences of exacerbation of SNHI are significant.

Conclusion

Many studies show some degree of SNHI associated with chronic OM. Reports vary regarding the significance of cholesteatoma, ossicular erosion, and duration of disease. It is difficult to draw conclusions owing to the nature of these clinical reports and the extremely heterogeneous patient populations.

The average degree of SNHI associated with OM is mild, but this finding may be misleading. There appears to be great variability between subjects. Reports of individual cases reveal that severe to profound SNHI is occasionally seen in patients with AOM and in patients with chronic OM.

The precise mechanism for SNHI as a consequence of OM is not known, but the greater effect on higher-frequency hearing, in conjunction with laboratory evidence, suggests that the cochlear damage is related to RW membrane permeability.

The effect of ototoxic topical antibiotics on hearing cannot be excluded in many of these studies.

In a large percentage of cases, the etiology of pediatric SNHI is unknown. One must consider the possibility of OM as the cause, particularly in patients with inner ear anomalies and in patients with delayed-onset unilateral SNHI.

Earlier, more aggressive treatment of OM (both acute and chronic) may be indicated in certain cases, for example, patients with inner ear anomalies, patients with new-onset SNHI or vestibular symptoms, and patients with preexisting SNHI.

References

Aviel A, Ostfeld E. Acquired irreversible sensorineural hearing loss associated with otitis media with effusion. Am J Otolaryngol 1982;3:217–22.

Billings KR, Kenna MA. Causes of pediatric sensorineural hearing loss. Arch Otolaryngol Head Neck Surg 1999;125:517–21.

Blakeley BW, Kim S. Does chronic otitis media cause sensorineural hearing loss? J Otolaryngol 1998;27:17–20.

Bluestone CD, Klein JO, editors. Otitis media in infants and children. 2nd ed. Hamilton (ON): BC Decker; 1995. p. 241–91.

Dommerby H, Tos M. Sensorineural hearing loss in chronic adhesive otitis. Arch Otolaryngol Head Neck Surg 1986;112:628–34.

Engel F, Blatz R, Schliebs R, et al. Bacterial cytolysin perturbs round window membrane permeability barrier in vitro: possible cause of sensorineural hearing loss in acute otitis media. Infect Immun 1998;66:343–6.

Goycoolea MV, Paparella MM, Goldberg B, et al. Permeability of the round window membrane in otitis media. Arch Otolaryngol 1980a;106:430–3.

Goycoolea MV, Paparella MM, Juhn SK, et al. Oval and round window changes in otitis media. Potential pathways between middle and inner ear. Laryngoscope 1980b;90:1387–91.

Harada T, Yamasoba T, Yagi M. Sensorineural hearing loss associated with otitis media with effusion. ORL J Otorhinolaryngol Relat Spec 1992;54:61–5.

Kaplan DM, Fliss DM, Kraus M, et al. Audiometric findings in children with chronic suppurative otitis media without cholesteatoma. Int J Pediatr Otorhinolaryngol 1996;35:89–96.

Kawauchi H, DeMaria TF, Lim DJ. Endotoxin permeability through the round window. Acta Otolaryngol (Stockh) 1988;457:100–15.

Kim CS, Kim HJ. Auditory brain stem response changes after application of endotoxin to the round window membrane in experimental otitis media. Otolaryngol Head Neck Surg 1995;4:557–65.

Levine BA, Shelton C, Berliner KI, et al. Sensorineural loss in chronic otitis media. Arch Otolaryngol Head Neck Surg 1989;115:814–6.

Lundman L, Santi PA, Morizono T, et al. Inner ear damage and passage through the round window membrane of *Pseudomonas aeruginosa* exotoxin A in a chinchilla model. Ann Otol Rhinol Laryngol 1992;101:437–44.

MacAndie C, O'Reilly BF. Sensorineural hearing loss in chronic otitis media. Clin Otolaryngol 1999;24:220–2.

Mutlu C, Odabasi AO, Metin K, et al. Sensorineural hearing loss associated with otitis media with effusion in children. Int J Pediatr Otorhinolaryngol 1998;46:179–84.

Noordzij JP, Dodson EE, Ruth RA, et al. Chronic otitis media and sensorineural hearing loss: is there a clinically significant relation? Am J Otol 1995;16:420–3.

O'Donoghue G, Balkany T, Cohen N, et al. Meningitis and cochlear implantation. Otol Neurotol 2002;23:823–4.

Paparella MM, Goycoolea MV, Meyerhoff WL. Inner ear pathology and otitis media. Ann Otol Rhinol Laryngol Suppl 1980;89:249–53.

Paparella MM, Morizono T, Le CT, et al. Sensorineural hearing loss in otitis media. Ann Otol Rhinol Laryngol 1984;93:623–9.

Rahko T, Karma P, Sipilä M. Sensorineural hearing loss and acute otitis media in children. Acta Otolaryngol (Stockh) 1989;108:107–12.

Schachern PA, Paparella MM, Goycoolea MV, et al. The permeability of the round window membrane during otitis media. Arch Otolaryngol Head Neck Surg 1987;113:625–9.

Spandow O, Anniko M, Hellström S. Inner ear disturbances following inoculation of endotoxin into the middle ear. Acta Otolaryngol (Stockh) 1989;107:90–6.

Vartiainen E, Karjalainen S. Factors influencing sensorineural hearing loss in chronic otitis media. Am J Otolaryngol 1987;8:13–5.

Vartiainen E, Vartiainen J. Age and hearing function in patients with chronic otitis media. J Otolaryngol 1995;24:336–9.

Chapter 69

LABYRINTHITIS

CHARLES D. BLUESTONE, MD

Labyrinthitis is usually a complication of otitis media (OM), which occurs when infection spreads into the cochlear and vestibular apparatus. But labyrinthitis can also be attributable to extension of infection from the subarachnoid space when meningitis occurs. When OM is the pathogenesis, the middle ear infection spreads through the round or oval window, but invasion may also take place from an infectious focus in an adjacent area, such as the mastoid antrum or petrous bone, or as a result of bacteremia. An abnormal communication between the middle and inner ears owing to a congenital or acquired defect (eg, trauma, cholesteatoma, tumor, or iatrogenic) is not an uncommon cause. When otogenic labyrinthitis develops, acute meningitis can occur with the ever-present danger of significant morbidity and mortality (Bluestone, 2003).

Classification

Schuknecht (1993) has reclassified labyrinthitis into three types:

- serous (toxic) labyrinthitis, in which there may be bacterial toxins or biochemical involvement but no bacteria are present
- suppurative (acute and chronic otogenic suppurative) labyrinthitis, in which bacteria have invaded the otic capsule
- meningogenic suppurative labyrinthitis, which is the result of invasion of bacteria from the subarachnoid space into the labyrinth. Labyrinthitis ossificans (labyrinthine sclerosis), in which there is replacement of the normal labyrinthine structures by fibrous tissue and bone, is the end stage of this complication, if arrested.

An alternative and acceptable classification of labyrinthitis today is the following (Bluestone et al, 2002):

- acute labyrinthitis
- subacute labyrinthitis
- chronic labyrinthitis
- labyrinthitis ossificans

Acute Labyrinthitis

This stage of labyrinthitis can be classified as being either acute serous or suppurative labyrinthitis, and each of these entities can be either localized or generalized.

Acute Serous Labyrinthitis

Acute serous labyrinthitis (also termed acute "toxic" labyrinthitis) is considered to be one of the most common complications of OM. Histopathologic studies in human temporal bones revealed evidence of serous labyrinthitis in most specimens from individuals who had OM (Paparella et al, 1972). Bacterial toxins from the infection in the middle ear may enter the inner ear, primarily through an intact round window or through a congenital defect between the middle ear and inner ear. The portal of entry may also be through an acquired defect of the labyrinth, such as from head trauma or previous middle ear or mastoid surgery. Biochemical changes within the labyrinth have also been found. The cochlea is usually more severely involved than the vestibular system. A review of audiograms of patients who had surgery for chronic OM revealed a significant degree of bone-conduction loss in the younger age groups (Paparella et al, 1980). Also, there were marked differences in the presence and degree of sensorineural hearing loss in the affected ear, compared with the normal ear, in patients of all age groups who had unilateral disease. They postulated that the high-frequency sensorineural hearing loss that frequently accompanies this disease is attributable to a pathologic insult to the basal turn of the cochlea. We reviewed the intratemporal complications of OM at our hospital that occurred between 1980 and 1995 and identified three children admitted with a diagnosis of acute serous labyrinthitis, which were complications of acute otitis media (AOM) (Goldstein et al, 1998).

Fluctuating sensorineural hearing loss may have several causes when OM is present, including acute serous labyrinthitis. However, this type of hearing loss has also been thought to be attributable to either endolymphatic hydrops (Paparella et al, 1979) or a perilymphatic fistula (Grundfast and Bluestone, 1978; Supance and Bluestone,

1983). A perilymphatic fistula has been associated with congenital middle and inner ear malformations (Weber et al, 1993). However, fluctuating/progressive sensorineural hearing loss can be attributable to a variety of other hereditary and acquired etiologies (Brookhouser et al, 1994).

Presenting Signs and Symptoms

The clinical presentation of a patient who has serous labyrinthitis (especially when a perilymphatic fistula is present) is sudden, progressive, or fluctuating sensorineural hearing loss or vertigo, or both, associated with OM or one or more of its complications or sequelae, such as mastoid osteitis. Vertigo may be the only presenting symptom. When serous labyrinthitis is a complication of OM and hearing loss is present, it is usually mixed, that is, with both conductive and sensorineural components. In some children who have recurrent middle ear infections, the hearing may be normal between episodes. In other children, only a mild or moderate sensorineural hearing loss will be present at all times. The presence of vertigo may not be obvious in children, especially infants. Older children may describe a feeling of spinning or turning, whereas younger children may not be able to verbalize the symptoms but manifest the dysequilibrium by falling, stumbling, or being clumsy. The vertigo may be mild and momentary, and it may tend to recur over months or years. Onset of vertigo, progressive sensorineural hearing loss, or both in a patient who has a preexisting hearing loss is frequently attributable to a fistula (Fitzgerald, 1996).

Spontaneous nystagmus may also be present, but the signs and symptoms of acute suppurative labyrinthitis, such as nausea, vomiting, and deep-seated pain, are usually absent. Fever, if present, is usually attributable to a concurrent upper respiratory tract infection or AOM. When congenital perilymphatic fistula is present, nystagmus may be observed during the course of the attack of AOM, in addition to the mixed hearing loss. I reviewed the medical records of 47 infants and children who had exploratory tympanotomy for possible fistula at our children's hospital and reported that 30 children (64%) had a past history of OM, and of these 30 patients, 28 (93%) had a fistula diagnosed at surgery (Bluestone, 1988).

Diagnostic Criteria

Classically, a labyrinthine fistula has been identified by performing a fistula test employing a Siegle pneumatic otoscope or by applying positive and negative external canal pressure using the pump-manometer system of an immittance audiometer. This test is considered positive if nystagmus or vertigo is produced by the application of the pressures. Electronystagmography is an objective way of documenting the presence or absence of the nystagmus as the findings of the fistula test may be misleading because there can be false-positive and false-negative results. The test can be done in the presence of a perforation of the tympanic membrane or tympanostomy tube. Fistulae are frequently associated with congenital or acquired defects in the temporal bone, such as the Mondini malformation. But the fistula test has poor sensitivity and specificity in identifying the usual fistula. When vertigo is associated with progressive or fluctuating sensorineural hearing loss, or both, or vertigo is the only complaint, a formal evaluation of balance can be helpful: any labyrinthine dysfunction can be diagnostic and can localize the affected side. Electrocochleography has been advocated to diagnose a fistula (Gibson, 1999), but this method has not been proven to be as sensitive and specific as desired.

Computed tomographic (CT) scans can be helpful in identifying defects of the temporal bone, such as a dilated vestibular aqueduct (Lee et al, 1999). In a study at our hospital, we reviewed the CT scans of 10 children (15 ears) with fistula confirmed at surgery and were able to identify an abnormality of the inner ear, middle ear, or both in 53% of the ears (Weissman et al, 1994).

We used the β_2-transferrin test to detect the presence of perilymph in the middle ear as a way to confirm the presence of a perilymphatic fistula. A sample of the suspect fluid in the middle ear was obtained at the time of exploratory surgery and was then assessed by an immunopathologic assay (Weber et al, 1994; Weber et al, 1995). The test appears specific but not sensitive. Also, a study by Buchman and associates (1999) found that the test did not identify perilymph but was positive when cerebrospinal fluid (CSF) was present. Thus, when the test is positive, it most likely confirms the presence of a CSF leak from the inner to the middle ear, and a more appropriate term for these malformations of labyrinthine windows is congenital perilymphatic/CSF fistula because the fluid emanating from the defect can be CSF (Bluestone, 1999). Currently, the most effective method to diagnose the presence of a perilymphatic fistula is at the time of exploratory middle ear surgery using the operating microscope (Bluestone, 2002b).

Management

When acute serous labyrinthitis develops during an attack of AOM, a tympanocentesis should be performed for microbiologic assessment of the middle ear effusion and a myringotomy to provide adequate drainage. If possible, a tympanostomy tube should also be inserted for more prolonged drainage and in an attempt to ventilate the middle ear. Antimicrobial agents with efficacy against *Streptococcus pneumoniae*, *Haemophilus influenzae*, and *Moraxella catarrhalis*, such as amoxicillin, should be administered. Other organisms, such as *Staphylococcus aureus* and *Pseudomonas*, have also been isolated from the middle ears of children who have acute labyrinthitis (Goldstein et al, 1998). Because these bacterial pathogens can be resistant to the standard recommended treatment of uncomplicated AOM with amoxicillin, an alternative antibiotic should be selected that will be more effective, which may require parenteral administration. When tympanocentesis is performed, selection of the antimicrobial agent can be culture directed. Following resolution of the OM, the signs and symptoms of the labyrinthitis should rapidly disappear. However, sensorineural hearing loss may persist. If the diagnostic assessment indicates a possible congenital or acquired defect of the labyrinth, an exploratory tympanotomy should be performed as soon as the middle ear is free of infection. The most common malformations are an abnormal round window and niche, such as a laterally facing round window, deformities of the stapes superstructure and footplate, deformed long process of the incus, or some combination of these congenital defects. More rarely, a congenital fissure between the round and oval windows is present (Supance and Bluestone, 1983; Weber et al, 1993). If a congenital malformation, with or without an obvious perilymphatic fistula, is found, it should be repaired using temporalis muscle grafts. Even when no defect of the oval or round window is identified, but a fistula is still suspected, the stapes footplate and round window should be covered with a connective tissue graft because a leak may not be present at the time of the tympanotomy but may recur (Grundfast and Bluestone, 1978; Supance and Bluestone, 1983). A tympanostomy tube should be reinserted if recurrent OM persists.

When acute mastoid osteitis, chronic suppurative OM, or cholesteatoma is present, definitive medical and surgical management of these conditions is essential in eliminating the labyrinthine involvement. A careful search for a labyrinthine fistula must be performed when mastoid surgery is indicated. However, a labyrinthectomy is not indicated for serous labyrinthitis. The surgical procedure to repair a perilymphatic/CSF fistula is described in detail in Bluestone (2002b).

When sensorineural hearing loss or vertigo, or both, develops during an attack of AOM or an episode of otitis media with effusion (OME), the patient should be carefully evaluated for the possible existence of serous labyrinthitis, which can be secondary to a congenital defect between the middle and inner ears. This combination is not uncommon, and failure to identify this complication can result in irreversible severe to profound hearing loss, making early diagnosis and prevention imperative. Because prevention of sensorineural hearing loss owing to other causes (such as congenital or viral causes) is not yet possible, our goal should be to prevent this loss of function in those children in whom it can be prevented. In addition, serous labyrinthitis may develop into acute suppurative labyrinthitis, which, in turn, can progress into meningitis (Bluestone, 2003).

Acute Suppurative Labyrinthitis

Suppurative (purulent) labyrinthitis may develop as a complication of OM or mastoiditis when bacteria spreads from the middle ear cleft into the labyrinth through the oval or round window; a preexisting temporal bone fracture; an area where bone has been eroded by cholesteatoma, tumor, or chronic infection; a congenital defect; or iatrogenic, as described above. The most common way in which bacteria enter the labyrinth is from the meninges during an attack of meningitis, but spread of infection by this route is usually not a complication of OM.

Acute suppurative labyrinthitis as a complication of OM is rare today with the widespread use of antibiotics, but this complication still occurs in both developing nations and in industrialized countries. When it occurs in children who have an episode of AOM and who are apparently treated appropriately and adequately, a congenital (or acquired) defect between the middle and inner ears must be ruled out to prevent further hearing loss and recurrence, which can be life-threatening owing to meningitis. Conversely, when a child develops bacterial meningitis, especially recurrent episodes, a congenital defect of the inner and middle ear must be ruled out. A congenital or acquired defect between the paranasal sinuses and the anterior cranial cavity can also cause meningitis. In our review of children who had intratemporal complications of OM at our hospital, we identified two patients who had a suppurative labyrinthitis during a recent 15-year period; one child had a congenital defect of the labyrinthine windows that was considered to be a perilymphatic/CSF fistula (Goldstein et al, 1998).

Presenting Signs and Symptoms

Sudden onset of vertigo, dysequilibrium, deep-seated pain, nausea and vomiting, and sensorineural hearing loss during an episode of AOM or an exacerbation of chronic suppurative OM signals the possibility that acute suppurative labyrinthitis has developed. Hearing loss is severe, and there is loss of the child's ability to repeat words shouted in the affected ear, with masking of sound in the opposite ear. Often spontaneous nystagmus and past-pointing can be observed. Initially, the quick component of the nystagmus is toward the involved ear, and there is a tendency to fall toward the opposite side. However, when there is complete loss of vestibular function, the quick component will be toward the normal ear. The patient may even be ataxic. Commonly, the onset of suppurative labyrinthitis may be followed by meningitis, which can be spread, causing another intracranial suppurative complication, such as cerebellar abscess. Thus, suppurative labyrinthitis is a serious complication of OM. The development of purulent labyrinthitis means that infection has spread to the fluids of the inner ear, and infection can then spread to the subarachnoid space through the cochlear aqueduct, vestibular aqueduct, or internal auditory canal.

Diagnosis

Magnetic resonance imaging (MRI) can be diagnostic of the labyrinthitis, and CT scans can identify congenital or acquired defects of the inner and middle ear that may have predisposed the child to spread of the infection from the middle ear to the labyrinth (and subarachnoid space). In the absence of associated meningitis, the CSF pressure and cell count are normal.

Management

When acute suppurative labyrinthitis occurs as a complication of OM and is not caused by meningitis (without OM), otologic surgery combined with intensive culture-directed, parenteral antimicrobial therapy is indicated. If this complication is attributable to AOM, immediate tympanocentesis (to identify the causative bacterial pathogen) and myringotomy with tympanostomy tube insertion (for adequate and prolonged drainage) are indicated, as described when serous labyrinthitis is present. If acute mastoid osteitis is present, a cortical (simple) mastoidectomy should be performed. However, because this complication can be secondary to cholesteatoma, tympanomastoidectomy is also required, and, in some cases, even a radical mastoidectomy or modified radical mastoidectomy may be required. A modified radical mastoidectomy may also be required when chronic suppurative OM is present without cholesteatoma, but a closed-cavity tympanomastoidectomy is more desirable (Bluestone, 2002a).

When meningitis occurs in association with suppurative labyrinthitis, then otologic surgery (eg, tympanomastoidectomy), other than a diagnostic and therapeutic tympanocentesis and myringotomy, may have to be delayed until the meningitis is under control and the child is able to tolerate a general anesthetic. But it is important to control the source of the infection in the middle ear and labyrinth as soon as possible. A labyrinthectomy should be performed only if there is complete loss of labyrinthine function, which is most likely irreversible, or if the infection has spread to the meninges in spite of adequate antimicrobial therapy. Initially, culture-directed parenteral antimicrobial agents appropriate to manage the primary middle ear and mastoid disease present should be administered. Because cholesteatoma and chronic suppurative OM are frequent causes of suppurative labyrinthitis, antimicrobial agents effective for gram-negative organisms, such as *Pseudomonas aeruginosa* and *Proteus*, are frequently required. The results of culturing the middle ear effusion, purulent discharge, or CSF are important in the selection of the most effective antibiotics.

Chronic Labyrinthitis

Chronic labyrinthitis is most commonly encountered as a complication of middle ear and mastoid disease when a cholesteatoma erodes the labyrinth, resulting in a fistula (Jang and Merchant, 1997). Osteitis may also cause bone erosion of the otic capsule. The fistula most commonly

occurs in the lateral semicircular canal and is filled by squamous epithelium of a cholesteatoma, granulation tissue, or fibrous tissue entering the labyrinth. The middle ear and mastoid are usually separated from the inner ear by the soft tissue at the site of the fistula, but when there is continuity, acute suppurative labyrinthitis may develop. However, chronic labyrinthitis may be caused by chronic suppurative OM or even chronic OME, especially if the child has a congenital defect between the middle and inner ear (congenital perilymphatic fistula).

Presenting Signs, Symptoms, and Diagnosis

The signs and symptoms of chronic labyrinthitis are similar to those of the acute forms of the disease (eg, sensorineural hearing loss and vertigo), except that their onset is more subtle. The disease is characterized by slowly progressive loss of cochlear and vestibular function over a prolonged period of time. The fistula test may be helpful in diagnosing a labyrinthine fistula, an MRI may reveal labyrinthitis, and CT scans may reveal a bony defect (Kvestad et al, 2001). When there is complete loss of function, there may be no signs or symptoms of labyrinthine dysfunction present.

Management

Because a cholesteatoma is the most common cause of this type of labyrinthitis, middle ear and mastoid surgery must be performed. For children with a labyrinthine fistula owing to a cholesteatoma, the preferred surgical procedure is a tympanomastoidectomy, but a modified radical mastoidectomy may be required. When labyrinthine function is still present, the cholesteatoma matrix overlying the fistula may or may not be left undisturbed depending on the extent of the disease because removal could result in total loss of function. Most surgeons advocate performing an intact canal wall procedure and removing the cholesteatoma matrix, either during the initial surgery or at a second-stage procedure.

Failure to diagnose this complication and perform the surgery may result in complete loss of cochlear and vestibular function with possible development of labyrinthine sclerosis or an acute suppurative labyrinthitis. The latter can cause a life-threatening intracranial complication, such as meningitis.

Labyrinthitis Ossificans (Labyrinthine Sclerosis)

This is the end stage of labyrinthitis, which is attributable to fibrous replacement or new bone formation (labyrinthitis ossificans) in part or all of the labyrinth, with resulting loss of labyrinthine function. Currently, this stage of labyrinthitis is most commonly the result of meningitis, not OM. But, as found in the review of CT scans by Weber and colleagues (1993), one child had labyrinthitis ossificans associated with a congenital peri-lymphatic fistula, presumably secondary to OM because meningitis had not occurred. Because this condition is the end stage of healing after acute or chronic labyrinthitis, prevention of disease of the middle ear is the most effective way to prevent this complication.

Labyrinthitis and Meningitis Related to Cochlear Implants and Inner Ear Malformations

Meningitis can result from an extension of infection in the labyrinth, which is caused by OM, when there is an abnormal communication between the middle and inner ears. Recently, the US Food and Drug Administration (FDA) issued a public health Web notification (2002) that recipients of cochlear implants are at risk for meningitis. The FDA noted that during a 14-year period, 91 cases of meningitis have been reported worldwide in patients who received implants, and 17 known deaths resulted from this infection. Most were children under the age of 7 years, but some adults also developed meningitis; the age of onset was from 21 months to 72 years. The pathogenesis of the episodes of meningitis remains uncertain, but the design of the implant and the surgical technique may be factors, and, importantly, the FDA recognizes that some deaf patients who are implant recipients may have congenital malformations of the inner ear that would make them at increased risk for meningitis. The manufacturers of the implants and implant surgeons are currently investigating the possible roles that the devices and the surgical techniques have in these attacks and methods of prevention (O'Donoghue et al, 2002). Indeed, after investigating this possibility, one implant (CLARION, Advanced Bionics) has been identified as a possible source of this complication and has recently been removed from the market, but the manufacturers of the implants and implant surgeons are continuing to evaluate other devices and surgical techniques. All otolaryngologists should be aware of methods to prevent meningitis both in patients who have been implanted or who are candidates for these devices and in all patients, regardless of age, who have sensorineural hearing loss associated with inner ear abnormalities. Also, patients who have recurrent meningitis, even without hearing loss or vertigo, may have a defect of the middle and inner ears.

In addition to surgery of the middle and inner ears (ie, iatrogenic), meningitis can occur in patients who have had injury to or tumors of the temporal bone or who have a congenital malformation of the labyrinth. In these cases, there is an abnormal communication between the inner ear and the middle ear cleft in which pathogens from the middle ear gain access to the labyrinth and the subarachnoid space, resulting in meningitis. As noted by the FDA, congenital malformations of the inner ear can be a cause of the meningitis, which resulted in the sensorineural hearing loss for which the patient received the cochlear implant. Even though most cases of meningitis that result in sensorineural hearing loss are bloodborne, OM may have been the cause. Labyrinthitis could have been the cause of the hearing loss, which could make the patient at risk for meningitis in the future. We had the misfortune to provide terminal care for a 6-year-old boy at our children's hospital who had had a cochlear implant at another institution and who developed fulminating pneumococcal meningitis and died. The histopathologic evaluation of his temporal bones provides an important clue to the possible pathogenesis of meningitis in some of these patients reported by the FDA. As described by Suzuki and colleagues (1998), he had bilateral Mondini malformations of his inner ears and had been implanted in his left ear, but he had OM and labyrinthitis in the contralateral, right, non-operative ear, which spread to the meninges, causing the meningitis. Thus, the cochlear implant was not involved in the pathogenesis of the meningitis, but the underlying inner ear anomaly was. Repair of his congenital labyrinthine fistula might have prevented this unfortunate and potentially preventable suppurative complication of OM.

Prevention

For prevention of labyrinthitis and meningitis in patients who have abnormalities of the inner ear—the possible role that a cochlear implant plays notwithstanding—the clinician should obtain a thorough history from patients and their families regarding antecedent head trauma or major middle and inner ear surgery. If the patient has had meningitis in association with an attack of AOM, the temporal bone anatomy should be evaluated. If there is no past history of OM, but the patient has had recurrent meningitis, the clinician should investigate the anatomy of the temporal bones, paranasal sinuses, and nasopharynx by CT scan. During an episode of AOM, the onset of the signs and symptoms associated with possible labyrinthitis, such as transient or permanent sensorineural hearing loss or vertigo, or both, and as described above, should alert the otolaryngologist to investigate the structure of the temporal bone.

Surgery

One method of prevention of meningitis in patients, especially infants and young children who have a cochlear implant or are candidates for implantation, is to prevent episodes of OM. Prompt treatment of attacks of AOM is warranted, and there is no justification to either delay or withhold antimicrobial therapy in these patients. Another method is to insert tympanostomy tubes in children who are otitis prone (Luntz et al, 2001). But every child who has sensorineural hearing loss may have an abnormal communication between the middle and inner ears, which should be identified and surgically repaired. Unfortunately, even though CT scans can be helpful in identifying these abnormalities, they are not sensitive (Weisman et al, 1994). Recurrent meningitis, even in a child who has normal hearing and normal findings on CT scans but who had AOM with each of the episodes of meningitis, may have a malformation. Indeed, Rupa and associates (2000) recently described just such a child who had no subsequent bouts of meningitis after surgical repair of the congenital middle ear defects in the oval window and promontory; clear fluid flowed from these sites. In this child, the surgeons elected to surgically obliterate the labyrinth, but a less radical procedure, such as using temporalis muscle grafts to close the middle ear defect(s) using a transcanal approach (Bluestone, 2002b), can be effective, especially when the patient has residual and serviceable hearing. Indications for assessment of the middle ear anatomy in patients undergoing cochlear implant surgery would be related to the etiology of the hearing loss, presence or absence of a past history of labyrinthitis or meningitis, and assessment, by imaging, of the anatomy of the middle and inner ears. The decision to perform an exploratory tympanotomy in other patients who are not candidates for cochlear implants but are suspected of having an abnormal communication between the middle and inner ears would be similar as described earlier in this chapter.

Vaccines

As recommended by the FDA, patients of all ages who have implants or who are candidates should receive the currently available safe and effective vaccines to prevent the most prevalent types of bacterial meningitis, *S. pneumoniae* and *H. influenzae*. The FDA public health Web notification reported that CSF culture results are available in 14 cases of meningitis in implant recipients, and the most common organisms were *S. pneumoniae* and *H. influenzae*. In six cases, the vaccination history against *S. pneumoniae* was known, and none of the patients were vaccinated. The FDA currently recommends the vaccination schedule listed in Table 69-1.

As I described previously, the new conjugated pneumococcal vaccine Prevnar is more effective for prevention of meningitis than for prevention of pneumococcal OM; the vaccine does reduce the attack rate of OM in otitis-prone infants and young children and does reduce the rate of tympanostomy tube placement (Bluestone, 2001). However, I believe that patients of *all* ages who have a cochlear implant or who are candidates should be vaccinated. Also, I now recommend that *all* patients, regardless of age, who have an inner ear acquired or congenital abnormality in which there is a communication between the inner ear and the middle ear cleft that is either documented or suspected should have vaccines against both *S. pneumoniae* and *H. influenzae*.

Summary and Conclusions

Even though it is estimated that since 1978, approximately 60,000 patients worldwide have received cochlear implants (Josefson, 2002), and only 52 cases of meningitis have been reported, it is the obligation of the otolaryngologist to attempt to prevent meningitis in all implant recipients and other patients who have not been implanted but who have a documented, or possible, abnormal communication between the inner and middle ears. Thus, I recommend the following:

- Everyone who has sensorineural hearing loss deserves a workup to determine the etiology, even when the patient has severe to profound deafness.
- Patients who develop sensorineural hearing loss of any degree during an attack of AOM should be evaluated for the possibility of labyrinthitis.
- A patient who has moderate to severe vertigo associated with an episode of AOM, even in the absence of sensorineural hearing loss, should be suspect for the presence of a defect between the middle and inner ears.
- Patients who have had meningitis in association with an episode of AOM and every patient who has had recurrent attacks of meningitis must have a workup to determine if the infection originated in the middle ear cleft.
- In addition to a thorough history and assessments of hearing, CT and even MRI should be included in the evaluation of patients who may have a labyrinthine defect.
- OM in patients who have cochlear implants should be prevented by prompt and effective treatment of each attack, and tympanostomy tube placement is advised for infants and young children who are otitis prone.
- Vaccines against the most common bacterial pathogens causing meningitis, *S. pneumoniae* and *H. influenzae*, should be administered to *all* patients who have, or will have, a cochlear implant and should also be recommended to all other individuals who have an abnormal communication between the middle and inner ears.

TABLE 69-1. Current Recommended Schedule of Vaccines for Prevention of Meningitis

Haemophilus influenzae conjugate vaccines for all children up to the age of 5 years

Heptovalent pneumococcal conjugate vaccine (Prevnar) for all children younger than 2 years and for children up to age 5 years who are at high risk of invasive pneumococcal disease

The 23-valent pneumococcal polysaccharide vaccines (Pnu-Immune 23, Pneumovax 23) for children over 2 years, adolescents, and adults who are at high risk for invasive pneumococcal disease

Heptovalent pneumococcal conjugate vaccine (Prevnar) for children 2 to 5 years of age who are at high risk of invasive pneumococcal disease, followed at least 2 months later by a 23-valent pneumococcal polysaccharide vaccine, which provides protection against a broader range of pneumococcal serotypes

Adapted from US Food and Drug Administration (2002).

- Because OM is the most likely antecedent event in the pathogenesis of meningitis in patients who have a middle and inner ear defect, surgical repair is indicated. If cochlear implant surgery is indicated, the repair can be performed at the time of the implantation.
- Because surgery that involves both the middle and inner ears is a known risk factor for potential meningitis, cochlear implants and the surgical technique to insert them may predispose these patients to this infection. Methods to limit the spread of infection from the middle to the inner ear should be investigated.

References

Bluestone CD. Otitis media and congenital perilymphatic fistula as a cause of sensorineural hearing loss in children. Pediatr Infect Dis J 1988;7(11 Suppl):141–5.

Bluestone CD. Implications of beta-2 transferrin assay as a marker for perilymphatic versus cerebrospinal fluid labyrinthine fistula [letter]. Am J Otol 1999;20:174–8.

Bluestone CD. Pneumococcal conjugate vaccine. Arch Otolaryngol Head Neck Surg 2001;127:464–7.

Bluestone CD. Mastoidectomy and cholesteatoma. In: Bluestone CD, Rosenfeld RM, editors. Surgical atlas of pediatric otolaryngology. Hamilton (ON): BC Decker; 2002a. p. 91–122.

Bluestone CD. Perilymphatic fistula and eustachian tube surgery. In: Bluestone CD, Rosenfeld RM, editors. Surgical atlas of pediatric otolaryngology. Hamilton (ON): BC Decker; 2002b. p. 123–32.

Bluestone CD. Prevention of meningitis: cochlear implants and inner-ear abnormalities. Arch Otolaryngol Head Neck Surg 2003:129:279–81.

Bluestone CD, Gates GA, Klein JO, et al. Chairman: committee report: terminology and classification of otitis media and its complications and sequelae. Ann Otol Rhinol Laryngol 2002;111 Suppl 188 (3 Pt 2):8–18.

Brookhouser PE, Worthington DW, Kelly WJ. Fluctuating and/or progressive sensorineural hearing loss in children. Laryngoscope 1994;104:958–64.

Buchman CA, Luxford WM, Hirsch BE, et al. Beta-2 transferrin assay in the identification of perilymph. Am J Otol 1999;20:174–8.

Fitzgerald DC. Perilymphatic fistula in teens and young adults: emphasis on preexisting sensorineural hearing loss. Am J Otol 1996;17:397–400.

Gibson WPR. Electrocochleography in the diagnosis of perilymphatic fistula: intraoperative observations and assessment of a new diagnostic office procedure. Am J Otol 1999;13:146–51.

Goldstein NA, Casselbrant ML, Bluestone CD, Kurs-Lasky M. Intratemporal complications of acute otitis media in infants and children. Otolaryngol Head Neck Surg 1998;119:444–54.

Grundfast KM, Bluestone CD. Sudden or fluctuating hearing loss and vertigo in children due to perilymph fistula. Ann Otol Rhinol Laryngol 1978;87:761–71.

Jang CH, Merchant SN. Histopathology of labyrinthine fistulae in chronic otitis media with clinical implications. Am J Otol 1997;18:15–25.

Josefson D. Cochlear implants carry risk of meningitis, agencies warn. BMJ 2002;325:298.

Kvestad E, Kvaerner KJ, Mair IWS. Labyrinthine fistula detection: the predictive value of vestibular symptoms and computed tomography. Acta Otolaryngol (Stockh) 2001;121:622–6.

Lee D, Stutz S, Coticchia J, Bluestone CD. Quiz case 2. Large vestibular aqueduct syndrome (LVAS). Arch Otolaryngol Head Neck Surg 1999;125:813–5.

Luntz M, Teszler CB, Shupak T, et al. Cochlear implantation in healthy and otitis-prone children: a prospective study. Laryngoscope 2001;111:1614–8.

O'Donoghue G, Balkany T, Cohen N, et al. Meningitis and cochlear implantation. Otol Neurotol 2002;23:823–4.

Paparella MM, Goycoolea MV, Meyerhoff WL. Inner ear pathology and otitis media: a review. Ann Otol Rhinol Laryngol 1980; 89:249–53.

Paparella MM, Goycoolea MV, Shea D, Meyerhoff WL. Endolymphatic hydrops in otitis media. Laryngoscope 1979;89:43–54.

Paparella MM, Oda M, Hiraida F, Brady D. Pathology of sensorineural hearing loss in otitis media. Ann Otol Rhinol Laryngol 1972;81:632–47.

Rupa V, Rajshekhar V, Weider DJ. Syndrome of recurrent meningitis due to congenital perilymphatic fistula with two different clinical presentations. Int J Pediatr Otorhinolaryngol 2000; 54:173–7.

Schuknecht HF. Pathology of the ear. 2nd ed. Philadelphia: Lea & Febiger; 1993.

Supance JS, Bluestone CD. Perilymph fistulas in infants and children. Otolaryngol Head Neck Surg 1983;91:663–71.

Suzuki C, Sando I, Fagan JJ, et al. Histopathological features of a cochlear implant and otogenic meningitis in Mondini dysplasia. Arch Otolaryngol Head Neck Surg 1998;124:462–6.

US Food and Drug Administration. FDA public health Web notification: cochlear implant recipients may be at greater risk for meningitis. Available at: www.fda.gov/cdrh/safety/cochlear.html (accessed Oct 17, 2002).

Weber PC, Bluestone CD, Kenna MA, Kelley RH. Correlation of beta-2 transferrin and middle-ear abnormalities in congenital perilymphatic fistula. Am J Otol 1995;16:277–82.

Weber PC, Kelly RH, Bluestone CD, Bassiouny M. Beta-2 transferrin confirms perilymphatic fistula in children. Otolaryngol Head Neck Surg 1994;110:381–6.

Weber PC, Perez BA, Bluestone CD. Congenital perilymphatic fistula and associated middle-ear abnormalities. Laryngoscope 1993;103:160–4.

Weissman JL, Weber PC, Bluestone CD. Congenital perilymphatic fistula: computed tomography appearance of middle ear and inner ear anomalies. Otolaryngol Head Neck Surg 1994;111:243–9.

Chapter 70

Cholesterol Granuloma of the Middle Ear and Mastoid ("Blue Ear")

A. Necmettin Akyıldız, MD, Yusuf K. Kemaloğlu, MD

Cholesterol granuloma (CG) is a nonspecific inflammatory response to the cholesterol crystals accumulated in the pneumatized bones when underaeration develops. These lesions, which are characterized by foreign body giant cells together with neovascularization and hemosiderin within a fibrous connective tissue under light microscopy (Figure 70-1), macroscopically look like soft brownish material containing shining golden-yellow specks (Biller and Linthicum, 2001; Bluestone and Klein, 1995; Nager and Vanderveen, 1976; Paparella and Lim, 1967; Sadé, 1979).

CG has been reported within the middle ear (ME) and mastoid and petrous portions of the temporal bone. Because the tympanic membrane otoscopically appears to be dark blue (steel blue) when CG is present within the ME, this entity has been named "blue ear" or idiopathic hemotympanum. In blue ear cases, involvement of the mastoid cells is almost invariably the rule. It is a generally accepted consideration that blue ear (ie, CG in the ME and mastoid) and only CG detected in the mastoid cells are sequelae of chronic otitis media with effusion (secretory otitis media [SOM]) (Biller and Linthicum, 2001; Bluestone and Klein, 1995; Nager and Vanderveen, 1976; Paparella and Lim, 1967; Sadé, 1979). Nevertheless, CG was also reported in subjects with chronic suppurative ear disease with or without cholesteatoma. Close associations of blue ear with retraction pockets and/or adhesive otitis media (OM) are depicted in Figure 70-2 (Jaisinghani et al, 1999; Özbilen et al, 1986; Özbilen et al, 1990; Özbilen et al, 1991; Sadé, 1979). Jaisinghani and colleagues (1999) reported significant correlations between retraction of the tympanic membrane and CG. In our previous reports, CG was found in both a refractory SOM group (patients who were not responding to either medical treatment and ventilation tube [VT] insertion and

who were still presenting with SOM after exclusion of the VT placed for at least 2 years [Table 70-1]) and those with retraction pocket or adhesive OM (Akyildiz, 1998a; Akyildiz, 1998b; Özbilen et al, 1986; Özbilen et al, 1990; Özbilen et al, 1991). CG was found in 14 of 43 (32%) subjects with refractory SOM (Akyildiz, 1998b). Further, it has been reported that blue ear and CG in the mastoid cells are associated with blockage of the eustachian tube and/or aeration routes between the mastoid cells and ME and a chronic granular mastoiditis (Akyildiz, 1998a Akyildiz, 1998b; Bluestone and Klein, 1995; Linthicum, 1971; Main et al, 1970; Özbilen et al, 1986; Özbilen et al, 1990; Özbilen et al, 1991; Sheey et al, 1969). The first author reported that blockage of the aditus was found in 72% (31/43) of his cases (Akyildiz, 1998b). Further, mucous metaplasia, together with effusion, was demonstrated in

FIGURE 70-1. Cholesterin crystals can be seen under the respiratory epithelium. Note the cellular infiltration around them. Courtesy of S. Özbilen. *Cholesterol clefts; **middle ear mucosa.

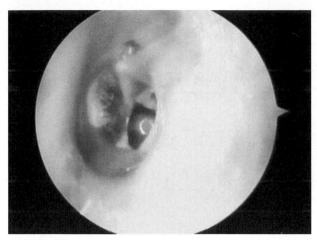

FIGURE 70-2. "Blue ear" with a deep retraction pocket in the posterior portion of the left tympanic membrane. Tympanosclerosis on the anterior portion was developed after extrusion of the second ventilation tube.

most of the subjects (Akyildiz, 1998b). We consider that these data support the contention that CG is associated with SOM and its sequelae.

Therefore, we can make the following statements: (1) as stated by Sadé (1979) and Bluestone and Klein (1995), if blue ear is seen in otoscopy in any case, it points out that this case suffers from a long-standing and refractory chronic ME effusion; hence, mastoid and middle ear surgery, in addition to VT insertion, is indicated in this case; and (2) if we find CG within the mastoid cells and/or antrum during any ear operation, we should understand that underaeration might have played a role in the process of the disease and that an obstruction in the aeration routes between the mastoid cells and ME could be possible.

On the other hand, CG in the petrous apex appears to be a different clinical entity presenting with vertigo, tinnitus, and hearing loss but not active ME disease. However, it has been considered that these lesions are also associated with obstruction of the air cells in the pneumatized petrous apex (Gherini et al, 1985; Goldofsky et al, 1991; Muckle et al, 1998). Because CG in the petrous apex is out of the scope of this chapter, no more attention will be given to it.

Etiology and Pathogenesis

Studies have provided the following data about the pathogenesis of CG: Main and colleagues (1970) observed CG formation, including iron deposits and hemorrhages, by obstructing the eustachian tube in the squirrel monkey for 6 to 12 months. But although they said that it was associated with underaeration of the ME, the reason why and how cholesterin crystals accumulated remained unknown (Main et al, 1970). According to Freidmann (1974), CG is

likely to result from hemorrhage within the mucosal tissue with resultant foreign body reaction. The negative pressure in the ME and mastoid cells may cause tears in the blood vessels and subsequently hemorrhage. The blood in the cavity, because it is unable to drain, is broken down to cholesterol, fibrin, and hemosiderin, and these products subsequently induce a foreign body reaction for CG formation (Biller and Linthicum, 2001; Goldofsky et al, 1991). Nevertheless, Sadé (1979) suggested that the negative pressure in the ME and mastoid cells is not high enough to cause such bleeding (Sadé, 1979). Sadé and colleagues (1980) showed that no evidence of bleeding was present in the ME mucosa. Sadé (1979) reported that lactoferrin (a glycoprotein with a molecular weight of 80,000 D, reversibly binding iron ions) was found in CG and chronically infected ME mucosa, and this glycoprotein may cause CG (Sadé, 1979). Niho (1986) considered that the pathogenesis of the cholesterol deposits is suspected to be fatty degeneration of the connective tissue. Another study on the origin of the cholesterin crystals is that of Miura and colleagues (2002). They found that a large amount of remaining mesenchyme, which was in continuity with the hematopoietic bone marrow in the locations in which CG was present, and that chronic effusion and inflammation of the eustachian tube were observed in all of the reported cases (Miura et al, 2002). These data support the contention that cholesterin crystals could be originated from the blood products even if negative pressure is not enough to cause vascular tears, as stated by Sadé (1979).

Clinical Features

Blue ear is a rare condition, mainly seen in children. As stated by Sadé (1979) and Bluestone and Klein (1995), it is the same disease with SOM, but it points to a more severe condition and even sequelae. That is, a history of long-standing SOM with or without recurrent otitis media, retraction and retraction pocket in the tympanic membranes, adhesive OM, negative pressure, B type tympanograms, and hearing loss (mainly conductive) are clinically detected in the majority of cases. Although asymptomatic cases were reported in the literature, all of

TABLE 70-1. Operative Findings during Mastoidectomy in 43 Patients with Refractory Secretory Otitis Media*

Finding	n (%)
Edema and hypertrophy	43 (100)
Cholesterol crystals	14 (32)
Blockage in aditus	31 (72)
Effusion	41 (95)
Mucous metaplasia	41 (95)

Adapted from Akyildiz N (1998b).
*Recurrence of secretory otitis media following extrusion of the tube after ventilation for 2 or more years.

our cases had at least a retracted tympanic membrane with negative pressure and hearing loss.

In addition, facial paralysis, vertigo, tinnitus, and sensorineural hearing loss may be present if the CG cyst extends to the petrous apex and/or if the lesion or the accompanying chronic suppurative ear disease with cholesteatoma destroys the bony barriers and affects the inner ear and facial nerve.

Differential Diagnosis

Differential diagnosis is particularly important for blue ear. It should be differentiated from a high jugular bulb, glomus tumors, a real hemotympanum, and sometimes barotrauma as they can cause blue discoloration in the tympanic membrane. Differential diagnosis is based on the history, physical examination, and radiologic assessment by computed tomography (CT), magnetic resonance imaging (MRI), and angiography.

In the presence of a high jugular bulb and glomus tumors, the blue discoloration occurs in the lower portion of the tympanic membrane. The pulsation in the drum is suggestive of glomus tumor. In these cases, CT of the temporal bone will be the best for diagnosis. Nevertheless, we do not consider that CT is indicated for each blue ear case. If pulsation is present and if the age, history, and physical findings of the case are not typical for a long-standing and refractory SOM, CT of the temporal bone is recommended. MRI and then angiography are indicated if there is a vascular lesion in CT. Differential diagnosis from a real hemotympanum is not problematic because these cases have an apparent history of trauma. Further, in these cases, the eardrum usually looks red in color, not dark blue, and sometimes perforation and lacerations in the external ear canal may be present.

Differential diagnosis for CG found in the mastoid cells during mastoid surgery is easily recognized by its typical macroscopic appearance, particularly if shining golden-yellow specks are present in a soft brownish material. Nevertheless, if the appearance of the granulation tissue is not typical, a malignancy may have to be ruled out.

If a CG cyst extends to the petrous apex, its differentiation from the petrous cholesteatoma and mucocele is particularly important. Both CT and MRI are recommended in these cases. Although some characteristic CT findings to differentiate CG from cholesteatoma and mucocele are suggested (Gherini et al, 1985; Goldofsky et al, 1991), MRI provides a more accurate diagnosis (Gherini et al, 1985; Goldofsky et al, 1991; Muckle et al, 1998; Lo, 1991). It was reported that CG presents a nonenhancing, smooth-walled, expansile lesion that is isodense with brain tissue in a patient with bilaterally well-pneumatized mastoids and petrous apex (Gherini et al, 1985; Lo, 1991). But cholesteatoma and mucocele are hypodense in CT. In MRI, CG is hyperintense in both T_1 and T_2, whereas cholesteatoma and mucocele are hypointense in T_1 but hyperintense in T_2 (Lo, 1991).

Management

As stated by Sadé (1979) and Bluestone and Klein (1995), the presence of blue ear points to refractory cases and chronic mucosal disease in the ME and mastoid cells. Hence, mastoid surgery and tympanoplasty, together with VT insertion, are the recommended therapy without giving any more medical treatment (Akyildiz, 1998a; Akyildiz, 1998b; Bluestone and Klein, 1995; Sadé, 1979). Nevertheless, medical therapy and only VT insertion were also suggested (Paparella, 1976; Takahashi et al, 1995). Because medical treatment for SOM was given to these cases several times previously, we consider that it is not necessary. Takahashi and colleagues (1995) suggested steroids for blue ear cases. In chronic effusion lasting more than 3 months, the authors prescribe antibiotics (amoxicillin with clavulanate or cefuroxime axetil for 10 days) and dexamethasone together (for days 1 and 2, 0.075 mg/kg/d; for days 3, 4, and 5, 0.00375 mg/kg/d; for days 6, 7, and 8, 0.75 mg/d if the patient weighs less than 40 kg or 1.5 mg/d if the patient weighs more than 40 kg; for days 9 and 10, half of the dosage of day 8) (Akyildiz, 1998b). But many patients relapsed even after VT insertions (Akyildiz, 1998b; Özbilen et al, 1986; Özbilen et al, 1990; Özbilen et al, 1991). Since 1983, the first author of this chapter and his team performed many mastoidectomies in the refractory cases presenting SOM after extrusion of the VT placed for 2 years. Almost all of these cases had dexamethasone at least once, and CG was found in many of them (Akyildiz, 1998a; Akyildiz, 1998b; Özbilen et al, 1986; Özbilen et al, 1990; Özbilen et al, 1991). One of the important factors for deciding on mastoidectomy was mastoid pneumatization. As stated by the researchers, mastoid pneumatization is important in the prognosis of SOM (Bayramoglu et al, 1997; Sadé and Fuchs, 1997). If it is poor and there is no improvement in mastoid aeration after VT insertion, we consider that mastoidectomy is indicated in cases of refractory SOM (Akyildiz, 1998b).

Surgical Technique

The key point for blue ear surgery is not only to clear CG from the ME and mastoid cells but also to establish aeration routes between the mastoid cells, ME, and eustachian tube. Hence, anterior tympanotomy (Holmquist and Bergström, 1978; Morimitsu et al, 1989) is indicated in most cases after a complete simple mastoidectomy and tympanoplasty by the tympanomeatal approach are performed. During the surgery, mucoid effusion in the ME and mastoid cells is encountered in many cases. As the first step of the operation, we do parasynthesis, aspirate the fluid (if any), and sometimes irrigate the ME cavity by saline solution. VT insertion is preferred to be performed in this stage, before elevation of the tympanomeatal flap. Subsequently, mastoid surgery combined with anterior tympanotomy (Morimitsu et al, 1989) is done. During anterior tympanotomy, the anterior attic bony plate (the cog) and a complete Körner's septum are major surgical handicaps that should be removed to provide a new and wide ventilating route by keeping the superior posterior meatal wall intact (Göksu et al, 1997; Hoshino, 1988; Morimitsu et al, 1989).

In the case of petrous apex involvement, if possible, removal of the entire CG is the best. However, drainage via the infracochlear approach is recommended when hearing preservation is desired (Goldofsky et al, 1991; Muckle et al, 1998).

References

Akyildiz N. Kolesterol granüloma. In: Kulak hastalıkları ve mikrocerrahisi. Vol. I. Ankara: Bilimsel Tıp Yayınevi; 1998a. p. 334–5.

Akyildiz N. Sekretuar otitis media. In: Kulak hastalıkları ve mikrocerrahisi. Vol. I. Ankara: Bilimsel Tıp Yayınevi; 1998b. p. 275–330.

Bayramoglu I, Ardic FN, Kara CO, et al. Importance of mastoid pneumatization on secretory otitis media. Int J Pediatr Otorhinolaryngol 1997;40:61–6.

Biller JA, Linthicum FH. Pathology case of the month. Cholesterol granuloma. Otol Neurotol 2001;22:569–70.

Bluestone CD, Klein JO. Complications and sequelae: intratemporal. In: Otitis media in infants and children. 2nd ed. Philadelphia: WB Saunders; 1995. p. 241–92.

Freidmann I. Pathology of the ear. London: Blackwell Scientific; 1974.

Gherini SG, Blackman DE, Lo WM, Solti-Bohman LG. Cholesterol granuloma of the petrous apex. Laryngoscope 1985;95:659–64.

Göksu N, Kemaloğlu YK, Köybaşıoğlu A, et al. Clinical importance of the Körner's septum. Am J Otol 1997;18:304–6.

Goldofsky E, Hoffman RA, Holliday RA, Cohen NL. Cholesterol cysts of the temporal bone: diagnosis and treatment. Ann Otol Rhinol Laryngol 1991;100:181–7.

Holmquist J, Bergström B. The mastoid air cell system in ear surgery. Arch Otolaryngol 1978;104:127–9.

Hoshino T. Surgical anatomy of the anterior epitympanic space. Arch Otolaryngol Head Neck Surg 1988;114:1143–5.

Jaisinghani VJ, Paparella MM, Schachern PA, Le CT. Tympanic membrane/middle ear pathologic correlates in chronic otitis media. Laryngoscope 1999;109:712–7.

Linthicum FH. Cholesterol granuloma (iatrogenic); further evidence of etiology, a case report. Ann Otol Rhinol Laryngol 1971;80:207–10.

Lo WM. Tumors of temporal bone and cerebellopontine angle. In: Som PM, Bergeron RT, Curtin HD, Reede DL, editors. Head and neck imaging. St. Louis: Mosby; 1991.

Main TS, Shimada T, Lim DJ. Experimental cholesterol granuloma. Arch Otolaryngol 1970;4:356–9.

Miura M, Sando I, Orita Y, Hirsch BE. Histopathologic study of the temporal bones and eustachian tubes of children with cholesterol granuloma. Ann Otol Rhinol Laryngol 2002;111:609–15.

Morimitsu T, Nagai T, Nagai M, et al. Long-term results of anterior tympanotomy for cholesteatoma. In: Tos M, Thomsen J, Peitersen E, editors. Proceedings of the Third Conference on Cholesteatoma and Mastoid Surgery. Amsterdam: Kugler Publications; 1989. p. 875–80.

Muckle RP, De la Cruz A, Lo WM. Petrous apex lesions. Am J Otol 1998;19:219–25.

Nager GT, Vanderveen TS. Cholesterol granuloma involving the temporal bone. Ann Otol Rhinol Laryngol 1976;85:204–9.

Niho M. Cholesterol crystals in the temporal bone and the paranasal sinuses. Int J Pediatr Otorhinolaryngol 1986;11:79–95.

Özbilen MS, Akyildiz N, Göksu N. Mastoid surgery in secretory otitis media. In: Sarcristan T, Alvarez-Vincet JJ, Andolf-Candela F, et al, editors. Proceedings of the XIV world congress of otorhinolaryngology, head and neck surgery. Amsterdam: Kugler & Ghedini Publications; 1990. p. 9–11.

Özbilen S, Akyıldız N, Köybaşıoğlu A. Mastoid surgery for middle ear effusion. In: Sadé J, editor. Secretory otitis media. Amsterdam: Kugler Publications; 1986. p. 557–60.

Özbilen S, Akyıldız N, Özgirgin N, et al. Mastoid surgery in secretory otitis media. Presented at the Politzer Society International Conference on Reality in Ear Surgery and Otoneurosurgery; 1991 June 16–21; Maastricht, Holland.

Paparella MM. Blue eardrum and its management. Ann Otol Rhinol Laryngol 1976;85 Suppl 25:293–5.

Paparella MM, Lim DJ. Pathogenesis and pathology of the "idiopathic" blue drum. Arch Otolaryngol 1967;85:249–58.

Sadé J. The blue drum (idiopathic haemotympanum) and cholesterol granulomas. In: Secretory otitis media and its sequelae. New York: Churchill Livingstone; 1979. p. 12–22.

Sadé J, Fuchs C. Secretory otitis media in adults: II. The role of mastoid pneumatization as a prognostic factor. Ann Otol Rhinol Laryngol 1997;106:37–40.

Sadé J, Halvey A, Klajman A, Mualem T. Cholesterol granuloma. Acta Otolaryngol (Stockh) 1980;89:233–9.

Sheey JL, Linthicum FH, Greenfiel EC. Chronic serous mastoiditis, idiopathic hemotympanum and cholesterol granuloma of the mastoid. Laryngoscope 1969;79:1189–217.

Takakashi H, Honjo W, Kurata K, Sugimaru T. Steroid and tube insertion for cholesterol granuloma: a preliminary study. In: Lim DJ, Bluestone CD, Casselbrant ML, et al, editors. Recent advances in otitis media: proceedings of the Sixth International Symposium. Hamilton (ON): BC Decker; 1995:414–6.

Chapter 71

SUBPERIOSTEAL ABSCESS/ BEZOLD'S ABSCESS

JOSEPH HADDAD JR, MD

The mastoid air cells connect to the middle ear cleft, and this extension suggests that most cases of suppurative otitis media (OM) are associated with some degree of inflammation of the mastoid air cells. The incidence of clinically significant mastoiditis, however, is rare in the antibiotic era. Nonetheless, mastoid infections still occur, and each year a busy practitioner may expect to see a few cases of acute mastoiditis. Of this small number, a smaller percentage still will be associated with subperiosteal abscess; an even smaller number may present as a Bezold's abscess. Although these infections are rare and no good recent data exist to quantify incidence of disease, it remains important to recognize the signs and symptoms to aid in diagnosis.

Subperiosteal Abscess

Acute mastoiditis frequently manifests as subperiosteal abscess, wherein purulent material from the mastoid empyema seeps from the mastoid bone into the potential space beneath the periosteum. Mastoid infections in general are rare now in the United States because of the frequent use of broad-spectrum antibiotics to treat acute otitis media. Therefore, the incidence of subperiosteal abscess is difficult to estimate.

The most common abscess site is postauricular. It forms as a result of hematogenous spread of infection through the small vascular channels in the suprameatal (Macewen's) triangle. When the infection erodes the outer cortex of the mastoid, above the insertion of the sternocleidomastoid muscle, a subperiosteal abscess develops. Inflammatory granulation tissue, which tends to occur when infection is present for more than 7 days, may form in the mastoid region, with blockage of the aditus ad antrum. This may contribute to disease progression and abscess formation.

Other sites that are rarely involved with abscess formation include the zygomatic region and sinodural angle.

These complications generally occur only if there is pneumatization of the mastoid in these regions, and this varies by age and individual mastoid pneumatization. Pneumatization begins soon after birth and is usually extensive by 2 years of age. A zygomatic subperiosteal abscess, if formed when there is infection in the zygomatic air cells, erodes through the cortical bone at the zygoma. It presents as a swelling above and in front of the ear and may be confused with a parotid abscess; the upper half of the auricle is displaced from the skull by the abscess.

Subperiosteal abscess is most commonly associated with marked displacement of the pinna anteriorly and inferiorly; the postauricular crease is obliterated, and fluctuance and erythema of the overlying skin are seen (Figure 71-1). Owing to the thickness of the periosteum, fluctuation may not be apparent in an early abscess.

Swelling may also be seen in the posterosuperior portion of the ear canal. Spontaneous rupture of the skin is sometimes seen, and otorrhea may be present. Systemic symptoms vary, with some patients presenting with fever and a toxic appearance and others with prolonged fever and occasional temperature spikes. Pain is variable and may be worse at night. The postauricular area may be tender to palpation.

A computed tomographic (CT) scan will demonstrate erosion of the bony mastoid cortex with a subperiosteal fluid collection (Figure 71-2). A CT scan is important in these cases as it determines the course of treatment and assists in planning surgical care. For instance, an early acute mastoiditis may present with swelling and erythema, and it may be difficult to determine on physical examination that an abscess is present. A CT scan will reveal the presence of an abscess, and this requires surgery rather than intravenous antibiotics and watchful waiting.

It should be kept in mind that there is a possibility for concurrent complications of OM. For instance, a brain abscess may be seen with mastoiditis and subperiosteal

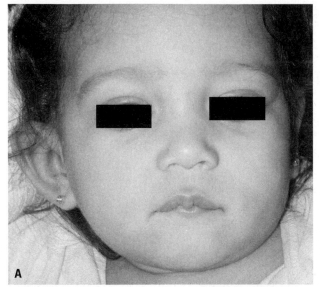

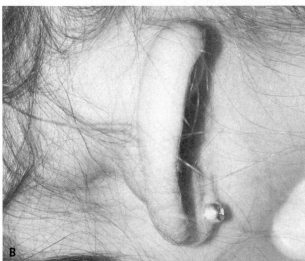

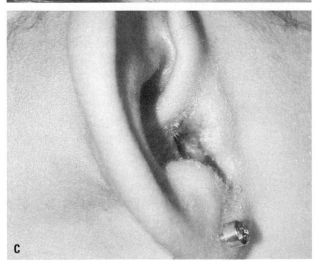

FIGURE 71-1. A 7-month-old girl with acute mastoiditis and a subperiosteal abscess. *A*, Preoperative photograph demonstrating marked auricular protrusion from the skull. *B*, Preoperative photograph showing postauricular erythema and edema. *C*, Intraoperative photograph showing edema and auricular protrusion.

abscess. A CT scan is diagnostic of this condition and helps guide therapy.

Because these infections are rare, it is difficult to give an age breakdown for incidence, but it is expected that a mastoid with a poorly developed air cell system is less likely to have abscess formation. Therefore, these infections should be much less common in infants.

Treatment requires surgical drainage of the abscess with a complete mastoidectomy and ear tube placement under general anesthesia. Whenever possible, it is helpful to obtain an audiogram prior to surgery. Myringotomy is performed first, with aspiration of fluid for culture using an Alden-Senturia trap or similar device. It is preferable to withhold antibiotics until the culture is taken. Intravenous antibiotics may then be started intraoperatively. A tube is placed through the myringotomy incision to allow for middle ear aeration and drainage.

The abscess is drained through a postauricular incision, made a few millimeters behind the postauricular crease. The incision is carried through the subcutaneous tissues and into the periosteum, which is raised from the mastoid bone by the abscess. The draining pus is cultured for aerobic and anaerobic bacteria. In most cases, an intact wall mastoidectomy is performed. The mastoid is thoroughly irrigated after drilling. Attention is paid to the aditus ad antrum, with removal of granulation tissue in this region to allow for good communication with the middle ear cleft. If there is significant edema of soft tissue over the mastoid, a small Penrose drain is left in place to facilitate resolution of infection. The wound is then closed with interrupted subcuticular chromic catgut sutures and interrupted nylon sutures to the skin, which are removed after 7 to 10 days.

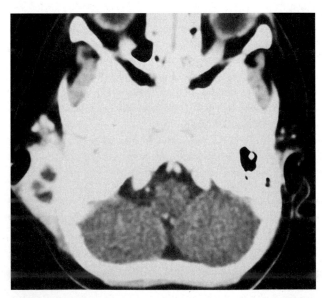

FIGURE 71-2. Computed tomographic scan of the 7-month-old girl from Figure 71-1, demonstrating mastoid opacification and a subperiosteal abscess.

Intravenous antibiotics are continued postoperatively until the cellulitis, fever, and systemic signs of infection resolve, which usually takes 3 to 5 days. Intravenous antibiotics are generally administered for 5 to 7 days. If doing well clinically after 5 to 7 days, the patient is then placed on oral antibiotics prior to discharge, for a total course of antibiotic treatment of 14 days. Amoxicillin-clavulanate or a broad-spectrum cephalosporin is generally used. Antibiotic eardrops are given for 5 to 7 days after surgery to help clear infection and maintain tube patency.

Bezold's Abscess

Purulent material from a mastoid infection may also spread below the pinna or into the neck behind the sternocleidomastoid muscle, the so-called Bezold's abscess. This infection, so named after Friedrich Bezold (1842–1908), arises from acute mastoiditis leading to perforation of the mastoid tip into the digastric groove with a resultant deep neck mass. The abscess is located deep and anterior to the mastoid tip, lateral to the mandible and extending inward toward the pharynx and down into the neck under the sternocleidomastoid muscle, and anterior and medial along the digastric muscle to the submaxillary triangle. The parotid gland may also be involved, and purulent drainage may be seen from the canal. To quote Bezold:

> Exceptionally large cells are often found in the adult…on the inner surface of the mastoid process, sometimes extending from the incisura mastoidea as far as the bulb of the jugular vein. Perforations at these places produce a very distinct clinical picture… The pus cannot reach the surface… No fluctuation can be felt. A moderately sensitive swelling develops rather suddenly in the lower surroundings of the mastoid process concealing its contours… The suppuration

spreads gradually in all directions…below the fascia of the neck. The pus may descend along the sheaths of the large vessels and may reach the larynx and even the mediastinum. The pus may descend…along the muscles of the vertebral column. A burrowing of pus leading to the formation of a retropharyngeal abscess was observed… A perforation of the tympanic membrane…did not precede the descensions of pus in the neck in 29 per cent of the cases I observed. Pneumococci were found most frequently to be the cause of the suppuration (Shambaugh, 1980).

A Bezold abscess is a very unusual complication of mastoiditis. It may present with neck pain, fever, and/or torticollis in a patient with acute or chronic OM.

Management of a Bezold's abscess includes mastoidectomy, in a fashion similar to that described for a subperiosteal abscess. Whenever possible, an audiogram should be attained preoperatively to assess hearing. The neck should be explored for drainage of the cervical abscess, with cultures of the purulent material taken for aerobic and anaerobic organisms. A small Penrose drain is left in place for approximately 48 hours or until drainage subsides. Intravenous antibiotics are continued until cervical cellulitis resolves, and culture-directed oral antibiotics are given for a total of 2 weeks postoperatively.

Suggested Reading

Bluestone CD, Klein JO, editors. Otitis media in infants and children. 3rd ed. Philadelphia: WB Saunders; 1999.

Dew LA, Shelton C. Complications of temporal bone infections. In: Cummings CW, Frederickson JM, Harker LA, et al, editors. Otolaryngology head and neck surgery. 3rd ed. St. Louis: Mosby; 1998. p. 3056–9.

Shambaugh GE, Glasscock ME, editors. Surgery of the ear. 3rd ed. Philadelphia: WB Saunders; 1980.

Chapter 72

PETROSITIS

CHARLES D. BLUESTONE, MD

Suppurative intratemporal (extracranial) complications of otitis media are still frequently encountered, not only in developing nations of the world but also in highly industrialized countries. Acute mastoiditis and facial paralysis occur most commonly; less frequent is acute labyrinthitis. Apical petrositis is a relatively rare suppurative complication today.

Epidemiology

At the Children's Hospital of Pittsburgh during the 15-year period from 1980 to 1995, only four children were admitted with this diagnosis. Three of these patients had simultaneous intracranial suppurative complications, such as dural sinus thrombosis (Goldstein et al, 1998). All of these children had this complication as a result of spread of an attack of acute otitis media.

Pathogenesis

Petrositis is secondary to an extension of infection from the middle ear and mastoid into the petrous portion of the temporal bone. All of the inflammatory and cellular changes described as occurring in the mastoid can also occur in the pneumatized petrous pyramid. About 80% of mastoids are aerated in adults, but only approximately 30% of petrous apex cells are aerated; about 7% can have asymmetric pneumatization of the petrous apex (Brachman and Giddings, 2001). Petrositis may be more frequent than appreciated by clinical and roentgenographic signs because there is communication of the petrosal gas cells with the mastoid–middle ear system. Pneumatization usually does not occur before age 3 years.

This suppurative complication of otitis media may be either acute or chronic. In the acute stage, there is extension of acute otitis media and mastoiditis into the pneumatized petrous air cells. The condition, like acute mastoiditis, is usually self-limited with resolution of the acute middle ear and mastoid infection, but, occasionally, the infection in the petrous portion of the temporal bone does not drain owing to mucosal swelling or because granulation is obstructing the passage from the petrous

air cells to the mastoid and middle ear. This results in acute petrous osteomyelitis (Chole and Donald, 1983; Stamm et al, 1984). The widespread use of antimicrobial agents has made this a rare complication. Chronic petrous osteomyelitis, however, can be a complication of chronic suppurative otitis media or cholesteatoma or both (Glasscock, 1972). Pneumatization of the petrous portion of the temporal bone does not have to be present because the infection can invade the area by thrombophlebitis, by osteitis, or along fascial planes (Allam and Schuknecht, 1968). When there is sixth nerve palsy and otitis media, in the absence of identifiable petrositis and without increased intracranial pressure, the palsy may be related to phlebitis along the inferior petrosal sinus (Homer et al, 1996). The infection may persist for months or years with mild and intermittent signs and symptoms or may spread to the intracranial cavity and result in one or more of the suppurative complications of ear disease, such as meningitis or extradural or intracranial abscess. The infection can also spread to the skull base with involvement of cranial nerves IX, X, and XI (Vernet's syndrome) (Motamed and Kalan, 2000).

Microbiology

The organisms that cause acute petrositis are the same as those that cause acute mastoid osteitis: *Streptococcus pneumoniae*, *Haemophilus influenzae*, and β-hemolytic streptococci. Chronic petrous osteomyelitis, however, may be caused by the bacteria associated with chronic suppurative otitis media and cholesteatoma, such as *Pseudomonas aeruginosa* or *Proteus* species. Rarely, *Mycobacterium tuberculosis* can be the offending bacterial organism (Hiranandani, 1967).

Diagnosis

The patient who develops acute petrositis usually presents with pain behind the eye, deep ear pain, persistent ear discharge, and sixth nerve palsy. This classic triad of pain behind the eye, aural discharge, and sixth nerve palsy is known as Gradenigo's syndrome (Gradenigo, 1907).

However, in the four patients who were admitted to the Children's Hospital of Pittsburgh during a recent 15-year period with this complication of otitis media, eye pain, deep ear pain, and persistent otorrhea were not all consistently present (Goldstein et al, 1998), which has been the experience in other reviews (Somers et al, 2001). Eye pain is attributable to irritation of the ophthalmic branch of the fifth cranial nerve. On occasion, the maxillary and mandibular divisions of the fifth nerve will be involved, and pain will occur in the teeth and jaw. A discharge from the ear is common with acute petrositis but may not be present with chronic disease. Paralysis of the sixth cranial nerve leading to diplopia is a late complication (Glasscock, 1972). Acute petrous osteomyelitis should be suspected when persistent purulent discharge follows a complete simple mastoidectomy for mastoid osteitis.

The diagnosis of acute petrous osteomyelitis is suggested by the unique clinical signs. Standard roentgenograms of the temporal bones may show clouding with loss of trabeculation of the petrous bone. The visualization is uncertain, however, because of normal variation in pneumatization (including asymmetry) and the obscuring of the petrous pyramids by superimposed shadows of other portions of the skull. Computed tomographic (CT) scans of the temporal bones can lead to diagnosis and should be obtained if there might be the possibility of an extension of infection into the cranial cavity. Thin-section (1.5 mm) axial and coronal CT scans with a bone algorithm are recommended (Coker and Jenkins, 2001). This complication must be distinguished from destructive lesions of the petrous apex owing to such conditions as cholesteatoma, cholesterol granuloma, arachnoid cysts, and chronic granulomatous disease; CT and magnetic resonance imaging can be diagnostic in distinguishing between these diseases (Chang et al, 2001; Hardjasudarma et al, 1995; Jackler and Parker, 1992; McHugh et al, 1994; Murakami et al, 1996). Radioisotope bone scan, which will show increased uptake in the petrous apex, has also been shown to be helpful (Gillanders, 1983; Motamed and Kalan, 2000).

Management

When acute petrositis is diagnosed, prompt and appropriate treatment is indicated to prevent spread into the intracranial cavity. Acute petrositis that is confined to the temporal bone and osteitis of the temporal bone is not evident on CT scans; tympanocentesis, which identifies the causative organism, culture-directed intravenous antimicrobial therapy, and tympanostomy tube placement may be effective in reversing the disease process. Thus, conservative management can be effective in selected cases, but surgical drainage of the mastoid and, in some patients, the readily available perilabyrinthine cells opened if there is osteitis of the petrous apex (other portions of the temporal bone) identified on the CT scans or if the patient fails to rapidly improve with conservative management (Al-Ammar, 2001; Bluestone, 2001; Minotti and Kountakis, 1999). The procedure should be a complete (simple, cortical) mastoidectomy that provides adequate drainage through the aditus ad antrum and free flow of irrigation fluid from the mastoid to the middle ear at the end of the procedure; a tympanostomy tube should also be placed. All four of the patients who had this diagnosis at the Children's Hospital of Pittsburgh (see above) were successfully treated with high-dose broad-spectrum intravenous antibiotic therapy and cortical (simple) mastoidectomy without entering the petrous apex; the petrous apex disease most likely drained into the mastoid cavity during the postoperative period. The three children with intracranial complications also had specific management of that complication (Goldstein et al, 1998).

Although some surgeons have advocated mastoidectomy for patients who have a sixth nerve palsy and otitis media but no demonstrable evidence of petrositis on CT scans (Homer et al, 1996), a more conservative approach (eg, tympanocentesis, tympanostomy tube insertion, and intravenous antimicrobial therapy) is a more appropriate initial therapeutic approach, reserving mastoidectomy for those patients who fail to rapidly improve.

In more severe cases of acute petrous osteomyelitis and acute mastoid osteitis, a more aggressive surgical approach to management may be required. The infracochlear approach is advocated by Coker and Jenkins (2001), in which a tympanomeatal flap is created through a postauricular approach. As an alternative, a transmastoid infralabyrinthine approach can be used, in which a complete mastoidectomy is performed and the infralabyrinthine gas cells are opened inferior to the posterior canal, superior to the jugular bulb, and medial to the facial nerve. If the infection has caused complete loss of cochlear and labyrinthine function, a petrosectomy through a radical mastoidectomy is also an alternative. Neely and Wallace (2001) recommend a staged approach, in which the first stage is a modified radical mastoidectomy (ossicular chain remains intact) and cell tracts to the petrous apex are opened if possible. If this procedure is not effective in reversing the disease process, a second stage is performed through the middle cranial fossa. For patients whose disease extends into surrounding structures, such as the pericarotid area, an infralabyrinthine retrofacial route has been successful in eliminating the disease (Somers et al, 2001). As an alternative for these complicated cases, the middle cranial fossa approach has been advocated (Chang, 2001; Hendershot et al, 1976).

References

Al-Ammar AY. Recurrent temporal petrositis. J Laryngol Otol 2001;115:316–8.

Allam AF, Schuknecht HF. Pathology of petrositis. Laryngoscope 1968;78:1813–32.

Bluestone CD. Extracranial complications of otitis media. In: Alper CM, Myers EN, Eibling DE, editors. Decision making in ear, nose and throat disorders. Philadelphia: WB Saunders; 2001. p. 40–2.

Brachman DE, Giddings NA. Drainage procedures for petrous apex lesions. In: Brachman DE, Shelton C, Arriaga MA, editors. Otologic surgery. 2nd ed. Philadelphia: WB Saunders; 2001. p. 466–77.

Chang CYJ. Petrous apex lesions. In: Alper CM, Myers EN, Eibling DE, editors. Decision making in ear, nose and throat disorders. Philadelphia: WB Saunders; 2001. p. 72–3.

Chole RA, Donald PJ. Petrous apicitis: clinical considerations. Ann Otol Rhinol Laryngol 1983;92:544–51.

Coker NJ, Jenkins HA. Atlas of otologic surgery. Philadelphia, WB Saunders; 2001.

Gillanders DA. Gradenigo's syndrome revisited. J Otolaryngol 1983;12:169–74.

Glasscock ME. Chronic petrositis. Ann Otol Rhinol Laryngol 1972; 81:677–85.

Goldstein NA, Casselbrant, ML, Bluestone CD, Kurs-Lasky M. Intratemporal complications of acute otitis media in infants and children. Otolaryngol Head Neck Surg 1998;119:444–54.

Gradenigo G. Ueber die paralyse des Nervus abducens bei Otitis. Arch Ohrenheil 1907;774:149–87.

Hardjasudarma M, Edwards RL, Ganley JP, et al. Magnetic resonance imaging features of Gradenigo's syndrome. Am J Otolaryngol 1995;16:247–74.

Hendershot EL, Wood JW, Bennhoff D. The middle cranial fossa approach to the petrous apex. Laryngoscope 1976;86:658–63.

Hiranandani LH. Tuberculous petrositis. Laryngoscope 1967;77: 1723–8.

Homer JJ, Johnson IJM, Jones NS. Middle ear infection and sixth nerve palsy. J Laryngol Otol 1996;110:872–4.

Jackler RK, Parker DA. Radiographic differential diagnosis of petrous apex lesions. Am J Otol 1992;13:561–74.

McHugh K, de Silva M, Isaacs D. MRI of petrositis in chronic granulomatous disease. Pediatr Radiol 1994;24:530–1.

Minotti AM, Kountakis SE. Management of abducens palsy in patients with petrositis. Ann Otol Rhinol Laryngol 1999;108:897–902.

Motamed M, Kalan A. Gradenigo's syndrome. Postgrad Med J 2000;76:559–60.

Murakami T, Tsubaki J, Tahara Y, et al. Gradenigo's syndrome: CT and MRI findings. Pediatr Radiol 1996;26:684–5.

Neely JG, Wallace MS. Surgery of acute infections and their complications. In: Brachman DE, Shelton C, Arriaga MA, editors. Otologic surgery. 2nd ed. Philadelphia, WB Saunders; 2001. p. 155–65.

Somers TJ, De Foer B, Govaerts P, et al. Chronic petrous apicitis with pericarotid extension into the neck in a child. Ann Otol Rhinol Laryngol 2001;110:988–91.

Stamm C, Pinto JA, Coser PL, Marigo C. Nonspecific necrotizing petrositis: an unusual complication of otitis in children. Laryngoscope 1984;94:1218–22.

Chapter 73

Epidural Abscess and Subdural Empyema

David H. Chi, MD

Intracranial otogenic complications require prompt recognition and treatment. Delays in diagnosis are associated with increased morbidity and mortality (Albers, 1999). Because these complications have become less common with the advances of antibiotic therapy, many physicians have had less experience in managing these cases. Nevertheless, a practicing otolaryngologist needs to be aware of the presentation and necessary treatment.

Acute and chronic otitis media (OM) result in intracranial complication in approximately 0.15% of cases (Jeanes, 1962). The most common intracranial complication is meningitis (Samuel et al, 1986). Subdural empyemas account for 8% of otogenic intracranial complications (Gower and McGuirt, 1983). The incidence of epidural abscesses or granulation tissue has not been studied in a series but is probably underreported when findings have been noted incidentally at the time of surgery. The importance of intracranial complications is that the mortality rate ranges between 13 and 55% (Smith and Hendrick, 1983). The neurologic sequelae are secondary to the local cerebral inflammation, vasculitis, and septic venous thrombosis induced by the irritation from pus; local edema and venous infarction result. If left untreated, the mass effect from the gradually edematous brain progresses to transtentorial herniation and death.

Etiology and Pathogenesis

The intimate relationship of the temporal bone with the middle and posterior fossae permits the extension of infection into the epidural and subdural spaces. Epidural abscesses or granulation develops when the pus or granulation tissue is between the dura and the adjacent temporal bone. Subdural empyemas accumulate within the potential space between the dura and the arachnoid membrane. Because the pus collects in a preformed space, the disease is an empyema instead of an abscess. This space is lined by a single layer of endothelial cells, and no septations exist except where the arachnoid granules are imbedded in the dura. Therefore, inflammatory processes may spread readily within the space. Typically, cholesteatoma or the infectious process erodes the bone adjacent to the dura and allows for direct expansion. Alternative routes for extension are through hematogenous spread via the bridging vessels. A temporal bone arachnoid granulation with its dural defect may also permit intracranial extension from mastoid sources (Nemzek and Swartz, 2003).

Presentation

Epidural Abscesses

The clinical presentation of epidural abscesses and granulation tissue is nonspecific. Patients may present with headaches, otorrhea, fever, and otalgia without meningeal irritation. The otorrhea with extradural abscesses is typically creamy, profuse, and pulsatile. Ipsilateral jugular vein compression may increase the rate of discharge. Cerebrospinal fluid pressure and cell counts are normal unless the patient has concomitant meningitis. The patient may also be completely asymptomatic, and the diagnosis is confirmed at the time of surgery for chronic OM or cholesteatoma.

Subdural Empyema

Subdural empyemas are an uncommon complication of OM in developed countries. The disease usually has a sinogenic source. One series reports that development of subdural abscesses with associated sinusitis occurred 2.5 times more compared with OM or mastoiditis (Hoyt and Fischer, 1991). In contrast, in developing countries, otogenic sources contribute to most cases of subdural abscesses (Pathak et al, 1990).

Unlike the variable appearance of a patient with an epidural abscess, a patient with a subdural empyema usually has a septic presentation. Headaches and fever are early symptoms and may be severe. Central nervous system findings include seizures, somnolence, photophobia, neck stiffness, and motor sensory deficits.

Management

Epidural Abscesses

A high index of suspicion is necessary for epidural abscesses, and radiographic imaging should be ordered. Temporal bone computed tomography (CT) may demonstrate bony defects over the sigmoid sinus (Figure 73-1), tegmen mastoideum, and tegmen tympani. Coronal imaging best demonstrates tegmen defects, whereas axial views delineate sigmoid or posterior fossa erosion. If questions of diagnosis exist with the CT, magnetic resonance imaging (MRI) is obtained. MRI may prove to be superior to CT in identifying intracranial purulent lesions and even in identifying small lesions of granulation and abscess not detected by CT. Large collections show a hyperintense signal in T_2-weighted images adjacent to a hypointense rim representing displaced dura (Meltzer et al, 1996) (Figure 73-2).

Prior to any ear surgery, when possible, an audiogram should be established to define baseline function. Intravenous antibiotics covering for the gram-positive and gram-negative bacteria and anaerobes should be initiated; cultures from surgery will determine any changes to the antibiotic therapy.

When an epidural abscess or granulation is expected or encountered, the bone over the tegmen and the sigmoid is thinned with the operative drill to examine the underlying dura. The bone does not necessarily have to be fully removed, but adequate exposure is necessary for thorough visualization. If, however, any question exists about disease deep to the bone, it is removed to expose the dura. If granulation tissue or abscess is encountered, the bone is drilled away until normal dura is seen. It is not essential to completely exenterate all of the granulation tissue, and care is

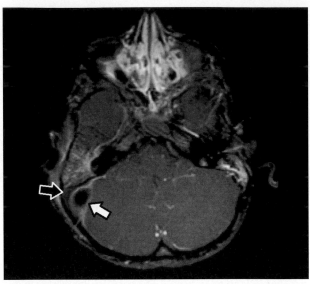

FIGURE 73-2. Magnetic resonance image of the same patient as in Figure 73-1 with right epidural abscess (*black arrow*) with associated sigmoid sinus thrombosis (*white arrow*).

taken not to violate the dura. Often granulation tissue or abscess overlying the sigmoid sinus may be associated with other complications, such as sigmoid sinus thrombophlebitis, that may lead to septic embolization, toxemia, jugular foramen syndrome, or otitic hydrocephalus.

Depending on the presence and extent of cholesteatoma, a modified radical or radical mastoidectomy may be performed. When a large cholesteatoma firmly adheres to the dura, the matrix may be left behind and allowed to remain contiguous with the mastoid cavity. A canal wall down mastoidectomy is performed. If the tympanic membrane is intact and the middle ear and mastoid disease is associated with inadequate ventilation, a tympanostomy tube is placed.

Subdural Empyema

The management of subdural empyema is under the guidance of neurosurgeons and depends on the status of the patient. Parenteral antibiotics and anticonvulsants are administered. Multiple antibiotics against gram-positive bacteria, gram-negative bacteria, and anaerobes are indicated initially until culture and sensitivity results are obtained. Appropriate initial coverage includes nafcillin, ceftriaxone, and metronidazole. Vancomycin may be substituted for those individuals with penicillin allergies. Antibiotics may then be adjusted as necessary based on organism identification and susceptibilities. A minimum of 3 weeks of intravenous antibiotics is recommended. Because the abscess is presumed to have extended through bone to reach the subdural space, the infection is treated as an osteomyelitis (Quick and Payne, 1972). The intravenous antibiotics are continued for 1 week after defervescence, and oral antibiotics are used for a total of 4 to 6 weeks.

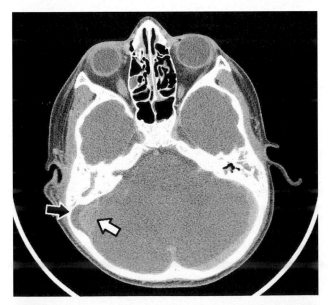

FIGURE 73-1. Axial computed tomographic scan of epidural abscess (*black arrow*) with extension over sigmoid sinus (*white arrow*).

A CT scan or an MRI is almost always diagnostic, but the absence of a typical radiographic lesion does not rule out an abscess (Hoyt and Fischer, 1991). The characteristic finding is that of a thin, low-density collection over the cerebral convexity (Figure 73-3). It may also extend into the interhemispheric fissure. The collection is with a rim of contrast enhancement. The neurologic status is assessed.

A lumbar puncture has a minimal role in the diagnosis of subdural empyema. The procedure carries the risk of brain herniation in a patient with an intracranial lesion with a mass effect and elevated intracranial pressure. Findings on CT that suggest a risk for herniation are midline shift, loss of the suprachiasmatic and basilar cisterns, loss of the superior cerebellar and quadrigeminal plate cisterns with sparing of the ambient cistern, and loss of the fourth ventricle.

Another limitation of a lumbar puncture is that the cerebrospinal fluid sample may be normal in patients with empyemas. Additionally, management is not altered when a broad antibiotic is initiated and neurosurgical drainage is performed. At the time of surgery, cultures may be obtained to identify organisms and check susceptibilities.

If the patient is unstable, surgery is limited to the neurosurgical drainage of the subdural infection and the otologic procedure is deferred until the patient is stabilized. If the subdural empyema is associated with acute OM, a myringotomy is performed at the bedside or concurrent with the neurosurgical procedure to evacuate the infection and obtain a culture.

Controversy exists over bur hole or craniotomy evacuation of the abscess. Advocates of craniotomy favor the exposure and complete drainage of pus. CT scans may localize the lesion but underestimate the collection. On exploration, it may be more loculated and tenacious then expected (Bannister et al, 1981). Others have reported increased survival and less recurrence with a craniotomy compared to bur holes (Wackym et al, 1990). Conversely, other series have demonstrated that multiple bur holes may effectively address the subdural infection with lower surgical morbidity than a craniotomy (Bok and Peter, 1993; deFalco et al, 1996). In children, percutaneous needle aspiration through an open fontanel or twist drill hole aspiration is another option to drain the infection without proceeding with a craniotomy.

If the patient is neurologically stable, the otolaryngologic procedure is performed following the neurosurgical drainage of the infection. A mastoidectomy is required to remove or exteriorize the otogenic source. The extent of the mastoid surgery depends on the associated disease and other complications that may be present. If the tympanic membrane is intact and the canal wall is preserved, a tympanostomy tube is inserted. Some physicians report that mastoid drainage is not necessary with otogenic subdural empyemas. Jeanes (1962) reports that only 65% percent of patients with subdural empyemas required mastoid

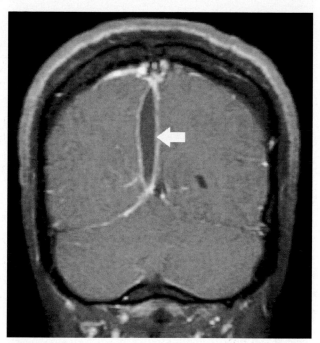

FIGURE 73-3. Coronal magnetic resonance image of parafalcine subdural empyema (*white arrow*). Courtesy of Barton F. Branstetter IV, MD, University of Pittsburgh.

surgery. On the other hand, Nealy (2001) advocates mastoid surgery because the otogenic subdural infections tend to be severe. Mastoid surgery is also recommended to prevent further seeding by the extracranial process.

Of note, some clinicians advocate a nonsurgical approach to subdural empyemas. Criteria for medical management are as follows: preserved mental status of the patient, nonfocal neurologic deficit, CT scan evidence of limited and localized collection of pus, and rapid clinical improvement (Mauser et al, 1985). The disadvantages of this nonsurgical approach are the potential long course of intravenous antibiotic therapy, inability to identify the organism and sensitivities, and need for close neurologic follow-up and repeat CT scans.

Favorable prognostic factors for patients who present with subdural empyemas include early diagnosis and referral, localized area of pus, preserved mental status, and early antibiotic therapy.

Failure to respond to surgical drainage may indicate inappropriate antibiotic treatment or inadequate abscess evacuation. The bacterial cultures are checked for any resistant organisms that may not have been adequately treated with the initial antibiotics. Appropriate adjustments are based on the susceptibilities. A repeat imaging study should be obtained to determine if persistent infection, insufficient drainage, or other complications are present. Based on the images, revision drainage is performed. In addition, an alternative source for the subdural infection should be considered. Because sinogenic subdural abscesses occur more commonly than those from otologic disease, a careful physical and radiographic examination may reveal the need to address simultaneous untreated sinus disease.

Complications of epidural and subdural abscesses include the local spread of infection, resulting in further intracranial sequelae. Meningitis, brain abscesses, otitic hydrocephalus, intracranial mass effect, osteomyelitis, and vascular thrombophlebitides may be present. Seventy-eight percent of patients in a series of 32 patients with subdural empyemas had a concomitant intracranial complication (Dill et al, 1995). Diagnoses and treatment of these different complications are discussed in other chapters.

Complications from surgical drainage include standard operative risks during middle ear surgery and mastoidectomy. Additionally, risks from removal of epidural granulation or abscess include cerebrospinal fluid leak from violation of dura. This may subsequently lead to meningitis. If extensive tegmen is removed, an encephalocele or myelomeningocele may result from the dural herniation. Excessive blood loss may occur during mastoidectomy involving granulation tissue. Blood volume up to 300 cc may be lost during the procedure, which may be significant in small children and those with coronary artery disease. Careful monitoring of estimated blood loss should be maintained to avoid complications from blood loss. Treatment of subdural abscesses introduces neurosurgical risks from brain hemorrhage, cerebrospinal fluid leak, meningitis, and cerebritis.

Conclusion

Although intracranial complications are uncommon, otogenic prompt recognition and treatment are important to limit morbidity and mortality. Epidural abscesses and granulation often occur with nonspecific signs and symptoms, and diagnosis is confirmed at the time of surgery. Treatment includes mastoid surgery, and its extent is determined by the amount of disease. Patients with subdural empyemas usually present with a more septic picture. Treatment consists of drainage of the subdural disease by a neurosurgeon with otologic surgery performed based on the medical stability of the patient.

References

Albers FW. Complications of otitis media: the importance of early recognition. Am J Otol 1999;20:9–12.

Bannister G, Williams B, Smith S. Treatment of subdural empyema. J Neurosurg 1981;55:82–8.

Bok APL, Peter JC. Subdural empyema: burr holes or craniotomy. J Neurosurg 1993;78:574–8.

deFalco R, Scarano E, Cigliano A, et al. Surgical treatment of subdural empyema: a critical review. J Neurosurg Sci 1996;40:53–8.

Dill SR, Cobbs CG, McDonald CK. Subdural empyema: analysis of 32 cases and review. Clin Infect Dis 1995;20:372–86.

Gower D, McGuirt WF. Intracranial complications of acute and chronic infectious ear disease: a problem still with us. Laryngoscope 1983;93:1028–33.

Hoyt DJ, Fischer SR. Otolaryngologic management of patients with subdural empyema. Laryngoscope 1991;101:20–4.

Jeanes A. Otogenic intracranial suppuration. J Laryngol Otol 1962;76:388–402.

Mauser HW, Ravijst RAP, Elderson A, et al. Nonsurgical treatment of subdural empyema. Case report. J Neurosurg 1985;63:128–30.

Meltzer C, Fukui M, Kanal E, Smirniotopoulos J. MR imaging of the meninges. Part I. Normal anatomic features and non-neoplastic disease. Radiology 1996;201:297–308.

Nealy G. Surgery of acute infections and their complications. In: Brackmann DE, Shelton C, Arriaga MA, editors. Otologic surgery. 2nd ed. Philadelphia: WB Saunders; 2001. p. 155–65.

Nemzek WR, Swartz JD. Temporal bone: inflammatory disease. In: Som PM, Curtin HD, editors. Head and neck imaging. 4th ed. St. Louis: Mosby; 2003. p. 1173–243.

Pathak A, Sharma BS, Mathuriya SN, et al. Controversies in the management of subdural empyema: a study of 41 cases with review of literature. Acta Neurochir (Wien) 1990;102:25–32.

Quick CA, Payne E. Complicated acute sinusitis. Laryngoscope 1972;82:1248–63.

Samuel J, Fernandes CMC, Steinberg JL. Intracranial otogenic complications: a persisting problem. Laryngoscope 1986;96:272–8.

Smith HP, Hendrick EB. Subdural empyema and epidural abscess in children. J Neurosurg 1983;58:392–7.

Wackym PA, Canalis RF, Feuerman T. Subdural empyema of otorhinological origin. J Laryngol Otol 1990;104:118–22.

Chapter 74

LATERAL SINUS THROMBOSIS AND OTITIC HYDROCEPHALUS

KENNY H. CHAN, MD

The otogenic cause of lateral sinus thrombosis (LST) is well recognized. The association between LST and otitic hydrocephalus is likewise sufficiently documented. Although large-scale series with extended follow-up for both of these entities are limited, this chapter aims at addressing these two clinical entities independently and in association with the pediatric population based on available information from the literature. Emphasis will be placed on the pathogenesis, presentation, diagnosis, and treatment of each of these entities. A great deal of information is drawn from the pseudotumor cerebri (PTC) literature because there is much more known about this broader topic and, at times, PTC and otitic hydrocephalus are used almost interchangeably.

Pathogenesis

Lateral Sinus Thrombosis

A host of causes for dural sinus thrombosis, including LST, have been identified in the literature (Table 74-1). Common etiologies and risk factors include systemic inflammatory diseases (eg, systemic lupus erythematosus and Behçet's disease), hypercoagulopathic states (eg, oral contraceptives and malignancies), trauma (eg, closed head trauma and temporal bone fracture), and bacterial infections (Biousse et al, 1999; Dickins and Graham, 1993; Ghorayeb et al, 1987; Taha et al, 1993).

TABLE 74-1. Etiologies of Lateral Sinus Thrombosis

Inflammatory diseases (eg, Behçet's disease)
Infectious diseases (eg, mastoiditis, cholesteatoma)
Coagulopathies
Oral contraceptives
Postsurgical (neuro-otologic, neurosurgical)
Closed head trauma and temporal bone fracture
Malignancies
Postpartum state
Unknown

Although the overwhelming majority of dural sinus thromboses secondary to otogenic causes occur in the lateral sinus, rare cases of thrombosis of the cavernous sinus have been reported (Doyle and Jackler, 1991). The literature is replete with case reports and small series of LST. One of the larger series was a 15-year review of 45 cases from Congella, South Africa (Samuel and Fernandes, 1987). Recent reports include a 15-patient series from Zurich, Switzerland (Holzmann et al, 1999), and a 9-patient series from Charlottesville, Virginia (Bradley et al, 2002). Complications of otitis media in the forms of acute mastoiditis and chronic mastoiditis secondary to cholesteatomas are the main culprits. It is generally accepted that the initiating step is thrombophlebitis of the dural sinus owing to contiguous infection of the mastoid. The process of thrombophlebitis leads to a mural thrombus. The lumen of the dural sinus is eventually occluded, and the infected thrombus may extend into the jugular foramen and beyond as well as be embolized into the systemic circulation.

Otitic Hydrocephalus

The term "otitis hydrocephalus" was coined by Symonds in 1931 (Bandyopadhyay, 2001). Otitic hydrocephalus in the neurology and neurosurgery literature is included within the broad umbrella of PTC (Table 74-2). Bandyopadhyay (2001) traced the evolution of the nomenclature and understanding of PTC in a succinct manner and commented that there is a great deal of controversy in

TABLE 74-2. Etiologies of Pseudotumor Cerebri

Decreased cerebrospinal fluid flow owing to meningeal diseases (eg, scarring following meningitis)
Occlusion of dural sinus, including lateral sinus (eg, otitic hydrocephalus)
Metabolic disorders (eg, corticosteroid use or withdrawal, hypoparathyroidism, Addison's disease)
Toxic (eg, hypervitaminosis A, lead, tetracycline, and idiosyncratic effect of various drugs)

terms of terminology and disease characterization (Table 74-3). In fact, the description of this entity prior to the advent of ventriculography in the 1930s is deemed unreliable. Nonetheless, Taylor was credited as the first to describe PTC patients with mastoid suppuration associated with double optic neuritis in 1890. The term PTC was first used by Nönne in 1904. In the latter half of the past century, the term benign intracranial hypertension was proposed by Foley in 1955 but was challenged by Buchheit and colleagues in 1969. Further advances of the entity were made by the advent of computed tomography (CT) and magnetic resonance imaging (MRI) techniques replacing pneumoencephalography.

To better understand the association between LST and PTC or otitic hydrocephalus, a brief discussion of the anatomy and physiology of the cerebrospinal fluid (CSF) in terms of formation, circulation, and absorption would be helpful. The choroid plexuses, located in the floor of the lateral, third, and fourth ventricles, are the centers for CSF formation. The flow of CSF begins at the main site of production, the lateral ventricles. From there, CSF traverses the third and fourth ventricles, the foramina of Magendie and Luschka, and then the perimedullary and perispinal subarachnoid spaces. Within the subarachnoid spaces, CSF flows rostrally and finally reaches the lateral and superior surfaces of the cerebral hemisphere, where most of the resorption takes place. The absorption of CSF is through the arachnoid villi, and they protrude most numerously into the superior sagittal and less so into the other dural sinuses.

The exact pathogenesis of PTC and therefore of otitic hydrocephalus is unknown. Earlier speculations included serous meningitis (Quincke, 1897), increased CSF in the subarachnoid space (Passot, 1913), hydrocephalus owing to the remote effects of bacterial toxins or otitis media (Warrington, 1914), vasomotor control of the intracranial vascular bed (Dandy, 1937), and venous engorgement resulting in cerebral edema (Gardner, 1939). Current understanding of the PTC pathogenesis includes the

following mechanism: increased production of CSF with no change in absorption, increased cerebral blood flow and an increase in cerebral blood volume, a change in the permeability of the blood-brain barrier with subsequent glial and neuronal edema, and increased resistance of CSF outflow through the arachnoid villi with little or no change in CSF production (Kosmorsky, 2001).

Clinical Presentation

Lateral Sinus Thrombosis

Otogenic LST is frequently seen as a disease of the pediatric age group. Samuel and Fernandes (1987) reported that 82% of their case series were under the age of 15 years. All of Holzmann and colleagues' series (1999) were of pediatric age.

The most common presentation includes headache and diplopia. Biousse and colleagues' series (1999) involved mainly adults with all types of cerebral venous thrombosis, including the lateral sinus. Its enormous sample size serves as an excellent illustration of the consequences of dural sinus thrombosis. Ninety-three percent had headaches and 41% had headaches for more than 1 month before correct diagnosis and appropriate treatment. Eighty-six percent had papilledema. Fifteen percent had sixth nerve palsies; the ratio between unilateral to bilateral was 3:1.

The otologic basis of the thrombosis also gives rise to fever, aural discharge, and mastoid tenderness. Although picket fence–type fever has been described, this pattern may likely be due to extension of the infectious and inflammatory process to the posterior fossa dura. Some of these patients may have clinical findings compatible with meningitis, hence causing a delay in diagnosis.

Otitic Hydrocephalus

One would expect a continuation and deterioration of signs and symptoms in otitis hydrocephalus compared with those of LST because of the effects of persistent elevated intracranial pressure, and these symptoms have been carefully documented by Wall (1991). Kosmorsky (2001) published a review article of PTC and detailed its clinical manifestation through an extensive literature search, particularly in the ophthalmology field. Although headache remains the most common presentation and is present in 75 to 99%, clearly 10% of the patients are asymptomatic. Although ophthalmologic manifestations in PTC are common, they have not been uniformly reported in cases of otitic hydrocephalus. The eye findings include monocular and binocular transient visual obscurations (momentary blackouts), diplopia from sixth nerve palsies, retrobulbar pain with eye movement, photophobia, visual field disturbance, and blindness. Although cognitive dysfunction in PTC has not been

TABLE 74-3. Evolution of Terminology Used for Pseudotumor Cerebri

Source	Year	Term Used
Taylor	1890	None
Quincke	1897	Serous meningitis
Nönne	1904	Pseudotumor cerebri
Passot	1913	Meningeal hypertension
Warrington	1914	Pseudotumor cerebri
Symonds	1931	Otitic hydrocephalus
Davidoff and Dyke	1937	Hypertensive meningeal hydrops
Dandy	1937	Intracranial pressure without brain tumor
Yaskin et al	1949	Papilledema of indeterminate etiology
Foley	1955	Benign intracranial hypertension
Corbett and Thompson	1989	Idiopathic intracranial hypertension

Adapted from Bandyopadhyay (2001) and Kosmorsky (2001).

shown, patients have been found to have increases in anxiety and depression (Table 74-4).

Diagnosis

Delayed diagnosis for both of these clinical entities can occur. Children are initially admitted to the medical service for a workup of headache or presumed meningitis. When papilledema is diagnosed, the ophthalmology or neurosurgery consultant may be called first. It is only when otitis, mastoiditis, and LST are brought to the forefront and linked that the otolaryngologist is called.

Lateral Sinus Thrombosis

Several physical findings are of particular interest to the otolaryngologist that may aid or raise the suspicion of the diagnosis of LST. Jugular foramen syndrome can develop from extension of the inflammatory process to the neural elements (cranial nerves IX, X, and XI). Extension of the process into the posterior fossa dura may cause swelling over the occiput (Griesinger's sign). When the jugular vein is occluded in the uninvolved side, the CSF pressure will rise (Toby-Ayer-Queckenstedt sign). Although these physical findings are of great historical interest, they are not always present or reliable. The more constant finding when LST has resulted in elevating intracranial pressure is papilledema.

The gold standard for the radiographic diagnosis of LST is to demonstrate the venous outflow tract during the venous phase of a cerebral angiogram. However, this more invasive technique has been replaced by the advent of neuroimaging techniques based on CT and MRI in the past two decades. Early description included a high-density lesion in the involved sinus on precontrast scans and a filling defect in the sinus on postcontrast scans (Ford and Sarwar, 1981). The "empty delta sign" as a manifestation of LST using contrast-enhanced CT was also described (Albers, 1991). At present, the combination of the abnormal signal intensity of MRI and the absence of flow in the lateral sinus using magnetic resonance angiography are common signs of the radiographic diagnosis of LST (Davison et al, 1997).

Otitic Hydrocephalus

Although LST is associated with otitic hydrocephalus, not all cases of LST will result in otitic hydrocephalus. Yet otogenic LST remains the cardinal diagnostic criterion of otitic hydrocephalus (Lenz and McDonald, 1984). The generally accepted criteria for the diagnosis of PTC are adapted because otitic hydrocephalus diagnostic criteria are not published (Table 74-5). There must be signs and symptoms of increased intracranial pressure. In addition to the clinical presentation of elevation of intracranial pressure, fundoscopic confirmation of papilledema and other ophthalmologic complications is required. There is an absence of focal signs on neurologic examination. There is an absence of ventricular system deformation and, obviously, other mass lesions by neuroimaging techniques. Elevated CSF pressure (> 200 mm H_2O) can be recorded. The subject is awake and alert.

A contrast-enhanced CT or MRI with magnetic resonance angiography is the first step in making the diagnosis. A thorough eye examination to document the degree of papilledema and any visual field defect by an ophthalmologist is preferred. After it has been determined that a lumbar puncture is safe, it should be performed to determine the opening pressure. In addition, the chemistry, cytology, and bacteriology of the content should be analyzed to rule out other causes, such as meningitis.

Treatment

Lateral Sinus Thrombosis

Intravenous antimicrobial therapy and surgery are the cornerstone therapy for LST. The choice of antimicrobial therapy is determined by the specific otogenic cause and the need to prescribe treatment that would penetrate into the central nervous system. Initial empiric choice should be a third-generation cephalosporin (ceftriaxone or cefotaxime) and vancomycin. If a cholesteatoma is present, the initial antimicrobial coverage should also include anaerobic coverage. Once the etiologic agent is identified and its susceptibility is determined, a specific drug or drug combination should be tailored. The expertise of an infectious disease consultant is most valuable because one is dealing with a central nervous system complication and resistant bacterial strains are encountered.

Surgical therapy is targeted first to address the underlying cause. In the case of an acute mastoiditis, a cortical

TABLE 74-4. Symptoms in Pseudotumor Cerebri

Headache
Eye
  Monocular and binocular transient obscurations
  Diplopia from sixth nerve palsies (unilateral or bilateral) and rarely from
    fourth and third nerve palsies
  Visual field disturbances (visual field loss to no light perception)
  Retrobulbar pain with eye movement
Intracranial noises
Shoulder and arm pain
Decreased smell
Other neurologic symptoms (dyscoordination, numbness, motor weakness)

TABLE 74-5. Criteria for the Diagnosis of Otitic Hydrocephalus

Presence of lateral sinus thrombosis
Signs and symptoms of elevated intracranial pressure
Absence of focal neurologic signs
Absence of ventricular system deformation by neuroimaging
Elevated cerebrospinal fluid pressure
Patient awake and alert

mastoidectomy is performed. With the presence of a cholesteatoma, the appropriate extirpation procedure needs to be performed. Attention is then focused on the lateral sinus itself. There is usually an abundance of granulation tissue surrounding the lateral aspect of the sinus, and this tissue needs to be removed gently to expose the thrombotic sinus. The surgical approach beyond this point has received a deal of discussion and debate in the literature mostly based on personal opinions and philosophies. It is reasonable to aspirate the sinus with a small-gauge needle to determine the contents of the sinus. It is also reasonable to incise the sinus to drain any purulent material in the sinus. Thrombus removal is probably too adventurous because injury of the medial wall will lead to central propagation of the infection and CSF leak. Ligation of the internal jugular vein may be reasonable in the face of septic embolism, but this phenomenon is extremely rare.

The treatment of LST with postoperative anticoagulation remains controversial. Holzmann and colleagues (1999) used intravenous heparin for their cohort of children. In a review of 19 cases of septic dural sinus thrombosis from their institution that were of all anatomic locations between 1940 and 1984 and a retrospective review of 136 cases published in the literature, Southwick and colleagues (1986) recommended intravenous antibiotics and early surgical drainage. Their retrospective analysis suggests that anticoagulation with heparin may reduce mortality only in carefully selected cases of septic cavernous sinus thrombosis (nonotogenic cause). Anticoagulation is not recommended in other forms of septic dural sinus thrombosis.

Otitic Hydrocephalus

The initial goal for the treatment of otitic hydrocephalus is identical to the treatment of LST in terms of intravenous antibiotics and surgical intervention. The secondary goal is to control the increased intracranial pressure primarily to prevent or at least control ophthalmologic complications. These measures include repeated lumbar punctures and drainage (daily or on alternate days) of sufficient CSF to maintain the pressures at normal or near-normal levels. It becomes impractical to perform repeated lumbar punctures in young children, and consideration for a lumbar drain may be necessary. Concomitant medical therapy may include a corticosteroid, oral hyperosmotic agents (glycerol or acetazolamide), and furosemide.

Although there are limited reports on otitic hydrocephalus cases needing a permanent surgical procedure owing to persistent papilledema and intractable headache, the literature is replete with indolent and advanced cases of PTC requiring additional surgical intervention. Both lumboperitoneal and ventriculoperitoneal shunts have been used. Although lumboperitoneal shunts are preferred by neurosurgeons, high failure rates have been reported. In addition to shunt failure and back or sciatic pain, mortality from infection in children has been reported. Ventriculoperitoneal shunts may not be the procedure of choice for the neurosurgeon because of the normal-size ventricles observed in this patient population, making placement technically challenging. In patients with PTC with progressive visual loss despite maximum medical therapy, optic nerve sheath decompression has been shown to be a safe and effective means of stabilizing visual acuity and the visual field (Banta and Farris, 2000).

Conclusion

Both PTC and otitic hydrocephalus are rare complications of otitis media but are still with us in the twenty-first century. Timely diagnosis is important because of their morbid consequences, and it is highly dependent on the clinician's index of suspicion. Once diagnosed, a team of clinicians may be required to achieve the best possible outcome. They may include an infectious diseases consultant, a neurologist, an ophthalmologist, and a neurosurgeon in addition to an otolaryngologist.

References

Albers FW. Lateral sinus thrombosis and computed tomography: the empty delta sign. ORL J Otorhinolaryngol Relat Spec 1991;53:45–7.

Bandyopadhyay S. Pseudotumor cerebri. Arch Neurol 2001;58:1699–701.

Banta JT, Farris BK. Pseudotumor cerebri and optic nerve sheath decompression. Ophthalmology 2000;107:1907–12.

Biousse V, Ameri A, Bousser MG. Isolated intracranial hypertension as the only sign of cerebral venous thrombosis. Neurology 1999;53:1537–42.

Bradley DT, Hashisaki GT, Mason JC. Otogenic sigmoid sinus thrombosis: what is the role of anticoagulation. Laryngoscope 2002;112:1727–9.

Buchheit WA, Burton C, Haag B, Shaw D. Papilledema and idiopathic intracranial hypertension: report of a familial occurrence. N Engl J Med 1969;280:938–42.

Dandy WE. Intracranial pressure without brain tumor: diagnosis and treatment. Ann Surg 1937;106:492–513.

Davison SP, Facer GW, McGough PF, et al. Use of magnetic resonance imaging and magnetic resonance angiography in diagnosis of sigmoid sinus thrombosis. Ear Nose Throat J 1997;76:436–41.

Dickins JR, Graham SS. Neurotologic presentation of sagittal sinus thromboses associated with oral contraceptive usage. Am J Otol 1993;14:644–7.

Doyle KJ, Jackler RK. Otogenic cavernous sinus thrombosis. Otolaryngol Head Neck Surg 1991;104:873–7.

Foley J. Benign forms of intracranial hypertension—'toxic' and 'otitic' hydrocephalus. Brain 1955;78:1–41.

Ford K, Sarwar M. Computed tomography of dural sinus thrombosis. AJNR Am J Neuroradiol 1981;2:539–43.

Gardner WJ. Otitic sinus thrombosis causing intracranial hypertension. Arch Otolaryngol 1939;30:253.

Ghorayeb BY, Yeakley JW, Hall JW 3rd, Jones BE. Unusual complications of temporal bone fractures. Arch Otolaryngol Head Neck Surg 1987;113:749–53.

Holzmann D, Huisman TA, Linder TE. Lateral dural sinus thrombosis in childhood. Laryngoscope 1999;109:645–51.

Kosmorsky G. Pseudotumor cerebri. Neurosurg Clin N Am 2001; 12:775–97.

Lenz RP, McDonald GA. Otitic hydrocephalus. Laryngoscope 1984; 94:1451–4.

Nönne M. Über Fälle von Symptomenkomplex 'Tumor cerebri' mit Ausgang in Heilung (pseudotumor cerebri). Z Nervenheilkd 1904;27:169–216.

Passot R. Méningitis et états méningés aseptiques d'origine otique [thesis]. Paris: G Steinheil; 1913. No.: 247.

Quincke H. Ueber Meningitis serosa und verwandte zustände. Dtsch Z Nervenheilkd 1897;9:149–68.

Samuel J, Fernandes CM. Lateral sinus thrombosis. J Laryngol Otol 1987;101:1227–9.

Southwick FS, Richardson EP Jr, Swartz MN. Septic thrombosis of the dural venous sinuses. Medicine (Baltimore) 1986;65: 82–106.

Taha JM, Crone KR, Berger TS, et al. Sigmoid sinus thrombosis after closed head injury in children. Neurosurgery 1993;32: 541–5; discussion 545–6.

Taylor F. The practice of medicine. London: J & A Churchill; 1890.

Wall M. Idiopathic intracranial hypertension. Neurol Clin 1991; 9:73–95.

Warrington WB. Pseudotumor. QJM 1914;7:93.

Chapter 75

MENINGITIS

ELLEN R. WALD, MD

Meningitis is an inflammation of the meninges. It may be caused by infectious agents (viruses, bacteria, fungi, parasites), chemical irritants (chemotherapeutic or radiographic materials injected into the cerebrospinal fluid), systemic medications (trimethoprim-sulfamethoxazole, nonsteroidal anti-inflammatory agents, etc), or, rarely, neoplasms (metastases or carcinomatosis). The subject of this chapter is meningitis, which is associated with infections of the middle ear.

Incidence

In the preantibiotic era, mastoiditis was a common complication of acute otitis media (AOM). In turn, intracranial complications of acute mastoiditis, including subdural and epidural abscess, sigmoid or lateral sinus thrombosis, brain abscess, and meningitis, were not rare. In the early antibiotic era, intracranial complications of acute mastoiditis were observed in 7.7 to 16.8% of cases (Luntz et al, 2001). Although currently mastoiditis is an infrequent complication of AOM, intracranial complications, including meningitis, still occur. A review of eight recent series of patients with mastoiditis published since 1995 (including cases that have occurred since 1980) showed the incidence of intracranial complications and meningitis to be 5.5% and 2.0%, respectively (De et al, 2002; Ghaffar et al, 2001; Go et al, 2000; Harley et al, 1997; Spratley et al, 2000; Tarantino et al, 2002; Vassbotn et al, 2002;) (Table 75-1).

Importance

Meningitis is an extremely serious infection of the central nervous system that is accompanied by a significant mortality rate and substantial morbidity. Depending on the age of the patient and etiology, mortality rates for bacterial meningitis vary from 3.0 to 7.7% (Arditi et al, 1998; Schuchat et al, 1997). Major neurologic sequelae include deafness, blindness, hydrocephalus, seizure disorders, motor problems (mono-, hemi-, or quadriplegia, paresis, or spasticity), and global retardation (IQ < 70). Minor neurologic sequelae include mild hearing loss, learning disabilities, language impairment, and modest decreases in intellectual ability (IQ between 70 and 90).

Etiology and Pathogenesis

The major pathogenetic mechanism for the development of acute meningitis is acute hematogenous dissemination from the nasopharynx as a portal of entry. The bacterial species that cause meningitis normally can be found colonizing the nasopharynx. Shortly after acquisition of the organism, and often in concert with a concurrent viral upper respiratory infection, a bacteremia occurs that seeds the meninges. Of the three common bacterial species that cause meningitis, *Haemophilus influenzae* type b (prior to licensure of the *H. influenzae* conjugate vaccine) had the greatest predisposition to seed the meninges (75% of bac-

TABLE 75-1. Recent Studies of Acute Mastoiditis in Children

Author	Years	No. of Patients	Mean Age (yr)	Intracranial Complications		
				Number (%)	Meningitis (%)	Others (*n*)
Vassbotn et al	1980–1993	57	3.6	1 (1.7)	0	Subdural abscess (1)
Harley et al	1982–1993	58	1.0	1 (1.7)	1 (1.7)	Meningitis (1)
Ghaffar et al	1983–1999	57	4.0	2 (3.5)	0	Sinus thrombosis (1)
Luntz et al	1984–1998	223	5.3	19 (8.5)	7 (3.1)	Meningitis (7), sinus thrombosis (7), subdural abscess (1), cerebellar abscess (1), perisinus empyema (3)
Go et al	1986–1998	118	6.0	8 (6.7)	1 (0.8)	Sinus thrombosis (6),* epidural abscess (4), meningitis (1)
Tarantino et al	1991–2000	40	4.5	0	0	
Sprately et al	1993–1998	43	4.6	5 (11.6)	3 (6.9)	Meningitis (3), sinus thrombosis (3)[†]
De et al	1995–2000	21	5.0	1 (4.8)	0	Sinus thrombosis (1)

*Five children had a single complication and three children had multiple complications.
[†]One patient had both meningitis and sinus thrombosis.

teremias were associated with a concurrent meningitis) and cause acute bacterial meningitis; *Neisseria meningitidis* is next most likely to seed the meninges (approximately 50% of cases of bacteremia are accompanied by meningitis) in the context of a bacteremia, and *Streptococcus pneumoniae* is least likely (< 2% of bacteremias result in the seeding of the meninges) (Shapiro et al, 1986). Although *S. pneumoniae* is least likely to seed the meninges when it causes a bacteremia, prior to licensure of the pneumococcal conjugate vaccine, it was the most likely bacterial species to give rise to occult bacteremia (nearly 100 times more common than *N. meningitidis* as a cause of occult bacteremia). The availability and widespread use of conjugate vaccines for *H. influenzae* type b and *S. pneumoniae* have already substantially impacted on the epidemiology of infections caused by these bacterial species and hopefully will continue to do so in the future (Dawson et al, 1999; Lin et al, 2003; Neuman and Wald, 2001).

Intracranial extension of infection from the middle ear may reach the central nervous system in one of three ways: progressive thrombophlebitis that begins in the veins that drain the middle ear or mastoid and spreads through the intact bone to the central nervous system, erosion of the bony walls of the middle ear or mastoid to cause infection by contiguous spread, and extension along preformed pathways that are congenital or acquired, such as the round window, dehiscent sutures, skull fracture, or the site of a cochlear implant (Bluestone and Klein, 1996).

Meningitis may be associated with infection of the middle ear under four circumstances: direct invasion, in which a suppurative focus in the middle ear spreads either through the mastoid bone or directly through the bony wall of the middle ear to involve the dura (which is contiguous) and finally the pia-arachnoid, to cause a generalized meningitis; spread of infection from the middle ear and mastoid through the inner ear to the meninges; as a sympathetic inflammatory response when there is bacterial infection of an adjacent area such as a subdural or brain abscess; and when a viral upper respiratory infection predisposes the patient to simultaneous and parallel infections of the middle ear and meninges, the former as a consequence of eustachian tube dysfunction and the latter from a bacteremic event, as described above (Table 75-2).

When there is direct invasion of the meninges from infection in the middle ear, there must be a simultaneous mastoiditis. The mastoiditis is usually obvious on physical examination but may, on occasion, be clinically silent. The bacterial agent is recovered from the spinal fluid, the characteristics of which are typical, as described below for cases of acute bacterial meningitis. The second mechanism that involves the spread of infection through the inner ear is believed to be extremely rare. When pathologic specimens from children with meningitis are examined, there is rarely any evidence (of osteitis or direct extension

of the infection from the middle ear to the central nervous system through soft tissue, labyrinth, or vasculature) that this pathogenetic mechanism is the mode of infection (Bluestone and Klein, 1996). When the third mechanism is the cause of inflammation in the meninges, the process is usually sterile, that is, an aseptic meningitis. In this case, the cell count in the spinal fluid is low (< 200 cells/mm^3), and lymphocytes frequently predominate. The glucose is typically normal. The final mechanism of meningitis in children with acute middle ear disease is by far the most common. In this case, there is no direct link between the middle ear infection and bacterial meningitis. It represents the overlap of a common infection (acute middle ear disease, to which the patient is predisposed by a viral upper respiratory infection in most cases) with an uncommon infection—bacterial meningitis—which frequently occurs in the context of a viral upper respiratory infection.

Clinical Presentation

The clinical presentation of children with acute bacterial meningitis varies with the age of the child. In children under age 1 year, fever and irritability will be nearly universal. The irritability very likely represents the discomfort-headache and neck stiffness as well as myalgias associated with fever. Often a paradoxical irritability is noted, that is, the infant complains least when resting in the crib and cries or moans incessantly when picked up or rocked, which presumably creates a stretch on the meninges. Lethargy, vomiting, and anorexia are very common. Poor fluid intake leads to dehydration. Generalized seizures occur in approximately 30% of children and often are the indication for seeking medical care. In about 50% of children, there has been a visit to the primary care doctor in the previous few days. Often an antibiotic was prescribed for a presumed focus of infection or occasionally simply because of the fever. There is no improvement in response to the antibiotic.

The older patient will usually complain of headache or neck pain. Fever and vomiting are often present. There may be progressive lethargy with poor oral intake. The alteration in consciousness may progress to coma. On admission to the hospital, there may be evidence of poor perfusion and shock. In the early hours of meningitis in the older child, there may be confusion and incoherency even before signs of meningeal irritation are obvious. Photophobia is fre-

TABLE 75-2. Pathogenesis of Concurrent Meningitis and Acute Otitis Media

Direct invasion by contiguous spread through the bony wall of the middle ear or mastoid

Spread from the middle ear to inner ear to spinal fluid

Sympathetic inflammatory response to infection in adjacent space

Simultaneous but unrelated events with viral upper respiratory infection as common risk factor

quently present. When ear disease or mastoiditis precedes the development of meningitis, there is frequently the complaint of otalgia and sometimes otorrhea.

Physical examination usually demonstrates signs of meningitis. In infancy, the fontanel may be full or bulging. It should be assessed with the infant in an upright position and not crying. Signs of meningeal irritation include positive Kernig's and Brudzinski's signs and evidence of photophobia. There may be focal neurologic deficits, such as cranial nerve palsies, hemiplegia, or hemiparesis, or there may be evidence of acute hearing loss. When otitis media is the risk factor for meningitis or is concurrent with bacterial meningitis, signs of acute middle ear inflammation are present on physical examination. These will usually include a bulging opacified tympanic membrane with red or yellow discoloration. Rarely, in cases of "missed mastoiditis," only middle ear effusion is present or the tympanic membrane may be completely normal.

In children with mastoiditis, there may be specific signs and symptoms on physical examination. There may be erythema and swelling behind or above the ear. When a subperiosteal abscess is present, there will be fluctuance in the postauricular area or there may be sagging of the posterosuperior wall of the eustachian tube. Otorrhea may be present.

Management Options

The most common clinical situation will be the child who presents with an apparently uncomplicated case of AOM and concurrent meningitis. In this instance, the likely bacterial etiology is either *S. pneumoniae* or *N. meningitidis* (Neuman and Wald, 2001). If the history is acute and there are no focal neurologic findings, the evaluation should consist of a complete blood count, blood culture, urine culture and analysis, and culture of the cerebrospinal fluid. In this case, there is no indication to perform an image of any kind before the lumbar puncture is performed. Most cases of acute bacterial meningitis will have more than 500 cells/mm^3, with a predominance of polymorphonuclear leukocytes (usually at least 85% combining mature and immature neutrophils), a low glucose level (almost always below 40 mg percent and usually below 20 mg percent), and a high protein level. Organisms may be seen on Gram stain. However, even if there are no organisms seen on the smear, treatment should be undertaken immediately. The antibiotic recommendations for the management of suspected acute bacterial meningitis include a third-generation cephalosporin, either intravenous cefotaxime (75 mg/kg/dose q6h) or ceftriaxone (50 mg/kg/dose q12h after a loading dose of 80–100 mg/kg/d), and vancomycin (15 mg/kg/dose q6h). The need to add vancomycin to the therapeutic regimen reflects a concern about the escalating prevalence of strains of *S. pneumoniae* that are resistant to penicillin and cephalosporins. Serum levels of vancomycin should be checked after the third dose. Peak levels of 35 to 40 µg/mL are desirable. If the bacterial species isolated from the cerebrospinal fluid is susceptible to cefotaxime, the vancomycin should be discontinued. If the bacterial species is resistant to cefotaxime, the usual recommendation is to continue treatment with both cefotaxime and vancomycin. Consideration may be given to adding rifampin (20 mg/kg as a single daily dose, intravenously or by mouth) or meropenem (40 mg/kg/d q8h). If AOM is present at the time of evaluation, a tympanocentesis should be performed to determine if the bacterial species infecting the middle ear and the spinal fluid are the same.

The value of adding dexamethasone to the therapeutic regimen of patients with bacterial meningitis has been controversial. Several studies reported in the late 1980s and early 1990s provided evidence that steroids, given just before or within a few minutes after antibiotics, were beneficial in protecting against deafness in children with bacterial meningitis owing to *H. influenzae* type b (Lebel et al, 1988; Odio et al, 1991; Schaad, 1993; Wald et al, 1995). The benefit of steroids has not been evaluated as extensively in cases of meningitis other than those caused by *H. influenzae* type b, although a meta-analysis of published data indicated a possible beneficial effect in cases of pneumococcal disease (McIntyre et al, 1997). Dexamethasone has not been shown to benefit overall neurologic outcome or mortality. Similarly, steroids have not been shown to be beneficial in children with meningitis owing to *N. meningitidis*, group B streptococcus, *Escherichia coli*, or viral meningitis. As meningitis owing to *H. influenzae* type b has been virtually eliminated, most experts have not advocated for the use of steroids in children presenting with probable bacterial meningitis. In late 2002, a study providing evidence of the beneficial effect of steroids in adults with pneumococcal meningitis was published (De Gans and van de Beek, 2002). Patients receiving steroids had a 50% reduction in mortality compared with the placebo group. There was, however, no improvement in neurologic outcome or outcome with regard to deafness. The bacteria that caused infection in this series were all susceptible to penicillin, and the antibiotic that was used was parenteral amoxicillin. The generalizability of this report, that is, its application to a pediatric population in which antibiotic-resistant bacterial pathogens are common and the antibiotic regimen includes an advanced-generation cephalosporin, is unclear.

When children present with meningitis that is associated with mastoiditis, considerations for antibiotic coverage should take into account the likely pathogens. Several large series of children with mastoiditis have been published in the last 6 years (De et al, 2002; Ghaffar et al, 2002; Go et al, 2000; Luntz et al, 2001; Harley et al, 1997; Spratley et al, 2000; Tarantino et al, 2002; Vassbotn et al, 2002). Establishing the precise microbiologic etiology of mastoiditis may be difficult because antibiotic therapy is frequently started when the child sees a primary physician and is diagnosed to have AOM. Even after the diagnosis of mastoiditis is recognized, parenteral antibiotics are frequently initiated before any samples are obtained for culture and sensitivity testing. Additional problems are created because some samples of material are obtained either from the external canal or by passing a swab through both the external canal and the tympanostomy tube. This last maneuver may exaggerate the recovery of *Pseudomonas aeruginosa* and *Staphylococcus aureus* from these patients. The precise interpretation of these isolates is not always straightforward. Taking all of these issues into account, a review of the microbiology of mastoiditis reveals interesting differences from the microbiology of uncomplicated AOM. In the latter condition, *S. pneumoniae* causes 30 to 40% of cases, nontypable *H. influenzae* causes 20 to 30% of cases, *Moraxella catarrhalis* causes 12 to 18% of cases, and *Streptococcus pyogenes* causes approximately 4% of cases. A review of eight studies that focused on 617 patients with acute mastoiditis identified the following bacterial species, in their relative order of prevalence: *S. pneumoniae* (76), *S. pyogenes* (28), *P. aeruginosa* (28), *S. aureus* (24), coagulase-negative *Staphylococcus* (14), *H. influenzae* (10), gram-negative enterics other than *Pseudomonas* (6), *Proteus mirabilis* (6), and *M. catarrhalis* (1) (De et al, 2002; Ghaffar et al, 2002; Go et al, 2000; Harley et al, 1997; Luntz et al, 2001; Spratley et al, 2000; Tarantino et al, 2002; Vassbotn et al, 2002) (Figure 75-1). Cultures were sterile in 30 to 50% of patients in each series. Meningitis was observed in 12 of 617 subjects with mastoiditis. With the enumerated bacterial species in mind, vancomycin and ceftazidime, cefepime, or meropenem are a reasonable combination with which to initiate antibiotics when meningitis complicates mastoiditis. The inclusion of ceftazidime, cefepime (Saez-Llorens and O'Ryan, 2001), or meropenem (Odio et al, 1999) rather than either cefotaxime or ceftriaxone relates to the superior activity that these agents have for *P. aeruginosa*. It is imperative to obtain specimens for culture from the cerebrospinal fluid, mastoid cavity, and middle ear as well as any purulent material that might be present in the subdural or epidural space. If at all possible, these specimens should be obtained before the initiation of antibacterial agents. If signs of mastoiditis are present when the patient is evaluated, it is appropriate to obtain a computed tomographic (CT) study of the brain and temporal bone soon after the patient is stabilized. These studies will delineate the presence of areas that may require drainage (subperiosteal, subdural, epidural, or brain abscess) or vascular foci of thrombosis (lateral sinus thrombosis, sagittal sinus thrombosis, and cavernous sinus thrombosis).

Recently, there has been recognition of an increased occurrence of bacterial meningitis as a complication of cochlear implants (Josefson, 2002). As cochlear implants are often placed in children with congenital malformations of the ear or who have previously had meningitis, there are several factors, other than the implant itself, that may contribute to the increased risk observed in these children. For example, there are reports of children with cochlear implants who have developed meningitis after the occurrence of AOM in the contralateral ear (Suzuki et al, 1998; Woolley et al, 1998). Worldwide, there are 91 reports of individuals developing meningitis after getting a cochlear implant (US Food and Drug Administration [FDA], 2002). This is out of approximately 60,000 people who have cochlear implants. Three manufacturers make FDA-approved cochlear implants that are used in the United States: Advanced Bionics Corporation in Sylmar, CA; Cochlear Corporation in Lane Cove, NSW, Australia; and MED-EL Corporation in Durham, NC. Of the 53 people in the United States who became ill with meningitis after getting a cochlear implant, 29 had the Advance Bionics CLARION device, 22 had the Cochlear Nucleus device, and 2 had the MED-EL Corporation device. Most of the infected individuals were younger than 7 years of age. The meningitis occurred anywhere from less than 24 hours to more than 6 years after the implant surgery. However, over 50% of the people developed meningitis within the first year of surgery. The organisms identified in 23 cases that occurred in the United States were *S. pneumoniae* (16), *H. influenzae* (4), *Streptococcus viridans* (2), and *E. coli* (1). The management of meningitis in these patients should be the same as for uncomplicated meningitis without mastoiditis.

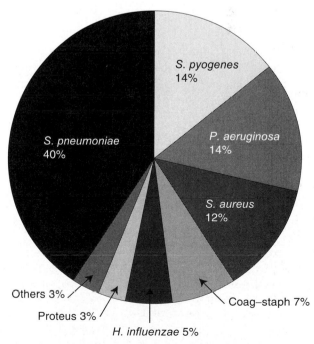

FIGURE 75-1. Relative proportion for each bacterial species in 617 patients with acute mastoiditis. Approximately 30 to 50% of the specimens showed no growth.

My Experience

When a diagnosis of probable meningitis is made, antibiotic therapy is initiated immediately after the evaluation has been completed. In the absence of signs and symptoms of mastoiditis, the drugs of choice are vancomycin and ceftriaxone (given in two divided doses). Steroids are used only in patients with meningitis that is presumed to be caused by typable *H. influenzae*. This might be prompted by the finding of pleomorphic gram-variable or gram-negative rods in the spinal fluid. Fluids are managed at a maintenance rate. If the child has presented with a seizure, anticonvulsants are initiated and a neurology consultation is sought. If the electroencephalogram (EEG) is normal, anticonvulsants are usually prescribed for approximately 6 months. If the EEG is abnormal, then the anticonvulsants are usually continued for at least 2 years and an image is obtained. In the absence of seizures or other complications, images are not necessary. The head circumference is measured daily. The fever will usually resolve after the first 4 to 5 days. For cases of meningococcal meningitis, therapy is continued for 5 to 7 days. For *H. influenzae*, antibiotic is continued for 7 to 10 days, and for *S. pneumoniae*, therapy is maintained for 10 to 14 days. In every instance, a shorter course of antibiotics is desirable if the course of illness is uncomplicated.

In children with meningitis complicating mastoiditis, vancomycin and cefepime will be initiated. As soon as there is bacteriologic proof of the cause of the infection, it may be possible to narrow the spectrum. A CT scan of the brain is usually desired to clarify the potential role of surgical intervention and to delineate the presence of sinus thrombosis. A CT scan of the temporal bone is appropriate if the middle ear is considered a possible source for the meningitis. Tympanocentesis or, more commonly, myringotomy and tympanostomy tube placement are appropriate to outline the microbiology of the ear disease and provide ventilation and decompression of the middle ear.

References

Arditi M, Mason EO Jr, Bradley JS, et al. Three year multicenter surveillance of pneumococcal meningitis in children: clinical characteristics and outcome related to penicillin susceptibility and dexamethasone use. Pediatrics 1998;102:1087–97.

Bluestone CD, Klein JO. Intracranial suppurative complications of otitis media and mastoiditis. In: Bluestone CD, Stool SE, Kenna MA, editors. Pediatric otolaryngology. Philadelphia: WB Saunders; 1996. p. 636–47.

Dawson KG, Emerson JC, Burns JL. Fifteen years of experience with bacterial meningitis. Pediatr Infect Dis J 1999;18:816–22.

De S, Makura ZG, Clarke RW. Paediatric acute mastoiditis: the Alder Hey experience. J Laryngol Otol 2002;116:440–2.

De Gans JD, van de Beek D. Dexamethasone in adults with bacterial meningitis. N Engl J Med 2002;347:1549–56.

Ghaffar FA, Wordemann M, McCracken GH Jr. Acute mastoiditis in children: a seventeen-year experience in Dallas, Texas. Pediatr Infect Dis J 2001;20:376–80.

Go C, Bernstein JM, de Jong AL, et al. Intracranial complications of acute mastoiditis. Int J Pediatr Otorhinolaryngol 2000;52:143–8.

Harley EH, Sdralis T, Berkowitz RG. Acute mastoiditis in children: a 12-year retrospective study. Otolaryngol Head Neck Surg 1997;116:26–30.

Josefson D. Cochlear implants carry risk of meningitis, agencies warn. BMJ 2002;325:298.

Lebel MH, Freij BJ, Syrogiannopoulos GA, et al. Dexamethasone therapy for bacterial meningitis: results of two double-blind, placebo-controlled trials. N Engl J Med 1988;319:964–71.

Lin PL, Michaels M, Mason EO Jr, et al. Incidence of invasive pneumococcal disease in children 3–36 months at a tertiary care center two years after licensure of the pneumococcal conjugate vaccine. Pediatrics 2003;111:896–9.

Luntz M, Bodsky A, Nusem S, et al. Acute mastoiditis—the antibiotic era: a multicenter study. Int J Pediatr Otorhinolaryngol 2001;57:1–9.

McIntyre PB, Berkey CS, King SJM, et al. Dexamethasone as adjunctive therapy in bacterial meningitis: a meta-analysis of randomized clinical trials since 1988. JAMA 1997;278:925–31.

Neuman HB, Wald ER. Bacterial meningitis in childhood at the Children's Hospital of Pittsburgh: 1988–1998. Clin Pediatr 2001;40:595–60.

Odio CM, Faingezicht I, Paris M, et al. The beneficial effects of early dexamethasone administration in infants and children with bacterial meningitis. N Engl J Med 1991;324:1525–31.

Odio CM, Puig JR, Feris JM, et al. Prospective, randomized investigator-blinded study of the efficacy and safety of meropenem vs cefotaxime therapy in bacterial meningitis in children. Meropenem Meningitis Study Group. Pediatr Infect Dis J 1999;18:581–90.

Saez-Llorens X, O'Ryan M. Cefepime in the empiric treatment of meningitis in children. Pediatr Infect Dis J 2001;20:356–61.

Schaad UB, Lips U, Gnehm HA, et al for the Swiss Meningitis Study Group. Dexamethasone therapy for bacterial meningitis in children. Lancet 1993;342:457–61.

Schuchat A, Robinson K, Wenger JD, et al. Bacterial meningitis in the United States in 1995. N Engl J Med 1997;337:970–6.

Shapiro ED, Aaron NH, Wald ER, Chiponis D. Risk factors for development of bacterial meningitis among children with occult bacteremia. J Pediatr 1986;109:15–9.

Spratley J, Silveira H, Alvarez I, Pais-Clemente M. Acute mastoiditis in children: review of the current status. Int J Pediatr Otorhinolaryngol 2000;56:33–40.

Suzuki C, Sando I, Fagan JJ, et al. Histopathological features of a cochlear implant and otogenic meningitis in Mondini dysplasia. Arch Otolaryngol Head Neck Surg 1998;124:462–6.

Tarantino V, D'Agostino R, Taborelli G, et al. Acute mastoiditis: a 10-year retrospective study. Int J Pediatr Otorhinolaryngol 2002;66:143–8.

US Food and Drug Administration. FDA public health Web notification: cochlear implant recipients may be at greater risk for meningitis. Available at: www.fda.gov/cdrh/safety/cochlear.html (accessed Oct 17, 2002).

Vassbotn FS, Lausen OG, Lind O, Moller P. Acute mastoiditis in a Norwegian population: a 20 year retrospective study. Int J Pediatr Otorhinolaryngol 2002;62:237–42.

Wald ER, Kaplan S, Mason E, et al. Dexamethasone therapy for bacterial meningitis in children. Pediatrics 1995;95:21–8.

Woolley AL, Jenison V, Stroer BS, et al. Cochlear implantation in children with inner ear malformations. Ann Otol Rhinol Laryngol 1998;107:492–500.

Chapter 76

CEREBRITIS AND BRAIN ABSCESS

KITIRAT UNGKANONT, MD

Cerebritis and brain abscesses are infections of the brain parenchyma that can cause serious morbidity and a high mortality rate. This was especially true in the preantibiotic era. The route of infection can be from the contiguous structures by direct invasion or through the valveless venous system of the face and paranasal sinus. Hematogenous spread from a distant site is common in the patient with congenital cyanotic heart disease (Bluestone and Klein, 1996). Common sources of brain abscess from otolaryngologic infection are sinusitis and otitis media (OM). Chronic OM with cholesteatoma is the most common cause of otogenic brain abscess (Bluestone and Klein, 2001).

Incidence

The incidence of intracranial complications of OM from recent studies in the antibiotic era was between 0.04 and 0.15% (Delbrouck et al, 1996). Kangsanarak and colleagues (1993) reviewed 17,144 cases of suppurative OM in Chiang Mai, Thailand, between 1983 and 1990 and found that the incidence of intracranial complication was 0.24%, among which brain abscess was 42% of the intracranial complications. In another report by Kangsanarak and colleagues (1995), the incidence of intracranial complication from acute otitis media (AOM) and chronic OM was 0.36%, and brain abscess was 33.3% of all of the intracranial complications. Yen and colleagues (1995) reviewed 122 cases of brain abscess between 1981 and 1994 and found that otolaryngologic sources accounted for 21.1% of all infections. Chronic OM and mastoiditis were the cause in 15.4% of otolaryngologic brain abscesses. Ratanasiri (1995) did a 10-year review of brain abscess in Thai children between 1981 and 1990. Fifty-four cases were diagnosed, and chronic OM was the source in 12.9%.

Importance

Early detection of otogenic brain abscess should be brought to the forefront because of its high mortality rate. In the review by Sennaroglu and Sozeri (2000) between 1968 and 1993, the mortality rate was 29% before 1976, when computed tomography (CT) was first available;

thereafter, the mortality rate was reduced to 10%. The mortality rates of brain abscess from chronic OM reported between 1981 and 1994 were 6.7% in Taiwan (Yen et al, 1995) and 14% in Thailand (Kangsanarak et al, 1993).

Etiology and Pathogenesis

Infection of the middle ear and mastoid can get to the brain tissue by direct invasion from osteitis or can cause other adjacent intracranial infection first, such as lateral sinus thrombosis or meningitis. Infection of the dura overlying the infected mastoid can be caused by a vascular pathway or erosion of the infected bone (Bluestone and Klein, 1996). The location of a bony defect is associated with the location of cerebritis/abscess in the brain. The common locations of otogenic brain abscess are in the temporal lobe on the same side of the infected ear and cerebellum (Bluestone and Klein, 1996; Kurien et al, 1998; Murthy et al, 1991; Sennaroglu and Sozeri, 2000; Yen et al, 1995). Erosion of the tegmen tympani results in a temporal lobe abscess, whereas erosion of Trautmann's triangle and the sigmoid sinus leads to cerebellar abscess (Murthy et al, 1991; Sennaroglu and Sozeri, 2000). Cholesteatoma is the most common cause of bony erosion, followed by granulation tissue in the mastoid. In the series of Kurien and colleagues (1998), all 36 cases with otogenic brain abscess had cholesteatoma. Cholesteatoma was found in 79 to 97.6% of the cases, with otogenic brain abscess in other reports (Kangsanarak et al, 1995; Sennaroglu and Sozeri, 2000; Yen et al, 1995).

Clinical Presentation

Symptoms and signs of intracranial complications usually occur about 1 month after an episode of AOM or an acute exacerbation of chronic OM (Bluestone and Klein, 1996). Ear symptoms consist of foul-smelling and purulent discharge. General symptoms are fever and headache. All of the 40 patients in the series of Sennaroglu and Sozeri (2000) had a headache for at least a week. In the initial stage of encephalitis/cerebritis, the clinical signs are fever, headache, vomiting, irritability, and change of consciousness. As the area of cerebritis becomes encapsulated, the focal signs appear. Temporal lobe abscesses are associated with visual field defects, aphasia, seizure, or a silent clinical picture. The signs of cerebellar abscess are vertigo, nystagmus, and ataxia. Papilledema or a bulging fontanel in young infants signifies increased intracranial pressure. A stiff neck may be found initially or later in the course if the abscess ruptures into the ventricular system (Brook, 1995).

Diagnosis

Before proceeding to any diagnostic tools, careful history taking and physical examinations are still of utmost importance to arouse suspicion of impending intracranial complications. The sudden appearance of fever and headache in a patient with chronic OM requires continuous monitoring of neurologic status as the clinical signs may change rapidly (Murthy et al, 1991). A proper diagnostic intervention at the right time is not only lifesaving but also helps to avoid crippling neurologic consequences. A CT scan is a very effective test in determining the size and location of the abscess. It becomes the mainstay of rapid diagnosis and follow-up. Brain abscess is identified as an area of low density surrounded by an enhancing ring of uniform thickness (Yen et al, 1995). Enzmann and colleagues (1979) did an experimental study in dogs and found that ring enhancement on the CT scan occurred in the stage of late cerebritis before the actual capsule formation. Magnetic resonance imaging (MRI) is also a diagnostic method of choice. It has been reported to have sensitivity and specificity superior to CT scan (Brook, 2002), especially for cerebritis and cerebral edema (Kendall, 1988). CT may be more available worldwide, so it is still more popular than MRI. Once the mass effect is shown by papilledema or is demonstrated in CT or MRI, lumbar puncture is not recommended. Cerebrospinal fluid culture is usually negative if there is no associated suppurative meningitis.

Bacteriology

The most predominant organisms recovered in otogenic brain abscess were anaerobes (*Bacteroides fragilis*, *Bacteroides* spp and anaerobic gram-negative rods) (Brook, 2002). Among the aerobic organisms, *Proteus mirabilis*, *Pseudomonas aeruginosa*, Enterobacteriaceae, and *Staphylococcus aureus* are the most common (Brook, 2002; Kurien et al, 1998). Srifuengfung and Dhiraputra (1993) reported anaerobic culture from brain abscesses in Siriraj Hospital, Thailand, in 1989: *Bacteroides* sp, *Fusobacterium* spp, nonsporing gram-positive bacilli, *Peptostreptococcus* spp, and *Clostridium* spp were identified.

Management

In the stage of encephalitis/cerebritis, antibiotic therapy only is useful, but once an abscess has formed, surgical drainage, combined with 4 to 8 weeks of antibiotics, is the treatment of choice. According to the bacteriology discussed above, initial empiric antimicrobial therapy should be based on the expected etiologic agents. Antibiotics of choice require good penetration through the blood-brain barrier. According to Brook (2002), empiric antibiotic therapy for brain abscess should include penicillin or metronidazole for anaerobes, chloramphenicol or third-generation cephalosporins for aerobic gram-negative organisms, and vancomycin for *S. aureus*. Ticarcillin plus clavulanic acid or a carbapenem can be an alternative as well. The initial empiric therapy can be adjusted specifically when the culture results are obtained.

Surgical drainage in otogenic brain abscess consists of neurosurgical drainage and mastoidectomy. Conventionally, neurosurgical drainage should be done first via a craniotomy, bur hole, or computer-assisted needle aspiration depending on the location of the abscess and the surgeon's expertise. Mastoid surgery will be done separately after the abscess has been drained in a clean neurosurgical field and the patient has been stabilized. The duration between the drainage and mastoidectomy varies from the same day (Kurien et al, 1998) to 2 weeks (Lundman, 1987).

In my department, we prefer to do mastoid surgery after the brain abscess is drained and the patient's vital signs have been stabilized. The duration between the two surgeries depends on the condition of the ear infection. Sometimes the mastoid needs to be drained urgently because of obstructing granulation tissue or polyps that prevent the ear discharge from coming out of the ear canal, and the infection has progressed to the eroded tegmen instead. Radical mastoidectomy with conchoplasty converts the infected ear into a "safe ear" in which office cleaning can be done frequently. Early mastoidectomy is also done in the patient with a concomitant complication, such as lateral sinus thrombosis or extradural abscess.

Conclusion

Cerebritis and brain abscess are serious complications of OM. The incidence has declined with the advent of antibiotics. Although the development of radiographic imaging has also helped to reduce the mortality rate, awareness of the problem, careful history taking, and physical examination, especially for neurologic signs, are essential to providing an accurate diagnosis and appropriate management.

References

Bluestone CD, Klein JO. Intracranial suppurative complications of otitis media and mastoiditis. In: Bluestone CD, Stool SE, Kenna MA, editors. Pediatric otolaryngology. Philadelphia: WB Saunders; 1996. p. 636–47.

Bluestone CD, Klein JO. Complications and sequelae: intracranial. In: Bluestone CD, Klein JO, editors. Otitis media in infants and children. 3rd ed. Philadelphia: WB Saunders; 2001. p. 299–381.

Brook I. Brain abscess in children: microbiology and management. J Child Neurol 1995;10:283–8.

Brook I. Infections of the central nervous system. In: Brook I, editor. Pediatric anaerobic infections. New York: Marcel Dekker; 2002. p. 145–67.

Delbrouck C, Mansbach AL, Blonbiau P. Otogenic thrombosis of the lateral sinus: report of a case in a child. Acta Otorhinolaryngol 1996;50:221–6.

Enzmann DR, Britt RH, Veager AS. Experimental brain abscess evolution: computed tomographic and neuropathologic correlation. Neuroradiology 1979;133:113–21.

Kangsanarak J, Fooanant S, Ruckphaopunt K, et al. Extracranial and intracranial complications of suppurative otitis media. report of 102 cases. J Laryngol Otol 1993;107:999–1004.

Kangsanarak J, Navacharoen N, Fooanant S, Ruckphaopunt K. Intracranial complications of suppurative otitis media: 13 years' experience. Am J Otol 1995;16:104–9.

Kendall BE. Magnetic resonance in diseases of the nervous system. Arch Dis Child 1988;63:1301–4.

Kurien M, Job A, Mathew J, Chandy M. Otogenic intracranial abscess: concurrent craniotomy and mastoidectomy—changing trends in a developing country. Arch Otolaryngol Head Neck Surg 1998;124:1353–6.

Ludman H. Complications of suppurative otitis media. In: Kerr AG, editor. Scott Brown's otolaryngology. 5th ed. London: Butterworth; 1987. p. 264–91.

Murthy PS, Sukumar R, Hazarika P, et al. Otogenic brain abscess in childhood. Int J Pediatr Otorhinolaryngol 1991;22:9–17.

Ratanasiri B. Ten year review of brain abscess in Children's Hospital, Bangkok, Thailand. J Med Assoc Thai 1995;78:37–41.

Sennaroglu L, Sozeri B. Otogenic brain abscess: review of 41 cases. Otolaryngol Head Neck Surg 2000;123:751–5.

Srifuengfung S, Dhiraputra C. Bacterial meningitis and brain abscess in Siriraj Hospital. J Infect Dis Antimicrob Agent 1993; 10:13–7.

Yen PT, Chan ST, Huang TS. Brain abscess: with special reference to otolaryngologic sources of infection. Otolaryngol Head Neck Surg 1995;113:15–22.

VIII. Sequelae of Otitis Media

Chapter 77

TYMPANIC MEMBRANE PERFORATION

STEN HELLSTRÖM, MD, PhD

Tympanic membrane (TM) perforations are a frequent cause of conductive hearing loss worldwide. Symptoms of TM perforation include mild conductive hearing loss, aural fullness, and mild tinnitus. Any symptoms of vertigo or severe sensorineural hearing loss could indicate damage to the inner ear. Any findings of a conductive hearing loss greater than 30 dB could mean an associated ossicular chain disruption.

Perforations Secondary to Otitis Media and Trauma

TM perforations can be acute or chronic. An acute perforation may occur secondary to an episode of acute otitis media (AOM) or in relation to trauma. The mechanism behind the traumatic injury to the TM is usually a sudden air pressure increase in the external ear canal or direct penetration of the TM by a foreign object. Most acute perforations will heal spontaneously, but with traumatic injuries, the healing rate will depend on the cause of the perforation. Thus, a penetrating injury of the TM caused by a hairpin or a cotton-tipped applicator or a pressure injury through a slap to the ear will heal in approximately 90% of the cases (Lindeman et al, 1987), whereas TM perforations evoked through a burn or blast injury, such as through explosives, will heal in only about 60 to 70% of injuries (Henry, 1945; Kerr and Byrne, 1975; Korkis, 1946). In addition to rupture of the TM, there may be ossicular damage within the middle ear, of which disruption of the incudomalleolar joint is the most common. Perforations caused by pressure-induced injuries are the most common source of injuries and include slaps or fist blows to the ear in sports (eg, in ball sports or water sports, the latter resulting from a hydraulic compression as water is forced into the external

auditory canal). More recently, it has also been shown that air-bag deployment contributes to pressure-induced injuries of the TM (McFeely et al, 1999). Slag burn damage is frequently seen in industry from welding or caustic agents. When hot metal fragments contact the TM, they usually not only penetrate but also pass into the mucosa of the middle ear cavity.

Spontaneous rupture of the TM is one of the most common complications secondary to AOM. Under these circumstances, the AOM is accompanied by acute drainage through the defect. There are no statistics available in clinical reports related to the frequency of spontaneous ruptures and spontaneous healing of the ruptured TM. In animal experiments with ears infected by *Streptococcus pneumoniae*, the frequency of draining ears in AOM was reported to be approximately 10% (Spratley et al, 2001). So far, there are no data that state that a certain bacterial species gives rise to a specific appearance of the TM perforation, except in tuberculosis, in which there appear to be more often a number of small perforations rather than a single perforation.

Classification of TM Perforations

Classification is performed according to the site, extent, and duration of the perforation. Regarding the site, the perforations occur mainly in the pars tensa and can be located in the anterosuperior, anteroinferior, posterosuperior, or posteroinferior quadrants. However, perforations may also occur in the pars flaccida.

The extent is related to the number of quadrants involved. The perforation can be limited to one quadrant, involve two or more quadrants but not all, or be a total perforation when all four quadrants are involved. The duration can, as already mentioned above, be acute or chronic. The chronic perforation is generally defined as a perforation that has persisted for more than 3 months.

Spontaneous Rupture in Otitis Media

An acute perforation associated with infection is small and heals spontaneously. Within hours, this perforation appears closed, and the TM is healed in a few days. One may question whether all of these spontaneously occurring perforations in AOM involve all layers of the TM or just the keratinizing squamous epithelium. In AOM, the extremely swollen lamina propria of the TM is flooded by a transudate filled with leukocytes—mainly neutrophils (Spratley et al, 2001). When performing a myringotomy in this condition, a gray-colored fluid will start to drain to the external auditory canal after having punctured the outer layer, the keratinizing squamous epithelium, and a much deeper puncture is needed to reach the middle ear cavity.

In years past, the predominant bacteria isolated in acute suppurative otitis media were *Streptococcus pyogenes* and *S. pneumoniae*. In particular, a fulminant infection with *S. pyogenes* was known to cause necrosis of the TM, resulting in a chronic perforation occupying two or more quadrants. Bacterial necrotizing toxins and degrading neutrophils, releasing proteolytic enzymes, cause destruction and subsequent perforations. This process mostly involves the central region of the TM in which the vascularity in general is very sparse (Hellström et al, 2003). With the advent of antibiotics, altered flora are frequently seen in the middle ear effusion material and the necrotizing TMs are less frequently seen.

Mechanisms Involved in the Healing Process of a TM Perforation

The TM is composed of three layers (Lim, 1995). In brief, the outermost layer, the keratinizing squamous epithelium, is continuous with the skin of the external auditory canal. Directly beneath it lies the middle fibrous layer, also known as the lamina propria. Finally, the inner mucosal layer is continuous with the mucosa of the tympanic cavity.

The powerful ability of the TM to heal mainly rests on the migratory capacity of the outer keratinizing squamous epithelium. Migration of the TM squamous epithelium is a well-recognized phenomenon. Ink dots placed near the center of the membrane will move in a centrifugal manner toward the periphery (Alberti, 1964; Litton, 1968). In a healing TM perforation, a hyperplastic squamous epithelium will close the perforation prior to the ingrowth of the connective tissue (Hellström et al, 1991; McIntire and Benitez, 1970; Stenfors et al, 1980). The healing process starts within hours after the injury. Vessels, normally seldom seen in the semitransparent portion of the TM, will appear at the border of the perforation. Initially, these vessels most probably represent dilated preexisting vessels,

but within 3 to 4 days, there will be an ingrowth of newly formed blood vessels (Hellström et al, 2003). The migrating squamous epithelium is characterized by a marked keratin production, which forms a spur, acting as a guide, ahead of the advancing epithelium. Once the keratinizing squamous epithelium is closed, it is thinned out, and then the rims of the fibrous layer reach each other with a final closing of the mucosal epithelium. Often the residual scar, as seen in the otomicroscope, will disappear rapidly, within weeks. In many aspects, the healing of a TM perforation resembles that of general wound healing. The wound healing process is a chain of inflammatory events, with an initial invasion of inflammatory cells followed by reparative and restoration phases.

Tissue Reactions in Myringotomized TM

In ears with AOM, the ruptures of the TM close even faster than in a perforated normal drum head. The early structural TM reactions to a myringotomy have been studied in an AOM model (Spratley et al, 2002). It was shown that in the inflamed middle ear infected by *S. pneumoniae*, the keratinocyte layer at the perforation layer reacted and increased in thickness 6 hours after the myringotomy. At 9 hours after the perforation, polymorphonuclear neutrophils, macrophages, and small lymphocytes intensely infiltrated the richly vascularized connective tissue layer. Four days after the myringotomy, most of the perforations were completely closed, and after 1 week, the TM structure was almost normalized. An identical myringotomy in a TM in a noninflamed middle ear showed a similar healing pattern but with a delayed response. The invasion of inflammatory cells did not occur until 1 to 2 days after the myringotomy, which should be compared with 6 to 12 hours in the infected middle ear. That the TM perforations seem to close faster in AOM was also shown in an earlier study (Magnuson et al, 1996). It was also observed that noninfected TMs developed myringosclerotic deposits earlier and more extensively (Spratley et al, 2002), which is also supported by clinical observations that myringosclerotic inlays seldom occur in spontaneously ruptured TMs in AOM. It was inferred from the study that the strong capacity for rapid healing in AOM, despite a concomitant collagen fiber disarrangement, implies a low risk for occurrence of residual perforations.

Chronic TM Perforations

An acute perforation may remain open and proceed to a permanent or chronic perforation. This may occur after repeated episodes or a single episode of suppurative AOM. In these cases, the epithelium of the outer surface and the mucosa of the inner epithelial lining will fuse into a transitional zone. This mucocutaneous junction appears to have lost its capacity for healing of the perforation (Spandow et al, 1996). This transitional zone will strip easily from the entire margin of the perforation—a procedure that is similar to chemical cauterization of the perforation rim with trichloroacetic acid or silver nitrate, performed in myringoplasties to enhance the epithelialization of the graft (Gladstone et al, 1995). Which specific mechanisms may cause a permanent perforation to develop have not yet been elucidated.

Recent exciting results from ongoing experimental studies on genetically altered animals, however, show that lack of plasminogen, an activator of proteases, will arrest the healing in TM perforations (Hellström et al, 2002). Moreover, when substituting plasminogen in this plasminogen-deficient species, the perforated TM will heal (Hellström et al, 2002). These results indicate that just as important as new formation of the keratinizing epithelium and the connective tissue elements is a preceding degradation of extracellular matrix components in the remodeling procedure. Retarded healing of TM perforations has also been observed after application of mitomycin C, an antineoplastic chemotherapeutic agent widely used in ophthalmology because of its ability to prevent closure of the trabeculectomy site in patients with glaucoma (Estrem and Batra, 1999; Kupin et al, 1995). Mitomycin C selectively interrupts deoxyribonucleic acid (DNA) replication and will inhibit mitosis and protein synthesis, which means that it could act through mechanisms similar to that in plasminogen deficiency—a lack of activation of proteases.

Growth Factors in Healing of TM Perforations

Regarding the healing process of perforated TMs, it is important to mention if any molecules, administered exogenously, have been shown to stimulate the healing process. Experience from wound healing research has suggested the possibility of accelerating healing of TM perforations with polypeptide growth factors and matrix moieties (Amoils et al, 1992a; Fina et al, 1993; Mondain et al, 1991; Mondain and Ryan, 1993). One of the first molecules to be shown to accelerate healing of TM perforations was hyaluronan (Laurent et al, 1988). Unfortunately, when tested clinically, hyaluronan was not superior in efficiency to closure by the paper patch technique (Laurent et al, 1991). Research on epidermal growth factor, topically applied for healing of experimental TM perforations, has been reported since 1990, with differing results (Amoils et al, 1992a; Dvorak et al, 1995; Lee et al, 1994). In a human trial on chronic TM perforations, no benefit was shown by use of topical application of epidermal growth factor (Ramsay et al, 1995). Fibroblast growth factors (FGFs) applied to TM perforations have been widely studied. However, neither basic FGF (bFGF) nor acidic FGF (aFGF) on the repair of TM perforations has produced a statistically significant higher closure rate compared with control treatment (Chauvin et al, 1999; Kaplan, 1984). Similar results have been obtained in studies testing platelet-derived growth factor, transforming growth factor β, and keratinocyte growth factor (Clymer et al, 1996; Soumekh et al, 1996; Yeo et al, 2000). Generally, most investigations in the field of growth factors and healing of TM perforations have been performed in animal models and as acute perforations. However, the topical application of polypeptide growth factors is being studied in experimental chronic perforations (Amoils et al, 1992b; Spandow and Hellström, 1993; Truy et al, 1995) and to see whether ototoxicity can be ruled out in clinical trials (Ma et al, 2002).

Enhanced Healing of Tympanic Membrane Performance by Stem Cells

Another area, which has recently started to be explored, is healing of TM perforations by use of embryonic stem cells (von Unge et al, 2003). In animal experiments, these stem cells were shown to enhance the healing, possibly by differentiation and integration into TM tissue. However, further experimental studies are needed to evaluate the clinical potential of applying stem cells on the perforated TM.

Perforations after Tympanostomy Tube Treatment and in Atrophic TMs

Except after an episode or episodes of AOM, perforations in relation to inflammatory conditions of the middle ear can occur after extrusion of a tympanostomy tube and in atrophic TMs. In a meta-analysis of the incidence of chronic perforations relative to tube type, the incidence was much higher for long-term tubes (Kay et al, 2001). Whereas short-term tubes had mean perforation rates of 2.2%, the incidence with long-term tubes was 16.6%. The biologic background as to why longstanding tympanostomy tubes seem to have a significantly higher rate of persistent perforations is not known, although it is feasible to assume that it might be a combination of a chronic inflammation dependent on or independent of an altered middle ear gaseous environment. Although it is tempting to suggest that long-term tympanostomy tubes should not be used, it is important to consider that they do have their own unique role, in particular for cases of prolonged eustachian tube dysfunction. Long-term tubes offer far longer periods of ventilation and decrease the need for frequent procedures under general anesthesia.

It is well agreed that long-standing otitis media with effusion may evolve into chronic otitis media and its sequelae, including persistent perforation (Tos, 1981). Otitis media with effusion will give rise to atrophic portions of the TM with or without retractions. In the atrophic areas, the lamina propria is weakened and contains few fibrous and elastic fibers, which make it thin, unelastic, and slack (Tos, 1984). These areas constitute a risk of permanent perforation with a very slight chance of healing. This should be, at least partly, due to an impaired vascular supply. These atrophic areas seem to have low biologic activity in general, which will be obvious if a tympanostomy tube is placed in these areas. This tube will be lost very rapidly, most probably owing to a reduced migratory activity of the keratinizing squamous epithelium normally trying to closely encircle the tube. Perforations in these atrophic areas will not heal spontaneously and will need a surgical myringoplasty to be closed.

Implications of Management

Spontaneous ruptures as well as myringotomy openings in AOM will most often heal rapidly and without any extensive scar tissues. When performing a myringotomy in a bulging TM, the incision should be performed in the anteroinferior quadrant, and one should make sure to penetrate all tissue layers of the TM. It should be pointed out that the middle ear tissue in AOM will not normalize faster after a myringotomy compared to a non-myringotomized ear. Therefore, this intervention should be restricted to cases not responding accurately to antibiotic treatment or when complications such as mastoiditis occur in relation to AOM.

A perforation that has persisted for 3 months is chronic and should be repaired to improve the hearing and to get a dry ear when exposed to water (eg, when taking a bath). In small perforations less than 3 mm in diameter, the first attempt to close the perforation could be through the paper patch technique (Golz et al, 2003) or by fat plug myringoplasty (Mitchell et al, 1997). These techniques should include the removal of the rim of the perforation prior to applying the paper patch or introducing the fat plug.

A larger perforation should be repaired by a conventional myringoplasty using fascia as the graft. This surgical procedure is well suited to be performed using local anesthesia. The use of single-flanged tympanostomy tubes should be restricted to children in risk groups as the incidence of permanent perforations is considerably larger with these tubes compared with the generally used double-flanged tubes. In children with previous episodes of otitis media effusion, the repair should not be performed until at an age when their middle ears are normalized and otitis media with effusion does not occur any longer.

Although there are promising results concerning the use of growth factors to stimulate the healing of TM perforations, there are still no such results from the clinical trials that will support the use of adjuvant medical therapy for repair of TM perforations.

Conclusion

TM perforations will occur secondary to various inflammatory conditions of the middle ear or in relation to trauma. Most perforations will heal spontaneously, but some will develop into persistent or chronic perforations. Although the healing process of a perforated TM has been quite well characterized, attempts to substitute molecules (eg, growth factors), which should enhance the healing, have so far not been rewarding. However, in the future, it should be possible to repair at least certain tympanic perforations by medical therapies without the need for surgical interventions.

References

Alberti PWRM. Epithelial migration in the tympanic membrane. J Laryngol Otol 1964;78:808–30.

Amoils CP, Jackler RK, Lusting LR. Repair of chronic tympanic membrane perforations using epidermal growth factor. Otolaryngol Head Neck Surg 1992a;107:669–83.

Amoils CP, Jackler RK, Milczuk H, et al. An animal model of chronic tympanic membrane perforation. Otolaryngol Head Neck Surg 1992b;106:47–55.

Chauvin K, Bratton C, Parkins C. Healing large tympanic membrane perforations using hyaluronic acid, basic fibroblast growth factor, and epidermal growth factor. Otolaryngol Head Neck Surg 1999;121:43–7.

Clymer MA, Schwaber MK, Davidson JM. The effects of keratinocyte growth factor on healing of tympanic membrane perforations. Laryngoscope 1996;106:280–5.

Dvorak DW, Abbas G, Ali T. Repair of chronic tympanic membrane perforations with long-term epidermal growth factor. Laryngoscope 1995;105:1300–4.

Estrem SA, Batra PS. Preventing myringotomy closure with topical mitomycin C in rats. Otolaryngol Head Neck Surg 1999;120:794–8.

Fina M, Baird A, Ryan A. Direct application of basic fibroblast growth factor improves tympanic membrane perforation healing. Laryngoscope 1993;103:804–9.

Gladstone HB, Jackler RK, Varav K. Tympanic membrane wound healing: an overview. Otolaryngol Clin North Am 1995;28:913–32.

Golz A, Goldenberg D, Netzer A, et al. paper patching for chronic tympanic membrane perforations. Otolaryngol Head Neck Surg 2003;128:565–70.

Hellström S, Bloom GD, Berghem L, et al. A comparison of hyaluronan and fibronectin in the healing of tympanic membrane perforations Eur Arch Otorhinolaryngol 1991;53:230–5.

Hellström S, Ny T, Li J, Eriksson P-O. Original discovery 2002. [In preparation]

Hellström S, Spratley J, Eriksson P-O, Pais-Clemente M. Tympanic membrane vessel revisited: a study in an animal model. Otol Neurotol 2003;24:494–9.

Henry GA. Blast injuries. Laryngoscope 1945;55:663–72.

Kaplan JZ. Acceleration of wound healing by a live yeast cell derivative. Arch Surg 1984;119:1005–8.

Kay DJ, Nelson M, Rosenfeld. Meta-analysis of tympanostomy tube sequelae. Otolaryngol Head Neck Surg 2001;124:374–80.

Kerr AG, Byrne JET. Concussive effects of bomb blast on the ear. J Laryngol Otol 1975;89:131–43.

Korkis FB. Rupture of the tympanic membrane of blast origin. J Laryngol 1946;61:367–90.

Kupin TH, Juzych MS, Shin DH, et al. Adjunctive mitomycin C in primary trabeculectomy in phakic eyes. Am J Ophthalmol 1995;119:30–9.

Laurent C, Hellström S, Fellenius E. Hyaluronan improves healing of experimental tympanic membrane perforations. Arch Otolaryngol Head Neck Surg 1988;114:1435–41.

Laurent C, Soderberg O, Anniko M, et al. Repair of chronic tympanic membrane perforations using application of hyaluronan or rice paper prostheses. ORL J Otorhinolaryngol Relat Spec 1991;53:37–40.

Lee AJ, Jackler RK, Kato BM, et al. Repair of chronic tympanic membrane perforation using epidermal growth factor: progress toward clinical application. Am J Otol 1994;15:10–8.

Lim DJ. Structure and function of the tympanic membrane: a review. Acta Otorhinolaryngol Belg 1995;49:101–15.

Lindeman P, Edström S, Granström G, et al. Acute traumatic tympanic membrane perforations. Arch Otolaryngol Head Neck Surg 1987;113:1285–7.

Litton WB. Epithelial migration in the ear: the location and characteristics of the generation centre revealed by utilizing a radioactive DNA precursor. Acta Otolaryngol Suppl (Stockh) 1968;240:1–39.

Ma Y, Zhao H, Zhou X. Topical treatment with growth factors for tympanic membrane perforations. Progress towards clinical application. Acta Otolaryngol (Stockh) 2002;122:586–99.

Magnuson K, Hermansson A, Hellström S. Healing of the tympanic membrane after myringotomy during *Streptococcus pneumoniae* otitis media. Ann Otol Rhinol Laryngol 1996;105:397–404.

McFeely WJ, Bojrab DI, Davis KG, Hegyi DF. Otologic injuries caused by airbag deployment. Otolaryngol Head Neck Surg 1999;113:62–7.

McIntire C, Benitez JT. Spontaneous repair of the tympanic membrane: histopathological studies in the cat. Ann Otol Rhinol Laryngol 1970;79:1129–31.

Mitchell RB, Pereira RH, Lazar RH. Fat graft myringoplasty in children—a safe and successful day-stay procedure. J Laryngol Otol 1997;111:106–8.

Mondain M, Ryan A. Histological study of the healing of traumatic tympanic membrane perforation after basic fibroblast growth factor application. Laryngoscope 1993;103:312–8.

Mondain M, Saffiedine S, Uziel A. Fibroblast growth factor improves the healing of experimental tympanic membrane perforations. Acta Otolaryngol (Stockh) 1991;111:337–41.

Ramsay HA, Hekkoinen EJ, Laurila PK. Effect of epidermal growth factor on tympanic membranes with chronic perforations: a clinical trial. Otolaryngol Head Neck Surg 1995;113:375–9.

Soumekh B, Hom DB, Levine S, et al. Treatment of chronic tympanic-membrane perforations with a platelet derived releasate. Am J Otol 1996;17:506–11.

Spandow O, Hellström S. Animal model for persistent tympanic membrane perforations. Ann Otol Rhinol Laryngol 1993;102:467–72.

Spandow O, Hellström S, Dahlström M. Structural characterization of persistent tympanic membrane perforations in man. Laryngoscope 1996;105:397–404.

Spratley J, Hellström S, Eriksson P-E, Pais-Clemente M. Myringotomy delays the tympanic membrane recovery in acute otitis media: a study in the rat model. Laryngoscope 2001;112:1474–81.

Spratley J, Hellström S, Eriksson P-O, Pais-Clemente M. Early structural tympanic membrane reactions to myringotomy: a study in an acute otitis media model. Acta Otolaryngol (Stockh) 2002;122:479–87.

Stenfors L-E, Carlsöö B, Winbladh B. Repair of experimental tympanic membrane perforations. Acta Otolaryngol (Stockh) 1980;90:332–41.

Tos M. Upon the relationship between secretory otitis in childhood and chronic otitis and its sequelae in adults. J Laryngol Otol 1981;95:1011–22.

Tos M. Atrophy of the tympanic membrane in surgery and pathology in the middle ear. In: Marquet JFE, editor. Proceedings of the International Conference on the Postoperative Evaluation in Middle Ear Surgery. Boston: Martinus Nijhoff; 1984. p. 170–6.

Truy E, Disant F, Morgon A. Chronic tympanic membrane perforation: an animal model. Am J Otol 1995;16:222–5.

von Unge M, Dirckx JJJ, Olivius NP. Embryonic stem cells enhance the healing of tympanic membrane perforations. Int J Pediatr Otorhinolaryngol 2003;76:215–9.

Yeo SE, Kim SW, Suh BD, et al. Effects of platelet-derived growth factor-AA on the healing process of tympanic membrane perforation. Am J Otolaryngol 2000;21:153–60.

Chapter 78

TYMPANOSCLEROSIS

STEPHANIE MOODY ANTONIO, MD, ANTONIO DE LA CRUZ, MD,
KAREN BORNE TEUFERT, MD

Tympanosclerosis (TS) is a common sequela of chronic or recurrent otitis media (OM) and surgery of the tympanic membrane or middle ear. It is often limited to the tympanic membrane and possesses little clinical significance. However, when TS involves the middle ear, it can result in ossicular fixation and conductive hearing loss. TS is characterized by the presence of white plaques or nodules in the fibrous layer of the tympanic membrane or the submucosa of the middle ear. It is a result of abnormal hyalinization, calcification, and ossification of involved tissues.

Description

The terms myringosclerosis (MS) and TS are often blurred in the literature. MS refers to white calcified plaques limited to the tympanic membrane. TS implies disease of the middle ear, although most authors use this term also to refer to disease of the tympanic membrane, such as that viewed by otoscopy. The diagnosis of MS is easily made during otomicroscopy. White patches of variable size appear to be limited to the tympanic membrane. The plaques tend to have sharp edges and a periphery of normal transluscent membrane to allow differentiation from a middle ear mass such as cholesteatoma.

TS may be seen through a thin and transluscent tympanic membrane but is more often discovered during surgery after raising a tympanomeatal flap or suspected because of conductive hearing loss. In the middle ear, TS may appear as small white-speckled thickened areas of middle ear mucosa, thickened plaques within the mucosa, or more extensive nodular lesions spanning the middle ear space and involving the ossicles. It is differentiated from cholesteatoma by its dull appearance, firmness, and often geometric borders (compared with the rounded smooth borders of cholesteatoma).

The coincidence of TS and MS is high (Jaisinghani et al, 1999). TS of the middle ear is difficult to identify through an intact tympanic membrane but should be suspected if the degree of hearing loss does not correlate with the appearance of the tympanic membrane or the clinical history. Differentiation of TS from otosclerosis in the presence of conductive hearing loss is suggested by a history of chronic OM. Computed tomography (CT) of the middle ear can suggest areas of abnormal calcification or ossification (Figure 78-1). Calcification of the tensor tympani tendon, stapedial tendon, and suspensory ligaments is fairly easy to see with CT (Figure 78-2). The diagnosis is best made during surgical exploration.

Incidence

The incidence of TS has been reported between 6.4 and 33% in subjects with chronic OM (Austin, 1988; Emmett and Shea, 1978; Maw, 1991; Morgan 1977; Sheehy and House, 1962). The incidence appears to increase with age (Daly et al, 1998; Maw, 1991) and with placement of tympanostomy tubes (Kay et al, 2001; Maw, 1991; Wielinga and Kerr, 1993). In the literature, a distinction is not usually made between disease limited to the drum and disease of the middle ear unless specific reference is made to the degree of conductive hearing loss, implying middle ear or ossicular involvement.

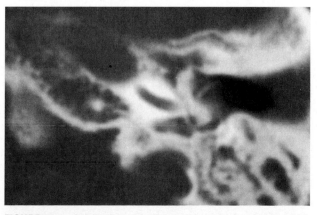

FIGURE 78-1. Axial computed tomographic scan showing the thick plaque of myringosclerosis obstructing the middle ear space.

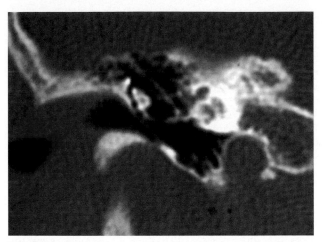

FIGURE 78-2. Coronal computed tomographic scan of a calcified tensor tympani tendon in a child with maximal conductive hearing loss. The ossicles are congenitally deformed. In addition to medial fixation of the malleus owing to the calcified tensor, there are bony adhesions to the scutum, which are likely congenital.

In a general pediatric clinic, one may expect to see MS or TS in a proportion of the patients. In a prospective study of 218 consecutive patients seen for otologic and nonotologic reasons in an outpatient pediatric otolaryngology clinic, 36 (16.5%) showed signs of MS or TS based on the office examination. Of these patients, 21 had undergone previous bilateral myringotomy and tube placement (Friedman et al, 2001). If specifically looking at a population of children with chronic OM, the incidence may be greater. In a cross-sectional study of 73 patients with more than 11 episodes of acute OM, the incidence of TS in 8- to 13-year-old patients was 26% (Stenstrom and Ingvarsson, 1995).

Of 1,210 patients with OM who underwent tympanoplasty and ossicular chain reconstruction between 1990 and 1998 at the House Ear Clinic, 17.6% had TS (House and Teufert, 2001). In a follow-up review of 203 patients from this study who had TS, the TS was located in the tympanic membrane in 45.8%, the middle ear in 8.4%, and the ossicles in 66.5%. Ossicular fixation was frequent; the malleus was fixed in 34.5%, the incus in 35.4%, and the stapes in 35.9% (Teufert and De La Cruz, 2002). Fixation of the malleus, incus, and stapes may occur in 16 to 55% (Wielinga and Kerr, 1993).

The incidence of TS increases with placement of tympanostomy tubes, with authors reporting an incidence of 28 to 61% (Wielinga and Kerr, 1993). Kay and colleagues (2001) performed a meta-analysis of 41 studies (including 7,197 ears) of tube placement and reported that the rate of TS after extrusion of tubes is 31.7%. There was no difference in the rates for short-term compared with long-term tube presence. The relative risk of TS after tubes compared with no surgery or myringotomy alone was 3.5% (Kay et al, 2001).

Pathogenesis

The etiopathogenesis is not completely understood, but several different mechanisms have been proposed. Triggers identified in association with TS include bacterial OM, serous OM, surgery, tympanostomy tubes, intratympanic hemorrhage, and perforation. TS is thought to be a progressive disorder that occurs in two or three stages (Wielinga and Kerr, 1993). The initial stage consists of a traumatic or inflammatory process leading to collagen damage and/or formation of granulation tissue. The second stage is characterized by fibroblast infiltration of the submucosa of the middle ear or lamina propria of the tympanic membrane with excessive production of collagen and hyalinization. In the final stage, calcification and ossification occur (Wielinga and Kerr, 1993). The early stages of TS may be reversible, and several authors have found that TS can disappear over time (Moller, 1984; Tos and Stangerup, 1989). In other cases, however, TS is thought to be a progressive disorder. In patients with a long history of ear disease and in adults compared with children, the incidence of TS is greater (Daly et al, 1998; Wielinga and Kerr, 1993)

The observation of an increased rate of TS after placement of pressure equalization tubes deserves special mention. The etiology is not known and continues to prompt interesting theories in the literature. Provocative factors include operative bleeding (Dawes et al, 1991; Parker et al, 1990), repeated tube placement (Maw, 1991), a foreign body reaction, or mechanical trauma (Lesser et al, 1988; Tos et al, 1983).

In an attempt to better understand TS, animal models have been developed (Forseni et al, 2002; Russell and Giles, 2002; Sprem et al, 2002). In a rat model, Wielinga and colleagues (2001) demonstrated edema, macrophage infiltration, and increased fibroblast activity in the lamina propria of the tympanic membrane within 1 week of eustachian tube obstruction. Eventually, the thickened lamina propria showed signs of degeneration and the appearance of calcareous deposits. In the subacute stage, fibrous tissue coexisted with avascular acellular hyalinized areas that had more extensive calcification. At longer time points, degeneration of the organized fibrous layer of the tympanic membrane continued with thickening of the lamina propria and further hyalinization and calcification. The progressive nature of TS was highlighted by Russell and Giles (2002). Rats with eustachian tube obstruction and resulting sterile OM were followed for 1 to 12 months. Histologic changes consistent with TS were seen within the submucosal connective tissue layer and progressed to involve all connective tissue sublayers of the tympanic membrane by 9 to 12 months. Calcium deposits were seen after 3 months in the submucosal layer and by 12 months in all layers. The normal structure of the radiate and circular layers of the lamina propria was lost within 9 to 12 months and replaced by thick deposits of calcium and haphazard arrangement of collagen (Russell and Giles, 2002).

Theories regarding the biochemical mechanisms of abnormal calcification include malfunctioning extracellular lysosomes and local immunologic hypersensitivity (Mann et al, 1980; Schiff et al, 1980). Flodin and others suggest that TS may be a result of bone macrophage differentiation to osteoclasts and subsequent ectopic bone production (Flodin, 2001; Forseni Flodin and Hultcrantz, 2002). The role of macrophages was also highlighted by Makiishi-Shimobayashi and colleagues (2001), who found osteopontin in the calcified tissues of patients with TS. The authors suggested that osteopontin is secreted by macrophages during an inflammatory process and that this protein acts as a flue between calcified deposits and stromal tissues.

Dursun and colleagues (1997) suggested that certain types of human leukocyte antigens (HLAs) may play a role in the pathogenesis of TS when they found elevated serum HLA-B35 and -DR3 in the patients with TS compared with a normal sample. A genetic linkage to atherosclerotic cardiovascular disease was suggested by Koc and Uneri (2002) when they identified a high rate of MS in atherosclerotic patients in comparison with a normal group.

Management

Myringosclerosis is usually inconsequential and requires no treatment. In the management of TS, an abnormal Rinne test and/or a conductive hearing loss of more than 30 dB are indications for surgery.

Myringosclerosis

Large plaques involving the tympanic membrane may result in fixation of the malleus and result in conductive hearing loss by inhibiting vibration and sound wave transmission. Note that this can be determined preoperatively by performing pneumatic otoscopy. Under high-power inspection, the manubrium should be freely mobile. If the manubrium is not mobile, it can be surmised that TS is interfering with sound conduction. Very thick plaques may interfere with middle ear ventilation (see Figure 78-1). In addition, extensive or thick MS left on the tympanic membrane remnant impairs graft healing after tympanoplasty for perforation. In these cases, MS plaques should be removed at the time of grafting. In addition to improving the graft take-rate, removal of MS allows better contact of a prosthesis with the new tympanic membrane and re-establishes a more normal vibratory capacity of the tympanic membrane. Removal of the MS in the anterosuperior quadrant of the tympanic membrane and/or sectioning of the anterior malleolar ligament may be necessary to obtain free malleolar movement.

To remove MS plaques, the plaque is outlined by perforation with a Rosen needle or sickle knife. It can then be removed without disturbing the remaining tympanic membrane or malleus. If performing a medial graft technique, the MS plaque is thinned by inserting a sharp pick and creating a plane between layers of MS or between MS and the fibrous layer of the tympanic membrane. Keeping a thin superficial layer, the underlying plaque is loosened and then removed with a cup forceps. This allows maximal preservation of the tympanic membrane while allowing a thin and flexible reconstruction.

TS of the Epitympanum

Fixation of the malleus or incus at the level of the epitympanum results in conductive hearing loss. Malleus fixation may also result from involvement of the tensor tympani tendon or anterior malleolar ligament. On finding a fixed ossicular chain, the point of fixation should be determined prior to attempting to mobilize the malleus or other ossicles. The incudostapedial joint is separated with a joint knife. Gentle palpation of the stapes, long process of the incus, and malleus determines which ossicles are fixed in the attic, oval window, or both. If attic fixation is present, the incus is separated from the malleus head and removed. If the malleus remains a point of fixation, the head is amputated with a malleus nipper at the level of the neck. (Simple mobilization of the malleus without removal of the head or attic wall is associated with a high rate of recurrent fixation.) The handle of the malleus now should be freely mobile. If the tensor tympani tendon is involved, it is sectioned. The sound-conducting mechanism is reconstructed with a partial ossicular replacement prosthesis (PORP) or total ossicular replacement prosthesis (TORP) depending on the presence or absence of the stapes superstructure. An alternative technique for attic fixation is removal of the outer attic wall (atticotomy) with ossicular mobilization. We prefer ossicular reconstruction because, in our experience, atticotomy alone frequently results in refixation. Scarring and refixation can be reduced by placement of Gelfilm or thin Silastic at mucosal or bony surfaces adjacent to mobilized ossicles.

Stapes Fixation

Tympanosclerotic fixation of the stapes may result from involvement of the stapedial tendon or the oval window niche. Surgical management of stapes fixation with TS is somewhat controversial. The risk of hydraulic cochlear damage by manipulation of the stapes and difficulty in removing tympanosclerotic plaques are cited as contraindications to surgical management (Smyth, 1972). The current literature supports surgical intervention, with options including stapes mobilization and stapedectomy (Albu et al, 2000; Gormley, 1987; Teufert and De La Cruz, 2002; Tos et al, 1990). One advantage of mobilization is the possibility of completing the surgery in one stage rather than with the two-stage technique required to perform stapedectomy in the presence of a perforation. One potential disadvantage to mobilization is the risk of refixation within a short time (Albu et al, 2000). In addition, sensorineural hearing loss may result from hydraulic displacement or perilymphatic fistula owing to mobilization (Albu et al, 2000; Smyth, 1972).

Stapedectomy offers perhaps less risk of sensorineural hearing loss than extensive dissection and associated manipulation of the oval window but requires a second stage after repair of perforation and resolution of chronic infection (Albu et al, 2000; Gormley, 1987; Smyth, 1972).

At the House Ear Clinic, TS involving the stapes is initially managed with stapes mobilization. Stapedectomy is reserved for those cases in which mobilization is unsuccessful. It is important to mobilize the stapes by removing the plaques and not by attempting to rock the stapes free. Rocking the stapes may result in fracture of the superstructure or the footplate and risks sensorineural hearing loss. A sharp Rosen needle, footplate hook, or laser is used to separate the tympanosclerotic plaques from the crura, promontory, and facial nerve. TS plaques are lifted in a posterior to anterior direction, not up or out, as this kind of movement may result in rupture of the annular ligament or dislocation of the stapes. Laser dissection is extremely helpful as it allows vaporization of TS with minimal ossicular displacement. The laser should not be used at the level of the facial nerve to avoid risk of thermal injury to the nerve. The stapes tendon should be left intact during the majority of the dissection to prevent excessive or abrupt movement of the stapes. Finally, if necessary, the stapes tendon is cut to view and free the posterior crus. If mobilization is successful and the mobile lateral chain remains in place, no further intervention is needed provided that good mobility has been achieved. If the incus is absent, the sound-conducting mechanism is reconstructed with a PORP.

If the mobilization is not successful and a perforation is present, the surgery is staged. A minimum of 6 to 12 months is allowed before the second-stage procedure to allow healing of the new graft and middle ear disease. During the second stage, mobilization is again attempted. If the stapes footplate still cannot be mobilized and the lateral chain is intact and mobile, a stapedectomy is performed. In the absence of an incus, a stapedectomy is reconstructed with a TORP placed on a perichondrial graft. Cartilage is placed between the tympanic membrane and the prosthesis to prevent extrusion.

Surgical Results

In our experience, hearing results after ossicular reconstruction for TS are good (Table 78-1) and complications are low. Compared with patients without TS undergoing

TABLE 78-1. Short- and Long-Term Hearing Results after Tympanoplasty for Tympanosclerosis

	Short-Term Air–Bone Gap ≤ 20 dB		Long-Term Air–Bone Gap ≤ 20 dB	
	n	%	n	%
Overall	181	64.6	109	67.9
Location of MS/TS				
Tympanic membrane	81	64.2	46	76.1
Middle ear	14	50	13	53.8
Location of fixation				
Malleus	64	65.6	37	70.3
Incus	65	69.2	41	68.3
Stapes	66	62.1	40	65.0
Type of procedure				
Stapedectomy	20	60.0	10	60.0
Stapes mobilization	46	63.0	30	66.7

Adapted from Teufert KB and De La Cruz A (2002).
MS = myringosclerosis; TS = tympanosclerosis.

ossicular chain reconstruction, the long-term postoperative air–bone gap was no different in the patients with TS (17.2 dB versus 17.4 dB) (Teufert and De La Cruz, 2002). Closure of the air–bone gap to less than 20 dB occurred in 67.9% of 109 patients with long-term follow-up. There was no effect on hearing results based on the location of TS: tympanic membrane, middle ear, or with or without ossicular fixation. Which ossicles were fixed also had no effect on good hearing outcome. The air–bone gap was closed to less than 20 dB in 70.3% of cases with malleus fixation, 68.3% with incus fixation, and 65% with stapes fixation. There was no difference in hearing results after stapedectomy versus stapes mobilization, with 60 and 63% of patients, respectively, having short-term closure of the air–bone gap to less than 20 dB. These results were stable at long-term follow-up in both groups (Teufert and De La Cruz, 2002).

In our experience, complications are unusual. There were no dead ears in this series. A high-frequency bone-conduction hearing loss of more than 10 dB was found in 1% (Teufert and De La Cruz, 2002).

Conclusion

TS appears to be the end product of recurrent acute or chronic ear infection and is of clinical significance only when it disrupts the ossicular chain movement. Very little is known about the etiology and pathology of this disease, and its surgical management remains controversial, especially when the stapes is involved. TS is managed according to its location and extension. Surgical treatment of TS is a safe procedure and is effective in the treatment of conductive hearing loss. The success rate of correcting conductive hearing loss was 67.9% in a series of patients operated on at the House Ear Clinic.

References

Albu S, Babighian G, Trabalzini F. Surgical treatment of tympanosclerosis. Am J Otol 2000;21:631–5.

Austin DF. Reconstructive techniques for tympanosclerosis. Ann Otol Rhinol Laryngol 1988;97:670–4.

Daly KA, Hunter LL, Levine SC, et al. Relationships between otitis media sequelae and age. Laryngoscope 1998;108:1306–10.

Dawes PJ, Bingham BJ, Rhys R, Griffiths MV. Aspirating middle ear effusions when inserting ventilation tubes: does it influence post-operative otorrhoea, tube obstruction or the development of tympanosclerosis? Clin Otolaryngol 1991;16:457–61.

Dursun G, Acar A, Turgay M, Calguner M. Human leukocyte antigens in tympanosclerosis. Clin Otolaryngol 1997;22:62–4.

Emmett JR, Shea JJ. Surgical treatment of tympanosclerosis. Laryngoscope 1978;88:1642–8.

Flodin MF. Macrophages and possible osteoclast differentiation in the rat bullar bone during experimental acute otitis media, with reference to tympanosclerosis. Otol Neurotol 2001;22:771–5.

Forseni Flodin M, Hultcrantz M. Possible inflammatory mediators in tympanosclerosis development. Int J Pediatr Otorhinolaryngol 2002;63:149–54.

Friedman EM, Sprecher RC, Simon S, Dunn JK. Quantitation and prevalence of tympanosclerosis in a pediatric otolaryngology clinic. Int J Pediatr Otorhinolaryngol 2001;60:205–11.

Gormley PK. Stapedectomy in tympanosclerosis. A report of 67 cases. Am J Otol 1987;8:123–30.

House JW, Teufert KB. Extrusion rates and hearing results in ossicular reconstruction. Otolaryngol Head Neck Surg 2001;125:135–41.

Jaisinghani VJ, Paparella MM, Schachern PA, Le CT. Tympanic membrane/middle ear pathologic correlates in chronic otitis media. Laryngoscope 1999;109:712–6.

Kay DJ, Nelson M, Rosenfeld RM. Meta-analysis of tympanostomy tube sequelae. Otolaryngol Head Neck Surg 2001;124:374–80.

Koc A, Uneri C. Genetic predisposition for tympanosclerotic degeneration. Eur Arch Otorhinolaryngol 2002;259:180–3.

Lesser TH, Williams KR, Skinner DW. Tympanosclerosis, grommets and shear stresses. Clin Otolaryngol 1988;13:375–80.

Makiishi-Shimobayashi C, Tsujimura T, Sugihara A, et al. Expression of osteopontin by exudate macrophages in inflammatory tissues of the middle ear: a possible association with development of tympanosclerosis. Hear Res 2001;153:100–7.

Mann W, Riede UN, Jonas I, Beck C. The role of matrix vesicles in the pathogenesis of tympanosclerosis. Acta Otolaryngol (Stockh) 1980;89:43–52.

Maw AR. Development of tympanosclerosis in children with otitis media with effusion and ventilation tubes. J Laryngol Otol 1991;105:614–7.

Moller P. Tympanosclerosis of the ear drum in children. Int J Pediatr Otorhinolaryngol 1984;7:247–56.

Morgan WC Jr. Tympanosclerosis. Laryngoscope 1977;87:1821–5.

Parker AJ, Maw AR, Powell JE. Intra-tympanic membrane bleeding after grommet insertion and tympanosclerosis. Clin Otolaryngol 1990;15:203–7.

Russell JD, Giles JJ. Tympanosclerosis in the rat tympanic membrane: an experimental study. Laryngoscope 2002;112:1663–6.

Schiff M, Poliquin JF, Catanzaro A, Ryan AF. Tympanosclerosis. A theory of pathogenesis. Ann Otol Rhinol Laryngol 1980;89:1–16.

Sheehy JL, House WF. Tympanosclerosis. Arch Otolaryngol Head Neck Surg 1962;76:151–7.

Smyth GD. Tympanosclerosis. J Laryngol Otol 1972;86:9–14.

Sprem N, Branica S, Dawidowsky K. Experimental hematotympanum—aspects to the tympanosclerosis development. Coll Antropol 2002;26:267–72.

Stenstrom C, Ingvarsson L. Late effects on ear disease in otitis-prone children: a long-term follow-up study. Acta Otolaryngol (Stockh) 1995;115:658–63.

Teufert KB, De La Cruz A. Tympanosclerosis: long-term hearing results after ossicular reconstruction. Otolaryngol Head Neck Surg 2002;126:264–72.

Tos M, Bonding P, Poulsen G. Tympanosclerosis of the drum in secretory otitis after insertion of grommets. A prospective, comparative study. J Laryngol Otol 1983;97:489–96.

Tos M, Lau T, Arndal H, Plate S. Tympanosclerosis of the middle ear: late results of surgical treatment. J Laryngol Otol 1990;104:685–9.

Tos M, Stangerup SE. Hearing loss in tympanosclerosis caused by grommets. Arch Otolaryngol Head Neck Surg 1989;115:931–5.

Wielinga EW, Kerr AG. Tympanosclerosis. Clin Otolaryngol 1993;18:341–9.

Wielinga EW, Peters TA, Tonnaer EL, et al. Middle ear effusions and structure of the tympanic membrane. Laryngoscope 2001;111:90–5.

Chapter 79

Dimeric Tympanic Membrane

STEN HELLSTRÖM, MD, PhD

Dimeric tympanic membrane (TM) refers to a condition with the formation of a neomembrane described as consisting of an outer keratinizing epithelium and an inner mucosal lining without the normal collagenous fiber layer between them. These dimeric TMs correspond to the atrophic areas, which may develop during long-standing otitis media (OM) and/or in healing of perforated TMs. These areas will form retractions and, in their most advanced forms, a collapsed atelectatic TM. Assuming that the atrophic areas of the TM are synonymous with a dimeric membrane, one may question whether a dimeric membrane is actually a bilayered membrane or whether the dimeric nomenclature relates to a phenomenon that merely involves qualitative changes of the fibrous layer.

Structure of the Normal TM

In a normal TM, in its pars tensa, the lamina propria is made of densely packed collagenous fibers. The fibers are highly organized in an outer radial and an inner circular layer (Lim, 1968a). Between the fibers and, in particular, adjacent to the basal membranes, below the epithelial linings, there is a considerable volume of extracellular matrix substances. The architecture of the pars tensa differs completely with regard to the lamina propria in comparison with the architecture of the pars flaccida, in which the lamina propria consists of a loose connective tissue (Lim, 1968b).

Despite many reports on the normal anatomy and structure of the human TM, few studies have evaluated the pathologic changes occurring in the TM in OM.

Formation of Retraction Pockets

Retraction pockets of the TM are frequently observed among patients with otitis media with effusion (OME) and occasionally persist even after the complete resolution of OME (Ars, 1995; Sadé, 1982; Tos et al, 1987; Yoon et al, 1990). We also know that the TMs with retraction pockets are a potential risk for the development of cholesteatoma (Sadé et al, 1981). However, little is known

about the mechanisms involved in the development of retraction pockets and why certain children without long-standing OME develop retraction pockets, whereas others with OME of similar duration do not.

Retractions of the TM are believed to occur owing to a combination of several pathologic processes (Ars, 1995; Helms, 1995), mainly suggested to involve dysfunction of the eustachian tube and its relation to OME. Under these circumstances, the gas diffusion mechanism in the middle ear cavity is impaired, resulting in sustenance of the negative pressure. Over a period of time, the inflammatory process results in destruction of the collagen fibers in the lamina propria and a weakening of the TM with the consequent retraction.

Retractions may occur in both the pars flaccida and the pars tensa and then, in particular, in the posterosuperior quadrant of the pars tensa. Ars and colleagues (1995) studied 100 human TMs in patients ages 3 to 82 years and noted 40% in the pars flaccida and 60% in the pars tensa, with 36% in the posterosuperior quadrant, 16% in the inferior half, and 8% in the anterosuperior quadrant.

Influence of Negative Pressure

When negative pressure develops in the middle ear cavity, the pars flaccida retracts first because of its elasticity. Its sensitivity to pressure is high, and it will retract in response to even minor changes. The amount of negative pressure that is damped by retraction of the pars flaccida, depends on the buffering action of the mastoid cavity.

In an earlier study on the rat middle ear cavity (Hellström and Stenfors, 1983), it was shown that only a few mm H_2O pressure changes retracted the pars flaccida and when the pars flaccida had retracted to its maximum—at about 50 mm H_2O—a further decrease in the middle ear pressure caused the relatively nonflexible pars tensa to retract. That there are minor pressure changes that will cause portions of the TM to retract has been shown by several authors (Buckingham and Ferrer, 1973; Sadé et al, 1976).

Considering that only minor changes of middle ear pressure are needed to cause retractions, why, specifically, the pars flaccida and the posterosuperior portion of the pars tensa? In studies on temporal bones from patients with purulent OM or OME, factors that may predispose for the development of retraction pockets were investigated (Ruah et al, 1992). The pars flaccida and the posterosuperior quadrant were shown to have a structural organization, which indicated that these areas may be of greater risk when subjected to long-standing negative middle ear pressure. However, in the presence of negative middle ear pressure, these anatomic weaknesses may not be sufficient for retraction pockets to appear unless an inflammatory process is present. It was concluded that the collagenolytic activity in a middle ear with purulent OM is much greater than that in OME. The results suggested that the persistence of the low-grade inflammation in OME or recurrent bouts of high-grade inflammation in purulent OM may lead to a progressive degradation of the fibrous layer of the tensa mainly at specific sites, ultimately leading to a slack atrophic area of the TM and the formation of a retraction pocket or perforation.

Structure of the Atelectatic TM

Histologically, the atelectatic TM was shown to consist of a thickened hyperkeratotic squamous epithelium and a flat mucosal epithelium facing the middle ear cavity (Kojima, 2001; Sadé, 1993). Between there was an edematous lamina propria infiltrated with round cells, mainly lymphocytes and plasmocytes. The typical collagenous layer, consisting of a strictly organized outer radial and an inner circular, was absent, and only in some cases randomly scattered remnants of fibrous material remained. Obviously, the atelectatic areas, which are observed as thin, slack TM portions in the otomicroscope, have a considerable thickness when analyzed in histologic sections. The structure of the atelectatic pars tensa should be compared with the structure of the pars flaccida, which also lacks an organized collagenous fibrous layer.

Interpreting these findings in relation to dimeric membranes, one must draw the conclusion that a dimeric TM is, in fact, a triple-layered membrane, like the normal TM, but the integrity of the collagenous layer is damaged.

Implications of Management

Retracted atelectatic TMs may present in a rather innocuous manner, being asymptomatic with normal or near-normal hearing. During these circumstances, the chronic TM pathology should be handled conservatively. The atelectatic areas may begin to accumulate squamous debris and need cleansing by an otorhinolaryngology specialist. However, when the disease progresses to complete atelectasis, ossicular erosion, and a severe conductive hearing loss, surgical intervention is needed.

The goals of surgery for atelectatic TMs are the restoration of an aerated middle ear and restored conductive hearing. This surgery should be planned and performed by an experienced otosurgeon. The surgery should involve the removal of all keratinizing epithelium invading the middle ear cavity, removal of infectious focus, and often a cartilage graft to reinforce the strength of the TM (Glasscock and Hart, 1992). The surgery often also includes the placement of a long-term ventilation tube.

Conclusion

A dimeric TM has been used as a synonym for a collapsing, atrophic portion of the TM in long-standing episodes of OME and recurrent bouts of purulent OM. This terminology should not be used because the dimeric TM, in reality, is triple layered but with a lamina propria lacking the organized collagenous architecture.

References

Ars B. Tympanic membrane retraction pocket. Acta Otorhinolaryngol Belg 1995;49:163–71.

Buckingham RA, Ferrer JL. Middle-ear pressure in a eustachian tube malfunction, manometric studies. Laryngoscope 1973;83:1585–93.

Hellström S, Stenfors L-E. The pressure equilibrating function of pars flaccida in middle ear mechanics. Acta Physiol Scand 1983;118:337–41.

Helms J. Retraction pocket/atelectatic middle ear. Int J Pediatr Otorhinolaryngol 1995;32 Suppl:159–61.

Kojima H. Thinning, retraction and adhesion of tense tympanic membrane. In: Takasaka T, Yuasa R, Hozawa K, editors. Proceedings of the 4th Extraordinary International Symposium on Recent Advances in Otitis Media. Bologna, Italy: Monduzzi Editore; 2001. p. 331–7.

Lim DJ. Tympanic membrane: electron microscopic observations. Part 1: pars tensa. Acta Otolaryngol (Stockh) 1968a;66:181–98.

Lim DJ. Tympanic membrane: electron microscopic observations. Part 2: pars flaccida. Acta Otolaryngol (Stockh) 1968b;66:532–51.

Ruah CB, Schachern PA, Paparella MM, Zelterman D. Mechanisms of retraction pocket formation in the pediatric tympanic membrane. Arch Otolaryngol Head Neck Surg 1992;118:1298–305.

Sadé J. Treatment of retraction pockets and cholesteatoma. J Laryngol Otol 1982;96:685–704.

Sadé J. Atelectatic tympanic membrane: histologic study. Ann Otol Rhinol Laryngol 1993;102:712–6.

Sadé J, Avraham S, Brown M. Atelectasis, retraction pockets and cholesteatoma. Acta Otolaryngol (Stockh) 1981;92:501–12.

Sadé J, Halevi A, Hadas E. Clearance of middle-ear effusions and middle ear pressures. Ann Otol Rhinol Laryngol 1976;85:58–62.

Tos M, Stangerup S-E, Larsen P. Dynamics of eardrum changes following secretory otitis media. Arch Otolaryngol Head Neck Surg 1987;113:380–5.

Yoon TH, Schachern PA, Paparella MM, Aeppli DM. Pathology and pathogenesis of tympanic membrane retraction. Am J Otolaryngol 1990;11:10–7.

Chapter 80

MIDDLE EAR ATELECTASIS

SVEN-ERIC STANGERUP, MD

Middle ear atelectasis describes a condition in which part or the entire eardrum is atrophic and "too large," similar to a deflated balloon. If the middle ear pressure is normal, the atelectatic part of the drum is easily seen, but in cases of eustachian tube dysfunction, negative middle ear pressure, and effusion, the atelectatic eardrum is maximally retracted and may resemble an adhesive otitis media (OM).

A retraction pocket is a localized atelectasis in combination with negative middle ear pressure. In contrast to adhesive OM, the atelectatic part of the drum does not adhere to the promontory. In cases in which the atelectasis is localized to the posterosuperior quadrant, the membrane may adhere to the long process of the incus (incudomyringopexy) or, in cases of resorption, to the long process of the incus to the stapes head (stapedomyringopexy). In cases of further resorption of the stapes crura, a platinomyringopexy may develop.

Usually, retractions of the pars flaccida (attic retractions) are not included in the definition of middle ear atelectasis but are graded by Tos and Poulsen (1980) as retraction types I to IV.

To describe the extension and localization of the atelectasis, we divide the pars tensa into four regions, of which the posterosuperior region is of clinical importance because of the well-defined pathology in this region

(Figure 80-1). Sadé and Berco (1976) divide atelectasis as partial (posterior part of the drum) or total and divide the degree of atelectasis into four stages: stage 1, drums obviously retracted but not yet touching the long process of the incus; stage 2, a collapsed drum, touching the long process of the incus or the stapes but not the promontory; stage 3, the drum is lying on the promontory but not adhering to it; and stage 4, the "adhesive type," in which the drum is adherent to the promontory.

We prefer to distinguish between retraction of the posterosuperior quadrant, which may extend into the sinuses of the posterior tympanum with accumulation of squamous debris (sinus cholesteatoma), and the diffuse atrophy, with retraction of the whole pars tensa, which may extend into the tympanic sinus, the hypotympanum, and the orifice of the eustachian tube, with accumulation of squamous debris (tensa retraction cholesteatoma).

Incidence

From a study in which a cohort of children was followed from age 4 years to 6 years with repetitive annual screening examinations, including otomicroscopy and tympanometry (Tos et al, 1984), the incidence of atrophy increased from 4% at age 4 years to 11% at age 16 years.

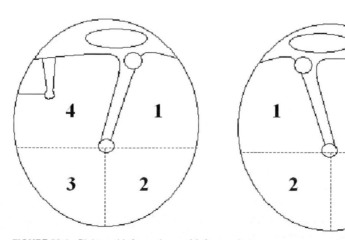

FIGURE 80-1. Right and left ear drum with four regions.

During the same period, the point prevalence of atrophy with retraction decreased from 4 to 0%, whereas the prevalence of atrophy with pexy increased from 0.3 to 3.2% at age 16 years. In total, the incidence of atelectasis is about 5.7% at school age, when the eustachian tube function is usually normalized. In children who had been treated for secretory OM, at follow-up 11 to 18 years after treatment, atrophy was found in 24%, atrophy with pexy in 10%, and adhesive OM in 4% (Tos et al, 1989). In a review article by Schilder (1999), atrophy was reported in 16 to 73% of ears with OM with effusion treated with ventilation tubes compared with 5 to 31% of ears with OM with effusion not treated with ventilation tubes. In the same study, the incidence of atelectasis was 10 to 37% in ears treated for OM with effusion with ventilation tubes.

Importance

In most cases with atelectasis of smaller parts of the drum, the hearing will be good and the patient will not have any problems. In cases of transient eustachian tube dysfunction, the hearing may deteriorate. In cases of purulent middle ear infection, the atrophic drum perforates easily, and because of poor healing capacity of the atrophic membrane, a chronic posterior or total perforation may be the outcome. Special attention should be paid to a patient with previous stable and asymptotic atelectasis if the ear starts to discharge. This is very often a sign of perforation and/or cholesteatoma development.

From a social point of view, an atelectatic drum may have job consequences, such as difficulty in obtaining flying and diving certificates because the atrophic drum may perforate during significant and sudden pressure changes.

In most cases in which the entire drum is atelectatic, the hearing will be compromised, and if the condition becomes unstable with accumulation of squamous debris and inflammation, the condition may evolve into sinus cholesteatoma or tensa retraction cholesteatoma (Tos, 1981).

Etiology and Pathogenesis

It is generally accepted that most eardrum pathology is a sequela from long-lasting secretory OM during early childhood leading to retraction and atrophy (Sadé and Berco, 1976; Schilder, 1999; Tos, 1981; Tos and Poulsen, 1980; Tos et al, 1984; Tos et al, 1989). From cohort studies with long-term follow-up examinations (Tos et al, 1984), it has been shown that there is a highly significant positive correlation between the degree of eustachian tube dysfunction through childhood and the development of eardrum pathology. When the drum has been retracted for a long time because of negative middle ear pressure, the lamina propria becomes thin and loses its elasticity (Akyildiz et al, 1993; Ars, 1991; Sadé, 1993; Sadé

and Berco, 1976; Yoon et al, 1990). When the eustachian tube function recovers at about 6 to 10 years of age and the middle ear pressure normalizes, the eardrum pathology becomes visible, especially atrophic and atelectatic parts of the drum. This explains why the incidence of eardrum pathology increases with the age of the child, despite a normalization of the eustachian tube function and subsequent normalization of the middle ear pressure.

Management

In atelectic ears with normal function of the eustachian tube and normal middle ear pressure, hearing will usually be within normal limits, but in some cases, the hearing may be considerably impaired. This is probably caused by other sequelae after long-lasting secretory OM, such as adhesions in the middle ear, fixation of the malleus, or resorption of the long process of the incus. A helpful tool to a more specific diagnosis is the pneumatic otoscope, with which the mobility of the malleus may be visualized. As already mentioned, acute middle ear infection is not common in the age group of patients with atelectasis, so in cases of ear discharge in a patient with previously stable and asymptotic atelectasis, this may be a sign of established cholesteatoma, and surgery is required.

In atelectatic ears with eustachian tube dysfunction and retraction, there is a risk that the atelectatic membrane becomes adherent to the incudostapedial joint and the promontory, which again may lead to ossicular resorption, accumulation of squamous debris, and development of sinus or tensa retraction cholesteatoma.

To prevent retraction of the atelectatic eardrum, equalization of the negative middle ear pressure is logical and important. This may be achieved by performing Valsalva's maneuver, extended Valsalva's maneuver, or nasal balloon inflation or by inserting a ventilation tube into the tympanic membrane (Table 80-1).

Valsalva's Maneuver

The Valsalva maneuver was described by the Italian doctor Antonio Maria Valsalva in 1704 originally as a method to expel pus from the tympanic cavity into the external auditory canal, but for many centuries, it has been used as a method to increase middle ear pressure. The maneuver is performed by pressing the air into the nasopharynx, with the mouth closed and the nostrils compressed by the fingers. If the patient is not able to inflate the middle ear by Valsalva's maneuver, then equalization may be achieved by what we call "extended Valsalva's maneuver."

Extended Valsalva's Maneuver

From clinical experience with Valsalva's maneuver, we developed a new method of autoinflation by which it is possible to improve the effectiveness of Valsalva's maneuver. We call the procedure the extended Valsalva's maneuver. Basically, it is performed in the same way as the ordinary Valsalva maneuver, but first the neck is stretched maximally by flexion forward and then the head is turned, positioning the ear to be inflated upward. In this position, the Valsalva maneuver is performed, increasing the chance of inflation in the elevated ear. When the opposite ear is to be inflated, the head is turned in the opposite position. If the extended Valsalva maneuver is unsuccessful, inflation using a nasal balloon (Otovent) may be successful. It has been shown that in children and adults unable to clear a negative middle ear pressure obtained during flight by performing Valsalva's maneuver, this could be achieved by nasal balloon inflation in 40 to 68% of cases (Stangerup et al, 1996).

Otovent Autoinflation

The Otovent set consists of a nose tube mounted with a special balloon. The nose tube is held airtight to one nostril, the opposite nostril is compressed with a finger, and, with the mouth closed, the balloon is inflated through the nose. During the inflation, a positive pressure of 600 dPa is created in the nose and nasopharynx, which may equalize the middle ear pressure via the eustachian tube because the normal opening pressure of the tube is about 400 dPa. The Otovent nasal balloon was originally developed as a method to improve middle ear ventilation in children suffering from eustachian tube dysfunction and secretory OM (Stangerup et al, 1992). If inflation fails, a ventilation tube should be inserted to prevent retraction and adhesion.

Ventilation Tubes

Inserting ventilation tubes in an atelectatic drum is problematic because of the poor height of the middle ear cavity. If the tube is placed in the atrophic part of the drum, it may be extruded within a few days. Usually, even in cases of diffuse atrophy of the pars tensa, the area superoanterior, just anterior to the processus brevis of the malleus, is the area of choice in which to insert the tube, preferably through a narrow incision. In a study by Luntz and colleagues (1991), ventilation tubes were inserted in 37 atelectatic ears, and then the tubes were sealed. In 4 ears, the retraction did not relapse, but in 33 ears, retrac-

TABLE 80-1. Treatment Paradigm in Atelectatic Ears

Hearing	Eustachian Tube Function	Stability	Treatment
Good	Good	Stable	No treatment
Good	Poor	Stable	Autoinflation
Poor	Poor	Stable	Autoinflation (tympanoplasty)
Poor	Good	Stable	Tympanoplasty (autoinflation)
Good	Good	Unstable*	Tympanoplasty (autoinflation)
Good	Poor	Unstable*	Tympanoplasty (autoinflation)
Poor	Poor	Unstable*	Tympanoplasty (autoinflation)

*Ears with retraction, inflammation, and accumulation of squamous debris.

tion redeveloped within 1 to 2 hours after the ventilating tube was sealed.

Explorative Tympanotomy and Tympanoplasty

Explorative tympanotomy is indicated in cases of atelectasis with normal eustachian tube patency if the hearing is significantly impaired. Often this will reveal fixation of the malleus or resorption of the long process of the incus.

In cases of severe retraction and instability (inflammation and accumulation of squamous debris in the retraction) and no effect of autoinflation, tympanoplasty is indicated. Some surgeons perform localized eversion or excision of the retraction pocket and grommet insertion (Blaney et al, 1999; Srinivasan et al, 2000). The success rate of this procedure is reported to be 74% with an observation period of 8 to 34 months. Excision combined with tympanoplasty for localized retractions of the tensa (Charachon et al, 1992; Yung, 1997) is reported to have an 80% success rate after 3 to 8 years of follow-up.

The problem with tympanoplasty in atelectatic ears with poor eustachian tube function/patency is that the drum recollapses, which has been reported to occur in 50% of the cases (Charachon et al, 1992; Yung, 1997). To avoid recollapse of the drum, tympanoplasty using cartilage palisades, to prevent postoperative retraction, has become popular, and the results seem to be good.

In our department, we advise patients to perform autoinflation about 2 weeks after tympanoplasty to ventilate the middle ear to avoid retraction and adhesion of the drum/graft to the promontory.

Conclusion

Atelectasis of the eardrum is a frequent finding in patients older than 7 years, primarily in subjects who had long-lasting secretory OM during early childhood. In most cases, the condition is harmless and without symptoms and treatment is not necessary, but in cases of poor eustachian tube function, the atelectatic membrane becomes retracted and may develop into sinus and tensa retraction cholesteatoma, which require tympanoplasty. In many cases, autoinflation by Valsalva's maneuver, extended Valsalva's maneuver, or inflation of a nasal balloon clears the negative middle ear pressure. If autoinflation fails, ventilation tube insertion or tympanoplasty may be necessary. Special attention should be paid to a patient with previous stable and asymptotic atelectasis if the ear starts to discharge. This may be a sign of perforation and/or cholesteatoma development.

References

Akyildiz N, Akbay C, Ozgirgin ON, et al. The role of retraction pockets in cholesteatoma development: an ultrastructural study. Ear Nose Throat J 1993;72:210–2.

Ars BM. Tympanic membrane retraction pockets. Etiology, pathology, treatment. Acta Otorhinolaryngol Belg 1991;45:265–77.

Blaney SP, Tierney P, Bowdler DA. The surgical management of the pars tensa retraction pocket in the child, results following simple excision and ventilation tube insertion. Int J Pediatr Otorhinolaryngol 1999;50:133–7.

Charachon R, Barthez M, Lejeune JM. Spontaneous retraction pockets in chronic otitis media, medical and surgical therapy. Ear Nose Throat J 1992;71:578–83.

Luntz M, Eisman S, Sadé J. Induced atelectasis of the middle ear and its clinical behavior. Eur Arch Otorhinolaryngol 1991;248:286–8.

Sadé J. Atelectatic tympanic membrane: histologic study. Ann Otol Rhinol Laryngol 1993;102:712–6.

Sadé J, Berco E. Atrophy of the tympanic membrane. Ann Otol Rhinol Laryngol 1976;85 Suppl 25:66–72.

Schilder AG. Assessment of complications of the condition and of the treatment of otitis media with effusion. Int J Pediatr Otorhinolaryngol 1999;49 Suppl 1:247–51.

Srinivasan V, Banhegyi G, O'Sullivan G, Sherman IW. Pars tensa retraction pockets in children: treatment by excision and ventilation tube insertion. Clin Otolaryngol 2000;25:253–6.

Stangerup SE, Sederberg-Olsen J, Balle V. Autoinflation as a treatment of tubal dysfunction and secretory otitis media. A randomized controlled study. Arch Otolaryngol Head Neck Surg 1992;118:149–52.

Stangerup SE, Tjernstrøm Ø, Harcourt J, et al. Barotitis in children after aviation; prevalence and treatment with Otovent. J Laryngol Otol 1996;110:625–8.

Tos M. Upon the relationship between secretory otitis in childhood and chronic otitis and its sequelae in adults. J Laryngol Otol 1981;95:1011–22.

Tos M, Poulsen G. Attic retractions following secretory otitis. Acta Otolaryngol (Stockh) 1980;89:479–86.

Tos M, Stangerup SE, Holm-Jensen S, Sørensen CH. Spontaneous course of secretory otitis and changes of the eardrum. Arch Otolaryngol 1984;110:281–9.

Tos M, Stangerup SE, Larsen PL, et al. The relationship between secretory otitis and cholesteatoma. In: Tos M, Thomsen J, editors. Cholesteatoma and mastoid surgery. Amsterdam: Kugler; 1989. p. 325–30.

Yoon TH, Schachern PA, Paparella MM, Aeppli DM. Pathology and pathogenesis of tympanic membrane retraction. Am J Otolaryngol 1990;11:10–7.

Yung MW. Retraction of the pars tensa: long term results of surgical treatment. Clin Otolaryngol 1997;22:323–6.

Chapter 81

ADHESIVE OTITIS MEDIA

GREGORY C. ALLEN, MD

Many definitions have been used to describe different types of inflammation in the middle ear and mastoid. As a result of various terminologies and classification systems, confusion has arisen among clinicians and researchers. The terminology used in definitions of middle ear pathology was discussed further in previous chapters of this book.

Adhesive otitis media (OM) is a result of healing after chronic inflammation of the middle ear. Chronic inflammation that may be present after prolonged middle ear effusion (MEE) leads to the ingrowth of fibroblasts and the formation of scar tissue in the middle ear space. The mucous membrane is thickened by proliferation of fibrous tissue, which frequently impairs the movement of the ossicles, resulting in a conductive hearing loss. Adhesive OM is common in children who have had recurrent acute or chronic otitis media with effusion (OME), atelectasis of the tympanic membrane (TM), or both. Because no data are available on the prevalence of adhesive OM in children, we are unable to establish the probability for development of adhesive OM in the child who has had MEE or atelectasis. In addition to impaired ossicular mobility, adhesive OM may result in ossicular discontinuity. The long process of the incus, because it has the most tenuous blood supply of all of the ossicular chain, is susceptible to erosion or rarefying osteitis. When there is severe localized atelectasis in the posterosuperior portion of the pars tensa of the TM, adhesive changes may bind the eardrum to the incus, stapes, and other surrounding middle ear structures and cause resorption of the ossicles. Once a retraction pocket occurs, cholesteatoma formation is also possible (Bluestone and Klein, 2002; Bluestone and Klein, 1988).

Prevention

Once adhesions between the TM and middle ear mucosa and ossicles have formed, treatment is quite difficult. As with many pathologic processes, prevention of the primary process is much easier. In a guinea pig model, tympanostomy tube placement after middle ear injury does prevent adhesive OM (Hashimoto, 2000). There is also evidence that placement of ventilation tubes in young children with recurrent acute OM and chronic OM helps to prevent adhesive OM (Valtonen et al, 2002). The identification of those patients who would most benefit from middle ear ventilation remains controversial.

Medical Therapy

Medical therapy is often ineffective in adhesive OM. Many different types of medical intervention have been tried, but few have shown benefit in randomized clinical trials. In untreated MEEs, a trial of antibiotics is often beneficial. If not previously used, a β-lactamase–stable antibiotic should be tried. Decongestants, topical and systemic, as well as antihistamines, have not been proven effective in adhesive OM, and the side effects of their use appear to outweigh any benefit (Flynn et al, 2002). Autoinsufflation may be of benefit in selected patients (Stangerup et al, 1992). (See also the chapter in this text, "Autoinflation for the Treatment of Otitis Media with Effusion.") Both oral and topical intranasal steroids alone or in combination with an antibiotic lead to a quicker resolution of OME in the short term, but there is no evidence of a long-term benefit from either (Butler and Van Der Voort, 2002). The treatment of OME is covered in Section IV: "Otitis Media with Effusion."

Surgical Therapy

Myringotomy and Ventilation Tubes

When medical therapy is ineffective, ventilation of the middle ear space by myringotomy with or without tube placement may be necessary. It has long been believed that prompt intervention with ventilation of the middle ear and mastoid may return the TM to its normal position (Buckingham and Ferrer, 1966). The ability of the TM to resume its normal position and consistency is often quite remarkable. If ventilation of the middle ear and mastoid, by surgical or medical means, does not reverse changes in the TM, then adhesive OM is present. The treatment of adhesive OM at this point is controversial. Some believe that the management of adhesive OM should primarily consist of observation alone unless worsening retraction or hearing loss occurs. Others think that prompt tympanoplasty is necessary to prevent further ossicular damage and conductive hearing loss. In either observation or surgical therapy, the present function of the eustachian tube is the most important determinant of pathologic progression. If eustachian tube function remains poor, it easily follows that the progression to ossicular discontinuity and/or cholesteatoma formation is quite probable. If eustachian tube function is improved, pathologic progression of adhesive OM may not occur.

Tympanoplasty

In the early stages of adhesive OM, when simple ventilation of the middle ear space with myringotomy and tube is not effective, tympanoplasty may be all that is necessary for treatment. It is important to keep in mind that simple tympanoplasty alone without improvement of eustachian tube function will lead only to retraction of the neotympanic membrane and subsequent recurrence of adhesive OM. For this reason, many strategies have been adopted to prevent re-retraction of the new TM. Placement of the ventilation tube at the time of tympanoplasty is one option, whereas others have adopted other methods to support the new TM. Cartilage-backed tympanoplasty is a popular treatment for the atelectatic and adhesive TM. A small disk of cartilage in the posterosuperior portion of the TM may prevent re-retraction, whereas, in other cases, a larger piece of cartilage is necessary. Conductive hearing loss is a concern in cartilage tympanoplasty, but increased conductive hearing loss of statistical significance has not been demonstrated (Dornhoffer, 1997). Monitoring of the middle ear status is also more difficult after cartilage tympanoplasty, and computed tomography may be necessary in cases of suspect cholesteatoma. Some have adopted the technique of replacing the entire TM with cartilage to prevent retraction. Believing that a larger effective middle ear space will help prevent negative middle ear pressure and TM retraction, some clinicians recommend mastoidectomy. In the presence of infection and inflammation, mastoidectomy is effective in clearing the inflammatory condition, but there is little evidence that increasing the effective middle ear space alone prevents TM retraction and the development of subsequent adhesions. Tympanomastoidectomy should therefore be reserved for cases of severe retraction and cholesteatoma and in which a chronic inflammatory condition exists, either with or without infection.

The treatment of chronic inflammatory conditions of the ear is a dynamic and ever-changing process. Without improvement of eustachian tube function or artificial ventilation, the above approaches to treatment of adhesive OM are destined to fail over time. It follows that in the treatment of children, when eustachian tube function can be expected to improve, it may be better to ventilate the middle ear and allow time for eustachian tube function to normalize. This can be done with or without tympanoplasty to normalize the position of the TM. In the adult, when the long-term prospect of improved eustachian tube function is unlikely, cartilage graft reconstruction of the TM with or without long-term middle ear ventilation is preferred.

Future Innovations

Control of the acute and chronic inflammatory reaction within the middle ear mucosa holds the future in the treatment of adhesive OM. Not only will the control of inflammatory mediators help to prevent adhesive OM, but control of inflammation and healing will also be quite helpful following surgical treatment of established disease.

References

Bluestone CD, Klein JO. Otitis media in infants and children. Philadelphia: WB Saunders; 1988.

Bluestone CD, Klein JO. Intratemporal complications and sequelae of otitis media. In: Bluestone CD, Stool SE, Alper CM, et al, editors. Pediatric otolaryngology. 4th ed. Philadelphia: WB Saunders; 2002. p. 737–8.

Buckingham RA, Ferrer JL. Reversibility of chronic adhesive otitis media with polyethylene tube, middle ear air-vent, kodachrome time lapse study. Laryngoscope 1966;76:993 1014.

Butler CC, Van Der Voort JH. Oral or topical nasal steroids for hearing loss associated with otitis media with effusion in children. Cochrane Database Syst Rev 2002;CD001935.

Dornhoffer JL. Hearing results with cartilage tympanoplasty. Laryngoscope 1997;107:1094–9.

Flynn CA, Griffin G, Tudiver F. Decongestants and antihistamines for acute otitis media in children. Cochrane Database Syst Rev 2002;CD001727.

Hashimoto S. A guinea pig model of adhesive otitis media and the effect of tympanostomy. Auris Nasus Larynx 2000;27:39–43.

Stangerup SE, Sederberg-Olsen J, Balle V. Autoinflation as a treatment of secretory otitis media. A randomized controlled study. Arch Otolaryngol Head Neck Surg 1992;118:149–52.

Valtonen HJ, Qvarnberg YH, Nuutinen J. Otological and audiological outcomes five years after tympanostomy in early childhood. Laryngoscope 2002;112:669–75.

Chapter 82

RETRACTION POCKETS

PEDRO CLARÓS MD, PHD

A tympanic membrane (TM) pocket is defined as a local retraction. It is a medial displacement of a portion of the atrophic eardrum toward the promontory or an invagination of a weakened TM inside the tympanic cavity.

Retraction pockets may cause cholesteatomas and ossicular chain problems to develop. Eustachian tube dysfunction can be part of the pathogenesis when a retraction pocket exerts negative pressure in the middle ear. When tubal dysfunction begins, the lamina propria and the TM lose their resistance. With time, the eardrum becomes thinner and transparent and falls toward the promontory.

Pathogenesis

Retraction pockets form for many reasons. The main cause is the presence of an inflammation in the upper airways and in the middle ear cleft mucosa. Factors such as negative pressure of the middle ear cleft, atrophy at the TM lamina propria, or dysfunction at the stratified squamous epithelium may also create retraction pockets (Clarós, 1976; Deguine, 1995; Kobayashi et al, 1994; Tanabe et al, 1999). Infection at the middle ear cleft injures the epithelial cells, provoking the adhesion of bacteria and maintaining the inflammation process.

Atrophy of the lamina propria never happens suddenly or in isolation. Instead, biochemical and biophysical mechanisms are at work. The biophysical mechanism can be explained by the rupture of the disulfate bridges by collagenases, which are liberated during the inflammation process. The biochemical mechanism can be explained by the viscoelastic properties of the lamina propria (Charachon et al, 1992).

With reference to the more specific weakness of the pars flaccida, the notch of Rivinus corresponds to the absence of the tympanic bone at the top of the tympanic frame. Here there is no annulus.

The stratified squamous epithelium is the site of two kinds of specific movement. The centrifugal keratin dispersion process involves the superficial layers and is particularly well suited to cleaning the external auditory canal. When disturbed, it provokes an accumulation of keratin into pockets.

Middle Ear Pressure

In normal conditions, three main elements control the middle ear cleft pressure: the fibrocartilaginous eustachian tube, the tympanic cavity and its mucosa, and the mastoid air cell system (Ars et al, 1997).

In a normal state, the fibrocartilaginous eustachian tube consists of a highly sophisticated valve through which gas flow enters or leaves the middle ear cleft. Three basic contingencies can occur: in normal conditions, a healthy mucosa and the eustachian tube offer an intermittent supply of gas transfer into the middle ear cleft. Nowadays, specialists agree that the gas transfer via the eustachian tube is poor in comparison with the gas exchanges between the middle ear cleft and the blood compartment, via the mucosa.

The quantity of gas introduced in the middle ear cleft is 1 μL times the frequency of deglutition (500 to 1,000 times a day). The interval of the intermittent opening of the lumen of the eustachian tube has been calculated to take place every 3 to 4 minutes (Ars and Ars-Piret, 1997).

The second contingency also appears in normal conditions and with healthy mucosa but under situations that can be considered exceptional, such as flying or diving. In these situations, the fibrocartilaginous eustachian tube constitutes a highly sophisticated security valve and plays a primary role in the balance of pressure in the middle ear cleft.

The third contingency involves the pathologic condition: when the mucosa suffers from inflammation, the eustachian tube minimizes the exchange of gases between the middle ear cleft and the nasopharynx (Sadé, 2000).

Tympanic Cavity and Its Mucosa

Oxygen and nitrogen are absorbed through the mucosa into the blood supply. Carbon dioxide and water vapor are transferred from the blood compartment into the tympanic cavity.

Two mechanisms help the tympanic cavity contribute to gas pressure balance in the middle ear cleft. The first mechanism is the compliance of the TM lamina propria. Compliance is ensured by the viscoelastic properties of the lamina propria and by the flexibility of the incudomalleo-lar joint (which functions as a static pressure receptor) to the TM, ensuring three-dimensional movement into the malleus. The second mechanism is the steady gas exchange through the mucosa. The diffusion depends on the cell properties of the mucosa, the diffusion rate of the gas, and how the vascular system behaves. The regular gas exchanges of the tympanic cavity are an expression of the similarity of the partial gas pressure in both compartments, either the tympanic cavity or mucosal lining tissue. The gas exchanges of the tympanic cavity depend on the relative speed of gas diffusion: absorption or elimination. The behavior of the vascular system also plays an important role in gas diffusion. Variations in the middle ear cleft blood flow associated with variations in the permeability of the vessels permit a wide adaptation to normal gas pressure fluctuations. The normal wide variations in the middle ear cleft pressure, in an interval of 24 hours, are related to vascular adaptations required by body position and sleep. The fluctuations in tympanic cavity pressure are controlled by the respiratory function.

The mastoid cell system contributes to the balance of gas pressure in the middle ear cleft by properties similar to those of the tympanic cavity. These properties give the mastoid air cell system the role of a pressure absorber. The mastoid air cell system is also related to pathologic situations. As size is important, we can conclude that the smaller the system, the quicker the deviation from normal pressures. The negative pressure that may be present between the tympanic cavity and the blood compartment through the local tissues may be compensated for by the gas contained in the mastoid air cell system. In relation to the vascular system, the mucosal surface area is increased by the high number of mucosal folds. These folds develop a mucosa surface, where vascularization is dense.

In normal conditions, a small mastoid in an adult is normal. However, it may be a consequence of an alteration in its development.

Classification

The TM retraction pocket fits into one of three criteria: topographic, quantitative, and qualitative. Topographic criteria refers to the location: the pars tensa or pars flaccida. Quantitative criteria refers to the dimension: partial or total. With reference to depth, we have to evaluate the extension, which allows regular control under the microscope and endoscopy. Qualitative criteria refers to the behavior of the pocket: self-cleaning or not, bone erosion, and fixation or nonfixation to the middle ear structures. To evaluate fixation, we use the Valsalva maneuver to transform the nonfixed retraction pocket into a ballooning TM or through suction of the pocket, which can be very painful. The presence of an additional stimulus can destabilize the present situation of the pocket (Ars, 1995).

Degree of Retraction Pockets

The grading of retraction pockets is the same, regardless of whether they occur on the Shrapnell membrane or over the posterosuperior part of the tympanum:

- Grade 1: A discrete retraction appears as a simple cavity in the pars flaccida or can be located as a depression over the pars tensa (Figure 82-1A). In either case, there is no contact with the deep structures of the middle ear. The ossicular chain is mantained intact. This deformity can be translated as an intratympanic depression and is a sign of alert.
- Grade 2: The retraction pocket is deeper and is clearly visible by otoscopy. Although it is mainly a pathologic state, the patient does not experience any functional disorder. These retraction pockets may touch the head and/or neck of the malleus (Shrapnell retraction pockets) or the long process of the incus (a posterosuperior retraction pocket) (Figure 82-1B). The most common location for incus erosion is the lenticular process. If the TM is not self-cleaning or an incus erosion exists, treatment is necessary, even if there is only simple aspiration of residual tissue. The contact with the stapes suprastructure can form an incudomyringostapediopexy.
- Grade 3: The retraction pocket adheres to the elements of the middle ear and is accompanied by destruction (Figure 82-1C). For lesions in the Shrapnell membrane, the pocket adheres to the head and/or neck of the malleus, and one part of the epitympanic (scutum) recess is eroded. For a posterosuperior retraction of the TM, the ossicular chain is injured with fixation or necrosis and there is a lysis of the posterosuperior part of the tympanic annulus. In these cases, surgery will likely be necessary as the area is not self-cleaning, and simple aspiration may not resolve the process.
- Grade 4: This grade is characterized by a profound retraction and the presence of tissue residuals that cannot be mobilized by a simple aspiration. In this phase, bone destruction of the annulus tympanicus and the ossicular chain exists (Figure 82-1D). Surgical treatment is necessary as this pocket is evolutive, is generally infected, and cannot be cured spontaneously. This grade constitutes the first phase of a confirmed cholesteatoma.

Characteristics of Retraction Pockets

Retraction pockets may be classified according to the following clinical and tympanomicroscopic characteristics:

- The pocket is stable. The risk of cholesteatoma is low. The histologic quality of the eardrum does not change. Audition is normal. The pocket may be reversible.
- The pocket is formed and uncertain. The risk of cholesteatoma exists. A progressive retraction or eardrum atrophy may develop. Audition is normal.
- The pocket is unstable. It is characterized by adhesion to the surrounding structures, erosion of the ossicular

chain and bony framework, accumulation of keratin owing to non–self-cleaning, and irritation owing to the presence of moist mucous polyps. The risk of cholesteatoma is high, and when the pocket presents all of these defects, a cholesteatoma begins to develop.

- Attic precholesteatoma. In this situation, the retraction of the Shrapnell membrane has responded with disturbed epithelium migration, accumulation of debris, crust formation, infection behind the crust, and proliferation of epithelium keratinization.

Symptoms associated with retraction pockets include otorrhea, infected debris, granulation tissue, bleeding and discomfort, painful acute inflammation, secondary hearing loss, and signs of fistula.

Prognosis

The prognosis value of a retraction pocket depends on the characteristics of the pocket and the surface on which it adheres.

The characteristics of the retraction pocket constitute its placement, its fixed or nonfixed character, its extension, its desquamative or nondesquamative character, and its association or not to inflammatory lesions in the form of granulomas. If the pocket is in the posterosuperior quadrant, it may affect the ossicular chain. If the pocket is fixed, either in the walls of the middle ear or in the tympanic sinus, the approach is difficult. If it is fixed over the ossicular chain, destruction of the long process of the incus or the the stapes suprastructure is possible.

Depending on the extension, the pocket may or may not be seen. If it lies in the attic, its extension does not permit its contours to be seen (Figure 82-2). This attic extension makes us believe in the existence of a cholesteatoma, and a computed tomographic (CT) scan could provide confirmation (Figure 82-3). If it is desquamative, the accumulation of tissue residual favors the formation of a cholesteatoma. When accompanied by granuloma, it may lead to otorrhea and denotes the evolutive character of this pocket.

Schematically, and without prejudging the area, the confirmation of one or various characteristics involves active surgical activity. It is important to underline the necessity of regular surveillance of a nonfixed simple pocket. The severe prognosis of certain pockets exists when they are anterosuperior with attic extensions and when they are anteroinferior, especially when they are total with complete tympanic retraction at the bottom of the middle ear cavity. In these cases just described, it is evident that a tubotympanic major dysfunction exists.

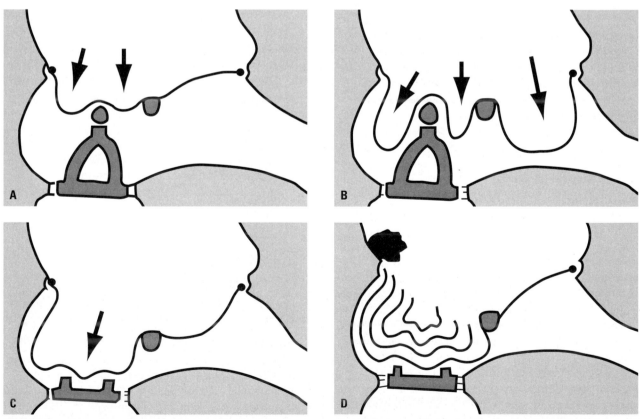

FIGURE 82-1. The degrees of retraction pockets are graded as Grade 1 when a discrete retraction appears in the pars flaccida or over the pars tensa (*A*), Grade 2 when retraction touches the head and/or neck of the malleus or the long process of the incus (*B*), Grade 3 when the retraction pocket adheres to the middle ear structure with destruction (*C*), and Grade 4 when there is profound retraction with bone destruction (*D*).

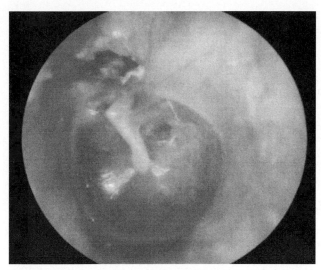

FIGURE 82-2. Otoscopic view of an attic retraction pocket. Its extension does not allow its contours to be seen.

When the patient is a child affected by immunologic instability, the prognosis is reserved as the pocket will evolve as a consequence of the intensity and frequency of the condition. In the adult, if one or various characteristics previously described appear, surgery is needed to avoid fixation of the pocket. If the pocket is already fixed, it will avoid lysis of the ossicular chain or the development of a cholesteatoma. In the adolescent or young adult, the prognosis is better as the pocket is more stable and an intervention can improve hypoacusia transmission.

Several local and regional variants may influence the prognosis: the velopalatine malformations and those cases of chronic inflammations with an allergic origin or infection of the upper respiratory airways.

Otoendoscopic Exploration of Retraction Pockets

Otoendoscopic exploration is useful for retraction pockets because it permits the diagnosis and follow-up and aids in the surgical procedure (Clarós, 2000).

Instrumentation

We use Storz instruments. With a direct vision teleotoscope (4 mm diameter and 10 cm in length), we can examine the TM and the retraction pockets.

For children or patients with a very narrow external ear canal, we recommend an otoendoscope of 2.7 mm diameter with angles of 0°, 30°, and 70°. The endoscopes are arranged on the instrument table in three colors, each indicating the angulation of the optical systems. To avoid fog, a demisting fluid is essential. Before use, the surgeon must thoroughly clean the lenses.

The light source should be 250 watts using a Y-shaped cable, with two outlets and one inlet that connect the generator and the endoscopes. The microcamera must be light and very sensitive and have a zoom lens that gives a close-up on the monitor. This microcamera is wrapped in a sterile covering or, if it is watertight, immersed in a decontaminating agent such as Ampholysine Plus for 15 minutes or stored in a box with tablets of formaldehyde. If possible, it is best sterilized in an autoclave with 2 kg pressure and for 15 minutes at 138°C.

The Storz microinstruments help explore the retraction pockets (specifically the microsuckers, microforceps, and microhook).

Otoendoscopic Findings

Otoendoscopy can be performed safely and comfortably. The essential features to be studied in the retraction pockets are as follows:

- The site. Is it marginal or nonmarginal? Retraction pockets are most often found in the posterior part of the pars tensa, where they may create a subligamentous pouch directed toward the posterior sulcus often with subtotal invagination of the pars tensa. Another frequent localization is in the epitympanic region.
- The quality of the invaginated epidermis. Is it dyskeratotic or not?
- The adhesion of the pocket in relation to the ossicles and the bony rim.

To measure the degree of adhesion, we recommend that the patient perform the Valsalva maneuver or we use a pneumatic otoscope. The balance of these three concepts allows us to consider any "dangerous criteria" of the retraction pockets (Bremond et al, 1990) when it is marginal, dyskeratotic, and adherent to the bony plane and if its evolution cannot be monitored (Figure 82-4).

In the follow-up of these retraction pockets, it is very useful to keep photographic records of each otologic control and to compare them.

The advantage of otoendoscopic exploration of the retraction pockets is that it provides precise assessment of boundaries of the pocket, their mobility, and the pouch

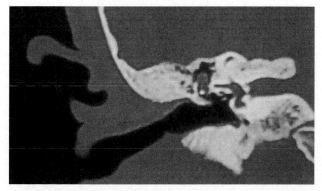

FIGURE 82-3. Computed tomographic scan of the patient with the attic retraction pocket in Figure 82-1.

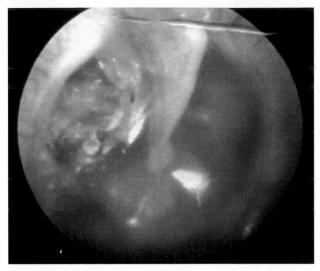

FIGURE 82-4. A typical retraction pocket that is marginal, dyskeratotic, and adherent to the bony plane.

site. Otoendoscopy is a vital technique in infancy and permits observation and detection of tympanic damages and those of the ossicular chain, which cannot be seen through other explorations.

Management of Retraction Pockets

Superficial retraction pockets with a good visible bottom and that are self-cleaning are not treated. Retraction pockets that are deeper, bigger, and well controlled under microscope exploration need only periodic cleaning to eliminate the keratin residuals. Shrapnell pockets, which are humid and non–self-cleaning, should be excised but limited to the adjacent skin. Any bone defect should be repaired with the aid of a chondroperichondrial graft. If the retraction pocket is associated with a bone lysis and with adherence of any of the middle ear structures or a cholesteatoma, a tympanoplasty is mandatory. In some cases, a transtympanic aerator in the anteroinferior quadrant will be necessary (Sadé, 1993).

Preventing a Cholesteatoma

Preventing a retraction pocket from becoming a cholesteatoma requires the following: elimination of keratin residuals from the hidden areas of the pocket, removal of skin from the wrong places, maintenance of a well-ventilated middle ear, and reconstruction or maintenance of an anatomic TM. Poor ventilation and the presence of granuloma tissue in the pocket or a bone defect are elements that can favor recurrence of a cholesteatoma or an iatrogenic cholesteatoma.

Surgery of Retraction Pockets

Surgery is indicated when a retraction pocket is considered a dangerous invagination by the criteria previously mentioned. Surgery includes providing the invaginations and their consequences, such as lysis of the incus and stapes or migration toward the facial recess region (Harner, 1995). The TM can be explored by using local anesthesia, lidocaine (2%) with adrenaline, in the posterior part of the external auditory canal supplemented by injecting the anterior part. Small pieces of cotton soaked in adrenaline will reduce bleeding. Via a transcanal approach, the pocket is excised totally, and the attic wall is reconstructed by a fragment of bone, cartilage, or other materials (Magnan et al, 1993).

Although costly, high-resolution CT should be used in studying a retraction pocket.

Surgical Technique

Retraction pocket surgery may be performed under local or general anesthesia. An incision is made at the retroauricular zone, and a vascular loop mantains the tissues in place. The tympanomeatal flap is slightly elevated toward the annulus. The flap is reflected over the attic retraction pocket or the sinus tympanum retraction pocket. With the aid of a cutting bur, the bony canal wall is widened from lateral to medial. In the case of attic retraction or attic cholesteatoma, the lateral wall of the attic is then drilled away, and the lateral attic is exposed. The extent of removal depends on disease extension. In a sinus retraction pocket or cholesteatoma, starting with a posterosuperior retraction of the pars tensa, the posterosuperomedial bone is removed, allowing for identification of the sinus tympanum, pyramidal process, and anterior part of vertical segment of the facial nerve, which is designated as the posterior annuloplasty. These bone removals permit marsupialization of the attic or sinus tympanum retraction. Care must be taken to avoid tearing the bottom of the retraction pocket or cholesteatoma. In patients with conductive hearing loss, ossiculoplasty may be performed after complete dissection. If necessary, a ventilation tube may be placed and a fascia graft performed with an overlay technique. Repairs of bony defect or removed bone in atticotomy or posterior sinusectomy are termed scutumplasty or posterior annuloplasty, respectively. Tragal or conchal cartilage is used for this reconstruction. In tensa retraction (adhesive otitis media) or early tensa cholesteatoma, the posterior atticotomy might be combined with posterior sinusectomy. If the disease seems to extend to the mastoid, endoscopes are used transmeatally or transcortically. If the cholesteatoma extensively occupies the mastoid, a classic mastoidectomy is made. Other inactive pathologic conditions such as effusion, cholesterol granuloma, and granulation are managed via endoscopic removal or with a minimal mastoidectomy.

The use of cartilage grafts has a number of associated difficulties. These include thickness, fixation, curvature, curling, and resorption. Excessively thick grafts may cause hearing loss by their weight or from reduction of middle ear depth and other adhesions. Tragal and lower conchal bowl grafts are the thickest examples. A thick graft is sometimes preferable in cases in which ossiculoplasty is impossible and maximum eardrum strength is needed. In these cases, the use of a portion of graft minimizes the chances of an eardrum collapse and will later permit the use of an air-conduction hearing aid if necessary (Adkins, 1990; Milewski, 1993).

If the graft borders are excessively thick over the scutum (Weber and Gantz, 1998), fixation may result in poor audiologic results (East, 1998). This can also occur in zones of ossification of the graft. The graft border beside the scutum is best trimmed to the minimum thickness when using a graft (Figure 82-5).

The graft shape should adapt well to the eardrum space. A graft can be either too flat or too curved. When a graft is being thinned, it can produce a folding away from the edges. This folding can be corrected by incision techniques but can at the same time create an excessive resorption of cartilage, which, in turn, may create a local pocket or cholesteatoma.

Use of composite grafts that reduce eardrum collapse and recurrent cholesteatoma has been successful. They are fundamental in the continuing move away from open cavity techniques as their use minimizes the risk of the four types of recurrent disease that are the principal objection to intact canal wall mastoidectomy.

Postoperative TM retraction pockets are mostly associated with cases of cholesteatoma managed by the intact canal wall technique (Charachon et al, 1992). In other words, a recurrent cholesteatoma may occur following any reconstructive procedure on a patient with chronic otitis media. There are three causes for postoperative retraction

pockets, which can be preventable: adhesions between the TM and structures medial to it, eustachian tube dysfunction, and atrophy of the reconstructed TM followed by atelectasis. The post-tympanoplasty retraction pockets are attributable to a ventilation problem in the pocket, either a tubal or mucosal type. Often a ventilation tube can stabilize the ear. In more serious cases, reinforcement with membrane cartilage is necessary. In these cases, the faulty tubal function requires the use of an open technique.

References

Adkins WY. Composite autograft for tympanoplasty and tympanomastoid surgery. Laryngoscope 1990;100:944–7.

Ars B. Tympanic membrane retraction pocket. Acta Otorhinolaryngol Belg 1995;49:163–71.

Ars B, Ars-Piret N. Morpho-functional partition of the middle ear cleft. Acta Otorhinolaryngol Belg 1997;51:181–4.

Ars B, Wuyts F, van de Heyning P, et al. Histomorphometric study of the normal middle ear mucosa. Preliminary results supporting the gas exchange function in the postero-superior part of the middle ear cleft. Acta Otolaryngol (Stockh) 1997;117:704–7.

Bremond G, Magnan J, Chays A, et al. Retraction pockets, pathological entity [in French]? Ann Otolaryngol Chir Cerviofac 1990;107:386–92.

Clarós P. Contribution à l'étude du cholestéatoma chez l'enfant et l'adolescent. Cah Otorhinolaryngol 1976;11:463–77.

Clarós P. Otoendoscopic exploration of retraction pockets. In: Magnan J, Chays A, editors. Proceedings of the Sixth International Conference on Cholesteatoma and Ear Surgery. Cannes: Label Productions; 2000. p. 549–51.

Charachon R, Barthez M, LeJeune JM. Spontaneous retraction pockets in chronic otitis media: medical and surgical therapy. Ear Nose Throat J 1992;71:578–83.

Deguine C. Pathogénèse du cholestéatome: apport de la photographie otoscopique. Rev Laryngol Otol Rhinol 1995;116:61–3.

East DM. Atticotomy with reconstruction for limited cholesteatoma. Clin Otolaryngol 1998;23:248–52.

Harner SG. Management of posterior tympanic membrane retraction. Laryngoscope 1995;105:326–8.

Kobayashi T, Masaru T, Yuji Y, et al. Pathogenesis of attic retraction pocket and cholesteatoma as studied by computed tomography. Am J Otol 1994;15:658–62.

Magnan J, Chays A, Florence A, Bremond G. Eradication of cholesteatoma by the closed technique—a report of 1000 cases. In: Nakano Y, editor. Cholesteatoma and mastoid surgery. Amsterdam: Kugler Publications; 1993. p. 663–5.

Milewski C. Composite graft tympanoplasty in the treatment of ears with advanced middle ear pathology. Laryngoscope 1993;103:1352–6.

Sadé J. Treatment of retraction pockets and cholesteatoma Eur Arch Otorhinolaryngol 1993;250:193–9.

Sadé J. The buffering effect of middle ear negative pressure by retraction of the pars tensa. Am J Otol 2000;21:20–3.

Tanabe M, Takahashi H, Honjo I, et al. Factors affecting recovery of mastoid aeration after ear surgery. Eur Arch Otolaryngol 1999;256:220–3.

Weber PC, Gantz BJ. Cartilage reconstruction of the scutum defects in canal wall-up mastoidectomies. Am J Otolaryngol 1998;19:178–82.

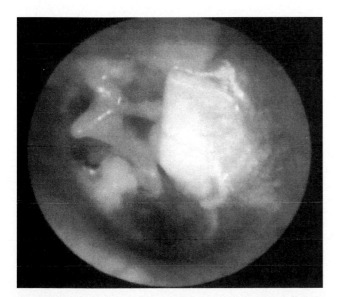

FIGURE 82-5. Otoscopic view, postsurgery, with a composite cartilage-fascia graft. The presence of cartilage in the posterosuperior area is evident.

Chapter 83

Cholesteatoma

Chris A. J. Prescott, CAJ, FRCS

Cholesteatoma is one of those diseases that maintain the mystique so essential to a successful specialty, in this case, otology. Cholesteatoma is a rather nasty disease with potentially fatal complications that, in general, can be diagnosed only by an otolaryngology specialist using special skills and sometimes even requiring surgical exploration for diagnosis. A concept that is seemingly simple to describe to the nonspecialist—squamous epithelium lines the outer surface of the eardrum, negative middle ear pressure creates a retraction pocket with squamous epithelium now lining the inside of the pocket, failure of migration of desquamated epithelium and formation of an expanding epithelioma in the middle ear, destruction of any bony structures with which it comes into contact, obstruction of natural drainage channels trapping infection and precipitating life-threatening complications (Figure 83-1)—cholesteatoma raises more unanswered questions and causes more heated debate than any other otologic disease, especially when it occurs in children.

Often one of the first questions asked concerns the name problem. The disease is characterized by accumulation of a pearly white substance in the middle ear, and this was thought by the earliest otologists to be cholesterol but is now known to be squamous epithelial debris. It was given the name "cholesteatoma," which is a more wondrous sounding name than mere "epithelioma" and has universally been retained.

The above simplistic explanation sounds good, but how does the squamous epithelium get into the middle ear cleft? There are several different mechanisms for this.

Congenital Cholesteatoma

Congenital cholesteatomas are not common. The squamous epithelium develops from nests of squamous cells that have been identified in human embryos in both the middle ear and in the temporal bone, particularly at its apex. Why they occur in these situations is not known.

Congenital cholesteatoma should be characterized by a "whitish" bulging in the middle ear behind an intact eardrum, and, as otoscopic expertise increases throughout the health professions, these are being increasingly seen. Often they are diagnosed only at myringotomy,

when squamous debris is found in the middle ear instead of the anticipated "glue" in a child booked for insertion of ventilation tubes for middle ear effusion. Astute recognition at otoscopy permits high-resolution computed tomography (CT) to delineate the extent of the cholesteatoma sac ("pearl") in the middle ear and exclude any other deposits in the temporal bone—as sometimes there can be multiple sacs—and allow planning for the surgical approach to remove the disease.

The precise incidence of congenital cholesteatoma is difficult to know because probably the majority of them are missed. They present later only after they have become infected or broken down, and their origin can no longer be determined with certainty. Cholesteatoma appearing to arise in an unusual site can be conjectured to have been congenital in origin. So-called "massive" cholesteatoma of the temporal bone was probably origi-

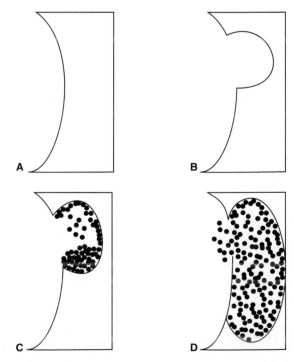

FIGURE 83-1. *A,* Some retraction. *B,* Retraction pocket formation. *C,* Pocket fills with squamous debris. *D,* Cholesteatoma invades middle ear.

nally a congenital cholesteatoma that expanded asymptomatically over many years until either some structure was eroded or infection arose that precipitated symptoms.

Acquired Cholesteatoma

The most common acquired cause is the progression of disease from a retraction pocket, which has been alluded to above and is discussed below. Another acquired cause is from migration of squamous epithelium inward from the margin of a perforation to invade and displace mucosal lining of the middle ear—a process that can sometimes be seen occurring. Whether the process is ever aggressive enough to cause frank cholesteatoma is uncertain. Certainly, cholesteatoma is found in association with a so-called central perforation, but usually in such cases, the disease is so far advanced that it is impossible to say whether it originated from epithelial migration or from a central retraction pocket, which would appear to be the more likely explanation. So-called marginal perforations usually have a retraction pocket origin.

Rarely, cholesteatoma can be found after traumatic implantation of squamous epithelium—usually surgical—when it takes the form of a squamous "pearl" in the middle ear.

The most common cause, progression from a retraction pocket in the eardrum, raises several unanswered questions, of which a few are as follows:

- Why do only some individuals form retraction pockets in response to negative middle ear pressure?
- Why do only some retraction pockets progress to cholesteatoma?
- Why are some retraction pocket cholesteatomas more aggressively invasive than others, particularly those arising in children compared with those arising in adults?
- Why do only some retraction pocket cholesteatomas excite an intense inflammatory reaction in surrounding tissue?
- Why do some retraction pocket cholesteatomas become infected and break down to behave as active chronic otitis media?

There are others. This suggests that cholesteatoma is still a fruitful field for otologic research.

Retraction pockets occur in several locations (Figure 83-2). There are unexplained geographic variations in the proportions of pars tensa versus pars flaccida cholesteatomas. In general, the posterosuperior portion of the pars tensa between the supporting structures of the handle of the malleus, tympanic ring, and posterior malleolar fold is the most common site of origin. As the pocket is sucked in, it creates the impression of a so-called "marginal" perforation—hence the dictum sometimes still heard that "a marginal perforation is an indicator of cholesteatoma."

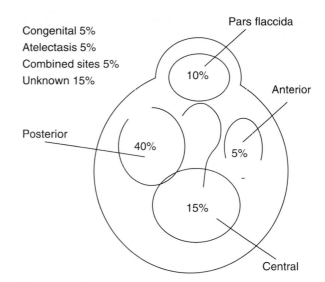

FIGURE 83-2. Sites of origin of cholesteatoma.

The different stages in development of retraction pocket cholesteatoma can be seen in a series of patients, but it is unusual to observe the progression of disease in an individual. This suggests that usually cholesteatoma formation takes place early in a retraction pocket if it is going to occur—the youngest child in my series was 2 years of age—and that an established retraction pocket free of cholesteatoma can frequently be stable.

This raises the question, "Can cholesteatoma be prevented by ventilation tubes?" Theoretically, this is an attractive option; anecdotally, it is possible, but certain rigorous conditions apply. The community has to be stable and affluent enough to afford regular prophylactic follow-up. All children in the community have to be examined at regular intervals from a young age so that middle ear effusions can be identified early. Ventilation tubes have to be inserted as soon as significant eardrum retraction, atrophy, or development of retraction pockets is identified and definitely before any adhesion to middle ear structures occurs. The children then have to be followed up past extrusion of the tube(s) with early reinsertion of ventilation tubes should a middle ear effusion recur. Follow-up must continue until the child is well past the age of recurrence of effusions. It is obvious that these conditions will apply to very few communities or probably to very few individuals.

Once a retraction pocket has formed, exactly why some maintain self-cleansing epithelial migration and others do not has not been adequately explained. In some way, this seems to be related to whether the retraction pocket forms an adhesion to any middle ear structures with which it comes in contact. There also has to be a change in the squamous epithelium from a rather passive layer to one that is more active with increased cell turnover in the epithelium and able to initiate processes resulting in inflammatory and other responses in contact tissues.

These little understood changes probably also relate in some way to the rapidity of progression and spread of the resulting cholesteatoma, although this is often not clearly obvious clinically as some small cholesteatomas can appear to have a very active epithelial matrix and some large cholesteatomas can appear to have a very inactive epithelial matrix. Aggressiveness of the cholesteatoma is another term often used, but this requires definition as it could relate to spread, destruction, inflammatory response, or all three—features that differ widely from one cholesteatoma to another.

Another feature that differs is the rate at which cholesteatomas become infected to thereafter behave as active chronic otitis media. There may be socioeconomic factors that influence this. Classically, one was supposed to be able to differentiate cholesteatoma from simple mucositis in a discharging ear from the smell and quantity of the discharge, but neither of these are reliable signs.

Presentation of the disease is difficult to describe because it often does not differ from other middle ear disease, discharge and/or hearing impairment being the most common symptoms. Destructive disease may present with complications such as deafness, vertigo, or facial palsy. Infection related to cholesteatoma always has the potential for presentation with mastoiditis and—again for which there is no real explanation—particularly for presentation with the intracranial complications of mastoiditis.

For the nonspecialist, what then should raise suspicion of cholesteatoma?

- Recognition of the presence of a "whitish" mass in the middle ear causing the eardrum to "bulge"—congenital cholesteatoma
- Failure of active chronic otitis media to respond to medical treatment—systemic antibiotic, dry mopping, and eardrops—after two to three courses of treatment; cholesteatoma is a surgical disease and does not respond to medical treatment
- The presence of a granulation tissue polyp in the deep ear canal, which is frequently associated with cholesteatoma

These findings are about all. Those with special training and experience with otoscopy may be able to recognize a retraction pocket, and a retraction pocket/perforation that is either posterosuperior/marginal or in the pars flaccida should be treated as suspicious. In practice, the majority of patients referred with a diagnosis of cholesteatoma because of the presence of a white mass in the eardrum turn out to have calcified scars.

Specialists do not have to be told how to diagnose cholesteatoma. Using whatever equipment is required/available, they examine the eardrum and as much of the middle ear as they can see, looking for the telltale presence of white squamous debris within the middle ear. As far as ancillary investigations are concerned, audiometry can be of assistance in determining whether there is ossicular destruction but is not reliable as the hearing can be normal in the presence of cholesteatoma wrapped around the ossicles and nearly normal even when there is extensive destruction. Radiologic examination is always a good topic for debate. High-quality CT scans can demonstrate soft tissue and bone destruction that could be cholesteatoma but may not be needed when cholesteatoma can be seen clinically as they have significant cost implications. Should the middle ear cleft and temporal bone be imaged prior to surgical exploration? On this, opinion is divided. Inexperienced surgeons need to know how much space they have in the mastoid for their approach to the mastoid antrum and aditus. Experienced surgeons tend not to need this but may want very high-resolution scans to demonstrate bony destruction of the middle and inner ear structures, especially when localized complications are present. When intracranial complications are present, imaging of adjacent intracranial structures is essential to determine the need for neurosurgical intervention.

With such a range of potential presentations, what are the likely scenarios, and what needs to be done for each?

Retraction Pocket Disease

The principles of managing retraction pocket disease that may or may not have progressed to cholesteatoma are as follows:

1. Examine the pocket in its entirety, cleaning it out thoroughly if required. When a retraction pocket is identified, the foremost question requiring an answer, no matter what the situation, is whether it has progressed to the stage of being a cholesteatoma. Otoscopy may provide the answer if the whole extent of the pocket can be seen. If not, it may be possible to see into the pocket with a thin-angled endoscope. If this is not available, examination with an operating microscope may permit adequate assessment, although sometimes this has to be done under anesthesia to permit the necessary tissue manipulation to see into the depths of the pocket. Sometimes limited surgery to expose the pocket may be required for adequate assessment.
2. Decide whether this is a pocket that is self-cleansing.
3. If self-cleansing, then follow up at regular intervals and decide at some point in time whether to excise the pocket and graft/reinforce the defect. Quite apart from the potential for progression to cholesteatoma, such a decision needs to be made in the interests of ossicular continuity and preservation of hearing. For some reason—we know the mechanism, but we do not know the why—squamous epithelium sucked in and wrapped around an ossicle eventually results in bone resorption. The long process of the incus is particularly vulnerable from a posterosuperior retraction

pocket and the body of the incus and head of the malleus from a pars flaccida retraction pocket.

4. If not self-cleansing, then decide whether the pocket can be maintained in a healthy state by regular cleaning or whether the pocket requires excision with grafting/support of the defect. In some individuals, an intermediate stage seems to exist in which a pocket contains squamous debris, but this can be easily cleared by microsuction (in a cooperative patient). For as long as this state can be maintained, these pockets can be observed in a patient who is not felt to be fit for definitive surgery provided that the whole extent of the pocket can be seen and the patient is able/willing to attend regular follow-up.

5. If the pocket has progressed to frank cholesteatoma, then surgical exploration is required: atticotomy and tympanomastoid surgery. Once a pocket contains inaccessible debris within its depths and/or this cannot be easily and completely cleared, then it should be regarded as a cholesteatoma and requires surgical removal. Surgery for cholesteatoma is discussed later. Several factors determine the type of surgery, of which the most obvious is the extent of disease, but this is often not the predominant determining factor.

Another of the unanswered questions is "How long does one watch a retraction pocket in a child?"

For a posterosuperior retraction pocket, if the pocket is one feature of retraction associated with middle ear effusion, then a ventilation tube should be inserted. If adhesion formation has not yet occurred, then the pocket should evert with middle ear ventilation. Close follow-up is required with early reinsertion of the ventilation tube should effusion recur after tube extrusion. Follow-up should continue until the child is well past the age of recurrence of effusions. Often the tympanic membrane will recover its structure and contour. Neglect in follow-up can result in a situation in which the retraction pocket recurs and can progress to cholesteatoma.

However, if adhesion has already occurred, then the pocket will not evert. In this situation, close follow-up is required with reinsertion of a ventilation tube whenever middle ear effusion recurs after tube extrusion. Once the middle ear is stable and maintaining ventilation, the decision has to be made whether to excise the retraction pocket. It is tempting to leave a stable pocket and simply observe it at regular intervals. The drawback to this approach is that in some individuals, the presence of squamous epithelium in contact with an ossicle promotes slow but steady destruction of the ossicle through increased osteoclastic activity within the bone—a process not necessarily associated with inflammation. The long and lenticular processes of the incus are particularly vulnerable. The best policy would appear to be excision and grafting of the pocket once the middle ear has stabilized.

Excision and grafting would also appear to be the best policy to adopt when first presentation is an established retraction pocket in an otherwise stable ear.

For a pars flaccida retraction pocket, a similar approach can be adopted provided that the full extent of the pocket can be seen. However, if the full extent of the pocket cannot be seen or if there is any suggestion of debris accumulation, then an atticotomy should be undertaken with reinforcement and grafting of the defect. A ventilation tube should be placed if there is either an effusion present or any possibility that an effusion will recur.

Having said this, if there is any sign that the cholesteatoma formation process has already started, then full cholesteatoma eradication surgery should be undertaken. Early cholesteatoma surgery offers the best chance for preservation/reconstruction of the ossicular conducting mechanism. The longer a cholesteatoma is "observed," the more ossicular destruction will occur and the less chance there is for hearing preservation.

Active Chronic Otitis Media

Although early recognition of the presence of a retraction pocket is the ideal, the practicality is that many of the pockets will have become infected and broken down prior to presentation, and the first indication of disease will be a chronic discharge from the ear: active chronic otitis media. In such circumstances, recognition of the presence of cholesteatoma becomes more difficult. The pocket now takes on the appearance of a perforation with a discharge, and the presence of squamous debris in the middle ear is easily overlooked. Standard treatment for active chronic otitis media (which is far more common than cholesteatoma)—systemic antibiotic, dry mopping, and eardrops—may or may not resolve the infection.

What indicators can be used to assist in suspicion of the presence of cholesteatoma? First and foremost is the dictum that any chronic discharging ear that cannot be resolved after two or three courses of treatment needs to be referred to determine the underlying cause of the chronic infection and, more specifically, to exclude cholesteatoma as the cause.

Another is the dictum that any perforation in the eardrum needs referral for assessment to determine whether this is a "safe" or an "unsafe" ear, that is, whether there is an underlying cholesteatoma. This is especially true if the perforation is in the pars flaccida or the posterosuperior quadrant of the pars tensa. However, cholesteatoma can be associated with perforations anterior to the handle of the malleus and with "central" perforations.

Chronic infection in a cholesteatoma can be associated with growth of a granulation tissue polyp, and although it is not the only cause for these, they should all be regarded as suspicious for underlying cholesteatoma. In the presence of chronic infection, experience—often with the assistance of microscopic examination and microsuction—is needed to make the diagnosis. The treatment is surgical, although often systemic antibiotics, dry mopping, and eardrops are used while waiting for surgery to "damp down" the infection and reduce the risk of complications occurring. Surgery for cholesteatoma will be discussed later.

Complications of Cholesteatoma

In summary, the following complications result from either the destructive nature of the disease, the obstructive nature of the disease, or a combination of both:

1. Destruction of the ossicular chain to cause conductive hearing impairment. This has been alluded to in the discussion of retraction pocket disease above. The more "aggressive" the character of the disease, the more extensive the destruction of the ossicles. The only part of the ossicular chain that appears to be relatively resistant to destruction is the footplate of the stapes. However, erosion can occur around its annular ligament, rendering it particularly vulnerable to dislocation during attempts to strip cholesteatoma matrix off remnants of crura and the footplate.

2. "Trapped" infection within the mastoid precipitating mastoiditis, which, in turn, precipitates intracranial complications of mastoiditis. It is this feature that makes cholesteatoma such a nasty disease: the fact that an undiagnosed or neglected cholesteatoma can rapidly progress to intracranial complications when it becomes infected, something that is far more common in less-developed than in well-developed countries.

3. Erosion of the fallopian canal to expose the facial nerve with the potential for facial palsy. Exposure of the nerve places it at risk of neuritis in the presence of infection or of injury during surgery when attempting to strip the overlying cholesteatoma matrix.

4. Erosion of the bony skeleton of the inner ear to cause balance disorders and sensorineural hearing impairment. Although the inner ear capsule can be eroded at any site with which cholesteatoma is in contact, the most vulnerable site is the bony covering of the lateral semicircular canal in the mastoid antrum. A fistula here places the labyrinth at risk of infection and a resulting "dead ear." (Infection should be placed in inverted commas because the clinical history often fails to suggest labyrinthitis when a dead ear is found related to a lateral semicircular canal fistula.) The labyrinth is also at risk during surgery when attempting to strip off cholesteatoma matrix overlying a fistula. If the membranous labyrinth is thought to have been injured, then grafting the fistula and giving the patient a course of high-dose steroid may "salvage" inner ear function.

5. Extension medially via a number of pathways around the inner ear to the petrous apex, where inflammation can create a localized "neighborhood" inflammation, the resulting neuritis complex being known as Gradenigo's syndrome.

6. Erosion of the bony skeleton of the middle ear cleft. Some of the consequences of this include the following:

   • Erosion of the tympanic ring, especially the scutum, which is that portion separating the ear canal from the attic area of the middle ear
   • Erosion of the bony wall between the ear canal and the mastoid to create a potential pathway for a fistula between the ear canal and the mastoid air cell complex
   • Erosion of the mastoid air cells—a useful diagnostic sign when seen radiologically
   • Erosion of the outer table of the mastoid cortex, creating a pathway for infection to present as a subperiosteal abscess, which, in turn, can break down to create a fistula between the skin and the mastoid air cell complex
   • Erosion of the bony covering of the sigmoid (lateral) sinus, exposing it to infection (thrombophlebitis, thrombosis, abscess, infected emboli) or to injury during surgery
   • Erosion of the bony covering of either middle fossa or posterior fossa dura, exposing the meninges to infection or injury during surgery

Surgery for Cholesteatoma

The definitive treatment of cholesteatoma is surgery. Briefly, there are three different surgical methods employed, although there are almost as many variations on these as there are otologists.

Atticotomy is a limited exposure of disease confined to the attic region of the middle ear. It may or may not involve dismantling and reconstructing the ossicular chain to remove disease wrapped around or deep to the ossicles. Sometimes attic disease will have extended into other parts of the middle ear, and surgery may then have to be extended to permit eradication of disease. At the end of the procedure, the "open" area may be fascia grafted and left exposed to the ear canal as a small atticotomy cavity or reconstruction of the bony defect created for exposure may be undertaken.

Once disease has extended backward beyond the attic region of the middle ear into the mastoid air cell system, then mastoid surgery is required in addition to attic surgery. This may take the form of open-cavity mastoid surgery, in which disease is removed from the mastoid, attic, and middle ear by creating a single cavity connecting all of these areas and opening the cavity into the ear canal by removing the superior and posterior bony walls of the ear canal. Modern open-cavity surgery involves some degree of reconstruction of both the tympanic membrane and the ossicular chain.

It may take the form of closed-cavity mastoid surgery in which disease is removed from the mastoid and the attic by connecting them into a single cavity. Separation from the ear canal is maintained by preserving the superior and posterior bony walls of the ear canal. Disease is removed from the middle ear using a combination of posterior and anterior tympanotomy approaches. After removal of all disease, the tympanic membrane and ossicular chain are reconstructed.

"Open" versus "closed" surgery is another field for much debate, again especially when the disease is present in children. The advantages of closed-cavity surgery are the potential for a reconstruction that is as close to normal anatomy as possible with a better chance of preserving or restoring hearing and a better chance of having a trouble-free ear as regards infection. The disadvantages are the greater degree of technical skill required and, because of this, the potential for leaving microscopic disease behind, which is undetectable by any other means apart from "second-look" surgery after a period of time that would allow such deposits to grow into residual disease. Second-look surgery is therefore mandatory because hidden disease can become infected and, once infected, rapidly progress to mastoiditis and its complications because all barriers that might otherwise contain the infection have been removed. Because anatomy has been restored but the underlying problem that precipitated cholesteatoma formation in the first place may not have been corrected, the potential exists for another retraction pocket to form and progress to a recurrence of cholesteatoma.

The advantages of open cavity surgery are that it is technically far easier to eradicate disease using this approach and that any disease that recurs will be visible and not trapped in a closed cavity. Visible disease in an open cavity is not likely to progress to mastoiditis and its complications even when the cavity becomes infected. The disadvantages are that it is not always possible to create a trouble-free cavity and it is very difficult to reconstruct a functioning sound-conducting ossicular system.

Once again—particularly in less-developed communities—the potential for life-threatening complications of infection in the presence of cholesteatoma has to be stressed because this plays a far greater role than any other factor in the decision regarding the type of surgery to be undertaken. In general, where expectation of poor follow-up exists or there is any perceived reluctance to permit or undergo second-look surgery, then open cavity surgery is the preferred option.

Surgeons develop their own ways of doing things, and this makes it difficult to prescribe an approach to surgery for cholesteatoma. A number of very practical principles follow:

1. Examine the ear under anesthesia to determine the nature and origin of the cholesteatoma.

2. No matter what the situation of the cholesteatoma, expose the mastoid cortex through a postauricular incision and drill an antral bur hole. Inspect the antrum and aditus to determine how far into the mastoid the cholesteatoma extends.

3. If the cholesteatoma is confined to the attic, then undertake an anterior atticotomy that is as extensive as required to eradicate disease from within the middle ear. Attempt ossicular reconstruction. Decide whether to reconstruct the bony scutum or leave an open, but grafted, atticotomy cavity. If the latter, then decide whether the exposed aditus requires reinforcing in addition to grafting. Graft the eardrum, attempting to restore a middle ear cavity in continuity with the eustachian tube. If this is not possible, then graft across the entire middle ear to try to ensure that there is no exposed mucosa after healing.

4. If cholesteatoma has invaded the mastoid, then decide whether to undertake open- or closed-cavity surgery. A compromise is available in which disease is eradicated using the open-cavity technique, and the cavity is then closed off from the middle ear by reconstructing the posterior and superior bony walls of the ear canal.

5. If closed-cavity surgery is undertaken, then it is important to realize that this is not conservative surgery. To remove all disease, the surgery has to be as radical as open-cavity surgery, the only difference being in the approaches used that permit preservation of the bony walls of the ear canal. It is probably this misconception that accounts for high residual disease rates in some centers. Any areas in which there is uncertainty as to the completeness of disease removal should be recorded in the operation notes, to be given special attention when looking for residual disease at second-look surgery. Tympanic membrane reconstruction is undertaken at the first surgery, but ossicular reconstruction can be deferred to the second surgery. If so, ossicles or remnants of ossicles can be stored in the mastoid cavity for later use.

6. If open-cavity surgery is undertaken, every effort should be made to ensure rapid and complete healing of the cavity to try to achieve a trouble-free ear afterward. A number of principles have been enunciated in this regard: shallow cavities, wide meatoplasties, cavity obliteration, middle ear reconstruction, etc. The single overriding factor is to ensure that there is no exposed mucosa in the healed cavity and to use whatever techniques that are practical to achieve this. The simplest technique is to harvest a huge fascia graft and, in addition to grafting the middle ear, extend the fascia graft to line the entire attic and mastoid cavity. Mucosa creates wet cavities, which are prone to infection. Middle ear and ossicular reconstruction should be attempted if possible at the first

surgery as the success rate for second attempts to restore a functioning sound conduction system is low. If contemplated, then ossicular remnants can be stored beneath the fascia graft for later use. Any areas in which it is thought that disease eradication is incomplete should be recorded in the operation notes, and these areas should be examined carefully at each follow-up visit. These are most likely to be in the oval window–sinus tympani–facial recess–round window area as most other areas can be adequately exposed by drilling and disease can be eradicated.

7. When surgery is undertaken in the presence of mastoiditis, the sigmoid (lateral) sinus should be exposed and "needled" to exclude thrombosis or intrasinus abscess and the middle cranial fossa dura should be exposed and explored to exclude an extradural abscess. Sometimes the posterior cranial fossa dura requires exposure as well. In the presence of intracranial sepsis, some neurosurgeons prefer a separate bur hole approach, whereas others prefer an approach through the mastoid. Frequently, the extent of soft tissue infection precludes the harvesting of adequate graft material. Prior to closure, extensive washing is required to remove any infected bone dust in an attempt to prevent wound infection, but because most incisions in these cases are made through infected tissue, many of these wounds become infected, and wound drainage is recommended.

Follow-up after Surgery

This is determined by the type of surgery undertaken. It is very easy to forget about the other ear, which requires a regular check to ensure that cholesteatoma is not developing.

In closed cavities—both atticotomy and mastoid—there always has to be suspicion of residual disease; therefore, planning for second-look surgery (and sometimes even third- and fourth-look surgery) is the major consideration. Second surgery provides an opportunity to correct any deficiencies in ossicular or tympanic membrane reconstruction. Early detection of recurrent retraction pockets is important, and, if detected, a decision has to be made whether to try to use a ventilation tube to prevent progression. Prompt recognition of infection is important with institution of vigorous intravenous antibiotic treatment and a very low threshold for surgical intervention.

With open cavities—both atticotomy and mastoid—a nicely grafted and well-healed cavity can be virtually trouble free, but, unfortunately, this state cannot always be attained. There is a long list of potential problems that can arise:

- In the early healing phase, granulomas can arise from the margins of meatoplasty flaps. If not removed, they can become adherent and heal as adhesion bands that can close off the cavity from view. Other adhesion bands can form in virtually any part of a cavity, trapping debris that can become a source of infection.

- Failure to control infection at surgery can lead to chronic infection in the healing cavity, which can delay healing for several months and is often the cause of a persistently troublesome cavity. British otology promotes the use of packing material soaked in the antiseptic bismuth iodoform paraffin paste for the postoperative cavity, and its use certainly seems to reduce the incidence of infection—particularly from coliform organisms—although the occasional sensitivity reaction to iodine will be seen. It does seem to have advantages over antibiotic-soaked packs, one of which is that it can be left in place for 2 to 3 weeks without causing problems.

- Areas of graft breakdown will expose mucosa, and the presence of mucosa leads to a wet cavity, which is prone to infection. Once exposed, it is almost impossible to remove mucosa without revision surgery.

- Residual disease can grow to form cholesteatoma matrix, lining areas of the cavity. Some surgeons deliberately leave the cholesteatoma matrix behind to act as a lining for the cavity. This is not recommended as keratotic debris accumulates in these areas, which can either act as a nidus for infection or, in some individuals, precipitate a granulomatous reaction in adjacent soft tissue.

- In some cavities, wax accumulation is a problem, and there does not seem to be an explanation as to why this should occur. Probably the meatoplasty technique has interfered with the normal outward migration pattern in the wax-secreting areas of the canal wall skin.

Careful examination of a troublesome cavity after cleaning should reveal the underlying cause(s) for the problem. Syringing is by far the most comfortable way to clean a cavity, but the water temperature has to be exactly body temperature. Systemic and topical therapy at best can introduce a measure of control of any infection, but, inevitably, the infection will flare up again. Once recognized, the problem area is best managed by revision surgery, and often this need only be very localized within the cavity; well-lined, well-healed areas do not need to be disturbed.

Conclusion

Skillful otoscopy by physicians undertaking regular "well child" examinations and recognition of any middle ear abnormalities will improve early detection of congenital cholesteatoma. Early recognition of eustachian tube dysfunction and appropriate management with use of ventilation tubes when indicated with close follow-up of such children until well past the age of recurrence of middle ear effusions should enable control of any retraction pocket formation before progression to cholesteatoma. Early recognition of frank cholesteatoma and appropriate surgical intervention are the key to hearing preservation and reduction of the complications of infection. Improving socioeconomic conditions and increasing awareness in communities about ear disease and hearing impairment and the need to seek attention early for any problems should improve the general state of "ear health" in communities. On the medical side, an awareness of the dictums that "any active chronic otitis media not responding to treatment needs referral for specialist opinion" and "any perforation or unrecognized abnormality in the eardrum needs referral for specialist opinion" should go a long way to reducing the devastating complications of cholesteatoma.

Suggested Reading

General

Sellars SL. The origins of mastoid surgery. S Afr Med J 1974;48:234–42.

Ventilation Tubes and Cholesteatoma

Rakover Y, Keywan K, Rosen G. Comparison of the incidence of cholesteatoma surgery before and after using ventilation tubes for secretory otitis media. Int J Pediatr Otorhinolaryngol 2000;56:41–4.

Roland NJ, Phillips DE, Rogers JH, Singh SD. The use of ventilation tubes and the incidence of cholesteatoma surgery in the paediatric population of Liverpool. Clin Otolaryngol 1992;17:437–9.

Comparison of the Biologic Behavior of Cholesteatoma in Adults and Children

Hildmann H, Sudhoff H. Cholesteatoma in children. Int J Pediatr Otorhinolaryngol 1999;49 Suppl 1:S81–6.

Pediatric Cholesteatoma

Iino Y, Imamura Y, Kojima C, et al. Risk factors for recurrent and residual cholesteatoma in children determined by second stage operation. Int J Pediatr Otorhinolaryngol 1998;46:57–65.

Prescott CAJ. Cholesteatoma in children—the experience at The Red Cross War Memorial Children's Hospital in South Africa 1988-96. Int J Pediatr Otorhinolaryngol 1999;49:15–9.

Silvola J, Palva T. One stage revision surgery for pediatric cholesteatoma: long-term results and comparison with primary surgery. Int J Pediatr Otorhinolaryngol 2000;56:135–9.

Shohet JA, DeJong AL. The management of pediatric cholesteatoma. Otolaryngol Clin North Am 2002;35:841–51.

Soldati D, Mudry A. Cholesteatoma in children: techniques and results. Int J Pediatr Otorhinolaryngol 2000;52:269–76.

Congenital Cholesteatoma

Nelson M, Roger G, Koltai PJ, et al. Congenital cholesteatoma: classification, management, and outcome. Arch Otolaryngol Head Neck Surg 2992;128:810–4.

Potsic WP, Samadi DS, Marsh RR, Westmore RF. A staging system for congenital cholesteatoma. Arch Otolaryngol Head Neck Surg 2002;128:1009–12.

Quantin L, Fernandez SC, Moretti J. Congenital cholesteatoma of external auditory canal. Int J Pediatr Otorhinolaryngol 2002;62:175–9.

Chapter 84

OSSICULAR DISCONTINUITY/FIXATION

JAMES S. BATTI, MD

This chapter reviews the whole host of known methods of reconstruction of the ossicular chain from the tympanic membrane (TM) to the oval window that are advocated in adults and children. Specific recommendations are provided for reconstruction in children when there is discontinuity or fixation of the ossicular chain.

Ossicular-related etiologies of conductive hearing loss can be congenital or acquired and are mainly attributable to either discontinuity or fixation. Ossicular discontinuity occurs in the following scenarios presented in order of frequency: eroded incudostapedial joint, absent incus, absent incus and stapes superstructure, and absent incus and stapes including the footplate (Hough, 1959). Any of these ossicular interruptions may include an absent malleus. Austin (1972) defined four groups in the absence of an intact incus: (1) malleus handle present, stapes superstructure present; (2) malleus handle present, stapes superstructure absent; (3) malleus handle absent, stapes superstructure present; and (4) malleus handle absent, stapes superstructure absent. Ossicular fixation most commonly occurs when the malleus head is ankylosed to the attic wall or when tympanosclerosis of the attic is present. Kartush (1994) modified Austin's classification of ossicular defects by adding two other groups related to ossicular fixation: ossicle head fixation with all ossicles present and stapes fixation with all ossicles present. Moretz (1998) added still another category, nonclassifiable, to describe unusual situations requiring ossiculoplasty that are not easily included in the other categories. These include a lateralized TM and some congenital abnormalities.

Chronic suppurative otitis media, with and without cholesteatoma, frequently results in disruption of the ossicular chain. Cholesteatoma is the most common acquired condition of the ear, secondary only to otitis media with effusion that requires surgical intervention. Cholesteatomas may develop from retraction pockets of the pars flaccida or at perforations of the TM or can be congenital behind an intact TM, without associated otitis media. Bone resorption from the cholesteatomas may occur owing to enzyme production by the expanding epithelial lining and lead to bony erosion of the ossicle, otic capsule, and mastoid. Eustachian tube dysfunction, causing changes in the TM, can apply pressure on the lenticular process of the incus, along with inflammation, and can also lead to ossicular erosion.

Immobility of an intact ossicular chain can be caused by fixation of the ossicles owing to tympanosclerosis, bony fixation to the surrounding structures, or congenital defects. Tympanosclerosis is a pathologic process in which degeneration of collagenous fibrous tissues occurs. Thickening of this homogeneous hyaline mass may occur, and, occasionally, the deposition of extracellular calcium and phosphate crystals may occur. Common areas for ossicular fixation to occur include the oval window with stapedius fixation, epitympanic fixation of the incus-malleus complex, tensor tympani tympanosclerosis, and tympanosclerosis involving the anterior mallear ligament. Tympanosclerosis is believed to occur in approximately 10% of cases of otitis media (Gibb and Pang, 1994).

Patient Selection

To achieve an adequate postoperative result, some preoperative clinical and audiologic features can be evaluated. The Bellucci (1973) system describes the state of infection: never infected, intermittent discharge, unremitting discharge, cleft palate, and nasopharyngeal deformities, whereas Austin's (1972) classification describes the availability of the malleus handle and stapes superstructure. Black (1992) described the state of infection using the surgical, prosthetic, infection, tissue, and eustachian factors or SPITE method of assessment, which uses both the Bellucci system and the Austin classification for ossiculoplasty prognosis. Significant factors preoperatively that predicted failure were surgical (complexity of surgery and if scutum and drum repair was needed), prosthetic (absence of the malleus and/or stapes, presenting a 50 dB air–bone gap or greater), infection (active chronic otorrhea or myringitis; the ear should be dry 6 to 24 months prior to surgery), and tissue (poor general condition, meatoplasty required; owing to the significance of the disease, poor mucosa of the middle ear) and eustachian tube dysfunction (middle ear effusion or a severely collapsed TM). Factors that failed to show statistically significant adverse effects in audiologic results included prior failed surgery, scutum defect repair without TM repair, myringoplasty, and staged surgery.

Loss of the stapes superstructure was found by Mills (1993) and by Smyth and Patterson (1985) to be associated with a poorer outcome in ossiculoplasty. To achieve success in ossiculoplasty, Smyth and Patterson (1985) concluded that the postoperative air-conduction average over the speech frequencies 0, 5, 1, 2, and 4 kHz must be < 30 dB or the interaural difference reduced to < 15 dB. Fifteen decibels corresponds to the cross-attenuation effect of the skull (Browning, 1986). If these criteria are not met, the patient will unlikely be aware of the audiometric improvement.

Options for Reconstruction of the Ossicular Chain

There are many options for ossicular reconstruction. They can be classified into three general groups. First, autograft prostheses include tissue harvested from the patient and used for reconstructing the ossicular chain. Examples of autografts include the patient's own ossicles or cartilage. Second, homograft prostheses are derived from human donor tissue, screened, and treated to avoid transmission of disease and are preserved for later use. Examples of homograft prostheses include the TM, ossicles, and cartilage. Although these tissues are natural, the alleged risk of transfer of infectious diseases, such as Creutzfeldt-Jacob disease and human immunodeficiency virus (HIV), is a potential risk but has never been reported after transplantation of tympano-ossicular grafts (Vercruysse et al, 2002). Third, artificial prostheses are synthetic and biocompatible; examples of these include high-density polyethylene sponge (Plastipore), aluminum oxide ceramic, and hydroxyapatite (Chole and Skarada, 1999).

Many reconstructive options are available depending on the type of ossicular dysfunction that occurs. Figure 84-1 represents the anatomic defect present when ossicular discontinuity is present and when all or part of the ossicles are present and the recommended options for repair.

Figure 84-2 provides options for reconstruction of the ossicular chain when ossicles are absent. Many of the preferred methods of reconstruction attempt to use the patient's own tissue. However, when this is not possible, prosthetic devices can be used depending on the ossicle(s) remaining. When prosthetic devices are used, they are classified according to the reconstruction desired. For example, incus prostheses are used when the malleus and

stapes are present, and incus-stapes prostheses are used when the stapes footplate is present along with an intact malleus. When the stapes superstructure is present, a partial ossicular replacement prosthesis (PORP) can be used, and when only the stapes footplate is available, a total ossicular replacement prosthesis (TORP) can be used.

Figure 84-3 provides options for reconstruction of the ossicular chain when fixation is present. When fixation of the incudomalleal or incudostapedial joints occurs, usually from tympanosclerosis, simple mobilization or an epitympanic bypass procedure can be performed. Albu and colleagues (2000) reviewed 115 patients with middle ear tympanosclerosis and concluded that in ossicular attic fixation, atticotomy and mobilization of the ossicles yielded better results than did the epitympanic bypass procedure. However, the difference did not reach statistical significance. Depending on the degree of fixation noted, we recommend an incus interposition procedure in severe cases, but each case must be individualized along with the patient's expectations of the procedure chosen.

Outcomes in Ossiculoplasty

Table 84-1 presents the outcomes with various methods of ossicular reconstruction by closure of the air–bone gap postoperatively and the associated extrusion rate.

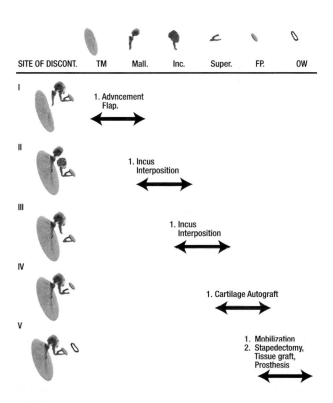

FIGURE 84-1. Recommended options for ossicular chain reconstruction (discontinuity, ossicles present). FP = footplate; OW = oval window; Super. = superstructure; TM = tympanic membrane.

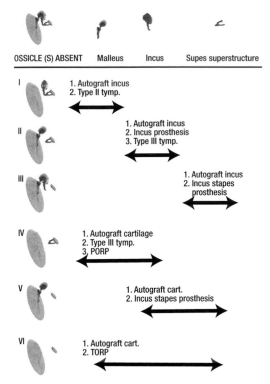

FIGURE 84-2. Recommended options for ossicular chain reconstruction (discontinuity, ossicles absent). PORP = partial ossicular replacement prosthesis; TORP = total ossicular replacement prosthesis; Tymp. = tympanosclerosis.

Reasons for Ossiculoplasty Failure

The first aim of a tympanoplasty is to remove middle ear disease. Many uncertainties in the hostile environment associated with surgery for chronic ear disease contribute to failure of the surgery, including eustachian tube dysfunction, middle ear adhesions, and mucosal disease. These abnormalities lead to retraction of the TM, atelectasis of the middle ear, middle ear effusion, and extrusion of the graft or prosthesis.

The second aim in tympanoplasty is to restore hearing. Unfortunately, the second goal is not easy to attain. Many factors may contribute to failure. These factors include anatomic problems related to the healing process after the first stage (ie, perforation or malposition of the new TM) or that may arise during or after the second stage (ie, perforation of the new TM with or without extrusion of the prosthesis).

A common etiology for perforation with or without extrusion of the prosthesis is dysfunction of the eustachian tube, which causes retraction of the graft and increases the tension of the prosthesis against the graft, which may be broken, causing a partial or complete extrusion of the prosthesis. One proposed method to decrease failure is to sever the tensor tympani tendon during ossicular reconstruction. This may give the TM a flatter configura-

tion and slight lateralization, thus facilitating placement of the prosthesis and decreasing the tendency of the TM to medialize in patients with substandard eustachian tube function (Slater et al, 1997).

Another common etiology is the direct contact between the prosthesis and the graft. This phenomenon may be caused by both sliding and reabsorption of the cartilage.

Functional failures may be attributable to too short a prosthesis, sliding of the prosthesis, fracture of the crura of stapes, or contraction and movement of the healing TM after the second stage. Each of these causes loss of connection between the footplate and the graft (Sellari-Franceschini et al, 1987).

Recommendations for Ossiculoplasty in Children

Few studies of ossicular reconstruction in children have been reported. Silverstein and colleagues (1986) reported 18 cases of ossicular reconstruction in children in which Plastipore TORPs and PORPs were used. Poor results were obtained with a 44% failure rate and a 17% extrusion rate. But Sheehy (1985), as well as Kessler and colleagues (1994), have reported the use of PORPs and TORPs in children with success rates similar to those of adults. In Kessler and colleagues' study, the mean age was 9.8 years.

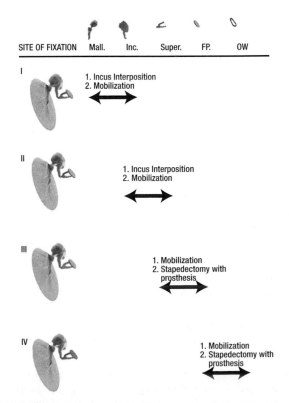

FIGURE 84-3. Recommended options for ossicular chain reconstruction (ossicular chain fixation). FP = footplate; OW = oval window; Super. = superstructure.

TABLE 84-1. Outcomes of Ossicular Reconstruction

Prosthesis	Hearing Loss < 20 dB at ≤ 1 Yr Postoperatively (%)	Hearing Loss < 20 dB at ≤ 1 Yr Postoperatively (%)	Extrusion (%)	Reference
Autograft				
Incus interposition	74		12.5	Nikolaou et al, 1992
	68			Jackson et al, 1983
PORP				
Incus replacement hydroxyapatite		83		Grote, 1990
	85			Wehrs, 1989
Incudostapedial joint		91	0	Schwetschenau and Isaacson, 1999
Plastipore	77	48	0	Colletti et al, 1987
	63		4	Bayazit, 1999
	49		10	Jackson et al, 1983
	73		7	Brackmann et al, 1984
		43	11	Smyth, 1982
Polyethylene	81	75	1	Slater et al, 1997
	40		50	Nikolaou et al, 1992
	78	89	0	Daniels et al, 1998
Ceramic	89		5	Nikolaou et al, 1992
Cartilage		65	0	Chole and Skarada, 1999
Hydroxyapatite/Plastipore		48	4	Macias et al, 1995
	43		4	Chole and Skarada, 1999
	71		7	Black, 1990
TORP				
Incus/stapes (hydroxyapatite/Plastipore)	50		4	Chole and Skarada, 1999
Incus/stapes (hydroxyapatite)		76	0	Grote, 1990
Plastipore	68	46	23	Colletti et al, 1987
	84			Brackmann and Sheehy, 1979
		55	8	Goldenberg, 1990
	43		4	Bayazit, 1999
Polyethylene	61		14	Nikolaou et al, 1992
	68	54	1	Slater et al, 1997
Ceramic	65		9	Nikolaou et al, 1997
Cartilage		65		Chole and Skarada, 1999
Hydroxyapatite/Plastipore	30		4	Chole and Skarada, 1999
		21	0	Macias et al, 1995
Malleus-footplate (hydroxyapatite)	73	71	0	Colletti and Fiorino, 1999
Tympanic membrane–footplate (hydroxyapatite)	75	60	0	Colletti and Fiorino, 1999
Hydroxyapatite/fluoroplastic	61	55	2	Daniels et al, 1998

PORP = partial ossicular replacement prosthesis; TORP = total ossicular replacement prosthesis.

Hearing results of an air–bone gap < 20 dB were noted in 54% of cases, with an extrusion rate of 13%. Tos and Lau (1989) evaluated autografts and homografts in children and found hearing results of 58% for an air–bone gap < 20 dB that remained stable. Owing to the lack of long-term use of middle ear prostheses in children, autograft materials are primarily used to reconstruct the ossicular chain (Chandrasekhar et al, 1995).

The most effective method of managing ossicular chain abnormalities is prevention of disease, that is, TM retraction treated with placement of a ventilation tube, cartilage graft, or both. The challenge and hesitancy to perform ossiculoplasty in children are primarily related to eustachian tube dysfunction with difficulty in controlling middle ear disease and cholesteatoma. With some reported failure rates higher in children than in adults, many would argue that ossicular reconstruction be postponed until a later age (Schwetschenau and Isaacson, 1999).

However, it must be emphasized that the same concepts and principles of successful tympanoplasty in adults and children should be followed. Once the child's ear is made safe and stable, ossicular reconstruction is the next goal and completes the restoration of normal middle ear function. Some express that children differ only in that they may be more likely to require postsurgical tympanostomy tube insertion to maintain a stable ear (Chandrasekhar et al, 1995).

Even though we have a paucity of studies that have evaluated short- and long-term outcomes of ossiculoplasty in children, the surgeon must have some guidelines for recommending these operations in the pediatric age group. Currently, we most frequently recommend incus interposition or a prosthesis in children when there has been no otitis media in ears without tympanostomy tubes for four or more seasons in both ears. Failure of the graft/prosthesis over time is usually the result of postoperative middle ear effusion, atelectasis, or both. Likewise, a similar ossicular reconstruction in children who have cholesteatoma removed from the middle ear is usually withheld until the middle ear is found to be free of disease (eg, at the time of "second-look" tympanotomy) because residual or recurrent cholesteatoma at the site of the reconstruction will usually result in failure of the graft or prosthesis. However, the timing and treatment option chosen for children should be individualized.

References

Albu S, Baabighian G, Trabalzini F. Surgical treatment of tympanosclerosis. Am J Otol 2000;21:631–5.

Austin DF. Ossicular reconstruction. Otolaryngol Clin North Am 1972;5:145–60.

Bayazit Y. Functional results of Plastipore prostheses for middle-ear ossicular chain reconstruction. Laryngoscope 1999;109:709–11.

Bellucci RJ. Dual classification of tympanoplasty. Laryngoscope 1973;83:1754–8.

Black B. Design and development of a contoured ossicular replacement prosthesis: clinical trials of 125 cases. Am J Otol 1990;11:85–9.

Black B. Ossiculoplasty prognosis: the SPITE method of assessment. Am J Otol 1992;13:544–51.

Brackmann DE, Sheehy JL. Tympanoplasty with TORPs and PORPs. Laryngoscope 1979;89:108–14.

Brackmann DE, Sheehy JL, Luxford WM. TORPs and PORPs in tympanoplasty: a review of 1042 operations. Otolaryngol Head Neck Surg 1984;92:32–7.

Browning GG. Clinical otology and audiology. London: Butterworths; 1986.

Chandrasekhar S, House J, Devgan U. Pediatric tympanoplasty. A 10 year experience. Arch Otolaryngol Head Neck Surg 1995;121:873.

Chole RA, Skarada DJ. Middle ear reconstructive techniques. Otolaryngol Clin North Am 1999;32:489–503.

Colletti V, Fiorino FG. Malleus to footplate prosthetic interposition: experience with 265 patients. Otolaryngol Head Neck Surg 1999;120:437–44.

Colletti V, Fiorino FG, Sittoni V. Minisculptured ossicle grafts versus implants: long-term results. Am J Otol 1987;8:553–9.

Daniels RL, Rizer FM, Schuring AG, Lippy WL. Partial ossicular reconstruction in children: a review of 62 operations. Laryngoscope 1998;108:1674–81.

Gibb AG, Pang YT. Current considerations in the etiology and diagnosis of tympanosclerosis. Eur Arch Otorhinolaryngol 1994;251:439–51.

Goldenberg RA. Hydroxylapatite ossicular replacement prostheses. Laryngoscope 1990;100:693–700.

Grote J. Reconstruction of the middle ear with hydroxyapatite implants: long-term results. Ann Otol Rhinol Laryngol 1990;144:12–6.

Hough J. Incudostapedial joint separation: Etiology, treatment and significances. Laryngoscope 1959;69:644.

Jackson CG, Glassock ME 3rd, Nissen AJ, et al. Ossicular chain reconstruction: the TORP and PORP in chronic ear disease. Laryngoscope 1983;93:981–8.

Kartush JM. Ossicular chain reconstruction: capitulum to malleus. Otolaryngol Clin North Am 1994;27:689–715.

Kessler A, Potsic WP, Marsh RR. Total and partial ossicular replacement prostheses in children. Otolaryngol Head Neck Surg 1994;110:302–3.

Macias JD, Glasscock ME 3rd, Widick MH, et al. Ossiculoplasty using the black hydroxylapatite hybrid ossicular replacement prostheses. Am J Otol 1995;16:718–21.

Mills RP. The influence of pathological and technical variables on hearing results in ossiculoplasty. Clin Otolaryngol 1993;18:202–51.

Moretz WH. Ossiculoplasty with an intact stapes: superstructure versus footplate prosthesis placement. Laryngoscope 1998;108:1–12.

Nikolaou A, Bourikas Z, Maltas V, Aidonis A. Ossiculoplasty with the use of autografts and synthetic prosthetic materials: a comparison of results in 165 cases. J Laryngol Otol 1992;106:692–4.

Schwetschenau EL, Isaacson G. Ossiculoplasty in young children with the Applebaum incudostapedial joint prosthesis. Laryngoscope 1999;109:1621–5.

Sellari-Franceschini S, Piragine F, Bruschini P, Berrettini S. TORPS and PORPS: causes of failure. Am J Otol 1987;8:551–2.

Sheehy J. Cholesteatoma surgery in children. Am J Otol 1985;6:170–2.

Silverstein H, McDaniel AB, Lichtenstein R. A comparison of PORP, TORP, and incus homograft for ossicular reconstruction in chronic ear surgery. Laryngoscope 1986;96:159–65.

Slater PW, Rozer FM, Schuring AG, Lippy WH. Practical use of total and partial ossicular replacement prostheses in ossiculoplasty. Laryngoscope 1997;107:1193–8.

Smyth G. Five year report on PORPs and TORPs. Otolaryngol Head Neck Surg 1982;90:343–6.

Smyth GD, Patterson CC. Results of middle ear reconstruction: do patients and surgeons agree? Am J Otol 1985;6:276–9.

Tos M, Lau T. Stability of tympanoplasty in children. Otolaryngol Clin North Am 1989;22:15–28.

Vercruysse JP, Offeciers FE, Somers T, et al. The use of malleus allografts in ossiculoplasty. Laryngoscope 2002;112:1782–4.

Wehrs RE. Incus replacement prostheses of hydroxylapatite in middle ear reconstruction. Am J Otol 1989;10:181–2.

Chapter 85

CONDUCTIVE HEARING LOSS

YAEL RAZ, MD

The auricle, external auditory canal, tympanic membrane (TM), and ossicular chain participate in localization, amplification, and transmission of sound to the cochlea. Disruption of this conductive mechanism at any point between the external meatus and the stapes footplate may result in conductive hearing loss. This chapter describes the general approach to the diagnosis and management of conductive hearing loss with a focus on otitis media (OM) and its sequelae. More detailed information regarding the management of specific causes of conductive hearing loss (acute otitis media [AOM], otitis media with effusion [OME], cholesteatoma, and ossicular discontinuity) is contained in respective chapters focused on these topics. Although OM and its sequelae account for the majority of conductive hearing loss, other causes, such as trauma, congenital anomalies, and neoplasms, must also be considered (Table 85-1).

OM and Conductive Hearing Loss

Acute Otitis Media

Conductive hearing loss is the most common complication of OM. There is a wide range in the character and severity of the hearing loss depending on the type of infection and degree of pathology. AOM may present with normal hearing or a mild to moderate conductive loss depending on the extent of middle ear effusion, myrinigitis, or mucosal edema. Conductive losses that occur as a result of AOM are often self-limited or reversible with appropriate treatment. However, AOM can result in long-term conductive hearing losses owing to chronic TM perforation, adhesive OM, or tympanosclerosis with ossicular fixation.

Otitis Media with Effusion

OME usually results in a conductive loss of 20 to 30 dB, although the degree of loss can vary depending on the character and quantity of the effusion (Bluestone and Klein, 2003). Recurrent or persistent OME can be managed with observation, medical therapy, or tympanostomy tubes. A trial of antibiotics is appropriate because a significant bacterial presence has been demonstrated by polymerase chain reaction, even when standard cultures are

negative (Post et al, 1995). Depending on the duration of the effusion and the severity of the hearing loss, tympanostomy tubes may be indicated. In the adult patient with OME who is significantly debilitated by the aural fullness and hearing loss, tympanostomy tubes may be inserted in the office without an initial trial of medical therapy.

TM Perforation

Both acute and chronic OM can result in perforation of the TM. Additionally, surgical therapy for recurrent AOM or OME (ie, tympanostomy tubes) may result in an iatrogenic perforation. The degree of hearing loss associated with a TM perforation depends on its location and extent. A small perforation may not have an appreciable effect on hearing, whereas large perforations may result in an air–bone gap of 20 to 30 dB. However, when there is a discontinuity in the ossicular chain, hearing acuity is greater in the presence of a perforation. In this setting, rather than serving as an amplifier, the TM poses an obstacle to sound transmission to the inner ear.

Acute perforations associated with AOM demonstrate a high rate of spontaneous closure, and observation is indicated for approximately 3 months. Chronic perforations (present for over 3 months) should be repaired to prevent entry of bacteria and to allow for bathing and swimming without precautions. In children, the timing of repair needs to be considered carefully as the perforation may be of therapeutic value in providing ventilation. Repair of a perforation when a child is still vulnerable to recurrent OM may result in the need for reperforating the newly grafted membrane to place a tympanostomy tube. Some authors have argued that there is no indication to delay tympanoplasty in children (Lau and Tos, 1986), whereas others suggest waiting until the age of 7 years to decrease the likelihood of OM (Sheehy and Anderson, 1980). Another reasonable option is to wait until the child has been free of infections for at least 1 year (Bluestone and Klein, 2003).

TM Retraction, Middle Ear Atelectasis, and Adhesive OM

TM retraction and middle ear atelectasis are due to eustachian tube dysfunction and resultant negative middle ear pressure. Retraction pockets are especially com-

TABLE 85-1. Etiologies of Conductive Hearing Loss

External ear	Iatrogenic	Penetrating foreign body
Cerumen impaction	Postoperative	Temporal bone fracture
Otitis externa	Traumatic cerumen removal	Ossicular dislocation
Cholesteatoma		Neoplasm
Keratitis obturans	**Tympanic membrane**	Squamous cell carcinoma
Foreign body	Perforation	Rhabdomyosarcoma
Exostosis	Otitis media	Otosclerosis
Osteoma	Iatrogenic (usually due to ventilation tubes)	Congenital ossicular hypoplasia/dysplasia
Trauma	Penetrating trauma	Ossicular fixation
Canal laceration	Barotrauma	Ossicular discontinuity
Auricular hematoma	Myringitis	Barotrauma
Temporal bone fracture	Retraction/eustachian tube dysfunction	Iatrogenic
Neoplasm		
Squamous cell carcinoma of the skin	**Middle ear**	**Inner ear**
Eosinophilic granuloma	Acute otitis media	Cochlear conductive loss
Atresia	Recurrent acute otitis media	Basilar membrane stiffness
Congenital	Otitis media with effusion	Enlarged vestibular aqueduct
Acquired	Adhesive otitis media	Superior canal dehiscence syndrome
Chondritis/perichondritis	Chronic otitis media	
	Cholesteatoma	**Combined**
	Tympanosclerosis	Anotia
	Trauma	Microtia

mon in the pars flaccida and the posterosuperior quadrant of the pars tensa. In these areas, the retraction pocket can drape over the ossicles resulting in erosion and ossicular discontinuity. Insertion of a tympanostomy tube may be helpful in reversing this process.

The atelectatic TM should be evaluated with pneumatic insufflation. Failure of the TM to separate from the promontory and the ossicular chain may be due to significant negative middle ear pressure. In the operating room, administration of nitrous oxide prior to myringotomy is helpful in these cases. However, it is also possible that the TM is bound to the underlying structures as a result of adhesive OM, a fibrous tissue proliferation that occasionally occurs in response to inflammation (Figure 85-1). Adhesive OM may result in a conductive loss owing to reduced compliance of the TM or reduced mobility of the ossicular chain. Establishing ventilation with a tympanostomy tube may not reverse this process. A tympanoplasty using cartilage to reinforce the TM may help to prevent ossicular damage owing to rarefying osteitis with resultant necrosis. However, patients with adhesive OM often retain excellent hearing. A reasonable alternative is close monitoring and intervention only in cases of accumulation of squamous debris or deterioration in hearing. In children, a rush to address this process at an age at which eustachian tube function is not well developed may result in recurrent middle ear atelectasis.

Cholesterol Granuloma

Cholesterol granuloma is another sequela of OM that may result in hearing loss (Figure 85-2). This process is characterized by foreign body reaction in an occluded space and may occur in the middle ear, mastoid, or petrous apex. When the granuloma involves the middle ear, the TM has a blue appearance, although the actual effusion is typically mustard colored. Middle ear cholesterol granulomas are characterized by viscous, granular effusions, which are difficult to clear with myringotomy and often require tympanoplasty and mastoid surgery (Bluestone and Klein, 2003).

Chronic Suppurative Otitis Media

Chronic suppurative otitis media (CSOM), with or without cholesteatoma, is often accompanied by erosion of

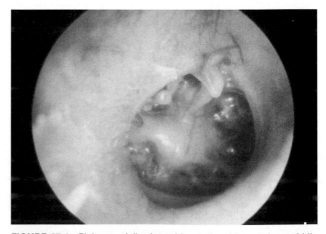

FIGURE 85-1. Right ear. Adhesive otitis media with complete middle ear atelectasis. The long process of the malleus is rotated inferiorly and contacts the promontory. The long process of the incus has necrosed, and the tympanic membrane is contacting the stapes capitulum. Clinical photographs courtesy of Barry Hirsch, MD, University of Pittsburgh, Pittsburgh, PA.

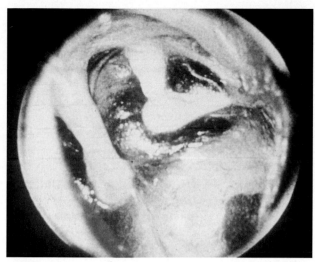

FIGURE 85-2. Left ear. Cholesterol granuloma resulting in a blue appearance of the tympanic membrane. Clinical photographs courtesy of Barry Hirsch, MD, University of Pittsburgh, Pittsburgh, PA.

the ossicles and conductive hearing loss. Ossicular fixation or discontinuity may be encountered. If the disease process itself does not result in ossicular discontinuity, the incus may need to be removed for full visualization and excision of a cholesteatoma, resulting in a complete conductive loss. Occasionally, hearing remains intact despite ossicular erosion and discontinuity because the cholesteatoma bridges the gap in the ossicular chain. This possibility should be discussed prior to surgery so that the patient has a reasonable expectation of the postoperative hearing outcome. In the presence of active middle ear and mastoid disease, an attempt at restoration of the ossicular chain is more likely to fail (Murphy, 2000), and strong consideration should be given to restoring hearing at a planned second-stage procedure.

Ossicular Discontinuity

Ossicular discontinuity can occur in the absence of cholesteatoma as a result of posterosuperior pars tensa retraction or adhesive OM with resultant rarefying osteitis. The most vulnerable site is the incudostapedial joint, usually secondary to necrosis of the long process of the incus. The incus is particularly susceptible because of its poor blood supply and because retraction pockets tend to form in the posterosuperior quadrant of the pars tensa, directly overlying the long process of the incus. For this reason, the posterosuperior quadrant is also a frequent site of acquired cholesteatoma, which may contribute to erosion of the ossicular chain and conductive hearing loss. When there is a discontinuity in the ossicular chain and the TM is intact, a maximal conductive loss (50 to 60 dB) will be seen. However, if a perforation is present, the loss may be less severe. Hypercompliance on impedance testing is suggestive of ossicular discontinuity.

Ossicular Fixation

Ossicular fixation secondary to adhesive OM, tympanosclerosis, congenital ossicular fixation, or otosclerosis must also be considered in the differential of conductive hearing loss. In this case, impedance testing may reveal decreased compliance. Tympanosclerosis occurs as a response to trauma or inflammation and is characterized by chalky white deposits within the TM. When this process is restricted to the eardrum (myringosclerosis), these hyaline deposits typically do not affect hearing. However, this process can extend to the middle ear and involve the ossicles, resulting in a conductive hearing loss. Fixation secondary to tympanosclerosis can be surgically released; however, refixation may pose a problem. Stapedectomy for tympanosclerosis is associated with a higher incidence of sensorineural hearing loss (Chole and Choo, 1998).

Ossicular fixation can also occur secondary to a congenital fixation of the malleus head, incus, or stapes. The most common anomaly is stapedial fixation (Teunissen and Cremers, 1993). Congenital stapedial fixation results from abnormal development and ossification of the annular ligament, which surrounds the stapes footplate. In otosclerosis, bone resorption and subsequent deposition across the annular ligament also result in stapedial fixation and a progressive conductive loss. Patients with congenital stapedial fixation can usually be distinguished from those with a juvenile onset of otosclerosis because their hearing loss is typically fixed and more severe and manifests at an earlier age (De La Cruz et al, 1999).

Evaluation

History and Physical Examination

A detailed history and physical examination are critical in guiding providers through the long list of differential diagnoses for conductive hearing loss. The onset, character, and severity of the hearing loss (constant or fluctuating, sudden or progressive) should be delineated. The history should also address previous otologic infections, associated otologic symptoms (aural fullness, pain, otorrhea), and the patient's (or parents') assessment of the degree of functional impairment. Additional issues that should be addressed when examining children include prenatal history, developmental milestones, school performance, and language development. Family history can point to hereditary causes of hearing loss and can prevent unwanted surprises in the operating room, such as a stapes gusher in a child with X-linked hereditary mixed hearing loss. A detailed review of systems may reveal involvement of other systems (ie, cardiac, renal), suggestive of a syndromic diagnosis.

Physical examination should include a complete head and neck examination with an eye for manifestations of a syndrome (abnormal facies, blue sclera). Otologic exam-

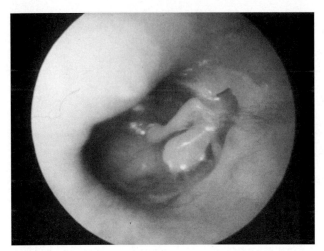

FIGURE 85-3. Left ear. Sculpted incus used to re-establish ossicular continuity. Clinical photographs courtesy of Barry Hirsch, MD, University of Pittsburgh, Pittsburgh, PA.

ination should include pneumatic otoscopy, which is often critical in assessing the middle ear for an effusion or distinguishing a reversible retraction from an adhesive process. The TM must be visualized in its entirety; retraction pockets and cholesteatoma may be obscured by cerumen, particularly in the epitympanum. Otomicroscopy enhances visualization and facilitates evaluation, particularly when aspiration or gentle palpation is required.

Audiologic Testing

Tuning fork testing, when feasible, can often give the provider a rapid means of assessing the nature and severity of hearing loss and can corroborate audiologic testing. When the hearing loss is associated with newly diagnosed AOM or OME, it is often appropriate to initiate a trial of medical therapy without obtaining a hearing test. However, if the condition persists or if resolution of the infection is not accompanied by a return to a normal baseline, a formal evaluation of hearing should be performed. In children, audiologic testing is performed in an age-appropriate fashion. Audiologists with experience in evaluating children can sometimes obtain masked air and bone, even in the toddler years. Immittance testing, including tympanometry and acoustic reflexes, is valuable in confirming clinical findings. Speech awareness or, if possible, speech reception thresholds should be obtained as well.

Laboratory Studies

Laboratory evaluation is guided by the findings revealed on history and physical examination. If there is a history of recurrent infections involving other systems, it may be appropriate to obtain studies of immune function. Allergy testing and evaluation for immotile cilia or sweat chloride testing are appropriate in selected patients. Other studies are ordered as dictated by clinical suspicion, including genetic testing.

Radiologic Imaging

In the pediatric population, conductive hearing loss without history or clinical evidence of OM should be evaluated with high-resolution temporal bone computed tomography (CT). Although a CT scan may assist in identifying the cause of the conductive defect, it is indicated primarily in evaluating the otic capsule and identifying abnormalities that might pose an increased risk at the time of surgery, particularly if a stapes procedure is considered. An enlarged vestibular aqueduct or a wide communication between the internal auditory canal and the cochlea is associated with an increased risk of a stapes gusher (De La Cruz et al, 1999). Identification of these abnormalities preoperatively may help to guide the decision-making process. Additionally, abnormalities in the course of the facial nerve are noted more frequently in the setting of congenital ossicular anomalies and can often be appreciated preoperatively with imaging studies.

Management of Conductive Hearing Loss

Otitis-Related Conductive Loss

The management of conductive hearing loss owing to infection or middle ear effusion is discussed in detail in the chapters on AOM, OME, and CSOM. There is some controversy in the literature regarding the extent to which conductive loss related to OM (and particularly OME) should be treated. Given the prevalence of AOM and OME, it is evident that many young children experience prolonged periods of conductive impairment at developmental stages that are critical for speech and language development. The long-term effects of this deficit are a matter of some debate, with some studies reporting no significant consequences (Rovers et al, 2000) and others reporting a deleterious effect on speech and language acquisition (Petinou et al, 2001). Given the absence of clear evidence on this matter, the provider must involve the patient and family in a discussion of the risks and benefits and formulate an individualized treatment plan.

Once infection and effusion have been addressed, re-examination with pneumatic otoscopy is critical. With the exception of transient hearing loss in the context of an uncomplicated acute infection, formal audiologic evaluation should be repeated once infection has been addressed and ventilation has been established. Otherwise, one might miss an underlying fixed loss owing to otosclerosis, a congenital ossicular anomaly, or a sequela of OM. A middle ear effusion can sometimes linger for weeks, causing a persistent conductive hearing loss on follow-up testing. These patients should be re-evaluated. If the effusion has not cleared after a period of 3 months, tympanostomy tubes should be considered.

Non–Otitis-Related Conductive Hearing Loss

In the setting of a stable conductive hearing loss without evidence of cholesteatoma and after acute infection and/or effusion have been ruled out, hearing restoration is an elective procedure. The patient, family, and physician need to weigh the risks and benefits of the available options, which usually include observation, aural rehabilitation, or surgery. In making this decision, many factors need to be taken into account, including the severity of the hearing loss, whether one or both ears are involved, the age of the patient, and the status of the eustachian tube function. Surgery is generally reserved for moderate to severe conductive losses with pure-tone averages > 30 dB and speech reception threshold > 35 dB (Briggs and Luxford, 1994).

Unilateral conductive losses in young children (less than 5 years old) can be managed with preferential seating, with or without amplification, and surgical management can be deferred until the child is old enough to participate in the decision-making process. There is a lack of consensus in the literature regarding the sequelae of untreated unilateral hearing loss. Many authors recommend a conservative approach for unilateral hearing loss. However, other studies point to a detrimental effect on school performance (Bess and Tharpe, 1984). Consequently, management recommendations regarding unilateral hearing loss have varied. Some surgeons encourage an early surgical approach to maximize binaural auditory input during the school years (Kessler et al, 1994). Others encourage delaying surgery until the child is less susceptible to OM, can participate in the decision-making process, and can perhaps tolerate exploration under local anesthesia. Most authors would agree that stapes surgery should not be performed in young children because increased susceptibility to OM in the perioperative period results in a higher risk of labyrinthitis and sensorineural hearing loss. If there is significant bilateral hearing loss, particularly in children, amplification must be instituted immediately, and surgical candidacy can then be assessed.

Exploratory Tympanotomy

There is no "cookbook" approach to exploration of the middle ear. Rather, the approach must be custom-tailored to the individual patient's anatomy and pathology. Many reconstructive techniques are available, and the best option is often the technique with which a particular surgeon has the most experience. The surgical approach (transcanal, postauricular, transmastoid) will depend on the patient's age and anatomy. Adults can often be explored under local anesthetic with intravenous sedation. Young children require a general anesthetic. If the patient requires ossiculoplasty as part of a larger operation for CSOM, consideration should be given to staging the ossiculoplasty until the middle ear condition stabilizes.

All three ossicles must be carefully palpated because multiple causes for conductive hearing loss may coexist. Re-exploration after failed stapes often reveals a secondary problem in the ossicular chain (Vincent et al, 1999). If ossicular discontinuity is encountered and the incus is usable, then incus interposition is a good option, associated with a low risk of extrusion or absorption (Figure 85-3). Many synthetic prostheses are available. Successful hearing outcomes depend less on the specific prosthesis used and more on adherence to certain critical principles. These include a columnar orientation of the reconstruction to maximize stability, interposition of cartilage between the TM and the prosthesis, and careful measurement of prosthesis length to avoid slippage or extrusion. Some authors argue that ossicular prostheses have a higher complication rate in children compared with adults (Silverstein et al, 1986). Perhaps in this population, stronger consideration should be given to using an incus interposition technique when possible.

When stapes fixation is encountered in conjunction with incudomalleolar anomalies, hearing results have been poorer (De La Cruz et al, 1999). In these cases, consideration should be given to hearing aids. Congenital middle ear abnormalities mandate extra caution with regard to the facial nerve because its course may be variable. Patients who are poor surgical candidates because of an underlying medical condition or because they have failed multiple previous attempts at reconstruction should be offered hearing aids. It is also prudent to defer surgery in select patients in whom exploration reveals significant abnormalities (ie, facial nerve directly overlying the oval window, aplasia of the oval window). Heroic efforts in the face of such significant anomalies, although sometimes transiently effective, are often associated with disappointing long-term hearing results (Lambert, 1990). In these settings, surgical correction should be attempted only after a thorough discussion with the patient and/or family to ensure appropriate expectations and a complete understanding of the risks and alternatives.

If chronic otorrhea precludes the use of air-conduction aids, then conventional bone-conduction aids or bone-anchored hearing aids (BAHAs) are a possibility. Bone-conduction hearing aids function through direct vibratory stimulation of the cochlea with a device placed behind the ear. These hearing aids can be held in place with glasses or a headband. They need to abut the skull with a tight fit, and this can create discomfort and pressure-related skin complications. The BAHA (Tjellstrom et al, 1981) snaps on to a titanium implant, which is osseointegrated into the mastoid cortex. This alleviates the discomfort associated with a headband, and patients report better sound fidelity (Bejar-Solar et al, 2000; Papsin et al, 1997). However, a minor surgical procedure is required to insert the titanium screw, and the patient must be prepared to clean and care for the implant site regularly. BAHAs should be considered in children with conductive hearing loss in an only hearing ear; in middle ear anomalies, such as stapedial fixation combined with incudomalleolar anomalies; and as an alternative to surgical reconstruction in canal atresia.

Special Considerations

Craniofacial Anomalies

Many craniofacial anomalies, including cleft palate and Down syndrome, are associated with middle ear/eustachian tube abnormalities that result in conductive hearing loss. Associated developmental defects pose a challenge to normal speech and language acquisition. This subset of patients requires a particularly aggressive approach to address OM to maximize their auditory input. Certain precautions must also be taken in caring for patients with craniofacial abnormalities. For example, in patients with Down syndrome, a radiologic assessment of cervical stability is indicated prior to surgical intervention. Branchiogenic syndromes such as Treacher Collins affect the mandibular arch and the ossicular chain, posing a potential risk of significant airway compromise at the time of surgery. Facial nerve anomalies are also more common and require an extra level of caution.

Underlying Hearing Loss

Otitis-related conductive hearing loss needs to be managed aggressively in patients with underlying hearing loss, whether it is a fixed conductive impairment or a sensorineural loss. A superimposed conductive loss may completely eliminate the already severely diminished auditory input. Patients with significant underlying hearing loss may be at a higher risk for OME (Janzen and Schaefer, 1984) and should be monitored on a regular basis, particularly if they derive some benefit from amplification.

Conclusion

This chapter summarizes the approach to evaluation and management of conductive hearing loss with an emphasis on the sequelae of OM. Critical points include the need for reassessment of otitis-related hearing impairment once the infection has resolved and normal ventilation has been established. The treatment plan must be tailored to the individual patient and take into account age, eustachian tube function, degree of hearing loss, and whether one or both ears are affected. Treatment options generally include observation, aural rehabilitation, and surgery. Elective surgical management of conductive hearing loss should be delayed until eustachian tube function has stabilized, particularly if stapes surgery is entertained. Children with craniofacial anomalies that affect speech and language or underlying sensorineural hearing loss require increased surveillance and prompt action if a conductive loss is detected.

References

Bejar-Solar I, Rosete M, de Jesus Madrazo M, Baltierra C. Percutaneous bone-anchored hearing aids at a pediatric institution. Otolaryngol Head Neck Surg 2000;122:887–91.

Bess FH, Tharpe AM. Unilateral hearing impairment in children. Pediatrics 1984;74:206–16.

Bluestone CD, Klein JO. Intratemporal complications and sequelae of otitis media. In: Bluestone CD, Alper CM, Arjmand EM, et al, editors. Pediatric otolaryngology. 4th ed. Philadelphia: WB Saunders; 2003. p. 687–763.

Briggs RJ, Luxford WM. Correction of conductive hearing loss in children. Otolaryngol Clin North Am 1994;27:607–20.

Chole RA, Choo MJ. Chronic otitis media, mastoiditis, and petrositis. In: Cummings CW, Fredrickson JM, Krause CJ, et al, editors. Otolaryngology head and neck surgery. 3rd ed. St. Louis: Mosby; 1998. p. 3026–46.

De la Cruz A, Angeli S, Slattery WH. Stapedectomy in children. Otolaryngol Head Neck Surg 1999;120:487–92.

Janzen VD, Schaefer D. Etiology of deafness in Robarts School for the Deaf. J Otolaryngol 1984;13:47–8.

Kessler A, Potsic WP, Marsh R. Total and partial ossicular replacement prostheses in children. Otolaryngol Head Neck Surg 1994;110:302–3.

Lambert PR. Congenital absence of the oval window. Laryngoscope 1990;100:37–40.

Lau T, Tos M. Tympanoplasty in children. An analysis of late results. Am J Otol 1986;7:55–9.

Murphy TP. Hearing results in pediatric patients with chronic otitis media after ossicular reconstruction with partial ossicular replacement prostheses and total ossicular replacement prostheses. Laryngoscope 2000;110:536–44.

Papsin BC, Sirimanna TK, Albert DM, Bailey CM. Surgical experience with bone-anchored hearing aids in children. Laryngoscope 1997;107:801–6.

Petinou KC, Schwartz RG, Gravel JS, Raphael LJ. A preliminary account of phonological and morphophonological perception in young children with and without otitis media. Int J Lang Commun Disord 2001;36:21–42.

Post JC, Preston RA, Aul JJ, et al. Molecular analysis of bacterial pathogens in otitis media with effusion. JAMA 1995;273:1598–604.

Rovers MM, Straatman H, Ingels K, et al. The effect of ventilation tubes on language development in infants with otitis media with effusion: a randomized trial. Pediatrics 2000;106:E42.

Sheehy JL, Anderson RG. Myringoplasty. A review of 472 cases. Ann Otol Rhinol Laryngol 1980;89:331–4.

Silverstein H, McDaniel AB, Lichtenstein R. A comparison of PORP, TORP, and incus homograft for ossicular reconstruction in chronic ear surgery. Laryngoscope 1986;96:159–65.

Teunissen EB, Cremers WR. Classification of congenital middle ear anomalies. Report on 144 ears. Ann Otol Rhinol Laryngol 1993;102:606–12.

Tjellstrom A, Lindstrom J, Hallen O, et al. Osseointegrated titanium implants in the temporal bone. A clinical study on bone-anchored hearing aids. Am J Otol 1981;2:304–10.

Vincent R, Lopez A, Sperling NM. Malleus ankylosis: a clinical, audiometric, histologic, and surgical study of 123 cases. Am J Otol 1999;20:717–25.

Chapter 86

EFFECTS OF OTITIS MEDIA ON CHILDREN'S SPEECH AND LANGUAGE

JOANNE E. ROBERTS, PhD

There continues to be debate over whether recurrent or persistent otitis media (OM) during the first few years of life increases a child's risk for later language and subsequent learning difficulties (Paradise, 1998; Roberts and Wallace, 1997; Ruben et al, 1998; Stool et al, 1994). The fluid in the middle ear that occurs with otitis media with effusion (OME) generally causes mild to moderate fluctuating conductive hearing loss that lasts until the fluid resolves. Since the mid-1960s, studies have reported that children who have experienced repeated or persistent OME in early childhood have lower scores on measures of speech and language skills and in academic achievement (Gravel and Wallace, 1992; Roberts et al, 2002; Shriberg et al, 2000; Teele et al, 1990), whereas other studies do not support this linkage (Paradise et al, 2000; Paradise et al, 2001; Peters et al, 1994; Roberts et al, 2000). This chapter describes how OME in early childhood may possibly affect children's language development, the importance of studying the linkages, the research studies examining the linkage of OME to language learning skills, and strategies and considerations for managing the child with frequent and/or persistent OME.

Importance of Studying the OME and Speech, Language Learning Linkage

OM, after the common cold, is the most frequent illness of early childhood (Lanphear et al, 1997; Schappert, 1992). Annual health care costs related to OM were $5.8 billion in 1998 (Bondy et al, 2000). One of the major reasons for medical management, including antibiotics and tympanostomy tubes, is to prevent any developmental consequences related to OME. Thus, whether OME causes developmental sequelae has highly significant implications for medical management and the well-being of young children. Further, the etiology of many speech and language delays (a slower rate of acquisition than expected), speech and language disorders (impairment in ability, comprehension, or production), and learning difficulties is not known, and the concern that a history of OME contributes to these difficulties has been raised.

Potential Linkage of OME to Later Speech, Language, and Learning

When a child has OME, the middle ear is inflamed, the tympanic membrane between the outer and middle ear is thickened, and fluid is present in the middle ear cavity. The middle ear transmits sound from the outer ear to the inner ear and then via the acoustic nerve to the brain. The fluid generally results in a mild to moderate conductive hearing loss, typically around 26 dB HL (equivalent to plugging your ears with fingers), but can vary from no hearing loss to a moderate loss (around 50 dB HL and hard to hear conversational speech). After the onset of an episode of OME, the fluid can persist for several weeks or even months.

A child who has a mild to moderate fluctuating hearing loss owing to an episode of OME will receive a partial or inconsistent auditory signal, which may result in misperceiving or not hearing words. It has been hypothesized that a child who experiences repeated and persistent episodes of OME and hearing loss may build up an inaccurate catalogue of words and be at a disadvantage for learning the rules of language, which ultimately affects the child's language and academic achievement, particularly in reading and other language-based subjects. It is also hypothesized that children who experience frequent changes in the intensity of signals, owing to a mild hearing loss, may "tune out" when an environment is noisy (eg, the television is on, other children are talking, an open classroom) and therefore develop attention difficulties for information heard in the environment. Recently, the consideration of the child's environment (eg, the responsiveness of the child's mother), as well as the multiple risk and protective factors that can affect children's language and learning, has provided new insight into the potential linkage of OME to children's later language and learning (Roberts and Wallace, 1997; Vernon-Feagans, 1999). Examples of risk factors include the presence of a disability that makes language processing difficult for the child and a child's mother having less than a high school degree. A very supportive and responsive home environment and a child with excellent vocabulary skills are examples of protective factors. Thus, it is proposed that the impact of OME on children's language and learning depends on the amount, timing, and laterality of OME episodes; the amount, timing, and laterality of hearing loss; a child's cognitive, linguistic, and perceptual abilities; the responsiveness and supportiveness of the child's home and child-care environments; and interactions among these variables.

Studies Examining the OME, Speech, Language, and Learning Linkage

During the past three decades, there have been an increasing number of original studies examining whether children who have frequent OME in early childhood score lower on measures of speech, language, and academic achievement than children without such a history. Earlier studies of the OME developmental linkage were retrospective in design using parent report or review of medical records, often collected by different medical providers, to document the frequency of OME. These data collection methods were more likely to contain measurement errors. More recent studies are prospective, with children's OME histories documented longitudinally from early infancy and repeated at specific sampling intervals. The prospective studies are more likely to have greater objectivity and accuracy over time, avoiding many of the methodologic limitations of previous studies.

Several prospective studies have found a relationship between a history of OM in early childhood and later speech and language skills during the preschool and early elementary school years (Gravel and Wallace, 1992; Roberts et al, 2002; Shriberg et al, 2000; Teele et al, 1984; Teele et al, 1990). Children who had more OME in early childhood scored lower in later measures of speech, receptive language, expressive language (Roberts et al, 2002; Teele et al, 1984; Wallace et al, 1988), and academic achievement (Gravel and Wallace, 1992; Teele et al, 1990). However, other studies examining the same language dimensions did not report a relationship between an early history of OME and later measures of receptive language, expressive language, vocabulary, syntax, or school achievement (Paradise et al, 2000; Paradise et al, 2001;

Peters et al, 1994; Teele et al, 1990). Only a few of these prospective studies have examined important factors that may affect the relationship between OME and later language and learning skills.

More recent prospective studies considered the impact of child and environmental factors, such as the extent of hearing loss a child experienced during early childhood, the educational level of the mother, and the responsiveness of the home environment on children's language development. For example, Paradise and colleagues (Feldman et al, 1999; Paradise et al, 2000) reported weak but significant correlations between OME in the first 3 years of life and language development (accounting for 1 to 3% of the variance in language skills), after controlling for many family background variables. Roberts and colleagues (1995, 1998, 2000) did not find a direct relationship between OME or hearing history and children's language skills between 1 and 5 years of age. They did find, however, that the caregiving environment (responsiveness of the child's home and child-care environments) mediated the relationship between children's history of OME and associated hearing loss and later communication development at 1 and 2 years of age but not in the later preschool or early elementary school years. That is, children with more OME and associated hearing loss tended to live in less responsive caregiving environments, and these environments were linked to lower performance in receptive and expressive language at 1 and 2 years of age. These and other ongoing prospective studies highlight the importance of examining the multiple factors that affect children's language development.

Several ongoing prospective studies are providing new and important information on the linkage of a history of OME in early childhood to later language difficulties. Three recent experimental studies (Maw et al, 1999; Rovers et al, 2000; Paradise et al, 2001) compared the effects of prompt versus delayed insertion of tympanostomy tubes (to drain the fluid) on language development. Both Paradise and colleagues (2001) and Rovers and colleagues (2000) found that prompt insertion of tympanostomy tubes did not improve children's language development. Maw and colleagues (1999) did find effects on language development 9 months after treatment with tympanostomy tubes. However, there were no longer differences between the groups 18 months after treatment.

Chronic OME and associated hearing loss in early childhood may be of particular concern for children from special populations who are already at risk for language and learning difficulties (Berman, 2001; Zeisel and Roberts, 2003). Children who have Down syndrome, fragile X syndrome, Turner's syndrome, Williams syndrome, Apert's syndrome, cleft palate, and other craniofacial differences often experience frequent and persistent OME in early childhood (Casselbrant and Mandel, 1999; Zeisel and Roberts, 2003). This increased risk for OME among special populations may be attributable to craniofacial structural abnormalities, hypotonia, or immune deficiencies. A few retrospective studies have reported that a history of OME further delays the speech and language development of children from special populations (Hubbard et al, 1985; Lonigan et al, 1992; Whiteman et al, 1986). Prospective studies documenting the linkages of OME to later development in young children from special populations are lacking and needed.

Several conclusions can be drawn from the research that was prospectively designed, documented OME beginning in infancy, and examined a range of outcomes. First, there is increasing support from prospective studies that for typically developing children, OME may not be a substantial risk factor for later developmental difficulties. Although a few studies report a very mild association between OME and later receptive and expressive language skills from infancy through entry into kindergarten, the effect size is generally very small, accounting for only about 1 to 4% of the variance. The clinical significance of this effect for language and learning is not clear. The quality of the caregiving environment at home and in child care plays a much more important role than OME in affecting children's later language. Second, data from several ongoing prospective studies using correlational and experimental designs and studies considering the many variables that may influence the linkage of OME to later development should provide important information. For example, given that hearing loss, rather than OME, is hypothesized to affect language learning, examining the degree of hearing loss experienced with OME during early childhood is critical. Further, examining factors, such as maternal responsiveness, that may mediate or moderate the impact of OME on children's language and learning is also essential. Third, further study of the impact of a history of OME and associated hearing loss on the language development of children from special populations is needed.

Management Strategies for Children with OME

Despite the lack of consensus, some children experiencing recurrent and persistent OME during the first few years of life may be at increased risk for later language and learning difficulties. Further, for many children from special populations (eg, children with Down syndrome, fragile X syndrome, cleft palate) who are at risk for both persistent OME in early childhood and for language and developmental difficulties, a history of chronic OME and persistent hearing loss may further contribute to language and learning difficulties. The strategies recommended below are appropriate for all children and are particularly important for children with persistent hearing loss owing to OME.

Consider the child Justin, described below, as you review the management strategies:

Justin is a 2 1/2-year-old male who has had four episodes of acute OME since 1 year of age. He has had OME for the past 4 months. He has begun to use some words communicatively, but his mother says he is just not as talkative as his older sister was when she was this age. His parents want to know whether the fluid in his ear is delaying his language and what they can do to help him.

Monitor for Hearing Loss

For children with chronic OME, identifying whether they have hearing loss is very important. The American Speech-Language-Hearing Association (1997) has published guidelines for screening the middle ear and hearing status of preschool and school-age children using acoustic immittance measures (tympanometry) and identification audiometry and for testing infants and developmentally younger children using acoustic immittance measures and either behavioral or electrophysiologic measures. There are differences of opinion about when children at risk for OME or with chronic OME should receive middle ear and hearing screenings. A child's hearing should be tested after 3 months of bilateral OME and/or four to six episodes of OME in a 6-month period with follow-up hearing screenings every 3 months until the effusion has resolved. Hearing should also be screened if parents have concerns about their children's hearing or if there are speech and language delays or a disorder. It is recommended that special populations of children below the age of 5 years who are at increased risk for OME (eg, children with Down syndrome, cleft palate) should be screened several times a year, particularly during the winter months. Additionally, for children enrolled in speech-language therapy who have chronic OME, screening of hearing and middle ear status should occur routinely as part of an ongoing intervention program.

Screen for Language and Other Developmental Delays

The language and developmental skills of children with persistent OME should be screened to determine if a child is showing a language delay. It is recommended that speech and language screenings occur after children have had 3 months of persistent OME, four to six episodes of OME in a 6-month period, whenever hearing loss is present, and/or when families or caregivers express concerns regarding a child's development. Children's speech and language skills can be screened as young as 6 months of age using tests such as the Early Language Milestone Scale (Coplan, 1987) or a parent report form such as the MacArthur Communication Development Inventories (Fenson et al, 1993). A child who fails a communication screening should be referred to a speech-language pathologist, whereas a child who fails a developmental screening should be referred to a psychologist, developmental pediatrician, or special educator.

Encourage a Responsive Language Learning Environment

Children who experience recurrent or persistent OME will benefit from a highly responsive language environment using strategies similar to those recommended for language development. Caregivers should respond to children's communication attempts, provide opportunities for children to participate in conversations, and elaborate on conversational topics. Games such as "peek-a-boo" or "I'm gonna get you" are fun for a child and teach children about conversational turn-taking. Activities that increase children's attention to sounds, words, and phrases, such as "Simon Says" or "The Wheels on the Bus," provide familiar phrases and limited new information. Reading with children also increases children's listening and language skills and introduces early literacy concepts that are important for learning to read. To encourage children's early language and literacy development, see Table 86-1 and Burns and colleagues (1999).

For a child who is experiencing hearing loss owing to OME, techniques used for children with hearing impairment to help a child better hear and understand speech may be useful. Environmental adaptations such as raising the intensity of the voice when talking, facing the child when talking, and seating a child toward the front of the room may be helpful to increase the level of speech. Also, activities that focus on auditory information and reinforce it with visual information should greatly increase children's attention. Further, decreasing background noise by turning off television sets or music may help a child concentrate on speech in the environment. See Table 86-1 for additional suggestions on how to promote children's listening skills.

Finally, some children with a history of OME may exhibit language and other developmental difficulties and may benefit from early intervention. A child should receive speech and language intervention if a speech delay or disorder is present, and intervention would decrease a child's impairment in speech or language. The use of personal or sound-field FM systems has been shown to be beneficial for some children with fluctuating and persistent hearing loss associated with OME. The speaker, such as a teacher, wears a small microphone and FM transmitter and the sound is sent to an earphone worn by the child or to a loudspeaker in the classroom.

Strategies for a Child with OME

For Justin, described earlier, who is experiencing repeated bouts of OME and whose parents have expressed some concerns about his language development, several strategies would be useful. First, Justin's hearing should be tested by an audiologist to determine if he has any hearing loss. If Justin has had 4 to 6 months of OME and a bilateral hearing loss (defined as 20 dB HL in the better ear), the Agency for Health Care Policy and Research guidelines (Stool et al, 1994) recommend that he receive tympanostomy tubes. If less hearing loss is present and the OME persists, Justin's hearing should be monitored every 3 months. Second, given Justin's parents' concern about his speech and lan-

---

TABLE 86-1. Language Learning Strategies for Children with Persistent Otitis Media with Effusion

Promote Language Learning
  Get down to your child's eye level when talking.
  Talk about familiar things in your child's environment (eg, pets, toys) and interests.
  Talk with your child during mealtimes, baths, and throughout the day.
  Play interactive games with your child to encourage talking, such as "pat-a-cake."
  Ask simple questions and pause for your child to respond.
  Respond to what your child is talking about immediately and with interest.
  Add to what your child is saying by using more words.
  Praise your child for talking even if the speech is unclear.
  Take your child many places (library, supermarket, the park) and talk about what you see.
  Say the names of things your child sees or plays with and describe things that happen.
  Talk with your child about what he/she did and will do, why things happen, and feelings.
  Encourage your child to talk to other children.
  Repeat language activities so that your child can learn what to expect.

Promote Listening
  Help children hear and understand your speech.
    Get within 3 feet of your child before speaking.
    Get your child's attention before speaking.
    Face your child and speak clearly with a normal tone and normal loudness.
    Use visual cues such as moving your hands and showing pictures in addition to using speech.
    Seat your child near adults and children who are speaking.
    Speak clearly and repeat important words, but use natural speaking tones and pattern.
    Check often to make sure your child understands what is being said.
    Stand still when talking to your child to decrease distractions.

  Decrease Background Noise
    Turn off unnecessary music and television in the background.
    Fix noisy appliances such as heaters or air conditioners.
    Limit play with noisy toys.
    Encourage teachers to create quiet areas such as dividers for small-group play and reading.
    Close windows and doors when it is noisy outside.

Promote Early Literacy Learning
  Read often to your child, describing and explaining pictures and referring to your child's own experiences ("Spot is like your dog.").
  Read slowly to your child, pausing at times to ask questions ("What will happen next?").
  Give your child books and magazines to look at.
  Read aloud traffic and store signs, labels on packages, and words on a menu.
  Let your child draw and write using crayons, markers, and pencils.
  Sing simple songs with repeated words and phrases.
  Talk about sounds and names of letters.
  Play sound, alphabet, and word games that focus on the beginning and ending sounds of words.
  Play word and listening games so that your child will listen to familiar patterns and fill in words.
  For older preschoolers, play rhyming games such as hat, cat, and bat.

Adapted from Roberts JE and Zeisel SA (2000).

guage, a speech-language pathologist should assess his speech and language skills. If the results of a speech and language assessment indicate a speech or language delay or disorder, Justin should be enrolled in speech-language therapy. Third, Justin's parents should receive information about the signs and symptoms of OME and hearing loss, factors that may increase the risk of Justin getting OME (eg, exposure to tobacco smoke), developmental milestones in language, and what they can do in their home and when interacting with Justin to make the environment as responsive and supportive of Justin's language development as possible. Reviewing with the family the language, listening, and literacy strategies listed in Table 86-1 and materials about OM written specifically for families (Roberts and Zeisel, 2000; Stool et al, 1994) would be very helpful.

Conclusion

In summary, the issue of whether recurrent OME affects the later acquisition of speech, language, and academic skills continues to be controversial. A few studies report a very mild association between OME and later development, but the clinical relevance of this association is unclear. It is clear that the quality of children's caregiving environment at home and in child care plays a much more important role than OME in affecting children's later development. However, some typically developing children, as well as children from special populations, may be at increased risk for later language and learning difficulties owing to a history of OME and associated hearing loss. Until further research can resolve whether a relationship between a chronic history of OME and later developmental skills exists, each child's hearing status, language skills, and development need to be considered in the management of young children with histories of OME.

References

American-Speech-Language-Hearing Association. Guidelines for audiologic screening. Rockville (MD): American Speech-Language-Hearing Association; 1997.

Berman S. Management of otitis media and functional outcomes related to language, behavior, and attention: is it time to change our approach? Pediatrics 2001;107:1175–7.

Bondy J, Berman S, Glazner J, Lezotte D. Direct expenditures related to otitis media diagnoses: extrapolations from a pediatric Medicaid cohort. Pediatrics 2000;105:E72.

Burns SM, Griffin P, Snow CE. Starting out right: a guide to promoting children's reading success. Washington (DC): National Academy Press; 1999.

Casselbrant ML, Mandel EM. Epidemiology. In: Rosenfeld RM, Bluestone CD, editors. Evidence-based otitis media. Hamilton (ON): BC Decker; 1999. p. 117–36.

Coplan J. The early language milestone scale. 2nd ed. Austin (TX): Pro-Ed; 1987.

Feldman HM, Dolloghan CA, Campbell TF, et al. Parent-reported language and communication skills at one and two years of age in relation to otitis media in the first two years. Pediatrics 1999;104:E52.

Fenson L, Dale P, Reznick S. MacArthur Communication Development Inventories. San Diego: Singular Publishing Group; 1993.

Gravel JS, Wallace IF. Listening and language at 4 years of age: effects of early otitis media. J Speech Hear Res 1992;35:588–95.

Hubbard TW, Paradise JL, McWilliams BJ, et al. Consequences of unremitting middle-ear disease in early life. N Engl J Med 1985;312:1529–34.

Lanphear BP, Byrd RS, Auinger P, et al. Increasing prevalence of recurrent otitis media among children in the United States. Pediatrics 1997;99:E1.

Lonigan CJ, Fischel JE, Whitehurst GJ, et al. The role of otitis media in the development of expressive language disorder. Dev Psychol 1992;28:430–40.

Maw R, Wilks J, Harvey I, et al. Early surgery compared with watchful waiting for glue ear and effect on language development in preschool children: a randomized trial. Lancet 1999;353:960–3.

Paradise JL. Otitis media and child development: should we worry? Pediatr Infect Dis J 1998;17:1076–83.

Paradise JL, Dollaghan CA, Campbell TF, et al. Language, speech sound production, and cognition in three-year-old children in relation to otitis media in the first three years of life. Pediatrics 2000;105:1119–30.

Paradise JL, Feldman HM, Campbell TF, et al. Effect of early or delayed insertion of tympanostomy tubes for persistent otitis media on developmental outcomes at the age of three years. N Engl J Med 2001;344:1179–87.

Peters SAF, Grievink EM, van Bon WHJ, Schilder AGM. The effects of early bilateral otitis media with effusion on educational attainment: a prospective cohort study. J Learn Disabil 1994;27:111–21.

Roberts JE, Burchinal MR, Jackson SC, et al. Otitis media in childhood in relation to preschool language and school readiness skills among black children. Pediatrics 2000;106:725–35.

Roberts JE, Burchinal MR, Medley LP, et al. Otitis media, hearing sensitivity, and maternal responsiveness in relation to language during infancy. J Pediatr 1995;126:481–9.

Roberts JE, Burchinal MR, Zeisel SA, et al. Otitis media, the caregiving environment, and language and cognitive outcomes at two years. Pediatrics 1998;102:346–52.

Roberts JE, Burchinal MR, Zeisel SA. Otitis media in early childhood in relation to children's school-age language and academic skills. Pediatrics 2002;110:696–706.

Roberts JE, Wallace IF. Language and otitis media. In: Roberts JE, Wallace IF, Henderson F, editors. Otitis media in young children: medical, developmental and educational considerations. Baltimore: Paul H. Brookes; 1997. p. 133–62.

Roberts JE, Zeisel SA. Ear infections and language development. Rockville (MD): American Speech-Language-Hearing Association and the National Center for Early Development and Learning; 2000.

Rovers MM, Straatman H, Ingels K, et al. The effect of ventilation tubes on language development in infants with otitis media with effusion: a randomized trial. Pediatrics 2000;106:E42.

Ruben RJ, Haggard MP, Bagger-Sjöbäck D, et al. Complications and sequelae. Recent advances in otitis media: report of the Sixth Research Conference. Ann Otol Rhinol Laryngol Suppl 1998;107:81–94.

Schappert SM. Office visits for otitis media: United States, 1975–90. Adv Data 1992;214:1–19.

Shriberg LD, Friel-Patti S, Flipsen P, Brown RL. Otitis media, fluctuant hearing loss, and speech-language outcomes: a preliminary structural equation model. J Speech Lang Hear Res 2000; 43:100–20.

Stool SE, Berg AO, Berman S, et al. Managing otitis media with effusion in young children. Clinical practice guidelines number 12. Rockville (MD): Agency for Health Care Policy and Research, Public Health Service, US Department of Health and Human Services; 1994. AHCPR Publication No.: 94-0622.

Teele DW, Klein JO, Chase C, et al. Otitis media in infancy and intellectual ability, school achievement, speech, and language at age 7 years. J Infect Dis 1990;162:685–94.

Teele DW, Klein JO, Rosner BA, The Greater Boston Otitis Media Study Group. Otitis media with effusion during the first three years of life and development of speech and language. Pediatrics 1984;74:282–7.

Vernon-Feagans L. Impact of otitis media on speech, language, cognition, and behavior. In: Rosenfeld RM, Bluestone CD, editors. Evidence-based otitis media. Hamilton (ON): BC Decker; 1999. p. 353–73.

Wallace IF, Gravel JS, McCarton CM, et al. Otitis media, auditory sensitivity, and language outcomes at one year. Laryngoscope 1988;98:64–70.

Whiteman BC, Simpson GB, Compton WC. Relationship of otitis media and language impairment in adolescents with Down syndrome. Ment Retard 1986;24:353–6.

Zeisel SA, Roberts JE. Otitis media in young children with disabilities. Infants and Young Children. 2003;16:106–19.

Chapter 87

TYMPANOPLASTY IN THE YOUNG CHILD

MIRKO TOS, MD, DMSc

In this chapter, the indications and surgical methods of tympanoplasty for noncholesteatomatous chronic otitis media (OM) in children are described and discussed. It is generally accepted that a cholesteatoma in a child should be operated on soon after diagnosis or even at suspicion for cholesteatoma in cases of a non–self-cleansing attic retraction, posterosuperior, or total pars tensa retraction. These conditions are called attic, sinus, and tensa retraction precholesteatomas, respectively (Tos, 1981; Tos, 1990).

In noncholesteatomatous chronic OM, there has been an ongoing debate on the indications for tympanoplasty in children and on the question of when to close the eardrum perforation. There have also been various opinions regarding when to perform mastoidectomy in connection with tympanoplasty. My views are based on 40 years of transcanal, "minimally invasive" tympanoplasty without mastoidectomy, with long-term follow-up of nearly all children (Drozdziewicz et al, 1999; Lau and Tos, 1986; Lau and Tos, 1988; Tos, 1993; Tos, 1995; Tos and Lau, 1989; Tos et al, 2000).

Indications for Tympanoplasty in Ears without Cholesteatoma

We have found that our results of tympanoplasty have been better in children than in adults and therefore the indications for surgery have been without any restriction to the age of the child. Other surgeons have reported on good results in children and closing perforations unrelated to age (Chandrasekhar et al, 1995; Ophir et al, 1987; Raine and Singh, 1983; Smyth and Hassard, 1980), and I share this view. During the last 20 years, the percentages of tympanoplasty in preschool children have increased in Denmark, mainly because of the desire for preschool-age children to swim. The median age of 7.8 years in our second series of 177 children operated on during a 15-year period (1980–1994) is lower (Drozdziewicz et al, 1999) than in the first 116 children operated on from 1968 to 1980; 26 of the children were 2 to 7 years old at the time of surgery (Lau

and Tos, 1986; Lau and Tos, 1988; Tos and Lau, 1989). The number of younger children with reperforation was not higher than in older children (Figure 87-1). Since 1995, the number of tympanoplasties on children has further increased, and the age at surgery has been further lowered.

The indication for tympanoplasty should be discussed and performed among the following subgroups of children:

- Children with perforation after grommet insertion. The perforation is usually not closed at an otolaryngology department but by the otolaryngologists outside the hospitals, who perform the grommet insertions, follow the patient, and close the small dry perforation 3 to 6 months after extrusion of the grommet. Because such grommet perforation does not cause any hearing loss or other problems, its closure should be postponed until the eventual secretory OM on the opposite side is cured. A positive Valsalva's maneuver on the perforation side is desired but not obligatory.

- Children with perforation after long-term ventilation tubes. The tubes are usually placed in an atrophic and

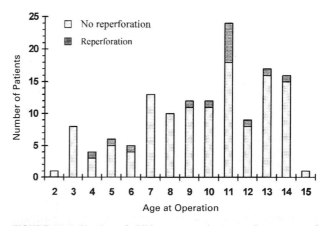

FIGURE 87-1. Number of children operated on at various ages and number of corresponding reperforations. Reproduced from Tos M et al (2000).

retracted eardrum, undergoing several previous grommet insertions. After removal of the long-term ventilation tube that has been blocked and surrounded by crusts, the atrophic drum will sometimes not heal because the vascular supply of the surrounding atrophic drum is not sufficient. If the ear is dry, such a perforation can be closed within 3 to 6 months after extrusion. A positive Valsalva's maneuver will be an advantage, but a negative Valsalva's maneuver is not a contraindication for tympanoplasty.

- Children with large perforations involving one, two, three, or all four quadrants. In the daily clinic, I characterize them as posterior, anterior, inferior subtotal, and total perforation. Posterior perforations can extend inferiorly, as can anterior perforations. A large inferior perforation can extend superiorly, involving the posterosuperior and anterosuperior quadrants, and become a subtotal perforation. There is a gradual transition between a subtotal and a total perforation, but it is not of surgical importance.

The ear may be dry, moist, slightly discharging, or heavily discharging. The dry perforations are closed at diagnosis if no active secretory or purulent OM on the opposite side is present.

The moist perforations with moist, secretory mucosa will usually be closed at diagnosis.

Often some granulation on the lateral side of the drum remnant—a myringitis—may be found, explaining the slight discharge at the dry middle ear mucosa. Early surgery of such cases is necessary and efficient. Mucociliary clearance will convey the mucus to the rhinopharynx and the mucosa will gradually improve, as is the normal procedure in all cases of secretory OM after grommet extrusion and spontaneous closure of the perforation. Our experience with such cases has been extremely good (Tos and Lau, 1989).

In slightly discharging or recurrently discharging ears, we will, after conservative treatment, perform a tympanoplasty. In heavily and constantly discharging ears in chronic granulating OM, we will, after unsuccessful conservative treatment, perform intact canal wall mastoidectomy with tympanoplasty in the same stage, with insertion of a thick retroauricular drainage and ventilating tube inserted into the mastoid cavity through a separate small incision (Tos, 1995). The surgery in the attic and the tympanic cavity is very conservative, and only the polyps and the granulation are removed.

Eustachian tube dysfunction does not change the indication for tympanoplasty or type of surgery. It has preoperatively been tested by Valsalva's maneuver only, postoperatively by tympanometry. Surprisingly enough, the long-term stability of tympanoplasty in ears with an intact ossicular chain and a preoperatively negative Valsalva's maneuver was as good as that in ears with a positive Valsalva's maneuver (Tos et al, 2000). General indications for tympanoplasty are the desire of the parents to have a dry perforation closed, recurrent infection of a dry perforation, granulations on the eardrum with perforation, hearing loss, bilateral perforations regardless of hearing acuity, closure of the perforation before inserting a hearing aid for perceptive hearing loss, and moist and discharging ears.

Contraindications

Except in cases of an acute purulent OM with pulsating secretion or a severe diffuse external otitis, there are no other contraindications to closing a perforation. In such situations, the closure is postponed until the acute changes in the middle ear have improved. Recurrent acute infection of the middle ear is, however, one of the most common indications for closure of the perforation. Sometimes the closure has to be performed soon after improvement of the acute changes to prevent a new infection from the ear canal.

Transcanal Approach and Age at Tympanoplasty

In children in general and in preschool children in particular, the application of the transcanal approach, without any incision laterally in the ear canal, is, in my opinion, of greatest importance and allows minimally invasive surgery. We have demonstrated that such conservative surgery can be performed successfully without any lateral incision and with no risk for postoperative ear canal stenosis or any other ear canal problems (Drozdziewicz et al, 1999; Lau and Tos, 1986; Lau and Tos, 1988; Tos, 1993; Tos and Lau, 1989; Tos et al, 2000). Many preschool children with previous middle ear diseases are uncooperative and do not allow any postoperative care. Therefore, the approach and the tympanoplasty should be adapted in such a way that no postoperative care is needed and the risk of lateral ear canal granulation formation and postoperative ear canal stenosis is eliminated. The transcanal approach with a fixed ear speculum (Figure 87-2) allows, by slight tilting in various directions, a sufficient view over the entire eardrum. Transcanal surgery may sometimes be technically difficult in preschool children; therefore, we place the task of performing tympanoplasty in the hands of the most experienced ear surgeons and do not use the children in training programs.

If the surgeon in some specific and difficult situations feels that a retroauricular approach is easier, it can be done.

Surgical Techniques

Several surgical techniques can be applied depending on the size of the perforation, thickness, and structure of the

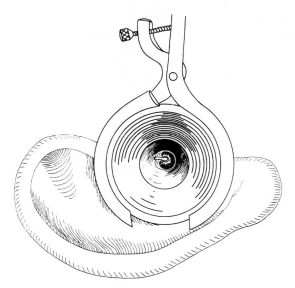

FIGURE 87-2. Transcanal approach with fixed ear speculum without any lateral incision of canal skin. Speculum is fixed with a speculum holder. Reproduced from Tos M (1993).

surrounding eardrum, approach, and surgeon's philosophy. Small grommet perforation can often be closed by scarification, removal of the edges of the perforation, or removal of the squamous epithelium from the edges of the perforation, followed by covering the perforation with a piece of Gelfoam, rice paper, or a small ball of gauze moistened with hydrocortisone ointment. Perforations of up to 2 mm in diameter can be closed by placement of a fatty lump taken from the ear lobule. After the perforation edge is scarified, the fatty lump is pushed through the perforation into the tympanic cavity and then pulled outward (Figure 87-3). Larger perforations can be closed with fascia or perichondrium placed as onlay or underlay grafts. Anterior perforations are closed with fascia by an onlay technique (Figure 87-4). An anterosuperior skin flap and a malleus flap are elevated and keratinized squamous epithelium is removed. Inferior perforations and total perforations are closed by applying an onlay technique as well (Figures 87-5 and 87-6). In these procedures, the middle ear mucosa is not touched at all, and we have not experienced blunting in our series (Drozdziewicz et al, 1999; Lau and Tos, 1986; Lau and Tos, 1988; Tos and Lau, 1989; Tos et al, 2000). Most surgeons prefer the underlay fascia grafting (Figure 87-7). Posterior perforations are always closed by underlay fascia grafting (Figure 87-8).

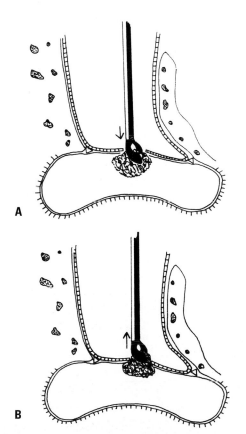

FIGURE 87-3. Placement of the fatty lump. *A,* The lump is brought into the cavity. *B,* It is pulled outward to be fixed inside the edges of the perforation. Reproduced from Tos M (1993).

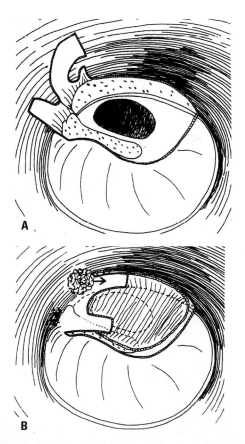

FIGURE 87-4. Onlay fascia grafting in anterior perforation. *A,* Malleus epithelial flap and anterosuperior skin flap are elevated and keratinized epithelium around the perforation is removed. *B,* After placement of the fascia, the flaps are replaced. Reproduced from Tos M (1993).

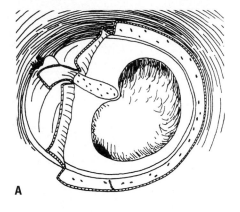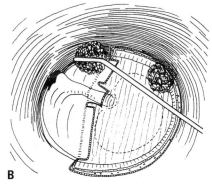

FIGURE 87-5. Onlay fascia grafting in inferior perforation. *A*, Incision is made 1 mm lateral to the annulus and the epithelium is removed. Superiorly small epithelial flaps are created. *B*, Fascia is placed onto the drum remnant and the epithelial flaps are replaced. Reproduced from Tos M (1993).

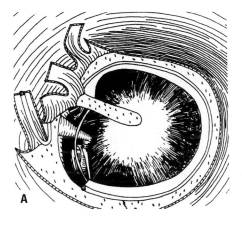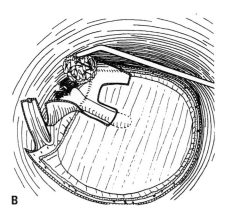

FIGURE 87-6. Onlay fascia grafting in total perforation. *A*, An incision 1 mm laterally to the annulus is made and the epithelium is removed. Superiorly, three epithelial flaps are elevated. *B*, The fascia is placed onto the annulus and the epithelial flaps are replaced. Reproduced from Tos M (1993).

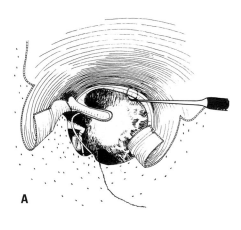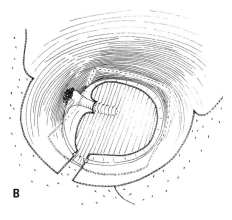

FIGURE 87-7. Underlay fascia grafting of a total perforation by the swing-door technique. *A*, The annulus and the superior epithelial flaps are elevated and the malleus handle is cleaned. *B*, The fascia is placed under the annulus and the flaps are replaced. Reproduced from Tos M (1993).

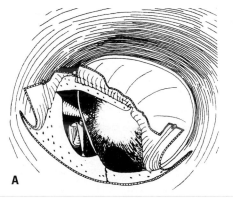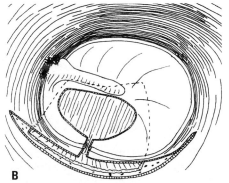

FIGURE 87-8. Underlay fascia grafting in posterior perforation. *A*, Skin is incised 3 mm lateral for the annulus and the drum remnants with the annulus elevated. *B*, Fascia is placed along the denuded malleus handle and the annulus is replaced. Reproduced from Tos M (1993).

References

Chandrasekhar SS, House JW, Devgan U. Pediatric tympanoplasty. A 10-year experience. Arch Otolaryngol Head Neck Surg 1995; 121:873–8.

Drozdziewicz D, Stangerup SE, Tos M, Trabalzini F. Long term results of surgery for sequelae to otitis media in children. In: Tos M, Thomsen J, Balle V, editors. Otitis media today. Amsterdam: Kugler Publications; 1999. p. 575–9.

Lau T, Tos M. Tympanoplasty in children. An analysis of late results. Am J Otol 1986;7:55–9.

Lau T, Tos. M. When to do tympanoplasty in children. Adv Otorhinolaryngol 1988; 40:156–61.

Ophir D, Porat M, Marshak G. Myringoplasty in the pediatric population. Arch Otolaryngol Head Neck Surg 1987;113:1288–90.

Raine CH, Singh SD. Tympanoplasty in children. A review of 114 cases. J Laryngol Otol 1983;97:217–21.

Smyth GDL, Hassard TH. Tympanoplasty in children. Am J Otol 1980;1:1–9.

Tos M. Upon the relationship between secretory otitis in childhood and chronic otitis and its sequelae in adults. J Laryngol Otol 1981;95:1011–22.

Tos M. Chronic otitis media and cholesteatoma. In: English GH, editor. Otolaryngology. Vol. 1. Philadelphia: Lippincott; 1990. p. 1–30.

Tos M. Manual of middle ear surgery. Vol. 1. New York: Thieme; 1993.

Tos M. Manual of middle ear surgery. Vol. 2. New York: Thieme; 1995.

Tos M, Lau T. Stability of tympanoplasty in children. Otolaryngol Clin North Am 1989;22:15–28.

Tos M, Ørntoft S, Stangerup SE. Results of tympanoplasty in children after 15 to 27 years. Ann Otol Rhinol Laryngol 2000;109: 17–23.

Chapter 88

State of Eustachian Tube Function in Tympanoplasty

Haruo Takahashi, MD, Seishi Hasebe, MD, Masaharu Sudo, MD

Researchers have extensively investigated the ventilatory functions of eustachian tubes (ETs) of ears with chronic otitis media (COM) undergoing tympanoplasty (Andreasson, 1977; Bluestone et al, 1978; Bluestone et al, 1979; Cohn et al, 1979; Flisberg, 1966; Fradis et al, 1987; Holmquist, 1968; Holmquist, 1969; Honjo, 1988; Honjo et al, 1989; MacKinnon, 1970; Magnuson, 1978; Sheehy, 1981; Siedentop et al, 1968; Sudo et al, 1999; Takahashi, 2001; Virtanen et al, 1980). Generally, the character of the dysfunction is different in ears with COM and ears with eardrum perforation versus those with cholesteatoma.

In this chapter, we introduce the characteristics of ET dysfunctions and discuss how they influence the outcome of tympanoplasty.

ET Functions of Ears with COM and Eardrum Perforation

According to the literature investigating the ventilatory functions of the ETs of patients with COM (Andreasson, 1977; Bluestone et al, 1979; Cohn et al, 1979; Flisberg, 1966; Fradis et al, 1987; Holmquist, 1968; Holmquist, 1969; Honjo, 1988; MacKinnon, 1970; Siedentop et al, 1968; Virtanen et al, 1980), the active ventilatory functions that correct middle ear pressure gradients (especially negative pressure) are generally poorer than normal, and the tubal passive opening pressure (OP) is relatively high in some ears with COM as some of the ETs are stenotic. In our investigations, OP was high in 23% of ears with COM (including 10% of highly stenotic or obstructed ETs), and the positive and negative middle ear pressure equalizing functions (PPEF and NPEF) were impaired in 23 and 47%, respectively (Honjo, 1988). This seems in part attributable to accumulated discharge in the tympanic cavity and ET but also in part to the anatomic predisposition of the ET in those patients.

Functions of Ears with COM and Cholesteatoma

The ETs of ears with cholesteatoma, particularly a retraction-type cholesteatoma, tend to be rather patulous, including 15 to 20% with abnormally low OP despite no remarkable differences in PPEF and NPEF compared with those without cholesteatoma (Honjo et al, 1989). Those patients with nearly patulous ETs (Magnuson, 1978) frequently have a sniffing habit and try to relieve themselves from unpleasant autophonia by sniffing, which closes the ET by inducing a profound negative pressure in the ET and in the middle ear. This can result in eardrum retraction and a retraction pocket or cholesteatoma formation. The incidence of sniff-induced cholesteatoma occurring in patients with nearly patulous ETs has been found to be unexpectedly high, ranging from 25 to 82% of patients with cholesteatoma (Kobayashi et al, 1996; Magnuson, 1978). In our experience, the incidence of sniff-induced cholesteatoma has been no less than 50%.

The Toynbee phenomenon may also play a role in cholesteatoma formation in which a considerable degree of negative pressure is induced in the middle ear by swallowing when both sides of the nose are obstructed owing to some reason, such as an upper respiratory tract infection (Sudo et al, 1999).

Influence of ET Ventilatory Function on the Outcome of Tympanoplasty

Patients undergoing tympanoplasty should have their ET ventilatory function examined preoperatively in all cases. The most suitable method of checking ventilatory function should be chosen according to the condition of the patients' ear. When there is an eardrum perforation, the inflation-deflation test is recommended. Sonotubometry can be used when there is no perforation and no fluid in the middle ear. If fluid is present in the middle ear, no ET function test will provide consistent results, but an inflation catheter can be used to determine whether the ET is patent or not. Also, computed tomography (CT) will show whether there is an air space in the bony portion of the ET. It is of some help to speculate on the ET function of the patient; if there is no air space, the ET function may be quite poor.

Both positive (Holmquist, 1968; Honjo, 1988; MacKinnon, 1970; Siedentop et al, 1968) and negative (Andreasson, 1977; Cohn et al, 1979; Fradis et al, 1987; Sheehy, 1981; Virtanen et al, 1980) correlations between ET function and the outcome of tympanoplasty have been reported, and there are no definite agreements concerning this issue; there is even an opinion regarding the significance of any preoperative ET function test (Sheehy, 1981).

This lack of consensus may be attributable in part to the fact that ventilation and pressure regulation of the middle ear are done not only by the ET but also by gas exchange through the mucosa in the middle ear, particularly the mastoid (Takahashi, 2001). The normal mucosa in the mastoid has a single layer of squamous epithelium with a rich distribution of capillaries just underneath it. This structure is similar to that of the alveolus in the lung and is advantageous for gas exchange (Figure 88-1). The gas exchange is a passive movement of gases through the mucosa between the blood and an air space (such as the mastoid), and all of the gases can move between them passively according to their partial pressure gradients. As a result, the total middle ear pressure tends to be kept at or near atmospheric pressure. Because the gas exchange function is basically the passive movements of gases, its impairment occurs when the movement of gases is disturbed. For example, the function can be impaired by an edematous mucosa or granulation or scar tissue in the middle ear by increasing the distance between the middle ear cavity and the capillaries. Most typically, the function stops when the middle ear is filled with an effusion or a granulation tissue, leaving no air space. In other words, an air space into which gases enter from the blood is neces-

sary in the middle ear for any gas exchange to occur (Table 88-1) (Takahashi, 2001). Thus, examining the aeration in the middle ear preoperatively, particularly in the mastoid, is as important as preoperatively testing ET function.

Clearance from the middle ear may be an even more important role of the ET than ventilation and pressure regulation. If only the ventilation and pressure regulation functions of the ET are impaired, they can be compensated for by the gas exchange function when the middle ear and mastoid are aerated. However, when the ET is completely obstructed, the middle ear cannot maintain its air space owing to accumulation of mucus or fluid (Takahashi, 2001). In our experience, the outcome of tympanoplasty is definitely poor in ears with a completely obstructed ET in which both the ventilatory and clearance functions of the ET are lost (Figure 88-2). Therefore, to preoperatively examine the patency of the ET using a tubal inflation catheter or some other method is indispensable, even if detailed ET function tests cannot be done.

Management of ET Dysfunction in Tympanoplasty

An overview of the strategy in the tympanoplasty for COM, including cholesteatoma, according to the state of ET function is described in Figure 88-3. In ears with a completely obstructed ET, preoperative treatment with antibiotics and/or otic drops containing antibiotics and steroids is worth trying for 1 to 2 months. In our experience, about half of the obstructed ETs recovered their patency after treatment. In the case of children, tympanoplasty for COM without cholesteatoma should be delayed until the patient is 10 years old because at earlier ages, the ET functions and immunity are generally immature. If the ET remains completely obstructed despite treatment, hearing is very likely to be affected. However, progressive lesions such as cholesteatoma should be resected completely in all cases.

When the ET is stenotic, similar preoperative treatments are recommended, but tympanoplasty will work most of the time if CT shows that the mastoid is aerated. If the ET is stenotic and the mastoid is not aerated but

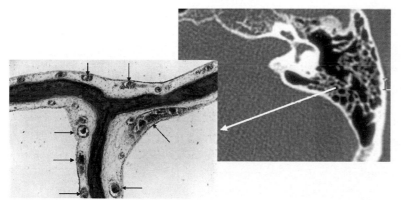

FIGURE 88-1. Computed tomographic image and light microscopic histology of a normal mastoid air cell (hematoxylin-eosin stain; original magnification ×100). Rich vascularity just underneath thin mucosa is seen (*arrows*).

TABLE 88-1. Correlation between the Presence or Absence of the Gas Exchange Function and the Presence or Absence of the Aeration (Air Space) in the Middle Ear (66 Ears with Otitis Media with Effusion)

	Gas Exchange Present	Gas Exchange Absent
Middle ear air space present	28	5
Middle ear air space absent	4	29

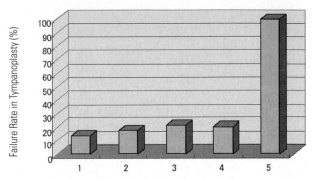

Grade of Eustachian Tube Function

FIGURE 88-2. Relation between preoperative eustachian tube function and outcome of tympanoplasty in 77 ears 6 months after tympanoplasty type I. Failure includes recurrence of otorrhea, drum perforation, or no improvement of hearing. Grade I: tubal opening pressure (OP), positive middle ear pressure equalizing function (PP), and negative middle ear pressure equalizing function (NP) were all good; grade II: two of the three tests (OP, PP, NP) were good; grade III: one of the three tests was good; grade IV: none of the three tests were normal; grade V: in addition to poor tubal ventilatory function of grade IV, dye clearance was also impaired, indicating complete obstruction of the eustachian tube. Numbers in parentheses indicate number of ears in each grade.

rather filled with soft tissue, insertion of a tympanostomy tube at or after tympanoplasty is recommended. In our experience, the type of tympanoplasty related to ET functions (medial versus lateral graft or cartilage graft underneath the eardrum) does not affect its outcome. Nothing is better than tympanostomy tube insertion or preoperative treatment for improving ET functions.

In cases of sniff-induced cholesteatoma, insertion of a tympanostomy tube during or after surgery is recommended in addition to a sufficient explanation and recommendation to the patient to cease the sniffing habit.

It is still controversial whether mastoidectomy should be done or not when the mastoid is filled with a soft tissue on the CT scan. This depends on the lesion in the mastoid; for example, the mastoid should be opened and cleaned in cases in which there is cholesteatoma, but we should know that we cannot expect that a postmastoidectomy cavity will revive as a functioning cavity exchanging gases. The cavity is usually filled with scar tissue after mastoidectomy (Takahashi, 2001).

In cases of tympanoplasty failure, the cause of the failure should be carefully analyzed. One of the causes may be failure of the pressure regulation system in the middle ear. Both ET and gas exchange function may be impaired in some cases, that is, the mastoid is filled with soft tissue and the active ventilatory functions of the ET are impaired. A sniffing habit may also cause a tympanoplasty failure. If no measures are taken to address the situation, for example, tympanostomy tube insertion, the same poor outcome is very likely to be expected after surgery even if the surgery is done according to proper techniques.

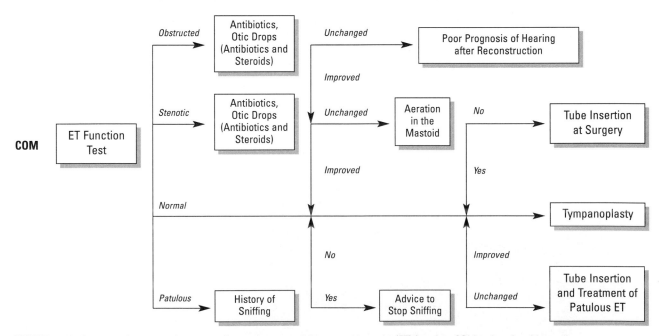

FIGURE 88-3. Strategy of tympanoplasty according to the state of the eustachian tube (ET) function. COM = chronic otitis media.

References

Andreasson L. Correlation of tubal function and volume of mastoid and middle ear space as related to otitis media. Acta Otolaryngol (Stockh) 1977;83:29–33.

Bluestone CD, Cantekin EI, Beery QC, Stool SE. Function of the eustachian tube related to surgical management of acquired aural cholesteatoma in children. Laryngoscope 1978;88:1155–64.

Bluestone CD, Cantekin EI, Douglas GS. Eustachian tube function related to the results of tympanoplasty in children. Laryngoscope 1979;89:450–8.

Cohn AM, Schwaber MA, Anthony LS, Jerger JF. Eustachian tube function and tympanoplasty. Ann Otol Rhinol Laryngol 1979; 88:339–47.

Flisberg K. Ventilatory studies on the eustachian tube. A clinical investigation of cases with perforated eardrums. Acta Otolaryngol Suppl (Stockh) 1966;219:1–82.

Fradis M, Podoshin L, Ben-David J. Eustachian tube function as a prognostic tool in tympanoplasty. In: Sadé J, editor. The eustachian tube. Amsterdam: Kugler Publications; 1987. p. 149–52.

Holmquist J. The role of the eustachian tube in myringoplasty. Acta Otolaryngol (Stockh) 1968;66:289–95.

Holmquist J. Eustachian tube function in patients with eardrum perforations following chronic otitis media. Acta Otolaryngol (Stockh) 1969;68:391–401.

Honjo I. Eustachian tube and middle ear diseases. Tokyo: Springer-Verlag; 1988.

Honjo I, Fujita A, Sato H, et al. Eustachian tube function in patients with cholesteatoma. In: Tos M, Thomsen J, Peitersen E, editors. Cholesteatoma and mastoid surgery. Amsterdam: Kugler & Ghedini; 1989. p. 455–8.

Kobayashi T, Jaginuma Y, Takahashi Y, Takasaka T. Incidence of sniff-induced cholesteatoma. Acta Otolaryngol (Stockh) 1996; 116:74–6.

MacKinnon DM. Relationship of pre-operative eustachian tube function to myringoplasty. Acta Otolaryngol (Stockh) 1970; 69:100–6.

Magnuson B. Tubal closing failure in retraction-type cholesteatoma and adhesive middle-ear lesions. Acta Otolaryngol (Stockh) 1978;86:408–17.

Sheehy JL. Testing eustachian tube function. Ann Otol Rhinol Laryngol 1981;90:562–4.

Siedentop KH, Tardy ME, Hamilton LR. Eustachian tube function. Arch Otolaryngol 1968;88:386–95.

Sudo M, Takahashi H, Tanabe M, et al. Toynbee phenomenon as a causative factor of middle ear disease. In: Tos M, Thomsen J, Balle V, editors. Otitis media today. The Hague: Kugler Publications; 1999. p. 287–90.

Takahashi H. The middle ear—the role of ventilation in disease and surgery. Tokyo: Springer-Verlag; 2001.

Virtanen H, Palva T, Janhiainen T. The prognostic value of eustachian tube function measurements in tympanoplastic surgery. Acta Otolaryngol (Stockh) 1980;90:317–23.

Chapter 89

PERSISTENT PERFORATION AFTER TYMPANOPLASTY

Ryo Yuasa, MD, Tomonori Takasaka, MD, PhD

Persistent perforation is one of the most common sequelae of tympanoplasty, and it may bring many undesirable consequences, including aural discharge, conductive hearing loss, and a handicap in swimming or hair washing. The surgeon's technical failure, incorrect surgical procedures, inappropriate indication for surgery, uncontrollable infection before and after the operation, and some unidentified factors within the patient are considered to be the causal factors of persistent perforation after the surgery. Most reperforations should be closed by revision surgery, except cases with a small dry perforation without aural discharge or any associated conductive hearing loss. However, the patient does not always agree to revision surgery. To repair the reperforation in the outpatient department (OPD), we developed a new, simple myringoplasty in 1989 as minimally invasive surgery (Yuasa et al, 1989; Yuasa et al, 1992). After describing the general aspects of "persistent perforation in tympanoplasty," the details and importance of this new, simple myringoplasty as the repair method in the OPD are presented in this chapter.

Incidence and Causes

Postoperative perforation after tympanoplasty occurs in 3 to 10% of cases in general (Cueva, 1999; Tos, 1980). The surgeon's technique, the surgical procedures, and the follow-up period may play important roles in this different rate of reperforation. On the other hand, the location of the perforation, the size of the perforation, and the age and sex of the patient do not affect the reperforation rate (Saito et al, 2001). The cause of the reperforation is considered to be different in each stage after surgery.

In the initial stage within the first few postoperative days, the major cause of reperforation is the detachment of the remnant tympanic membrane (TM) and the graft. This problem may result from a technical failure of the surgeon (Tos et al, 2000), such as the transplantation of an inadequately sized graft or inadequate postoperative packing. High pressure in the middle ear caused by diffu-

sion of nitrous oxide during general anesthesia can also be one of the causes (Neidhardt et al, 1992) but is infrequent (Perreault et al, 1981).

In the second stage of the postoperative period, from 1 month to 1 year, reperforation may frequently be caused by the necrosis of the graft, which is believed to be brought on by uncontrollable serious infection caused by specific organisms such as methicillin-resistant *Staphylococcus aureus*, *Pseudomonas aeruginosa*, or tuberculosis. Insufficient eradication of active diseases in the middle ear cleft and/or mastoid cavity, particularly in the case of cholesteatoma in the tympanic cavity, may result in the failure of the perforation to close. The ear with so-called "eosinophilic otitis media" associated with bronchial asthma has a high possibility of reperforation because a large amount of the thick effusion displaces the graft externally (Nagamine et al, 2002).

Persistent perforation may occur in an atrophic part of the regenerated TM in the later stage (more than 1 year postoperatively), probably caused by acute otitis media in this period (Kartush et al, 2002).

Eustachian tube dysfunction may not be a causal factor of postoperative perforation (Gardner and Dornhoffer, 2002); however, it may result in the sequelae as otitis media with effusion or adhesive otitis media with or without cholesterol granuloma. In cases with myringotomy or ventilation tube insertion for these diseases, a persistent perforation sometimes occurs as a consequence (Kay et al, 2001).

Management and Treatment of Persistent Perforation in Tympanoplasty

Because the causal factors of persistent perforation after tympanoplasty are different according to the period of its occurrence, the management and the treatment of reperforation are described according to the order of the occurrence.

Initial Stage: Within 1 Week after the Operation

Graft problems at this early stage may occur by dislocation of the graft and may cause persistent perforation in the future. When dislocation of the graft is discovered, it should be repositioned as soon as possible. In the conventional method, it is technically difficult to inlay the dislocated graft again without revision surgery, even if it is discovered in the early postoperative period. On the other hand, such graft problems can be discovered and easily corrected in the OPD by introducing a simple underlay myringoplasty following Yuasa's method (Yuasa, 1997), described previously.

Second Stage: Between 1 Week and Several Months Postoperatively

Secondary infection or recurrent infection may be the most common causal factor of reperforation in this period. The secondary infection by contamination should be absolutely avoided, especially from the opposite ear in bilateral cases. In addition to general administration of antibiotics sensitive to the causal microorganisms, local treatment, such as repeated irrigation of the ear with povidone-iodine (polyethylene iodine) solution, is also important for this purpose. On the other hand, active inflammation remaining in the middle ear or in the temporal bone after the first operation may also bring reperforation and persistent aural discharge. Therefore, a complete eradication of diseases in the ear is necessary in cases with active and extensive inflammatory diseases. However, the exact indication for complete eradication of the inflammatory diseases in the ear, that is, complete mastoidectomy, still remains unclear (Balyan et al, 1997). No evident difference was found in the postoperative results between cases with and without mastoidectomy (Mishiro et al, 2001).

Stable Period: After Controlling the Infection

After control of the postoperative infection, the reperforation will be dry and stable in size. In this condition, paper patch can be attempted with many kinds of materials, such as cellophane, gentamicin ointment seal, and chitin sheet. Although the effectiveness of a patch for traumatic perforation has been noted (Amadasun, 2002), its effectiveness for persistent perforation after ear surgery seems to be doubtful. Therefore, in general, revision surgery will be indicated in this stable period after 6 months or more postoperatively. However, revision surgery is contraindicated if the cause of reperforation is clear, such as cholesteatoma in the middle ear, "eosinophilic otitis media," and other specific infections of the middle ear.

Revision Surgery for Repair of Reperforation

The simple myringoplasty according to Yuasa's method is applicable for persistent perforation after tympanoplasty as the first choice of method for revision surgery in the OPD.

Important Surgical Procedures for Prevention of Persistent Perforation after Tympanoplasty

As mentioned above, the surgeon's technical failure, including incorrect procedures, may play an important role in the causal factors of persistent perforation after tympanoplasty. Therefore, important surgical procedures for prevention of reperforation are described in this section.

After detaching the canal skin from the posterior bony canal, the outer epithelial layer of the remnant of the eardrum should be peeled from its medial fibrous layer continuously with the canal skin. If a graft is placed on the bare surface of the fibrous layer, where a small part of epithelial layer is left remaining, the remnant outer epithelial layer can develop under the transplanted graft and can cause persistent perforation or sometimes form a pearly cyst (cholesteatoma) in the new TM in the postoperative course.

When the perforation is total or anteriorly located, a complete inlay and fixation of the graft are important for preventing the detachment of the graft from the vascular bed. Use of fibrin glue can help ensure the fixation of the graft.

Increased intratympanic pressure by nitrous oxide should be controlled at the grafting during general anesthesia.

If aural discharge is present and persists preoperatively, bacteriologic investigation should be performed and adequate antibiotics should be given before and after the surgery. Irrigating the middle ear before the surgery is also important for controlling infection.

When an active infection as purulent discharge or infected granulation tissue is present in the middle ear and/or mastoid air cells, eradication of these diseases including mastoidectomy should be considered to avoid postoperative perforation and its persistence.

Simple Myringoplasty with Use of Fibrin Glue (Yuasa's Method) for Revision Surgery as Closure of Persistent Perforation in Tympanoplasty

A new, simple myringoplasty with the use of fibrin glue was developed in 1989 (Yuasa et al, 1989) and has been widely accepted as the first choice of method and minimally invasive procedure for closure of persistent perforation of the eardrum in our country (Maeta et al, 1998; Yuasa, 1997). This method can also be applied for persistent perforation after tympanoplasty because it can be performed and repeated in the OPD for most cases of persistent perforation with minimal invasion. To apply this method for reperforation, preservation of a piece of graft material is recommended even when the conventional method is applied at the first operation.

Anesthesia

Local anesthesia is generally applied in this method, except for children under 10 years. Patients with some associated risks, such as bronchial asthma, cardiopulmonary disorders, hypertension, or diabetes, can also be indicated with fewer complications.

First, the remnant of the eardrum is anesthetized with a few small cotton balls with "anesthetic solution" (20 g of lidocaine, 20 g of phenol, 20 g of menthol, and 20 mL of glycerin in 100 mL of solution). About 15 minutes later, the remnant eardrum changes to a whitish color. In this condition, the perforation margin can be cut and removed without any pain. When an incision on the posterior canal skin is required for special cases, as described in the next section, 0.5 to 1.0 mL of 1% lidocaine is injected into the meatal skin. The retroauricular region is also anesthetized with an injection of 2 mL of 1% lidocaine to harvest the subcutaneous connective tissue or the areolar temporalis fascia for the graft material.

Surgical Procedures

For general cases, cut and remove the anesthetized margin of the perforation. The anesthetized margin of the perforation is cut and removed with a fine pick through an ear speculum to make a vascular bed for grafting (Figure 89-1). No skin incision is generally required in the meatal skin in this procedure.

Harvest the subcutaneous connective tissue for the transplant material. Subcutaneous tissue or areolar temporalis fascia harvested from the retroauricular region after local anesthesia is used for the graft. Subcutaneous connective tissue is preferred to temporalis muscle fascia in this method because thick subcutaneous connective tissue is better at adapting to the vascular bed than a thin fascia graft.

Trim the graft. The harvested graft material is trimmed to twice the diameter of the perforation. A portion of the remaining graft material is kept in the freezer at between −18°C and −20°C to be used for repairing any reperforation in the postoperative course. The procedure for this repair is explained in the section on postoperative care.

Underlay and affix the graft. The trimmed graft is stretched in the middle ear cleft and placed in the center of the perforation. Then the stretched graft is lifted and attached to the inner side of the remnant TM so that the perforation is completely closed by the graft. After checking to ensure contact of the graft to the margin of the perforation, a few drops of fibrin glue (autologous fibrin glue has recently been developed and used for this purpose to prevent any unknown viral infection) (Park,

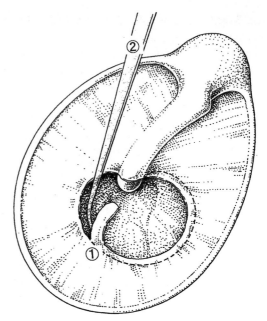

FIGURE 89-1. The anesthetized margin of the perforation is cut and removed with a fine pick through an ear speculum to make a vascular bed.

1994) are applied at the contact area (Figure 89-2).

In this method, no packing is necessary in either the middle ear cleft or the external ear canal. Therefore, improved hearing immediately after the operation can be achieved, and the condition of the graft can be continuously observed through the postoperative course. This is a great advantage for the patient who has eardrum perforation in the only hearing ear or in the better hearing ear.

Special Cases

Cases with Total Defect of the Eardrum

For the ear with a total defect of the TM, this method can also be indicated using two different-sized grafts. A smaller one is placed on the anteroinferior margin as for the annulus and the other one is the graft for closure, attaching to the smaller one (Figure 89-3).

Cases with a Curved External Canal

When the anteroinferior margin of the perforation is difficult to observe, an endaural incision is required to obtain a suitable observation angle. Use of an endoscope may also be helpful in such cases for both observation and accomplishment of the surgical procedures (Usami et al, 2001).

Cases with a Marginal Perforation

If the perforation is located in the posterior margin of the eardrum, the posterior canal skin should be elevated from the bony meatus to insert the graft between them. At the same time, it is important to observe whether the epidermis invades the middle ear or the epitympanum.

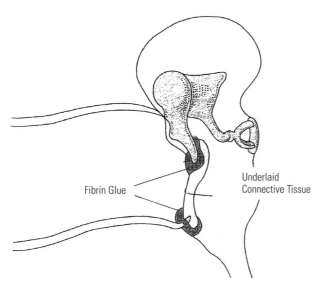

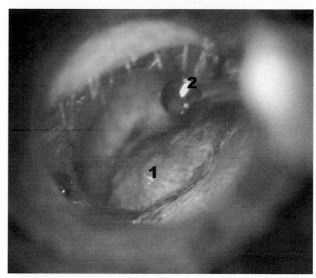

FIGURE 89-2. After checking to ensure contact of the graft to the margin of the perforation, a few drops of fibrin glue are applied at the contact area.

Cases with the Malleus Handle Touching the Promontory

If the malleus handle touches the promontory, it should be cut and removed by a malleus nipper with minimum invasion to the ossicular chain and the inner ear.

Complications

Because this method is minimally invasive, very few serious complications have been reported. Therefore, bilateral, same-day surgery for bilateral perforated chronic otitis

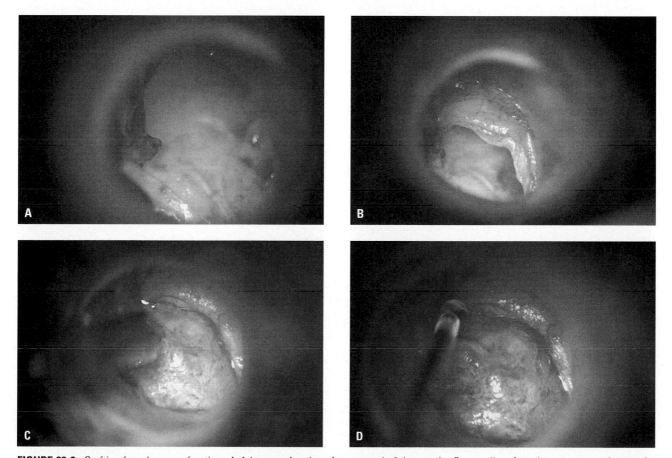

FIGURE 89-3. Grafting for a large perforation. *A,* A large perforation after removal of the margin; *B,* a small graft to the anteroposterior margin; *C,* a large graft lifted with fine forceps; *D,* two pieces of graft fixed with fibrin glue.

media can be safely performed by introducing this method (Sakagami et al, 2000). The most common complication after surgery is a mild dizziness, nausea, and vomiting, which generally disappear after several hours without requiring treatment. Therefore, the patient should not drive a car immediately after the operation, and one night of hospitalization is recommended (Megerian et al, 2000). In addition to this aural complication, bradycardia may occur during surgery. To avoid this condition, 0.5 mg of atropine sulfate as the adult dose should be subcutaneously injected 30 minutes before the operation.

Postoperative Care

Regular Checkup of the Condition

Because no material is packed in the meatus after the operation in this method, the postoperative condition can be directly observed immediately after the operation. Thus, it is possible to correct postoperative problems at an early stage if necessary. The details are described in the next section.

Repair of Reperforation

If some problems, such as reperforation or insufficient connection, do occur, they can be discovered at an early stage and corrected in the OPD. Autologous frozen connective tissue is used for repairing a reperforation using the same procedure as the previous operation. However, as no skin incision is required, this second procedure can easily be performed in the OPD without any complications. By introducing this method for repair with autologous frozen material, the postoperative success rate greatly increases, as shown in the next section.

Postoperative Results

Postoperative Condition of the Graft (Otoscopic Findings)

In this method, the condition of the graft can be observed immediately after the operation. The conditions of the transplanted graft change during the postoperative course as follows: preoperative reperforation (Figure 89-4A), epithelialization in the second week (Figure 89-4B),

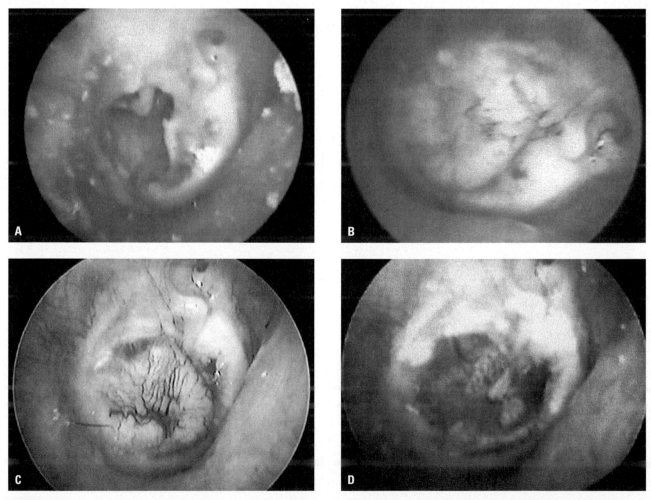

FIGURE 89-4. The conditions of the transplanted graft change during the postoperative course as follows: *A*, preoperative reperforation; *B*, epithelialization in the second week; *C*, evident vascularization in a couple of months; and *D*, a thinner graft in 6 months postoperatively.

evident vascularization in a couple of months (Figure 89-4C), and a thinner graft in 6 months postoperatively (Figure 89-4D).

Postoperative Hearing

Postoperative hearing is easily forecast by a preoperative paper patch and can be achieved to this hearing level in almost all cases. The improved hearing level immediately after the operation continues and, in general, gradually improves within the first postoperative year (Figure 89-5).

Long-Term Follow-Up of the Condition of the Graft (Rate of Reperforation)

In our experience, 87.7% of 4,079 cases had no problem with the graft during a 1-year postoperative period. The remaining 12.3% of cases had a reperforation, including a small-sized one, of which 57.7% occurred within 1 month postoperatively. The problems that occurred within 1 month are considered to be attributable to technical reasons. These postoperative problems can easily be corrected with the use of the autologous frozen tissue obtained in the previous operation, as described in the section on postoperative care. After this postoperative repair with frozen autologous graft material, the total success rate for closure of the perforation rose to 94.6%. This success rate for closure of the perforation is similar to the data for the conventional method. The remaining 5.4% includes cases in which the perforation was left untreated (4.7%) because the patient did not return to our hospital. Fewer than 1% of cases in which the perforation did not close by these methods underwent the conventional inlay method.

Cases with Repeated Perforation

Even after repeated repairs of the recurrent perforation, 0.7% of cases still had perforation, which underwent the conventional myringoplasty by the inlay (sandwich) method with complete success. After following this order of treatment—first Yuasa's method, then the repair of any reperforation with autologous frozen tissue in the OPD, and then the conventional method for the fewer than 1% of unsuccessful cases—the final success rate was 95.3%. The remaining 4.7% could not be followed up for more than 6 months postoperatively.

Conclusion

Persistent perforation has been shown to occur in 3 to 10% of cases after tympanoplasty in previous studies. Technical failure of the surgeon is believed to be the most frequent cause. Incorrect procedures and indications, uncontrollable infection, and unknown factors within the patient (such as immunodeficiency) are considered to be the other causes of persistent perforation after tympanoplasty.

Dysfunction of the eustachian tube may not affect persistent reperforation; however, it may bring middle ear effusion or adhesion of the graft with or without cholesterol granuloma. Persistent perforation may often bring many disadvantages to the patient, such as persistent aural discharge, conductive hearing loss (including influences to the inner ear in some cases), and a handicap in swimming and hair washing.

Most cases with persistent perforation should be closed by revision surgery after a postoperative follow-up period of more than 6 months, except cases with a very small, dry perforation without any complications. However, the patient does not always agree to revision surgery. To obtain agreement for surgical closure of the persistent perforation in tympanoplasty, a simple myringoplasty with use of fibrin glue according to the Yuasa method is applicable for repair in the OPD and is recommended as the first choice of method for this purpose in most cases with reperforation after tympanoplasty as minimally invasive surgery.

Because the frozen autologous graft material can be effectively used for repeated perforations, a piece of graft material should be kept frozen after the previous operation to be used in revision surgery according to Yuasa's method, even when the conventional method is applied for the previous operation. In very few cases (fewer than 1%), reperforation cannot be closed by repeated application of Yuasa's method in the OPD. For such cases, conventional revision surgery should be employed.

Treatment for persistent perforation in tympanoplasty should be chosen depending on the period of its occurrence and the order of procedures: reposition of the detached graft in the earliest period, control of infection in the next period, paper patch expecting spontaneous closure, Yuasa's simple myringoplasty in the OPD, and conventional revision surgery as the final approach.

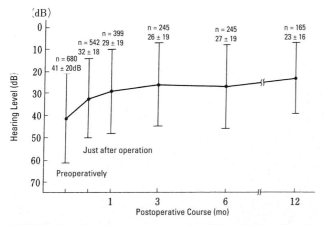

FIGURE 89-5. The improved hearing level immediately after the operation continues and, in general, gradually improves within the first postoperative year.

References

Amadasun JE. An observational study of the management of traumatic tympanic membrane perforations. J Laryngol Otol 2002;116:181–4.

Balyan FR, Celikkanat S, Aslan A, et al. Mastoidectomy in non-cholesteatomatous chronic suppurative otitis media: is it necessary? Otolaryngol Head Neck Surg 1997;117:592–5.

Cueva RA. Areolar temporalis fascia: a reliable graft for tympanoplasty. Am J Otol 1999;20:709–11.

Gardner E, Dornhoffer JL. Tympanoplasty results in patients with cleft palate: an age- and procedure-matched comparison of preliminary results with patients with cleft palate. Otolaryngol Head Neck Surg 2002;126:518–23.

Kartush JM, Michaelides EM, Becvarovski Z, et al. Over-under tympanoplasty. Laryngoscope 2002;112:802–7.

Kay DJ, Nelson M, Rosenfeld RM. Meta-analysis of tympanostomy tube sequelae. Otolaryngol Head Neck Surg 2001;124:374–80.

Maeta M, Saito R, Nakagawa F, et al. A clinical comparison of orthodox myringoplasty and a simple method with fibrin glue [in Japanese]. Nippon Jibiinkoka Gakkai Kaiho 1998;101:1062–8.

Megerian CA, Reily J, O'Connell FM, Heard SO. Outpatient tympanomastoidectomy: factors affecting hospital admission. Arch Otolaryngol Head Neck Surg 2000;126:1345–8.

Mishiro Y, Sakagami M, Takahashi Y, et al. Tympanoplasty with and without mastoidectomy for noncholesteatomatous chronic otitis media. Eur Arch Otorhinolaryngol 2001;258:13–5.

Nagamine H, Iino Y, Kojima C, et al. Clinical characteristics of so called eosinophilic otitis media. Auris Nasus Larynx 2002;29:19–28.

Neidhardt A, Bachour K, Pequignot M, et al. An analgesic strategy for tympanoplasties. Cah Anesthesiol 1992;40:43–7.

Park MS. Autologous fibrin glue for tympanoplasty. Am J Otol 1994;15:687–9.

Perreault L, Rousseau P, Garneau JF, et al. Gas diffusion in the middle ear during anesthesia for tympanoplasty. Can Anaesth Soc J 1981;28:136–10.

Saito T, Tanaka T, Tokuriki M, et al. Recent outcome of tympanoplasty in the elderly. Otol Neurotol 2001;22:153–7.

Sakagami M, Mishiro Y, Tsuzuki K, et al. Bilateral same day surgery for bilateral perforated chronic otitis media. Auris Nasus Larynx 2000;27:35–8.

Tos M. Stability of myringoplasty based on late results. ORL J Otorhinolaryngol Relat Spec 1980;42:171–81.

Tos M, Stangerup SE, Orntoft S. Reasons for reperforation after tympanoplasty in children. Acta Otolaryngol Suppl (Stockh) 2000;543:143–6.

Usami S, Iijima N, Fujita S, et al. Endoscopic-assisted myringoplasty. ORL J Otorhinolaryngol Relat Spec 2001;63:287–90.

Yuasa R. A new underlay myringoplasty with use of fibrin glue as minimally invasive surgery. In: Sanna M, editor. Cholesteatoma and mastoid surgery. Rome: Cic Edizioni Internazionali; 1997. p. 854–8.

Yuasa R, Saijo S, Tomioka Y, et al. Office closure of eardrum perforation with fibrin glue [in Japanese]. Otolaryngol Head Neck Surg (Tokyo) 1989;61:1117–22.

Yuasa R, Suetake M, Kaneko Y, Kambayashi J. A new simple myringoplasty with fibrin glue. In: Yanagihara N, Suzuki J, editors. Transplants and implants in otology. Amsterdam: Kugler Publications; 1992. p. 207–10.

Chapter 90

VENTILATION TUBES IN ASSOCIATION WITH TYMPANOPLASTY

MICHAEL M. PAPARELLA, MD

A primary indication for tympanoplasty is otitis media (OM), and I have found ventilation tubes (VTs) to be an indispensable adjunct to tympanoplasty for treatment of the continuum of OM (Figure 90-1). When tympanoplasty follows physical trauma, of course, use of VTs is unnecessary. A VT can be considered to be a passive substitute for a dysfunctional eustachian tube, the primary function of which is ventilation of the middle ear cleft and the secondary function of which is passive drainage, to compensate for hypofunctional mucociliary drainage. Certainly, a "passive," inert prosthesis cannot be expected to mimic precisely the action (muscular and mucociliary) of a functioning eustachian tube. Eustachian tube dysfunction represents a fundamental and most important mechanism in the pathogenesis of OM. However, as we have learned from many studies in animals and in patients, the various forms of OM can and do occur along a continuum, with initiating etiologic factors relating to multifactorial inheritance. After a brief introduction of this continuum and of the flexible surgical approach to treatment of OM, a discussion follows of the use of VTs as adjuncts to tympanoplasty.

Types of Tubes and Techniques for Placement (Use and Abuse)

All VTs provide the same function of passive ventilation and drainage. Various materials and types have been used by many, successfully. I have found silicone rubber tubes to be most useful because, although they are stiff, their malleability eases introduction. Although I have developed and used various types and sizes, two sizes are commonly used: a regular small one with a 1.1 mm diameter and a large one with a 1.5 mm diameter and a large inner flange for obstinate cases, particularly of mucoid OM and/or chronic OM (Juhn et al, 1977). These tubes have a very short lumen, which presents less chance for obstruc-

tion. As has been described in published reports, and as I have seen on many occasions, long T tubes logically have a greater likelihood of becoming obstructed, as well as a much higher incidence of perforation, which usually requires subsequent tympanoplasty.

The best place for insertion of a VT, I have found, is in the anterosuperior quadrant adjacent to the manubrium of the malleus. A tube should not be placed on a "hill," such as the promontory, but in a "valley," such as the protympanum near the middle ear outlet of the eustachian tube. Because atelectasis of the tympanic membrane is a common concomitant of OM, I obviously look for a location in a valley rather than on a hill. Another location or space is the hypotympanum beneath the anteroinferior quadrant, but never in the posterosuperior quadrant, to avoid middle ear/ossicular structures. As simple as it may seem, it is critically important to be certain that the inner flange is in the middle ear, to avoid rapid and embarrassing extrusion.

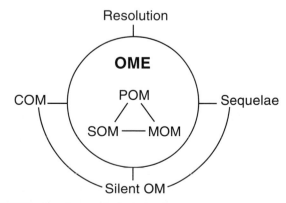

FIGURE 90-1. Schematic diagram of the continuum of otitis media (OM) and the interaction of its various forms. COM = chronic otitis media; MOM = mucoid otitis media; OME = otitis media with effusion; POM = purulent otitis media; SOM = serous otitis media.

"Abuse" of VT use has been described in published reports, and, as with any tool, abuse is possible. However, I have found misunderstanding of the use of VTs to be prevalent. I cite two common examples. One is the "high incidence" of post-tubal implant otorrhea, which I find to be a minor problem in our patients (fewer than 3%). If one understands the continuum and how otitis media with effusion (OME) evolves, especially how mucoid OM leads to classic chronic OM characterized by pathologic tissue (especially granulation tissue), it is easy to see that otorrhea results from an expression of the underlying pathologic condition and not from foreign-body reaction to the tube per se.

Another prevalent concept appearing in studies (especially pediatric studies) would deny use of tubes even in the presence of chronic OME because the hearing is normal or loss is not too severe, and/or because behavioral communication disorders or educational dysfunction do not seem to ensue later (usually still during childhood, according to longitudinal studies). In the collection of human temporal bones in our otopathology laboratory at the University of Minnesota, there are specimens from approximately 600 cases of OM, and many of these patients had clinical records to correlate functional with pathologic findings. I wish that those authors with the notion that damage does not ensue would have time to study this collection; they would definitely find (as I and many others have described in published reports) that chronic OME and especially mucoid OM can lead to chronic OM, including chronic silent OM, and to many other sequelae later in life, often in adults, which the longitudinal studies to date have not addressed or included. Moreover, we have seen and treated many adult patients with serious problems of OM that stem from OM in childhood. Besides otologic findings of chronic OM, a lateral Law's view screen of the mastoid will often show a hypoplastic, sclerotic mastoid. Frequently, these patients will undergo a period of quiescence or inactivity at age 10 or 12 years and then in their adult years will develop either full-blown episodes of chronic OM and chronic mastoiditis or a variety of sequelae in the middle and/or inner ear.

Chronic Otitis Media with Effusion and Use of Ventilation Tubes

It is relevant to mention briefly the use of VTs for OME. We would all agree that their use is applicable only when chronicity is established after 2 or 3 months.

Again, I find that secretory or mucoid otitis media (MOM) is the primary form of OME that can lead to chronic OM and mastoiditis and chronic silent OM. Tubes are placed in position as described above, and a #1 tube is used in all cases. Adenoidectomy is an adjunct of

the procedure if indicated clinically. If the problem becomes persistent and the tubes are extruded early, this means that active pathologic conditions of fluid and sometimes tissue are developing beneath the tympanic membrane, and then one can evolve, in chronic obstinate cases of MOM, to the use of a #2 VT with the larger diameter of 1.5 mm.

Chronic Silent OM and Middle Ear/Inner Ear Interaction

We have found that chronic silent OM is a common finding, both in our collection of human temporal bones in the otopathology laboratory and in patients. The most common example of this would be where MOM evolves into chronic OM characterized by granulation tissue that can fill the mastoid and middle ear in children or in adults. We also see examples of cholesteatoma that were not identified because of an intact, apparently normal-appearing tympanic membrane. Chronic silent OM refers to chronic pathologic conditions characterized by various sequelae in the middle ear, including granulation tissue, cholesterin granulation tissue, and cholesteatoma that exists behind an intact tympanic membrane. The classic definition of chronic OM in textbooks includes a history or findings of perforation and otorrhea, but many examples of intractable pathologic tissue can occur behind an intact tympanic membrane and may, in addition to pathologic changes in tissue, include a variety of sequelae involving the ossicles and the middle ear space (Djeric et al, 1994; Paparella et al, 1984).

Another important concept to consider when using VTs with tympanoplasty is the existence of interactions between the inner ear and middle ear. Here, too, I have found ample evidence in animal and in human temporal bones, as well as in clinical examples, of dysfunction developing in the inner ear from pathologic conditions in the middle ear. The round window membrane, which is 0.065 mm thick, is essentially permeable. Almost anything that is placed in the middle ear can be reflected with some change in the perilymph of the scala tympani or deeper in the labyrinth. Sensorineural hearing loss and vestibular findings can be common sequelae of chronic OM. The normal human cochlear duct is approximately 31 mm long, and approximately half of that length exists in the basal turn, which is silent and not tested with routine audiometry. Nevertheless, there are many studies, in animals and in humans, that demonstrate that this is a real problem and, of course, I see this quite commonly in the clinic. Here, too, it is important to consider VTs in such patients (Paparella et al, 1970).

In patients with chronic silent OM, it is important to consider eradicating the pathologic conditions and recreating the middle ear space. This can be done by incising the tensor tympani, lateralizing the malleus, enlarging the diameter of the middle ear by atticotomy, and removing the posterior bony meatus. Use of Silastic and then use of a VT after eradication of pathologic tissue creates an air-containing middle ear. If a patient shows evidence of interaction of the middle ear with the inner ear, it is relevant, after cleaning pathologic tissues away from the round window niche, to graft that area with collagen and Gelfoam (packed Gelfoam alone has been found to be efficacious) and then to reconstruct the middle ear, eradicate pathologic conditions, and, once again, use a VT to avoid further development of pathologic conditions or damage from barometric conditions, which can contribute to difficulties from interactions of the middle and inner ear (Vambutas and Paparella, 1999).

Flexible Surgical Approach and the Continuum of OM

When I look at the pathogenesis and pathology of the various forms of OM of the continuum, I find that it is not desirable to use a stereotypical surgical approach to treat these diseases. For example, I observed that in many courses in dissection of temporal bone throughout the world, one method is taught to treat, for example, pathology of the middle ear and mastoid. I find that a flexible approach is conservative and sufficient to treat all of these forms of OM on the basis of an understanding of the continuum and its pathogenesis. I have found children who have had radical mastoidectomy that could have been avoided. I have never performed radical mastoidectomy for chronic OM or chronic mastoiditis in a child but would rather do a flexible, conservative approach, such as will be described, to achieve an aerated, noninfectious middle ear cleft.

Usually, if such a child has evolved from MOM to chronic OM, typically, a small endaural incision will allow elevation of a tympanomeatal flap, assessment of pathologic conditions in the middle ear, eradication of granulation tissue and other pathologic tissue, and reconstruction of the middle ear, enlarging it in diameter as well as depth, using Silastic, applying grafting if the ear is atelectatic or requires a graft, and then inserting a VT in the anterosuperior quadrant, as mentioned earlier. This, with antibiotics pre- and postoperatively as necessary, has provided a safe, dry ear in all of our children so as not to require a radical mastoidectomy for many years because this more conservative approach suffices to manage the pathologic conditions in such instances.

In a real sense, every patient who has surgery to treat OM, particularly chronic OM, has an "exploratory" tympanotomy. This means that, no matter whether computed tomographic scans were ordered or other diagnostic tests were provided preliminarily, one is never sure of pathologic conditions unless one assesses not only the pathologic tissue but also changes to ossicles and other contents of the middle ear and mastoid. It is common for surprises and new findings to occur, and one must identify the anatomic pathologic conditions and cope with this as conservatively as possible using a flexible surgical approach.

Another important consideration in the pathogenesis of OM and in use of the flexible approach to treat the continuum of OM would be obstructive sites. We have found, in our collection of temporal bones and particularly in patients, that obstructive sites that appear to occur on a genetic basis are commonly part of the pathogenesis of OM. For example, a patient may have a narrowed protympanum, a very high promontory, or a deep oval or round window niche. There can be an obstructive site at that point. Certainly, atelectasis that attaches itself to the promontory would be another example. The manubrium is often retracted and is often attached to the promontory. Understanding this aids judicious placement of VTs.

The next obstructive site would be the isthmus or gateway to the attic. Obstructive sites can occur in the anterior, middle, or posterior attic region, and, of course, obstructive sites can occur in the aditus ad antrum, which, of course, led to the classic Bondy modified radical mastoidectomy for treatment of cholesteatoma. Then, too, obstructive sites can occur in various aspects of the mastoid air-cell system. Another secondary consideration for obstructive sites would be that we find, in children and adults with chronic OM particularly, that the middle ear cleft itself seems to be hypodeveloped, along with hypopneumatization of the mastoid air-cell system. There can therefore be a low-hanging tegmen mastoideum or tegmen tympani. An important consideration is obstruction that can exist in the external auditory canal. Very often, there is a very tortuous, narrowed, obstructive external auditory canal, and with inflammation of the canal, this can add to OM and vice versa. All of these considerations of pathology and anatomy need to be taken into consideration when using the flexible approach and VTs.

Steps in the flexible approach, which would usually include use of a VT, would include exploratory tympanotomy and then an endaural approach (small, medium, or large) if there are sufficient pathologic conditions. This universal endaural approach allows the flexible approach to take place. Other steps of the flexible approach include—most importantly—canalplasty (both posterior and superior), reconstruction and enlargement of the middle ear, atticotomy, and mastoidotomy (one should look in the mastoid to see if there are any actual pathologic conditions that require eradication), tympanoplasty, and mastoidectomy as indicated (if the mastoid is sclerotic, one should not use an intact wall postauricular mastoidectomy because the dangers outweigh the benefits in terms of treatment, and one would only end up with a small mastoid in any case). When a mastoidectomy is done, whether through a closed or an open approach, it is possible in a large mastoid cavity to drill mastoid cortical bone posteriorly, superiorly, and inferiorly and, in many cases, to reduce the mastoid cavity to 50% or more of its normal space.

If the patient has an extensive canalplasty or an open-cavity tympanomastoidectomy, we find a Thiersch graft 10 days later to be essential to obtain a properly dry, healed ear as soon as possible. The packing, sutures, and granulations are carefully removed, and a Thiersch graft is applied to the unhealed raw surfaces in the mastoid cavity or in the large canalplasty as required, 10 days postoperatively. Often the ear will be dry within a couple of weeks. This is a same-day procedure that can be done in the office or usually in the outpatient operating room under local or general anesthesia as needed (Harvey et al, 1992; McClain and Paparella, 1995; Paparella, 1982).

Exploratory Tympanotomy

After using VTs for chronic OME, if the problem persists and there is an adequate ear canal, one should consider exploratory tympanotomy to assess such pathologic conditions as granulation tissue, to eradicate it, to enlarge the middle ear space, if needed, using Silastic lining, and then to consider a VT. This is the next conservative step (Paparella and Koutroupas, 1982).

Blue Eardrum

In 1929, the concept of "the blue eardrum" was described by Shambaugh and identified as a separate disease entity (Shambaugh, 1929). Later, this entity was referred to as "idiopathic hemotympanum" (O'Donnell, 1941). We have found, from subsequent studies, that a blue or a purple eardrum is simply a long-term manifestation or sequela of chronic serous OM characterized by cholesterin granuloma that can occupy the middle ear cleft and produce this color. Thus, this is another example of chronic silent OM, and in the process of eradication, it may be sufficient to eradicate the pathologic tissue on the middle ear through an endaural approach, or, if needed, a mastoidectomy can be done in association with it. In addition to enlarging the middle ear, it is important to use a VT; typically, one with a #2 or larger lumen would be used after tympanoplasty and, if needed, mastoidectomy for so-called blue eardrum or "idiopathic hemotympanic membrane" (Paparella, 1976; Paparella and Lim, 1967).

Atelectasis

Another common sequela of OME is atelectasis. Atelectasis refers to an atrophic tympanic membrane that is retracted or collapsed, often attached to the mucoperios-

teum or the promontory without a middle ear space. In such instances, these patients may have a problem with effusions from the middle ear, but they cannot be treated because there is no space for a tube to be placed; thus, it is readily extruded. If the patient has a functional deficit (eg, a conductive loss of sufficient magnitude, a residual conductive loss after aerating the middle ear with VTs, or a suspected or existing attic cholesteatoma), a simple corrective procedure has been used in many patients to date.

This procedure consists of re-establishing the mesotympanic space, strengthening the tympanic membrane by an underplant fascial graft, incising the tensor tympani and enlarging the mesotympanum, extirpating any pathologic tissue, re-establishing ossicular continuity with a partial or total ossicular replacement prosthesis (PORP, TORP), and inserting a VT in the anterosuperior drumhead along with silicone sheeting lining the middle ear. A Gelfilm support structure allows placement of a graft between the Gelfilm and the underlying atrophic tympanic membrane (Paparella, 1979; Paparella and Jung, 1981).

Many physicians have advocated cartilage, which is stiff, as a graft in patients with atelectasis. This does not, however, preclude eustachian tube dysfunction and pathologic conditions evolving from the mucoperiosteum subsequent to surgery. Here, too, a VT is essential to avoid underlying pathologic conditions (Figure 90-2).

Tympanoplasty I, II, III, IV, and V

Whenever tympanoplasty is performed for chronic OM, it can be anticipated that eustachian tube dysfunction will occur both subsequent to tympanoplasty and prior to tympanoplasty as an important part of the pathogenesis. In the early days, we made quantitative measurements of eustachian tubes and ultimately found them not to be useful; this testing was discontinued many years ago. Whenever there is a remnant of the anterior drumhead, in addition to tympanoplastic reconstruction and reconstruction of the middle ear, a VT is routinely used in the anterosuperior quadrant, as mentioned above. If a patient is having a type III or IV tympanoplasty (or even more rarely a type V tympanoplasty, which we discontinued years ago), a VT is more difficult to use because of the small space in the middle ear and because often there is no remnant of a tympanic membrane in such patients. These are typically patients who might have, for example, an open-cavity tympanomastoidectomy in addition to having type III or IV tympanoplasty. In such patients, we have found, in select cases, that it may be advisable to insert a tube through an intact graft after it is well healed, for 4 to 6 months postoperatively, although this is not usually necessary. A VT is most efficacious if it is used at the same time as the tympanoplasty is performed.

We have found that by far the most common cause of failure of tympanoplasty is post-tympanoplasty atelecta-

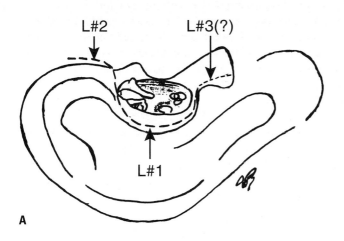

A

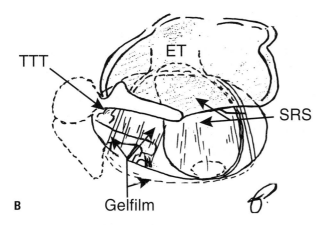

B

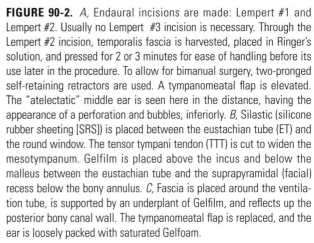

FIGURE 90-2. *A,* Endaural incisions are made: Lempert #1 and Lempert #2. Usually no Lempert #3 incision is necessary. Through the Lempert #2 incision, temporalis fascia is harvested, placed in Ringer's solution, and pressed for 2 or 3 minutes for ease of handling before its use later in the procedure. To allow for bimanual surgery, two-pronged self-retaining retractors are used. A tympanomeatal flap is elevated. The "atelectatic" middle ear is seen here in the distance, having the appearance of a perforation and bubbles, inferiorly. *B,* Silastic (silicone rubber sheeting [SRS]) is placed between the eustachian tube (ET) and the round window. The tensor tympani tendon (TTT) is cut to widen the mesotympanum. Gelfilm is placed above the incus and below the malleus between the eustachian tube and the suprapyramidal (facial) recess below the bony annulus. *C,* Fascia is placed around the ventilation tube, is supported by an underplant of Gelfilm, and reflects up the posterior bony canal wall. The tympanomeatal flap is replaced, and the ear is loosely packed with saturated Gelfoam.

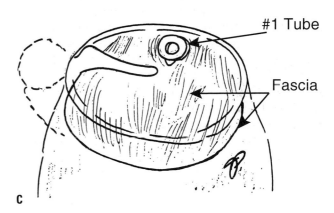

C

sis. Thus, patients who have an excellent result who do not come back for follow-up visits may have recurrent disease requiring revision of the surgery. For example, if the tube extrudes a year or two later, and the patients return with atelectasis, they require either reinsertion of a VT in the clinic or, if the problem is severe enough, revision of the tympanoplasty, again with insertion of a VT. This has happened so many times that it proves beyond a doubt that eustachian tube dysfunction after tympanoplasty continues to be a major problem, as it does primarily in the vast majority of patients who require tympanoplasty for chronic OM and chronic mastoiditis and/or chronic silent OM. These many observations have led to two important facts: it is important for the patient to return for follow-up care every 6 or 12 months as indicated, and in such patients, a larger #2 tube (1.5 mm) is preferable for long-term ventilation.

Tympanomastoidectomy

There were, historically and as defined in the literature, three classic forms of mastoidectomy: simple mastoidectomy, modified radical mastoidectomy, and radical mastoidectomy. Since the development of tympanoplasty in

the 1950s by Wüllstein and Zöllner, we have found that those classic forms have literally disappeared. For example, we never do radical mastoidectomy for chronic OM and chronic mastoiditis. There is still rarely a case for simple mastoidectomy, although not many have occurred in the postantibiotic era.

Three types of tympanomastoidectomy have replaced the three classic types. The simple mastoidectomy has become the closed-cavity or intact wall tympanomastoidectomy or so-called "posterior tympanotomy," a term applied by Europeans. It consists of a complete simple mastoidectomy, enlargement of the facial recess, and postauricular tympanoplasty without canalplasty. We have found that the intact bridge tympanomastoidectomy (IBM) beautifully replaces the previous modified radical or classic Bondy mastoidectomy. It consists of open-cavity tympanomastoidectomy, canalplasty, enlargement of the middle ear, reconstruction of the bridge to optimize reconstruction of the middle ear and ossiculoplasty, and reduction of the mastoid, along with eradication of pathologic tissue. A VT is routinely used in this procedure (Sajjadi and Paparella, 1996). The open-cavity tympanomastoidectomy replaces the classic radical mastoidectomy and is desirable in all cases to allow proper healing to take place and optimize possibilities of retention or improvement of hearing. I have found that VTs, either #1 or #2, are often used in all of those three types of tympanomastoidectomy. I commonly perform the IBM or open-cavity procedure, but, usually, closed-cavity procedures consist of an endaural approach, as mentioned above, and usually a radical mastoidectomy is not required in children, particularly when they have a hypoplastic mastoid air-cell system.

Partial and Total Ossicular Replacement Prostheses

Frequently, I find that the incus is destroyed in cases of chronic OM, particularly in patients who have evolved from mucoid to chronic OM. This appears to be the most common lesion of the ossicles. Typically, the next ossicle to be damaged would be the stapes, and much less often the malleus. Thus, in association with tympanoplasty or tympanomastoidectomy, I commonly use TORPs or PORPs. Once again, it is important to enlarge and reconstruct the middle ear. This is particularly benefited by the IBM approach. As mentioned above, whenever doing tympanoplasty or tympanomastoidectomy, I find that the use of a VT is most important in the anterosuperior quadrant and in the protympanum space, as described.

I have seen many patients who have had extrusions of PORPs and TORPs over the years, but the most common cause is that they do not come back for follow-up, and a VT that might have been inserted perhaps 5 years previously has since become occluded. Then they developed post-tympanoplasty atelectasis, and the PORP or TORP has been extruded. It is rare that extrusion of the TORP or PORP is on the basis of a foreign-body reaction, but it is by far most common that it is caused by post-tympanoplasty atelectasis.

Conclusion

The above reinforces the importance of use of VTs with TORPs and PORPs and in many forms of tympanoplasty and/or reconstruction of the middle ear in dealing with the continuum of OM. Eustachian tube dysfunction is an important factor in patients pre- and post-tympanoplasty.

An understanding of the pathogenesis and the pathology will encourage, first, use of a flexible approach and, second, in patients who require it, consideration of a VT in association with tympanoplasty for atelectasis and when tubal dysfunction is a problem or is strongly suspected.

References

Djeric DR, Schachern PA, Paparella MM, et al. Otitis media (silent): a potential cause of childhood meningitis. Laryngoscope 1994;104:1453–60.

Harvey SA, Paparella MM, Sperling NM, Alleva M. The flexible (conservative surgical) approach for chronic otitis media in young children. Laryngoscope 1992;102:1399–403.

Juhn SK, Paparella MM, Goycoolea MV, et al. Pathogenesis of otitis media. Ann Otorhinolaryngol 1977;86:481–92.

McClain A Jr, Paparella MM. Flexible surgical approach for treating otitis media. Minn State J Otolaryngol 1995;1:52–63.

O'Donnell JH. "Blue drum" or idiopathic hemotympanum in children. BMJ 1941;2:86.

Paparella MM. Blue ear drum and its management. Ann Otol Rhinol Laryngol 1976;85 Suppl 25:293–5.

Paparella MM. "How I do it"—otology and neurology: tympanoplasty for atelectatic ears. Laryngoscope 1979;89:1345–6.

Paparella MM. Panel discussion: pathogenesis of otitis media: current treatment of otitis media based on pathogenesis studies. Laryngoscope 1982;92:292–6.

Paparella MM, Brady DR, Hoel R. Sensori-neural hearing loss in chronic otitis media and mastoiditis. Trans Am Acad Ophthalmol Otolaryngol 1970;74:108–15.

Paparella MM, Jung TTK. Experience with tympanoplasty for atelectatic ears. Laryngoscope 1981;91:1472–7.

Paparella MM, Jung TTK, Mancini F, et al. Silent otitis media. In: Lim DJ, Bluestone CD, Klein JO, Nelson JD, editors. Recent advances in otitis media with effusion—proceedings of the Third International Symposium. Toronto: BC Decker; 1984.

Paparella MM, Koutroupas S. Exploratory tympanotomy revisited. Laryngoscope 1982;92:531–4.

Paparella MM, Lim DJ. Pathogenesis and pathology of the "idiopathic" blue ear drum. Arch Otolaryngol 1967;85:249–58.

Sajjadi H, Paparella MM. Intact-bridge mastoidectomy: operative techniques. Oper Tech Otolaryngol Head Neck Surg 1996;7:55–61.

Shambaugh GE. The blue drum membrane. Arch Otolaryngol 1929;10:238–40.

Vambutas A, Paparella MM. Tympanoplasty. Otolaryngol Clin North Am 1999;32:505–12.

IX. *Miscellaneous Topics on Otitis Media*

Chapter 91

IMAGING IN OTITIS MEDIA

JANE L. WEISSMAN, MD, JAMES C. ANDERSON, MD

Computed tomography (CT) and magnetic resonance imaging (MRI) play an important role in the evaluation of otitis media and its complications. CT excels at delineating fine cortical bone (mastoid septations, tegmen tympani). MRI better delineates intracranial complications. Often the two studies are complementary.

Techniques

Both CT and MRI can best be used by tailoring the examinations to the appropriate clinical setting. Although standard scanning can be used in the majority of cases, decisions as to the extent of coverage (neck or intracranial imaging), use of contrast, and use of certain MRI techniques will be helped by knowledge of clinical concerns.

CT is the study of choice to evaluate the mastoid cortex and septae, Körner's septum, tegmen tympani, and ossicles. Slices are 1 mm thick (or thinner) with no interslice gap, or they can be overlapping. Axial and coronal views are acquired, with the axial images obtained in the plane of the lateral semicircular canal.

The fine osseous structures of the temporal bone are well evaluated with current spiral (helical) CT scanning. Recent technical improvements include multidetector CT scanners with capabilities of submillimeter imaging, faster scan times, and a wider area of scan coverage with each rotation of the CT gantry. Additionally, isotropic imaging (the ability to view image data in any plane, without loss of clinically relevant image detail) may alleviate the need to scan in both axial and coronal planes (Caldemeyer et al, 1999). These improvements allow better images to be obtained in patients who have difficulty remaining motionless or are unable to be positioned for direct coronal imaging. Scanning of some children may be able to be performed without the use of sedation owing to the faster scan time. Intravenous iodinated contrast is generally not needed for CT evaluation of the osseous structures but may be needed if intracranial complications are being sought.

MRI becomes important if intracranial complications are suspected, facial palsy is present, or there is otoscopic evidence for hemorrhage. Evaluation of the entire brain with T_1-weighted and T_2-weighted or fluid-attenuated inversion recovery (FLAIR) sequences is performed. FLAIR is an MRI sequence that allows better visualization of areas of high signal on T_2-weighted images by canceling out the signal from normal cerebrospinal fluid, which is also bright and could obscure subtle areas of brain edema. Additionally, thinner (3 mm or less) axial T_1- and T_2-weighted images of the temporal bones, posterior fossa, and middle cranial fossa are obtained. Gadolinium-enhanced scans in the coronal and axial planes with T_1 weighting are also generated. Magnetic resonance venography (MRV) may be used to help evaluate for thrombosis of the sigmoid sinus (Chakeres et al, 1996).

Complications of Acute Otomastoiditis

CT findings in uncomplicated acute otomastoiditis include opacification of the mastoid air cells and middle ear. Usually, it is not possible to determine if the material is obstructed secretions, pus, edematous mucosa, granulation tissue, or a combination of these materials.

Imaging findings of the complications of acute otomastoiditis can be divided into primary temporal bone complications, extracranial complications, and intracranial complications. Primary temporal bone complications include coalescence (erosion of the mastoid septae), erosion of the mastoid cortex, petrous apicitis, and labyrinthitis. Extracranial complications include subperiosteal abscess and Bezold's abscess. Intracranial complications include epidural abscess, mastoiditis, cerebritis, cerebral abscess, and dural venous thrombosis. The appearance of each on CT and MRI is discussed, along with criteria for choosing the optimal study.

Coalescence of the mastoid is often the first CT finding after mastoid and middle ear opacification (Figure 91-1). Careful evaluation of the mastoid septae and com-

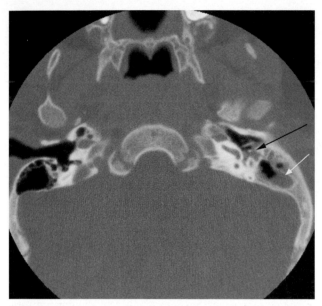

FIGURE 91-1. Axial computed tomographic scan: partial opacification of middle ear (*black arrow*) and mastoid air cells (*white arrow*), owing to inflammation.

parison with the opposite side can help, but asymmetry in aeration of the mastoids is common. The mastoid cortex should be scrutinized to evaluate for erosions that may raise suspicion for intra- or extracranial extension of infection from the mastoid air cells. MRI is somewhat insensitive for detecting coalescence or cortical erosion, revealing only the opacification of the air cells.

Petrous apicitis is important to recognize as it, too, can lead to intracranial extension of disease. The differential diagnosis and specific entities are discussed later and are summarized in Table 91-1. CT will reveal findings similar to those seen in the mastoid air cells, with debris and disruption of bony septae. If any clinical concern for intracranial extension is present (including the classic Gradenigo's syndrome triad of otomastoiditis, sixth nerve palsy, and pain in the distribution of the fifth cranial nerve) with findings of petrous apicitis on CT, MRI is needed to explore for intracranial complications. MRI

findings in petrous apicitis without intracranial extension include enhancement of the petrous apex and may have, in some cases, enhancement of the meninges and Meckel's cave (Swartz, 1996). Although uncommon with current antibiotic treatment, petrous apicitis should always be kept in mind as it can occur with acute or chronic otitis media, immediately or after delay following mastoidectomy, and may occur independently of mastoiditis.

Labyrinthitis in the setting of acute otomastoiditis may occur via spread of infection across the round or oval window. MRI is better suited to identify this complication. Gadolinium-enhanced T_1-weighted images demonstrate enhancement within the membranous labyrinth in the acute setting (Swartz, 1996). Precontrast T_1-weighted images are necessary to distinguish between hemorrhage and enhancement (Weissman et al, 1992) (Figure 91-2).

The earliest imaging findings of extracranial complications are erosions of the mastoid cortex, seen best on CT, and swelling in the overlying soft tissues. Distinction between abscess and edema in the soft tissue around the mastoid is important as it may indicate extension of infection from the mastoid but can also be seen in the setting of a thrombosis of a mastoid emissary vein. The most common location of extracranial abscess formation attributable to direct extension from the mastoids is postauricular, owing to the thin bone in this region. Anterior extension through the preauricular mastoid cortex will lead to abscess along the root of the zygomatic bone. Bezold's abscess and erosion through the mastoid tip are rare but potentially life threatening. Infection may spread inferiorly along the sternocleidomastoid muscle and into the mediastinum or may extend superiorly to the base of the skull or even to the vertebrae. Recognizing this by imaging is vital as these may not be evident on clinical examination (Castillo et al, 1998). Intravenous contrast is helpful to identify and define the extent of abscess (Figure 91-3).

Two scenarios direct the choice of imaging investigations of intracranial complication. One is in unexplained meningitis, especially in children. CT examination of the temporal bones with special attention to the tegmen and

TABLE 91-1. Magnetic Resonance Studies Pre- and Postgadolinium Enhancement

| Diagnosis | Bone Destruction | CT | MRI | | |
			T_1	T_2	Gadolinium Enhancement
Effusion	No	Air-fluid levels nonspecific if opacified	Variable	Variable, generally high	No
Granulation tissue	Usually no	Tissue density	Variable, generally intermediate	Generally high	Yes, intensely
Cholesterol granuloma	May show expansile characteristics	May be hyperdense	High	High	Yes
Cholesteatoma	Yes	Typically in Prussak's space	Low to intermediate, heterogeneous	High, heterogeneous	No
Epidermoid (congenital cholesteatoma)	Yes	Variable location, tissue density	Low to intermediate	High	No

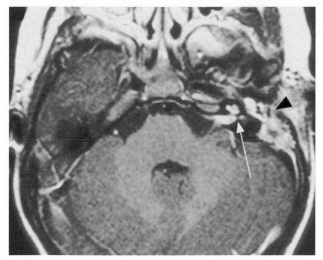

FIGURE 91-2. Magnetic resonance image of labyrinthitis: T_1-weighted image with gadolinium reveals enhancement of the labyrinth and internal auditory canal (*white arrow*), secondary to inflammation of middle ear and mastoids (*black arrowhead*).

sigmoid sinus plate should be undertaken. The second is in patients with known otomastoiditis with clinical signs of intracranial complications. In this setting, MRI is considered the study of choice, with MRV performed as well to assess the dural sinuses.

The multiplanar capabilities of MRI are helpful in identifying small intracranial abscesses and may show meningeal enhancement in meningitis. Abscess may occur in the middle cranial fossa following erosion of the tegmen or of the anterior cortex of the petrous pyramid. Posterior fossa is involved when the bone of Trautmann's triangle, over the sigmoid sinus plate or the posterior cortex of the petrous pyramid, is eroded (Swartz, 1996). Epidural abscess may occur by direct extension; however, subdural and parenchymal abscesses more commonly occur secondary to thrombophlebitis.

The diagnosis of venous sinus thrombosis can be difficult. Even with MRI, the diagnosis of dural sinus occlusion can be difficult because of variations in anatomy and venous flow. A combination of pre- and postcontrast MRI and MRV is considered state-of-the-art imaging for diagnosing sigmoid sinus thrombosis. There are pitfalls even with this combination of imaging, including slow flow in large veins and sinuses, arachnoid granulations that may cause filling defects, and dramatic, but normal, asymmetry of the sinuses (Swartz and Harnsberg, 1998) (Figure 91-4).

Chronic Otomastoiditis Complications

Findings and complications in chronic otomastoiditis include tympanic membrane retraction, middle ear effusion, granulation tissue, cholesterol granuloma, acquired cholesteatoma, and ossicular erosions or fixation (Swartz,

1996). These can occur alone or in combination and may be superimposed on acute otomastoiditis complications. Hearing loss, either conductive or sensorineural, may be associated with these complications.

Tympanic membrane retraction, although well seen with otoscopic examination, can be seen with CT when the membrane is thickened. The tympanic membrane is inconspicuous in its normal state.

Effusions are diagnosed on imaging by demonstration of an air-fluid level. Two planes of imaging are helpful to differentiate from other material by verifying free-fluid movement. Thus, direct coronal imaging rather than single-plane imaging with reformatted images is needed. When complete opacification is present, this differentiation may not be possible: CT attenuation or Hounsfield numbers are unreliable as the fluid may be variable in its components and the density of the contents of very small air cells may be impossible to measure. MRI studies pre- and postgadolinium enhancement can differentiate between middle ear effusion, mucosal inflammation, granulation tissue, cholesterol granuloma, and cholesteatoma. Fluid may have variable T_1- and T_2-weighted intensities but is generally hyperintense on both owing to material with the fluid. Fluid will not enhance (see Table 91-1).

Bony erosion cannot be used as the sole criterion to differentiate granulation tissue from cholesteatoma, although the location of erosion may help. Granulation tissue will image as high signal intensity on T_2-weighted images and enhances intensely. Granulation tissue can occur along with other complications, including cholesteatoma.

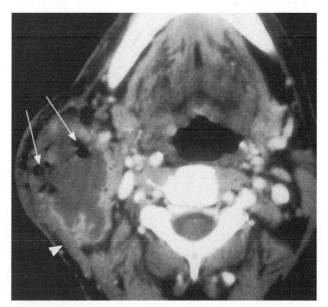

FIGURE 91-3. Contrast-enhanced computed tomographic scan demonstrates Bezold's abscess in the right neck inferior to mastoid tip and deep to the sternocleidomastoid muscle (*white arrowhead*). Note air within abscess from previous aspiration attempt (*white arrows*).

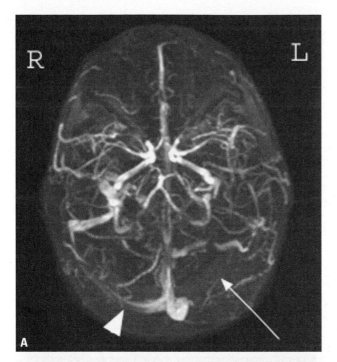

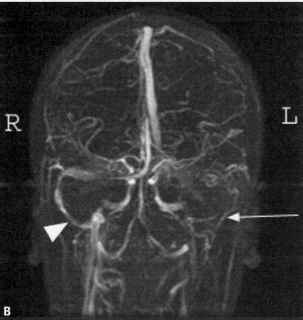

FIGURE 91-4. Magnetic resonance venography maximum-intensity projection (MIP) images. *A,* Cranial-caudal MIP; *B,* anterior-posterior MIP. Lack of flow in left transverse sinus and sigmoid sinus owing to thrombosis (*white arrows*). Compare with normal right transverse sinus and sigmoid sinus (*white arrowheads*).

Cholesterol granuloma has several aliases, including cholesterol cyst, giant cholesterol cyst, chocolate cyst, and blue-domed cyst. In the petrous apex, these may have a dramatic expansile appearance. They are generally described as being hyperintense on both T_1- and T_2-weighted images. Enhancement may be difficult to determine owing to the high signal on precontrast images.

Acquired cholesteatoma can be a diagnostic challenge particularly when it occurs in an atypical location. CT is the initial study of choice. The classic pars flaccida location is best seen on coronal CT to demonstrate the location in Prussak's space and subtle erosion of the scutum. Erosion of the ossicles may also be seen. Masses in this location may extend into the mastoid air cells via the aditus ad antrum. The pars tensa cholesteatomas typically occur in the facial recess and sinus tympani (Maroldi et al, 2001). These structures are best visualized in the axial plane (Swartz, 1996). Although CT is generally sufficient, if the tegmen tympani or sinus plate shows defects, then MRI is useful to determine if epidural extension or temporal lobe herniation has occurred. MRI may also be helpful when the middle ear cavity is filled with soft tissue (Veillon et al, 2000). Cholesteatoma does not enhance with gadolinium; thus, MRI can be helpful in differentiating granulation tissue from cholesteatoma when no bone destruction is present (Figure 91-5).

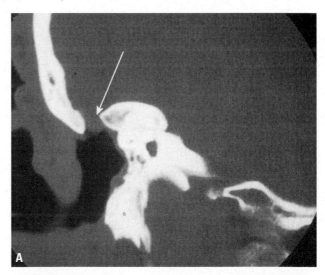

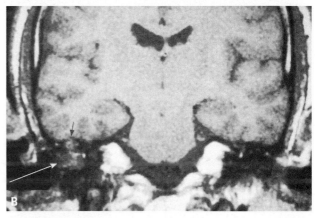

FIGURE 91-5. *A,* Coronal computed tomographic scan with erosion of the tegmen by a cholesteatoma (*white arrow*). *B,* Coronal T_1-weighted magnetic resonance image in the same patient with more of the cholesteatoma demonstrated (*white arrow*) and with extension through the tegmen (*black arrow*).

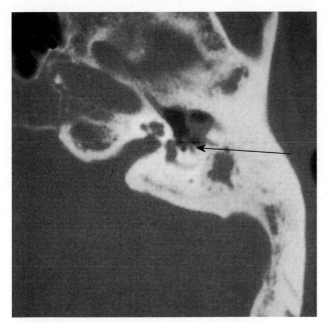

FIGURE 91-6. Axial computed tomographic scan: cholesteatoma with erosion into horizontal semicircular canal (*black arrow*).

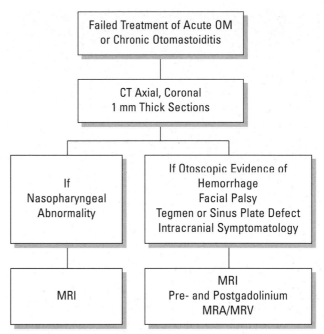

FIGURE 91-7. Imaging algorithm. Adapted from Swartz JD and Harnsberger HR (1998).

Cholesteatoma can lead to several other complications that imaging can aid in diagnosing, including labyrinthitis, conductive hearing loss, and facial nerve paralysis. Labyrinthitis and labyrinthine fistulae can occur secondary to cholesteatoma owing to erosion most commonly into the lateral semicircular canal. Labyrinthitis is best imaged with MRI, as described earlier under acute complications; however, CT is useful to visualize the erosion of the semicircular canal.

CT is the modality of choice for evaluating conductive hearing loss secondary to ossicle erosion and facial nerve canal bone erosion, aiding in pinpointing the area of involvement. CT can reveal erosion of the incudostapedial joint and stapes superstructure; however, subtle ossicular erosion may not be detected even with high-quality imaging (Swartz and Harnsberger, 1998) (Figure 91-6).

For evaluation of facial nerve involvement, CT is directed at studying the integrity of the facial nerve canal and looking for mass adjacent to the midtympanic segment of the facial nerve. Subtle erosions may be difficult to visualize owing to the normally thin bone overlying portions of the facial nerve; however, most erosion is readily apparent (Swartz, 1996). MRI with gadolinium can help confirm nerve involvement, with enhancement of the nerve seen when the canal is eroded.

Conductive hearing loss may occur in the setting of cholesteatoma or noncholesteatomatous chronic otitis media. In noncholesteatomatous chronic otitis media, the hearing loss may be attributable to ossicular erosions or fixation. The distal incus and stapes are most commonly involved, but the malleus head or incus body can be involved. Fixation can occur because of fibrous tissue,

true tympanosclerosis, and new bone formation. Imaging in both the axial and coronal planes is needed to best evaluate all parts of the ossicular chain (Swartz, 1996).

Imaging in otitis media and otomastoiditis is best used to help evaluate the complications of failed acute and chronic otomastoiditis. Use of CT, MRI, or both may be needed and can be guided by specific clinical concerns. Figure 91-7 provides a basis for an imaging workup.

References

Caldemeyer KS, Sandrasegaran K, Shinaver CN, et al. Temporal bone: comparison of isotropic helical CT and conventional direct axial and coronal CT. AJR Am J Roentgenol 1999;172:1675–82.

Castillo M, Albernaz VS, Mukherji SK, et al. Imaging of Bezold's abscess. AJR Am J Roentgenol 1998;171:1491–5.

Chakeres DW, Oehler M, Schmalbrock P, Slone W. Temporal bone imaging. In: Som PM, Curtin HD, editors. Head and neck imaging. 3rd ed. St. Louis: Mosby-Year Book; 1996. p. 1319–50.

Swartz JD. Temporal bone inflammatory disease. In: Som PM, Curtin HD, editors. Head and neck imaging. 3rd ed. St. Louis: Mosby-Year Book; 1996. p. 1391–414.

Swartz JD, Harnsberger HR, editors. Imaging of the temporal bone. 3rd ed. New York: Thieme Medical Publishers; 1998.

Maroldi R, Farina D, Palvarini L, et al. Computed tomography and magnetic resonance imaging of pathologic conditions of the middle ear. Eur J Radiol 2001;40:78–93.

Veillon F, Riehm S, Roedlich MN, et al. Imaging of middle ear pathology. Semin Roentgenol 2000;25:2–11.

Weissman JL, Curtin HD, Hirsch BE, Hirsch WL Jr. High signal from the otic labyrinth on unenhanced magnetic resonance imaging. AJNR Am J Neuroradiol 1992;13:1183–7.

Chapter 92

Otitis Media in Newborn Infants

Elizabeth D. Barnett, MD

Otitis media (OM) occurs in the newborn infant as an isolated infection or may be associated with sepsis, meningitis, or other systemic illness. Diagnostic criteria for acute otitis media (AOM) are the same as for older infants and children: the presence of middle ear fluid plus one or more signs of acute illness. The spectrum of pathogens causing middle ear disease in the first few weeks of life reflects pathogens causing sepsis in neonates, with a transition in the first weeks of life to middle ear pathogens common in older children. The assessment of the newborn infant with OM involves evaluating signs and symptoms of systemic illness and the appearance of the tympanic membrane (TM). Treatment involves consideration of pathogens likely to cause sepsis in newborns and those likely to cause OM in older infants and children.

Ear of the Newborn Infant

The ear canal of the newborn is often filled with vernix caseosa. The ear canals are pliable and collapse easily. It is difficult to distinguish the TM from the edge of the canal because of the extreme oblique angle at which the TM is positioned, almost in the same plane as the canal wall. The mobility of the TM in newborn infants is difficult to assess because it may be mistaken for movement of the wall of the ear canal (Jaffe et al, 1970). By 1 month of age, the TM assumes a position relative to the ear canal more typical of the older child (Bluestone and Klein, 2001).

The middle ear in full-term healthy infants may be filled with fluid in the first hours of life but is well aerated, with normal middle ear pressure, within the first 24 to 72 hours of life (Keith, 1975). Infants with nasotracheal or endotracheal tubes are at higher risk of having middle ear effusion in the newborn period (Berman et al, 1978; Persico et al, 1985). Autopsy studies demonstrate that amniotic fluid, meconium, cellular material with mucus, and purulent fluid may be found in the middle ear of newborn infants (De Sa, 1973; Piza et al, 1989).

Middle Ear Effusion in Neonates

Prospective evaluation of newborn infants helps define the baseline status of the middle ear in healthy and vulnerable newborns. Poor mobility of the TM on pneumatic otoscopy, suggesting middle ear effusion, was found in 18 of 101 healthy Navajo newborns (18%) examined in a newborn nursery in Gallup, New Mexico (Jaffe et al, 1970). Examination of 125 infants admitted to a neonatal intensive care unit identified middle ear effusion in 30% (Balkany et al, 1978). A study of low birth weight (< 2,300 g) infants examined three times weekly until discharge found OM (defined as TM abnormality on examination from intensive care unit, confirmed by finding fluid or pus in the middle ear at myringotomy) in three infants (incidence of 2%) (Warrant and Stool, 1971). The variation in incidence of middle ear fluid in these studies likely reflects the variability in resolution of fluid present in the middle ear at birth, the different times the infants were examined relative to time of birth, and the different risk factors for middle ear disease in newborn infants.

Microbiology of Middle Ear Infection in Neonates

OM in infants under 2 weeks of age, or in infants who remain hospitalized for prolonged periods after birth, may be caused by organisms associated with sepsis in newborns, such as group B streptococcus, enteric gram-negative bacilli, and *Staphylococcus*. Gram-negative bacilli, including *Pseudomonas aeruginosa*, were the most common organisms cultured from purulent middle ear effusions in an autopsy series; β-hemolytic streptococcus was also identified. All infants in this study had pneumonia or meningitis; thus, the finding of organisms associated with neonatal sepsis was not unexpected (De Sa, 1973). *P. aeruginosa* has also been cultured from purulent drainage from the middle ear in an infant thought to have acquired the organism during a water birth (Parker and Boles, 1997). Group A streptococcus, *Klebsiella pneumoniae*, and other organisms have been identified in the middle ear of newborns. Tuberculosis of the middle ear and of the middle ear and parotid gland have been reported in preterm infants from Hong Kong and Turkey (Ng et al, 1995; Senbil et al, 1997). The mothers of these infants had active pulmonary tuberculosis. A high index of suspicion for unusual organisms such as *Mycobacterium tuberculosis* is necessary under appropriate circumstances.

The most common pathogens causing AOM in newborns, especially those 2 weeks of age and older, are those causing OM in older infants and children, such as *Streptococcus pneumoniae* and *Haemophilus influenzae*. Nozicka and colleagues (1999) performed tympanocentesis in 40 previously healthy, nontoxic-appearing infants 0 to 8 weeks of age with OM. Middle ear cultures were positive in 25 of 40 infants (62.5%), with *S. pneumoniae* and *Moraxella catarrhalis* the most common organisms identified. Organisms identified in five studies of OM in newborn infants can be found in Table 92-1.

Diagnosis of Otitis Media in Newborn Infants

AOM is defined as the presence of middle ear effusion plus one or more signs of systemic illness. In newborns, the signs of systemic illness may be subtle and include fever, irritability, poor feeding, a runny nose, and lethargy. Pneumatic otoscopy remains the modality of choice for diagnosis of middle ear effusions. Examination of the middle ear is challenging in the newborn because of the position of the TM and the difficulty in assessing its movement (Eavey et al, 1976). The TM may be thickened, with limited mobility in the first few days of life (Cavanaugh, 1987). The position and appearance of the middle ear resemble that of the older child by about 1 month of age.

Tympanometry is of limited value in examination of the middle ear in newborn infants. It is difficult to obtain

a seal in the ear canal with the instrument, and the pliability of the canal may be problematic. Even when fluid is identified by aspiration, a flat tympanogram may not be present in the newborn (Pestalozza and Cusmano, 1980). Acoustic reflectometry may be useful in identification of middle ear fluid in the very young infant as insertion into the ear canal or establishment of a seal is not needed, although systematic study of this technique has not been done in this age group (Barnett et al, 1998).

Management of Newborn Infants with Otitis Media

Febrile or otherwise ill-appearing infants 2 weeks of age or younger who have middle ear effusion may have infection owing to organisms associated with neonatal sepsis, such as enteric gram-negative bacilli or group B streptococcus. Appropriate management of these infants is directed toward identifying the organism by culturing blood, urine, cerebrospinal fluid, or middle ear fluid. A penicillin and an aminoglycoside or a third-generation cephalosporin are appropriate antibiotics for ill or very young infants with OM. For infants who have not left the nursery owing to prolonged illness or prematurity, selection of antimicrobial agents to cover nosocomial organisms is appropriate.

The possibility of bacteremia occurring in association with OM is a concern when assessing very young infants with OM. The prevalence of bacteremia in 832 infants 3 to 12 months of age with fever and OM was 3.7% in a Boston study carried out prior to universal immunization of infants with either *H. influenzae* or pneumococcal conjugate vaccines (Schutzman et al, 1991). A more recent study of 40 infants 0 to 12 weeks of age with OM identified 2 of 15 febrile infants with positive bacterial cultures from sites other than the middle ear: a 2-week-old infant had an *Escherichia coli* urinary tract infection and a 7-week-old infant had pneumococcal bacteremia (Nozicka et al, 1999). None of the afebrile infants in the study had bacte-

TABLE 92-1. Microbiology of Otitis Media in Newborn Infants

Author	Site (Year)	Age Range	Patients, N	Streptococcus pneumoniae	Haemophilus influenzae	Escherichia coli	Staphylococcus	Group B Streptococcus	Group A Streptococcus	Klebsiella pneumoniae	Other	Sterile
Bland, 1972	Honolulu (1970–71)	0–6 wk	18	1 (6)	3 (17)	7 (39)	5 (28)				2 (12)	
Tetzlaff et al, 1977	Dallas (1974–76)	0–5 wk	42*	13 (31)	11 (26)	5 (12)		1 (2)	1 (2)	2 (5)	11 (26)	4 (10)
Balkany et al, 1978	Denver (1975–76)	0–4 mo	34	9 (29)	5 (16)	2 (6)	11 (35)			2 (6)	2 (6)	6 (18)
Shurin et al, 1976	Boston (1976)	0–6 wk	17	4 (24)	2 (12)			2 (12)	1 (6)	1 (6)		7 (41)
Nozicka et al, 1999	Milwaukee (1994–95)	0–8 wk	40*	6 (15)	1 (3)	2 (5)	9 (23)		3 (8)	2 (5)	10 (25)	15 (38)

*Some infants had more than one organism identified.

rial pathogens isolated from blood, urine, or cerebrospinal fluid. Infants with OM who are younger than 2 weeks of age and those 2 to 8 weeks of age with fever, underlying illness, prematurity, or ill appearance are at increased risk of serious bacterial illness, and evaluation should be targeted toward evaluation and treatment of systemic infection.

Healthy, full-term infants who are diagnosed with AOM when older than 2 weeks of age are likely to have middle ear infection owing to organisms similar to those that cause OM in older children. Treatment with an oral antibiotic and outpatient management with close follow-up would be appropriate for previously healthy, nontoxic-appearing, afebrile infants 2 to 8 weeks of age with OM (Nozicka et al, 1999).

Infants with persistent middle ear effusion who remain ill despite antimicrobial therapy and those for whom no other source of infection can be identified may be candidates for needle aspiration of the middle ear so that the middle ear fluid may be cultured. Aspiration of the middle ear of the newborn is more difficult technically than in older children and requires the assistance of an otolaryngologist.

Prognosis of Middle Ear Effusion in Newborns

Infants experiencing OM early in life are at increased risk for repeated episodes of OM and for chronic otitis media with effusion (OME) (Marchant et al, 1984; Nozicka et al, 1999; Teele et al, 1989). Early colonization of the infant nasopharynx with *S. pneumoniae*, *H. influenzae*, and *M. catarrhalis* is also associated with increased risk of AOM and OME (Faden et al, 1997). Strategies for reduction of middle ear disease in infants and older children must be targeted toward preventing the first episode, as well as reducing risk factors for recurrent disease.

Prevention of Otitis Media in the Very Young Infant

Prevention of OM in infants may be accomplished by reducing risk factors associated with OM. Risk factors that can be modified include day care, lack of breast-feeding, prone sleep position, pacifier use, and exposure to cigarette smoke. Other risk factors, such as sibling history of OM, anatomic and genetic factors, and the immunologic status of the host, are not possible to alter (Bluestone and Klein, 2001). Introduction of conjugate pneumococcal vaccines in infancy beginning as early as 6 weeks of age may reduce OM, recurrent OM, and use of tympanostomy tubes in older children but is unlikely to have a direct impact on disease in newborns. Reduction of carriage of pneumococcus in the nasopharynx of household contacts immunized with pneumococcal conjugate vaccine may, however, reduce exposures of neonates to pneumococcus.

Low cord blood pneumococcal antibody has been shown to be associated with more episodes of AOM over the first year of life (Becken et al, 2001). In theory, maternal immunization with pneumococcal vaccine could reduce neonatal disease owing to pneumococcus. Prevention of influenza (through maternal immunization) and respiratory syncytial virus (in premature, chronically ill, or fragile newborns) can reduce OM owing to these viral pathogens. Vaccines against nontypable *H. influenzae* and *M. catarrhalis* may be available in the future but will need to be used in neonates or have an impact on reducing nasopharyngeal carriage in the community to have a significant impact on disease in the youngest infants.

Conclusion

OM in ill or febrile infants and those in the first 2 weeks of life may be associated with sepsis owing to typical pathogens of neonatal sepsis or infection. Evaluation and treatment of these infants involve assessment for neonatal pathogens and treatment with parenteral antibiotics to cover these organisms. Previously healthy infants 2 weeks of age and older with OM who are afebrile and appear well are likely to have disease owing to the pathogens likely to cause OM in older children and may be treated as outpatients with appropriate antibiotics and close follow-up.

References

Balkany TJ, Berman SA, Simmons MA, Jafek BW. Middle ear effusions in neonates. Laryngoscope 1978;88:398–405.

Barnett ED, Klein JO, Hawkins KA, et al. Comparison of spectral gradient acoustic reflectometry and other diagnostic techniques for detection of middle ear effusion in children with middle ear disease. Pediatr Infect Dis J 1998;17:556–9.

Becken ET, Daly KA, Lindgren BR, et al. Low cord blood pneumococcal antibody concentrations predict more episodes of otitis media. Arch Otolaryngol Head Neck Surg 2001;127:517–22.

Berman SA, Balkany TJ, Simmons MA. Otitis media in the neonatal intensive care unit. Pediatrics 1978;62:198–201.

Bland RD. Otitis media in the first six weeks of life: diagnosis, bacteriology, and management. Pediatrics 1972;49:187–97.

Bluestone CD, Klein JO. Otitis media in infants and children. 3rd ed. Philadelphia: WB Saunders; 2001.

Cavanaugh RM Jr. Pneumatic otoscopy in healthy full-term infants. Pediatrics 1987;75:520–3.

De Sa DJ. Infection and amniotic aspiration of middle ear in stillbirth and neonatal deaths. Arch Dis Child 1973;48:872–80.

Eavey RD, Stool SE, Peckham GJ, et al. How to examine the ear of the neonate. Clin Pediatr (Phila) 1976;15:338–41.

Faden H, Duffy L, Wasielewski R, et al. Relationship between nasopharyngeal colonization and the development of otitis media in children. J Infect Dis 1997;175:1440–5.

Jaffe BF, Hurtado F, Hurtado E. Tympanic membrane mobility in the newborn (with seven months' follow-up). Laryngoscope 1970;80:36–48.

Keith RW. Middle ear function in neonates. Arch Otolaryngol 1975;101:376–9.

Marchant CD, Shurin PA, Turczyk VA, et al. Course and outcome of otitis media in early infancy: a prospective study. J Pediatr 1984;104:826–31.

Ng PC, Hiu J, Fok TF, et al. Isolated congenital tuberculosis otitis in a pre-term infant. Acta Paediatr 1995;84:955–6.

Nozicka CA, Hanly JG, Beste DJ, et al. Otitis media in infants aged 0-8 weeks: frequency of associated serious bacterial disease. Pediatr Emerg Care 1999;15:252–4.

Parker PC, Boles RG. *Pseudomonas* otitis media and bacteremia following a water birth. Pediatrics 1997;99:653.

Persico M, Barker GA, Mitchell DP. Purulent otitis media—a "silent" source of sepsis in the pediatric intensive care unit. Otolaryngol Head Neck Surg 1985;93:330–4.

Pestalozza G, Cusmano G. Evaluation of tympanometry in diagnosis and treatment of otitis media of the newborn and of the infant. Int J Pediatr Otorhinolaryngol 1980;2:73–82.

Piza JE, Gonzalez MP, Northrop CC, Eavey RD. Meconium contamination of the neonatal middle ear. J Pediatr 1989;115:910–4.

Schutzman SA, Petrycki S, Gleisher GR. Bacteremia with otitis media. Pediatrics 1991;87:48–53.

Senbil N, Sahin F, Caglar MK, et al. Congenital tuberculosis of the ear and parotid gland. Pediatr Infect Dis J 1997;16:1090–1.

Shurin PA, Pelton SI, Klein JO. Otitis media in the newborn infant. Ann Otol Rhinol Laryngol 1976;85:216–22.

Teele DW, Klein JO, Rosner B, et al. Epidemiology of otitis media during the first seven years of life in children in Greater Boston: a prospective, cohort study. J Infect Dis 1989;160:83–94.

Tetzlaff TR, Ashworth C. Nelson JD. Otitis media in children less than 12 weeks of age. Pediatrics 1977;59:827–32.

Warrant WS, Stool SE. Otitis media in low-birth-weight infants. J Pediatr 1971;79:740–3.

Chapter 93

ACUTE OTITIS MEDIA AND OTITIS MEDIA WITH EFFUSION IN THE IMMUNOCOMPROMISED CHILD

BRITTA RYNNEL-DAGÖÖ, MD, PHD

In children with recurrent and/or persistent pyogenic infections of the respiratory tract that may not respond as expected to treatment, an immunodeficiency disorder must be considered. Infections are also common in pediatric transplant patients and in children with chronic debilitating diseases. These children are often on immunosuppressive drugs and require special attention.

The pathogenesis of acute otitis media (AOM) is multifactorial. Dysfunction of the eustachian tube and an immature immune system in early childhood are two dominating factors. In immunologic disorders, mainly antibody deficiencies, recurrent episodes of AOM (RAOM) are a common and early phenomenon (Rosen et al, 1999). Immunodeficiencies and immunosuppression are rare conditions but are important for the clinician to recognize to obtain early and accurate treatment.

Little is known about otitis media with effusion (OME) in the immunocompromised child.

Upper Respiratory Tract and the Middle Ear

The upper airways are outlined (or possibly lined) by a respiratory epithelium with goblet cells and cilia and are further protected by innate and acquired immunity, both systemic and local. The local secretory immune system is under complex immunoregulatory control (Brandtzaeg et al, 1999). The initial induction of B cells is believed to take place in the organized mucosa-associated lymphoid tissue, which consists of lymphoid organs such as the palatine tonsils and the nasopharyngeal tonsil in Waldeyer's ring. The primed B cells are seeded out through lymph and

blood vessels to secretory tissues such as the airway mucosa and the salivary glands, where they differentiate into immunoglobulin (Ig)-producing plasma cells. The host–parasite interactions in the nasopharynx with bacterial colonization and antigen uptake in the lymphoid tissue (the adenoid) have an impact on the maturation of both local and systemic immunity. Nasopharyngeal carriage of bacteria in childhood is also a potential mechanism for pathogenesis because bacteria might invade the eustachian tube and the middle ear and cause disease. There is a direct communication from the nasopharynx through the eustachian tube to the middle ear, which is virtually sterile—a phenomenon that is poorly understood.

The mucosal membrane of the middle ear is thin and transparent and consists of a one-layered, squamous epithelium. There are a few goblet cells and no glands. The middle ear mucosa has a very limited secretory ability.

In an animal model of OM, Goldie and coworkers (1990) studied vascular leakage into the middle ear after inoculation with pneumococci. The IgG-to-IgA ratio in the fluid on day 3 indicated that the fluid was mainly derived from serum. In the very early phase of purulent OM in an earlier healthy ear, the defense mechanisms are derived from the blood. A large body of evidence has been accumulated that supports the role of serum antibody in protecting the middle ear cavity from disease.

Immaturity of the Immune System in Otitis-Prone Children

After birth, the incidence of AOM is low when maternally acquired antibodies are still relatively high in infants.

RAOM is found in about 5% of all children in the age group of 6 months to 2 years (Ingvarsson et al, 1982). Several studies have shown a defective or immature immune system with significantly lower levels of specific antibody activity against common pneumoccal serotypes in children with RAOM (Freijd et al, 1985; Harsten et al, 1989). Lower specific antibody activity against P6—the highly conserved outer membrane protein from nontypable *Haemophilus influenzae*—in serum has been reported in a significant number of highly otitis-prone children (Yamanaka and Faden, 1993).

A successful immune response to any infectious agent depends on activation of the appropriate set of immune effector functions and cytokine-producing cells. We studied interleukin (IL)-1β, IL-6, and tumor necrosis factor-α levels in nasopharyngeal secretions. Children with recurrent episodes of OM had significantly lower nasopharyngeal IL-1β levels than did healthy children (Lindberg et al, 1994). There is thus evidence for a minor immunologic defect or a slow maturation of immunity in a number of children with RAOM.

Passive immunization for prevention has been demonstrated in only two relatively small clinical trials using high-titered polyclonal human antibody (Englund and Glezen, 2001).

Host Defenses in Abnormal Hosts

Primary Specific Immunodeficiency

Many immunodeficiency diseases are inherited. Defective antibody formation is the most common abnormality, and this group of diseases presents clinically with recurrent pyogenic infections (Rosen et al, 1999). Table 93-1 summarizes the various types of host defense disorders that increase the susceptibility to infections, including AOM in the majority of cases (Patel and Ogra, 1997).

Selective IgA Deficiency

About 1 in 700 whites have no demonstrable serum IgA. Many of these individuals have no apparent disease, whereas others have chronic and recurrent sinusitis and otitis media.

Selective IgG Subclass Deficiency

The most common presenting illness is frequent upper and lower respiratory tract infections. IgG subclass deficiency is often associated with selective IgA deficiency. It should be noted that the diagnosis is difficult because the normal commercially available laboratory measurements are not well standardized.

Transient Hypogammaglobulinemia in Infancy

Maternal IgG is actively transferred to the fetus in the late phase of pregnancy. Ig levels in the infant disappear after birth, and the child's own production starts. The time of initiation and the rate of production of Ig varies considerably. In premature children and in some full-term infants, the serum Ig concentration may be very low—within an "immunodeficient range." The antibody production may be delayed for as long as 36 months, when normal levels of Ig are reached. This might be the case seen in some highly otitis-prone children with RAOM from 6 months to about 3 years of age.

Immunodeficiency Associated with Other Diseases

In many congenital and hereditary conditions, immunodeficiencies have been described. In patients with Down syndrome, RAOM is often observed. In patients with Turner's syndrome, recurrent infections are common.

Assessment and Treatment of Patients Suspected of Having a Primary Immunodeficiency

Early diagnosis and treatment are vital and may prevent the otherwise inevitable devastating damage that may occur, especially to the lungs. Thus, when there are persistent and recurrent infections, including failure to thrive or persistent diarrhea, which do not respond as expected to antibiotics and other treatments such as

TABLE 93-1. Host Defense Disorders and Typical Infections Relating to the Upper Respiratory Tract

Host Defense	Defective in	Infections
Nasal turbinates Mucociliary clearance	Endotracheal intubation	Sinusitis
Cilia	Ciliary dyskinesia syndrome	Otitis media, sinusitis
Mucus blanket	Cystic fibrosis	Sinusitis
Immunoglobulins		
Secretory IgA, IgA, and IgG subclasses	IgA deficiency Agammaglobulinemia Hypogammaglobulinemia IgG subclass deficiency	Otitis media, sinusitis Otitis media, sinusitis
IgE	Hyper IgE syndrome (Job's syndrome)	
Cellular		
Neutrophils		
Decreased count	Chemotherapy Congenital neutropenia	Otitis media, mastoiditis
Motility	Motility disorders	Otitis media, sinusitis
Function	Chronic granulomatous disease	Ulcerative stomatitis
Lymphocytes		
Decreased count	Acquired immune deficiency syndrome (AIDS)	Oral candidiasis, otitis media, sinusitis
Function	Chronic mucocutaneous candidiasis	Oral candidiasis
	Severe combined immunodeficiency	Oral candidiasis, sinusitis
	Wiskott-Aldrich syndrome	Otitis media, sinusitis
Complement	C3, C5 deficiency	Otitis media, sinusitis

insertion of ventilating tubes for RAOM, an immunodeficiency must be considered (Rosen et al, 1999). This is particularly important if family members have similar susceptibility to infections. A careful history will often reveal other types of infection proneness, including episodes of pneumonia or soft tissue infections.

In these infection-prone children, a first screening has to be performed with examination of blood and quantitative measurement of serum Ig concentrations: IgA, IgM, IgG, IgG subclasses, and IgE.

However, functional antibody deficiency may be present despite normal IgG or IgG subclass levels. Conversely, deficient levels of a single subclass of IgG may be found in individuals who have effective specific antibody production and are clinically normal. Our policy is thus to cooperate with clinical immunologists and pediatricians when it comes to interpretation of the measurements and when active immunologic treatment has to be considered.

Ig replacement is now accepted for patients who have significantly diminished serum IgG levels and/or demonstrated defects in antibody production. Ig replacement therapy by subcutaneous infusion of gammaglobulin is used increasingly and is of special value for children. It is possible to give high and effective doses that are well tolerated and with a very low frequency of systemic adverse reactions (Gardulf et al, 1991). There will still be a need for treatment for AOM and otorrhea, which will be performed according to recommendations for children with RAOM without immunodeficiency.

Secondary Immunodeficiency in the Immunocompromised Host

Besides the primary immunodeficiencies, the major causes of increased risk for infection are transplantation of bone marrow or solid organs, immunosuppressive drugs, malnutrition, or chronic diseases such as diabetes mellitus and cystic fibrosis (Hugles and Pizzo, 2000). Also, an implanted foreign body may be an increased risk. Children with malignancy may be severely compromised by immunodeficiency caused by the disease, the therapy, or both.

Transplantation of bone marrow, liver, kidney, and heart (heart-lung) has achieved acceptance as a therapeutic modality for selected diseases and at medical centers with specialized competence. Sucessful organ transplantation requires a profound modification of the recipient's immune response to prevent graft rejection. Because immunosuppression is directed primarily against a T-cell response, the pattern of infections is predictable and comprises mainly opportunistic infections.

Defects in the normal host response may be reflected in the clinical manifestations. An anemic and neutropenic patient may have AOM without erythema and congestion of the tympanic membrane. Fever is, however, also a sensitive and specific sign in patients treated with corticosteroids or anticancer drugs.

Many normal childhood viral illnesses are well tolerated and do not require special treatment. Otitis media and routine upper respiratory tract infections can be treated in the outpatient setting, although fever and symptoms prolonged beyond the usual course require further investigation and contact with the patient's regular pediatrician.

References

Brandtzaeg P, Baeckevold ES, Farstad IN. Regional specialization in the mucosal immune system: what happens in the microcompartments? Immunol Today 1999;20:141–50.

Englund JA, Glezen WP. Passive immunization for the prevention of otitis media. Vaccine 2001;19:116–21.

Freijd A, Oxelius V-A, Rynnel-Dagöö B. A prospective study demonstrating an association between plasma IgG2 concentrations and susceptibility to otitis media in children. Scand J Infect Dis 1985;17:115–20.

Gardulf A, Hammarström L, Smith E. Home treatment of hypogammaglobulinemia with subcutaneous rapid transfusion. Lancet 1991;338:162–6.

Goldie P, Hellström S, Johansson U. Vascular events in experimental otitis media: a comparative study. ORL J Otorhinolaryngol Relat Spec 1990;52:104–12.

Harsten G, Prellner K, Heldrup J, et al. Recurrent acute otitis media. A prospective study of children during the first three years of life. Acta Otolaryngol (Stockh)1989;107:111–9.

Hugles N, Pizzo PhA. Infections in immunocompromised host. In: Behrman RE, Kliegman RM, Jensen HB, editors. Nelson textbook of pediatrics. 16th ed. Philadelphia: WB Saunders; 2000. p. 780–8.

Ingvarsson L, Lundgren K, Olofson B. A prospective study of acute otitis media in children. 2. Incidence in an urban population. Acta Otolaryngol Suppl (Stockh) 1982;388:29–52.

Lindberg K, Rynnel-Dagöö B, Sundquist K. Cytokines in nasopharyngeal secretions, evidence for defective Il-1β production in children with recurrent episodes of acute otitis media. Clin Exp Immunol 1994;97:396–402.

Patel JA, Ogra PL. Host defence. In: Johnsson JT, You VL, editors. Infectious diseases and antimicrobial therapy of the ears nose and throat. Philadelphia: WB Saunders; 1997. p. 18–35.

Rosen FS, Eibl M, Roifman C, et al. Primary immunodeficiency diseases report of IUIS scientific committee. Clin Exp Immunol 1999;118 Suppl 1:1–28.

Yamanaka N, Faden H. Low serum IgG antibody levels specific for P6 of nontypable *Haemophilus influenzae* in otitis-prone children. J Pediatr 1993;113:524–9.

Chapter 94

ACUTE OTITIS MEDIA/ OTITIS MEDIA WITH EFFUSION IN CHILDREN WITH CLEFT PALATE

RUDOLF LEUWER, MD

Clefting of the lip and hard and soft palate is a frequent inborn deformity occurring in 2 to 3 cases per 1,000 births (Godbersen, 1997). It is seen in multiple variations and causes both esthetic and functional disorders. Clefts of the soft palate may result in hearing, speech, and swallowing disorders. Hence, treatment of a child with a cleft palate is an interdisciplinary task, with a substantial share by the otolaryngologist.

The incidence of otitis media with effusion (OME) in cleft palate children is about 97% (Grant et al, 1988). However, in a study of 250 patients, Honjo (1988) did not observe any cases of acute otitis media (AOM). It is still unclear whether the extent of middle ear disease depends on the type of cleft (Handzic-Cuk et al, 2001; Honjo, 1988). Nevertheless, the early and long-term therapy of OME is important to reduce the risk of persistent hearing loss (Godbersen, 1997).

Pathogenesis of OME in Children with Cleft Palate

Several factors may be involved in the pathogenesis of OME in children with cleft palate:

Prerepair Factors

A mechanical obstruction of the nasopharyngeal ostium is considered a possible reason for the high incidence of OME in children with cleft palate. Two different factors may contribute to this block: Godbersen (1997) showed that before surgical adaptation of the soft palate, the free palatal vela can itself mechanically obstruct the nasopha-ryngeal ostium of the eustachian tube. But even after veloplasty, hyperplasia of the adenoids could also cause a persisting obstruction of the ostium.

Cohen and colleagues (1994) demonstrated that myogenesis in fetal cleft palate specimens differs from normal. Although our own electrophysiologic observations in adults (Leuwer et al, 1999) indicate that a primary lack of function of the tensor veli palatini muscle seems unlikely, Cohen and colleagues (1994) observed an impaired organization of the individual muscle fibers, especially near the medial epithelial edge. Hence, the active tubal function, that is, the muscular compliance of the eustachian tube, can be impaired independently of surgery.

Factors Occurring after Cleft Palate Repair

During veloplasty, the integrity of the hamulus and the tensor veli palatini muscle is at risk. Thus, the muscular compliance of the eustachian tube can be impaired after surgery (Leuwer et al, 1999). The muscular compliance is a complex function of the tensor veli palatini muscle, and contraction of the profound portion of the tensor muscle only causes the opening of the cranial third of the tubal diameter (the so-called Rüdinger's security channel). At the same time, contraction of the superficial portion of the same muscle compresses the Ostmann's fatty tissue and thus the lower two-thirds of the tubal diameter. Mucosal folds in the lower portion of the tubal diameter support a propulsion mechanism toward the nasopharynx during compression (Sando et al, 1994). Hence, the muscular compliance implies the simultaneous aeration and drainage of the middle ear by contraction of the tensor veli palatini muscle.

Independent Factors

Paradise and colleagues (1994) could show that eustachian tube dysfunction is not the only pathogenic factor involved in the development of OME in cleft palate patients. In their study, breast milk nutrition provided variable protection against otitis media in these children. They inferred that infective or noninfective inflammation of the upper respiratory tract could contribute to the pathogenesis of OME. However, the precise mechanism of this factor remains unclear.

Management Options

General Considerations

Independent of the special situation of children with cleft palate, many nonsurgical and surgical treatments have been described to directly influence eustachian tube function. All of these studies had different criteria and are not comparable. There is no evidence from randomized, controlled trials that any of the different treatments described represent an effective causative therapy and reduce further interventions.

Interventions for Eustachian Tube Dysfunction

Because the clefting velum may obstruct the nasopharyngeal ostium, palate repair can improve eustachian tube function and thus middle ear status (Bluestone, 1983). However, the prevalence of OME after veloplasty still remains at about 70% (Robinson et al, 1992), and a very early closure does not significantly change the need for ventilation tubes (Nunn et al, 1995). More important than the time of intervention is the choice of surgical technique. The tendons of the superficial and the profound portions of the tensor veli palatini muscle inserting or being adjacent to the pterygoid hamulus play an important role in muscular function. This function substantially depends on the integrity of the hamulus (Barsoumian et al, 1988). Recently, Kane and colleagues (2000) published a prospective study about hamulotomy. They compared two different groups, one with and one without hamulus fracture during palatoplasty. The mean follow-up time was 1 year. Tympanostomy tubes were placed in 106 of 161 patients. The results of their study did not reveal any differences between the two groups concerning postoperative auditory brainstem response testing, time of tube extrusion, or effusion culture results. However, this study must be critically discussed. Inasmuch as most of the children of both groups had to be treated with tympanostomy tubes, one cannot expect any otologic difference. Besides taking into account the natural development of the eustachian tube with growth, the observation period of 1 year is not long enough. Handzic-Cuk and colleagues (2001) emphasized that because of the immature neuromuscular control, the tensor does not become completely functional before the age of 7 years. Looking at our own long-term findings, deliberate or accidental hamulotomy results in an impairment of tensor function and must be strictly avoided during veloplasty (Leuwer et al, 1999). Bütow and colleagues (1991) described a new surgical technique to improve eustachian tube function after intravelar veloplasty. They developed a special suture sling to bilaterally connect the tensor veli palatini muscle under maximal tension. This suture sling requires an intact hamulus. Nevertheless, as there has been no further discussion regarding the long-term results of this surgical procedure, this method cannot be generally suggested.

The question of whether adenoidectomy should or should not be performed is still subject to discussion. In my opinion, the risk of an increased postoperative velopharyngeal insufficiency should prevent the otolaryngologist from adenoidectomy (Haapanen et al, 1993).

Another possible aspect for the management of OME in children with cleft palate could be the lack of the mucosal blanket in the tubal lumen. Very recently, Chandrasekhar and colleagues (2002) published the results of an animal experiment using surfactant to reduce eustachian tube passive opening pressure. Although their results and those of other groups are encouraging, there is still no evidence that this treatment can be transferred to the therapy of children with OME. Ambroxol is a commonly used drug that stimulates the production of pulmonary surfactant by the alveolar type II pneumocytes. Passali and Zavattini (1987) performed a randomized multicenter study in 435 children and adults with OME with a mean duration of symptoms of 26.5 days. They reported a significant positive effect of this treatment on the middle ear. It must be pointed out that during this study, patients were allowed to continue antihistamine or decongestant treatment. Taking into consideration the lack of well-defined outcome criteria of this study and the long-term eustachian tube dysfunction in children with cleft palate, I am still reluctant to recommend ambroxol for the adjuvant treatment of OME.

Role of Tympanostomy Tubes

OME is present in virtually all children with cleft palate (Handzic-Cuk et al, 2001). The high incidence of persistent OME even after palatal surgery means that an otolaryngologist prior to and regularly after surgical treatment should evaluate these patients (Nunn et al, 1995). Reliable restoration of hearing by insertion of tympanostomy tubes is recommended by most authors (Grant et al, 1988). However, it has to be emphasized that active tubal function is not changed by the insertion of ventilation tubes (van Heerbeek et al, 2001). On the other hand, in a study of 81 cleft palate children, Smith and colleagues (1994) demonstrated that eustachian tube function normalizes in 78% of patients within a follow-up of 10 years after cleft palate repair. However, this group concludes that their aggressive surgical treatment with tympanostomy tubes is at least partly responsible for the excellent long-term hearing results. Seagle and colleagues (1998) examined 112 children after cleft palate surgery at ages 5 to 9 years. No single child had received tympanostomy tubes. Only a minority (31%) had ever been treated with antibiotics. Their results were surprising: 58 children had tympanograms indicating abnormalities and only 19 presented with pathologic findings in handheld otoscopy. Their North American control group that had been liberally treated with antibiotics and tympanostomy tubes showed even worse results. Seagle and colleagues (1998) point out that universal early placement of tympanostomy tubes to alleviate hearing problems has to be critically studied when taking into consideration that insertion of tympanostomy tubes itself may lead to abnormal otologic conditions.

My Recommendations

The time of choice for surgical procedures with cleft palate patients has always been a matter of discussion (Kirschner et al, 2000). Besides this controversial debate, according to the standards of the interdisciplinary German Cleft Palate Craniofacial Association at Hamburg University Medical School, each preschool child with cleft palate has to be assessed by an otolaryngologist at least twice a year, beginning in early infancy. This assessment always includes microscopic otoscopy, tympanometry, and hearing tests. If middle ear effusion persists for more than 3 months, tympanostomy tubes are inserted. However, we should hesitate to routinely practice tube insertion, considering the problems of repeated use of general anesthesia and the risk of persistent otorrhea or permanent tympanic membrane perforation. Nevertheless, we have to be aware that adequate treatment of middle ear pathology in children with cleft palate prevents structural and functional impairments such as persistent hearing loss, atelectasis, and cholesteatoma.

References

Barsoumian R, Kuehn DP, Moon JB, Canady JW. An anatomic study of the tensor veli palatini and dilator tubae muscles in relation to eustachian tube and velar function. Cleft Palate Craniofac J 1998;35:101–10.

Bluestone CD. Eustachian tube function: physiology, pathophysiology, and role of allergy in pathogenesis of otitis media. J Allergy Clin Immunol 1983;72:242–51.

Bütow KW, Louw B, Hugo SR, Grimbeck RJ. Tensor veli palatini muscle tension sling for eustachian tube function in cleft palate. Surgical technique and audiometric examination. J Craniomaxillofac Surg 1991;19:71–6.

Chandrasekhar SS, Connelly PE, Venkatayan N, et al. Intranasal metered dose aerosolized surfactant reduces passive opening pressure of the eustachian tube: comparison study in two animal models. Otol Neurotol 2002;23:3–7.

Cohen SR, Chen LL, Burdi AR, Trotman CA. Patterns of abnormal myogenesis in human cleft palates. Cleft Palate Craniofac J 1994;31:345–50.

Godbersen GS. Das Kind mit Lippen-, Kiefer-, Gaumen-Spalte. Laryngorhinootologie 1997;76:562–7.

Grant HR, Quiney RE, Mercer DM, Lodge S. Cleft palate and glue ear. Arch Dis Child 1988;63:176–9.

Haapanen ML, Veija M, Pettay M. Speech outcome in cleft palate patients with simultaneous primary palatal repair and adenoidectomy. Acta Otolaryngol (Stockh) 1993;113:560–2.

Handzic-Cuk J, Cuk V, Gluhinic M, et al. Tympanometric findings in cleft palate patients: influence of age and cleft type. J Laryngol Otol 2001;115:91–6.

Honjo I. Eustachian tube and middle ear diseases: middle ear disease and eustachian tube in patients with cleft palate. Tokyo: Springer; 1988.

Kane AA, Lo LJ, Yen BD, et al. The effect of hamulus fracture on the outcome of palatoplasty: a preliminary report of a prospective, alternating study. Cleft Palate Craniofac J 2000;37:506–11.

Kirschner RE, Randall P, Wang P, et al. Cleft repair at 3 to 7 months of age. Plast Reconstr Surg 2001;105:2127–32.

Leuwer R, Henschel M, Sehhati-Chafai-Leuwer S, et al. A new aspect on the development of chronic middle ear diseases in patients with cleft palate. Laryngorhinootologie 1999;78:115–9.

Nunn DR, Derkay CS, Darrow DH, et al. The effect of very early cleft palate closure on the need for ventilation tubes in the first years of life. Laryngoscope 1995;105:905–8.

Paradise JL, Elster BA, Tan L. Evidence in infants with cleft palate that breast milk protects against otitis media. Pediatrics 1994; 94:853–60.

Passali D, Zavattini G. Multicenter study on the treatment of secretory otitis media with ambroxol. Importance of a surface-tension-lowering substance. Respiration 1987;51:152–9.

Robinson PJ, Lodge S, Jones BM, et al. The effect of palate repair on otitis media with effusion. Plast Reconstr Surg 1992;89:640–5.

Sando I, Takahashi H, Matsune S, Aoki H. Localization of function in the eustachian tube: a hypothesis. Ann Otol Rhinol Laryngol 1994;103:311–4.

Seagle MB, Nackashi JA, Kemker FJ, et al. Otologic and audiologic status of Russian children with cleft lip and palate. Cleft Palate Craniofac J 1998;35:495–9.

Smith TL, DiRuggiero DC, Jones KR. Recovery of eustachian tube function and hearing outcome in patients with cleft palate. Otolaryngol Head Neck Surg 1994;111:423–9.

van Heerbeek N, Ingels KJ, Snik AF, Zielhuis GA. Eustachian tube function in children after insertion of ventilation tubes. Ann Otol Rhinol Laryngol 2001;110:1141–6.

Chapter 95

ACUTE OTITIS MEDIA/ OTITIS MEDIA WITH EFFUSION IN CRANIOFACIAL SYNDROMES

UDAYAN K. SHAH, MD

The otolaryngologist plays an important role in the care of syndromic children. The prevalence of otitis media (OM) in early childhood means that the otolaryngologist may be among the first providers of medical care who have the opportunity to make a syndromic diagnosis. Appreciating the possibly relevant syndromes for a given child allows for a broader medical consideration by preventing incomplete care. Missing a syndromic connection can place a child at risk for medical or surgical complications in the course of "routine" care, for example, by injuring a weak cervical spinal cord in a child with Down syndrome (DS). The study of craniofacial syndromes (CFSs) and OM is therefore both instructive, by demonstrating the interplay of specific etiologic factors for OM in a given syndrome, and practical, by permitting the comprehensive management of middle ear health in the context of multiple handicaps. The "heuristic" importance—what a named syndrome teaches us about a patient—means that there is clinical value in thinking of syndromic associations in those children who may have some, but not all, features of a given syndrome (Shah et al, 1998).

This chapter first reviews several syndromes that epitomize the multifactorial nature of OM in children with CFS. Cleft palate (CP), the 22q deletion syndromes (velocardiofacial and DiGeorge), trisomy 21 (DS), and the CHARGE syndrome (coloboma of the eye, heart anomaly, choanal atresia, retardation, and genital and ear anomalies) are discussed in detail. These and other important syndromes are listed in Table 95-1. The general management philosophy for the care of acute otitis media (AOM) and otitis media with effusion (OME) in children with CFS is then shared.

An exhaustive enumeration of the many CFSs associated with OM is beyond the scope of this chapter. Several excellent references provide current information for the clinician (National Center for Biotechnology Information; Sakashita et al, 1996).

Cleft Palate

Otologic disorders have been noted in children with CP since the late 1800s (Bluestone, 1971). Clefting of the facial complex is associated with nearly 400 syndromes (Reyes et al, 1999). The most familiar is the Pierre Robin syndrome/sequence (cleft palate, micrognathia, and glossoptosis). Palatal clefts may be obvious, in the hard or soft palate, or occult, as in the submucous CP. The diagnosis of CP may be made by inspection, palpation, and/or fiberoptic endoscopy. The identification of a submucous CP is made by noting the presence of a bifid uvula, a muscular diathesis of the palate (at the zona pellucida), and notching of the posterior border of the hard palate (Reyes et al, 1999).

CP, whether or not associated with other skull base or facial anomalies, is often accompanied by OM. Greater than two-thirds of children with CP may have OM, as opposed to non-CP children, and the OM is more likely to persist beyond the age of 6 years, the age at which children without CP normalize their eustachian tube (ET) function (Kemaloglu et al, 1999; Reyes et al, 1999). Serous OM, in general, tends to develop more rapidly and last longer in children with CP. Structural factors contributing to OM in CP center on poor ET function owing to an abnormally positioned ET orifice, obstruction at the aural and/or pharyngeal ends of the ET, a narrow opening of the ET, ET structure, abnormal muscular control of ET ventilation, and the lack of an intact palatal partition allowing nasopharyngeal reflux of bacteria and may correlate with the timing and type of palatal surgery (Bluestone, 1971; Kemaloglu et al, 1999; Reyes et al, 1999; Takasaki et al, 2000).

Management of OM in CP is initially expectant and preventive, in part by attempts at prone or head-up positioning (American Academy of Pediatrics, 2002) or considering antibiotic prophylaxis, but primarily by early placement of tympanostomy tubes, also called pressure

TABLE 95-1. Syndromes That Epitomize the Multifactorial Nature of Otitis Media in Children with Craniofacial Syndromes

Syndrome/Disease	Implications				
	Airway	Cardiac	Central Nervous System	Otologic	Other
CHARGE	Choanal atresia	Cardiovascular anomalies	Learning; mental retardation, developmental		Genitourinary; growth
Crouzon's	Macrognathia			Ossicular anomalies	Craniosynostosis, exophthalmos, facial skeletal anomalies
DiGeorge		Cardiovascular anomalies		Ossicular anomalies; aberrant facial nerve and vestibulocochlear hypoplasia	Thymic hypoplasia or aplasia, esophageal atresia
Fetal alcohol	Cleft palate	Congenital heart defects	Microcephaly, learning, mental retardation, behavioral disorders	Susceptible to recurrent otitis media	Growth deficiency, abnormal facies, ptosis
Goldenhar's	Micrognathia			Small mastoid, external auditory canal atresia	
Noonan's	Micrognathia, cleft palate	Cardiovascular anomalies		Auricular and ossicular anomalies	Ptosis, skeletal anomalies
Treacher-Collins	Micrognathia, cleft palate			Ossicular anomalies, small middle ear cavity	Eyelid coloboma, abnormal facies
Pierre Robin	Cleft palate, retrognathia, glossoptosis	Cardiovascular anomalies	Mental retardation, hydrocephaly, microcephaly		Congenital cataracts, retinal detachment
Velocardiofacial	Retrognathia, larynx, cleft palate, pharyngeal hypotonia	Cardiovascular anomalies	Learning, developmental		Ocular anomalies, neonatal hypocalcemia Aberrant internal carotid artery anatomy in nasopharynx mandates caution for adenoidectomy

equalization (PE) tubes, to enhance ME ventilation. The early insertion of PE tubes is facilitated at our institution by our management scheme for CP, which entails surgical repair of a cleft lip if it is present at 3 months of age, palatal surgery at 8 to 10 months, and surgery at 6 to 7 years for the alveolus, allowing for proactive (some would say "prophylactic") PE tube insertion. This "high-risk" approach is supported by current guidelines for OM care via the American Academy of Pediatrics (2002). Although in some cases, the "usual" criteria for PE tubes are not met, either by duration of fluid or objective determination of hearing impairment related to OM, I believe that these children benefit from the relatively minor intervention of PE tube insertion that stabilizes their otologic health.

ET function tends to improve after palatal closure but may never completely normalize (Bluestone, 1971; Smith et al, 1994). In my experience with unilateral CP, ET function continues to be impaired to some degree on the cleft side, even after palatal repair.

I avoid adenoidectomy for management of OM in CP, owing to the potential for postadenoidectomy velopharyngeal insufficiency (VPI). When required, partial adenoidectomy (leaving tissue in the midline or leaving tissue inferiorly, away from the choanae) has been effective in improving OM while avoiding VPI.

22q Deletion Syndromes

Velocardiofacial Syndrome

Deletions of portions of the short arm of chromosome 22 may present either as velocardiofacial syndrome (VCFS) or as DiGeorge syndrome. The incidence of VCFS is roughly 1 in 4,000 live births. Shprintzen first described VCFS in 1978 (Reyes et al, 1999) in children with palatal abnormalities, middle ear disease, and hearing loss. The major criteria today for diagnosis of VCFS are clefting of the secondary palate, hypernasal speech, pharyngeal hypotonia, structural heart anomalies, dysmorphic facial appearance, slender hands and fingers, and learning disabilities. Less common findings are short stature, inguinal or umbilical hernias, hypospadias, and scoliosis (Ford et al, 2000). Ocular, laryngeal, feeding/swallowing, and immunodeficiencies have been recently identified.

VCFS is one of the more common CFSs that include clefting. As many as 8% of isolated CP patients have VCFS, and 98% of VCFS patients have a palatal cleft, most often a submucous CP (two-thirds of patients) rather than an overt cleft (one-fourth of patients) (Ford et al, 2000).

Deletions of portions of chromosome 22q11.2 (83% of individuals with VCFS) show by the fluorescence in situ hybridization (FISH) assay. Those who phenotypically have VCFS but have a negative FISH may have a point mutation or a rearrangement of sequences between the documented breakpoints. The deletions may be transmitted in an autosomal dominant manner or may represent either a de novo deletion or a translocation.

The prevalence of middle ear disease in VCFS ranges from 22 to 47% (Finkelstein et al, 1993; Reyes et al, 1999). The etiology of OM in VCFS may be attributable to the abnormal craniofacial anatomy, CP, and ET dysfunction (Reyes et al, 1999). The role of adenoid hypertrophy is controversial as adenoid tissue is often absent or minimal in size. Hearing loss is attributable to OME, middle ear ossicular anomalies, narrow external auditory canals (EACs), and/or sensorineural deafness.

Reyes and colleagues (1999) did not find a difference in OM incidence owing to the type of palatal abnormality or chromosomal deletion. In fact, the prevalence of middle ear disease in VCFS was comparable to that seen in isolated CP. Interestingly, they also found that age did not affect the prevalence of middle ear disease.

Management of OM in VCFS requires an appreciation of comorbid conditions. The subtlety of some clinical stigmata may warrant a genetics evaluation. Earlier myringotomy and tube insertion are helpful for these patients (Reyes et al, 1999).

Adenoidectomy is problematic in VCFS for two reasons. First, the vascular anatomy of the nasopharynx is abnormal, with medial displacement of the internal carotid and vertebral arteries. Nasopharyngeal endoscopy found 31% of patients to have abnormal pulsation of the posterior or lateral pharyngeal wall in VCFS (Reyes et al, 1999). Magnetic resonance angiography is recommended preoperatively to avoid vascular injury during pharyngeal surgery because the absence of pulsations laterally in the pharyngeal walls does not necessarily mean that the vascular anatomy is normal. In addition, the removal of even small adenoid tissue may result in VPI. Careful pre- and intraoperative evaluation for VPI is recommended, either by palpation of the hard and soft palate and/or observation of the uvula and palate during phonation, radiography, or endoscopy. When adenoidectomy is performed, partial adenoidectomy keeping tissue superiorly (posteriorly) is recommended to prevent postoperative VPI (Reyes et al, 1999).

DiGeorge Syndrome

Children with DiGeorge syndrome are like those with VCFS in that they have a chromosomal deletion in the 22q11 region. Diagnosis and differentiation between VCFS and DiGeorge are clinical because there is a wide range of phenotypic presentation, and FISH may not be able to detect the deletion. DiGeorge syndrome demonstrates the effect of maldeveloped third and fourth pharyngeal pouches and is also therefore termed pharyngeal pouch syndrome or thymic aplasia/hypoplasia. DiGeorge syndrome demonstrates the combined role of structural and immunologic factors in OM. A microdeletion in the region of chromosome 22q11, N25, is considered to be the main cause, although deletions in the 10p region have also been seen (Ganbo et al, 1999). DiGeorge patients have a hypoplastic or aplastic thymus and parathyroid glands (which may result in immunodeficiency and/or hypocalcemic seizures) and may have great vessel malformations, congenital heart disease, and esophageal atresia. Facial findings are hypertelorism, a short philtrum, an antimongoloid slant of the eyes, a bifid uvula, and low-set, often notched ears. Vestibulocochlear malformations and an anomalous facial nerve course have been seen. DiGeorge patients are susceptible to viral and bacterial infections because the T-lymphocyte response to immunogenic stimuli is reduced, with a decreased number of T cells, including those located in the middle ear (Ganbo et al, 1999).

Earlier consideration is given in DiGeorge syndrome to PE tube insertion, especially given the cellular immunodeficiency, which limits antibiotic effectiveness against AOM. Adenoidectomy must heed the potential for medially malpositioned internal carotid and/or vertebral arteries, as in VCFS.

CHARGE Syndrome

Children with the CHARGE syndrome exemplify the management of OM in the setting of multiple communication deficits. Pagon and colleagues (1981) presented the CHARGE "association" as a constellation of ocular coloboma, heart anomalies, choanal atresia, retarded growth and/or development, genital hypoplasia, and ear anomalies. The incidence of CHARGE is estimated to be 1 in 10,000 in the United States. Defects in renal and cranial nerve function are also now appreciated to be prevalent among these children. Children who meet some but not all criteria for CHARGE syndrome may be considered, for the purposes of otologic treatment and prognosis, to be similar to children who strictly fit the inclusion criteria (Shah et al, 1998). The deaf-blind issues that impair learning are compounded by cognitive and motor delays and have prompted earlier intervention for OM.

CHARGE children are otitis prone owing to an abnormal skull base and, in some cases, may have immune deficiencies similar to those of DiGeorge children. Otologic and audiologic evaluations are impeded by narrow and "floppy" ear canals. Amplification and speech and language habilitation are further complicated, as in many other syndromic children, by prolonged early hospitalization and ongoing care of medical comorbidities. The frequent OM in CHARGE children requires compensatory adjustment of hearing aid levels, causes difficulty with hearing aid fit owing to misshaped auricles, and causes visual field deficits. Neurocognitive delays mean that early hearing assessment must rely more often on electrical measures such as testing for the auditory brainstem response and/or otoacoustic emissions rather than on behavioral testing. Most children with CHARGE syndrome at some point require otologic management of middle ear disease, usually with tympanostomy tubes. Nasopharyngeal regurgitation in young children with CHARGE syndrome may result in a higher rate of post-tube otorrhea. Management with otic drops and office débridement can prevent tube occlusion, thereby preserving hearing levels and preventing OM. Tube removal may be required when otorrhea is very difficult to manage, and conductive hearing loss may then require amplification. If adenoidectomy is considered for the care of OM, an aberrant skull base shape and the potential for neuromuscular palatal weakness, predisposing the patient to postadenoidectomy VPI, must be considered.

Ossicular anomalies are not uncommon. Incompletely developed or fused ossicles and severe tympanic membrane atelectasis may require further surgical or audiologic management after tympanostomy tube insertion (Dhooge et al, 1998). Sensorineural hearing loss is commonly seen and is usually managed with amplification.

Trisomy 21 (Down Syndrome)

Trisomy 21, DS, is the most common aneuploid chromosomal disorder causing mental retardation. It occurs in 1 in 600 to 1 in 1,000 live births in the United States and is the most familiar CFS seen by most otolaryngologists (Centers for Disease Control and Prevention, 1994; Shott et al, 2001). This trisomy of chromosome 21 was first described in 1866 by J. Langdon Down, who characterized "mongolism" as exhibiting a broad facies, short stature, mental retardation, and widely spaced canthi. The chromosomal trisomy is usually attributable to meiotic nondysjunction in 95% of children with trisomy 21 (47,XX, +21), whereas translocations and mosaicism contribute to the rest (Antonarrakis, 1991).

Hearing loss is seen in 39 to 89% of DS children compared with 2.5% of the general population (Marttila, 1986; Roizen et al, 1993). This hearing loss is usually attributable to OM and is therefore bilateral and conductive (Dahle and McCollister, 1986).

OM in DS is primarily attributable to ET dysfunction and is thought to be caused by the following:

- baseline hypotonicity
- impaired function of the tensor veli palatini (Schwartz and Schwartz, 1978)
- anatomic differences consisting of
  - a sharper angle of entry of the ET into the nasopharynx in DS children compared with normal children
  - a narrower nasopharynx (Brown et al, 1989; Shott et al, 2001)
  - a more cylindrical shape of the ET
  - less pliable tori

Care for OM is complicated in DS owing to EAC anomalies (narrow EAC, cerumen impaction, and "floppy" EAC) and middle ear anomalies (ossicular malformations, narrow middle ear space). Auricular anomalies and EAC stenosis can impede hearing and make otoscopy difficult (Dahle and McCollister, 1986). Meatoplasty and/or canalplasty have been shown to be beneficial after age 3 years for difficult cases by Pappas and colleagues (1994). Medical, surgical, and anesthetic management of AOM and OME is further complicated in DS by skull base, cervical spine, and neurodevelopmental problems; an abnormal craniofacial skeleton; soft tissue redundancy and hypotonia; the increased risk of malignancy; and endocrinologic and immunologic problems (Shott et al, 2001).

Early consideration of myringotomy with tube insertion in DS is warranted because of the poor ET function and the need to optimize communication by treating conductive hearing loss (CHL). Cognitive development is all the more critical to reinforce early in life for DS owing to the early senescence that these patients experience. Intravenous antibiotics and mastoidectomy are reserved for complications of OM or refractory cases. Preoperative computed tomography is particularly important in such cases to identify surgically relevant temporal bone anatomy, especially narrower bony confines of the temporal bone and associated facial nerve and ossicular anomalies (Bilgin et al, 1996; Glass et al, 1989; Harda and Sando, 1981; Igarishi et al, 1977; Shibahara and Sando, 1989).

Stenotic EACs may make placement of the tympanostomy tube challenging and at times impossible. Care of PE tubes in DS is also difficult owing to stenotic ear canals, cerumen impaction, thickened aural discharge, increased incidence of upper respiratory tract infection, and a persistent perforation rate after tube extrusion that may be high (Iino et al, 1999; Selikowitz, 1993a). Poor ET function may predispose the DS child to post-tympanostomy tube otorrhea owing to loss of the "middle ear air cushion." Once tympanostomy tubes are in place, poor ET function may predispose the DS child to reflux of nasopharyngeal secretions into the middle ear. Aural débridement, antibiotic eardrops, feeding in the upright position, and medical management of acid reflux may prevent the need to remove the tympanostomy tubes. In addition to OME/AOM causing CHL, CHL can also be caused by middle ear mesenchyme in DS (Bilgin et al, 1996; Harda and Sando, 1981). Frequent otolaryngologic care, approximately every 3 months, is therefore recommended (Pappas et al, 1994; Roizen et al, 1993). Earlier tube replacement after extrusion is recommended. Aggressive postoperative care and audiologic evaluation will secure optimal outcomes, as demonstrated in Pappas and colleagues (1994), who compared the effects of EAC reconstruction, amplification, and auditory-oral–based speech and language therapy in DS. They found that the therapy group showed age-appropriate early language skills, whereas the control group (who received their intervention after their first birthday) exhibited generalized language delays with a noticeable gap between their receptive and expressive language skills.

Adenoidectomy in DS may be considered earlier in the management of OM owing to the improvement in airway and nasal secretions that may be seen.

Perioperative Risks in Trisomy 21

Airway risk is higher in DS owing to midfacial and mandibular hypoplasia, relative macroglossia, adenotonsillar hypertrophy, pharyngeal hypotonia, tracheomalacia and subglottic stenosis, increased secretions and frequent upper respiratory tract infections, central sleep apnea, and obesity. Long-standing airway obstruction can lead to cor pulmonale and/or pulmonary hypertension (Jacobs et al, 1996; Johnson, 1992). In addition, up to one-third to half of the children with DS suffer from congenital heart disease.

The high incidence of subclinical hypothyroidism in DS warrants preoperative laboratory evaluation (Johnson, 1992; Rubello et al, 1995; Selikowitz et al, 1993b). Preoperative cervical spine radiographs have proven helpful in some instances to assess atlantoaxial instability or subluxation in DS children with neurologic symptoms of cervical spinal cord compromise. Currently, asymptomatic DS children do not require cervical spine radiographs or clearance before surgery, even with adenoidectomy (American Academy of Pediatrics, 2001). However, given the high prevalence of atlantoaxial instability in this group (around 15%), extra caution is warranted during head turning or neck manipulation. Such precautions include smaller than usual or no shoulder rolls, strapping the head and body to the operating table and tilting the bed rather than turning the head for exposure during PE tube insertion, and intubation or airway manipulation with a cervical collar worn by the patient or with the head and neck stabilized as if the cervical spinal cord were unstable.

Therapy: General Comments

The "multiple hits" that CFS persons face in OM generally require a longer period of care of OM, beyond the age of 6 years, when ET function is expected to normalize in most other children.

When the CFS involves an immunodeficiency, antibiotic therapy may need to be considered earlier or for longer periods of time. Culture-directed therapy may be required, with middle ear fluid obtained at the time of PE tube placement or earlier, via office tympanocentesis. CFS children may benefit from earlier tympanostomy tube placement because OME is more likely to be refractory to observation and antibiotic therapy.

The decision to recommend PE tubes requires weighing social and educational function with regard to hearing and communication, language development, the need for other procedures, prior antibiotic use and effectiveness in clearing AOM, the season, and audiologic measures. For example, observation of OME is acceptable for a CFS child with good function and without recent AOM, with serous OM and flat tympanograms, and with mild hearing loss, in the summer. In the winter, I would have a low threshold for recommending PE tube placement, usually after two consecutive episodes of AOM, in a child with a CFS. Their predilection to OME mandates close watch over the potential for short- and long-term complications, whether they are anatomic (middle ear) or communicative.

When PE tubes are required, children with CFS may require overnight observation as concomitant anomalies increase their anesthetic risk and require additional monitoring or therapy. Longer-acting tympanostomy tubes may be considered earlier. My usual progression for tube types for middle ear ventilation moves from silicone Paparella-type 1.0 mm inner diameter tubes for the first two sets, then Reuter Bobbin fluoroplastic 1.14 mm inner diameter or angled Armstrong grommet tubes, and then, as my largest tube, the silicone Paparella-type 1.27 mm tube. When using the Paparella tubes, I trim the lateral tag so that debris does not accumulate on this. Very retracted tympanic membranes sometimes require the more firm fluoroplastic Reuter Bobbin or beveled Armstrong tube type, using the rigid flange to dissect between the promontory and the medial layer of the tympanic membrane. I do not like using T tubes because of the narrow and long lumen: this seems prone to more frequent clogging, and I have concerns about the large medial flanges predisposing to a persistent tympanic membrane perforation and the potential for discomfort from the tube shaft hitting the EAC skin.

Children with CFS may experience such severe post-tube otorrhea that tube removal is considered. Amplification for CHL is useful in such cases once the tympanic membrane has healed.

The American Academy of Pediatrics' Section on Otolaryngology and Bronchoesophagology recommends follow-up by the otolaryngologist within the month after placement, evaluation of baseline hearing status, and interval examinations by the pediatrician or otolaryngologist not longer than every 6 months. Children with CFS may require closer interval examinations (American Academy of Pediatrics, 2002). Follow-up by the otolaryngologist is required until the tympanic membrane has healed, ET function normalizes, and hearing is restored.

Adenoidectomy may be considered for management of OM, with the first set of PE tubes for children with obstructive breathing or recurrent sinusitis or after the second set of PE tubes. Some syndromes (eg, VCFS) require caution during adenoidectomy owing to aberrant internal carotid artery anatomy.

Conclusion

The care of the child with CFS and OM requires appreciation not only of ET dysfunction but also of the specific syndromic comorbidities as they pertain to medical and surgical management of fluid in the ear. The care of the CFS child with OM exemplifies the need for comprehensive and multidisciplinary care. The multiple communication deficits that may exist make optimizing otologic status critical to optimizing language, developmental and social integration, and education.

References

American Academy of Pediatrics, Committee on Genetics. Health supervision for children with Down syndrome. Pediatrics 2001;107: 442–9.

American Academy of Pediatrics, Section on Otolaryngology and Bronchoesophagology. Follow-up management of children with tympanostomy tubes. Pediatrics 2002;109:328–9.

Antonarrakis SE. Parental origin of the extra chromosome in trisomy 21 as indicated by analysis of DNA polymorphisms. N Engl J Med 1991;324:872–6.

Bilgin H, Kasemsuwan L, Schachern PA, et al. Temporal bone study of Down syndrome. Arch Otolaryngol Head Neck Surg 1996; 122:271–5.

Bluestone CD. Eustachian tube obstruction in the infant with cleft palate. Ann Otol Rhinol Laryngol 1971;80 Suppl 2:1–30.

Brown PM, Lewis GT, Parker AJ, Maw AR. The skull base and nasopharynx in Down syndrome in relation to hearing impairment. Clin Otolaryngol 1989;14:241–6.

Centers for Disease Control and Prevention. Down syndrome prevalence at birth—United States, 1983–1990. MMWR Morb Mortal Wkly Rep 1994;43:617–22.

Dahle AJ, McCollister FP. Hearing and otologic disorders in children with Down syndrome. Am J Ment Defic 1986;90:636–42.

Dhooge I, Lemmerling M, Lagache M, et al. Otological manifestations of CHARGE association. Ann Otol Rhinol Laryngol 1998;107:935–41.

Finkelstein Y, Zohar Y, Nachmani A, et al. The otolaryngologist and the patient with velo-cardio-facial syndrome. Arch Otolaryngol Head Neck Surg 1993;119:563–9.

Ford LC, Sulprizio SL, Rasgon BM. Otolaryngological manifestations of velo-cardio-facial syndrome: a retrospective review of 35 patients. Laryngoscope 2000;110:362–7.

Ganbo, TI, Sando I, Balaban CD, et al. Inflammatory response to chronic otitis media in DiGeorge syndrome: a case study using immunohistochemistry on archival temporal bone sections. Ann Otol Rhinol Laryngol 1999;108:756–61.

Glass RBJ, Yousefzadeh DK, Roizen NJ. Mastoid abnormalities in Down syndrome. Pediatr Radiol 1989;19:311–2.

Harda T, Sando I. Temporal bone histopathologic findings in Down syndrome. Arch Otolaryngol Head Neck Surg 1981; 107:96–103.

Igarashi M, Takahashi M, Alford BR, Johnson PE. Inner ear morphology in Down syndrome. Acta Otolaryngol (Stockh) 1977; 83:175–81.

Iino Y, Imamura Y, Haridai S, Tanaka Y. Efficacy of tympanostomy tube insertion for otitis media with effusion in children with Down syndrome. Int J Pediatr Otorhinolaryngol 1999;49:143–9.

Jacobs IN, Gray RF, Todd NW. Upper airway obstruction in children with Down syndrome. Arch Otolaryngol Head Neck Surg 1996;122:945–50.

Johnson JT. Instructional courses, American Academy of Otolaryngology-Head and Neck Surgery. Vol. 5. St. Louis: Mosby Year Book; 1992.

Kemaloglu YK, Kobayashi T, Nakajima T. Analysis of the craniofacial skeleton in cleft children with otitis media with effusion. Int J Pediatr Otorhinolaryngol 1999;47:57–69.

Marttila TI. Results of audiometrical screening in Finnish schoolchildren. Int J Pediatr Otorhinolaryngol 1986;11:39–46.

National Center for Biotechnology Information. Available at: http://www.ncbi.nlm.nih.gov/Omim (accessed July 6, 2003).

Pagon RA, Graham JL Jr, Zonana J, Yong S. Coloboma, congenital heart disease, and choanal atresia with multiple anomalies: CHARGE association. J Pediatr 1981;99:223–7.

Pappas DG, Flexer C, Shackelford L. Otological and habilitative management of children with Down syndrome. Laryngoscope 1994;104:1065–70.

Reyes MRT, LeBlanc EM, Bassila MK. Hearing loss and otitis media in velo-cardio-facial syndrome. Int J Pediatr Otorhinolaryngol 1999;47:227–33.

Roizen NJ, Wolters C, Nicol T, Blondis TA. Hearing loss in children with Down syndrome. J Pediatr 1993;123:S9–12.

Rubello D, Pozzan GB, Casara D, et al. Natural course of subclinical hypothyroidism in Down syndrome: prospective study results and therapeutic considerations. J Endocrinol Invest 1995;17: 35–40.

Sakashita T, Sando I, Kamerer DB. Congenital anomalies of the external and middle ears. In: Bluestone CD, Stool SE, Kenna MA, editors. Pediatric otolaryngology. 3rd ed. Philadelphia: WB Saunders; 1996. p. 333–70.

Schwartz DM, Schwartz RH. Acoustic impedence and otoscopic findings in young children with Down syndrome. Arch Otolaryngol Head Neck Surg 1978;104:652–6.

Selikowitz M. A five-year longitudinal study of thyroid function in children with Down syndrome. Dev Med Child Neurol 1993a; 35:396–401.

Selikowitz M. Short-term efficacy of tympanostomy tubes for secretory otitis media in children with Down syndrome. Dev Med Child Neurol 1993b;35:511–5.

Shah UK, Ohlms LA, Neault MW, et al. Otologic management in children with the CHARGE association. Int J Pediatr Otorhinolaryngol 1998;44:139–47.

Shibahara Y, Sando I. Congenital anomalies of the eustachian tube in Down syndrome. Ann Otol Rhinol Laryngol 1989;98:543–7.

Shott SR, Joseph A, Heithaus D. Hearing loss in children with Down syndrome. Int J Pediatr Otorhinolaryngol 2001;61:199–205.

Smith TL, Diruggiero D, Jones K. Recovery of eustachian tube function and hearing outcome in patients with cleft palate. Otolaryngol Head Neck Surg 1994;111:423–9.

Takasaki K, Sando I, Balaban CD, Ishijima K. Postnatal development of eustachian tube cartilage: a study of normal and cleft palate cases. Int J Pediatr Otorhinolaryngol 2000;52:31–6.

Chapter 96

OTITIS MEDIA AND ITS COMPLICATIONS IN CONGENITAL AURAL ATRESIA

ROBERT F. YELLON, MD

All varieties of otic pathology can occur in congenital aural atresia. It is likely (although unproven) that the incidence of otitis media (OM) in congenital aural atresia is higher than that seen in the general population because aural atresia often occurs in conjunction with multiple congenital anomalies. As part of the constellation of congenital anomalies that frequently coexist with congenital aural atresia, anomalies of the skull base, palate, and eustachian tube (ET) are quite common in the hemifacial microsomias of oculoauriculovertebral (Goldenhar's) syndrome and the CHARGE association (coloboma of the eye, heart anomaly, choanal atresia, retardation, and genital and ear anomalies). The not uncommon paresis or paralysis of the ipsilateral palate in these children (Figure 96-1) would be expected to impair ET function, thus predisposing them to OM. This ipsilateral paresis or paralysis indicates that the extent of the congenital anomalies sometimes extends beyond the temporal bone and auricle. Aural atresia also frequently occurs in association with bilateral syndromes such as Treacher Collins or Nager's syndrome. Cleft palate and its associated ET dysfunction are often a component of these syndromes.

The degree of pneumatization and aeration of the temporal bone in congenital aural atresia may be another prognostic factor for postoperative OM following aural atresia repair. One would assume that a higher degree of pneumatization and aeration would be inversely correlated with the chances for OM, whereas a limited amount of pneumatization and aeration would portend poor chances for an excellent long-term result owing to possible chronic OM. Temporal bones with severe hypopneumatization usually are not candidates for reconstruction because of both limited surgical access and poor ET function. The Jahrsdoerfer (1978) grading system for judging the chances for a successful hearing result in aural atresia reconstruction does take pneumatization of the middle ear into account, and patients with good pneumatization are awarded a higher, more favorable score. However, the exact contribution of the degree of pneumatization to the incidence of OM in aural atresia is not known.

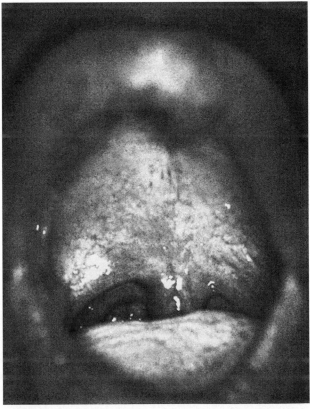

FIGURE 96-1. Unilateral palatal paralysis associated with unilateral congenital aural atresia. This ipsilateral palatal paralysis indicates that the extent of the congenital anomalies in congenital aural atresia may extend beyond the auricle and temporal bone. Eustachian tube dysfunction and an increased incidence of OM would be expected in this patient.

Diagnosis of OM in Congenital Aural Atresia

A difficult point of discussion is how to detect OM that occurs in a patient with congenital aural atresia who has not had surgery. Without computed tomography (CT), magnetic resonance imaging, or at least mastoid radiography, the diagnosis is difficult to make in the absence of an ear canal and tympanic membrane for direct visualization. The presence of periauricular pain may help make the diagnosis, as may the presence of fever or elevation of the neutrophil count. Postauricular redness and swelling or fluctuation are obvious signs of complications of OM in aural atresia. However, for mild, uncomplicated cases of OM occurring in patients with aural atresia who have not undergone surgery, the incidence is unknown.

OM and Complications in Congenital Aural Atresia

It is clear that OM and any of its complications may occur in aural atresia without surgery or may follow surgical reconstruction. Treatments of OM and its complications in congenital aural atresia are, in general, the same as the standard treatments for these conditions with the following caveats. Reconstructive surgery for congenital aural atresia usually follows microtia reconstruction at the age of 4 to 7 years. However, surgery for OM and its complications may be performed at any age if the disease process is severe enough to warrant surgical intervention. Treatment of OM and specific types of complications in congenital aural atresia should follow the guidelines for treatment of these conditions described in the other chapters of this book. It is important to take into account the possible alterations in anatomy such as the lateral and anterior displacement of the facial nerve that is frequently seen in congenital aural atresia. One would more frequently obtain CT studies to help predict the altered anatomy prior to surgical intervention and to rule out complications such as bone erosion or occult cholesteatoma. An otologist experienced in congenital ear surgery should be involved if possible.

In the discussion below, the literature reporting OM and its complications in aural atresia will be discussed and divided into OM that was detected in ears without surgery, intraoperatively, and following reconstruction. Although infections of the reconstructed ear canal are clearly related to surgery, it is not clear whether middle ear and mastoid infections and their associated complications are a result of or are increased by the surgery or would have occurred anyway in the atretic ear without surgery. The surgical reconstruction allows a portal for visualization and detection of OM that would have gone undetected in the absence of severe pain or complications.

Historically, Krampitz (1912) was the first to report a case of purulent OM in a case of microtia in 1912. However, the patient was reported to have a small but patent ear canal. In 1931, Fraser reported the presence of OM in the temporal bone specimen of a patient with aural atresia. In 1955, Ireland and Bryce reported a case of an atretic ear that had recurrent discharge through a dehiscence in the ear canal that drained through a cervical fistula. Ruben and colleagues (1969) reported the presence of bilateral OM in the atretic temporal bones of a girl with Treacher Collins syndrome who died of other causes.

Close and Scholl (1982) reported a case of coalescent mastoiditis with subperiostial abscess requiring mastoidectomy in a child with aural atresia. Zalzal (1987) reported a case of acute mastoiditis in an atretic ear complicated by sigmoid sinus thrombosis that required ligation of the jugular vein, revision mastoidectomy, and evacuation of the infected thrombus in the sigmoid sinus.

Alterations in anatomy can lead to unusual presentations of OM in aural atresia. Figure 96-2 shows the CT scan of the temporal bone of a child with aural atresia, chronic staphylococcal otorrhea, anacusis, and CHARGE association. When prolonged culture and sensitivity–directed intravenous antimicrobial agents did not alleviate the otorrhea, radical mastoidectomy with temporalis muscle flap

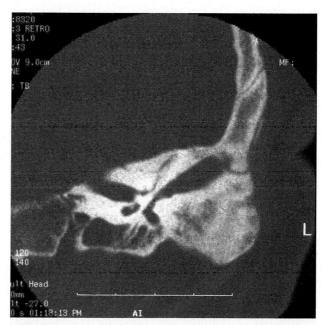

FIGURE 96-2. Coronal computed tomographic scan of the temporal bone of a child with aural atresia and chronic staphylococcal otorrhea that was unresponsive to intravenous antimicrobial agents. Radical mastoidectomy with temporalis muscle flap obliteration of the cavity was performed. Histopathologic examination of tissue removed revealed ectopic salivary tissue. It is unlikely that nonsurgical treatment would ever have stopped the otorrhea secondary to the ectopic salivary tissue. This case illustrates how alterations in anatomy may lead to unusual presentations of otitis media in congenital aural atresia.

obliteration of the cavity was performed. During the mastoidectomy, yellowish tissue was removed, which histopathologic examination revealed to be ectopic salivary tissue. Thus, it is unlikely that nonsurgical treatment would ever have stopped the otorrhea secondary to the ectopic salivary tissue.

Gill (1969; 1971) was the first to report the finding of OM intraoperatively. He reported a 50% incidence of finding OM in a series in 113 reconstructed congenital ears. His findings ranged from mild changes such as granulation tissue to frank pus with bone erosion. He reported one case of acute mastoiditis in 113 surgical cases of aural atresia. Only 2 of these cases had clinical signs of OM preoperatively. No author other than Gill (1969; 1971) has reported such a high incidence of OM identified at the time of surgery. Weigand (1975) reported findings of chronic OM in 2 of 26 surgical cases, and Jahrsdoerfer (1978) reported such findings in only 1 of 20 operative cases.

Following aural atresia reconstruction, OM with effusion can persist and require myringotomy and tube insertion. Recurrent acute otitis media (AOM) may likewise require tube insertion. Once a tube has been placed, or if a perforation occurs in the reconstructed tympanic membrane, it can obviously act as a portal of infection from the outside environment. Chang and colleagues (1994) reported a 4% incidence of otorrhea following atresia reconstruction. Figure 96-3 shows the CT scan of a girl with acute mastoiditis following aural atresia repair who had a tube placed for recurrent AOM. On two separate occasions, the tube became blocked, and she developed acute mastoiditis that required mastoidectomy and tube replacement.

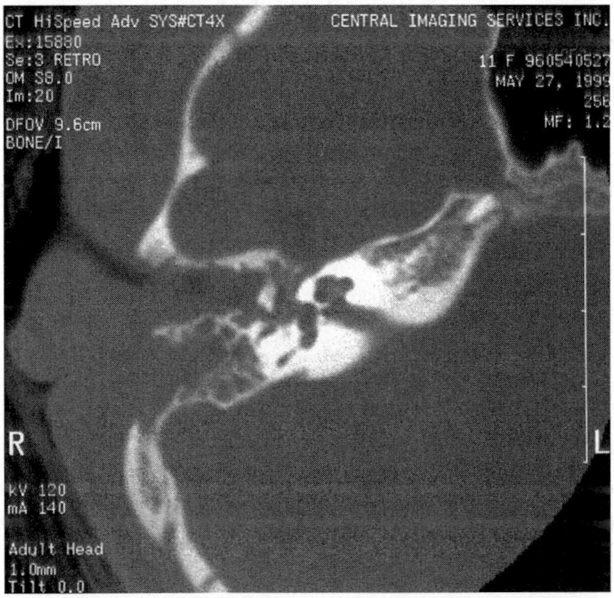

Adhesive OM is also possible following congenital aural atresia reconstruction. As discussed by Lambert (1998), audiologic results may decline following bouts of OM owing to fibrosis or ossicular erosion or possibly suppurative labyrinthitis.

Cholesteatoma in Congenital Aural Atresia

Congenital cholesteatomas in atretic ears may also become infected. These congenital cholesteatomas usually, but not always, occur in stenotic ear canals and are considered to be canal cholesteatomas. Such canal cholesteatomas may erode bone and extend into the mastoid or middle ear. Primary middle ear cholesteatomas may also occur from embryonic rests of epithelial tissue. Hoenk and colleagues (1969) reported a case of congenital cholesteatoma medial to the atretic plate. In all patients with congenital aural atresia, both early (first year of life) and late (4 to 5 years old) CT studies should be obtained as part of an investigation to determine whether reconstruction is possible and to monitor for possible growth of congenital cholesteatomas. Nishimura and colleagues (1989) reported five cases of intractable retroauricular abscesses associated with congenital cholesteatomas arising in patients with microtia and congenital aural atresia. These cases required surgery to remove the cholesteatoma in addition to drainage of the abscesses.

FIGURE 96-3. Computed tomographic scan of the temporal bone of a child who previously underwent aural atresia repair and tympanostomy tube placement who developed acute mastoiditis on two occasions following blockage of the tube requiring tube replacement and tympanomastoidectomy.

Ear Canal and Mastoid Cavity Infections following Aural Atresia Reconstruction

For completeness, it should be noted that ear canal infections occur frequently following aural atresia reconstruction, and this often leads to meatal stenosis. Canal infections and meatal stenosis can occur postoperatively in up to one-third of surgically repaired cases of aural atresia (Jahrsdoerfer, 1978). Meatal stenosis may also occur in the absence of infection. Meatal stenosis may respond to triamcinolone injections. The incidence of meatal stenosis appears to be decreased by the use of pedicled skin flaps in the reconstructed meatus (Jahrsdoerfer, 1978; Nishizaki et al, 1999). The technique of aural atresia reconstruction may influence the incidence of postoperative infectious complications. The canal wall down approach described by Shih and Crabtree (1993) and Schuknecht (1989) appears to predispose patients to more infections and meatal stenoses than the anterior approach (no mastoidectomy) described by Jahrsdoerfer (1978). Thus, the anterior approach is preferred whenever possible.

Conclusion

The diagnosis and treatment of OM in congenital aural atresia remain quite challenging. The alterations in anatomy from the congenital anomaly and from reconstructive surgery can lead to unusual presentations of OM and its complications in these patients. The clinician must rely on the combination of laboratory, microbiologic, and radiographic studies; clinical signs and symptoms; and good judgment to make the correct diagnosis and plan appropriate therapy.

References

Chang SO, Min YG, Kim CS, Koh TY. Surgical management of congenital aural atresia. Laryngoscope 1994;104:606–11.

Close LG, Scholl PD. Coalescent mastoiditis in a case of congenital aural atresia. Int J Pediatr Otorhinolaryngol 1982;4:69–76.

Fraser JS. Maldevelopments of the auricle, external acoustic meatus and middle ear. Arch Otolaryngol 1931;13:1–27.

Gill NW. Congenital atresia of the ear. J Laryngol Otol 1969;83: 551–87.

Gill NW. Congenital atresia of the ear. J Laryngol Otol 1971;85: 1251–4.

Hoenk BE, McCabe BF, Anson BJ. Cholesteatoma auris behind a bony atresia plate. Arch Otolaryngol 1969;89:470–7.

Ireland PE, Bryce DP. Cervical fistula associated with unilateral congenital aural atresia. Arch Otolaryngol 1955;62:262–5.

Jahrsdoerfer RA. Congenital atresia of the ear. Laryngoscope 1978; 88:1–48.

Krampitz P. Uber einige seltenere Formen von Missbildungen des Gehororgans, Z Ohrenheilk Krankheit Luftweg Ohrenheil 1912;65:44–52.

Lambert PR. Congenital aural atresia: stability of surgical results. Laryngoscope 1998;108:1801–5.

Nishimura Y, Minatogawa T, Kumoi T. Intractable retroauricular abscess associated with microtia and aural atresia—some views in relation to the congenital cholesteatoma and microtia. Ann Plast Surg 1989;23:74–80.

Nishizaki K, Masuda Y, Karita K. Surgical management and its post-operative complications in congenital aural atresia. Acta Otolaryngol Suppl (Stockh) 1999;540:42–4.

Ruben RJ, Toriyama M, Dische MR, et al. External and middle ear malformations associated with mandibulofacial dysostosis and renal abnormalities: a case report. Ann Otol Rhinol Laryngol 1969;78:605–24.

Schuknecht HF. Congenital aural atresia. Laryngoscope 1989; 99:908–17.

Shih L, Crabtree AJ. Long-term surgical results for congenital aural atresia. Laryngoscope 1993;103:1097–102.

Weigand ME. [The concept of endaural tympanoplasty for severe congenital atresia auris.] Laryngorhinootologie 1975;54:148–54.

Zalzal GH. Acute mastoiditis complicated by sigmoid sinus thrombosis in congenital aural atresia. Int J Pediatr Otorhinolaryngol 1987;14:31–9.

Chapter 97

Exclusively Unilateral Recurrent Acute Otitis Media or Otitis Media with Effusion

David H. Chi, MD, Cuneyt M. Alper, MD

Acute otitis media (AOM) and otitis media with effusion (OME) are usually bilateral diseases. The majority of the risk factors for AOM or OME apply to both ears. However, the timing and severity of infection during an episode of otitis media (OM) show variability. At any instant, an infection or effusion can be experienced or observed as unilateral. Although infections or effusion in one ear, sparing the other, is not rare, most of the unilateral infections alternate between both ears in the long term.

The focus of treatment for AOM or OME in the majority of cases is the patient and not the individual ear. Although the history of the disease or the appearance of each ear may seem to be different, a decision for treatment is reached for the patient based on criteria that ignore the laterality of the disease.

Although systemic medical treatment does not differentiate ears, any surgical treatment brings the option to individualize the treatment for each ear. Despite this possibility, surgical treatment for both ears is generally identical. The underlying rationale for using the same treatment for both ears is that the risk factors for the development or persistence of an episode of AOM or OME must be similar bilaterally in the majority of conditions. The potential consequence of withholding surgical treatment on the contralateral, normal ear based on a better history or appearance at the time of planning is that disease may develop on the untreated side, requiring a second procedure. This withholding of intervention introduces the liability of additional surgery, problems of authorization for a second procedure, and increased costs. Thus, both ears are treated similarly in most cases, despite the knowledge or suspicion of unilateral disease.

Exceptions exist to the decision of bilateral treatment for OME and recurrent AOM when exclusively unilateral disease is present. This chapter discusses the factors that affect the individual ear differently, summarizes known conditions that require only unilateral treatment, highlights important underlying diagnoses that are associated with unilateral disease, and attempts to set recommendations for the criteria for individualized management of ears in OM.

Identification and treatment of exclusively unilateral OM require a definition of this entity. However, there are no established criteria for the diagnosis of exclusively unilateral disease. A time limit has not been set for a patient to have unilateral OM to call it "exclusively" unilateral disease. Thus, the clinician faces a challenge of recognizing the patient with unilateral OM and determining the appropriate treatment. We suggest a definition of exclusively unilateral OM as the criteria of no episode of recurrent AOM or OME in the contralateral ear for 2 or more years.

The importance of managing patients with exclusively unilateral OM lies in three issues. First, unilateral OM may be a manifestation of an underlying neoplastic, possibly malignant, process, especially in adults. Second, one ear of a patient may have structural or functional abnormalities that may need to be identified to better understand and treat the disease in that particular ear. Third, proper selection of cases that require only unilateral treatment minimizes subjecting the contralateral ear to unnecessary surgery and its potential complications or sequelae in that ear.

Incidence

There are no data on the incidence of exclusively unilateral disease. The exact incidence of AOM and OME is unknown, let alone the incidence of unilateral disease.

Epidemiologic studies have demonstrated a high incidence of OM in the pediatric population. Overall, 19 to 62% of children had had at least one episode of AOM by age 1 year and 50 to 84% by age 3 years (Casselbrant and Mandel, 1999). AOM presents bilaterally in about 80% of children younger than 2 years of age. In older children, the percentages decrease. A little more than half of the children during the fourth year of life and slightly less than half of the children during the fifth and sixth years had bilateral OM. By the seventh year, about one-third of children present with bilateral disease (Stangerup and Tos, 1986).

The exact incidence of episodes of OME is not known because the disease is asymptomatic and underdiagnosed. Monthly pneumotoscopy and tympanometry examinations of 2- to 6-year-old children in day care demonstrated middle ear effusion (MEE) in 53 to 61% of children (Casselbrant et al, 1985). Others have reported an incidence of MEE of 26% in 387 7-year-old children (Lous and Fiellau-Nikolajsen, 1981).

The proportion of unilateral versus bilateral OM may be derived from the subjects enrolled in clinical trials. Well-recognized studies have stratified subjects at enrolment with respect to their laterality to randomize subjects with similar severity of the disease. In a recent study, Paradise and colleagues (2003) randomized children with unilateral and bilateral MEE for early and late ventilation tube insertion. Among 6,350 children younger than 2 months of age who were enrolled and followed for 3 years, 407 children were enrolled to the study with a history of 2 months or more with MEE. Bilateral effusions were present in 37% of the children, whereas unilateral effusion was in 63%. Whereas 22% of the children had bilateral continuous effusions for up to 9 months, 13.4% of the children had continuous unilateral effusion at 3 months. In the late ventilation tube group at 9 months, there was continuous unilateral effusion in 12.2% of the children. Discontinuous effusion was present in 74.4% of the children during the study period, but there is no information as to whether these discontinuous effusions shifted sides.

Another study (Hogan et al, 1997) followed 97 infants with monthly otoscopy and tympanometry for 3 years. The average duration of unilateral effusion was 5 months, whereas it was 8 to 9 weeks for bilateral effusions. Analysis of the data showed that there was a low probability of changing between unilateral states (from the left to the right ear being affected or the reverse), there was a comparatively high probability of remaining in a bilateral state (either free of effusion or with bilateral effusion), and about half of the unilateral states reverted to normal (effusion free) after just one observation. Although this study suggests no change of effusion between the sides, the average duration of the effusion is too short to conclude that treating individual ears in unilateral disease would be appropriate.

All of the information gathered from these studies above is limited by the fact that although recurrent AOM or OME may be unilateral at any time point, most of these studies do not distinguish children who have had exclusively unilateral disease. Moreover, these studies identifying unilateral disease do not differentiate if the disease is alternating between the two ears.

Important information from epidemiologic studies is that children younger than age 6 years are prone to continue to develop OM in either ear. Thus, it is appropriate to treat the contralateral unaffected ear in this age group.

Etiology and Pathogenesis

Most of the known risk factors for recurrent AOM or OME are expected to affect both ears concurrently. Risk factors including age, prematurity, gender, race, allergy and immunity, genetic predisposition, and certain craniofacial abnormalities, such as Down syndrome, affect both ears. Other risk factors, such as season, upper respiratory infections, attendance at day care, passive smoking, bottle-feeding, socioeconomic status, and pacifier use, affect both ears simultaneously.

On the other hand, there are potential factors that may account for the increased risk of an infection or effusion on only one side. The common factor in the pathogenesis of recurrent AOM or OME is eustachian tube dysfunction. There are rare conditions for selective dysfunction of one eustachian tube such as from altered structure of the tube or obstruction of one tube. Mechanical obstruction causing eustachian tube dysfunction may be related to nasal, nasopharyngeal, or intratemporal obstruction or masses. When the anatomic obstruction involves the tube, it can be intraluminal, periluminal, or peritubal.

A summary differential diagnosis of possible etiologic factors for unilateral disease is in Table 97-1. Syndromes typically affect a person bilaterally, but certain other craniofacial syndromes with asymmetric structural and functional abnormalities, such as branchio-oto-renal syndrome (Ceruti et al, 2002) and Goldenhar's syndrome, may affect one ear more than the other. Although not commonly observed, patients with a unilateral cleft palate also have a probable higher risk of ear disease on the ipsilateral side. One of the main reasons that these conditions do not necessarily result in exclusively unilateral disease is the effect of other risk factors in the same child that lead to OM on the less affected ear.

TABLE 97-1. Etiopathogenesis of Unilateral Otitis Media

Congenital
    Branchio-oto-renal syndrome
    Goldenhar's syndrome
    Unilateral cleft palate
Inflammatory
    Unilateral rhinosinusitis
    Asymmetric adenoid hypertrophy
Neoplasms
    Nasopharyngeal carcinoma
    Sinonasal neoplasms
    Juvenile nasopharyngeal angiofibroma
Trauma
    Nasal foreign body
    Iatrogenic (adenoidectomy, pharyngeal flap)
Miscellaneous
    Mass in middle ear (cholesteatoma)

Asymmetric eustachian tube or mastoid anatomy may also contribute to unilateral disease. A study was conducted (Sirikci et al, 2001) to determine whether a relationship exists between mastoid size and auditory tube angle and chronic ear disease. Computed tomographic (CT) scans of the affected ears of 24 patients with unilateral chronic OM were compared with those of the healthy contralateral ears and the ears of 12 healthy controls. Whereas there was no significant difference in the auditory tube angle between the diseased and normal ears in the patients with unilateral chronic OM, significant differences existed in the auditory tube angle between the ears of patients with OM and the healthy controls.

Unilateral differences may be exacerbated by edema from infection and allergy. Unilateral initial infections may progress to persistent low-grade inflammation or infection that becomes chronically active without involvement of the contralateral ear.

Other etiologies are benign and malignant nasopharyngeal lesions that cause asymmetric obstruction of one eustachian tube. The clinician needs to rule out the presence of a nasopharyngeal malignancy in an adult and young adults who present with unilateral OM. Also, in pediatric patients, the clinician needs to determine when to suspect and evaluate for a nasopharyngeal mass. The index of suspicion in children with nasopharyngeal carcinoma (NPC) is low. In the United States, the annual incidence is approximately one to two cases per million under the age of 30 years (Jenkin et al, 1981). Moreover, in the presentation of OME, cervical lymphadenopathy is common in children. This similar presentation of rare NPCs along with typical AOM or OME forces the clinician to make judicious decisions.

A mass in the middle ear may obstruct the lateral portion of the eustachian tube, contributing to its dysfunction and subsequent OM. The obstruction may be secondary to granulation or a foreign body. Enlarging congenital cholesteatoma at the anterosuperior quadrant of the middle ear may cause eustachian tube obstruction and secondary MEE. It may be seen through the tympanic membrane or be evident at the time of middle ear exploration in refractory OM.

Iatrogenic causes also need to be considered. A child with prior adenoidectomy or pharyngeal surgery may have trauma to the torus tubarius and subsequent scarring, leading to unilateral eustachian tube dysfunction. Also, incomplete asymmetric adenoid removal may potentially lead to unilateral eustachian tube obstruction.

Diagnosis

History

The most important aspect of assessing a patient with unilateral recurrent AOM is obtaining a thorough history. Information begins with the patient's age. Any adult with new onset of unilateral OME requires office flexible nasopharyngoscopy to exclude a nasopharyngeal malignancy. Other important components of the patient history include unilateral nasal obstruction, epistaxis, epiphora, rhinorrhea, anosmia, facial pain, facial numbness, smoking and alcohol history, fever, night sweats, and weight loss. The otologic history should include prior history of OM and duration of effusion. The index of suspicion for nasopharyngeal malignancy is much lower in a patient with chronic unilateral disease than in an older child or adult with no prior or distant history of ear infections who develops unilateral disease. Other factors of patient history involve an accurate account of unilateral disease. The patient often presents to an otolaryngologist with only a history of recurrent AOM. If questions of exclusive unilaterality exist, good communication between the referring physician and the otolaryngologist is important and may require the review of old records to confirm the accuracy of laterality. In addition, surgical history should be noted for head and neck surgery, radiation, ear surgery, and prior adenoidectomy.

Physical Examination

Physical examination findings also determine appropriate evaluation. The presence of an effusion is confirmed. Also, the status of the ear is assessed and checked for retractions, middle ear mass, and perforation. The nose is examined for unilateral rhinorrhea, epistaxis, and mass. The oral cavity and pharynx are assessed for any suspicious lesions, clefts, and palate elevation. A thorough cranial nerve examination is also performed to evaluate for cranioneuropathies such as facial numbness and oculomotor dysfunction. Cervical examination evaluates for lymphadenopathy. Audiologic and tympanometric evaluation should be performed according to the guidelines for diagnosis and management of recurrent AOM and OME.

Any adult who presents with unilateral OME, regardless of the absence of additional history or physical examination findings, warrants office flexible nasopharyngoscopy to evaluate for NPC. A mass in the nasopharynx requires further evaluation with biopsy, imaging studies, and complete upper aerodigestive tract endoscopy. Appropriate treatment is coordinated with a multidisciplinary approach based on the pathology and extent of the lesion.

Children with exclusively unilateral disease present a clinical dilemma of when to evaluate for nasopharyngeal pathology. A child who presents with any unilateral nasal symptoms or physical examination findings deserves an evaluation of the nasopharynx. The presence of NPC has been reported in children of elementary school age (Ong and Tan, 2000). The clinical presentation of childhood NPC is similar to that of adults. Bilateral cervical disease is present in 50% of cases (Martin and Shah, 1995).

A male adolescent child with recurrent unilateral epistaxis with nasal obstruction and unilateral AOM or OME may have juvenile nasopharyngeal angiofibroma. Physical examination may demonstrate a reddish mass with bowing of the septum. Larger lesions may cause facial asymmetry. This presentation warrants a CT scan. No biopsy is necessary and is avoided because of the vascularity of the tumor. Diagnosis is made based on clinical and CT findings and confirmed after surgical resection.

Treatment

Adult Patients

If no mass is seen in the nasopharynx, the patient should be treated for unilateral AOM or OME, as described in previous chapters (Figure 97-1). If the decision is made to proceed with tympanostomy tubes after failure of medical therapy, unilateral tube placement should be performed. A unilateral tympanostomy tube is recommended because the symptoms and examination may be followed in an adult. Moreover, tubes in adults may be performed with local anesthesia in the office without the risks and costs of general anesthesia.

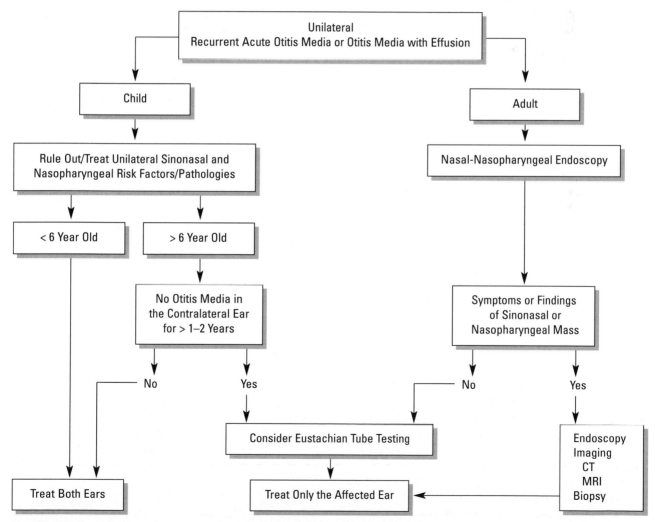

FIGURE 97-1. Algorithm of treatment of recurrent acute otitis media or otitis media with effusion. CT = computed tomography; MRI = magnetic resonance imaging.

Pediatric Patients

If the child does not have a history or physical examination suggestive of a nasopharyngeal mass or does not have a mass on endoscopy, the child is managed as though he or she has bilateral disease, as described in previous chapters. The only difference is that tympanostomy tubes are recommended after the effusion has been present for 6 months for persistent unilateral disease, instead of at 3 months for bilateral disease. The contralateral ear is normal and unaffected, allowing for increased time for resolution of the effusion without adverse effects on hearing.

Once the child meets the criteria for surgery, bilateral myringotomy and tympanostomy tube placement are performed for children under age 6 years of age (see Figure 97-1). The rationale for tympanostomy tubes in both the affected and unaffected ears is that children younger than 6 years old with unilateral disease are at risk of developing AOM or OME in the contralateral ear and that the antibiotics may have prophylactically treated the uninvolved ear from developing infection or effusion. Children who are over the age of 6 years receive tympanostomy tubes in the affected ear only as they are considered to have "outgrown" the need for tubes, based on epidemiologic studies, in the unaffected ear but still have problems with eustachian tube dysfunction on the affected side. Many children eligible for ventilation tube placement at age 6 years or above have a history of prior tubes. It is not unusual that the interval between the insertion of ventilation tubes is too brief to determine that the OM is exclusively unilateral. In such patients with only unilateral ear disease during the short interval without tubes, it is safer to place tubes on both sides. Although there are no studies or set recommendations, it seems that to be relatively convinced that an ear is not going to get an infection or effusion and that a ventilation tube is probably not necessary, the ear has to be free of OM for at least 1, and preferably 2, years.

Children may be a candidate for unilateral tympanostomy tubes when they continue to have unilateral disease and the contralateral normal ear is disease free for over 1 to 2 years. Prior to surgery, eustachian tube testing may be performed to document the opening pressure and active function of the unaffected side (see Figure 97-1). Normal contralateral function will support the decision to treat only the diseased ear.

Children who have bilateral nasal airway obstructive symptoms should undergo adenoidectomy at the time of tube insertion. Prior to adenoid removal, the nasopharynx is visualized for any suspicious masses that may obstruct the ipsilateral eustachian tube orifice. Biopsies are taken and sent as a fresh specimen if a lesion is encountered.

After the extrusion of the initial set of tubes, if the patient has persistent unilateral recurrent AOM or OME, a second set of tubes is placed and adenoidectomy is performed regardless of size (Paradise et al, 1990). During the adenoidectomy, the nasopharynx is carefully visualized to evaluate for any suspicious mass. Appropriate biopsy is performed when necessary.

If the second set of tubes extrudes and the patient has recurrent AOM or OME, the option of long-term tube placement is considered. Also, if the child continues to have exclusive unilateral disease, the clinician may consider treating only the affected side. Prior to treatment, eustachian tube testing is recommended to confirm unilateral dysfunction as a criterion to guide any future decision for unilateral tympanostomy tube insertion.

Conclusion

Exclusively unilateral recurrent AOM or OME requires the clinician to rule out the factors affecting only one ear, including the presence of a nasopharyngeal mass. Once ruled out, the clinician may consider treating only the affected ear in an adult or in a child only if there is a long history of unilateral disease.

References

Casselbrant ML, Brostoff LM, Cantekin EI, et al. Otitis media with effusion in preschool children. Laryngoscope 1985;95:428–36.

Casselbrant ML, Mandel EMM. Epidemiology. In: Rosenfeld RM, Bluestone CD, editors. Evidence-based otitis media. Hamilton (ON): BC Decker; 1999. p. 117–36.

Ceruti S, Stinckens C, Cremers CW, Casselman JW. Temporal bone anomalies in the branchio-oto-renal syndrome: detailed computed tomographic and magnetic resonance imaging findings. Otol Neurotol 2002;23:200–7.

Hogan SC, Stratford KJ, Moore DR. Duration and recurrence of otitis media with effusion in children from birth to 3 years: prospective study using monthly otoscopy and tympanometry. BMJ 1997;314:350–3.

Jenkin DRT, Anderson JR, Jereb B, et al. Nasopharyngeal carcinoma—a retrospective review of patients less than thirty years of age. Cancer 1981;47:360–6.

Lous J, Fiellau-Nikolajsen M. Epidemiology of middle ear effusion and tubal dysfunction: a one year prospective study comprising monthly tympanometery in 387 non-selected seven year old children. Int J Pediatr Otorhinolaryngol 1981;3:303–17.

Martin WMD, Shah KH. Carcinoma of the nasopharynx in young patients. Int J Radiat Oncol Biol Phys 1995;28:991–9.

Ong YK, Tan HKK. Nasopharyngeal carcinoma in children. Int J Pediatr Otorhinolaryngol 2000;55:149–54.

Paradise JL, Bluestone CD, Rogers KD, et al. Efficacy of adenoidectomy for recurrent otitis media in children previously treated with tympanostomy tube placement: results of parallel randomized and nonrandomized trials. JAMA 1990;263:2066–73.

Paradise JL, Feldman HM, Campbell TF, et al. Early versus delayed insertion of tympanostomy tubes for persistent otitis media: developmental outcomes at the age of three years in relation to prerandomization illness patterns and hearing levels. Pediatr Infect Dis J 2003;22:309–14.

Sirikci A, Bayazit YA, Bayram M, Kanlikama M. Significance of the auditory tube angle and mastoid size in chronic ear disease. Surg Radiol Anat 2001;23:91–5.

Stangerup SE, Tos M. Epidemiology of acute suppurative otitis media. Am J Otolaryngol 1986;7:47–54.

Chapter 98

OTITIS MEDIA IN TEENAGERS AND ADULTS

BARRY E. HIRSCH, MD, FACS

Otitis media (OM) is a clinical problem that may be encountered in adolescents and adults. The highest incidence of OM is in children under 5 years of age. The frequency of episodes of OM significantly diminishes after the age of 7 years but still occurs sporadically and remains more prevalent during the winter months. As children get older, they are exposed to ongoing immunologic challenges from the environment and other people. Depending on their geographic location, adolescents and adults can become sensitized to a host of antigens and develop hypersensitivity signs and symptoms manifested by sinonasal and middle ear disease.

It is difficult to accurately report the incidence of OM in adults. It has been estimated that 3 to 15% of patients with OM referred to otolaryngology clinics are adults (Oppenheimer, 1975; Sadé, 1979). In a study by Yung and Arasaratnam (2001), it was reported that in a population of 350,000, there were 53 adult patients who required myringotomy tubes. These patients underwent nasal endoscopy, and 35.8% were identified with signs or symptoms of chronic rhinosinusitis. They also noted that a significant portion of this group had a strong history of atopy.

Pathogenesis

The development and function of the eustachian tube in early childhood have a tremendous impact on the subsequent status of the tympanic membrane (TM), ossicles, middle ear space, and mastoid aeration. Children with poor tubal function have a lower threshold for recurrent or chronic ear disease. Permanent sequelae may develop, causing changes in the integrity and position of the TM, ossicles, and middle ear space, predisposing older children and adults to recurrent ear infections, TM perforation, conductive hearing loss, development of cholesteatoma, and possible chronic suppurative OM.

Obtaining a complete current and past medical history is important in understanding the etiology of ear com-

plaints and findings. A patient providing a history of recent illness with ear pain, fever, and decreased hearing and identifying an inflamed, bulging TM has OM. Although not very common without a history of previous ear problems, acute otitis media (AOM) does occur in this population.

The information obtained from the patient's past medical history should include not only their otologic history but other issues such as trauma, recent travel, allergy symptoms and treatment, medications, significant medical problems, current illness in their family, smoking habits, and current living conditions. Allergic rhinitis can cause obstruction, fluid accumulation, and bacterial infections, resulting in sinusitis and OM with effusion (OME) (Skoner, 2000). Similar to young children exposed to other children in day care, adolescents and young adults are more prone to exposure of infectious organisms, such as infectious mononucleosis, from their fellow students in high school or college. The presence of palatine tonsillar hypertrophy and nasal and oral pharyngitis frequently causes referred otalgia and eustachian tube dysfunction, which may predispose toward the development of OM.

Consideration should also be given toward gastroesophageal reflux having a causal relation to chronic ear disease. Although not a common source of eustachian tube dysfunction, successful antireflux treatment has resulted in reversal of middle ear disease (Poelmans et al, 2001). Patients who are immunocompromised are at risk for developing OM. Inadequate surveillance of virulent and more innocuous organisms permits them to cause rapidly progressive or more insidious infections, respectively. Patients known to have human immunodeficiency virus (HIV) infection should be carefully examined for evidence of middle ear disease. This is also pertinent to patients who are immunocompromised for other reasons, such as those with uncontrolled diabetes mellitus or systemic malignancy and those receiving chemotherapy for treatment of these diseases.

Diagnosis

Attention to detail in the physical examination of the ears and head and neck is imperative in the assessment of disease of the middle ear. Although the TM will be intact in patients with acute, recurrent, or serous OM, critical inspection and interpretation of what is observed provide insight into the etiology and anticipated treatment. Physical findings include the color, position, symmetry, mobility, integrity, and stability of the TMs. Findings suggestive of an infectious process consist of erythema and/or vascular injection of skin of the medial bony canal, the TM, and vessels along the malleus handle. Bulging of an opaque TM in this setting implies a transudate or exudate under pressure, expanding the middle ear space. Pulsation in synchronicity with cardiac contractions also suggests a middle ear with an inflamed and hypervascular mucosa.

The differential diagnosis for the etiology of pulsation of the TM also includes transmission from an intact dura from a dehiscent defect in the bony tegmen of the epitympanum. A middle fossa meningoencephalocele making contact with the head of the malleus/body of the incus transmits intracranial pulsations through the ossicular chain to the TM. Similarly, clinicians should be very suspicious of observing pulsations of a noninflamed TM with clear fluid in the middle ear space (serous OM). The possibility of a dehiscence of the dura resulting in cerebrospinal fluid in the mastoid and middle ear air system should be considered. It is rare for children to present with these findings. Tegmen defects typically occur in patients with a history of head trauma or following previous mastoid surgery or, rarely, spontaneously in patients with hydrocephalus and/or the propensity for tegmen thinning with ongoing dural pulsations.

Other TM findings include retraction and focal or diffuse atrophy of the TM. The latter may indicate a healed TM following myringotomy tube extrusion or a disease-related perforation. Myringosclerosis may be present, indicating a previous history of recurrent or chronic OM. This scope of involvement can be limited to a small area of the TM or infiltrate the entire drum with fixation of the malleus and extend into the fibrous annulus. Pneumatic otoscopy is an important diagnostic tool that helps to determine the mobility, integrity, and position of the TM.

A complete head and neck examination is necessary for patients with new onset of symptoms. The nasal passages should be inspected for evidence of inflammation, significant congestion or obstruction, polyps, or rhinorrhea. The nasopharynx should be inspected in any new patient, especially someone with unilateral serous effusion. It is important to verify that the adenoids have atrophied (or are absent following previous removal) and that there are no other masses or tumors causing eustachian tube obstruction. Inspection can be accomplished by indirect nasopharyngoscopy with a small mirror through the oral cavity or by transnasal endoscopy using a rigid or flexible fiberoptic endoscope. The oral cavity is examined for hypertrophy or disease of the palatine tonsils. The posterior pharyngeal wall may show evidence of lymphoid islands suggestive of nasopharyngeal drainage, primary infection, or allergic naso- and oropharyngitis. The hypopharynx and larynx are evaluated, looking for signs of gastric reflux (inflammation of the arytenoids, false vocal folds, or posterior glottic chink). The neck is palpated to identify evidence of abnormal masses, pathologic lymph node enlargement, or hypertrophy or masses within the thyroid gland.

Adults who present with new-onset serous OM require a full head and neck examination, with special attention to the nasopharynx. Despite the fact that OM does occur in adults, pathology of the nasopharynx must be ruled out to avoid missing a potentially serious source of origin. This is particularly important in patients with a unilateral serous effusion. Flexible fiberoptic or rigid endoscopy is warranted if an indirect examination is not feasible with a mirror. If there is concern regarding any mass in the nasopharynx or fullness or obliteration of the fossa of Rosenmüller, computed tomography or magnetic resonance imaging of the skull base should be done in anticipation of performing a biopsy.

Preliminary assessment of hearing should be performed with tuning fork testing. Teenagers and adults, as opposed to young children, should be able to provide reliable feedback regarding their perception of localization and magnitude of the sound. The results from this part of the physical examination help to determine the presence and magnitude of a conductive hearing loss. Lateralization of either the 256 Hz or 512 Hz fork (Weber's test) to the involved ear implies a conductive hearing loss. (This can also be a manifestation of severe sensorineural hearing loss in the contralateral ear.) A negative Rinne test (bone conduction greater than air conduction) with the 512 Hz fork suggests a conductive hearing loss of at least 20 dB. These findings should be recorded in the patient's chart for the purpose of assessing outcome after treatment or intervention. Tuning fork testing, alone, should suffice for patients known to the physician and for whom a diagnosis has been established.

A complete audiogram should be obtained for patients being evaluated for recurrent ear problems or for those in whom surgical intervention is anticipated. This provides a baseline for which future progression and outcome can be compared. Patients with an established history of recurrent or chronic OME returning for ventilation or placement of a myringotomy tube do not need a repeat audiogram if they are deemed to be reliable and their own assessment of their hearing follows patterns experienced in the past.

Management

Similar to young children, teenagers and adults can experience AOM, which is often unilateral. Adolescent and adult patients having ongoing problems with recurrent effusions or ear infections are managed differently than patients of similar age who present with their first episode. The physician and patient often have a good understanding as to which treatment has been effective in the past. If recurrent infection has responded to antibiotics, then it is reasonable to take this line of therapy. Patients who have required ventilation of the middle ear should have a myringotomy performed. If the frequency of episodes is rare and situational, such as following an upper respiratory infection or barotrauma from an air flight, then a myringotomy alone will suffice. Patients with poor or marginal eustachian tube function will likely require placement of a myringotomy tube as well. In contrast to children, this is performed as an office procedure.

Intervention is determined based on the degree of pain the patients are experiencing and the findings on physical examination. A myringotomy can provide relief of pain and may prevent spontaneous rupture of the TM. Anesthesia is provided with the use of topical phenol, but this is often insufficient owing to inadequate penetration of an inflamed and thickened TM. If a myringotomy is still warranted in this setting, injection of a local anesthetic (lidocaine with epinephrine) is done prior to the drainage procedure. Patients in these age groups often present with involvement in one ear. If a myringotomy tube is necessary and the contralateral ear is normal, treatment is directed only toward the side of involvement. This is in contrast to children with recurrent OM who require middle ear ventilation. If a child is to undergo a general anesthetic for recurrent OM, it is most typical that ventilation tubes are placed into both ears. This management decision is reasonable because children are more prone to bilateral ear disease, and it averts the need for a possible subsequent general anesthetic should the noninvolved ear develop disease.

On occasion, patients with a history of chronic ear problems can complain of hearing loss and have mild retraction of the TM with seemingly clear visibility of the promontory, suggesting no effusion, and conductive hearing loss identified with tuning forks and on audiometric testing. A natural assumption is that the hearing problem resides within the ossicular chain. A diagnostic myringotomy should be performed to ensure that fluid in the middle ear is not accounting for this loss. This is of particular relevance when patients have a history of allergic rhinitis. They may have a clear but very thick mucoid effusion in the middle ear. Despite the TM having sluggish mobility and the middle ear appearing to be free of fluid, tenacious mucoid can be a surprising finding, and once it is aspirated and removed and a myringotomy tube is placed, the conductive hearing loss is typically resolved. Patients with severe allergic sinonasal and pulmonary disease frequently have involvement of the middle ear. The source of pathology and obstruction is thought to be the mucosa of the nasopharyngeal portion of the eustachian tube (Bernstein, 1993). Patients who do not respond to topical and systemic immunotherapy may require long-term ventilation with myringotomy tubes (Fireman, 1997).

The organisms encountered in adults with AOM are the same as those cultured from children. The three most prevalent bacteria are *Streptococcus pneumoniae*, *Haemophilus influenzae*, and *Moraxella catarrhalis*. Infections can also be caused by *Streptococcus pyogenes* and *Staphylococcus aureus*. Although the infection may be of viral origin, treatment is given with systemic antibiotics. Amoxicillin with clavulanic acid provides coverage to all organisms, assuming that resistance has not developed. Second-generation cephalosporins such as cefuroxime and cefprozil, or a third-generation formulation such as cefpodoxime, are often prescribed in penicillin-allergic patients who have taken similar formulations without complications. Other options include the quinolones (ciprofloxacin, levofloxacin), macrolides (azithromycin, clarithromycin), and the combinations of trimethoprim-sulfamethoxazole or erythromycin-sulfisoxazole.

Patients who do not show some improvement after 36 to 48 hours of medication may have OM from a resistant organism. Obtaining a culture of the middle ear fluid is necessary to make this determination. If a myringotomy had not been done, doing so will give access toward obtaining a culture and likely provide significant relief if the infection and symptoms have progressed despite 2 days of treatment. Again, local injection may be necessary to provide anesthesia because topical phenol may not be effective.

Sudden onset of ear pain may be attributable to bullous myringitis. There may be more than one bullae present. Aspiration of the fluid or air containing bullae provides immediate relief. Older literature suggested that this finding was indicative of infection caused by *Mycoplasma pneumoniae*. Bullous myringitis alone may be of viral origin but is often associated with OM. Marais and Dale (1997) summarized the results of three separate studies of patients with bullous myringitis and middle ear aspirates. They reported the same organisms as identified in AOM, *S. pneumoniae*, *H. influenza*, and β-hemolytic streptococcus. The blistering of the TM may be a variant of AOM, justifying the use of oral antibiotics. Unless there is evidence of otorrhea and myringitis, topical antibiotic eardrops are not prescribed.

Adult patients with marginal eustachian tube dysfunction are prone to recurrent or chronic serous OM when nasal congestion, inflammation, or secretions compromise the aeration function of tubal opening. This may also be attributable to inherent mucosal abnormalities within the tubal lumen. If this is not of infectious origin, patients can benefit from the use of topical and systemic decongestants. Patients with chronic rhinitis and an allergic component are given a trial of intranasal steroid spray. This may provide sufficient control of nasal mucosal edema and secretions to maintain adequate tubal function. Derebery and Berliner (1998) have written a thorough review of otologic manifestations and treatment of allergic disorders.

In most clinical situations, if medical therapy fails, middle ear aeration can be achieved by performing a myringotomy and placing a ventilation tube. The type of myringotomy tube is dictated by the chronicity and frequency of middle ear effusion or infections. Relatively short-term pressure equalization is accomplished with a small diameter tube such as a Tiny Tytan (Medtronic Xomed, Jacksonville, FL). The need for long-term ventilation can be achieved with a myringotomy tube designed with a larger flange placed within the middle ear. This can be in the form of a T tube or large-diameter disk such as a Per-Lee tube (Figure 98-1) (Medtronic Xomed). Both of the latter tubes entail a higher risk of TM perforation should they extrude.

Teenagers and adults who continue having middle ear problems from their childhood years can pose diagnostic and management challenges. The status of the TM may limit or compromise the needed intervention if disease recurs. Dense myringosclerosis affecting most of the TM may prohibit placement of a myringotomy tube. Myringosclerosis and tympanosclerosis are often the result of chronic middle ear disease and represent subsequent scarring and calcification. These patients often have additional conductive hearing loss that may warrant intervention. If a myringotomy tube cannot be placed using topical or local anesthesia, the procedure may require general anesthesia.

Severe atrophy of the TM is also commonly seen in the setting of eustachian tube dysfunction, repeated tube

placements, and ongoing negative middle ear pressure. Recurrent fluid and a conductive hearing loss may develop in an ear having a flimsy, thin, retracted membrane. There is often a potential small area for placing a ventilation tube in the anterosuperior quadrant just lateral to the eustachian tube orifice in the middle ear. The patient may be able to facilitate aeration by forcing air up the eustachian tube (Valsalva's maneuver). A small myringotomy can be enlarged with an empty alligator forceps. Care should be taken to avoid using a large suction, such as a number 7, which may tear the remaining TM, creating a perforation that is too large. Ears with chronic OM may develop adhesive OM, precluding ventilation and successful restoration of the middle ear. This scenario may require two-stage reconstruction of the ear using Silastic sheeting during the first procedure.

Another problem that can occur in patients with long-standing eustachian tube dysfunction is the development of a retraction pocket. These can be located in the attic, the posterosuperior quadrant, or centrally in the pars tensa. These patients still can experience recurrent OM or serous effusion. Careful examination of the ear should be done to look for evidence of cholesteatoma. Tuning fork testing and an audiogram are obtained to determine the presence and magnitude of a conductive hearing loss. If a large conductive hearing loss is present, suspicion is raised for an attic pocket containing cholesteatoma, causing erosion of the head of the malleus and the body of the incus. A large air–bone gap with a posterosuperior retraction pocket suggests erosion of the long process of the incus. Particular caution is needed when there is mild retraction of the TM onto the incudostapedial joint. On rare occasions, placement of a ventilating tube may help to lateralize the TM, pulling it off a natural type III tympanoplasty. Although the intention of tube placement is to free the middle ear of fluid and provide ventilation to the middle ear, a near maximal conductive hearing loss can result from this well-intentioned procedure. The physician should be aware of this possibility and should make the patient aware with informed consent.

Conclusion

Chronic or recurrent OM in teenagers and adults is often a continuation of problems secondary to eustachian tube dysfunction originating in childhood. If children do not "grow out" of their chronic or recurrent episodes of chronic OM, they typically remain predisposed to ongoing problems. Over time, the TM may become atrophic, have chronic retraction and myringosclerosis, and possibly develop adhesive scarring in the middle ear and subsequent problems with the ossicular chain, causing conductive hearing loss. The evaluation and management of a persistent TM perforation, conductive hearing loss, and the development of cholesteatoma are covered in other

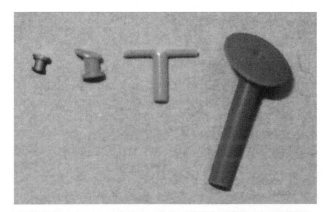

FIGURE 98-1. Four myringotomy tubes used for middle ear ventilation. *From left to right:* the Tiny Tytan provides short-term ventilation for a few months. The Armstrong beveled grommet typically lasts for 9 to 12 months. A T tube and a Per-Lee tube can remain for many years.

chapters in this book. AOM can have its initial onset in an adult and its treatment regimen directed in a similar manner to that in children. The residual serous effusion typically resolves within a few weeks. In contrast, in children it can take from 1 to 3 months to completely resorb the fluid from the middle ear. A persistent unilateral effusion merits confirmation that the nasopharynx is normal. New-onset ear infections may be a manifestation of the patient being immunocompromised. If medications fail to eliminate the middle ear fluid, then performing a myringotomy with tube placement should relieve the pressure and hopefully restore hearing to its baseline level. Patients with allergic sinonasal disease should have their medical therapy optimized to maximize appropriate function of the eustachian tube. In contrast to children, consideration for bilateral intervention in teenagers and adults is based on the status of each ear rather than anticipating that both ears will become involved. Variations in tube design allow the surgeon to adapt the intervention to meet long-term ventilation needs as dictated by the likely chronicity of middle ear pathology.

References

Bernstein JM. The role of IgE-mediated hypersensitivity in the development of otitis media with effusion: a review. Otolaryngol Head Neck Surg 1993;109:611–20.

Derebery MJ, Berliner KI. Allergy for the otologist. External canal to inner ear. Otolaryngol Clin North Am 1998;31:157–73.

Fireman P. Otitis media and eustachian tube dysfunction: connection to allergic rhinitis. J Allergy Clin Immunol 1997;99 Suppl:787–97.

Marais J, Dale BA. Bullous myringitis: a review. Clin Otolaryngol 1997;22:497–9.

Oppenheimer RP. Serous otitis: a review of 922 cases. Eye Ear Nose Throat Mon 1975;54:316–8.

Poelmans J, Tack J, Feenstra L. Chronic middle ear disease and gastroesophageal reflux disease: a causal relation? Otol Neurotol 2001;22:447–50.

Sadé J. Secretory otitis media and its sequelae. New York: Churchill Livingstone; 1979.

Skoner DP. Complications of allergic rhinitis. J Allergy Clin Immunol 2000;105 Suppl:605–9.

Yung MW, Arasaratnam R. Adult-onset otitis media with effusion: results following ventilation tube insertion. J Laryngol Otol 2001;115:874–8.

Chapter 99

Effect of Season in the Treatment of Acute Otitis Media and Otitis Media with Effusion

Carlton J. Zdanski, MD

Acute otitis media (AOM) and otitis media with effusion (OME) are disease processes with multiple risk factors, including their well-known association with preceding or concomitant upper respiratory tract infection (URI). Many studies show a parallel in the seasonal variation of both AOM and OME and URI, with increases in the incidence of each disease in the fall, winter, and spring months. Treatment options vary for both AOM and OME and are, in part, determined by the severity and duration of disease. The impact that any changes in risk factors might have on the disease are therefore important in therapeutic decision making. This is particularly true in "borderline" cases, in which the balance in the decision between medical and surgical management might be more easily affected by changes in risk factors than in cases of greater severity and duration, in which treatment options may be more limited.

Incidence

The seasonal predilection of AOM and OME in children is well documented. Multiple studies show an increase in the incidence of both AOM and OME in the fall, winter, and spring seasons with a nadir in the incidence in the summer months (Alho et al, 1993; Bluestone and Klein, 2001; Casselbrant et al, 1984; Casselbrant et al, 1985; Chonmaitree and Heikkinen, 1997; Engel et al, 1999; Henderson et al, 1982; Ruuskanen et al, 1991; Sly et al, 1980; Tos and Poulsen, 1979; Vesa et al, 2001). The odds ratio for season as a risk factor for AOM ranged from 1.4 to 1.47 in the spring, fall, and winter versus 1.0 in the summer months (Alho et al, 1993). For OME, rates vary from up to 29% in the fall and winter to 0 to 19% in the summer months (Table 99-1).

This seasonal pattern of AOM and OME mirrors the pattern seen with viral URI, and there is widespread agreement that there is an association between the presence of a preceding or concomitant viral URI and AOM and OME (Casselbrant et al, 1985; Chonmaitree and Heikkinen, 1997; Engel et al, 1999; Henderson et al, 1982; Ruuskanen et al, 1991; Tos and Poulsen, 1979). Tos and Poulsen (1979) reported that the "frequency of catarhalia is minimal in the healthy ears and very large in the constantly affected ears" (ie, URI symptoms are less common in patients without OME and are more common in patients with OME). Henderson and colleagues (1982) also found "a close relation between the occurrence of viral respiratory infections and acute OME." Engel and colleagues (1999) reported a higher incidence of OME in winter and that 60% of cases of OME were associated with common cold symptoms. Casselbrant and colleagues (1985) stated that "the seasonal variation in the point prevalence of OME was related to the seasonality of URI episodes," noting that 35% of children with URI had concomitant OME, whereas only 11% of those without URI had OME.

TABLE 99-1. Prevalence (%) of Otitis Media with Effusion by Season

Study (Year)	Fall/Winter/Spring	Summer
Tos and Poulsen (1979)	11.3–14.6	7.2
Sly et al (1980)	29	6
Casselbrant et al (1984)	25	0–7
Engel et al (1999)	24–29	19

Additional evidence supports the association of viral URI and AOM. Vesa and colleagues (2001) found a "close association between respiratory viruses causing URIs and AOM with rhinoviruses and respiratory syncytial virus (RSV) being the most important both in frequency and association with AOM." Other viruses associated with AOM include influenza virus A (Vesa et al, 2001), parainfluenza virus 3 (Vesa et al, 2001), adenovirus (Vesa et al, 2001), and coronavirus (Bluestone and Klein, 2001). The causative role of viral URI in the development of eustachian tube dysfunction and both OME and AOM is supported by multiple studies of human subjects infected with both rhinovirus and influenza A virus (Bluestone, 1999). It is clear from these studies as well that different viruses have varying abilities to cause eustachian tube dysfunction, AOM, and OME (Bluestone, 1999; Chonmaitree and Heikkinen, 1997; Henderson et al, 1982).

The weight of the evidence clearly supports a key role for URI in the pathogenesis of AOM and OME. Possible mechanisms include direct viral infection (Pitkaranta et al, 1998; Vesa et al, 2001), aspiration of nasopharyngeal microorganisms secondary to the high negative middle ear pressure induced by viral URI (Bluestone, 1999; Buchman et al, 1995), eustachian tube dysfunction from inflammation secondary to infection or allergy (Bluestone, 1999), and alterations in local host defense such as decreased mucociliary clearance time (Doyle et al, 1994), suppression of polymorphonuclear leukocyte function (Chonmaitree and Heikkinen, 1997), release of cytokines and inflammatory mediators (Chonmaitree and Heikkinen, 1997).

Given this evidence supporting viral URI in the pathogenesis of AOM and OME, several strategies for the prevention of OM have been advocated (Chonmaitree and Heikkinen, 1997; Erramouspe and Heyneman, 2000; Henderson et al, 1982). Administration of the influenza A vaccine prior to the flu season results in up to a 32 to 36% reduction in AOM (Clements et al, 1995; Heikkinen et al, 1991) and a possible reduction (28%) in OME (results not significant) (Clements et al, 1995). The development of an RSV vaccine may provide additional reductions.

Streptococcus pneumoniae is the most common bacterial cause of AOM. Strategies that prevent infection with *S. pneumoniae* should decrease the overall rate of AOM. Administration of the pneumococcal vaccine Prevnar decreases the number of episodes of AOM by 7.0% (Black et al, 2000), and the vaccine is recommended by the American Academy of Pediatrics for all children ≤ 23 months of age and children at "high risk" for invasive pneumococcal disease 24 to 59 months of age (American Academy of Pediatrics, 2000). Additional antistreptococcal measures such as xylitol gum or syrup, which inhibits the growth and epithelial cell adhesion of *S. pneumoniae* and decreases the number of episodes of AOM in children attending day care but has availability and delivery issues, certainly merit further research (Erramouspe and

Heyneman, 2000). Finally, immunoprophylaxis may benefit high-risk populations by decreasing the number of URI events. However, more investigation is needed (Van Cauwenberge et al, 1999).

My Experience

Patients with recurrent AOM and OME are a relatively heterogeneous group. Management of the clinical problem should be tailored to reflect the diversity of the patients encountered.

Nonsurgical interventions should be attempted prior to surgical management provided that no compelling factors (ie, infectious complication, speech delay, sensorineural hearing impairment with worsened hearing sensitivity secondary to OME, etc) mandate more expeditious surgical intervention. Modification of risk factors should be attempted if they do not place the family under undue stress. Aggressive management of allergic disease—when present—should also be attempted. Although no definitive data support these interventions, it certainly makes good intuitive sense.

Administration of Prevnar and, in older patients, Pneumovax is warranted in patients who meet surgical indications or who suffer complications secondary to invasive streptococcal disease. Although the full benefit may not be seen until the next season, the future benefit with respect to treatment of recurrent infections (complications, antibiotic use, additional future surgery) certainly warrants this intervention. Administration of a yearly influenza A immunization prior to the influenza season to patients who have been surgical candidates in the past or who are leading a clinical course toward surgery is also warranted. These proactive interventions are definitely indicated in special patients (craniofacial patients, those who have suffered complications from disease, those who have undergone surgery for recurrent AOM or OME, those with immune deficiency or compromise). Future investigations may prove other measures (an effective RSV vaccine, xylitol or another locally active substance, immunoprophylaxis) to be effective in the prevention of recurrent AOM and OME in various settings, but I do not recommend them at present.

Once nonsurgical interventions have been exhausted, surgical interventions should be considered. These may include myringotomy, myringotomy and pressure equalization (PE) tube placement, and adenoidectomy or combinations of these procedures depending on the surgeon's philosophy and the particular needs of the patient and family. As outlined in the present chapter, the prevalence of OME and the prevalence of AOM are less in summer months and greater in fall, winter, and spring. This would imply that the threshold for surgical intervention is different for different seasons. Simple short-term observation of patients with "borderline" indications for surgery is warranted in the late winter and early spring season, whereas the same patient in late summer or early fall might cause more concern and may engender a more aggressive approach. For example, for a child with three episodes of AOM in 6 months presenting in early fall who has exhausted medical management, I would recommend bilateral myringotomy and PE tube placement, whereas for the same child presenting in late spring, I would recommend an additional period of observation as long as the child is otitis free. An additional example would be a 4 year old with OME for 3 months and a conductive hearing loss presenting in late fall (recommend bilateral myringotomy and PE tubes) versus the same child presenting in late spring (I recommend observation for an additional month if no speech or language issues are present) versus the same child (OME for 3 months and hearing loss) who is on the swim team who had difficulties with tube otorrhea previously secondary to water exposure (consider bilateral myringotomies and adenoidectomy instead of tubes, recognizing that there is a chance that tubes may be necessary later).

Finally, a word about the seasonality of otorrhea associated with PE tubes. Episodes of otorrhea occurring in the winter months may be more likely to be the result of AOM as a consequence of URI and those occurring in the summer months may more likely be the consequence of water exposure (Rosenfeld and Isaacson, 1999). Whether water precautions prevent (or cause) tube otorrhea is beyond the scope of this chapter. However, etiologic agents of tube otorrhea may be somewhat predictable based on the history of the antecedent event (URI versus water exposure, both of which may be influenced by the season). Empiric therapy may then be guided by these clues. Whether URI (associated with *S. pneumoniae*, *Haemophilus influenzae*, and *Moraxella catarrhalis*) or water exposure (associated with *Pseudomonas aeruginosa* and *Staphylococcus aureus*) is the cause, treatment should be appropriate, as detailed elsewhere (Rosenfeld and Isaacson, 1999).

References

Alho OP, Kilkku O, Hannu O, et al. Control of the temporal aspect when considering risk factors for acute otitis media. Arch Otolaryngol Head Neck Surg 1993;119:444–9.

American Academy of Pediatrics, Committee on Infectious Diseases. Policy statement: recommendations for the prevention of pneumococcal infections, including the use of pneumococcal conjugate vaccine (Prevnar), pneumococcal polysaccharide vaccine, and antibiotic prophylaxis (RE9960). Pediatrics 2000;106:362–6.

Black S, Shinefield H, Fireman B, et al. Efficacy, safety and immunogenicity of heptavalent pneumococcal conjugate vaccine in children. Pediatr Infect Dis J 2000;19:187–95.

Bluestone CD. Eustachian tube function and dysfunction. In: Rosenfeld RM, Bluestone CD, editors. Evidence-based otitis media. Hamilton (ON): BC Decker; 1999. p. 148–51.

Bluestone CD, Klein JO. Otitis media in infants and children. 3rd ed. Philadelphia: WB Saunders; 2001.

Buchman CA, Doyle WJ, Skoner DP, et al. Influenza A virus–induced acute otitis media. J Infect Dis 1995;172:1348–51.

Casselbrant ML, Brostoff LM, Cantekin EI, et al. Otitis media with effusion in preschool children. Laryngoscope 1985;95:428–36.

Casselbrant ML, Okeowo PA, Flaherty MR, et al. Prevalence and incidence of otitis media in a group of preschool children in the United States. In: Lim DJ, Bluestone CD, Klein JO, Nelson JD, editors. Recent advances in otitis media with effusion. Hamilton (ON): BC Decker; 1984. p. 16–9.

Chonmaitree T, Heikkinen T. Role of viruses in middle ear disease. Ann N Y Acad Sci 1997;830:143–57.

Clements DA, Langdon L, Bland C, Walter E. Influenza A vaccine decreases the incidence of otitis media in 6- to 30-month-old children in day care. Arch Pediatr Adolesc Med 1995;149:1113–7.

Doyle WJ, Skoner DP, Hayden F, et al. Nasal and otologic effects of experimental influenza A virus infection. Ann Otol Rhinol Laryngol 1994;103:59–69.

Engel J, Anteunis L, Volovics A, et al. Risk factors of otitis media with effusion during infancy. Int J Pediatr Otorhinolaryngol 1999;48:239–49.

Erramouspe J, Heyneman CA. Treatment and prevention of otitis media. Ann Pharmacother 2000;34:1452–68.

Heikkinen T, Ruuskanen O, Waris M, et al. Influenza vaccination in the prevention of acute otitis media in children. Am J Dis Child 1991;145:445–8.

Henderson FW, Collier AM, Sanyal MA, et al. A longitudinal study of respiratory viruses and bacteria in the etiology of acute otitis media with effusion. N Engl J Med 1982;306:1377–83.

Pitkaranta A, Virolainen A, Jero J, et al. Detection of rhinovirus, respiratory syncytial virus, and coronavirus infections in acute otitis media by reverse transcriptase polymerase chain reaction. Pediatrics 1998;102:291–5.

Rosenfeld RM, Isaacson GC. Tympanostomy tube care and consequences. In: Rosenfeld RM, Bluestone CD, editors. Evidence-based otitis media. Hamilton (ON): BC Decker; 1999. p. 315–36.

Ruuskanen O, Arola M, Heikkinen T, Zeigler T. Viruses in acute otitis media: increasing evidence for clinical significance. Pediatr Infect Dis J 1991;10:425–7.

Sly RM, Zambie MF, Fernandes DA, Fraser M. Tympanometry in kindergarten children. Ann Allergy 1980;44:1–7.

Tos M, Poulsen G. Tympanometry in 2 year old children: seasonal influence on frequency of secretory otitis and tubal function. ORL J Otorhinolaryngol Relat Spec 1979;41:1–10.

Van Cauwenberge P, Berdeaux G, Morineau A, et al. Use of diagnostic clusters to assess the economic consequences of rhinopharyngitis in children in Italy and France during winter. Clin Ther 1999;21:404–21.

Vesa S, Kleemola M, Blomqvist S, et al. Epidemiology of documented viral respiratory infections and acute otitis media in a cohort of children followed from two to twenty-four months of age. Pediatr Infect Dis J 2001;20:574–81.

Chapter 100

Nosocomial Otitis Media: Hospital and Pediatric Intensive Care Unit– Acquired Disease

Craig S. Derkay, MD, Nariman Dash, MD

The pediatric intensive care unit (PICU) offers a multi-disciplinary approach to critical care for patients with complicated medical and surgical problems. Children meeting the admission criteria for this facility frequently suffer from acute respiratory distress, neurologic insults, cardiovascular compromise, major traumatic injuries, or multiorgan failure. Although the emergence of pediatric intensive care over the last three decades has resulted in a significant decrease in the morbidity and mortality of critically ill pediatric patients (Tilford et al, 1998), it has also become a breeding ground for a number of difficult-to-treat nosocomial infections. The occult nature of many of these infections frequently results in a delay in definitive diagnosis. This delay may result in prolonged PICU admissions with increased morbidity and cost.

Fever

Fever is a frequently encountered clinical sign in pediatric hospitals. Febrile patients are often immunocompromised, have multiple indwelling devices, and share a common area with other infected patients. Fever, as a sign of inflammation, may be infectious or noninfectious in origin (Rangel-Frausto et al, 1995). In fact, in the setting of fever of unknown origin, only 36% of cases represent an infectious process (Petersdorf and Beeson, 1961). Neoplasms, collagen vascular diseases, or idiopathic sources such as "drug fevers" typically cause the remaining cases. Also, despite a common misconception, the degree of fever does not reflect the severity of an infectious process (Clark et al, 1991). Because fever can represent a serious life-threatening condition, however, it is paramount to identify its origin. The initial workup should focus on the

history, physical examination, risk factors, and likelihood of a particular disease process.

Sepsis

Sepsis may result when infections go unrecognized or there is a delay in diagnosis. Microbial pathogens elicit an immune response by host cells, and the resulting chemical cascade is responsible for the clinical manifestation of sepsis (Zimmerman and Dietrich, 1987). Sepsis has increased in incidence over the past two decades in the PICU population (Jafari and McCracken, 1992). The primary goal in the treatment of sepsis is the eradication of the responsible organisms. Sepsis resulting from an abscess or an infected indwelling medical device requires drainage of the abscess or removal of the indwelling device and treatment with appropriate intravenous antibiotics. Hemodynamic instability, if present, must be promptly identified and managed.

Otitis Media as a Source of Sepsis

Although pneumonia and urinary tract infections account for the majority of nosocomial infections, otitis media (OM) has frequently been recognized as a silent source of sepsis in a subset of PICU patients (Persico et al, 1985). OM in the PICU is associated with a longer intensive care unit (ICU) course and prolonged use of parenteral antibiotics (Derkay et al, 1989). OM may go unrecognized owing to the presence of other complicated medical problems. The few studies that have addressed this issue (Derkay et al, 1989; Donowitz, 1986; Persico et al, 1985) have demonstrated a strong relationship between the development of OM and the presence of nasotracheal and nasogastric tubes.

Middle ear effusion (MEE) is an immediate complication of almost every nasotracheal intubation in high-risk patients (Figure 100-1). Persico and colleagues (1985) reported MEE in 87% of patients 5 days following nasal intubation and in 100% of patients within 10 days of nasal intubation. Berman and colleagues (1978) reported similar results in the neonatal intensive care unit (NICU). Eighty percent of patients who were nasotracheally intubated developed OM during their NICU course. Sixty-three percent of all cases of OM diagnosed in the NICU were in nasally intubated patients. In addition, the authors found that intubated patients who did not develop OM were on broad-spectrum antibiotics for other reasons.

Risk Factors for the Development of OM

Derkay and colleagues (1989) undertook a prospective study of 107 PICU and respiratory care unit (RCU) children to assess the prevalence and potential risk factors for the development of OM. Thirty-one percent of patients who met the study criteria developed OM, which was associated with the presence of both feeding and breathing tubes in 70% of cases. Among different surgical and medical services, the liver transplant service had the highest prevalence of OM (71%), which may reflect the altered immune status of these patients. Children who developed OM stayed, on average, 11.7 days longer in the PICU or RCU than children without OM. The children with OM frequently received more types of antibiotics and were treated for longer periods of time than their non-OM counterparts. Tympanocentesis confirmed otoscopic diagnosis in 97% of ears and was associated with defervescence within 24 hours.

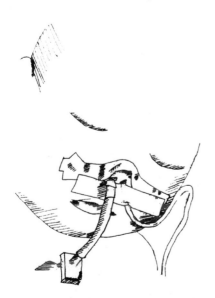

FIGURE 100-1. Nasotracheal intubation.

Eustachian Tube Dysfunction and Nasopharyngeal Pathogens

The two major predisposing factors for middle ear pathology are eustachian tube dysfunction and the presence of nasopharyngeal pathogens (Proctor, 1979). Nasotracheal intubation frequently accompanied by nasogastric intubation for nutritional supplementation results in nasopharyngeal edema and stasis (Bluestone and Klein, 1983). Local mucosal irritation and edema contribute to narrowing of the eustachian tube and eventual obstruction at the level of the nasopharynx. Negative middle ear pressure develops following eustachian tube obstruction. Ineffective neuromuscular function secondary to paralytic agents or intrinsic to the patient results in dysfunctional swallowing and accumulation of nasopharyngeal secretions. A large nasotracheal tube in a small pediatric nasopharynx leads to further stasis of secretions and localized inflammation. Ultimately, the intermittent change in diameter or position of the nasotracheal tube allows for eustachian tube opening and aspiration of nasopharyngeal organisms into a negatively pressurized middle ear space. This proposed mechanism may explain the frequency of OM on the intubated side (Persico et al, 1985) and the observed increase in OM following repeated episodes of nasotracheal intubation.

The diameter of the nasotracheal tube is directly related to the pathogenesis of tube-related OM (Persico et al, 1985). Smaller tubes, such as nasogastric tubes, are likely to result in less nasopharyngeal edema and stasis. Nasogastric tubes, however, have been shown to promote gastroesophageal reflux in ventilated patients despite reflux precautions (Orozco-Levi et al, 1995). It is also known that simulated reflux through the application of pepsin and hydrochloric acid to the nasopharynx has resulted in significant eustachian tube dysfunction in animal models (Heavner et al, 2001). Therefore, although not previously studied, nasogastric intubation-related gastroesophageal reflux may contribute to eustachian tube dysfunction in this patient population.

Sinusitis

Similar to OM, sinusitis is a clinically silent process associated with sepsis that is frequently overlooked in the intubated patient (O'Reilly et al, 1984). Fassoulaki and Pamouktsoglou (1989) reported that 87% of patients without sinus disease as documented by computed tomography developed sinusitis 8 days after nasotracheal intubation. Although orally intubated patients can develop sinusitis, most studies support an increased risk associated with nasal intubation (Bach et al, 1992; Michelson et al, 1992). Also, the maxillary sinuses of nasally intubated patients tend to harbor pathologic organisms more frequently than those of orally intubated patients (Michelson et al, 1992). Bos and colleagues (1989) reported three cases of pediatric sinusitis associated with sepsis in the PICU. Despite negative radiographic evidence of sinusitis, surgical drainage revealed pus and led to resolution of associated sepsis. Therefore, local inflammation resulting from nasopharyngeal instrumentation appears to increase the incidence of not only OM but also sinusitis.

Indwelling Medical Devices

Tracheotomy patients who are frequently admitted to the PICU or RCU also frequently suffer from chronic OM (Beste et al, 1999). Tracheotomy patients who required mechanical ventilation are more likely to develop OM than tracheotomy patients breathing spontaneously (Derkay et al, 1989). It is likely that nasopharyngeal edema, reflux, and ineffective neuromuscular function, which are frequently found in this patient population, are similarly responsible for eustachian tube dysfunction.

Certain bacteria display an affinity for indwelling medical devices. They typically produce a proteinaceous biofilm, which increases their adherence and provides protection from host defenses. Additionally, bacteria may divide at a reduced rate within the biofilm. This slowing of cell turnover provides protection from certain cell wall–specific antibiotics that rely on high cell turnover rates for killing bacteria (Dougherty and Simmons, 1989). A nasotracheal tube coated with bacteria contained within a protective biofilm can provide a constant source of pathogens capable of causing OM. For this reason, it is recommended, whenever medically possible, to remove the offending foreign bodies as part of the treatment for nosocomial OM in the hospitalized patient.

The presence of a bacteria-laden fluid within the middle ear cleft in conjunction with a nasopharyngeal foreign body introduces a combination that may be difficult to eradicate. In fact, many nasally intubated patients go on to develop acute OM despite treatment with potent, broad-spectrum antibiotics. The high concordance rate (80%) between bacteria isolated from MEE and blood cultures in the septic patients illustrates the potential impact of this situation on patient outcomes (Persico et al, 1985). There are, however, discrepancies in the results of middle ear cultures obtained from ICU patients among different studies. Patient age and treatment with antibiotics at the time of tympanocentesis may account for some of the disparities.

Despite the variations in culture results, however, it appears that there is a shift toward gram-negative pathogens in this patient population. The middle ear pathogens identified in septic PICU or NICU children include *Staphylococcus epidermidis, Staphylococcus aureus, Klebsiella pneumoniae, Escherichia coli,* and *Enterobacter* species (Berman et al, 1978). *Moraxella catarrhalis* bacteremia should be considered in febrile young children

with evidence of OM, especially in the presence of an underlying immunodeficiency (Abuhammour et al, 1999).

Treatment Algorithm

Although several studies have addressed the role of OM in the PICU setting, no similar studies are available for other inpatients. Patients with severe or neglected OM can present with mastoiditis, osteitis, facial nerve paralysis, or intracranial complications. Immunocompromised children such as those on chemotherapy for neoplastic disease or those with human immunodeficiency virus (HIV) or other immunosuppressed states are at greater risk for recurrent or severe middle ear infections and can present with systemic complications related to their OM (Shapiro and Novelli, 1998). Prompt diagnosis is warranted to prevent rapid progression. Lack of overt signs for acute otitis media (AOM) should not delay therapy. Otitis media with effusion (OME), although it appears benign, is often a bacterial disease and requires appropriate antibiotic management in complicated cases. Our treatment algorithm is significantly different in this setting than for an asymptomatic MEE discovered on physical examination in the outpatient setting. Nontoxic, afebrile patients can be treated with a short course of broad-spectrum antibiotics followed by close observation. If there are signs of clinical worsening or no improvement is noted after finishing antibiotics, then surgical treatment to include tympanocentesis with culture is then considered. A similar approach is employed in the febrile child with MEE in the setting of other possible sources of infection and those with fever but a documented blood pathogen that is unlikely to be of middle ear origin. Similarly, when MEE is present in a febrile child with a more likely source such as an infected catheter, the catheter should be removed and empiric antibiotics used first before proceeding with tympanocentesis and culture. However, when in doubt, one should not hesitate to sample the MEE for additional pathogens if the clinical situation is confusing or deteriorating.

Physical Examination

Evaluation should begin with a complete history and physical examination. Facial features should be examined closely because craniofacial anomalies signal potential otologic disorders. The external auditory canal should be inspected by pulling the auricle posteriorly and pushing the tragus anteriorly. Any obstructing cerumen should be removed. A pneumatic otoscope with an adequate light source should be used. The largest speculum that passes through the canal provides the best view of the tympanic membrane (TM) and a seal for pneumatic examination. Color, position, vascularity, and mobility of the TM are key in the diagnosis of MEE. A normal TM is often translucent and moves briskly on pneumatic otoscopy. OME results in decreased TM mobility and obscuring of middle ear landmarks. Unlike the diagnosis of AOM with a red and bulging TM, accurate diagnosis of OME requires more experience and practice. Handheld acoustic reflectometry or tympanometry may be a helpful adjunct in this setting.

Myringotomy/Tympanocentesis

In all septic or symptomatic patients with hospital-acquired OM, it is necessary to obtain fluid from behind the TM. This can be done either by myringotomy or tympanocentesis. First, any obstructing cerumen or debris is removed from the ear canal and the TM is inspected. The anterior-inferior quadrant is preferred for tympanocentesis because it avoids the ossicles and chorda tympani. It is also less vascular and less innervated than other quadrants. Commercially available, disposable tympanocentesis sets include all necessary materials (Figure 100-2). A sterile trap device is attached to an 18- or 21-gauge, 3½-inch straight spinal needle and wall suction. Most patients in the PICU and NICU do not require physical restraining; however, conscious sedation on the otherwise awake child is recommended. The largest otoscope speculum that will comfortably fit the external auditory canal is used and the anterior-inferior quadrant is identified. A few drops of topical anesthetic or an otowick impregnated with 8 to 32% tetracaine are placed into the external auditory canal and allowed time to take effect, generally at least 15 minutes. Alternatively, phenol can be applied topically to the proposed puncture site with a small cotton-tipped applicator. Betadine or 70% ethanol followed by saline rinses should be used to sterilize the ear canal and prevent contamination of the specimen. The tympanocentesis needle is then inserted until it is just short of the TM. With the operator's hand steadied against the patient's head, the needle is pushed just through the TM, the middle ear is quickly aspirated, and the needle is promptly withdrawn. The quantity of material aspirated is typically small and is often caught in the needle hub or tubing. To retrieve the sample, a small volume of nonbacteriostatic saline is gently suctioned

through the tubing or syringe and the entire sample is sent for Gram stain and culture. Broad-spectrum systemic antibiotics and ototopical, nonototoxic antibiotic drops are applied pending final culture results.

When considering myringotomy under general anesthesia for treatment and sampling of OM in a septic child, an operating microscope with a 250 mm focal length lens is used. An appropriate-size speculum is selected. The auricle is retracted posteriorly while the speculum is introduced. The external auditory canal is then débrided of cerumen. The TM is then visualized and a site for myringotomy is chosen. Betadine or 70% alcohol solution is used to sterilize the external auditory canal to limit the culturing of ear canal contaminants. The myringotomy knife is grasped with the tips of the fingers and away from the line of vision to maximize the operative field of vision. A small radial incision is made in the anterior-inferior quadrant providing that there are no vascular anomalies (Figure 100-3). Middle ear fluid is evacuated using a sterile trap mechanism (Tymp-tap, Xomed-Treace, Jacksonville, FL). The color and consistency of the fluid are noted and sent for Gram stain and appropriate cultures.

Alternatively, a handheld otoscope or portable microscope could be used to perform myringotomy without general anesthesia using the technique described above for tympanocentesis. There may also be a role for using a microscope outfitted with a carbon-dioxide flash-scan laser to perform myringotomy and obtain middle ear fluid in children who may benefit from an additional period of temporary ventilation (an average of 3 weeks) (Bent et al, 2001). Again, broad-spectrum antibiotics and nonototoxic ototopical antibiotic drops should be initiated to cover potential pathogens from Gram stain results and modified later based on culture results.

Occasionally, an aural polyp may be encountered, which provides a valuable opportunity to obtain tissue

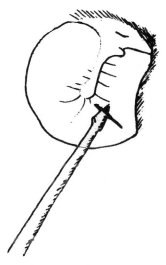

FIGURE 100-3. A small radial incision is made in the anterior-inferior quadrant.

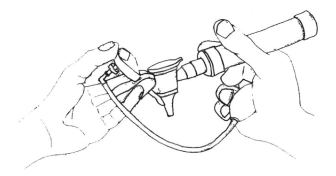

FIGURE 100-2. Channel-directed tympanocentesis speculum.

for diagnosis of rare disorders in a debilitated patient (ie, Langerhans' cell histiocytosis or leukemia), and should be biopsied and sent for histologic examination.

Despite similarities between AOM and closed-space abscess, aspiration alone has proven to be of limited value in clearance of AOM or MEE. Although aspiration temporarily decompresses the middle ear and provides material for diagnosis and culture, the opening seals quickly, preventing ongoing ventilation. In febrile or septic patients with no identifiable source of infection, middle ear fluid should be sampled to guide treatment. However, if such a patient has a history of recurrent OM, persistent MEE, or a complication of OM, then placement of a tympanostomy tube is advised to provide longer-term ventilation and drainage. The threshold for tube placement in this setting is more liberal (fewer than three infections in 6 months or four infections in 12 months, less than 3 months with a bilateral and less than 6 months with a unilateral effusion) than for the uncomplicated, ambulatory patient. Fluid characteristics collected at the time of myringotomy can assist in the decision-making process. Recovery of thick, mucoid MEE, as seen in "glue ears," may necessitate placement of a tympanostomy tube to provide for a longer period of ventilation.

Conclusion

Nosocomial infections result in a significant amount of morbidity and mortality. Most commonly, these infections affect the pulmonary system. However, OM remains a significant problem, particularly in the PICU with an intubated child. The nearly universal finding of MEE among nasally intubated patients mandates frequent pneumatic otoscopy for accurate diagnosis. In the presence of MEE and signs of sepsis, myringotomy or tympanocentesis should be performed and nasotracheal and nasogastric tubes changed to oral tubes if medically possible.

References

Abuhammour WM, Abdel-Haq NM, Asmar BI, Dajani AS. *Moraxella catarrhalis* bacteremia: a 10-year experience. South Med J 1999;92:1071–4.

Bach A, Boehrer H, Schmidt H, Geiss HK. Nosocomial sinusitis in ventilated patient. Nasotracheal versus orotracheal intubation. Anesthesia 1992;47:335–9.

Bent JP, April MM, Ward RF. Atypical indications for OtoScan laser-assisted myringotomy. Laryngoscope 2011;111:87–9.

Berman SA, Balkany T, Simmons MA. Otitis media in the neonatal intensive care unit. Pediatrics 1978;62:198–201.

Beste DJ, Conley SF, Milbrath MM. Prevalence of chronic otitis media with effusion in pediatric tracheotomy population: a retrospective review. Pediatr Pulmonol 1999;28:194–8.

Bluestone CD, Klein JO. Otitis media with effusion, atelectasis, and eustachian tube dysfunction. In: Bluestone CD, Stool SE, editors. Pediatric otolaryngology. Philadelphia: WB Saunders; 1983. p. 397–401.

Bos AP, Tibboel D, Hazebroek FW, et al. Sinusitis: hidden source of sepsis in postoperative PICU patients. Crit Care Med 1989;17:886–8.

Clark DE, Kimelman J, Raffin TA. The evaluation of fever in the intensive care unit. Chest 1991;100:213–30.

Derkay CS, Bluestone CD, Thompson AE, Kardatske D. Otitis media in the pediatric intensive care unit: a prospective study. Otolaryngol Head Neck Surg 1989;100:292–9.

Donowitz LG. High risk of nosocomial infections in the pediatric intensive care patient. Crit Care Med 1986;14:26–8.

Dougherty SH, Simmons RL. Endogenous factors contributing to prosthetic device infections. Infect Dis Clin North Am 1989;3:199–209.

Fassoulaki A, Pamouktsoglou P. Prolonged nasotracheal intubation and its association with inflammation of paranasal sinuses. Anesth Analg 1989;69:50–2.

Heavner SB, Hardy SM, White DR, et al. Transient inflammation and dysfunction of the eustachian tube secondary multiple exposures of simulated gastroesophageal refluxant. Ann Otol Rhinol Laryngol 2001;110:928–34.

Jafari HS, McCracken GH Jr. Sepsis and septic shock for clinician. Pediatr Infect Dis J 1992;11:739–49.

Michelson A, Schuster B, Kamp HD. Paranasal sinusitis associated with nasotracheal and orotracheal long-term intubation. Arch Otolaryngol Head Neck Surg 1992;118:937–9.

O'Reilly MJ, Reddick EJ, Black W, et al. Sepsis from sinusitis in nasotracheally intubated patients—a diagnostic dilemma. Am J Surg 1984;147:601–4.

Orozco-Levi M, Torres A, Ferrer M, et al. Semirecumbent position protects from pulmonary aspiration but not completely from gastroesophageal reflux in mechanically ventilated patient. Am J Respir Crit Care Med 1995;152:1387–90.

Persico M, Barker GA, Mitchell DP. Purulent otitis media—a "silent" source of sepsis in the pediatric intensive care unit. Otolaryngol Head Neck Surg 1985;93:330–4.

Petersdorf RG, Beeson PB. Fever of unexplained origin: report on 100 cases. Medicine 1961;40:1.

Proctor B. Etiology of otitis media. In: Weit RJ, Coulthard SW, editors. Otitis media—proceedings of the Second National Conference on Otitis Media. Columbus (OH): Ross Laboratories; 1979. p. 21–5.

Rangel-Frausto MS, Pittet D, Costigan M, et al. The natural history of the systemic inflammatory response syndrome (SIRS). JAMA 1995;273:117–23.

Shapiro NL, Novelli V. Otitis media in children with vertically acquired HIV infection. Int J Pediatr Otorhinolaryngol 1998;45:69–75.

Tilford JM, Roberson PK, Lensing S, Fiser DH. Differences in pediatric ICU mortality over time. Crit Care Med 1998;26:1737–43.

Zimmerman JL, Dietrich KA. Current perspectives on septic shock. Pediatr Clin North Am 1987;34:131–63.

Chapter 101

PERSISTENT/ RECURRENT OTALGIA

MARK E. WHITAKER, MD, BARRY E. HIRSCH, MD, FACS

Otalgia, or ear pain, is a common symptom of acute otitis media (AOM). In very young patients, the sensation of otalgia may be conveyed only as irritability, sleeplessness, or rubbing at the ear. Otalgia usually resolves quickly when patients are treated with appropriate therapy. In this chapter, treatment of otitis-related otalgia is discussed. Further, the evaluation and management of persistent and/or recurrent otalgia despite adequate treatment of AOM are covered. Finally, the management of otalgia in patients without evidence of middle ear disease is included. This is a common occurrence, yet the true incidence is quite difficult to ascertain. It is reported that approximately 50% of patients complaining of otalgia have a nonotologic etiology as the source (Paparella and Jung, 1991). In treating these patients, obtaining an accurate diagnosis is crucial to developing an effective treatment plan. This becomes even more important because some patients with significantly morbid diseases may present solely with otalgia.

Anatomy

Sensory innervation to the auricle, surrounding skin, and temporal bone is derived from cranial nerves V, VII, IX, and X, as well as the second and third cervical spinal nerves. The auriculotemporal branch of the third division of the trigeminal nerve provides sensory innervation for the tragus, anterior, and superior regions of the auricle and external auditory canal and lateral surface of the tympanic membrane (TM) (Table 101-1). The trigeminal nerve is the most common source of referred otalgia. This is attributable to the fact that it has the longest extracranial course with the most extensive distribution (Thaller and De Silva, 1987). The facial nerve provides sensory innervation to the posterior and posterior superior auricle on its lateral surface as well as the adjacent posterior wall of the external auditory canal medially toward the posterosuperior TM. The glossopharyngeal nerve provides sensory innervation to a portion of the posterior portion of the external auditory canal, lateral surface of the TM, and the majority of the mastoid air cells and eustachian tube. The medial aspect of the TM receives sensory innervation from the tympanic branch of the glossopharyngeal nerve (Jacobson's nerve). The auricular branch of the vagus (Arnold's) nerve innervates a portion of the posterior canal wall, the floor of the external auditory canal, and the corresponding external surface of the TM. The upper cervical nerves (C2, C3) supply the sensory innervation to the posterior surface of the auricle and a portion of the skin overlying the mastoid.

Classification

Otalgia may be classified as primary or referred. Primary otalgia is attributable to a process directly involving the auricle or temporal bone. Referred otalgia stems from a process in a nearby structure. Table 101-2 provides a differential diagnosis of primary otalgia. In most cases, the

TABLE 101-1. Innervation Sites Related to Otalgia

Nerve	Innervation Sites
Cranial nerve V (trigeminal)	Tragus, anterior, and superior regions of the auricle and external auditory canal, and lateral surface of the tympanic membrane
Cranial nerve VII (facial)	Posterior and posterosuperior auricle on its lateral surface, posterior wall of the external auditory canal
Cranial nerve IX (glossopharyngeal)	Posterior external auditory canal, medial surface and portion of the lateral surface of the tympanic membrane, mastoid air cells, and eustachian tube
Cranial nerve X (vagus)	Floor of the external auditory canal, posterior canal wall, and corresponding lateral surface of the tympanic membrane
Upper cervical nerves (C2,C3)	Posterior surface of the auricle and skin overlying the mastoid

TABLE 101-2. Differential Diagnosis of Primary Otalgia

External ear
  Otitis externa
  Myringitis
  Cerumen impaction
  Foreign body
  Auricular perichondritis or chondritis
  Relapsing polychondritis
  Frostbite
  Traumatic tympanic membrane perforation
  Herpes infection
  Malignant or benign lesion of the external canal
Middle ear and mastoid
  Acute otitis media
  Acute mastoiditis
  Facial nerve inflammation (Ramsay Hunt syndrome and Bell's palsy)
  Benign and malignant tumors of the temporal bone
  Complications of otitis media and mastoiditis
    Meningitis
    Brain abscess
    Subperiosteal abscess
    Venous sinus thrombophlebitis
    Petrous apicitis

causes of primary otalgia will be easily identified. Herpes zoster is one exception to this rule. This often presents with pain; however, the onset of vesicles may be delayed. Table 101-3 provides a differential diagnosis of referred otalgia.

History

A thorough history is indispensable when evaluating patients with recurrent or persistent otalgia. General information regarding the duration and quality of the pain as well as any radiation of pain must be noted. Although determining the duration of the pain may not help differentiate primary from referred otalgia, it may help with the differential diagnosis. Also, any relationship of the pain to activities such as chewing or swallowing may implicate the temporomandibular joint or pharynx, respectively. A history of dyspepsia may prompt further questioning regarding gastroesophageal reflux. Inquiry pertaining to related otorrhea, diminished auditory acuity, tinnitus, vertigo, facial paralysis, or a history of otologic surgery may help confirm suspicion of primary otalgia. Inquiry regarding trauma to the pinna, external auditory canal, or TM, including trauma from cotton tip applicators, helps to substantiate primary otalgia as well. A history of water exposure to the external auditory canal such as aural irrigations, water sports, or recent use of a sauna or hot tub may help identify an appropriate etiology of the pain. Other associated symptoms that must be queried include weight loss, odynophagia, vision changes, facial numbness, purulent rhinorrhea, and voice changes. Specific inquiry seeking a history of immunosuppressive illness or therapy or existence of an autoimmune disorder raises the suspicion of an infectious etiology or relapsing

polychondritis, respectively. Indeed, a thorough history of all of these regions helps the clinician. Just as important is the need for a complete head and neck examination.

Physical Examination

In managing patients with persistent or recurrent otalgia, a thorough examination of the head and neck is necessary to ensure that no other contributing sources of pain are present that may have been overlooked at the time of the initial examination when the patient was evaluated and treated for otitis media (OM). To this end, examination of the pinna is performed to determine the presence of ulcerations or inflammation that may represent cutaneous malignancies or chondritis. The postauricular region is examined for blunting of the postauricular sulcus and for mastoid tenderness that may indicate acute mastoiditis. The otoscopic examination is focused not

TABLE 101-3. Differential Diagnosis of Referred Otalgia

Oral/dental
  Exposed root surfaces
  Pulpitis or pulpal necrosis
  Periapical infection
  Periodontal infection
  Impacted teeth
  Traumatic occlusion
  Ill-fitting dental appliance
  Recent adjustment of arch wires
  Atypical facial pain
  Craniomandibular disorders
  Mucocutaneous disorders
Pharynx
  Inflammatory disorders
  Tonsillitis and peritonsillar abscess
  Post-tonsillectomy pain
  Eagle's syndrome
Larynx and esophagus
  Epiglottitis
  Laryngitis
  Perichondritis or chondritis
  Arthritis of cricoarytenoid joint
  Hiatal hernia
  Gastroesophageal reflux
  Infection or foreign body in esophagus
Neurologic disorders
  Trigeminal neuralgia
  Glossopharyngeal neuralgia
  Postherpetic neuralgia
Headaches
Cervicogenic pain
  Myofascial pain dysfunction
  Disorders involving the cervical spine (C2–C3)
Neoplastic disease
  Nonotogenic carcinoma, sarcomas, and metastatic disease
Other
  Traction or inflammation involving cerebrovascular blood supply (cervical myalgia)
  Thyroiditis
  Angina
  Aneurysm of great vessels

only on the TM and middle ear but also on the external canal. Findings of canal edema, inflammation, and tenderness raise concern for otitis externa. The external auditory canal is examined for ulcerations or granular masses that may represent malignancy or necrotizing otitis externa. Examination of the TM and middle ear is more precisely examined with a binocular microscope if available. The TM is examined for myringitis, perforation, OM, and cholesteatoma. However, a dry TM perforation or cholesteatoma without inflammation generally does not cause pain. Pneumatic otoscopy should also be performed to aid in detection of middle ear effusion. Tuning fork testing is performed to screen for a conductive or sensorineural hearing loss on the side of concern. Any finding on tuning fork testing is confirmed with formal audiometry. The remainder of the head and neck is then examined. Examination of the oral cavity and oropharynx is indicated to evaluate dental status or occlusion or to identify the presence of inflammation or malignancy. The floor of the mouth, tonsil, and tongue base should be palpated for mass lesions that may not be identified on visual inspection alone. Flexible fiberoptic evaluation of the nasopharynx, hypopharynx, and larynx looking for signs of gastric reflux, inflammation, and malignancy is prudent. The parotid and neck are palpated for masses. The temporomandibular joint must also be palpated and assessed for pain on palpation, crepitus, and limitation of jaw opening. A thorough neurologic examination is also performed with particular attention to the cranial nerves that contribute to sensory innervation of the ear, namely cranial nerves V, VII, IX, and X. Trigeminal nerve dysfunction would manifest as weakness of the muscles of mastication and hypesthesia of the face, cornea, and/or ear canal. The facial nerve is assessed for paralysis or paresis. Glossopharyngeal and vagus nerve involvement would present as hoarseness or aspiration. Finally, examination for decreased gag reflex and vocal cord function is performed. Vestibular function is also examined by evaluation of the eyes for both spontaneous nystagmus and for deviation with pneumatic otoscopy (fistula test). Romberg's test and gait testing are also performed.

Primary Otalgia

Sources of primary otalgia may be divided into etiologies originating from the external ear or the middle ear and mastoid. The external auditory canal is examined for inflammation, vesicles, or evidence of ulceration or osteomyelitis. The clinician should maintain suspicion for carcinoma that may be misinterpreted as granulation tissue. Most cases of primary otalgia are readily identified by the clinician. The more serious conditions that are considered include the complications of OM and mastoiditis. These complications that may contribute to otalgia include petrositis, subperiosteal abscess, extradural or perisinus abscess, venous sinus thrombosis, and brain abscess. Complete discussion of these complications is deferred to the chapter that is dedicated to this subject.

Management of Primary Otalgia

Patients complaining of otalgia emanating from the ear and mastoid generally have identifying features on examination that confirm the diagnosis. Management of disease processes of the external ear is beyond the scope of this chapter. We focus on otalgia related to OM. In the setting of AOM, the administration of appropriate antibiotics is the mainstay of treatment. Symptoms should improve within 48 to 72 hours (Bluestone, 1998). Administration of over-the-counter analgesics and antipyretics, as well as warm compresses, may also lessen the intensity of the symptoms. Consideration for recommending decongestants should be given, especially in association with a concomitant upper respiratory infection. Antihistamines can be of benefit in the patient with suspected allergic rhinitis. They may, however, cause an undesirable drying effect on secretions. Analgesic drops (benzocaine/antipyrine) may be applied to the affected ear two to four drops four times daily as needed, but, generally, they are not necessary in uncomplicated AOM given the expected expeditious resolution of pain with the use of oral analgesics. A tympanocentesis with an 18-gauge spinal needle may be indicated in those patients who do not respond appropriately to antibiotics. This treatment may also be necessary for newborns, immunocompromised patients, and patients with a suspected complication of OM. A tympanocentesis provides a means of obtaining a culture to direct therapy and often immediate short-term relief of otalgia. A small tympanocentesis will close rapidly; therefore, for longer-lived relief of otalgia, a formal myringotomy should be considered. A scheduled follow-up examination should take place in 24 to 48 hours in high-risk patients such as the newborn or immunocompromised patients to ensure response to therapy. In the case of persistent pain associated with fever, headache, or meningismus, further evaluation is warranted to identify the potential development of complications of AOM or mastoiditis.

Eustachian tube dysfunction is another common cause of primary otalgia. In the case of an obstructive etiology (functional or mechanical), the eustachian tube is less effective at ventilating the middle ear. This may cause an elevated negative pressure in the middle ear. Patients may complain of otalgia, aural pressure, and hearing loss, as well as popping or crackling noises. This may or may not be related to an upper respiratory tract infection. Treatment consists of decongestants, antihistamines, and middle ear inflation with Valsalva techniques. In children, Otovent (Invotec International, Jacksonville, FL), used three times daily, may be considered to assist with middle ear ventilation. An evaluation for underlying causes such as adenoid hypertrophy should be performed if the symptoms are of a more chronic nature. Finally, a myringotomy and tube may be indicated if medical management fails.

Referred Otalgia

Patients complaining of ear pain and found to have a normal otologic examination should be suspected of having referred otalgia. These patients may present with either acute or chronic pain. In the vast majority of patients, acute pain is referred from the orofacial region by way of the trigeminal nerve. Multiple dental conditions may contribute to otalgia, including impacted teeth, periapical or periodontal infection, or exposed dental roots. To confirm this diagnosis, tapping on the teeth during the examination to elicit pain or using a local nerve block with lidocaine can be used. Further dental causes of pain include poor dental occlusion, ill-fitting dentures, or recent tightening of orthodontic appliances. The oral examination must also detect evidence of acute or recurrent herpes infection or lichen planus. Other facial causes of acute otalgia would include maxillary sinusitis, nasal infections, and parotiditis.

Referred otalgia from the larynx and pharynx occurring from acute processes is usually attributable to an inflammatory etiology. The glossopharyngeal nerve conveys referred pain from the tonsils and pharynx through the tympanic branch of the ninth cranial nerve. Common disorders in this region contributing to otalgia include pharyngitis, tonsillitis, peritonsillar abscess, and retropharyngeal abscess. Oral and pharyngeal ulcers, possibly of viral origin, are another source of acute otalgia. Post-tonsillectomy pain is commonly associated with otalgia to the extent that patients are generally counseled preoperatively to anticipate this referred pain. Another pharyngeal source to be considered is an elongated styloid process, which may produce Eagle's syndrome. This is characterized by sharp, stabbing pain that is provoked by swallowing, turning the head, or carotid compression and is often noted in post-tonsillectomy patients. Transoral palpation through the tonsillar fossa helps confirm the diagnosis. Therapy generally consists of surgical excision of the styloid process if symptoms persist. In the region of the larynx, viral or bacterial epiglottitis, laryngitis, perichondritis, chondritis, and arthritis of the cricoarytenoid joint may contribute to otalgia. Esophageal disorders may also cause otalgia, including esophageal foreign body, inflammation, gastroesophageal reflux, and hiatal hernia.

Causes of otalgia presenting with a more chronic duration include craniomandibular disorders such as temporomandibular joint pain and atypical facial pain. The temporomandibular joint may be confirmed as a source by eliciting pain and tenderness during palpation of the temporomandibular joint during mandibular range of motion. Myofascial pain dysfunction is noted by detecting trigger points during transoral palpation of the pterygoid muscles and the coronoid process of the mandible. Once confirmed, treatment includes a regimen of a soft diet, analgesics, and warm compresses. Evaluation by an oral surgeon is necessary to assess dental occlusion and to determine whether a dental appliance or surgery is indicated. In contrast, atypical facial pain usually has a normal physical examination. These patients present with a unilateral, continuous, deep, boring pain that is generally unresponsive to medical therapy. A trial of tricyclic antidepressants or gabapentin may be of benefit to some patients.

Neurologic disorders, which are also considered chronic causes of otalgia, must be considered even though they are rare. Trigeminal neuralgia generally presents in patients between 35 and 50 years of age. Women are affected more commonly than men, with a ratio of 3 to 2. The symptoms consist of sharp, lancinating pain in the distribution of the second and third divisions of the trigeminal nerve lasting seconds to minutes at a time. Certain triggers that may be related to the pain include a light touch, vibration, or a breeze. The physical examination in these patients will be normal. The differential diagnosis for this symptom complex includes myofascial pain, postherpetic neuralgia, cluster headache, temporal arteritis, multiple sclerosis, and tumor. Magnetic resonance imaging (MRI) is indicated in patients being evaluated for trigeminal neuralgia because this presentation of pain may represent a mass lesion in the middle or posterior fossa (Bullitt et al, 1986). The management of trigeminal neuralgia is conservative, progressing from medical management to surgery or stereotactic radiosurgery (Kondziolka et al, 2002). Multiple medications have been recommended based on uncontrolled observations, including phenytoin, clonazepam, valproic acid, and gabapentin. However, carbamazepine has been proven efficacious in several controlled studies (Sinderup and Jensen, 2002).

Glossopharyngeal neuralgia presents as recurrent episodes of unilateral, sharp, stabbing pain occurring in the tonsil, lateral pharyngeal wall, posterior third of the tongue, or middle ear. Similar to trigeminal neuralgia, a trigger zone usually elicits episodes initiated by swallowing, yawning, or coughing. Some episodes have been known to be associated with bradycardia, syncope, or seizure (Ferrante et al, 1995). The physical examination is unremarkable; however, care must be made during examination to rule out the presence of carcinoma. Medical therapy may consist of various combinations of medications starting with carbamazepine. Surgical intervention is reserved for failure to respond to medical therapy.

Geniculate neuralgia presents with sharp pain within the ear. Patients generally localize the pain by pointing to the external auditory canal. This pain is thought to originate in the geniculate ganglion or the sensory division of the facial nerve, the nervus intermedius. In these patients, a malignant neoplasm must be ruled out, and MRI is indicated to evaluate the course of the facial nerve from the brainstem to the stylomastoid foramen (Thompson and Hirsch, 1998). Carbamazepine, valproic acid, and antidepressants have been described for geniculate neuralgia. When conservative medical therapy fails, surgery may be considered. This involves a middle fossa craniotomy and sectioning of the nervus intermedius and geniculate ganglion (Pulec, 2002).

Postherpetic neuralgia is characterized by severe burning pain in the region of the affected cranial nerves. Cranial nerves V, IX, and X are implicated, and the pain may be referred to the cutaneous regions supplied by these nerves, namely the face, mastoid, neck, and occipital regions. The wider distribution of this pain helps differentiate this type of neuralgia from geniculate neuralgia. Herpes zoster is caused by the reactivation of dormant varicella-zoster virus that is present within the spinal or cranial nerve ganglia. The reactivated virus transmigrates in a segmental fashion along affected nerves, resulting in a localized painful vesicular eruption of the skin along the distribution of the nerve. The pain and vesicles of acute herpes zoster typically resolve within 2 to 3 weeks. The pain of postherpetic neuralgia, however, persists beyond this timeframe. Patients over 50 years of age are deemed at risk and therefore require more intensive therapy than the symptomatic treatment that is recommended for younger patients. The treatment regimen for acute herpes zoster may include the use of antiviral agents, corticosteroids, topical therapy, and antidepressants. The initial treatment for postherpetic neuralgia includes nonsteroidal anti-inflammatory analgesics and tricyclic antidepressants. Further treatment may require anticonvulsant medications and referral to a neurologist. In the treatment of postherpetic neuralgia, aggressive treatment early in the disease is indicated. As time progresses, the ability to satisfactorily treat the pain diminishes.

Headaches must be considered within the discussion of chronic causes of referred otalgia. Each of the three major types of headache (vascular, tension, and inflammatory) may contribute to otalgia. The classification and description of the types of headache are beyond the scope of this chapter. It must be noted that each type causes a specific pattern of cephalalgia and constellation of symptoms.

Patients who complain of otalgia should be questioned regarding their history of headaches and offered appropriate treatment if the symptoms are the likely source.

Other causes of otalgia remote from the head and neck have been reported (Wazen, 1989). It is felt that diseases of the tracheobronchial tree or mediastinum may transmit pain to the ear by way of the vagus nerve. Several pathologic processes have been reported as causes of referred otalgia, including thyroiditis, angina, and aneurysmal dilatation of the great vessels. Treatment of otalgia in these cases is directed toward the primary cause. Persistent pain in the presence of consistent normal physical examination warrants psychiatric evaluation.

In conclusion, the treatment of otalgia may be a simple undertaking, or it may be quite complex and frustrating. A good understanding of the anatomy of the head and neck with particular emphasis on the cranial nerves is necessary. If no etiology can be determined, imaging of the head and skull base is warranted with a contrast-enhanced MRI. A readiness to consult with specialists in the fields of oral and maxillofacial surgery, neurology, neurosurgery, and, occasionally, psychiatry provides the patient with comprehensive evaluation and management.

References

Bluestone CD. Role of surgery for otitis media in the era of resistant bacteria. Pediatr Infect Dis J 1998;17:1090–8.

Bullitt E, Tew JM, Boyd J. Intracranial tumor in patients with facial pain. J Neurosurg 1986;64:865–71.

Ferrante L, Artico M, Nardacci B, et al. Glossopharyngeal neuralgia with cardiac syncope. Neurosurgery 1995;36:58–63.

Kondziolka D, Lunsford LD, Flickinger JC. Stereotactic radiosurgery for the treatment of trigeminal neuralgia. Clin J Pain 2002;18:42–7.

Paparella MM, Jung TTK. Odontalgia. In: Paparella MM, Shumrick DA, Gluckman JL, Meyerhoff WL, editors. Otolaryngology. 3rd ed. Philadelphia: WB Saunders; 1991. p. 1237–42.

Pulec JL. Geniculate neuralgia: long-term results of surgical treatment. Ear Nose Throat J 2002;81:30–3.

Sinderup SH, Jensen TS. Pharmacotherapy of trigeminal neuralgia. Clin J Pain 2002;18:22–7.

Thaller SR, De Silva A. Otalgia with a normal ear. Am Fam Physician 1987;36:29–36.

Thompson SW, Hirsch BE. Otalgia from near and far. Emerg Med 1998;30:52–70.

Wazen JJ. Referred otalgia. Otolaryngol Clin North Am 1989; 22:1205–15.

Chapter 102

PERSISTENT OR RECURRENT NEGATIVE MIDDLE EAR PRESSURE

OTAVIO B. PILTCHER, MD, PhD, CUNEYT M. ALPER, MD

Middle ear pressure (MEP) changes owing to a number of factors. Individual differences, as well as physiologic and environmental changes and stimuli, determine the temporal changes in MEP. Each individual (in fact, each ear) has a certain range of variation within the normal conditions and a different rate and extent of developing negative MEP owing to the effect of the determining factors.

Normal MEP range is considered to be between +50 mm H_2O and −100 mm H_2O. Although it is not unusual for individuals to experience brief periods of negative MEP under normal physiologic and environmental variations, recurrence or persistence of extended periods of negative MEP may lead to subjective discomfort and/or result in middle ear effusion (MEE) or infection, as well as complications or sequelae. A huge individual variability in the rate and extent that negative MEP would develop with physiologic and environmental changes and individual differences in the risk of development of effusion, infection, complications, or sequelae limit the ability of physicians to set a criterion for the duration and extent of significant negative pressure to define "persistent" or "recurrent" negative MEP. However, this chapter attempts to present and discuss the etiologic factors in the development of negative MEP, its clinical significance and criteria, and potential methods of management. A rational approach to middle ear (ME) underpressure requires the distinction of potential clinical presentations associated with negative MEP (Table 102-1). Note that for each clinical presentation, the negative MEP may be incidental, recurrent, or persistent.

Incidence

Negative MEP is considered a prevalent finding in the general population. Casselbrant and colleagues (1985) reported negative pressures in 66% of a group of 2- to 6-

year-old preschool children. The prevalence of negative MEP was 34% among institutionalized Brazilian children and 7% in schoolchildren referred owing to general hearing screening failure (Marttila, 1986). A lower prevalence of negative MEP in older children (49% at age 5 years to 4% at age 16 years) was reported (Stangerup et al, 1994). Negative MEP has been shown to follow colds in up to two-thirds of previously healthy children, consistent with the higher incidence during the viral upper respiratory infection (URI) seasons (autumn and winter). Great daily variability in MEP and a high rate of spontaneous resolution of negative MEP are well documented (Lildholdt, 1980; Moody et al, 1998; Winther et al, 2002). Based on the available data, it is not possible to determine the exact incidence or prevalence among the different clinical categories proposed in Table 102-1.

Pathogenesis

Factors associated with recurrent or persistent negative MEP are listed in Table 102-2. Baseline structural, anatomic, and physiologic factors, as well as transient factors, play a role in the development of negative MEP.

For a better understanding of the variations in the development of negative MEP, it is helpful to review some

TABLE 102-1. Potential Clinical Presentation of Subjects with Negative Middle Ear Pressure

Normal ears with incidental negative middle ear pressure

Normal ears with subjective discomfort (children, adolescents, and adults)

Ears that develop acute otitis media or otitis media with effusion secondary to negative middle ear pressure

Ears with preexisting atelectasis/retraction pocket/cholesteatoma

Ears that develop hearing loss or balance problems with negative middle ear pressure

Ears with negative middle ear pressure after tympanoplasty

TABLE 102-2. Factors Associated with Persistent or Recurrent Negative Middle Ear Pressure

Long-lasting/baseline factors
  Anatomic/neurologic/developmental problems (eg, craniofacial anomalies, cleft palate, etc)
  Maturation problems (eg, eustachian tube angle length, efficiency of muscle opening)
  Nasal obstruction
  Adenoid hypertrophy
  Sniff-related negative middle ear pressure
  Chronic inflammatory processes (eg, rhinosinusitis, adenoiditis)
  Nasal allergies
  Small/underpneumatized mastoid
Transient/recurrent factors
  Upper respiratory infection
  Viral otitis media (possibly a virus triggers the negative pressure before bacteria get there)
  Barotrauma (eg, flying/diving)
  Pacifier/type of bottle-feeding

concepts of ME anatomy and physiology. The ME cleft is a relatively rigid gas pocket containing gases: N_2, O_2, CO_2, and water vapor. Although the ME communicates intermittently with the external environment when the eustachian tube (ET) opens, there is a constant gas exchange across the ME mucosa. The opening of the ET results in a pressure difference–driven bolus exchange of gases between the nasopharynx and the ME. Transmucosal gas exchange is via equalization of the partial pressures of each gas between the ME and venous blood. Although mucosal thickness, area, and mucosal blood flow all affect the overall gas exchange rate, each gas has a unique exchange coefficient, which is the main determining factor (Doyle et al, 1999). Although it takes a few minutes for CO_2 to equalize across the ME mucosa, an hour or two is necessary for O_2, and several days are necessary for N_2 to equalize (Alper et al, 1996). Interestingly, the sum of partial pressures of all gases in the venous blood (and in the absence of ET openings eventually in the ME) is less than the atmospheric pressure. If there was no connection between the ME and the outside, the partial pressures of all gases in the ME would eventually equilibrate with the venous blood, and the MEP would, as a result, decrease to about –600 to –700 mm H_2O. Because the equilibrium of CO_2 and O_2 occurs within the first few hours, the rate of exchange of N_2 would determine the fate of the MEP in the absence of the ET opening. Again, it would take several days for the MEP to go to below –600 mm H_2O. There seems to be a critical MEP at around –200 to –300 mm H_2O, where transudation of fluid into the ME occurs (Alper et al, 2000a). Although gas exchange continues over days, the increased volume of fluid reducing the remaining volume of gas in the ME cleft prevents the MEP from dropping too fast to below –600 mm H_2O. Therefore, even before the pressure reaches below –400 mm H_2O, the ME is usually filled with effu-

sion (Alper et al, 1996). The earlier the ear starts to accumulate effusion, the higher the MEP stays; the later it starts and the slower transudation occurs, the lower the MEP reaches.

There are probably significant individual differences in the rate of decrease in the MEP and the threshold and rate of development of MEE. Although there are differences in physiologies and responses to stimuli leading to variability in the threshold at which effusion develops, there is a critical threshold for each individual (and perhaps each individual ear) at which MEP can persist for extended periods of time without the development of MEE.

For the strict definition of persistent negative MEP, an ear should remain at a negative pressure level without developing MEE. As stated above, on average, it should not be at a pressure below –200 to –300 mm H_2O. We also stated that if the ET is not opening, the pressure will not stay at any specific level. There must be entry of gas into the ME to keep the ME pressure at a specific level (Alper and Doyle, 1999; Alper et al, 2000b). Therefore, persistent negative MEP means that the ET is regularly opening to supply gas into the ME but at a much lower frequency than normal, barely keeping the MEP above the threshold of development of MEE (Alper et al, 1999a). One exception to that, which needs to be studied further, is a thinned tympanic membrane (TM) with increased transtympanic gas exchange to the extent that it balances the rate of gas loss through the mucosal gas exchange, keeping the MEP at a constant negative level.

The more common scenario, for the reasons listed above, is to have recurrent negative MEP. This clinical presentation is much more likely because the reversible nature of the changes in the physiologic and environmental conditions or stimuli may allow MEP to remain at levels for durations that do not lead to the transudation of effusion. We are excluding from the focus of discussion some or most of the ears that cannot withhold the pressures at a level or duration to prevent the development of MEE. Although the subjects who can maintain an aerated ME or who develop MEE are distinguished after the fact, the past history of each individual with similar occurrences of periods of negative MEP may give a clue to the potential outcome.

In addition to the rare causes of ET obstruction/dysfunction caused by tumors and congenital disorders, the most common direct and indirect risk factors for the development of recurrent ME underpressure are acute and chronic inflammatory diseases of the upper respiratory tract (viral URIs, acute or chronic rhinosinusitis, allergic rhinitis, nasal obstruction, and sniffing). The inflammatory processes may interfere with the ME gas balance by causing ET dysfunction and impeding ME mucosal gas exchange. Nasal obstruction could also be associated with chronic rhinosinusitis and allergic rhinitis, resulting in a negative pressure in the nasopharynx that prevents the

ME from equilibrating its pressure with the atmospheric pressure. Sniff-induced negative MEP has the same pathophysiology. The presence of adenoids may be responsible for negative MEP owing to obstruction of the nasopharynx and/or inducing inflammation (inflammatory mediators and as a source of virus and bacteria).

Among the causes of recurrent negative MEP, URIs are the major cause, followed by barotrauma. In the first case, ME underpressure is induced by ET dysfunction and ME mucosal inflammation owing to the presence of viruses and pathogenic bacteria (*Streptococcus pneumoniae* and *Haemophilus influenzae*) in the nasopharynx. Clinical evidence supports this correlation and suggests that preexistence of good ET function may be protective against development of negative MEP during viral infections (Moody et al, 1998). Studies with army pilots do not corroborate this conclusion for barotrauma because good function preflight did not influence the prevalence of this ME process (Ashton and Watson, 1990). Probably the same degree of MEP deregulation predisposes the individual to or perpetuates otitis media (OM) depending on the factors concurrently present, including viral infection, inflammation, and ET anatomy and function.

One other mechanism to increase the chance of development of MEE during a viral URI is the higher chance of reflux of nasopharyngeal secretions containing virus and bacteria through the ET into the ME during those rare ET openings because of the larger pressure gradient between the ME and the nasopharynx. When a viral URI is the initial insult leading to worsening of ET function, the chance of a viral load entering the ME is higher. This entry can lead to inflammation and resulting transudation and exudation. Inflammation of the ME mucosa itself leads to an increased blood flow and a more rapid gas exchange, resulting in a steeper drop of MEP (Alper et al, 1999b).

The significance of the mastoid in the ME gas balance has been constantly debated. Whereas some researchers believe in its importance as a gas reservoir, buffer, and pressure regulator, others question the evidence that proves those functions (Doyle, 2000; Raveh et al, 1999). Many hypotheses have been postulated to explain the reported association between mastoid size and ME disease. Although once developed it may also contribute to the ear disease, it seems that small mastoid size is a consequence of poor ET function and recurrent or persistent middle ear disease.

Management

The identification of the etiology responsible for the development of ME underpressure, the presence or absence of subjective complaints, complications or sequelae, the patient's age, and the season should help determine whether the patient requires treatment. The goal would be to prevent acute otitis media (AOM) or

otitis media with effusion (OME) secondary to the ME underpressure, as well as prevent possible complications or sequelae, such as severe retraction of the TM (incus necrosis/retraction pockets), balance disturbance, and hearing loss. Subjective complaints such as autophony, tinnitus, and a sense of pressure or ear pain are potential presentations for which treatment may be considered.

The approach to the management of ME underpressure should start with determining whether the affected ear has developed any sequelae or complications. If the subject does not have any complaints (when negative MEP is an incidental finding) and the ears are normal and without sequelae, nothing should be done, and no follow-up is necessary. If the ear is normal and there are only subjective complaints (not severe and for a short duration), the identification and control of the risk factors in addition to the explanation of the problem and its prognosis are generally enough. Evaluation may include audiometry and tympanometry, as well as follow-up for the persistence of the complaints.

For patients with negative MEP who frequently develop AOM or OME; those who have preexisting or concurrent atelectasis/retraction pocket/cholesteatoma; those who present with severe or prolonged ear pain, hearing loss, or balance disturbance; or those who have a history of prior ear surgery (tympanoplasty), a closer follow-up is necessary, and an intervention should be considered (Table 102-3).

Prevention

Evidence of a causal relationship between viral URI and negative MEP, and consequently OM, has resulted in strategies that prevent or treat viral infections. It was demonstrated that although most children develop negative MEP during a viral URI, the great majority have spontaneous resolution and do not need any treatment. Subjects who develop recurrent AOM and or chronic OME or present with previous atelectasis, retraction pockets, or chronic OM may benefit from attempts to prevent viral infections. Unfortunately, attempts to identify an early sign or symptom on which to base the timing of prophylactic intervention to prevent OM during a viral URI has not been successful. There were also no predictors for the occurrence of poor tubal function, ME

TABLE 102-3. Management of Negative Middle Ear Pressure

Prevention (vaccines, hygiene, and avoiding known precipitating factors such as pacifiers, bottle-feeding, sniffing, smoking, allergenic ambient control)

Insufflation methods (Valsalva's maneuver, Otovent)

Medical management (surface tension–lowering substances, bioactive substances, topical and systemic decongestants, topical sodium cromoglycate, antihistamines, anticholinergics, corticosteroids, systemic antihistamines, anti-inflammatory steroids and nonsteroids, antiviral drugs)

Surgery (myringotomy, laser-assisted myringotomy, ventilation tubes, mastoidectomy)

underpressure, and earache (Doyle et al, 1999; Moody et al, 1998; Palmu et al, 2002).

Influenza A vaccine reduced the incidence of OM in children older than 6 months of age when applied once a year before the influenza season (Heikkinen et al, 1991). Unfortunately, there is no consensus whether all children or just the specific high-risk groups should be immunized. Presently, in the United States, immunization of all children 6 to 23 months of age and their household caretakers, as well as out-of-home caregivers, is recommended. Respiratory syncytial virus (RSV) and parainfluenza vaccines are still being developed and await further tests.

An alternative strategy may be administration of systemic and topical antiviral drugs (the neuraminidase inhibitors oseltamivir and zanamivir) after the onset of signs or symptoms of a viral URI. The duration and severity of influenza virus infection were significantly diminished in adults who used those medications at the beginning of the infectious process. One study showed a reduction in ME underpressure and, consequently, fewer ME complications (Heikkinen et al, 1991). The use of zanamivir among children was also tested, with similar results (Whitley et al, 2001). Although approved by the US Food and Drug Administration, the utility of this antiviral drug for other URIs (RSV, parainfluenza) remains unclear. Among children, it is difficult to differentiate a true influenza virus infection from other common URIs. The specificity of zanamivir for the influenza virus may result in a large proportion of unnecessary prescriptions. Older antiviral medications should not be considered viable alternatives. Investigational antihuman rhinovirus agents, including intranasal tremacamra, intranasal AG7088, and oral pleconaril, may warrant further studies.

Avoidance and control of other factors that may be directly or indirectly involved in the regulation of MEP may also be potential targets. Elimination of the use of pacifiers and discouraging bottle-feeding may prevent development of negative pressure in the nasopharynx and, consequently, in the ME in susceptible children. The habit of sniffing may also be targeted by addressing the underlying triggering factors, such as allergic or vasomotor rhinitis or sinusitis.

Insufflation

A management option for negative MEP originates from the nineteenth century, when Deleau and later Politzer advocated insufflation of air through the ET with or without catheterization, respectively. Recently, ME inflation has been revived for the prevention and treatment of negative MEP and its consequences. Unfortunately, clinical trials using this technique have reported contradictory results. Whereas some authors (Stangerup, 1998; Stangerup et al, 1994) advocate its use for different types of ME disease (barotrauma, OME), others found lower success rates in trials on animal models (Alper and

Doyle, 1999; Alper et al, 1999a; Alper et al, 1999b; Alper et al, 2000b). Adequate frequency of inflations to maintain normal MEP is quite variable among individuals. The efficacy of potential regimens and adjuvant medical therapies to augment the inflation has not been studied. As with any other chronic disease, treatment requires compliance with the recommendations.

An important concern with the autoinflation method is the potential risk of contaminating the ME with pathogenic viruses and bacteria from the nasopharynx during inflation maneuvers. Because negative MEP is more likely to develop during a viral URI, use of inflation maneuvers may bring a higher risk of OM when they are needed the most. It may be speculated that worsened ET ventilation function with edema and obstruction during a viral URI may actually be temporarily beneficial by permitting better ET protective function. Any inflation attempt may hamper this improved protective function of the ET during a viral URI.

The second major concern is the lack of ability to use or compliance in using autoinflation devices (Otovent) in the young children who need this treatment the most. Currently, the most promising use of autoinflation seems to be for barotrauma and in older children when there is continued negative MEP after the resolution of active signs and symptoms of cold.

Medical Management

Different experimental models have been used to test the possible effects of surface tension–lowering substances (Chandrasekhar et al, 2002). Surfactants are believed to decrease the mean opening pressure of the ET and help with the influx of gas bolus. In addition to defining an ideal way of use (instilled, rinsed, or nebulized), there is still the need for testing in a more complex and multifactorial model, including a test against placebo. Surfactants seem a reasonable option to enhance ME ventilation, but they may diminish the ET protection function. Because topical decongestants do not have a positive effect on ET function in children, their use is not justified and should be discouraged (Chandrasekhar et al, 2002). β-Adrenoreceptor agonists were tried in a few experimental studies. Some investigators suggested that isoprenaline acted on the ET by causing secretion of surface tension–lowering substances (Turner and Darden, 1996). Although decongestants (α-adrenoreceptor agonists), antihistamines (H$_1$ receptor antagonists), or a combination of both have been known to decongest the mucosa of the ET and ME by causing vasoconstriction, no results support the regular use of these drugs for the treatment of negative MEP or OM.

Other treatment options for allergic rhinitis (topical drugs such as sodium cromoglycate, antihistamines, anticholinergics, and corticosteroids) may also be important but have not yet been proven to be of any benefit in relieving ME underpressure. Although reasonable, there is no proof that corticosteroids or nonsteroidal anti-inflammatory drugs reduce or prevent ME underpressure development and its consequences.

Recently, some herbal and other alternative treatments have been tried to control the inflammatory process, but no results regarding MEP have been measured. As with all medications, well-designed trials must be performed with enough power to establish new treatment methods for negative MEP.

Surgical Treatment

The principle of bypassing problems with ME ventilation comes from the observation in the eighteenth century that TM perforation stabilized the ME disease. More than 200 years later, the impact of ventilation tubes (VTs) on the prevention and treatment of various forms of ME disease has been well established. On the other hand, there is a lack of studies on its use for negative MEP. It is clear that an opening in the TM would immediately solve the problem of negative MEP. Various methods of creating an opening in the TM include tympanocentesis, myringotomy (with knife or laser), or myringotomy and VT insertion. The relative ineffectiveness of analgesia with topical anesthesia limits the justified use of myringotomy to very few symptomatic subjects or special indications. Because it may be justified in a bulging eardrum, any subject with severe ear pain owing to significant negative MEP may need a myringotomy. Unfortunately, the duration of a patent opening after myringotomy is very short, limited from hours to days. Therefore, in anticipation of a longer duration of negative MEP, alternative methods are sought.

Laser-assisted myringotomy is proposed to achieve an opening in the TM that will last for several weeks. Although the duration of a patent opening may not be adequate for the resolution of inflammation in the ME and prevention of recurrence in the ears with OME, laser-assisted myringotomy may be a treatment alternative for patients who suffer from symptomatic negative MEP for an extended period of time.

For persistent or recurrent negative MEP, VT insertion may be a better option. However, although rare, potential risks, sequelae, and complications of VTs should limit their use to ears with well-established, persistent, or recurrent negative MEP with signs of atelectasis, retraction pockets, or a trend for development of cholesteatoma.

Some surgeons believe that mastoidectomy may be indicated for chronic negative pressure, resulting in a long history of chronic OME, retraction pockets, or recurrent otorrhea that is unresponsive to all other treatment methods. Mastoidectomy can be considered in the presence of TM and ME complications despite previous VT insertions. Recently, surgical implantation of a permanent mastoid cannula was described but received limited enthusiasm (Young, 1998).

When enlarged, adenoids are acknowledged as an etiologic factor in ET dysfunction, but evidence supports the contention that the most important aspect of the adenoids is as the source of pathogenic bacteria. Despite the fact that obstruction of the nasopharynx may cause negative MEP, many studies have failed to demonstrate any relationship between the size of the adenoid and the occurrence of ME underpressure and OME. There are no specific studies looking at the effect of tonsillectomy in the prevention and treatment of ME underpressure. However, lack of efficacy for chronic OME or recurrent AOM also may be generalized to this condition.

Selection of Treatment Method

Clinically, if negative MEP resolves without resulting in OME or other sequelae, the only concern would be the discomfort to the subject. In small children, it is difficult to differentiate AOM from a red and bulging TM owing to crying. Although experienced otoscopists can rule out OM in this scenario, it is possible that such a child may be labeled with the diagnosis of AOM. As a result, recurrent negative MEP may be responsible for the diagnosis of recurrent AOM in a subset of children. Although these children may do quite well after the VT placement, the "improvement" may be related to prevention of variation in the MEP, not AOM episodes. This fact highlights the importance of accurate diagnosis of AOM or OME but fails to address a reasonable aproach to children with negative MEP, who may frequently be experiencing significant discomfort that affects their behavior or sleep.

It should not be forgotten that most patients with ME underpressure have it temporarily and with a high rate of spontaneous resolution. In the absence of symptoms, the presence of negative MEP may be incidental during a routine examination with pneumatic otoscopy. In any asymptomatic patient, generalized retraction of the eardrum suggestive of negative MEP that does not have signs of sequelae may be ignored. However, children with chronic negative MEP may be more susceptible to ME complications (AOM and OME). In this case, they should be followed closely, and the different associated etiologic factors must be investigated and treated if possible. On the other hand, although asymptomatic, any ear with the signs of TM atelectasis or retraction pocket should be followed to assess the persistence and progression of the negative MEP and its sequelae. When there is severe atelectasis or deep retraction pockets, ears should be closely monitored, and insertion of VTs should be strongly considered even though the individuals may be asymptomatic. In the presence of a retraction pocket that extends beyond the visual field, unless there is a strong suspicion of cholesteatoma, a VT should be inserted to assess whether the retracted portion of the TM will resume the normal anatomic position or at least the entire depth becomes visible. In ears in which the depth of the retraction pocket remains invisible, a computed tomographic (CT) scan should be ordered to proceed with a tympanoplasty with or without a cartilage graft to make the ear safe. In ears with evidence or a strong suspicion of cholesteatoma, a CT scan should be obtained first for the surgical planning.

An ear with a retracted TM that is associated with subjective complaints may require an audiologic and tympanometric evaluation. In the absence of sequelae or complications of negative MEP, management of symptomatic subjects should be tailored according to their past history. In older children and adults, there may be an adequate history on the outcome of prior episodes of negative MEP. In subjects with no prior history of OM, a supportive approach is appropriate. In subjects with severe episodes with prolonged durations of symptomatic negative MEP or resulting OM, medical, insufflation, and surgical options should be considered.

Even in considerably symptomatic individuals who do not have any sign of atelectasis, retraction pocket, or cholesteatoma formation, VT insertion should be avoided. However, teenagers and adults with recurrent or persistent negative MEP may present with a significant degree of complaints. We cannot compare the dramatic presentations of these individuals with what infants or young children are experiencing. Having seen how intolerable adults find the MEP changes, one wonders what infants may be experiencing. Although the physician's approach to such presentations of teenagers and adults tends to be supportive by suggesting waiting for the resolution, a patient's strong demand for a cure to his or her problem may require VT insertion. In any child at the age when he or she can successfully perform autoinflation (ie, using an Otovent device), this method should be encouraged prior to the VT insertion. Although some reports suggest compliance with Otovent treatment in children as young as 3 years of age, this author's experience is discouraging in children younger than 4 to 5 years of age.

The presence of sequelae or complications in symptomatic subjects should be managed as outlined above for asymptomatic subjects. For those with recurrent/chronic ME underpressure who develop AOM or chronic OME with TM and mastoid complications (atelectasis, chronic mastoiditis, cholesteatoma), VT insertion with or without adenoidectomy becomes a possible option. The selection of a mastoidectomy as a treatment for chronic ME underpressure is still debated but remains an alternative in the face of VT failure and development of complications (retraction pockets, cholesteatoma, or chronic discharge).

For ears that develop persistent or recurrent negative MEP after tympanoplasty or if the insufflation methods are not tolerated or successful, VT insertion may be considered. If a revision surgery becomes necessary owing to development of atelectasis or retraction pockets, cartilage graft or lateral graft techniques with or without concurrent VT placement may be considered. In ears with established poor ET dysfunction, these surgical options may be considered during the first tympanoplasty.

Conclusion

Negative MEP is usually transient, leading to either spontaneous resolution or progression to various forms of OM. Whereas the former does not need any treatment, the latter is managed in a manner specific to the type and severity of OM. Ears known to progress to OM may be managed with the perspective of prophylaxis before the OM develops. Ears with prolonged or recurrent negative MEP that leads to symptoms or sequelae require a therapeutic approach. Owing to the high spontaneous resolution rate of this entity, surgery should be kept as the last option for cases with complications or sequelae, and persistent or recurrent negative MEP should be managed with watchful waiting or insufflation methods.

References

Alper CM, Ardic FN, Doyle WJ. The effects of changing middle ear pressure and gas partial pressure on mucosal blood flow and vascular permeability in the chinchilla. Auris Nasus Larynx 2000a;27:105–11.

Alper CM, Doyle WJ. Repeated inflation does not prevent otitis media with effusion in a monkey model. Laryngoscope 1999;109:1074–80.

Alper CM, Doyle WJ, Seroky JT. Higher rates of pressure decrease in inflamed compared to noninflamed middle ears. Otolaryngol Head Neck Surg 1999b;121:98–102.

Alper CM, Swarts JD, Doyle WJ. Middle ear inflation for the diagnosis of otitis media with effusion. Auris Nasus Larynx 1999a;26:479–86.

Alper CM, Swarts JD, Doyle WJ. Prevention of otitis media with effusion by repeated air inflation in a monkey model. Arch Otolaryngol Head Neck Surg 2000b;126:609–14.

Alper CM, Tabari R, Seroky JT, Doyle WJ. Magnetic resonance imaging of otitis media with effusion caused by functional obstruction of the eustachian tube. Ann Otol Rhinol Laryngol 1996;106:422–31.

Ashton DH, Watson LA. The use of tympanometry in predicting otic barotrauma. Aviat Space Environ Med 1990;61:56–61.

Casselbrant ML, Brostoff LM, Cantekin EI, et al. Otitis media with effusion in preschool children. Laryngoscope 1985;95:428–36.

Chandrasekhar SS, Connelly PE, Venkatayan N, et al. Intranasal metered dose aerosolized surfactant reduces passive opening pressure of the eustachian tube: comparison study in two animal models. Otol Neurotol 2002;23:620–1.

Doyle WJ. Experimental results do not support a gas reserve function for the mastoid. Int J Pediatr Otorhinolaryngol 2000;52:229–38.

Doyle WJ, Alper CM. A model to explain the rapid pressure decrease after air-inflation of diseased middle ear. Laryngoscope 1999;109:70–8.

Doyle WJ, Alper CM, Seroky JT. Trans-mucosal inert gas exchange constants for the monkey middle ear. Auris Nasus Larynx 1999;25:5–12.

Chapter 103

Management of Acute Otitis Media or Mastoiditis in Children with Cochlear Implants

Hans-Georg Kempf, MD, PhD

For more than 20 years, cochlear implantation (CI) has been performed in children and adults in many major and minor centers all over the world. Modern CI provides digital technology with an intracochlear electrode array and different stimulation patterns (Lenarz and Battmer, 1996).

The surgical technique is well established and related to an extensive examination of the candidates preoperatively. Severe disasters concerning the operative procedure and the postoperative outcome are rare (Hofman and Cohen, 1995; Kempf et al, 1997). Complications in cochlear implantation are defined as minor (no or conservative treatment), major (revision surgery, meningitis, implant loss, facial nerve injury), intraoperative (gusher, obliteration), early (immediately and up to 3 months postoperatively), and delayed (more than 3 months postoperatively, eg, cholesteatoma, electrode dislocation, device failure). The following sections show data of complications after CI and recommended procedures with a special focus on infection-related problems in implanted children, for example, acute otitis media (AOM) and mastoiditis.

Incidence and Findings in Complications after CI

Short- and long-term complications in pediatric CI are rare but can lead to loss of the implant.

Our own clinical study of 366 implanted children evaluated the complication rate postoperatively and during follow-up. Their ages ranged from 1 to 14 years, and they were operated on between 1987 and 1997 in Hannover, Germany. In most of the cases, a Nucleus 22 mini-implant (Cochlear Corp., Englewood, CO) was used. Additionally, since 1994, the Clarion 1.0 and 1.2 (Advanced Bionics Corp., Sylmar, CA) and, since 1997, the Nucleus 24M implants have been implanted. Most of the children lost their hearing due to meningitis ($n = 200$) or were congenitally deaf. Additionally, the data on infectious complications of 331 adult cochlear implant patients were included to compare the incidence of infectious complications in children and adults. During the follow-up period of up to 8 years, AOM occurred in 11 children in the implanted ear and in 9 children in the contralateral ear, resulting in a rate of 5.6%. Seven ears were opened by myringotomy. Five ears were opened by a retroauricular approach, and in all of them, acute mastoiditis with pus was found. In these cases, scar tissue and thickened mastoidal mucosa were removed. The antrum was reopened, and a small retroauricular drainage tube was inserted and kept in place for up to 5 days. No further complications occurred during follow-up. In one girl, labyrinthitis with loss of implant performance was observed after rubella vaccination. The reimplantation procedure was complicated by severe ossification of the implanted cochlea. In two additional cases, severe infection in the implant bed developed, and, despite local and conservative treatment, the devices had to be removed (Table 103-1). The electrode was kept inside the cochlea. In one case, successful reimplantation was performed 1 year later. The second child was reimplanted 6 months later without further problems.

Severe Complications after CI

In general, CI is a safe and reliable otosurgical procedure. The rate of severe complications is low compared with other surgical procedures. Comparing our own data

TABLE 103-1. Infectious Complications after Cochlear Implant Surgery

Complication	Children (n = 366)		Adults (n = 331)	
	Number	%	Number	%
Meningitis	0	0	0	0
Acute otitis media	20	5.5	5	1.5
Severe infection with explantation	2	0.5	3	0.9
Cholesteatoma	1	0.25	19	5.7
Mastoiditis	5	1.25	7	2.1
Labyrinthitis	1	0.25	3	0.9

(Kempf et al, 1997) with those from the multicenter study of Hoffman and Cohen (1995), the same range of major complications occurred (Table 103-2). The low rate of severe complications is related to several issues. In most of the centers, a standard surgical procedure for all patients is used by a small number of surgeons. However, owing to the large number of patients, CI is a routine surgical procedure and a complete program involving the whole team (Lehnhardt, 1991; Lenarz, 1994; Lenarz et al, 1997). Major postoperative problems—wound infections, flap problems, and electrode dislocation—should be treated with special techniques (Laszig, 1996; Lehnhardt, 1991; Myamoto et al, 1996) to avoid explantation and/or intracranial complications. On the other hand, infectious complications related to AOM occur more frequently in children compared with adults (see Table 103-1).

AOM and CI

A deaf child with AOM should not be implanted. The surgical procedure should be cancelled and performed 2 to 3 weeks after treatment with antibiotics, nose drops, and antiphlogistic drugs. AOM or acute mastoiditis on the implanted ear should be treated as routinely as in unimplanted ears. Antibiotics should be administered intravenously for a few days longer than normal. Luntz and colleagues (1996) reported a series of 50 children with CI and reported the incidence of AOM pre- and postoperatively: 74% had AOM before and 16% after implantation.

The incidence and severity of AOM decreased after implantation. The authors point out that a history of recurrent AOM should not inordinately delay CI.

Mastoiditis after CI

There is a small but not an increased risk for a child developing acute mastoiditis in the implanted ear. In the case of mastoiditis, the mastoid can also be opened without risk for the implant, as reported by Marangos and colleagues (1996) and proven by my own experience (Kempf et al, 2000). If there is a severe infection, including in the implant bed, removal of the device is necessary and provides the only chance of healing (Figures 103-1 and 103-2). The electrode should remain in the cochlea, thus keeping the intracochlear space open. As shown in several reported cases, a successful reimplantation on the affected side is possible, for example, after 1 year. During the reimplantation procedure, the electrodes can be inserted into the cochlea in the same way. After healing, hearing performance will rise again. A severe delay of speech development and hearing competence may be seen.

Prevention of Infections/Complications

Adenoidectomy and use of ventilation tubes before implantation as well as careful subtotal mastoidectomy during cochlear implant surgery in children can probably reduce the incidence of AOM after implantation. During cochlear implant preinvestigation in children, the nasopharynx is routinely examined and the adenoids are removed. In cases of serous otitis media, grommets are inserted to improve ventilation of the middle ear spaces (Lenarz, 1994). In cases of chronic mastoiditis detected during cochlear implant surgery, a subtotal mastoidectomy is recommended without implantation. This gives an excellent chance of restoration of the mucosa. In a second-stage surgery, implantation can be performed after 6 months under improved mastoid conditions. The surgical field is prepared and the implantation is possible in an ear without infection and with an excellent anatomic situation.

TABLE 103-2. Comparison of Complication Rate in Pediatric Cochlear Implantation

	Hoffman and Cohen (1995; n = 1,905)		MHH (n = 366, < 3 mo)		MHH (n = 366, > 3 mo)	
	n	%	n	%	n	%
Flap complications	30	1.57	10	3.66	1	0.27
Electrode dislocation	25	1.31	0	0	1	0.26
Facial nerve stimulation	18	0.94	4	1.12	7	1.89
Facial nerve injury	11	0.58	0	0	0	0
Electrode malinsertion	11	0.58	0	0	0	0

Adapted from Hoffmann and Cohen (1995).

MHH = Medical University Hannover (Department of Otolaryngology, Germany).

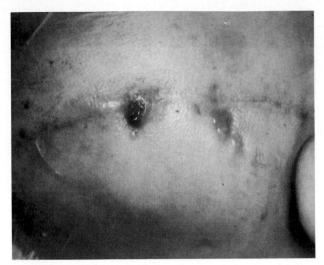

FIGURE 103-1. Severe wound infection 6 weeks after cochlear implantation in a 3-year-old child.

Meningitis after CI

There is no clinical evidence that an implanted ear bears an increased risk of developing labyrinthitis with subsequent meningitis. In some centers, very few cases of meningitis after cochlear implantation were observed in the last few years without a clear correlation to the type of implant or electrode system used. Cases of meningitis after CI are treated as in specialized pediatric departments with a combination of intravenously administered antibiotics. Owing to the fact that pneumococci and *Haemophilus influenzae* are the leading microorganisms, a vaccination against both pathogens is recommended for implanted children.

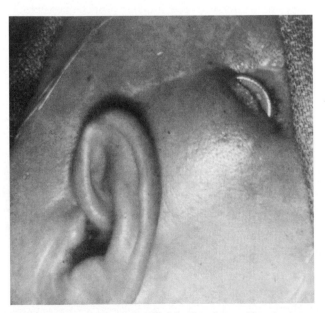

FIGURE 103-2. Flap necrosis with infection after cochlear implantation 18 months after first surgery.

Among cochlear implant candidates, there might be patients who have abnormal middle and/or inner ear conditions such as inner ear malformations, atretic mastoid with meningocele, chronic otitis media, or petrous bone fracture (Bendet et al, 1998). In such cases, the insertion of a foreign body could bring the risk of an existing or potential intracranial communication or when the ear is prone to infection. As shown in adults (Issing et al, 1996) and in children (Bendet et al, 1998; Weber et al, 1995), using a specific technique with lateral petrosectomy and fat obliteration of the remaining space, a very safe local situation can be achieved. By obliterating and isolating the tympanomastoid cleft from the outer environment with permanent closure of the external ear canal, a broader spectrum of patients can be implanted safely. On the other hand, singular case reports also show the possibility of suppurative labyrinthitis and meningitis following chronic otitis media from the contralateral ear that was not implanted but is malfunctioning (Suzuki et al, 1998).

Conclusion

As expected for a pediatric population, AOM and mastoiditis can occur in the implanted ear and in the contralateral side. Early detection of the infection, consequent conservative treatment with antibiotics, and, if necessary, operative opening of the mastoid can prevent infection of the device bed with subsequent implant loss. Children with cochlear implants should be handled with care. Also, minor complaints should be examined by a specialist to detect the risk of a complication as early as possible. Extensive information of the parents and good contact to implantation centers (eg, hotline contact) can prevent most of the disturbances and make pediatric CI as safe as such a technology can be.

Acknowledgment

This work was supported by a grant from the Deutsche Forschungsgemeinschaft DFG to HGK (Ke 657/3-1).

References

Bendet E, Cerenko D, Linder TE, Fisch U. Cochlear implantation after subtotal petrosectomies. Eur Arch Otorhinolaryngol 1998;255:169–74.

Hoffman RA, Cohen NL. Complications of cochlear implant surgery. Ann Otol Rhinol Laryngol Suppl 1995;166:420–2.

Issing PR, Schoenermark M, Kempf HG, Lenarz T. Indications for middle ear obliteration within the scope of cochlear implant management. Laryngorhinootologie 1996;75:727–31.

Kempf HG, Johann K, Weber BP, Lenarz T. Complications in cochlear implant surgery in children. Am J Otol 1997;18 Suppl: 62–3.

Kempf HG, Stöver T, Lenarz T. Mastoiditis and acute otitis media in children with cochlear implants: recommendations for medical management. Ann Otol Rhinol Laryngol Suppl 2000;185:25–7.

Laszig R. Komplikationen bei Cochlear Implants im Kindesalter. HNO 1996;44:119–20.

Lehnhardt E. Intracochlear placement of Cochlear implant electrodes in soft surgery technique. HNO 1991;41:356–9.

Lenarz T. Cochlear Implant bei Kindern: Konzept, Auswahlkriterien, operatives Vorgehen und Ergebnisse. In: Lenarz T, Lehnhardt E, Bertram B, editors. Cochlear Implant bei Kindern. Stuttgart: Thieme; 1994. p. 4–15.

Lenarz T, Battmer R. Das Clarion Cochlear Implant—technische Grundlagen, erste klinische Erfahrungen und Ergebnisse. Laryngorhinootologie 1996;75:1–9.

Lenarz T, Hartrampf R, Battmer RD, et al. Die Cochlear-Implant Versorgung bei Kleinkindern. Laryngorhinootologie 1997; 75:719–26.

Luntz M, Hodges AV, Balkany T, et al. Otitis media in children with cochlear implants. Laryngoscope 1996;106:1403–5.

Marangos N, Aschendorff A, Laszig R. Management of acute otitis media or mastoiditis on the implanted side [abstract]. In: Proceedings of the 3rd European Symposium on Paediatric Cochlear Implantation; 1996; Jun 3–8; Hannover, Germany.

Myamoto RT, Young M, Myres WA, et al. Complications of pediatric cochlear implantation. Eur Arch Otorhinolaryngol 1996;253:1–4.

Suzuki C, Sando I, Fagan JI, et al. Histopathological features of a cochlear implant and otogenic meningitis in Mondini dysplasia. Arch Otorhinolaryngol Head Neck Surg 1998;124:462–6.

Weber BP, Lenarz T, Dietrich B, Dillo W. Cochlear implantation into a malformed cochlea with a rare footplate defect. Laryngorhinootologie 1996;75:319–25.

Chapter 104

TUBERCULOUS OTITIS MEDIA

SOHAM ROY, MD

Tuberculous otitis media (OM) has decreased in incidence since the introduction of antituberculous drugs in the latter part of the twentieth century. Early in the twentieth century, up to 18% of all cases of chronic suppurative OM were attributed to tuberculosis; this has dropped to current rates of less than 1% (Greenfield et al, 1995). More recent literature suggests that the incidence of tuberculous OM represents 0.05 to 0.9% of all cases of chronic OM (Skolnik et al, 1986).

Although the exact incidence of tuberculous OM is not known, as few as 93 cases over 5 years have been reported; it is likely that the exact incidence is underreported as the correct diagnosis is frequently delayed. It is thought that the decrease in incidence is attributable to the advent of antituberculous drugs and the addition of multidrug regimens for resistant tuberculosis. However, as a result of recent increases in human immunodeficiency virus (HIV) infection rates, the incidence of pulmonary tuberculosis has increased since the mid-1980s, with a resultant dramatic increase in the incidence of tuberculous OM in recent years, mostly in larger urban populations (Greenfield et al, 1995). As a result, clinicians should be aware of the signs and symptoms of tuberculous infection for refractory cases of chronic OM.

Tuberculosis is an infection of *Mycobacterium tuberculosis* communicated traditionally through aerosolized respiratory secretions. Although most of those infected become asymptomatic carriers of the disease (without clinical findings but still purified protein derivative [PPD] positive), immunocompetent hosts have a 5 to 10% lifetime risk of developing clinical symptoms. People infected with tuberculosis and concomitant HIV carry a 10% annual risk of developing clinical tuberculosis (Byer and Dupuis, 1995). Most of these patients will present with pulmonary disease, but a small percentage will go on to develop extrapulmonary tuberculosis.

Tuberculous OM is most often caused by *M. tuberculosis*, although atypical mycobacteria (*M. avium, M. bovis, M. fortuitum*) have also been reported. Three major mechanisms have been proposed for the seeding of ear disease in tuberculous infections. First, tuberculous OM may result from hematogenous or lymphatic spread from concurrent pulmonary infection. Ascending infection from the nasopharynx may send *M. tuberculosis* retrograde through the eustachian tube, and it is possible to have direct inoculation of tuberculosis through a tympanic membrane (TM) perforation. It has been speculated that *M. bovis* infection in unpasteurized milk refluxing through the eustachian tube was the etiology behind the high incidence of aural tuberculosis in children early in the twentieth century (Kirsch et al, 1995). Currently, approximately 50% of patients with tuberculous OM will also have pulmonary tuberculosis identified on chest radiography (Cleary and Batsakis, 1995). Middle ear disease usually occurs in conjunction with active pulmonary tuberculosis. It may also occur in the absence of clinically symptomatic pulmonary disease, although this is rare. The clinician treating a chronic draining ear should be alert to the signs and symptoms of tuberculous OM as it is often overlooked in the differential diagnosis.

Clinical Findings

A documented history of tuberculosis exposure is very rare in patients who present with a chronic draining ear that has been unresponsive to traditional antibiotic and topical therapy. However, a history of prior active tuberculosis is relatively common in patients with otitic tuberculosis (40–65% in a different series) (Greenfield et al, 1995; Lee and Drysdale, 1993). Therefore, patients with an unresponsive draining ear should be questioned in detail about any previous history of or exposure to tuberculosis. The results of skin testing and chest radiography can be widely varied. Chest radiography may be normal in 50% of cases (Kirsch et al, 1995), whereas PPD results are positive in a high percentage of patients with tuberculous OM (78–100%).

The clinical diagnosis of tuberculous OM is difficult because very few patients will present with the "classic" features of painless otorrhea and pale granulation tissue through multiple perforations in the TM. The most consistent finding in all series in the literature is chronic otorrhea. Even when the TM appears intact, the eardrum is granular or thickened and draining (Lee and Drysdale, 1993). Chronic otorrhea that is unresponsive to conventional treatment for chronic suppurative OM should raise suspicion for tuberculous infection.

Tuberculous OM has a wide spectrum of clinical presentations, but cases often have common features. The typical constellation of clinical findings in aural tuberculosis includes painless aural discharge and conductive hearing loss, which may progress to profuse otorrhea with profound hearing loss. However, in rare cases, tuberculous OM may present without drainage or a TM perforation. Otalgia is considered by most experts to be an infrequent presentation, although it has been described in up to 50% of cases. This seems to be associated with an acute presentation of tuberculous infection with a sudden onset of otorrhea, or it may occur from deep-seated granulation tissue in the mastoid cavity (Farrugia et al, 1997). Because of the rarity of this disease and the widely variable clinical presentation, the time from first presentation to confirmation of a diagnosis ranges from less than a year to many years in some reports (Greenfield et al, 1995).

Classically, otoscopic findings of multiple perforations and "pale granulation tissue" emanating from the middle ear were thought to be pathognomonic for tuberculous middle ear disease. However, recent literature has not confirmed these earlier descriptions. Instead, physical examination typically confirms a single subtotal or total perforation (77%) of the TM (Kirsch et al, 1995). Granulation tissue is frequently found on the surface of the TM remnant or extruding through the perforation from the middle ear mucosa. Ossicular destruction may be present; destruction of the long process of the malleus has been identified in up to 30% of patients and is considered by some authors to be pathognomonic for tuberculous OM. The otorrhea in aural tuberculosis is classically described as thin, watery, and profuse. A polyp in the external auditory canal may be present in anywhere from 13 to 100% of cases. Most authors agree that identification of a polyp in the external auditory canal should raise suspicion for tuberculous OM (Greenfield et al, 1995).

Cervical lymphadenopathy may present in 5 to 10% of patients with tuberculosis of the middle ear. Early-onset and persistent lymphadenopathy that does not respond to treatment for chronic OM should increase suspicion for tuberculous infection. The lymphadenopathy is almost always nontender. Draining sinus tracts or fistulae through the skin will occur in up to 20% of cases (Cleary and Batsakis, 1995). Other constitutional symptoms such as weight loss, night sweats, and hemoptysis are generally absent in isolated middle ear tuberculosis but are often found in patients with active pulmonary tuberculosis. The remainder of the head and neck examination is usually unremarkable.

Diagnosis

Diagnosis of tuberculous OM is frequently delayed in isolated middle ear disease without systemic findings as it is often diagnosed clinically as an unresponsive chronic suppurative OM. Further confounding an early diagnosis is the common finding of a superimposed bacterial infection. Specifically, patients with tuberculous OM will have cultures that first isolate *Pseudomonas*, *Streptococcus*, *Staphylococcus*, or *Klebsiella* in up to 80% of cases. The presence of pathogenic bacteria may prevent correct identification of *M. tuberculosis* by tissue biopsy or culture (Linthicum, 2002; Saunders and Albert, 2002). In addition, any previous use of topical antibacterial drops containing neomycin may inhibit growth of *M. tuberculosis* and result in false-negative acid-fast bacilli (AFB) stains and cultures.

Cultures of middle ear otorrhea and tissue biopsy are positive for *M. tuberculosis* in low numbers of patients. Smears for AFB are positive in only up to 20% of cases, whereas cultures specific for mycobacteria are positive in anywhere from 5 to 44% of cases (Kirsch et al, 1995). Nonetheless, the first step toward diagnosis of tuberculous OM includes AFB stains and culture of otorrhea. If stains and culture of otorrhea fail to confirm *M. tuberculosis* but the clinical suspicion remains high, then histologic examination of granulation tissue is required for the confirmation of acid-fast organisms. Tissue biopsies can often be obtained from cooperative patients in an outpatient setting. However, histologic evaluation may have a false-negative rate of up to 10% on the first attempt, emphasizing the need for a high index of suspicion and repeat biopsies if tuberculous infection is strongly suspected. More recent literature suggests that polymerase chain reaction testing of tuberculous otorrhea may provide a more rapid and higher yield of diagnosis when low numbers of organisms are present, although this type of testing is not widely available. Overall, even with a thorough investigation for tuberculosis, including chest radiography, PPD skin testing, and stains and cultures of otorrhea, tuberculous OM might be confirmed in only 26% of all cases (Kirsch et al, 1995). Often in these cases, the patient may undergo surgery for chronic suppurative OM before the definitive diagnosis is confirmed.

Because of the wide variety of clinical findings in tuberculous OM, the following guidelines can be suggested for diagnosis: Clinical signs and symptoms should always be reviewed in cases of unresponsive chronic OM, looking for unusual clinical features as described above. If atypical clinical findings are identified, repeated cultures for mycobacteria and AFB stains should be obtained. However, because mycobacterial counts are often low in extrapulmonary tuberculosis, biopsies of granulation tissue should always be obtained if clinical suspicion persists along with chest radiographs and PPD skin testing.

Radiology

High-resolution computed tomography (CT) scanning of the temporal bones is the most useful imaging modality in suspected tuberculous OM. Plain films and magnetic resonance imaging are of lesser utility. Typically, CT findings include sclerosis of the mastoid cavity and opacification of the middle ear and mastoid air cells. Destruction of the ossicles and, in particular, erosion of the handle of the malleus are common (Cavallin and Muren, 2000). Increased density of the cortical mastoid bone is often identified in conjunction with areas of increased radiolucency where bone resorption has occurred (Greenfield et al, 1995). Similarly, destruction of the facial canal may be identified in patients with facial paralysis. These findings are often confused with cholesteatoma and may mimic findings in carcinoma of the temporal bone. Extension of the disease process into surrounding soft tissues of the neck, parotid, and skull base may be seen in more advanced cases. Bony destruction within the otic capsule may be identified when sensorineural hearing loss has occurred (Hoshino et al, 1994).

Complications

Osseous destruction by mycobacterial infection can result in inner ear erosion with labyrinthine canal fistula, facial paralysis, or "cold" (nontender) mastoid abscess. Facial paralysis is a common complication of tuberculous OM. Tuberculous infection should be suspected in cases of chronic OM without cholesteatoma when facial paralysis occurs. The incidence of facial paralysis in tuberculous OM is estimated to be 21% of cases, although some series have identified facial paralysis in up to 40% of patients (Farrugia et al, 1997). Facial paralysis is more common in children and is usually unilateral even in cases of bilateral disease (Bitsori et al, 1999; Farrugia et al, 1997; Shaida and Siddiqui, 1998). Conductive hearing loss from both ossicular and TM destruction is commonplace. Sensorineural hearing loss is much less common but may occur after local destruction of the bony otic capsule and resultant labyrinthine fistula formation. Sensorineural hearing loss often persists after treatment for the infection, especially when treatment was begun late in the course of the disease. Intracranial complications from tuberculous infection are rare as dura appears to be resistant to direct spread of tuberculosis (Grewal et al, 2000).

Treatment

Delays in diagnosis often result in treatment being initiated late. However, the importance of making an early and correct diagnosis cannot be overemphasized as early medical treatment is usually curative and surgery can often be avoided. Furthermore, facial paralysis may become permanent the longer treatment is delayed (Chernoff and Parnes, 1992).

The primary treatment of tuberculous OM is medical therapy. The advent of effective multidrug treatment regimens against tuberculosis has made it possible to cure this disease without extensive surgery. Surgery may occasionally be performed for chronic otomastoiditis prior to the correct diagnosis being confirmed, and AFB are identified only incidentally in the postoperative specimen. A postoperative wound breakdown after tympanomastoid surgery is highly suspicious for tuberculous OM (Lee and Drysdale, 1993; Pulec and Deguine, 1999).

Initial treatment in uncomplicated cases of tuberculous OM includes a regimen of antituberculous chemotherapeutic agents used to treat pulmonary tuberculosis. Typically, the regimen consists of four-drug therapy, daily isoniazid (INH), rifampin, pyrazinamide, and ethambutol for 14 days, and then therapy is reduced to twice a week for an additional 6 weeks. Treatment should be directed by an infectious disease specialist who is experienced in the management of tuberculosis. After the first 2 months of treatment, INH and rifampin are given for an additional treatment period of up to 9 months, depending on the clinical response. Multidrug-resistant tuberculosis (MDR TB) has become an increasing problem because of concurrent HIV infection and poor patient compliance with the initial treatment regimen. MDR TB requires inpatient hospitalization and treatment; chemotherapeutic agents are determined by organism sensitivity and resistance from appropriate cultures. In MDR TB, intravenous streptomycin and quinolones are frequently added to the treatment regimen. Once appropriate medical therapy is initiated, chronic otorrhea will usually resolve within 2 months, although it may persist for up to 5 months; at least 6 months of medical therapy is typically required for long-term cure even after resolution of the otorrhea. INH toxicity may result in liver injury; thus, liver enzymes should be monitored throughout the course of treatment. Rifampin toxicity is rare and occurs only at higher doses, whereas streptomycin may be both vestibulotoxic and ototoxic, which are dose related.

The role of surgery in tuberculous OM has diminished with the improvement in antituberculous chemotherapy regimens (Saunders and Albert, 2002). Now surgical treatment is largely limited to management of complications such as subperiosteal abscess, facial nerve paralysis, postauricular fistula formation, and removal of bony sequestrum. Mastoidectomy and tympanoplasty as surgical therapy in addition to chemotherapy have not shown any statistical improvement in resolution of otorrhea and granulation tissue over medical treatment alone. However, after a full course of medical therapy and resolution of middle ear otorrhea and granulation tissue, tympanoplasty for persistent TM perforation and ossicular chain reconstruction after ossicular destruction are possible to restore hearing and TM function (Bhalla et al, 2001; Greenfield et al, 1995; Kirsch et al, 1995; Linthicum, 2002; Saunders and Albert, 2002). Surgical decompression of the facial nerve can result in a more rapid return of facial function after tuberculous infection is confirmed.

Conclusion

Tuberculous OM is a rare disease but is increasing in incidence in large urban populations. Because tuberculous OM clinically can mimic chronic suppurative OM, clinicians should have a high index of suspicion when patients fail to respond to conventional medical therapy. Diagnosis may be confirmed by skin testing, chest radiographs, and culture and staining of otorrhea, but histologic confirmation may be required by a biopsy of middle ear granulation. There is a high incidence of false-negative testing for tuberculous OM, so the clinician must be persistent in making a difficult diagnosis. Early diagnosis is paramount to a good clinical outcome. Treatment with multiple antituberculous chemotherapeutic agents is usually curative, although surgery may be required for complications, which are rare.

References

Bhalla RK, Jones TM, Rothburn MM, Swift AC. Tuberculous otitis media—a diagnostic dilemma. Auris Nasus Larynx 2001; 28:241–3.

Bitsori M, Galanakis E, Kokori H, et al. Tuberculous mastoiditis in a child. Eur J Pediatr 1999;158:435.

Byer R, Dupuis L. Tuberculosis, public health and civil liberties. Annu Rev Public Health 1995;16:307–26.

Cavallin L, Muren C. CT findings in tuberculous otomastoiditis. A case report. Acta Radiol 2000;41:49–51.

Chernoff WG, Parnes LS. Tuberculous mastoiditis. J Otolaryngol 1992;21:290–2.

Cleary KR, Batsakis JG. Mycobacterial disease of the head and neck: current perspective. Ann Otol Rhinol Laryngol 1995;104:830–3.

Farrugia EJ, Raza SA, Phillipps JJ. Tuberculous otitis media—a case report. J Laryngol Otol 1997;111:58–9.

Greenfield BJ, Selesnick SH, Fisher L, et al. Aural tuberculosis. Am J Otol 1995;16:175–82.

Grewal DS, Hathiram BT, Agarwal R, et al. Otitic hydrocephalus of tubercular origin: a rare cause. J Laryngol Otol 2000;114:874–7.

Hoshino T, Miyashita H, Asai Y. Computed tomography of the temporal bone in tuberculous otitis media. J Laryngol Otol 1994;108:702–5.

Kirsch CM, Wehner JH, Jensen WA, et al. Tuberculous otitis media. South Med J 1995;88:363–6.

Lee PY, Drysdale AJ. Tuberculous otitis media: a difficult diagnosis. J Laryngol Otol 1993;107:339–41.

Linthicum Jr FH. Tuberculous otitis media. Otol Neurotol 2002;23:235–6.

Pulec JL, Deguine C. Tuberculous chronic otitis media. Ear Nose Throat J 1999;78:820.

Saunders NC, Albert DM. Tuberculous mastoiditis: when is surgery indicated? Int J Pediatr Otorhinolaryngol 2002;65:59–63.

Shaida A, Siddiqui N. Imaging quiz case 2. Tuberculous mastoiditis causing a facial palsy. Arch Otolaryngol Head Neck Surg 1998;124:341–3.

Skolnik PR, Nadol JB Jr, Baker AS. Tuberculosis of the middle ear: review of the literature with an instructive case report. Rev Infect Dis 1986;8:403–10.

Chapter 105

Treatment of Otitis Media in the Managed Care Environment

Charles M. Myer III, MD

The prevalence and cost of treatment of otitis media (OM) in the pediatric age group have a profound effect on the current health care system. During the past decade, there has been an increase in day-care attendance, an increase in the incidence of acute otitis media (AOM), a subsequent increase in the use of antimicrobial agents in the treatment of OM, a parallel increase in drug resistance among the causative bacterial agents, and a resultant increase in the cost of treatment, both directly and indirectly. These changes have taken place during a time when managed care has increased substantially. Therefore, it is imperative that clinicians understand how these changes in the management of OM interact with changes in our health care system.

Other than well-child care, AOM is the leading reason for pediatric physician visits in the United States. It has been estimated that the diagnosis of OM accounted for about 10 million visits in 1975 and subsequently almost 25 million visits in 1990 (Rosenfeld, 1996). In all likelihood, this diagnosis is even more common today. The greatest increase in physician visits occurred in those children under 2 years of age (224%), but there were smaller increases in all age groups up until the age of 10 years. No increases were seen in children over 10 years of age or in adults (Schappert, 1992). Approximately 80% of children will have experienced at least one episode of AOM by the time they reach 3 years of age (Carlson and Seay, 1999). In the United States alone, over 20 million episodes of AOM occur each year (Dagan, 2000).

With AOM accounting for approximately half of all pediatric diagnoses made and with antimicrobial therapy being used with almost each infection, the impact that this condition has on our current health care system, including managed care, is startling (Carlson and Seay, 1999). The direct and indirect costs for treatment of this condition are estimated at approximately 5 billion dollars per year in the United States (Gates, 1999). To make a significant impact on the cost associated with OM, disease prevention must play a prime role in the overall plan to achieve cost reduction. Helping physicians and parents understand the risk factors associated with OM is valuable in attempting to minimize the number of cases of this infectious disease. Unfortunately, some of the risk factors associated with OM are not controllable, including its prevalence in children under 2 years of age, male gender, genetic predisposition, children with older siblings, early onset of OM, low socioeconomic status, inhalant allergies, ethnic background, craniofacial malformation, and immature or impaired immunologic function (Klein, 2000).

However, there are conditions that can be controlled within a household that may minimize the number of episodes of OM. Although it may not be possible to eliminate more than several of these potential factors associated with OM in any one individual, the cumulative benefit of such an educational process may be significant in terms of cost savings for the overall health care system (Bluestone and Klein, 1996).

Over the past two decades, health care coverage in the United States has been dictated by growth of the "managed care environment." As such, third-party payers often have dictated which primary care physicians patients may choose, if they may see a specialist, which specialist they may see, and, frequently, which drugs may be used to treat OM. This system has attempted to make the primary care physician the "managing partner" in all health care matters involving an individual patient. Thus, access to specialists and some current methods of treatment may have been limited. Unfortunately, no studies exist that demonstrate the superiority of this form of care as opposed to that which took place previously. It is with this background that this chapter is presented, detailing the impact of managed care on the care of the patient with AOM and otitis media with effusion (OME).

Decreasing Exposure to Antibiotics

The management of OM begins with an accurate diagnosis by the clinician that is appropriately communicated to parents using correct terminology. Specifically, physicians must understand the difference between AOM and OME. In fact, patients with AOM almost always present with signs and symptoms of acute infection, which are frequently systemic and are lacking in children with OME. Although middle ear effusion (MEE) and hearing loss are present in both conditions in almost all situations, the presence of systemic signs and symptoms is limited to those children with acute disease. When children are seen following treatment of AOM, MEE is frequently present for several months. It is crucial that the clinician communicate this to families using appropriate terminology so that their expectation is not for administration of another antimicrobial agent. Administration of unnecessary antimicrobial agents can be minimized by avoiding follow-up visits of AOM at the traditional 2-week mark, where MEE is commonly expected. When children return at this time, physicians often indicate to parents that the child still has "an infection" when, in fact, there is an effusion present. In this situation, the expectation of the parent and, consequently, the physician is administration of an antimicrobial agent. In almost all situations, this translates into a second-line agent that is more expensive and has a broader antimicrobial spectrum. Multiplied by millions of patient care visits, the cost to the health care system can be staggering in terms of monetary expenses in addition to an increase in bacterial resistance. Thus, accurate diagnosis must be accompanied by clear and understandable transmission of this information to families so as to minimize their expectations for unnecessary antimicrobial agents. Furthermore, physicians would be wise to delay follow-up of these patients after treatment of an episode of AOM to minimize the unnecessary administration of an antimicrobial agent for the treatment of MEE that is likely to be present. In the asymptomatic child, one might consider seeing the patient approximately 6 or 8 weeks following initiation of treatment instead of the traditional 2 weeks to minimize the risk of prescribing antimicrobial agents unnecessarily.

As indicated previously, the cost (Gates, 1999) associated with OM can be minimized by an accurate diagnosis. In addition to using the appropriate terminology, physicians must improve their skills in the diagnosis of OM to ensure accuracy. A study using simulation technology demonstrated that pediatricians were correct only about 50% of the time in differentiating between the physical findings of AOM and OME. Otolaryngologists, on the other hand, were correct approximately

75% of the time in their diagnosis of these conditions. With this in mind, it is important for both primary care physicians and otolaryngologists to work on their diagnostic skills continuously as diagnostic accuracy will minimize administration of antimicrobial therapy unnecessarily (Pichichero and Poole, 2001). The use of tympanocentesis as a diagnostic procedure should be considered also, especially in children with severe otalgia, those who are seriously ill, or those who appear toxic. In addition, this technique may be helpful in those patients who exhibit an unsatisfactory response to antimicrobial therapy, those who develop OM while receiving antimicrobial therapy for another indication, those with a confirmed or potential suppurative complication, and when OM develops in a newborn, a sick neonate, or an immunologically deficient patient, any of whom may harbor an unusual organism and for whom an alternative antimicrobial agent may be necessary (Bluestone and Klein, 1996).

As indicated previously, rational use of antimicrobial therapy begins with making the proper diagnosis. I firmly believe that the unnecessary and inappropriate use of antimicrobial therapy in the treatment of OM is most glaring in the treatment of an effusion inaccurately diagnosed as AOM. Before choosing an antimicrobial agent, the physician must remember that there is a favorable natural history associated with most episodes of AOM and some children may be suitable for observation alone. Specifically, approximately 80% of AOM episodes improve spontaneously within a few days, and eight children must receive antimicrobial therapy to improve one. If close follow-up can be ensured, suppurative complications often seen with AOM are not increased with initial observation (Rosenfeld et al, 2001).

Vaccination

One of the more recent developments for prophylaxis of OM is the conjugate pneumococcal vaccine. The true purpose of this vaccine is the prevention of invasive pneumococcal disease such as meningitis and sepsis. In addition, there will be some degree of protection from *Streptococcus pneumoniae* OM, and, consequently, there will be fewer tympanostomy tubes placed. Unfortunately, physicians frequently try to influence their patients to take this vaccine because of the potential otologic benefits, discounting the intent of this vaccine for the prevention of serious disease. In some cases, because parents may view vaccines with skepticism, the vaccine is not taken because of the parental perception of OM as a relatively minor problem for which the risk of a vaccine is not warranted. Physicians should educate parents regarding the true intent of the vaccine to increase the likelihood that the vaccine is given. Any benefit that a patient receives in diminishing the incidence of OM is helpful, but this should not be the major reason for receiving the pneumococcal vaccine (Klein, 2000).

Individualizing Antibiotic Choices

Although general guidelines can be established, one must individualize whether a patient should receive antimicrobial therapy at the time of diagnosis or if a period of observation is appropriate. Because most children with AOM under 2 years of age have lower rates of clinical and bacteriologic resolution, it is generally recommended that these patients receive treatment early on. Similarly, patients who appear toxic (severe otalgia and fever greater than 39°C orally) would derive benefit from early treatment also (Rosenfeld et al, 2001).

Another means of decreasing exposure to antibiotics and thus minimizing the development of bacterial resistance would be to treat for shorter periods of time. Again, those patients who are quite young or seriously ill generally derive benefit from treatment for at least 7 to 10 days as opposed to restricting treatment to 5 days or fewer. Similarly, if one is unsure of the diagnosis of AOM in a patient older than 2 years of age, one might consider delaying therapy if good follow-up can be ensured. In general, the use of amoxicillin as a first-line agent is appropriate, considering high-dose therapy in those children who are under 2 years of age, those who are in day-care settings, and those who have been treated within the past month with an antimicrobial agent. Because most studies are relatively small and because there is a good spontaneous resolution rate for AOM, clinical investigations rarely show a difference between different antimicrobial agents for the treatment of AOM (Rosenfeld et al, 2001). However, one may choose a broad-spectrum agent for AOM relapses, treatment failures, or complicated cases, developing a protocol similar to the algorithm developed by the Drug-resistant *Streptococcus pneumoniae* Therapeutic Working Group (Dowell et al, 1999). Understanding the role of antimicrobial therapy to limit inappropriate prescribing is key to minimizing cost expenditure for the treatment of OM. It has been shown that up to 50% of parents will try to influence the pediatrician to prescribe antibiotics when drugs are not indicated. Unfortunately, approximately 33% of pediatricians admit that they have complied with parental wishes at least occasionally (McCracken, 1999). Not only do parents ask for antibiotics for their child, they also often ask for a specific agent, usually one that is relatively broad spectrum (Klein, 2000). Through advertising and previous experience with their physician, parents have been conditioned to believe that antimicrobial agents are necessary to cure all infectious and inflammatory processes (Carlson and Seay, 1999). As a result, bacterial resistance rates are increasing, and, coincidentally, the cost to treat OM is increasing substantially as well.

Third-Party Constraints

Although physicians and parents may influence some of the problems associated with the treatment of OM, insurers also play a significant role by the development of restrictive formularies and cost containment measures that may impact the treatment of AOM. The constraints may limit the antimicrobial choices of physicians, and, as a result, physicians may be forced to select a drug that is not optimal for their particular patient. Where effectiveness and safety of various drugs are relatively similar, patient compliance becomes one of the prime factors in choosing an agent. If a third-party payer limits physician choice based strictly on cost, the physician may not be able to prescribe that agent that will ensure compliance and effective administration of the drug. As a result, drug therapy may fail because of compliance issues, not infectious disease issues.

Prophylaxis Avoidance

Antimicrobial prophylaxis has been used for many years to minimize the development of AOM (Bluestone and Klein, 1996). Although this may be effective for the individual patient, one must consider what the cost may be for society as bacterial resistance rates increase. Use of prophylaxis should be individualized and limited to amoxicillin and sulfisoxazole in general. Use should be limited to the respiratory season, and, if infections continue on a year-round basis, surgical intervention may be more appropriate than continuation of prophylaxis. Alternatively, if prophylaxis is chosen, one might choose to limit administration of the prophylactic agent to episodes of actual upper respiratory infections, thus further limiting exposure of the patient and, hopefully, minimizing the development of resistant bacterial organisms.

Surgical Intervention

As an alternative to antimicrobial prophylaxis for the treatment of recurrent AOM, ventilating tube placement should be considered. The overall cost to the population may be less with surgical treatment if one considers the diminished cost (Gates, 1999) associated with fewer physician visits, fewer antibiotic prescriptions, and the time lost from work. In addition to recurrent AOM, other general indications for tympanostomy tube insertion include persistent MEE refractory to antimicrobial therapy (3 months when bilateral or 6 months when unilateral); persistent episodes of MEE in which the criteria do not meet the definition noted previously but the cumulative duration is considered excessive, such as an effusion present for 6 of the previous 12 months; intracranial or intratemporal complications; eustachian tube dysfunction characterized by pain, hearing loss, vertigo, tinnitus, or severe retraction; and barotrauma (Bluestone and Klein, 1996). Additionally, adenoidectomy may be effective in certain patients for the prevention of recurrent episodes of OM. In most situations, this is reserved for patients who have had a prior set of ventilating tubes but may be considered in the young patient receiving an initial set of tubes when there is significant nasal obstruction. Tonsillectomy may play some role in the treatment of children with OM, but its efficacy is less certain and, in general, the risk-to-benefit ratio does not favor tonsillectomy as a primary form of treatment for OM (Paradise et al, 1999).

Conclusion

AOM accounts for a large portion of all pediatric physician visits and antimicrobial prescriptions. Studies have shown, however, that the spontaneous cure rate for AOM treated with analgesics differs little from the cure rate for OM treated with antibiotics, especially in children over 2 years of age. As a result, the concept of withholding antimicrobial therapy for certain patient populations has been advocated. One must keep in mind both the economic and noneconomic costs associated with the decision to withhold therapy, specifically the development of antibiotic resistance, by combining improved diagnostic skills with better treatment regimens so that patients can receive excellent care at a decreased cost, an appropriate goal in this era of managed care.

References

Bluestone CD, Klein JD. Otitis media, atelectasis and eustachian tube dysfunction. In: Bluestone CD, Stool SE, Kenna MA, editors. Pediatric otolaryngology. 3rd ed. Philadelphia: WB Saunders; 1996. p. 383–582.

Carlson D, Seay R. Drug therapy: AOM program focuses on antibiotics usage. Drug Benefit Trends 1999;11:40–2, 45–7.

Dagan R. Clinical significance of resistant organisms in otitis media. Pediatr Infect Dis J 2000;19:378–82.

Dowell SF, Butler JC, Giebink GS, et al. AOM: management and surveillance in an era of pneumococcal resistance—a report from the Drug-resistant *Streptococcus pneumoniae* Therapeutic Working Group. Pediatr Infect Dis J 1999;18:1–9.

Gates GA. Otitis media—the pharyngeal connection. JAMA 1999;282:987–9.

Klein JD. Management of otitis media: 2000 and beyond. Pediatr Infect Dis J 2000;19:383–7.

McCracken GH Jr. Prescribing antimicrobial agents for treatment of AOM. Pediatr Infect Dis J 1999;18:1141–6.

Paradise JL, Bluestone CD, Colborn DK, et al. Adenoidectomy and adenotonsillectomy for recurrent otitis media: parallel randomized clinical trials in children not previously treated with tympanostomy tubes. JAMA 1999;282:945–53.

Pichichero ME, Poole MD. Assessing diagnostic accuracy and tympanocentesis skills in the management of otitis media. Arch Pediatr Adolesc Med 2001;155:1137–42.

Rosenfeld RM, Casselbrant ML, Hannley MT. Implications of the AHRQ evidence report on AOM. Otolaryngol Head Neck Surg 2001;125:440–8.

Rosenfeld RM. An evidence-based approach to treating otitis media. Pediatr Clin North Am 1996;43:1171–81.

Schappert SM. Office visits for otitis media: United States, 1975–90. Adv Data 1992;214:1–19.

Chapter 106

Cost-Effectiveness in Treatment of Otitis Media

Glenn S. Takata, MD, MS, Linda S. Chan, PhD

Cost-effectiveness analysis (CEA) as an analytic method has not been fully used in assessing treatment alternatives for otitis media (OM) in the published literature. To conduct CEA, treatment outcome and cost data must both be available to determine if any desirable effects of treatment outweigh the resources used to effect that treatment. Elsewhere in this book, evidence on the efficacy of OM treatments is described, but study design issues weaken the validity and generalizability of those findings. Studies have been published that estimate the cost of OM to society, but these estimates are not linked to OM outcomes. Although the ultimate test of treatment alternatives for OM rests on their cost-effectiveness in the patient care setting, the cost-effectiveness literature for treatment of OM that exists is limited and unlikely to lead to generalizable, informed decisions on treatment for large numbers of individual patients or societal health policy.

Study design deficiencies make it difficult to generalize findings on the efficacy of OM treatment alternatives for use in CEA despite attempts to control experimental conditions and relevant clinical factors. The initial dilemma for OM treatment lies in the observation that the term OM encompasses a wide array of conditions whose definitions are not consistent among the community of researchers and clinicians who study and treat OM. To facilitate generalization of a study's findings for direct use in clinical practice or in CEA, it is necessary to agree on definitions for the condition being evaluated, for example, acute otitis media (AOM), recurrent otitis media (ROM), chronic otitis media, otitis media with effusion (OME), persistent OME, or other OM-related conditions. Unfortunately, such agreement has not been reached. Other factors may also be of importance to treatment outcome, including, but not limited to, the age of the patient, comorbid conditions, and socioeconomic factors. The efficacy studies examining the impact of these factors are few considering the general acceptance of their import and the large number of studies that have been published. Further-

more, the same outcomes are not measured in all studies. Moreover, when similar outcomes are present, definitions often differ. The paucity of outcome data from OM treatment efficacy studies that address these three very basic methodologic issues makes it difficult to conduct meaningful CEAs on OM treatment. In contrast, the important issues of OM-specific health status and OM-specific outcome preferences have been studied by Rosenfeld and colleagues (1997), Alsarraf and colleagues (1998), Bisonni and colleagues (1991), Oh and colleagues (1996), and Bergus and Lofgren (1998).

Several estimates have been made on the societal cost of OM in the United States. In a recent evidence analysis, it was estimated that the total national cost of AOM in 1995 was $2.98 billion, taking into account direct and indirect costs and including episodes of OME and chronic OM resulting from AOM (Takata et al, 1999). Gates (1996) placed the annual national total cost of AOM at $3.15 billion in the 0- to 4-year age group in the early or mid-1990s. Stool and Field (1989) put the cost of OM at $2.4 to 3.3 billion in the 0- to 6-year age group in the mid- or late 1980s. Gates (1996) and Stool and Field (1989) included some indirect as well as direct costs in their estimates. Using figures provided by Berman and colleagues (1997), the annual medical cost of persistent middle ear effusion for children aged 0 to 1 year old in Colorado would have been $1.37 to $4.92 billion. Stool and colleagues (1994), using claims data from health insurers, estimated that the national total cost of OME was $1.09 billion in 1991. Despite the possible weaknesses of these estimates (Takata et al, 1999), the costs of OM are generally considered high. However, none of these studies link these costs to OM treatment outcomes. In addition, several studies have estimated the costs of various components of OM care, including Berman and colleagues (1997), Kaplan and colleagues (1997), Alsarraf and colleagues (1999), Niemelä and colleagues (1999), and Bondy and colleagues (2000), in addition to the cost analyses described below.

Cost-Effectiveness Analysis

Even if one assumes that OM treatments are efficacious in controlled, experimental conditions and although we have demonstrated that society spends a considerable amount of money on OM treatment, do we know if a particular treatment will work in the uncontrolled clinical setting and yield desirable outcomes that outweigh the cost of the treatment? CEA, defined by Garber and colleagues (1996) as "a method designed to assess the comparative impacts of expenditures on different health interventions," can be designed to accomplish such a reality-based assessment to inform decisions on choosing between OM treatment alternatives. Some may worry that CEA sacrifices individual well-being to societal well-being, but Garber and colleagues (1996) noted that "the overall welfare of society is a function of individual preferences [where] individuals maximize a well-defined preference function [that is] their 'utility' or sense of well-being." Cost-utility analysis (CUA) incorporates patient preferences of outcomes into CEA.

How can we evaluate if a CEA is of high quality? A consensus of experts convened by the US Public Health Service to standardize the conduct of CEA to allow for comparison between studies recommended that a "Reference Case" analysis be included in all CEAs (Gold et al, 1996). The general considerations of the Reference Case are paraphrased as follows for the treatment of OM:

- The Reference Case perspective is societal.
  - Effectiveness incorporates both benefits and harms of OM treatment alternatives.
  - Study boundaries should be broad enough to encompass the range of children affected by the OM treatment alternative and all types of cost and health consequences.
  - The time horizon should be long enough to include all relevant future effects of the OM treatment alternative.
  - The decision to include a cost or health effect in a CEA should involve a reasonable balance between expense and difficulty and potential importance in the analysis.
- The Reference Case should compare the OM treatment alternative to existing practice and to other relevant alternatives, such as best available, viable low cost, or "do nothing." If the intensity of the alternative in terms of duration or frequency is relevant, it should be included in the analysis.
- The resource consumption estimates and relevant effects of the OM treatment alternatives should be estimated for the group of children actually affected by the treatment.

Specific considerations regarding outcomes, costs, discounting, uncertainty, and reporting guidelines for the Reference Case are detailed by Gold and colleagues (1996).

One must also keep in mind that CEA is not equivalent to cost-minimization analysis (CMA), cost-consequence analysis (CCA), or cost-benefit analysis (CBA) (Torrance et al, 1996). CMA assumes that the effectiveness of the treatment alternatives is equivalent, so the emphasis of the analysis is on costs. In CCA, the costs and consequences of treatment are listed separately for each alternative without linking the two. CBA translates all treatment outcomes into dollar equivalents and compares them with costs that are also in dollar equivalents.

Otitis Media CEA

The literature for economic evaluations of therapies for treating OM includes 11 studies published since 1965. One of these studies was undertaken in Nigeria (Amadasun, 1997) and is not described here in further detail because of potential differences in medical care costs and practices between that country and the United States. Five studies explicitly addressed treatments for AOM (Branthaver et al, 1997; Callahan, 1988; Landholt and Kotschwar, 1994; Oh et al, 1996; Weiss and Melman, 1988). Two studies addressed ROM (Banz et al, 1998; Bisonni et al, 1991), two addressed persistent OME (Berman et al, 1994; Hartman et al, 2001), and one addressed unspecified OM (Lieu et al, 2000).

The population characteristics and interventions of the 10 studies are summarized in Tables 106-1 and 106-2. Except in the broadest terms, the five economic evaluations of antibiotic treatments for AOM have little in common apart from the fact that they all evaluated antibiotics and that four of the studies used decision-analysis models. In four studies, amoxicillin-clavulanate was compared with one or more other antibiotic therapies. In the fourth study (Weiss and Melman, 1988), amoxicillin was compared with cefaclor. Only two of the studies specified the dosage and schedule of antibiotic treatments. Oh and colleagues (1996) looked at second-line therapy, whereas the others looked at first-line therapy. The two economic evaluations of recurrent OM assessed two very different treatment comparisons. Bisonni and colleagues (1991) evaluated tympanostomy tubes versus antibiotics, whereas Banz and colleagues (1994) evaluated ribosomal immunotherapy, an uncommon treatment option, versus no intervention. Both studies on persistent OME looked at tympanostomy tubes and no intervention as initial treatment, but Berman and colleagues (1994) also looked at antibiotics and corticosteroids. Lieu and colleagues (2000) looked at the effect of pneumococcal vaccine on unspecified OM. Most of the observation periods were relatively short, and only one study looked at quality-adjusted life-days (Oh et al, 1996) and one looked at longer-term outcome (Hartman et al, 2001). In those studies that mentioned a time frame, only one looked at the total life span (Lieu et al, 2000).

Analytic Methods in Otitis Media CEA

The salient elements of the analytic approach used in the 10 studies are summarized in Table 106-3. Five used CMAs, whereas two used CUAs and three used CEAs. Three of the five CUA and CEAs presented the societal perspective. Three of the CMAs, which were framed as CEAs with the assumption of equal outcomes, were reported to be from the societal perspective. Indirect costs were included in five of the studies, and six included the side effects of treatment. The cost of therapy and treatment efficacy estimates were derived from various sources. None of the studies examined or estimated the costs of long-term sequelae of failed treatments such as recurrences of illness, surgery, or patient hearing loss, but Hartman and colleagues (2001) looked at language development. Seven of the studies did sensitivity analyses, in some cases rather limited, to test the robustness of their results. Although Banz and colleagues (1994) clearly state that their study was funded by the manufacturer, it is not clear if that was the case in the other studies.

Results of Otitis Media CEA

Findings as to the most cost-effective antibiotic therapy for AOM differ (see Table 106-1). In the CUA study, cefaclor seemed to be more cost-effective than amoxicillin-clavulanate or erythromycin-sulfamethoxazole as second-line therapy (Oh et al, 1996). In the CEA study, it was concluded that cefaclor was more cost-effective than amoxicillin, amoxicillin-clavulanate, and erythromycin-sulfisoxazole (Branthaver et al, 1997). In the cost-minimization studies, amoxicillin was judged less costly than cefaclor in one study (Weiss and Melman, 1988), trimethoprim-sulfamethoxazole was less costly than four alternative antibiotics in another (Callahan, 1988), and amoxicillin-clavulanate and cefpodoxime-proxetil were cost-neutral in another study (Landholt and Kotschwar, 1994). The specific results of the AOM studies differ as well. Oh and colleagues (1996) found that cefaclor and amoxicillin-clavulanate produced nearly identical quality-adjusted life-days but that direct treatment costs with cefaclor were 10% lower per patient than the direct costs of amoxicillin-clavulanate. Conversely, Weiss and Melman (1988) concluded that cefaclor yielded a 5% higher treatment cost per patient than amoxicillin. Finally, Branthaver and colleagues (1997) reported no differences in the direct costs per patient of five antibiotic therapies, including amoxicillin, amoxicillin-clavulanate, and cefaclor, but that cefaclor and trimethoprim-sulfamethoxazole produced a higher cure rate. These conflicting findings make it unclear whether the treatment cost of cefaclor is higher than, lower than, or the same as the treatment cost of amoxicillin and other antibiotics.

In the CUA/CEAs of recurrent OM, Bisonni and colleagues (1991) found that antibiotic chemoprophylaxis

TABLE 106-1. Summary of Study Population Characteristics, Interventions, and Results of Cost Analyses of Therapies for Acute Otitis Media

Baseline Characteristics	Oh et al (1996)	Branthaver et al (1997)	Landholt and Kotschwar (1994)	Weiss and Melman (1988)	Callahan (1988)
Location/site/date	Canada/unspecified/1992	Rockville, MD/staff model HMO/1990	US/unspecified/1991–1993	US/unspecified/1987–1988?	Ft. Hood, TX/military hospital/1987
Patient age	2 mo–18 yr	0–7 yr	6 mo–12 yr	Unspecified	Unspecified
Interventions	Second-line antibiotics: C 40 mg/kg ÷ tid; AC 40 mg/10 mg/kg ÷ tid; ES 50 mg/150 mg/kg ÷ tid (duration unspecified)	First-line antibiotics: A, AC, C, ES, or TS (dose, schedule, duration unspecified)	First-line antibiotics: AC 40 mg/kg ÷ tid for 10 d; CP 10 mg/kg ÷ bid for 10 d	First-line antibiotics: A or C (dose, schedule, and duration unspecified)	First-line antibiotics: A, C, ES, AC, or TS; Second-line antibiotic: AC for first-line failures (dose, schedule, duration unspecified except C: tid × 10 d or bid × 10 d or bid × 5 d)
Observation period	30 d	8 wk	30 d?	Unspecified	Unspecified
Health outcome(s)	QALD	Cure/no cure	OM severity score Cure/no cure	Cure/no cure	Cure/no cure
Baseline results	QALDs/case, cost/QALD (1994 USD): C: 28.15, $3.84; AC: 27.98, $4.25; ES: 28.03, $4.28	Cost/case (USD): not different cure rates: TS and C highest, ES lowest; Cost-effectiveness: TS highest, AC lowest	Costs/episode (1994 USD) (comparable cure rates) (1994): AC: $108.55, CP: $109.29 statistically insignificant	Cost/case (USD) (comparable cure rates) (1997): A: $68.57, C: $72.83 statistically significant?	Cost/patient (1997 USD) (comparable cure rates) (1997): A: $6.44, ES: $10.80, TS: $40.64, C: $14.17 (bid × 10 d), AC: $188.08

A = amoxicillin; AC = amoxicillin-clavulanate; C = cefaclor; CP = cefpodoxime; ES = erythromycin-sulfisoxazole; HMO = health maintenance organization; OM = otitis media; QALD = quality-adjusted life-days; TS = trimethoprim-sulfamethoxazole.

TABLE 106-2. Summary of Study Population Characteristics, Interventions, and Results of Cost Analyses of Therapies for Recurrent Otitis Media, Persistent Otitis Media with Effusion, and Unspecified Otitis Media

Baseline Characteristics	ROM		Persistent OME		Unspecified OM
	Bisonni et al (1991)	Banz et al (1994)	Berman et al (1994)	Hartman et al (2001)	Lieu et al (2000)
Location/site/date	US/unspecified/unspecified	France/unspecified/ 1993	Colorado/unspecified/ 1992	The Netherlands/ unspecified/1998–1999	US/unspecified/ 1997
Patient age	Unspecified	Unspecified	13 mo	19 mo	Birth cohort
Interventions	Preventive treatment: tubes* or AB	Preventive treatment: RI or NI	First-line treatment: OBS, AB, CO, CO + AB, or VT; 3-wk follow-up: non-VT options for first-line failures; 6-week follow-up: VT for 3-wk failures	First-line treatment: VT or NI	Pneumococcal vaccine: routine infant or no vaccine
Observation period	unspecified	6 winter mo	6 mo	1 yr	Birth to death
Health outcome(s)	Cure/no cure	AOM in 6 mo	Cure/no cure	Time without effusion, language development	OM episodes averted
Baseline results	Cost/case (USD): tubes*: $396.44; AB: $281.30; Utility (0–1, ie, less to more desirable): tubes: 0.9325; AB: 0.9476	Cost/case (French francs): RI: 1364 francs; NI: 2134 francs	Cost/case (USD): CO + AB/AB: $720.12; VT: $1372.17	Cost/patient (1998 USD): VT: $454; NI: $120	Cost/averted OM episode (1997 USD): routine infant: $160 ($58/vaccine dose)

*Tubes = polyethylene tubes inserted into tympanic membrane with antibiotics for 1 week and up to two tube reinsertions and six visits and antibiotic eardrops for recurrences.

AB = antibiotics for 7 to 10 days followed by chemoprophylaxis for 6 months with failures treated with tubes, AOM = acute otitis media; CO = corticosteroid; NI = no intervention; OBS = observation; OM = otitis media; OME = otitis media with effusion; RI = ribosomal immunotherapy; VT = ventilating tubes (with follow-up at 1 month and 6 months).

had a favorable cost per patient and a slightly favorable utility compared with tympanostomy tubes, and Banz and colleagues (1994) found that ribosomal immunotherapy was more cost-effective than no intervention. Costs appeared to be the dominant factor in the tympanostomy tube versus chemoprophylaxis CUA. The ribosomal immunotherapy baseline results did not change with the severity of the ROM.

In the cost analysis of persistent OME after AOM, Berman and colleagues (1997) concluded that the alternative of corticosteroids plus antibiotics at the initial visit with antibiotics for treatment failures at the 3-week follow-up and tympanostomy tubes at the final 6-week follow-up was the most cost-effective and that tympanostomy tubes used at the initial visit were the least cost-effective, assuming equal outcomes. These results appeared to hold within the 95% confidence limits of the treatment efficacy rates. Hartman and colleagues (2001) found that no intervention had a lower cost for the same outcome compared with tympanostomy tubes for first-line treatment of persistent OME.

The CEA on the impact of pneumococcal vaccine on aversion of unspecified OM resulted in a reasonable cost under the assumptions of the study. In particular, it estimated a vaccine cost of $58 per dose (Lieu et al, 2000). However, varying the study assumptions did result in changes in the cost per averted OM episode.

Conclusions from Otitis Media CEA

The evaluative economic literature on treatments for OM is too small, its methodologies too varied, and its findings too inconsistent to provide a clear-cut guide for choosing the most cost-effective therapies. For example, in the case of antibiotics and AOM, one possible reason for the inconsistencies in results is that the total treatment costs of antibiotics such as amoxicillin and cefaclor may not be greatly different. Two of the five studies discussed here did claim that there appeared to be nonsignificant differences in the total treatment costs of alternative antibiotics (Oh et al, 1996; Weiss and Melman, 1988). Even the two studies that favored one antibiotic over another did not report large differences in efficacy and treatment costs, and it is conceivable that true efficacy rates and direct treatment costs do not differ materially among several of the antibiotic alternatives.

As with any economic analysis, whether one accepts the findings depends on the modeling of the treatment alternatives and the validity of the cost and efficacy assumptions. In the area of OM, the validity of treatment efficacy data is hindered by the various study design issues mentioned earlier. We advise readers to evaluate the model, cost, and efficacy assumptions of the original articles cited in this chapter before making practice or policy decisions based on the necessarily brief discussion presented here.

TABLE 106-3. Key Methodologic Characteristics of Otitis Media Cost Analyses

Methodologic Factor	Characteristics	AOM (n = 5)	ROM (n = 2)	Persistent OME (n = 2)	Unspecified OM (n = 1)
Methodology	CUA	a	f		
	CEA	b	g		j
	CMA	c, d, e		h,i	
Analytic technique	DA	a, b, d, e	f, g	h	j
	RCT			i	
	RDA	b, c			
Perspective	Societal	a, b, c, d		i	j
	Health payor		f, g	h	j
	Hospital	e			
	Patient	c	g	h	
Indirect costs in analysis	Included	d	g	h, i	j
	Not included	a, b, c, e	f		
Side effects in analysis	Included	a, b, c	f, g		j
	Not included	d, e		h,i	
Utilization estimate source	Literature	e	g	h,i	
	National data		g		
	HMO/hospital data	b, e	f		j
	Authors' data	b, c, d			
	MD survey	a	g		
Unit cost estimate source	Literature			h	
	Authors' data	c, d			
	International data		g		
	National/state data		g	h, i	
	HMO/hospital data	a, b, e	f	i	j
Efficacy estimate source	Literature	a, d, e	f, g	h	j
	National/local data				j
	HMO/hospital data	b			
	Authors' data	c		i	
	Expert panel				j
	Authors' estimate		g		
	MD survey	a			
Sensitivity analysis	Conducted	a, d	f, g	h, i	j
	Not conducted	b, c, e			

AOM = acute otitis media; CCA = cost-consequence analysis; CEA = cost-effectiveness analysis; CMA = cost-minimization analysis; CUA = cost-utility analysis; DA = decision analysis; HMO = health maintenance organization; OM = otitis media; OME = otitis media with effusion; RCT = randomized, controlled trial; RDA = retrospective data analysis; ROM = recurrent otitis media. a = Oh et al, 1996; b = Branthaver et al 1997; c = Landholt and Kotschwar, 1994; d = Weiss and Melman, 1988; e = Callahan, 1988; f = Bisonni et al, 1991; g = Banz et al, 1994; h = Berman et al, 1994; i = Hartman et al, 2001; j = Lieu et al, 2000.

Several research issues should be addressed in future CEAs of therapies for OM:

- CUAs or CEAs should be performed rather than CMAs unless the assumption of equivalent outcomes is well established.
- Large national representative databases should be used for determining medical care use and prices.
- A societal perspective should be adopted, and indirect illness and treatment costs should be incorporated in evaluative studies.
- A standard generic measure of the health benefits of treatment, such as quality-adjusted or healthy life-years (or days), should be adopted and used in CEAs to allow comparability of study results. Quality of life in OM has recently become a research issue (Alsarraf et al, 1998; Rosenfeld et al, 1997).
- The costs and health benefits of treatment failures and complications and long-term sequelae should be recognized and incorporated into evaluations of treatments for OM.

Acknowledgment

We thank Richard Ernst, PhD, for giving us permission to use materials from his prior review of the cost literature on AOM that was included in an evidence report on the management of AOM (Takata et al, 1999). However, the authors of this chapter are fully responsible for its contents.

References

Alsarraf R, Jung CJ, Perkins J, et al. Otitis media health status evaluation: a pilot study for the investigation of cost-effective outcomes of recurrent acute otitis media treatment. Ann Otol Rhinol Laryngol 1998;107:120–8.

Alsarraf R, Jung CJ, Perkins J, et al. Measuring the indirect and direct costs of acute otitis media. Arch Otolaryngol Head Neck Surg 1999;125:12–8.

Amadasun JE. The cost effective medical treatment of suppurative otitis media in a Nigerian environment. West Afr J Med 1997; 16:185–7.

Banz K, Schwicker D, Thomas AM. Economic evaluation of immunoprophylaxis in children with recurrent ear, nose, and throat infections. Pharmacoeconomics 1994;6:464–77.

Bergus GR, Lofgren MM. Tubes, antibiotic prophylaxis, or watchful waiting: a decision analysis for managing recurrent acute otitis media. J Fam Pract 1998;46:304–10.

Berman S, Byrns PJ, Bondy J, et al. Otitis media-related antibiotic prescribing patterns, outcomes, and expenditures in a pediatric Medicaid population. Pediatrics 1997;100:585–92.

Berman S, Roark R, Luckey D. Theoretical cost-effectiveness of management options for children with persisting middle-ear infusions. Pediatrics 1994;93:353–63.

Bisonni RS, Lawler FH, Pierce L. Recurrent otitis media: a cost-utility analysis of simulated treatment using tympanostomy tubes vs. antibiotic prophylaxis. Fam Pract Res J 1991;11:371–8.

Bondy J, Berman S, Glazner J, Lezotte D. Direct expenditures related to otitis media diagnoses: extrapolations from a pediatric Medicaid cohort. Pediatrics 2000;105:E72.

Branthaver B, Greiner DL, Eichelberger B. Determination of cost-effective treatment of acute otitis media from HMO records. Am J Health Syst Pharm 1997;54:2736–40.

Callahan CW. Cost effectiveness of antibiotic therapy for otitis media in a military pediatric clinic. Pediatr Infect Dis J 1988;7: 622–5.

Garber AM, Weinstein MC, Torrance GW, Kamlet MS. Theoretical foundations of cost-effectiveness analysis. In: Gold MR, Siegel JA, Russell LB, Weinstein MC, editors. Cost-effectiveness in health and medicine. New York: Oxford University Press; 1996. p. 25–53.

Gates GA. Cost-effectiveness considerations in otitis media treatment. Otolaryngol Head Neck Surg 1996;114:525–30.

Gold MR, Siegel JA, Russell LB, Weinstein MC, editors. Cost-effectiveness in health and medicine. New York: Oxford University Press; 1996.

Hartman M, Rovers MM, Ingels K, et al. Economic evaluation of ventilation tubes in otitis media with effusion. Arch Otolaryngol Head Neck Surg 2001;127:1471–6.

Kaplan B, Wandstrat TL, Cunningham JR. Overall cost in the treatment of otitis media. Pediatr Infect Dis J 1997;16(2 Suppl): S9–11.

Landholt TF, Kotschwar TR. A pharmacoeconomic comparison of amoxicillin/clavulanate and cefpodoxime proxetil in the treatment of acute otitis media. Clin Ther 1994;16:327–33.

Lieu TA, Thomas RG, Black SB, et al. Projected cost-effectiveness of pneumococcal conjugate vaccination of healthy infants and young children. JAMA 2000;283:1460–8.

Niemelä M, Uhari M, Möttönen M, Pokka T. Costs arising from otitis media. Acta Pædiatr 1999;88:553–6.

Oh PI, Maerov P, Pritchard D, et al. A cost-utility analysis of second-line antibiotics in the treatment of acute otitis media in children. Clin Ther 1996;18:160–82.

Rosenfeld RM, Goldsmith AJ, Tetlus L, Balzano A. Quality of life for children with otitis media. Arch Otolaryngol Head Neck Surg 1997;123:1049–54.

Stool SE, Berg AO, Berman S, et al. Otitis media with effusion in young children. Clinical practice guideline number 12. Rockville (MD): Agency for Health Care Policy and Research, Public Health Service, US Department of Health and Human Services; July 1994. AHCPR Publication No.: 94-0622.

Stool SE, Field MJ. The impact of otitis media. Pediatr Infect Dis J 1989;8 Suppl:S11–4.

Takata GS, Chan LS, Shekelle PG, et al. Management of acute otitis media. Final evidence report. Rockville (MD): Agency for Health Care Policy and Research, Public Health Service, US Department of Health and Human Services; 1999.

Torrance GW, Siegel JE, Luce BR. Framing and designing the cost-effectiveness analysis. In: Gold MR, Siegel JA, Russell LB, Weinstein MC, editors. Cost-effectiveness in health and medicine. New York: Oxford University Press; 1996. p. 54–81.

Weiss JC, Melman ST. Cost-effectiveness in the choice of antibiotics for the initial treatment of otitis media in children: a decision analysis approach. Pediatr Infect Dis J 1988;7:23–6.

Chapter 107

Treatment of Otitis Media in Regions with Limited Health Care

Amanda Leach, PhD, Peter Morris, FRACP, PhD

Little is known of the epidemiology of otitis media (OM) in developing countries and disadvantaged populations. Where studies have been conducted, the rates of the most severe form of OM (chronic suppurative otitis media [CSOM]) are often high (Ologe and Nwawolo, 2002; Rupa et al, 1999). The World Health Organization (WHO) recommends that a rate in excess of 4% defines a population with a massive public health problem requiring urgent attention (WHO/CIBA Foundation Workshop, 1996).

The health transition seen in the Western world, driven by public health reforms over the past 150 years, is now taking place in developing nations. Improved economic and social processes are gradually being translated into improvements in health. For some regions, apparent declines in the rates of CSOM have also been reported from cross-sectional survey data (Giles and Asher, 1991; Hamilton et al, 1980; Zakzouk and Hajjaj, 2002). The authors have attributed the improvements to raised awareness and school- or community-based ear health programs. This is certainly feasible. The evidence for the effectiveness of interventions for CSOM was recently comprehensively reviewed by Acuin and colleagues (2000). They found that topical antibiotics with aural toilet were the most effective treatment for resolution of otorrhea in the short term (odds ratio: 0.31; 95% confidence interval [CI]: 0.23, 0.43). High-quality studies with longer-term outcomes (including tympanic membrane healing) have not been reported.

The WHO Integrated Management of Childhood Illness (IMCI) strategy, which has been initiated in over 48 countries, currently recommends a simple approach to the management of ear infections. This includes a diagnostic algorithm that is independent of otoscopy (Gove, 1997). Antibiotic treatment is limited to 5 days, and a child without pain or discharge is considered not to have an ear infection. The restrictive nature of these clinical care guidelines very clearly illustrates the overwhelming influence of limited resources.

Disadvantaged Populations

Developing countries are not the only place where high rates of CSOM are found. Our own experience comes from working with Aboriginal children living in remote communities of the Northern Territory in Australia. These children continue to experience overwhelmingly high rates of CSOM. In a recent survey of 29 communities throughout the Northern Territory, 25% of young Aboriginal children had either CSOM or acute otitis media (AOM) with perforation, 31% had bilateral otitis media with effusion (OME), and only 7% of children had bilaterally normal middle ears (Leach et al, 2002). The enormous inequalities in health status between Aboriginal and non-Aboriginal Australians reflect a complex history of social and economic marginalization and disempowerment. This chapter describes the many challenges to the delivery of effective ear health care in this setting.

As living standards improve and as opportunities for better education and employment become available to Aboriginal people, health status will rise. There remains, however, an urgent need for the many children with CSOM and associated hearing loss to receive more immediate attention. For many years, there has been confusion surrounding the evidence for the effectiveness of medical or audiologic interventions in these children. Recent summaries of well-designed studies describe clear, although sometimes modest, benefits for the effectiveness of antibiotic regimens. The new conjugated pneumococcal vaccine is also expected to contribute to prevention of OME, AOM, AOM with perforation, and CSOM.

Disease Burden

Many factors contribute to poor health outcomes. In biologic terms, the greatest risk factor for early onset and persistence of OM is bacterial colonization of the nasopharynx (Leach et al, 1994). Early age of infection is, in turn, the result of early and frequent exposure to high doses of multiple bacterial pathogens, usually from siblings or other young household contacts. This vicious circle of early exposure, persistent colonization, and chronic disease is perpetuated by overcrowded and poor living conditions (particularly lack of washing facilities), limited access to appropriate health care services, and the low priority of non–life-threatening or chronic health conditions. For some children, the impact of other factors, such as eustachian tube dysfunction, may be critical.

Limited health care services are continually challenged by the high rates of other illnesses. The enormous health inequalities between Aboriginal and non-Aboriginal Australians are reflected by the 20-year difference in life expectancy (Australian Bureau of Statistics, 1997). For all major causes of death and ill health, Aboriginal rates far exceed those of non-Aboriginal Australians. Of specific relevance to the topic of OM are the extremely high rates of invasive pneumococcal disease (2%) (Krause et al, 2000) and chronic suppurative lung disease (5%).

Diagnosis

The diagnosis of OM is complex (Figure 107-1), and definitions vary widely throughout the world and across epidemiologic and clinical studies. These differences in definition have important implications for management and service delivery.

We believe that the most urgent need of high-risk populations is to reduce the rates of CSOM. We have found that the most important diagnostic predictor of perforation is bulging of the tympanic membrane (P. Morris,

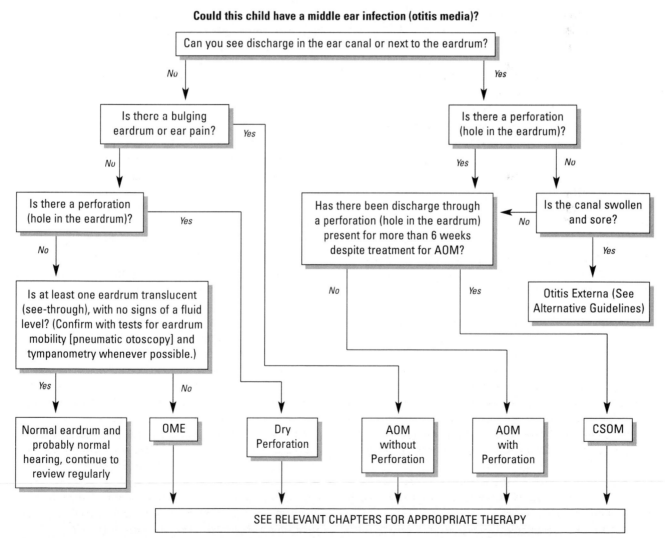

FIGURE 107-1. Algorithm for the diagnosis of OM. Reproduced with permission from Morris P et al (2001). AOM = acute otitis media; CSOM = chronic suppurative otitis media; OME = otitis media with effusion.

unpublished PhD thesis, 1998). Additional signs and symptoms, such as pain, redness, fever, or irritability, may or may not be present. In our experience, they are generally absent in this population. Initial perforations are very small. Healing and reperforation are common events. Once discharge becomes established through a larger perforation, treatment is much less likely to be successful. Persistent discharge leads to increases in the size of the perforation. In some children, the whole tympanic membrane and adjacent ossicles may be eroded. With this in mind, we recommend the following practical definitions of the most important categories of OM:

- OME is the presence of fluid behind an intact tympanic membrane without signs or symptoms consistent with suppurative infection.
- AOM without perforation is the presence of fluid behind an intact eardrum plus bulging, redness, fever, ear pain, or irritability. Bulging of the tympanic membrane is the most common indicator of AOM without perforation.
- AOM with perforation is the presence of fluid behind the tympanic membrane plus pus in the ear canal within the last 7 days, active discharge for less than 6 weeks, or discharge through a very small perforation (< 2% of the tympanic membrane).
- CSOM is the presence of active discharge through a perforation (> 2% of the tympanic membrane) for more than 6 weeks despite appropriate treatment for AOM with perforation.

The importance of obtaining both a good history to ascertain the duration of the illness and a clear view of the tympanic membrane is emphasized.

Strategic Integrated Approach to Child Health Care in Developing Countries

In developing countries with extremely limited resources, the following recommendations are all likely to be good health "buys":

- primary prevention strategies (improved home hygiene facilities and practices)
- campaigns for cheaper vaccines
- audiologic and behavioral measures that reduce the disadvantages associated with hearing loss (clear speech, gaining child's attention, checking comprehension, etc)
- antibiotics (possibly longer courses at higher doses) for the very young child with recurrent AOM with perforation
- careful assessment of CSOM with cleaning and antibiotic or antiseptic application over a long period with planned follow-up

Unfortunately, many of these recommendations have not been evaluated in well-designed studies in high-risk populations.

As discussed earlier, the WHO Department of Child and Adolescent Health and Development developed a strategy for the IMCI for use in developing countries where health resources are limited. This can be accessed at <http://www.who.int/child-adolescent-health/New_Publications/IMCI/IMCI_Info_English/pdf/inform.html> (Gove, 1997).

This strategy clearly illustrates the challenges facing health workers in regions with limited resources. Its implementation involves training and provision of locally adapted guidelines in IMCI, improved health systems, and improved family and community practices. Although a strategic integrated approach is promoted, the diagnosis and treatment of ear problems receive limited attention. Recommendations are restricted to diagnoses possible without the use of otoscopy. Acute ear infection is diagnosed on the basis of ear discharge for fewer than 14 days or ear pain. Five days of antibiotic (as for pneumonia) is recommended. A diagnosis of chronic ear infection is made where ear discharge has occurred for more than 14 days and ear wicking is the only recommended therapy. Where there is no pain or no ear discharge, no treatment is recommended.

Medical Management

Many randomized, controlled trials (RCTs) and several meta-analyses show a benefit of antibiotics in the treatment of AOM (without perforation) and OME. These trials have been conducted in low-risk populations where rates of natural cure are high and few perforations occur (Rosenfeld and Bluestone, 1999). There are no published RCTs from high-risk populations. Despite this, there is a large amount of information relevant to these children, yet comprehensive summaries are hard to find.

In 2001, the Office of Aboriginal and Torres Strait Islander Health published *Recommendations for Clinical Care Guidelines on the Management of Otitis Media in Aboriginal and Torres Strait Islander Populations* (<http://www.health.gov.au/oatsih/pubs/omp.htm>) (Morris et al, 2001). The guidelines are based on an update of a systematic review of existing evidence (Couzos et al, 2001). The aim is to provide clinicians with the information they need to deliver high-quality care for Aboriginal and Torres Strait Islander children. The level of evidence for each recommendation is given with explicit links to the original evidence studies. The guidelines also include seven algorithms for management and are unique in addressing all forms of OM (OME, chronic OME, AOM without perforation, AOM with perforation, and CSOM).

Comorbidities such as bronchitis, persistent nasal discharge, pneumonia, skin sores, or trachoma are also common in Aboriginal children. Opportunities to intervene in the progression of many problems at one time should be recognized by the health care provider. The guidelines have addressed this in the practical treatment plan with specific recommendations for the management of OM where comorbidities occur.

Although the guidelines provide excellent information on diagnosis, prognosis, and treatment, their impact on ear health service delivery has not been evaluated. All health clinics that provide care for Aboriginal and Torres Strait Islander people have received copies. However, it is well documented that dissemination of information in this way has a limited impact on practice. Assistance with implementation should also be considered an important part of the guideline production process.

Recently Completed RCTs in High-Risk Populations

We have recently completed a placebo-controlled RCT of long-term antibiotics (amoxicillin, 50 mg/kg/d, tid for up to 24 weeks) for the treatment of OME and the prevention of AOM and CSOM. One hundred and one babies under the age of 12 months and with bilateral OME were randomized. Ear examinations (video pneumatic otoscopy) and nasopharyngeal swab collection occurred every 2 to 4 weeks for up to 24 weeks. A success was defined as bilaterally aerated ears at two successive (monthly) examinations. Forty-nine babies were randomized to placebo and 52 to amoxicillin. There were 5 successes and 96 failures: 49 of 49 in the placebo group and 47 of 52 in the amoxicillin group (relative risk [RR]: 0.9; [95% CI: 0.83, 0.99], risk difference: −9.6% [95% CI: −18, −1.1], number needed to treat [NNT] = 10, Fisher exact $p = .057$). Eighty-two babies did not have a perforation at the end of their enrolment in the study and 19 had perforations: 14 of 49 (29%) in the placebo group and 5 of 52 (10%) in the amoxicillin group (RR: 0.34 [95% CI: 0.14, 0.8], risk difference = −19% [95% CI: −3.6, −34], NNT = 5, Fisher exact $p = .021$). Seventy-one babies did not have a perforation during therapy, and 29 (29%) had at least one perforation detected during therapy: 18 of 49 (37%) placebo recipients and 11 of 52 (21%) receiving amoxicillin (RR: 0.58 [95% CI: 0.3, 1.09], risk difference = −16% [95% CI: −33, 2], NNT = 6.4, Fisher exact $p = .12$). From this study, we have concluded that antibiotics have a significant benefit for severe OM in Aboriginal children and that the relative benefits are consistent with previous studies.

Audiologic Management

Hearing assessment is recommended for children with suspected hearing loss or with bilateral OM for longer than 3 months. Individual amplification systems and school classroom sound-field amplification systems are options for reducing the effects of persistent hearing loss in Aboriginal children. Families and teachers should be advised of the need for visual prompts, reduced background noise, and clear speech. Speech therapists should be involved in the management of children with speech and language delay whenever they are available.

Surgical Treatment in High-Risk Populations

Grommet surgery is a popular intervention for reversing the hearing loss associated with OME. Chronic otorrhea is a potential complication but is relatively rare in low-risk populations. In Aboriginal children, a case series of 60 procedures in 35 children documented early extrusion or infection in 38% of ears (A. Foreman, unpublished data, 1997). For these children, a transition from a mild hearing loss (mean 25 dB, range 10–40 dB) associated with OME to a moderate hearing loss (mean 35 dB, range 20–55 dB) associated with CSOM is possible. Many others report a similar experience in settings where suppurative diseases are common.

A descriptive study of operations for middle ear disease (excluding grommets) on Aboriginal patients reported a success rate of 53%; increasing age was the only variable predictive of success (Mak et al, 2000). Successful outcomes were more likely in adults and children aged > 10 years. However, success is defined surgically, and this does not take into account the importance of hearing for language acquisition and learning in young children.

Education

This is always the most important part of the primary health care consultation. Effective education should not be restricted by cost. Families should be informed of the likely impact of OM on their child's hearing, speech, language, and behavioral development. It should be explained that the level of hearing loss may vary over time and that the child may hear conversation or a raised voice only as a whisper on some days. Families also need to be informed of the need for long-term interventions, including medical treatment. Topical antibiotics may be required for as long as 16 weeks if CSOM develops. Behavioral strategies such as engaging the child's attention and using clear speech can reduce the impact of a mild hearing loss. Families also need to be aware of the importance of personal hygiene in preventing the spread of germs among small children (Roberts et al, 2000) and of the additional risk to small babies of becoming infected early in life through exposure to young children with persistent nasal discharge and a high density of bacterial pathogens.

In high-risk populations in which more than 4% of children may have CSOM, the option to involve schools

TABLE 107-1. Key Messages for Primary Health Care Providers in High-Risk Populations

Families should be informed that children are at greatly increased risk of severe OM.

Families should be encouraged to attend the local health clinic as soon as possible whenever a child develops ear pain or discharge.

Frequent ear examinations are recommended even when the child is well. Use pneumatic otoscopy or tympanometry whenever possible.

Antibiotics are recommended for children with AOM (identified by bulging ear drum or recent perforation). Antibiotics should be continued until the bulging and discharge have resolved.

CSOM should be diagnosed only in children who have persistent discharge through a perforation despite appropriate treatment for AOM with perforation. Effective treatment of CSOM requires a long-term approach to regular dry mopping of ear discharge followed by the application of topical antibiotics or antiseptics.

All children with persistent bilateral OM (all types) for greater than 3 months should have their hearing assessed.

Families of children with significant hearing loss (> 20 dB) should be informed of the benefits of improved communication strategies and hearing aids.

AOM = acute otitis media; CSOM = chronic suppurative otitis media; OM = otitis media.

in medical and audiologic management should be considered. School-based programs such as classroom sound-field amplification and delivery of medications have the capacity to significantly improve ear health (Smith et al, 1996) and reduce the disadvantages associated with hearing loss. Such arrangements may need intersectoral support from local or regional policy makers.

Conclusions

Children living in some developing countries and disadvantaged populations continue to suffer unacceptably high rates of severe OM (AOM with perforation and CSOM). In addition, the interventions available to families may be limited by their cost or the presence of other competing priorities. Despite these complexities, improvements in the quality of primary health care provided in the first 2 years of life are likely to have substantial impact (Table 107-1). Greater attention must be given to effective communication of the benefits associated with different interventions. Discussions with families about how interventions might be adopted should also be encouraged. Even when recommendations are not able to be followed as prescribed, this type of approach is likely to provide long-term benefits to affected families and their communities.

References

Acuin J, Smith A, Mackenzie I. Interventions for chronic suppurative otitis media. Cochrane Syst Rev 2000;CD000473.

Australian Bureau of Statistics. Deaths 1996. Canberra: Australia Cat No 3302.0, 1997.

Couzos S, Metcalf S, Murray R, et al. Systematic review of existing evidence and primary care guidelines on the management of otitis media in Aboriginal and Torres Strait Islander populations. Canberra: Office for Aboriginal and Torres Strait Islander Health; 2001.

Giles M, Asher I. Prevalence and natural history of otitis media with perforation in Maori school children. J Laryngol Otol 1991;105:257–60.

Gove S. Integrated management of childhood illness by outpatient health workers: technical basis and overview. The WHO working group on guidelines for integrated management of the sick child. Bull World Health Organ 1997;75 Suppl 1:7–24.

Hamilton M, McKenzies-Pollock M, Heath M. Aural health in 227 Northland school and preschool children. N Z Med J 1980;91: 59–62.

Krause VL, Reid SJ, Merianos A. Invasive pneumococcal disease in the Northern Territory of Australia, 1994–1998. Med J Aust 2000;173 Suppl:S27–31.

Leach A, Boswell J, Asche V, et al. Bacterial colonization of the nasopharynx predicts very early onset and persistence of otitis media in Australian Aboriginal infants. Pediatr Infect Dis J 1994;13:983–9.

Leach AJ, Morris PS, McCallum G, et al. What will Prevnar do for chronic suppurative otitis media in indigenous Australian children? International Symposium on Pneumococci and Pneumococcal Diseases; 2002 May 4; Anchorage.

Mak D, MacKendrick A, Weeks S, Plant AJ. Middle-ear disease in remote Aboriginal Australia: a field assessment of surgical outcomes. J Laryngol Otol 2000;114:26–32.

Morris P, Ballinger D, Leach A, et al. Recommendations for clinical care guidelines on the management of otitis media in Aboriginal and Torres Strait Islander populations. Canberra: Office of Aboriginal and Torres Strait Islander Health; 2001.

Ologe FE, Nwawolo CC. Prevalence of chronic suppurative otitis media (CSOM) among school children in a rural community in Nigeria. Niger Postgrad Med J 2002;9:63–6.

Roberts L, Smith W, Jorm L, et al. Effect of infection control measures on the frequency of upper respiratory infection in child care: a randomized, controlled trial. Pediatrics 2000;105:738–42.

Rosenfeld R, Bluestone CD. Evidence-based otitis media. Toronto: BC Decker; 1999.

Rupa V, Jacob A, Joseph A. Chronic suppurative otitis media: prevalence and practices among rural South Indian children. Int J Pediatr Otorhinolaryngol 1999;48:217–21.

Smith A, Hatcher J, Mackenzie I, et al. Randomised controlled trial of treatment of chronic suppurative otitis media in Kenyan schoolchildren. Lancet 1996;348:1128–33.

WHO/CIBA Foundation Workshop. Prevention of hearing impairment from chronic otitis media; 1996 Nov 19; London. WHO/PDH/98.4.

Zakzouk SM, Hajjaj MF. Epidemiology of chronic suppurative otitis media among Saudi children—a comparative study of two decades. Int J Pediatr Otorhinolaryngol 2002;62:215–18.

Chapter 108

PARENTAL COUNSELING IN OTITIS MEDIA

JAIMIE DE ROSA, MD, KENNETH M. GRUNDFAST, MD, FACS, FAAP

Otitis media (OM) is, on the one hand, a pervasive and troublesome childhood health problem and, on the other hand, so common as to be an expected part of growing up. The incidence of OM appears to have increased in recent years. According to the National Center for Health Statistics, the diagnosis of OM in the United States has increased from about 10 million visits in 1975 to almost 25 million in 1990. The cost of managing childhood OM in the United States is estimated to be around 5 billion dollars (Gates, 1996a). Moreover, approximately 30 million prescriptions are written annually for oral antibiotics to treat OM, representing one-fourth of all prescriptions for oral antibiotics (Bluestone, 1989). Therefore, childhood OM is common and costly and can affect children and their families, depending on the way in which ear infections are treated. Because there are many different ways to treat OM and parents should have some choice among various options for treating their children's ear infections, the more that parents know and understand about OM, the better the overall management for the child can be.

Management of OM can be viewed as a three-part relationship among the parent as primary caregiver, primary care physician (usually a pediatrician), and otolaryngologist, all of whom are involved in making decisions that affect care of the child (Grundfast and Carney, 1989). Communication among parent, primary care physician, and otolaryngologist is of paramount importance. Unfortunately, the words used to describe the middle ear disorders that affect children can be confusing: the same words can convey different meanings to various individuals involved in the care of a child. When physicians use imprecise and confusing words in describing to parents their observations during an ear examination and the diagnosis being made for a child during an office visit, parents easily become confused and frustrated. For example, when a child returns for a follow-up examination 2 weeks after diagnosis of acute otitis media (AOM) and the pediatrician who observes fluid in the middle ear says that the child's ear is "still infected," the parent often expects that a second course of antibiotic should be given because that was the treatment provided at the previous visit when the "ear infection" was initially diagnosed. But if the parent questions the pediatrician, the physician might explain that there are no signs of AOM detected and that the diagnosis is simply persistent serous effusion, which often does not need treatment with antibiotic. Perhaps even worse, when a pediatrician tells a parent that the ear "still looks gunky" or "looks icky," then the parents might wonder about the disorder that the child has and how the current condition is related to previous conditions the child has had.

The diagnosis of OM encompasses a continuum of disorders, including acute infection within the middle ear as well as persistent middle ear effusion (Rosenfeld, 1996). Clearly defining the specific disorder being treated helps the physician communicate effectively with the parent. Some succinct and easily understandable terms used to describe different types of OM are defined below.

AOM means that infection has developed recently within the middle ear. Typical symptoms of AOM are fever, irritability, and pain in the affected ear. Typical signs are a red, bulging opaque eardrum, sometimes with a yellowish hue in certain areas, that has reduced mobility when tested with a pneumatic otoscope (Bluestone, 1989). AOM usually follows an acute upper respiratory infection (Gates, 1996a), and published reports show that AOM affects at least 50% of children by age 1 year, 65% by age 2 years, and 70% of children by age 3 years (Bluestone, 1998; Rosenfeld, 1996). Nevertheless, both physicians and caregivers should be reassured that most cases of AOM resolve promptly with appropriate treatment and are rarely accompanied by complications (Gates, 1996a). Because so many children have at least one episode of AOM and because the infections usually resolve without complication or sequelae, AOM is viewed by parents and physicians as an expected part of growing up, much like upper respiratory infections. They can be frequent and troublesome but not a major risk to the overall health and well-being of the child.

Recurrent AOM (RAOM) defines the condition characterized by acute ear infections that are occurring often. Although there may not be universal agreement among physicians about how many acute ear infections are ordinary and expected versus how many are occurring too often, there is some consensus that a child who has four or more episodes of AOM within 6 consecutive months might be in need of intervention to reduce the frequency of the ear infections. Children with RAOM suffer repeatedly from the symptoms of pain and sleeplessness that accompany the ear infections. Adding to the stress of the acute illness, working parents of children who suffer from RAOM often have to get up at night to care for a child in pain, take unscheduled absences from work to bring the child to a doctor, spend time going to a pharmacy to get medications, and then miss additional time from work to take the child to follow-up doctor visits. The sensitive and caring physician should be aware of the family stress from RAOM and consider the impact of the recurring childhood illness on parents. When choosing among alternatives for the management of RAOM, the primary care physician should gather information from the parents about how the child's ear infections are affecting family members and consider which treatment fits best with the needs of the parents and is the most appropriate for the child.

Persistent otitis media with effusion (POME) can be defined as middle ear effusion persisting more than 3 months after initial detection. Approximately 90% of effusions resolve within 3 months without treatment (Gates et al, 1985; Rosenfeld, 1996). POME, also known as "glue ear," usually follows a symptomatic AOM but can occur without any prior symptoms.

Parental Confusion

Many parents have difficulty comprehending the different aspects of the continuum of OM. That is, parents do not easily understand that there is a difference between AOM that usually is treated with antibiotic and persistent middle ear effusion that does not need treatment with an antibiotic. When a primary care physician fails to explain to a parent the difference between AOM and OME, then the parent can become confused about the rationale for a recommended treatment or the reluctance of a physician to prescribe medication. Quite likely, the failure of primary care physicians and otolaryngologists to spend the time to carefully explain to parents exactly what has been observed during the ear examination and what disorder has been diagnosed has engendered some of the skepticism parents occasionally express about the seemingly conflicting types of advice they receive about how best to treat ear infections. Some frustrated parents say that their primary care doctor keeps treating ear infections with "too much medicine," and they suspect that tubes in the ears should have been recommended sooner. Conversely, some parents feel that ear specialists (otolaryngologists) are too quick to recommend inserting tubes in children's ears without clearly explaining the indications for inserting tubes and the alternative methods of management. A description of the options that should be explained in counseling parents about the treatment of ear infections follows below.

Medical Management

When a child with RAOM has resolution of effusion between acute infections, then treating each individual infection with a full course of antibiotics certainly is reasonable and appropriate (Bluestone, 1989). If the episodes of AOM occur with a frequency deemed to be excessive by the parents and the primary care physician, then an antibiotic can be given daily in a prophylactic dose for the purpose of diminishing the frequency of acute infections. However, giving a full course of antibiotics multiple times and giving low-dose antibiotics daily is not without risk. Such frequent use of antibiotics can lead to growth of organisms resistant to commonly used antibiotics. Further, although in the United States, treating AOM with antibiotics is customary, it is worth remembering that AOM usually resolves spontaneously so that "watchful waiting," rather than antimicrobial therapy, is also an option (Pirozzo and Del Mar, 2001). Nowadays, parents should be counseled about the benefits and risks of antimicrobial therapy, and parents need to be told about the problems now arising with the emergence of strains of bacteria resistant to antibiotics.

Surgical Management

Surgical interventions for OM include tympanocentesis, myringotomy, tympanostomy tube placement, and/or adenoidectomy. Tympanocentesis is indicated when the otolaryngologist or pediatrician needs to identify the organisms present within middle ear fluid either for research purposes or when there is a need to know the specific organism causing the middle ear infection (Rosenfeld, 1996). Myringotomy can be done to drain infected fluid from the middle ear, or, if performed in combination with insertion of a tube, the myringotomy can be done to improve middle ear ventilation. Usually, a myringotomy incision will heal within 24 to 48 hours. Indications for myringotomy include the following: to alleviate pain associated with AOM, to obtain a sample of middle ear fluid for Gram's stain and culture, and to provide drainage of infected middle ear fluid when there is a manifest or impending complication of AOM such as mastoiditis, labyrinthitis, or facial paralysis. Myringotomy and tympanostomy tube placement are effective in diminishing the frequency of AOM and maintaining improved hearing when there has been conductive hearing loss associated with persistent middle ear effusion. Adenoidectomy, when performed to treat OM, helps to reduce the bacterial load contributing to middle ear disease. In the past, the enlarged adenoid was erroneously believed to contribute to chronic middle ear effusion by obstructing the pharyngeal orifice of the eustachian tube (Gates, 1996a; Gates, 1996b; Gates et al, 1988; Maw, 1985; Pirozzo and Del Mar, 2001). However, the size of the adenoid is not a factor in deciding whether removal of adenoids will be helpful in the management of OM. Specifically, there is no role for adenoidectomy in a child with AOM (Paradise et al, 1999). A child with RAOM or POME should undergo adenoidectomy at the initial myringotomy and tympanostomy tube placement only if the child also has nasal obstruction. For children with RAOM who require a repeat myringotomy and tympanostomy tube placement, adenoidectomy is recommended, regardless of adenoid size (Bluestone, 1998). In those children with chronic OME who require repeat myringotomy with tympanostomy tube placement, adenoidectomy is recommended (Bluestone, 1989; Paradise et al, 1990). Although adenoidectomy has been proven useful in the treatment of OM, the above recommendations reflect the fact that adenoidectomy is not without risk as endotracheal intubation is required, and there is increased risk of bleeding and postoperative discomfort. Therefore, the possible benefit of adenoidectomy for the child with RAOM or persistent middle ear effusion must be weighed against the risks, especially in the very young child. There is no role for tonsillectomy in the treatment of OM (Deutseh, 1996; Neill et al, 2002).

When a child with OM is referred to an otolaryngologist, there is a need for the parents, the primary care physician, and the otolaryngologist to arrive at a common understanding regarding the severity of the child's ear problems. Then all need to agree on the next best step in management. The involved physicians have a responsibility to counsel the parents appropriately.

Responsibility of the Primary Care Physician

Prior to referral to the otolaryngologist, the pediatrician should counsel the parents or caregivers appropriately. The pediatrician or family physician has a responsibility to allay parents' fears and put in perspective the impact that ear infections can have on a child. The primary care physician should discuss the natural history of OM and inform the parents that ear infections commonly occur during childhood, usually resolve by around age 4 years, and are easily managed with medicine, surgery, or both. Further, the primary care physician should let the parents know that ear infections rarely cause serious complications, long-term hearing loss, or other significant sequelae (Curry et al, 2002). Because there are many alternatives for management of OM, the pediatrician or family physician has a responsibility to apprise parents of the options for management and then consider the wishes of the parents in choosing among the alternatives for management. See Table 108-1 for further counseling.

When parents express a fear that ear infections might cause their child to permanently lose hearing, impede speech development, or impair the child's cognitive abilities, the primary care physician should be familiar with relevant scientific reports published in reputable medical journals. For example, Paradise and colleagues (2001) reported in the *New England Journal of Medicine* the results of a randomized controlled study showing that there is no significant adverse effect on child development at age 3 years if a child with persistent middle ear effusion waits 9 months before having a tympanostomy tube inserted to improve hearing (see also Stephens, 2001). However, the results of this study have been carefully scrutinized and widely discussed. Specifically, some critics have raised concerns that the failure to show a difference between the groups may be partly attributable to the fact that the delayed-tube group may have had unilateral effusions or resolution of the effusion during the 9 months. Accordingly, until further studies substantiate the lack of benefit for insertion of tubes, many primary care physicians and otolaryngologists likely will continue to recommend insertion of ventilating tubes for children who are seemingly at risk for delays in speech development.

The pediatrician should also be aware of and ready to discuss with the family any impact that the child's ear infections may be having on family life (Froom et al, 2001). For example, getting the sick child to the doctor's office is not an easy task for many families. Some caregivers are forced to miss work when bringing a child to the doctor's office, perhaps thereby incurring lost wages. Also, a child's acute ear infections may be causing sleepless nights for parents and, consequently, increased emotional stress.

The primary care physician also has a responsibility to counsel the parents about steps that they can take to reduce the frequency of ear infections. Children in day care with six or more children have an incidence of OM higher than other children. Although it is unlikely that these children can avoid day care altogether, enrolling the child in a day-care setting with fewer children may help reduce the frequency of ear infections. Tobacco smoke exposure in the household also increases the risk for OM in a child. The pediatrician should also encourage parents to wean their children off pacifiers as early as possible and to discourage bottle propping in the supine position. Both can increase reflux into the nasopharynx, through the eustachian tube, and into the middle ear. Children should also be up to date on all vaccinations. The pediatrician should discuss with the parents the factors that increase the risk for OM in children and provide realistic methods to reduce the child's risk of infection.

TABLE 108-1. Top 10 Frequently Asked Questions

1. My doctor said that my child has fluid in the middle ear. Does this mean that he has an infection?
   Not necessarily. Acute otitis media, otherwise known as a middle ear infection, means that there is both fluid (effusion) and acute inflammation in the ear. This is often because of bacteria, which can be treated with antibiotics. However, there are times when the effusion is not infected. In these cases, the effusion will usually go away with time.

2. My child was given antibiotics three times in the past month for his ears. Does that mean he had three ear infections?
   Not always. Some pediatricians will prescribe several courses of antibiotics for the same ear infection. It is important that parents ask the doctor the reason for each antibiotic therapy. It is also wise to keep a record of all of the times your child has had an ear infection and the treatments given.

3. Are there any ways in which we can reduce how often our child gets ear infections?
   Yes. Children with recurrent ear infections may be influenced by environmental factors that can be altered to improve their health:
   - If your child is bottle-fed, keep him from drinking while on his back.
   - Also, try to wean your child from pacifier use as soon as possible.
   - Keep your child's vaccinations up to date.
   - Remove environmental allergens, including cigarette/cigar smoke and pets.
   - If possible, place your child in day-care centers caring for a small number of children.

4. My doctor told me that we could either wait a few months to see if my child's ear fluid goes away or have tubes placed now. Will my child suffer irreversible damage by waiting?
   No. Although many parents worry that they are preventing normal child development (especially speech) by "watchful waiting," the most current data show that this is not true. There is no detrimental effect on early childhood development if one waits 6 months prior to myringotomy and tympanostomy tube placement.

5. If my child has tubes placed, will that *cure* his ear infections?
   No. Myringotomy and tympanostomy tube placement may help to reduce the frequency and the severity of ear infections, but they are still possible.

6. My otolaryngologist recommended that my child get a myringotomy and tympanostomy tube placement *and* an adenoidectomy. My child only has problems with his ears, so why do the adenoids need to come out too?
   Adenoids are located in the back of the nose, close to the eustachian tubes, which help drain the middle ear. The adenoids can hold bacteria, which travel up the eustachian tubes and infect the middle ear, causing infections. Removing the adenoids can reduce the number of ear infections.

7. My child has tubes in his ears and now has clear liquid draining from both ears. He does not have a fever but recently had a cold. Does he have an ear infection?
   Probably not. Otorrhea (draining ears) is a normal consequence of tube placement, especially when a child has had a recent upper respiratory tract infection. In fact, the tube allows a passageway for the liquid to drain, helping to prevent ear pain and, possibly, an ear infection.

8. My child has tubes in his ears. Why did my doctor say that I had to keep his ears dry?
   Anyone with tympanostomy tubes must take precautions from getting too much water in the ears. This is because water can get from the outside into the middle ear through the tube. If the water is dirty, this can increase the risk of ear infections. Therefore, earplugs are recommended for any type of water contact, including bathing and swimming.

9. My child had tympanostomy tubes placed last month. Why does he still need to go to the otolaryngologist?
   Once the tubes have been placed, most otolaryngologists will check the child's ears and hearing routinely for at least the next year. This is to ensure that the child's ear health improves and that there are no other problems with the ears.

10. How do my child's ear tubes come out?
    Depending on the type of tube placed, they usually fall out on their own within 6 months to $1\frac{1}{2}$ years. If, after approximately 2 years, the tube(s) is still in the eardrum, the otolaryngologist will often recommend removal in either the office or the operating room.

Prior to referral to an otolaryngologist, the pediatrician must evaluate a child with OM for any abnormalities or illnesses that negatively impact the resolution of OM (Isaacson and Rosenfeld, 1996). Specifically, children with Down syndrome, craniofacial anomalies, cleft palate, and immunodeficiency, Eskimos, and/or Native Americans have OM that is either more severe or more difficult to resolve. Children should also be evaluated for environmental and food allergies.

When the primary care physician has determined that referral to an otolaryngologist is warranted, it is important to explain carefully to the parents why the child is being referred to a consultant and what is to be expected when the child is evaluated in the office of the otolaryngologist. Usually, a child is referred to an otolaryngologist because the primary care physician believes that surgery might be indicated. However, even though the otolaryngologist has

the ability to do surgery, the otolaryngologist should not be viewed by the primary care physician or portrayed to the parent simply as the "doer" of surgery. Specifically, the parent should have the understanding that their child is going to be evaluated by an otolaryngologist who may work closely with an audiologist so that additional information can be obtained and an opinion offered. The consulting otolaryngologist is a surgeon experienced in the management of childhood ear problems and is capable of performing the appropriate surgery if needed.

The primary care physician also has a responsibility of communicating effectively with the otolaryngologist to whom the child has been referred. This means that a telephone call or a written summary of relevant information about the child's otologic problems should go to the consulting otolaryngologist. Unfortunately, this is a step that often is neglected by too many primary care physicians. A clear and concise summary of the child's illness should include the following:

- The total number of episodes of AOM that have occurred during the 3, 6, and 12 months prior to the referral
- The date on which each AOM was diagnosed, indicating in which ear the infection occurred
- The treatment provided for each infection and the response to treatment
- A summary of additional concerns, such as the child's delay in speech development, slowness to meet developmental milestones, or specific parental concerns and apprehensions

Responsibility of the Otolaryngologist

The otolaryngologist has a responsibility to carefully examine the child's ears and then complete a full head and neck examination. Then, before formulating an opinion and making recommendations, the otolaryngologist may decide to test the child's hearing. Although the otolaryngologist is a surgeon with the ability to operate on children, not all children need surgery. An otolaryngologist is the expert on ear and hearing disorders and is the consultant who can best render an opinion on the next step in management when a primary care physician concludes that medical management alone has not been successful. When a child has had a hearing test during the visit to the ear specialist, the otolaryngologist or an audiologist has the responsibility of explaining to the parents the results of the audiologic testing and the significance of the results. Most parents can understand the difference between conductive and sensorineural hearing loss when the distinction is explained. Moreover, parents deserve to know the effect that ear infections have had on their child's ear hearing. Similarly, most parents can understand how tympanograms are obtained and interpreted, and the tympanograms help to reaffirm the pneumatic otoscopic assessment of the tympanic membrane's mobility.

Sometimes, the most appropriate next step for a child is surgery, whereas, at other times, judicious watchful waiting is more appropriate. Nowadays in the United States, parents tend to like "quick fixes" and have become accustomed to giving medicine to treat and sometimes to prevent ear infections. Similarly, parents today sometimes are in favor of having surgery done on their child to reduce the frequency of ear infections or to improve hearing, even though surgical intervention might not necessarily be warranted. Therefore, the otolaryngologist has the responsibility of putting in perspective for the parent the relative benefits and risks of surgery. This means that the otolaryngologist has to be prepared to spend time explaining to parents how surgery can be helpful and how surgery can result in untoward outcomes or complica-

tions. The otolaryngologist who is articulate and empathic will always take the time to provide clear explanations for the parent, thereby allaying unwarranted fears. Unfortunately, a hurried and uncaring otolaryngologist who is "just too busy" to provide clear explanations can exacerbate parental fears, which, in turn, can lead to subtle pressure on the otolaryngologist to proceed with surgery when some other option might suffice.

If the otolaryngologist and parent(s) agree that the child should undergo surgery, preoperative counseling is imperative. First, the surgeon must describe the surgical procedure that is going to be done in a way that the caregiver can easily comprehend. Furthermore, possible risks from surgery must be discussed. For example, the parents should be aware that there can be a persistent tympanic membrane perforation once the tympanostomy tube has fallen out (0 to 4% for short-term tubes and 12 to 25% for long-term tubes) (Isaacson and Rosenfeld, 1996). Moreover, the parents should understand the length of time that the tubes are expected to remain in the ears (6 to 15 months for short-term tubes and 1.5 to 2 years for long-term tubes). Parents should be aware that if the tubes stay in the ears for too long (usually more than 2 years), removal is often necessary, in either the office or the operating room. The site often depends on the child and the type of tube. The parents should also be made aware that some children require a second surgery for OM.

Counseling the parents and pediatricians about what to expect after tympanostomy tubes have been placed is vital. Otorrhea is an expected consequence in children with tubes who have an upper respiratory tract infection (Grundfast and Carney, 1989). Many parents observe the liquid draining from their child's ears after tympanostomy tube placement and assume that the child has an infection. Because the otorrhea through a tympanostomy tube usually is concomitant with a viral upper respiratory infection, most otolaryngologists recommend treatment only with topical otic drops rather than with antibiotics. However, parents require reassurance that draining of the middle ear via the tube is good. Children with tympanostomy tubes will have to adhere to strict water precautions, such as wearing ear plugs when swimming or bathing to prevent dirty water (and bacteria) from entering the middle ear space (Isaacson and Rosenfeld, 1996). In addition, the parents should learn prior to surgery that the child with tympanostomy tubes will require close follow-up with the otolaryngologist for at least 1 year. Specifically, the otolaryngologist will examine the child and obtain a hearing test within the first month after tubes have been inserted.

Conclusion

Because there has been so much controversy for such a long time about how best to treat OM, parents deserve clear explanations when presented with the various options for management of their children's ear infections. The primary care physician needs to exchange information with the otolaryngologist so that they can work together to ensure that parents understand when watchful waiting is best, when medical treatment is needed, or when the time has come to have surgery. Because there are many options for treatment and the differences among the various treatments may be subtle or negligible, parents should have the ability to make informed choices and play a role in the care of their children's ear infections.

References

Bluestone CD. Recent advances in pediatric otolaryngology: modern management of otitis media. Pediatr Clin North Am 1989;36:1371–85.

Bluestone CD. Role of surgery for otitis media in the era of resistant bacteria. Pediatr Infect Dis J 1998;17:1090–8.

Curry MD, Mathews HF, Daniel HJ, et al. Beliefs about and response to childhood ear infections: a study of parents in eastern North Carolina. Soc Sci Med 2002;54:1153–65.

Deutseh ES. Tonsillectomy and adenoidectomy—changing indications. Pediatr Clin North Am 1996;43:1319–35.

Froom J, Culpepper L, Green LA, et al. A cross-national study of acute otitis media: risk factors, severity, and treatment at initial visit. Report from the International Primary Care Network (IPCN) and the Ambulatory Sentinel Practice Network (ASPN). J Am Board Fam Pract 2001;14:406–17.

Gates GA. Cost-effectiveness considerations in otitis media treatment. Otolaryngol Head Neck Surg 1996a;114:525–30.

Gates GA. Sizing up the adenoid. Arch Otolaryngol Head Neck Surg 1996b;122:239–40.

Gates GA, Avery CA, Prihoda TJ. Effect of adenoidectomy upon children with chronic otitis media with effusion. Laryngoscope 1988;98:58–63.

Gates GA, Wachtendorf C, Hearne EM, Holt GR. Treatment of chronic otitis media with effusion: results of tympanostomy tubes. Am J Otolaryngol 1985;6:249–53.

Grundfast KM, Carney CJ. Ear infections in your child. New York: Warner Books; 1989.

Isaacson G, Rosenfeld RM. Care of the child with tympanostomy tubes. Pediatr Clin North Am 1996;43:1183–91.

Maw AR. Age and adenoid size in relation to adenoidectomy in otitis media with effusion. Am J Otolaryngol 1985;6:245–8.

Neill RA, Scoville C, Belden J. What are the indications for tonsillectomy in children? J Fam Pract 2002;51:314.

Paradise JL, Bluestone CD, Colborn DK, et al. Adenoidectomy and adenotonsillectomy for recurrent acute otitis media. JAMA 1999;282:945–53.

Paradise JL, Bluestone CD, Rogers KD, et al. Efficacy of adenoidectomy for recurrent otitis media in children previously treated with tympanostomy-tube placement. JAMA 1990;263:2066–73.

Paradise JL, Feldman HM, Campbell TF, et al. Effect of early or delayed insertion of tympanostomy tubes for persistent otitis media on developmental outcomes at the age of three years. N Engl J Med 2001;344:1179–87.

Pirozzo S, Del Mar C. Should watchful waiting be used more often for acute otitis media? Arch Pediatr Adolesc Med 2001;155:1097.

Rosenfeld RM. An evidence-based approach to treating otitis media. Pediatr Clin North Am 1996;43:1165–79.

Stephens MB. Does delaying placement of tympanostomy tubes have an adverse effect on developmental outcomes in children with persistent middle ear effusions? J Fam Pract 2001;50:651.

INDEX